21st EDITION
GUNS ILLUSTRATED®
1989

Edited by Harold A. Murtz
and the Editors of Gun Digest

DBI BOOKS, INC.

About Our Covers

The "art and science" of shotgun slug shooting has taken huge leaps forward in the past few years, and one of the leaders in this technology has been Ballistic Research Industries, developers of both extremely efficient slugs and new slug guns.

Our front cover shows BRI's current generation pump slug gun, the "BRI Special." It's based on the Mossberg Model 500 Trophy Slugster but has improvements such as a rifled 24-inch stainless steel barrel with porting and scope mount, walnut butt with high straight comb, walnut slide handle, quick-detachable sling swivel studs, and a higher quality recoil pad. It's available only in 12-gauge with 3-inch chamber, and only from BRI.

Shown with the new gun is a selection of the excellent BRI slug ammunition in two styles—sabot (cutaways at right, 12 and 20 gauge) and Gualandi (cutaways below the gun, available in 12-, 16-, 20- and 410-gauge). These slugs are sold either as loaded ammunition or as components.

Our back cover highlights the prototype "BRI Special" Mossberg Model 5500 MK II automatic shotgun. It will be available with a rifled, 24-inch ordnance-steel barrel finished inside and out with Mossberg's MARINECOAT metal coating, scope mount, high, straight-comb walnut butt and walnut forend, quick-detachable swivel studs, and a high quality recoil pad. The gun is chambered only for 12-gauge 3-inch shells. Like its slide-action mate, this "BRI Special" is available only from Ballistic Research Industries, although a similar smooth-bored version will be offered by Mossberg later this year. BRI president Bob Sowash used this gun and BRI Sabot Bullets to bring down that beautiful caribou in the Alaskan wilderness.

A full report on the latest in slugs and slug guns appears on page 17 of this edition.

Photos by John Hanusin.

GUNS ILLUSTRATED STAFF

EDITOR
Harold A. Murtz

ASSISTANT TO THE EDITOR
LiJo Anderson

EDITORIAL/PRODUCTION ASSISTANT
Maria L. Connor

CONTRIBUTING EDITOR
Clay Harvey

GRAPHIC DESIGN
James P. Billy
Mary MacDonald

MANAGING EDITOR
Pamela J. Johnson

PUBLISHER
Sheldon L. Factor

DBI BOOKS, INC.

PRESIDENT
Charles T. Hartigan

VICE PRESIDENT & PUBLISHER
Sheldon L. Factor

VICE PRESIDENT—SALES
John G. Strauss

TREASURER
Frank R. Serpone

Copyright © MCMLXXXVIII by DBI Books, Inc., 4092 Commercial Ave., Northbrook, Illinois 60062. All rights reserved. Printed in the United States of America.

No part of this publication may be reproduced, stored in a retrieval system, or transmitted in any form or by any means, electronic, mechnical, photocopying, recording, or otherwise, without the prior written permission of the publisher.

The views and opinions contained herein are those of the authors. The editor and publisher disclaim all responsibility for the accuracy or correctness of the authors' views.

Manuscripts, contributions and inquiries, including first class return postage, should be sent to the GUNS ILLUSTRATED Editorial Offices, 4092 Commercial Ave., Northbrook, IL 60062. All material received will receive reasonable care, but we will not be responsible for its safe return. Material accepted is subject to our requirements for editing and revisions. Author payment covers all rights and title to the accepted material, including photos, drawings and other illustrations. Payment is at our current rates.

CAUTION: Technical data presented here, particularly technical data on handloading and on firearm adjustment and alteration, inevitably reflects individual experience with particular equipment and components under specific circumstances the reader cannot duplicate exactly. Such data presentations, therefore, should be used for guidance only and with caution. DBI Books, Inc. accepts no responsibility for results obtained using this data.

Arms and Armour Press, London, G.B., exclusive licensees and distributors in Britain and Europe; New Zealand; Nigeria, South Africa and Zimbabwe; India and Pakistan; Singapore, Hong Kong and Japan. Capricorn Link (Aust.) Pty. Ltd. exclusive distributors in Australia.

ISBN 0-87349-026-6   Library of Congress Catalog #69-11342

CONTENTS

FEATURES

Single Actions With A Foreign Accent
Jim Thompson 4

The 425 Express
Cameron Hopkins 11

Slug Gun Update
Jon R. Sundra 17

S&W's Classic Hunter
Stanley Trzoniec 23

LeMat
Rick L. Fines 28

Double Rifles Aren't Dead!
Tom Turpin 32

20 Years With the 44 Magnum
B.A. Hawks 39

Cast Bullets for Hunting
Howard E. French 48

The Cheney Plains Rifle
Rex Thomas 55

AMT's Auto Mag II
Jim Gosnell 60

Shooting The French 1935 Pistols
Oscar Tamenne 66

Mastering the Blackpowder Shotgun
Sam Fadala 72

On The Firing Line
Clay Harvey 77

Remington's Top Gun: The Rolling Block Rifle
Norm Wiltsey 85

Russia's Garand: The Tokarev Rifle
Robert T. Shimek 91

H&R's 25 ACP Pistol
Donald M. Simmons 97

DEPARTMENTS

GUNDEX 102
Handguns—U.S. & Imported 110
Rifles—U.S. & Imported 153
Shotguns—U.S. & Imported 205
Blackpowder Guns 235
Air Guns 253
Ammunition Tables 277

British Cartridge Ballistics 280
Chokes & Brakes 281
Metallic Sights 282
Scopes & Mounts 285
Spotting Scopes 295
Directory of the Arms Trade 297

SINGLE ACTIONS
With A Foreign Accent

The Super Dakota, or Super Dakota Magnum, is similar in concept to Uberti's Buckhorn, an enlarged Colt-inspired revolver with no equivalent among the classic Colts.

For slappin' leather and all around fun shooting, there's a wide choice of "cowboy" guns that'll fit nearly every budget. Here's a look at those made on the Continent.

by JIM THOMPSON

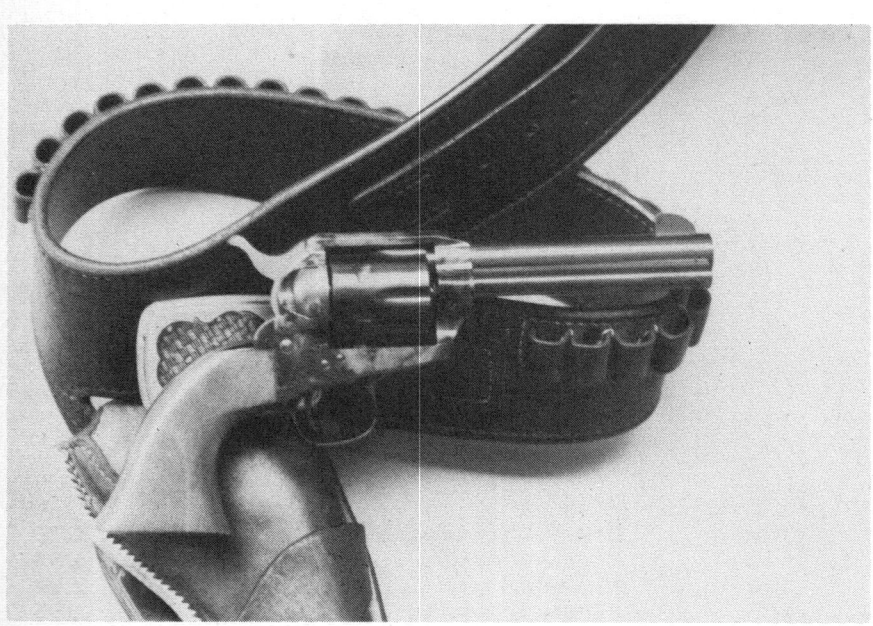

EMF's Dakota shot better with its 45 ACP cylinder than the author anticipated. The gun looks "right" with the traditional Lawrence rig shown.

WESTERN SINGLE ACTION revolvers are nothing more nor less than a steel memory of violence past. Their romance is mostly fictional, but they really did witness the winning of the last of the West and the taming of the rest. And the pistols did settle a lot of disputes, drive a lot of nails, keep peace in some very savage places.

One buys today's Western-style single actions more with the heart, eyes, and perhaps an assortment of glands than with the brain. The shortcomings of the ancient thumb-buster are universally known ... slow to load, odd linkages based on flat springs, incredibly long hammer fall, triggers a little too tender, marginal safety until recent wedge and revolving base-pin safeties, and still marginal if they're not used or understood ... and they're all true.

Just as true are the great strengths of these famous sidearms. Old-timers will tell you these old critters had virtually no internal part that couldn't

Some of Uberti's target models, like this Buckhorn Target from Benson Firearms, are frequently mistaken at first glance for Rugers.

F.I.E.'s Tanfoglio-built Texas Ranger (right, with 6½-inch barrel) and Little Ranger (lower left, 3¼-inch) are in the Buffalo Scout line. The "standard" Buffalo Scout (upper left) has a 4¾-inch tube. Excam also markets a similar line of Tanfoglio pistols.

be hammered and cut from a horseshoe nail or old wagon spring. A man could point and shoot with a single action, drawing it from the leather and firing while someone else was between heartbeats, that you could strike a man full force with your Colt or Remington or drive a nail and not compromise the pistol at all. Those things are true, too.

Save perhaps for the little 3-3½-inch barreled Sheriff's Models, classic single action purchases have been pretty much emotional and nostalgic decisions, rather than practical ones, for at least 50 years. There's only one thing they can be made to do better than any other handgun, and that's deliver a first shot from proper leather in absolute minimum time. Nobody else with anything else approaches Thell Reed or Steve Benson or a half-dozen other experts who can deliver a shot from a signal, into a lethal area, in $1/10$-second or less. This requires proper walk'n'draw or Buscadero gear, but *nobody* in IPSC or other "combat shooting" even comes close. But even that has precious little to do with why these pistols are purchased and revered.

These pistols stink of the West, even if the closest they've ever been is Hartford, Connecticut. They look right. They feel right. Four clicks to full cock, big bullets, and hell-bent-for-leather. That's why people buy them.

Truth be known, standard single actions are no longer a stock item with Colt, and are produced mainly as commemoratives. Read that as expensive and ornate. If your budget is not limitless and you must have a new single action to shoot and look at, it will probably have to come from Italy or Germany.

Today's armchair cowboy has a far greater choice of armament than he would've had 100 years ago. Even the percussions and all manner of odd long guns are made today in greater profusion than the originals ever were. That's good news for those of us who don big hats and heavy boots and walk a little more bowlegged than our time on horseback really justifies.

There's nothing new about copies of single actions. The Spanish produced some mediocre copies even before World War I. Hy Hunter contracted with Sauer to make a slightly updated copy in the 1950s. These continued into the 1970s as the Great Western brand, then Hawes pistols, by that time "Rugerized" with floating firing pins but still with flat springs. Navy Arms' Val Forgett started the drive toward true replicas through a late '50s contract with Aldo Uberti of Gardone Val Trompia, Italy, in which 2000 Colt "Navy" M1851 copies were specified. Other importers contracted with firms in Belgium to produce the 1860 "Army" Colt replicas, among others. The Italian Armi Jager products, called "Dakotas," were Colt cartridge clones, and were marketed by Intercontinental Arms in the late 1960s.

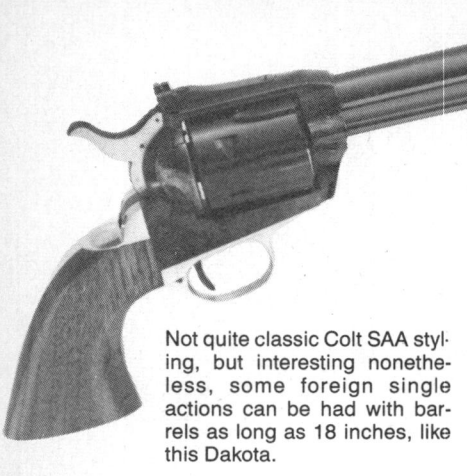

Not quite classic Colt SAA styling, but interesting nonetheless, some foreign single actions can be had with barrels as long as 18 inches, like this Dakota.

The Target Cattleman from Mitchell Arms bears more than a passing resemblance to Ruger's home-grown 357 Blackhawk. They're two handsome guns.

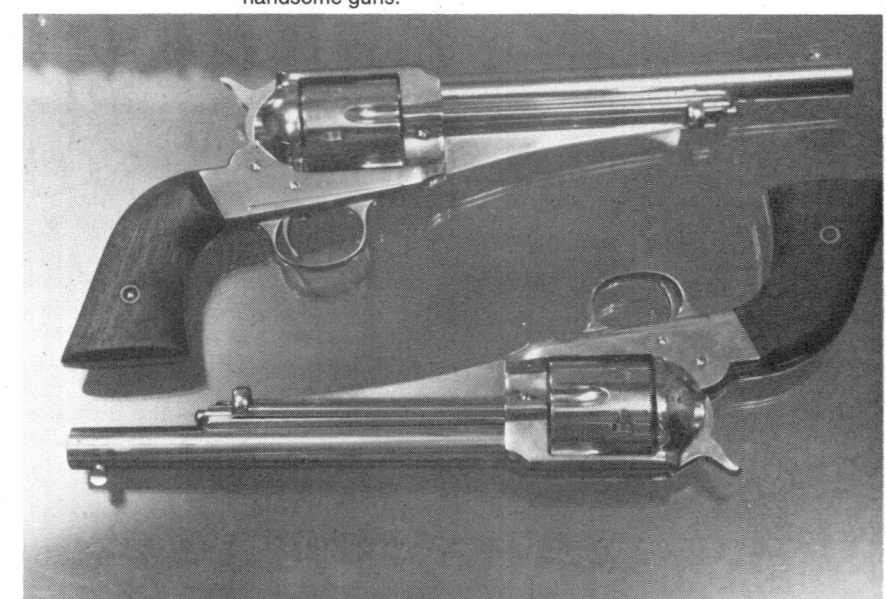

The author's Uberti "Outlaws" are chambered for 357 Magnum and 45 Colt, both nickel plated. With apologies to George Patton, they are being fitted with the gaudiest mother of pearl stocks money can buy.

By the early '70s, every major variant of anything that could remotely have been called a "cowboy gun" was on the market and going strong, including German and Italian copies of the post-WWII 22-caliber Scout pistols.

Because of GCA '68's safety requirements, something very odd started to happen: 1. A gun law actually had a small positive impact (we in the trade call this "the exception which proves the rule"); and 2. Given a respectable memory and a little care, finally, after 100 years, it became at least nominally safe to carry hawgleg gun with six rounds in the cylinder.

By 1977, demand and supply had reached the point where new models like the Interarms Virginian Dragoon could draw on a genuinely cosmopolitan expertise to produce a pistol whose parts were mostly made by Uberti in Italy, finished and calibrated by Hammerli in Switzerland, sometimes assembled there, later assembled here, all based on an American design some 104 years old at the time. Interarms was the first to specify stainless steel on an Uberti product, and last generation Virginian Dragoons were "Rugerized" to the extent of employing coil mainsprings.

These foreign products are good and the selections are deep. They're literally good enough to bear the original Colt name, and, in fact, Ron Keysor, in the January '87 issue of *American Rifleman,* (p.46) notes that Uberti made most of the Colt restrike percussions sold under Colt's own name.

Some of the cowboys guns from Europe are not replicas at all, but new models for magnum calibers, puffed up proportionally and gracefully from originals that were insufficiently robust for the bigbore 44 Magnum.

Others, from Uberti and Armi Jager, duplicate construction details and finish in a manner so reverent to the originals of the 19th century that only the presence of Italian proofs and importer logos allow easy distinction between New England manufacture and Italian duplication. Some of the "special editions" include historical markings, charcoal blue, elegant renditions of long-extinct tool processes that bespeak a special eye for detail well beyond an ordinary engineer's. In fact, many of my Ubertis have literally looked more like Colts than my Colts of the last 25 years or so.

Just as with my Colts, though, I am inclined to follow the procedures my pistolsmith taught me on any little

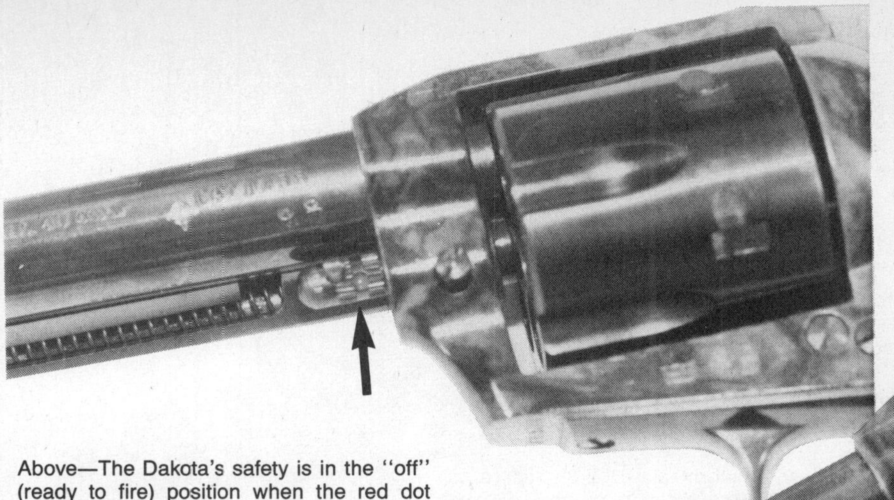

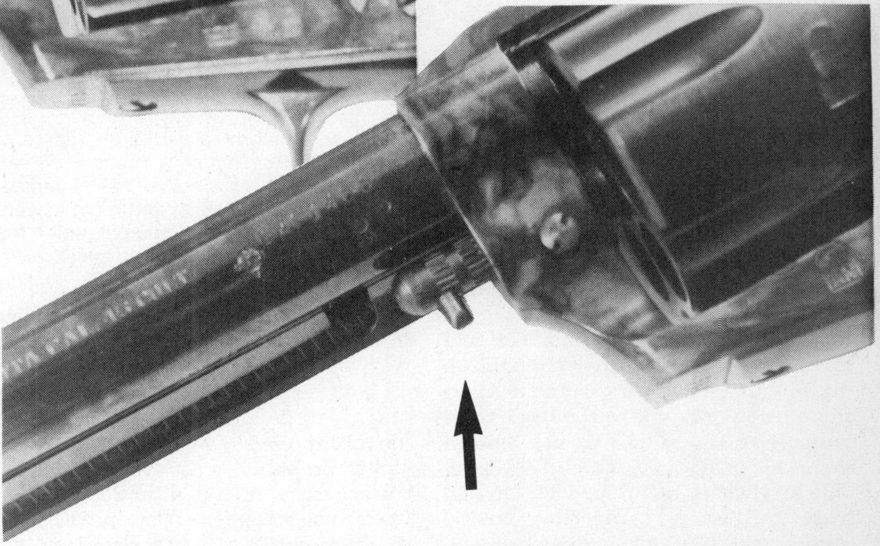

Above—The Dakota's safety is in the "off" (ready to fire) position when the red dot shows. Right—with the safety "on" (hammer retarded beyond primer), the small handle points down. This is a novel approach to a single action safety.

The author found the Dakota a fun 45 to shoot. Here, he's just hit a 12-inch gong at long range with the 45 ACP cylinder in place.

glitch of feel or fit, especially with the cylinder bolt. This can score an ugly vertical scratch in a cylinder if not properly smoothed. Anything having to do with the trigger or hammer notches I refer to John Student, 6054 Farmdale, North Hollywood, CA 91606. Hammer fall, in particular, has much to do with the accuracy of these hawglegs, since even the best of us cannot hold still forever. If it has seemed to a single action owner that his gun gets "more accurate" with age, it's usually because the hammer is mashing or grinding off tiny burrs every time its dropped, thereby dropping faster with age. This means the shooter may lose his opportunity to read his ammo box instructions between the time he squeezes the trigger and actual ignition of the primer. I've learned to have John do the "slicking" up front, preventing problems for the life of the pistol.

I've owned about 70 of these pistols, and had an equal amount of glitches in proportion to the Colts I've owned over the years, mostly from the same causes. Worst of these tend to be excessively polished chambers, which cause recoil plate jams when cartridges slide back from recoil; strange springs (easily solved with careful stone work by a 'smith); miscellaneous cylinder oddities, including undersized or oversized chambers and a Colt with no real machining on the index notches. Only the last is not easily solved with some swift expedient. Excessively polished chambers can be dealt with in the short run by using unpolished brass handloads, in the long run with moderately gentle touches of #400 grit emory paper. But cylinder glitches must go back to the manufacturer or importer. If, for some reason, this sounds like a lot of problems, I have several pages of common glitches on modern double-action revolvers. This design was for willful, tough men, under arduous conditions, and though the pistols won't do a lot of things, you almost have to abuse them to cause a serious malfunction.

This article covers four foreign single action makers: Tanfoglio Fratelli, Uberti, and Armi Jager of Italy, and Weihrauch in Germany. It is wise for the American consumer to remember that foreign guns are carefully proofed in detail by law before they can be sold or exported. This includes not just proof firing, but certification of metallurgy, safety devices, size specification, and overall conformance to a manufacturer's own quality control standards. As a result, I have never owned any proofed foreign firearm which would not function or which I felt to be unsafe. I cannot make such a statement about any nation which does not have a uniform proof law, and have, in fact, had many expensive firearms not so proofed fail to function right out of the box, brand new. European proof codes do not guarantee perfection. They warrant safety and com-

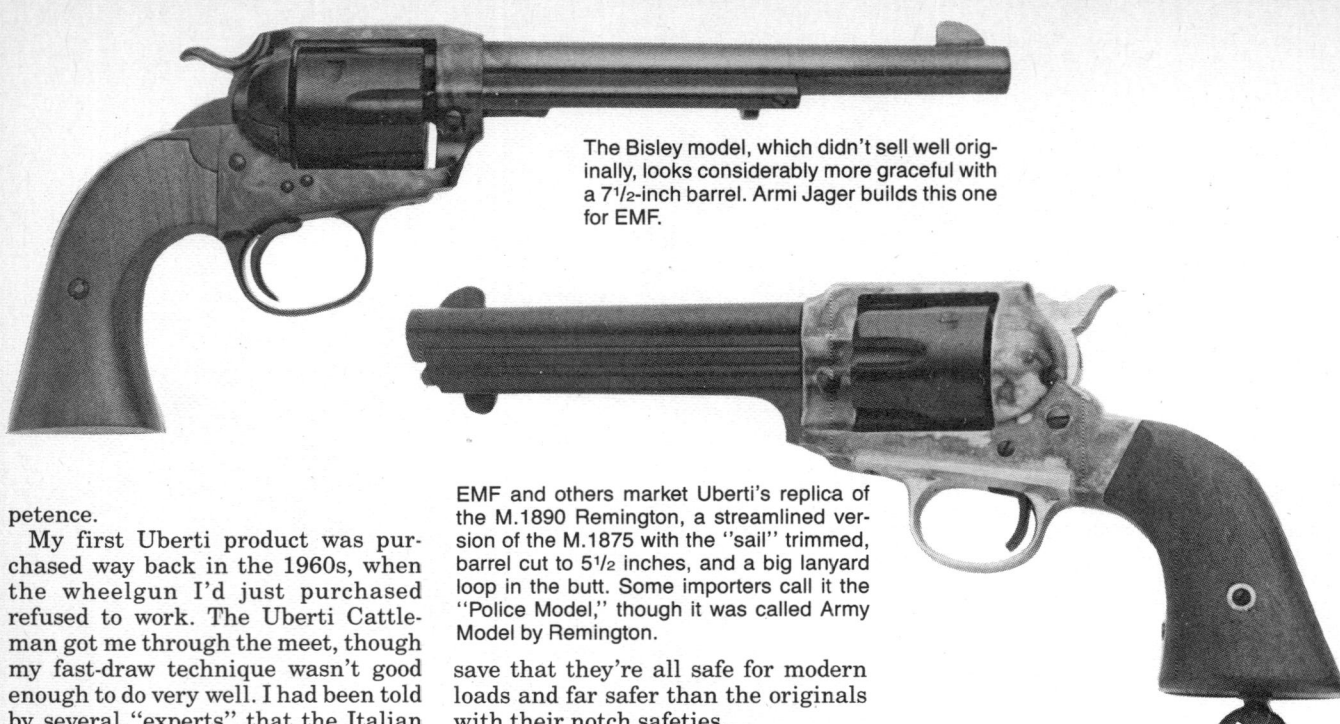

The Bisley model, which didn't sell well originally, looks considerably more graceful with a 7½-inch barrel. Armi Jager builds this one for EMF.

petence.

My first Uberti product was purchased way back in the 1960s, when the wheelgun I'd just purchased refused to work. The Uberti Cattleman got me through the meet, though my fast-draw technique wasn't good enough to do very well. I had been told by several "experts" that the Italian thumb-buster was downright dangerous. Truth was, it was better than competent, though I was not fond of the brass backstrap, which I later replaced with a refinished strap and trigger guard off a horribly rusted Colt. I mounted hard rubber grips on the hybrid thus produced, since the Italian one-piece units wouldn't properly fit the American backstrap very well, and it was amazing how many people commented on my nice "Colt."

Uberti

The Uberti single actions comprise three families: The Cattleman, a slightly modified Colt P clone with variants from the 3½-inch barreled Sheriff's Model to 18-inch carbines. There are blue options and finish material choices include stainless steel, oddments of furniture options, and include the 22-caliber "Stallions"; the "Buckhorns" are puffed-up enlargements of the old Model P for the 44 Magnum cartridge, and are often available with a 44-40 accessory cylinder; and the "Outlaws," Remington copies comprising the Model 1875 and its progeny, the Model 1890 Army, sometimes called the "Police Model," with its reduced underbarrel "sail" and shorter 5½-inch barrel.

The Ubertis are offered in the usual finish and barrel length permutations, and adjustable sight, flattop models are offered in the Cattleman and Buckhorn lines. Stainless versions are also available from some distributors.

The guns generally act rather like their Colt and Remington forebears,

EMF and others market Uberti's replica of the M.1890 Remington, a streamlined version of the M.1875 with the "sail" trimmed, barrel cut to 5½ inches, and a big lanyard loop in the butt. Some importers call it the "Police Model," though it was called Army Model by Remington.

save that they're all safe for modern loads and far safer than the originals with their notch safeties.

I got excellent performance from the stainless 5½-inch-barreled target model supplied by Mitchell Arms. The sights probably account for much of the accuracy, though after 250 rounds, I notice no scrapes or friction traces on the hammer/frame interface, tending to suggest rapid, unencumbered hammer fall. This is always a good sign in a single action and a boost to accuracy.

I could not equal this performance with the standard large-frame Mitchell "Buckhorn"-style 44 Magnum. A fellow gun club member casually asked to test the pistol, assumed the gymnastic "Creedmoor" position, and loaded up six Federal #44A 240-grain jacketed hollowpoints. After much smoke and flame cleared, he'd made a single hole at 25 yards I'd normally associate with a 12-gauge slug, and left with the remark, "Gee, I sure like these new *Rugers*."

My Outlaws were bought for the very most sentimental reason: to replace a couple of authentic models sold in 1969 to finance my daughter Anna's delivery into this world. Even back then, the Colts were worth enough to cover that contingency and a raft of other bills. Like my originals, the 357 and 45 Colt I purchased from EMF were nickel plated, and true to the originals, the Remington copies outshot both the New England Colts and their Italian clones.

Some old-timers claim the straight shooting of the old Remington black-powder guns was due to that big sail under the barrel acting as a stiffener and heat sink, the tighter cylinder/barrel gap, and the longer standard barrel. But I think it's most likely due to greater overall rigidity and faster lock time than Colts or copies, although I must concede—as the apochryphal reports of the 19th Century always said—that the big sail under the barrel is a genuine asset if the ancient horse pistol requires use as a club. Wyatt Earp supposedly bashed Dodge City drunks with a Model 1875, and for that particular purpose, no other design is quite as functional.

Just as with the originals, my copies shoot high with a normal sight picture under 100 yards, so I have learned to show less sight in the topstrap gash at shorter ranges. I regularly use both of these flashy pistols to ring the 300-yard gong at the range, a lot more fun than the tedium and discipline of punching itty-bitty holes in bullseye targets. The Outlaws' bores run tight, which I found out by experience, rather than by slugging the bore on my 45. A friend brought some very hairy handloads along to the range, implanted with the .451-inch Hornady #4518 bullet, superbly accurate in automatics but supposedly under diameter for 45 Colt revolvers. The Outlaw handled them with alacrity and superb accuracy.

Two odd bits of information that apply equally to authentic and replica Remingtons of the classic era: 1. The cylinders are over 1/16-inch shorter

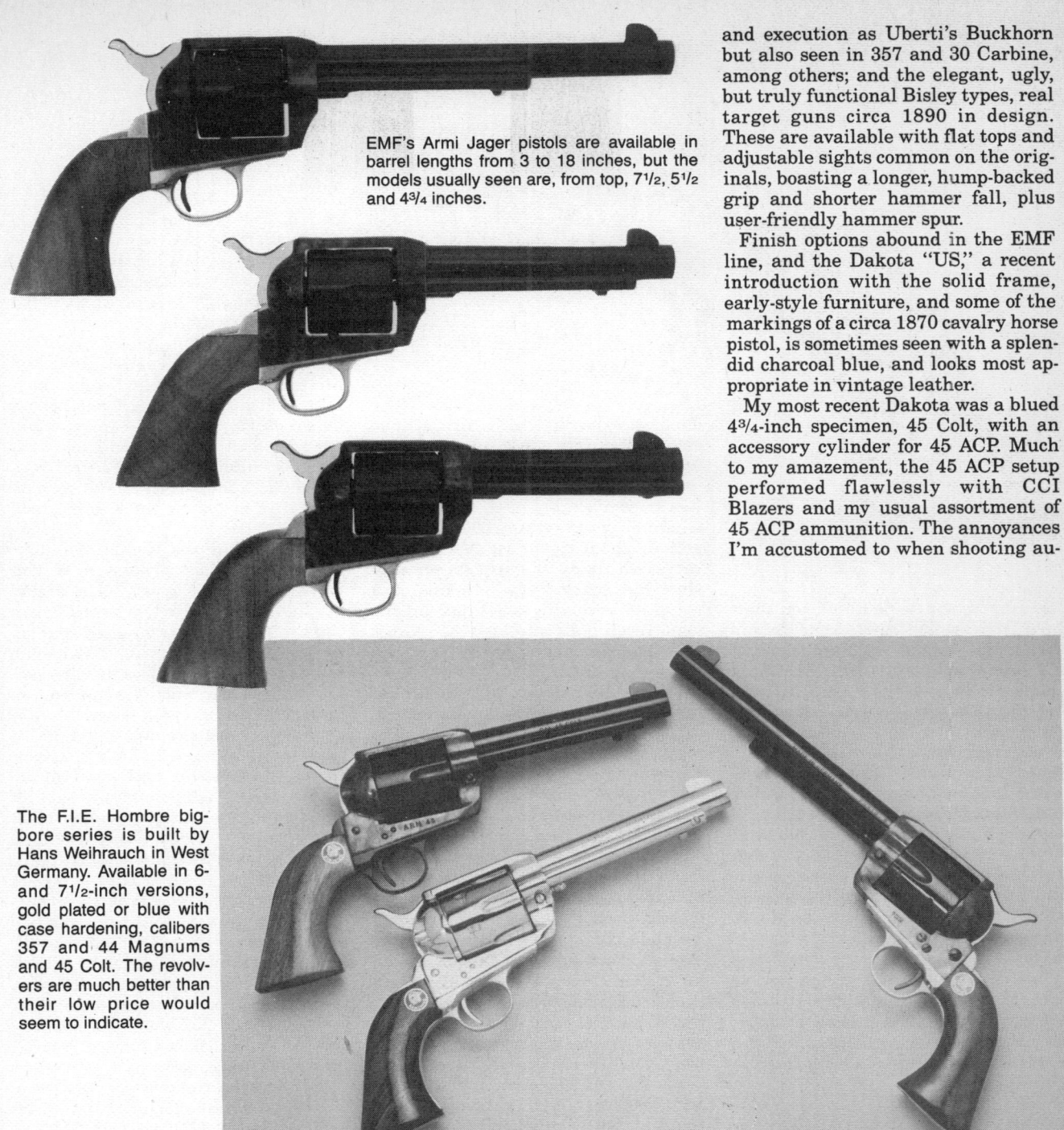

EMF's Armi Jager pistols are available in barrel lengths from 3 to 18 inches, but the models usually seen are, from top, 7½, 5½ and 4¾ inches.

The F.I.E. Hombre big-bore series is built by Hans Weihrauch in West Germany. Available in 6- and 7½-inch versions, gold plated or blue with case hardening, calibers 357 and 44 Magnums and 45 Colt. The revolvers are much better than their low price would seem to indicate.

and execution as Uberti's Buckhorn but also seen in 357 and 30 Carbine, among others; and the elegant, ugly, but truly functional Bisley types, real target guns circa 1890 in design. These are available with flat tops and adjustable sights common on the originals, boasting a longer, hump-backed grip and shorter hammer fall, plus user-friendly hammer spur.

Finish options abound in the EMF line, and the Dakota "US," a recent introduction with the solid frame, early-style furniture, and some of the markings of a circa 1870 cavalry horse pistol, is sometimes seen with a splendid charcoal blue, and looks most appropriate in vintage leather.

My most recent Dakota was a blued 4¾-inch specimen, 45 Colt, with an accessory cylinder for 45 ACP. Much to my amazement, the 45 ACP setup performed flawlessly with CCI Blazers and my usual assortment of 45 ACP ammunition. The annoyances I'm accustomed to when shooting au-

than on Colts, and while they present no difficulties with 357 and 44-40, will cause problems with full-length (1.6-inch) 45 Colt loadings which will jam against the forcing cone; and 2. The hammer configuration and geometry is different enough from Colt's that shooters accustomed to the more common wheelgun may miss the spur entirely in fast draw or other "hurry-up" exercises.

Armi Jager

Armi Jager pistols are all Colt copies or Colt inspired. There are more standard chamberings in this line, imported to the U.S. exclusively by EMF, than with Uberti, and the pistols comprise three groups: The Dakota, a rather vast group of straightforward Model P clones with a much improved rotating base pin safety; the Magnum Dakota, virtually the same concept

tomatic rounds from revolvers just didn't happen. In fact, owing to tighter tolerances all around, the pistol shot much better with the stubby ACP hull than with my favorite 45 Colt loads. I was especially pleased that the roughed-up chambers held the cases firmly in place without the need for retaining clips or spring gizmos (which either get in the way or don't work). Similar rigs from EMF al-

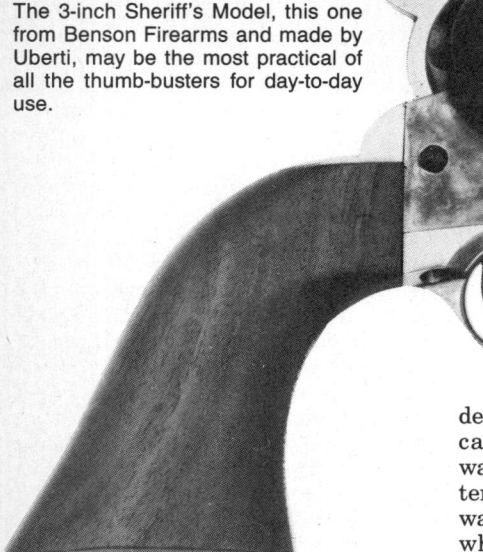

The 3-inch Sheriff's Model, this one from Benson Firearms and made by Uberti, may be the most practical of all the thumb-busters for day-to-day use.

low 9mm Luger to be fired from their 38/357 guns, and 32/20 from the big 30 Carbine "Magnum" frame model.

I am eager to run a Bisley through its paces. This model, especially with a 7½-inch barrel, flat top, and adjustable sights, is a more practical pistol than its prettier stablemates, which is why Ruger recently added the style to their line. Not only is that extra pinky not left dangling as if oh-so-properly sipping a cup of tea, but the hammer and hammer fall action is slicker and faster. These variants also *seem* to exhibit more detailed attention to lockwork fit and interface than the standard Dakotas.

Generally, Armi Jager's pistols are not quite as slick out of the box as Uberti's, which is why my Dakotas are 'smithed even before I shoot them. But the materials are good and the systems are solid. And the feel is right.

F.I.E.

F.I.E. (Firearms Import and Export) markets two basic single action variants, the Tanfoglio-produced Ranger/Buffalo Scout 22s and the German Weihrauch-built Hombre series in 357, 45 Colt, and 44 Magnum. Excam also markets a similar line of Tanfoglio 22 units as "Tanarmis." These guns can be had in a wide variety of finishes and grip styles, with a good choice of acessories. The pistols are quite different from each other.

My buffalo Scout was a "Yellow Rose," a petite, pretty little bauble, gold-plated with ivory composition grips. Both 22 LR and 22 WMR cylinders were nestled in a nicely lined case. Machine work on externals wasn't particularly good, but the internals were near perfect. Trigger pull was uncomfortably close to the point where heavy breathing could trip the action—about 2 pounds; nice for accuracy with the little gun's speedy lock time but scary anywhere but at a range. A revolving steel disc on the right recoil plate swell can be rotated over the firing pin for use as a positive safety, and I *used* it.

This is the most durable gold plating I have ever seen on any firearm. It stood up better than most nickel plate.

The pistol shot good groups; the Federal 22 WMR hollowpoints didn't do as well as the standard velocity 22 LR Federal Champions, but still fine. This isn't a bullseye pistol. It's a fine, fancy can-destroyer *par excellence,* and it was for that purpose that I mostly used this little gem. Recoil isn't a factor, so if the hands are quick enough, a can tossed by the left can be hit quickly by a right-hand swung Scout once or more rather easily. Just remember, this is still a single action, so don't freeze the arm's movement when you squeeze the trigger, or you'll miss. Pan, as if you were taking an action picture with a camera, and you'll hit with ridiculous ease.

Fun is what these pistols are about, and if there were awards for such frivolous stuff, this 22 should win one.

F.I.E.'s Hombre is another kind of animal entirely. German-made, German it looks. No-nonsense square corners, 5 ounces more metal than the standard Colt, a massive cylinder and cleverly executed base pin safety and "Rugerish" floating firing pin. The general impression is as if Hans Weihrauch had simply taken a large block of ordnance steel and eliminated all those parts and places not essential to a Western-style single action. The philosophical progeny of Sauer's single actions, functionally similar to Uberti's big Buckhorn, it escapes me how a firearm of this quality can be sold for a profit at a list price of under $250.

I challenged this pistol with the stiffest factory 357 loads I could find and some maximum handloads. I kept tearing it apart looking for looseness or excessive wear for almost 1000 rounds. The pistol shot best with heavier bullets like the Federal 180-grain SWC, though stiff handloads on the brink of maximum also grouped well.

One aspect of the Hombre I finally noticed was the precision of the threads on the screws. I am accustomed to single actions requiring tightening every few hundred rounds, to the extent that I do it without thinking. The Hombre, despite use just on the sane side of abuse, never loosened up, and I took it apart half a dozen times or more, which generally accelerates a single action's tendency to wiggle around and get sloppy. Thread speed seems to run about the same as on the Italian specimens, but everything fits very securely.

The Hombre, though not as graceful or as "Western" as its Italian counterparts, may be the most practical of the Colt spinoffs, owing to the floating firing pin and generally high overall quality, particularly in view of its price. The case hardening is the real thing, the hardwood grips are for real, and my 6-inch 357 showed less abrasion in its internals than I expect of full-caliber single actions.

At the turn of the century, there was only one single action commonly available on the U.S. market—Colt's—and a worker who made, typically, $35-$50 per month could own one for about $20.00. Today, a consumer who makes 20-50 times that raw dollar income can choose from about 80 variants of about a half-dozen basic designs of cartridge single actions. All of these cost a far lower proportion of his income than a worker 90 years ago had to sacrifice for a design which, even then, was a long-in-the-tooth legend. Not only is the classic single action not dead, it's more alive than ever. Just being made under different roofs.

●

The 425 Express

by CAMERON HOPKINS

Author with a record class Giant Oryx taken in Namibia's Kalahari Desert with the prototype 425 Express rifle. This animal is remarkably tough and hard to kill.

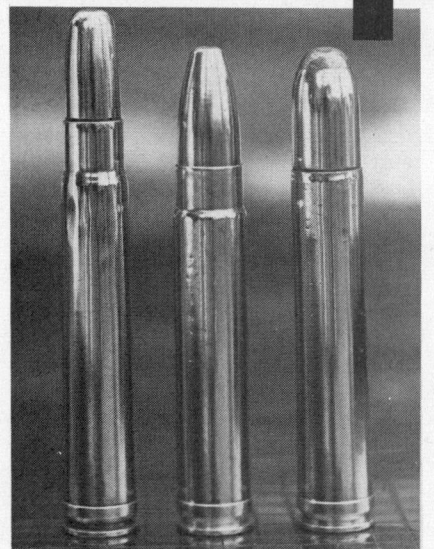

The 425 Express (center) takes the middle ground between the 375 H&H Magnum (left) and the 458 Winchester Magnum. The 375 shoots a 300-gr. bullet, the 458 a 500-gr., and the 425 splits the difference with a 400-gr. projectile. The 425 is 30 percent more powerful than the 375.

Looking for something new in a hunting cartridge? Here's something a bit different that bridges the gap between the 375 and 458 that's suitable for both African game as well as home-grown critters, and you don't need a custom-length action.

HUNTERS ENJOYED the best years of cartridge development in the decade spanning the mid-50s to the mid-60s. Other than a few fits and starts, like the 8mm Remington Magnum in 1978, nothing much new has come along since this banner time of cartridge invention. You've got such mundane matters as putting a rim on the 308 Winchester and calling it the 307, but you can hardly put that in the same league with, say, the introduction of the 7mm Remington Magnum in 1962.

You can almost safely say that we had a new cartridge every year from 1955 to 1965. There's just one gap, 1961:

1955 . . . . 243 Win.
1956 . . . . 458 Win. Mag.
1957 . . . . 280 Rem. Mag.
1958 . . . . 338 Win. Mag.
1959 . . . . 358 Norma Mag.
1960 . . . . 308 Norma Mag.
1962 . . . . 7mm Rem. Mag.
1963 . . . . 300 Win. Mag.
1964 . . . . 225 Win. Mag.
1965 . . . . 350 Rem. Mag.

And these are just the highlights. The 340 Weatherby (1962), 358 Winchester (1955), 223 Remington (1957), 222 Remington Magnum (1958) are a

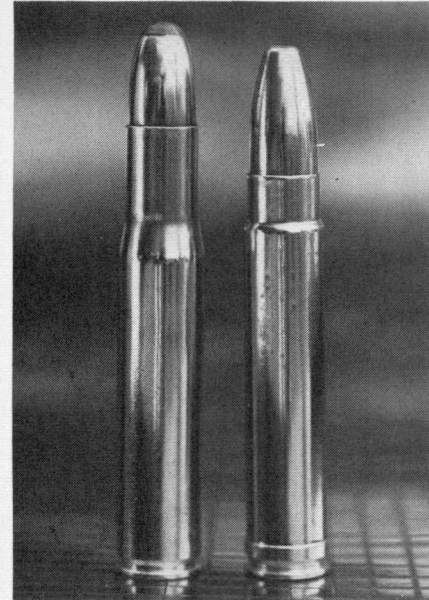

The 404 Rimless Nitro Express (left) was the inspiration for the 425 Express. It's confusing, but both actually use .423-in. bullets.

For such an odd size of .423-in., the new Express has quite a few bullets available. Front to back: 400-gr. "Bear Claw" softpoint; 400-gr. "Monolithic Solid"; 400-gr. Woodleigh steel jacketed solid; 400-gr. Barnes softpoint; and 400-gr. "Sledgehammer" solid.

few more. Yes, those were the good years.

Other than the 22-250 (an old wildcat) coming out of hibernation in 1969 and the 375 Winchester in 1978, not much has stirred in the ballistic labs. Now, 32 years after the 458 Winchester and 76 years after the 375 Holland & Holland Magnum, comes a breath of fresh air to this stale climate of the status quo. A new hunting cartridge called the 425 Express was born in 1987. The 425 Express is a standard-length round with two loadings: a 350-grain spitzer at 2550 fps and a 400-grain roundnose at 2450 fps. It is designed to bridge the gulf between the large-bore 458 Magnum and the medium-bore 375 Magnum.

The genesis of the 425 Express was the convergence of two ideas. Two experimenters in California had conceived a .423-inch bore hunting cartridge by combining the bullet from the obsolete 404 Jeffrey with the 300 Winchester Magnum case. Then word reached the Golden State that Bill Ruger was investigating the introduction of six proprietary new cartridges to bear the Ruger name on the headstamp. Rumor had it that Mr. Ruger was looking for a medium-large cartridge for his new line of hunting rounds.

It has been said that Bill Ruger has long been envious of Roy Weatherby and the various Weatherby proprietary cartridges. Also, of the Big Three rifle makers, only Ruger does not have his name on a cartridge. There are all sorts of Winchester magnums and Remington magnums, but not a single Ruger magnum.

Working with Federal Cartridge Company's marketing manager, Mike Bussard, the two wildcatters set about evaluating the new cartridge which, at the time, held the working designation of 425 Ruger Express. A prototype rifle was built on the Ruger 77 action and a special run of 350-grain spitzer bullets were ordered from Cor Bon Custom Bullets.

The cartridge was to fit a standard length action for an overall loaded length of 3.340-inches. The reason is two-fold: first and foremost, the Ruger 77 is not made in a magnum length, which is why Ruger does not chamber the 375 H&H in the gun (it's available in the No. 1 single shot); secondly, a 30-06-size cartridge requires a shorter bolt throw to load a fresh round from the magazine, and this facilitates reliable operation of the rifle under the pressure of the hunt. The designers were acutely aware that the 425 Express is a big game cartridge, and that means a man's life could depend on feeding reliability in the face of a charging Kodiak bear or enraged elephant. Short-stroking the bolt, which is a problem with the magnum-length cartridges, could be fatal.

Given the design parameters, the wildcatters found two potential cases for the basis of the 425 Express. The 458 Winchester was itself designed to fit a standard length action, so that was a prime candidate. But the 300 Winchester Magnum case also fits a standard action, yet offers a longer overall case, the difference coming in the neck of the 300. Designer Whit Collins, after consulting with prototype rifle maker John French, decided on the 300 case with a length of 2.552-

Noted handgun authority J.D. Jones lets drive with the 425 Express. He's firing a full-charge load with 400-gr. bullet. He describes the recoil as a "shove" and likens it to the kick of a 375 H&H.

Recovered bullets from big game illustrate the comparative performance of the 425 (center) with the 375 (left) and 458. The 425 slugs are every bit as big, if not bigger, than the 45-cal. 510-gr. softnose bullets.

inches versus the 2.500-inch length of the 458 case.

The shoulder angle was set at 32 degrees in order to provide maximum case capacity for powder while at the same time insuring reliable feeding from the magazine. The shoulder angle plays a role in the complex mechanics of powder burning rate, piston area, bore expansion ratio and other esoteric matters of internal ballistics.

The result is a remarkably efficient cartridge. Small adjustments give unusual improvements to the ballistics, the sign of effective design. While most magnum rounds show a Power Efficiency Rating of 30-35 percent, the Express has a P.E.R. of 35-45 percent. To give you an idea of how this translates into the real world, consider that the 425 Express carries as much energy at 1300 yards as a 41 Magnum has at the muzzle!

The heavy hitting Express had never been conceived as a tack-driver for picking out gnat's eyes. You simply do not need any better than tea-cup accuracy out of a rifle that churns up 5200 ft./lbs. of muzzle energy. The experimenters had agreed that a 2-inch group at 100 yards would be just fine for hitting game that resembles a Hyundai Excel with horns.

Lo and behold, the 400-grain round-nose bullets are awfully close to $1/2$-MOA, well within the magic sub-MOA that accuracy buffs consider essential.

Independent testing by James E. Fender confirmed that the 425 Express prototype rifle puts the big 400-grain slugs into less than an inch at 100 yards. Jim's best group measured $7/8''$ x $5/8''$, four shots at 100 yards (Jim got excited when he saw one ragged hole after four shots and flinched a called flyer for the fifth round.)

As we hunters know, accuracy is a factor of both rifle and cartridge, so the construction of the prototype rifle on the Ruger 77 action is certainly relevant. The barrel is a Douglas premium blank with a 1:14-inch twist cut to 22 inches. It has an octagonal profile with an integral recoil lug and it is glass bedded into a Fiberpro composite stock of synthetic materials. The barrel is free-floated past the recoil lug.

Six bullet makers offer .423-inch bullets and between them there is a surprisingly wide assortment for such an obscure bore size. The standard weight is 400 grains with all six offering at least two versions each, ranging from a solid bronze bullet, A-Square's Monolithic design, to a heavy copper-jacketed solid from Barnes to a semi-spitzer soft point from Trophy Bonded Bullets. In all, there are 15 different bullets, 13 in 400 grains and two 350 grainers.

Only Barnes and Cor Bon offer 350-grain spitzers, which are the best bullets for North American hunting with the lone exception of Kodiak bear. The 400-grain softs would be better for the giant bear of the north, but the 350-grain spitzers are better for elk and moose. There is not much point in hitting deer or antelope with 5200 ft./lbs. of energy, but the 425 Express obviously could kill these animals.

Loading these bullets can be accomplished with either the 300 Win. Mag. or the 458 Win. Mag. cases. Each has its benefits. The 458 case may simply be run in a Redding sizing die and emerges formed to the Express dimensions. No sweat, no different in procedure than sizing a 458 case in its own die. The drawback is that the 458 case is only 2.500-inches in length instead of the proper 2.552-inch.

In order to obtain the correct case, you must fire-form 300 Win. Mag. cases or go through two passes in a Redding size die. Redding offers two tapered expander plugs, graduated to step up the 30-caliber neck to 423 in

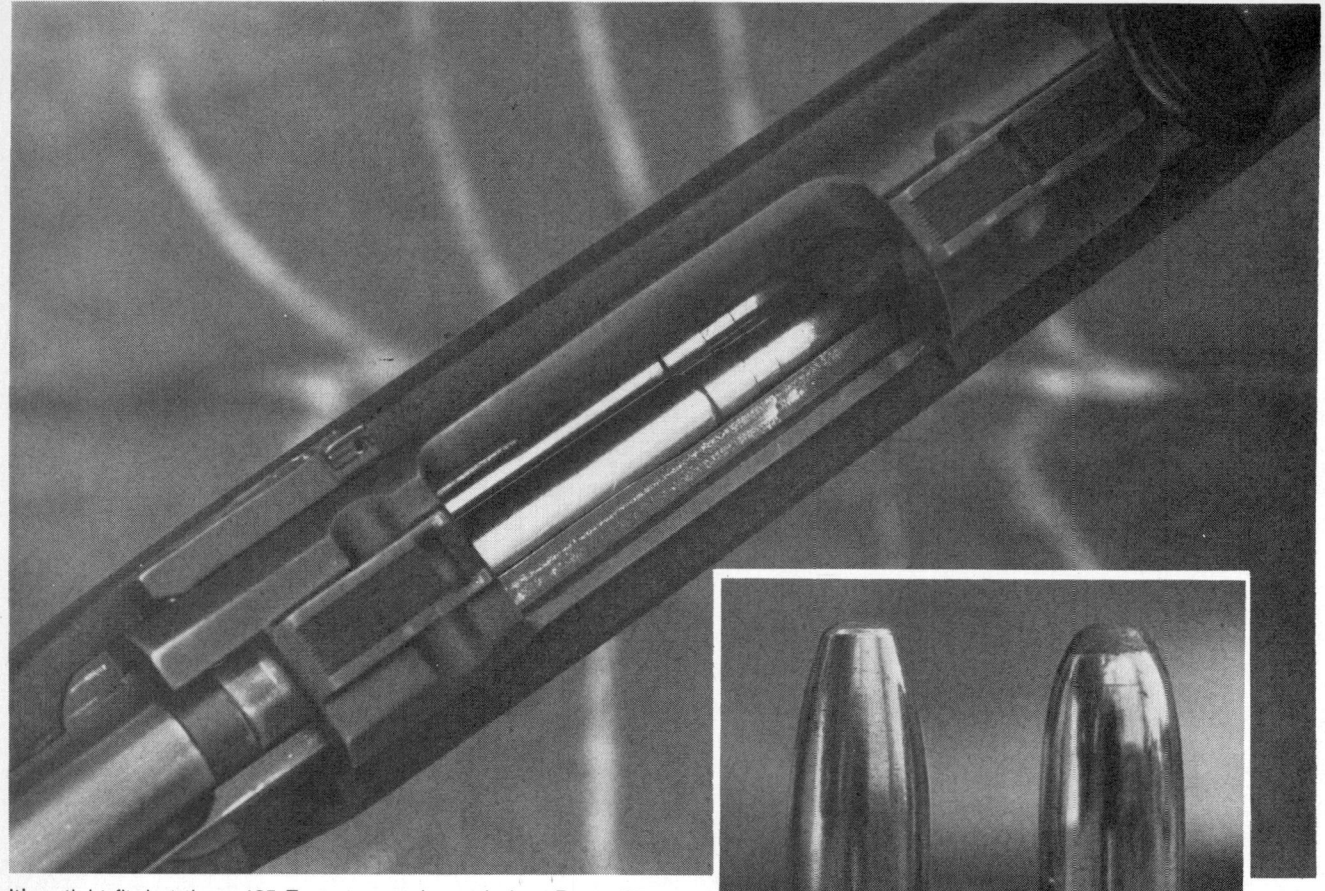

It's a tight fit, but three 425 Express rounds nestle in a Ruger 77 magazine. The loaded Express measures 3.340-in., same as the 30-06, and therefore fits a standard-length action.

Note the different case neck lengths. The 300 Win. Mag. (left) has a neck .052-in. longer than the 458 Win. Mag. when both are formed to 425 Express. Either works just fine, but the 300 case is preferred because it grips the bullet tighter.

increments. You can't expand that much in one stroke.

Fire forming is accomplished by loading the case with 18-20 grains of WW 231. Then fill the case with either cornmeal or some of the new "shot buffer" granules used in reloading shotshells. Cap the case with a wax plug to keep everything from falling out. Trim the case to 2.552-inch before fire forming because otherwise the case forms into the chamber's throat and will not fit a 423-inch trimmer pilot if you try to trim after fire forming.

Now that you have either sized 458 cases or fire-formed the 300 cases, the reloading is straight forward. Happily, the inherent accuracy of the 425 Express allows you to load the charges for the highest velocity without sacrificing accuracy. Some cartridges give you an "either/or" option of either top velocity or top accuracy, but you can have both with the Express.

A word of caution is in order before addressing specific loads for the Express. The following loads and those shown in the nearby table have been carefully prepared and test-fired. Each extracted case was miked for case head expansion with no swelling whatsoever found. Though there are no pressure signs like flattened primers or ejector impressions on the head, the author specifically cautions that the top loads listed, and the ones following, should be reduced by 10 percent and slowly approached in 2-grain increments while watching carefully for pressure signs. The handloader must understand that load development in wildcat cartridges must be done with even greater care than standard rounds due to the lack of supporting data in recognized reloading manuals. Neither the author nor GUNS ILLUSTRATED assumes any responsibility for results obtained with this reloading data, due to the variations in individual components and techniques of individual handloaders.

The best load for the 400-grain bullets is 73 grains of H-4895 with a Federal #215 Large Magnum Rifle primer. This load clocks 2422 fps from a 22-inch Douglas barrel. It is suspected that velocity should touch 2500 fps from a 24 inch barrel, but that has not been confirmed.

The best load for the 350-grain spitzers is 77 grains of Accurate Arms #2460 with the same Federal #215 primer. The 22-inch test barrel yields 2539 fps with this load for 5011 ft./lbs. of muzzle energy.

A Burris Scout Scope sits atop the reserve iron sights in Ruger detachable rings. The barrel's quarter-rib has Ruger's nifty base slots. This 2¾× scope offers a wide field of view and quick target acquisition.

A Leupold 6× M-8 Compact scope perches in Ruger rings on the Model 77's integral base slots. This is the long range sight of the prototype rifle's "tri-sight" system—two scopes and the irons.

Speaking of muzzle energy, you should ignore this largely irrelevant figure stolen from the professors of physics. While the mass times velocity squared divided by a constant might indeed reveal the "pure" physics, it has no bearing on the killing power of a rifle cartridge. Sir Issac Newton never hunted elk.

A far better indicator of relevant hunting ballistics is the formula devised by African ivory hunter Pondoro Taylor, resulting in the Taylor Knock Out Value, an index which corresponds to the real world of big game hunting. The trouble with the pure physics formula is that it asks you to square the velocity, which might appeal to the Weatherby fanciers, but totally ignores bore diameter, which rankles the Keith followers. The Taylor calculation balances bullet weight, velocity and bore diameter equally.

The 425 Express, according to the laboratory eggheads, is 14 percent more powerful than the 458 Winchester Magnum and 12 percent more powerful than the 375 H&H Magnum. (Yes, the eggheads would have you believe the 375 is "more gun" than the 458.) This is misleading. Here is what the Taylor formula says:

Cartridge	Energy	Taylor Knock Out
375 H&H Mag. (300 gr./2600 fps)	4,504	41
425 Express (400 gr./2400 fps)	5,117	58
425 Express (350 gr./2600 fps)	5,255	55
458 Win. Mag. (500 gr./2000 fps)	4,442	63

Now that's more like it! The 425 Express, with 400 grainers is 30 percent more lethal than the 375 H&H and 8 percent less powerful than the 458 Magnum. Most hunters with experience at killing big game should agree that these figures more closely represent reality in the field.

Though the eggheads might have bamboozeled us with "paper energy," there are two scientific aspects of hunting bullets that are indeed relevant. The figures for sectional density and ballistic coefficient both indicate "real world" performance based on complex mathematical calculations about a bullet's form and flight.

The ballistic coefficient refers to a bullet's ability to overcome wind resistance. Translation: how flat-shootin' it is. The higher the number the better.

The 425 Express has higher BCs in both 350- and 400-grain bullets than either the 375 H&H or the 458 win. Mag.

Bullet/Caliber	BC
500 gr./458	.297
300 gr./375	.282
400 gr./425	.361
350 gr./425	.323

The sectional density refers to how well a bullet retains its energy and velocity. For hunters, the sectional density also reflects the extent of penetration in game animals. A commonly cited example is the 175-grain 7mm bullet and the 180-grain 30-caliber bullet, both of which have nearly identical weights, but the 7mm has an SD of .310 while the 308 bullet has an SD of .271 making the 7mm, theoretically, a better penetrator.

Sectional density is the ratio of a bullet's weight and its diameter. The higher the number the better.

Bullet/Caliber	SD
500 gr./458	.341
300 gr./375	.305
400 gr./425	.319
350 gr./425	.279

The ballistic coefficient and sectional density figures take on significance when analyzing trajectory. And the most important aspect of trajectory is "point blank range," or the distance at which the cartridge can be fired with a spot-on hold at game ani-

Leading custom bullet makers offer .423-in. bullets. Barnes and Cor Bon have the 350-gr. types, but the others stick with 400-gr. slugs originally intended for the 404 Rimless Nitro Express.

mals, without "holding over" or compensating for bullet drop. The point blank range computations for the 425 Express are based on an acceptable impact point of plus-or-minus 6 inches.

The 350-grain spitzer bullet has a maximum point blank range of 350 yards with a zero at 280 yards. At this telescope setting, the bullet strikes 4.67 inches high at 100 yards, spot-on at 280 yards and less than 6 inches low at 350 yards.

The 400-grain roundnose bullet, Barnes' softnose in this case, has a maximum point blank range of 300 yards with a zero at 260 yards. Here, the bullet impacts 4.56 inches high at 100 yards.

All bullet testing for the Express has been conducted on large African game because the designers firmly believe that wet newspaper, clay, sand, duct seal and other artificial mediums are not only irrelevant but also misleading. It is little consolation to know that your bullet with plow through 36 inches of pine boards when you find it swerves from glancing heavy bone. There is only one valid test for hunting bullets—killing game.

The prototype Express safaried in Namibia and South Africa in 1987 and tallied up 11 kills. The author hunted with noted handgun authority Massad Ayoob who, after seeing the 425 in action and, after a disappointing failure with his 375 H&H on a kudu bull, remarked: "I never thought I'd feel under-gunned with a three-seven-five, but that 425 Express is a real killer!"

Does the 425 Express recoil horribly? Not according to several test shooters. J.D. Jones, handgun hunter and developer of wildcat handgun hunting cartridges, fired the prototype rifle and said it was "about like a 375." This was a common comment as most shooters felt the recoil to be equal to that of the old British medium bore. One shooter said the recoil "is a lot less punishing than my 338 Magnum." It is more of a heavy shove than a sharp jab.

Accurate, reliable, hard-hitting. The 425 Express might be the first new cartridge of interest to big game hunters since those glorious days of 30 years ago when we had a new cartridge almost every year for ten years.

425 Express Handloads

400-grain bullet (Barnes roundnose)

Powder Charge	Velocity (fps)	Energy (ft./lbs)	TKO*
73 grs. H-4895	**2422**	**5212**	**58**
73 grs. IMR-4895	2308	4132	56
75 grs. IMR-4895	2368	4982	57
71 grs. IMR-4064	2283	4630	55
74 grs. IMR-4064	2366	4973	57
76 grs. IMR-4064	2371	4994	57
70 grs. AA-2460	2263	4550	55
72 grs. AA-2460	2305	4720	56
76 grs. AA-2460	2399	5113	58
72 grs. WW-760	2056	3755	50
74 grs. WW-760	2120	3993	51
76 grs. WW-760	2154	4122	52

350-grain bullet (Cor-Bon spitzer)

Powder Charge	Velocity (fps)	Energy (ft./lbs.)	TKO*
77 grs. AA-2460	**2539**	**5011**	**54**
75 grs. AA-2460	2476	4767	52
77 grs. IMR-4064	2502	4866	53
79 grs. IMR-4064	2536	4999	54
73 grs. IMR-4320	2396	4463	51
75 grs. IMR-4320	2459	4700	52
75 grs. IMR-4895	2452	4674	52
76 grs. IMR-4895	2455	4685	52
75 grs. WW-760	2189	3725	46
77 grs. WW-760	2209	3793	47
76 grs. H-4895	2462	4712	52
77 grs. H-4895	2492	4827	53

*Taylor Knock-Out Value as described by the author in the text. Bold print indicates the author's suggested load with each bullet.

NOTE: Velocities were recorded 12 feet from the muzzle on a PACT chronograph. The test barrel is a 22-inch Douglas with a 1:14 twist. All loads use Federal #215 Large Rifle Magnum primers. The cases are 300 Win. Mag. from Federal, fire-formed to 425 Express specifications.

425 Express Ammo

Loaded Ammunition

The Hunting Shack
P.O. Box 7465
Missoula, MT 59807
(406) 728-3263

A-Square
Rt.1, Simmons Rd.
Madison, IN 47250
(812) 273-3633

Bullets for Handloaders

A-Square
Rt. 4, Simmons Rd.
Madison, IN 47250
(812) 273-3633

Barnes Bullets
P.O. Box 215
American Fork, UT 84003
(801) 756-4222

Woodleigh Bullets
800 W. Maple Lane
Bensenville, IL 60106
(312) 595-2792

Professional Hunter Sply.
P.O. Box 608
Ferndale, CA 95536
(707) 786-9460

Cor-Bon Custom Bullets
P.O. Box 10126
Detroit, MI 48210
(313) 894-2373

Trophy Bonded Bullets
7704 Kingsley
Houston, TX 77087
(713) 645-4499

Handloading Dies

Redding Reloading
114 Starr Rd.
Cortland, NY 13045
(607) 753-3331

SLUG GUN UPDATE

It wasn't until just a few years ago that the hunter forced to use shotgun slugs for big game had much of a chance of actually hitting his target. Now, there are three domestic ammo makers offering accurate slug loads, and the gunmakers are giving us rifled barrels to shoot them.

by **JON R. SUNDRA**

Sundra's test gun battery consisted of, from left: Winchester 1300 Deer Gun with rifled barrel; Franchi 48-AL smoothbore; Remington 870 SP with Aimpoint 1000; High Standard/E.R. Shaw rifled barrel, with Bushnell 3-9x; and Ithaca's Deerslayer II with Leupold 6x Compact.

Our Big Three ammunition makers (Remington, Federal and Winchester) offer only Foster-type rifled slugs which the author contends are outclassed by several newcomers.

THERE WAS A TIME when the yearly advancements in shotgun slugs and slug guns could be covered in depth on the back of a business card... with room to spare! No more. Today we're talking one of the most dynamic areas of the shooting sports. Take this year, for example: Three major U.S. gun makers—Ithaca, Mossberg and U.S. Repeating Arms—have introduced *rifled* 12-gauge slug guns. Further contributing to the activity, E.R. Shaw, the original developer of the rifled slug barrel, continues to do a booming business fitting barrels and furnishing blanks to both industry and the gunsmithing trade. And the Hastings folks, importers of the French-made Paradox rifled barrels, keep expanding their line of aftermarket accessory barrels for the more popular shotguns.

GUNS ILLUSTRATED 1989 17

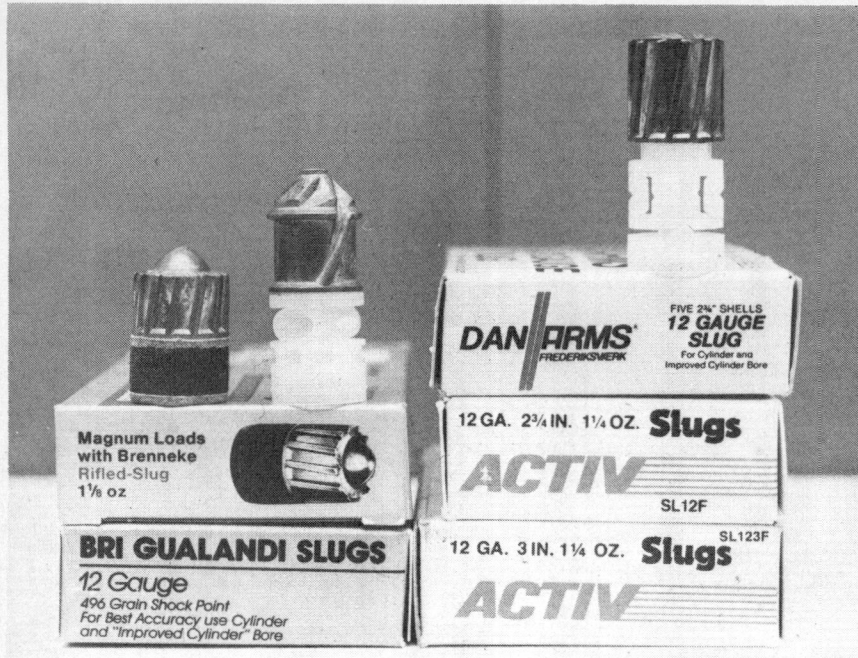

At left is the original Brenneke rifled slug, the design of which dates back to the mid-1890s, and has its base wad screwed to the base. The Italian-made Gualandi (center) and Servo (right), as loaded by Activ and Danarms, are decided improvements.

mount scopes and thus take advantage of the increased range and performance now available to them.

So much for a summary of the high points. Let's now look at some of these new goodies in more detail starting with the guns.

With Ithaca being back in business, the new company has renamed the old reliable Model 37 pump, calling it the Model 87 to commemorate the gun's 50th year of production. In revamping the 87 line, Ithaca chose to go with an optional rifled-barrel version of their well-known Deerslayer. Called Deerslayer II, this new Ithaca has the distinction of being the only "solid frame" rifled slug gun. Unlike the Winchester Model 1300 and Mossberg's Super Slugster, both of which retain their barrel interchangeability feature, Ithaca has chosen to thread their rifled barrels into the receiver; they have that option because theirs is steel while those of its competitors are of aluminum alloy. By permanently threading the 25-inch spout to the receiver, Ithaca loses the versatility of barrel interchangeability, but gains—at least theoretically—in accuracy. All other things equal, a threaded barrel's tighter, more solid mating with the receiver should provide a higher level of accuracy, assuming a conventional receiver-mounted scope.

Ithaca, however, is offering two scope-mounting options. The receiver is drilled and tapped to accept conventional bases, plus there's a steel quarter-rib up on the barrel which serves as a base for the adjustable open sight, as well as scope mounts a la the Ruger

On the ammo scene, the BRI people, originators of the streamlined 50-caliber sabot round, have introduced a 20-gauge, as well as a 12-gauge, 3-inch Magnum version of their revolutionary ... *cartridge* I'd guess you'd call it. Federal recently increased the diameter of their 12-gauge Foster-type slugs from .695- to .729-inch to match the cylinder bore of a 12 gauge gun, thereby increasing accuracy. Activ and Remington now have high-steppin' magnum versions of their 12-gauge slug loadings; Activ a 2¾-inch and Remington a 3-inch version.

Accessory-wise, firms like Aimpoint and B-Square have expanded their offerings of scope mounts to fit most of the popular shotguns without gunsmithing, so shooters can more easily

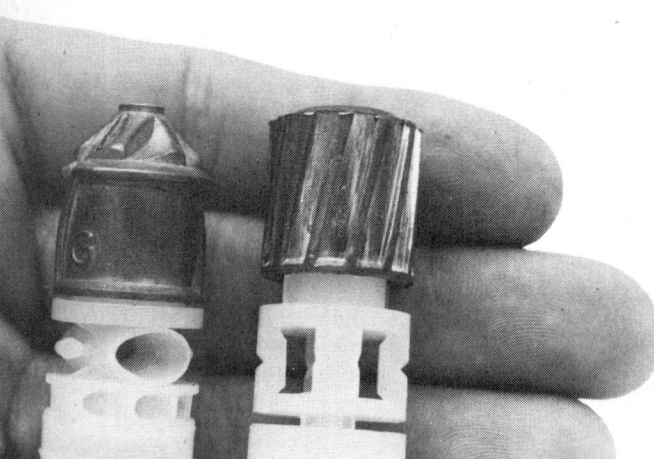

The Gualandi slug at left does not perform as well in rifled bores as the Activ/Danarms, according to Sundra. Both are made in Italy.

Winchester's Model 1300 rifled Deer Gun was a pre-production sample and was not drilled and tapped for scope mounts. Regular production guns will be drilled and tapped, however.

Sundra's test Remington 870 SP Slug Gun was used with the Hastings Paradox interchangeable rifled barrel. An Aimpoint 1000 sight was used in Aimpoint mounts.

Author puts the Ithaca Deerslayer II through its paces. Unlike the Winchester and Mossberg guns, the Deerslayer's barrel is threaded into the receiver, thus precluding the use of other barrels.

No. 1. A barrel-mounted scope makes a lot of sense for interchangeable-barrel guns, but not much for a fixed-tube job like the Deerslayer II. Still, the option's there.

We chose to go with the receiver mount on which we clamped a Leupold 6x Compact in Weaver rings. With scope in place, our test gun weighed 8 pounds, 2 ounces. Like all 87s (and the several million Model 37s already out there), the Deerslayer II features bottom ejection which makes it as well suited for southpaws as it is for right-handers. The buttstock is of the Monte Carlo trap style to furnish more facial support for scope use. For their rifled slug gun, U.S. Repeating Arms called on their popular slide action Model 1300 which they've jazzed up with a Win-Tuf laminated stock and a matte-blue, non-reflective metal finish. Barrel length is 24 inches; nominal weight $6^{3/4}$ pounds, though our sample was closer to 7 pounds.

For this year's guns, USRAC's George Rockwell says only conventional open sights will be offered, but the receiver will be drilled and tapped for scope mount bases. Our pre-production sample, however, was not drilled and tapped so we had to do our testing with the open sights. For 1989, however, George tells us that a barrel extension mount will most likely be incorporated on the production guns. The extension mount is simply a scope mount base attached to the barrel, but which extends back over the receiver to allow the mounting of normal-eye-relief scopes. With the mount being integral with the barrel, the advantage alluded to earlier is afforded—accessory barrels can be interchanged while retaining zero. Of course, with USRAC having interchangeable choke tubes, only one Winchoke-equipped accessory barrel is needed to provide total versatility for upland game, waterfowl and big game.

As for Mossberg's version of the rifled shotgun, theirs is based on the Model 500, the only gun produced these days by the North Haven firm (albeit in enough permutations to fill the company's current 28-page catalog). Unfortunately, we had to satisfy ourselves with information taken from that catalog on what Mossberg is calling its Trophy Slugster because as of editorial deadline no guns were available for testing.

Like the proposed 1989 version of the Winchester Model 1300, the Trophy Slugster's 24-inch rifled barrel will wear an extension scope mount, thereby retaining interchangeability between a zeroed-in barrel for big game and a smoothbore with Accu Chokes for everything else. As with Ithaca's Deerslayer II and USRAC's Model 1300 Deer Gun, the Mossberg will have a 3-inch chamber allowing the use of either $2^{3/4}$ or 3-inch shells. The Trophy Slugster goes a step further in specialization, however, by providing a high-comb buttstock specifically designed for scope use; in fact, there will be no iron sights provided on the Trophy Slugster, that's how confident Mossberg is that everyone will want to mount a scope.

For areas where rifled bores are not allowed—a subject we'll touch upon later—Mossberg is offering the identical Model 500 in smoothbore version. In either configuration, the Trophy Slugster weighs in at $7^{1/4}$ pounds, complete with the recoil pad and QD swivel studs furnished.

So that we'd have as many manufacturers as possible represented for this update, we had E.R. Shaw fit one of their rifled barrels to an old High Standard pump gun, then drill and tap the receiver for Redfield mounts—one of the many gunsmithing services they provide to accompany their mail order barrel-fitting operation. Representing the growing line of Hastings after-market rifled barrels, we alternated one of their 20-inch Paradox tubes for a Remington 870 with the original smoothbore spout that came on the gun, in this case a Model 870 SP (Special Purpose) slug gun.

For a second smoothbore we opted

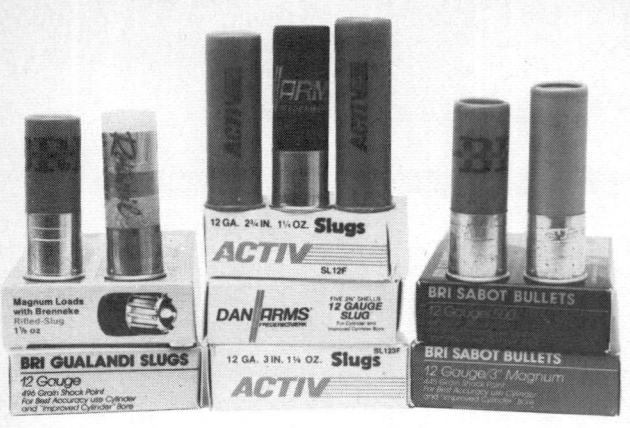

The alternatives to the American Foster-type slugs are these numbers as loaded by BRI, Activ and Danarms. All of them perform better than the Fosters.

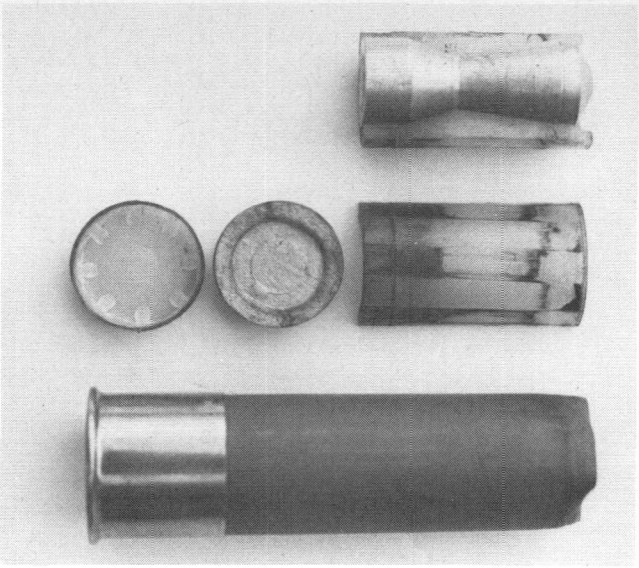

BRI's unique sabot encases a streamlined 50-caliber projectile inside a two-piece nylon sleeve which falls away after exiting the muzzle. A recovered sabot (center) shows rifling marks.

for the Italian-made Franchi AL-48 which wore a 23-inch slug barrel, i.e., reamed Cylinder bore and wearing open sights. The Franchi was the only semi-auto used and the only gun not having a 3-inch chamber. Its Browning-type long recoil action really softens recoil, something that was much appreciated during long sessions at the bench.

Though we had just about every commercial slug load on hand—standard and magnums, sabots, Brenneke and Foster-types—for this update, we wanted to concentrate more on the rifled barrels and those recent ammo developments mentioned at the outset: BRI's 3-inch Magnum Sabot and the 3-inch magnums of Activ, Remington and Federal.

Of our Big Three ammo producers, all of whom load the Foster-type slug (named after the originator), only Remington continues to size their cup-shaped chunk of lead to .695-inch, supposedly to preclude muzzle damage should it be fired through a Full-choke barrel. Problem is that being about .035-inch undersize for the nominal .729-inch Cylinder bore of a 12-gauge gun, the squat slugs can get kinda' cockeyed as they obturate. Bottom line is that they exit the muzzle with less uniform coaxial alignment than if they were dimensioned to match the bore in the first place. That's my theory anyway, based on the bench testing of several hundred rounds of Remington slug ammo through a dozen or more guns, both smoothbore and rifled. Why Federal and Winchester have concluded that sizing their slugs to .730-inch won't present problems for them, while Remington apparently does, I can't say.

Appropriately enough, we tested Remington's 3-inch Magnum slugs through their own Model 870 SP, using both the original smoothbore tube and the rifled Hasting's Paradox accessory barrel. For sights, we mounted an Aimpoint 1000 in Aimpoint's own, no-gunsmithing side mount which uses the two cross-pin holes that hold the 870's trigger assembly in place. It works well, but looks like hell.

Through the original 870 SP smoothbore tube that came with the gun, Remington's Slugger 3-inch Magnums clocked a sizzling 1690 fps through the 20-inch barrel. Group size from benchrest averaged about 9 inches at 75 yards (the distance used for all the Foster-type loads and for those guns sporting iron sights. The rest of the shooting was done at 100 yards). Through the Paradox 20-inch rifled spout, groups averaged 7 inches and velocities 45 fps less than through the bunny barrel—1640.

We also ran Remington's 2¾-inch standard and Magnum loads through both 870 barrels with the Hastings turning in the best groups—6 to 7 inches with the 3-inch Magnums. As a basis for comparison, we fired the 2¾-inch Remington loads through the smoothbore Franchi along with some of Federal's fodder with about the same results: 7-9-inch groups at 75 yards. Allowing an inch or two for the open sights compared to the Aimpoint, both guns and ammo performed about equally.

The Aimpoint, incidentally, makes a lot of sense for a slug gun. With the typical shot averaging much less than 100 yards, the lack of magnification doesn't present a big problem; in fact, it's almost offset by that illuminated dot that can really put you on target quickly. I just may use one this season, if I get a chance to hunt in a slug-only area.

Though Federal's 1¼-ounce 3-inch Magnum load performs better now that they've increased the diameter of the slug, I still couldn't get it to shoot as well as the Winchester stuff. I don't know what it is they do differently out there in East Alton, but over the past 4 years that I've been into slug guns, Winchester's fodder invariably shoots the best of the Foster-types. Some of my colleagues have reported consistent 5 and 6-inch 75-yard groups with both Federal and Remington ammo, but I have never gotten either to shoot that well. And out to 75 yards the Winchester stuff shoots as well out of the bunny barrels as it does through the rifled types.

In keeping with past experiences, the BRI-Gualandi fodder shot right with the Winchester stuff, but only through the smoothbores. That's okay though, because that's how it's supposed to work. The BRI folks import the Italian-made Gualandi slug and load it in their Soquel, California, plant right alongside the 50-caliber Sabots for that overwhelming majority of slug gun shooters who use smoothbores. Not that you can't use the Sabot loads in smooth tubes; the Gualandi's simply outperform them.

It's only when you team up the BRI Sabot loads with the rifled tube that

Even with iron sights, Winchester's Model 1300 with rifled barrel turned in groups like this at 75 yards with the BRI Sabots.

At 75 yards, the BRI Gualandi slugs performed well out of the Remington SP, definitely accurate enough to bring down a deer.

things start to happen. The scope-equpped High Standard/Shaw and the Ithaca Deerslayer II turned in 3 to 4-inch 100-yard groups routinely. Both guns seemed to shoot equally well. Even with the iron sights on the Winchester 1300 I managed groups under 4 inches from 75-yards.

In every case, however, the 2¾-inch BRI Sabots outperformed the 3-inch Magnums. Not by a lot, mind you, but by an inch or so on average. The shorter loads chronographed 1275 fps through the 25-inch Ithaca barrel, while the magnums clocked 1425. Even with the magnums, though, those 5-inch groups at 100 yards make for a 100-yard-plus deer gun.

Also consistent with past experiences, the slug loads of Activ Industries, that up-and-coming shotshell maker in Kearneysville, West Virginia, continue to shoot exceptionally well no matter what gun I put them through. This Brenneke-type projectile, with its attached base wad/cushion, is made in Italy (like the Gualandi) and loaded by Activ. The Danarms people (501 Office Center, Ft. Washington, PA 19034), import the same slug and load it at their ammo factory in Denmark. The result is two brands of ammo loaded with the same slug which perform similarly—which is to say, *great*! Through the Franchi and Remington smoothbores, through the Hastings, Winchester, Ithaca and Shaw rifled barrels, it was all the same to these two loadings.

The Ithaca Deerslayer II turned in these excellent 100-yard groups with both Activ and Danarms ammunition.

We're talking 6 to 7-inch groups from a scoped smoothbore at 100 yards and 5 to 6-inch groups through a rifled tube. Velocity for the 1¼-ounce slugs through the Winchester 1300's 24-inch rifled barrel proved to be 1445 fps

GUNS ILLUSTRATED 1989 **21**

These 100-yard groups are not uncommon when using a rifled barrel and the BRI Sabots. These sub-3-inch groups were fired through a Shaw barrel.

Today's slug gun hunter has had a whole new dimension of performance opened to him in just the last few years. However, check your local hunting laws before using a rifled shotgun.

for the Danarms fodder and 1480 for Activs. The smoothbores averaged only slightly higher.

The new 3-inch Activ Magnum averaged just over 140 fps faster than the short stuff, but didn't group quite as well. Still, I wouldn't hesitate to recommend any of the three loadings for deer and black bear on out to 100 yards.

The only Brenneke-type slug that did not shoot up to past standards was the Brenneke itself, loaded by Rotweil of West Germany. We didn't have as much of the Brenneke ammo on hand as we did the others, but the 8 to 10-inch groups we punched with a rifled bore from 75 yards, and 7 to 8-inch groups from a smoothbore, were about 20 percent larger than we had gotten with previous lots of ammo.

The data resulting from firing several hundred rounds for this article simply confirmed past conclusions: There are more accurate and versatile slug loads available than the Foster types loaded by our Big Three companies. With factory production rifled shotguns now a reality, I think Federal, Remington and Winchester would do well to start thinking about improving their respective products or content themselves as being also-rans.

As great as the BRI Sabots shoot through rifled bores, the performance of loads now being offered by Activ, Danarms and Gualandi aren't too far behind accuracy-wise... and they do it in smoothbores which today surely accounts for at least 98 percent of the slug guns out there. As for maximum range and flatness of trajectory, however, the BRI Sabots win hands down if one's thinking beyond 90 or 100 yards.

On the legality of rifled slug barrels, I'm told that Ohio, Michigan and Wisconsin have yet to rule on them. New York recently okayed it but that doesn't guarantee the hold-outs will follow suit. In the meantime, if you haven't yet done any experimenting with the new brands and types of slug loads now available, you're in for one helluva surprise. ●

IT SEEMS LIKE every big-bore-forty-four has its own marketing strategy. Ruger's Super Redhawk features brute strength by way of heavy investment castings in highly critical areas. The Dan Wesson series has a fine array of interchangeable barrels fine tuned to the most discriminating shooter. Smith & Wesson's claim to fame is her tough Model 29, mentioned what seems zillions of times already by way of close association with a cocky detective named Harry Callahan.

Over the years we've seen variations on a theme all brought forward by request or design to fit a particular need or job. The Model 29 is an excellent case in point. What started out as a gleam in Elmer Keith's eye has now progressed from carbon steel to stainless steel to the recently introduced Classic Hunter covered in this report. From her vivacious underlug barrel to her sexy non-fluted cylinder, this particular model is aimed at one pretty specific market—the field hunter. But let's back up a bit for some insight into the Model 29s colorful history.

I don't think many will contest the fact that Elmer Keith was the person instrumental in achieving his goal of "upgrading" the 44 Special to magnum status. Starting the ball rolling some 35 years ago, he spread his desires to people in high places at both Smith & Wesson and Remington Arms.

Smith & Wesson's New Classic Hunter

This new offering from the folks who brought us Dirty Harry's gun of choice should be just the ticket for the handgun hunter who wants something just a little different, right from the factory. It's a handsome brute that performs as good as it looks.

by STANLEY W. TRZONIEC
Photos by the author

What almost seems like a backward way of doing things, Keith initially talked to execs at Remington in hopes of getting them to produce a heavy 44-caliber loading. Consisting of a 250-grain bullet powered by 18.5 grains of 2400, the Remington folks were receptive to the idea. However, they had second thoughts of stoking some of the older triple locks with that particular loading. It was then that Keith suggested that the case be made about 1/10-inch longer (same as the 38 versus 357, introduced in 1935) so those out there with less than their share of God given intelligence would not try stuffing the loads up the pipe of older 44 Specials. Again, the answer was yes, but Remington would be a lot happier if a new gun was introduced to better serve the purpose.

The behind-the-scenes action was starting to gain steam and in 1954 the first toolroom gun was assembled for feasibility testing. Things worked out for the better, and almost 18 months later—in December, 1955— the first full production guns were starting to come down the line. Available with a 6½-inch barrel, blued or nickel, the guns met with moderate success.

Since then, we've seen a multitude of changes, modifications, finishes and materials used in the making of today's Model 29. We've seen it go from a "four screw" to a "three screw" sideplate model, a small run of 5-inch barrels, threading on the extractor changed from right to left hand to prevent its unscrewing outward during recoil. New cylinder stops were on the board in 1961 and in 1970 production was increased dramatically by 400 percent just by a movie showing a hot rod police officer doing his duty with a Model 29 on his shoulder! Stainless steel was (is) in vogue, so in 1980 we witnessed 629s coming out of the Springfield plant in great numbers. In all, from that 1955 introduction, dozens of variations and modifications were made, making the Model 29 44 Magnum the gun it is today.

Happy with the success rate of the 357 L-frame guns introduced in recent times, Smith went about to bring on line the same type of gun design-wise in 44 bore. Termed the Classic Hunter, she is presently available in blue only, 6-inch barrel and, for a change, has Hogue rubber grips as standard equipment. Please remember, this Classic Hunter is an *addition* to the Model 29 lineup; all other models currently made will remain in production for those shooters who may still want to use more traditional guns. Price, as this is written, will be around $475.00, retail.

When you first look at this gun you are impressed. Even just laying there on the dealer's counter gets the blood boiling. The Classic Hunter is different in appearance. No, not a radical

One of the distinctive features of the new S&W Classic Hunter is the smooth, unfluted cylinder. Though it looks stronger than a fluted cylinder, handloaders should note that it really isn't; home-brews should be kept to the same intensity as normal loads.

change mind you, for she is still the basic N-frame 44 Magnum that we all have become familiar with over the years. Perhaps, rather than the traditional looks, its the un-traditional look that gets your attention.

First off, the cylinder will catch your eye. It is unfluted, smooth to the touch and a very handsome addition to the gun. In keeping with the rounded lines of the barrel, that cylinder is there more for additional weight (or heft) than anything else. For the hunter coming on sight of a big game animal, this added mass will be appreciated, especially after a long and

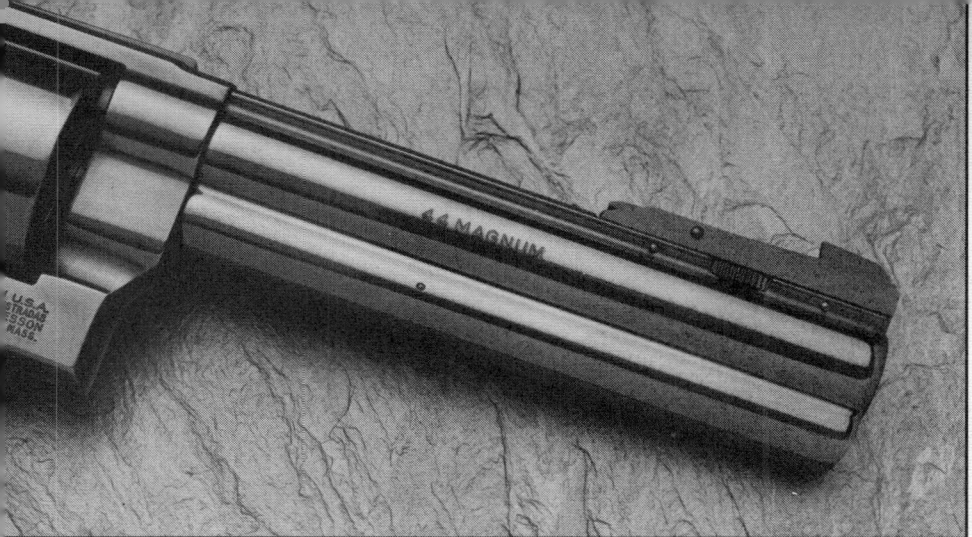

The full-length underlug of the Classic Hunter gives a muzzle-heavy feel to the gun and adds to its good looks. The overall high polish is excellent and greatly enhances the appearance.

The rear sight on the Classic Hunter is the old faithful S&W style that is adjustable for both windage and elevation. The top of the frame and barrel are matted and grooved to reduce reflections. Both trigger and hammer are of the wide target style.

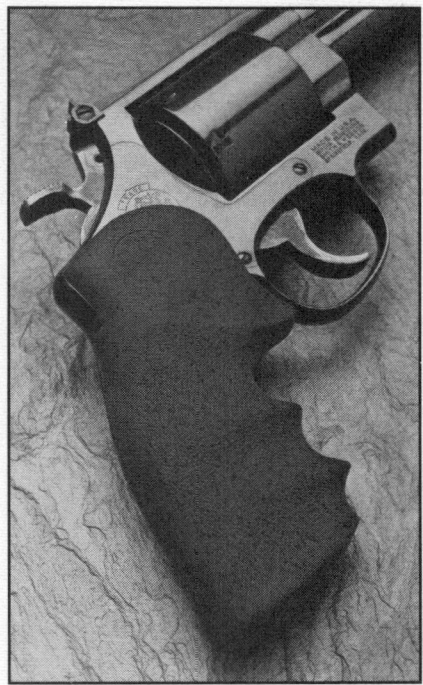

For the first time in S&W history, the grips are from an outside vendor. The Hogue Monogrip is all rubber, has a non-slip surface, and has finger grooves built in. This is another eye-catching feature of this new handgun.

sometimes winded stalk.

With this non-fluted cylinder, it should be stressed here and now that handloaders who think they can pump up their favorite reloads to higher velocities (and pressures) had better think again. Though this new cylinder *looks* stronger, in reality there is no difference in engineered dimensions between this Classic Hunter and standard Model 29 fluted cylinders. Cylinder walls, distance between charge holes and bolt cuts are all the same. In fact, I am starting to hear rumblings relative to the fact that because the cylinder is slightly heavier, it now may be possible that on rapid double-action employment for prolonged sessions over extended periods, the force necessary to stop this momentum at every charge hole could accelerate wear on cylinder bolt cuts, thereby setting the timing off somewhat. Only time, usage and possible recall notices could bear this out. So, it goes without saying that only industry standard commercial ammunition or handloads within that range should be used. If you present Model 29 is happy with what you are now feeding it, stay with the same menu.

The second part of this new look is the barrel. Termed a "heavy barrel" by many, it is to a certain extent, as in heavy weight—not in diameter as in target barrels. Due in part to an integral underlug, when picked up by the grip, first impressions do point to that of a target gun; definitely muzzle heavy. The barrel is polished bright like the rest of this premium gun, and it has a cut to protect the extractor rod and a nicely detailed top rib on which is set an adjustable front sight.

Four position in nature, I believe this type of sight was first introduced on longer $10^{5/8}$-inch Smiths a few years back. This variation was a silhouette-type Model 29. Later we saw this same type of sight on L-frame 586 and 686 357s. In any event, the sight is keyed for ranges from 50 to 150 yards while using a 240-grain projectile. Though I think it's a swell idea to put this type of front sight on a handgun, to me it is like driving in the fog above the speed limit. You are over extending yourself. This gun and cartridge, in even the very best hands (and eyes), is a 50- to 100-yard gun at best. For my type of shooting here in New England, it looks like if I want to fool around with the settings, numbers 1 and 4 would be best. Out hunting, it would be another story; use one setting and compensate for bullet drop, for I'm afraid even in stand hunting you're not going to have time to change from one sight setting to another if something pops up in front of you.

The front blade is Patridge in style,

the rear blade is void of a white outline and, regardless of any shortcomings mentioned above, the combination gives a good sight picture. Rear sights are standard Smith & Wesson, and are adjustable for both windage and elevation. By the way, Smith does include an Allen wrench and a special tool for use on either sighting fixture for changes. The hammer is target style, very handy in the woods for cocking with gloves on. The trigger is also of target style, wide and grooved, and as this gun is meant to be fired single action, we don't have to worry about "finger roll" off the face as is often desired in double-action shooting.

Last, a set of rubber Hogue Monogrips are included with this Classic Hunter. This is the first time a Smith & Wesson has been made and shipped with a pair of grips other then those made (from wood) right there on the premises. Like anything else, grips tend to be very subjective in both appeal and use, and, if for some reason they don't fit your hand or style, what you'll have to do to get the regular Smith target grips to fit is to order a "stock pin" from the parts department. This is the little crosspin that fits into the hole on the bottom of the grip frame; its function is to keep the wood grips from shifting under recoil. The Hogue grips are semi-soft to the touch, have a non-slip texture. They are easily removed for cleaning by simply removing the base screw and slipping them downward and off. The attaching stirrup stays on the gun, centering the Monogrip as it is reattached.

In order to get a better insight on how this new offering performs in the field, a simple range plan was set up. Instead of running through countless combinations of various bullets, primers, cases and propellants, I picked one load—22.0 grains of 2400—topped off with a good assortment of popular 240-grain hunting bullets. This load was Elmer Keith's favorite with heavy bullets so with some of the variables taken care of, we could concentrate on just one—outright bullet performance. Checking my inventory of bullets, I found samples of 240-grain offerings from Hornady, Speer, Sierra and Remington. For those who have not gotten the word, Remington is back in the component business and with a shipment of 240-grain semi-jacketed hollow points fresh in from the plant in Arkansas, I was ready to go.

As much as I tried to stay within hunting guidelines in bullet selection for this big Smith, there were cross-

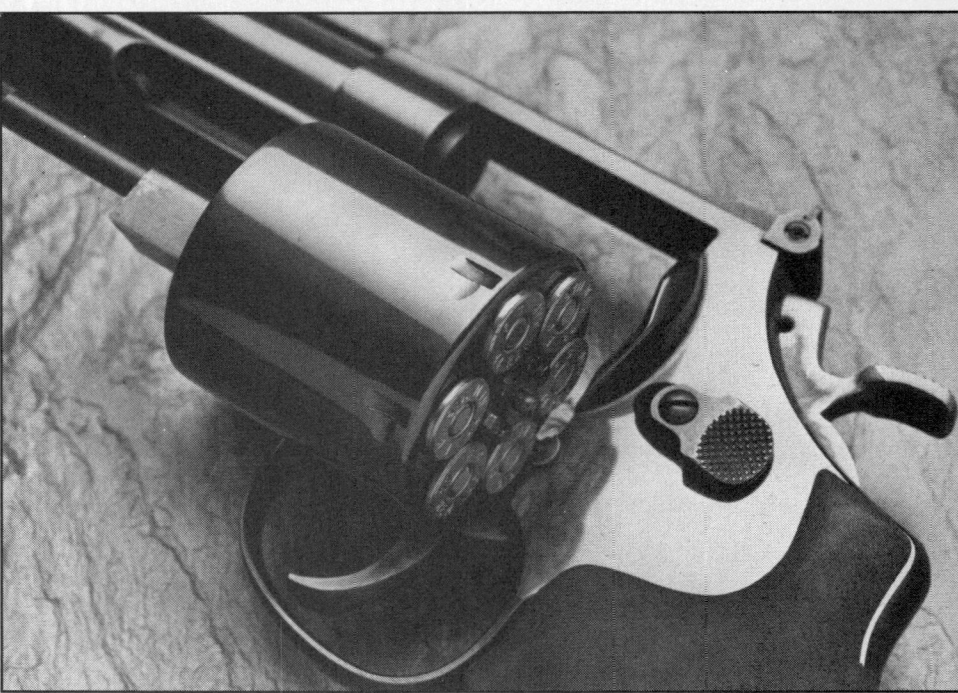

Over the years S&W handguns have seen many modifications and the Classic Hunter shows another—the cylinder chambers are not counter-bored. With modern ammunition being as reliable as it is, this seems to make sense.

overs where I used both silhouette and hunting styles. Of these, Hornady's JTC-SIL and Sierra's slightly heavier 250-grain FPJ got the nod. They were included in the testing.

Cases were all Federal, ditto on the primers. Their #155 Magnum primers were used to insure complete ignition. All cases, even though they were brand new, were run through the sizing die, then slightly belled and primed. For uniformity, all cases were charged in one sitting, thus discounting any weather problems (hot, cold, humidity) from upsetting the final charge ratio. Lyman's trusty #55 powder measure was used, and every fifth round checked for weight on the RCBS #304 scale. Crimping was heavy to not only prevent bullet move-

Bullet/Style	O.A.L. (in.)	Velocity (fps)	Accuracy (in.)
Range Results 44 Magnum S & W Classic Hunter 240 Grain Bullets			
Hunting			
Hornady HP	1.630	1351	2.50
Remington SJHP	1.590	1389	2.25
Sierra JHC	1.590	1372	2.37
Speer JSP	1.580	1378	2.00
Speer JMHP	1.590	1379	2.00
Remington factory	1.580	1296	2.00
Hunting/Silhouette			
Hornady JTC-SIL	1.600	1389	1.87
Sierra FPJ*	1.580	1355	1.75
Lead			
Hornady SWC	1.650	1447	2.75
Speer SWC	1.650	1428	3.00

*This bullet weighs 250 grains. All Federal cases were used, with Federal #155 Magnum primers.
Reduce all loads by at least 10 percent before using them in your gun.

The front sight is adjustable for four positions and was borrowed from S&W's long-barreled Model 29. It's a neat feature, but of little use to the hunter.

At the range, Trzoniec found the Classic Hunter to be a good performer at the 50-yard mark. To get consistent results, he clamped the gun in the Ransom Rest. The gun shoots as good as it looks!

ment from recoil, but to keep velocities in line. For hunters reading this article, the test distance was 50 yards, not 25, to get a better picture of gun/bullet performance. And, to add some integrity to all this, the Classic Hunter was locked down in a Ransom Rest and all velocities clocked over a Southwest Instruments chronograph. The results of this testing are shown in a table nearby.

I don't think it was much of a surprise to see that the "silhouette-hunting"-type bullets edged out straight hunting-type projectiles in the accuracy department. In order for you to remain competitive in these events, everything, including bullets, must be in the highest state of tune. With regular bullets, however, both Speer entries led the pack, followed by Remington, Sierra and Hornady. Lead bullets were erratic, as the best I could muster was $2^{3}/_{4}$- to 3-inch groups, even though they had the highest velocities. And, speaking of velocities, note how consistent all the loads were across the board. The surprise of the day was Remington factory ammo, blasting out of the muzzle slightly slower than my handloads, and grouping into tight 2-inch circles. Since these figures represent groups fired from a machine rest, hopefully it doesn't take long for the educated field hunter to realize that at 100 yards, freehand and breathing hard from a long stalk, his groups are going to be larger. All I can say is practice, practice, practice! Nevertheless, I see great potential for this new Smith & Wesson Classic Hunter.

For those shooters wanting a heavier N-framed 44 Magnum, this is going to be a first choice. Handgun hunters will jump with joy over the fact that for once someone thought of them in both additional weight and moisture resistant grips. Whether or not this gun fits any of your needs is up to you, but the fact of the matter is that Smith & Wesson has brought another Model 29 on line. That should make us all happy!

Following the lead of the Distinguished Magnum 357s, the Model 29 Classic Hunter is almost a twin in outward appearance. Buyers can interchange wood stocks with the addition of a small cross-pin.

The Navy Arms LeMat replica is superbly finished and unlike any Colt or Remington replica. This is a Civil War-era revolver that shoots nine 44-cal. balls and a shotgun barrel full of whatever a resourceful Confederate cavalryman could stuff down that big hole.

Disassembly is not quite as simple as with a wedge-system Colt, but it's nothing to make life especially difficult. Note the threads toward the rear of the cylinder/shotgun barrel which keep things together.

LeMat

Some good ideas come along at the wrong time. Dr. LeMat's revolver was unique and innovative, but it would be hard to imagine a worse time for any gun to have lasting impact.

by RICK L. FINES

DR. LEMAT'S CREATION could do everything Colt's and Remington's best revolvers could do—but the LeMat could do it nine times instead of six. If nine 44-caliber balls didn't get the job done, the LeMat's fat cylinder revolved around a shotgun barrel that could be selected with a flick of the thumb. With Queen Victoria's England fighting wars all over the globe, the Europeans violently disagreeing and a bit of shooting going on in the American West, one would think that a revolver with the LeMat's firepower would have found buyers waiting in line. It never happened. Some good ideas come along at the wrong time. Dr. LeMat's revolver was unique and innovative, but it would be hard to imagine a worse time or a worse place than the American Civil War and the Confederacy for any gun design to have lasting impact. Still, it's surprising that the LeMat concept wasn't

The firing selector is shown thumbed to the shotgun barrel fire position. With the shot tube selected, no rear sight is available—or needed for a target smaller than a large horse. The selector is pulled back to fire the ball-loaded cylinder.

picked up by one of the dozens of handgun manufacturers of the late 19th century.

As a replica, the Navy Arms LeMat is a breath of fresh black powder smoke. For about 30 years, longer than the originals were in production, more Colt and Remington copies have come out of Italy than ever left the factories at Hartford or Ilion. Except for differences in quality, they have all looked much the same. This Navy Arms LeMat replica looks like nothing designed in any Yankee armory.

Like the Gatling gun, the LeMat was the invention of a doctor. Patented in the U.S. in 1856 by Dr. Jean Alexandre Francois LeMat of New Orleans, the first LeMat revolvers were said to have been turned out by John Krider of Philadelphia. Later, with the Civil War on the horizon, Dr. LeMat was aided by Pierre Gustave Toutant Beauregard, a Union Army officer, also from New Orleans, who later "went South," became one of the C.S.A.'s best-known generals and, later, a successful Reconstruction politician. Dr. Charles F. Girard was instrumental in establishing LeMat production in Paris, France, and later assumed business control of the LeMat venture.

Reference sources differ, with suggestions that some LeMats were produced at Birmingham, England, and some in France. Others say the LeMats were all carried across the Channel from France to England, where they were proofed and accepted by C.S.A. purchasing agents, then shipped to Bermuda in British-flag merchant ships, run through the Union's naval blockade of Confederate ports, and finally landed in the Confederate States.

Dr. LeMat's arms were made in two 44-caliber variations with 65-caliber smooth-bore barrels, a 32 with a 41-caliber smooth-bore tube, and a revolving carbine. Differences were minor, and related to the loading lever latch, trigger guard and barrel release details.

The French influence clearly shows in the LeMat design, as the percussion LeMat lockwork and all other design features are virtually identical to the French LeFaucheux pinfire revolvers.

Following the American Civil War, commercial production continued on a very limited scale in France and Belgium, with a notable lack of commercial success. It would seem that leftover parts were assembled and the design was forgotten.

The Navy Arms LeMat replicas come in three versions called the Cavalry, Army and Navy Models, all differing slightly, as did the originals. At 3½ pounds empty, the LeMat is quite a handful, but doesn't feel as heavy as the 55-ounce heft would suggest. Balance is quite good—only a scale would tell the shooter how heavy the LeMat really is. The only adverse handling quality relates to the hammer spur—it's a bit clumsy to thumb back without shifting one's grip, and requires a good bit of strength.

The feel of the LeMat is similar to that of a Colt Dragoon-sized replica. After handling the LeMat, an 1860 Army-sized revolver seems more like a pocket pistol. While complaints relating to bulk and handling qualities might have been a detriment on paper, the incredible advantage of 10 quick shots—when most military arms fired one at a time—would have ruled out any real objections from people who made a living shooting at other people.

The LeMat concept is remarkably simple. The shotgun barrel is actually a greatly oversized cylinder pin, and is firmly and deeply threaded to the revolver frame. Because the cylinder pin is so large, there's room for nine 44-caliber chambers. Takedown is not quite as simple as with the familiar Colt wedge system, in that a spring-retained pin must be withdrawn at the lower front of the frame, then the rifled barrel must be unscrewed and pulled forward and over the shotgun barrel. The threads that retain the rifled barrel are located on the forward band and engage mating threads at the tip of the shot barrel. The cylinder is then pulled forward and away from the shot barrel. The hammer is fitted with a pivoting nose piece which is left in the conventional position to fire the nine 44 chambers, and flipped up to fire the percussion cap on the shot barrel. The rammer is conventional, save for being mounted on the side of the barrel for want of another place to put it. A detachable ramrod, which seems too short to be useful, is carried within the rammer lever for use in stuffing the shot barrel.

The unique LeMat design is most surprising in that the design enjoyed no success following the South's surrender. In an era when percussion revolvers were still in common use, and when virtually every arms patent was gleefully infringed, an improved LeMat would have been an answer to all sorts of questions asked in the American West and in the far reaches of Victoria Regina's British Empire. The

Top—A nine-shot 44-cal. revolver with a shotgun tube for close encounters might sound as though wheels would be needed to move the piece. Not so. Overall LeMat handling characteristics are about the same as for a Colt Dragoon. Above—The 20th-century rubber band holding the loading lever in place addresses the fact that the loading lever retention spring wanted to fall off.

top-break revolver technology of the early cartridge era would have been simple to adapt to the LeMat concept. We can only wonder at what a LeMat-styled Smith & Wesson top-break, nine-shot 44/20 gauge would have done to Colt Peacemaker sales.

Most Confederate-made revolvers were, like modern black powder handguns, direct copies of Colt/Remington designs. Other Confederate arms, like modern third-world armament, amounted to whatever could be found that would shoot. Suggestions that the LeMat was a "standard" Confederate sidearm are fanciful, considering the few LeMats that managed to slip through the very effective Union Naval blockade. Only a few thousand LeMat revolvers were contracted for and estimates suggest that, at best, a few hundred made it to General Lee's troops.

Like all Navy Arms products, the LeMat replica isn't just well done—the execution is superb. Because the LeMat is assembled and tested in the U.S., the usual several dozen Italian proof marks are absent. The top of the barrel is nicely roll engraved "Col. LeMat," and surrounded with a scroll design. "44 cal" is scrolled on the right side of the 7½-inch octagonal rifled barrel. The deeply stamped "Navy Arms, Ridgefield, N.J. U.S.A." is caried discreetly, in very small letters, on the left side of the barrel, but is concealed by the loading lever. The overall effect does not announce REPLICA, as with most modern black powder arms, but does discourage fakers from "aging" this fine replica.

Finish is blue, with color case-hardened hammer, trigger and barrel firing selector. Grips are dense, crisply diamond-checkered walnut, tightly fitted, with an eggshell oil finish and no checkering run-outs.

The only mechanical criticisms relate to the original design—not to the Navy Arms rendition. The entire rammer/loading lever was something of an afterthought to the original pinfire French design. A spring clip retains the loading lever in the stowed

Discharging the shot barrel is a memorable experience; any adversary should have had the good sense to run or surrender . . . It's surprising that the novel design wasn't more popular during the Civil War, and after.

Navy Arms offers three variations of the LeMat revolver, top to bottom, Army, Navy and Cavalry.

position. The clip is secured to the side of the barrel with a screw seated in a shallow, tapped hole. On the test sample LeMat, the screw was so short that it engaged only one thread, and was impossible to properly tighten without risk of stripping. The concern about losing parts from this expensive replica—on loan—accounts for the garish, 20th-century rubber band visible near the muzzle in the nearby shooting photos. The loading lever never really felt happy with its task, pivoted from an off-center position on the side of the barrel.

Before stripping the LeMat, I noticed the lack of bolt cuts in the cylinder and wondered how positive chamber indexing was achieved. Pulling the revolver apart solved that mystery. While the hand and ratchet are about the same as found in any other revolver, a small spring-loaded pin engages a detent near each of the nine chambers as the LeMat is cocked. I doubt that this arrangement is as durable as Colt/Remington practice, but it also means that no dragging bolt will etch an unsightly ring around the deep blue on the cylinder.

Though the LeMat holds a great deal of powder, ball and shot, the chambers are not the bottomless holes of the Walker class. A 15-grain charge of FFFg black powder, behind a Speer .451-in. round ball, seemed appropriate. Rather than the traditional smear of grease or lard at the front of the cylinder to prevent all nine chambers from emptying at once, I used Wonder Wads and eliminated some of the gooey mess. The smooth-bore tube was loaded with something other than the suggested Navy Arms load of a single 65-caliber round ball. Considering that the original LeMat was intended to fire shot from that big hole, it seemed reasonable to do so with this replica. Besides, I didn't have any balls that size. A half-dozen #4 shot pellets with a greasy wad of cotton waste did a good job and was more representative of what a Rebel cavalryman would have stuffed down that hole.

It's a good thing it doesn't have to be done as often, because loading the LeMat requires a good bit more patience than more mundane Colt-style revolvers. The balls almost—but don't quite line up with chambers and the rammer. Remember to hold your mouth right. Because of the oddly articulated afterthought loading lever, the result is more deformation of the lead balls than would be the case with other style replicas.

These comments are not to suggest that Navy Arms did a bad manufacturing job, or that Dr. LeMat designed a lemon. Considering that LeMat had to contend with Frenchmen, Englishmen, the small matter of a Union naval blockade and full-scale war, it's amazing that he managed to do as well as he did.

The .451-in. ball, wad and 15-grain FFFg charge left about ¼-inch of space to spare after the charge was firmly rammed into place. Navy Arms suggests that no more than a 25-grain FFFg charge be fed to the smoothbore tube, but the literature that came with the LeMat made no specific suggestion for the 44 barrel. Other Navy Arms literature suggests 20 to 30 grain FFFg black powder loads for Colt or Remington-type revolvers, so my 15-grain dose imposed no great strain on the LeMat or the shooter.

With my light loads and the heavy LeMat, recoil was slight and the LeMat was pleasant to shoot. Sights were typical of the era—terrible—with a blued bead front and a hammer notch at the rear. With the shot barrel selector flipped up, the rear sight is obscured. It would be difficult to suggest that a sight is needed with that shot barrel. Because of a ball deformation and rudimentary sights, no effort was made to prove that the LeMat was capable of chasing a Colt Gold Cup off the range. This replica is an exercise in history and engineering that "might have been"—not something with which to punch paper.

Navy Arms makes not only a replica of one of the rarest and most interesting Confederate arms, the LeMat is among the most superbly crafted replicas I have ever examined. I'm certain the C.S.A. purchasing agents would have accepted all the LeMats that Val Forgett could supply. Considering that Navy Arms' trademark is the logo of the Confederate States Navy, the C.S.A. purchasing agents would have felt right at home. ●

by TOM TURPIN

The author and his mighty Cape buffalo where he fell. These old bulls live in the thickest bush and a good, heavy-caliber double rifle like this Heym 470 is as close to ideal as one can get for digging them out.

DOUBLE RIFLES Aren't Dead!

Long favored by African hunters, the double rifle was almost at the brink of extinction a few years ago. Now that commercial ammunition is once again available, the noble double is making a slow but sure comeback.

THERE ARE VARIOUS types of firearms that, merely upon hearing the type, immediately conjure up visions of historical usage. When one hears "Single Action Army," or "Peacemaker," or "Frontier," the thought process automatically turns to cowboys. When a Winchester lever-action rifle is mentioned, one thinks immediately of a saddle carbine and riding the range. The passing mention of a Kentucky rifle elicits thoughts of Daniel Boone and coon-skin caps. So it is with the double rifle as well.

When one hears, sees, or even thinks about those twin rifled tubes and sausage-long cartridges, only one thought can possibly come to mind—Africa and charging jumbo, cape buffalo and rhino!

Each of these firearms have seen a resurgence of interest among the shooting public during the past few years. The single-action revolver, after lying dormant for a number of years except within the collector field, was

All ready for a day in the African bush, this hunter is armed with a large-caliber double rifle and is ready for anything from impala to dinosaur.

Gun writer Jim Woods demonstrates the proper method of preparing for a quick reload with a double rifle. Note the two 470 N.E. rounds held between the fingers of his left hand. After a quick left and right, it is a simple matter to break open the action with the right hand, let the ejectors kick out the empties, and quickly drop the two rounds with the left hand. With practice, double rifles are quick to reload.

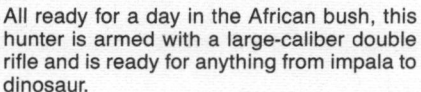

Craig Boddington, editor or Petersen's *Hunting Magazine,* regularly carries this 470 double when on safari. Built by C.W. Andrews in the 1920s, it's still in excellent condition.

reintroduced by Bill Ruger. Not long after Ruger's success, many companies followed suit and offered copies of the famous Colt to the trade. Even the original manufacturer, Colt, reintroduced the handgun to the public.

Lever-action rifles, thanks to Marlin, Savage and Winchester (later USRAC), never died completely. However, we have also witnessed a renewed interest in this type rifle.

The Kentucky rifle, along with other famous types of muzzleloaders, has really come of age again. Many states are now offering special hunting seasons limited to the old charcoal burners or modern replicas thereof.

We can now add the double rifle as well. When, several years ago, Kynoch announced that they would no longer manufacture ammunition for the traditional British double rifles, it was thought by many, perhaps most, to be the death knell for that type of rifle. With ammo no longer being made for the 577 Nitro Express, 470, 500/465, 450/400 and many others, their usefulness as a hunting rifle waned considerably. There remained considerable collector interest, both in the rifles and in the ammo, but practical usage came to a screeching halt. A few, primarily professional hunters, who had squirreled away sufficient stocks of ammo to last awhile, continued to use their doubles. Most hunters of dangerous game, however, converted to bolt-action express rifles chambered for the 458 Winchester or 460 Weatherby Magnum.

During the hiatus, the double never really died, but came very close. A few Continental gunmakers, primarily German, Austrian and Belgian, continued to produce a few doubles, although most often in the over/under version rather than the traditional side-by-side type. They were also usually chambered for smaller calibers, with the 9.3x74R, a metric caliber comparable to the 375 H&H flanged, being about the largest caliber available. A few of the old British calibers were chambered in rifles turned out by individual gunmakers, but very few indeed. The world renowned British firms that survived turned out the occasional double, usually chambered for the 458 Winchester, but the heyday for these guns was basically over.

In the past 3 or 4 years however, we have seen a number of newly manufactured double rifles on the market. Many are chambered for the 375 H&H

An example of a contemporary double rifle from Europe, this Heym is chambered for the 9.3 × 74R cartridge. This sidelock exhibits traditional Germanic styling.

Author Turpin (left) and hunting companion Jim Duffy taking a break on safari in Zimbabwe. Turpin is armed with a 470 double rifle, while Duffy is carrying a custom Winchester Model 70 in 375 H&H.

One of the finest (and most expensive) double rifles ever made is this F.W. Heym gun. It was number three in the "Guns of the Big Five" series, sponsored by Safari Club International. It was auctioned at SCI's annual convention and went for an astonishing $65,000.

Austria. As far as I am aware, the second to do so was the West German factory of F.W. Heym. The Belgian firms Lebeau Corally and Domoulin also added the 470 to their line of doubles. Others followed shortly thereafter. All in all, the double rifle is experiencing a revival in popularity as a using rifle, and there are many excellent reasons why it should. These reasons are so good that I don't believe it would have ever practically died had ammo continued to be available.

Why didn't the availability of doubles chambered for the 458 Winchester cartridge save the popularity of the double as a hunting rifle? When or 458 Winchester, both rimless cartridges and, as such, somewhat unsuitable for double rifles. Many, however, are being chambered for the "obsolete" rimmed British cartridges, primarily the 470 Nitro Express. One of the most popular and effective of the Nitro Express calibers, the 470 died a premature death only because of the unavailability of ammunition.

This situation changed when Jim Bell of Brass Extrusion Laboratories Ltd. began offering loaded 470 ammo to the market. Jim had been making new brass cases for the 470 and many other obsolete calibers for several years. That helped, of course, but didn't solve the problem. The availability of loaded ammunition however, was another story. It breathed a spark of life into the 470 that is getting stronger with each passing year. When loaded ammo became available, we began seeing more and more new double rifles appearing on the market.

To my knowledge, the first factory to offer newly manufactured double rifles chambered for dangerous game calibers, was Franz Sodia of Ferlach, Winchester introduced the 458, it was intended to duplicate 470 ballistics, although in my experience, it never quite made it. Still, the 458 is a dangerous-game caliber and in wide use in Africa and elsewhere. The reason is quite simple. It is simply a matter of a rimmed case vs. a rimless case. The double rifle is basically a life insurance policy for dangerous-game hunting. As such, it must function properly. Several companies made doubles chambered for rimless cartridges, and they built the rimless extractor as good as it can be made. However, none

One of the best places in the U.S. to start looking for a quality double rifle is with this man, George Caswell of Champlin Firearms. Caswell always has a large selection of the guns on hand, as well as other quality rifles and shotguns.

were as good and as positive, nor could they be, as a rimmed-case extractor. Pressure is also considerably higher in the 458 than with the 470, and bolt guns can safely withstand significantly higher chamber pressures than a double rifle. No, double rifles and rimmed cases go together like ham and eggs.

For someone accustomed to using a bolt action rifle, or, lever action and single shots for that matter, there are a few differences with double rifles that one should know and understand.

First of all, a double rifle, much like a woman, is very fickle. They are not nearly as forgiving as most other rifle types. A double rifle is regulated by its maker, that is the barrels are adjusted to place a shot from each barrel as close as possible to each other at a given range. This is done with one powder, one bullet weight, one case, and one primer. Change any one of the components of the load, or more often, use another load, and chances are very good, if not certain, that the gun will not shoot each barrel together. Simple things, done as a matter of routine with other types of rifles, like adding a recoil pad, can and usually do adversely affect the grouping of a double rifle.

Even the manner in which a double rifle is shot affects the groups. The barrels are regulated by the maker by firing the right barrel first, followed by firing the left barrel within 10 seconds. By doing it this way, the right barrel is regulated cold, and the left barrel is regulated after any expansion or warpage caused by heat generated by the firing of the right barrel has taken place. If the shooter fires the left barrel first, or waits between shots until the gun has cooled, there is a distinct possibility that regulation will be off considerably.

The accuracy of a double rifle, when compared to a bolt-action repeater, is not all that good. Most bolt guns, right out of the box, will deliver three-shot groups, measured center-to-center, of $1^{1}/_{2}$ to 2 inches or so at 100 yards range. A little tinkering and load development will generally better the out-of-the-box groups by $^{1}/_{2}$-inch or so, and sometimes more. Precious few double rifles can duplicate this kind of performance. A large-bore double rifle that will place a left and right shot within 2 to $2^{1}/_{2}$ inches of each other at a 50-yard range is quite good. One that does much better than that is exceptional. Large-bore doubles, 458 and up, are generally regulated at 50 yards. Smaller bores, 375 and under, are sometimes regulated at longer ranges. As regulation is a manual process, if one is buying a new double, the regulation parameters can normally be specified. If the buyer wants the regulation done with a particular brand of ammo, or a particular bullet weight, etc., those wishes can normally be accommodated.

If all this sounds like a condemnation of the double rifle, believe me it is not intended. It is certainly true that a double rifle is not as accurate as other types, is far more fickle toward ammunition, much less versatile, and significantly more expensive. All those points are facts that cannot be argued. Truth is truth, no matter how you try to color it. For these reasons, in most hunting situations, a good bolt-action magazine rifle is superior to a double. There are other situations, however, where the double rifle has no equal.

The double rifle has some advantages that no bolt gun can duplicate. First is the speed with which a good double can be brought into action. There are basically two reasons for this, one of which is possible on a bolt gun and the other not. The first is the safety release. Almost all double rifles have the shotgun-type tang safety. It is practically automatic that, as the rifle is being mounted to the shoulder, the shooter thumbs the safety off. Most bolt guns require considerably more effort to release the safety, although some are equipped with a tang safety similar to the shotgun type. The second feature that makes the double faster is one of balance. All doubles that I have ever handled were beautifully balanced and lightning fast to bring to bear on a target. Like a little double-barreled quail gun, it almost gets on target by itself.

When hunting in heavy brush, quick snap shots are often required and in this situation the double rifle is second to none. The major advantage is the ability to get off two *aimed* shots quickly.

Craig Boddington with his trophy white rhino. His rifle on this hunt was a Heym Model 88B Safari, chambered for the 470 Nitro Express.

A second major advantage of the double is the speed with which two a-i-m-e-d shots can be taken. There is nothing to manipulate; all that is necessary is to recover from the recoil of the first shot, then fire the second. An argument has often been made that a shooter can manipulate the bolt while recovering from the recoil and therefore shoot two aimed shots as fast as with a double. Theoretically, I suppose this is true. However, it would take many hours of practice to attain that level of expertise. I shoot a bolt gun a lot, far more than the average shooter, and there is no way that I can do it. Frankly, I don't know anyone who can.

A third major advantage is reliability. I am the first to admit that a good bolt-action rifle is very reliable and a breakdown or malfunction is rare. It does happen though. A bolt gun has but one trigger, one firing pin, one magazine spring,—one of everything. If the one available does break, the rifle is out of action until it can be replaced or repaired. The double, on the other hand, has basically two of everything. Even in the rare event that one

This currently-made Perugini-Visini Model Selous double rifle is available in a variety of calibers and carries a rather heady price tag of just over $20,000.

When firing a double rifle from the bench, not the most pleasant experience in the world, always pad the fore-end with your hand in this manner. Doing otherwise will likely cause erratic accuracy.

firing pin does break, there is another, ready to go. Of course, the double is now a single shot, but that is much better than nothing.

All of these advantages are really only significant when the hunter is after dangerous game in heavy cover. In a situation where the pursued can suddenly become the pursuer, and has the strength, fortitude and temperament to carry it through, these differences can literally mean the differences between life and death or serious injury. In such instances, a double rifle of suitable caliber has no equal in a sporting firearm.

Perhaps the greatest recommendation for the double rifle comes from the professional hunters in Africa. These gentlemen spend more time among dangerous game in one season than the average hunter does in two to three lifetimes. They are, on the average, working stiffs, just like the rest of us. The fact that a double rifle costs a sizeable chunk of a year's income for them does not preclude the purchase of one. After all, the double is the tool of their trade, and not only are they responsible for protecting their own hide, but also that of their client and staff as well. No, a good double is a necessity for doing business, just like a Land Rover, tentage, etc.

Looking back on the heyday of East African safaris, the list of users of double rifles are like a "Who's Who" of professional hunters. Donald Ker and Syd Downey, founders of the famous safari company of Ker & Downey were both users of double rifles. Myles Turner, one of their best PHs, also used a double. John Taylor, old Pondoro himself, makes a convincing argument in his writings for the essentiality of a double. His arguments were based upon many years experience in the field, averaging 11 hunting months each year. The list goes on and on. There were a few well known PHs that did not use double rifles, most notably Cdr. Blount and Harry Selby, both of whom used 416 Rigby magazine rifles. That they each had long and successful careers is a lasting tribute to their skills. In fact, last I heard, Harry Selby was still plying his skills as a PH, and still carrying his trusted 416.

Starting at somewhere around $10,000 and going upward from there, a double rifle is not exactly a bargain basement item. Even at that lofty figure, we are in the lower end of the double rifle spectrum. I have seen a number of double rifles listed at double

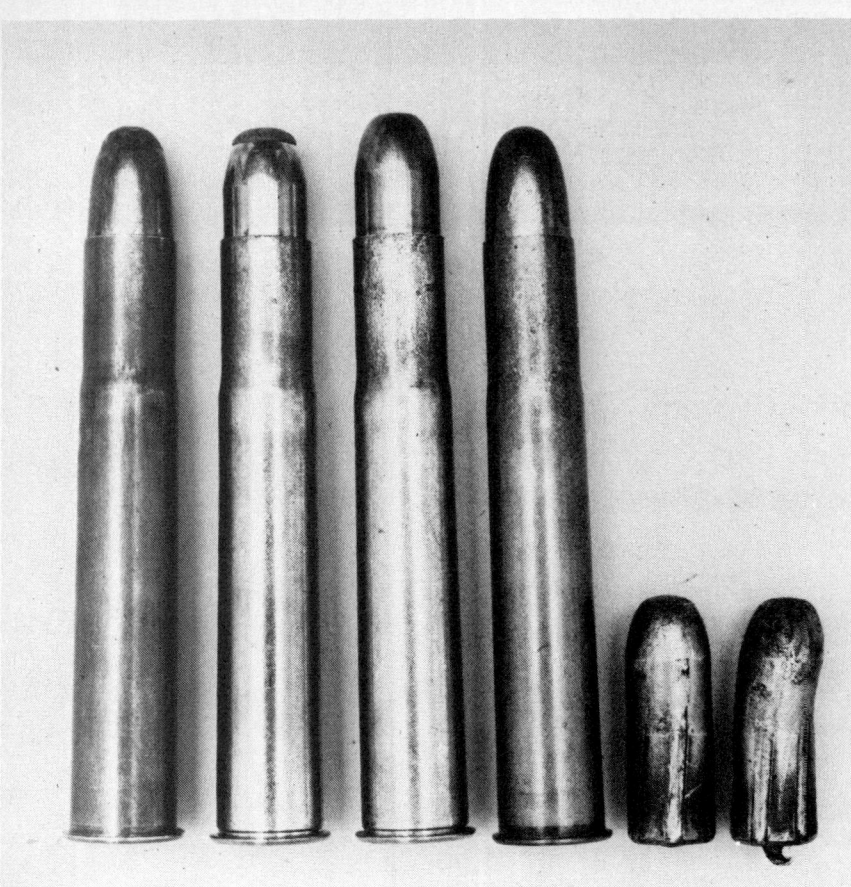

Four different loadings of the 470 Nitro Express, from left: Kynoch 500-gr. soft point, B.E.L.L. 500-gr. soft point, B.E.L.L. 500-gr. solid, and Kynoch 500-gr. solid. The two bullets at right are 500-gr. Woodleigh solids that were recovered from a rhino.

Double rifles are also available in the less costly boxlock style. This Perugini-Visini Model Victoria-D in 458 Win. Mag. sells for only about $12,500.

by the bull. I had him, dead to rights, at about 30 yards. He had no idea that anyone was within a hundred miles of him, a tribute to the skills of my PH, Nigel Theisen, and our trackers Munetsi and Million. Yet, there was a feeling of something very subjective, that the double rifle belonged in this situation. It was most satisfying, taking this mighty animal with an appropriate and historically correct rifle. Would it have been any less satisfying had I used a bolt gun? I cannot say.

All in all, the double rifle does have its place in the game fields of the world. Where the brush is thick and the ranges short, a double rifle will hold its own with any rifle made. Add to that situation, facing an animal that can take on anything with an equal chance of coming out the winner, and the double rifle becomes more than just a luxury. I won't say it is essential, as John Taylor did for several situations, but I will say that it increases the odds of a successful outcome for the hunter. In such situations, perhaps the purchase of a good

that figure and even higher. Can the hunter going on a once-in-a-lifetime safari justify the expenditure of such a sum? Or, for that matter, the hunter that goes on safari for two or three weeks every year? Of course, the answer to that question is no. One can do quite well on the occasional safari with a bolt-action magazine rifle of suitable caliber. It is only in the hands of the professional hunter, one who spends several months each year in the bush with dangerous game, and who has the responsibility of protecting his clients, that the question is debatable.

Having said that, the realities of the situation do not always carry the day. If one wishes to travel to the African bush armed with a double rifle, and either already has one in their battery, or can afford to purchase one, why not? In my last trip to the dark continent, I was armed with my pet David Miller 270 for plains game hunting and a Heym 470 Nitro Express double rifle for cape buffalo. Could I have done as well with a bolt gun in 375 H&H or 458 Winchester? I think the answer to that question is undeniably yes. Would I have experienced the same feelings when stalking the mighty bovine? I think the answer to that question is undeniably no. As it turned out, I was not charged

double rifle is the cheapest insurance that one can buy. Added to that is the fact that double rifles generally appreciate in value, rather than depreciate. Can you imagine a situation where you invest in insurance and have the potential of realizing a gain on your investment? With double rifles, you certainly can.

Is it function or nostalgia that make a safari and a double rifle go together like peanut butter and jelly? Frankly, it's a bit of both, although the percentages will probably weigh heavily in favor of nostalgia. Of course, there is nothing wrong with that, so long as we don't forget that the function of a double rifle is what created the nostalgia to start with. When faced with the prospect of digging dangerous game out of heavy cover, I'm convinced that nothing is better for the task than a heavy-caliber double rifle. ●

20 YEARS With The 44 Magnum

by B.A. HAWKS

It's a blaster, no doubt about it. But after two decades of use the author still fairly dotes on the round and it's his choice for handgun hunting.

I FIRST BECAME enamored of the 44 Remington Magnum cartridge as a pubescent, acne-afflicted youngster, never mind when. Tales of its man-eating recoil cowed me more than a little, so the first gun so-reamed to find its way into the modest Hawks collection was a rifle. To be specific, a Marlin 336-T. Don't remember that one? It presaged Marlin's revival of the 1894 short-action and was not really a satisfactory marriage. As I recall, the lifter was a two-piece affair on those 336s in order for the stubby round to feed acceptably in the 30-30-length action. It's the only 336 I can recall ever displaying mechanical malfeasance. I don't remember how well it shot but if its grouping abilities had been laudable, I would.

I went to Korea, leaving the little 44 in the cabinet alongside a Czech-built 8x57 Mauser with a ruined bore, a Mossberg turnbolt 22 rimfire, and a nifty Marlin 39-A "Golden Mountie" which my school chum talked me out of and still owns. Whilst overseas, I began to study firearms in earnest, bussing from post to post, searching dusty Army libraries for books on guns and

Hawks nailed this 13-point Ohio buck with the new S&W Classic Hunter at 77 yards. It weighed 213 pounds and scored 170 points as a nontypical trophy.

Dr. Jack Amato and his first pig, shot with a 4-inch S&W Model 629 and one 180-gr. Starfire factory load.

Young shooter Jeff Miller handles the big Ruger Redhawk with aplomb. The recoil is heavy, but doesn't hinder his accurate shooting.

hunting. I bought and read every gun periodical available, cover to cover. I acquired my first reloading manual, a Speer Number something-or-other, and *digested* it; I'd been poring over that tome for 7 months before I ever reloaded a round. (And so do I advise anyone interested in taking up handloading, though no one ever seems to listen to me.)

I began my home-brew efforts in the summer of 1968, immediately upon my return stateside. Even after all my reading I made some minor mistakes. It's always better to be instructed in the rudiments by someone knowledgeable. Alas, I was unacquainted with anyone at the time who knew a primer was an explosive device, not a first-grader's reading material.

Somewhere in there I bought my first 44 Maggie sixgun, and with some degree of trepidation. However, Elmer Keith had convinced me that—contrary to claims made by the likes of Charlie Askins—I could probably fire the thing without rendering my wrist bones useless cartilage. Elmer was right. I survived the ordeal not only intact but none the worse for wear.

At the time, I was serving Uncle Samuel by participating in one-hand competition with the 45 automatic. I'd been taught by the Army always to wear both eye and ear protection while shooting, a germ of wisdom writers of the bygone era had attempted to instill, however insufficiently. The non-com coaches for the XVIII Air Borne Corps pistol team had no such difficulty. Thus was I wearing good muff-type sound-attenuation devices when I cut loose with a 44 that initial time.

My vehicle was the venerable Ruger Super Blackhawk. Its heft and plow-handle grip design made it reasonably comfortable to shoot. I did so. Often. With that gun I produced my first sub-half-inch five-shot cluster from the bench at 25 yards. Was I impressed! The gun wouldn't *average* that of course, but it would go right under an inch with its pet load for three five-shot strings. The second article I ever sold featured that wonderful old "Super Bee," was entitled "The Magnums and 296," and was printed in the spring of 1974.

During those early years I flirted with various 44 Magnum sixguns, including the almost impossible to afford Smith & Wesson Model 29s. Unfortunately I have misplaced the targets fired by those long-ago test guns. There were also more 44 rifles, including a Ruger Carbine or three, a couple of Marlin 1894s, and a pair of Remington 788 bolt-guns. None of them was especially noteworthy in the precision department; all were ultimately swapped off.

After becoming a gun scribe, I began to keep meticulous records. They tell me that to this time I've fired 33 handguns on which I have stored data, maybe a half-dozen more that are but dim recollections. I've punched many a hole in target paper with those guns, ventilated a critter or two, worked up more than one handload from scratch. I'm certain you want to hear about it.

The Maggie in the Hunting Fields

I've used various 44 wheelguns to slay whitetail deer, wild boar and mouflon sheep. Only two required finishing shots. A mouflon ram hit a bit too far back at 70 yards galloped out to 110 or so, stopped, stood there a moment very sick. From the kneel I angled another one into him. Same spot, opposite side. He ran a few more steps; then I did it properly, boring a 44-cali-

Grady Shields is pleased with these targets that are typical of the 44 Magnum. Three strings fired with 240-gr. Federal JHPs hover in the 1-inch range, while the top right load (240-gr. Winchester JHP) printed nearly three times that!

ber hole through his lungs and dumping him in his tracks. Chances are he was tired anyway. Not an exemplary performance, but the fault lies at *my* feet, not the caliber's, not the 180-grain Federal hollow point that I used, nor yet the superb Ruger Redhawk that launched the slug.

A boar hog took two hits, though the first one—a Freedom Arms 300-grain jacketed soft point—smashed both shoulder joints as he whizzed by broadside, plopping him on his snoot in the late-winter leaves. (A high-shoulder shot is ideal for *stopping* an animal, but leaves a bit to be desired in *killing* one quickly.) I turned off his lamp with a *coup de grace* to the ticker.

More typical was the monster 13-point whitetail buck I killed last year hunting with Jack Amato in Ohio. The big old buck (213 pounds on the hoof, weighed, not guessed) was ghosting along a trail in the snow—likely looking for a receptive doe—when I spotted him. Using what I have been told is the first Smith & Wesson Classic Hunter Model 29 to be applied to big game, I sent along a 240-grain Federal jacketed hollow point. He was standing 77 yards away when the bullet reached him, perforating his rib box and sailing on through to kick up a divot on his far side. He dashed 85 yards in a half-circle through deep woods and collapsed as he tried to negotiate a steep grade.

Dave Pickens and I searched for an hour before finding him. But find him we did. Stone dead. He scored 170 points (green) as a nontypical. Fine Ohio buck, that one.

The three foregoing illustrations are indicative of 44 Magnum field performance. Stick a bullet in the right spot at ranges around 100 yards or less and the animal joins its predecessors with facility; tuck that slug far astray and a mess is wrought. Just as with any other powerful cartridge. Well directed, a 44 Magnum handgun will put meat in the larder.

Although the subject is moot, I like a quick-expanding bullet on ungulates of modest heft. Once the weight eases up into the 250 to 300-pound neighborhood then a stouter, longer bullet is called for. Many experienced hunters opine that since few (if any) handgun bullets can be relied upon to expand in flesh, and those that do can't always be depended on to dig deeply, the way to go is with a wide flat point of extreme sectional density (read *weight*). That way a 44-caliber wound channel from sternum to stern or side to side is the consistent result of a solid hit. Such thought has merit. Nonetheless, since I've never recovered a 180-grain jacketed hollow point from any animal I have shot personally, for deer-sized fauna I intend to stick to good expanding bullets unless a specific experiment is being conducted.

And now it's time to descant on the various 44 Magnum hardware currently offered. After said expatiation, I'll proffer my opinions as to which gun to buy, should one or two of you be interested. Onward.

Dan Wesson

Although Dan Wesson is the unequivocal leader in metallic silhouette competition, I came to the marque late in my life. In fact, my first 44-chambered DW sixgun joined my household just last year. Widely heralded for its accuracy, the DW is also renowned for its sturdiness and superb single-action trigger pull. Does it deserve such accolades?

Well, the stout construction is obvious. Weight is 48 ounces—3 pounds—unloaded. Its frame is burly, the six chambers surrounded by considerable steel, the ratchet teeth impressive and precisely cut. The bolt is broad shouldered, the hand (or pawl) robust. Aside from the grip escutcheons and the grip screw (which runs up through the bottom of the panel, not laterally as on, for example, Smith & Wesson Model 29 variants), I've had no parts breakage or chronic loosening. The

Dan Wesson 44 Magnum.

rear sight element doesn't appear to me to be as sturdy as those of some other brands, but none of my three test guns has ever given me any trouble in that area. (But then I've never dropped a DW onto its rear sight, either.)

As I'm sure you're aware, DW six-guns feature readily interchangeable barrels. A feeler gauge is provided along with a multi-functional tool to enable said barrel switching. The system works and doubtless contributes considerably to the vaunted DW accuracy.

So how accurate are they? Of the 33 44 Magnum handguns I've tested, slots number three, seven, and 13 go to Dan Wesson revolvers. The most precise of the trio, an 8-inch version, averaged 1.095 inches from the bench at 25 yards, which translates to 4.18 minutes of angle. The load was Federal's wonderful 240-grain jacketed hollow point, lot 13B-7436. Runner-up was the 240 Hornady JHP at 1.20 inches for four five-shot strings. Pretty good?

My second best DW showed a 1.33-inch aggregate of three five-shot groups with the same Federal offering. That particular gun is fitted with a ported 6-inch barrel, white-insert front sight, and has a wish-off trigger.

The least accurate of the bunch was another 8-incher, this one going into 1.41 inches with Federal's 180-grain jacketed hollow points, averaging five groups. Taking the best load in all three guns, the overall average comes to 1.28 inches. Damned good.

Problem areas? Well, none of the DW grip styles provided with my test guns fit my hand very well, nor yet did a Pachmayr replacement unit. And sometimes a barrel nut "shoots" itself so tightly into place that it's tough to get it loose when it's time to change barrels. And a stainless steel barrel included with one of my Pistol Paks was not properly threaded, so wouldn't seat correctly in any of my frames. Aside from those minor faux pas, there were few warts on the Dan Wessons I tested.

Desert Eagle

The IMI-built Desert Eagle is the only 44 Magnum autoloader currently manufactured, to my knowledge. It's a big, burly, heavy, ill-balanced, well-made, homely, cumbersome, readily scopable, brilliantly accurate handgun. When fitted with Millett sights and the optional (and superb) adjustable trigger, all is copacetic. The standard sights, though easily seen and capable of adequate optical precision, cannot be brought to taw, at least in my hands and with my vision. Since the front element is dovetailed into the barrel, I suppose it can be replaced with a unit of the proper height. If so, I reckon I could live without the Millett sighting system since the standard rear sight is laterally drift adjustable.

The trigger, however, is another matter entirely. So weighty is the "normal" trigger's pull, so gritty its articulation, so lengthy its travel—both before and after release—that it is virtually impossible to shoot the gun accurately except from a rest. Although it's an expensive option, don't leave home without the adjustable trigger option. Period.

Given good iron sights (or a scope) and the optional trigger, is the Desert Eagle an acceptable hunting arm? You bet! It's more accurate than most revolvers, holds nine rounds instead of five or six, doesn't kick much (due to several factors), is beautifully fabricated and reliable. What more could you ask?

Good balance? Feel? Fret-free portability? Finesse? Forget it. Like I said, the gun is big, weighs as much as a grain elevator, has the rapier-like edge of an anvil. So what? Balance, feel, concealability, and grace are not what the Desert Eagle's all about. It's about brute force, functioning when the going gets tough, a serious mein. It offers all those and more.

In its 6-inch-barreled rendition, the aluminum-framed Eagle tips the beam at 52 ounces; the all-steel item

Hunter John Neese took this nice hog with his 44 Magnum Desert Eagle auto and never felt under-gunned.

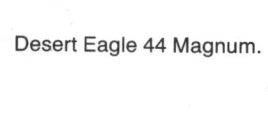
Desert Eagle 44 Magnum.

hefts 10 ounces more. Pretty heavy. (How much a long-barreled, scope-sighted, fully-loaded Desert Eagle might weigh I won't even guess, but I suspect it would be enough to spavin the most substantial of horses.)

Action articulation is by gas, and there is a rotating bolt for secure locking. All in all, an impressive example of solidity. And mass.

The Eagle comes in 357 and 41 Magnums as well as the 44, and I wouldn't be a bit surprised to see it proffered in 454 Casull one day. It certainly should be strong enough. We'll see. There are stainless steel versions, bright and satin nickel, even models with gilt adornments. Both 10 and 14-inch barrels are cataloged. A scope mount is listed and is unique in my experience in that it lets its wielder retain the use of iron sights merely by peering beneath the mount itself! Ingenious.

I have tested two Desert Eagle 44s and one 357. All of them gave impressive accuracy, but especially the big bores. The aluminum-framed gun printed 1.36 inches at 25 yards with 220 Federal MCP ammo, went into 1.49 inches for four strings with Speer's 200-grain Lawman hollow point. My sample steel-framed piece—lousy trigger and all—managed an impressive 1.56-inch aggregate with the 180 Federal JHP while functioning perfectly, though the factory advises against the use of lightweight bullets.

I topped the aluminum number with a crystal-clear Burris 1x pistol scope with 3-minute dot reticle. At 100 yards, the gun groups between 6 and 8 inches regularly, using a plethora of loads. Offhand, I can burst water-filled gallon jugs at the same range with metronomic regularity. Conspiring to make such shooting easy are the superior trigger pull, that marvelous no-magnification Burris scope, and the accuracy inherent in the Desert Eagle design. Believe me: The Eagle is some gun.

Problems? A few. Only a weightlifter can muscle back that massive and stiffly-sprung slide, especially when a scope is in place (requiring the manipulator to pinch-grip the thing). Only two weightlifters can depress the slide release when it is holding the action open; the release lever wants enlarging. My aluminum-framed pistol displays an exasperating proclivity for tossing one flyer per five-shot string, usually at 5 o'clock but not always. Many, many times it will stuff four bullets into one hole—or awfully close to it—only to pitch one toward the basement. Even so, the above group averages *include* all those flyers. The level of accuracy that might be realized should those errant bullets be brought into the fold boggles the mind.

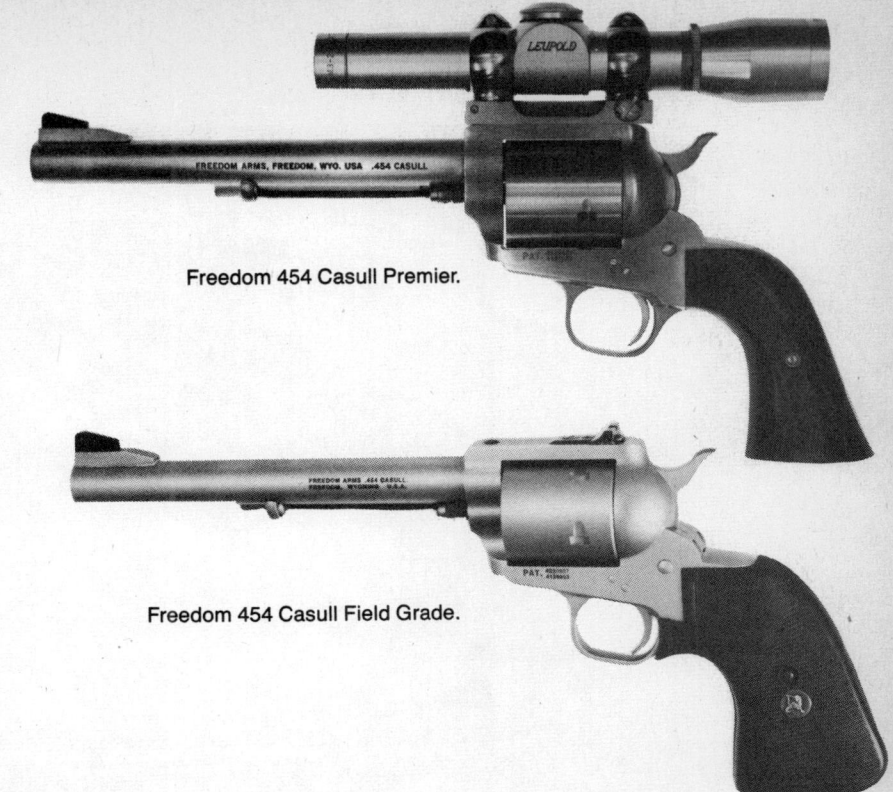

Freedom 454 Casull Premier.

Freedom 454 Casull Field Grade.

Freedom Arms Casull

The Freedom Arms Casull is built in Freedom, Wyoming. By elves. Or so you'd suspect from its quality. No handgun turned out today, from any land, can rival its undiluted excellence of fabrication, in my opinion. Not only is it built like Swiss watches *used* to be built, but its handling qualities are extraordinary, its balance a delight, its accuracy as good as anything in its class. The FA Casull is expensive, make no mistake—about 2½ times the tariff on such as a Smith Model 29 or a Ruger Redhawk. That's only a bit more than such ballyhooed and expensive sixguns as Colt's Python and Single Action Army, neither of which is in the Casull's league in any other respect.

Although the FA single action has gained considerable notoriety as the vehicle for the impressive 454 Casull Magnum cartridge, it is also turned out in 44 Magnum and 45 Colt. Retail price is $1,095 with adjustable sights, just under a grand with non-adjustable sighting equipment.

What about the FA makes it so hot, and especially so expensive? Tolerances: There practically are none. Assembly: All joints mesh with such perfection as to appear to be merely scribed lines, not actual matings of metal. In addition, the grips mate with the straps as if painted on. Further: The chambers are bored in direct line with the barrel on each revolver for utmost accuracy. The triggers are better than on many double-action designs famed for their crispness, and a factory-performed action job is an inexpensive option.

More things to like. When you snap open the loading gate, it goes SNAP!, like that. Positively. When you shut it it goes CLUNK!, like that. Like closing the breech on a Fox Sterlingworth twenty-bore double. Ah, precision. Craftsmanship. Quality. Nothing else compares, from anyone, anywhere, at any price, at least not in handgun form.

I currently have three Casull five-shooters. Two are 454s, the third a 4¾-inch 44 Mag. This latter will group the 240 Hornady JHP into 1.54 inches at 25 yards, an average of four groups. The 200 Hornady hollow point goes 1.65. If this doesn't seem overly impressive let me hasten to note that I have done little load-development work with the bonny gun. But I will. And I'll wager a cup of tea that it will print inside 5 minutes once I do. Maybe better.

Any blemishes? Well, I'd love for it to take six shots but that ain't in the cards. One of the reasons the Casull is so hell-for-strong is its beefy *five-shot* cylinder. It's a tradeoff I can live with. The moral: If Freedom Arms Casulls have problem areas, I ain't discovered them.

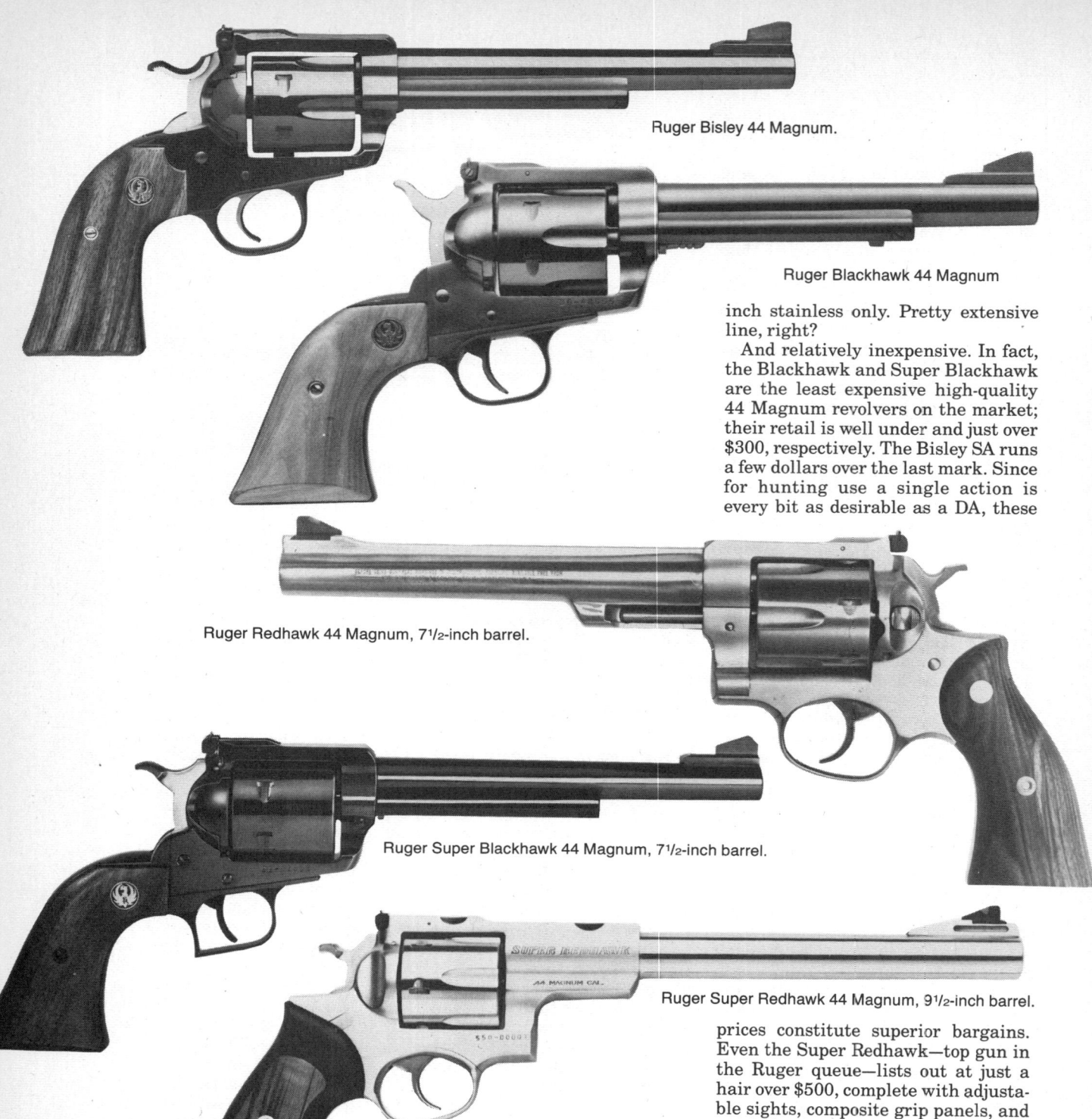

Ruger Bisley 44 Magnum.

Ruger Blackhawk 44 Magnum

Ruger Redhawk 44 Magnum, 7½-inch barrel.

Ruger Super Blackhawk 44 Magnum, 7½-inch barrel.

Ruger Super Redhawk 44 Magnum, 9½-inch barrel.

Ruger

Sturm, Ruger and Company offers more types and configurations of 44 sixguns than any other outfit. A quick perusal of their line would uncover the standard Blackhawk single action (their lightest and most compact model), the Super Blackhawk SA (both stainless and blue), the single-action Bisley permutation, the double-action Redhawk (stainless or blue, 5½ or 7½-inch barrel length), and the brutish Super Redhawk, 7½ and 9½ inch stainless only. Pretty extensive line, right?

And relatively inexpensive. In fact, the Blackhawk and Super Blackhawk are the least expensive high-quality 44 Magnum revolvers on the market; their retail is well under and just over $300, respectively. The Bisley SA runs a few dollars over the last mark. Since for hunting use a single action is every bit as desirable as a DA, these prices constitute superior bargains. Even the Super Redhawk—top gun in the Ruger queue—lists out at just a hair over $500, complete with adjustable sights, composite grip panels, and quick-detachable scope mounts. Ruger has a corner on value.

But are they any count? Unquestionably. They almost never wear out, seldom go out of time (I am tempted to say "never," since I've not see one so afflicted), and are generally smooth functioning. I'd bet a Studebaker that a Redhawk will outlast any double-action 44 extant. The single actions are likely more enduring of magnum loads than any competitor save the Casull, and possibly the Desert Eagle.

Grip designs on all except the Super

Blackhawk and Blackhawk are quite ergonomic, fitting most hands well without aftermarket assistance. The Redhawk and the Bisley are particularly notable in this regard.

And boy, will Rugers shoot! The most precise 44-caliber revolver I ever tested was the earlier-mentioned old-model Super Blackhawk, which averaged .97-inch at 25 yards with 26.7 grains of Winchester 296 under the 200 Hornady JHP. Decanting 23.0 grains of the same propellant and stuffing atop the case some now-defunct 236-grain Norma jacketed hollow points provided a 1-inch aggregate for three five-shot strings.

My two other old model Super Bees averaged 1.22 and 1.37 inches. That puts them in fifth and eleventh places of all 33 guns I've tested. The Bisley 44 I tried recently printed 1.18 inches with 24.0 grains of 296 pushing the 240 Sierra JHC, putting it in fifth place among all my 44s, past and present. Good? There's more.

My two most precise Ruger Redhawks—one a stainless 7½-inch version, the other a 5½-inch blue—went into 1.26 and 1.36 inches respectively, for the sixth and ninth spots. Yet another stainless 7½-inch model averaged 1.47 inches. My Super Redhawk grouped right at 1½ inches at 25 yards and averaged 3.78 inches at *100* (that's 3.61 MOA), the premier performance I've received from a revolver at that range. (My scoped Redhawk is nigh as good at 3.96 inches, or 3.78 MOA).

Want more? Okay. Of the 13 Ruger 44 Magnum revolvers I have tested, 100 percent averaged 1¾ inches or under and 62 percent went below 1½ inches. Impressed? You should be. No other brand of which I have tried *at least six samplings* will approach that record. None.

Problems? Trigger pulls. Ruger is not, nor ever has been, noted for trigger quality out of the box. So I have ace gunsmith Mike Merker of The Base Camp (2407 West 5th Street, Washington, NC, 27889, 919/946-3113) work my single-action triggers over for me. He does a masterful job, as does his boss Chris Latta.

Bob O'Connor, one of my hunting cronies, handles the attention I deem requisite on my various Redhawks. However, if several samples of that model are handled and dry-fired before buying, one with a crisp pull will usually surface.

Aside from trigger pull quality, Rugers generally fit acceptably, present few unsightly tool or casting marks, and work well. One nationally-known gun writer told me of a Super Black-

Dr. Don Creed likes his 6-inch nickel Model 29 with 2x Leupold for whitetails. He takes a deer or two each year with this gun and swears by the 180-gr. Federal JHPs.

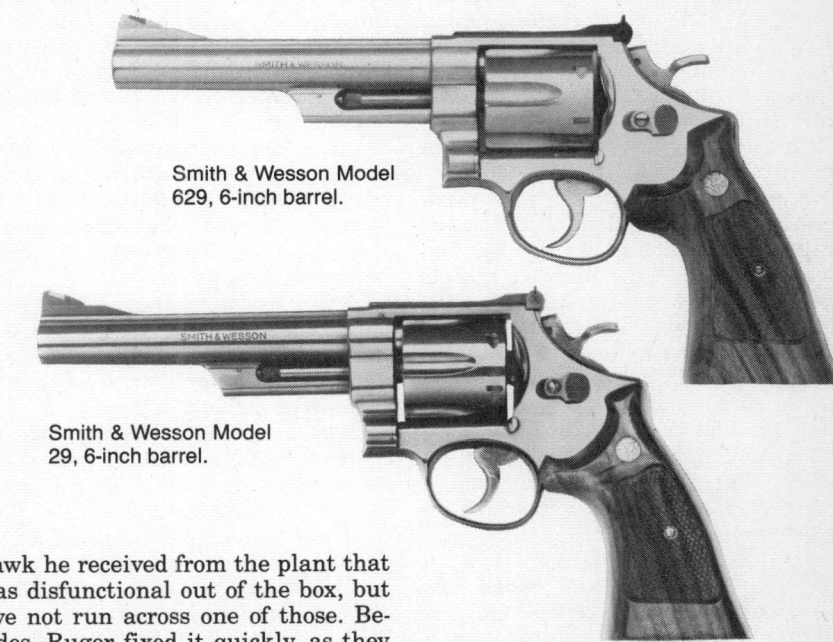

Smith & Wesson Model 629, 6-inch barrel.

Smith & Wesson Model 29, 6-inch barrel.

hawk he received from the plant that was disfunctional out of the box, but I've not run across one of those. Besides, Ruger fixed it quickly, as they would for *any* customer. But I admit it shouldn't have happened.

There you have it. To synopsize: Rugers are reliable, long-lived, superbly accurate, well made, affordable, backed by a respected name, and hold their value quite well should you fauch for something new. A Ruger is never a mistake.

Smith & Wesson

Smith & Wesson produced the first 44 Magnum revolver in conjunction with Remington Arms Company, who built the ammunition. (Smith also initiated the 357 and 41 Magnums. At times the grand old firm has been quite progressive; at other times they can be a fusty lot.) As everyone knows, Elmer Keith had a major role in the birthing process as well, and went on to do his part in assuring the nascent load's acceptance.

All S&W 44 Magnum revolvers bear the same model number, or one with a single numerical addition. For example, the Model 29 comes in both blued and nickeled format while the Model 629 is the stainless version. The new Classic Hunter is yet another Model 29 variant, not a separate designation. This is unprecedented for the staid New England company. For example, there are various 22 rimfire models, numerous 38 Specials (Model 10, 36, 52, etal), an amplitude of 357s (Model 13, 19, 27, 28, 581, ad infinitum), more than one 9mm (Model 39, 439, 59, 669). And so forth. Even the 41 Magnum—much less popular than any of the foregoing—has worn two different model designations, not counting the stainless-indicating numeral "six," either. Not so the 44. Everything begins or ends with the appellation "29."

To their credit, S&W forty-fours boast exceptionally clean single-action triggers, often (but not always) very nice double-action pulls as well. All 44 Mags wear fine adjustable sights, a solid barrel rib, two-point lockup—fore and aft—and either full-sized target grips or Hogue combat stocks. Quality of craftsmanship varies from gun to gun and ranges from good to excellent, with the best examples difficult to improve upon.

Smith 44 sixguns are lighter than most other double actions. This fact carries with it a dual persona. On the one hand, a 4-inch M29 (in particular) is pleasant to tote all day in a belt rig, with even the longer barreled models being of comfortably exiguous heft. Conversely, this lack of avoirdupois makes the guns more obstreperous to fire; they buck right smart unless toned down a bit by a gas-venting process. The new Classic Hunter allays recoil somewhat by the addition of a full-length barrel underlug and a non-fluted cylinder, both of which increase weight.

Accuracy is usually present in spades. For example, the second best 44 accuracy I ever received, and the top performance I ever wrung from a revolver of *any* caliber with *factory* ammunition, came from a 4-inch Model 629. Three five-shot strings (witnessed) showed a 1.04-inch aggregate at 25 yards using 240 Federal hollow points, of course. (Those incredible Federal loads are so accurate I now handload only for special purposes. If I want simply to test a new 44 Magnum handgun for accuracy I rely on three loads, in order of preference: 240 Federal JHP, 180 Federal JHP, and the 240 Hornady JHP. Newer lots of the 200 Speer JHP are also showing up well.)

A 44 Magnum in full recoil can be intimidating to the uninitiated shooter, but it won't break your wrist as some rumors claim.

My $8^{3/8}$-inch nickel Model 29—fitted up with a Burris 1.5-4x scope—went into twelfth spot on my all-time list by virtue of a 1.39-inch mean using the abovementioned 240 Federal ammo. My $10^{5/8}$-inch blued M29 and I collaborated with a 2.5-7x Burris, 24.0 grains of 296, and the 240 Nosler jacketed hollow point to turn in a three-group average at 100 yards of 3.82 inches (3.65 MOA), the second tightest I've received from any repeating handgun at that yardage.

Of the 10 Smiths on which I have data, eight managed to slip under 2 inches at the 25-yard line with one recipe or another. Forty percent of them went inside 1½ inches.

There are some problems with the Smith family. One, there seems to be an immoderate gun-to-gun variation in accuracy and overall quality. This tendency is much less pronounced today than it was just a couple of years ago, but I'll have to wait and see if the current trend continues. Two, many Model 29s display an alarming tendency to "skip," and a panoply of them unlock themselves upon firing (i.e., the bolt withdraws from its notch in the cylinder, leaving the cylinder free to rotate partially). Three, according to many, many knowledgeable gunners, Model 29s show an inclination toward going out of time under the stress of absorbing continuous

Developing handloads for the 44 Magnum will pay big dividends, allowing you to tailor your loads to your gun. The Lee 1000 tool shown turns out quality reloads at reasonable cost.

magnum punishment. I've never had this happen, but then I doubt I ever put 500 full-bore rounds through one specific S&W 44. It is something to bear in mind if you intend to do much shooting.

Other 44 Magnum Handguns

There are on the firearms scene other 44 Magnum-chambered short guns. In general, I advise that they be avoided for the most part although one or more of them may offer a simulacrum of acceptable features and quality. I've had experience with a pair of Interarms Virginian Dragoons, a Llama Super Commanche, and an Astra stainless steel double action. All of them would fire when I tugged on their triggers, and usually managed to hit the target so long as it wasn't especially miniscule or far away. Neither of the Dragoons would print under 2¼ inches at 25 yards with any load tried, though one would come quite close. My test Astra averaged exactly 2.25 inches with Federal's 180-grain number, but its runner-up fodder went into 3.60 inches! The Llama was in 32nd place among my 20 years worth of 44 Magnum handguns, grouping 2.73 inches for three five-shot strings with 180 Federal stuff, and 2.75 inches with the 240 Hornady JHP. Such "precision" renders me decidedly plangent.

Since Llama and Astra DA revolvers are not too far arrear of the Smith & Wesson Model 29 in price, I cannot for the life of me recommend either of them unless the prospective purchaser has been scrimping and saving for years. In that instance, said buyer wouldn't be able to shoot often anyway—finances would preclude it—so I suppose either of the above would suffice after a fashion. But remember the admonishment regarding the sow's ear and the silk purse.

Were I offered a Virginian Dragoon at a bargain-basement price, I *would* consider it. The guns are sturdy and appear to be well made. It was always a mystery to me why they wouldn't group.

A specialty item such as the Thompson/Center Contender is, of course, a different ball game from the foregoing, being nicely made and boasting impressive accuracy. It's just that I can't conjure up much use for a single-shot 44 Magnum when the T/C

The author prefers 180-gr. bullets for use on animals up to 250 pounds. Bigger critters need bigger bullets, however.

can be had in such potent chamberings as the 7-30 Waters and 35 Remington, both of which will outreach the best of 44s.

For those febrile souls among you who are champing at the bit to own and tend a 44 Magnum handgun, and are intent on making a wise and cost-effective selection, I'll now propound on that issue in the hopes that my two decades of experience will assist me in offering an antipyretic to your heated exuberance. Here they are, the . . .

Picks of the Litter

For hunting use a single action has advantages over the double action designs, primarily compactness, light weight, and ease of replacing one or two fired cases without dumping the entire contents of the cylinder on the ground. For we fumble-fingered folk, such is an undeniable boon. If cost were an object—and for most of us it is—I would choose a Ruger Blackhawk then treat it to a trigger job and have all its screws Lok-Tited in place. Ditto if I wanted the lightest 44 possible, perhaps for a trail gun. Should I be able to stretch the budget another $50, I'd jump on the Ruger Bisley and live happily ever after.

If cost were no obstacle I'd toss my money into Freedom Arms' hat, knowing that I would likely never live long enough to wear the gun out and that my dovecote of hunting compadres would envy me openly and cease to accuse me of feckless behavior. Only a man of taste and substance would aspire to a Casull, or be able afford one!

For a primary *scoped* hunting arm, I'd be torn between the new Super Redhawk and the plain-Jane Redhawk. If iron sights were to be utilized on occasion, the Redhawk would get the nod. For scope use *only* it's a toss-up but the Super would likely win out.

If I planned to wear a 44 Magnum handgun all day as an adjunct to a rifle as primary armament, my first, second and third choices would be a 4-inch Smith & Wesson 629, Model 29 nickel, or Model 29 blue. There would be only one likely competitor, the Ruger Blackhawk. I think I'd go with the Smith if I didn't intend to shoot it much. For putting hundreds of rounds down its chute, the Ruger is the better selection.

The Desert Eagle is a wild-card choice. I'd be quite happy with it as a primary hunting tool, not so pleased as a secondary sidearm. Too heavy.

For defense use, I lean to the 4-inch Model 629/29 again if I'm going to have to wear the thing. If I will be toting it in my vehicle or camping it beside my bed, the Ruger 5½-inch Redhawk would be my pick if full-house magnum ammo was to be stuffed up its flue. With mid-range ammo, I could live nicely with either the Model 29 or the short Redhawk. Again, the Desert Eagle is a contender here, but only under very specific conditions.

Were I reduced to *one* 44 Maggie, both for use in the field and to protect the hearth, I'd put my money on a 5½-inch Ruger Redhawk and grin.

So say I.

Jim Roberts fired this Llama 44 and found it to his liking. Although not as accurate as some of the "major brands," it is a viable alternative if money is in short supply.

Cast Bullets For Hunting

In many cases, cast bullet loads perform as well as jacketed types and you get more bang for your dollar. Here are some interesting tests using home-made loads in popular calibers.

by HOWARD E. FRENCH

FOR CENTURIES the lead bullet was used by hunters to kill virtually any land mammal, from elephant to rabbit. Then, when smokeless gunpowder came on the scene, it was found that the lead slug, round ball or conical, could not stand up to the velocities generated by this new powder. The French, who developed the first smokeless powder, used a solid bronze bullet in their first military smokeless powder cartridge to avoid any disturbance of the bore—with this bullet there obviously could not be *any* leading of the barrel. This new cartridge revolutionized military thinking. The American 45-70, with its 405- or 500-grain bullet immediately became obsolete as did the arms of every other nation. Every country in the world

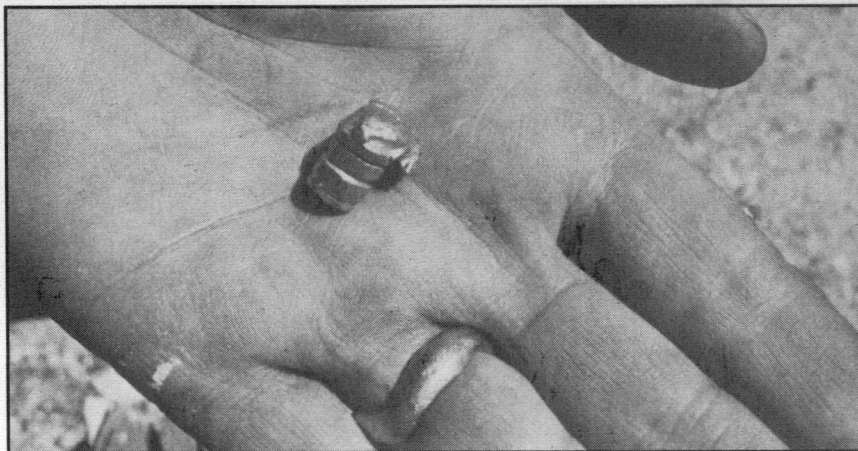

This 375 H&H cast bullet, with the NEI soft-lead-point, had most of the pure lead expanded, then torn off during penetration. Obviously, there was plenty of hard lead in the base to make it continue to penetrate, just like a jacketed bullet.

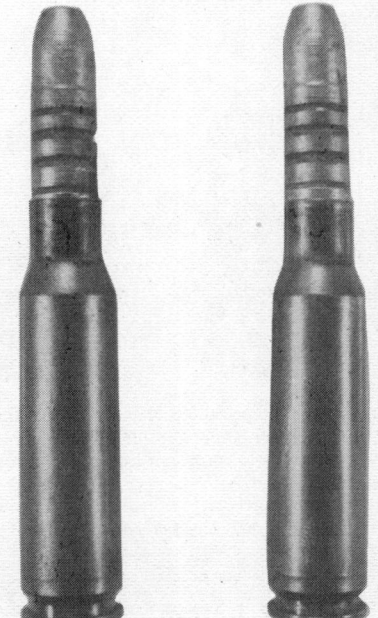

Case at left had the neck expanded with a die made specifically for cast bullet use, the bullet fitting neatly inside the case, ready for seating. The bullet in the case on the right teeters at the mouth because the expander button of the sizing die was intended for jacketed bullets.

During his testing, French found that cast 458 Win., 45-70, 375 H&H and 30-caliber bullets expanded if they hit something hard (a ¾-inch board), or had soft noses (like the NEI duplex slug which had a pure lead nose welded to a hard lead alloy base). The larger 45-caliber bullets would have been deadly even if they did *not* expand.

soon had smokeless powder military arms using jacketed bullets.

Naturally, civilians also bought commercial versions of military arms. The extremely flat trajectory of the smokeless round, compared to that of blackpowder arms, made them the toast of the shooting field. Karamojo Bell used the 303 British round as well as the 7x57mm Mauser, along with other arms, to kill over 1000 elephant! The long 6.5mm and 7x57mm bullets had great penetration and many shooters liked them for use on dangerous game.

Sometimes, however, these bullets had too much penetration. Hunters after deer, sheep, pronghorn and other smaller animals, didn't need a bullet that would perforate an elephant's skull. They wanted a bullet that would still give flat trajectory, but also expand just like the lead blackpowder bullets did. After all, those soft lead blackpowder bullets did expand in game animals. Even after smokeless rounds ruled the day, many hunters in India still used 577-caliber blackpowder arms (with lead-bulleted cartridges) because they considered them more effective on tiger than the newer arms.

Cast bullet penetration was tested in various media, such as the dampened newsprint seen here, as well as in clay and clay and damp paper interspersed with wood.

GUNS ILLUSTRATED 1989 49

The NEI 375 H&H soft-lead-point bullet (left) compared to a Hornady jacketed bullet; both weighed 270 grains and were fired at the same velocity. Both expanded well. Conclusion: At realistic ranges, cast bullets work well!

Cast bullets for 45-caliber arms included the NEI 420-grain, left, Lyman's 385-grain solid (center) and the Lyman 324-grain hollow-point (right). Sharp-nosed bullets *must not* be used in tube-fed lever actioned rifles.

At the left is a Lyman "M" die insert used to expand cases for specific use with cast bullets. It slightly over-expands the mouth of the case to insure proper bullet seating. Standard die insert (right) works well with jacketed bullets but is *not* as satisfactory with cast bullets.

The author found that his "Old Reliable" Shiloh rifle in 45-70 could easily handle all weights of 45-caliber bullets. And that includes the massive 500-grain slug!

So, bullet makers responded, not just with solid, military-style bullets, but also with hollowpoints, soft nose, partition bullets, bullets with special thick bases, lead cores soldered in place, plastic points...well, you name it.

Of course, these bullets have been successful, downing game animals all over the world. However, just the other day, I was looking at prices of jacketed hunting bullets in my local gun shop. Popular 30-caliber bullets are close to 15 cents each, $3.00 for enough bullets to fill a 20 round box of shells. Naturally, this is only part of the cost of assembling a loaded car-

BRNO 375 H&H rifle, topped with a Zeiss scope, handled cast bullets very well. By cutting down on velocity this caliber can be used effectively on North American game without hammering the shooter at each shot. At right is a 4-round, 50-yard group of ¾ inch, the 5th round stretching things out to 1⅜ inches. The bullet was an NEI 270 grainer.

At 50 yards this 458 Win. stoked with Lyman 384-grain bullets travelling at 1949 fps, with a muzzle energy of 3238 foot pounds, produced this group of 1½ inches, with even better groups having been fired. A potent load.

tridge. I assume that you have brass cases on hand but you also have to buy primers as well as pay the ever escalating price of powder. Nonetheless, reloading is still a saving over buying factory-loaded ammo. For 15 cents apiece you get a "standard" bullet, but the "specialty" bullets are much more expensive. Big bore bullets? They can cost up to 44 cents each for standard slugs while custom bullets far exceed this price. Heck, you can pay several dollars apiece for some custom bullets! No doubt these bullets are worth their cost if you're planning to hunt large and dangerous game; but, most American shooters are after deer or deer-sized animals which don't require such exotic projectiles.

It makes you wonder how the average reloading shooter, using jacketed bullets, can afford that all-important practice with his rifle before going on a hunt. Of course, there is another group of hunters, the ones that use cast bullets for both practice as well as hunting. They can afford much more inexpensive practice than the hunter/reloader using jacketed bullets, and, these cast-bullet shooters may well perform better in the field as a result of their extra practice.

When you look back at the old-time hunters who used lead bullets, some of the velocities and muzzle energies they got with their loads were not what we would call "hot," even though they downed many an animal. For bigger animals these hunters used bigger bullets. The old-time elephant rifles had top velocities of just about 1600 fps (feet per second) while the smaller-bore rifles were normally under 2000 fps. Many well known blackpowder arms tossed a bullet about 1300 fps and managed to put many a trophy on the wall, or meat in the larder.

Today things are different. With smokeless powder we can shoot cast bullets much faster than the old blackpowder rounds could. Conical cast bullets can be shot at velocities well over 2000 fps without leading the bore of a rifle or big-bore handgun. How? Gas checks protect the base of the bullet, and the bullet itself can be heat treated to make it harder; there are composite bullets that expand like a jacketed load, and there are bullets cast with both lead and copper for superior ballistics. In addition, current bullet lubricants are far better than those used just a few years ago.

I pulled from my bookshelves a copy of the *Lyman Ideal Hand Book Number 34*; it has no printing date but was probably published in 1946, just after WW II. In looking at the cast bullets shown for 30-caliber rifles, it was amazing to see just how few bullets were offered compared to what Lyman now has available. The same was true for other calibers as well. The heyday of cast bullet shooting terminated near the end of the 19th century and rapidly went downhill when smokeless guns appeared. Today, things are totally different, and with the increased use of cast bullets, we are offered many newly designed moulds to cast bullets for all types of shooting.

Now I'm not going to put down some of the older rifles, be they muzzleloaders or breechloaders, as some of them possess an accuracy level that's still outstanding. But let's take a closer look. Many of the old loads used in match shooting required that the bullet be eased down the bore, from the muzzle (in both muzzleloaders as well as breechloaders), or be carefully inserted from the breech into the rifling by means of a special tool. (This method pre-engraved the rifling onto the bullet.) Dandy accuracy, but not desirable for the modern hunter who wants a cast-bullet cartridge that loads just as easily as a jacketed-bullet type and delivers comparable shooting performance on game. Without question these goals can easily be met. In short, the lead bullet can be far more powerful today than ever before.

I picked several different calibers to test with cast bullets; included were the 30-30 chambered in a Savage bolt action, the 308 Winchester in a Remington Model 700, 375 H&H Magnum in a Brno bolt rifle, 45-70 in a Marlin lever action rifle (as well as another 45-70 in a modern Shilo Sharps falling block), and a Mauser '98 custom rifle chambered for the 458 Win. Mag.

With these calibers and cast bullets, you could take on any North American animal, including grizzly! There is no question that the 458 Winchester can drive a cast 500-grain bullet at the same velocity as a jacketed bullet and, of course, it can also use lighter loads. Now, a 500-grain bullet at over 2000 fps can easily drop a grizzly. With lighter loads the 458 Magnum is pleasant to shoot and can take smaller animals with deadly efficiency.

On the other hand if you don't own a big bore, a cast-bullet-loaded 30-30 easily comes up to the muzzle energy of factory jacketed bullets and can be used for taking deer-sized game. A factory loaded 30-30 with a 170-grain jacketed bullet at 2200 fps has a muzzle energy of 1830 foot pounds. A cast 199-grain (NEI #197308GC) bullet at 2062 fps has a muzzle energy of 1879 foot pounds! Not bad for the cast bullet!

When you get to the bigger calibers, the 375 H&H, as well as the 45-70, also deliver cast bullet performances that range from mild on up to spectacular!

If you think that's good, you can even cast rifle bullets of two different lead alloys for better, more controlled expansion. Of course, this is not new as blackpowder shooters had such bullets, but usually only for match shooting. Today, NEI (Northeast Industrial Inc.) makes moulds for the 375, 458 or 45-70 in two parts. One is a normal mould and will cast a full dimensioned bullet ready to size and reload. However, the second mould casts only the nose of the bullet (with a reduced base that allows it to be encapsulated within the harder breech section during a second casting). The nose-only portion is called the SLP, meaning *soft lead point*.

An NEI 420-grain cast 458 Magnum slug caused quite a blast when it hit this clay medium. The soft-point-lead bullet *really* opened up.

To make the soft-lead-point projectile you must first cast pure lead into the nose section of this special mould. This soft lead "half-projectile" is then placed into the nose of the second full-diameter mould, to allow pouring in the base alloy to fuse both parts. To insure that both the nose and the base will be "soldered" together you must heat the mould with the soft lead nose section in place, using a propane or other torch for about 15 to 20 seconds. Then quickly move the mould to your lead furnace and cast the hard lead or linotype into the mould. If the nose portion is properly heated you get a soft-nosed bullet with the hard lead of the lower base completely fused to the upper base of the soft lead nose portion. Done properly, the bullet will be homogenously welded together. You can't twist them apart with pliers!

When fired, the soft lead of that duplex bullet will expand nicely on impact. Depending on velocity, you can get a perfectly mushroomed bullet, or, if going a bit faster, the soft lead will expand, until it's torn off the hard base. The hard lead base continues to penetrate just like some modern, jacketed loads. Sort of a poor man's Nosler Partition slug. NEI also makes a mould that allows you to cast a bullet core inside a jacket made from copper tubing.

Basically, there are two main worries with cast bullets—velocity and the hardness of the lead alloy. Bullets that are too soft can lead the bore, yet, if they are cast of extremely hard material, you can easily disrupt the nose of the bullet or even have the bullet disintegrate. Velocities of just over 2000 fps seem about right for properly alloyed cast bullets. In other words a good cast bullet is one that won't lead the bore but is still soft enough to expand in the animal.

In firing both jacketed factory ammunition and cast lead bullets from a 30-30 and a 308 into water-soaked newsprint, I found that penetration was about the same with either type of bullet. However, in a few cases

when the cast bullet did not expand, those bullets penetrated much farther than the jacketed slug. Not particularly desirable, as you would like expansion, but the added penetration could be helpful.

The 375 H&H

In the 375 H&H there was no attempt to match penetration of lead bullets with jacketed rounds—the factory ammunition was just too powerful. However, in one test, a jacketed 270-grain Hornady bullet was loaded to the same velocity as a dual-cast NEI soft-lead-point bullet. Penetration of the jacketed and cast bullets in damp newsprint was nearly the same. The Hornady bullet retained 84 percent of its original weight while the cast bullet held 76 percent of its weight. Both bullets expanded well at a velocity of 1871 fps. In checking the *Hornady Handbook,* the 1871 fps velocity of the jacketed bullet would indicate that the bullet had traveled, in effect, some 200 yards from the muzzle before before it hit our test medium and expanded.

Factories routinely show expanded bullets in this same manner; they simply reduce the amount of propellent until the bullet is traveling at the velocity it would normally have in a long range hunting situation, say at 300 yards, then they fire it into their test medium at close range.

During my tests the cast bullet was propelled at its normal muzzle velocity for that load and obviously only indicated what it would accomplish at close range. My cast bullet loads were mild and could be speeded up to more impressive velocities and bullet expansion.

To show this, the 375 H&H cast NEI soft-lead-core bullet was speeded up to 2128 fps; the base held together, even though the nose was torn apart, and the base portion pentrated and exited 26 inches of damp newsprint. When the bullet was cast of solid, hard lead it had about the same penetration and retained 91 percent of its original weight. Obviously, some of these bullets were dug out of the hard sand behind the damp newsprint, which also indicates just how tough these bullets were. I certainly would expect such a load to be effective on most game animals.

While this same bullet could also be used in a 375 Winchester, it would not be suitable for use in a lever-action rifle because of that sharply-pointed nose. The recoil alone could cause the sharp point of one bullet to fire the primer of the cartridge in front of it in a tubular magazine. Never use pointed bullets in any tube-fed rifle.

Going to a more conventional 375-caliber cast bullet, I tried a Lyman gas-checked type (#375449AX) which weighs 283 grains and has a flat nose—ideal for use in a lever-action 375 Winchester. In the 375 H&H it was easy to get 1887 fps and a muzzle energy of 2237 foot pounds!

According to Lyman, a similar bullet of 264 grains can be driven to 1700 to 1800 fps with a muzzle energy of 1899 foot pounds (at 1800 fps) in a 375 Winchester rifle. That compares favorably with the factory 375 Winchester which has a 250-grain bullet driven at 1900 fps with a muzzle energy of 2005 foot pounds.

The 45-70

The 45-70 bullets are so numerous that you can find just about any style you want. I chose the famous Lyman Gould hollowpoint (#457122), a favorite of hunters in the 19th century, as well as a Lyman 384-grain gas check (#457483), the NEI 420-grain gas check (#425458GC) and one of the heavier bullets, a Lyman 512-grain gas check (#457132). While the 500-grain bullet is considered a "standard" weight for the 45-70, my own cast bullets gained an extra 12 grains with the lead alloy I was using.

The Marlin Model 1895 has Micro-Groove rifling and cast bullet velocities should be kept under 1800 fps for best results. As a result, the fast-stepping hollowpint 324-grain Gould bullet didn't shoot well with my loads although it might have perked up with a different powder charge. The Lyman 384-grain bullet shot quite well for close range use as my load put four rounds in less than 1¼ inches at 50 yards. This load, at 1641 fps, penetrated 23 inches of damp paper as well as a ¾-inch plywood board! The Marlin is a modern action designed for the loads put out by major arms factories but will not handle cartridges loaded with a 500-grain bullet. These slugs are just a bit too long to feed from magazine into the chamber.

I had another 45-70, an Old Reliable Shiloh Rifle Co., that would handle almost any 45-caliber bullet except the NEI 420 as this load would not chamber in the rifle. In checking with Wolf Droege of Shiloh Rifle Co., he said I had an early rifle and that the guns they are making today would handle any bullets. Despite this news I, like most reloaders, was determined to try this load in my rifle. I seated the bullet a bit deeper, then ran the load up into a 45 ACP taper crimp die. Voila, it worked perfectly and the round chambered!

The Sharps has a 30-inch barrel which allowed me to gain a few extra feet per second when compared to the Marlin's carbine-length barrel. In the Sharps I was also able to use the 512-grain loads; however, the Sharps took more kindly to the 324-grain Gould

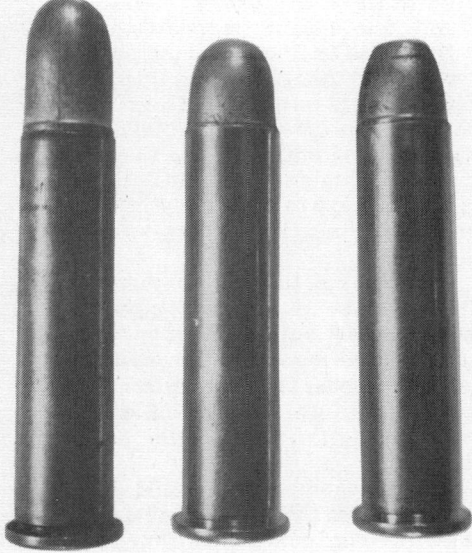

Bullets for the 45-70 are easy to come by as this cartridge has been popular for so many years. Left to right, 512 grain, 384 grain and the Gould 324-grain hollowpoint.

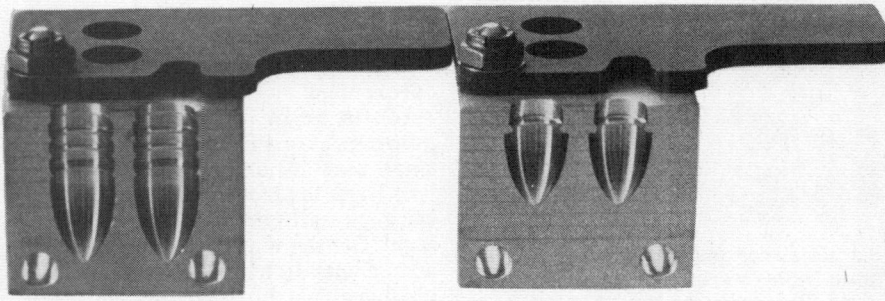

NEI moulds for soft-lead-points come in two sections, one for the soft point itself (right). The full-length mould can be used to cast a solid bullet for normal shooting without using the special soft lead insert.

hollowpoint load and shot better groups. Penetration with bigger 384-, 420- and 512-grain bullets was spectacular. All these loads penetrated 26 inches of damp newsprint. No, the solid lead bullets didn't expand, but there was no reason that they should. Clearly that big 45-caliber bullet does not need to expand! Going into an animal it has a greater diameter than most small-bore bullets, even if they are fully mushroomed!

The 458 Magnum

With the 458 I did not try the 512-grain cast bullet for penetration. I didn't need to. I once put a 500-grain solid jacketed bullet into a Cape Buffalo that seemed to literally pull the veldt from under his hooves!

The 458 Magnum cast bullets showed even more power than the 45-70 loads. The 384- and 420-grain bullets gave 3239 and 4312 foot pounds of energy. Penetration? It was more than you would need, and the expansion of soft-lead-nose bullets was impressive. The solid 420-grain went through 26 inches of damp sand. The bullet looked almost ready to be reloaded again!

A Word of Caution

I guess everyone has their own ideas on how to reload hunting ammunition. I happen to be the cautious sort of reloader. One time, while dove hunting, I picked up some 12-gauge hulls from a shooter near me. The rims on all the cases were blown apart. I asked him if this was normal. "On my extra-special reloads it is," he replied. I found another spot to hunt. Another time a shooter at a range handed me a box of 20, 45-70 empty cases, each with the primer blown, and asked me if this was normal. His rifle? One lovingly produced by Christian Sharps when blackpowder was in its heyday. I remarked that I had never seen a blown primer with blackpowder. The shooter said that to clean up the blackpowder smoke, he had added just a touch of smokeless powder (enough to blow up a modern Colt 45 pistol) against the primer, before filling the case with the finest blackpowder he could find. Another time I arrived at a range after they had just removed the barrel of a rifle from the ground in front of the 50-yard target. The bullet may still be whistling around this earth. The rest of the rifle wasn't worth looking at, and they were still picking pieces of stock from the shooter's arm.

That's why I'm a cautious reloader. I don't have the vaguest idea of how many rounds I have reloaded myself, with never a problem. If you are going to reload, *pay attention to the loading manuals.* Lyman has *The Cast Bullet Handbook* and RCBS has a relatively new book, *Cast Bullet Manual.* For ongoing help, *The Fouling Shot*, the journal of the Cast Bullet Association, is another source of information. In addition, if I want a load for a particular bullet that I can't find in a reloading manual, as a computer owner, I run a computer program call *Load From A Disk*, which gives powders, velocities and pressures. This is helpful as you can always pick a load giving lower pressures that would be suitable for cast bullets. If you collect reloading manuals, some of the earlier ones will give you a great deal of helpful information. Old Lyman Handbooks, Sharpe's massive compilation of facts in his *Complete Guide to Handloading*, as well as books by Whelen and other well-known writers are full of valuable cast bullet information.

Before you begin to shoot cast bullets in your rifle clean the bore thoroughly. Not just a lick and a switch through the barrel, but a good, thorough cleaning. This is particularly true when using small-bore guns. The big 45 and 375 calibers aren't as fussy as the smaller bores such as the 30-30 and 308 Winchester. Bits of jacket material in the bore play hell on cast bullets. First, clean the bore with a bore paste (I like Corbin's). Next, I thoroughly clean both the bore and chamber with a degreaser to make certain that the bore paste is completely removed. Then I clean again with a conventional bore solvent. Believe me, this can make the difference in accuracy when using cast bullets.

Once your rifle is cleaned and you are ready to reload your ammo take a good look at the brass cases. I make certain that they are in as good shape as the ones I use for loading with jacketed bullets. My brass is strictly trimmed to industry standards and I fully resize each case. Some people recommend that your brass should be sized to just snugly fit the rifle's chamber. I don't buy that. Maybe for varmint shooting, but when I use my rifle for a big game animal hunt, I want that case to flow freely into the chamber, just like store-bought ammo.

In expanding the necks of the cases I always use an expanding button made for cast bullets. They open the case up a bit more than the standard button made for jacketed bullets. This allows you to seat the cast bullet easily without injuring the bullet or the gas check.

I always chamber each round of ammunition into the rifle it's going to be used in, before going on any hunt. I do this with factory ammunition, reloads assembled with jacketed bullets and, particularly, with ammo loaded with cast bullets. With bolt-action rifles it's usually easy to remove the firing pin so that you can check the ammunition at home. With other types of actions, such as a lever gun, I test them at the range, with the muzzle pointed down range.

While we have talked about big game hunting loads, this is only a small part of hunting. Many hunters like light loads with cast bullets for taking small game and birds, where legal. Consequently, whether you are armed with light loads or some of the big-bore cast bullet loads that will take any animal, those home-grown cast bullets will serve you in any hunting field. ●

Both the Lyman 283 grain (left) and NEI 270-grain (right) were used in the 375 H&H round. They easily fed through the action of the author's BRNO rifle. These slugs can also be used to turn out cast-bullet 375 Winchester ammo.

The Cheney Plains Rifle

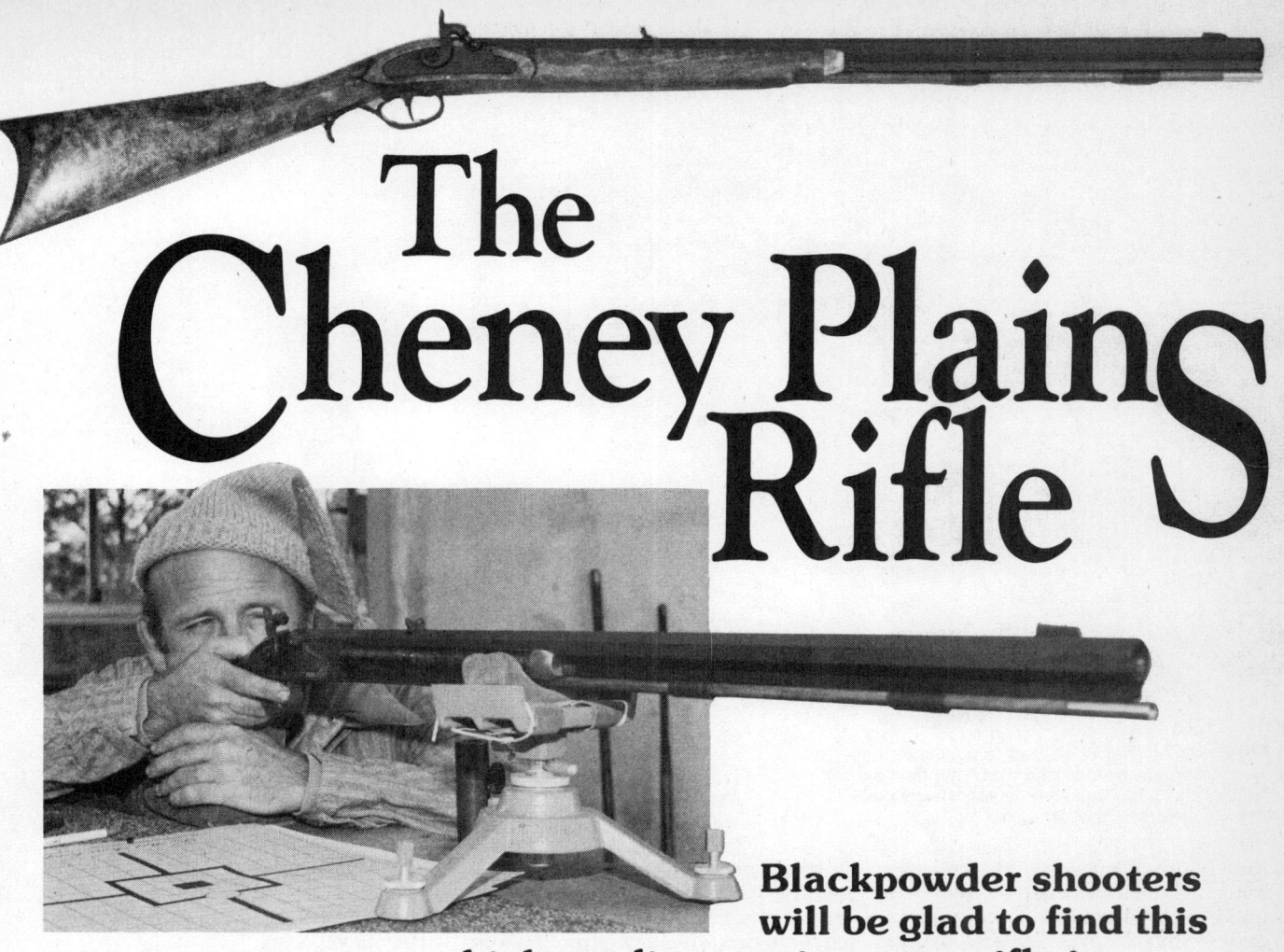

Mark Cheney shooting one of his Leman Plains Rifle creations. The rifle is available in either 50 or 54 caliber, and with browned steel or brass furniture.

Blackpowder shooters will be glad to find this high quality, semi-custom rifle is available at a mass-production price. And, this gun shoots as good as it looks!

by REX THOMAS

THE PAST 10 YEARS or so have been rewarding ones for me, thanks to blackpowder firearms. It was about that long ago that I first developed a serious interest in primitive firearms. I did so because I wanted a new challenge in big game hunting. I won't go into the whys or the wherefores in great detail. It's enough to say that I had reached a point with modern firearms where taking some game animals had become too easy.

I've always felt that hunting big game is a very personal thing that should be done on a very intimate "close enough to touch" level. If you love the pure satisfaction that comes from the hunt and not the kill, as I do, then you know what I'm talking about. In the past 10 years of blackpowder hunting, I've had the good fortune to take many big game animals, including several four-point mule deer, a record book antelope and a mountain lion. I even have plans this year for moose and mountain goat and somewhere down the road, I'm going to take a bull elk. Black bear still elude me after three attempts without ever drawing a bead on a bruin.

Much of my hunting experience has been an evolution in learning as much as I could about blackpowder firearms. Like most hunters who somehow find themselves interested in blackpowder, I started with simple and rather inexpensive rifles that I now class as mass-produced firearms.

There are a lot of them around made by such companies as Thompson/Center, Lyman, and CVA. These are sort of the working man's guns in blackpowder circles, much like a Remington or Winchester bolt-action rifle is in centerfire circles. You can buy workhorse guns or you can move up or down a level or two in quality and buy whatever kind of rifle might fit your hunting or shooting needs, as well as your pocketbook.

I've owned and hunted with rifles from all the companies just mentioned. I still have some of their rifles in my gunrack today, and there are many fond memories wrapped up in various outings with them.

Several years ago, I decided to move

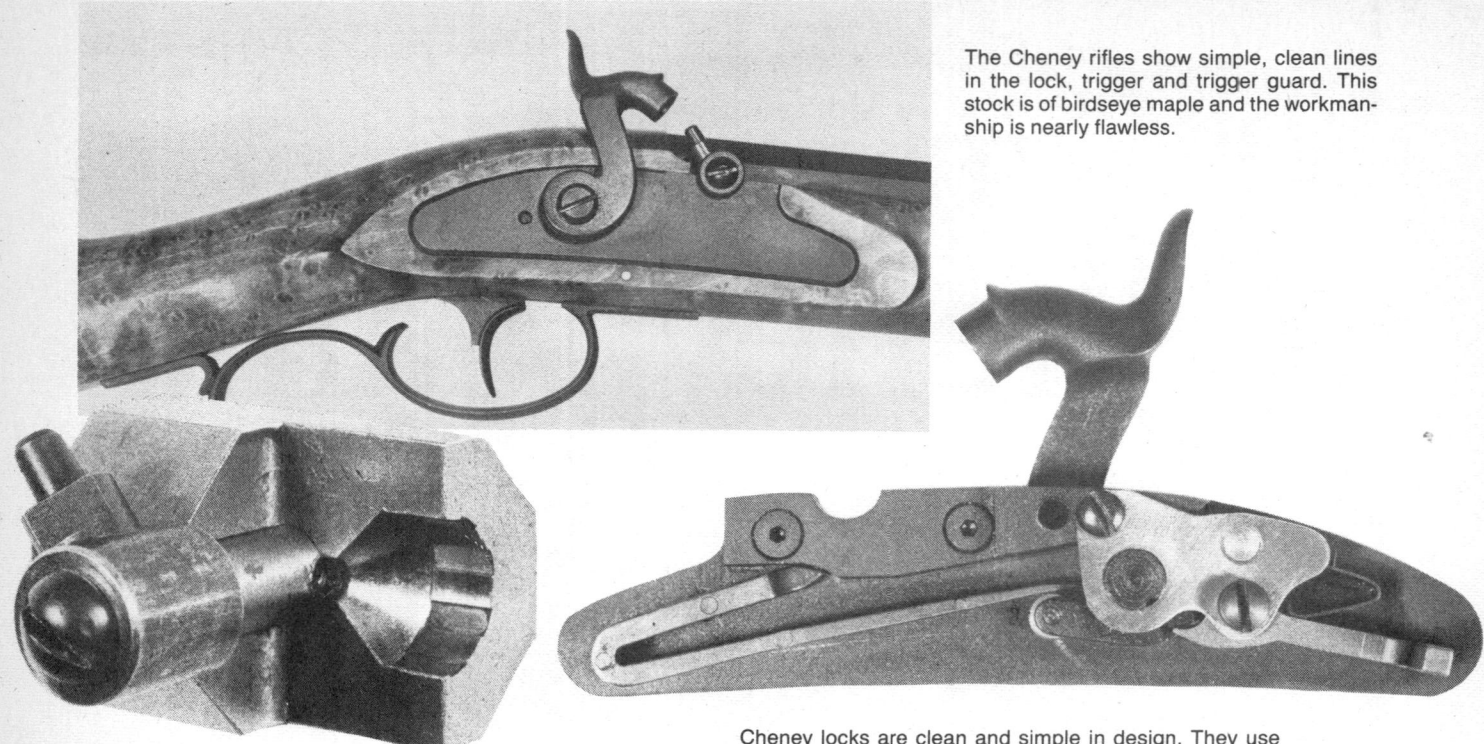

The Cheney rifles show simple, clean lines in the lock, trigger and trigger guard. This stock is of birdseye maple and the workmanship is nearly flawless.

Cheney locks are clean and simple in design. They use two leaf springs and a unique "roller" on the mainspring. The parts are engineered for years of trouble-free service.

A cut-away of Cheney's breech plug snows that the bolster is a hollow tube that extends clear through the plug. A flash hole is perfectly centered at the end of the barrel.

into another realm of blackpowder hunting and firearms. There are a number of what I like to call "semi-custom" blackpowder riflemakers in this country. Many, like Hatfield Rifle Works, Ozark Mountain Arms and Oregon Trail Riflesmiths have been written about before. Such rifle makers share some common characteristics, including a rather limited number of rifles made annually; hand-made quality; a limited number of true craftsmen working away in unique small factories or shops; and a quality rifle at a realistic price, usually in the $400 to $700 range.

Recently, I found another fine rifle maker practically in my own backyard—Mark Cheney of Cheney Firearms. I'm surprised I didn't find him some time ago because he's been building blackpowder rifles for several years now, but he is only of late beginning to attain the recognition he deserves. The company is owned and operated by Mark Cheney, a true craftsman who has been making either blackpowder rifles or various modern gun parts for many years. I've spent the better part of a year getting to know Mark, watching him work in his shop, test firing rifles with him at the range and so on. What I have learned is that here is a man with an amazing understanding of rifle mechanics, functional gun design, firearms history, wood and metal finishing, ballistics, the laws of physics and so much more.

Mark presently makes both a half-stock and full-stock percussion Plains Rifle designed in the tradition of well-known riflemaker Henry Leman. Cheney rifles are available in either 50 or 54 caliber only, browned steel or brass. By the time you read this, you will be able to order Cheney's rifles in flintlock or percussion. I've had a look at the flintlock he will use and it's a beauty. It's meticulously crafted to be reliable, easy to maintain, and as near waterproof as a flintlock can be. If you are into flintlocks, this one will be worth waiting for.

In the last decade, I've become very discriminating about what I like and don't like. To me, high quality means several things, including good looks, proper balance, superior components, excellent fit and finish, total reliability and shooting excellence. In blackpowder arms, all of this has to come together at once. Cheney's rifle is one of very few that achieves superior marks from me in all of the above mentioned areas. Take it for what it's worth. I've examined, handled, shot, hunted with and written about many blackpowder rifles in the last several years and this one is well worth the surprisingly few dollars you will have to pay to get one.

The rifle that Mark built for me is a 54-caliber half-stock with browned steel rather than brass. My rifle is typical of what he produces daily in his shop here in northern Utah—no special treatment just because I'm a writer and that's the way I like things done.

The barrel is cut from solid round bar stock and is drilled between centers, reamed, rifled and polished. It measures 1 inch from flat to flat and 30 inches in length. The muzzle is crowned and the breechplug is installed concentric to the center line of the bore. Inside, the bore is cut with eight lands and grooves and it has a one turn in 70-inch twist—excellent for round ball, maxi-balls or Buffalo Bullets.

Worthy of special mention here is the design of the breechplug. The bolster, or drum, runs clear through the lower portion of the barrel and a flash hole is perfectly centered at the end of the barrel. An Allen screw holds the drum permanently in alignment from the opposite side of the lock. The advantage in this system is that the spark and hot gasses from the cap are

Mark Cheney, founder of the company, inspects a rough-cut half-stock before machining and fitting the metal.

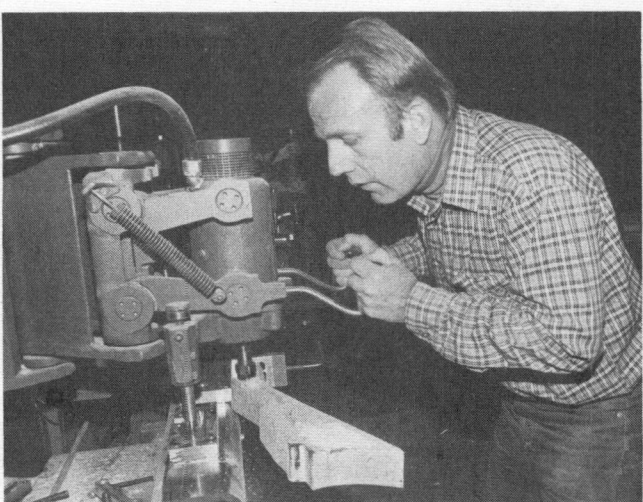

Ultra-high speed routers that are keyed to metal templates allow Cheney to make a perfect wood to metal fit in the lock area.

Much of the initial shaping of wood parts is done on high-speed belt sanders, which reduces time required to complete a rifle.

forced into smaller and smaller tubes and out at the center of the powder charge at the bottom of the barrel. This allows even "flash" ignition and better utilization of the powder charge. In other systems, the ignition is like a slow fuse (one grain of powder lined up against another) until it comes in contact at the side of the barrel with the full powder charge. This seems to be a less efficient method of ignition. Cheney consistently gets 12 to 14 percent greater muzzle velocity with his system over other barrels with conventional breechplugs. And, he also gets less deviation in velocity from any string of shots during test firing. This translates into better accuracy and he believes it is all due to his unique breechplug system.

The stock on any Cheney rifle is made from hard northern maple. Cheney uses highly figured birdseye or burl maple that would probably be graded as "AA" selection grade. This is a couple of steps above what you would normally expect on a muzzle loading rifle for this price, but I find the quality of the wood to be in harmony with the overall quality of the rifle.

Metal parts, including the lockplate and hammer, buttplate and toeplate, trigger, trigger guard, tenons, barrel rib, sights and barrel are all first sand blasted and then browned in a hot

GUNS ILLUSTRATED 1989 **57**

bath process. The finish is non-reflective and as even as you could hope for on even high grade rifles or shotguns.

The Cheney lock is unique for a couple of reasons. To begin, Cheney manufactures his own lock. The design uses two traditional leaf springs. The mainspring and tumbler contact is via a roller bearing mounted in the tumbler. The tumbler bearing surfaces are the largest I've seen on any lock. The safety, or half-lock, and sear surfaces are precision cut and then hand honed for smooth, trouble-free operation.

The marriage of wood to metal in Cheney's Plains Rifle is one area that Cheney takes great pride in, and rightfully so. Utilizing ultra-high speed routers set up on very expensive master templates, rifle stocks can be custom fitted to locks, triggers, barrels and buttplates with little or no hands-on labor required. This process works remarkably well only as long as the metal parts are consistent, and Cheney takes great pains to ensure that they are. I had the chance to see these very expensive routers in action and can tell you that there's no way a better fit could be obtained through using only hand tools.

Cheney uses a special, reddish-brown phenolic resin stain derived from linseed and tung oils that deeply penetrates the stock. At least three coats are applied and treated stocks are partially dried in special heat chambers between coats. From here on, Cheney is a bit mysterious about the final finishing of his stocks, but he attains a very smooth, hand-rubbed look akin to the work you might expect from a custom-stock maker like Reinhart Fajen, Inc. Cheney says that if the stock on his rifles takes some abuse through a hard hunting season, it can be easily and quickly restored by applying products like Birchwood Casey's Tru Oil.

A rib is soldered to the bottom of the barrel and two tenons hold a brass tipped, hickory ramrod in place under the barrel. Cheney supplies a special cleaning jag with each rifle that is specially made to fit the breech or lower portion of the barrel. This is a very important factor often overlooked by other blackpowder gun makers. The life of the barrel can be extended when you have the right tools to do a proper and thorough cleaning job. The barrel is pinned to the stock with two brass pins in tradi-

pounds) with no creep. Another reason is his sights. At first glance, they seem crude but when you line up on a target, you quickly realize that the thin front blade and clean cut notch in the rear sight make for an excellent sight picture. I also found that the hammer and nipple line up perfectly, often a problem with other rifles and one that can create ignition problems.

Mark and I spent a number of hours on the rifle range testing the ballistics of my rifle with an Oehler 33 chronograph and testing for accuracy. To begin, we fired 10 shots to break in the barrel and then swabbed it out and started our tests. Mark had developed a recommended load for his 54-caliber rifles over the years so we conducted our studies using it, which consists of 100 grains of FFFg powder, a Speer .530-inch roundball, pillow ticking patch lubed with Hoppe's #9 and a CCI #11 cap. Ballistic studies of this load revealed an average muzzle velocity of 1902 fps. Standard deviation after five rounds was only 18 fps. I've found a much greater standard deviation with other blackpowder rifles. Checking this data against Lyman's ballistic charts showed a 13 percent increase in velocity over Lyman's

One of Cheney's assistants applies the necessary "elbow grease" in the final shaping phase of a stock.

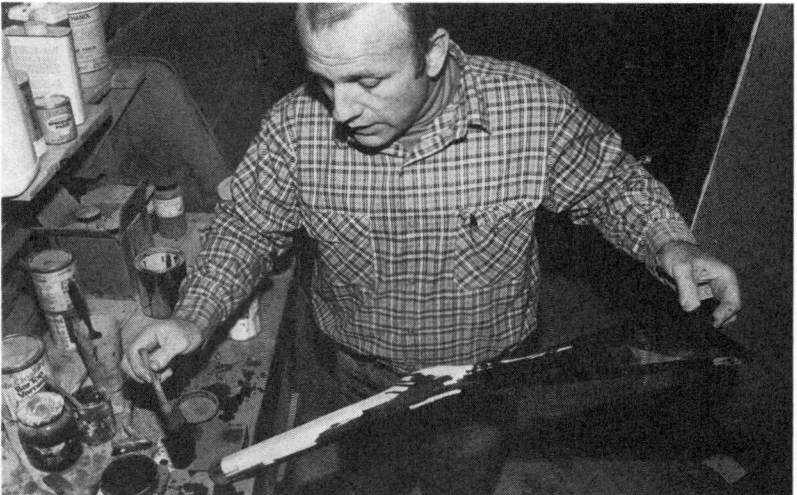

Cheney uses a phenolic resin type of varnish, applying several coats that penetrate deeply. His finishing process is very similar to that used on musical instruments and high quality furniture.

After the stock is inletted and rough fit to the metal parts comes the stage of preparation and assembly that gives Cheney's rifles that professional look. Much of the final shaping is on high-speed belt sanders and it takes an experienced craftsman to produce a work of art rather than just a big pile of sawdust. There's also a lot of filing and hand sanding that must be done before the stock gets to the stain and finish process.

tional style, and a pewter forend cap at the tip of the stock lends a final touch of class.

To handle one of Cheney's Plains Rifles is to experience good balance, to appreciate functional design and to know the difference between a mere tool and a craftsman's near work of art. Not only do Cheney rifles look and feel superior, but they also shoot remarkably well. Part of the reason for this is clean trigger pull (set at 4

tests.

In addition, we set up targets at 50 yards and fired five-shot groups. I was surprised, if not overwhelmed, at what I came up with. Several five-shot groups using the above load turned in average groups of only 1 1/4 inches. My best group was a mere 3/4-inch. I've shot a number of center fire rifles with open sights that couldn't shoot nearly this well, not to mention numerous blackpowder rifles that I felt good about if they would hold together with 2-inch groups at that distance. There was no reason to try and improve on such a load, but I do intend to do more studies when time and weather will allow with maxi-balls and Buffalo Bullets.

It's very likely that you have never heard of the Cheney Plains Rifle, even though it has been around for the past few years. It's never been listed in any firearms directory but it has been picked up within the past several months by Cabela's. They recognize it for the high quality rifle it is at an affordable price. You can contact Mark Cheney and ask for further information or order your rifle directly through him at Cheney Firearms Co., P.O. Box 321, Woods Cross, UT 84087. Mark currently prices his Plains Rifle at $449.00.

In my years of experience with blackpowder rifles, I'm confident this is one of the very finest replicas made today, by any U.S. riflemaker. Knowing the quality of the components, how well the rifle is put together and how accurately it shoots, I've already decided it's going with me later this year when I head to the far north for moose and mountain goat.

Having absolute confidence in your rifle is vital to success and the Cheney Plains rifle is one you and I can rely on for many years to come. There's no doubt in my mind this one will be around long enough to pass along to one of my sons, and possibly even one of his sons.

A chronograph helped prove that Cheney barrels give higher muzzle velocities than "standard" barrels. There is also minimal velocity deviation, a factor in improved accuracy.

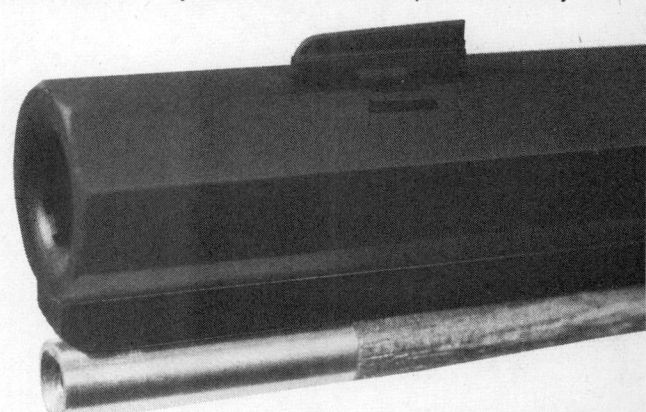

The front sight (above) is somewhat traditional in that it's drift-adjustable for windage. The upper part of the blade is thinned down for finer sighting. The buckhorn rear sight (below) is also drift-adjustable for windage. It has a thin cut in the bottom of the notch.

Cheney Plains Rifle Data

Caliber	50 or 54
Barrel	30″ (1″ flats) rifled
Rifling	Hook-cut .010″ to .012″ deep
Twist	1 turn in 70″
Ignition	Percussion or flintlock
Lock	Leaf springs, roller bearing tumbler
Stock	Birdseye northern maple (full-stock or half-stock)
Sights	Blade front, buckhorn rear, drift adjustable
Furniture	Browned steel or brass
Finish	Hot browned steel Hand-rubbed oil
Overall Length	47¼″
Weight	50 caliber — 9 lbs. 54 caliber — 8½ lbs.
Features	Single set trigger High grade maple stock Custom fit cleaning jag supplied
Price: Percussion or flintlock	$449.00

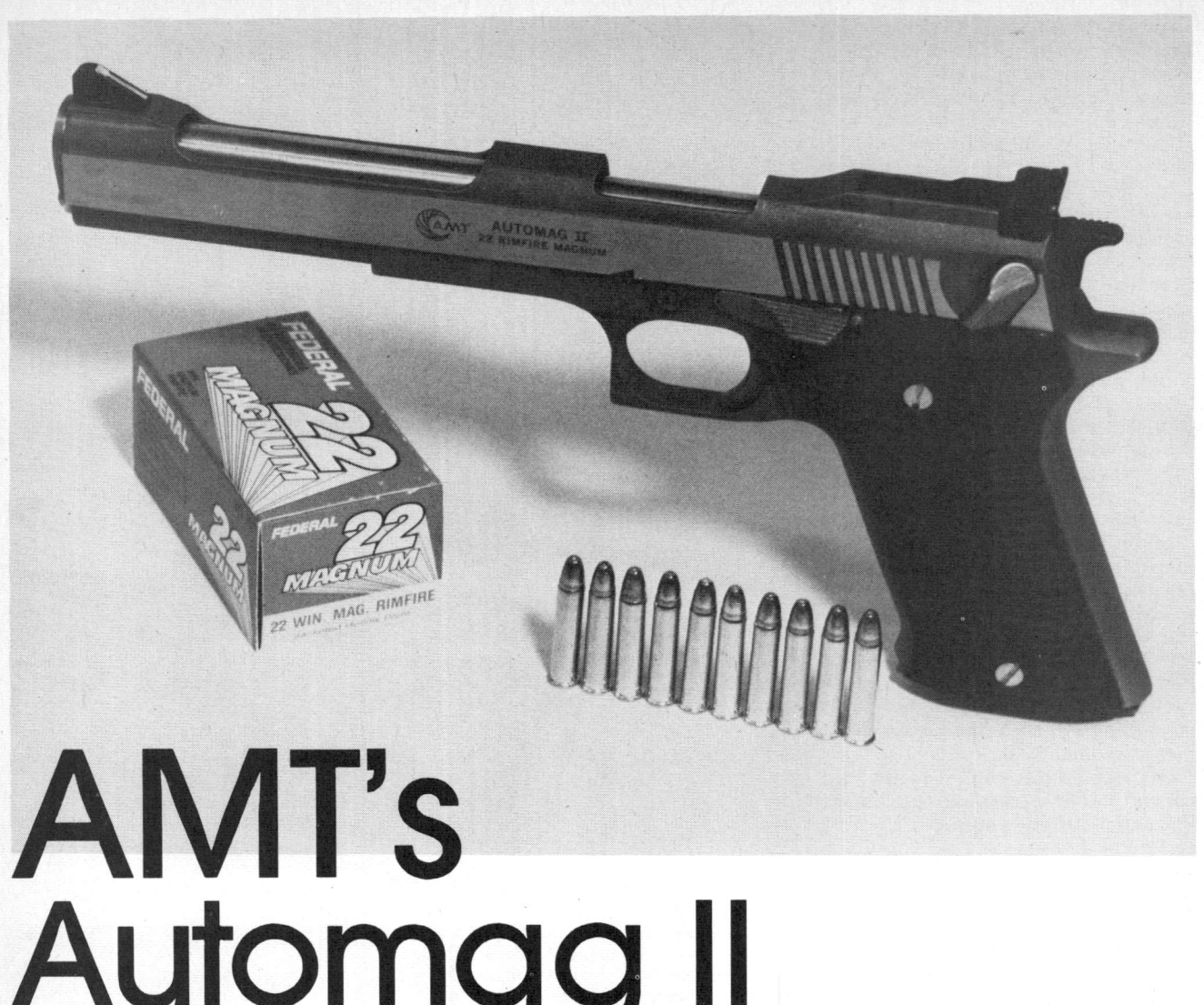

AMT's Automag II
a refreshingly new pistol

Here's a look at the first truly successful auto pistol that chambers the powerful 22 WMR cartridge. In shooting over 3000 rounds, the author's gun didn't miss a beat.

by JIM GOSNELL

Ask FOR THE UNUSUAL in the world of guns and chances are that someone will hand you an AMT Automag II. No, this isn't a wild "Buck Rogers Space Gun" or something that Dirty Harry will want to carry. Rather, it's a functional as well as good looking handgun which fills a definite void in the firearms industry. The feature making this stainless steel wonder unique is that it is the first truly successful semi-auto handgun designed for the 22 WMR cartridge, a rimfire round which has been around for close to 30 years.

AMT (Arcadia Machine and Tool, Inc.) is no stranger to stainless steel. The 44 Automag was their creation as

Gosnell found the Automag II to handle well in his tests. The excellent Millett sights contributed to the gun's accuracy potential. Below left—The front sight has a blaze-orange insert, while the rear (left) uses white around the notch, and is fully adjustable. Hammer-block safety is below the sight.

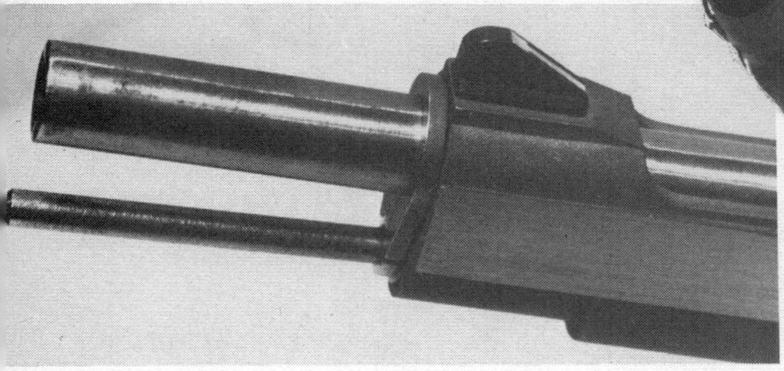

was the Hardballer, which is a stainless copy of the Colt Government 45 ACP. They also offer a long-slide version of the Hardballer for "Pin" competition and a shortened model for concealed carry. The line-up also includes the Backup, which is a small auto offered in either 22 Long Rifle or 380 ACP, as well as other stainless steel handguns and rifles chambered for the 22 Long Rifle.

Appearance of the Automag II is pleasing, looking somewhat more slender than its big-bore cousins and the finish is "first cabin." The frame and the top of the slide have a gray matte finish while the sides of the slide are brushed and bright. This, along with the grooved black plastic grips, provides a very attractive contrast. The jury is still out, however, on the open-top slide which was done to save weight, I suspect, and to aid in cooling of the barrel. It might look a little cleaner without that cut-out. There are no sharp corners to snag things on, which adds to the "user-friendly" characteristics of this handgun. When I first picked the gun up I noticed that it fit very well in my hand and it has excellent balance. Operation of the safety, the slide release, and cocking of the hammer are all accomplished easily without shifting the gun in my hand. Slide operation is a breeze with the comfortable grip providing ample leverage.

The trigger guard is squared off to provide a finger rest for the support hand. This is a feature made popular by many of the big-bore combat autos and, though cosmetically appealing, it is a feature that I prefer not to use since I have a tendency to pull the gun down when using the finger rest. Quite a number of people have enjoyed success using the finger rest but, try as I might, I just can't seem to get consistent control of the gun by using it.

As if the Automag II didn't have enough going for it, the guys at AMT topped it off with excellent Millett sights. If you are among those who

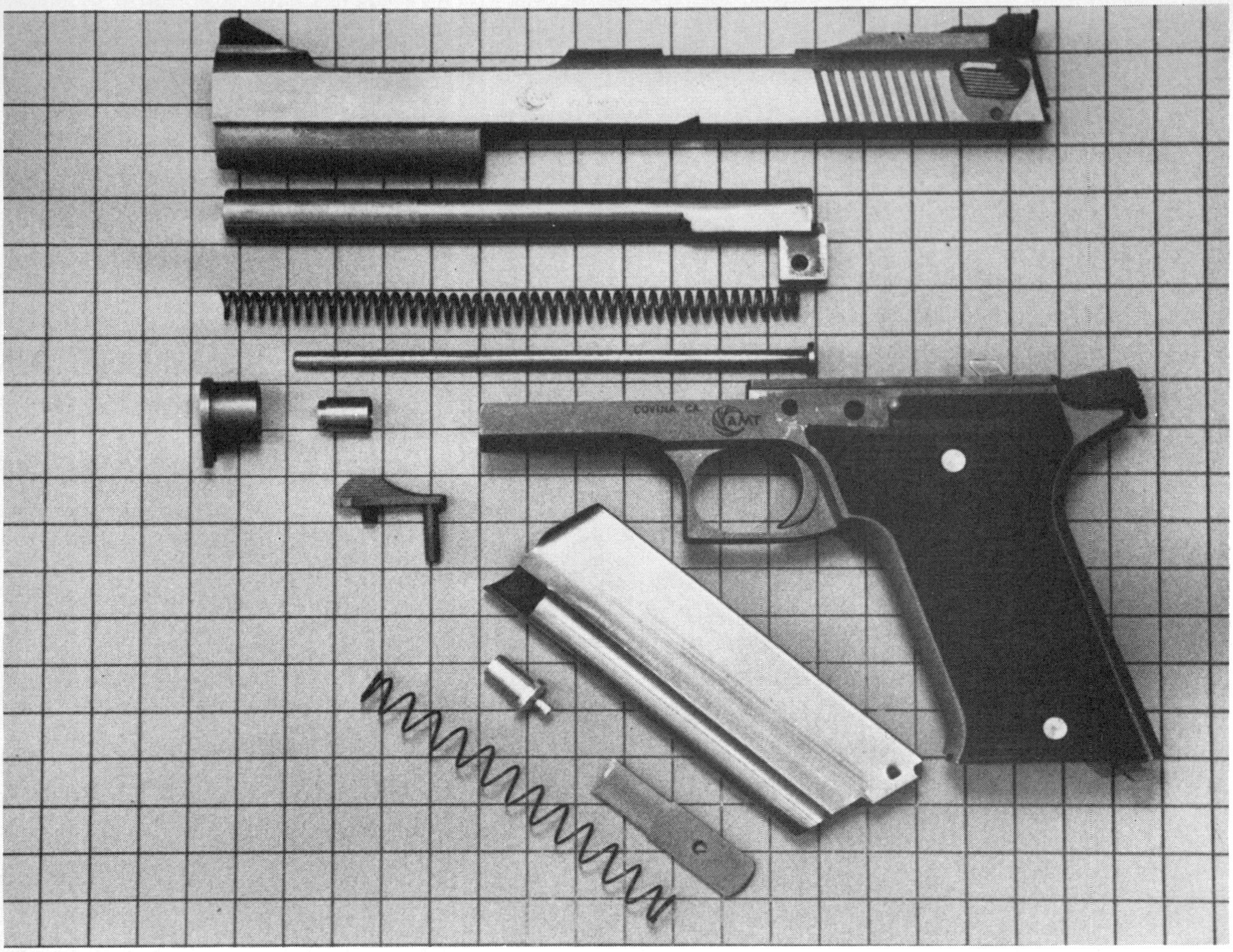

Field-stripping the Automag II is quick and simple. Counting the magazine as one unit, there are only nine basic parts when stripped. Grid is ½-inch squares.

The Automag II magazine holds 10 rounds of 22 WMR but Gosnell found it much easier on his thumb to load only eight shots. Magazine release is on the butt of the grip.

have never had the opportunity to use Millett sights, you are really missing one of the joys of handgunning. The blaze-orange ramp front and white outline "longhorn" rear just seem to line up naturally. The rear sight is fully adjustable for windage and elevation and the screws are large enough that you don't need a watchmaker's screwdriver to make the adjustments. Finally, for those of us who seem to forget which direction to turn the screws for correction, the sight is marked with arrows to assist.

Another good feature on this gun is the safety. When activated, a steel bar rolls out beyond the firing pin to prevent contact by the hammer. Operation of the safety is very positive with equal pressure required to place it in either on or off position. With the safety on, the gun can be dry fired. This makes for some excellent practice sessions but, as with the handling of any firearm, be positive that the gun is unloaded before pulling that trigger.

The magazine release is located on the heel of the grip and is large enough for easy, positive operation. Personnally, I'd love to see this gun with a 1911-type release on the side of the grip. Maybe that's asking too much, but it sure would be a nice touch. The magazine holds 10 rounds but forcing the 9th and 10th rounds in proves to be somewhat of a chore. For comfort's sake I have been loading the clips with 8 rounds.

Lately, most handguns seem to leave the factory with rather heavy triggers and the Automag II is no exception. I would guess this has something to do with the growing number of product liability suits. Mine broke at 11 pounds, which explains the 4-inch groups that I got when I first shot the gun! I was beginning to think that a hydraulic assist would be needed, but a local gunsmith worked the gun over and the trigger now breaks at a very crisp 5 pounds. What an improvement! But be warned that the Automag II is not a simple gun internally and only a *competent* gunsmith should attempt to do any trigger work on it.

From a function standpoint, the design of the Automag II was no easy task. Due to a late peak pressure of the 22 WMR, the case mouth tends to stick in the chamber causing extraction problems. Larry Grossman, designer of the Automag II, solved this problem by drilling 18 holes at 90 degrees to the chamber in a series of three rows of six holes each. A sleeve was then welded over the chamber with just enough clearance to allow gases to pass from the first set of holes back to the next two rows, thus equalizing the chamber pressure. Fired cases clearly show powder stains from the chamber holes. Absolutely brilliant and, best of all, it works! And, I have yet to experience any fouling of the holes.

There's no doubt that we have a fine gun here, so let's take a look at what we're going to feed it. As stated earlier, the 22 WMR has been around for nearly three decades. Although it was designed as a rifle cartridge, the first gun on the market was the Ruger Single-Six. As a matter of fact, Ruger had their gun available before Winchester released the ammunition! The 22 WMR is one of those cartridges that sparks controversy every time someone mentions it and, in this writer's opinion, it has received a considerable amount of unwarranted bad publicity. In just about every debate concerning the 22 WMR the same four negative points surface: it's too loud; it's too expensive to shoot; it's too destructive on small game; it's not accurate. Now, let's take a look at these complaints on an individual basis.

1. Too loud. No one in their right mind would shoot any firearm without proper ear protection. Even a 22 is capable of causing permanent hearing loss. In today's atmosphere of

Author found RWS and Federal's new 50-grain ammunition to give the best accuracy. The Federal load shoots under 1-inch groups like this at 25 yards.

Right—Federal now makes two bullet weights for the 22 WMR, the 40-grain (left) and 50-grain (with the wider bullet band), both jacketed hollowpoints. Above—It's tough to tell the difference between the 40- and 50-grain boxes—No. 757 is the heavier bullet.

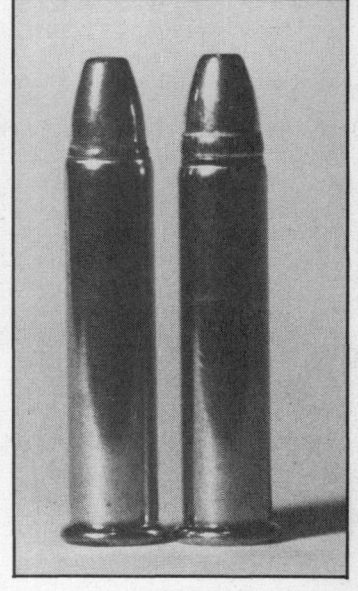

health awareness it amazes me that anyone would shoot without ear protection. So, that argument doesn't hold water.

2. It's too expensive to shoot. If compared to a 22 Long Rifle, sure, it's more expensive but that's not quite fair. The 22 WMR is a lot more, ballistically, than a Long Rifle. Let's look at it compared to the 38 Special which, next to the 22 Long Rifle, is America's favorite plinking round and, on the average, lists for $15.00 per box. The 22 WMR lists for $6.70, which is less than half that of the 38. It is more costly than the Long Rifle, but you do get more bang for your buck here.

I know, you reload your 38s and it costs you one hell of a lot less than $15.00 a box. So, let's take a peek at it from that angle as well. Using list prices again, you still have to shell out between $3.75 and $7.00 per box for components, depending on the bullet and powder used, and this does not include the cost of brass or your time. If you are loading on a single-stage press it takes a considerable amount of time just to load one box, let alone 3 or 4 boxes for some weekend plinking. Not having to reload and chase brass can be worth quite a bit. I have been

able to find 22 WMR at a local sporting goods store for $4.25 per box and, by doing a little shopping, I'm sure that you'll be able to find some pretty fair prices in your area. In my book, the 22 WMR is still pretty cheap to shoot unless you plan to shoot several hundred rounds a day. Don't get me wrong—I do enjoy reloading, I just like shooting better.

3. Too destructive on small game. For the most part, I have found this to be a myth as well. Used in a handgun, the 22 WMR is almost ballistically identical, if not somewhat superior, to the 22 Long Rifle when used in a rifle. Hence, we have the power of a 22 rifle carried neatly on the hip and I have found damage is minimal in taking small game with the 40-grain FMJ. When used to its full potential in a rifle, the 22 WMR can be destructive on animals such as squirrels, especially when a hollow point is used. My suggestion here is to make a head shot. I'm quite pleased with the performance of the 40-grain FMJ and use it almost exclusively.

4. Poor accuracy. Here again we have an unwarranted black cloud hanging over the 22 WMR. I own a Smith & Wesson Model 48 (in 22 WMR) which has printed ½-inch groups at 25 yards and, fed properly, the Automag II holds a close second to it. Granted, my Model 48 is a target-quality gun sporting an 8⅜-inch barrel, but we are talking about the round being inherently inaccurate. To my way of thinking, that sure blows

Good looks, fine handling characteristics and flawless functioning all combine to make the Automag II perfect for taking small game and a great plinker. Because it's made of stainless steel, maintenance is less of a problem.

There are only four makers of 22 WMR ammunition—Federal, Winchester, RWS and CCI. FMJ, JHP bullets (40- and 50-grain) and shot cartridges (except RWS) are available.

that rumor out of the water.

Currently, the only ammo makers producing 22 WMR are Federal, CCI, Winchester and RWS. All are made with a 40-grain bullet with the choice of FMJ or hollow point. Federal has just recently released a new 50-gr. hollow point which shows great promise. Federal, CCI, and Winchester brands are readily available in most areas while the RWS is a might scarce. On a local search for the RWS, I came up empty handed but was finally able to locate some through Dave Cumberland at The Old West Scrounger in Montague, California. If you are having trouble locating anything in the way of ammunition, especially the odd-ball calibers, there is an excellent chance that Dave has just what you are after.

A note enclosed with the Automag II indicates that there might be a problem with the gun malfunctioning when using CCI ammunition loaded with flake powder. I didn't experience any such problem but should you find this to be true, CCI will replace your ammunition with their current run which is being loaded with ball-type powder. As a matter of fact, I didn't find any round that failed to cycle the gun with the single exception of the CCI shot cartridge, and I fully expected that.

When shooting the various types of ammunition over my Oehler 33 Chronograph, I found most to average about 1400 fps. The fastest proved to be the RWS at 1495 and the Federal at 1460. Not bad considering a 22 Long Rifle 40 grain is still short of 1300 fps out of a 20-inch tube. My gun seems to show a preference for both the RWS and the new Federal 50-grain ammo, both printing just under an inch at 25 yards. The Federal 50-grain number clocks in at 1250, quite

Uncle Mike's #5 Sidekick holster fits the Automag II nicely. Their belt, extra clip holder and pouch make for a nice outfit to carry the gun.

a bit slower than it's little 40-grain brother. Still, muzzle energy is about the same and, since it's accurate, I'll stick with it.

Another Automag II owner I talked with said that his particular gun favors CCI. This goes to show that guns of the same brand and model can be very individualistic. It is important that you try all brands of ammunition available in order to determine what works best in your gun. With the trigger job, all of the ammunition tested prints under 2 inches using a sand bag rest. I have managed a few offhand groups under 2 inches using the Federal 50-grain loads.

As with any new-on-the-market handgun, finding a holster can be a trying experience. My search turned up Uncle Mike's #5 Sidekick which fits the Automag nicely. I bought one in camouflage along with a belt, extra clip holder, and a pouch which will hold two boxes of ammo. This rig has proved to be a real winner when it comes to utility and economy. It is light in weight and very comfortable to wear. Combined with the Automag II, it can't be beat for small game hunting trail use.

In testing the Automag II, I have put over 3000 rounds through the gun and the only malfunction was an occasional failure of the slide to remain open after the last shot. If you get the impression that I'm a great fan of the 22 WMR and the Automag II, you're right on target. This is a perfect marriage, making a good cartridge that much better.

It's been a long time coming but the Automag II *has* arrived and let's hope it's here to stay. We now have a fine handgun for small game and varmints as well as plinking. The best part is that it is just plain fun! ●

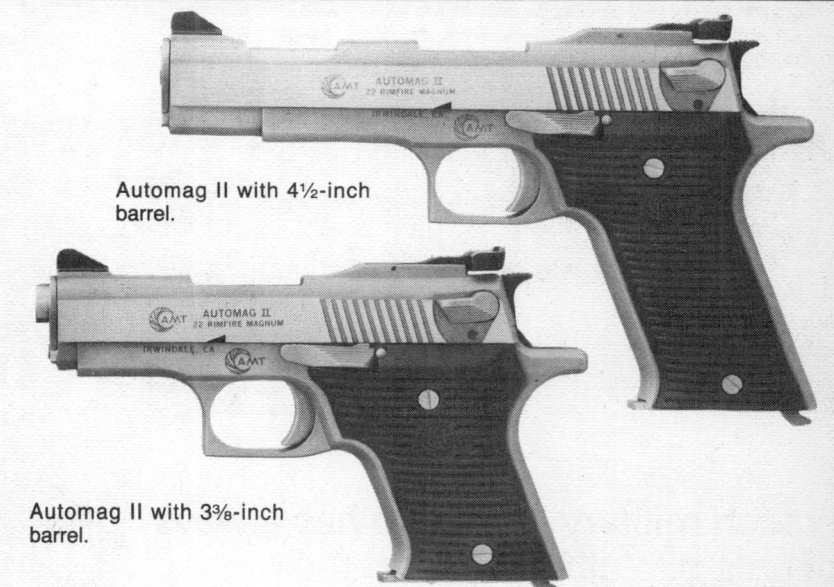

Automag II with 4½-inch barrel.

Automag II with 3⅜-inch barrel.

New Models

There were quite a few new things to see at the SHOT Show this year, but I had a nice surprise when I stopped by the AMT booth. Since the introduction of the 6-inch model, AMT now has two new versions of the Automag II and they're just what the doctor ordered.

The first new model should be available by the time you read this, with a release time in mid- to late May. It is a 4½-inch version with the same magazine capacity as the 6-inch. This will be a great sidearm. It'll be to carry and, unless I miss my guess, will not suffer much in the ballistics department from the 6-inch model. With the shorter barrel, this gun looks a little more balanced than it's brother with the longer nose. I have a strong suspicion that I have found *my* trail gun!

The next version out will have a 3⅜-inch barrel and a magazine capacity of seven rounds. AMT is looking to penetrate the defence and the police back-up market quite a bit deeper with this model. Even with the shorter grip this gun fits very comfortably in my large hand. This gun will be easy to conceal and should do very well in it's intended market. It should be available around September of 1988.

List price for both of these new models is said to be the same as the original gun—$329.00.

Shooting the French M1935 Pistols

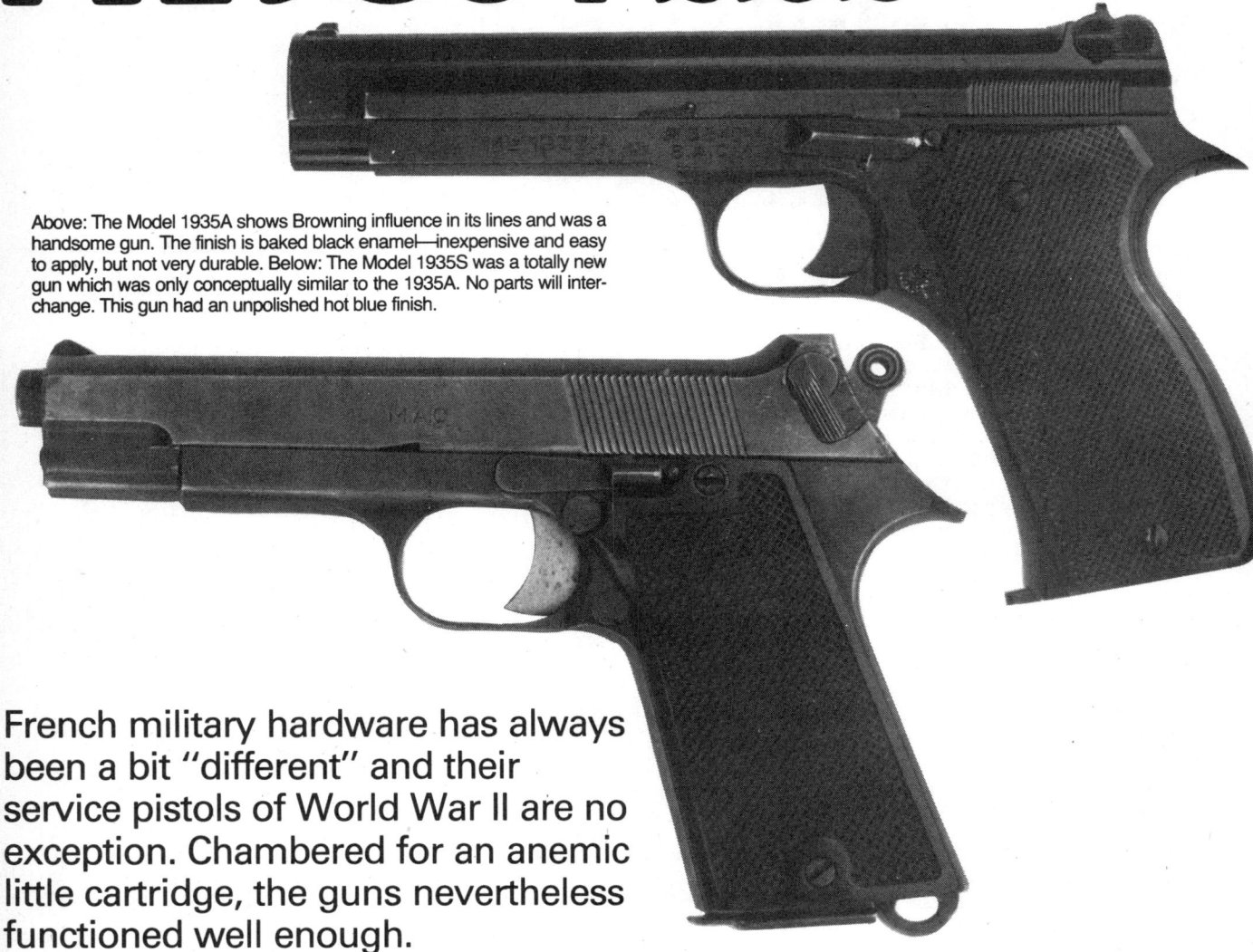

Above: The Model 1935A shows Browning influence in its lines and was a handsome gun. The finish is baked black enamel—inexpensive and easy to apply, but not very durable. Below: The Model 1935S was a totally new gun which was only conceptually similar to the 1935A. No parts will interchange. This gun had an unpolished hot blue finish.

French military hardware has always been a bit "different" and their service pistols of World War II are no exception. Chambered for an anemic little cartridge, the guns nevertheless functioned well enough.

by OSCAR TAMENNE

IN 1934, WHEN FRANCE finally settled down to choosing a proper standard pistol for her armed services, no one could have questioned why she was doing so. French martial handguns of the pre-war era were a motley lot: the only modern, moderately-powerful pistols were M1928 LeFrancais autos in 9mm Browning Long caliber... and of these, there existed only a handful, bought years before as evaluation pieces. Otherwise, the French military relied upon quantities of Savage and Star 32 ACP pocket automatics, and upon an indecent number of Ruby-type pocket "cheapies" which had been ordered during the darkest days of World War I. Even France's near-prehistoric 8mm M1892 Ordnance revolvers were still to be found, though usually with rear-echelon units. And so, when the French—Depression-crippled as were others, but mindful of developments across the Rhine—decided to re-equip all three of their services during the decade 1930-1940, the standard handgun was one of the items scheduled for review.

The review took the form of a government-sponsored design competition which took place in 1935-36. Prerequisites for entry into this com-

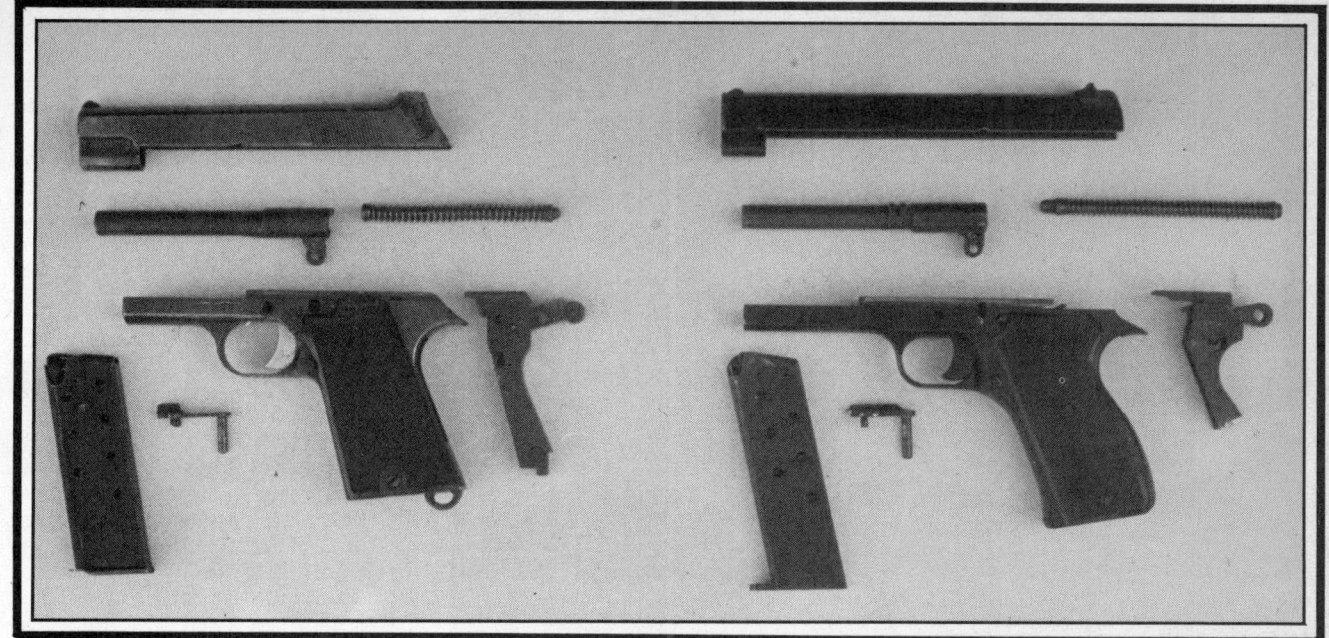

This comparative field-strip reveals the similarity of layout between the 1935S (left) and 1935A pistols. Both had modular firing mechanisms similar to the Russian Tokarev autoloader.

The Model 1935S safety (top) turned to this vertical position to render the gun "safe." This is clumsy and not at all secure. Safety of the 1935A (left) is slightly more convenient to the hand but is even less secure than the A-model.

petition were few, but were enough to discourage a majority of potential competitors. A modular, drop-in firing mechanism, consisting of the ejector, hammer, sear, hammer-spring, and sear-spring, was one of these requirements: Russia's Tokarev was the sole production pistol to be designed around such a system, and so this requirement rendered ineligible virtually all available designs of the period.

A second requirement for submissions concerned caliber, which was to be 7.65 L pour Pistolet, known today as 7.65 French Long. This round was a true oddball among pistol cartridges, a derivative of the WWI-vintage 30 Pederson cartridge. (Remember the Pederson? It was intended to be used in the famous Pederson device, designed to give semi-auto capability to '03 Springfield rifles.) Apparently, the French had been much impressed when, in the 1920s, John M. Browning had demonstrated a light rifle designed around the Pederson, and so they'd developed this cartridge as their next pistol and submachinegun round. Hence, the requirement for 7.65 Long chambering when France issued her 1934 handgun specs. This only further served to alienate would-be competitors, since there are problems attached to designing a gun around a still-experimental cartridge not available in one's own country (as both Bergmann and Luger had discovered years earlier in the U.S. 1905 pistol trials). It is to this day hard to see why the 7.65 Long so enthralled the French, since its ballistics—87-grain .308-inch FMJ projectile at 1175 fps—were nothing spectacular.

Predictably, only a limited number of prototypes was forthcoming in answer to the government's specification. FN of Belgium submitted one, as did the French national arsenal at St. Etienne. But it was a Charles Petter-designed entry by SACM (also a French concern) which captured the fancy of the military evaluators. This pistol featured a locked-breech, Browning-style action and was small for a service sidearm. It was less than 7½ inches long with its 4.3-inch barrel and weighed only 26 ounces. It was also a handsome little beast and the Browning influence was obvious in its lines. The gun worked well, and included in its engineering all the aforementioned prerequisites. The French ordered the gun into production as the Model 1935A and actual deliveries

A major difference between the A and S models was in the locking systems. The 1935A (left) used Browning-style locking lugs; the '35S exchanged these for a simple-to-machine shoulder.

from the SACM (Societe Alsacienne des Constructions Mecaniques) plant commenced in 1938.

The rate of production was, however, slow, due mainly to the amount of complex machine tooling needed to make it. Added to which, a single firm simply could not be responsible for all of France's handgun needs. Hence, as of late 1938, a call went out for a redesign of the '35A to create a gun which could be made more quickly. It was intended to enroll a number of firms in the production of the revamped arm. The St. Etienne arsenal took up the challenge and, within a surprisingly short time, materialized with the MAS (Manufacture d'Armes de St. Etienne) Model 1935S . . . which was essentially a whole new pistol. Only the general configuration was the same as the 1935A's: The gun retained the *concepts* of a locked-breech system and a modular firing mechanism and a safety that blocked the hammer from the firing pin and a loaded chamber indicator. But specifics of these systems were changed, as were other things, particularly the locking mechanism, which became a simple barrel-mounted shoulder in place of the Browning-style lugs. Over-all length decreased slightly, but the weight was upped 2 ounces. Few parts interchanged; even the eight-shot magazines differed.

Plans were made to have this new arm built at no fewer than three arsenals: SACM, already building the 1935A; SAGEM, Societe d'Applications Generales Electriques et Mecaniques; and the "home" arsenal at St. Etienne. MAC (Manufacture d'Armes de Chatellerault) was to contribute to the effort also, by producing a variant sub-type, the M1935S M1, which featured a slightly reconfigured safety. With four builders thus cooperating, it was hoped to reach an annual production figure of 36,000 pistols. Then came the disaster of June 1940 and all of France's rearmament programs came to a sudden, German-mandated end. Only 3,500 M1935A and 1,400 M1935S handguns had been completed and distributed among France's three services.

The Nazis, being ever the packrats of the service pistol world, were quick to swipe every 1935A they came upon. (For whatever reason, they ignored the M35S, though they certainly had lesser items in service as of 1940.) In addition, not four months after France's capitulation, M1935A production was resumed, this time under German direction and for use by the Wehrmacht. Some 40,000 pistols, renamed "Pistole 625 (f)" and in some cases lacking the standard magazine safety, rolled off the assembly lines over the next 3½ years. To this day, no one knows just where in the German military they served. One thing is fairly certain: the '35As were never issued to front-line combat units. The problems in obtaining "Pistole-Patrone Kaliber 7.65 Lang," as the Nazis termed the M35's unique cartridge, were just too great. Issue to support units, where ammo resupply would not often be required, is suspected.

Following the cessation of hostilities in Europe, M1935A production at SACM resumed for a second time . . . now for the post-war French Army. (The notion of totally supplanting the A-model with the S- had been discarded.) Model 1935S and S M1 manufacture was re-initiated also, though neither of the S-variant guns had been built for over 5 years. Sufficient pistols were subsequently com-

The S-model rear sight (right) was somewhat better than the A's. To be sure, the 1935A's was better configured, being properly squared off, but it was so small that it could barely be used.

pleted to permit extensive M1935 use during the Indo-Chinese and Algerian campaigns, actions which resulted in the loss of a shocking percentage of these post-war-produced pistols. Only in February of 1950 did M35 manufacture finally cease, due to adoption by the French of an up-scaled, up-calibered variant of the 1935S, the MAS 1950, in 9mm Parabellum chambering. A total of about 75,000 M1935 handguns of all types had been completed.

The little 7.65 Long-bored pistols did not last long in service following introduction of the MAS 1950. As of the early '60s, quantities of both post-war S models as well as As could be had through the mails from U.S. import houses, usually for scandalously low prices. Caliber is what limited the value: only French surplus military fodder—steel-cased and sometimes unreliable—was available for the would-be shooter, since no U.S. firm ever loaded the 7.65 Long round and since machining cases down from 32 S&W Long was tedious. A second impediment to sales was the usual, and quite unjustified, American contempt for French handguns, a prejudice dat-

Test ammo used by the author was custom-made rounds (left) which are created from reworked 32 S&W brass, and (right) 1947-vintage French military cartridges in 32-round boxes.

The original French military fodder used by the author was a curse. Hang-fires and near-squibs were commonplace, resulting in the large 25-meter groups shown here.

Above—The 1935S M1 displays a typical 3-inch 25-meter group shot with Godfrey ammo. Below—The 1935A printed this 2½-inch, 25-meter group, also with Godfrey loads. These 90-grain bullets chronographed only 920 fps but functioning was flawless.

ing from the First War when the Republique's Ruby-style automatics did look pretty sad alongside our 1911s. The result was that few M35s ever made it out to a firing range, and fewer still were ever exercised seriously, to discover just what they could and couldn't do. What has come down to us today is that the little pistols are "gentle to shoot." But little else has been said.

What are the 35A and 35S like on the range? That was something this author decided to find out, utilizing a Nazi-marked SACM M1935A pistol loaned by collectors' arms dealer Syd Rachwal, and a post-war M1935S sent by National Automatic Pistol Collectors' Association President Tom Knox. Test ammunition consisted primarily of custom-crafted, Boxer-primed fodder, but a small quantity of original French rounds, made in 1947, was included also to ensure "authentic" test results.

Trials of the M1935A, which bore the characteristic black enamel finish, commenced with a mechanical accuracy check from 25 meters using five of the custom cartridges. Shooting proved to be a challenge because the trigger pull was absurdly heavy, added to which the trigger surface seemed poorly configured. It was easy to cut one's finger endlessly on that "crescent moon" edge. Still, results were surprising: 2½-inch groups could be printed, though obtaining five good letoffs with that beast of a trigger was a chore. At least one called flyer marred most accuracy efforts. A single five-shot 50-meter effort was also made which gave a group of 5 inches center-to-center. That represents very-good class accuracy from an unaltered fighting pistol.

Results with the French surplus fodder were not so promising. Hangfires and near-squibs were commonplace. I averaged one flintlock-style ignition and one noticeably-underpowered shot per five shot string. As a result of these misadventures, groups were unacceptably large ... like 5 inches at 25 meters. Trials with the steel-cased French fodder were thus not continued for long and I returned to the custom cartridges, which never once flintlocked or squibbed on me.

Model 1935A characteristics, other than accuracy, ranged from "fine" to "unacceptable." Functionality was perfect, the gun giving 100-percent reliability with both the custom and the original rounds, when the latter ignited properly. Controllability was merely adequate, and by no means optimum for a 32. In three tries at the "six shots in three seconds from ten meters on an Option silhouette" controllability test, I "maxed" only once. Shooting a possible on this exercise should be easy with a 32! This was due to the troublesome trigger and to the light-reflecting black paint on what were already smallish sights. Handling wasn't what it should be either. Quick magazine changes, which should have been easy with the 1911-style thumb-button, were hampered by a magazine which wouldn't drop clear. One had to wonder, too, about the security of that oh-so-exposed (when on Safe) thumb lever. I personally recommend chamber-empty as the safe carry mode with an M1935 . . . for security—and other reasons.

MAS 1935S trials were carried out with the previously-described postwar-issue gun. According to owner Tom Knox, this arm had a particularly interesting, and slightly shady, past. It had fallen into the hands of some unscrupulous artisan who had stamped the piece with a spurious Nazi Kriegsmarine mark, then sold the resulting fake to an unfortunate collector for a handsome sum. There never was a Nazi M35S, please recall, which is why the poor victim had never before seen such a "treasure" . . . In any event, this hot-blued version of the Brooklyn Bridge (M35Ss were not painted like the A models) ultimately wound up in the Knox collection, bought as a recognized fake, where it remains to this day as a curiosity. Hence, the availability of such a "rarity" as a test piece for this article.

Groups with the S M1 ran a consistent 3 inches at 25 meters with the reloads, which is good-class accuracy. A single 50-meter effort went into 6¼ inches. The French loads printed 5¼ inches or so at 25 meters amidst the usual hang-fires and half-power ignitions. Groupability was thus only marginally inferior to what had been experienced with the M1935A.

Reliability was another matter. Throughout trials of the 35A, it had been apparent that the custom ammo had been loaded somewhat lighter than the French military fodder, though this mattered not at all to the highly catholic M1935A, which had perked away happily with either round. But the 35S M1 was far more selective in its tastes than its older brother had been. This gun would function not at all with the custom ammo (which chronographed 920 fps average with its 90-grain bullet), but instead would feed only the French military ammo (1096 fps average for its 87-grain pill, assuming five good ignitions). Alas, in the absence of a second 35S or 35S M1 test piece, it proved impossible to determine whether this fastidiousness was a standard 1935S trait or merely a quirk of the test sample.

Model 35S M1 characteristics, other than accuracy/reliability, seemed improved over those of the M1935A. A workable trigger was presented albeit with lots of creep, but a decent 5-pound letoff, and bigger, less reflective sights were provided. Too, grip-to-barrel angle was not so sharp as with the 35A. Furthermore, magazines dropped freely, so that reloads became very quick, and a more accessible hammer was installed, that thumb-cocking might be facilitated. By no means, however, were all changes benign—the new hammer bit the author's hand viciously. Nor were all 35A inadequacies addressed because I still cut my finger on the crescent-moon trigger, and the safety was still vulnerable when in "Safe" position.

It is easy to conclude here by condemning the French M35s on one basis or another: their cartridge, especially, was less than battle-worthy, and they possess other qualities that—to today's shooter—seem ergonomically ill-considered. Yet, viewed from a different perspective, the Petter-designed M1935s were anything but failures. In contrast to a number of WWII pistols, the 1935s basic design survived the war and went on to do creditable things. France's present-day service auto, the M1950 is, as we said earlier, little more than an upscaled M1935S. And even the "ultimate" SA auto, the fabulous SIG 210, was profoundly influenced by the French '35s. All of which is quite noteworthy coming from a little pistol we gunwriters still occasionally poke fun at in print.

At 50 meters, the best accuracy was with the Model 1935A and custom ammo—a 5-inch group. The S-model gun turned in a 6¼-inch group at the same distance.

Mastering The

Waterfowl *can* be taken with a front-stuffer! Hunters Greg and Gene Thompson take a minute to admire the author's 10-gauge Navy Arms shotgun. With the right loads and procedures it'll shoot as well as a modern gun.

THE ALL-ROUND hero of shooting irons for the American pioneer and homesteader was the shotgun. The blackpowder sootbelcher could put dinner on the table Saturday and ward off an "infringment of privacy" on Sunday when unwanted guests came to call on the cabin. A can of blackpowder in the back room, some lead to melt down, a few percussion caps, and the shooter was ready to fill the air with the buzz of little lead bees. Wads could be made from various handy materials, too; you didn't have to use commercial fodder for effective close-range results.

Cubed shot was not the answer to long-range pattern density, to be sure, and swan shot—melted lead dropped through a sieve and cooled in water—(the pellets ended up having a

The blackpowder double is, of course, a hammergun, and it may take some shooters a little time to get used to earring the hammers back for each shot. This adds to the fun!

Blackpowder Shotgun by SAM FADALA

Many shooters are discovering that the blackpowder shotgun can be just as potent as the modern types, but these sootburners sometimes need special attention to be really efficient.

swan-like tail) wouldn't compete for prizes in today's trap competition either. But, game wasn't that sophisticated and trouble often showed up on the doorstep, so the blackpowder shotgun did its job in solid fashion. Besides, it might be loaded with good commercial pellets, too, especially the buckshot sizes, and then the gun patterned very well, and it had plenty of power. The blackpowder shotgun, today's or yesterday's version, has about as much ballistic punch as our modern factory loads. So there was never a lack of authority.

The blackpowder muzzleloader changed its character like a chameleon changes its color. The old buck 'n' ball load was one possibility, and still is. There were two distinct types of buck and ball loadings. One I don't like and never recommend. It's a single ball with shot on top of it. The other I do recommend. It uses a properly loaded single lead ball, patched to hold it downbore, in one barrel, while the other barrel is loaded with shot, again in a correct proportion with the powder charge. Here was and is versatility! If a rabbit jumps out, you use the shot-loaded bore. If a deer presents itself, the ball is fired. Small shot with a modest powder charge is loaded for quail, larger shot with more powder for ducks, geese and turkeys.

Calling the modern blackpowder shotgun wildly popular today would be stretching the longbow, as they used to call exaggerating. There are a number of modern downwind shooters who use the charcoal burning shotgun, certainly, but the shooting fraternity at large has never caught onto the fact that here is a firearm with all of the old-time fascination, plenty of blackpowder challenge in its loading techniques, but at the same time, a lot of power with good pattern possibility. The joy of bagging game with the rabbit-eared percussion shotgun is real and deep-seated. The totally practical fellow who prefers buying a trout instead of catching one won't like the sport, but the rest of us thrive on it.

However, you have to master the blackpowder shotgun just as you would any other tool. It's a lot of fun to throw a cloud of smoke at the fast-disappearing tail of a cock pheasant, or experience the healthy (but non-punishing) thrust of the smokepole going

An easy method of carrying components in the field is to load separate empty 35mm film cans with the proper amounts of powder and shot. Here, the powder is being dropped down-bore.

The over-powder wad is introduced into one of the muzzles and will be run home with the fiberglass ramrod.

off as a mallard wings by the blind. But after a little of that with nothing but holes in the air to show for the fun, the blackpowder scattergun finds itself left in the closet while the modern gun is taken on the hunt. My first experience with the sootburner left me with plans of burying mine in the garden so I'd never have to look at it again.

I was sage hen hunting. These big gray birds rise from the field as if they had 2 pounds of potatoes tied to their feet, but the long-winged grouse can actually accelerate much faster than it appears, and they are missed regularly by hunters who actually count their shotshells instead of saying, "I think I hit about every bird I shot at!" I was having a bad time of it. There were lots of birds, but they weren't being harvested into my game bag. Follow-up shots were necessary, too. I was using plenty of shot and plenty of powder, but I was not a master of the blackpowder scattergun.

A season later, if I recall correctly, and if I'm not stretching the longbow myself, I bagged about a dozen birds with 14 shots. The difference wasn't luck, nor were the birds flying slower. I'd caught onto some of the fine points concerning the double-barreled caplock shotgun. That year, my wad column included a modern plastic cup. My patterns went from 45 percent to about 60 percent. The gun was still no good past 30 yards or so, but at least when I centered a bird in the pattern, it wasn't dusted; it was dropped cleanly. Experimentation with various wad columns led me to a load comprised of powder charge, over-powder wad (to retain pressure on the powder charge for better burning), the modern plastic wad, shot, and a single, thin over-shot wad.

You'll hear and read that the blackpowder shotgun really doesn't need choke in order to gain a good pattern. For the most part, that's as scientific as wetting your finger and holding it into the air to determine wind velocity. A Cylinder-bored muzzleloader barrel will give you about 45 percent patterns, just as a modern shotgun will. You can improve upon the pattern with one-piece plastic wads, but even with these there is no guarantee that the patterns will be *dense*. And you can also alter the ratio between shot and powder to further improve the pattern. Remember that a plastic wash can be left in the bore from using the modern one-piece wad. I found that Shooter's Choice solvent got rid of this wash in my guns. However, plastic wads will not properly fit all muzzleloader shotguns.

I'd also worked with my loads to bring improvement. The blackpowder scattergun has been long loaded in a volume for volume manner. This method has *nothing* to do with weight of either powder charge or shot charge. It simply means that one measure is used for both the powder and the shot, giving the same *bulk* volume of each. It is a workable loading method and I have used it for years. How-

Fadala finds that FFg powder is just right for his 12-gauge shotgun. Experimentation is the key to success.

The shot charge is dropped down the barrel. The other barrel has already been loaded, as indicated by the film can lid inserted in the muzzle.

Next, the over-shot was is inserted into the muzzle then rammed home with the ramrod. Once both barrels are loaded, be sure to remove the can lid!

ever, I did experience a modest density improvement in the pattern by altering this volume-for-volume load in favor of shot, using a *reduced* powder charge with the same amount of shot previously fired. The overbalance in favor of shot made for a denser pattern, but lower pellet velocity.

Mastering the blackpowder shotgun requires patterning and safe experimentation, using only those maximum loads (or less) as recommended by the gunmaker. Any wad which increases the inertia of the load, for example, making it more difficult for the charge to escape the bore, provides a strong possibility of *raised pressure*, so experimentation is done only with the sanction of the gunmaker, who knows what his shotgun will withstand, pressure-wise. However, the bore of the shotgun is so large that pressures are generally very low, the gases having a huge area to react upon. So you can experiment, but you must do so safely. Two sources of blackpowder shotgun loads are the *Gun Digest Black Powder Loading Manual* and the *Hodgdon Data Manual*, No. 25.

My experimentation carried me one step further. I sent my favorite blackpowder scattergun to a fellow who specialized in choking muzzleloaders. Myron Olson (phone 605/886-9787) still does this sort of work. The name "scattergun" is strictly a friendly monicker for the shotgun. When a shotgun really does scatter its shot all over the place, it's time to correct the problem. The jug choke Olson installed on my gun brought it from 45 percent patterns (60 percent with special wad columns) all the way to 80 percent, or very close to it, out of each barrel. Since I was hunting big birds and ducks, that's just what I wanted.

The good news is that we now have a commerical blackpowder double-barreled shotgun with Full and Full chokes. Navy Arms offers it in their Model T&T, No. TRA200. After making the shotgun shoot with much more effective patterns, I was "mastering" the gun just fine. In fact, I found very little field difference in game harvesting between the smokepole and the modern shotshell, with, of course, the exception of loading speed and ease, which are all in favor of the modern gun.

Mastery, as the reader can see, is more in gun preparation than shooter prep. The percussion shotgun has a relatively fast lock time, not as fast as the modern gun, but it does not require any special long leads in order to bring shot pattern and target together. A fast *and sustained* swing is necessary for best results, but that point could attach readily to the modern shotgun as well as the old-timer.

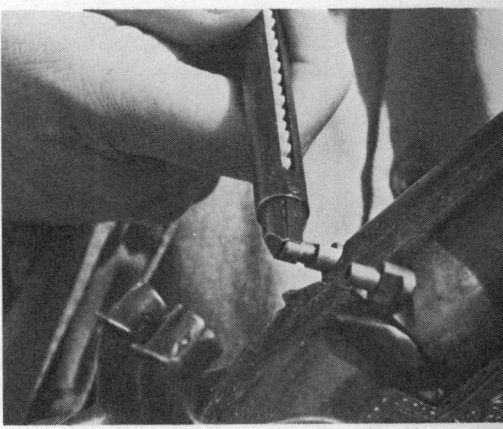
When both barrels have been loaded, a capper is used to install a cap on the nipples.

The fowler—flintlock ignition—is a different story. The ones I've fired have reasonable lock time, but they do require a little more lead to make up for a slower lapse between the trigger pull and pellets emerging from the muzzle. No major concern, really. You won't find many flintlock shotguns around. The caplock is king.

The 12 gauge is the most popular bore size. I have a 10 I admire a lot and a 12, and I've owned a 20 and a 24 gauge. The 12 will really do it all, from quail to geese, but anyone wanting the extra shot charge afforded by the 10 can't go wrong with that gauge.

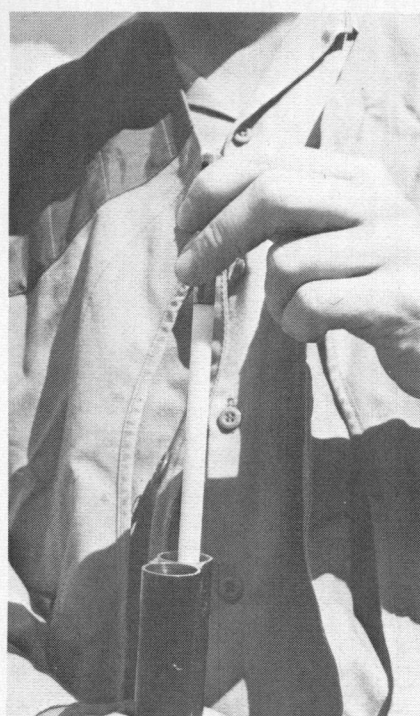

Fadala has found that a fiberglass ramrod will take a lot of abuse without bending or breaking. The wad column should be seated firmly.

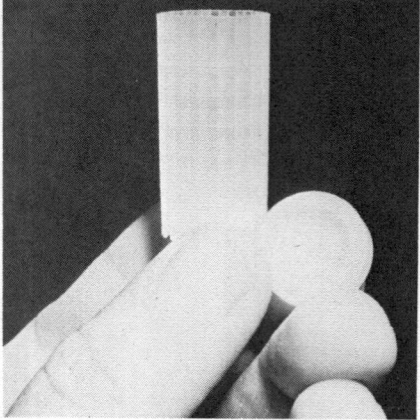

Ballistic Products, Inc. sells a plastic wad system that has worked well in Fadala's tests. The wad and sealing unit provided excellent pattern and ballistics.

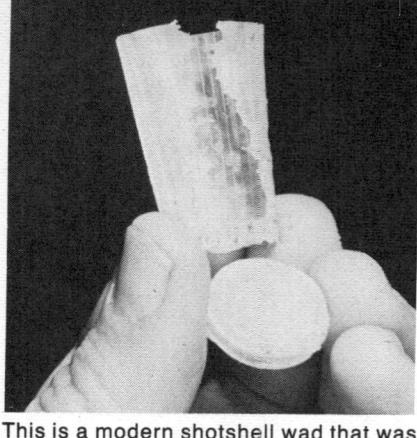

This is a modern shotshell wad that was used in a blackpowder shotgun. It showed that there was a rough spot in the bore which was cutting through the plastic.

In fact, today's 12s and 10s are generally 13s and 11s. The bore dimension is gauged to accept the modern wad size. Therefore, the 12 gauge blackpowder bore is about the same inner measure as the inside of a modern 12 gauge shotgun hull, and the same goes for the 10. The actual bore sizes vary, and the shooter must check his own muzzleloading shotgun to see what size wads it requires.

My own shotguns, the one bored Full and Full by Olson, and my Navy Arms Full/Full model, are today loaded primarily with standard wads. These wads don't leave a plastic wash in the bore because they are not plastic. And they produce excellent patterns. I did have some trouble with cushion fiber wads at first. Reduction of the powder charge improved the shot pattern, leading me to believe, incorrectly, that it had been high velocity which ruined the pattern in the first place. But that was not true. The pattern was "blown" because the gas from the powder charge was destroying the over-powder cushion fiber wad. Once that was corrected, by simply installing an over-powder wad downbore prior to seating the cushion wad, patterns were fine, and loads were once again in the high velocity realm.

How high? My shotguns, both well-made of top-grade materials, are allowed stout powder/shot charges. I have chronographed my 12 gauge recently with 1½ ounces of shot at about 1200 feet per second muzzle velocity, not that far behind the modern factory shotgun shell of the "baby magnum" type. The key to coming up with the best field load for the muzzleloader lies in three areas. First, never exceed the maximum load allowed by the manufacturer for his gun. Second, balance shot and powder, varying acceptable wad components, until the pattern is best. Pattern is the key to performance. I've seen shotgun patterns with soccer ball size holes and it takes no imagination to visualize a quail being missed or just "feather-singed" with a gap like that. Third, stay with FFg granulation, Fg, or Pyrodex RS. I prefer FFg or RS in my 12 gauge, RS or Fg in my 10. I see no need for FFFg in the shotgun.

Patterning is not difficult to do. Get ahold of some large paper, such as butcher paper. Four long slats (narrow boards), perhaps 4 to 5 feet tall are needed. Nail the paper between the wood slats, back off 40 yards and fire for the center of the paper. Lay a 30-inch cardboard cutout over the densest part of the pattern and draw a circle around its edges. Count the pellets within that 30-inch circle. Divide by the number of pellets in your load and you have your pattern percentage. If your load held 400 pellets and 250 of them are within the 30-inch circle, your gun is shooting a little over 60 percent. That can be called a Modified choke.

Personal mastery of the muzzleloader shotgun also means learning how to handle it in the field. After arriving at a load which patterns best, by juggling all components safely (powder charge, shot charge, size of shot and wad column) I make up readyloads for the hunt. My prepared loads are no more than empty 35mm film containers. Some hold shot. An equal number hold the pre-measured powder charge. I keep them in separate pockets of my field coat, shot in the left-hand side, powder in the right-hand side. Wads go in other pockets. Then there is no fiddling with loose powder or shot in the field.

You shoot. Ear the hammers back. Clear any cap debris from the nipples. Blow down the bores to insure the extinguishing of any latent sparks. Pop the top off a powder container. Drop the charge. Insert the correct wads, shot, and over-shot wad. Cap. And you're ready to fire again. The ignition of the side-by-side percussion shotgun is excellent. The design allows a straight route for the flash from the cap to find the powder charge in the breech. I can't recall a single misfire or hangfire in the hunting field with my blackpowder shotguns.

So the faithful servant of the pioneer and settler is back to serve again, in modern hands. Blackpowder shotgunning is rewarding, enjoyable, romantic—just plain fun. But the good part is that the smokepole scattergun is also efficient in the hands of a shotgunner who has mastered it, having the gun choked if it is choke-less, or buying a choked model to begin with, finding the best-patterning load for it, and carrying pre-measured loads into the field to avoid any loading problems. It's too bad that more shooters haven't discovered the old sootburning muzzleloader. It was around before rubber tires and it will probably still be here after commercial space flights. ●

On The Firing Line

by CLAY HARVEY

Contributing Editor Harvey casts his critical eye on a number of new and recent developments, all of which proved interesting—only some more than others. Here's the docket:

- F.I.E.'s Rimfire Single Actions
- Winchester Model 70 Winlite
- Ruger Mini Thirty
- Browning Stainless Stalker
- Casull 454 Field Grade
- A-Square Hannibal
- A.A. Arms AP9 Pistol
- Colt 10mm Delta Elite
- Anschutz Exemplar Rimfire

F.I.E. Buffalo Scouts in differing finishes.

F.I.E. Rimfire Single Actions

Since Colt dropped their Frontier Scout line of single-action 22 rimfires, Ruger has become the primary supplier of such sixguns. The only problem is that Ruger revolvers, while not exorbitantly expensive, are not cheap either. Enter F.I.E., of Hialeah, Florida.

Offered are the Buffalo Scout, Yellow Rose (a gold-plated Buffalo Scout), the Little Ranger, and the Texas Ranger. All, except for the gilded version, are quite inexpensive, and even that shiny number sells for around $150 according to my most recent price sheet.

The Buffalo Scout and Yellow Rose are crafted in Italy by Tanfoglio. The former is available in chrome finish, blue, and blue-and-gold, with the latter the dearest at about a hundred bucks retail. Convertible versions (with an extra 22 WMR cylinder) are tendered for only $20 more.

The Italian sixguns feature a drift-adjustable rear sight, floating firing pin, and a hammer-block safety system. The chrome version wears polymer grip panels of "target" style, complete with thumbrest. Its screws are blued for contrast. The gilt number comes standard with both cylinders, blued screws, and a set of walnut grips.

Built entirely in America, according to F.I.E., are the Little Rangers and the Texas Rangers. These are also listed with an extra cylinder as an option, and differ from the European guns primarily by a slight difference in their safety mechanism, the fact that they are made only in blue form, that their rear sight is a trough in the topstrap (in Colt fashion), and by virtue of gold-plated screws to add pizazz. The imported guns are cataloged only with 4¾-inch barrels, whereas the

GUNS ILLUSTRATED 1989 **77**

F.I.E. Texas Rangers (left and right) and the Little Ranger with round butt (bottom).

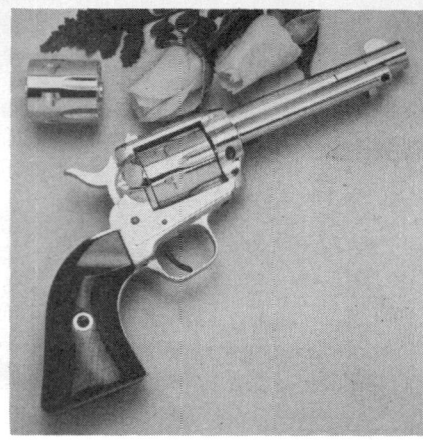

F.I.E. Yellow Rose is gold plated.

American items can be had in 3¼-inch (with bird's head grips), 4¾-inch, 6½-inch, and 9-inch configurations. The most expensive of these is the convertible, of course, and it lists at about $120.

I have tested all iterations in the Ranger series, from the Little Ranger to the long-Tom. In their price range, they are unsurpassed for quality. Since they have true fixed sights, there was a windage problem with two of them, but that is not unique to F.I.E.! Considering their low initial cost, I still consider it a bargain to toss $20 at a gunsmith to bring the sights to taw, either by bending the front sight blade or turning in the barrel.

Trigger pull quality varied from not so hot on the long-barreled gun to excellent on the 4¾-inch version. The other two were average: a bit creepy, gritty and none too light. But again, a good gunsmith can remedy such for a pittance, although it would likely void F.I.E.'s warranty. Thus, for a total expenditure of maybe $165, *including* the cost of the handgun, one would have a dual-cylinder revolver that hits point of aim, boasts a good trigger pull, and is as safe as most any single-action design extant.

All that adds up to a bargain in my book.

Winchester Model 70 Winlite

I have been a fan of the Winchester Model 70 for all of my adult years. Although the stock styling of the post-1964 iterations did not fill me with euphoria, I was not especially disenchanted with the action. The pre-'64 numbers looked a little handsomer, and had cut checkering (however poorly done), but they were as heavy as a forklift, long of barrel except in the Featherweight version, and I'd never found them to be uncommonly accurate. The newer Model 70s, except for their reprehensible impressed checkering and lamentable hog-trough forend channels, were okay in my book.

In the late 1970s, Olin finally got it right. Cut checkering was reintroduced, dark walnut graced most M70 permutations, stock styling was at least as *graceful* as the pre-'64s if not much less *bulky*. And then a couple of years later came the new Model 70 Featherweight. Ah, rapture. The stock was slender, gorgeous, comfortable. Its checkering pattern was as attractive as any that ever graced a factory gun, and better than most. Not only that, it was well executed, with diamonds that looked like diamonds, points that were pointed up, and few runovers in sight. Sigh. It was love at first sight.

Then along came factory synthetic stocks. At first, I hated them, being a walnut-and-steel foozle. But they grew on me. When camo-painted ones hit the gun racks, I was converted. In my view, synthetics were as handsome as any wood-stocked rifle, just in a different way. (Some guys might *prefer* blonds, other brunettes; who but a dolt would cast out a well-turned redhead based solely on the hue of her coiffure?)

Besides, synthetic stocks were (and are) more functional than wood. They can be "checkered," had in any color (even made to resemble wood), are nigh unbreakable, and, most importantly, are so resistant to moisture absorption or release that they're as inert as anything can be. Why is that important? After you've missed (or worse, wounded) the buck of your dreams because of a divaricated zero, you won't have to ask that question.

Virtually every gun maker offers a synthetic stock nowadays, whether built in-house or acquired from a vendor. The Winchester version is dubbed the "Winlite." So, is it light? Well, kinda. Note that in the foregoing paragraph, I did not list among a synthetic's attributes exiguous heft. That's because they are not always lighter than wood, and what difference there is isn't pronounced. While some synthetic rifles—most notably the Ultra Light Arms—are indeed airweight specimens, such is the result of more than one design aspect, not merely the stock.

Winchester's Winlite stock (confected by McMillan) is not uncommonly light, but it is quite handsome. Constructed of hand-laid fiberglass, its styling is functional if not especially recoil-reducing. (Too much drop.) "Checkering" is not provided, but the pebbled external finish is relatively slip-free.

Metalwork, alas, is flossy-glossy, and will warn any game in the vicinity of your presence. Will the factories never learn?

Non-magnum Winlites wear a stock that mimes in shape the Model 70 Featherweight, complete with schnabel forend. In the belted chamberings, the forend is not unlike that on a Model 70 Sporter. There is no cheekpiece on either Winlite model. All I have seen have been gifted with recoil pads; some have worn hinged floorplates, some blind magazines. The current catalog depicts a gun with a floorplate. All Winlite synthetic stocks carry a lifetime warranty.

According to the 1988 catalog, the Winlite is proffered in 270 Winchester, 280 Remington, and 30-06 among the standard chamberings. The belted numbers are 7mm Remington, 300 Winchester, and 338 Winchester Magnums.

I have tested a trio of Winlites, all three in belted persuasion. Items of note: quality of fabrication varied little from gun to gun, was uniformly excellent; the trigger pulls, after adjustment by yours truly using the method provided by the trigger design, were all superb; the safety lever worked smoothly on all three, much more so than Model 70s of years past; the hinged floorplates wiggled and wobbled like an emu on ice.

The stocks were comfortable to snuggle up to, provided excellent feel and balance, had just the right pistol grip curve for the Harvey hand. However . . . assuaging the debilitating effects of recoil is not their forte. The 7mm Magnum bopped my shoulder about like an A-Square Hannibal 375 Holland & Holland I was shooting on the same day. My gunning crony, barrister Grady Shields, agreed. The 300 Magnum pounded me unmercifully, making shooting it accurately (or even shoddily) a loathsome chore unless I used shoulder protection. (Such as letting Grady do the shooting.) The 338 beat me to a pulp, ground me up, spit me out. If I do any further shooting with either of the latter, they will be fitted with a muzzle brake, period! A 270 or 280 should engender no such a level of disquietude.

How was accuracy? Good, excellent, and barely passing, in order of caliber from the Big Seven up. I'll elaborate. My 7mm Magnum will print under 1½ inches on demand with its pet handload of 72.2 grains of IMR 4831 beneath a 115 Speer hollow point, ignition by CCI 250. With Federal's 165 Premium SPBT, the average was slightly better, 1.43 inches. The 150-grain softpoint Federal fodder went 1.54 inches for an average of three five-shot strings.

My 300 Magnum was the premium performer of the threesome; in fact, it was the most accurate 300 I have ever tested. With 180 Norma softpoints, it provided an aggregate for four five-shot strings of a tight 1.18 inches, with two groups going well under an inch! Runner-up was the 180 Federal softpoint at 1.66, with the 190 Hornady boattail just aft with 1.71 for its mean. (Incidentally, not only was the Norma ammo exquisitely precise, it was the fastest 180-grain load clocked, getting 2940 fps instrumental at 12.5 feet. Great hunting load.)

Conversely, the 338 was the least accurate I have run across. It barely squeezed below 2 inches with Federal's 210-grain Premium Partition loading, averaging 1.995 for four strings. Bridesmaid was 68.0 grains of IMR 4350 and the 250 Nosler Partition, for 2663 fps and a 2.08-inch group average. Seventy-one grains of IMR 4831 and the same bullet yielded just over 2700 fps at the nozzle and 2.37-inch accuracy. (And misery at the buttplate!)

The Big Seven and the 300 functioned fine, thanks, but the 338 gave feeding problems. Most of the time said disfunctioning was due to the belt of one cartridge snagging that of the one beneath it in the magazine. The bolt nose would then drive the upper one forward, dragging the lower one along. Everything would come to a screeching halt when the nose of the top round impacted the feed ramp. This not unique to Model 70s; my Remington 8mm Magnum is just as bad. One reason I don't care much for belted loads.

But I do care for the Model 70 Winlite. So far, it has established itself as my second favorite synthetic-stocked rifle brand. And the Number Two slot ain't bad, especially when Number One is filled by a gun costing three times as much. Few flies on the Winlite.

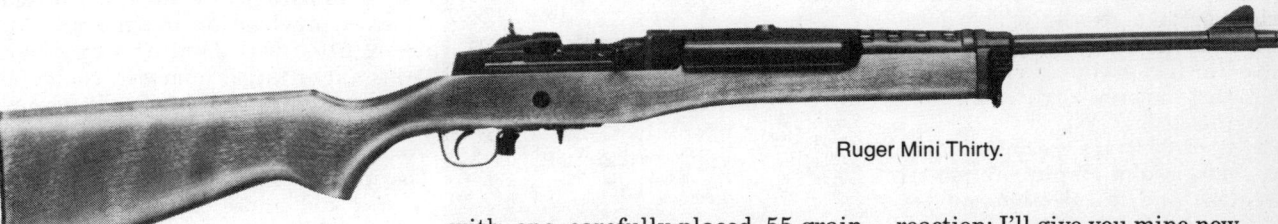

Ruger Mini Thirty.

Ruger Mini 30

When Ruger abandoned the XGI 7.62 NATO some years back, aficionados of that company's semi-automatic rifle line were crestfallen. When would they have access to a deer-capable rifle bearing the Ruger phoenix? (Some folks allow it's an eagle, but I know a phoenix when I see one.) Now, the 223 Remington is viewed by some nimrods as adequate for deer-sized game, and the Mini-14 series is reamed to that little round, so where's the rub? The 223 will certainly kill a deer—I've done so myself, with one carefully-placed 55-grain softpoint—but the fact that a hub cap can be removed with a Randall knife does not make it the proper tool for the job. The 223 is for experts, not duffers, neophytes, nor yet Ollie Ordinary.

Enter the Ruger Mini 30. The what? In case you came in late, the Mini 30 is Ruger's answer to the seeker of whitetail deer in the woods, replacing (Ruger hopes) the late lamented 44 Carbine, and erasing any latent desire for the defunct XGI that may remain abroad in the land. Can this pugnacious upstart shoulder such a weighty burden, supplanting one long-respected gun while stiff-arming its stillborn agnate into oblivion? Only time will tell about the public's reaction; I'll give you mine now.

The militaryesque Mini 30 is likely as good at waylaying a departing whitetail as its cousin, the 44 Carbine. It will probably prove to be more accurate, gun to gun, and as handy in the brush. Will it anchor a buck as decisively? Maybe. Maybe not. I have taken no game with a Mini 30, a fair amount with 44 Magnum handguns. The little 30-bore has its work cut out.

The Mini is reamed for the 7.62 x 39mm Russian cartridge, a bitty critter that is alleged to kick 123-grain missiles along in the 2400 fps vicinity. Not exactly laggard, but not Mach III, either. And that little 123-grain projectile is none too heavy for a 30 caliber; in fact, most hunters consider that varmint heft. One thing I've learned: What is good for vermin at one speed is often fine for bigger game at a different (slower) one. For what it's worth, I would have no qualms at all about shooting a whitetail with the 7.62 x 39 so long as I could hold the range to 150 yards or under.

Aside from the diameter of its bore, the Mini 30 is pretty much the familiar Mini-14 Ranch Rifle. It comes from New Hampshire wearing a hardwood stock, plastic buttplate and handguard, a folding peep rear sight, and the traditional Ruger integral scope-mount system. The detachable box magazine holds but five rounds; at this time no large-capacity version is available from Ruger. (Eagle International is reportedly working to correct this situation for aftermarket buyers.)

I purchased my sample Mini 30 at retail, so it was no factory-massaged ringer. It turned out to be the most accurate Ruger paramilitary auto I have fired. Using a handbook dose of Hodgdon's H335 behind a 125-grain softpoint, I received a 2.49-inch aggregate for three five-shot strings at 100 yards. That, friends, is just fine. It required many an hour at the loading bench, but so what?

Factory ammo, whether ball or hunting type, was, uh. . . unrewarding. Best was some Chinese military stuff, grouping just under 5 inches for the mean. PMC factory softpoints were pretty fast, clocking just under 2300 fps from the short 18½-inch barrel, but accuracy was not noteworthy at 5.17 inches. Although faster, PMC FMJ stuff was wildly inaccurate, "grouping" nearly 10 inches at the 100-yard mark. Pretty sad.

The little gun perked with everything. No miscues of any kind. *I* fouled up, missing a heavy, wide-racked buck which I had outmaneuvered, outwitted, and outwaited. Had him dead to rights, alas a bit farther away than was ideal. I flat missed him. More than once. Not the Ruger's fault. This fall will be different.

In case you are ambivalent, let me set it in stone: I like the Mini 30, am dithyrambic about is lilliputian cartridge. I suspect Ruger will sell a bunch of them.

Browning Stainless Stalker

I discussed the Browning A-Bolt at some length in this space in the 1986 edition of GUNS ILLUSTRATED. So why this treatment? Two reasons: To fill you in on my past 3 years with various A-Bolts; to inform you of the newest Browning bolt-action development.

The nascent Stainless Stalker has all the normal A-Bolt attributes, which include the three-lug bolt, short 60-degree bolt rotation, scissored magazine spring, routed forend channel to save weight, hinged floorplate with its detachable box magazine, tang safety, soft rubber buttpad on all models and calibers, and the cartridge depressor beneath the bolt to enable slick operation. Nothing new here. What is new is a barrel and receiver of matte-finished stainless steel (to reduce glare and prevent rusting), and a composite stock.

The stock deserves special mention. It is comprised of graphite-reinforced fiberglass and is injection molded. That means it comes from the mold not only ready to receive a barreled action, but with sharp checkering already in place at forend and pistol grip, enabling a firm gripping surface. Further, the stock is not painted, but is solid black all the way through. Result: There is no "finish" to flake or peel off, nor yet to ding or dent as on a wooden handle. Of course, as with all synthetic stocks, dimensional changes due to moisture absorption or release are things of the past. These stocks are as close to inert as your brother-in-law.

Available calibers do not exactly constitute a panoply, with only the 270 Winchester, 7mm Remington Magnum, and 30-06 available at this time. I'll wager a sou that will change quickly, but for the nonce such chamberings should handle nicely the average venerer's chores.

Now for the promised update on three annum's worth of work with various A-Bolts. To date, I have tested

Harvey used a Browning A-Bolt to down this "cow horn" buck on the coast of North Carolina.

fairly extensively the following centerfire chamberings: 223 Remington (Medallion), 243 Winchester (Hunter), 257 Roberts (Hunter), 25-06 Remington (Hunter), 270 Winchester (Camo Stalker), 7mm-08 Remington (Hunter), 280 Remington (Medallion), 7mm Remington Magnum (Stainless Stalker and Medallion), 30-06 Springfield (Medallion). Of those ten rifles, all would group with one load or another under 1½ inches at 100 yards, for an average of three or more five-shot strings. *No other brand of sporter that I have tested at least five examples of can make that claim.* None. Zero. No matter their cost, country of origin, caliber. Further, of the ten guns above, three would average under an inch—the 7-08, 270 Camo, and the Medallion 7mm Mag. Even more surprising, the 270 would do so with *factory ammo!* (Federal's 130-grain soft point boattail Premium, to be specific.)

Are you impressed? You should be stunned! I was. Such consistency of precision is unprecedented in the sporter-rifle field. Bear in mind that none of these rifle was tuned in any way—bedding was untouched, triggers adjusted only by the limited means provided by the factory. All were fitted with hunting scopes, not varmint or target numbers. No handload was developed specifically for any rifle, but were standard recipes I had used in other guns of similar chambering.

As I said: unprecedented.

One of the ten guns, the Stainless Stalker, gave functioning difficulties. When its hinged floorplate was snapped into place with vigor, the top round would occasionally pop up out of the magazine, then on out of the rifle onto the benchtop. Once in a while that same gun would relinquish its grip on the rim of a cartridge case upon extraction, withdrawing it halfway from the chamber, then riding over its rim, leaving the case stranded. Lest you find that isolated example sufficient reason to objurgate A-Bolts in general, let me mention that there is no brand of firearm on the market—again, regardless of price—with which I have not had some serious bout of misfunctioning at one time or other. The A-Bolt's 10 percent

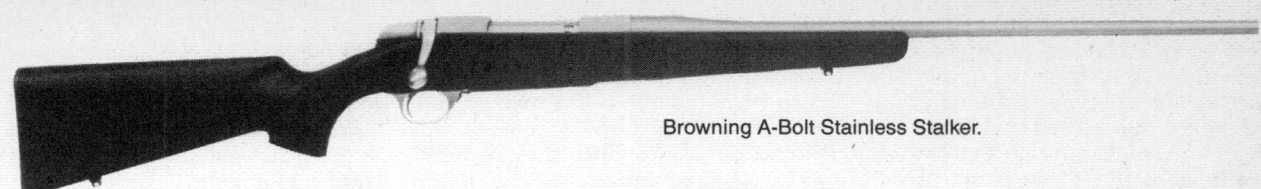

Browning A-Bolt Stainless Stalker.

problem rating is head and shoulders above all but the Ruger 77s in my experience, so far as reliability is concerned.

I would not hesitate to hunt anywhere at any time with a Browning A-bolt, so long as I could match my chambering to the job at hand. Considering its modest price and array of models and cartridges, it is the sleeper of the bolt-action rifle market. I stand unequivocally in its corner.

Casull 454 Field Grade

Just last year I became acquainted with what many shooters consider to be the finest revolver in the world, and what undoubtedly *is* the most powerful factory-loaded revolver cartridge in existence, the awesome 454 Casull. I'll admit to being a bit apprehensive when I first touched off a shot; I'd heard the recoil was fierce. It was. Not totally unmanageable, mind you, but decidedly asperous.

Another item of note: The gun was very, very accurate. Fired from the bench at 25 yards, groups with Freedom Arms' 300-grain jacketed softpoint factory provender averaged under 1¼ inches! The only other load I had access to at the time—the 260-grain stuff—went 1.44 inches. Good?

The craftsmanship on my sample 6-inch Casull was distinguished. All square edges were square, all curves curved, few tool marks were in evidence. The grip panels fit as if hewn from the same material as the straps; metal-to-metal joinings appeared not so much as joints but as thin scribed lines. Nobby, indeed, the Casull five-shooter.

But, whew!... expensive! *Really* expensive. Outfitted the way my test gun was—with an action job and replaceable forcing cone bushing—the tally came to $1349. Wow.

Other would-be Casull owners took one look at that window sticker and uttered stronger epithets than "wow." The sound of all those wallets snapping shut was a tocsin to the powers that govern Freedom Arms. The inner circle went into a huddle. After suitable incantations had been performed and the accountants consulted, a new incarnation was born. It bore the time-worn "Field Grade" appellation, was heralded as a much less expensive version of the vaunted Premier Grade.

How much less expensive? The unadorned Field Grade (meaning not fitted out with such trappings as mentioned above, which are available to the well-heeled, just as on the Premier

Freedom Premier Grade.

Freedom 454 Field Grade.

Grade) goes out the door at $795. Hey, that *is* less expensive, isn't it! But is it *inexpensive*? No, it is not. But damn, is it GOOD.

The new permutation wears a handsome matte finish, Pachmayr neoprene grips, and the same level of workmanship as its more expensive sibling. It is also available with the famed T'SOB scope mounts and a Leupold 2x scope in matching "silver" hue. My test gun (which was the second one to leave the factory on its way to a gun writer, though I'm not supposed to tell) came so equipped, and in addition was treated to the 3-pound trigger job, a $59 option, and worth it.

Quality was everything I'd been promised, and more. There is no revolver on the market so finely fabricated as the Freedom Arms Casull, even in its plebeian Field Grade guise. But will it shoot? In a word, yes.

Armed with all four factory offerings, I hied my carcass to the range, besat myself at a 100-yard rifle benchrest, and proceeded to sandpaper my right palm to an angry crimson not unlike that assumed by my son Chris when he wants to be fed. (The culprit is the rubber grips; the standard grips of the Premier Grade do not tenderize one's mitt in such unmannerly fashion.) After the smoke cleared I had a fistful of targets to measure. I did so.

The 260-grain Freedom Arms softpoint emerged victorious by a sub-

Author used the 454 Casull to kill this 200-pound porker with one shot.

stantial margin, grouping three five-shot strings into an impressive 4.07 inches, or 3.89 minutes of angle. That corresponds roughly to 1-inch groups at the normal 25-yard handgun-testing distance. Runner-up was the 240-grain jacketed hollow point at 5.31 inches, with the milder "medium-velocity" factory load of the same heft going 5.48 inches. Carrying the drag was the 300-grain soft point, at 8.85 inches for the mean.

I fired one more string with the hot 240-grain number, from the kneeling position at the hundred mark. The result was a vertical 7½-inch spread, with four going into 4½ inches. Not particularly incondite, that performance, if I do say so.

For the record, the Freedom Arms Casull is the finest hunting revolver attainable. It provided the third best accuracy I've ever received from any centerfire handgun tested at 100 yards, and with factory ammo at that. The factory-loaded 454 hits as hard at *200* yards as do the best 44 Magnum loads at the *muzzle*.

Whether all this is worth the tariff is up to the individual to decide. You want my opinion? Okay; I *bought* my Field Grade, and at the normal dealer rate, not a huge discount as befits my station and rugged good looks. But Jim Morey did throw in the trigger job. I'm no pushover.

A. A. Arms AP9 9mm

A. A. Arms, Inc. (P. O. Box 25610-272, Mint Hill, NC, 28212, 704/545-5565), offers an unusual 9mm handgun not unlike the Intratec Assault Pistol in configuration. It boasts a fixed barrel, 20-round magazine (inserted at the front of the trigger guard, not into the butt), a ventilated barrel shroud or cover, a "figure-eight" front sight adjustable for both windage and elevation (however crudely), a polymer one-piece grip-frame/trigger guard assembly, a tubular receiver inside which reciprocates the massive bolt, and a large, easy-to-see rear sight.

The new gun has several things going for it, and a few warts. Foremost among its assets is its businesslike mien; it resembles a machine pistol. Thus, its intimidation factor cannot be overlooked when considering it for self defense. (Anyone who would deliberately go up against a firearm displaying such an intense level of vitiosity would have to be either very competent or incredibly stupid.) Furthermore, teenage boys *love* the AP9 at first glance; it might aid in tearing your 14-year-old away from his video game and out to the range, thus fomenting lust for the shooting sports in his breast.

Accuracy is another strong suit. In fact, my test AP9 is the most accurate centerfire selfloader I have tested. With its most precise fodder—a handload of 9.2 grains of Hercules Blue Dot, the 100 Speer JHP, CCI 500 primers, Remington brass—three five-shot 25-yards groups averaged 1.23 inches! No centerfire auto in my experience is even in that league. Second place load was the fine 90-grain Hornady JHP, at 1.36 inches for three strings, with third spot going to the new 124 Federal full-metal-jacket flat nose, at 1.58 inches. Even this last level of grouping is unprecedented, although I have tried one or two 9mms that would come close. (But *close* ain't *equal*.)

Reliability wants discussion. So

Young Jeff Miller was enticed into shooting mostly by the looks of the A.A. Arms AP9.

long as full-jacketed, round-nose ammo of at least 115 grains is used, the AP9 will perk happily along. Switch to anything under 115 grains in heft, or to a flat nose or hollowpoint (with one exception), and the gun will grind to a halt every shot or two. Period. That fact limits its utility as a defense or hunting gun dramatically.

The one exception mentioned above is the 124-grain Federal Nyclad hollow point. For close-range work, this load might well do the job. It fed reliably in my test gun. One serious caveat: Please note that I specified "close range." Why? Because the Nyclad rendition was so inaccurate in my sample that only three or four shots of every five would print on a 12-inch square target at 25 yards. Still, for home defense, that load is viable in my AP9.

So how, you ask, did I shoot all those groups if the gun won't feed hollow points? I single-loaded them. Every one. I work hard for my money.

The tubular steel receiver just asks to be drilled and tapped to accept a scope. The accuracy of the piece suggests that it could well connect on woodchuck-sized vermin to perhaps 100 yards if so equipped. The rub is that a nimrod would have to use his gun as a single shot, which is complicated by the fact that there is no bolt hold-open device. Problems, problems.

And the warts? The trigger finger piece is far too narrow. Worse, its leading edges are sharp. Worse yet, the pull is heavy and grating. All this means severe discomfort to the trigger finger pretty dang quick. A factory-provided trigger shoe—to be installed by the shooter, if desired—would be a welcome anodyne.

The AP9 is a bit more complicated to disassemble for cleaning than is the case with most 9mm autos. So it takes a bit longer, and requires more careful attention upon reassembly. Big deal.

The safety lever is in the same spot relative to the shooting thumb (of a right hander) as it is on the Colt Government Model. It is large, easy to manipulate, smooth-edged. I like it.

The AP9 is not a holster gun. In fact, a holster made for it would resemble a suitcase or gym bag. It is for carrying, not wearing. Nonetheless, for sticking under a car seat (where legal), or on the seat beside you (ditto), there are few handguns on the market that would provide as much security (by way of firepower) as a fully-loaded (21 shots) AP9. And *that* is its forte.

Oh, the cost. I have no retail information at this time, but I've seen the AP9 proffered in gunshops. The highest asking price was $300. That's right, three-hundred bucks! One dealer quoted his at less than $250, so I'm not certain there is a suggested retail. But even at three C-notes, the AP9 is a super deal.

Now, if they'll just modify that trigger, and either make them up in 45 ACP or insure that they'll accept all 9mm bullets types, I predict that A. A. Arms will have much trouble...keeping up with orders.

Colt Delta Elite 10mm

Colt's much ballyhooed Delta Elite Government Model is not big news because of the gun, but because of its chambering. Colt—much to their credit—was the first major maker to offer the 10mm Auto cartridge in a repeating handgun. (The producers of the infamous Bren 10 were not, by any definition, "major.")

For a few years, due to problems attendant with the nascent cartridge's vehicle and its builder, it appeared as if the promising new auto pistol cartridge was not going to make the commercial grade. Norma was sitting on a pile of ammo, gnashing their teeth; Bren 10 admirers had guns (sometimes), but no magazines for same. Things were not rosy. Then, Boom!, Colt rattled their sabres and rode in with the cavalry.

Into the venerable and beloved Government Model they poked the potent cartridge. Double recoil springs were utilized, as well as polymer parts here and there, but basically the old warhorse was unchanged. The Delta Elite version is a highly polished rendition, wearing neoprene combat wraparound grips, a three-white-dot high-profile sighting system, special markings on its slide, and a long trigger. Magazine capacity is seven rounds.

So what makes it special? The 10mm cartridge. I chronographed all four currently available factory rounds in one of my Delta Elites. To wit: 155 Hornady JHP, 1298 fps instrumental velocity at 12.5 feet (for 580 foot pounds); 170 Hornady JHP, 1244 fps (584 foot pounds); 170 Norma JHP (Lot 09622), 1157 fps (505 foot pounds); 200 Norma FMJ (Lot 10601), 1014 fps (456 foot pounds). Using 13.8

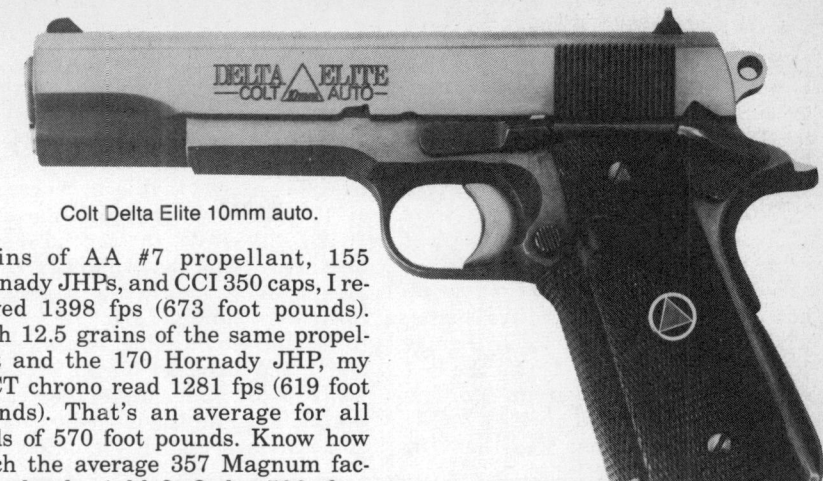

Colt Delta Elite 10mm auto.

grains of AA #7 propellant, 155 Hornady JHPs, and CCI 350 caps, I received 1398 fps (673 foot pounds). With 12.5 grains of the same propellant and the 170 Hornady JHP, my PACT chrono read 1281 fps (619 foot pounds). That's an average for all loads of 570 foot pounds. Know how much the average 357 Magnum factory load yields? Only 500 foot pounds, according to Federal data. Make no mistake about it, the 10mm is one puissant load.

And in my Colts, accurate as well. In my first gun, a First Edition "Commemorative," 170 Norma factory fodder provided an aggregate for five five-shot groups at 25 yards of only 2.17 inches! That's the best I've ever managed to wring from a standard Government Model in any chambering, and much better than the last Gold Cup I tested. The 200-grain Norma rendition was less impressive giving 3.26 inches for six strings. For fun, I fired a 10-round group with each load at 100 yards. The 170 Norma hollowpoint went 13.4 inches; the 200 truncated cone FMJ clustered all 10 into 13.6. Not bad for an untuned autoloader.

My second Delta, a test piece from Colt, average thus: 155 Hornady JHP, 2.84 inches for four groups at 25 yards; 170 Hornady JHP, 3.49 inches for four groups; 170 Norma JHP, 4.36 inches for three strings; 200 Norma FMJ 3.68 inches for three groups. The 170 Hornady JHP pushed by 12.5 of AA #7 produced a 3.55-inch agg for three five-shot strings. Not so good as my First Edition, but certainly not shoddy, and about par for an out-of-the-box Colt GM.

No malfunctions marred either gun's performance, which is most unusual in my experience with current GMs, at least when chambered for 45 ACP. The slide is very difficult to retract, due to the stiff springs. The 10mm Delta is thus no gun for the average untrained distaff shooter or youngster, unless they have a helluva grip. Recoil, as you might surmise, is heavy. Not uncontrollable, but noticeably stouter than that of a 45 ACP.

Fabrication quality on both my specimens was clearly superior to that normally provided by Colt these days. Everything fit; all parts meshed smoothly; trigger pulls were better than average. Even the checkering on the guide bushings was competently done! Amazing. I am smitten by Colt's newest thoroughbred.

Anschutz Exemplar 22 LR

The Anschutz Exemplar isn't, as one gun magazine has claimed, the first pistol the German arms maker has marketed, not by a long shot. It is, however, the firm's most recent sortie into that niche. Chambered for 22 Long Rifle (and there is a WMR version), the handgun comes with target sights, a 9.85-ounce trigger pull, a left-handed Match 64 action, and a detachable-box five-round magazine. The stock is of good walnut, stippled fore and aft, and fits the hand quite comfortably. The rear sight is readily removable, and the receiver is grooved to accept a scope mount.

Barrel length is 10 inches; a 14-inch

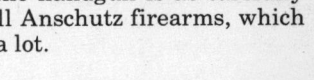

Anschutz Exemplar.

version (bedubbed the Model XIV) is available as well. New this year is the Exemplar Left, which has the bolt handle on its *right* side, for left-handed shooters. Listed heft is 3.35 pounds for the 10-inch iterations, 4.15 for the long-nosed model. The 22 Hornet has also been added, and is said to weigh 4.35 pounds. Anschutz also offers a shoulder rig for toting the gun in the field.

Since the basic Model 64 rifle action is familiar to most gunners, there is little reason to dwell on it. Suffice to say that the handgun is as carefully built as all Anschutz firearms, which is saying a lot.

All Anschutz rifles shoot well. Most of them shoot *exceptionally* well. The new Exemplar pistol fulfills its expectations completely. To date, I have fired only three brands of ammunition in my sample gun—Eley Tenex, Federal Champion, and an elderly batch of Winchester Mark II Match. Not a single 25-yard five-shot group (fired from benchrest, of course) has measured as *large* as one-half inch. Nope, not one. The average of five strings with the Eley stuff was .3096-inch, or 1.18 minutes of angle. Using the Federal Champion, the aggregate for four groups went .35-inch (1.34-MOA). Bringing up the rear was the Winchester load, printing .37-inch (1.41-MOA). Not far to the rear, was it?

At 100 yards, Eley Tenex printed a 1.56-inch average, which amounts to 1.49-MOA. During 25 years of gun testing, I have had exactly four rimfire rifles exceed that level of precision at 100 yards. One was an Anschutz 1522-D 22 WMR, the second a little Mannlicher-stocked Anschutz 22 LR Model 1418, another a Heckler & Koch autoloading M770 with 22 Long Rifle conversion unit in place, the fourth a Winchester Model 9422-M, a WMR iteration. Remember, those were rifles, and the only four—of the many I have tested, including such high-ticket items as Kimber and KDF—that would shade the Exemplar.

So how many rimfire handguns have I used that would better (or even match) the accuracy so easily provided by my sample Exemplar? None. Not even the superlative Thompson/Center Contender. For metallic silhouette competition, or dotting a squirrel's eye at 60 paces, the new Anschutz has no peer, let alone a superior.

All this has its price, but not an exorbitant one. Current retail is about $395. For such precision, that's practically a gift.

The Exemplar is exemplary.

A-Square Hannibal.

A-Square Hannibal

Genial, erudite, charismatic Art Alphin hails out of Madison, Indiana, where he assembles some of the finest and most esoteric hunting rifles to be found. Art turns out two different items, the Hannibal and the Caesar, the latter built on a much-modified Remington Model 700 action. The guns I have here for testing are both Hannibals. Let's talk about them.

An A-Square Hannibal starts life as a surplus Pattern-17 Enfield action, which is magnafluxed and hardness tested, trued up where needed, then refinished and matte blued. Art screws on an A-Square barrel, which is stiffer than most normal tubes—and heavier—and which he claims has a faster twist rate than standard for increased bullet stability. The bolt handle is swept outward and rearward, to make quick manipulation easier. Open or receiver sights are available, the former in several forms. My 375 H&H, for example, wears a three-leaf, wide-vee express sight dovetailed into a steel ramp.

Aside from the obvious high level of workmanship and attention to detail, A-Square rifles are notable for their unusual "Coil-Chek" stock configuration. Mr. Alphin designed the stock to attenuate felt recoil by as much as 50 percent. How? Through a large cross-sectional butt area, ventilated soft-rubber recoil pad, a thick comb, longer-than-normal length of pull, robust heft, and a carefully arrived at pistol grip shape. Do all these things work as advertised? Yes, so far as I can tell. Explain? Sure.

Neither of my two Hannibals is uncomfortable to fire, even from prone, for at least 20 shots at a sitting. With some factory ammunition, I have fired 60 rounds in an afternoon's testing with little ill effect. Exactly which of the stock's characteristics most allays the backthrust, I dunno; I suspect all of them work in concert. If I had to point my finger at only one attribute, I'd choose the immoderate weight as being most expeditious in reducing perceived kick.

So how heavy is an A-Square? It depends. Art will pretty much build what you want. My test 375 tips the beam at 11¾ pounds scoped, slung, and fully loaded. My 340 Weatherby Magnum is only about a pound lighter.

Aside from being agreeable to shoot, even when chambered to one of the horrendously potent cartridges Alphin offers (such as the 375 and 378 Weatherby Magnums, the 416 Rigby, 450 Ackley Magnum, 460 Weatherby, and even the awe-inspiring 500 A-Square, which propels a 707-grain solid at a claimed 2250 fps!), A-Square rifles are notable for their reliability under any conditions, their nigh unbelievable wood-to-metal fit, and their fine trigger pulls.

Both my test rifles proved totally reliable in functioning so long as I paid attention to loaded overall cartridge length. Extraction was positive; ejection forceful. In fact, neither gun displayed any verjuice whatever.

Accuracy? The 340 Weatherby provided the tightest grouping with factory ammo of any medium-bore (from 32 to 375 caliber) rifle I have ever shot. And it was consistent. With A-Square's 250-grain pointed softpoint boattail, four five-shot 100-yard strings ran to 1.45 for the average. (Closest I've ever come to that was when testing editor Murtz's Whitworth 375, at 1½ inches on the button.) Further, the 200 Weatherby soft-points printed 1.50 for three groups, with the 250 Weatherby round nose hitting 1.59. Like I said, consistent.

The 375 was consistent as well, but not nearly so precise. Using A-Square 300-grain softpoint boattails, the aggregate came to 2.35 inches for three groups. Next best was the 300-grain Monolithic Solid at 2.59, with third slot going to the "Dead Tough" softpoints, which grouped 2.71 inches. Both loads are from A-Square's lengthy list of factory-loaded cartridges.

As a rifle for long-distance dialing of large North American fauna, my 340 would be the berries. It has all the requisite precision, and with the 200 Weatherby softpoint starting at 3135 fps at the muzzle, it shoots flat as a Kansas interstate. The 375, although not as accurate, would still be my choice of guns in that chambering should I win the sweepstakes and zip myself off to Africa.

A-Square rifles are not bargain-basement items, retailing for somewhere in the $1500 to $2000 neighborhood, depending on options. So if you, like me, are wallowing in the quagmire of penury, they might be out of your reach. If, on the other hand, your wallet runneth over, give one of Art's rifles a long look. Chances are you won't regret it. ●

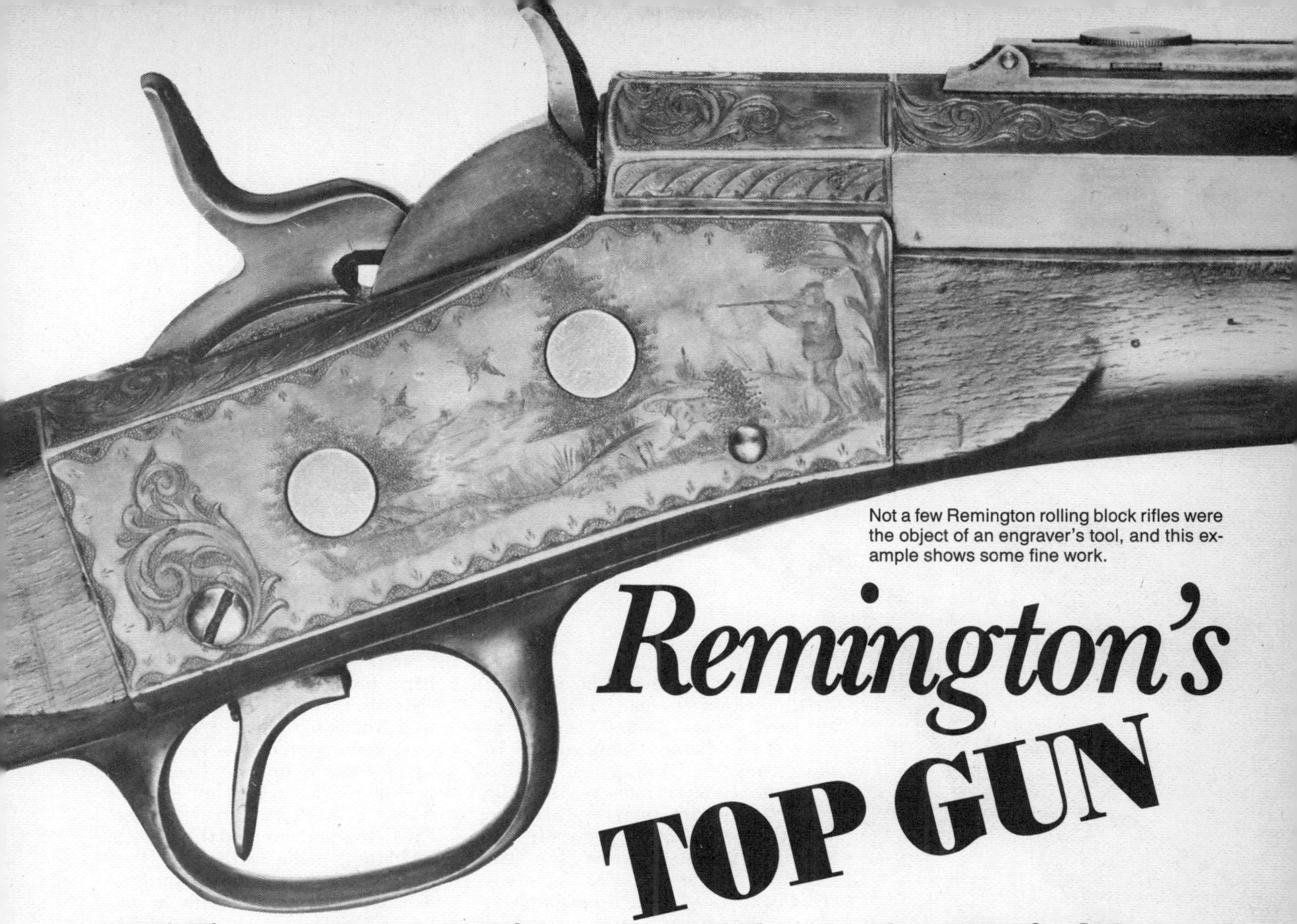

Not a few Remington rolling block rifles were the object of an engraver's tool, and this example shows some fine work.

Remington's TOP GUN
The Rolling Block Rifle

The rolling block design was made from 1866 to 1933 and is credited with saving the Remington company from financial ruin after the Civil War. It was a heck of a gun!

by NORMAN B. WILTSEY

Eliphalet Remington founded the Remington Arms Co. in 1816 in what is now Ilion, New York. He died August 12, 1861, and left the business to his sons Philo, Sam and Eliphalet.

APRIL OF 1865 was a time for shrewd re-evaluation and careful planning for an uncertain future at the Remington Arms factory in Ilion, New York. The three Remington brothers, Philo, Sam, and Eliphalet III, had been caught far out on a financial limb when the end of the Civil War resulted in the abrupt cancellation of lucrative government contracts.

Characteristically, the hard-pressed and hard-working brothers didn't even consider bankruptcy, although they had a perfect setup for such a tricky maneuver. (There is no business problem that a bucket of honest sweat can't drown). That was the private slogan of these rather remarkable Americans.

The Remington Agricultural Works, a separate company under the name

The Remington-Geiger split-breech actioned rifle, patented by Leonard Geiger in 1861. This was the forerunner of the famous rolling block rifles, using a Rider-improved design.

The Remington-Hepburn No. 3 Improved Creedmoor rifle. It was designed by a Remington employee and was made in many variations. The No. 3 Creedmoor was probably the highest form of the Hepburn.

of Remington Brothers, was not legally involved in the business affairs of the Arms Company. The brothers could have let the Arms Company go under and concentrated on making farm and industrial machinery, absorbing a few of their workers into the Agricultural Works and discharging the rest of the force. To Philo, Sam, and Eli such a move was unthinkable, even if dictated by stern necessity. Instead, they threw their boundless energy, limited resources and canny know-how into producing the best breech-loading rifle yet manufactured—the soon-to-be famous Remington rolling block.

Remington's search for the best breechloader in the world dated back to 1862 when Philo Remington brought inventor Leonard M. Geiger to the Ilion factory. As a result, 20,000 carbines equipped with Geiger's split breech, through which the hammer struck a rimfire cartridge, were manufactured by the Savage Arms Company of Middleton, Conn., under license, and on Remington-designed machines. Federal troops received the new breechloader early in 1865 and used them with deadly effect in the last climactic battles of the Civil War.

But the split breech, with the inherent weakness of such a mechanism, was not the answer to the insistent demand for a breechloader of simple yet rugged construction. Remington expert Joseph Rider, inventor in 1859 of the first double-action revolver, worked diligently with Geiger to develop a new and improved version of the Geiger breechloading carbine. Early models of the result of their joint efforts received a rigid trial at the Springfield (Mass.) Arsenal. There, in head-on competition with 65 other makes including the Sharps and the Henry, the Geiger-Rider carbines flunked dismally. Disheartened, the Remington representatives returned the rejected guns to the factory. Doggedly, Joseph Rider went to work to iron out the bugs in the design. He made the task his personal project and worked at it day and night.

Shortly after General Lee's surrender at Appomattox on April 9, 1865, ending the Civil War, Rider dispelled the gloom shrouding the idle Remington factory by announcing that the new rifle was now ready for production. Typically, the Remington brothers promptly decided to stake everything on the new gun. Work on it started at once.

Technically, the Rider rolling breech-block was a vast improvement over any breechloader then on the market. Alden Hatch, in *Remington Arms In American History,* writes: "The breech was immensely strong, easy to operate and as nearly foolproof as a gun can be." The first modern breechloaders made, Remington rolling block rifles were manufactured from 1866 to 1933. Many American shooters 50 years or over have used a Remington of this type at one time or another in their lives. (I received one in 22 caliber on my 14th birthday. It was a jewel in every way).

The firing pin operated through the breechblock, made of the best steel .69-inch thick. A single backward motion of the thumb opened the breech, extracted the spent cartridge. Safety was assured by a lever which secured the hammer while the gun was open and locked the breech after it was closed. Cartridge inserted, a forward flip of the thumb closed the breech and the rifle was ready for firing. For the first time in firearms history a single-shot breechloader could be loaded and fired at a fairly rapid rate. With practice, on ordinary shooter could get off a shot every 4 seconds. Hunters and soldiers quickly attained an average rate of 17 shots per minute.

As with all great inventions, the Remington rolling block rifle was simply and soundly based on scientific principles. It was quite literally impossible to blow out the breech. The hammer striking the back of the breechblock added strength to the breech itself at the instant of discharge. As Joseph Rider had predicted, "the greater the recoil, the greater the security attained." Rider's startling statement was amply proved at Liege, Belgium, where one of the new 50-70 Remingtons was tested at the government proving house. Director Alphonse Polain reported that the gun was loaded with 750 grains of

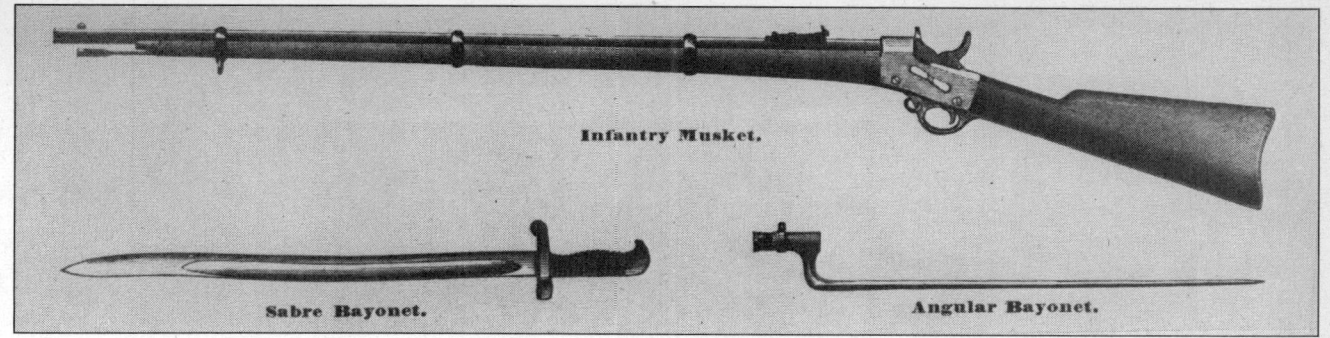

A large number of rolling blocks was sold to the Egyptian government for use by their armed forces. Two types of bayonets were available for these guns—the saber and the angular socket.

powder (normal charge 70 grains), 40 balls and two wads. "Nothing extraordinary" happened to the rifle when this tremendous load was fired. Director Polain laconically noted in his official report: "The barrel could not have received a stronger charge, as the last one filled its entire length."

Other rigorous tests included soaking the gun in sea water for 24 hours, firing 2500 rounds without cleaning the bore, firing the rifle without the stock, and firing filed-down cartridges that would burst in the barrel. One daring tester left a ramrod in the barrel, backed by a heavy powder load, and shot it out. The No. 1 model took all the tests without a single failure in operation or a burst barrel.

By then the Remingtons were fully aware that they had the best breechloading rifle in the world; the problem was to convince the buying public of that fact. Chance gave the No. 1 the initial boost of publicity it needed; chance in the person of a Texas cattleman named Nelson Story.

Story had struck it rich in to Montana gold camps. He high-tailed it back to Texas and invested most of his sizable stake in 3000 longhorn cattle. Thirty hardbitten cowboys—ex-Confederate cavalrymen—eagerly signed up to drive the herd 1500 miles to Montana. Story planned to sell half the herd to beef-hungry miners at $50 a head—twice what he'd paid for them—and start a ranch in the rich Montana grazing lands with the remaining 1500. He did just that, but would never have made it through Wyoming if he hadn't providentially discovered the new Remington breechloader en route.

At Fort Leavenworth, Kansas, the commanding officer warned Nelse that the Sioux chiefs Red Cloud and Crazy Horse were on the warpath and had declared their Wyoming hunting grounds barred to all white men. To reach Montana, Story and his men would have to trail their cattle straight through the Sioux lands guaranteed to them by solemn treaty. "Turn back," urged the worried C.O. "You can't fight a thousand Indians—and you certainly can't outrun them. The best that can happen to you is to lose your herd and your wagons; the worst, your life and the lives of all your men."

Nelse shrugged. "At my age, a man has to figure he's immortal or he'll never amount to a damn. I'm too deep in the game to play scared poker now. We'll go through—or die a-tryin'!"

"You're a stubborn fool, Story!," the officer replied testily. "But, since you're hellbent to commit suicide, you might as well take some of those red devils with you. We're testing a new breechloading rifle here. First shipment to arrive in the West. Damndest gun I ever saw, fast and smooth. The Sioux are used to facing muzzleloaders. When they run into practically steady fire from these breechloaders, they might just figure it 'big white-man medicine' and back off. We have enough extras to arm your men. Worth trying anyhow."

Story agreed that indeed it was worth trying. He tested the new rifle on the fort firing range and was delighted with its range, accuracy and speed of operation. He bought 30 of the new Remingtons and 100 rounds of brass centerfire 50-70 cartridges for each gun. So armed, Nelse figured that his straight-shooting ex-soldiers packed enough firepower to blast their way through to Montana, no matter what the odds against them.

The summer of 1865 was shading into autumn when Story moved boldly up the Bozeman Trail into dangerous Sioux territory. The dust kicked up by his wagons and cattle advertised the herd's presence to every Indian within 30 miles.

After easily repelling a minor raid near Fort Reno, Story and his rugged outfit were later attacked in force by the Sioux under the redoubtable Crazy Horse himself. Nelse estimated the Indians at about 500 warriors. They swept in recklessly on the ringed wagons of the white men, took the first volley without flinching, and raced on expecting to overrun the handful of Texans before they could reload their rifles. But the Remingtons poured out such a steady volume of fire the headlong charge of the mounted warriors wavered and broke. Crazy Horse signalled his braves to begin the classic Indian circling maneuver, gradually closing in until the moment arrived for a final overwhelming rush. But this, too, failed. Sioux casualties mounted as the staccato barking of the Remingtons never slackened. With nearly a third of his band dead or wounded, Crazy Horse called off the attack—the white man's new medicine was too strong.

Twice more roving bands of Sioux attacked the wagon train, and twice they were beaten off with heavy losses before Story got through to Montana with the loss of but one man. Nelse gave all the credit for the amazing feat to the new Remington breechloaders. "Without 'em, Crazy Horse and his warriors would have ridden right over us in that first rush," he admitted.

Word of Story's exploit and glowing tribute to the No. 1 reached the Remington factory and the brothers were quick to utilize the publicity value to the utmost. As a result, the new breechloader became popular with hunters and soldiers all over the West. Yet, the mass sales necessary for real profit did not materialize and the specter of financial ruin still haunted the war-expanded Remington plant at Ilion. Although government Ordnance experts rated the No. 1 the best breechloader in existence, the postwar economic slump resulted in the cancellation of large gun orders from

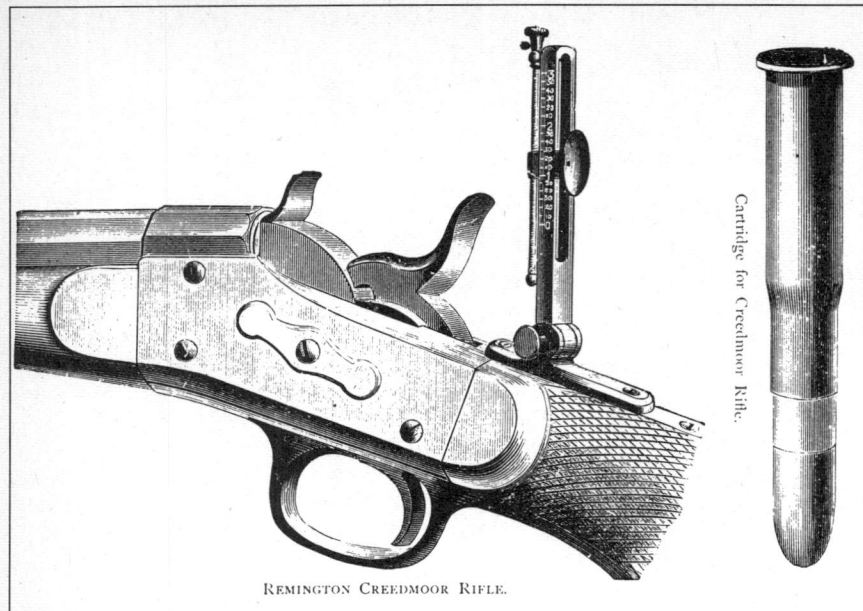

The Remington rolling block Creedmoor rifle had a tang-mounted Vernier rear sight. It was named after the Creedmoor Rifle Range on Long Island, New York.

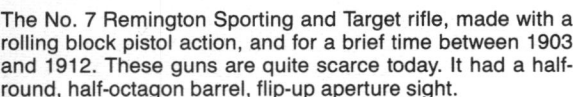

The No. 7 Remington Sporting and Target rifle, made with a rolling block pistol action, and for a brief time between 1903 and 1912. These guns are quite scarce today. It had a half-round, half-octagon barrel, flip-up aperture sight.

the Army. The Navy and Marine Corps bought a few guns but not enough to pull the Remington factory out of the red.

At this time America was flooded with war surplus guns of all makes and models, selling for a few dollars apiece to the undiscriminating buyers who made up the bulk of the market. Realizing that they could not compete with these cheap firearms, the Remington brothers held a strategy meeting and decided to send Sam to Europe to sell the No. 1 on the Continent. A natural salesman, Sam placed large orders for Remingtons in many European countries. Surviving a harrowing ordeal in Prussia when a gun in the hands of the King himself misfired, salesman Sam drove on to new honors. At the 1867 Imperial Exposition in Paris, a group of ordnance experts from ten leading nations unanimously picked the Remington as the best rifle in the world. Proud Sam received from Marshal Canrobert the Exposition's Silver Medal, the supreme award for military and sporting arms.

Moving on to Cairo, the dynamic American closed a deal with Ismael Pasha, Khedive of Egypt, for a large order of rifles for the new Egyptian army then being reorganized by the American General Stone. The former Confederate General was quick to endorse the Khedive's choice of the "Yankee" weapon. Ismael Pasha presented Sam with a fine scimitar of Damascus steel, and later, when the guns arrived precisely on schedule, topped his first gift with a parcel of land in Cairo. Eventually Sam built a tidy little "palace" on his land, but never gained the leisure to live in it. But his whirlwind selling campaign in Europe had assured the No. 1 of international success and that was all that mattered to him.

From 1866 to 1873 the Remington rolling block rifle remained unchallenged as the most popular all-round sporting rifle of its day, with the Sharps its closest competitor. In the latter year Winchester came out with the soon-to-be famous '73 lever-action repeating rifle. Chambered for the 44-40 centerfire cartridge which also fit the 44 Colt revolver, the Winchester quickly outsold the single-shot Remington. Yet, for both big game hunting and target shooting, the new Winchester could not compete with the Remington, now produced in 44-90-400 caliber as well as 50-70. Both guns far outranged the Winchester, outclassed it in accuracy and packed a far deadlier killing punch. The 44-90, in particular, was favored by so many Buffalo hunters that it became known from the Rio Grande to the Yellowstone as the "Remington Buffalo Rifle."

General George A. Custer was among the many ardent hunters who preferred the Remington. In 1872, impressed by the performance of the rolling block rifles as tested by troops in the field, Custer ordered a 50-70 Sporting Rifle of the finest (F) grade, priced at $91.50. The General wrote the Remingtons an enthusiastic letter datelined:

Headquarters, Fort Abraham Lincoln, D.T. October 5, 1873.
Messrs' Remington & Sons:
Dear Sirs—Last year I ordered from your firm a Sporting Rifle, caliber 50. I received the rifle a short time prior to the departure of the Yellowstone Expedition. The Expedition left Fort Rice the 20th of June, 1873, and returned to Fort Abraham Lincoln, Sept. 21, 1873. During the period of three months I carried the rifle

referred to on every occasion and the following list exhibits but a portion of the game killed by me: Antelope 41, buffalo 4, blacktail deer 4, American deer 3, white wolf 2 . . .

"The number of animals killed is not so remarkable as the distance at which the shots were executed. The average distance at which the 41 antelope were killed was 250 yards . . . I rarely obtained a shot at an antelope under 150 yards, while the range extended from that distance up to 630 yards.

"With the expedition were professional hunters employed by the Government to obtain game for the troops. Many of the officers and men also were excellent shots . . . I was the only person who used one of your Rifles, which, as may be properly be stated, there were pitted against it breech-loading rifles of almost every description, including many of the Springfield breech-loaders altered to Sporting Rifles. With your Rifle I killed far more game than any other single party, professional or amateur, while the shots made with your rifle were at longer range and more difficult shots than made by any other rifles in the command. I was more than ever impressed by the many superior qualities possessed by the system of arms manufactured by your firm . . .

    I am truly yours,
    Geo. A. Custer
    Brevet Major General U.S. Army

Custer carried his Remington Sporting Rifle into his last battle at the Little Bighorn on June 25, 1876. Sgt. J.M. Ryan, who supervised the burial detail 3 days after the battle, stated that "under the General's body were four or five brass cartridge shells; they were what he used in his Remington rifle."

No history of the Remington rolling block rifle would be complete without mention of the famed Creedmoor rifle, which rated for years as the best target rifle in America. The Creedmoor takes its name from the Creedmoor Rifle Range on Long Island, New York; the first such range in America and site of the first international shooting match between American and European marksmen.

In September of 1874, six American members of the American Rifle Club—a subsidiary organization of the National Rifle Association—met the Irish team in a widely heralded shooting match. The Irish marksmen, with their meticulously made muzzle-loading match rifles, had defeated the British, Canadian, and Australian teams and sought to add American top marksmen to their string of victories in order to further validate their claim to the world championship. Their guns, made by John Rigby, famous Dublin gunsmith, were equipped with Vernier elevation sights and wind-gauge scales. Rigby himself was a member of their team.

Six Americans were selected by means of elimination trial shoots to contest the formidable Irish team. Three rounds were to be shot at 800, 900 and 1000 yards. Remington and Sharps supplied the Americans with rifles; three 44-90-550 Remingtons and three Sharps of identical caliber. L.L. Hepburn, foreman of the Remington Mechanical Dept., designed the Remington entry around the rolling block action and named it the Creedmoor Rifle in honor of the Long Island range where the great match was to take place.

The American team was composed of Lt. Henry Fulton (Remington); C.W. Yale (Sharps); Col. John (Old Reliable) Bodine (Remington); Col. H.A. Gildersleeve (Sharps); L.L. Hepburn (Remington); Gen. J.S. Dakin (Sharps).

The Irish team was composed of Dr. J.B. Hamilton, John Rigby, Capt. Walker, James Wilson, J.K. Milner, and Edmund Johnson.

A large crowd attended the match, hoping that the Americans would win or at least give a good account of themselves against the world renowned Irish sharpshooters.

Alden Hatch describes the start of the match as follows: "The team captains tossed for choice of stands and the Irish won. They surprised everyone by choosing stands 16 and 17, which were considered less desirable than 19 and 20, which went to the Americans. Number 18 was left vacant to avoid confusion. The squads took their places, marked for them by red flags, facing an immense rectangle of shaven lawn. The targets were 800 yards away, backed by massive mounds of earth, and they shimmered in a mirage of heat waves.

The targets were the English standard of that era, measuring 12 inches by 6. The square black bullseye was 3 by 5 inches, the "center" was 6 by 6 inches. This left a space 6 by 3 inches on each side called an "outer." A bullseye counted four points, a center three and an outer two. Thus, the highest possible score for a round of 15 shots was 60, and a perfect score for a team of six was 360.

Lt. Fulton led off for the Americans in the 800-yard first round. Lying on his back in the odd "stance" used by many top marksmen of the period, Fulton scored five bullseyes and a center with his first six shots.

Dr. Hamilton and J.K. Milner made the best scores for the Irish team on the opening round; Hamilton scoring 13 bullseyes out of 15 shots. Milner had the best run of consecutive bulls at 11. While none of the Americans were as brilliant individually as Hamilton and Milner, the Yanks shaded them as a team. Final score for the first round was America 326, Ireland 317.

At 900 yards the Irishmen scored 312 to the Americans' 310. Milner,

The Remington Light Baby Carbine had a saddle ring on the left side of the receiver and was issued to U.S. Cavalry units.

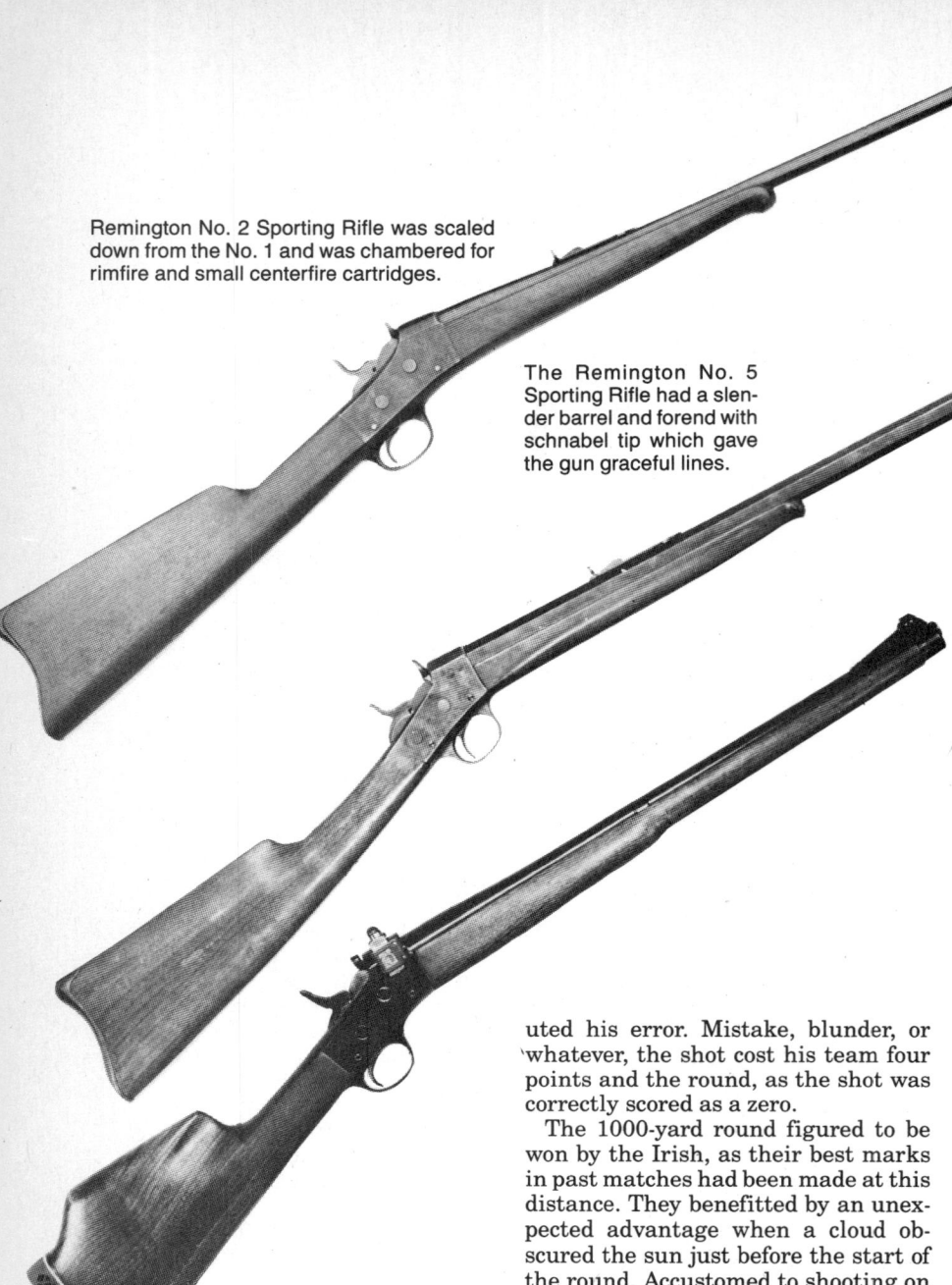

Remington No. 2 Sporting Rifle was scaled down from the No. 1 and was chambered for rimfire and small centerfire cartridges.

The Remington No. 5 Sporting Rifle had a slender barrel and forend with schnabel tip which gave the gun graceful lines.

Because of their great strength, many rolling block actions were converted into sporting rifles in any number of modern calibers. In the late 1950s, actions and complete rifles could be bought for under $10!

like Lt. Fulton, an ardent exponent of the prone-back shooting position, lost a bullseye in this round by scoring on the wrong target. Lying on his back with the butt of his rifle resting on his armpit, Milner held the gun muzzle between his toes. This posture inevitably narrowed his field of vision drastically and to that fact must be attributed his error. Mistake, blunder, or whatever, the shot cost his team four points and the round, as the shot was correctly scored as a zero.

The 1000-yard round figured to be won by the Irish, as their best marks in past matches had been made at this distance. They benefitted by an unexpected advantage when a cloud obscured the sun just before the start of the round. Accustomed to shooting on sunless days in misty Ireland, the invaders from Erin ran off their shots rapidly before the lucky cloud drifted past, and finished their round well ahead of the Americans.

Grimly, with three shots apiece left to fire, Lt. Fulton and Col. Bodine steeled down to shoot. Fulton, a bit jittery, scored three centers. Col. Bodine, the nerveless "Old Reliable" of the American team, scored bullseyes on his first two shots. At this point, with one shot to go, the total scores stood Ireland 931, America 930. The match and unofficial world championship hung on Bodine's last shot.

The day was oppressively hot and, before taking his position for his last shot, Bodine asked for a bottle of ginger beer. The bottle exploded in his hand as he was opening it, cutting him severely. Calmly, the Colonel wrapped his handkerchief around his badly cut hand and assumed his favorite prone firing position. Spectators held their breath and Bodine's white handkerchief-bandage turned sopping red before he squeezed off the shot. The Remington barked—and a relieved cheer went up from the crowd as, on target 19, the marker's white disk rose to cover the bullseye. Final score: America 934, Ireland 931, America winning the match by three points.

Although the American margin of victory was slight and unfortunately tainted by the fact that Milner had fired at the wrong target, the match proved that American marksmen and American breechloaders could hold their own with Europe's best marksmen firing muzzleloaders produced by one of the world's master gunsmiths.

The Remington brothers and Remington workmen were especially jubilant at the result, as Remingtons narrowly outscored the rival Sharps 468 to 466. The Hepburn-designed Creedmoor rifle was produced as a regular model later that year. The first model had a straight grip and curved buttplate. Later models had pistol grips and slightly curved buttplates. The heavy octagon barrels were equipped with Vernier sights and wind gauges. The Remington catalog of 1875 lists the Creedmoor as selling for $108. Destined for immediate popularity, it remained the first choice of discriminating marksmen for many years. Connoisseurs of classic firearms cherish the Creedmoor today, nearly 100 years after Remington ceased its manufacture in 1890. In the field of target shooting it ranked as highly with marksmen as did the famous Remington Buffalo Rifle of the 1870s and 1880s. Together, they helped mightily in the making of American history. ●

Russia's Garand

The Story of the Tokarev Rifle

The SVT-40 in its element—as a sniper rifle in the hands of a woman sniper. Note the standard 3.5x scope and the unique mount. *(Reprinted with permission, from Peter R. Senich, The German Sniper 1914-1945, p. 117 © 1977 by Bison Books, published by Chartwell Books, Inc.)*

TRIVIA QUESTION: If the United States, with its 4,028,000 Garands in service, fielded more major-caliber semi-auto battle rifles than any other country involved in WW II, what nation was second in this regard? Many would guess Germany, but the answer is Russia. Yes, archaic ol' Russia, ostensibly so technologically backward and industrially crippled by Stalinism that she literally invited attack, even by a country that knew well the folly of making war on two fronts at once. Russia built and issued an imposing 2,000,000 full-powered self-loading rifles between the years 1936 and 1945 . . . and that is a deliberate underestimation, since it ignores the AVS-36 rifles built and shipped to field units between 1936

With war looming on the not-so-distant horizon, many countries found their military hardware lacking in the 1930s, and most chose to update their smallarms in some way. Mother Russia adopted the Tokarev design in two variations that proved successful . . . to a point.

by ROBERT T. SHIMEK

A thin sheet-metal piston cover "protects" the operating rod, piston and gas cylinder. A hard blow to the cover could easily put the gun out of action, though.

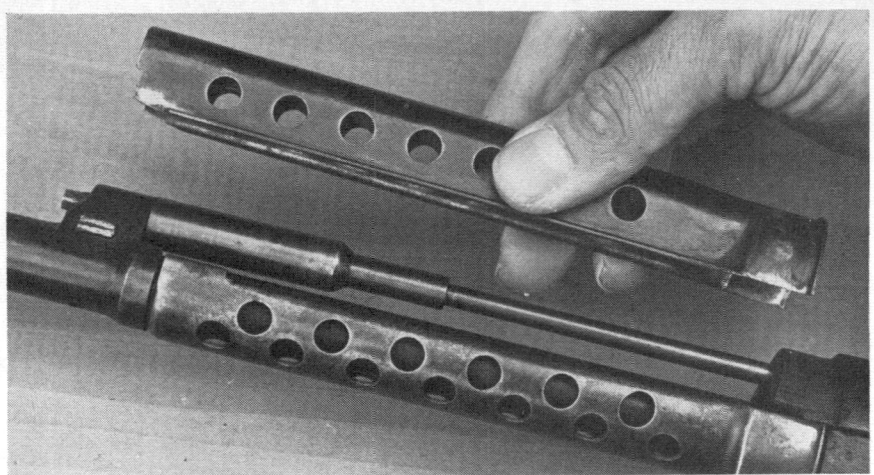

and 1938. By contrast, Germany never completed more than 600,000 G.41/G.43 rifles. Even if you insist upon adding to this figure the 7.92 mm Kurz-chambered assault rifles, you still don't get 2,000,000 units. We don't know exactly how many *sturmgewehre* were made, but no estimate I've seen was anywhere near 1,400,000 guns.

What sort of gun made up the bulk of the USSR's 2,000,000 self-loading rifles? The Tokarev rifle, in its SVT-38 and SVT-40 variants, was Russia's staple self-loader. Designed contemporarily with our own M-1, the Tok as "Russia's Garand"... or at least, Russia's *attempt* at a Garand. Thus it constitutes a fascinating subject for study, as well as a lesson in what might have happened had decision makers in our military but made a critical mistake or two in overseeing our own 1930s semi-auto rifle program.

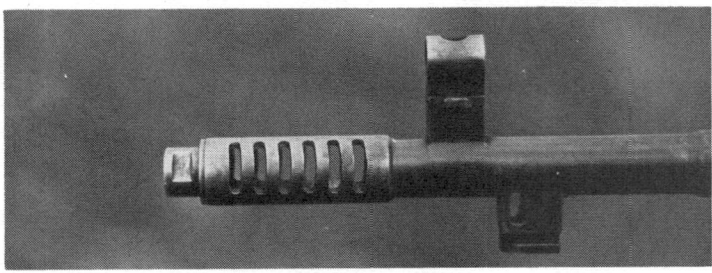

The six-slot muzzle brake seems to work very well. Teamed with the gas-operated action, it reduces recoil to easy-to-manage proportions. After 1941, the muzzle brake had only two baffles.

The author testing the Tokarev from the bench. Recoil was inordinately light in this gun, even though the cartridge—the 7.62x54R—is a full-power round roughly equivalent to our own 30-06.

The Tokarev semi-automatic rifle—we can deal with the Models 38 and 40 collectively, since they're so similar—was a product of the genius of Fedor Tokarev, creator of the ultra-rugged and dependable TT-30/TT-33 Soviet service pistol. Tokarev's intent in designing his auto rifle was replacement of the "lemon" self-loader the Soviets had unwisely selected for limited production in 1936. This "lemon," the Simonov-engineered AVS-36, was proving to be a disaster afield: The mechanism was dirt-sensitive and stoppage-prone, and the elective full-auto mode caused excessive wear. Also, according to one source, muzzle blast was horrific, thanks to the design of the muzzle brake.

Tokarev, in his researches, made special efforts to avoid the problems of the '36. He engineered a new gas-operated action that relied for locking on a bolt that cammed downward into a recess in the receiver floor; this system differed from the AVS-36's "vertically-moving locking block" arrangement, and it worked better. The Tokarev action was also well sealed, so as to prevent entrance of dirt and debris, in that there was no wide-open track for the operating handle, as on AVS-36. Too, a six-baffle muzzle-brake was incorporated, so as to deal better with blast, and the full-auto mode was eliminated.

The result, initially, was the SVT-38, a 10-shot, detachable-box-magazine-fed battle rifle that measured a longish 48¼ inches (compared to our Garand's 43 inches) and weighed 8¾ pounds empty (the U.S. M-1 tipped the scales at 9½ pounds). Interesting Model 38 features included a gas regulation system by which the amount of gas operating the action might be controlled; this was pretty advanced stuff for a personal rifle of the 1930s, though Browning had come up with the concept some years before. Also of interest was the two-piece stock, and the integral scope rails on the receiver (apparently, more-than-acceptable accuracy was expected). The gun was even impressive visually, courtesy of that muzzle brake and those hand-guard-mounted ventilation ports. But there were other characteristics that prophesied a less-than-favorable future for the M38: The 7.62x54R car-

92 GUNS ILLUSTRATED 1989

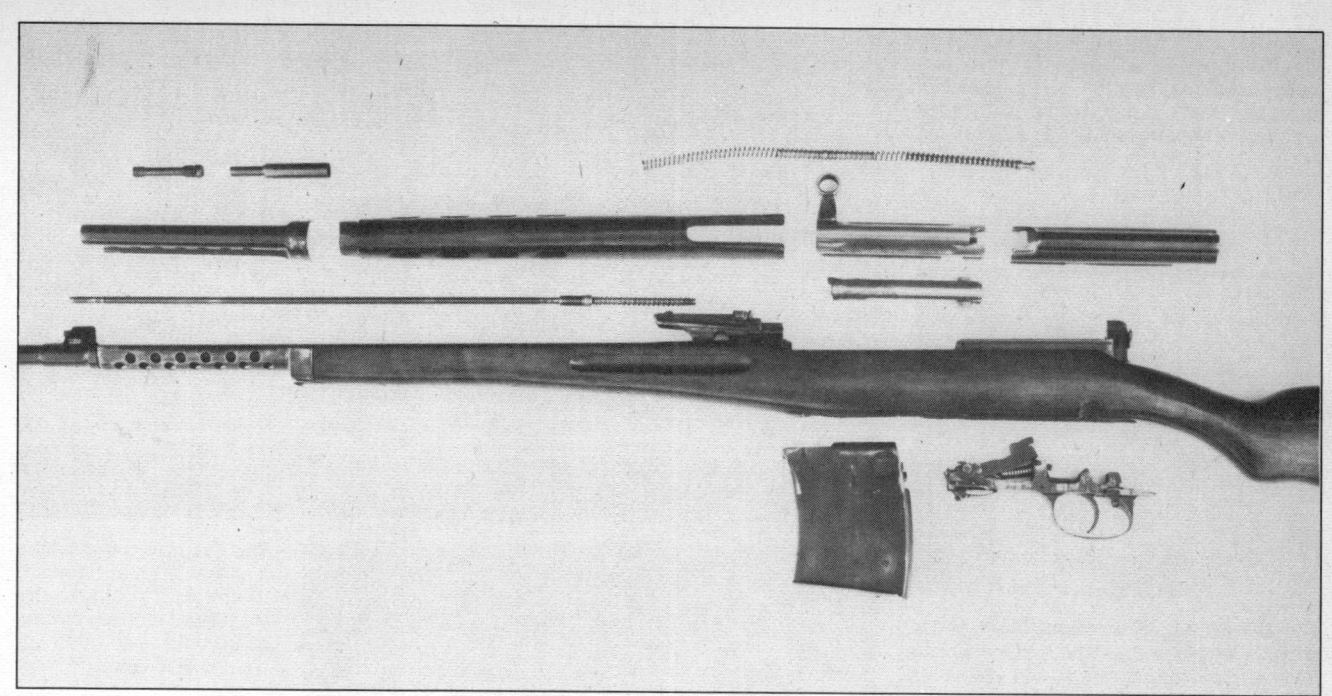
Field-stripping the Tokarev seemed elementary to the author. It can be done quickly and requires only a cartridge for a tool. Whatever the Russians' "field maintenance problems" were, field-stripping wasn't one of them!

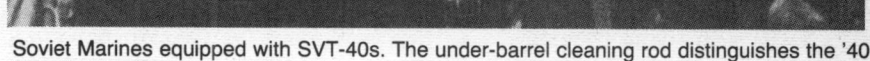
Soviet Marines equipped with SVT-40s. The under-barrel cleaning rod distinguishes the '40 from the SVT-38.
Reprinted with permission, from John Weeks, Infantry Weapons, *p. 95, Ballantine's Illustrated History of the Violent Century, Weapons Book No. 25, published by Ballantine Books, Inc. © 1971 by John Weeks.)*

Soviet propagandists made little effort to conceal the fact that the Red Army was taking self-loading rifles into service.
(Reprinted with permission, from S.L. Mayer (editor), The Russian War Machine 1917-1945, *p. 117. © 1977 by Bison Books, published by Chartwell Books, Inc.)*

tridge, being a rimmed effort, promised feeding problems; also, the flutes lining the chamber indicated that help was needed during extraction.

It was at this point that Simonov, designer of AVS-36, reappeared on the scene. The AVS-36 had been re-engineered so as to eliminate its faults, Simonov claimed, and the arm could be returned to production, eliminating the need for setting up an SVT-38 production line. There is evidence to suggest that Simonov had done just as he claimed. But by this time, 1939, the Soviet Defense Committee, chaired by Stalin, had committed to the SVT and production proceeded with Five-Year-Plan passion. Large numbers of the new rifles rolled off the assembly lines within a short period of time and, by the inauguration of hostilities with Finland in 1939, the SVT-38 was on its way to becoming a major type. With the Winter War, however, came the shattering of illusions. The '38, while not as malfunction-prone as the AVS-36, proved fragile and not amenable to

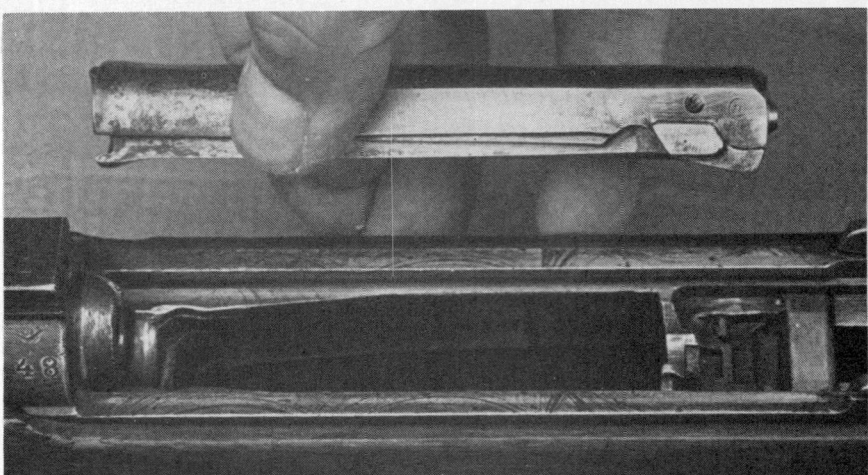

The Tokarev locking system involves a wedge on the rear bottom of the bolt which drops into a recess in the receiver floor during lock-up. Metal finishing was a bit crude.

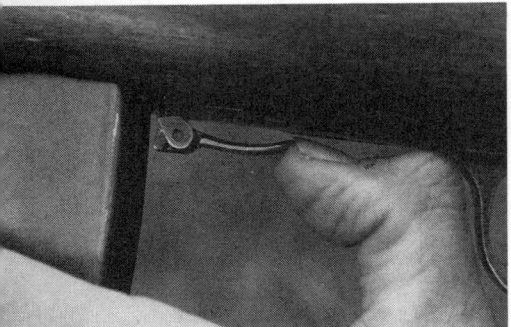

The SVT-40 magazine release looks, and is, absurdly fragile. It's also hard to manipulate quickly. SVT magazines are in *very* short supply and can bring three-figure prices.

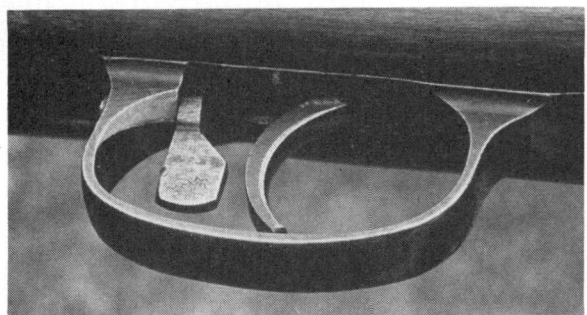

The Tokarev safety is neither sophisticated nor quick to operate. It blocks the trigger and requires a clumsy 90-degree rotation upward to disengage.

maintenance afield, even though frequent maintenance was critical to Tokarev reliability. Furthermore, the gun was too heavy, and those "nature-of-the-beast" rimmed-cartridge-in-an-auto-rifle feeding bobbles plagued the action.

Plainly, there were some design inadequacies here and so, as of 1940, an improved successor to the SVT-38 materialized. This was the SVT-40, which strove nobly to "fix" the shortcomings evidenced by the '38 without interrupting production any more than necessary. The new gun extensively altered the furniture of the old and strengthened some internal parts, though basic engineering remained unchanged. The stock alterations involved a change from two-piece to one-piece configuration, replacement of the '38's two barrel bands with a one-band system, relocation of the cleaning rod from right-side-exterior of stock to the more conventional under-barrel, inside-the-stock location, and reconfiguration of the metal piston cover. Internal modifications included the addition of some production expedients, as well as the strengthening alluded to above. Furthermore, it was decided to acquire the desired level of reliability afield by limiting the issue of Tokarev rifles to "special soldiers"—NCOs, snipers, and elite troops—who could be expected to give the level of maintenance the Tok required. The malfunctions engendered by the rimmed cartridge could be countenanced, in the interest of not interrupting production.

It is here that our story becomes unclear. We know that SVT-40 Tokarevs began leaving the factories as of their year of designation, but what is less clear is just when Model 38 production stopped. Some authorities insist that the last '38s left the factories in the year 1940, but recent scholarship suggests that SVT-38s were still being made as of 1942. We'll probably never know, since the Russians to this day do not speak freely regarding events surrounding the "Great Fatherland War."

The SVT-40 was too late to join its Model SVT-38 brothers in the struggle for Finland (and too late to be captured by the Finns, as were so many '38s). But by the time of Operation Barbarossa, M40 was ensconced as a major type. As had been planned, primary use was by non-commissioned officers in infantry units, by elite soldiers like ski troops and marines, and by snipers. The Tok was especially suitable for sniping, because the self-loading action required none of the position-revealing manipulation by hand that a bolt-gun requires. The gun was also suitable for sniping because many of Russia's snipers were women. Lest this give you cause for amusement, be advised that the USSR's second deadliest sniper, with kills well into the three-figure range, was a woman! A woman, however toughened by military training, appreciated the gentle kick of an auto rifle; she also appreciated the Tok's reasonable 8½-pound weight, which made the gun tolerable to carry, even with the standard 3.5x telescope installed. Hence, the Tok found particular acceptance among snipers—of both genders. It also found some acceptance among the Germans who, being ever short of semi-auto rifles, utilized the Tok as a "capture n' reissue" weapon.

Sniper service could not suffice to keep the Tokarev design alive, however. As a heavy-duty battle rifle, even in "responsible" supervisory or elite hands, the gun was a bust. Reliability was still a problem, and the SVT proved far too fragile for the hand-to-hand combat of the Eastern Front. Hence, early on, the infantry began phasing the Tok out of service, which is one ignominious fate for what seemed the most advanced fighting rifle in the Soviet inventory. Development of shortened carbine and selective-fire ("AVT-40") versions could not save the gun. By January, 1945, plans were afoot to stop production of the gun, though these were not acted upon immediately. By the time manufacture did stop, presumably near war's end, a production total of

The Germans also liked the SVT-40 and used them whenever they could be found. Officers, of course, claimed first dibs. Curiously, the Wehrmacht seemed oblivious to the guns' shortcomings.
(Reprinted with permission, from Peter R. Senich, The German Sniper 1914-1945, *p. 417. © 1982 by Peter Senich, published by Paladin Press.)*

Norma 180-gr. soft-point ammo rated at 2624 fps is the only factory-new 7.62x54R fodder available today. It performed flawlessly in the test Tokarev.

Ski troops were also among the "elite" soldiers authorized Tokarevs. Conditions on the Russian front were horrendous for both men and machine—and both were expected to function well.
(Reprinted with permission, from Otto Preston Chaney, Jr., Zhukov Marshall of the Soviet Union, *p. 88, Ballantine's Illustrated History of the Violent Century, War Leader Book No. 28, published by Ballantine Books. © 1974 by Random House, Inc.)*

about 1,400,000 units had been reached. This represents a minor effort by Soviet standards.

Examine a Tokarev rifle today and some of the reasons for the rifle's troubles are at once apparent. My test sample Tok, a 1941-built SVT-40 model loaned by friend Larry Tieger, impressed me immediately with its fragility. The stock was so slim; by comparison to a Garand's beefy furniture, the Tok's wood seemed toy-like. Similarly, the SVT's thin-walled, ventilation-holed handguard stunned me with its delicacy. And as for metal surfaces, the Model 40 showed sheet metal—thin sheet metal—in so critical an area as the piston cover, which protects the piston and operating rod. Even the controls were dainty beyond credibility. The magazine catch looked so delicate it seemed destined for service on a dressing table jewelry box, not on an article intended for heavy combat. And the magazine was well-exposed to damage.

Internally, the impression of fragility faded somewhat. There were 62 parts—more, but not a lot, than on the Garand and Gewehr 43. Quality, at least as evidenced by the test piece, was outstanding, better than on Garands I've seen, better by far than on the G.43. Finish was a combination of polished, in-the-white steel and well-applied rust-blue, typical pre-war standard in the USSR and comparable to what was being made in Western Europe at the time.

Firing tests of the sample SVT-40 confirmed some of what history records regarding Tok performance, but failed to evidence other characteristics long associated with the gun. Recoil from this arm, when firing Norma 180-grain soft-point factory loads said to produce 2624 fps, was mild; the Tokarev is among the gentlest full 30-caliber battle rifles this author has fired. Plainly, that Tok action is a kick-reducer par excellence, and I wouldn't be surprised to find out that the muzzle brake helps. My test piece was equipped with the original six-baffle brake, not with the two-baffle model which was adopted in 1941. I had no trouble at all discerning why women snipers liked the gun.

Otherwise, I fear my test results were at variance with what I'd expected. Accuracy was merely adequate,

GUNS ILLUSTRATED 1989 **95**

The author shooting the Tokarev off-hand. The gun consistently put five shots into 4 inches from 100 yards—not exactly spectacular accuracy.

like 4 inches for five shots from 100 yards, and that isn't what one ordinarily expects from a sniping rifle. The bore of my test piece was moderately pitted, however, and that doubtless affected my results. I must also concede that I had a devilish time using the issue open sights. My eyes tired easily whenever I tried to hold a sight-picture, probably because of the small size of both rear "U" and front post.

Functioning was a surprise too, though for good rather than ill. The SVT fed, fired, and ejected the Norma soft-point round-noses like it had been made for them. Interestingly, ejection was forward. "If you miss 'im with the bullet, you get 'im with the case," commented one wag. Of course, the military fodder worked well too. There were no bobbles at any time during the course of about 100 test rounds fired. I make it a point not to stress a collector-class arm any more than is necessary to gain a valid shooting impression; hence only the 100 rounds.

Other Tokarev particulars evaluated included the thumb safety and field-strip sequence. The former didn't impress me: mechanically, it was crude (the safety blocks the trigger) and operation seemed clumsy because you rotate the lever 90 degrees by pushing all the way through the trigger guard with the trigger finger. Field-strip was more to my liking. It was quick, easy (much easier than a Garand), and required only a cartridge as a tool. Not even cursorily-trained soldiers could have had much trouble taking down this rifle. Detail strip didn't look that imposing either. Alas, history does not record just what the field-maintenance headaches associated with the Tokarev were, hence my inability to evaluate this matter.

This, then, is the story of the Tokarev automatic rifle, and I'm not sure which of several morals to draw from it—"Don't build semi-auto rifles around rimmed cartridges"; "Don't make delicate instruments for combat use"; "Don't be hasty to commit yourself to a new-wave fighting rifle." But the tale certainly invites "what if" speculations. What if the Tok had been eminently successful? Would Germany have been turned more quickly? And what of the effect on Soviet weapons development? Surely, we wouldn't have seen all those pistol-calibered submachineguns ... or the tactics their use mandated.

What if we Americans had made errors in automatic rifle development similar to those made by the Russians? How would we have fared in WW II with only bolt-rifles and submachineguns as shoulder arms? Now *there's* speculation of a most unpleasant kind. ●

The author wishes to thank Dr. Edward Clinton Ezell, Curator, Division of Armed Forces History, National Museum of American History, Smithsonian Institution, for his kind assistance in updating Tokarev production totals and manufacturing history for this article.

Photo Credit Publishers

Ballantine Books, Inc.
Div. of Random House, Inc.
201 E. 50th St.
New York, NY 10022
212/751-2600

Bison Books Corp.
15 Sherwood Place
Greenwich, CT 06830
203/661-9551

Paladin Press
P.O. Box 1307
Boulder, CO 80306
303/443-7250

Harrington & Richardson's 25 ACP AUTO PISTOL

Harrington & Richardson had a "flawed" reputation for making some pretty bad revolvers, but their short-lived automatic was a real jewel. The quality was outstanding, but the public just couldn't get past the bad name the company had gotten.

by DONALD M. SIMMONS

Harrington & Richardson Arms Company has an undeserved reputation as a manufacturer of "cheap" revolvers. This onus is not only unfair, but it's not even true; H&R came from a long and honorable line of gun manufacturing, producing a broad line of revolvers, shotguns and rifles. Frank Wesson, brother of Daniel B. Wesson, founder of Smith & Wesson, started his own arms company in Worcester, Massachusetts just prior to the American Civil War. In 1871, Frank Wesson entered into a partnership with his nephew Gilbert H. Harrington, forming Wesson & Harrington Arms Co. Gilbert Harrington left Wesson in 1875 and joined William A. Richardson, creating Harrington & Richardson Arms Co. H&R was incorporated in 1888, forming the Harrington & Richardson Arms Corporation. In 1973, H&R moved from its parent city of Worcester to Gardner, Massachusetts.

During my lifetime, H&R produced well-made, inexpensive, medium-powered revolvers. In 1912, H&R entered the field of automatic pistol manufacturing. Before we go into this venture, let's talk a little about the cartridge they were to use in their new pistol.

In 1904, firearms design genius John Moses Browning wrote to Remington's Union Metallic Cartridge Co. asking William "U.M.C." Thomas to make him a new type of automatic pistol cartridge in 25 caliber. Mr. Thomas obliged and the 25 ACP (Automatic Colt Pistol) was created. This impotent round has, undoubtedly, been chambered in more different pistols than any other centerfire cartridge.

It is this 25 ACP cartridge that Harrington & Richardson used in their first automatic pistol marketed in 1912. Colt Patent Firearms Company of Hartford, Connecticut, had already been making the Browning-designed, 25-caliber automatic pistol, their Model N, for 4 years. Overseas in Belgium, the firm of Fabrique Nationale (FN) had been manufacturing the same pistol as Colt from 1906. The only difference between the two pistols was that the Colt had a manual safety, while the FN pistol didn't. So the concept of a vest pocket automatic was not new to the shooting public at the time of H&R's entry into the auto pistol field.

Harrington & Richardson went overseas for the design of their first automatic pistol, and purchased the American rights from Webley & Scott to make it. The actual model of this pistol was the brainchild of William J. Whiting, Webley & Scott's superintendant. He designed the entire W&S line of self-loading pistols, starting with their big 455 auto and working down through the 38/9mm, 380, 32 and finally the 25s. Webley & Scott eventually sold two different 25s, the exposed hammer model in 1911 and, in 1920, the so called "hammerless," to which the H&R was the predecessor.

H&R always called their autos "self-loading" which is certainly better terminology than the universal "automatic," but today the word has been accepted and "automatic" in a pistol means a single round fired for each

GUNS ILLUSTRATED 1989 97

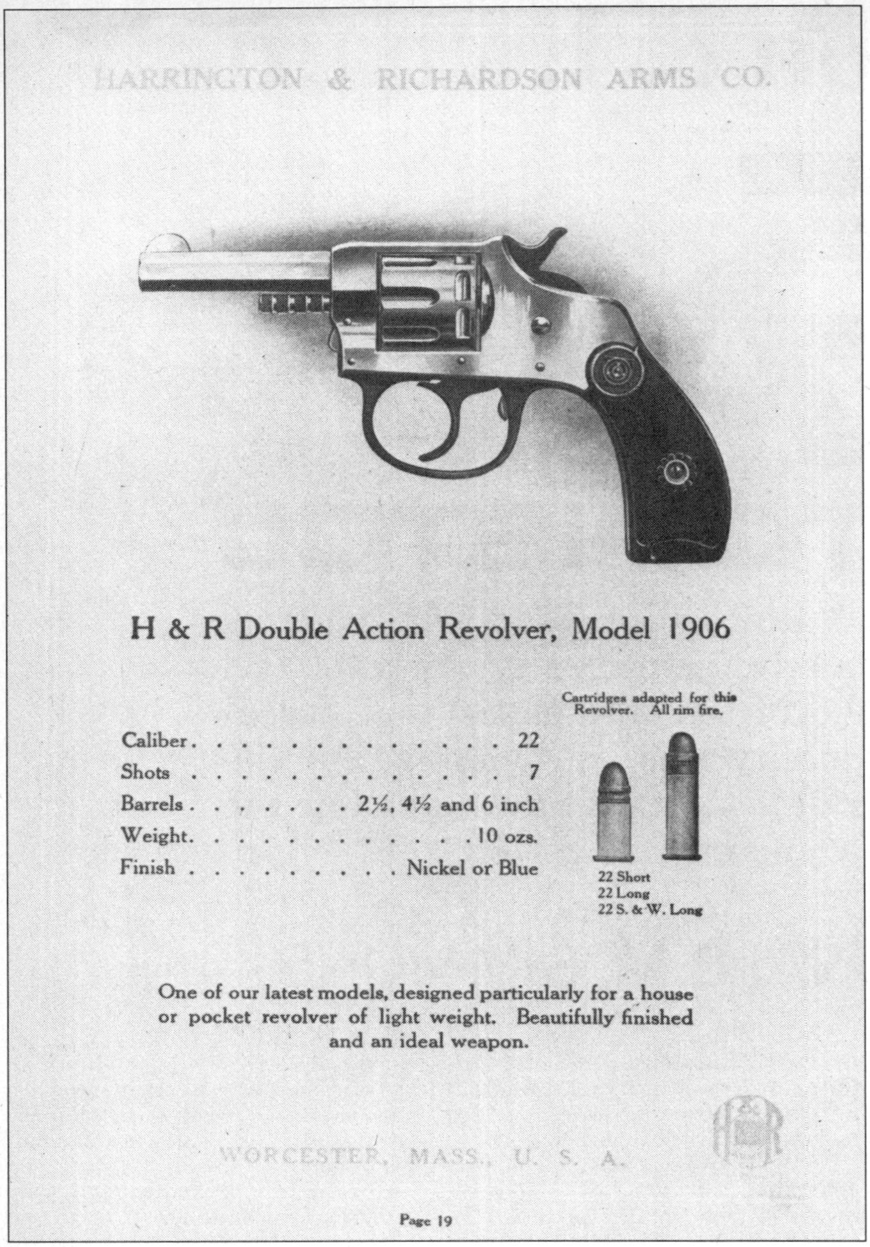

H & R Double Action Revolver, Model 1906

Caliber 22
Shots 7
Barrels . . . . . . 2½, 4½ and 6 inch
Weight . . . . .10 ozs.
Finish . . . . Nickel or Blue

Cartridges adapted for this Revolver. All rim fire.
22 Short
22 Long
22 S. & W. Long

One of our latest models, designed particularly for a house or pocket revolver of light weight. Beautifully finished and an ideal weapon.

WORCESTER, MASS., U. S. A.

Page 19

The villain of the Harrington & Richardson story was the inexpensive double-action solid-frame revolvers that made up a large portion of their line. These guns gave the company an unsavory name.

pull of the trigger. They also called their pistol "hammerless," which is not technically correct. Their auto had a concealed hammer.

The Harrington & Richardson auto appears at first glance to be very simple, but this is an illusion not borne out by the facts. Externally, there are only four user-controlled points: the trigger, manual safety, slide pulls, and the magazine catch for discharging the pistol's magazine. The gun had no grip safety as in Colt's Model N and no sights at all. Internally we find a very complicated disconnector system not at all like the one eventually used in the "hammerless" Webley & Scott, and a manual safety that locks the trigger, which is not the best place to make a firearm secure. (The firing pin is the last thing before the cartridge's primer and it is this part that is the safest to block). Even the magazine catch is complicated and requires an extra locking hole in the magazine's body. The overall machining is superb, the fits are so tight that one is hard put to see the joining lines. Compared to its peer, the Colt Model N 25 ACP of 1908, the H&R represents a machinist's nightmare. There is no way that the cost of fabrication of the two different pistols could be comparable—so much for simplicity; it is only skin deep!

There is great strength and reliability built into the Harrington & Richardson automatic pistols. One of the first autos that I ever owned was a second-hand H&R 25 that I bought at W.S. Brown in Pittsburgh, Pennsylvania, in 1939 for the munificent sum of $7.50. In all the years that I owned this fine pistol, serial number 2823, it never misfired, jammed or had feed problems, and I used every kind of ammo I could get my hands on—grubby 25-round boxes from Germany, corrosive rounds from overseas, as well as our own obsolete domestic ammunition.

The pistol's takedown is not only easy but is also extremely quick, which gives the shooter no chance to beg off cleaning the piece after a session at the range. The factory gives the following takedown instructions:

"To take apart. Place safety in down position, and if there are any cartridges in the magazine, remove magazine. Cock hammer by drawing breech block (slide) way back and allowing it to spring forward. While in

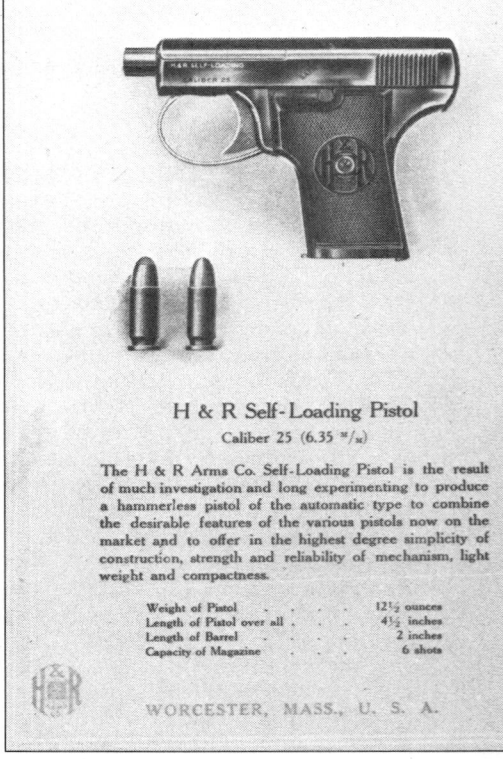

This page from a 1913 Harrington & Richardson catalog shows the little 25 ACP pistol. The company preferred to call the gun a "self-loader," and of "hammerless" design when, in fact, it had a concealed hammer.

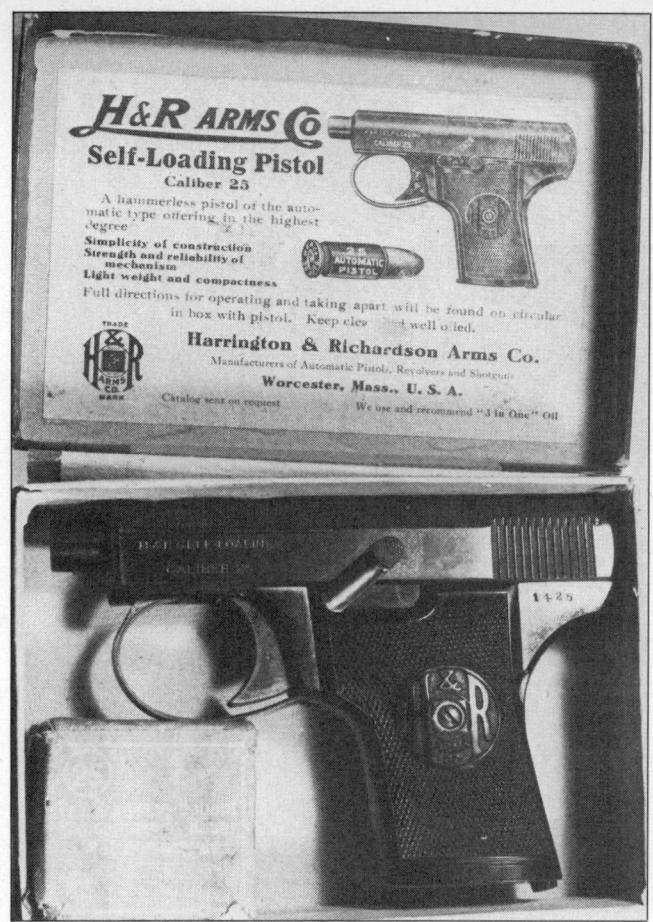

This is what "new in the box" is all about to collectors. This is serial number 1425, complete with an original box of 25 ACP ammo. The box label says to keep the gun well oiled and recommends "3 in One" oil.

This front page of the instruction booklet shows the gun and both FMJ and softpoint ammunition available. The H&R logo used in the copy is interesting, wasn't often used.

Left and right views of a very early H&R 25 auto, serial number 429. This example has seen a fair bit of use judging from the condition of the finish. Difficult to see in the photo is the blank patent date in the right side markings.

the rearward position note that there is no cartridge in the chamber to avoid an accident. Place finger through the bow of the trigger guard and pull toward muzzle, until the guard is freed. After end of guard toward butt is free, the breech block and the barrel can be withdrawn, sliding them together toward the muzzle. After separating from the frame, the barrel can be lifted from the breech block." That's all there is to the takedown and it takes less than 15 seconds.

There is little doubt that the H&R is light at 12.13 ounces empty and 13.12 ounces loaded. The Colt outweighs the H&R by a full ounce, but the parent Webley & Scott weighs only a scant 10.6 ounces empty. The H&R factory gave the following statistics:

Weight of Pistol—12 1/2 ounces
Length of Pistol Overall—4 1/2 inches (4.45″)
Length of barrel—2 inches (2.15″)
Capacity of Magazine—6 shots

Variations

At first glance the Harrington & Richardson auto doesn't seem to have many variations, but on digging a little deeper we find enough to keep the most avid gun collector happy. The standard finish is polished blue with a polished in-the-white trigger guard; the trigger and safety lever are both case-hardened. The most common magazine is nickel plated with the follower blued, but a few H&R 25 autos have an entirely blued magazine. These seem to be on the early-issue pistols, but this is not always the case—on my H&R 25, s/n 1680, we find a blued magazine. There is also a blued magazine in pistol s/n 429. There is a rumor that an all-nickel H&R 25 exists, but I have never seen one that looked like it left the factory that way. All of the advertising literature that I have seen fails to mention the availability of nickel plating. I think that an all-nickel H&R is a myth. The color of the baked rubber grip pieces seems to vary from the common shiny black to an occasional brown tone. One of my collector friends thinks he has the answer to the brown grips. His theory is that those pistols that have been in a hock shop or gun store window have been exposed to the rays of the sun and over a period of time have been faded to a brown color. This seems reasonable, especially when you find pistols with one grip black (the down side) and the other brown (the up side) when on display.

The next change was a far reaching one—the number of lands and grooves changed. The original H&R 25 barrel had five lands and grooves with right-hand twist, one turn in 12 inches. These five-grooved barrels are found at least to s/n 1700 and no higher than s/n 3400. In the interim, you may find either five or six grooves. On the five-groove rifling, the land's width is .070-inches, while on the other the land measures .030-inch.

There is another rumor which has no basis of fact—that the slide pulling grooves vary from gun to gun. There is only one correct number, and that is 13 slide grooves from s/n 1 through the terminal serial s/n 16630. On the other hand, the later H&R 32 ACP auto did exhibit a change in the type and number of slide pulls! The "hammerless" Webley & Scott had only 12 grooves per side.

The slide markings on the Harrington & Richardson went through a change in logo, and the earlier marking from s/n 1 through s/n 60 was as follows:

Right:
HARRINGTON & RICHARDSON ARMS CO.
WORCESTER, MASS. U.S.A.
PAT AUG. 20:07 APRIL 9 & 13 1909

Left:
H&R SELF-LOADING
CALIBER 25

This pair of H&R 25s is unusual in that they are consecutively numbered—8302 and 8303. It's exciting to find consecutive guns of any kind!

The later pistols from s/n 60 to s/n 9000 were marked.
Right:
HARRINGTON & RICHARDSON ARMS CO.
WORCESTER, MASS. U.S.A.
PAT AUG. 20:07 APRIL 13:09
Left:
H&R SELF-LOADING
CALIBER 25

Pistols with serial numbers above 9000 had a brand new stamp in which the blank left by the removal of the early April date was eliminated.
Right:
HARRINGTON & RICHARDSON ARMS CO.
WORCESTER, MASS. U.S.A.
PAT AUG. 20 1907 APRIL 13 1909
Left:
H&R SELF-LOADING
CALIBER 25

There is an interesting theory about the blank space in the middle logo, and that is that Harrington & Richardson expected to receive one more U.S. patent in April of 1909. However, it was never to come and when the stamp had the date ground off and the stamp had to be redone, the space disappeared. We do know that Colt received a sample H&R auto, s/n 20, which was turned over to Carl Ehbets, Colt's patent attorney and designer, a rare combination of skills. Mr. Ehbets noted that the new pistol seemed to infringe on A.C. Wright's U.S. patent #556367 in the area of the pivoting trigger found on the Colt/Browning 25 auto Model N.

Above—Field stripping the H&R 25 was simple and straightforward. It stripped into only four basic pieces, so maintenance was not a problem.

The Webley & Scott "hammerless" 25 ACP followed the H&R gun, and was designed by the same man, William J. Whiting, Webley & Scott's superintendent at the time.

Two types of magazines are found with H&R 25 auto pistols, the most common nickel-plated (left) and the blued version.

This information may have scared off H&R from trying to have their trigger patented. Strangely, Colt seemed to worry more about the little H&R company than they did about the flood of cheap pinned-trigger junk that was being imported from Spain during the period between World War I and World War II. Also strange is the fact, in light of the above, that Colt went on to make a staggering 416,000 of the Model N from 1908 to 1946, while H&R made a scant 16,630 pistols from 1912 to 1916. The little H&R company had less than 4/1000th of 1 percent of the domestic vest pocket pistol market—not exactly the lion's share!

Harrington & Richardson serial numbered a goodly number of components in their 25 auto. The gun has the so-called legal serial number on the left rear of the frame. Inside, the barrel and slide each have either the last three digits or the whole serial number. The sear bar is also numbered to the gun. These numbers make the authenticity of the parts easier to establish and always please a collector. Most U.S.-made pistols don't exhibit this large a number of serials. The classic of serial numbering can be seen on a German-made Mauser 98 rifle of the pre-World War I period, where even the little guard screws had the last two digits of the serial number on them!

The Harrington & Richardson 25 caliber automatic was a well-made gun that just never got over the bad image that H&R had made for itself. Its machining rivaled that found in peacetime Lugers. In looking back, it is obvious that the H&R auto couldn't be made to compete with the cheaper to make Colt Model N—it was just a question of how long H&R could afford to keep a "loss leader" in their line. The answer was for 4 years. I hope the myth that the excellent Harrington & Richardson auto was made overseas has been put to rest forever. It's as American as apple pie. H&R would come back after World War I with their 32 ACP automatic pistol. It was also designed by Whiting of Webley & Scott, but it, too, was doomed to public rejection.

The years have swallowed up the little H&R 25 caliber auto, but it was a unique design and showed that the maker of the "Saturday Night Specials" could also make a highly complicated and difficult to fabricate firearm. ●

The author wishes to thank the following collectors who helped in the preparation of this article: Sid Aberman; Len Hunter; Ernie Lang; Dr. Howard Mathews; Dan Stern.

The author was able to examine the following H&R 25 ACP guns in his research for this article:

37	7656
56	7658
241	8302
429	8303
513	10724
646	10771
1425	10915
1680	11711
3271	13510
3435	16037
4894	

GUNDEX®

A listing of all the guns in the catalog, by name and model, alphabetically and numerically.

Auto Handguns—Service & Sport ... 110-129	Bolt Action & Single Shot Shotguns . 230-232
Competition Handguns 129-135	Military & Police Shotguns 232-234
Revolvers—Service & Sport 135-143	Black Powder Pistols 235-238
Single Action Revolvers 144-149	Black Powder Revolvers 239-242
Miscellaneous Handguns 149-153	Black Powder Muskets, Rifles 242-251
Centerfire Military Auto Rifles 153-160	Black Powder Shotguns 252-253
Centerfire Sporting Auto Rifles 161-162	Air Pistols 253-258
Centerfire Lever, Slide & Misc 162-166	Airsoft Handguns 259-260
Centerfire Bolt Actions 166-181	Air Rifles 260-272
Centerfire Single Shots 181-183	Airsoft Rifles 272-273
Drillings, Combos, Double Rifles . . . 183-186	Paint Ball Handguns 274-275
Rimfire Auto Rifles 186-191	Paint Ball Rifles 275-276
Rimfire Lever & Slide Actions 192-193	Ammunition 277-280
Rimfire Bolt Actions & Single Shots . 194-199	Chokes & Brakes 281
Competition Rifles 199-204	Metallic Sights 282-284
Auto Shotguns 205-208	Scopes & Mounts 285-294
Pump Shotguns 209-211	Spotting Scopes 295-296
Over/Under Shotguns 212-222	Directory of the Arms Trade 297-320
Side-By-Side Shotguns 222-229	

A

AMAC Long Range Rifle, 153
AMT Automag II Pistol, 110
AMT Back-Up Pistol, 110
AMT Lightning Pistol, 110
AMT Lightning Small Game, 186
AMT Lightning 25/22 Rifle, 186
AMT 45 Hardballer, Long Slide, 110
AP-74 Auto Rifle, 187
ARS/Farco Air Shotgun, 262
Action Arms AT-84 DA Pistol, 110
Air Arms Bora Air Rifle, 260
Air Arms Camargue Air Rifle, 261
Air Arms Firepower Air Rifle, 260
Air Arms Khamsin Air Rifle, 260
Air Arms Mistral Air Rifle, 261
Air Match Model 600 Air Pistol, 253
AirShot BSA Airsporter-S Rifle, 261
AirShot BSA Airsporter Stutzen, 261
AirShot BSA Mercury, Super Rifles, 261
AirShot BSA Meteor, Super Rifles, 261
AirShot BSA Scorpion Pistol, 253
AirShot BSA Supersport Standard, Custom, 262
AirShot Survival Air Carbine, 262
Ethan Allen Pepperbox, 238
American Arms AKY39, AKF39 Rifles, 153
American Arms Bristol O/U, 212
American Arms Camper Special, 230
American Arms EP380 Pistol, 111
American Arms PK22 Pistol, 111
American Arms Silver, Silver II O/Us, 212
American Arms Single, Waterfowl Shotguns, 230
American Arms TT9MM Pistol, 110
American Arms Turkey Special Double, 222
American Arms Turkey Special O/U, 212
American Arms Turkey Special Single, 230
American Arms Waterfowl Double, 222
American Arms Waterfowl Special O/U, 212
American Arms York, Derby Doubles, 222
American Arms ZC380 Pistol, 111
American Derringer Model 1, 150
American Derringer Model 3, 150
American Derringer Model 4, 150
American Derringer Model 6, 150
American Derringer Model 7, 150

American Derringer Semmerling LM-4, 149
American Derringer Texas Commemorative, 150
Anschutz Achiever Rifle, 194
Anschutz Bavarian CF Rifle, 167
Anschutz Bavarian RF Rifle, 194
Anschutz Deluxe 525 Auto, 187
Anschutz Exemplar Pistol, 150
Anschutz Mark 2000 Target, 199
Anschutz 54.18 MS, 54.18 MSL Silhouette Rifles, 200
Anschutz 64-MS, 64-MS Left Hand, 64-MS FWT Rifles, 199
Anschutz 1403D Match Rifle, 200
Anschutz 1416/1516 Deluxe Rifles, 194
Anschutz 1418D/1518D Deluxe Rifles, 194
Anschutz 1422D/1522D Classic Rifles, 194
Anschutz 1422D/1522D Custom Rifles, 194
Anschutz 1700 Classic, 167
Anschutz 1700 Custom, 167
Anschutz 1803D Match, 199
Anschutz 1808ED, 1808EDL Super Running Target, 200
Anschutz 1827B Biathlon, 200
Anschutz 1907, 1907-L Match Rifles, 200
Anschutz 1910 Super Match II, 200
Anschutz 1911, 1911-L Match Rifles, 200
Anschutz 1913, 1913-L Super Match, 200
Anschutz 2001 Match Air Rifle, 262
Arizaga Model 31 Double, 223
Armoury R140 Hawkin Rifle, 247
Armscor AK22 Auto Rifle, 187
Armscor Model 14P Rifle, 194
Armscor Model 20P Rifle, 187
Armscor Model 30 Pump Shotgun, 209
Armscor Model 30R Riot Shotgun, 232
Armscor Model 1500 Rifle, 194
Armscor Model 1600 Auto Rifle, 187
Armscor 38 Revolver, 135
Armsport 1050 Double, 223
Armsport 1225/1226 Folding O/U, 212
Armsport 2700 O/U, 212
Armsport 2700 O/U Goose Gun, 212
Armsport 2751 Gas Auto, 205
Armsport 2755 Pump Shotgun, 209
Armsport 2782 Turkey Gun, 183
Armsport 2801 Bolt Action, 167
Armsport 2900 Tri-Barrel Shotgun, 212
Army 1851 Revolver, 240
Army 1860 Revolver, 241
A-Square Caesar Rifle, 166
A-Square Hannibal Rifle, 166
Astra A-60 Pistol, 111
Astra A-90 Auto Pistol, 111
Astra Constable Pistol, 111
Astra Model 44, 45 Revolvers, 135
Astra 357 Magnum Revolver, 135
Australian Automatic Arms SAP Pistol, 111
Australian Automatic Arms SAR Rifle, 154
Auto-Ordnance Model 1927A-3, 187
Auto-Ordnance Thompson M1, 154
Auto-Ordnance 27A-1, 1927A-5, 154
Auto Ordnance 1911-A1 Pistol, 111

B

BF Arms Single Shot Pistol, 129
BGJ Magnum Double, 223
BRI Special Rifled Shotgun, 209
BRI/Benelli 123-SL-80 Shotgun, 205
BRNO CZ 75 Pistol, 113
BRNO CZ 83 DA Pistol, 113
BRNO CZ 85 Pistol, 113
BRNO CZ 581 O/U, 213
BRNO Model ZH 301 O/U, 214
BRNO Model 500 O/U, 213
BRNO Super Express O/U, 184
BRNO Super O/U, 213
BRNO ZH Series 300 Combo, 184
BRNO ZKB 680 Fox Bolt Action, 168
BRNO ZKK 600, 601, 602 Bolt Actions, 168
BRNO ZKM 452 Rifle, 195
BRNO ZP149, ZP349 Doubles, 223
Baby Bretton O/U Shotgun, 213
Baby Dragoon Model 1848, 1849 Pocket Wells Fargo Revolvers, 240
Barrett Light 50 Model 82, 154
Beeman Beta Air Rifle, 263
Beeman Carbine Model C1, 264
Beeman Mini P-08 Pistol, 111
Beeman Model P-08 Pistol, 112
Beeman P1 Magnum Air Pistol, 253
Beeman R1 Air Rifle, Carbine, 265
Beeman R1 Laser Air Rifle, 264
Beeman R7 Air Rifle, 264
Beeman R8 Air Rifle, 265
Beeman R10 Air Rifle, 265
Beeman/Feinwerkbau C60 Rifle, 263
Beeman/Feinwerkbau FWB 65 Mk.I, 254
Beeman/Feinwerkbau FWB 65 Mk.II, 254
Beeman/Feinwerkbau F300-S Running Boar, 263
Beeman/Feinwerkbau Model 2 COFD, 254
Beeman/Feinwerkbau Model 2 Mini-2, 254
Beeman/Feinwerkbau Model 90 Pistol, 255
Beeman/Feinwerkbau 124/127 Magnum, 262
Beeman/Feinwerkbau 300-S Match, 263
Beeman/Feinwerkbau 300-S Mini-Match, 263
Beeman/Feinwerkbau 300-S Universal Match, 263
Beeman/Feinwerkbau 601 Air Rifle, 263
Beeman/Feinwerkbau 601 Running Target, 263
Beeman/Feinwerkbau 2000, Mini-Match Target, 201
Beeman/Feinwerkbau 2600 Target, 201
Beeman/HW Model 60J Rifle, 167
Beeman/HW Model 60J-ST Rifle, 195
Beeman/HW Model 660 Match Rifle, 200
Beeman/HW 35L/35EB Sporters, 264
Beeman/HW 55SM, 55MM, 55T Rifles, 264
Beeman/HW 77 Rifle, Carbine, 264
Beeman/Harper Aircane, 263
Beeman/Krico Model 320, 195
Beeman/Krico Model 340 Silhouette, 201
Beeman/Krico Model 400, 420, 167
Beeman/Krico Model 620, 720, 167
Beeman/Krico Model 640 Super Sniper, 201
Beeman/Krico Model 640 Varmint, 167
Beeman/Krico Model 700L Deluxe, 167
Beeman/Unique D.E.S. 69 Target, 129
Beeman/Unique 2000-U Match, 129
Beeman/Webley Hurricane Pistol, 254
Beeman/Webley Omega Air Rifle, 264
Beeman/Webley Tempest Pistol, 254
Beeman/Webley Vulcan II Deluxe, 264
Beeman/Weihrauch HW-60 Target, 201
Beeman/Weihrauch HW-70 Pistol, 254
Benelli M1 Super 90 Field Shotgun, 205
Benelli M1 Super 90 M&P, 232
Benelli Montefeltro Super 90, 205
Benjamin 242/247 Air Pistols, 255
Benjamin 342/347 Air Rifles, 265
Beretta A-303 Auto Shotgun, 205
Beretta AR70 Rifle, 154
Beretta Express S689, SSO Double Rifles, 184
Beretta Model 21 Pistol, 112
Beretta Model 84, 85, 87, 89 Pistols, 112
Beretta Model 92F Pistol, 113
Beretta Model 950BS Pistol, 112
Beretta Model 950EL Pistol, 112
Beretta SO-5, SO-6 O/Us, 213
Beretta 500 Series Bolt Actions, 168
Beretta 626, 627 Doubles, 223
Beretta 682, 687 Sporting Clays Shotguns, 213
Beretta 686, 687 O/Us, 213
Beretta 1200F Shotgun, 205
Beretta 1200FP Shotgun, 232
Bernardelli Auto Carbine, 187
Bernardelli Model 60 Pistol, 112
Bernardelli Model 69 Target Pistol, 130
Bernardelli PO 18, Combat Pistols, 112
Bernardelli Series Roma Doubles, 223
Bernardelli Series S. Uberto Doubles, 223
Bernardelli System Holland H., 223
Black Watch Scotch Pistol, 235
Black Widow Paint Ball Gun, 275
Browning A-Bolt Camo Stalker, 168
Browning A-Bolt Gold Medallion, 169
Browning A-Bolt Hunter, Medallion Rifles, 168
Browning A-Bolt Left Hand, 168
Browning A-Bolt Micro Medallion, 168
Browning A-Bolt Pronghorn Antelope, 169
Browning A-Bolt Short Action, 168
Browning A-Bolt Stainless, Composite Stalkers, 168
Browning A-Bolt 22 Gold Medallion, 195
Browning A-Bolt 22 Rifle, 195
Browning A-500 Auto Shotgun, 206
Browning Auto-5 Gold Classic, 206
Browning Auto-5 Light 12, 20, Sweet 16, 205
Browning Auto-5 Magnum 12, 206
Browning Auto-5 Magnum 20, 206
Browning Auto-22 Grade VI, 188
Browning Auto-22 Rifle, 188
Browning B-80 Plus Auto, 206
Browning B-80 Upland Special, 206
Browning BDA-380 DA Pistol, 114
Browning BL-22 Lever Action, 192
Browning BLR Model 81 Lever Action, 162
Browning BPS Ladies, Youth Shotguns, 209
Browning BPS Shotgun, 209
Browning BPS Stalker, 209
Browning BT-99 Trap, 230
Browning Big Game BAR, 161
Browning Buck Mark Silhouette, 113
Browning Buck Mark Varmint, 113
Browning Buck Mark 22 Pistol, 113
Browning Citori O/U, 214

Browning Citori O/U Trap, Skeet Models, 214
Browning Citori Superlight, 214
Browning Gold Classic O/U, 214
Browning High-Power Rifle, 161
Browning Hi-Power Pistol, 123
Browning Limited Edition Waterfowl Superposed, 214
Browning Magnum Auto Rifle, 161
Browning Model 12 Shotgun, 209
Browning Model 71 Rifle, 162
Browning Model 1885, 181,
Bryco Model 25 Pistol, 114
Bryco Model 38 Pistol, 114
Bryco Model 48 Pistol, 114
Bushmaster Auto Pistol, 114
Bushmaster Auto Rifle, 154

C

CP Full Tilt Paint Ball Gun, 275
CVA Brittany II Shotgun, 252
CVA Colonial Pistol, 236
CVA Express Rifle, 251
CVA Frontier, Mountain Rifles, 247
CVA Hawken, St. Louis Rifles, 247
CVA Kentucky Rifle, 245
CVA Missouri Ranger Rifle, 247
CVA New Model Pocket Remington, 241
CVA O/U Carbine-Rifle, 251
CVA Pennsylvania Long Rifle, 243
CVA Philadelphia Percussion Derringer, 236
CVA Siber Pistol, 237
CVA Squirrel Rifle, 244
CVA Third Model Colt Dragoon, 239
CVA Trapper Shotgun, 252
CVA Vest Pocket Derringer, 238
CVA 1858 Remington Target, 240
Cabanas Espronceda IV, 195
Cabanas Laser Rifle, 195
Cabanas Leyre Rifle, 195
Cabanas Master, Varmint Rifles, 195
Calico Model 100 Carbine, 188
Calico Model 100-P Pistol, 114
Calico Model 100-S Sporter, 188
Century Centurion 14 Sporter, 169
Century Enfield Sporter #4, Jungle Sporter, 169
Century Swedish Sporter #38, 169
Century Weekender Sporter Rifle, 196
Century Mfg. Model 100 SA, 144
Champlin Bolt Action Rifle, 169
Charleville Flintlock Pistol, 235
Charter AR-7 Explorer, 188
Charter Arms Bulldog, 136
Charter Arms Bulldog Pug, 136
Charter Arms Bulldog Tracker, 136
Charter Arms Off-Duty, 136
Charter Arms Pathfinder, 136
Charter Arms Police Bulldog, 136
Charter Arms Police Undercover, 136
Charter Arms Target Bulldog, 136
Charter Arms Undercover, 136
Cheney Plains Rifle, 244
Chipmunk Silhouette Pistol, 130
Chipmunk Single Shot Rifle, 196
Churchill Bolt Action Rifles, 169
Churchill Highlander, Regent Bolt Actions, 169
Churchill Monarch O/U, 215
Churchill Regent Combo, 184
Churchill Regent O/U, 215
Churchill Regent Trap, Skeet, 215

Churchill Royal Double, 223
Churchill Windsor Double, 224
Churchill Windsor O/U, 215
Cimarron Artillery Model SA, 144
Cimarron Old Model SA, 144
Cimarron Sheriff Model SA, 144
Cimarron U.S. Cavalry Revolver, 144
Cimarron 1866 Half-Magazine Carbine, 163
Cimarron 1873 Button Half-Magazine, 163
Cimarron 1873 30 Express Rifle, 163
Classic Model 101 Field I, II, Waterfowler, 215
Classic Model 101 Sporter, 215
Classic Model 101 Trap, Skeet, 215
Classic Model 201 Double, 224
Colt AR-15A2 Carbine, 154
Colt AR-15A2 Delta H-BAR, 155
Colt AR-15A2 H-BAR, 155
Colt Combat Commander Pistol, 115
Colt Combat Elite Mk IV/Series 80, 115
Colt Delta Elite 10mm Pistol, 114
Colt Gold Cup National Match, 130
Colt Gov't. Model Mk IV/Series 80, 114
Colt King Cobra, 137
Colt Lightweight Commander Mk IV/Series 80, 115
Colt Mustang Plus II, Mustang 380, Mustang Pocket Lite, 115
Colt Officer's ACP Mk IV/Series 80, L.W., 114
Colt Python, 137
Colt Single Action Army, 144
Colt 380 Gov't. Model, 115
Commando Arms Carbine, 155
Command Post Airsoft Grease Gun, 273
Command Post Airsoft MP5-A3 Carbine, 272
Command Post Airsoft 04 Pistol, 259
Command Post Airsoft 09 Pistol, 259
Command Post Airsoft 12, 272
Command Post Airsoft 13 Pistol, 259
Command Post Airsoft 14 Rifle, 273
Command Post Airsoft 15 Rifle, 273
Command Post Airsoft 45 Pistol, 260
Command Post Airsoft 57 Pistol, 260
Command Post Airsoft 59 Pistol, 260
Command Post Airsoft 645 Pistol, 259
Command Post Airsoft 870, 273
Command Post Gas Auto Mag Pistol, 259
Command Post M-11 Gas Pistol, 259
Command Post M-60A1, 272
Command Post Tracer Scorpion Pistol, 260
Command Post Uzi Pump, 272
Command Post XM-177E2, M-16 Airsoft Carbine, 273
Competitor Single Shot Pistol, 130
Confederate Tucker & Sherrard, 239
Cook & Brother Confederate Carbine, 250
Coonan 357 Magnum Pistol, 115
Cosmi Auto Shotgun, 206
Crosman AIR 17 Rifle, 266
Crosman Model 66 Powermaster, 265
Crosman Model 84 COFD Match Rifle, 265
Crosman Model 338 Air Pistol, 255
Crosman Model 357, 1357 Air Pistols, 255
Crosman Model 760 Pumpmaster, 266
Crosman Model 781 Single Pump, 266

Crosman Model 788 BB Scout, 267
Crosman Model 1322, 1377 Air Pistols, 255
Crosman Model 2100 Classic, 267
Crosman Model 2200 Magnum, 267
Crosman Model 3100 Rifle, 266
Crosman Model 3357 Spot Marker Pistol, 255
Crosman Model 6100 Challenger, 267
Crosman Model 6300 Challenger, 267
Crosman Model 6500 Challenger, 267
Crosman Z-77 Air Carbine, 266
Crosman/Anschutz Model 380, 266
Crosman/Blaser Conversion Kit, 255
Crosman/Skanaker Match Pistol, 255
Crucelegui Hermanos Model 150, 224
Custom Paint Ball Gun, 275

D

Daewoo AR100 Auto Rifle, 155
Daewoo AR110C Auto Carbine, 155
Daisy Legacy 2201, 2211, 2221 Single Shots, 196
Daisy Legacy 2202, 2212, 2222 Repeaters, 196
Daisy Legacy 2203, 2213 Auto Rifles, 188
Daisy Legacy 2231 Combo Single Shot, 196
Daisy Legacy 2232 Combo Repeater, 196
Daisy Model 188 BB Pistol, 256
Daisy Model 840 Air Rifle, 267
Daisy Power Line 44 Air Revolver, 256
Daisy Power Line 92 Pistol, 256
Daisy Power Line 717, 747 Air Pistols, 256
Daisy Power Line 753 Target, 267
Daisy Power Line 777 Pellet Pistol, 256
Daisy Power Line 814, 914 Rifles, 268
Daisy Power Line 856 Pump-Up Rifle, 268
Daisy Power Line 860 Pump-Up, 268
Daisy Power Line 880 Pump-Up, 268
Daisy Power Line 900 Pellet Repeater, 268
Daisy Power Line 922, 970, 920, 268
Daisy Power Line 953, 268
Daisy Power Line 1200 COFD Pistol, 256
Daisy Youthline 95, 105, 111 Rifles, 267
Daisy Youth Line 1500 Air Pistol, 256
Daisy 1938 Red Ryder Commemorative, 269
Dakota Bisley SA, 144
Dakota Single Actions, 145
Dakota 1875 Outlaw, 145
Dakota 1890 Police, 145
Dakota Arms 76 Classic Rifle, 170
Dakota Arms 76 Safari Rifle, 170
Charles Daly Diamond Skeet, 216
Charles Daly Diamond Trap O/U, 216
Charles Daly Field III O/U, 216
Charles Daly Hawken Rifle, 247
Charles Daly Superior II O/U, 216
Davis Derringer, 150
Davis P-32 Auto Pistol, 115
Desert Eagle 357 Pistol, 116
Detonics Combat Master Mk VI, Mk I, 116
Detonics Janus Scoremaster Pistol, 130
Detonics Scoremaster Target, 130
Detonics Servicemaster Pistol, 116
Dixie Abilene Derringer, 237

Dixie Brass Frame Derringer, 237
Dixie Delux Cub Rifle, 246
Dixie Hawken Rifle, 248
Dixie Indian Gun, 243
Dixie LePage Dueller, 237
Dixie Lincoln Derringer, 236
Dixie Magnum Percussion Shotgun, 252
Dixie Model 1863 Springfield Musket, 250
Dixie Model 1873 Lever Action, 163
Dixie Northwest Trade Gun, 248
Dixie Overcoat Pistol, 236
Dixie Pennsylvania Pistol, 235
Dixie Percussion Wesson Rifle, 248
Dixie Philadelphia Derringer, 237
Dixie Queen Anne Flintlock, 235
Dixie Screw-Barrel Pistol, 237
Dixie Squirrel Rifle, 243
Dixie Tennessee Mountain Rifle, 243
Dixie Third Model Dragoon, 239
Dixie Tornado Target Pistol, 238
Dixie W. Parker Pistol, 236
Dixie Wyatt Earp Revolver, 242
DuBiel Bolt Actions, 170

E

E.M.F. Henry Carbine, 163
El Gamo 126 Super Match, 269
El Gamo 128 Match Rifle, 269
Elgin Cutlass Pistol, 238
Encom Mk. IV Assault Pistol, 116
Encom MP-9, MP-45 Pistols, 116
Erma Model ESP 85A Pistol, 116
Erma Sporting Revolver, 137

F

FAMAS Air Rifle, 269
FAS AP604 Air Pistol, 257
FAS Model 601, 602, 603 Pistols, 131
FAS Model 604 Air Pistol, 257
F.I.E. Arminius Revolvers, 137
F.I.E. Buffalo Scout SA, 145
F.I.E. D-86 Derringer, 151
F.I.E. GR-8 Black Beauty, 188
F.I.E. Hamilton & Hunter, 230
F.I.E. Hombre SA, 146
F.I.E. Little Ranger SA, 145
F.I.E. Model 122 Bolt Rifle, 197
F.I.E. S.S.S. Single, 230
F.I.E. Super Titan II Pistol, 117
F.I.E. Texas Ranger SA, 145
F.I.E. The Best A27B Pistol, 117
F.I.E. Titan Tiger, 137
F.I.E. Titan II Pistol, 117
F.I.E. Titan 25 Pistol, 117
F.I.E. TZ-75 Pistol, 117
F.I.E. Yellow Rose Revolver, 145
F.I.E./Franchi Alcion S, 216
F.I.E./Franchi LAW 12, 233
F.I.E./Franchi Model 48/AL Auto, 206
F.I.E./Franchi Para Carbine, 188
F.I.E./Franchi Prestige, Elite Autos, 207
F.I.E./Franchi SAS 12, 233
F.I.E./Franchi Slug Gun, 206
F.I.E./Franchi SPAS 12 Pump/Auto, 233
F.I.E./Maroccini Priti O/U, 216
FN-LAR Competition Auto, 155
FN-LAR Heavy Barrel 308 Match, 155
FN-LAR Paratrooper 308 Match 50, 64, 155
FN 308 Model 50-63, 155
FNC Auto Rifle, 155

FX-1 Air Rifle, 269
FX-2 Air Rifle, 269
Falcon Portsider Pistol, 116
Feather AT-9 Auto Carbine, 156
Feather AT-22 Auto Carbine, 189
Feather Guardian Angel Pistol, 151
Feather Mini-AT Pistol, 117
Federal XC-220 Carbine, 189
Federal XC-900/XC-450 Carbines, 156
Ferlib Model F VII Double, 224
Finnish Lion Target Rifle, 201
Auguste Francotte Bolt Action Rifle, 170
Auguste Francotte Double Rifles, 184
Auguste Francotte Doubles, 224
Freedom Arms Boot Gun, 146
Freedom Arms Mini Revolver, 146
Freedom Arms Percussion Mini Revolver, 242
Freedom Arms 454 Casull, 146
French-Style Dueling Pistol, 237

G

Galil Model ARM Rifle, 156
Galil 308 Auto Rifle, 156
Garbi Model Special, 225
Garbi Model 51B, 224
Garbi Model 60, 225
Garbi Model 62A, 62B, 225
Garbi Model 71, 225
Garbi Model 100, 225
Garbi Model 101, 225
Garbi Model 102, 225
Garbi Model 103A, 103B, 225
Garbi Model 200, 225
GAT Air Pistol, 257
GAT Air Rifle, 269
Glock 17 Auto Pistol, 117
Glock 19 Auto Pistol, 117
Goncz High-Tech Carbine, 156
Goncz High-Tech Long Pistol, 118
Grendel Model P-10 Pistol, 118
Grendel SRT Compact Rifle, 170
Griswold & Gunnison Revolver, 241

H

Hammerli Model 150, 152 Free Pistols, 131
Hammerli Model 212 Pistol, 118
Hammerli Model 232-1, 232-2 Rapid Fire, 131
Hammerli Standard 208, 211, 215 Pistols, 131
Harper's Ferry 1806 Pistol, 236
Hatfield Squirrel Rifle, 243
Hatfield Uplander Shotgun, 226
Hawken, St. Louis, Deluxe, Hunter Rifles, 248
Heckler & Koch HK-91A2, A3, 156
Heckler & Koch HK-93A2, A3, 156
Heckler & Koch HK-94A2, A3, 157
Heckler & Koch HK-300 Rifle, 189
Heckler & Koch HK-630, HK-770, HK-940, 161
Heckler & Koch PSG-1 Marksman, 201
Heckler & Koch P7-K3 Pistol, 118
Heckler & Koch P7-M8, P7-M13 Pistols, 118
Heckler & Koch P9S Pistol, 118
Heckler & Koch P9S Target Model, 118
Heckler & Koch SL6, SL7 Auto Rifles, 161
Heckler & Koch VP70Z Pistol, 118
Helwan Brigadier Pistol, 119

Heym 88B Safari Double Rifle, 184
Holmes Model 88 Shotgun, 233
Holmes MP-22 Assault Pistol, 119
Holmes MP-83 Assault Pistol, 119
Hopkins & Allen Boot Pistol, 238
Hopkins & Allen Brush Rifle, 246
Hopkins & Allen Pa. Hawken Rifle, 245
Hopkins & Allen Percussion Shotgun, 252
Hopkins & Allen Underhammer Rifles, 246
Howa Lightning Rifle, 171
Howa Model 1500 Hunter Rifle, 171
Howa Model 1500 Rifle, 171
Howa Model 1500 Trophy Rifle, 171

I

Illinois Arms Model 180 Auto Carbine, 189
Interarms Model 22 ATD Rifle, 189
Intratec Scorpion Pistol, 119
Intratec TEC Companion Derringer, 151
Intratec TEC-9, TEC-9S Pistols, 119
Intratec TEC-9M, TEC-9MS Pistols, 119
Ithaca Deerslayer II Rifled Shotgun, 209
Ithaca Model 5E Trap Single, 230
Ithaca Model 87 Deerslayer, 209
Ithaca Model 87 Deluxe Pump, 210
Ithaca Model 87 DSPS M&P, 233
Ithaca Model 87 Hand Grip, 233
Ithaca Model 87 Supreme, 209
Ithaca Model 87 Ultralight, 210
Ithaca-Navy Hawken Rifle, 248
Ithaca X-Caliber Pistol, 151

J

Jennings J-22 Pistol, 120
Iver Johnson Enforcer Pistol, 119
Iver Johnson Li'l Champ Rifle, 197
Iver Johnson Model 3112 Rifle, 189
Iver Johnson PM30HB Carbine, 157
Iver Johnson Targetmaster Pump, 192
Iver Johnson TP22, TP25 Pistols, 120
Iver Johnson Wagonmaster Lever, 192

K

Kentuckian Rifle, Carbine, 243
Kentucky Flintlock Pistol, 236
Kentucky Flintlock Rifle, 243
Kentucky Percussion Pistol, 236
Kentucky Percussion Rifle, 243
Kimber Big Game Rifle, 171
Kimber Model 82 Sporter, 172
Kimber Model 82, 84 CF Super America, 171
Kimber Model 82, 84 RF Super America, 197
Kimber Model 82B Rifle, 197
Kimber Model 84 Sporter, 171
Kimber Predator Pistol, 151
Kodiak Double Rifle, 251
Korriphila HSP 701 DA Pistol, 120
Korth Auto Pistol, 120
Korth Revolver, 137
Krieghoff K-80 International Skeet, 216
Krieghoff K-80 Pigeon, 216
Krieghoff K-80 Skeet Set, 216
Krieghoff K-80 Sporting Clays, 216
Krieghoff K-80 Trap, Skeet, 216
Krieghoff KS-5 Trap, 231

L

L.A.R. Grizzly Win Mag Mk I Pistol, 120

L.A.R. Grizzly Win Mag 8" 10 Pistol, 120
Lebeau-Courally Boxlock Double, 226
Lebeau-Courally Sidelock Double, 226
Lebeau-Courally Sidelock Double Rifle, 185
LeMat Army Model Revolver, 242
LeMat Cavalry Model Revolver, 242
LeMat Naval Style Revolver, 242
Ljutic BiGun, Four Barrel Skeet, 217
Ljutic LJII Pistol, 151
Ljutic LTX Super Deluxe, 231
Ljutic Mono Gun, 231
Ljutic Recoilless Space Rifle, 181
Ljutic Recoilless Space Shotgun, 231
Ljutic T.C. LM-6 O/U, 217
Llama Comanche III, 138
Llama Compact Frame Pistol, 121
Llama Large Frame Pistol, 121
Llama M-82 Pistol, 121
Llama Small Frame Pistol, 121
Llama Super Comanche IV, V, 138
London Model 1851 Revolver, 240
London Armory Enfield Musketoon, 249
London Armory 2-Band 1858 Enfield, 249
London Armory 3-Band 1853 Enfield, 249
Lyman Great Plains Rifle, 244
Lyman Plains Pistol, 235
Lyman Trade Rifle, 245

M

MAS 223 Auto Rifle, 157
Mandall/Cabanas Pistol, 151
Mandall/Zanardini Double Rifle, 185
Mark X American Field Series Rifles, 172
Mark X LTW Sporter Rifle, 172
Mark X Viscount Rifle, 172
Marksman Model 17 Air Pistol, 257
Marksman Model 29 Air Rifle, 269
Marksman Model 55 Air Rifle, 270
Marksman Model 70 Air Rifle, 270
Marksman Model 1010 Repeater Pistol, 257
Marksman Model 1740 Air Rifle, 270
Marksman Plainsman 1049 COFD Pistol, 257
Marlin Golden 39AS Rifle, 192
Marlin Model 9 Camp Carbine, 161
Marlin Model 15Y Little Buckaroo, 198
Marlin Model 25 Rifle, 197
Marlin Model 25M Rifle, 198
Marlin Model 25MB Midget Magnum, 198
Marlin Model 39TDS Carbine, 193
Marlin Model 45 Carbine, 161
Marlin Model 55 Goose Gun, 231
Marlin Model 60 Rifle, 190
Marlin Model 70HC Rifle, 190
Marlin Model 70P Papoose, 190
Marlin Model 75C Rifle, 190
Marlin Model 780 Rifle, 197
Marlin Model 781 Rifle, 197
Marlin Model 782 Rifle, 197
Marlin Model 783 Rifle, 197
Marlin Model 995 Rifle, 190
Marlin 30AS Lever Action, 163
Marlin 336CS Lever Action, 163
Marlin 336LTS Carbine, 163
Marlin 444SS Lever Action, 164
Marlin 1894CL Lever Action, 164
Marlin 1894CS Lever Action, 164
Marlin 1894M Carbine, 192
Marlin 1894S Lever Action, 164
Marlin 1895SS Lever Action, 164
Mauser Model 225 Rifle, 172
Mauser Model 300 SL Air Rifle, 270
Maximum Single Shot Pistol, 152
Mercury G1032 Double, 226
Merkel 47E, 47S, 147E, 147S, 247S, 347S, 447S, 226
Merkel 200E, 201E, 203E, 303E, 217
Mini-Mark X Rifle, 172
Mississippi Model 1841 Rifle, 250
Mitchell AK-22 Auto Rifle, 190
Mitchell AK-47, H.B., Rifle, 157
Mitchell MAS/22 Rifle, 191
Mitchell M-16/22 Rifle, 191
Mitchell M-59 Rifle, 158
Mitchell M-76 Counter-Sniper, 157
Mitchell Arms SA Revolvers, 146
Mitchell Galil/22 Rifle, 190
Model 007 Assault Paint Ball Gun, 276
Model 007, Sport, Tournament Paint Ball Pistols, 274
Model 85 Paint Ball Machine Pistol, 274
Model 3357 DA Paint Ball Pistol, 274
Moore & Patrick Flint Dueler, 237
Morini CM-80 Super Competition, 131
Mossberg Model 500 Bullpup, 234
Mossberg Model 500 Camo Pump, 210
Mossberg Model 500 Mariner, 233
Mossberg Model 500 Security, 233
Mossberg Model 500 Sporting Pump, 210
Mossberg Model 500 Trophy Slugster, 210
Mossberg Model 590 Military, 234
Mossberg Model 835 Ulti-Mag, 210
Mossberg Model 5500 Mk. II, 207

N

Navy Arms Charleville, 242
Navy Arms Country Boy Rifle, 245
Navy Arms Duckfoot, 238
Navy Arms Fowler Shotgun, 252
Navy Arms Henry Carbine, 164
Navy Arms Henry Iron Frame, 164
Navy Arms Henry Military Rifle, 164
Navy Arms Henry Trapper, 164
Navy Arms Hunter Shotgun, 252
Navy Arms LePage Dueller, 237
Navy Arms Model 83/93 Bird Hunter, 217
Navy Arms Model 95/96 Sportsman, 217
Navy Arms Model 105 Shotgun, 231
Navy Arms Model 410 O/U, 217
Navy Arms Rolling Block, 182
Navy Arms Snake Eyes, 238
Navy Arms T&T Shotgun, 252
Navy Arms 1858 Remington-Style Revolver, 241
Navy Arms 1863 Springfield, 250
Navy Model 1851 Revolver, 240
Navy Model 1861 Revolver, 241
Navy-Sheriff 1851 Revolver, 240
New England Firearms D/A Revolvers, 138
New England Firearms Handi-Gun, 231
New England Firearms Pardner, 231
New England Firearms 10-Ga. Single, 231
New Model 1858 Army Revolver, 240
New Orleans Ace, 238
Ninja Paint Ball Gun, 275
Norinco Officer's Nine Carbine, 158
North American Mini-Revolvers, 146

O

Omega Auto Pistol, 121
Omega Folding Double, 226
Omega Standard, Deluxe Folding O/Us, 217

P

PMI Custom Paint Ball Gun, 276
Pachmayr Dominator Pistol, 121
Pachmayr/Perazzi MX-20 O/U, 217
Pardini Fiocchi Free Pistol, 132
Pardini Fiocchi PIO Match Air Pistol, 257
Pardini Fiocchi Rapid Fire Match Pistol, 132
Pardini Fiocchi Standard Pistol, 132
Pardini Fiocchi 32 Match Pistol, 132
Parker DHE Double, 227
Parker-Hale Enfield Pattern 1858 Naval Rifle, 249
Parker-Hale Enfield 1853 Musket, 249
Parker-Hale Enfield 1861 Musketoon, 249
Parker-Hale Model 81 African Rifle, 173
Parker-Hale Model 81 Classic, 172
Parker-Hale Model 87 Target Rifle, 202
Parker-Hale Model 1000 Standard, 173
Parker-Hale Model 1100 Lightweight, 172
Parker-Hale Model 1100M African Magnum, 173
Parker-Hale Model 1200 Super Bolt, Clip, 173
Parker-Hale Model 2100 Midland, 173
Parker-Hale Volunteer Rifle, 250
Parker-Hale Whitworth Military Target Rifle, 250
Parker-Hale 600 Series Doubles, 226
Partisan Avenger Pistol, 121
Pennsylvania Full Stock Rifle, 244
Perazzi Grand American 88 Special, 218
Perazzi Mirage Skeet Set, 218
Perazzi Mirage Special, Sporting, 218
Perazzi MX1, MX1B Sporting, 218
Perazzi MX3 Special Single, O/U, 218
Perazzi MX4 O/U, 218
Perazzi MX8/MX8 Special Trap, Skeet, 218
Perazzi MX12, MX20 Hunting, 218
Perazzi TM1 Special Trap, 218
Perugini-Visini Classic Double, 226
Perugini-Visini Liberty Double, 226
Perugini-Visini Selous Double Rifle, 185
Perugini-Visini Victoria Double Rifle, 185
Phelps Heritage 1, Eagle 1, 147
Philadelphia Percussion Derringer, 236
Piotti Model King Extra, 227
Piotti Model King No. 1, 227
Piotti Model Lunik, 227
Piotti Model Monte Carlo, 227
Piotti Model Piuma, 227
Pocket Police 1862 Revolver, 241
Poly Tech AK-47/S Auto Rifle, 158
Poly Tech AKS-762 Rifle, 158
Poly Tech M-14/S Auto Rifle, 158
Pursuit Paint Ball Rifle, 276
Pursuit PMI I Paint Pistol, 274
Pursuit Rapid Fire Paint Pistol, 274

R

RPM XL Single Shot Pistol, 152
RSR/Anschutz Woodchucker Rifle, 198
RWS/Diana Model 5G Air Pistol, 258
RWS/Diana Model 5GS Air Pistol, 258
RWS/Diana Model 6M Match Pistol, 257
RWS/Diana Model 10 Match Pistol, 258
RWS/Diana Model 24, 34 Rifles, 270
RWS/Diana Model 36, 38 Rifles, 270
RWS/Diana Model 45 Air Rifle, 270
RWS/Diana Model 52 Rifle, 270
RWS/Diana Model 75KT 01 Running Boar, 270
RWS/Diana Model 75T 01 Air Rifle, 270
Rahn Deer Series, 173
Rahn Elk Series Rifle, 173
Rahn Himalayan Rifle, 173
Rahn Safari Rifle, 173
Ranger Model 1911A1 Pistol, 122
Raven MP-25 Pistol, 122
Record Champion Air Pistol, 258
Record Jumbo Air Pistol, 258
Remington Model Seven, 175
Remington Model Seven Custom KS, 175
Remington Model Seven FS, 175
Remington Model 11-87 Premier, 207
Remington Model 11-87 Premier Trap, 207
Remington Model 11-87 Premier Skeet, 207
Remington Model 11-87 Special Purpose Deer Gun, 207
Remington Model 11-87 Special Purpose Magnum, 207
Remington Model 541-T Rifle, 198
Remington Model 552BDL Rifle, 191
Remington Model 572BDL Fieldmaster, 193
Remington Model 581-S Sportsman, 198
Remington Model 700ADL, ADL/LS, 174
Remington Model 700BDL, 174
Remington Model 700BDL Left Hand, 174
Remington Model 700BDL Varmint Special, 174
Remington Model 700 Classic, 173
Remington Model 700 Custom KS Mountain Rifle, 174
Remington Model 700 FS Rifle, 174
Remington Model 700 Gun Kit, 174
Remington Model 700 Mountain Rifle, 174
Remington Model 700 RS Rifle, 174
Remington Model 700 Safari, 174
Remington Model 870 Brushmaster Deluxe, 210
Remington Model 870 Express, 210
Remington Model 870 High Grade, 210
Remington Model 870 Small Gauges, 210
Remington Model 870 Special Field, 211
Remington Model 870 Special Purpose Deer, 210
Remington Model 870 Special Purpose Magnum, 211
Remington Model 870 TC Trap, 211
Remington Model 870 Wingmaster, Brushmaster, Deer Gun, 210
Remington Model 870P Police, 234
Remington Model 1100 Auto, 207
Remington Model 1100 LT-20, Small Gauge, 208
Remington Model 1100 Special Field, 208
Remington Model 1100 Tournament Skeet, 208
Remington Model 1100 20 Ga., Deer Gun, 208
Remington Model 1100D Tournament, 208
Remington Model 1100F Premier, 208
Remington Model 7400 Auto, 162
Remington Model 7600 Pump, 164
Remington Parker AHE Double, 227
Remington Sportsman 78, 175
Remington XP-100 Custom Long Range Pistol, 152
Remington XP-100 Silhouette Pistol, 132
Remington XP-100 Varmint Special, 152
Remington 40-XB-BR, 202
Remington 40-XB KS Varmint Special, 202
Remington 40-XB Rangemaster CF, 202
Remington 40-XC, 40-XC KS National Match, 202
Remington 40-XR Position Rifle, 202
Remington 40-XR Rimfire Custom Sporter, 198
Rigby-Style Target Rifle, 251
Rizzini Boxlock Double, 227
Rizzini Sidelock Double, 228
Rogers & Spencer Revolver, 241
Rossi Model 59, 62 SA Pump, 193
Rossi Model 62 SAC Carbine, 193
Rossi Model 68, 68/2 Revolvers, 138
Rossi Model 88, 88/2 Revolvers, 138
Rossi Model 92 Puma SRS, 165
Rossi Model 92 Saddle Ring Carbine, 165
Rossi Model 511 Sportsman's 22 Revolver, 138
Rossi Model 851, 951 Revolvers, 138
Rossi Model 971 Revolver, 138
Rossi Overland Double, 228
Rossi Squire Double, 228
Rottweil '72 American Skeet, 218
Ruger GP-100 Revolver, 139
Ruger Mini-14/5F Folding Stock, 159
Ruger Mini-14/5R Ranch Rifle, 158
Ruger Mini Thirty Rifle, 158
Ruger Mk II Bull Barrel, 132
Ruger Mk II Gov't. Target, 132
Ruger Mk II Standard Auto, 122
Ruger Mk II Target Model, 132
Ruger Model 77R, 175
Ruger Model 77RL Ultra Light, 176
Ruger Model 77RLS Ultra Light Carbine, 176
Ruger Model 77RS Magnum, 175
Ruger Model 77RS Tropical, 175
Ruger Model 77RSI International, 175
Ruger Model 77V Varmint, 175
Ruger Model 77/22 Rifle, 198
Ruger New Model Bisley, 147
Ruger New Model Blackhawk, 147
Ruger New Model Single-Six, 147
Ruger New Model Super Blackhawk, 147
Ruger New Model Super Single-Six, 147
Ruger No.1A Light Sporter, 182
Ruger No.1B Single Shot, 181
Ruger No.1H Tropical Rifle, 182
Ruger No.1RSI International, 182
Ruger No.1S Medium Sporter, 181
Ruger No.1V Special Varminter, 182
Ruger P-85 Pistol, 122
Ruger Redhawk Revolver, 139
Ruger Red Label O/U, 218
Ruger Small Frame New Model Bisley, 147
Ruger Super Redhawk, 139
Ruger 10/22 Carbine, 191
Ruger 10/22 Sporter, 191
Ruger 44 Old Army Revolver, 242

S

S.A.B. Renato Gamba Doubles, 228
SAE Commando Air Rifle, 271
SAE Jet 900 Air Rifle, 271
SAE Model 66C O/U, 219
SAE Model 70 O/U, 219
SAE Model 73 Air Rifle, 271
SAE Model 92 Air Rifle, 270
SAE Model 209E Double, 228
SAE Model 210S Double, 228
SAE Model 340X Double, 228
SIG P-210-2 Auto Pistol, 123
SIG P-210-6 Auto Pistol, 123
SIG-Sauer P-220 DA Pistol, 123
SIG-Sauer P-225 DA Pistol, 123
SIG-Sauer P-226 DA Pistol, 123
SIG-Sauer P-230 DA Pistol, 123
SKB Model 200, 400 Doubles, 228
SKB Model 505, 605, 219
SKB Model 885 Trap, Skeet, 219
SKB Model 1300 Auto Shotgun, 208
SKB Model 1900 Auto Shotgun, 208
SKB Model 1900 Trap Shotgun, 208
SKB Model 3000 Auto Shotgun, 208
Safari Arms Enforcer Pistol, 122
Safari Arms Matchmaster Pistol, 122
Sako Carbine, 176
Sako Deluxe Sporter, 177
Sako Fiberclass Sporter, 176
Sako Heavy Barrel, 176
Sako Hunter Left Hand, 176
Sako Hunter, LS Rifle, 176
Sako Mannlicher-Style Carbine, 176
Sako Safari Grade, 176
Sako Super Deluxe Sporter, 177
Sako Triace Match Pistol, 133
Samurai Paint Ball Gun, 276
San Marco 10 Ga. O/U, 219
Santfl Schuetzen Target Rifle, 251
Sauer Model 90, Safari Rifles, 177
Sauer Model 200 Rifle, 177
Sauer-Franchi O/Us, 219
Savage Model 24 Combo, 185
Savage Model 24-C, 185
Savage Model 24-V, 185
Savage Model 69-RXL, RXG Pumps, 234
Savage Model 99C Lever Action, 165
Savage Model 110B, 177
Savage Model 110E, 177
Savage Model 110F, 177
Savage Model 389 Combo, 185
Savage-Stevens 311, 311 Waterfowl, 229
Scarab Skorpion Pistol, 123
W&C Scott Bowood Deluxe, 229
W&C Scott Chatsworth Grande Luxe, 229
W&C Scott Kinmount Game Gun, 229

Second Model Brown Bess, 242
Seecamp LWS 32 Pistol, 122
Sharp U-FP Air Pistol, 258
C. Sharps New Model 1875 Rifle, 182
C. Sharps 1875 Classic Sharps, 182
Sheridan Blue, Silver Streak Rifles, 271
Sheridan COFD Air Rifle, 271
Sheridan HB Pneumatic Pistol, 258
Sheriff 1851 Revolver, 240
Shiloh Sharps Sporting Rifles 1, 3, 182
Shiloh Sharps The Jaeger Rifle, 182
Shiloh Sharps 1862 Confederate Carbine, 251
Shiloh Sharps 1863 Military Rifle, Carbine, 250
Shiloh Sharps 1863 Sporting Rifle, 251
Shiloh Sharps 1874 Business, Carbine, Saddle Rifles, 183
Shiloh Sharps 1874 Long Range Rifle, 182
Shiloh Sharps 1874 Military Rifle, 183
Shiloh Sharps 1874 Montana Roughrider, 183
Sile Deluxe Percussion Shotgun, 253
Sile Field King Super Light, Hunter, Slug Master, 220
Sile Field Master II O/U, 219
Sile Folding Hunter, 232
Sile Protector Single, 232
Sile Sky Stalker O/U, 220
Sile Trap, Field, Skeet Kings, 220
Sile Valley Combo Gun, 186
Simson/Suhl Model 85 EJ, 220
Smith & Wesson Model 10, 139
Smith & Wesson Model 10 H.B., 139
Smith & Wesson Model 13, 65, 139
Smith & Wesson Model 15, 139
Smith & Wesson Model 17 K-22, 140
Smith & Wesson Model 19, 140
Smith & Wesson Model 25, 140
Smith & Wesson Model 27, 140
Smith & Wesson Model 29 Classic Hunter, 140
Smith & Wesson Model 29 Silhouette, 133
Smith & Wesson Model 29, 629, 140
Smith & Wesson Model 31, 140
Smith & Wesson Model 34, 63, 141
Smith & Wesson Model 36, 37, 141
Smith & Wesson Model 38, 141
Smith & Wesson Model 41 Match, 133
Smith & Wesson Model 41 Pistol, 133
Smith & Wesson Model 49, 649, 141
Smith & Wesson Model 52, 133
Smith & Wesson Model 57, 657, 141
Smith & Wesson Model 60, 141
Smith & Wesson Model 64, 141
Smith & Wesson Model 66, 141
Smith & Wesson Model 67, 141
Smith & Wesson Model 422 Pistol, 124
Smith & Wesson Model 439, 639, 124
Smith & Wesson Model 459, 659, 124
Smith & Wesson Model 469, 669, 124
Smith & Wesson Model 581, 586, 686, 141
Smith & Wesson Model 645 Pistol, 124
Smith & Wesson Model 745, 133
Sniper Mk. II Paint Ball Gun, 276
Sokolovsky 45 Automaster, 133
Spectre Auto Carbine, 159
Spectre Auto Pistol, 125
Spiller & Burr Revolver, 242
Splatmaster 102 Marking Pistol, 275
Sportarms Model HS21S SA, 147
Sportarms Model HS38S Revolver, 142

Sportarms Tokarev Model 213 Pistol, 125
Springfield Armory BM-59, 159
Springfield Armory M1-A, 159
Springfield Armory M1-A Super Match, 203
Springfield Armory M1 Garand, 160
Springfield Armory M-6 Scout, 186
Springfield Armory M-21 Sniper, 203
Springfield Armory Model 22 Rifle, 159
Springfield Armory Model 700 BASR, 203
Springfield Armory SAR-48, 159
Springfield Armory 1911-A1 Combat Commander, 125
Springfield Armory 1911-A1 Defender Pistol, 125
Springfield Armory 1911-A1 Pistol, 125
Star Model BM, BKM Pistols, 125
Star Model PD Pistol, 126
Star Model 30M, 30PK Pistols, 125
Steel City Double Deuce Pistol, 126
Steel City War Eagle Pistol, 126
Sterling HR-81/HR-83 Air Rifles, 271
Stevens Model 67 Pump Shotguns, 211
Stevens 311-R Guard Gun, 234
Steyr A.U.G. Rifle, 160
Steyr-Mannlicher Luxus, 178
Steyr-Mannlicher Match UIT, 203
Steyr-Mannlicher Model M, Professional, 177
Steyr-Mannlicher Model S, S/T, 178
Steyr-Mannlicher Model SL, L, 178
Steyr-Mannlicher SSG Marksman, SSG PII, 203
Steyr-Mannlicher SSG Match, 203
Steyr-Mannlicher Varmint SL, L, 178
Stoeger/IGA Double, Coach Gun, 229
Stoeger/IGA O/U, 220
Stoeger/IGA Single, 232
Super Six Golden Bison Revolver, 148

T

Tanarmi Baby TA90 Pistol, 126
Tanarmi Model TA76 SA, 148
Tanarmi Model TA90 Pistol, 126
Tanner Standard UIT Rifle, 204
Tanner 50 Meter Free Rifle, 204
Tanner 300 Meter Free Rifle, 203
Targa GT22, GT32, GT 380 Pistols, 127
Targa GT22T Target Pistol, 127
Targa GT26 Pistol, 127
Targa GT27 Pistol, 126
Targa GT380XE Pistol, 126
Taurus Model 65, 66, 142
Taurus Model 73, 142
Taurus Model 80, 142
Taurus Model 82, 142
Taurus Model 83, 142
Taurus Model 85, 142
Taurus Model 86 Master, 134
Taurus Model 689 Revolver, 143
Taurus PT58 Pistol, 127
Taurus PT-92AF Pistol, 127
Taurus PT-99AF Pistol, 127
Techni-Mec SPL 640, 642 Folding O/Us, 220
Techni-Mec SR 692 EM O/U, 220
Texas Longhorn Border Special, 148
Texas Longhorn Grover's Improved No. 5, 148
Texas Longhorn R.H. SA, 148
Texas Longhorn Sesquicentennial Model, 148

Texas Longhorn The Jezebel, 152
Texas Longhorn West Texas Flat Top Target, 148
Texas Paterson 1836, 239
Theoben-Prometheus Air Rifle, 272
Theoben Sirocco Classic, Grand Prix, 271
Theoben Sirocco Eliminator, 272
Thompson/Center Cherokee Rifle, 247
Thompson/Center Contender, 153
Thompson/Center Contender Carbine, 183
Thompson/Center Hawken Rifle, 247
Thompson/Center New Englander Rifle, 246
Thompson/Center New Englander Shotgun, 253
Thompson/Center Penna. Hunter, 244
Thompson/Center Renegade Hunter, 246
Thompson/Center Renegade Rifle, 246
Thompson/Center Super 14 Contender, 134
Thompson/Center TCR '87, 183
Tippmann SMG-60 Paint Ball Gun, 276
Tradewinds H-170 Auto, 208
Tradewinds Model 260-A Rifle, 191
Traditions Hunter, Frontier Rifle, Carbine, 248
Traditions Penna., Shenandoah Rifles, 244
Traditions Trapper, Frontier Scout Rifles, 245
Traditions Trapper Pistol, 238
Trail Guns Kodiak 10 Ga. Shotgun, 253
Tryon Rifle, 246
Tryon Trailblazer Rifle, 244

U

USAS-12 Auto Shotgun, 234
Uberti Confederate Tucker & Sherrard, 239
Uberti Henry Rifle, 165
Uberti Inspector Revolver, 143
Uberti Model 1861 Navy, 240
Uberti Phantom Silhouette Pistol, 134
Uberti Rolling Block Carbine, 183
Uberti Rolling Block Pistol, 153
Uberti Santa Fe Hawken, 245
Uberti 1st Model Dragoon, 239
Uberti 2nd Model Dragoon, 239
Uberti 3rd Model Dragoon, 239
Uberti 1858 Army Revolving Carbine, 249
Uberti 1862 Pocket Navy, 241
Uberti 1866 Red Cloud Commemorative, 165
Uberti 1866 Sporting Rifle, 165
Uberti 1866 Trapper's Model Carbine, 165
Uberti 1866 Yellowboy Carbine, 165
Uberti 1866 Yellowboy Indian Carbine, 165
Uberti 1873 Buckhorn Revolving Carbine, 166
Uberti 1873 Buckhorn SA, 149
Uberti 1873 Buntline SA, 149
Uberti 1873 Cattleman Revolving Carbine, 166
Uberti 1873 Cattleman SAs, 149
Uberti 1873 Sporting Rifle, 165
Uberti 1873 Stallion SA, 149
Uberti 1875 Outlaw SA, 149
Uberti 1875 Revolving Carbine, 165

GUNDEX

Uberti 1890 Outlaw SA, 149
Ultra Light Model 20, 24, 178
Ultra Light Model 20 REB Pistol, 153
Ultra Light Model 20S, 178
Ultra Light Model 28, 178
UZI Carbine, 160
UZI Mini Carbine, 160
UZI Pistol, 127
UZI Mk.I Paint Ball Pistol, 275

V

Valmet Hunter Auto, 162
Valmet M-76 Auto Rifle, 160
Valmet M-78 Auto Rifle, 160
Valmet 412S Combo, 186
Valmet 412S Double Rifle, 186
Valmet 412S Field O/U, 220
Valmet 412ST Trap, Skeet, 220
Varner Favorite Single Shot, 199
Victory Model MC5 Pistol, 128
Voere Model 1007/1013 Rifles, 199
Voere Model 2115 Rifle, 191
Voere 2155, 2165 Rifles, 178

W

Walker 1847 Percussion, 239
Walther American PPK Pistol, 128
Walther American PPK/s Pistol, 128
Walther CP COFD Air Pistol, 258
Walther Free Pistol, 134
Walther GSP, GSP-C, 134
Walther GX-1 Match, 204
Walther LGR Running Boar Air Rifle, 272
Walther LGR Universal Match Air Rifle, 272
Walther Model TPH Pistol, 128
Walther OSP Rapid Fire, 134
Walther P-5 Pistol, 128
Walther P-38 Pistol, 128
Walther P-88 Auto Pistol, 128
Walther PP Pistol, 128
Walther Running Boar Match, 204
Walther U.I.T. BV Universal, 204
Walther U.I.T. Match, 204
Weatherby Athena O/U, 221
Weatherby Athena Trap, 232
Weatherby Eighty-Two Auto, 208
Weatherby Euromark Rifle, 179
Weatherby Fibermark Rifle, 179
Weatherby Lazermark Mark V Rifle, 179
Weatherby Mark V Rifle, Left Hand, 179
Weatherby Mark XXII Clip Model, 191
Weatherby Mark XXII Tube Model, 191
Weatherby Orion O/U, 220
Weatherby Vanguard Fiberguard, 179
Weatherby Vanguard VGL, 179
Weatherby Vanguard VGX, VGS, 179
Weaver Arms Nighthawk, 160
Dan Wesson Model 8-2, 14-2, 143
Dan Wesson Model 9-2, 15-2, 32M, 143
Dan Wesson Model 22, 143
Dan Wesson Model 40 Silhouette, 134
Dan Wesson Model 41V, 44V, 143
Whitworth Express Rifle, 180
Wichita Classic Pistol, 135
Wichita Classic Rifle, 180
Wichita Hunter, International Pistol, 135
Wichita Mk-40 Silhouette, 135
Wichita Silhouette Pistol, 135
Wichita Silhouette Rifle, 204
Wichita Varmint Rifle, 180
Wildey Auto Pistol, 129
Wilkinson Linda Pistol, 129
Wilkinson Sherry Pistol, 129
Winchester American Flyer, Combo, 221
Winchester Defender Pump, 234
Winchester Model 23 Classic, 229
Winchester Model 23 Custom, 229
Winchester Model 23 Light Duck, Golden Quail, 229
Winchester Model 70 Lightweight, 180
Winchester Model 70 Winlite, 180
Winchester Model 70XTR Featherweight, 181
Winchester Model 70XTR Sporter, 180
Winchester Model 70XTR Super Express, 180
Winchester Model 94 Big Bore Side Eject, 166
Winchester Model 94 Side Eject, 166
Winchester Model 94XTR Deluxe, 166
Winchester Model 94XTR 7x30 Waters, 166
Winchester Model 101 Diamond Grade Target, 221
Winchester Model 101 Pigeon Grade, 221
Winchester Model 101 Waterfowl Winchoke, 221
Winchester Model 101 Winchoke O/U, 221
Winchester Model 1300 Rifled Deer Gun, 211
Winchester Model 1300 Turkey, 211
Winchester Model 1300 Waterfowl, 211
Winchester Model 1300XTR Featherweight, 211
Winchester Model 9422XTR Pistol Grip, 193
Winchester Model 9422XTR Rifle, 193
Winchester Model 9422MXTR Rifle, 193
Winchester Pistol Grip Pump Security, 234
Winchester Quail Special, 221
Winchester Ranger Auto Shotgun, 208
Winchester Ranger Bolt Rifle, 181
Winchester Ranger Pump, Combo, 211
Winchester Ranger Pump, Youth, 211
Winchester Ranger Side Eject Carbine, 166
Winchester Stainless Marine Pump, 234

Z

Pietro Zanoletti 2000 Field, 222
A. Zoli Angel Field Grade, Condor, 222
A. Zoli Delfino S.P. O/U, 222
A. Zoli O/U Combo, 186
Zouave Percussion Rifle, 250

HANDGUNS—AUTOLOADERS, SERVICE & SPORT

Includes models suitable for several forms of competition and other sporting purposes.

AMT 45 ACP HARDBALLER LONG SLIDE
Caliber: 45 ACP.
Barrel: 7".
Length: 10½" over-all.
Stocks: Wrap-around rubber.
Sights: Fully adjustable rear sight.
Features: Slide and barrel are 2" longer than the standard 45, giving less recoil, added velocity, longer sight radius. Has extended combat safety, serrated matte rib, loaded chamber indicator, wide adjustable trigger. From AMT.
Price: $499.00

AMT Long Slide

AMT AUTOMAG II AUTO PISTOL
Caliber: 22 WMR, 10-shot magazine.
Barrel: 3⅜", 4½", 6".
Weight: About 23 oz. **Length:** 9⅜" over-all.
Stocks: Smooth black composition.
Sights: Blade front, Millett adjustable rear.
Features: Made of stainless steel. Gas-assisted action. Exposed hammer. Slide flats have brushed finish, rest is sandblast. Squared triggerguard. Introduced 1986. From AMT.
Price: $329.00

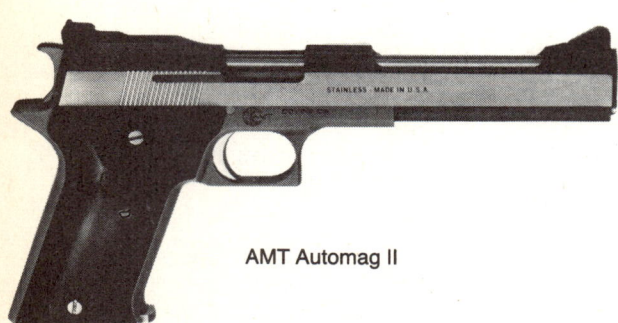

AMT Automag II

AMT LIGHTNING AUTO PISTOL
Caliber: 22 LR, 10-shot magazine.
Barrel: Tapered or Bull—6½", 8½", 10"; Bull—5".
Weight: 45 oz. (6½" barrel). **Length:** 10¾" over-all (6½" barrel).
Stocks: Checkered wrap-around rubber.
Sights: Blade front, Millett adjustable rear.
Features: Made of stainless steel. Uses Clark trigger with adjustable stops; receiver grooved for scope mounting; trigger guard spur for two-hand hold; interchangeable barrels. Introduced 1984. From AMT.
Price: 5" bull, 6½" tapered or bull $289.00
Price: 8½", tapered or bull $289.00
Price: 10", tapered or bull $289.00

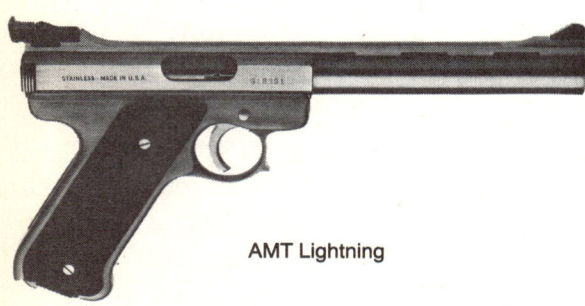

AMT Lightning

AMT "BACKUP" AUTO PISTOL
Caliber: 22 LR, 8-shot magazine; 380 ACP, 5-shot magazine
Barrel: 2½".
Weight: 18 oz. **Length:** 4.25" over-all.
Stocks: Checkered Lexon.
Sights: Fixed, open, recessed.
Features: Concealed hammer, blowback operation; manual and grip safeties. All stainless steel construction. Smallest domestically-produced pistol in 380. From AMT.
Price: 22 LR or 380 ACP $237.00

AMT 45 ACP HARDBALLER
Caliber: 45 ACP.
Barrel: 5".
Weight: 39 oz. **Length:** 8½" over-all.
Stocks: Wrap-around rubber.
Sights: Adjustable.
Features: Extended combat safety, serrated matte slide rib, loaded chamber indicator, long grip safety, beveled magazine well, adjustable target trigger. All stainless steel. From AMT
Price: $465.00
Price: Government model (as above except no rib, fixed sights) $403.00

AMT Backup

ACTION ARMS AT-84 DA PISTOL
Caliber: 9mm Para., 15 shots; 41 Action Express, 10 shots.
Barrel: 4.72".
Weight: 35.3 oz. **Length:** 8.1" over-all.
Stocks: Checkered walnut.
Sights: Blade front, rear drift-adjustable for windage.
Features: Double action; polished blue finish. Introduced 1987. Imported from Switzerland by Action Arms Ltd.
Price: $525.00
Price: Model 84P (3.66" bbl., 7.24" o.a.l., weighs 32.1 ozs., and has 13/8-shot magazine) $525.00

AMERICAN ARMS TT9MM AUTO PISTOL
Caliber: 9mm Para., 9-shot magazine.
Barrel: 4.5".
Weight: 32 oz. **Length:** 8" over-all.
Stocks: Grooved plastic
Sights: Fixed.
Features: Single-action mechanism. Blue finish. Imported from Yugoslavia by American Arms, Inc. Introduced 1988.
Price: $288.00

HANDGUNS—AUTOLOADERS, SERVICE & SPORT

AMERICAN ARMS EP380 AUTO PISTOL
Caliber: 380 ACP, 7-shot magazine.
Barrel: 3½".
Weight: 25 oz. **Length:** 6½" over-all.
Stocks: Checkered wood.
Sights: Fixed.
Features: Double action. Made of stainless steel. Slide-mounted safety. Imported from West Germany by American Arms, Inc. Introduced 1988.
Price: $540.00

AMERICAN ARMS PK22 D/A AUTO PISTOL
Caliber: 22 LR, 8-shot magazine.
Barrel: 3.3".
Weight: 22 oz. **Length:** 6.3" over-all.
Stocks: Checkered plastic.
Sights: Fixed.
Features: Double action. Polished blue finish. Slide-mounted safety. Made in the U.S. by American Arms, Inc.
Price: $199.00

ASTRA A-90 DOUBLE-ACTION AUTO PISTOL
Caliber: 9mm Para. (15-shot), 45 ACP (9-shot).
Barrel: 3.75".
Weight: 40 oz. **Length:** 7" over-all.
Stocks: Checkered black plastic.
Sights: Square blade front, square notch rear drift-adjustable for windage.
Features: Double or single action; loaded chamber indicator; combat-style trigger guard; optional right-side slide release (for left-handed shooters); automatic internal safety; decocking lever. Introduced 1985. Imported from Spain by Interarms.
Price: Blue $450.00

ASTRA CONSTABLE AUTO PISTOL
Caliber: 22 LR, 10-shot; 380 ACP, 7-shot.
Barrel: 3½".
Weight: 26 oz.
Stocks: Moulded plastic.
Sights: Adj. rear.
Features: Double action, quick no-tool takedown, non-glare rib on slide. 380 available in blue, stainless steel, or chrome finish. Engraved guns also available—contact the importer. Imported from Spain by Interarms.
Price: Blue, 22 .... $325.00
Price: Chrome, 22 .... $330.00
Price: Blue, 380 .... $305.00

AUTO-ORDNANCE 1911A1 AUTOMATIC PISTOL
Caliber: 9mm Para., 38 Super, 9-shot; 41 Action Express, 8-shot; 45 ACP, 7-shot magazine.
Barrel: 5".
Weight: 39 oz. **Length:** 8½" over-all.
Stocks: Checkered plastic with medallion.
Sights: Blade front, rear adj. for windage.
Features: Same specs as 1911A1 military guns—parts interchangeable. Frame and slide blued; each radius has non-glare finish. Made in U.S. by Auto-Ordnance Corp.
Price: 45 cal. $344.95
Price: 9mm, 38 Super, 41 A.E. $381.95

> Consult our Directory pages for the location of firms mentioned.

BEEMAN MINI P-08 AUTO PISTOL
Caliber: 380 ACP (5-shot).
Barrel: 3.5".
Weight: 22½ oz. **Length:** 7⅜" over-all.
Stocks: Checkered hardwood.
Sights: Fixed.
Features: Toggle action similar to original "Luger" pistol. Slide stays open after last shot. Has magazine and sear disconnect safety systems. Imported from West Germany by Beeman.
Price: $389.50

AMERICAN ARMS ZC380 AUTO PISTOL
Caliber: 380 ACP, 8-shot magazine.
Barrel: 3.75".
Weight: 26 oz. **Length:** 6.5" over-all.
Stocks: Checkered plastic.
Sights: Fixed.
Features: Single-action mechanism. Polished blue finish. Imported from Yugoslavia by American Arms, Inc. Introduced 1988.
Price: $288.00

Astra A-90 Pistol

Astra A-60 Double Action Pistol
Similar to the Constable except in 380 only, with 13-shot magazine, slide-mounted ambidextrous safety. Available in blued steel only. Introduced 1980.
Price: $400.00

AUSTRALIAN AUTOMATIC ARMS SAP PISTOL
Caliber: 223, 20- or 30-shot magazine.
Barrel: 10.5".
Weight: 5.9 lbs. **Length:** 20.5" over-all.
Stocks: Checkered composition.
Sights: Protected post front, revolving aperture rear adjustable for windage.
Features: Gas operated with short-stroke mobile cylinder. Hammer forged barrel with chrome chamber and bore. Imported from Australia by Kendall International.
Price: $750.00

Auto-Ordnance 1911A1

CAUTION: PRICES CHANGE. CHECK AT GUNSHOP.

HANDGUNS—AUTOLOADERS, SERVICE & SPORT

BEEMAN MODEL P-08 AUTO PISTOL
Caliber: 22 LR, 8-shot magazine.
Barrel: 4".
Weight: 25 oz. **Length:** 7¾" over-all.
Stocks: Checkered hardwood.
Sights: Fixed.
Features: Has toggle action similar to original "Luger" pistol. Slide stays open after last shot. Imported from West Germany by Beeman.
Price: $389.50

Beeman P-08

BERNARDELLI PO18 DA PISTOL
Caliber: 9mm Para., 16-shot magazine.
Barrel: 4.8".
Weight: 36.3 ozs. **Length:** 6.2" over-all.
Stocks: Checkered, contoured plastic standard; walnut optional.
Sights: Low profile combat sights.
Features: Manual thumb safety, half-cock, magazine safties, auto-locking firing pin block safety; ambidextrous magazine release. Introduced 1987. From Mandall Shooting Supplies.
Price: With plastic grips $595.00

Bernardelli PO 18

BERNARDELLI MODEL 60 AUTO PISTOL
Caliber: 22 LR, 10-shot; 32 ACP, 9-shot; 380 ACP, 7-shot.
Barrel: 3½".
Weight: 26½ oz. **Length:** 6½" over-all.
Stocks: Checkered plastic with thumbrest.
Sights: Ramp front, white outline rear adj. for w. & e.
Features: Hammer block slide safety; loaded chamber indicator; dual recoil buffer springs; serrated trigger; inertia-type firing pin. Imported from Italy by Mandall Shooting Supplies.
Price: $289.95

BERETTA MODEL 84/85 DA PISTOLS
Caliber: 380 ACP, 13-shot magazine; 22 LR, 7-shot (M87).
Barrel: 3.82".
Weight: About 23 oz. (M84/85), 20.8 oz. (M87). **Length:** 6.8" over-all.
Stocks: Glossy black plastic (wood optional at extra cost).
Sights: Fixed front, drift-adjustable rear.
Features: Double action, quick take-down, convenient magazine release. Introduced 1977. Imported from Italy by Beretta USA.
Price: Model 84 (380 ACP) $456.00
Price: Model 84 wood grips $484.00
Price: Model 84 nickel finish $512.00
Price: Model 85 nickel finish $406.00
Price: Model 85 plastic grips $378.00
Price: Model 85 wood grips $392.00
Price: Model 87, 22 LR, 7-shot magazine $412.00
Price: Model 87 Long Barrel, 22 LR, single action $427.00
Price: Model 89 Sport Wood, single action, 22 LR $525.00

Beretta Model 87

BERETTA MODEL 950 BS AUTO PISTOL
Caliber: 22 Short, 6-shot; 25 ACP, 8-shot.
Barrel: 2.5".
Weight: 9.9 oz. (22 Short, 10.2 oz.) **Length:** 4.5" over-all.
Stocks: Checkered black plastic.
Sights: Fixed.
Features: Single action. Thumb safety; tip-up barrel for direct loading/unloading, cleaning. From Beretta U.S.A.
Price: Blue, 25 .... $152.00
Price: Blue, 22 .... $152.00
Price: EL model (gold etching) $217.00

Beretta Model 950 BS-4

Beretta Model 21 Pistol
Similar to the Model 950 BS. Chambered for 22 LR and 25 ACP. Both double action. 2.5" barrel, 4.9" over-all length. 7-round magazine on 22 cal.; 8-round magazine on 25 cal; 22 cal. available in nickel finish. Both have walnut grips. Introduced in 1985.
Price: 22 cal $215.00
Price: 22 cal, nickel finish $238.00
Price: 25 cal $215.00
Price: EL model, 22 or 25 .... $250.00

Beretta Model 21

HANDGUNS—AUTOLOADERS, SERVICE & SPORT

BERETTA MODEL 92F PISTOL
Caliber: 9mm Parabellum, 15-shot magazine.
Barrel: 4.9".
Weight: 34 oz. **Length:** 8.5" over-all.
Stocks: Checkered black plastic; wood optional at extra cost.
Sights: Blade front, rear adj. for w.
Features: Double-action. Extractor acts as chamber loaded indicator, squared trigger guard, grooved front and back straps, inertia firing pin. Matte finish. Introduced 1977. Imported from Italy by Beretta USA.
Price: With plastic grips $596.00
Price: With wood grips $616.00

BRNO CZ 83 DOUBLE ACTION PISTOL
Caliber: 32, 15-shot; 380, 13-shot.
Barrel: 3.7".
Weight: 26.5 oz. **Length:** 6.7" over-all.
Stocks: Checkered black plastic.
Sights: Blade front, rear adj. for w.
Features: Double-action; ambidextrous magazine release and safety. Polished or matte blue. Imported from Czechoslovakia by Saki International.
Price: $425.00

BROWNING BUCK MARK 22 PISTOL
Caliber: 22 LR, 10-shot magazine.
Barrel: 5½".
Weight: 32 oz. **Length:** 9½" over-all.
Stocks: Black moulded composite with skip-line checkering.
Sights: Ramp front, rear adj. for w. and e.
Features: All steel, matte blue finish, gold-colored trigger. Buck Mark Plus has laminated wood grips. Made in U.S. Introduced 1985. From Browning.
Price: Buck Mark $189.75
Price: Buck Mark Plus $227.75

Browning Buck Mark Silhouette
Same as the Buck Mark except has 9⅞" heavy barrel with .900" diameter; hooded front sight with interchangeable posts, Millett Gold Cup 360 SIL rear on a special top sighting plane. Grips and fore-end are black multi-laminated wood. Introduced 1987.
Price: $309.95

Beretta Model 92F

BRNO CZ 75 AUTO PISTOL
Caliber: 9mm Para., 15-shot magazine.
Barrel: 4.7".
Weight: 35 oz. **Length:** 8" over-all.
Stocks: Checkered wood.
Sights: Blade front, rear adj. for w.
Features: Double action; blued finish. Imported from Czechoslovakia by Saki International.
Price: $599.00

BRNO CZ-85 Auto Pistol
Same gun as the CZ-75 except has ambidextrous slide release and safety levers, is available in 9mm Para. and 7.65, contoured composition grips, matte finish on top of slide. Introduced 1986.
Price: $655.00

Browning Buck Mark Silhouette

Browning Buck Mark Varmint
Same as the Buck Mark except has 9⅞" heavy barrel with .900" diameter and full-length scope base (no open sights); black multi-laminated wood grips, with optional fore-end. Over-all length is 14", weight is 48 oz. Introduced 1987.
Price: $279.95

Browning Buck Mark Varmint

Consult our Directory pages for the location of firms mentioned.

Browning Hi-Power

BROWNING HI-POWER 9mm AUTOMATIC PISTOL
Caliber: 9mm Parabellum, 13-shot magazine.
Barrel: 4 21/32".
Weight: 32 oz. **Length:** 7¾" over-all.
Stocks: Walnut, hand checkered, or black Polyamide.
Sights: ⅛" blade front; rear screw-adj. for w. and e. Also available with fixed rear (drift-adj. for w.).
Features: External hammer with half-cock and thumb safeties. A blow on the hammer cannot discharge a cartridge; cannot be fired with magazine removed. Fixed rear sight model available. Ambidextrous safety available only with matte finish, moulded grips. Imported from Belgium by Browning.
Price: Fixed sight model, walnut grips $449.95
Price: 9mm with rear sight adj. for w. and e., walnut grips $491.95
Price: Standard matte black finish, fixed sight, moulded grips, ambidextrous safety $414.95

CAUTION: PRICES CHANGE. CHECK AT GUNSHOP.

HANDGUNS—AUTOLOADERS, SERVICE & SPORT

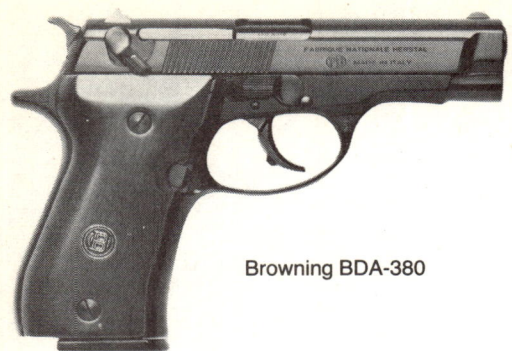

Browning BDA-380

BROWNING BDA-380 DA AUTO PISTOL
Caliber: 380 ACP, 13-shot magazine.
Barrel: 3 13/16".
Weight: 23 oz. **Length:** 6¾" over-all.
Stocks: Smooth walnut with inset Browning medallion.
Sights: Blade front, rear drift-adj. for w.
Features: Combination safety and de-cocking lever will automatically lower a cocked hammer to half-cock and can be operated by right or left-hand shooters. Inertia firing pin. Introduced 1978. Imported from Italy by Browning.
Price: Blue. $429.95
Price: Nickel $452.95

BRYCO MODEL 38 AUTO PISTOLS
Caliber: 22 LR, 6-shot magazine.
Barrel: 2.8".
Weight: 15 oz. **Length:** 5.3" over-all.
Stocks: Polished resin-impregnated wood.
Sights: Fixed.
Features: Safety locks sear and slide. Choice of satin nickel, bright chrome or black Teflon finishes. Introduced 1988. From Jennings Firearms.
Price: 22 LR, 32 ACP $99.95
Price: 380 ACP $129.95

BRYCO MODEL 25 AUTO PISTOL
Caliber: 25 ACP, 6-shot magazine.
Barrel: 2.5".
Weight: 11 oz. **Length:** 5" over-all.
Stocks: Polished resin-impregnated wood.
Sights: Fixed.
Features: Safety locks sear and slide. Choice of satin nickel, bright chrome or black Teflon finishes. Introduced 1988. From Jennings Firearms.
Price: $89.95

BRYCO MODEL 48 AUTO PISTOLS
Caliber: 22 LR, 32 ACP, 380 ACP, 6-shot magazine.
Barrel: 4".
Weight: 19 oz. **Length:** 6.7" over-all.
Stocks: Polished resin-impregnated wood.
Sights: Fixed.
Features: Safety locks sear and slide. Choice of satin nickel, bright chrome or black Teflon finishes. Announced 1988. From Jennings Firearms.
Price: 22 LR, 32 ACP $99.95
Price: 380 ACP $129.95

BUSHMASTER AUTO PISTOL
Caliber: 223, 30-shot magazine.
Barrel: 11½" (1-10" twist).
Weight: 5¼ lbs. **Length:** 20½" over-all.
Stocks: Synthetic rotating grip swivel assembly.
Sights: Post front, adjustable open "Y" rear
Features: Steel alloy upper receiver with welded barrel assembly, AK-47-type gas system, aluminum lower receiver, one-piece welded steel alloy bolt carrier assembly. From Bushmaster Firearms.
Price: $339.95
Price: With matte electroless nickel finish $379.95

CALICO MODEL 100-P AUTO PISTOL
Caliber: 22 LR, 100-shot magazine.
Barrel: 6".
Weight: 3.7 lbs. (loaded). **Length:** 17" over-all.
Stocks: Moulded composition.
Sights: Adjustable post front, notch rear.
Features: Aluminum alloy frame; flash suppressor; pistol grip compartment; ambidextrous safety. Uses same helical-feed magazine as M-100 Carbine. Introduced 1986. Made in U.S. From Calico.
Price: $249.95

Calico Model 100-P

Colt Government Model

COLT GOV'T MODEL MK IV/SERIES 80
Caliber: 9mm, 38 Super, 45 ACP, 7-shot.
Barrel: 5".
Weight: 38 oz. **Length:** 8½" over-all.
Stocks: Checkered walnut.
Sights: Ramp front, fixed square notch rear.
Features: Grip and thumb safeties and internal firing pin safety, grooved trigger. Accurizor barrel and bushing.
Price: Blue, 45 ACP $565.95
Price: Bright stainless, 45 ACP $659.95
Price: 9mm, blue only $569.95
Price: 38 Super, blue $569.95
Price: Stainless steel, 45 ACP $599.95

Colt 10mm Delta Elite
Similar to the Government Model except chambered for 10mm auto cartridge. Has three-dot high profile front and rear combat sights, rubber combat stocks with Delta medallion, internal firing pin safety, and new recoil spring/buffer system. Blue only. Introduced 1987.
Price: $626.95

COLT OFFICERS ACP MK IV/SERIES 80
Caliber: 45 ACP, 6-shot magazine.
Barrel: 3½".
Weight: 34 oz. **Length:** 7¼" over-all.
Stocks: Checkered walnut.
Sights: Ramp blade front with white dot, square notch rear with two white dots.
Features: Trigger safety lock (thumb safety), grip safety, firing pin safety; grooved trigger; flat mainspring housing. Also available with lightweight alloy frame and in stainless steel. Introduced 1985.
Price: Matte finish $549.95
Price: Blue $565.95
Price: L.W., matte finish $565.95
Price: Stainless $599.95
Price: Bright stainless $659.95

HANDGUNS—AUTOLOADERS, SERVICE & SPORT

Colt Combat Elite MK IV/Series 80
Similar to the Government Model except in 45 ACP only, has stainless frame with ordnance steel slide and internal parts. High profile front, rear sights with three-dot system, extended grip safety, beveled magazine well, rubber combat stocks. Introduced 1986.
Price: $689.95

COLT COMBAT COMMANDER AUTO PISTOL
Caliber: 45 ACP, 7-shot; 38 Super Auto, 9mm Luger, 9-shot.
Barrel: 4¼".
Weight: 36 oz. **Length:** 7¾" over-all.
Stocks: Checkered walnut.
Sights: Fixed, glare-proofed blade front, square notch rear.
Features: Grooved trigger and hammer spur; arched housing; grip and thumb safeties.
Price: Blue, 9mm $569.95
Price: Blue, 45 .... $565.95
Price: Blue, 38 Super $569.95

Colt Combat Elite

Colt Lightweight Commander Mark IV/Series 80
Same as Commander except high strength aluminum alloy frame, wood panel grips, weight 27½ oz. 45 ACP only.
Price: Blue $565.95

COLT 380 GOVERNMENT MODEL
Caliber: 380 ACP, 7-shot magazine.
Barrel: 3¼".
Weight: 21¾ oz. **Length:** 6" over-all.
Stocks: Checkered composition.
Sights: Ramp front, square notch rear, fixed.
Features: Scaled down version of the 1911A1 Colt G.M. Has thumb and internal firing pin safeties. Introduced 1983.
Price: Blue $365.95
Price: Nickel $406.95
Price: Coltguard $386.95

Colt 380 Government

Colt Mustang Plus II
Similar to the 380 Government Model except has the shorter barrel and slide of the Mustang. Blue finish only. Introduced 1988.
Price: $365.95

Colt Mustang 380, Mustang Pocket Lite
Similar to the standard 380 Government Model. Mustang has steel frame (18.5 oz.), Pocket Lite has aluminum alloy (12.5 oz.). Both are ½" shorter than 380 GM, have 2¾" barrel. Introduced 1987.
Price: Mustang 380, blue $365.95
Price: As above, nickel $406.95
Price: As above, Coltguard $386.95
Price: Mustang Pocket Lite, blue $369.95

COONAN 357 MAGNUM PISTOL
Caliber: 357 Mag., 7-shot magazine.
Barrel: 5".
Weight: 42 oz.
Length: 8.3" over-all.
Stocks: Smooth walnut.
Sights: Open, adjustable.
Features: Unique barrel hood improves accuracy and reliability. Many parts interchange with Colt autos. Has grip, hammer, half-cock safeties. From Coonan Arms.
Price: Model B (linkless barrel, interchangeable ramp front sight, new rear sight) $650.00

Coonan 357 Magnum

DAVIS P-32 AUTO PISTOL
Caliber: 32 ACP, 6-shot magazine.
Barrel: 2.8".
Weight: 22 oz. **Length:** 5.4" over-all.
Stocks: Laminated wood.
Sights: Fixed.
Features: Choice of black Teflon or chrome finish. Announced 1986. Made in U.S. by Davis Industries.
Price: $87.50

Davis P-32

CAUTION: PRICES CHANGE. CHECK AT GUNSHOP.

HANDGUNS—AUTOLOADERS, SERVICE & SPORT

DETONICS "SERVICEMASTER" AUTO PISTOL
Caliber: 45 ACP, 7-shot magazine.
Barrel: 4¼".
Weight: 32 oz. **Length:** 7⅞" over-all.
Stocks: Pachmayr rubber.
Sights: Fixed combat.
Features: Stainless steel construction; thumb and grip safeties; extended grip safety. Polished slide flats, rest matte.
Price: $975.00

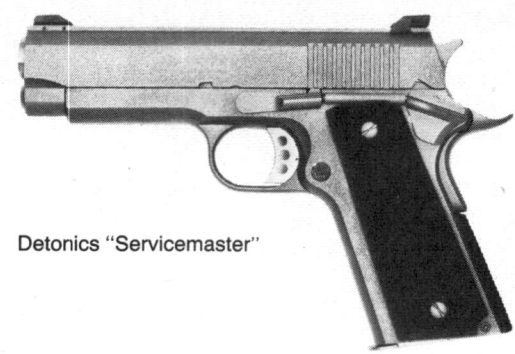
Detonics "Servicemaster"

DETONICS "COMBAT MASTER" MK VI, MK I
Caliber: 45 ACP, 6-shot magazine.
Barrel: 3½".
Weight: 29 oz. **Length:** 6¾" over-all, 4½" high.
Stocks: Checkered walnut.
Sights: Combat type, fixed and adj. sights avail.
Features: Has a self-adjusting cone barrel centering system, beveled magazine inlet, "full clip" indicator in base of magazine; standard 7-shot (or more) clip can be used in the 45. Throated barrel and polished feed ramp. Introduced 1977. From Detonics.
Price: MK I, matte finish, fixed sights $725.00
Price: MK VI, polished stainless, adj. sights $795.00

DESERT EAGLE MAGNUM PISTOL
Caliber: 357 Mag., 9-shot; 41 Mag., 44 Mag., 8-shot.
Barrel: 6", 10", 14", interchangeable.
Weight: 357 Mag.—52 oz. (alloy), 62 oz. (steel); 41 Mag., 44 Mag.—56 oz. (alloy), 66.9 oz. (stainless).
Length: 10¼" over-all. (6" bbl.).
Stocks: Wrap-around soft rubber.
Sights: Blade on ramp front, combat style rear. Adjustable available.
Features: Rotating three-lug bolt; ambidextrous safety; combat-style trigger-guard; adjustable trigger optional. Military epoxy finish. Satin, bright nickel, hard chrome, polished and blued finishes available. Imported from Israel by Magnum Research Inc.
Price: 357, 6" bbl., standard pistol $589.00
Price: As above, alloy frame $589.00
Price: As above, stainless steel frame $629.00
Price: 41 Mag., 6", standard pistol $699.00
Price: 41 Mag., alloy frame $699.00
Price: 41 Mag., stainless steel frame $739.00
Price: 44 Mag., 6", standard pistol $717.00
Price: As above, alloy frame $717.00
Price: As above, stainless steel frame $750.00

Desert Eagle 357

ENCOM MK IV ASSAULT PISTOL
Caliber: 45 ACP, 30-shot magazine.
Barrel: 4.5", 6", 8", 10" optional.
Weight: 6 lbs. **Length:** 12.6" over-all (4.5" barrel).
Stocks: Black composition.
Sights: Fixed.
Features: Semi-auto fire only. Side-loading magazine. Interchangeable barrels. Optional retractable stock available with 18½" barrel. Made in the U.S. by Encom America, Inc. Introduced 1988.
Price: $279.95

Encom Mk. IV

ENCOM MP-9, MP-45 ASSAULT PISTOLS
Caliber: 9mm, 45 ACP, 10, 30, 40 or 50-shot magazine.
Barrel: Interchangeable 4½", 6", 8", 10", 18", 18½".
Weight: 6 lbs. (4½" bbl.). **Length:** 11.8" over-all (4½" bbl.).
Stocks: Retractable wire stock.
Sights: Post front, fixed Patridge rear.
Features: Blowback operation, fires from closed breech with floating firing pin; right or left-hand models available. Made in U.S. From Encom America, Inc.
Price: 9mm or 45 ACP, standard pistol $275.00
Price: As above, Mini Pistol (3½" bbl.) $250.00
Price: Carbine (18½" bbl., retractable wire stock) $390.00

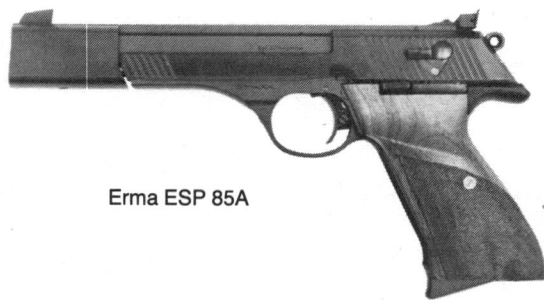
Erma ESP 85A

ERMA SPORTING PISTOL MODEL ESP 85A
Caliber: 22 LR, 8-shot, 32 S&W Long, 5-shot.
Barrel: 6".
Weight: 41 oz. **Length:** 10" over-all.
Stocks: Checkered walnut with thumbrest and adjustable left- or right-hand shelf.
Sights: Interchangeable blade front, micro. rear adjustable for windage and elevation.
Features: Interchangeable caliber conversion kit; adjustable trigger, trigger stop. Comes with lockable carrying case. Imported from West Germany by Competition Arms, Inc. Introduced 1988.
Price: .... NA

FALCON PORTSIDER AUTO PISTOL
Caliber: 45 ACP, 7-shot magazine.
Barrel: 5".
Weight: 38 oz. **Length:** 8½" over-all.
Stocks: Checkered walnut.
Sights: Fixed combat.
Features: Made of 17-4 stainless steel. Enlarged left-hand ejection port, extended ejector, long trigger, combat hammer, extended safety, wide grip safety. Introduced 1986. From Falcon Firearms.
Price: $580.00

HANDGUNS—AUTOLOADERS, SERVICE & SPORT

F.I.E. "THE BEST" A27B PISTOL
Caliber: 25 ACP, 6-shot magazine.
Barrel: 2½".
Weight: 13 oz. **Length:** 4⅝" over-all.
Stocks: Checkered walnut.
Sights: Fixed.
Features: All steel construction. Has thumb and magazine safeties, exposed hammer. Blue finish only. Introduced 1978. Made in U.S. by F.I.E. Corp.
Price: $154.95

F.I.E. "TZ-75" DA AUTO PISTOL
Caliber: 9mm Parabellum, 15-shot magazine; 41 Action Express, 11-shot magazine.
Barrel: 4.72".
Weight: 35.33 oz. **Length:** 8.25" over-all.
Stocks: Smooth European walnut. Checkered rubber optional.
Sights: Undercut blade front, open rear adjustable for windage.
Features: Double action trigger system; squared-off trigger guard; rotating slide-mounted safety. Introduced 1983. Imported from Italy by F.I.E. Corp.
Price: $424.95
Price: Satin chrome with red outline sights $444.95

F.I.E. "TITAN 25" PISTOL
Caliber: 25 ACP, 6-shot magazine.
Barrel: 2⁷⁄₁₆".
Weight: 12 oz. **Length:** 4⅝" over-all.
Stocks: Smooth walnut.
Sights: Fixed.
Features: External hammer; fast simple takedown. Made in U.S.A. by F.I.E. Corp.
Price: Blue $74.95
Price: Dyna-Chrome $84.95
Price: 24K gold with bright blue frame, smooth walnut grips $99.95

F.I.E. "TITAN II" PISTOLS
Caliber: 32 ACP, 380 ACP, 6-shot magazine; 22 LR, 10-shot magazine.
Barrel: 3⅞".
Weight: 25¾ oz. **Length:** 6¾" over-all.
Stocks: Checkered nylon, thumbrest-type; walnut optional.
Sights: Adjustable.
Features: Magazine disconnector, firing pin block. Standard slide safety. Available in blue or chrome. Introduced 1978. Imported from Italy by F.I.E. Corp.
Price: 32 or 380, blue $209.95
Price: 32 or 380, chrome $224.95
Price: 22 LR, blue $154.95

FEATHER MINI-AT AUTO PISTOL
Caliber: 22 LR, 20-shot magazine.
Barrel: 6".
Weight: 30 oz. **Length:** 15¼" over-all.
Stocks: Moulded composition.
Sights: Protected blade front, adjustable notch rear.
Features: Matte black finish. From Feather Enterprises. Introduced 1987.
Price: $219.95

F.I.E. "SUPER TITAN II" PISTOLS
Caliber: 32 ACP, 12-shot; 380 ACP, 11-shot.
Barrel: 3⅞".
Weight: 28 oz. **Length:** 6¾" over-all.
Stocks: Smooth, polished walnut.
Sights: Adjustable.
Features: Blue finish only. Introduced 1981. Imported from Italy by F.I.E. Corp.
Price: 32 or 380 .... $249.95

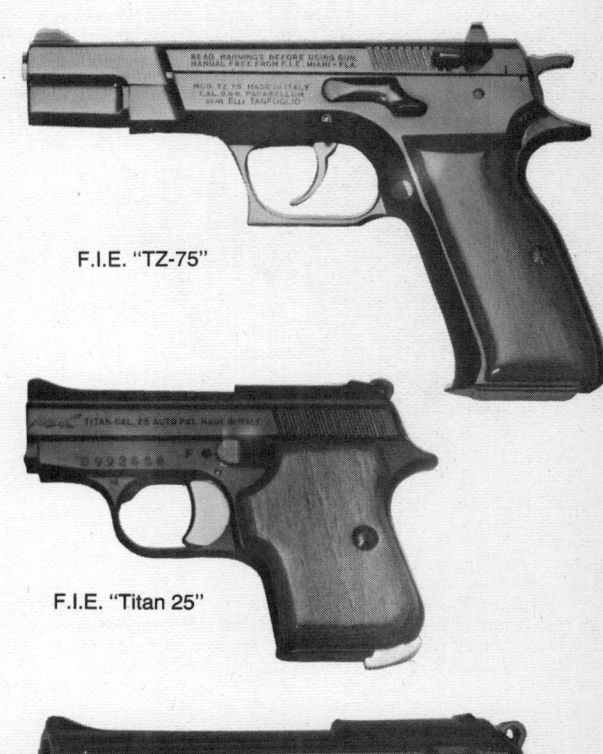

F.I.E. "TZ-75"

F.I.E. "Titan 25"

F.I.E. Titan II

Glock 19

GLOCK 17 AUTO PISTOL
Caliber: 9mm Para., 17-shot magazine.
Barrel: 4.48".
Weight: 21.8 oz. (without magazine). **Length:** 7.40" over-all.
Stocks: Black polymer.
Sights: Dot on front blade, white outline rear adj. for w. and e.
Features: Polymer frame, steel slide; double-action trigger with "Safe Action" system; mechanical firing pin safety, drop safety; simple take-down without tools; locked breech, recoil operated action. Adopted by Austrian armed forces 1983. NATO approved 1984. Imported from Austria by Glock, Inc.
Price: With extra magazine, magazine loader, cleaning kit $511.60
Price: Model 17L (6" barrel) $740.53

Glock 19 Auto Pistol
Similar to the Glock 17 except has a 4" barrel, giving an over-all length of 6.9" and weight of 21.2 oz. Magazine capacity is 15 rounds. Introduced 1988.
Price: $511.60

CAUTION: PRICES CHANGE. CHECK AT GUNSHOP.

HANDGUNS—AUTOLOADERS, SERVICE & SPORT

GONCZ HIGH-TECH LONG PISTOL
Caliber: 9mm Para., 30 Mauser, 38 Super, 18- and 32-shot magazine; 45 ACP, 10- and 20-shot magazine.
Barrel: 4", 9.5".
Weight: 3 lbs., 10 oz. (with 4" barrel). **Length:** 10½" over-all (with 4" barrel).
Stocks: Alloy grooved pistol grip.
Sights: Front adjustable for elevation, rear adjustable for windage.
Features: Fires from closed bolt; floating firing pin; safety locks the firing pin. All metal construction. Barrel threaded for accessories. Matte black oxide and anodized finish. Designed by Lajos J. Goncz. Introduced 1985. From Goncz Co.
Price: With 9½" barrel... $350.00
Price: With 4" barrel... $340.00

Goncz High-Tech Pistol

GRENDEL P-10 AUTO PISTOL
Caliber: 380 ACP, 10-shot magazine.
Barrel: 3".
Weight: 15 oz. **Length:** 5.3" over-all.
Stocks: Checkered polycarbonate metal composite.
Sights: Fixed.
Features: Double action only with a low inertia safety hammer system. Magazine loads from the top. Matte black, electroless nickel or green finish. Introduced 1987. From Grendel, Inc.
Price: Black finish.. $150.00
Price: Green finish.. $155.00
Price: Electroless nickel.. $165.00

Grendel P-10

HAMMERLI MODEL 212 HUNTER'S PISTOL
Caliber: 22 LR
Barrel: 4.9".
Weight: 31 oz. **Length:** 8.5" over-all.
Stocks: Checkered walnut.
Sights: White dot front adjustable for elevation, rear adjustable for windage.
Features: Semi-automatic based on the Model 208, intended for field use. Uses target trigger system which is fully adjustable. Comes with tool kit. Imported from Switzerland by Osborne's Supplies. Introduced 1984.
Price: About... $1,471.00

Hammerli 212

HECKLER & KOCH P7M8 AUTO PISTOL
Caliber: 9mm Parabellum, 8-shot magazine.
Barrel: 4.13".
Weight: 29 oz. **Length:** 6.73" over-all.
Stocks: Stippled black plastic.
Sights: Fixed, combat-type.
Features: Unique "squeeze cocker" in front strap cocks the action. Gas-retarded action. Squared combat-type trigger guard. Blue finish. Compact size. Imported from West Germany by Heckler & Koch, Inc.
Price: P7M8... $881.00
Price: P7M13 (13-shot capacity, matte black finish, ambidextrous magazine release, forged steel frame).................................. $1,099.00

Heckler & Koch P7K3 Auto Pistol
Similar to the P7M8 and P7M13 except chambered for 380 ACP, 8-shot magazine. Uses an oil-filled buffer to decrease recoil. Introduced 1988.
Price: $881.00
Price: 22 LR conversion unit..................................... $428.00

Heckler & Koch P7-M8

HECKLER & KOCH VP 70Z DOUBLE ACTION AUTO
Caliber: 9mm Para., 18-shot magazine.
Barrel: 4½".
Weight: 32½ oz. **Length:** 8" over-all.
Stocks: Black stippled plastic.
Sights: Ramp front, channeled slide rear.
Features: Recoil operated, double action. Only 4 moving parts. Double column magazine. Imported from West Germany by Heckler & Koch, Inc. Limited availability.
Price: $399.00
Price: Extra magazine... $27.00

HECKLER & KOCH P9S DOUBLE ACTION AUTO
Caliber: 45 ACP, 7-shot magazine.
Barrel: 4".
Weight: 31 oz. **Length:** 7.6" over-all.
Stocks: Checkered black plastic.
Sights: Open combat type.
Features: Double action; polygonal rifling; delayed roller-locked action with stationary barrel. Loaded chamber and cocking indicators; cocking/decocking lever. **Limited quantity available.** Imported from West Germany by Heckler & Koch, Inc.
Price: P-9S Combat Model, 45 ACP............................... $1,299.00
Price: P9S Target Model, 45 ACP................................. $1,382.00

HANDGUNS—AUTOLOADERS, SERVICE & SPORT

Helwan "Brigadier"

HELWAN "BRIGADIER" AUTO PISTOL
Caliber: 9mm Parabellum, 8-shot magazine.
Barrel: 4.5".
Weight: 32 oz. **Length:** 8" over-all.
Stocks: Grooved plastic.
Sights: Blade front, rear adjustable for windage.
Features: Polished blue finish. Single action design. Cross-bolt safety. Imported by Interarms.
Price: $249.00

HOLMES MP-83 ASSAULT PISTOL
Caliber: 9mm, 16- or 32-shot; 10mm, 12- or 25-shot; 45, 10- or 20-shot.
Barrel: 6".
Weight: 3½ lbs. **Length:** 14½" over-all.
Stocks: Walnut grip and fore-end.
Sights: Post front, open adj. rear.
Features: All steel construction, blue finish. Deluxe package includes gun, foam-lined travel case, Zytel stock, black metal vent, barrel shroud, extra magazine and sling. From Holmes Firearms.
Price: $500.00
Price: Deluxe $525.00
Price: Caliber conversion kit $220.00

Holmes MP-22 Assault Pistol
Similar to the MP-83 except chambered for 22LR, 32-shot capacity. Weighs 2½ lbs., has bolt-notch safety.
Price: $450.00
Price: Deluxe $525.00

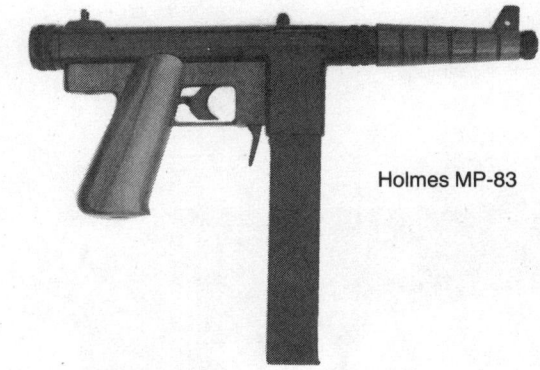

Holmes MP-83

Intratec TEC-9

INTRATEC TEC-9 AUTO PISTOL
Caliber: 9mm Para., 36-shot magazine.
Barrel: 5".
Weight: 50 oz. **Length:** 12½" over-all.
Stock: Moulded composition.
Sights: Fixed.
Features: Semi-auto, fires from closed bolt; firing pin block safety; matte blue finish. Comes wih 1" black nylon sling. From Intratec.
Price: $247.95
Price: TEC-9S (as above, except stainless) $306.95

Intratec TEC-9M Pistol
Similar to the TEC-9 except smaller. Has 3" barrel, weighs 44 oz.; 20-shot magazine.
Price: $226.95
Price: TEC-9MS (as above, stainless) $286.95

INTRATEC SCORPION AUTO PISTOL
Caliber: 22 LR, 30-shot magazine.
Barrel: 4".
Weight: 30 oz. **Length:** 11 3/16" over-all.
Stocks: Moulded composition.
Sights: Protected post front, rear adjustable for windage and elevation.
Features: Ambidextrous cocking knobs and safety. Matte black finish. Accepts any 10/22-type magazine. Announced 1988. Made in U.S. by Intratec.
Price: $154.95

Intratec Scorpion

IVER JOHNSON ENFORCER MODEL 3000 AUTO
Caliber: 30 M1 Carbine, 15- or 30-shot magazine.
Barrel: 9½".
Weight: 4 lbs. **Length:** 17" over-all.
Stocks: American walnut with metal handguard.
Sights: Gold bead ramp front. Peep rear.
Features: Accepts 15 or 30-shot magazines. From Iver Johnson.
Price: Blue finish $333.20

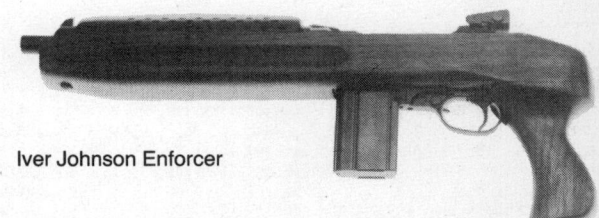

Iver Johnson Enforcer

CAUTION: PRICES CHANGE. CHECK AT GUNSHOP.

HANDGUNS—AUTOLOADERS, SERVICE & SPORT

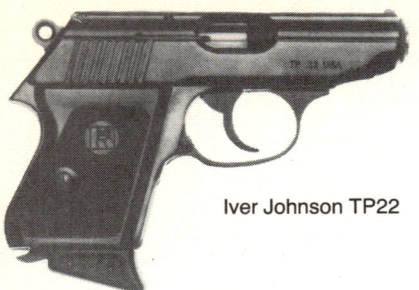

Iver Johnson TP22

IVER JOHNSON TP22, TP25 AUTO PISTOL
Caliber: 22 LR, 25 ACP, 7-shot magazine.
Barrel: 2.85".
Weight: 14½ oz. **Length:** 5.39" over-all.
Stocks: Black checkered plastic.
Sights: Fixed.
Features: Double action; 7-shot magazine. Introduced 1981. Made in U.S. From Iver Johnson's.
Price: Either caliber, blue $191.65
Price: As above, nickel $206.12

JENNINGS J-22 AUTO PISTOL
Caliber: 22 LR, 6-shot magazine.
Barrel: 2½".
Weight: 13 oz. **Length:** 4$^{15}/_{16}$" over-all.
Stocks: Walnut on chrome or nickel models; checkered black Cycolac on Teflon model.
Sights: Fixed.
Features: Choice of bright chrome, satin nickel or black Teflon finish. Introduced 1981. From Jennings Firearms.
Price: About $69.95

Jennings J-22 Pistol

KORRIPHILA HSP 701 DA AUTO PISTOL
Caliber: 9mm Para., 38 W.C., 38 Super, 45 ACP, 9-shot magazine in 9mm, 7-shot in 45.
Barrel: 4" (Type I), 5" (Type II, III).
Weight: 35 oz.
Stocks: Checkered walnut.
Sights: Ramp or target front, adj. rear.
Features: Delayed roller lock action with Budichowsky system. Double/single or single action only. Very limited production. Imported from West Germany by Osborne's. Introduced 1986.
Price: About $3,400.00

Korriphila HSP 701

Korth Auto Pistol

KORTH SEMI-AUTOMATIC PISTOL
Caliber: 9mm Parabellum, 13-shot magazine.
Barrel: 4½".
Weight: 35 oz. **Length:** 10½" over-all.
Stocks: Checkered walnut.
Sights: Combat-adjustable.
Features: Double action; 13-shot staggered magazine; forged machined frame and slide. Matte and polished finish. Introduced 1985. Imported from West Germany by Osborne's.
Price: About $3,715.00

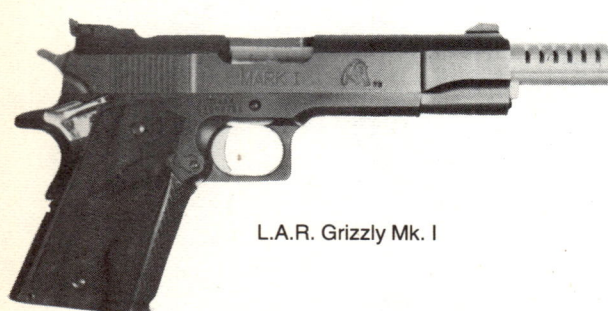

L.A.R. Grizzly Mk. I

L.A.R. GRIZZLY WIN MAG MK I PISTOL
Caliber: 357 Mag., 357/45, 10mm, 45 Win. Mag., 45 ACP, 7-shot magazine.
Barrel: 5.4", 6.5".
Weight: 51 oz. **Length:** 10½" over-all.
Stocks: Checkered rubber, non-slip combat-type.
Sights: Ramped blade front, fully adjustable rear.
Features: Uses basic Browning/Colt 1911-A1 design; interchangeable calibers; beveled magazine well; combat-type flat, checkered rubber mainspring housing; lowered and back-chamfered ejection port; polished feed ramp; throated barrel; solid barrel bushings. Available in satin hard chrome, matte blue, Parkerized finishes. Announced 1983. From L.A.R. Mfg. Inc.
Price: 45 Win. Mag. $675.00
Price: 357 Mag. $699.00
Price: Conversion units (357 Mag.) $149.00
Price: As above, 45 ACP $132.00

L.A.R. Grizzly Win Mag 8" & 10"
Similar to the standard Grizzly Win Mag except has lengthened slide and either 8" or 10" barrel. Available in 45 Win. Mag., 45 ACP, 357/45 Grizzly Win. Mag., 10mm or 357 Magnum. Introduced 1987.
Price: 8", 45 ACP, 45 Win. Mag., 357/45 Grizzly Win. Mag. $1,250.00
Price: As above, 10" $1,313.00
Price: 8", 357 Magnum $1,275.00
Price: As above, 10" $1,337.00

HANDGUNS—AUTOLOADERS, SERVICE & SPORT

Llama Large Frame Auto

LLAMA LARGE FRAME AUTO PISTOL
Caliber: 38 Super, 45 ACP.
Barrel: 5″
Weight: 40 oz. **Length:** 8½″ over-all.
Stocks: Checkered walnut.
Sights: Fixed.
Features: Grip and manual safeties, ventilated rib. Imported from Spain by Stoeger Industries.
Price: Blue..$352.00
Price: Satin chrome, 45 ACP only..............................$471.00

LLAMA COMPACT FRAME AUTO PISTOL
Caliber: 9mm Para., 9-shot, 45 ACP, 7-shot.
Barrel: 4 5/16″.
Weight: 37 oz.
Stocks: Smooth walnut.
Sights: Blade front, rear adjustable for windage.
Features: Scaled-down version of the Large Frame gun. Locked breech mechanism; manual and grip safeties. Introduced 1985. Imported from Spain by Stoeger Industries.
Price: Blue only...$352.00

Llama Small Frame Auto

LLAMA SMALL FRAME AUTO PISTOLS
Caliber: 22 LR, 32, 380.
Barrel: 3 11/16″.
Weight: 23 oz. **Length:** 6½″ over-all.
Stocks: Checkered plastic, thumb rest.
Sights: Fixed front, adj. notch rear.
Features: Ventilated rib, manual and grip safeties. Model XV is 22 LR, Model IIIA is 380. Both models have loaded indicator; IIIA is locked breech. Imported from Spain by Stoeger Industries.
Price: Blue, 22 LR,...$290.00
Price: Blue, 32, 380...$299.00
Price: Satin chrome, 22 LR or 380............................$377.00

OMEGA AUTO PISTOL
Caliber: 38 Super (9-shot), 10mm, 45 ACP (7-shot).
Barrel: 5″, 6″.
Weight: 45.3 oz. (6″ barrel).
Stocks: Pachmayr checkered rubber.
Sights: Blade front, fully adjustable rear.
Features: Convertible between calibers; ported barrels. Based on 1911-A1 but with improved barrel lock-up. Introduced 1987. From Springfield Armory.
Price: Single caliber, 38 Super, 10mm or 45 ACP.................$849.00

LLAMA M-82 DA AUTO PISTOL
Caliber: 9mm Para., 15-shot magazine.
Barrel: 4¼″.
Weight: 39 oz. **Length:** 8″ over-all.
Stocks: Matte black polymer.
Sights: Blade front, rear drift adjustable for windage. High visibility three-dot system.
Features: Double-action mechanism; ambidextrous safety. Introduced 1987. Imported from Spain by Stoeger Industries.
Price:...$751.00

PACHMAYR DOMINATOR PISTOL
Caliber: 22 Hornet, 223, 7mm-06, 308, 35 Rem., 45 Rem., 44 Mag., single shot.
Barrel: 10½″ (44 Mag.), 14″ all other calibers.
Weight: 4 lbs. (14″ barrel). **Length:** 16″ over-all (14″ barrel).
Stocks: Pachmayr Signature system.
Sights: None furnished; drilled and tapped for scope mounting.
Features: Bolt-action pistol on 1911A1 frame. Comes as complete gun. Introduced 1988. From Pachmayr.
Price: Either barrel..$524.50

Omega Auto

Partisan Avenger

PARTISAN AVENGER AUTO PISTOL
Caliber: 45 ACP, 30-shot magazine.
Barrel: 6¼″.
Weight: 5 lbs., 7 oz. **Length:** 11″ over-all.
Stocks: Smooth composition.
Sights: Protected blade front, fixed rear.
Features: Semi-auto only. Fires from a closed bolt. Uses standard M-3 "Grease Gun" magazine. Introduced 1988. Made in U.S. From Patriot Dist. Co.
Price:...$445.00

HANDGUNS—AUTOLOADERS, SERVICE & SPORT

RANGER 1911A1 45 AUTO PISTOL
Caliber: 45 ACP, 7-shot magazine.
Barrel: 5".
Weight: 38 oz. **Length:** 8½" over-all.
Stocks: Checkered walnut.
Sights: Glare-proof front, square-notch rear drift-adj. for windage.
Features: Made in U.S. from 4140 steel and other high-strength alloys. Barrel machined from a forged billet. Introduced 1988. From Federal Ordnance, Inc.
Price: Standard model $427.95
Price: With extended slide release and safety $436.95
Price: With ambidextrous slide release and safety $446.95

Ranger 1911A1

RAVEN MP-25 AUTO PISTOL
Caliber: 25 ACP, 6-shot magazine.
Barrel: 2 7/16".
Weight: 15 oz. **Length:** 4¾" over-all.
Stocks: Smooth walnut or ivory-colored plastic.
Sights: Ramped front, fixed rear.
Features: Available in blue, nickel or chrome finish. Made in U.S. Available from Raven Arms.
Price: $69.95

RUGER P-85 AUTOMATIC PISTOL
Caliber: 9mm Para., 15-shot magazine.
Barrel: 4.50".
Weight: 32 oz. **Length:** 7.84" over-all.
Stocks: Grooved "Xenoy" composition.
Sights: Square post front, square notch rear adj. for windage, both with white dot inserts.
Features: Double action with ambidextrous slide-mounted safety which blocks firing pin and disengages firing mechanism. Slide is 4140 chrome-moly steel, frame is a lightweight aluminum alloy, both finished matte black. Ambidextrous magazine release. Introduced 1986.
Price: $295.00
Price: P-85 C (comes with plastic case, extra magazine) ... $325.00

Raven MP-25

Ruger P-85

Ruger Mark II Stainless

RUGER MARK II STANDARD AUTO PISTOL
Caliber: 22 LR, 10-shot magazine.
Barrel: 4¾" or 6".
Weight: 36 oz. (4¾" bbl.). **Length:** 8 5/16" (4¾" bbl.).
Stocks: Checkered hard rubber.
Sights: Fixed, wide blade front, square notch rear adj. for w.
Features: Updated design of the original Standard Auto. Has new bolt hold-open device, 10-shot magazine, magazine catch, safety, trigger and new receiver contours. Introduced 1982.
Price: Blued (MK 4, MK 6) $199.80
Price: In stainless steel (KMK 4, KMK 6) $266.40

SAFARI ARMS MATCHMASTER PISTOL
Caliber: 45 ACP, 6-shot magazine.
Barrel: 5".
Weight: 40 oz. **Length:** 8.7" overall.
Stocks: Checkered plastic.
Sights: Combat adjustable.
Features: Beavertail grip safety, ambidextrous extended safety, extended slide release, combat hammer, threaded barrel bushing; throated, ported, tuned. Finishes: blue, Parkerize, matte. Also available in a lightweight version (30 oz.) and stainless steel. Available from Olympic Arms, Inc.
Price: $595.00

Safari Arms Enforcer Pistol
Shortened version of the Matchmaster. Has 3.8" barrel, over-all length of 7.7", and weighs 40 oz. (standard weight), 27 oz. in lightweight version. Other features are the same. From Olympic Arms, Inc.
Price: $595.00

SEECAMP LWS 32 STAINLESS DA AUTO
Caliber: 32 ACP Win. Silvertip, 6-shot.
Barrel: 2", integral with frame.
Weight: 25 cal. 12 oz., 32 cal. 10.5 oz. **Length:** 4⅛" over-all.
Stocks: Black plastic.
Sights: Smooth, no-snag, contoured slide and barrel top.
Features: Aircraft quality 17-4 PH stainless steel. Inertia operated firing pin. Hammer fired double action only. Hammer automatically follows slide down to safety rest position after each shot—no manual safety needed. Magazine safety disconnector. Polished stainless. Introduced 1980. From L.W. Seecamp.
Price: $290.00

HANDGUNS—AUTOLOADERS, SERVICE & SPORT

SCARAB SKORPION AUTO PISTOL
Caliber: 9mm Parabellum, 32-shot magazine.
Barrel: 4.63".
Weight: 3.5 lbs. **Length:** 12.25" over-all.
Stocks: Stained polymer.
Sights: Fixed, open.
Features: Semi-auto fire only. Ambidextrous cocking knobs. Comes with one magazine, front hangar and leather hand strap, imitation sound suppressor, padded carrying case, flash hider, leather shoulder strap, 22 LR sub-caliber conversion. Made in U.S. Announced 1988. From Armitage International, Ltd.
Price: **$279.50**

Scarab Skorpion

SIG P-210-2 AUTO PISTOL
Caliber: 7.65mm or 9mm Para., 8-shot magazine.
Barrel: 4¾".
Weight: 31¾ oz. (9mm) **Length:** 8½" over-all.
Stocks: Checkered black composition.
Sights: Blade front, rear adjustable for windage.
Features: Lanyard loop; matte finish. Conversion unit for 22 LR available. Imported from Switzerland by Osborne's, SIGARMS and Mandall Shooting Supplies.
Price: P-210-2 Service Pistol (SIGARMS, Mandall) .. **$1,485.00 to $1,895.00**
Price: P-210-2 (Osborne's), about. **$1,400.00**
Price: 22 Cal. Conversion unit (Osborne's), about. **$825.00**

SIG P-210-6 AUTO PISTOL
Caliber: 9mm Para., 8-shot magazine.
Barrel: 4¾".
Weight: 36.2 oz. **Length:** 8½" over-all.
Stocks: Checkered black plastic; walnut optional.
Sights: Blade front, micro. adj. rear for w. & e.
Features: Adjustable trigger stop; target trigger; ribbed front stap; sandblasted finish. Conversion unit for 22 LR consists of barrel, recoil spring, slide and magazine. Imported from Switzerland by Osborne's and SIGARMS, Inc.
Price: P-210-6 (SIGARMS). **$1,754.00**
Price: 22 Cal. Conversion unit (Osborne's) **$1,035.00**
Price: As above, from SIGARMS **$719.00**
Price: P-210-6 (Osborne's). **$1,800.00**

SIG P-210-6

SIG-SAUER P-220 "EUROPEAN" AUTO PISTOL
Caliber: 9mm, 38 Super; 45 ACP. (9-shot in 9mm and 38 Super, 7 in 45).
Barrel: 4⅜".
Weight: 28¼ oz. (9mm). **Length:** 7¾" over-all.
Stocks: Checkered black plastic.
Sights: Blade front, drift adj. rear for w.
Features: Double action. De-cocking lever permits lowering hammer onto locked firing pin. Squared combat-type trigger guard. Slide stays open after last shot. Imported from West Germany by SIGARMS, Inc.
Price: "European" **$632.50**
Price: "American" (side-button magazine release, 45 ACP only) **$687.50**

SIG-SAUER P-225 DA AUTO PISTOL
Caliber: 9mm Parabellum, 8-shot magazine.
Barrel: 3.8".
Weight: 26 oz. **Length:** 7 3/32" over-all.
Stocks: Checkered black plastic.
Sights: Blade front, rear adjustable for windage.
Features: Double action. De-cocking lever permits lowering hammer onto locked firing pin. Squared combat-type trigger guard. Shortened, lightened version of P-220. Imported from West Germany by SIGARMS, Inc.
Price: **$715.00**

SIG-Sauer P-220

SIG-SAUER P-226 DA Auto Pistol
Similar to the P-220 pistol except has 15-shot magazine, 4.4" barrel, and weighs 26½ oz. 9mm only. Imported from West Germany by SIGARMS, Inc.
Price: Blue. **$742.50**
Price: Electroless nickel **$819.50**
Price: K-Kote (Polymer) finish **$764.50**

SIG-SAUER P-230 DA AUTO PISTOL
Caliber: 32 ACP, 8-shot; 380 ACP, 7-shot.
Barrel: 3¾".
Weight: 16 oz. **Length:** 6½" over-all.
Stocks: Checkered black plastic.
Sights: Blade front, rear adj. for w.
Features: Double action. Same basic action design as P-220. Blowback operation, stationary barrel. Introduced 1977. Imported from West Germany by SIGARMS, Inc.
Price: **$495.50**
Price: In stainless steel (P-230 SL). **$577.50**

SIG-Sauer P226

CAUTION: PRICES CHANGE. CHECK AT GUNSHOP.

HANDGUNS—AUTOLOADERS, SERVICE & SPORT

SMITH & WESSON MODEL 422 AUTO
Caliber: 22 LR, 10-shot magazine.
Barrel: 4½", 6".
Weight: 22 oz. (4½" bbl.) **Length:** 7½" over-all (4½" bbl.).
Stocks: Checkered plastic (Field), checkered walnut (Target).
Sights: Field — serrated ramp front, fixed rear; Target — Patrige front, adjustable rear.
Features: Aluminum frame, steel slide, brushed blue finish; internal hammer. Introduced 1987.
Price: 4½", 6", fixed sight. $198.00
Price: As above, adjustable sight $234.50

Smith & Wesson 422

SMITH & WESSON MODEL 439 DOUBLE ACTION
Caliber: 9mm Luger, 8-shot magazine.
Barrel: 4".
Weight: 30 oz. **Length:** 7⅝" over-all.
Stocks: Checkered walnut.
Sights: Serrated ramp front, square notch rear is fully adj. for w. & e. Also available with fixed sights.
Features: Rear sight has protective shields on both sides of the sight blade. Frame is aluminum alloy. Firing pin lock in addition to the regular rotating safety. Magazine disconnector. Comes with two magazines. Ambidextrous safety standard. Introduced 1980.
Price: Blue, from $472.00
Price: Adjustable sight, from $498.50
Price: Model 639 (stainless), from $523.50

Smith & Wesson Model 659

SMITH & WESSON MODEL 459 DOUBLE ACTION
Caliber: 9mm Luger, 14-shot magazine.
Barrel: 4".
Weight: 30 oz. **Length:** 7⅝" over-all.
Stocks: Checkered high-impact nylon.
Sights: ⅛" square serrated ramp front, square notch rear is fully adj. for w. & e. Also available with fixed sights.
Features: Alloy frame. Rear sight has protective shields on both sides of blade. Firing pin lock in addition to the regular safety. Magazine disconnector. Comes with two magazines. Ambidextrous safety standard. Introduced 1980.
Price: Blue, from $501.50
Price: Adjustable sight, from $528.00
Price: Model 659 (stainless), from $553.00

Smith & Wesson Model 469 Mini-Gun
Basically a cut-down version of the Model 459 pistol. Gun has a 3½" barrel, 12-round magazine, over-all length of 6¹³⁄₁₆", and weighs 26 oz. Also accepts the 14-shot Model 459 magazine. Cross-hatch knurling on the recurved-front trigger guard and backstrap; magazine has a curved finger extension; bobbed hammer; sandblast blue finish with pebble-grain grips. Ambidextrous safety standard. Introduced 1983.
Price: $478.50
Price: Stainless Model 669. . . . . $522.50

Smith & Wesson Model 469

Consult our Directory pages for the location of firms mentioned.

SMITH & WESSON MODEL 645 DOUBLE ACTION
Caliber: 45 ACP, 8-shot magazine.
Barrel: 5".
Weight: 37.5 ozs. **Length:** 8⅝" over-all.
Stocks: Checkered high-impact nylon.
Sights: Red ramp front, rear drift-adjustable for windage, or fully adjustable.
Features: Double action. Made of stainless steel. Has manual hammer-drop, magazine disconnect and firing pin safeties. Cross-hatch knurling on the recurved front trigger guard and backstrap; bevelled magazine well. Introduced 1985.
Price: Fixed sight. $622.00
Price: Adjustable sight $649.00

Smith & Wesson Model 645

HANDGUNS—AUTOLOADERS, SERVICE & SPORT

Spectre D/A

SPECTRE DOUBLE ACTION AUTO PISTOL
Caliber: 9mm Para., 30-shot magazine.
Barrel: 8".
Weight: 2.2 lbs. **Length:** 13.7" over-all.
Stocks: Black composition grip.
Sights: Post front, flip rear.
Features: Double action mechanism fires from closed bolt. Introduced 1987. Imported by Mitchell Arms, Inc.
Price: $670.00

SPORTARMS TOKAREV MODEL 213
Caliber: 9mm Parabellum, 8-shot magazine.
Barrel: 4.5".
Weight: 31 oz. **Length:** 7.6" over-all.
Stocks: Grooved plastic.
Sights: Fixed.
Features: Blue finish, hard chrome optional. 9mm version of the famous Russian Tokarev pistol. Made in China by Norinco; imported by Sportarms of Florida. Introduced 1988.
Price: Blue, about $259.75
Price: Hard chrome, about $329.75

SPRINGFIELD ARMORY 1911-A1 AUTO PISTOL
Caliber: 9mm or 45 ACP, 8-shot magazine.
Barrel: 5".
Weight: 2¼ lbs. **Length:** 8½" over-all.
Stocks: NA.
Sights: Blade front, rear drift-adjustable for windage.
Features: All forged parts, including frame, barrel, slide. All new production. Custom slide and parts available. Introduced 1985. From Springfield Armory.
Price: Complete pistol, Parkerized $362.00
Price: Complete pistol, blued $383.00
Price: 45 to 9mm conversion kit, Parkerized $169.00
Price: As above, blued $177.00

Springfield Armory 1911-A1

Springfield Armory 1911-A1 Defender
Similar to the standard 1911-A1 except has fixed combat-style sights, bevelled magazine well, extended thumb safety, bobbed hammer, walnut stocks, serrated front strap, and comes with two stainless steel magazines. Available in 45 ACP only, choice of blue or Parkerized finish. Introduced 1988.
Price: Blue $454.00
Price: Parkerized $434.00

Springfield Armory 1911-A1 Combat Commander
Similar to the standard 1911-A1 except slide and barrel are ½" shorter. Comes with bobbed hammer and walnut stocks. Available in 45 ACP only; choice of blue or Parkerized finish. Introduced 1988.
Price: Blue $467.00
Price: Parkerized $447.00

Springfield Combat Commander

STAR MODEL 30M & 30PK DOUBLE-ACTION PISTOLS
Caliber: 9mm Para., 15-shot magazine.
Barrel: 4.33" (Model M); 3.86" (Model PK).
Weight: 40 oz. (M); 30 oz. (PK). **Length:** 8" over-all (M); 7.6" (PK).
Stocks: Checkered black plastic.
Sights: Square blade front, square notch rear click-adjustable for windage and elevation.
Features: Double or single action; grooved front and backstraps and trigger guard face; ambidextrous safety cams firing pin forward; removable backstrap houses the firing mechanism. Model M has steel frame; Model PK is alloy. Introduced 1984. Imported from Spain by Interarms.
Price: Model M or PK $510.00

STAR BM, BKM AUTO PISTOLS
Caliber: 9mm Para., 8-shot magazine.
Barrel: 3.9".
Weight: 25 oz.
Stocks: Checkered walnut.
Sights: Fixed.
Features: Blue or chrome finish. Magazine and manual safeties, external hammer. Imported from Spain by Interarms.
Price: Blue, BM and BKM $360.00
Price: Chrome, BM only $375.00

Star Model 30 PK

CAUTION: PRICES CHANGE. CHECK AT GUNSHOP.

HANDGUNS—AUTOLOADERS, SERVICE & SPORT

STAR MODEL PD AUTO PISTOL
Caliber: 45 ACP, 6-shot magazine.
Barrel: 3.94".
Weight: 28 oz. **Length:** 7 7/16" over-all.
Stocks: Checkered walnut.
Sights: Ramp front, fully adjustable rear.
Features: Rear sight milled into slide; thumb safety; grooved non-slip front strap; nylon recoil buffer; inertia firing pin; no grip or magazine safeties. Imported from Spain by Interarms.
Price: Blue.. $395.00

Star Model PD Pistol

STEEL CITY "DOUBLE DEUCE" PISTOL
Caliber: 22 LR, 7-shot; 25 ACP, 6-shot.
Barrel: 2½".
Weight: 18 oz. **Length:** 5½" over-all.
Stocks: Rosewood.
Sights: Fixed.
Features: Double-action; stainless steel construction with matte finish; ambidextrous slide-mounted safety. From Steel City Arms, Inc.
Price: 22 or 25 cal $289.95

STEEL CITY "WAR EAGLE" PISTOL
Caliber: 9mm Para., 15-shot magazine.
Barrel: 4", 6".
Weight: NA. **Length:** NA.
Stocks: Rosewood.
Sights: Fixed and adjustable.
Features: Double action; matte-finished stainless steel; ambidextrous safety. Announced 1986.
Price: $550.00

Steel City Double Deuce

TANARMI TA90 DA AUTO PISTOL
Caliber: 9mm Parabellum, 15-shot magazine.
Barrel: 4.75".
Weight: 35 oz. **Length:** 8.25" over-all.
Stocks: Checkered neoprene rubber.
Sights: Blade front, white outline rear.
Features: Improved version of the Czech CZ75. Chrome plated barrel and trigger, extended slide release lever. Available in matte blue or matte chrome. Imported from Italy by Excam.
Price: Matte blue $415.00
Price: Matte chrome $430.00

Tanarmi Baby TA90 Auto Pistol
Similar to the standard TA90 except has ¾" shorter barrel/slide, ½" shorter grip. Barrel length 4", weight is 30 oz., 12-shot magazine.
Price: Matte blue $430.00
Price: Matte chrome $450.00

Tanarmi TA90

TARGA GT380XE PISTOL
Caliber: 380 ACP, 11-shot magazine.
Barrel: 3.88".
Weight: 28 oz. **Length:** 7.38" over-all.
Stocks: Smooth hardwood.
Sights: Adj. for windage.
Features: Blue finish. Ordnance steel. Magazine disconnector, firing pin and thumb safeties. Introduced 1980. Imported by Excam.
Price: 380 cal., blue...................................... $235.00

TARGA MODEL GT27 AUTO PISTOL
Caliber: 25 ACP, 6-shot magazine.
Barrel: 2 7/16".
Weight: 12 oz. **Length:** 4 5/8" over-all.
Stocks: Smooth walnut.
Sights: Fixed.
Features: Safety lever take-down; external hammer with half-cock. Assembled in U.S. by Excam, Inc.
Price: Blue... $75.00
Price: Chrome.. $80.00

Targa GT380XE

HANDGUNS—AUTOLOADERS, SERVICE & SPORT

Targa GT26 Auto Pistol
Similar to the GT27 except has steel frame, push-button magazine release and magazine disconnect safety. Contoured smooth walnut grips. Satin blue finish. Imported from Italy by Excam, assembled in U.S.A.
Price: $115.00

Targa GT26

TARGA MODELS GT22, GT32, GT380 AUTO PISTOLS
Caliber: 22 LR, 10-shot; 32 ACP or 380 ACP, 6-shot magazine.
Barrel: 4⅞".
Weight: 26 oz. **Length:** 7⅜" over-all.
Stocks: Walnut.
Sights: Fixed blade front; rear drift-adj. for w.
Features: Chrome or blue finish; magazine, thumb, and firing pin safeties; external hammer; safety lever take-down. Imported from Italy by Excam, Inc.
Price: 22 cal., blue $200.00
Price: 22 cal., nickel $215.00
Price: 32 cal., blue $200.00
Price: 32 cal., chrome $215.00
Price: 380 cal., blue $212.00
Price: 380 cal., chrome $220.00
Price: 380 cal., chrome, engraved $245.00
Price: 380 cal., blue, engraved $235.00

TARGA GT22T TARGET AUTO
Caliber: 22LR, 12-shot.
Barrel: 6".
Weight: 30 oz. **Length:** 9" over-all.
Stocks: Checkered walnut, with thumbrest.
Sights: Blade on ramp front, rear adjustable for windage.
Features: Blue finish. Finger-rest magaznine. Imported by Excam.
Price: $200.00

Targa GT380

TAURUS MODEL PT-92AF AUTO PISTOL
Caliber: 9mm Para., 15-shot magazine.
Barrel: 4.92".
Weight: 34 oz. **Length:** 8.54" over-all.
Stocks: Brazilian walnut.
Sights: Fixed notch rear. Three-dot sight system.
Features: Double action, exposed hammer, chamber loaded indicator. Inertia firing pin. Blue finish. Imported by Taurus International.
Price: $381.51
Price: Satin nickel finish $393.38

Taurus PT-99AF Auto Pistol
Similar to the PT-92 except has fully adjustable rear sight, smooth Brazilian walnut stocks and is available in polished blue or stain nickel. Introduced 1983.
Price: Polished blue $408.74
Price: Satin nickel $422.23

Taurus PT99AF

TAURUS MODEL PT58 AUTO PISTOL
Caliber: 380 ACP, 13-shot magazine.
Barrel: 4.01".
Weight: 30 oz.
Stocks: Brazilian walnut.
Sights: Integral blade on slide front, notch rear. Three-dot system.
Features: Double action with exposed hammer; inertia firing pin. Introduced 1988. Imported by Taurus International.
Price: Blue $359.90
Price: Satin nickel $366.45

UZI® PISTOL
Caliber: 9mm Parabellum, 45 ACP.
Barrel: 4.5".
Weight: 3.8 lbs. **Length:** 9.45" over-all.
Stocks: Black plastic.
Sights: Post front with white dot, open rear click adjustable for windage and elevation, two white dots..
Features: Semi-auto blow-back action; fires from closed bolt; floating firing pin. Comes in a moulded plastic case with 20-round magazine; 25 and 32-round magazines available. Imported from Israel by Action Arms. Introduced 1984.
Price: $579.00

UZI Pistol

CAUTION: PRICES CHANGE. CHECK AT GUNSHOP.

HANDGUNS—AUTOLOADERS, SERVICE & SPORT

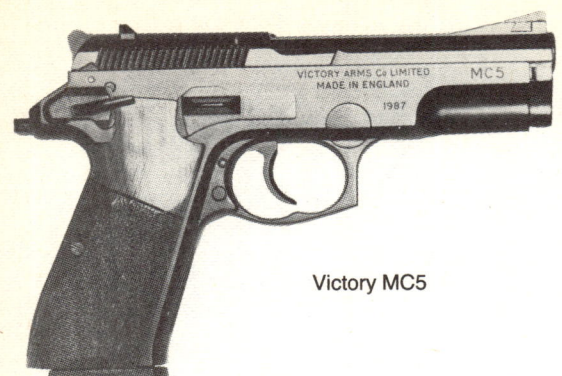

Victory MC5

VICTORY MC5 AUTO PISTOL
Caliber: 9mm Para., 38 Super (17-shot magazine), 41 Action Express (12-shot), 45 ACP (10-shot).
Barrel: 4", 6", 7½", interchangeable.
Weight: 45 oz. **Length:** 8½" over-all (4⅜" barrel).
Stocks: High-impact plastic.
Sights: Patridge three-dot system; ramped non-snag front, rear adjustable for windage with different heights available.
Features: Double-action auto; chamber loaded indicator; exposed hammer; ambidextrous safety, magazine catch, slide release; open-top slide. Introduced 1988. Imported from England by Magnum Research, Inc.
Price: MC5 .... $459.00
Price: Extra barrels $100.00
Price: Extra magazines $25.00

WALTHER PP AUTO PISTOL
Caliber: 22 LR, 8-shot; 32 ACP, 380 ACP, 7-shot.
Barrel: 3.86".
Weight: 23½ oz. **Length:** 6.7" over-all.
Stocks: Checkered plastic.
Sights: Fixed, white markings.
Features: Double action; manual safety blocks firing pin and drops hammer; chamber loaded indicator on 32 and 380; extra finger rest magazine provided. Imported from Germany by Interarms.
Price: 22 LR $815.00
Price: 32 .... $795.00
Price: 380 .... $815.00
Price: Engraved models .... On Request

Walther PP Auto Pistol

Walther American PPK Auto Pistol
Similar to Walther PPK/S except weighs 21 oz., has 6-shot capacity. Made in the U.S. Introduced 1986.
Price: Stainless, 380 ACP only $515.00
Price: Blue, 380 ACP only $515.00

Walther American PPK/S Auto Pistol
Similar to Walther PP except made entirely in the United States. Has 3.27" barrel with 6.1" length over-all. Introduced 1980.
Price: 380 ACP only $515.00
Price: As above, stainless $515.00

WALTHER P-38 AUTO PISTOL
Caliber: 22 LR, 9mm Para., 8-shot.
Barrel: 4¹⁵⁄₁₆" (9mm), 5¹⁄₁₆" (22 LR).
Weight: 28 oz. **Length:** 8½" over-all.
Stocks: Checkered plastic.
Sights: Fixed.
Features: Double action; safety blocks firing pin and drops hammer; chamber loaded indicator. Matte finish standard, polished blue, engraving and/or plating available. Imported from Germany by Interarms.
Price: 22 LR $995.00
Price: 9mm $895.00
Price: Steel frame $1,225.00
Price: Engraved models .... On Request

Walther P-38 Auto Pistol

Walther P-5 Auto Pistol
Latest Walther design that uses the basic P-38 double-action mechanism. Caliber 9mm Para., barrel length 3½"; weight 28 oz., over-all length 7".
Price: $999.00

WALTHER P-88 AUTO PISTOL
Caliber: 9mm Para., 15-shot magazine.
Barrel: 4".,
Weight: 31½ oz. **Length:** 7⅜" over-all.
Stocks: Checkered black composition.
Sights: Blade front, rear adj. for w. and e.
Features: Double action with ambidextrous decocking lever and magazine release; alloy frame; loaded chamber indicator; matte finish. Imported from Germany by Interarms.
Price: $1,165.00

WALTHER MODEL TPH AUTO PISTOL
Caliber: 22 LR, 6-shot magazine.
Barrel: 2¼".
Weight: 14 oz. **Length:** 5⅜" over-all
Stocks: Checkered black composition.
Sights: Blade front, rear drift-adjustable for windage.
Features: Made of stainless steel. Scaled-down version of the Walther PP/PPK series. Made in U.S. Introduced 1987. From Interarms.
Price: $350.00

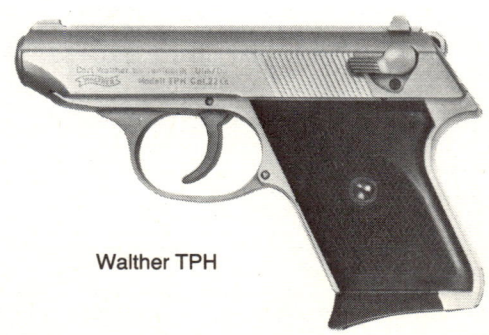

Walther TPH

HANDGUNS—AUTOLOADERS, SERVICE & SPORT

Wildey Auto

WILDEY AUTOMATIC PISTOL
Caliber: 9mm Win. Mag., 45 Win. Mag., 475 Wildey Mag., 357 Peterbuilt.
Barrel: 5″, 6″, 7″, 8″ (45 Win. Mag.); 8″, 10″ (475 Wildey Mag.). Interchangeable.
Weight: 64 oz. (5″ barrel). **Length:** 11″ over-all (7″ barrel).
Stocks: Checkered hardwood.
Sights: Ramp front, fully adjustable rear.
Features: Gas-operated action. Made of stainless steel. Has three-lug rotary bolt. Double action. Made in U.S. by Wildey, Inc.
Price: $895.00

WILKINSON "LINDA" PISTOL
Caliber: 9mm Para., 31-shot magazine.
Barrel: 8⁵⁄₁₆″.
Weight: 4 lbs., 13 oz. **Length:** 12¼″ over-all.
Stocks: Checkered black plastic pistol grip, maple fore-end.
Sights: Protected blade front, aperture rear.
Features: Fires from closed bolt. Semi-auto only. Straight blowback action. Cross-bolt safety. Removable barrel. From Wilkinson Arms.
Price: $324.93

Wilkinson "Sherry"

WILKINSON "SHERRY" AUTO PISTOL
Caliber: 22 LR, 8-shot magazine.
Barrel: 2⅛″.
Weight: 9¼ oz. **Length:** 4⅜″ over-all.
Stocks: Checkered black plastic.
Sights: Fixed, groove.
Features: Cross-bolt safety locks the sear into the hammer. Available in all blue finish or blue slide and trigger with gold frame. Introduced 1985.
Price: $149.95

COMPETITION HANDGUNS

Models specifically designed for classic competitive shooting sports.

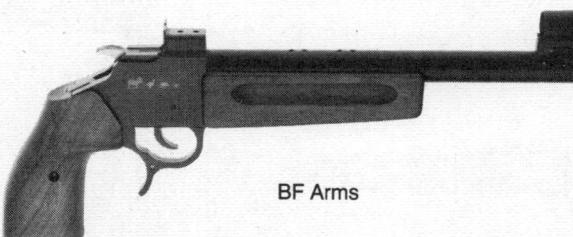

BF Arms

B F ARMS SINGLE SHOT PISTOL
Caliber: 7mm Super Mag., 7mm/375 Super Mag., 32-20, 30 Herrett, 357 Mag., 357 Max.
Barrel: 10″.
Weight: 46 oz.
Stocks: Ambidextrous, oil-finished walnut with fore-end.
Sights: Hooded front, fully adjustable match rear.
Features: Falling block short-stroke action. Wilson air-gauged match-grade barrel. Flat black oxide finish. Drilled and tapped for standard scope mounts. Made in U.S. by B F Arms. Introduced 1988.
Price: Silhouette, with sights $285.00
Price: Hunter, no sights $259.50

Beeman/Unique 69

BEEMAN/UNIQUE D.E.S. 69 TARGET PISTOL
Caliber: 22 LR, 5-shot magazine.
Barrel: 5.91″.
Weight: 35.3 oz. **Length:** 10.5″ over-all.
Stocks: French walnut target-style with thumbrest and adjustable shelf; hand-checkered panels.
Sights: Ramp front, micro. adj. rear mounted on frame; 8.66″ sight radius.
Features: Meets U.I.T. standards. Comes with 260-gram barrel weight; 100, 150, 350 gram weights available. Fully adjustable match trigger; dry firing safety device. Imported from France by Beeman.
Price: Right-hand $1,065.00
Price: Left-hand $1,060.00

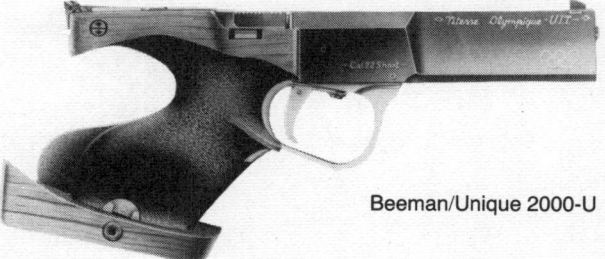

Beeman/Unique 2000-U

BEEMAN/UNIQUE MODEL 2000-U MATCH PISTOL
Caliber: 22 Short, 5-shot magazine.
Barrel: 5.9″.
Weight: 43 oz. **Length:** 11.3″ over-all.
Stocks: Anatomically shaped, adjustable, stippled French walnut.
Sights: Blade front, fully adjustable rear; 9.7″ sight radius.
Features: Light alloy frame, steel slide and shock absorber; five barrel vents reduce recoil, three of which can be blocked; trigger adjustable for position and pull weight. Comes with 340-gram weight housing, 160-gram available. Imported from France by Beeman. Introduced 1984.
Price: Right-hand $1,198.00
Price: Left-hand $1,260.00

CAUTION: PRICES CHANGE. CHECK AT GUNSHOP.

COMPETITION HANDGUNS

Bernardelli Model 69

Chipmunk Silhouette

BERNARDELLI MODEL 69 TARGET PISTOL
Caliber: 22 LR, 10-shot magazine.
Barrel: 5.9″.
Weight: 38 oz. **Length:** 9″ over-all.
Stocks: Wrap around, hand-checkered walnut with thumbrest.
Sights: Fully adjustable and interchangeable target-type.
Features: Conforms to U.I.T. regulations. Has 7.1″ sight radius, .27″ wide grooved trigger with 40-45 oz. pull. Manual thumb safety and magazine safety. Introduced 1987. From Mandall Shooting Supplies.
Price: $289.95

CHIPMUNK SILHOUETTE PISTOL
Caliber: 22 LR.
Barrel: 14⅞″.
Weight: About 2 lbs. **Length:** 20″ over-all.
Stock: American walnut rear grip.
Sights: Post on ramp front, peep rear.
Features: Meets IHMSA 22-cal. unlimited category for competition. Introduced 1985.
Price: $149.95

COLT GOLD CUP NAT'L MATCH MK IV/Series 80
Caliber: 45 ACP, 7-shot magazine.
Barrel: 5″, with new design bushing.
Weight: 39 oz. **Length:** 8½″.
Stocks: Blue—Checkered walnut, gold plated medallion; stainless has black walnut.
Sights: Ramp-style front, Colt-Elliason rear adj. for w. and e., sight radius 6¾″.
Features: Arched or flat housing; wide, grooved trigger with adj. stop; ribbed-top slide, hand fitted, with improved ejection port.
Price: Blue $729.95
Price: Stainless $783.95
Price: Bright stainless $835.95

Colt Gold Cup Series 80

COMPETITOR SINGLE SHOT PISTOL
Caliber: 22 LR, 223, 7mm TCU, 7mm Int., 30 Herrett, 357 Maximum, 41 Mag., 44 Mag., 454 Casull, 375 Super Mag. Others on special order.
Barrel: 10.5″, 14″.
Weight: NA **Length:** NA
Stocks: Smooth walnut with thumb rest.
Sights: Ramp front, open adjustable rear.
Features: Interchangeable barrels of blue ordnance or bright stainless steel; ventilated barrel shroud; receiver has integral scope mount. Introduced 1987. From Competition Arms, Inc.
Price: With 10.5″ bbl. $562.50
Price: With 14″ bbl. $578.50
Price: Extra barrels, 10.5″, standard calibers $93.75
Price: Special calibers, add $62.50

Competitor Single Shot

DETONICS SCOREMASTER TARGET PISTOL
Caliber: 45 ACP, 451 Detonics Magnum, 7-shot magazine.
Barrel: 5″ heavy match barrel with recessed muzzle; 6″ optional.
Weight: 42 oz. **Length:** 8⅜″ over-all.
Stocks: Pachmayr checkered with matching mainspring housing.
Sights: Blade front, Low-Base Bomar rear.
Features: Stainless steel; self-centering barrel system; patented Detonics recoil system; combat tuned; ambidextrous safety; extended grip safety; National Match tolerances; extended magazine release. Comes with two spare magazines, three interchangeable front sights, and carrying case. Introduced 1983. From Detonics.
Price: 45 ACP or 451 Mag., 6″ barrel $1,150.00
Price: As above, 5″ barrel $1,110.00

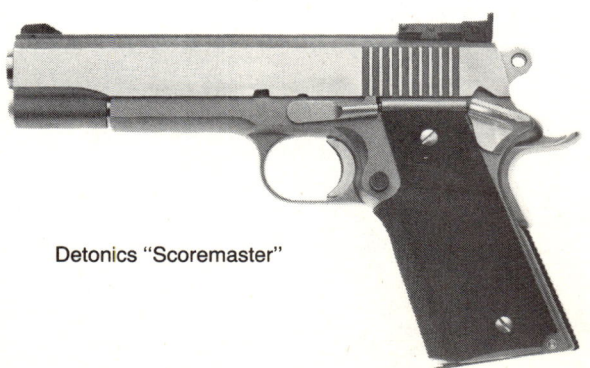

Detonics "Scoremaster"

Detonics Janus Scoremaster Pistol
Similar to the standard Scoremaster except in 45 ACP only and comes with extra 5.6″ compensated barrel and is easily convertible. With longer barrel, the front sight is mounted on the specialist compensator. Over-all length with 5.6″ barrel is 10″, weight is 46 oz. Adjustable Millett rear sight, hand-serrated custom front. Has 8-shot magazine. Made of stainless steel with polished slide flats. Introduced 1988.
Price: $1,650.00

COMPETITION HANDGUNS

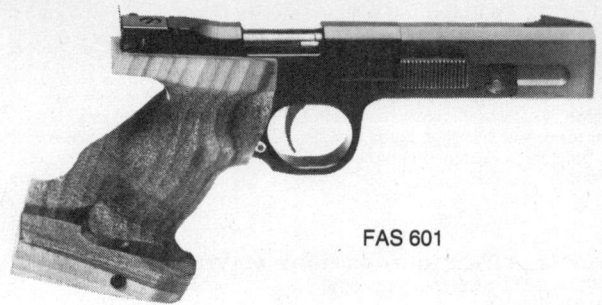

FAS 601

FAS 602 MATCH PISTOL
Caliber: 22 LR, 5-shot.
Barrel: 5.6".
Weight: 37 oz. **Length:** 11" over-all.
Stocks: Walnut wrap-around; sizes small, medium or large, or adjustable.
Sights: Match. Blade front, open notch rear fully adj. for w. and e. Sight radius is 8.66".
Features: Line of sight is only 11/32" above centerline of bore; magazine is inserted from top; adjustable and removable trigger mechanism; single lever takedown. Full 5 year warranty. Imported from Italy by Mandall and Osborne's.
Price: From Osborne's, about $895.00
Price: From Mandall....................................... $1,095.00

FAS 601 Match Pistol
Similar to SP 602 except has different match stocks with adj. palm, shelf, 22 Short only for rapid fire shooting; weighs 40 oz., 5.6" bbl.; has gas ports through top of barrel and slide to reduce recoil; slightly different trigger and sear mechanisms.
Price: From Osborne's, 601, 603, about...................... $1,050.00
Price: From Mandall....................................... $1,095.00

HAMMERLI MODEL 150 FREE PISTOL
Caliber: 22 LR, single shot.
Barrel: 11.3".
Weight: 43 ozs. **Length:** 15.35" over-all.
Stocks: Walnut with adjustable palm shelf.
Sights: Sight radius of 14.6". Micro rear sight adj. for w. and e.
Features: Single shot Martini action. Cocking lever on left side of action with vertical operation. Set trigger adjustable for length and angle. Trigger pull weight adjustable between 5 and 100 grams. Guaranteed accuracy of .78", 10 shots from machine rest. Imported from Switzerland by Osborne's, Mandall Shooting Supplies and Beeman.
Price: About (Mandall)... $1,699.50
Price: With electric trigger (Model 152), about (Mandall)......... $1,799.50
Price: Model 150 (Osborne's).................................. $1,850.00
Price: Model 152 (Osborne's).................................. $1,980.00
Price: Model 150 (Beeman, right hand)......................... $1,980.00
Price: Model 152 (Beeman, right hand)......................... $2,105.00

Hammerli 152

Hammerli 208

HAMMERLI STANDARD, MODELS 208, 211, 215
Caliber: 22 LR.
Barrel: 5.9", 6-groove.
Weight: 37.6 oz. (45 oz. with extra heavy barrel weight). **Length:** 10".
Stocks: Walnut. Adj. palm rest (208), 211 has thumbrest grip.
Sights: Match sights, fully adj. for w. and e. (click adj.). Interchangeable front and rear blades.
Features: Semi-automatic, recoil operated. 8-shot clip. Slide stop. Fully adj. trigger (2¼ lbs. and 3 lbs.). Extra barrel weight available. Imported from Switzerland by Osborne's, Mandall Shooting Supplies, Beeman.
Price: Model 208, approx. (Mandall)........................... $1,399.50
Price: Model 211, approx. (Mandall)........................... $1,295.00
Price: Model 215, approx. (Mandall)........................... $1,295.00
Price: Model 208 (Osborne's), about........................... $1,555.00
Price: Model 211 (Osborne's), about........................... $1,515.00
Price: Model 215 (Osborne's), about........................... $1,226.00
Price: Model 208 (Beeman)................................... $1,580.00
Price: Model 211 (Beeman)................................... $1,413.00
Price: Model 215 (Beeman)................................... $1,175.00

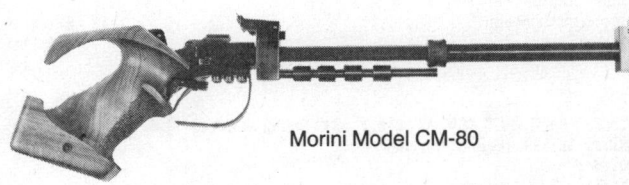

Morini Model CM-80

HAMMERLI MODEL 232 RAPID FIRE PISTOL
Caliber: 22 Short, 6-shot.
Barrel: 5", with six exhaust ports.
Weight: 44 oz. **Length:** 10.4" over-all.
Stocks: Stippled walnut; wraparound on Model 232-2, adjustable on 232-1.
Sights: Interchangeable front and rear blades, fully adjustable micrometer rear.
Features: Recoil operated semi-automatic; nearly recoilless design; trigger adjustable from 8.4 to 10.6 oz. with three lengths offered. Wraparound grips available in small, medium and large sizes. Imported from Switzerland by Osborne's, Beeman, Mandall. Introduced 1984.
Price: Model 232-1, (Osborne's), about........................ $1,285.00
Price: Model 232-2, (Osborne's), about........................ $1,330.00
Price: Model 232-1 (Beeman)................................. $1,300.00
Price: Model 232-2 (Beeman)................................. $1,490.00

MORINI MODEL CM-80 SUPER COMPETITION
Caliber: 22 Long Rifle, single shot.
Barrel: 10", free floating.
Weight: 30 oz., with weights. **Length:** 21.25" over-all.
Stocks: Walnut, adjustable or wrap-around in three sizes.
Sights: Match; square notch rear adjustable for w. and e.; up to 15.6" radius.
Features: Adjustable grip/frame angle, adjustable barrel alignment, adjustable trigger weight (5 to 120 grams), adjustable sight radius. Comes with 20-shot test target (50 meters) and case. Introduced 1985. Imported from Italy by Osborne's.
Price: Standard... $1,100.00
Price: Deluxe... $1,400.00

CAUTION: PRICES CHANGE. CHECK AT GUNSHOP.

COMPETITION HANDGUNS

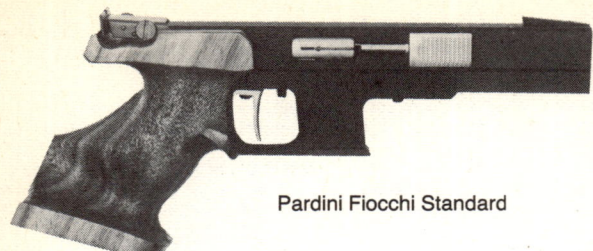
Pardini Fiocchi Standard

PARDINI FIOCCHI STANDARD PISTOL
Caliber: 22 LR, 5-shot magazine.
Barrel: 4.9".
Weight: 37 ozs. **Length:** 11.7" over-all.
Stocks: Match-type stippled walnut.
Sights: Match-type undercut blade front, fully adjustable open rear.
Features: Match trigger. Matte blue finish. Comes with locking case. Imported from Italy by Fiocchi of America.
Price: $868.75

PARDINI FIOCCHI RAPID FIRE MATCH
Caliber: 22 Short, 5-shot magazine.
Barrel: 5.1".
Weight: 34.5 ozs. **Length:** 11.7" over-all.
Stocks: Stippled walnut, match-type.
Sights: Post front, fully adjustable rear.
Features: Alloy bolt. Has 14.9" sight radius. Imported from Italy by Fiocchi of America.
Price: $893.75

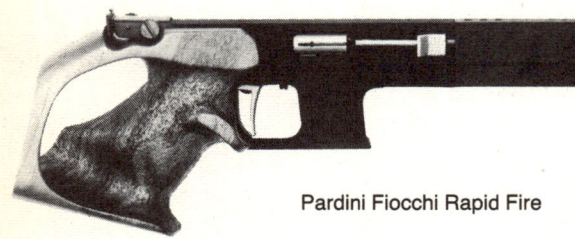
Pardini Fiocchi Rapid Fire

PARDINI FIOCCHI 32 MATCH PISTOL
Caliber: 32 S&W Long, 5-shot magazine.
Barrel: 4.9".
Weight: 38.7 ozs. **Length:** 11.7" over-all.
Stocks: Stippled walnut match-type with adjustable palm shelf.
Sights: Match. Undercut blade front, fully adjustable open rear.
Features: Match trigger. Recoil compensation system. Imported from Italy by Fiocchi of Amercica.
Price: $906.25

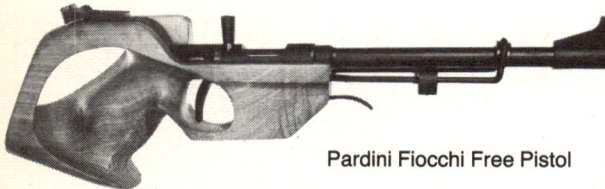
Pardini Fiocchi Free Pistol

PARDINI FIOCCHI FREE PISTOL
Caliber: 22 LR, single shot.
Barrel: 4.9".
Weight: 37 ozs. **Length:** 11.7" over-all.
Stocks: Walnut, special hand-fitting free-pistol design.
Sights: Post front, fully adjustable open rear.
Features: Rotating bolt-action design. Has 8.6" sight radius. Imported from Italy by Fiocchi of America.
Price: $962.50

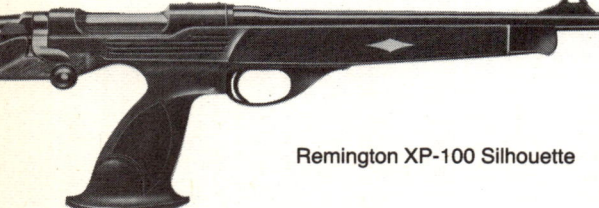
Remington XP-100 Silhouette

REMINGTON XP-100 SILHOUETTE PISTOL
Caliber: 7mm BR Remington, 35 Remington, single shot.
Barrel: 14¾".
Weight: 4⅛ lbs. **Length:** 21¼" over-all.
Stock: Brown nylon, one piece, checkered grip.
Sights: None furnished. Drilled and tapped for scope mounts.
Features: Universal grip fits right or left hand; match-type grooved trigger, two-position thumb safety.
Price: 7mm BR Rem $380.00
Price: 35 Rem $393.00

Ruger Government Target

RUGER MARK II TARGET MODEL AUTO PISTOL
Caliber: 22 LR, 10-shot magazine.
Barrel: 6⅞".
Weight: 42 oz. **Length:** 11⅛" over-all.
Stocks: Checkered hard rubber.
Sights: .125" blade front, micro click rear, adjustable for w. and e. Sight radius 9⅜". Introduced 1982.
Price: Blued (MK-678) $249.75
Price: Stainless (KMK-678) $316.35

Ruger Mark II Bull Barrel
Same gun as the Target Model except has 5½" or 10" heavy barrel (10" meets all IHMSA regulations). Weight with 5½" barrel is 42 oz., with 10" barrel, 52 oz.
Price: Blued (MK-512, MK-10) $249.75
Price: Stainless (KMK-512, KMK-10) $316.35

Ruger Mark II Government Target Model
Same gun as the Mark II Target Model except has higher sights and is roll marked "Government Target Model" on the right side of the receiver below the rear sight. Identical in all respects to the military model used for training U.S. armed forces except for markings. Comes with factory test target. Introduced 1987.
Price: Blued (MK678G) $288.60

COMPETITION HANDGUNS

SAKO TRIACE MATCH PISTOL
Caliber: 22 Short, 22 Long Rifle, 32 S&W Long, 6-shot magazine.
Barrel: 5.9″.
Weight: 44.3 oz. to 48.3 oz. (depending on caliber). **Length:** 11.0″ over-all.
Stocks: Fully adjustable walnut.
Sights: Blade front, micrometer adjustable rear.
Features: Semi-auto match pistol comes in three calibers. Trigger is adjustable for sear engagement, weight of pull, free travel and position. Comes with carrying case, tool/cleaning kit, two magazines. Imported from Finland. Available from Osborne's
Price: Three-caliber system, about $2,800.00

Smith & Wesson 29 Silhouette

SMITH & WESSON MODEL 29 SILHOUETTE
Caliber: 44 Magnum, 6-shot.
Barrel: 10⅝″.
Weight: 58 oz. **Length:** 16³⁄₁₆″ over-all.
Stocks: Over-size target-type, checkered Goncalo Alves.
Sights: Four-position front to match the four distances of silhouette targets; micro-click rear adjustable for windage and elevation.
Features: Designed specifically for silhouette shooting. Front sight has click stops for the four pre-set ranges. Introduced 1983.
Price: $510.00

SMITH & WESSON 22 AUTO PISTOL MODEL 41
Caliber: 22 LR, 10-shot clip.
Barrel: 7″.
Weight: 43½ oz. **Length:** 12″ over-all.
Stocks: Checkered walnut with thumbrest, usable with either hand.
Sights: Front, ⅛″ Patridge undercut; micro click rear adj. for w. and e.
Features: ⅜″ wide, grooved trigger with adj. stop.
Price: S&W Bright Blue $536.00

Smith & Wesson Model 41

SMITH & WESSON 38 MASTER MODEL 52 AUTO
Caliber: 38 Special (for mid-range W.C. with flush-seated bullet only), 5-shot magazine.
Barrel: 5″.
Weight: 40.5 oz. with empty magazine. **Length:** 8⅝″ over-all.
Stocks: Checkered walnut.
Sights: ⅛″ Patridge front, S&W micro click rear adj. for w. and e.
Features: Top sighting surfaces matte finished. Locked breech, moving barrel system; checked for 10-ring groups at 50 yards. Coin-adj. sight screws. Dry firing permissible if manual safety on.
Price: S&W Bright Blue $694.00

SMITH & WESSON 22 MATCH HEAVY BARREL M-41
Caliber: 22 LR, 10-shot clip.
Barrel: 5½″ heavy.
Weight: 44½ oz. **Length:** 9″ over-all.
Stocks: Checkered walnut with modified thumbrest, usable with either hand.
Sights: ⅛″ Patridge on ramp base. S&W micro click rear adj. for w. and e.
Features: ⅜″ wide, grooved trigger; adj. trigger stop.
Price: S&W Bright Blue, satin matted top area $536.00

SMITH & WESSON MODEL 745 AUTO
Caliber: 45 ACP, 8-shot magazine.
Barrel: 5″.
Weight: 38.75 oz. **Length:** 8⅝″ over-all.
Stocks: Checkered walnut.
Sights: Serrated ramp front, square notch high visibility rear adj. for w.
Features: Stainless steel frame, blued slide, hammer, trigger, sights. Comes with two magazines. Introduced 1987.
Price: $699.00

Smith & Wesson Model 52

Sokolovsky Automaster

SOKOLOVSKY 45 AUTOMASTER
Caliber: 45 ACP, 6-shot magazine.
Barrel: 6″.
Weight: 3.6 lbs. **Length:** 9½″ over-all.
Stocks: Smooth walnut.
Sights: Ramp front, Millett fully adjustable rear.
Features: Intended for target shooting, not combat. Semi-custom built with precise tolerances. Has special "safety trigger" next to regular trigger. Most parts made of stainless steel. Introduced 1985. From Sokolovsky Corp.
Price: $4,500.00

CAUTION: PRICES CHANGE. CHECK AT GUNSHOP.

COMPETITION HANDGUNS

TAURUS MODEL 86 MASTER REVOLVER
Caliber: 38 Spec., 6-shot.
Barrel: 6" only.
Weight: 34 oz. **Length:** 11¼" over-all.
Stocks: Over-size target-type, checkered Brazilian walnut.
Sights: Patridge front, micro. click rear adj. for w. and e.
Features: Blue finish with non-reflective finish on barrel. Imported from Brazil by Taurus International.
Price: $257.38
Price: Model 96 Scout Master, same except in 22 cal. $257.38

Taurus Model 86 Master

Thompson/Center Super 14 Contender

THOMPSON/CENTER SUPER 14 CONTENDER
Caliber: 22 LR, 222 Rem., 223 Rem., 6mm TCU, 7mm TCU, 7 x 30 Waters, 30-30 Win., 35 Rem., 357 Rem. Maximum, 44 Mag., single shot.
Barrel: 14".
Weight: 45 oz. **Length:** 17¼" over-all.
Stocks: T/C "Competitor Grip" (walnut and rubber).
Sights: Fully adjustable target-type.
Features: Break-open action with auto safety. Interchangeable barrels for both rimfire and centerfire calibers. Introduced 1978.
Price: $345.00
Price: With Armour Alloy II finish $415.00
Price: Extra barrels, blued $155.00
Price: As Above, Armour Alloy $195.00

UBERTI "PHANTOM" SA SILHOUETTE
Caliber: 357 Mag., 44 Mag.
Barrel: 10½".
Weight: NA. **Length:** NA.
Stocks: Walnut target-style.
Sights: Blade on ramp front, fully adj. rear.
Features: Hooked trigger guard. Introduced 1986. Imported by Benson Firearms, Uberti USA.
Price: $539.00

WALTHER FREE PISTOL
Caliber: 22 LR, single shot.
Barrel: 11.7".
Weight: 48 ozs. **Length:** 17.2" over-all.
Stocks: Walnut, special hand-fitting design.
Sights: Fully adjustable match sights.
Features: Special electronic trigger. Matte finish blue. Introduced 1980. Imported from Germany by Interarms.
Price: $1,750.00

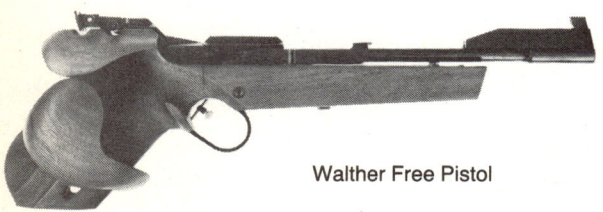
Walther Free Pistol

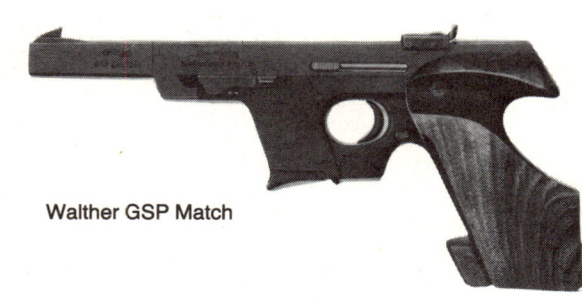
Walther GSP Match

WALTHER GSP MATCH PISTOL
Caliber: 22 LR, 32 S&W wadcutter (GSP-C), 5-shot.
Barrel: 5¾".
Weight: 44.8 oz. (22 LR), 49.4 oz. (32). **Length:** 11.8" over-all.
Stocks: Walnut, special hand-fitting design.
Sights: Fixed front, rear adj. for w. & e.
Features: Available with either 2.2 lb. (1000 gm) or 3 lb. (1360 gm) trigger. Spare mag., bbl. weight, tools supplied in Match Pistol Kit. Imported from Germany by Interarms.
Price: GSP $1,300.00
Price: GSP-C $1,500.00
Price: 22 LR conversion unit for GSP-C $800.00
Price: 22 Short conversion unit for GSP-C $825.00
Price: 32 S&W conversion unit for GSP-C $975.00

Walther OSP Rapid-Fire Pistol
Similar to Model GSP except 22 Short only, stock has adj. free-style hand rest.
Price: $1,475.00

DAN WESSON MODEL 40 SILHOUETTE
Caliber: 357 Maximum, 6-shot.
Barrel: 6", 8", 10".
Weight: 64 oz. (8" bbl.) **Length:** 14.3" over-all (8" bbl.).
Stocks: Smooth walnut, target-style.
Sights: ⅛" serrated front, fully adj. rear.
Features: Meets criteria for IHMSA competition with 8" slotted barrel. Blue or stainless steel.
Price: Blue, 6" $508.32
Price: Blue, 8" $525.19
Price: Blue, 10" $543.41
Price: Stainless, 6" $568.97
Price: Stainless, 8" slotted $595.13
Price: Stainless, 10" $609.03

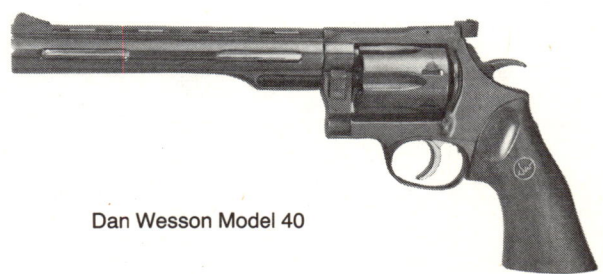
Dan Wesson Model 40

COMPETITION HANDGUNS

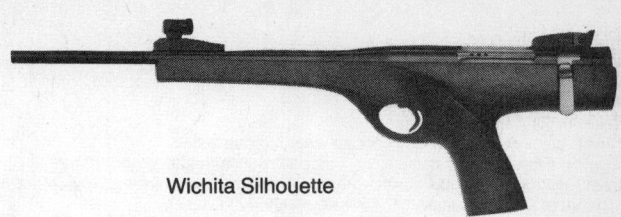
Wichita Silhouette

WICHITA SILHOUETTE PISTOL
Caliber: 22-250, 7mm IHMSA, 308. Other calibers available on special order. Single shot.
Barrel: 14 15/16".
Weight: 4½ lbs. **Length:** 21 3/8" over-all.
Stocks: American walnut with oil finish. Glass bedded.
Sights: Wichita Multi-Range sight system.
Features: Comes with left-hand action with right-hand grip. Fluted bolt, flat bolt handle. Action drilled and tapped for Burris scope mounts. Non-glare satin blue finish. Wichita adjustable trigger. Introduced 1979. From Wichita Arms.
Price: Center grip stock $900.00
Price: As above except with Rear Position Stock and target-type Lightpull trigger $975.00

WICHITA MK-40 SILHOUETTE PISTOL
Caliber: 22-250, 7mm IHMSA, 308 Win. F.L. Other calibers available on special order. Single shot.
Barrel: 13", non-glare blue; .700" dia. muzzle.
Weight: 4½ lbs. **Length:** 19 3/8" over-all.
Stocks: American walnut with oil finish.
Sights: Wichita Multi-Range sighting system.
Features: Aluminum receiver with steel insert locking lugs, measures 1.360" O.D.; three locking lug bolts, three gas ports; flat bolt handle; completely adjustable Wichita trigger. Introduced 1981. From Wichita Arms.
Price: $800.00

WICHITA CLASSIC PISTOL
Caliber: Any, up to and including 308 Win.
Barrel: 11¼", octagon.
Weight: About 5 lbs.
Stocks: Exhibition grade American black walnut. Checkered 20 lpi. Other woods available on special order.
Sights: Micro open sights standard. Receiver drilled and tapped for scope mount.
Features: Receiver and barrel octagonally shaped, finished in non-glare blue. Bolt has three locking lugs and three gas escape ports. Completely adjustable Wichita trigger. Introduced 1980. From Wichita Arms.
Price: $2,950.00
Price: Engraved, in walnut presentation case $4,850.00

WICHITA HUNTER, INTERNATIONAL PISTOL
Caliber: 22 LR, 22 Mag., 7mm INT-R, 7x30 Waters, 30-30 Win., 32 H&R Mag., 357 Mag., 357 Super Mag., single shot.
Barrel: 10½".
Weight: International — 3 lbs., 13 oz.; Hunter — 3 lbs., 14 oz.
Stocks: Walnut grip and fore-end.
Sights: International — target front, adjustable rear; Hunter has scope mount only.
Features: Made of 17-4PH stainless steel. Break-open action. Grip dimensions same as Colt 45 auto. Safety supplied only on Hunter model. Extra barrels are factory fitted. Introduced 1983. Available from Wichita Arms.
Price: International $484.95
Price: Hunter $484.95
Price: Extra barrels $265.00

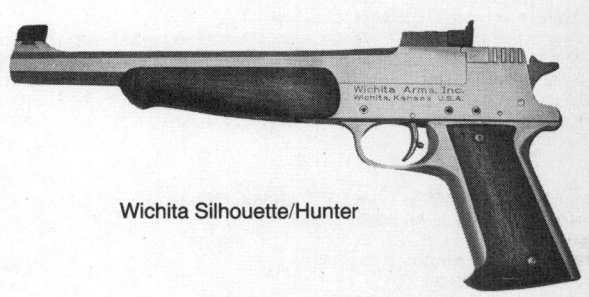
Wichita Silhouette/Hunter

HANDGUNS—DOUBLE ACTION REVOLVERS, SERVICE & SPORT

Includes models suitable for hunting and competitive courses for fire, both police and international.

Armscor 38

ARMSCOR 38 REVOLVER
Caliber: 38 Spec.
Barrel: 4".
Weight: 32 oz.
Stocks: Checkered Philippine mahogany.
Sights: Ramp front, rear adj. for windage.
Features: Ventilated rib; polished blue finish. Introduced 1986. Imported from the Philippines by Pacific International Merchandising Corp.
Price: $139.95

ASTRA 357 MAGNUM REVOLVER
Caliber: 357 Magnum, 6-shot.
Barrel: 4", 6", 8½".
Weight: 40 oz. (6" bbl.) **Length:** 11¼" (6" bbl.).
Stocks: Checkered walnut.
Sights: Fixed front, rear adj. for w. and e.
Features: Swing-out cylinder with countersunk chambers, floating firing pin. Target-type hammer and trigger. Imported from Spain by Interarms.
Price: 4", 6" $295.00
Price: 8½" $305.00

Astra Model 44, 45 Double Action Revolver
Similar to the 357 Mag. except chambered for 44 Mag. or 45 Colt. Barrel length of 6" only, giving over-all length of 11 3/8". Weight is 2¾ lbs. Introduced 1980.
Price: 44 Mag., 6", stainless. $425.00

CAUTION: PRICES CHANGE. CHECK AT GUNSHOP.

HANDGUNS—DOUBLE ACTION REVOLVERS, SERVICE & SPORT

CHARTER ARMS POLICE BULLDOG
Caliber: 32 H&R Mag., 38 Special, 6-shot.
Barrel: 4", 4" straight taper bull.
Weight: 21 oz. **Length:** 9" over-all.
Stocks: Hand checkered American walnut; square butt.
Sights: Patridge-type ramp front, notched rear (adjustable on 32 Mag.).
Features: Spring loaded unbreakable beryllium copper firing pin; steel frame; accepts +P ammunition; full length ejection of fired cases.
Price: Blue, 32 Mag. $208.00
Price: Blue, 38 Spec. $201.00
Price: Stainless steel, 38 Spec. only $263.00

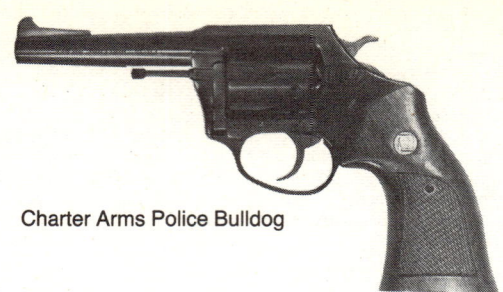
Charter Arms Police Bulldog

CHARTER ARMS BULLDOG
Caliber: 44 Special, 5-shot.
Barrel: 2½", 3".
Weight: 19 oz. **Length:** 7¾" over-all.
Stocks: Checkered walnut, Bulldog.
Sights: Patridge-type front, square-notch rear.
Features: Wide trigger and hammer; beryllium copper firing pin.
Price: Service Blue 3" $211.00
Price: Stainless steel $267.00
Price: Service blue, 2½" $211.00
Price: Stainless steel, 2½" $270.00
Price: Stainless steel, 3", neoprene grips $267.00

Charter Arms Bulldog Tracker
Similar to the standard Bulldog except chambered for 357 Mag., has adjustable rear sight, 2½", 4" or 6" bull barrel, ramp front sight, square butt checkered walnut grips on 4" and 6"; Bulldog-style grips on 2½". Available in blue finish only.
Price: $214.00

Charter Arms Stainless Bulldog

CHARTER ARMS TARGET BULLDOG
Caliber: 357 Mag. or 44 Spec., 5-shot.
Barrel: 4".
Weight: 21 oz. **Length:** 9" over-all.
Stocks: Square butt.
Sights: Blade front, rear adj. for w. and e.
Features: Shrouded barrel and ejector rod. All-steel frame. Introduced 1986.
Price: 357 Mag. $232.00
Price: 44 Spec. $240.00

CHARTER ARMS BULLDOG PUG
Caliber: 44 Special, 5-shot.
Barrel: 2½".
Weight: 19 oz. **Length:** 7¼" over-all.
Stocks: Bulldog walnut or neoprene.
Sights: Ramp front, notch rear.
Features: Shrouded ejector rod; wide trigger and hammer spur. Introduced 1986.
Price: $234.00

CHARTER ARMS UNDERCOVER REVOLVER
Caliber: 38 Special, 5-shot; 32 S & W Long, 6-shot.
Barrel: 2", 3".
Weight: 16 oz. (2") **Length:** 6¼" (2").
Stocks: Checkered walnut.
Sights: Patridge-type ramp front, notched rear.
Features: Wide trigger and hammer spur. Steel frame. Police Undercover, 2" bbl. (for 38 Spec. +P loads) carry same prices as regular 38 Spec. guns.
Price: Polished Blue $195.00
Price: 32 S & W Long, blue, 2" $195.00
Price: Stainless, 38 Spec., 2" $252.00

Charter Stainless Off-Duty

Charter Arms Off-Duty Revolver
Similar to the Undercover except 38 Special only, 2" barrel, Mat-Black nonglare finish. This all-steel gun comes with Red-Dot front sight and choice of smooth or checkered walnut or neoprene grips. Also available in stainless steel. Introduced 1984.
Price: Mat-Black finish $164.00
Price: Stainless steel $219.00

Charter Arms Pathfinder
Same as Undercover but in 22 LR or 22 Mag., and has 2", 3" or 6" bbl. Fitted with adjustable rear sight, ramp front. Weight 18½ oz.
Price: 22 LR, blue, 3" $204.00
Price: 22 LR, square butt, 6" $237.00
Price: Stainless, 22 LR, 3" $257.00
Price: 2", either caliber, blue only $204.00

Charter Arms Police Undercover
Similar to the standard Undercover except 2" barrel only, chambered for the 32 H&R Magnum and 38 Spec. (6-shot). Patridge-type front with fixed square notch rear. Blue finish or stainless steel; checkered walnut grips. Also available with Pocket Hammer and with steel frame. Introduced 1984.
Price: Standard hammer, 32 Mag., blue $198.00
Price: Pocket Hammer, 32 Mag., blue $202.00
Price: Standard hammer, 38 Spec., blue $195.00
Price: Pocket Hammer, 38 Spec., blue $198.00
Price: Standard hammer, 38 Spec., stainless $252.00
Price: Pocket Hammer, 38 Spec., stainless $256.00

HANDGUNS—DOUBLE ACTION REVOLVERS, SERVICE & SPORT

COLT KING COBRA REVOLVER
Caliber: 357 Magnum, 6-shot.
Barrel: 2½", 4", 6" (STS); 4", 6" (BSTS); 4", 6" (blue).
Weight: 42 oz. (4" bbl.). **Length:** 9" over-all (4" bbl.).
Stocks: Checkered rubber.
Sights: Red insert ramp front, adj. white outline rear.
Features: Stainless steel; full length contoured ejector rod housing, barrel rib; matte finish. Introduced 1986.
Price: STS, 2½", 4", 6" $414.95
Price: BSTS 4", 6" $449.95
Price: Blue, 4", 6" $389.95

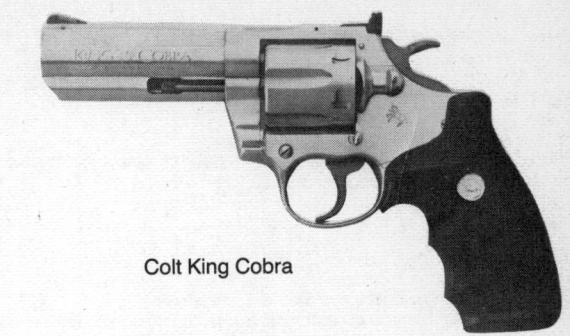
Colt King Cobra

COLT PYTHON REVOLVER
Caliber: 357 Magnum (handles all 38 Spec.), 6-shot.
Barrel: 2½", 4", 6" or 8", with ventilated rib.
Weight: 38 oz. (4" bbl.). **Length:** 9¼" (4" bbl.).
Stocks: Checkered walnut, target type.
Sights: ⅛" ramp front, adj. notch rear.
Features: Ventilated rib; grooved, crisp trigger; swing-out cylinder; target hammer.
Price: Blue, 2½", 4", 6", 8" $729.95
Price: Stainless, 2½", 4", 6" $835.95
Price: Bright stainless, 2½", 4", 6" $859.95

Colt Python 357

ERMA SPORTING REVOLVER
Caliber: 22 LR, 32 S&W Long, 357 Mag.
Barrel: 4", 5½", 6".
Weight: 44 to 48 oz. **Length:** 9½" overall (4" barrel).
Stocks: Stippled walnut service-type and adjustable match grip.
Sights: Interchangeable blade front, micro. adjustable rear for windage and elevation.
Features: Polished blue finish. Comes with both grip styles. Adjustable trigger. Imported from West Germany by Competition Arms, Inc. Introduced 1988.
Price: .... NA

Erma Sporting

F.I.E. "TITAN TIGER" REVOLVER
Caliber: 38 Special.
Barrel: 2" or 4".
Weight: 27 oz. **Length:** 6¼" over-all. (2" bbl.)
Stocks: Checkered plastic, Bulldog style. Walnut optional.
Sights: Fixed.
Features: Thumb-release swing-out cylinder, one stroke ejection. Made in U.S.A. by F.I.E. Corp.
Price: Blue $169.95

F.I.E. "ARMINIUS REVOLVERS"
Caliber: 38 Special, 357 Magnum, 32 S&W, 22 Magnum, 22 LR.
Barrel: 2", 3", 4", 6".
Weight: 35 oz. (6" bbl.). **Length:** 11" over-all (6" bbl.).
Stocks: Checkered plastic; walnut optional.
Sights: Ramp front, fixed rear on standard models, w. & e. adj. on target models.
Features: Thumb-release, swing-out cylinder. Ventilated rib, solid frame, swing-out cylinder. Interchangeable 22 Mag. cylinder available with 22 cal. versions. Imported from West Germany by F.I.E. Corp.
Price: .... $154.95 to $239.95

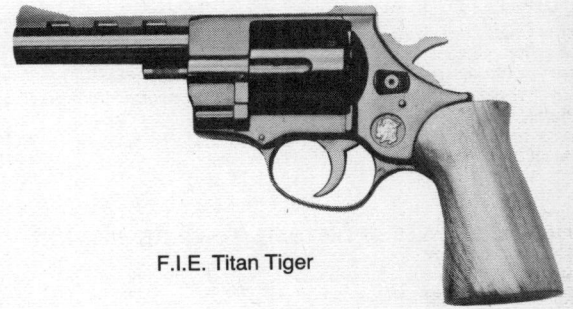
F.I.E. Titan Tiger

KORTH REVOLVER
Caliber: 22 LR, 22 Mag., 357 Mag., 9mm Parabellum.
Barrel: 3", 4", 6".
Weight: 33 to 38 oz. **Length:** 8" to 11" over-all.
Stocks: Checkered walnut, sport or combat.
Sights: Blade front, rear adjustable for windage and elevation.
Features: Four interchangeable cylinders available. Major parts machined from hammer-forged steel; cylinder gap of .002". High polish blue finish. Presentation models have gold trim. Imported from Germany by Osborne's, Beeman.
Price: Polished (Osborne's), about $2,045.00
Price: From Beeman .... $1,936.00 to $2,800.00

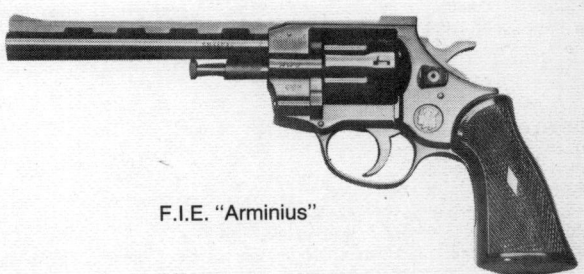
F.I.E. "Arminius"

CAUTION: PRICES CHANGE. CHECK AT GUNSHOP.

HANDGUNS—DOUBLE ACTION REVOLVERS, SERVICE & SPORT

LLAMA COMANCHE III REVOLVERS
Caliber: 357 Mag.
Barrel: 4", 6".
Weight: 28 oz. **Length:** 9¼" (4" bbl.).
Stocks: Checkered walnut.
Sights: Fixed blade front, rear adj. for w. & e.
Features: Ventilated rib, wide spur hammer. Satin chrome finish available. Imported from Spain by Stoeger Industries.
Price: Blue finish $301.00
Price: Satin chrome $357.00

Llama Super Comanche IV, V Revolver
Similar to the Comanche except: large frame, 357 (Comanche V) or 44 Mag. (Comanche IV), 4", 6" or 8½" barrel only (357 Mag), 6", 8½" (44 Mag.); 6-shot cylinder; smooth, extra wide trigger; wide spur hammer; over-size walnut, target-style grips. Weight is 3 lbs., 2 ozs. Blue finish only.
Price: 44 Mag. $393.00
Price: 357 Mag. $414.00

NEW ENGLAND FIREARMS DA REVOLVERS
Caliber: 22 LR (9-shot), 32 H&R Mag. (5-shot).
Barrel: 2½" or 4".
Weight: 25 oz. (22 LR, 2½"). **Length:** 7" over-all (2½" bbl.).
Stocks: American walnut.
Sights: Fixed on 2½" models, fully adjustable on 4".
Features: Choice of blue or nickel finish. Introduced 1988. From New England Firearms Co.
Price: .... NA

Llama Super Comanche

ROSSI MODEL 68 REVOLVER
Caliber: 38 Spec.
Barrel: 2", 3".
Weight: 22 oz.
Stocks: Checkered wood.
Sights: Ramp front, low profile adj. rear.
Features: All-steel frame, Thumb latch operated swing-out cylinder. Introduced 1978. Imported from Brazil by Interarms.
Price: 38, blue, 3" $183.00
Price: M68/2 (2" barrel) $183.00
Price: 3", nickel $193.00

ROSSI MODEL 971 REVOLVER
Caliber: 357 Mag., 6-shot.
Barrel: 4", heavy.
Weight: 36 oz. **Length:** 9" over-all.
Stocks: Checkered Brazillian hardwood.
Sights: Blade front, fully adjustable rear.
Features: Full length ejector rod shroud; matted sight rib; target-type trigger, wide-checkered hammer spur. Introduced 1988. Imported from Brazil by Interarms.
Price: $249.00

ROSSI MODEL 88 STAINLESS REVOLVER
Caliber: 32 S&W, 38 Spec., 5-shot.
Barrel: 2", 3".
Weight: 22 oz. **Length:** 7.5" over-all.
Stocks: Checkered wood, service-style.
Sights: Ramp front, square notch rear drift adjustable for windage.
Features: All metal parts except springs are of 440 stainless steel; matte finish; small frame for concealability. Introduced 1983. Imported from Brazil by Interarms.
Price: 3" barrel $210.00
Price: M88/2 (2" barrel) $210.00

ROSSI MODEL 511 SPORTSMAN'S 22 REVOLVER
Caliber: 22 LR, 6-shot.
Barrel: 4".
Weight: 30 oz. **Length:** 9" over-all.
Stocks: Checkered wood.
Sights: Orange-insert ramp front, fully adj. square notch rear.
Features: All stainless steel. Shrouded ejector rod; heavy barrel; integral sight rib. Introduced 1986. Imported from Brazil by Interarms.
Price: $235.00

ROSSI MODEL 951 REVOLVER
Caliber: 38 Special, 6-shot.
Barrel: 3", 4", vent. rib.
Weight: 30 oz. **Length:** 9" over-all.
Stocks: Checkered hardwood, combat-style.
Sights: Colored insert front, fully adjustable rear.
Features: Polished blue finish, shrouded ejector rod. Medium-size frame. Introduced 1985. Imported from Brazil by Interarms.
Price: M951, blue $235.00
Price: M851 (as above, stainless) $249.00

Rossi Model 971

Rossi Model 88 Stainless

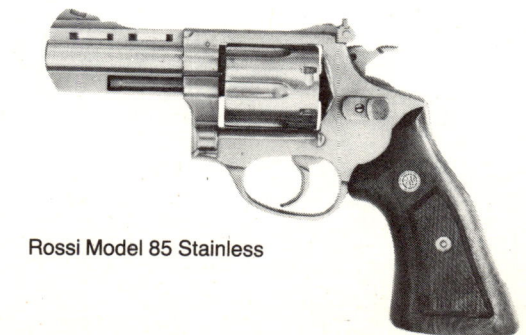

Rossi Model 85 Stainless

CAUTION: PRICES CHANGE. CHECK AT GUNSHOP.

HANDGUNS—DOUBLE ACTION REVOLVERS, SERVICE & SPORT

RUGER GP-100 REVOLVERS
Caliber: 357 Magnum, 6-shot.
Barrel: 4" (heavy), 6", and 6" heavy.
Weight: About 40 oz. **Length:** 9.3" over-all (4" bbl.).
Stocks: Ruger Cushioned Grip (live rubber with Goncalo Alves inserts).
Sights: Interchangeable front blade, fully adj. rear.
Features: Uses all new action and frame incorporating improvements and features of both the Security-Six and Redhawk revolvers. Full length ejector shroud. Satin blue and stainless. Introduced 1986.
Price: GP-141 (4" heavy bbl.) $360.40
Price: GP-160 (6" bbl.) $360.40
Price: GP-161 (6" heavy bbl.) $360.40
Price: KGP-141 (stainless, 4" heavy bbl.) $392.20
Price: KGP-160 (stainless, 6" bbl.) $392.20
Price: KGP-161 (stainless, 6" heavy bbl.) $392.20

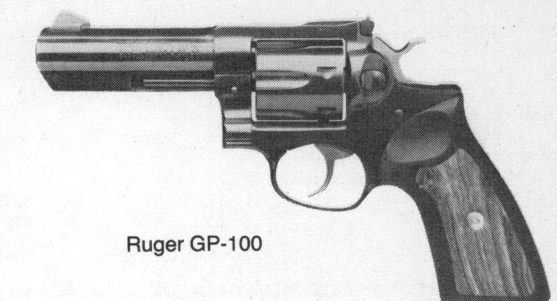
Ruger GP-100

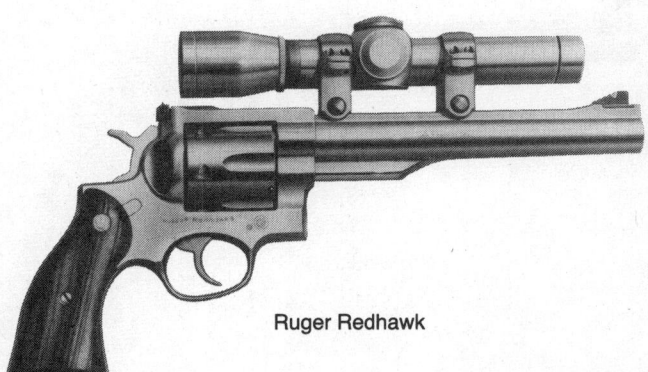
Ruger Redhawk

RUGER REDHAWK
Caliber: 41 Mag., 44 Rem. Mag., 6-shot.
Barrel: 5½", 7½".
Weight: About 54 oz. (7½" bbl.). **Length:** 13" over-all (7½" barrel).
Stocks: Square butt Goncalo Alves.
Sights: Interchangeable Patridge-type front, rear adj. for w. & e.
Features: Stainless steel, brushed satin finish, or blued ordnance steel. Has a 9½" sight radius. Introduced 1979.
Price: Blued, 41 Mag., 44 Mag., 5½", 7½" $397.00
Price: Blued, 41 Mag., 44 Mag., 7½", with scope mount, rings $430.00
Price: Stainless, 41 Mag., 44 Mag., 5½", 7½" $447.50
Price: Stainless, 41 Mag., 44 Mag., 7½", with scope mount, rings ... $482.50

Ruger Super Redhawk Revolver
Similar to the standard Redhawk except has a heavy extended frame with the Ruger Integral Scope Mounting System on the wide top strap. The wide hammer spur has been lowered for better scope clearance. Incorporates the mechanical design features and improvements of the GP-100. Choice of 7½" or 9½" barrrel, both with ramp front sight base with Redhawk-style interchangeable insert sight blades, adjustable rear sight. Comes with Ruger "Cushioned Grip" panels of live rubber and Goncalo Alves wood. Satin polished stainless steel, 44 Magnum only. Introduced 1987.
Price: KSRH-7 (7½"), KSRH-9 (9½") $510.00

SMITH & WESSON M&P Model 10 REVOLVER
Caliber: 38 Special, 6-shot.
Barrel: 2", 4".
Weight: 30½ oz. **Length:** 9¼" over-all.
Stocks: Checkered walnut, Service. Round or square butt.
Sights: Fixed, ramp front, square notch rear.
Price: Blued $305.00
Price: Nickeled, 4" only $315.50

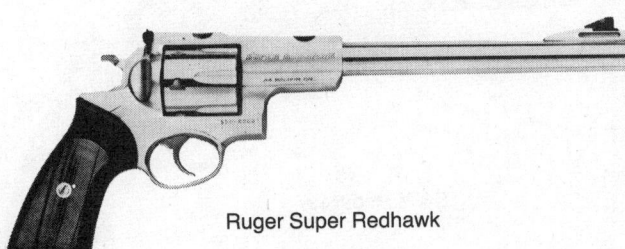
Ruger Super Redhawk

Smith & Wesson 38 M&P Heavy Barrel Model 10
Same as regular M&P except: 4" heavy ribbed bbl. with ramp front sight, square rear, square butt, wgt. 33½ oz.
Price: Blued $305.00
Price: Nickeled $315.00

SMITH & WESSON Model 13 H.B. M&P
Caliber: 357 and 38 Special, 6-shot.
Barrel: 3" or 4".
Weight: 34 oz. **Length:** 9 5/16" over-all (4" bbl.).
Stocks: Checkered walnut, service.
Sights: ⅛" serrated ramp front, fixed square notch rear.
Features: Heavy barrel, K-frame, square butt (4"), round butt (3").
Price: Blue $310.00
Price: Model 65, as above in stainless steel $337.00

S&W Model 10-H.B.

SMITH & WESSON MODEL 15 COMBAT MASTERPIECE
Caliber: 38 Special, 6-shot.
Barrel: 2", 4", 6", 8⅜".
Weight: 32 oz. **Length:** 9 5/16" (4" bbl.).
Stocks: Checkered walnut. Grooved tangs.
Sights: Front, Baughman Quick Draw on ramp, micro click rear, adjustable for w. and e.
Price: Blued, 2", 4", 6" $330.50
Price: Blue, 8⅜" $341.50

S&W Model 13

CAUTION: PRICES CHANGE. CHECK AT GUNSHOP.

HANDGUNS—DOUBLE ACTION REVOLVERS, SERVICE & SPORT

SMITH & WESSON MODEL 17 K-22 MASTERPIECE
Caliber: 22 LR, 6-shot.
Barrel: 4", 6", 8⅜".
Weight: 39 oz. (6" bbl.). **Length:** 11⅛" over-all.
Stocks: Checkered walnut, service.
Sights: Patridge front with 6", 8⅜", serrated on 4", S&W micro. click rear adjustable for windage and elevation.
Features: Grooved tang, polished blue finish.
Price: 4", 6" bbl. $347.50
Price: 8⅜" bbl. $391.00

S&W Model 19

SMITH & WESSON 357 COMBAT MAGNUM Model 19
Caliber: 357 Magnum and 38 Special, 6-shot.
Barrel: 2½", 4", 6".
Weight: 36 oz. **Length:** 9 9/16" (4" bbl.).
Stocks: Checkered Goncalo Alves, target. Grooved tangs.
Sights: Front, ⅛" Baughman Quick Draw on 2½" or 4" bbl., Patridge on 6" bbl., micro click rear adjustable for w. and e.
Features: Also available in nickel finish.
Price: S&W Bright Blue, adj. sights, from $319.50

SMITH & WESSON MODEL 25 REVOLVER
Caliber: 45 Colt, 6-shot.
Barrel: 4", 6", 8⅜".
Weight: About 46 oz. **Length:** 11⅜" over-all (6" bbl.).
Stocks: Checkered Goncalo Alves, target-type.
Sights: S&W red ramp front, S&W micrometer click rear with white outline.
Features: Available in Bright Blue or nickel finish; target trigger, target hammer. Contact S&W for complete price list.
Price: 4", 6", blue $408.00
Price: 8⅜", blue or nickel $415.50

S&W Model 25

SMITH & WESSON 357 MAGNUM M-27 REVOLVER
Caliber: 357 Magnum and 38 Special, 6-shot.
Barrel: 4", 6", 8⅜".
Weight: 45½ oz. (6" bbl.). **Length:** 11 5/16" (6" bbl.).
Stocks: Checkered walnut, Magna. Grooved tangs and trigger.
Sights: Serrated ramp front, micro click rear, adjustable for w. and e.
Price: S&W Bright Blue, 4" $429.50
Price: As above, 6" $403.00
Price: 8⅜" bbl., sq. butt, target hammer, trigger, stocks $410.00

S&W Model 29

SMITH & WESSON 44 MAGNUM Model 29 REVOLVER
Caliber: 44 Magnum, 44 Special or 44 Russian, 6-shot.
Barrel: 4", 6", 8⅜", 10⅝".
Weight: 47 oz. (6" bbl.), 44 oz. (4" bbl.). **Length:** 11⅜" overall (6" bbl.).
Stocks: Oversize target type, checkered Goncalo Alves. Tangs and target trigger grooved, checkered target hammer.
Sights: ⅛" red ramp front, micro click rear, adjustable for w. and e.
Features: Includes presentation case.
Price: S&W Bright Blue or nickel, 4", 6" $458.50
Price: 8⅜" bbl., blue $468.50
Price: 10⅝", blue only (AF) $510.00
Price: Model 629 (stainless steel), 4", 6" $485.00
Price: Model 629, 8⅜" barrel $501.50

S&W "Classic Hunter"

SMITH & WESSON MODEL 29 "CLASSIC HUNTER"
Caliber: 44 Magnum, 6-shot.
Barrel: 6" heavy with full-length lug.
Weight: 52 oz.
Stocks: Hogue soft neoprene.
Sights: Click adjustable front, rear adjustable for windage and elevation.
Features: Non-fluted cylinder; blue finish. Introduced 1988.
Price: .... $474.50.

SMITH & WESSON 32 REGULATION POLICE Model 31
Caliber: 32 S&W Long, 6-shot.
Barrel: 2", 3".
Weight: 18¾ oz. (3" bbl.). **Length:** 7½" (3" bbl.).
Stocks: Checkered walnut, Magna.
Sights: Fixed, 1/10" serrated ramp front, square notch rear.
Features: Blued.
Price: $337.00

S&W Model 31

HANDGUNS—DOUBLE ACTION REVOLVERS, SERVICE & SPORT

SMITH & WESSON 1953 Model 34, 22/32 KIT GUN
Caliber: 22 LR, 6-shot.
Barrel: 2", 4".
Weight: 24 oz. (4" bbl.). Length: 8⅜" (4" bbl. and round butt).
Stocks: Checkered walnut, round or square butt.
Sights: Front, serrated ramp, micro. click rear, adjustable for w. & e.
Price: Blued $338.50
Price: Model 63, as above in stainless, 4" $371.50

SMITH & WESSON 38 CHIEFS SPECIAL & AIRWEIGHT
Caliber: 38 Special, 5-shot.
Barrel: 2", 3".
Weight: 19½ oz. (2" bbl.); 13½ oz. (AIRWEIGHT). Length: 6½" (2" bbl. and round butt).
Stocks: Checkered walnut, round or square butt.
Sights: Fixed, serrated ramp front, square notch rear.
Price: Blued, standard Model 36 .... $312.00
Price: As above, nickel $322.50
Price: Blued, Airweight Model 37 .... $331.00
Price: As above, nickel $344.00

Smith & Wesson Bodyguard Model 49, 649 Revolvers
Same as Model 38 except steel construction, weight 20½ oz.
Price: Blued, Model 49 .... $331.50
Price: Stainless Model 649 .... $377.50

SMITH & WESSON 41 MAGNUM Model 57 REVOLVER
Caliber: 41 Magnum, 6-shot.
Barrel: 4", 6" or 8⅜".
Weight: 48 oz. (6" bbl.). Length: 11⅜" (6" bbl.).
Stocks: Oversize target type checkered Goncalo Alves.
Sights: ⅛" red ramp front, micro. click rear, adj. for w. and e.
Price: S&W Bright Blue or nickel 4", 6" $406.50
Price: 8⅜" bbl. $421.00
Price: Stainless, Model 657, 4", 6" $433.00
Price: As above, 8⅜" $448.00

SMITH & WESSON MODEL 64 STAINLESS M&P
Caliber: 38 Special, 6-shot.
Barrel: 2", 4".
Weight: 34 oz. Length: 9⁵⁄₁₆" over-all.
Stocks: Checkered walnut, service style.
Sights: Fixed, ⅛" serrated ramp front, square notch rear.
Features: Satin finished stainless steel, square butt.
Price: $331.50

SMITH & WESSON MODEL 66 STAINLESS COMBAT MAGNUM
Caliber: 357 Magnum and 38 Special, 6-shot.
Barrel: 2½", 4", 6".
Weight: 36 oz. Length: 9⁹⁄₁₆" over-all.
Stocks: Checkered Goncalo Alves target.
Sights: Front, Baughman Quick Draw on ramp, micro click rear adj. for windage and elevation.
Features: Satin finish stainless steel.
Price: From $363.00

SMITH & WESSON MODEL 586 DISTINGUISHED COMBAT MAGNUM
Caliber: 357 Magnum.
Barrel: 4", 6", 8⅜", full shroud.
Weight: 46 oz. (6"), 41 oz. (4").
Stocks: Goncalo Alves target-type with speed loader cutaway.
Sights: Baughman red ramp front, four-position click-adj. front, S&W micrometer click rear (or fixed).
Features: Uses new L-frame, but takes all K-frame grips. Full length ejector rod shroud. Smooth combat-type trigger, semi-target type hammer. Trigger stop on 6" models. Also available in stainless as Model 686. Introduced 1981.
Price: Model 586, blue, 4" $367.00
Price: Model 586, nickel, from $378.00
Price: Model 686, stainless, from $394.00
Price: Model 581, fixed sight, blue, 4" $335.50
Price: Model 681, fixed sight, stainless $362.00
Price: Model 586, 6", adj. front sight, blue $407.00
Price: As above, 8⅜" $423.50
Price: Model 686, 6", adj. front sight $430.50
Price: As above, 8⅜" $447.00

SMITH & WESSON BODYGUARD MODEL 38
Caliber: 38 Special, 5-shot.
Barrel: 2".
Weight: 14½ oz. Length: 6⁵⁄₁₆" over-all.
Stocks: Checkered walnut.
Sights: Fixed serrated ramp front, square notch rear.
Features: Alloy frame; internal hammer.
Price: Blued $350.50
Price: Nickeled $363.00

Smith & Wesson Model 60 Chiefs Special Stainless
Same as Model 36 except: 2" bbl. and round butt only.
Price: Stainless steel $357.00

S&W Model 649

S&W Model 57

SMITH & WESSON MODEL 67 K-38 STAINLESS COMBAT MASTERPIECE
Caliber: 38 Special, 6-shot.
Barrel: 4".
Weight: 32 oz. (loaded). Length: 9⁵⁄₁₆" over-all.
Stocks: Checkered walnut, service style.
Sights: Front, Baughman Quick Draw on ramp, micro click rear adj. for windage and elevation.
Features: Stainless steel. Square butt frame with grooved tangs.
Price: $360.00

S&W Model 686

CAUTION: PRICES CHANGE. CHECK AT GUNSHOP.

HANDGUNS—DOUBLE ACTION REVOLVERS, SERVICE & SPORT

SPORTARMS MODEL HS38S REVOLVER
Caliber: 38 Special, 6 shot.
Barrel: 3", 4".
Weight: 31.3 oz. **Length:** 8" overall (3" barrel).
Stocks: Checkered hardwood; round butt on 3" model, target-style on 4".
Sights: Blade front, adjustable rear.
Features: Polished blue finish; ventilated rib on 4" barrel. Made in West Germany by Herbert Schmidt; imported by Sportarms of Florida.
Price: About $150.00

TAURUS MODEL 66 REVOLVER
Caliber: 357 Magnum, 6-shot.
Barrel: 3", 4", 6".
Weight: 35 oz.
Stocks: Checkered walnut, target-type. Standard stocks on 3".
Sights: Serrated ramp front, micro click rear adjustable for w. and e. Red ramp front with white outline rear on stainless models only.
Features: Wide target-type hammer spur, floating firing pin, heavy barrel with shrouded ejector rod. Introduced 1978. From Taurus International.
Price: Blue.. $233.45
Price: Satin nickel $243.92
Price: Stainless steel....................................... $296.41
Price: Model 65 (similar to M66 except has a fixed rear sight and ramp front), blue, 3" or 4" only $216.47
Price: Model 65, satin nickel, 3" or 4" only.............. $227.60

TAURUS MODEL 73 SPORT REVOLVER
Caliber: 32 S&W Long, 6-shot.
Barrel: 3", heavy.
Weight: 22 oz. **Length:** 8¼" over-all.
Stocks: Oversize target-type, checkered Brazilian walnut.
Sights: Ramp front, notch rear.
Features: Imported from Brazil by Taurus International.
Price: Blue $193.92
Price: Satin nickel $211.10

TAURUS MODEL 80 STANDARD REVOLVER
Caliber: 38 Spec., 6-shot.
Barrel: 3" or 4".
Weight: 31 oz. (4" bbl.). **Length:** 9¼" over-all (4" bbl.).
Stocks: Checkered Brazilian walnut.
Sights: Serrated ramp front, square notch rear.
Features: Imported from Brazil by Taurus International.
Price: Blue.. $187.90
Price: Satin nickel $199.39

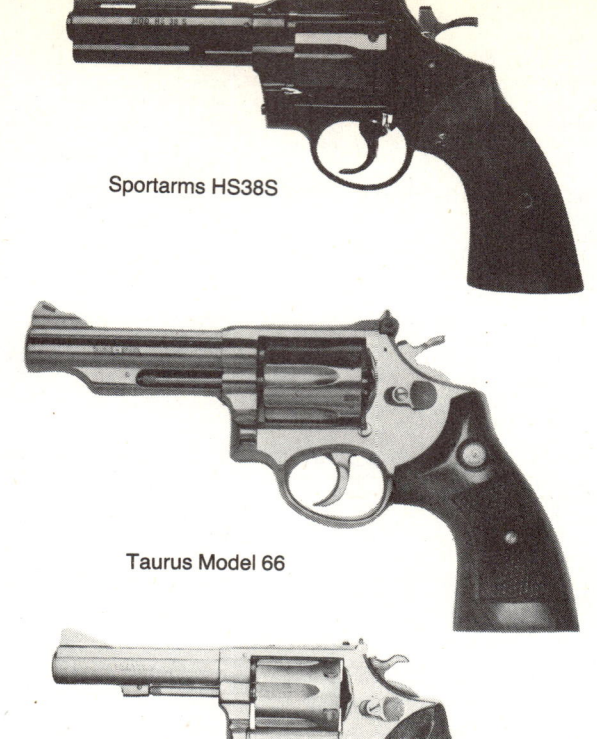

Sportarms HS38S

Taurus Model 66

Taurus Model 83

TAURUS MODEL 82 HEAVY BARREL REVOLVER
Caliber: 38 Spec., 6-shot.
Barrel: 3" or 4", heavy.
Weight: 33 oz. (4" bbl.). **Length:** 9¼" over-all (4" bbl.).
Stocks: Checkered Brazilian walnut.
Sights: Serrated ramp front, square notch rear.
Features: Imported from Brazil by Taurus International.
Price: Blue, about $187.90
Price: Satin nickel, about $199.39

TAURUS MODEL 83 REVOLVER
Caliber: 38 Spec., 6-shot.
Barrel: 4" only, heavy.
Weight: 34½ oz.
Stocks: Over-size checkered walnut.
Sights: Ramp front, micro. click rear adj. for w. & e.
Features: Blue or nickel finish. Introduced 1977. Imported from Brazil by Taurus International.
Price: Blue.. $197.82
Price: Satin nickel $208.15

Taurus Model 82

Taurus Model 85

TAURUS MODEL 85 REVOLVER
Caliber: 38 Spec., 5-shot.
Barrel: 2", 3".
Weight: 21 oz.
Stocks: Checkered walnut.
Sights: Ramp front, square notch rear.
Features: Blue, satin nickel finish or stainless steel. Introduced 1980. Imported from Brazil by Taurus International.
Price: Blue.. $199.88
Price: Satin nickel, 3" only $214.43
Price: Stainless steel....................................... $253.09

HANDGUNS—DOUBLE ACTION REVOLVERS, SERVICE & SPORT

TAURUS MODEL 669 REVOLVER
Caliber: 357 Mag., 6 shot.
Barrel: 4", 6".
Weight: 37 oz. (4" bbl.)
Stocks: Checkered walnut, target type.
Sights: Serrated ramp front, micro. click rear adjustable for windage and elevation.
Features: Wide target-type hammer, floating firing pin, full length barrel shroud. Introduced 1988. Imported by Taurus International.
Price: Blue.. $241.85
Price: Stainless... $304.80

Taurus Model 669

UBERTI "INSPECTOR" REVOLVER
Caliber: 32 S&W Long, 38 Spec., 6-shot.
Barrel: 3", 4", 6".
Weight: 24 oz. (3" bbl.). **Length:** 8" over-all (3" bbl.).
Stocks: Checkered walnut.
Sights: Blade on ramp front, fixed or adj. rear.
Features: Blue or chrome finish. Introduced 1986. Imported from Italy by Benson Firearms, Uberti USA.
Price: Blue, fixed sights $429.00
Price: Blue, adj. sights, 4", 6" only $465.00
Price: Chrome, fixed sights $459.00
Price: Chrome, adj. sights, 4", 6" only $499.00

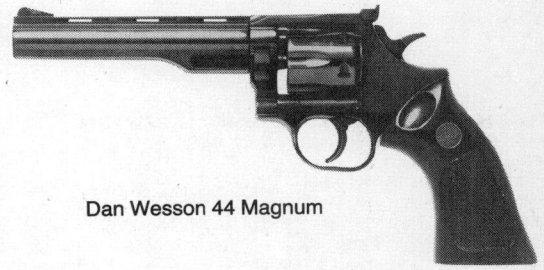
Uberti Inspector

DAN WESSON MODEL 41V & MODEL 44V
Caliber: 41 Mag., 44 Mag., 6-shot.
Barrel: 4", 6", 8", 10"; interchangeable.
Weight: 48 oz. (4"). **Length:** 12" over-all (6" bbl.).
Stocks: Smooth.
Sights: 1/8" serrated front, white outline rear adjustable for windage and elevation.
Features: Available in blue or stainless steel. Smooth, wide trigger with adjustable over-travel; wide hammer spur. Available in Pistol Pac set also.
Price: 41 Mag., 4", vent. $412.80
Price: As above except in stainless $461.98
Price: 44 Mag., 4", blue. $431.45
Price: As above except in stainless $507.30

Dan Wesson 44 Magnum

Dan Wesson 9-2, 15-2 & 32M Revolvers
Same as Models 8-2 and 14-2 except they have adjustable sight. Model 9-2 chambered for 38 Special, Model 15-2 for 357 Magnum. Model 32M is chambered for 32 H&R Mag. Same specs and prices as for 15-2 guns. Available in blue or stainless. Contact Dan Wesson for complete price list.
Price: Model 9-2 or 15-2, 2½", blue $337.64
Price: As above except in stainless $366.07

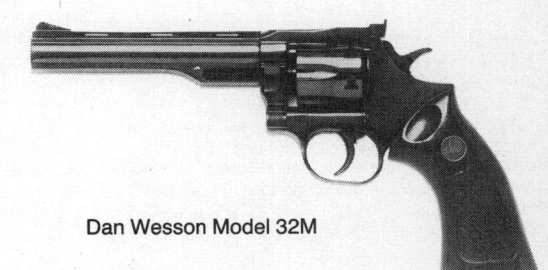
Dan Wesson Model 32M

DAN WESSON MODEL 22 REVOLVER
Caliber: 22 LR, 22 WMR, 6-shot.
Barrel: 2½", 4" 6", 8", 10"; interchangeable.
Weight: 36 oz. (2½"), 44 oz. (6"). **Length:** 9¼" over-all (4" barrel).
Stocks: Checkered; undercover, service or over-size target.
Sights: 1/8" serrated, interchangeable front, white outline rear adjustable for windage and elevation.
Features: Built on the same frame as the Dan Wesson 357; smooth, wide trigger with over-travel adjustment, wide spur hammer, with short double-action travel. Available in Brite blue or stainless steel. Contact Dan Wesson for complete price list.
Price: 2½" bbl., blue $337.64
Price: As above, stainless $366.07
Price: With 4", vent. rib, blue $369.97
Price: As above, stainless $398.41
Price: Stainless Pistol Pac, 22 LR. $689.01

DAN WESSON MODEL 8-2 & MODEL 14-2
Caliber: 38 Special (Model 8-2); 357 (14-2), both 6-shot.
Barrel: 2½", 4", 6", 8"; interchangeable.
Weight: 30 oz. (2½"). **Length:** 9¼" over-all (4" bbl.).
Stocks: Checkered, interchangeable.
Sights: 1/8" serrated front, fixed rear.
Features: Interchangeable barrels and grips; smooth, wide trigger; wide hammer spur with short double action travel. Available in stainless or Brite blue. Contact Dan Wesson for complete price list.
Price: Model 8-2, 2½", blue $267.15
Price: As above except in stainless $311.38
Price: Model 714-2 Pistol Pac, stainless $516.68

CAUTION: PRICES CHANGE. CHECK AT GUNSHOP.

HANDGUNS—SINGLE ACTION REVOLVERS

Both classic six-shooters and modern adaptations for hunting and sport.

CENTURY MODEL 100 SINGLE ACTION
Caliber: 30-30, 375 Win., 444 Marlin, 45-70, 50-70.
Barrel: 6½", 8" (standard), 10", 12". Other lengths to order.
Weight: 6 lbs. (loaded). **Length:** 15" over-all (8" bbl.).
Stocks: Smooth walnut.
Sights: Ramp front, Millett adj. square notch rear.
Features: Highly polished high tensile strength manganese bronze frame, blue cylinder and barrel; coil spring trigger mechanism. Calibers other than 45-70 start at $1,500.00. Introduced 1975. Made in U.S. From Century Gun Dist., Inc.
Price: 8" barrel, 45-70 .... $780.00
Price: 10" barrel, 45-70 .... $810.00
Price: 12" barrel, 45-70 .... $840.00

Century Model 100

CIMARRON U.S. CAVALRY MODEL SINGLE ACTION
Caliber: 45 Colt
Barrel: 7½"
Weight: 42 oz. **Length:** 13½" overall
Stocks: Walnut.
Sights: Fixed.
Features: Has "A.P. Casey" markings; "U.S." plus patent dates on frame, serial number on backstrap, trigger guard, frame and cylinder, "APC" cartouche on left grip; color case-hardened frame and hammer, rest charcoal blue. Exact copy of the original. Imported by Cimarron Arms.
Price: $459.00

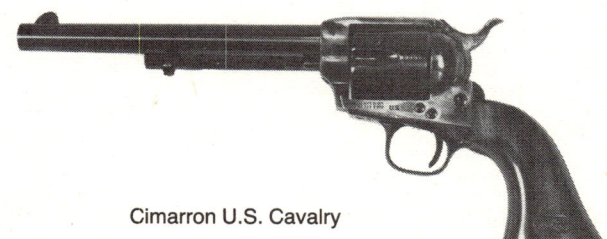
Cimarron U.S. Cavalry

Cimarron Artillery Model Single Action
Similar to the U.S. Cavalry model except has 5½" barrel, weighs 39 oz., and is 11½" over-all.
Price: $459.00

CIMARRON SHERIFF MODEL SINGLE ACTION
Caliber: 22 LR, 22 WMR, 38 Spec., 357 Mag., 44 WCF, 45 Colt.
Barrel: 4".
Weight: 38 oz. **Length:** 10" over-all.
Stocks: Walnut.
Sights: Fixed.
Features: Patent dates on frame; serial number on backstrap, trigger guard, frame and cylinder. Modern or old-style blue. Uses blackpowder frame. Imported by Cimarron Arms.
Price: $389.00

CIMARRON "OLD MODEL" SINGLE ACTION
Caliber: 22 LR, 22 WMR, 38 WCF, 357 Mag., 44 WCF, 45 Colt.
Barrel: 3", 4", 4¾", 5½", 7½".
Weight: 39 oz. **Length:** 10" over-all (4" barrel).
Stocks: Walnut.
Sights: Blade front, fixed or adjustable rear.
Features: Uses "old model" blackpowder frame with "Bullseye" ejector. Imported by Cimarron Arms.
Price: Standard model $389.00
Price: "A" engraving (30 percent coverage) $589.00
Price: "B" engraving (50 percent coverage) $699.00
Price: "C" engraving (100 percent coverage) $1,099.00

COLT SINGLE ACTION ARMY REVOLVER
Caliber: 45 Colt, 6-shot.
Barrel: 3", 4¾", 5½", 7½", 10".
Weight: 37 oz. (5½" bbl.). **Length:** 10⅞" over-all (5½" bbl).
Stocks: Black composite rubber with eagle and shield crest.
Sights: Fixed. Grooved top strap, blade front.
Features: Blue with color case-hardened frame or all nickel with walnut stocks. Available in limited quantities through the Colt Custom Shop only.
Price: From $1,045.00

Cimarron Sheriff Model

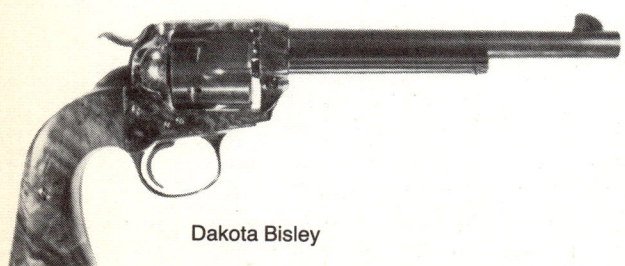
Dakota Bisley

DAKOTA BISLEY MODEL SINGLE ACTION
Caliber: 22 LR, 22 WMR., 32-20, 32 H&R Mag., 357, 30 Carbine, 38-40, 44 Spec., 44-40, 45 Colt, 45 ACP.
Barrel: 4⅝", 5½", 7½".
Weight: 37 oz. **Length:** 10½" over-all with 5½" barrel.
Stocks: Smooth walnut.
Sights: Blade front, fixed groove rear.
Features: Colt-type firing pin in hammer; color case-hardened frame, blue barrel, cylinder, steel backstrap and trigger guard. Also avail. in nickel, factory engraved. Imported by E.M.F.
Price: All calibers, bbl. lengths $540.00
Price: Combo models—22 LR/22 WMR, 32-20/32 H&R, 357/9mm, 44-40/44 Spec., 45 Colt/45 ACP $600.00
Price: Nickel, all cals. $640.00
Price: Engraved, all cals., lengths $700.00

HANDGUNS—SINGLE ACTION REVOLVERS

DAKOTA SINGLE ACTION REVOLVERS
Caliber: 22 LR, 22 WMR., 357 Mag., 30 Carbine, 32-20, 32 H&R Mag., 38-40, 44-40, 44 Spec., 45 Colt, 45 ACP.
Barrel: 3½", 4⅝", 5½", 7½", 12", 16¼".
Weight: 45 oz. **Length:** 13" over-all (7½" bbl.).
Stocks: Smooth walnut.
Sights: Blade front, fixed rear.
Features: Colt-type hammer with firing pin, color case-hardened frame, blue barrel and cylinder, brass grip frame and trigger guard. Available in blue or nickel plated, plain or engraved. Imported by E.M.F.
Price: 22 LR, 30 Car., 357, 44-40, 45 Colt, 4⅝", 5½", 7½".........$480.00
Price: 22 LR/22 WMR, 45 Colt/ 45 ACP, 32-20/32 H&R, 357/9mm, 44-40/44 Spec., 5½", 7½"...............$580.00
Price: 357, 44-40, 45, 12".............$520.00
Price: 357, 44-40, 45, 3½"............$520.00

Dakota Single Action

DAKOTA 1875 OUTLAW REVOLVER
Caliber: 357, 44-40, 45 Colt.
Barrel: 7½".
Weight: 46 oz. **Length:** 13½" over-all.
Stocks: Smooth walnut.
Sights: Blade front, fixed groove rear.
Features: Authentic copy of 1875 Remington with firing pin in hammer; color case-hardened frame, blue cylinder, barrel, steel backstrap and brass trigger guard. Also available in nickel, factory engraved. Imported by E.M.F.
Price: All calibers..........$485.00
Price: Nickel................$520.00
Price: Engraved..............$600.00

Dakota 1890 Police Revolver
Similar to the 1875 Outlaw except has 5½" barrel, weighs 40 oz., with 12½" over-all length. Has lanyard ring in butt. Calibers 357, 44-40, 45 Colt. Imported by E.M.F.
Price: All calibers..........$500.00
Price: Nickel................$540.00
Price: Engraved..............$600.00

Dakota 1890 Police

F.I.E. "TEXAS RANGER" REVOLVER
Caliber: 22 LR, 22 WMR.
Barrel: 4¾", 6½", 9".
Weight: 31 oz. (4¾" bbl.). **Length:** 10" over-all.
Stocks: American walnut.
Sights: Blade front, notch rear.
Features: Single-action, blue/black finish. Introduced 1983. Made in the U.S. by F.I.E.
Price: 22 LR, 4¾"............$104.95
Price: As above, convertible (22 LR/22 WMR)......$124.95
Price: 22 LR, 6½"............$104.95
Price: As above, convertible (22 LR/22 WMR)......$124.95
Price: 22 LR, 9".............$104.95
Price: As above, convertible (22 LR/22 WMR)......$124.95

F.I.E. "Texas Ranger"

F.I.E. "Little Ranger" Revolver
Similar to the "Texas Ranger" except has 3¼" barrel, birdshead grips. Introduced 1986. Made in U.S. by F.I.E.
Price: 22 LR................$104.95
Price: 22 LR/22 WMR convertible.............$124.95

F.I.E. "Little Ranger"

F.I.E. "Buffalo Scout"

F.I.E. "BUFFALO SCOUT" REVOLVER
Caliber: 22 LR/22 WMR.
Barrel: 4¾".
Weight: 32 oz. **Length:** 10" over-all.
Stocks: Black checkered nylon, walnut optional.
Sights: Blade front, fixed rear.
Features: Slide spring ejector. Blue, chrome, gold or blue with gold backstrap and trigger guard models available. Imported from Italy by F.I.E.
Price: Blued, 22 LR..........$89.95
Price: Blue, 22 convertible...$110.95
Price: Chrome, 22 LR.........$104.95
Price: Chrome, convertible...$126.95
Price: "Yellow Rose," gold, 22 convertible......$149.95

F.I.E. "Yellow Rose" Limited Edition Revolver
Same gun as the "Buffalo Scout" revolver except is completely 24 karat gold plated and has ivory polymer grips scrimshawed with a map of Texas, the Texas state flag and a single yellow rose highlighted with green leaves. Comes in a French fitted presentation case of American walnut, lined and fitted with contrasting velvet. Polished brass-plated hinge and lock. From F.I.E. Introduced 1987.
Price:................$349.95

CAUTION: PRICES CHANGE. CHECK AT GUNSHOP.

HANDGUNS—SINGLE ACTION REVOLVERS

F.I.E. "HOMBRE" SINGLE ACTION REVOLVER
Caliber: 357 Mag., 44 Mag., 45 Colt.
Barrel: 6" or 7½".
Weight: 45 oz. (6" bbl.).
Stocks: Smooth walnut with medallion.
Sights: Blade front, grooved topstrap (fixed) rear.
Features: Color case hardened frame. Bright blue finish. Super-smooth action. Introduced 1979. Imported from West Germany by F.I.E. Corp.
Price: $249.95
Price: 24K gold plated $429.95

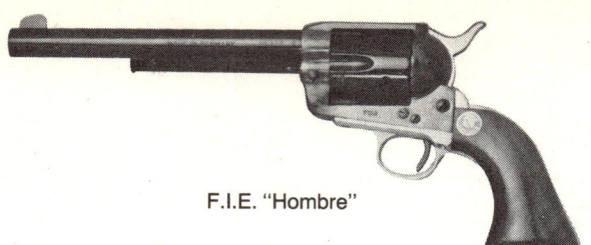

F.I.E. "Hombre"

FREEDOM ARMS 454 CASULL
Caliber: 44 Mag., 45 Colt, 454 Casull, 5-shot.
Barrel: 4¾", 6", 7½", 10".
Weight: 50 oz. **Length:** 14" over-all (7½" bbl.).
Stocks: Impregnated hardwood.
Sights: Blade front, notch or adjustable rear.
Features: All stainless steel construction; sliding bar safety system. Lifetime warranty. Made in U.S.A.
Price: Fixed sight $995.00
Price: Adjustable sight $1,085.00
Price: Field Grade, adjustable sight, (matte stainless finish, Pachmayr Presentation grips, 4¾", 7½", 10") $795.00
Price: Field Grade, fixed sight, 4¾" only $725.00

Freedom 454 Field Grade

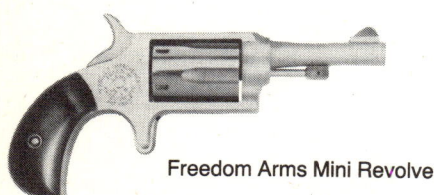

Freedom Arms Mini Revolver

FREEDOM ARMS MINI REVOLVER
Caliber: 22 Short, Long, Long Rifle, 5-shot; 22 WMR., 4-shot.
Barrel: 1".
Weight: 4 oz. **Length:** 4" over-all.
Stocks: Impregnated hardwood.
Sights: Blade front, notch rear.
Features: Made of stainless steel, simple take down; half-cock safety; floating firing pin; cartridge rims recessed in cylinder. Comes in gun rug. Lifetime warranty. Also available in percussion — see black powder section. From Freedom Arms.
Price: 22 LR, 1" barrel $139.20
Price: 22 WMR, 1" barrel $160.45

Freedom Arms Boot Gun
Similar to the Mini Revolver except 22 WMR only, has 3" barrel, weighs 5 oz. and is 5⅞" over-all. Has over-size grips, floating firing pin. Made of stainless steel. Lifetime warranty. Comes in rectangular gun rug. Introduced 1982. From Freedom Arms.
Price: 22 WMR $199.95

MITCHELL SINGLE ACTION ARMY REVOLVERS
Caliber: 22 LR, 357 Mag., 44 Mag., 45 Colt, 6-shot.
Barrel: 4¾", 5½", 6", 6½", 7½", 10" 12", 18".
Weight: NA. **Length:** NA.
Stocks: One-piece walnut.
Sights: Serrated ramp front, fixed or adjustable rear.
Features: Color case-hardened frame, brass backstrap, balance blued; hammer block safety. Stainless steel and dual cylinder models available. Imported by Mitchell Arms.
Price: Fixed sight, 22 LR, 4¾", 5½", 7½" $259.95
Price: As above, 357,45 .... $264.95
Price: As above, 44 Mag. $269.95
Price: Adjustable sight, 22 LR, 4¾", 5½", 7½" $265.00
Price: As above, 357, 45 .... $279.95
Price: As above, 44 Mag. $284.95
Price: Stainless steel, 22 LR, 4¾", 5½", 7½" $299.00
Price: As above, 357 Mag. $319.95
Price: 44 Mag./44-40, dual cylinder, 4¾", 6", 7½" ... $319.95
Price: 22 LR/22 Mag., dual cylinder, 4¾", 5½", 7½" . $275.00
Price: Silhouette Model, 44 Mag., 10", 12", 18" $299.95

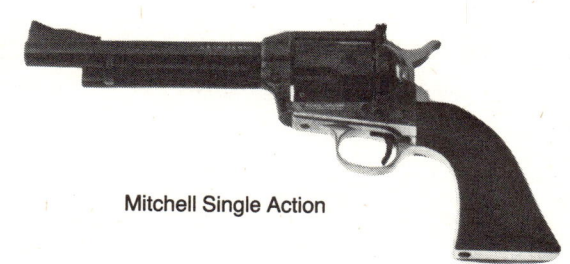

Mitchell Single Action

Consult our Directory pages for the location of firms mentioned.

North American Mini

NORTH AMERICAN MINI-REVOLVERS
Caliber: 22 S, 22 LR, 22 WMR., 5-shot.
Barrel: 1⅛", 1⅝", 2½".
Weight: 4 to 6.6 oz. **Length:** 3⅝" to 6⅛" over-all.
Stocks: Laminated wood.
Sights: Blade front, notch fixed rear.
Features: All stainless steel construction. Polished satin and matte finish. From North American Arms.
Price: 22 Short, 1⅛" bbl. $135.00
Price: 22 LR, 1⅛" bbl. $136.00
Price: 22 LR, 1⅝" bbl. $137.00
Price: 22 WMR, 1⅝" bbl. $156.00
Price: 22 WMR, 2½" bbl. $171.00

HANDGUNS—SINGLE ACTION REVOLVERS

PHELPS HERITAGE I, EAGLE I REVOLVERS
Caliber: 444 Marlin, 45-70, 6-shot.
Barrel: 8" or 12".
Weight: 5½ lbs. **Length:** 19½" over-all (12" bbl.).
Stocks: Smooth walnut.
Sights: Ramp front, adjustable rear.
Features: Single action; polished blue finish; safety bar. From E. Phelps Mfg. Co.
Price: Heritage I (45-70), Eagle I (444 Marlin) 8" barrel, about **$680.00**
Price: As above, 12" barrel, about **$700.00**

Ruger N.M. Blackhawk

Ruger N.M. Bisley Blackhawk

Ruger Small Frame New Model Bisley
Similar to the New Model Single-Six except frame is styled after the classic Bisley "flat-top." Most mechanical parts are unchanged. Hammer is lower and smoothly curved with a deeply checkered spur. Trigger is strongly curved with a wide smooth surface. Longer grip frame designed with a hand-filling shape, and the trigger guard is a large oval. Dovetail rear sight drift-adjustable for windage; front sight base accepts intechangeable square blades of various heights and styles. Available with an unfluted cylinder and roll engraving, or with a fluted cylinder and no engraving. Weight about 41 oz. Chambered for 22 LR and 32 H&R Mag., 6½" barrel only. Introduced 1985.
Price: **$286.38**

RUGER NEW MODEL SUPER SINGLE-SIX CONVERTIBLE REVOLVER
Caliber: 22 LR, 6-shot; 22 WMR in extra cylinder.
Barrel: 4⅝", 5½", 6½", or 9½" (6-groove).
Weight: 34½ oz. (6½" bbl.). **Length:** 11¹³⁄₁₆" over-all (6½" bbl.).
Stocks: Smooth American walnut.
Sights: Improved Patridge front on ramp, fully adj. rear protected by integral frame ribs.
Features: New Ruger "interlocked" mechanism, transfer bar ignition, gate-controlled loading, hardened chrome-moly steel frame, wide trigger, music wire springs throughout, independent firing pin.
Price: 4⅝", 5½", 6½", 9½" barrel **$245.03**
Price: 5½", 6½" bbl. only, stainless steel **$308.58**

SPORTARMS MODEL HS21S SINGLE ACTION
Caliber: 22 LR or 22LR/22 WMR combo, 6 shot.
Barrel: 5½".
Weight: 33.5 oz. **Length:** 11" over-all.
Stocks: Smooth hardwood.
Sights: Blade front, rear drift adjustable for windage.
Features: Available in blue or chrome with imitation stag or wood stocks. Made in West Germany by Herbert Schmidt; imported by Sportarms of Florida.
Price: 22 LR, blue, "stag" grips, about **$80.00**
Price: 22LR/22 WMR Combo, chrome, wood stocks, about **$120.00**

RUGER NEW MODEL SUPER BLACKHAWK
Caliber: 44 Magnum, 6-shot. Also fires 44 Spec.
Barrel: 7½" (6-groove, 20" twist), 10½".
Weight: 48 oz. (7½" bbl.) 51 oz. (10½" bbl.). **Length:** 13⅜" over-all (7½" bbl.).
Stocks: Genuine American walnut.
Sights: ⅛" ramp front, micro click rear adj. for w. and e.
Features: New Ruger interlocked mechanism, non-fluted cylinder, steel grip and cylinder frame, square back trigger guard, wide serrated trigger and wide spur hammer.
Price: Blue (S-47N, S-411N) **$330.23**
Price: Stainless (KS-47N, KS-411N) **$360.75**

RUGER NEW MODEL BLACKHAWK REVOLVER
Caliber: 30 Carbine, 357 Mag./38 Spec., 41 Mag., 44 Mag., 45 Colt, 6-shot.
Barrel: 4⅝" or 6½", either caliber, 5½" (44 Mag. only), 7½" (30 Carbine, 45 Colt only).
Weight: 42 oz. (6½" bbl.). **Length:** 12¼" over-all (6½" bbl.).
Stocks: American walnut.
Sights: ⅛" ramp front, micro click rear adj. for w. and e.
Features: New Ruger interlocked mechanism, independent firing pin, hardened chrome-moly steel frame, music wire springs throughout.
Price: Blue, 30 Carbine (7½" bbl.), BN31 .... **$275.00**
Price: Blue, 357 Mag. (4⅝", 6½") BN34, BN36 .... **$286.10**
Price: Blue, 357/9mm (4⅝", 6½") BN34X, BN36X **$299.70**
Price: Blue, 44 Mag. (5½") S45N **$330.23**
Price: Blue, 41 Mag., 44 Mag., 45 Colt (4⅝", 6½") BN41, BN42, BN44, BN45 .... **$286.10**
Price: Stainless, 357 Mag. (4⅝", 6½") KBN34, KBN36 .... **$352.43**

Ruger New Model Bisley
Similar to standard New Model Blackhawk except the hammer is lower with a smoothly curved, deeply checkered wide spur. The trigger is strongly curved with a wide smooth surface. Longer grip frame has a hand-filling shape. Adjustable rear sight, ramp-style front. Available with an unfluted cylinder and roll engraving, or with a fluted cylinder and no engraving. Fixed or adjustable sights. Chambered for 357, 41, 44 Mags. and 45 Colt; 7½" barrel; over-all length of 13". Introduced 1985.
Price: **$340.77**

Ruger Bisley Single-Six

Ruger New Model Single-Six Revolver
Similar to the Super Single-Six revolver except chambered for 32 H&R Magnum (also handles 32 S&W and 32 S&W Long). Weight is about 34 oz. with 6½" barrel. Barrel lengths: 4⅝", 5½", 6½", 9½". Introduced 1985.
Price: **$235.32**

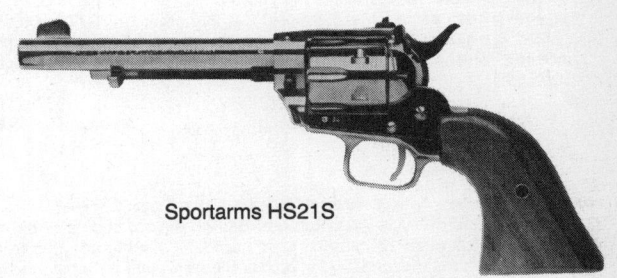
Sportarms HS21S

CAUTION: PRICES CHANGE. CHECK AT GUNSHOP.

HANDGUNS—SINGLE ACTION REVOLVERS

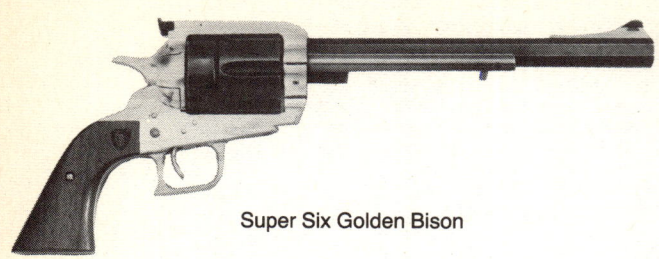

Super Six Golden Bison

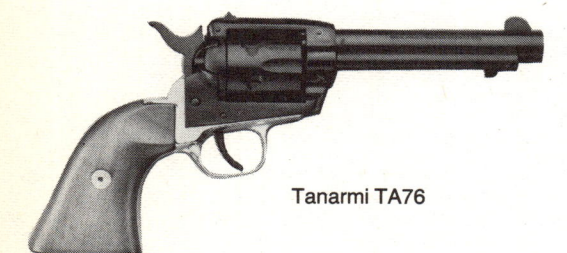

Tanarmi TA76

SUPER SIX GOLDEN BISON 45-70 REVOLVER
Caliber: 45-70, 6-shot.
Barrel: 8″, 10½″, octagonal.
Weight: 5 lbs., 12 oz. (8″ bbl.) **Length:** 15″ over-all (8″ bbl.).
Stocks: Smooth walnut.
Sights: Blaze orange blade front on ramp, Millett fully adjustable rear.
Features: Cylinder frame and grip frame of high tensile Manganese bronze; hammer of Manganese bronze with a hardened steel pad for firing pin contact; all coil springs; full-cock, cross-bolt interlocking safety and traveling safeties. Choice of antique brown or blue/black finish. Lifetime warranty. Comes in a fitted black walnut presentation case. Made in the U.S. by Super Six Limited.
Price: Golden Bison (8″ bbl.) $1,895.00
Price: Golden Bison Bull (10½″ bbl.) $1,995.00

TANARMI S.A. REVOLVER MODEL TA76
Caliber: 22 LR, 22 WMR, 6-shot.
Barrel: 4¾″, 6″ or 9″.
Weight: 32 oz. **Length:** 10″ over-all.
Stocks: Walnut.
Sights: Blade front, rear adj. for w. & e.
Features: Manual hammer block safety. Imported from Italy by Excam.
Price: 22 LR, blue 4¾″ $95.00
Price: Combo, blue, 4¾″ $105.00
Price: 22 LR, chrome, 4¾″ $99.00
Price: Combo, chrome, 4¾″ $121.00
Price: Combo, blue, 6″ $115.00
Price: Combo, blue, 9″ $115.00

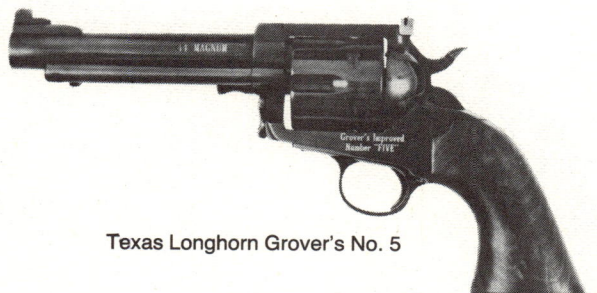

Texas Longhorn Grover's No. 5

TEXAS LONGHORN GROVER'S IMPROVED NO. FIVE
Caliber: 44 Magnum, 6-shot.
Barrel: 5½″.
Weight: 44 oz. **Length:** NA.
Stocks: Fancy AAA walnut.
Sights: Square blade front on ramp, fully adjustable rear.
Features: Music wire coil spring action with double locking bolt; polished blue finish. Hand-made in limited 1,200-gun production. Grip contour, straps, over-sized base pin, lever latch and lockwork identical copies of Elmer Keith design. Lifetime warranty to original owner. Introduced 1988.
Price: $985.00

TEXAS LONGHORN RIGHT-HAND SINGLE ACTION
Caliber: All centerfire pistol calibers.
Barrel: 4¾″.
Weight: NA. **Length:** NA.
Stocks: One-piece fancy walnut, or any fancy AAA wood.
Sights: Blade front, grooved top-strap rear.
Features: Loading gate and ejector housing on left side of gun. Cylinder rotates to the left. All steel construction; color case-hardened frame; high polish blue; music wire coil springs. Lifetime guarantee to original owner. Introduced 1984. From Texas Longhorn Arms.
Price: South Texas Army Limited Edition — hand-made, only 1,000 to be produced; "One of One Thousand" engraved on barrel. $1,500.00

Texas Longhorn Arms Texas Border Special
Similar to the South Texas Army Limited Edition except has 3½″ barrel, birds-head style grip. Same special features. Introduced 1984.
Price: $1,500.00

Texas Longhorn Arms Cased Set
Set contains one each of the Texas Longhorn Right-Hand Single Actions, all in the same caliber, same serial numbers (100, 200, 300, 400, 500, 600, 700, 800, 900). Ten sets to be made (#1000 donated to NRA museum). Comes inhand-tooled leather case. All other specs same as Limited Edition guns. Introduced 1984.
Price: $5,750.00
Price: With ¾-coverage "C-style" engraving $7,650.00

Texas Longhorn Arms West Texas Flat Top Target
Similar to the South Texas Army Limited Edition except choice of barrel length from 7½″ through 15″; flat-top style frame; ⅛″ contoured ramp front sight, old model steel micro-click rear adjustable for w. and e. Same special features. Introduced 1984.
Price: $1,500.00

Texas Longhorn Sesquicentennial Model Revolver
Similar to the South Texas Army Model except has ¾-coverage Nimschke-style engraving, antique golden nickel plate finish, one-piece elephant ivory grips. Comes with hand-made solid walnut presentation case, factory letter to owner. Limited edition of 150 units. Introduced 1986.
Price: $2,500.00

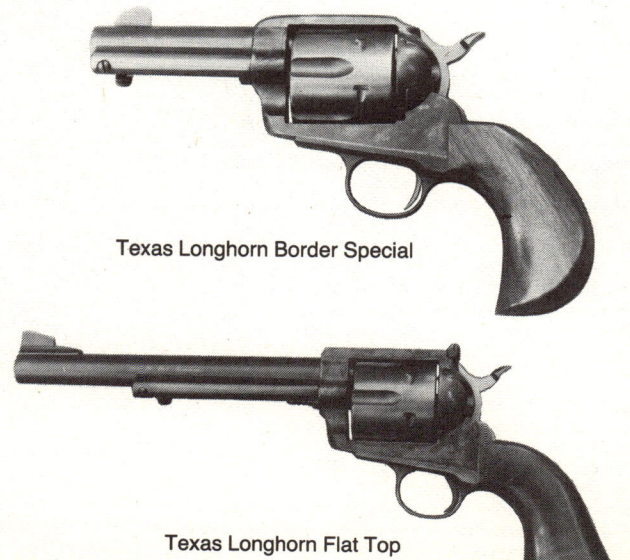

Texas Longhorn Border Special

Texas Longhorn Flat Top

HANDGUNS—SINGLE ACTION REVOLVERS

UBERTI 1873 CATTLEMAN SINGLE ACTIONS
Caliber: 22 LR, 22 WMR, 32-20, 38 Spec., 38-40, 357 Mag., 44 Spec., 44-40, 45 Colt, 6-shot.
Barrel: 4¾", 5½", 7½"; 44-40, 45 Colt also with 3".
Weight: 38 oz. (5½" bbl.). **Length:** 10¾" over-all (5½" bbl.).
Stocks: One-piece smooth walnut.
Sights: Blade front, groove rear; fully adjustable rear.
Features: Steel or brass backstrap, trigger guard; color case-hardened frame, blued barrel, cylinder. Imported from Italy by Benson Firearms, Uberti USA.
Price: Steel backstrap, trigger guard, fixed sights $375.00
Price: As above, adj. sight $399.00
Price: Brass backstrap, trigger guard, fixed sights $345.00
Price: As above, adj. sight $375.00

Uberti Cattleman

Uberti 1873 Buckhorn Single Action
A slightly larger version of the Cattleman revolver. Available in 44 Magnum or 44 Magnum/44-40 convertible, otherwise has same specs.
Price: Steel backstrap, trigger guard, fixed sights $385.00
Price: As above, brass $355.00
Price: Convertible (two cylinders) add $40.00

Uberti 1873 Buntline Single Action
Available in 357 Mag., 44-40 or 45 Colt (Cattleman frame), 44 Mag./44-40 convertible (Buckhorn frame) with 18" barrel. Weight is 3.6 lbs. with an over-all length of 23". Same sight and frame options as Cattleman and Buckhorn.
Price: Steel backstrap, trigger guard, fixed sight $409.00
Price: As above, adj sight. $435.00
Price: Brass backstrap, trigger guard, fixed sight.................. $379.00
Price: As above, adj. sight $409.00
Price: Convertible, add $65.00
Price: Shoulder stock $135.00

UBERTI 1890 ARMY "OUTLAW" REVOLVER
Caliber: 357 Mag., 44-40, 45 Colt, 6 shot.
Barrel: 5½".
Weight: 37 oz. **Length:** 12½" over-all.
Stocks: American walnut.
Sights: Blade front, groove rear.
Features: Replica of the 1890 Remington single-action. Brass trigger guard, rest is blued. Imported by Benson Firearms, Uberti USA.
Price: $369.00
Price: Nickel plated $409.00

UBERTI 1875 SA ARMY "OUTLAW" REVOLVER
Caliber: 357 Mag., 44-40, 45 Colt, 6-shot.
Barrel: 7½".
Weight: 44 oz. **Length:** 13¾" over-all.
Stocks: Smooth walnut.
Sights: Blade front, notch rear.
Features: Replica of the 1875 Remington S.A. Army revolver. Brass trigger guard, color case-hardened frame, rest blued. Imported by Benson Firearms, Uberti USA.
Price: $355.00
Price: Nickel plated $395.00

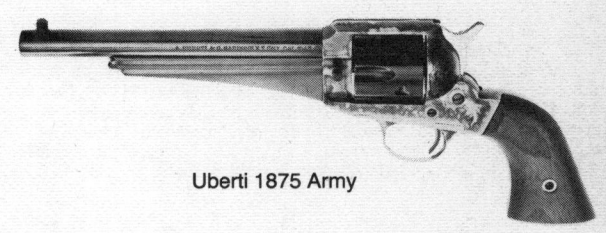
Uberti 1875 Army

UBERTI 1873 STALLION SINGLE ACTION
Caliber: 22 LR/22 WMR convertible.
Barrel: 4¾", 5½", 6½", round.
Weight: 36 oz. **Length:** 10¾" over-all.
Stocks: One-piece walnut.
Sights: Blade front, groove rear or ramp front, adjustable rear.
Features: Smaller version of the Cattleman with same frame options. Imported from Italy by Benson Firearms, Uberti USA.
Price: Steel backstrap, trigger guard, fixed sights $375.00
Price: As above, adj. sight $399.00
Price: Brass, fixed sights $345.00
Price: As above, adj. sight $375.00
Price: Stainless, fixed sight $425.00
Price: As above, adj. sight $450.00

Uberti 1873 Stallion

HANDGUNS—MISCELLANEOUS

Specially adapted single-shot and multi-barrel arms.

American Derringer Semmerling

AMERICAN DERRINGER SEMMERLING LM-4
Caliber: 9mm Para., 7-shot magazine; 45 ACP, 5-shot magazine.
Barrel: 3.625".
Weight: 24 oz. **Length:** 5.2" over-all.
Stocks: Checkered plastic on blued guns, rosewood on stainless guns.
Sights: Open, fixed.
Features: Manually-operated repeater. Height is 3.7", width is 1". Comes with manual, leather carrying case, spare stock screws, wrench. From American Derringer Corp.
Price: Blued... $1,250.00
Price: Stainless steel $1,500.00

CAUTION: PRICES CHANGE. CHECK AT GUNSHOP.

HANDGUNS—MISCELLANEOUS

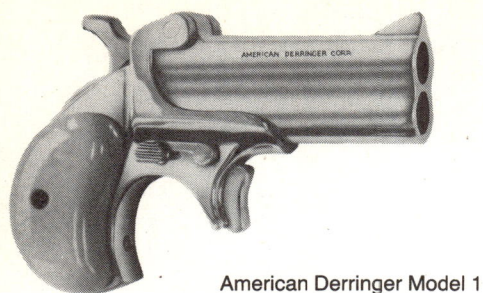
American Derringer Model 1

AMERICAN DERRINGER MODEL 1
Caliber: 22 LR, 22 WMR, 22 Hornet, 223 Rem., 30 Luger, 30-30 Win., 32 ACP, 38 Super, 380 ACP, 38 Spec., 9x18, 9mm Para., 357 Mag., 357 Maximum, 10 mm, 41 Mag., 38-40, 44-40 Win., 44 Spec., 44 American, 44 Mag., 45 Colt, 45 ACP, 410-ga. (2½").
Barrel: 3".
Weight: 15½ oz. (38 Spec.). **Length:** 4.82" over-all.
Stocks: Rosewood, Zebra wood.
Sights: Blade front.
Features: Made of stainless steel with high-polish or satin finish. Two shot capacity. Manual hammer block safety. Introduced 1980. Available in almost any pistol caliber. Contact the factory for complete list of available calibers and prices. From American Derringer Corp.
Price: 22 LR or WMR $218.00
Price: 22 Hornet, 223 Rem. $369.00
Price: 38 Spec. $187.50
Price: 357 Maximum $250.00
Price: 357 Mag. $225.00
Price: 9x18, 9mm, 380, 38 Super $172.50
Price: 10 mm $218.00
Price: 44 Spec, 44 American $275.00
Price: 38-40, 44-40 Win., 45 Colt, 45 Auto Rim $275.00
Price: 30-30, 41, 44 Mags., 45 Win. Mag. $369.00
Price: 45-70, single shot $312.00
Price: 45 Colt, 410, 2½" $312.00
Price: 45 ACP, 10mm Auto $218.00

AMERICAN DERRINGER MODEL 3
Caliber: 38 Special.
Barrel: 2.5".
Weight: 8.5 oz. **Length:** 4.9" over-all.
Stocks: Rosewood.
Sights: Blade front.
Features: Made of stainless steel. Single shot with manual hammer block safety. Introduced 1985. From American Derringer Corp.
Price: $115.00

American Derringer Model 4
Similar to the Model 1 except has 4.1" barrel, over-all length of 6", and weighs 16½ oz.; chambered for 3" 410-ga. shotshells or 45 Colt. Can be had with 45-70 upper barrel and 3" 410-ga. or 45 Colt bottom barrel. Made of stainless steel. Manual hammer block safety. Introduced 1985.
Price: 3" 410/45 Colt (either barrel) $350.00
Price: 3" 410/45 Colt or 45-70 (Alaskan Survival model) ... $369.00

American Derringer Model 7
Similar to Model 1 except made of high strength aircraft aluminum. Weighs 7½ oz., 4.82" o.a.l., rosewood stocks. Available in 22 LR, 32 S&W Long, 32 H&R Mag., 380 ACP, 38 Spec., 44 Spec. Introduced 1986.
Price: 22 LR or 38 Spec. $187.50
Price: 38 S&W, 380 ACP, 32 S&W Long $157.50
Price: 32 H&R Mag. $172.50
Price: 44 Spec. $500.00

American Derringer Model 6
Similar to the Model 1 except has 6" barrels chambered for 3" 410 shotshells or 45 Colt, rosewood stocks, 8.2" o.a.l. and weighs 21 oz. Shoots either round for each barrel. Manual hammer block safety. Introduced 1986.
Price: High polish or satin finish $369.00
Price: Gray matte finish $350.00

American Derringer Texas Commemorative
A Model 1 Derringer with solid brass frame, stainless steel barrel and stag grips. Available in 38 Special, 44-40 Win., 44 American or 45 Colt. Introduced 1987.
Price: $285.00

ANSCHUTZ EXEMPLAR BOLT ACTION PISTOL
Caliber: 22 LR, 5-shot; 22 WMR, 22 Hornet, 5-shot.
Barrel: 10", 14".
Weight: 3½ lbs. **Length:** 17" over-all.
Stock: European walnut with stippled grip and fore-end.
Sights: Hooded front on ramp, open notch rear adjustable for w. and e.
Features: Uses Match 64 action with left-hand bolt; Anschultz #5091 two-stage trigger set at 9.85 oz. Receiver grooved for scope mounting; open sights easily removed. Introduced 1987. Imported from West Germany by PSI.
Price: 22 LR $375.00
Price: 22 LR, left-hand $405.00
Price: 22 LR, 14" barrel $419.50
Price: 22 Hornet $758.00

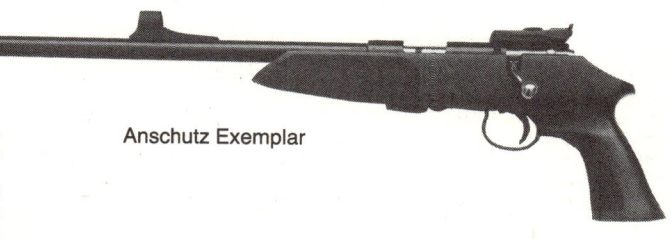
Anschutz Exemplar

Consult our Directory pages for the location of firms mentioned.

Davis Derringer

DAVIS DERRINGERS
Caliber: 22 LR, 22 WMR, 25 ACP, 32 ACP.
Barrel: 2.4".
Weight: 9.5 oz. **Length:** 4" over-all.
Stocks: Laminated wood.
Sights: Blade front, fixed notch rear.
Features: Choice of black Teflon or chrome finish; spur trigger. Introduced 1986. Made in U.S. by Davis Industries.
Price: $64.90

HANDGUNS—MISCELLANEOUS

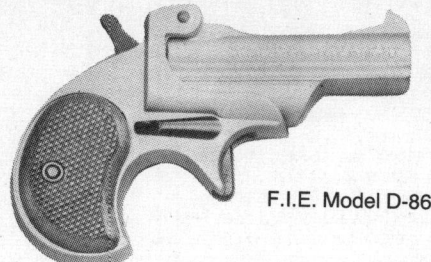
F.I.E. Model D-86

F.I.E. D-86 DERRINGER
Caliber: 38 Special.
Barrel: 3".
Weight: 14 oz.
Stocks: Checkered black nylon, walnut optional.
Sights: Fixed.
Features: Dyna-Chrome or blue finish. Spur trigger. Tip-up barrel; extractors. Made in U.S. by F.I.E. Corp.
Price: With nylon grips $94.95
Price: With walnut grips $114.95

FEATHER GUARDIAN ANGEL PISTOL
Caliber: 9mm Parabellum.
Barrel: 2".
Weight: 17 oz. **Length:** 5½" over-all.
Stocks: Black composition.
Sights: Fixed.
Features: Uses a pre-loaded two-shot drop-in "magazine." Stainless steel construction; matte finish. From Feather Enterprises. Announced 1988.
Price: $169.95

Feather Guardian Angel

INTRATEC TEC COMPANION DERRINGER
Caliber: 32 H&R Mag., 38 Spec., 357 Mag., 2 shot.
Barrel: 3".
Weight: 13 oz. **Length:** 4⅝" over-all.
Stock: Moulded composition.
Sights: Blade front, fixed rear.
Features: Double action; swing-out barrels; one-stroke ejector; automatic selector; trigger/hammer block safety; matte black finish. From Intratec.
Price: $114.95

Intratec TEC-38

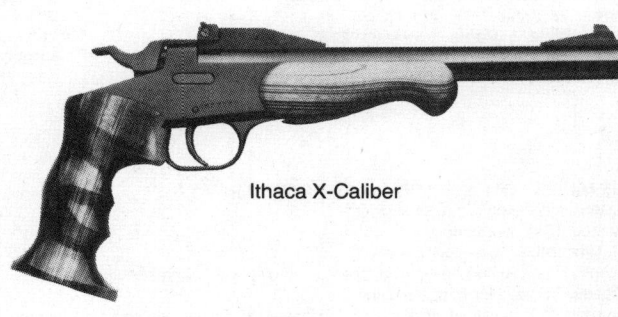
Ithaca X-Caliber

ITHACA X-CALIBER SINGLE SHOT
Caliber: 22 LR, 223 Rem., 35 Rem., 357 Mag., 357 Max., 44 Mag.
Barrel: 10", 15".
Weight: 3¼ lbs. **Length:** 15" over-all (10" barrel).
Stocks: Goncalo Alves grip and fore-end on Model 20; American walnut on Model 30.
Sights: Blade on ramp front; Model 20 has adjustable, removeable target-type rear. Model 30 has step-adjustable Deerslayer and is grooved for scope mounting.
Features: Dual firing pin for RF/CF use. Model 20 has polished blue finish, Model 30 has matte teflon finish and comes with sling.
Price: Model 20, Model 30, 10" or 15" $256.00

Kimber Predator

KIMBER PREDATOR PISTOL
Caliber: 221 Fireball, 223 Rem., 6mm TCU, 6 x45, 7mm TCU; single shot.
Barrel: 15¾".
Weight: About 5½ lbs. **Length:** NA
Stock: AA claro walnut (Hunter); French walnut (Supergrade).
Sights: None furnished. Accepts Kimber scope mount system.
Features: Uses the Kimber Model 84 mini-Mauser action. Supergrade has ebony fore-end tip, 22 l.p.i. checkering. Introduced 1987.
Price: Hunter.. $995.00
Price: Supergrade $1,195.00

LJUTIC LJ II PISTOL
Caliber: 22 WMR.
Barrel: 2¾".
Stocks: Checkered walnut.
Sights: Fixed.
Features: Double action; ventilated rib; side-by-side barrels; positive on/off safety. Introduced 1981. From Ljutic Industries.
Price: $1,199.00

MANDALL/CABANAS PISTOL
Caliber: 177, pellet or round ball; single shot.
Barrel: 9".
Weight: 51 oz. **Length:** 19" over-all.
Stock: Smooth wood with thumb rest.
Sights: Blade front on ramp, open adjustable rear.
Features: Fires round ball or pellets with 22 blank cartridge. Automatic saftety; muzzle brake. Imported from Mexico by Mandall Shooting Supplies.
Price: $125.00

CAUTION: PRICES CHANGE. CHECK AT GUNSHOP.

HANDGUNS—MISCELLANEOUS

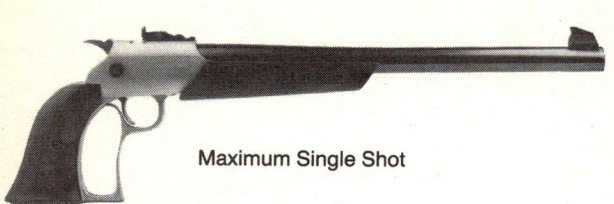
Maximum Single Shot

MAXIMUM SINGLE SHOT PISTOL
Caliber: 22 Hornet, 22 BR, 223 Rem., 22-250, 6mm BR, 6mm-223, 243, 250 Savage, 6.5mm-35, 7mm TCU, 7mm BR, 7mm-35, 7mm INT-R, 7mm-08, 7mm Rocket, 7mm Super Mag., 30 Herrett, 308 Win., 32-20, 357 Mag., 357 Maximum, 358 Win., 44 Mag.
Barrel: 8¾", 10½", 14".
Weight: 61 oz. (10½" bbl.), 67 oz. (14" bbl.). **Length:** 15", 18½" over-all (with 10½" and 14" bbl., respectively).
Stocks: Smooth walnut stocks and fore-end.
Sights: Ramp front, fully adjustable open rear.
Features: Falling block action; drilled and tapped for M.O.A. scope mounts; integral grip frame/receiver; adjustable trigger; Douglas barrel (interchangeable); Armoloy finish. Introduced 1983. Made in U.S. by M.O.A. Corp.
Price: 8¾", 10", 14" $499.00
Price: Extra barrels $129.00
Price: Scope mount $39.00

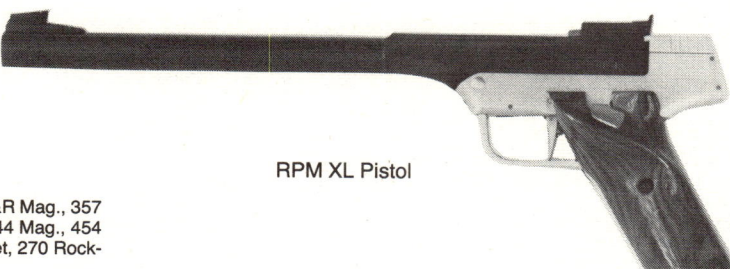
RPM XL Pistol

RPM XL SINGLE SHOT PISTOL
Caliber: 22 LR, 22 WMR, 225 Win., 25 Rocket, 6.5 Rocket, 32 H&R Mag., 357 Max., 357 Mag., 30-30 Win., 30 Herrett, 357 Herrett, 41 Mag., 44 Mag., 454 Casull, 375 Win., 7mm UR, 7mm Merrill, 30 Merrill, 7mm Rocket, 270 Rocket, 270 Max., 45-70.
Barrel: 8" slab, 10", 10¾", 12", 14" bull; 450" wide vent. rib, matted to prevent glare.
Weight: About 60 oz. **Length:** 12¼" over-all (10¾" bbl.).
Stocks: Smooth walnut with thumb and heel rest.
Sights: Front .125" blade (.100" blade optional); Millett or ISGW rear adj. for w. and e.
Features: Polished blue finish, hard chrome optional. Barrel is drilled and tapped for scope mounting. Cooking indicator visible from rear of gun. Has spring-loaded barrel lock, positive hammer block thumb safety. Trigger adjustable for weight of pull and over-travel. For complete price list contact RPM.
Price: Regular ¾" frame, right-hand action $585.00
Price: As above, left-hand action $610.00
Price: Wide ⅞" frame, right-hand action only $635.00
Price: Extra barrel, 8"-10¾" $180.00
Price: Extra barrel, 12"-14" $250.00

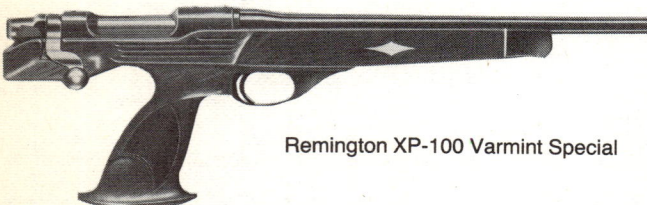
Remington XP-100 Varmint Special

REMINGTON XP-100 "VARMINT SPECIAL"
Caliber: 223 Rem., single shot.
Barrel: 10½", ventilated rib.
Weight: 60 oz. **Length:** 16¾".
Stock: Brown nylon one-piece, checkered grip with white spacers.
Sights: Tapped for scope mount.
Features: Fits left or right hand, is shaped to fit fingers and heel of hand. Grooved trigger. Rotating thumb safety, cavity in fore-end permits insertion of up to five 38 cal., 130-gr.metal jacketed bullets to adjust weight and balance. Included is a black vinyl, zippered case.
Price: Including case, about $373.00

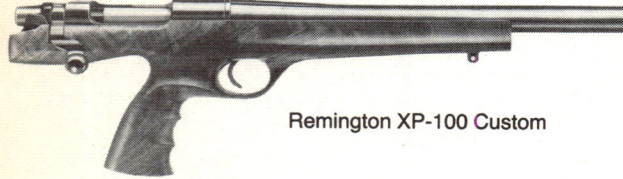
Remington XP-100 Custom

Remington XP-100 Custom Long Range Pistol
Similar to the XP-100 "Varmint Special" except chambered for 223 Rem. (heavy barrel), 7mm-08 Rem. and 35 Rem.; comes with sights—interchangeable blade on ramp front, fully adjustable Bo-Mar rear. Custom Shop 14½" barrel, Custom Shop English walnut stock in right- or left-hand configuration. Action tuned in Custom Shop. Weight is under 4½ lbs. Introduced 1986.
Price: $907.00

TEXAS LONGHORN "THE JEZEBEL" PISTOL
Caliber: 22 Short, Long, Long Rifle, single shot.
Barrel: 6".
Weight: 15 oz. **Length:** 8" over-all.
Stocks: One-piece fancy walnut grip (right or left hand), walnut fore-end.
Sights: Bead front, fixed rear.
Features: Hand-made gun. Top-break action; all stainless steel; automatic hammer block safety; music wire coil springs. Barrel is half round, half octagon. Announced 1986. From Texas Longhorn Arms.
Price: About $250.00

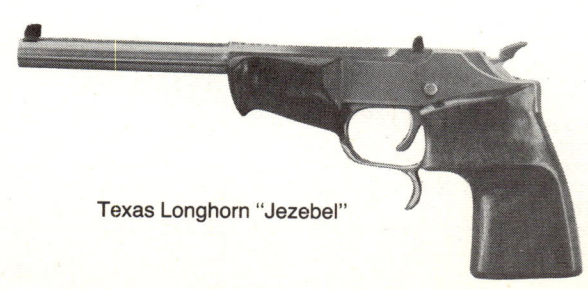
Texas Longhorn "Jezebel"

HANDGUNS—MISCELLANEOUS

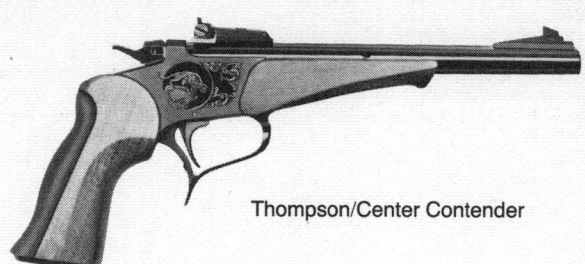
Thompson/Center Contender

THOMPSON/CENTER ARMS CONTENDER
Caliber: 7mm TCU, 30-30 Win., 22 S, L, LR, 22 WMR, 22 Hornet, 223 Rem., 30 Carbine, 9mm Para., 7 x 30 Waters, 32 H&R Mag., 32-20 Win., 357 Mag., 357 Rem. Max., 44 Mag., 45/410, single shot.
Barrel: 10", tapered octagon, bull barrel and vent. rib.
Weight: 43 oz. (10" bbl.). **Length:** 13¼" (10" bbl.).
Stocks: T/C "Competitor Grip." Right or left hand.
Sights: Under-cut blade ramp front, rear adj. for w. & e.
Features: Break-open action with auto-safety. Single-action only. Interchangeable bbls., both caliber (rim & centerfire), and length. Drilled and tapped for scope. Engraved frame. See T/C catalog for exact barrel/caliber availability.
Price: Blued (rimfire cals.) $335.00
Price: Blued (centerfire cals.) $335.00
Price: With Armour Alloy II finish $405.00
Price: With internal choke $410.00
Price: As above, vent. rib $425.00
Price: Extra bbls. (standard octagon) $145.00
Price: Bushnell Phantom scope base $13.50
Price: 45/410, vent. rib, internal choke bbl. $165.00

UBERTI ROLLING BLOCK TARGET PISTOL
Caliber: 22 LR, 22 WMR., 22 Hornet, 357 Mag., single shot.
Barrel: 9⅞", half-round, half-octagon.
Weight: 44 oz. **Length:** 14" over-all.
Stocks: Walnut grip and fore-end.
Sights: Blade front, fully adj. rear.
Features: Replica of the 1871 rolling block target pistol. Brass trigger guard, color case-hardened frame, blue barrel. Imported by Benson Firearms, Uberti USA.
Price: $305.00

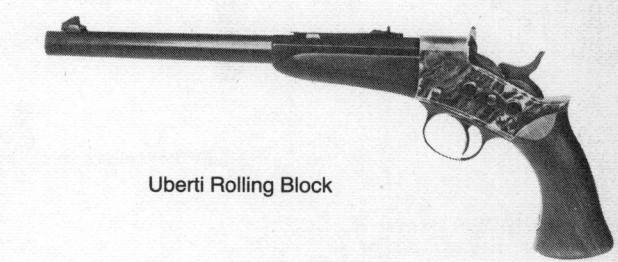
Uberti Rolling Block

ULTRA LIGHT ARMS MODEL 20 REB HUNTER'S PISTOL
Caliber: 22-250 thru 308 Win. standard. Most silhouette calibers and others on request. 5-shot magazine.
Barrel: 14", Douglas No. 3.
Weight: 4 lbs.
Stock: Composite Kevlar, graphite reinforced. Du Pont Imron paint in green, brown, black and camo.
Sights: None furnished. Scope mount included.
Features: Timney adjustable trigger; two position, three-function safety; benchrest quality action; matte or bright stock and metal finish; right or left-hand action. Shipped in hard case. Introduced 1987. From Ultra Light Arms.
Price: $1,300.00

Ultra Light Model 20

CENTERFIRE RIFLES—MILITARY STYLE AUTOLOADERS

Suitable for, and adaptable to, certain kinds of competitions as well as sporting purposes, such as hunting.

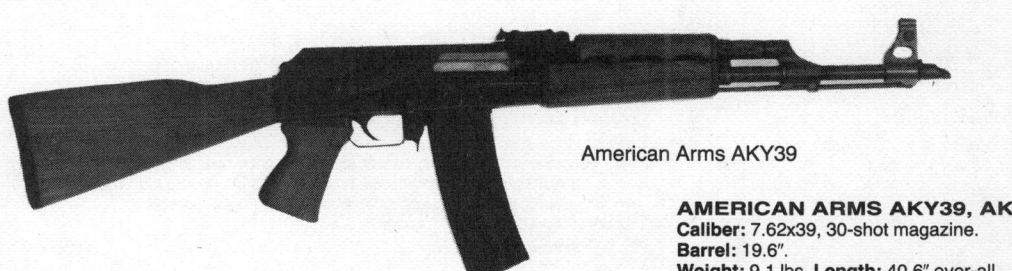
American Arms AKY39

AMAC LONG RANGE RIFLE
Caliber: 50 BMG.
Barrel: 33", fully fluted, free floating.
Weight: 30 lbs. **Length:** 55.5" over-all.
Stock: Composition. Adjustable drop and comb.
Sights: Comes with Leupold Ultra M1 20x scope.
Features: Bolt-action long range rifle. Comes with Automatic Ranging Scope Base. Adjustable trigger. Rifle breaks down for transport, storage. From Iver Johnson.
Price: $8,500.00

AMERICAN ARMS AKY39, AKF39 RIFLES
Caliber: 7.62x39, 30-shot magazine.
Barrel: 19.6".
Weight: 9.1 lbs. **Length:** 40.6" over-all.
Stock: Teakwood (AKY39), folding metal (AKF39).
Sights: Hooded post front, open adjustable rear. Flip-up Tritium night sights front and rear.
Features: Matte blue finish on metal, oil-finished wood. Imported from Yugoslavia by American Arms, Inc.
Price: Wood stock (AKY30) $595.00
Price: Folding metal stock (AKF39) $625.00

CAUTION: PRICES CHANGE. CHECK AT GUNSHOP.

CENTERFIRE RIFLES—MILITARY STYLE AUTOLOADERS

AUTO-ORDNANCE MODEL 27 A-1 THOMPSON
Caliber: 45 ACP, 30-shot magazine.
Barrel: 16".
Weight: 11½ lbs. **Length:** About 42" over-all (Deluxe).
Stock: Walnut stock and vertical fore-end.
Sights: Blade front, open rear adj. for w.
Features: Recreation of Thompson Model 1927. Semi-auto only. Deluxe model has finned barrel, adj. rear sight and compensator; Standard model has plain barrel and military sight. From Auto-Ordnance Corp.
Price: Deluxe $716.00
Price: Standard (horizontal fore-end) $716.00
Price: 1927A5 Pistol (M27A1 without stock; wgt. 7 lbs.) $622.50
Price: Lightweight model $631.50

AUSTRALIAN AUTOMATIC ARMS SAR RIFLE
Caliber: 223, 5- or 20-shot magazine.
Barrel: 16.25".
Weight: 7.5 lbs. **Length:** 35.8" over-all.
Stock: Fixed composition.
Sights: Protected post front, revolving aperture read adjustable for windage.
Features: Gas operated with short-stroke mobile cylinder. Hammer forged barrel with chrome chamber and bore. Imported from Australia by Kendall International.
Price: $775.00

Thompson M1

Auto-Ordnance Thompson M1
Similar to the Model 27 A-1 except is in the M-1 configuration with side cocking knob, horizontal fore-end, smooth un-finned barrel, sling swivels on butt and fore-end. Matte black finish. Introduced 1985.
Price: $625.00

BUSHMASTER AUTO RIFLE
Caliber: 223, 30-shot magazine
Barrel: 18½".
Weight: 6¼ lbs. **Length:** 37.5" over-all.
Stock: Rock maple.
Sights: Protected post front adj. for elevation, protected quick-flip rear peep adj. for windage; short and long range.
Features: Steel alloy upper receiver with welded barrel assembly; AK-47-type gas system, aluminum lower receiver; silent sling and swivels; bayonet lug; one-piece welded steel alloy bolt carrier assembly. From Bushmaster Firearms.
Price: With maple stock $384.95
Price: With nylon-coated folding stock $394.95
Price: Matte electroless finish, maple stock $394.95
Price: As above, folding stock $394.95

Bushmaster Auto Rifle

BERETTA AR70 SPORTER RIFLE
Caliber: 223, 8- and 30-shot magazines.
Barrel: 17.2".
Weight: 8.3 lbs. **Length:** 38" over-all.
Stock: Black high-impact plastic.
Sights: Blade front, diopter rear adjustable for windage and elevation.
Features: Matte black epoxy finish; easy take-down. Comes with both magazines, cleaning kit, carrying strap. Imported from Italy by Beretta U.S.A. Corp. Introduced 1984.
Price: $800.00

Barrett Light-Fifty

BARRETT LIGHT-FIFTY MODEL 82A-1
Caliber: 50 BMG, 11-shot detachable box magazine.
Barrel: 33".
Weight: 35 lbs. **Length:** 63" over-all.
Stock: Uni-body construction.
Sights: None furnished.
Features: Semi-automatic, recoil operated with recoiling barrel. Three-lug locking bolt; six-port harmonica-type muzzle brake. Bipod legs and M-60 mount standard. Fires same 50-cal. ammunition as the M2HB machine gun. Introduced 1985. From Barrett Firearms.
Price: Parkerized $5,995.00

Colt AR-15A2

COLT AR-15A2 CARBINE
Caliber: 223 Rem.
Barrel: 16".
Weight: 5.8 lbs. **Length:** 35" over-all (extended).
Stock: Telescoping aluminum.
Sights: Post front, adjustable for elevation, flip-type rear for short, long range, windage.
Features: 5-round detachable box magazine, flash suppressor, sling swivels. Forward bolt assist included. Introduced 1985.
Price: Limited availability $769.95

CENTERFIRE RIFLES—MILITARY STYLE AUTOLOADERS

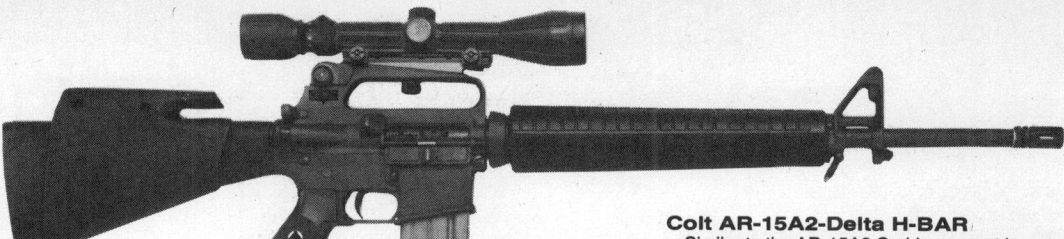

Colt AR-15A2 Delta H-BAR

Colt AR-15A2-Delta H-BAR
Similar to the AR-15A2 Carbine except has standard stock, is refined and inspected by the Colt Custom Shop. Comes with a 3-9x rubber armored scope and removeable cheek piece, adjustable scope mount, black leather military-style sling, cleaning kit, and hard carrying case. Pistol grip has Delta medallion. Introduced 1987.
Price: $1,359.95

Colt AR-15A2 H-BAR
Similar to the AR-15A2 Delta H-BAR except has heavy barrel, 800-meter M-16A2 rear sight adjustable for windage and elevation, case deflector for left-hand shooters, target-style nylon sling. Introduced 1986.
Price: $869.95

COMMANDO ARMS CARBINE
Caliber: 45 ACP.
Barrel: 16½".
Weight: 8 lbs. **Length:** 37" over-all.
Stock: Walnut buttstock.
Sights: Blade front, peep rear.
Features: Semi-auto only. Cocking handle on left side. Choice of magazines—5, 20, 30 or 90 shot. From Gibbs Guns.
Price: Mark 9 or Mark 45, blue $259.00
Price: Nickel plated $304.00

Daewoo AR110C Auto Carbine
Similar to the MAX-1 except has a folding buttstock giving over-all length of 38.9" (extended), 28.7" (folded). Weight is 7.5 lbs.; barrel length is 18.3". Has hooded post front sight, adjustable peep rear. Uses AR-15/M-16 magazines. Introduced 1985. Imported from Korea by Pacific International.
Price: $399.95

Daewoo AR100

DAEWOO AR100 AUTO RIFLE
Caliber: 5.56mm (223), 30-round magazine.
Barrel: 17".
Weight: 6.5 lbs. **Length:** 38.4" over-all (butt extended).
Stock: Retractable.
Sights: Post front, adjustable peep rear.
Features: Machine-forged receiver; gas-operated action; uses AR-15/M-16 magazines. Introduced 1985. Imported from Korea by Pacific International.
Price: $429.95

FN-LAR Competition

FN-LAR COMPETITION AUTO
Caliber: 308 Win., 20-shot magazine.
Barrel: 21" (24" with flash hider).
Weight: 9 lbs., 7 oz. **Length:** 44½" over-all.
Stock: Black composition butt, fore-end and pistol grip.
Sights: Post front, aperture rear adj. for elevation, 200 to 600 meters.
Features: Has sling swivels, carrying handle, rubber recoil pad. Consecutively numbered pairs available at additional cost. Imported by Gun South, Inc.
Price: $3,179.00

FN-LAR Paratrooper 308 Match 50-64
Similar to FN-LAR competition except with folding skeleton stock, shorter barrel, modified rear sight. Imported by Gun South, Inc.
Price: $3,239.00

FN-LAR Heavy Barrel 308 Match
Similar to FN-LAR competition except has wooden stock and fore-end, heavy barrel, folding metal bipod. Imported by Gun South, Inc.
Price: With wooden, stock $4,175.00
Price: With synthetic stock $3,776.00

FN 308 Model 50-63
Similar to the FN-LAR except has 18" barrel, skeleton-type folding buttstock, folding cocking handle. Introduced 1982. Imported from Belgium by Gun South, Inc.
Price: $3,239.00

FNC AUTO RIFLE
Caliber: 223 Rem.
Barrel: 18".
Weight: 9.61 lbs.
Stock: Synthetic stock.
Sights: Post front; flip-over aperture rear adj. for elevation.
Features: Updated version of FN-FAL in shortened carbine form. Has 30-shot box magazine, synthetic pistol grip, fore-end. Introduced 1981. Imported by Gun South, Inc.
Price: Standard model $2,204.00
Price: Paratrooper, with folding stock $2,322.00

FNC Auto Rifle

CAUTION: PRICES CHANGE. CHECK AT GUNSHOP.

CENTERFIRE RIFLES—MILITARY STYLE AUTOLOADERS

Federal XC-900/XC-450

FEDERAL XC-900/XC-450 AUTO CARBINES
Caliber: 9mm Para., 32-shot magazine; 45 ACP.
Barrel: 16.5" (with flash hider).
Weight: 8 lbs. **Length:** 34½" over-all.
Stock: Detachable tube steel; adjustable stock optional.
Sights: Hooded post front, peep rear adjustable for w. and e.
Features: Quick takedown for transport, storage. All heli-arc welded steel construction. Made in U.S. by Federal Engineering Corp.
Price: Phosphate finish, either cal. $513.50
Price: As above, with adj. stock. $561.54
Price: With teflon finish, nylon covered fore-end, hard-chrome bolt . $610.94
Price: As above, with adj. stock. $656.44

FEATHER AT-9 AUTO CARBINE
Caliber: 9mm Parabellum, 32-shot magazine.
Barrel: 16".
Weight: 5 lbs. **Length:** 33½" overall (stock extended).
Stock: Telescoping wire, composition pistol grip.
Sights: Hooded post front, adjustable aperture rear.
Features: Semi-auto only. Matte black finish. From Feather Enterpirses. Announced 1988.
Price: $499.95

Galil Auto Rifle

GALIL 308 AR SEMI-AUTO RIFLE
Caliber: 308 Win., 25-shot magazine.
Barrel: 18.5".
Weight: 9.6 lbs. **Length:** 39" over-all (stock extended).
Stock: Tube-type metal folding stock.
Sights: Post-type front, flip-type "L" rear.
Features: Gas operated, rotating bolt. Cocking handle, safety and magazine catch can be operated from either side. Introduced 1982. Imported from Israel by Action Arms Ltd.
Price: $849.00
Price: As above in 223 (16.1" bbl., 36.5" o.a.l., 35-shot magazine). . . $795.00

Galil Model ARM Semi-Auto Rifle
Similar to the standard AR models except comes with folding bipod with integral wire cutter, vented hardwood handguard and carrying handle. Other specs are the same. Introduced 1987.
Price: 223 . . . . $875.00
Price: 308 . . . . $940.00

Goncz Carbine

GONCZ HIGH-TECH CARBINE
Caliber: 9mm Para., 30 Mauser, 38 Super, 18- and 32-shot magazine; 45 ACP, 10- and 20-shot magazine.
Barrel: 16.1".
Weight: 4 lbs., 2 oz. **Length:** 31" over-all.
Stock: Grooved alloy pistol grip, black high-impact plastic butt. Walnut optional at extra cost.
Sights: Front adjustable for e., rear adjustable for w.
Features: Fires from closed bolt; floating firing pin; safety locks the firing pin; all metal construction; barrel threaded for accessories. Matte black oxide and anodized finish. Designed by Lajos J. Goncz. Introduced 1985. From Goncz Co.
Price: $385.00
Price: With halogen light. $500.00
Price: With laser sight system $1,495.00

Heckler & Koch HK-91

HECKLER & KOCH HK-91 AUTO RIFLE
Caliber: 308 Win., 5- or 20-shot magazine.
Barrel: 17.71".
Weight: 9½ lbs. **Length:** 40¼" over-all.
Stock: Black high-impact plastic.
Sights: Post front, aperture rear adj. for w. and e.
Features: Delayed roller-lock action. Sporting version of West German service rifle. Takes special H&K clamp scope mount. Imported from West Germany by Heckler & Koch, Inc.
Price: HK-91 A-2 with plastic stock. $932.00
Price: HK-91 A-3 with retractable metal stock. $1,098.00
Price: HK-91 scope mount with 1" rings. $346.00

Heckler & Koch HK-93 Auto Rifle
Similar to HK-91 except in 223 cal., 16.13" barrel, over-all length of 35½", weighs 7¾ lbs. Same stock, fore-end.
Price: HK-93 A-2 with plastic stock. $932.00
Price: HK-93 A-3 with retractable metal stock. $1,098.00

CENTERFIRE RIFLES—MILITARY STYLE AUTOLOADERS

Heckler & Koch HK-94

HECKLER & KOCH HK-94 AUTO CARBINE
Caliber: 9mm Parabellum, 15-shot magazine.
Barrel: 16".
Weight: 6½ lbs. (fixed stock). **Length:** 34¾" over-all.
Stock: High-impact plastic butt and fore-end or retractable metal stock.
Sights: Hooded post front, aperture rear adjustable for windage and elevation.
Features: Delayed roller-locked action; accepts H&K quick-detachable scope mount. Introduced 1983. Imported from West Germany by Heckler & Koch, Inc.
Price: HK-94-A2 (fixed stock) $932.00
Price: HK-94-A3 (retractable metal stock) $1,098.00
Price: 30-shot magazine.. $33.75
Price: Clamp to hold two magazines $25.00

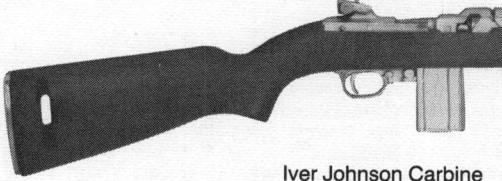
Iver Johnson Carbine

IVER JOHNSON PM30HB CARBINE
Caliber: 30 U.S. Carbine.
Barrel: 18" four-groove.
Weight: 6½ lbs. **Length:** 35½" over-all.
Stock: Glossy-finished hardwood or walnut.
Sights: Click adj. peep rear.
Features: Gas operated semi-auto carbine. 15-shot detachable magazine. Made in U.S.A.
Price: Blue finish, hardwood stock $265.00
Price: Blue finish, walnut stock $291.50
Price: Paratrooper.. $291.50

MAS 223 Auto

MAS 223 SEMI-AUTO RIFLE
Caliber: 223, 25-shot magazine.
Barrel: 19.2".
Weight: About 8 lbs. **Length:** 29.8" over-all.
Stock: Rubber-covered adjustable check piece converts to left- or right-hand shooters.
Sights: Adjustable blade front with luminescent spot for night use, aperture adj. rear.
Features: Converts to left- or right-hand ejection. Armored plastic guards vital parts, including sights. Civilian version of the French FAMAS assault rifle. Introduced 1986. Imported from France by Century Arms.
Price: With spare parts kit, bipod, sling, spare magazine, about ... $1,295.00

Mitchell AK-47

MITCHELL AK-47 SEMI-AUTO RIFLE
Caliber: 223, 308, 7.62x39, 30-shot magazine.
Barrel: 19.6".
Weight: 9.1 lbs. **Length:** 40.6" over-all with wood stock.
Stock: Teak.
Sights: Hooded post front, open adj. rear.
Features: Gas operated semi-automatic. Last-round bolt hold-open. Imported from Yugoslavia by Mitchell Arms.
Price: Wood stock $675.00
Price: With folding metal stock $698.00

Mitchell Heavy Barrel AK-47
Same gun as the standard AK-47 except has heavy finned barrel, heavy fore-end, fully adjustable day or night sights. Available with or without folding, detachable bipod.
Price: $995.00

Mitchell M-76

MITCHELL M-76 COUNTER-SNIPER RIFLE
Caliber: 7.9 mm.
Barrel: 21.8". Muzzle brake, flash hider.
Weight: 10.9 lbs. **Length:** 44.6" over-all.
Stock: Teak.
Features: Uses AK-47 action. Optional scope, night sight, mounts available. Imported from Yugoslavia by Mitchell Arms.
Price: $1,525.00

CAUTION: PRICES CHANGE. CHECK AT GUNSHOP.

CENTERFIRE RIFLES—MILITARY STYLE AUTOLOADERS

MITCHELL M-59 SEMI-AUTO RIFLE
Caliber: 7.62x39, 10-shot magazine.
Barrel: 18".
Weight: 9 lbs. **Length:** 44" over-all.
Stock: Walnut.
Sights: Hooded post front, open adj. rear.
Features: Gas-operated likeness of the SKS rifle. Imported from Yugoslavia by Mitchell Arms.
Price: $666.00

NORINCO OFFICER'S NINE CARBINE
Caliber: 9mm Parabellum, 25-round magazine.
Barrel: 16.1".
Weight: 8.4 lbs. **Length:** 24.4" over-all (stock folded).
Stock: Folding metal.
Sights: Post-type front, flip-type rear.
Features: Blue finish. Similar to the famous Israeli submachine gun. Imported from China by Pacific International. Introduced 1988.
Price: $459.95

Poly Tech AK47/S

POLY TECH AK-47/S AUTO RIFLE
Caliber: 7.62x39, 30-shot magazine; optional 5-, 20- 40-shot box magazines, 75-round drum magazine available.
Barrel: 16⅜".
Weight: 8.2 lbs. **Length:** 34⅜" over-all.
Stock: Oil-finished Chiu wood.
Sights: Protected post front, leaf rear graduated to 800 meters.
Features: Semi-auto version of the original AK-47. Receiver is machined from bar stock. Chrome lined barrel, chromed gas piston; phosphated bolt and bolt carrier. Spring-loaded firing pin. Comes with three 30-shot magazines, cleaning kit, web sling, oil bottle and an original AK-47-pattern bayonet. Imported from China by Poly Technologies, Inc.
Price: $579.95

Poly Tech AKS-762 Folding Stock Rifle
Similar to the AKS-762 Wood Stock rifle except has side-folding skeleton stock. Semi-auto version of the Chinese Type 56-2 assault rifle. No bayonet mount.
Price: $449.95

Poly Tech M-14/S

POLY TECH M-14/S AUTO RIFLE
Caliber: 7.62mm NATO, 20-shot box magazine.
Barrel: 22" (without flash hider).
Weight: 9.2 lbs. **Length:** 43 ³⁄₁₀" over-all.
Stock: Oil-finished Chinese walnut, fiberglass handguard (walnut optional).
Sights: Square blade front, click adjustable aperture rear.
Features: Semi-auto only. Receiver is machined from chrome-moly steel. Chrome lined barrel, chromed gas piston. Parkerized finish. Announced 1988. Imported from China by Poly Technologies, Inc.
Price: $709.95

POLY TECH AKS-762 AUTO RIFLE
Caliber: 7.62x39, 30-shot magazine; optional 5-, 20- and 40-shot, 75-round drum magazines available.
Barrel: 16⅜".
Weight: About 8.4 lbs. **Length:** 34⅜" over-all.
Stock: Oil-finished Chiu wood.
Sights: Hooded post front, leaf rear graduated to 800 meters.
Features: Semi-auto version of the Chinese Type 56 (AKM) rifle. Chrome-lined barrel, chromed gas piston, phospated bolt and bolt carrier, rest blued. Spring-loaded firing pin. Comes with detachable Type 56 spike bayonet, sling, cleaning kit, oil bottle. Imported from China by Poly Technologies, Inc.
Price: Wood or folding metal stock $419.95

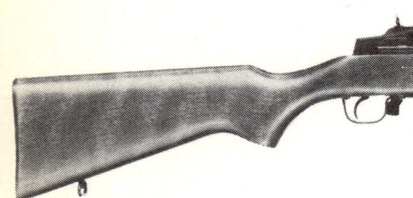

Ruger Mini Thirty

RUGER MINI-14/5R RANCH RIFLE
Caliber: 223 Rem., 5-shot detachable box magazine.
Barrel: 18½".
Weight: 6.4 lbs. **Length:** 37¼" over-all.
Stock: American hardwood, steel reinforced.
Sights: Ramp front, fully adj. rear.
Features: Fixed piston gas-operated, positive primary extraction. New buffer system, redesigned ejector system. Ruger S100RH scope rings included. 20-shot magazines available from Ruger dealers, 30-shot magazine available only to police departments and government agencies.
Price: Mini-14/5R, blued $437.00
Price: Mini-14/5RF, blued, folding stock $515.00
Price: K Mini-14/5R, stainless $478.50
Price: K Mini-14/5RF, stainless, folding stock $541.00

Ruger Mini Thirty Rifle
Similar to the Mini-14 Ranch Rifle except modified to chamber the 7.62x39 Russian service round. Weight is about 7 lbs., 3 oz. Has 6-groove barrel with 1-10" twist, Ruger Integral Scope Mount bases and folding peep rear sight. Detachable 5-shot staggered box magazine. Blued finish. Introduced 1987.
Price: $437.00

CENTERFIRE RIFLES—MILITARY STYLE AUTOLOADERS

Ruger Mini-14/5F

Ruger Mini-14/5F Folding Stock
Same as the Ranch Rifle except available with folding stock, checkered high impact plastic vertical pistol grip. Over-all length with stock open is 37¾", length closed is 27½". Weight is about 7¾ lbs.
Price: Blued ordnance steel, standard stock, Mini-14/5 .... $437.00
Price: Stainless, K-Mini 14/5 .... $447.00
Price: Blued, folding stock, Mini-14/5 F $483.50
Price: Stainless, folding stock, K-Mini-14/5 F $514.50

Spectre Carbine

SPECTRE AUTO CARBINE
Caliber: 9mm Para., 30-shot magazine.
Barrel: 16.5".
Weight: 5.3 lbs. **Length:** 35.5" over-all (stock extended).
Stock: Folding metal.
Sights: Post front, two-position flip rear.
Features: Double- or single-action fire; 50-shot magazine available. Introduced 1987. Imported by Mitchell Arms, Inc.
Price: $680.00

SPRINGFIELD ARMORY SAR-48 RIFLE
Caliber: 7.62mm NATO (308 Win.), 20-shot magazine.
Barrel: 21".
Weight: 9.9 lbs. **Length:** 43.3" over-all.
Stock: Fiberglass.
Sights: Adjustable front, adjustable peep rear.
Features: New production. Introduced 1985. From Springfield Armory.
Price: Standard model $899.00
Price: "Bush" rifle, 18" barrel $899.00
Price: Heavy Barrel rifle $899.00
Price: Model 22, 22 LR trainer $760.00
Price: Para model, folding stock $969.00

Springfield Armory SAR-48 Bush

Springfield Armory M1A

SPRINGFIELD ARMORY M1A RIFLE
Caliber: 7.62mm NATO (308), 243 Win., 5-, 10- or 20-shot box magazine.
Barrel: 25 1/16" with flash suppressor, 22" without suppressor.
Weight: 8¾ lbs. **Length:** 44¼" over-all.
Stock: American walnut or birch with walnut colored heat-resistant fiberglass handguard. Matching walnut handguard available.
Sights: Military, square blade front, full click-adjustable aperture rear.
Features: Commercial equivalent of the U.S. M-14 service rifle with no provision for automatic firing. From Springfield Armory. Military accessories available including 3-9x56 ART scope and mount.
Price: Standard M1A rifle, about $782.00
Price: Match Grade, about $998.00
Price: Super Match (heavy premium barrel), about $1,231.00
Price: M1A-A1 Assault Rifle, walnut stock, about $859.00
Price: As above, folding stock, about $874.00

Springfield Armory BM-59 Alpine

SPRINGFIELD ARMORY BM-59
Caliber: 7.62mm NATO (308 Win.), 20-shot box magazine.
Barrel: 17.5".
Weight: 9¼ lbs. **Length:** 38.5" over-all.

Stock: Walnut, with trapped rubber butt pad.
Sights: Military square blade front, click adj. peep rear.
Features: Full military-dress Italian service rifle. Available in selective fire or semi-auto only. Refined version of the M-1 Garand. Accessories available include: folding alpine stock, muzzle brake/flash suppressor/grenade launcher combo, bipod, winter trigger, grenade launcher sights, bayonet, oiler. Extremely limited quantities. Introduced 1981.
Price: Standard Italian model, about $1,248.00
Price: Alpine model, about $1,435.00
Price: Alpine Paratrooper model, about $1,624.00
Price: Nigerian Mark IV model, about $1,365.00

CAUTION: PRICES CHANGE. CHECK AT GUNSHOP.

CENTERFIRE RIFLES—MILITARY STYLE AUTOLOADERS

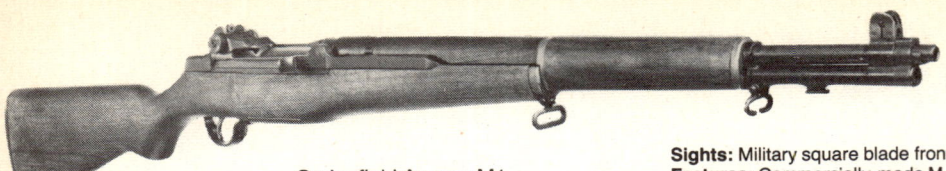

Springfield Armory M1

SPRINGFIELD ARMORY M1 GARAND RIFLE
Caliber: 308, 30-06, 8-shot clip.
Barrel: 24".
Weight: 9½ lbs. **Length:** 43½" over-all.
Stock: Walnut, military.
Sights: Military square blade front, click adjustable peep rear.
Features: Commercially-made M-1 Garand duplicates the original service rifle. Introduced 1979. From Springfield Armory.
Price: Standard, about $761.00
Price: National Match, about $897.00
Price: Ultra Match, about.. $1,033.00
Price: M1-D Sniper, no scope or mount, about $1,033.00
Price: M1-T26 "Tanker," walnut stock, about $797.00
Price: As above, folding stock, about $774.00
Price: Standard M-1 Garand with Beretta-made receiver, about ... $1,510.00

STEYR A.U.G. AUTOLOADING RIFLE
Caliber: 223 Rem.
Barrel: 20".
Weight: 8½ lbs. **Length:** 31" over-all.
Stock: Synthetic, green. One-piece moulding houses receiver group, hammer mechanism and magazine.
Sights: 1.5x scope only; scope and mount form the carrying handle.
Features: Semi-automatic, gas-operated action; can be converted to suit right or left-handed shooters, including ejection port. Transparent 30- or 40-shot magazines. Folding vertical front grip. Introduced 1983. Imported from Austria by Gun South, Inc.
Price: Right or left-hand model.. $1,362.00

Steyr A.U.G. Rifle

UZI Carbine

UZI® CARBINE
Caliber: 9mm Parabellum, 41 Action Express, 45 ACP.
Barrel: 16.1".
Weight: 8.4 lbs. **Length:** 24.4" (stock folded).
Stock: Folding metal stock. Wood stock available as an accessory.
Sights: Post-type front, "L" flip-type rear adj. for 100 meters and 200 meters. Both click-adjustable for w. and e.
Features: Adapted to meet BATF regulations, this semi-auto has the same qualities as the famous submachine gun. Made by Israel Military Industries. Comes in moulded carrying case with sling, magazine, sight adjustment key. Exclusively imported from Israel by Action Arms Ltd. 9mm introduced 1980; 45 ACP introduced 1985; 41 A.E. introduced 1987.
Price: $698.00

UZI® Mini Carbine
Similar to the UZI Carbine except shorter receiver dimensions and has a forward-folding metal stock. Available in 9mm Para. or 45 ACP; 19.75" barrel; over-all length of 35.75" (26.1" folded); weight is 7.2 lbs. Introduced 1987.
Price: $698.00

Valmet M-76

Valmet M78 Semi-Auto
Similar to M76 except chambered only for 308 Win., has 24¼" heavy barrel, weighs 11 lbs., 43¼" over-all; 20-shot magazine; bipod; machined receiver. Length of pull on wood stock dimensioned for American shooters. Rear sight adjustable for w. and e., open-aperture front sight; folding carrying handle. Imported from Finland by Valmet.
Price: $999.00

VALMET M-76 STANDARD RIFLE
Caliber: 223, 15 or 30-shot magazine, or 308, 20-shot magazine.
Barrel: 16¾".
Weight: About 8½ lbs. **Length:** 37¾" over-all.
Stock: Wood, synthetic or folding metal type; composition fore-end.
Sights: Hooded adjustable post front, peep rear with luminous night sight.
Features: Semi-automatic only. Has sling swivels, flash suppressor. Bayonet, cleaning kit, 30-shot magazine, scope adaptor cover optional. Imported from Finland by Valmet.
Price: Wood stock $699.00
Price: Folding stock... $825.00
Price: Synthetic stock $795.00

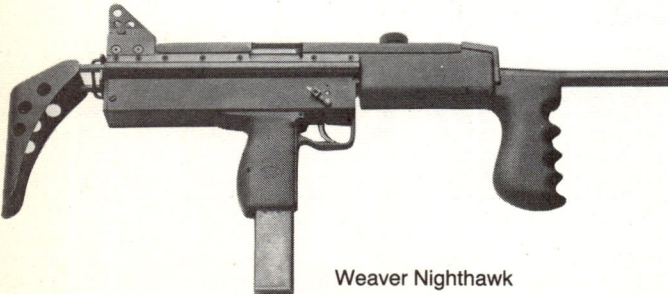

Weaver Nighthawk

WEAVER ARMS NIGHTHAWK
Caliber: 9mm Para., 25-shot magazine.
Barrel: 16.1".
Weight: 7 lbs. **Length:** 26½" (stock retracted).
Stock: Retractable metal frame.
Sights: Hooded blade front, adjustable peep V rear.
Features: Semi-auto fire only; fires from a closed bolt. Has 21" sight radius. Black nylon pistol grip and finger-groove front grip. Matte black finish. Introduced 1983. From Weaver Arms Corp.
Price: $525.00

CENTERFIRE RIFLES—SPORTING AUTOLOADERS

Includes models for hunting, adaptable to and suitable for certain competition.

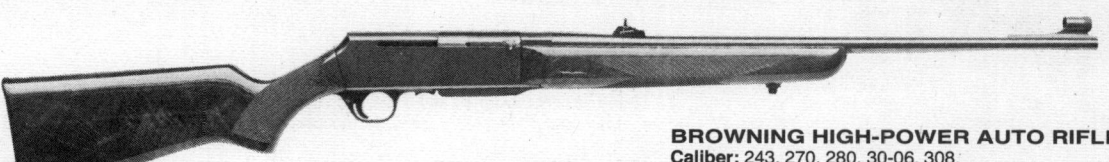
Browning High Power Rifle

BROWNING HIGH-POWER AUTO RIFLE
Caliber: 243, 270, 280, 30-06, 308.
Barrel: 22" round tapered.
Weight: 7⅜ lbs. **Length:** 43" over-all.
Stock: French walnut p.g. stock (13⅝"×2"×1⅝") and fore-end, hand checkered.
Sights: Adj. folding-leaf rear, gold bead on hooded ramp front, or no sights.
Features: Detachable 4-round magazine. Receiver tapped for scope mounts. Trigger pull 3½ lbs. Imported from Belgium by Browning.
Price: Grade I, with sights $574.95
Price: Grade I, no sights $559.95

Browning Big Game BAR
Similar to the standard BAR except has silver-gray receiver with engraved and gold inlaid whitetail deer on the right side, a mule deer on the left; a gold-edged scroll banner frames "One of Six Hundred" on the left side, the numerical edition number replaces "One" on the right. Chambered only in 30-06. Fancy, highly figured walnut stock and fore-end. Introduced 1983.
Price: $3,550.00

Browning Magnum Auto Rifle
Same as the standard caliber model, except weighs 8⅜ lbs., 45" over-all, 24" bbl., 3-round mag. Cals. 7mm Mag., 300 Win. Mag., 338 Win. Mag.
Price: Grade I, with sights $634.95
Price: Grade I, no sights $619.95

Heckler & Koch HK630

HECKLER & KOCH HK770 AUTO RIFLE
Caliber: 308 Win., 3-shot magazine.
Barrel: 19.6".
Weight: 7½ lbs. **Length:** 42.8" over-all.
Stock: European walnut. Checkered p.g. and fore-end.
Sights: Vertically adjustable blade front, open, fold-down, rear adj. for w.
Features: Has the delayed roller-locked system and polygonal rifling. Magazine catch located at front of trigger guard. Receiver top is dovetailed to accept clamp-type scope mount. Imported from West Germany by Heckler & Koch, Inc. Limited availability.
Price: $797.00
Price: HK630, 223 Rem $784.00
Price: HK940, 30-06 .... $917.00

Heckler & Koch SL6

HECKLER & KOCH SL7 AUTO RIFLE
Caliber: 308 Win., 3-shot magazine.
Barrel: 17".
Weight: 8 lbs. **Length:** 39¾" over-all.
Stock: European walnut, oil finished.
Sights: Hooded post front, adjustable aperture rear.
Features: Delayed roller-locked action; polygon rifling; receiver is dovetailed for H&K quick-detachable scope mount. Introduced 1983. Imported from West Germany by Heckler & Koch, Inc. Limited availability.
Price: $797.00
Price: Model SL6 (as above except in 223 Rem.) $784.00

Marlin Model 45

MARLIN MODEL 9 CAMP CARBINE
Caliber: 9mm Parabellum, 12-shot magazine (20-shot available).
Barrel: 16½", Micro-Groove® rifling.
Weight: 6¾ lbs. **Length:** 35½" over-all.
Stock: Walnut-finished hardwood; rubber butt pad; Mar-Shield® finish.
Sights: Ramp front with bead with Wide-Scan® hood, adjustable open rear.
Features: Manual bolt hold-open; Garand-type safety, magazine safety; loaded chamber indicator; receiver drilled, tapped for scope mounting. Introduced 1985.
Price: $294.95

Marlin Model 45 Carbine
Similar to the Model 9 except chambered for 45 ACP, 7-shot magazine. Introduced 1986.
Price: $294.95

CAUTION: PRICES CHANGE. CHECK AT GUNSHOP.

CENTERFIRE RIFLES—SPORTING AUTOLOADERS

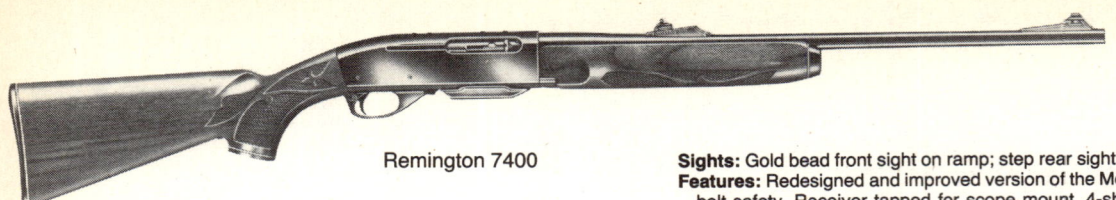

Remington 7400

REMINGTON MODEL 7400 AUTO RIFLE
Caliber: 243 Win., 270 Win., 280 Rem., 308 Win. and 30-06, 4-shot magazine.
Barrel: 22" round tapered.
Weight: 7½ lbs. **Length:** 42" over-all.
Stock: Walnut, deluxe cut checkered p.g. and fore-end.
Sights: Gold bead front sight on ramp; step rear sight with windage adj.
Features: Redesigned and improved version of the Model 742. Positive cross-bolt safety. Receiver tapped for scope mount. 4-shot clip mag. Introduced 1981.
Price: About $440.00
Price: Carbine (18½" bbl., 30-06 only) $440.00
Price: D Grade, about $2,291.00
Price: F Grade, about $4,720.00
Price: F Grade with gold inlays, about $7,079.00

Valmet Hunter

VALMET HUNTER AUTO RIFLE
Caliber: 223, 15-, 30-shot magazines; 243, 9-shot magazine; 308, 5- 9- and 20-shot magazines.
Barrel: 20½".
Weight: 8 lbs. **Length:** 42" over-all.
Stock: American walnut butt and fore-end. Checkered palm-swell p.g. and fore-end.
Sights: Blade front, open flip-type rear.
Features: Uses semi-auto Kalashnikov-type gas-operated action with rotating bolt. Stock is adjustable for length via spacers. Optional cleaning kit, sling, ejection buffer, scope mount. Introduced 1986. Imported from Finland by Valmet.
Price: $795.00

CENTERFIRE RIFLES—LEVER, SLIDE & MISC.

Both classic arms and recent designs in American-style repeaters for sport and field shooting.

Browning Model 71

BROWNING MODEL 71 LEVER ACTION RIFLE
Caliber: 348 Win., 4-shot magazine.
Barrel: 20" (Carbine), 24" (Rifle).
Weight: 8 lbs., 2 oz. (Rifle). **Length:** 45" over-all (Rifle).
Stock: Select walnut, pistol grip type, classic-style fore-end. Flat metal butt-plate. Satin finish.
Sights: Hooded front, open buckhorn rear.
Features: Reproduction of the Winchester Model 71 with half-length magazine tube, uncheckered wood; blue finish. High Grade model has extra quality wood with high gloss finish and fine checkering. Barrel and magazine are blued, receiver and lever are grayed and have scroll engraving with gold plated big game. Production limited to 3,000 Rifles, 3,000 Carbines. Introduced 1987. Imported from Japan by Browning.
Price: Grade I, Rifle or Carbine $599.95
Price: High Grade, Rifle or Carbine $979.95

Browning BLR

BROWNING BLR MODEL 81 LEVER ACTION RIFLE
Caliber: 222, 223, 22-250, 243, 257 Roberts, 7mm-08, 308 Win. or 358 Win., 4-shot detachable magazine.
Barrel: 20" round tapered.
Weight: 6 lbs. 15 oz. **Length:** 39¾" over-all.
Stock: Checkered straight grip and fore-end, oil finished walnut. Gold bead on hooded ramp front; low profile square notch adj. rear, or no sights.
Sights: Gold bead on hooded ramp front; low profile square notch adj. rear.
Features: Wide, grooved trigger; half-cock hammer safety. Receiver tapped for scope mount. Recoil pad installed. Imported from Japan by Browning.
Price: With sights $472.50
Price: No sights $457.50

CENTERFIRE RIFLES—LEVER, SLIDE & MISC.

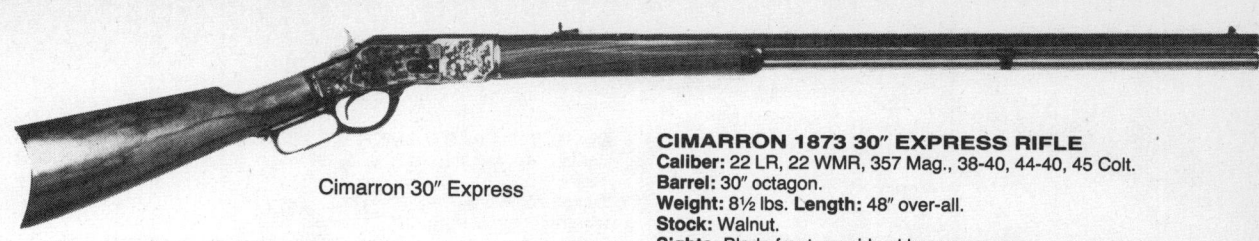
Cimarron 30" Express

CIMARRON 1873 30" EXPRESS RIFLE
Caliber: 22 LR, 22 WMR, 357 Mag., 38-40, 44-40, 45 Colt.
Barrel: 30" octagon.
Weight: 8½ lbs. **Length:** 48" over-all.
Stock: Walnut.
Sights: Blade front, semi-buckhorn ramp rear.
Features: Color case-hardened frame; choice of modern blue-black or charcoal blue for other parts. Barrel marked "Kings Improvement." From Cimarron Arms.
Price: $695.00

Cimarron 1873 "Button" Half-Magazine
Similar to the 1873 Express except has 24" barrel with half-magazine.
Price: $695.00

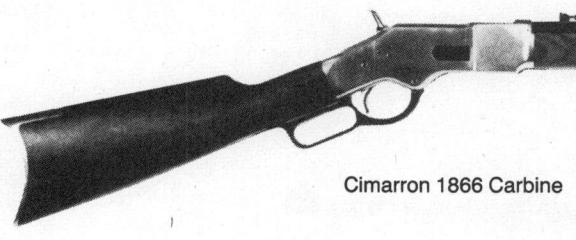
Cimarron 1866 Carbine

CIMARRON 1866 HALF-MAGAZINE CARBINE
Caliber: 22 LR, 22 WMR, 38 Spec., 38-40, 44-40.
Barrel: 24".
Weight: 7½ lbs. **Length:** 43" over-all.
Stock: Walnut.
Sights: Blade front, original-type folding rear.
Features: Half-magazine style (button). Choice of modern blue-black or old-style charcoal blue. From Cimarron Arms.
Price: $595.00

Dixie Model 1873

DIXIE ENGRAVED MODEL 1873 RIFLE
Caliber: 44-40, 11-shot magazine.
Barrel: 20", round.
Weight: 7¾ lbs. **Length:** 39" over-all.
Stock: Walnut.
Sights: Blade front, adj. rear.
Features: Engraved and case hardened frame. Duplicate of Winchester 1873. Made in Italy. From Dixie Gun Works.
Price: $595.00
Price: Plain, blued carbine $495.00

E.M.F. HENRY CARBINE
Caliber: 44-40 or 44 rimfire.
Barrel: 21".
Weight: About 9 lbs. **Length:** About 39" over-all.
Stock: Oil stained American walnut.
Sights: Blade front, rear adj. for e.
Features: Reproduction of the original Henry carbine with brass frame and buttplate, rest blued. From E.M.F.
Price: Standard $1,380.00
Price: Engraved $1,598.00

Marlin 336CS

MARLIN 336CS LEVER ACTION CARBINE
Caliber: 30-30 or 35 Rem., 6-shot tubular magazine.
Barrel: 20" Micro-Groove®.
Weight: 7 lbs. **Length:** 38½" over-all.
Stock: Select American black walnut, capped p.g. with white line spacers. Mar-Shield® finish.
Sights: Ramp front with Wide-Scan™ hood, semi-buckhorn folding rear adj. for w. & e.
Features: Hammer-block safety. Receiver tapped for scope mount, offset hammer spur; top of receiver sand blasted to prevent glare.
Price: Less scope $325.95

Marlin 30AS Lever Action Carbine
Same as the Marlin 336CS except has walnut-finished hardwood p.g. stock, 30-30 only, 6-shot. Hammer-block safety.
Price: $320.95

Marlin 336LTS

Marlin 336LTS Lever Action Carbine
Similar to the 336CS except has 16¼" barrel, weighs 6½ lbs., and over-all length of 34⅜". Rubber rifle butt pad. Introduced 1988.
Price: $325.95

CAUTION: PRICES CHANGE. CHECK AT GUNSHOP.

CENTERFIRE RIFLES—LEVER, SLIDE & MISC.

Marlin 1894S

MARLIN 1894S LEVER ACTION CARBINE
Caliber: 41 Magnum, 44 Special, 44 Magnum, 45 Colt, 10-shot tubular magazine
Barrel: 20" Micro-Groove®.
Weight: 6 lbs. **Length:** 37½" over-all.
Stock: American black walnut, straight grip and fore-end. Mar-Shield® finish. Rubber rifle butt pad.
Sights: Wide-Scan® hooded ramp front, semi-buckhorn folding rear adj. for w. & e.
Features: Hammer-block safety. Receiver tapped for scope mount, offset hammer spur, solid top receiver sand blasted to prevent glare.
Price: $357.95

Marlin Model 1894CL Rifle
Similar to the 1894S except chambered for 25-20 Win. and 32-20 Win. Has 6-shot magazine, 22" barrel with standard rifling, over-all length of 38¾", weight of 6¼ lbs. Introduced 1988.
Price: $383.95

Marlin Model 1894CS Carbine
Similar to the standard Model 1894S except chambered for 38 Special/357 Magnum with 9-shot magazine, 18½" barrel, hammer-block safety, brass bead front sight. Introduced 1983.
Price: $357.95

Marlin 1894CL

Marlin Model 1894CL Classic
Similar to the 1894CS except chambered for 25-20 and 32-20 Win. Has 6-shot magazine, 22" barrel with 6-groove rifling, brass bead front sight, adjustable semi-buckhorn folding rear. Hammer block safety. Weighs 6¼ lbs., over-all length of 38¾". Introduced 1988.
Price: $383.95

MARLIN 444SS LEVER ACTION SPORTER
Caliber: 444 Marlin, 5-shot tubular magazine.
Barrel: 22" Micro-Groove®.
Weight: 7½ lbs. **Length:** 40½" over-all.
Stock: American black walnut, capped p.g. with white line spacers, rubber rifle butt pad. Mar-Shield® finish; swivel studs.
Sights: Hooded ramp front, folding semi-buckhorn rear adj. for w. & e.
Features: Hammer-block safety. Receiver tapped for scope mount; offset hammer spur.
Price: $385.95

MARLIN 1895SS LEVER ACTION RIFLE
Caliber: 45-70, 4-shot tubular magazine.
Barrel: 22" round.
Weight: 7½ lbs. **Length:** 40½" over-all.
Stock: American black walnut, full pistol grip. Mar-Shield® finish; rubber buttpad; q.d. swivel studs.
Sights: Bead front with Wide-Scan® hood, semi-buckhorn folding rear adj. for w. & e.
Features: Hammer-block safety. Solid receiver tapped for scope mounts or receiver sights; offset hammer spur.
Price: $385.95

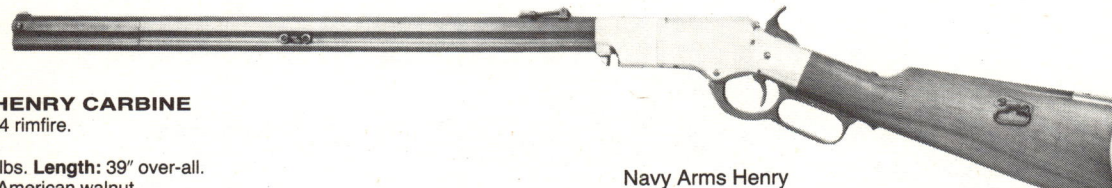

Navy Arms Henry

NAVY ARMS HENRY CARBINE
Caliber: 44-40 or 44 rimfire.
Barrel: 24".
Weight: About 8¼ lbs. **Length:** 39" over-all.
Stock: Oil-stained American walnut.
Sights: Blade front, rear adj. for e.
Features: Reproduction of the original Henry carbine with brass frame and buttplate, rest blued. Will be produced in limited edition of 1,000 standard models, plus 50 engraved guns. Made in U.S. by Navy Arms.
Price: Standard $769.00
Price: Engraved $1,849.00

Price: Iron Frame rifle (similar to Carbine except has blued frame) . $933.00
Price: Military Rifle (similar to Carbine except has sling swivels, different rear sight) $769.00
Price: Trapper model (16½" bbl., 7¼ lbs., 34½" o.a.l.) $769.00

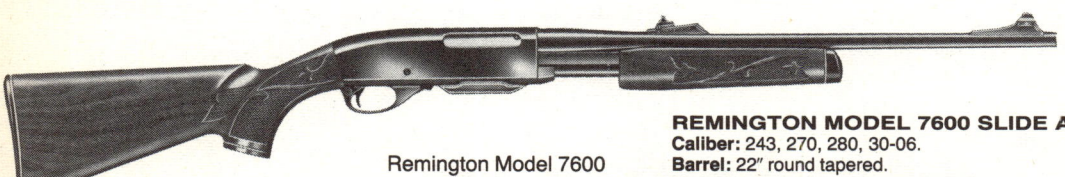

Remington Model 7600

REMINGTON MODEL 7600 SLIDE ACTION
Caliber: 243, 270, 280, 30-06.
Barrel: 22" round tapered.
Weight: 7½ lbs. **Length:** 42" over-all.
Stock: Cut-checkered walnut p.g. and fore-end, Monte Carlo with full cheekpiece.
Sights: Gold bead front sight on matted ramp, open step adj. sporting rear.
Features: Redesigned and improved version of the Model 760. Detachable 4-shot clip. Cross-bolt safety. Receiver tapped for scope mount. Also available in high grade versions. Introduced 1981.
Price: About $400.00
Price: Carbine (18½" bbl., 30-06 only) $400.00

Consult our Directory pages for the location of firms mentioned.

CENTERFIRE RIFLES—LEVER, SLIDE & MISC.

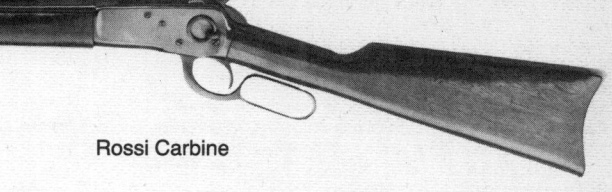
Rossi Carbine

ROSSI SADDLE-RING CARBINE M92 SRC
Caliber: 38 Spec./357 Mag., 44 Spec./44-40, 44 Mag., 10-shot magazine.
Barrel: 20".
Weight: 5¾ lbs. **Length:** 37" over-all.
Stock: Walnut.
Sights: Blade front, buckhorn rear.
Features: Recreation of the famous lever-action carbine. Handles 38 and 357 interchangeably. Has high-relief puma medallion inlaid in the receiver. Introduced 1978. Imported by Interarms.
Price: $282.00
Price: Blue, engraved $327.00
Price: 44 Spec./44 Mag. (Model 65) $297.00

Rossi Puma M92 SRS Short Carbine
Similar to the standard M92 except has 16" barrel, over-all length of 33", in 38/357 only. Puma medallion on side of receiver. Introduced 1986.
Price: $282.00

Savage Model 99C

SAVAGE 99C LEVER ACTION RIFLE
Caliber: 243 or 308 Win., detachable 4-shot magazine.
Barrel: 22", chrome-moly steel.
Weight: 8 lbs. **Length:** 41¾" over-all.
Stock: Walnut with checkered p.g. and fore-end, Monte Carlo comb.
Sights: Hooded ramp front, adjustable ramp rear sight. Tapped for scope mounts.
Features: Grooved trigger, top tang slide safety locks trigger and lever. Brown rubber butt pad, q.d. swivel studs, push-button magazine release.
Price: $459.00

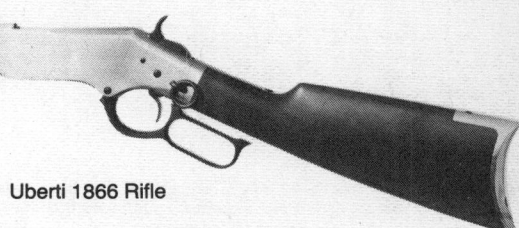
Uberti 1866 Rifle

UBERTI MODEL 1866 SPORTING RIFLE
Caliber: 22 LR, 22 WMR, 38 Spec., 44-40.
Barrel: 24¼", octagonal.
Weight: 8.1 lbs. **Length:** 43¼" over-all.
Stock: Walnut.
Sights: Blade front adj. for w., rear adj. for e.
Features: Frame, buttplate, fore-end cap of polished brass, balance charcoal blued. Imported by Benson Firearms, Uberti USA.
Price: $759.00
Price: Yellowboy Carine (19" round bbl.) $629.00
Price: Yellowboy "Indian" Carbine (engraved receiver, "nails" in wood) $709.00
Price: 1866 "Red Cloud Commemorative" Carbine $709.00
Price: 1866 "Trapper's Model" Carbine (16" bbl.) $629.00

UBERTI 1875 ARMY TARGET REVOLVING CARBINE
Caliber: 357 Mag., 44-40, 45 Colt, 6 shot.
Barrel: 18".
Weight: 4.9 lbs. **Length:** 37" over-all.
Stock: Walnut.
Sights: Ramp front, rear adj. for elevation.
Features: Polished brass trigger guard and buttplate, color case-hardened frame. Carbine version of the 1875 revolver. Imported by Benson Firearms, Uberti USA.
Price: Blue barrel, cylinder $529.00
Price: Nickeled barrel, cylinder $645.00

UBERTI HENRY RIFLE
Caliber: 44-40.
Barrel: 24¼", half octagon.
Weight: 9.2 lbs. **Length:** 43¾" over-all.
Stock: American Walnut.
Sights: Blade front, rear adj. for e.
Features: Frame, elevator, magazine follower, buttplate are brass, balance blue (also available in polished steel). Imported by Benson Firearms, Uberti USA.
Price: $845.00
Price: Henry Carbine (22¼" bbl.) $845.00

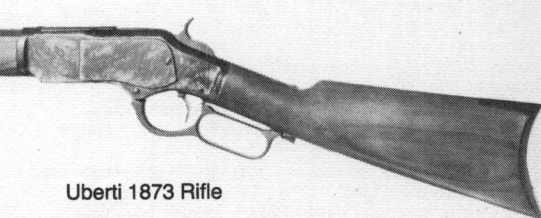
Uberti 1873 Rifle

UBERTI 1873 SPORTING RIFLE
Caliber: 22 LR, 22 WMR, 38 Spec., 357 Mag., 44-40, 45 Colt.
Barrel: 24¼", octagonal.
Weight: 8.1 lbs. **Length:** 43¼" over-all.
Stock: Walnut.
Sights: Blade front adj. for w., open rear adj. for e.
Features: Color case-hardened frame, blued barrel, hammer, lever, buttplate, brass elevator. Imported by Benson Firearms, Uberti USA.
Price: $830.00
Price: 1873 Carbine (19" round bbl.) $769.00
Price: 1873 Carbine, nickel plated $889.00
Price: 1873 "Trapper's Model" Carbine (16" bbl.) $769.00

CAUTION: PRICES CHANGE. CHECK AT GUNSHOP.

CENTERFIRE RIFLES—LEVER, SLIDE & MISC.

UBERTI 1873 CATTLEMAN REVOLVING CARBINE
Caliber: 22 LR/22 WMR, 38 Spec., 357 Mag., 44-40, 45 Colt, 6-shot.
Barrel: 18".
Weight: 4.4 lbs. **Length:** 34" over-all.
Stock: Walnut.
Sights: Blade front, groove rear, or adjustable target.
Features: Carbine version of the single-action revolver. Brass buttplate, color case-hardened frame, blued cylinder and barrel. Imported by Benson Firearms, Uberti USA.
Price: Fixed Sight...$459.00
Price: Target sight...$495.00
Price: 22 convertible (two cyls.) fixed sight...............$489.00
Price: As above, target sights..................................$529.00

WINCHESTER MODEL 94 SIDE EJECT RIFLE
Caliber: 30-30, (12" twist), 6-shot tubular magazine.
Barrel: 16", 20".
Weight: 6½ lbs. **Length:** 37¾" over-all.
Stock: Straight grip walnut stock and fore-end.
Sights: Hooded blade front, semi-buckhorn rear. Drilled and tapped for receiver sight and scope mount.
Features: Solid frame, forged steel receiver; side ejection, exposed rebounding hammer with automatic trigger-activated safety transfer bar. Introduced 1984.
Price: 30-30, about..$299.00
Price: With 1.5-4.5x Bushnell scope, mounts................$342.00
Price: Trapper model (16" bbl., 30-30), about...............$274.00
Price: As above, 45 Colt, 44 Mag./44 Spec., about.........$296.00
Price: With Win-Tuff laminated hardwood stock.............$299.00
Price: Long Barrel Rifle (24" bbl., long fore-end)............$286.00

Uberti 1873 Buckhorn 44-Cal. Revolving Carbine
Similar to 1873 Cattleman Carbine except slightly larger proportions. Available in 44 Mag. or 44 Mag./44-40 convertible.
Price: Fixed sights..$469.00
Price: Target sights..$509.00
Price: Convertible (two cylinders), fixed sights..............$515.00
Price: Convertible, target sights................................$549.00

WINCHESTER MODEL 94 BIG BORE SIDE EJECT
Caliber: 307 Win., 356 Win., 6-shot magazine.
Barrel: 20".
Weight: 7 lbs. **Length:** 38⅝" over-all.
Stock: Monte Carlo-style American walnut. Satin finish.
Sights: Hooded ramp front, semi-buckhorn rear adjustable for w. & e.
Features: All external metal parts have Winchester's deep blue high polish finish. Rifling twist 1 in 12". Rubber recoil pad fitted to buttstock. Introduced 1983. Made under license by U.S. Repeating Arms Co.
Price: About..$299.00

Winchester Ranger Side Eject Carbine
Same as Model 94 Side Eject except has 5-shot magazine, American hardwood stock and fore-end, no front sight hood. Introduced 1985.
Price: About..$244.00
Price: With 4x32 Bushnell scope, mounts, about............$278.00

Winchester Model 94XTR

Winchester Model 94 XTR Deluxe Rifle
Similar to the Winchester Model 94 Side Eject except has better walnut butt and fore-end with special XTR cut checkering, solid rubber butt pad, satin finish. Roll-engraved barrel legend. High polish blue finish. Introduced 1988.
Price:..$426.00

Winchester Model 94XTR Side Eject, 7x30 Waters
Same as Model 94 Side Eject except has 24" barrel, chambered for 7x30 Waters, 7-shot magazine, over-all length of 41¾" and weight is 7 lbs. Barrel twist is 1-12". Rubber butt pad instead of plastic. Introduced 1984.
Price: About..$312.00

CENTERFIRE RIFLES—BOLT ACTIONS

Includes models for a wide variety of sporting and competitive purposes and uses.

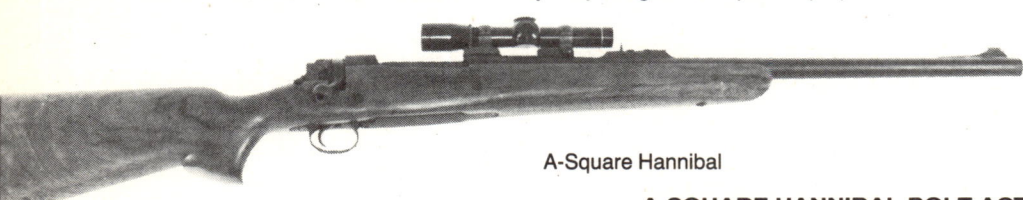
A-Square Hannibal

A-SQUARE CAESAR BOLT ACTION RIFLE
Caliber: Group I—270, 30-06, 9.3x62; Group II—7mm Rem. Mag., 300 Win. Mag., 338 Win. Mag., 416 Taylor, 458 Win. Mag.; Group III—300 H&H, 300 Wea., 8mm Rem. Mag., 340 Wea., 9.3x64, 375 H&H, 375 Wea., 416 Hoffman, 450 Ackley.
Barrel: 20" to 26" (no-cost customer option).
Weight: 8½ to 11 lbs.
Stock: Claro walnut with hand-rubbed oil finish; classic style with A-Square Coil-Chek® features for reduced recoil; flush detachable swivels. Customer choice of length of pull.
Sights: Choice of three-leaf express, forward or normal-mount scope, or combination (at extra cost).
Features: Matte non-reflective blue, double cross-bolts, steel and fiberglass reinforcement of wood from tang to fore-end tip; Mauser-style claw extractor; expanded magazine capacity. Right or left hand. Introduced 1984. Made in U.S. by A-Square Co., Inc.
Price: Group I calibers...$1,575.00
Price: Group II calibers..$1,650.00
Price: Group III calibers...$1,650.00

A-SQUARE HANNIBAL BOLT ACTION RIFLE
Caliber: Group I—270, 30-06, 9.3x62; Group II—7mm Rem. Mag., 300 Win. Mag., 338 Win. Mag., 416 Taylor, 458 Win. Mag.; Group III—300 H&H, 300 Wea., 8mm Rem. Mag., 340 Wea., 9.3x64, 375 H&H, 375 Wea., 416 Hoffman, 450 Ackley; Group IV—338 A-Square, 378 Wea., 416 Rigby, 404 Jeffrey, 460 Short A-Square, 460 Wea., 500 A-Square.
Barrel: 20" to 26" (no-cost customer option).
Weight: 8½ to 11 lbs.
Stock: Claro walnut with hand-rubbed oil finish; classic style with A-Square Coil-Chek® features for reduced recoil; flush detachable swivels. Customer choice of length of pull.
Sights: Choice of three-leaf express, forward or normal-mount scope, or combination (at extra cost).
Features: Matte non-reflective blue, double cross-bolts, steel and fiberglass reinforcement of wood from tang to fore-end tip; Mauser-style claw extractor; expanded magazine capacity. Right hand only. Introduced 1983. Made in U.S. by A-Square Co., Inc.
Price: Group I calibers...$1,410.00
Price: Group II calibers..$1,480.00
Price: Group III calibers...$1,540.00
Price: Group IV calibers...$1,600.00

CENTERFIRE RIFLES—BOLT ACTIONS

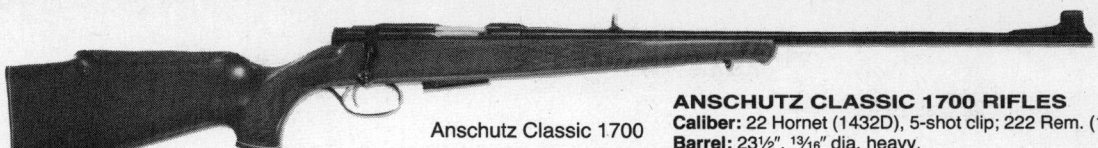
Anschutz Classic 1700

ANSCHUTZ CLASSIC 1700 RIFLES
Caliber: 22 Hornet (1432D), 5-shot clip; 222 Rem. (1532D), 2-shot clip.
Barrel: 23½", ¹³⁄₁₆" dia. heavy.
Weight: 7¾ lbs. **Length:** 42½" over-all.
Stock: Select European walnut with checkered pistol grip and fore-end.
Sights: None furnished, drilled and tapped for scope mounting.
Features: Adjustable single stage trigger. Receiver drilled and tapped for scope mounting. Introduced 1988. Imported from Germany by PSI.
Price: 22 Hornet $1,099.00
Price: 222 Rem. $1,099.00

ANSCHUTZ BAVARIAN BOLT ACTION RIFLE
Caliber: 22 Hornet, 222 Rem., detachable clip.
Barrel: 24".
Weight: 7¼ lbs. **Length:** 43" over-all.
Stock: European walnut with Bavarian check rest. Checkered p.g. and fore-end.
Sights: Hooded ramp front, folding leaf rear.
Features: Uses the improved 1700 Match 54 action with adjustable trigger. Drilled and tapped for scope mounting. Introduced 1988. Imported from Germany by Precision Sales International.
Price: $1,099.00

Anschutz Custom 1700 Rifles
Similar to the Classic models except have roll-over Monte Carlo cheekpiece, slim fore-end with Schnabel tip, Wundhammer palm swell on pistol grip, rosewood grip cap with white diamond insert. Skip-line checkering on grip and fore-end. Introduced 1988. Imported from Germany by PSI.
Price: 22 Hornet $1,099.00
Price: 222 Rem. $1,099.00

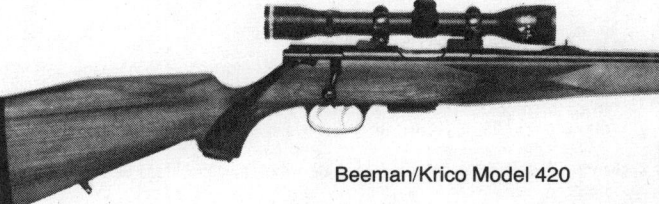
Beeman/HW 60J

BEEMAN/HW 60J BOLT ACTION RIFLE
Caliber: 222 Rem.
Barrel: 22.8".
Weight: 6.5 lbs. **Length:** 41.7" over-all.
Stock: Walnut with cheekpiece; cut checkered p.g. and fore-end.
Sights: Hooded blade on ramp front, open rear.
Features: Polished blue finish; oil-finished wood. Imported from West Germany by Beeman. Introduced 1988.
Price: $688.00

ARMSPORT 2801 BOLT ACTION RIFLE
Caliber: 243, 308, 30-06, 7mm Rem. Mag., 300 Win. Mag.
Barrel: 24".
Weight: 8 lbs.
Stock: European walnut with Monte Carlo comb.
Sights: Ramp front, open adj. rear.
Features: Blue metal finish, glossy wood. Introduced 1986. Imported from Italy by Armsport.
Price: $575.00

Beeman/Krico Model 420

Beeman/Krico Model 620/720 Bolt Action Rifle
Similar to the Model 600/700 except has 20.75" barrel, weighs 6.8 lbs., and has full-length Mannlicher-style stock with metal Schnabel fore-end tip; double set trigger with optional match trigger available. Receiver drilled and tapped for scope mounting. Imported from West Germany by Beeman.
Price: Model 620 (243 Win.) $1,830.00
Price: Model 720 (270 Win.) $1,820.00
Price: Model 720 (30-06) $1,845.00

BEEMAN/KRICO MODEL 400 BOLT ACTION RIFLE
Caliber: 22 Hornet, 5-shot magazine.
Barrel: 23.5".
Weight: 6.8 lbs. **Length:** 43" over-all.
Stock: Select European walnut, curved European comb with cheekpiece; solid rubber butt pad; cut checkered grip and fore-end.
Sights: Blade front on ramp, open rear adjustable for windage.
Features: Detachable box magazine; action has rear locking lugs, twin extractors. Available with single or optional match and double set trigger. Receiver grooved for scope mounts. Made in West Germany. Imported by Beeman.
Price: $1,225.00
Price: Model 420 (as above except 19.5" bbl., full-length Mannlicher-style stock, double set trigger) $1,425.00

Beeman/Krico Model 640 Varmint

BEEMAN/KRICO MODEL 640 VARMINT RIFLE
Caliber: 222 Rem., 4-shot magazine.
Barrel: 23.75".
Weight: 9.6 lbs. **Length:** 43½" over-all.
Stock: Select European walnut with high Monte Carlo comb, Wundhammer palm swell, rosewood fore-end tip; cut checkered grip and fore-end.
Sights: None furnished. Drilled and tapped for scope mounting.
Features: Free-floating heavy bull barrel; double set trigger with optional match trigger available. Imported from West Germany by Beeman.
Price: $1,697.00

BEEMAN/KRICO MODEL 700L DELUXE RIFLE
Caliber: 17 Rem., 222, 223, 22-250, 243, 308, 7x57, 7x64, 270, 30-06, 9.3x62, 8x68S, 7mm Rem. Mag., 300 Win. Mag., 9.3x64.
Barrel: 24" (26" in magnum calibers).
Weight: 7.5 lbs. **Length:** 44" over-all (24" barrel).
Stock: Traditional European style, select fancy walnut with rosewood Schnable fore-end, Bavarian cheekpiece, 28 lpi checkering.
Sights: Hooded front ramp, rear adjustable for windage.

Features: Butterknife bolt handle; gold plated single-set trigger; front sling swivel attached to barrel with ring; silent safety. Introduced 1983. Made in West Germany. Imported by Beeman.
Price: Model 700, magnum calibers $1,953.00

CAUTION: PRICES CHANGE. CHECK AT GUNSHOP.

CENTERFIRE RIFLES—BOLT ACTIONS

Beretta 500 Series

BRNO ZKB 680 FOX BOLT ACTION RIFLE
Caliber: 22 Hornet, 222 Rem., 5-shot magazine.
Barrel: 23½".
Weight: 5 lbs. 12 oz. **Length:** 42½" over-all.
Stock: Turkish walnut, with Monte Carlo.
Sights: Hooded front, open adj. rear.
Features: Detachable box magazine; adj. double set triggers. Imported from Czechoslovakia by Saki International.
Price: $499.00

BERETTA 500 SERIES CUSTOM BOLT ACTION RIFLES
Caliber: 222, 243, 308 (M501); 30-06.
Barrel: 23," to 24".
Weight: 6.8 to 8.4 lbs. **Length:** NA
Stock: Close-grained walnut with oil finish, hand checkering.
Sights: None furnished; drilled and tapped for scope mounting.
Features: Model 500 — short action; 501 — medium action. All models have rubber butt pad. Imported from Italy by Beretta U.S.A. Corp. Introduced 1984.
Price: Model 500 and 501 .... $725.00

BRNO ZKK 600, 601, 602 BOLT ACTION RIFLES
Caliber: 30-06, 270, 7x57, 7x64 (M600); 223, 243, 308 (M601); 8x68S, 375 H&H, 458 Win. Mag. (M602), 5-shot magazine.
Barrel: 23½" (M600, 601), 25" (M602).
Weight: 6 lbs., 3 oz. to 9 lbs., 4 oz. **Length:** 43" over-all (M601).
Stock: Walnut.
Sights: Hooded ramp front, open folding leaf adj. rear.
Features: Adjustable set trigger (standard trigger included); easy-release floorplate; sling swivels. Imported from Czechoslovakia by Saki International.
Price: ZKK 600 Standard $599.00
Price: As above, Monte Carlo stock $649.00
Price: ZKK 601 Standard $549.00
Price: As above, Monte Carlo stock $599.00
Price: ZKK 602, Monte Carlo stock $749.00
Price: As above, standard stock $689.00

Browning Short Action A-Bolt
Similar to the standard A-Bolt except has short action for 22-250, 243, 257 Roberts, 7mm-08, 308 chamberings. Available in Hunter or Medallion grades. Weighs 6½ lbs. Other specs essentially the same. Introduced 1985.
Price: Medallion, no sights $502.95
Price: Hunter, no sights $432.95
Price: Hunter, with sights $487.95

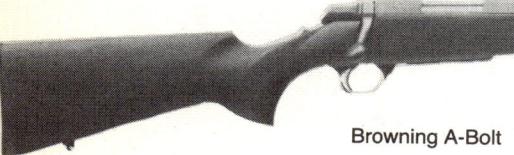
Browning A-Bolt

Browning A-Bolt "Stainless Stalker"
Similar to the Hunter model A-Bolt except receiver is made of stainless steel; the rest of the exposed metal surfaces are finished with a durable matte silver-gray. Graphite-fiberglass composite textured stock. No sights are furnished. Available in 270, 30-06, 7mm Rem. Mag. Introduced 1987.
Price: $551.95
Price: Composite Stalker (as above with checkered stock) $432.95

Browning A-Bolt Left Hand
Same as the Medallion model A-Bolt except has left-hand action and is available only in 270, 30-06, 7mm Rem. Mag. Introduced 1987.
Price: $524.95

BROWNING A-BOLT RIFLE
Caliber: 25-06, 270, 30-06, 280, 7mm Rem. Mag., 300 Win. Mag., 338 Win. Mag., 375 H&H Mag.
Barrel: 22" medium sporter weight with recessed muzzle; 26" on mag. cals.
Weight: 6½ to 7½ lbs. **Length:** 44¾" over-all. (Magnum and standard), 41¾" (short action).
Stock: Classic style American walnut; recoil pad standard on magnum calibers.
Features: Short-throw (60°) fluted bolt, three locking lugs, plunger-type ejector; adjustable trigger is grooved and gold plated. Hinged floorplate, detachable box magazine (4 rounds std. cals., 3 for magnums). Slide tang safety. Medallion has glossy stock finish, rosewood grip and fore-end caps, high polish blue. Introduced 1985. Imported from Japan by Browning.
Price: Medallion, no sights $502.95
Price: Hunter, no sights $432.95
Price: Hunter, with sights $487.95
Price: Medallion, 375 H & H Mag., with sights $587.95

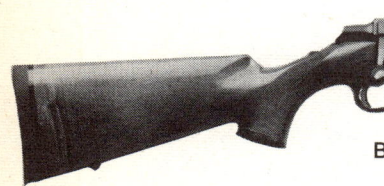
Browning Micro Medallion

Browning A-Bolt Micro Medallion
Similar to the standard A-Bolt except is a scaled-down version. Comes with 20" barrel, shortened length of pull (13⁵⁄₁₆"); three-shot magazine capacity; weighs 6 lbs., 1 oz. Available in 243, 308, 7mm-08, 257 Roberts, 22-250. Introduced 1988.
Price: No sights $502.95

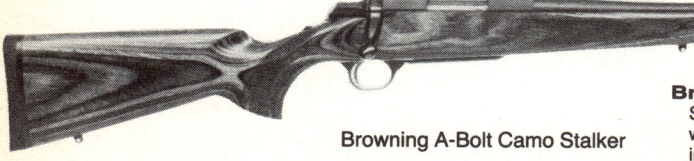
Browning A-Bolt Camo Stalker

Browning A-Bolt "Camo Stalker"
Similar to the Hunter model A-Bolt except the stock is of multi-laminated wood that has been stained varying shades of black and green; cut checkering; metal parts have a matte, non-glare finish. No sights are furnished. Available in 270, 30-06, 7mm Rem. Mag. Introduced 1987.
Price: $459.95

CENTERFIRE RIFLES—BOLT ACTIONS

Browning A-Bolt Pronghorn Antelope Issue
Same specifications as standard A-Bolt except available only in 243 Win. and has detailed engraving on the receiver flats, floorplate, trigger guard and at the rear of the barrel. Each side of the receiver has a different pronghorn study in 24 karat gold plating. Stock is a high grade of walnut with skipline checkering and a pearl border and high gloss finish. Brass spacers separate the rosewood caps and recoil pad. Limited edition of 500 rifles. Introduced 1987.
Price: $1,240.00

Browning A-Bolt Gold Medallion
Similar to the standard A-Bolt except has select walnut stock with brass spacers between rubber recoil pad and between the rosewood grip cap and fore-end tip; gold-filled barrel inscription; palm-swell pistol grip, Monte Carlo comb, 22 lpi checkering with double borders; engraved receiver flats. In 270, 30-06, 7mm Rem. Mag. only. Introduced 1988.
Price: $624.95

Century Centurion 14

CENTURY CENTURION 14 SPORTER
Caliber: 303 British, 7mm Rem. Mag., 300 Win. Mag., 5-shot magazine.
Barrel: 24".
Weight: NA. **Length:** 43.3" over-all.
Stock: Walnut-finished European hardwood. Checkered p.g. and fore-end. Monte Carlo comb.
Sights: None furnished.
Features: Uses modified Pattern 14 Enfield action. Drilled and tapped for scope mounting. Blue finish. From Century International Arms.
Price: 303, about $225.95
Price: Magnum calibers, about $251.95

Century Swedish

CENTURY SWEDISH SPORTER #38
Caliber: 6.5 x 55 Swede, 5-shot magazine.
Barrel: 24".
Weight: NA. **Length:** 44.1" over-all.
Stock: Walnut-finished European hardwood with checkered p.g. and fore-end; Monte Carlo comb.
Sights: Blade front, adjustable rear.
Features: Uses M38 Swedish Mauser action; comes with Holden Ironsighter see-through scope mount. Introduced 1987. From Century International Arms.
Price: About $212.95

Century Enfield

CENTURY ENFIELD SPORTER #4
Caliber: 303 British, 10-shot magazine.
Barrel: 25.2".
Weight: NA. **Length:** 44.5" over-all.
Stock: Beechwood with checkered p.g. and fore-end, Monte Carlo comb.
Sights: Blade front, adjustable aperture rear.
Features: Uses Lee-Enfield action; blue finish. Introduced 1987. From Century International Arms.
Price: $185.95
Price: Jungle Sporter (20½" bbl.) $207.95

CHAMPLIN RIFLE
Caliber: All std. chamberings, including 458 Win. and 460 Wea. Many wildcats on request.
Barrel: Any length up to 26" for octagon. Choice of round, straight taper octagon, or octagon with integral quarter rib, front sight ramp and sling swivel stud.
Weight: About 8 lbs. **Length:** 45" over-all.
Stock: Hand inletted, shaped and finished. Checkered to customer specs. Select French, Circassian or claro walnut. Steel p.g. cap, trap buttplate or recoil pad.
Sights: Bead on ramp front, 3-leaf folding rear.
Features: Right-hand Champlin action, tang safety or optional shroud safety, Canjar adj. trigger, hinged floorplate.
Price: From $5,400.00

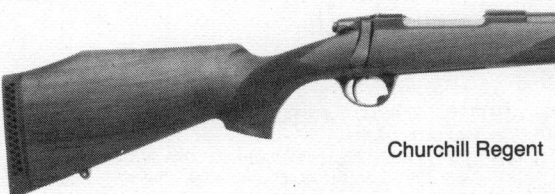
Churchill Regent

CHURCHILL BOLT ACTION RIFLE
Caliber: 243, 25-06, 270, 308, 30-06 (4-shot magazine), 7mm Rem. Mag., 300 Win. Mag. (3-shot).
Barrel: 22" (7mm Rem. Mag. has 24").
Weight: 7½ lbs. **Length:** 42½" over-all with 22" barrel.
Stock: European walnut, checkered p.g. and fore-end. Regent grade has Monte Carlo, Highlander has classic design.
Sights: Gold bead on ramp front, fully adj. rear.
Features: Positive safety locks trigger; oil-finished wood; swivel posts; recoil pad. Imported by Kassnar Imports, Inc. Introduced 1986.
Price: Highlander, without sights, either cal. $350.00
Price: As above, with sights $380.00
Price: Regent, without sights $549.00
Price: As above, with sights $579.00

Churchill Highlander Bolt Action Rifle
Similar to the Regent except has a classic-style stock of standard-grade European walnut. Highlander Combo includes rifle without iron sights, q.d. swivels, cobra-style sling, rings, bases, and 3-9x32 scope.
Price: Highlander with sights $379.00
Price: Highlander Combo $409.00
Price: Highlander without sights $349.00

CAUTION: PRICES CHANGE. CHECK AT GUNSHOP.

CENTERFIRE RIFLES—BOLT ACTIONS

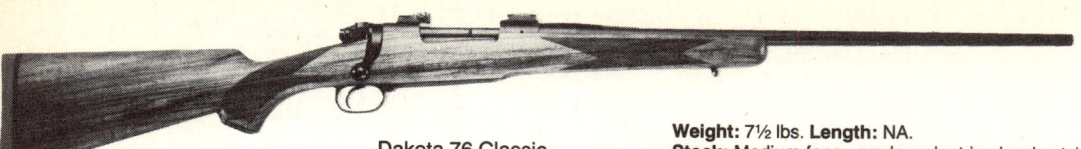

Dakota 76 Classic

DAKOTA 76 CLASSIC BOLT ACTION RIFLE
Caliber: 257 Roberts, 270, 280, 30-06, 7mm Rem. Mag., 338 Win. Mag., 300 Win. Mag., 375 H&H, 458 Win. Mag.
Barrel: 23".
Weight: 7½ lbs. **Length:** NA.
Stock: Medium fancy grade walnut in classic style. Checkered p.g. and fore-end; solid butt pad.
Sights: None furnished; drilled and tapped for scope mounts.
Features: Has many features of the original Model 70 Winchester. One-piece rail trigger guard assembly; steel grip cap. Adjustable trigger. Many options available. Introduced 1988. From Dakota Arms, Inc.
Price: From $1,750.00

Dakota 76 Safari

DAKOTA 76 SAFARI BOLT ACTION RIFLE
Caliber: 338 Win. Mag., 300 Win. Mag., 375 H&H, 458 Win. Mag.
Barrel: 23".
Weight: 8½ lbs. **Length:** NA.
Stock: Fancy walnut with ebony fore-end tip; point-pattern with wrap-around fore-end checkering.
Sights: Ramp front, standing leaf rear.
Features: Has many features of the original Model 70 Winchester. Barrel band front swivel, inletted rear. Cheekpiece with shadow line. Steel grip cap. Introduced 1988. From Dakota Arms, Inc.
Price: From $2,750.00

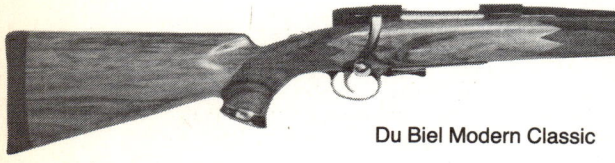

Du Biel Modern Classic

Du BIEL ARMS BOLT ACTION RIFLES
Caliber: Standard calibers 22-250 thru 458 Win. Mag. Selected wildcat calibers available.
Barrel: Selected weights and lengths. Douglas Premium.
Weight: About 7½ lbs.
Stock: Five styles. Walnut, maple, laminates. Hand checkered.
Sights: None furnished. Receiver has integral milled bases.
Features: Basically a custom-made rifle. Left or right-hand models available. Five-lug locking mechanism; 36-degree bolt rotation; adjustable Canjar trigger; oil or epoxy stock finish; Presentation recoil pad; jeweled and chromed bolt body; sling swivel studs; lever latch or button floorplate release. All steel action and parts. Introduced 1978. From Du Biel Arms.
Price: Rollover Model, left or right-hand .... $ 2,500.00
Price: Thumbhole, left or right hand $2,500.00
Price: Classic, left or right hand $2,500.00
Price: Modern Classic, left or right hand...................... $2,500.00
Price: Thumbhole Mannlicher, left or right hand $2,500.00

Francotte Rifle

AUGUSTE FRANCOTTE BOLT ACTION RIFLES
Caliber: 243, 270, 7x64, 30-06, 308, 300 Win. Mag., 338, 7mm Rem. Mag., 375 H&H, 416 Rigby, 458 Win. Mag.
Barrel: 23½" standard; other lengths on request.
Weight: 7.61 lbs. (medium cals.), 11.1 lbs. (magnum cals.).
Stock: Fancy European walnut. To customer specs.
Sights: To customer specs.
Features: Basically a custom gun, Francotte offers many options. Imported from Belgium by Armes de Chasse.
Price: .... NA

Grendel SRT

GRENDEL SRT COMPACT RIFLE
Caliber: 308 Win., 9-shot magazine.
Barrel: 20" (Models 20F [fluted], 20L [not fluted]), 24" (Model 24, not fluted).
Weight: 6.7 lbs. (Model 20F). **Length:** 40.8" over-all (Model 20F), open; folds to 30" length.
Stock: Folding Du Pont Zytel reinforced with glass fiber.
Sights: None furnished. Integral scope bases.
Features: Uses Sako A-2 action. Muzzle brake. Fore-end has a rod for sling swivel and will accept M-16 clip-on bipod. Uses Sako scope mount. Introduced 1987. From Greendel, Inc.
Price: SRT-20F (fluted barrel) $510.00
Price: SRT-20L (non-fluted) $480.00
Price: SRT-24 (non-fluted) $480.00

CENTERFIRE RIFLES—BOLT ACTIONS

Howa Hunter

Howa Model 1500 Hunter Rifle
Similar to the Grade II except has checkered hardwood stock without recoil pad; available in 223, 243, 270, 30-06, 7mm Rem. Mag., with sights. Introduced 1987.
Price: $440.00

HOWA M1500 TROPHY BOLT ACTION RIFLE
Caliber: 223, 22-250, 243, 270, 30-06, 308, 7mm Rem. Mag., 300 Win. Mag., 338 Win. Mag.
Barrel: 22" (24" in magnum calibers.).
Weight: 7½-7¾ lbs. Length: 42" over-all (42½" for 270, 30-06, 7mm).
Stock: American walnut with Monte Carlo comb and cheekpiece; 18 l.p.i. checkering on p.g. and fore-end.
Sights: Hooded ramp gold bead front, open round-notch rear adj. for w. & e. Drilled and tapped for scope mounts.
Features: Trigger guard and magazine box are a single unit with a hinged floorplate. Comes with q.d. swivel studs. Composition non-slip buttplate with white spacer. Magnum models have rubber recoil pad. Introduced 1979. Imported from Japan by Interarms.
Price: $465.00

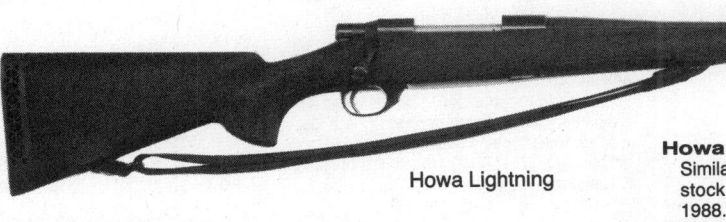
Howa Lightning

Howa Model 1500
Similar to the standard 1500 except has a 22" heavy barrel and fully adjustable trigger. Chambered for 22-250 and 223. Weighs 9 lbs. 5 oz. Skipline checkering, q.d. swivels. Introduced 1982.
Price: Parkerized, oil finished stock $515.00

Howa Lightning Rifle
Similar to the Howa Trophy model except comes with lightweight Carbolite stock; weighs 7 lbs. Available in 270, 30-06, 7mm Rem. Mag. Introduced 1988.
Price: 270, 30-06 .... $465.00
Price: 7mm Rem. Mag. $480.00

Kimber Big Game

KIMBER BIG GAME RIFLE
Caliber: 270, 280, 7mm Rem. Mag., 30-06, 300 Win. Mag., 338 Win. Mag., 375 H&H.
Barrel: 22" (24" for magnum).
Weight: About 7¾ lbs. Length: 42" over-all (22" bbl.).
Stock: Claro walnut; Custom Classic and Super America have AAA fancy claro or straight grain English walnut.
Sights: None furnished.
Features: Three styles available—Classic, Custom Classic, Super America. Mauser-style extractor; Model 70-type override trigger design, ejector, three-position safety; Mauser-style bolt stop; Featherweight M70 barrel profile (except 338, 375). Introduced 1988.
Price: Classic $985.00
Price: Custom Classic $1,230.00
Price: Super America $1,385.00

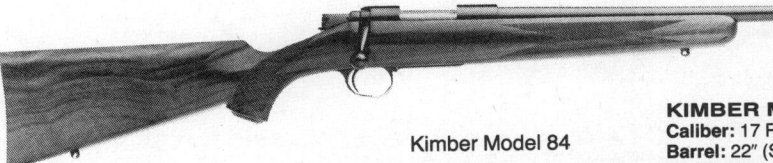
Kimber Model 84

Kimber Model 82, 84 Super America
Super-grade version of the Models 82 and 84. Has a Classic stock only of specially selected, high-grade, California claro walnut, with Continental beaded cheekpiece and ebony fore-end tip; borderless, full-coverage 20 lpi checkering; Niedner-type checkered steel buttplate. Options include barrel quarter-rib with a folding leaf sight, skeleton grip cap, checkered bolt knob. Available in 22 Long Rifle, 22 Magnum, 22 Hornet, 17 Rem., 221 Rem., 222 Rem., 223 Rem.
Price: Model 82, 22 Long Rifle, less 4x scope $1,150.00
Price: Model 82, 22 Hornet, less scope $1,195.00
Price: Model 84, 223 Rem. $1,285.00

KIMBER MODEL 84 SPORTER
Caliber: 17 Rem., 221 Fire Ball, 222 Rem., 223 Rem., 5-shot magazine.
Barrel: 22" (Sporter), 24" (Varmint).
Weight: About 6¼ lbs. Length: 40½" over-all (Sporter).
Stock: Two styles available. "Classic" is Claro walnut with plain, straight comb; "Custom Classic" is of fancy select grade Claro walnut, ebony fore-end tip, Niedner-style buttplate. All have 18 lpi hand cut, borderless checkering, steel grip cap, checkered steel buttplate.
Sights: Hooded ramp front with bead, folding leaf rear (optional).
Features: All new Mauser-type head locking bolt action; steel trigger guard and hinged floorplate; Mauser-type extractor; fully adjustable trigger; chrome-moly barrel. Three-position safety (new in '87). Round-top receiver drilled and tapped for scope mounting. Varmint gun prices same as others. Introduced 1984. Contact Kimber for full details.
Price: Classic stock, no sights $885.00
Price: Continental (222, 223 only) $985.00
Price: Custom Classic stock, no sights $1,130.00
Price: Kimber scope mounts, from $48.00
Price: Open sights fitted (optional) $55.00

CAUTION: PRICES CHANGE. CHECK AT GUNSHOP.

CENTERFIRE RIFLES—BOLT ACTIONS

KIMBER MODEL 82 SPORTER
Caliber: 22 Hornet, 3-shot flush-fitting magazine; 218 Bee, 25-20, single shot.
Barrel: 22½", 6 grooves; 1-in-14" twist; 24" heavy.
Weight: About 6¼ lbs. **Length:** 42" over-all.
Stock: Three styles available. "Classic" is Claro walnut with plain, straight comb; "Custom Classic" is of fancy select grade Claro walnut, ebony fore-end tip, Niedner-style butt-plate. All have 18 lpi hand cut, borderless checkering, steel grip cap, checkered steel buttplate.
Sights: Hooded ramp front with bead, folding leaf rear (optional).
Features: All steel construction; twin rear horizontally opposed locking lugs; fully adjustable trigger; rocker-type safety. Receiver grooved for Kimber scope mounts. Available in true left-hand version in selected models. Introduced 1982. Contact Kimber for full details.
Price: Classic stock, no sights (left hand also avail.) $795.00
Price: Continental $895.00
Price: Custom Classic, no sights (left hand also avail.) $1,040.00
Price: Kimber scope mounts, from $48.00
Price: Open sights fitted (optional) $55.00

MARK X AMERICAN FIELD SERIES
Caliber: 22-250, 243, 25-06, 270, 7x57, 7mm Rem. Mag., 308 Win., 30-06, 300 Win. Mag.
Barrel: 24".
Weight: 7 lbs. **Length:** 45" over-all.
Stock: Genuine walnut stock, hand checkered with 1" sling swivels.
Sights: Ramp front with removable hood, open rear sight adjustable for windage and elevation.
Features: Mauser-system action. One piece trigger guard with hinged floor plate, drilled and tapped for scope mounts and receiver sight, hammer-forged chrome vanadium steel barrel. Imported from Yugoslavia by Interarms.
Price: With adj. trigger, sights $550.00
Price: 7mm Rem. Mag., 300 Win. Mag $565.00

Mark X LTW

Mark X LTW Sporter Bolt Action Rifle
Similar to the standard Mark X except comes with lightweight Carbolite composition stock, 20" barrel; weighs 7 lbs. Available in 270, 30-06, 7mm Rem. Mag. Introduced 1988.
Price: 270, 30-06 . . . . $465.00
Price: 7mm Rem. Mag. $480.00

Mark X Viscount Rifle
Same gun and features as the Mark X Sporting Rifle except has stock of European hardwood. Imported from Yugoslavia by Interarms. Reintroduced 1987.
Price: $440.00
Price: 7mm Rem. Mag., 300 Win. Mag $455.00

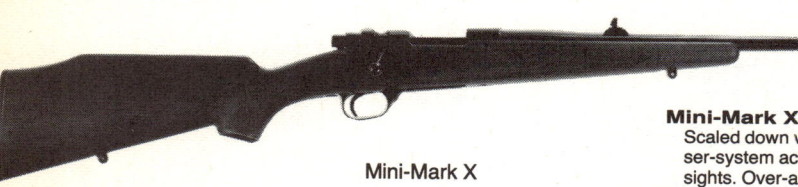

Mini-Mark X

Mini-Mark X Rifle
Scaled down version of the Mark X Sporting Rifle. Uses miniature M98 Mauser-system action, chambered for 223 Rem.; 20" barrel with open adjustable sights. Over-all length of 39¾", weight 6.35 lbs. Drilled and tapped for scope mounting. Checkered hardwood stock. Adjustable trigger. Introduced 1987. Imported from Yugoslavia by Interarms.
Price: $460.00

MAUSER 225 BOLT ACTION RIFLE
Caliber: 243, 25-06, 270, 7x57, 308, 30-06, 4-shot magazine (standard); 257 Wea., 270 Wea., 7mm Rem. Mag., 300 Win. Mag., 300 Wea., 308 Norma Mag., 375 H&H, 3-shot magazine (magnum).
Barrel: 24" (standard), 26" (magnum).
Weight: About 8 lbs. **Length:** 44½" over-all (24" bbl.).
Stock: Oil finished, hand checkered European walnut with Monte Carlo. Recoil pad and swivel studs standard.
Sights: None furnished. Drilled and tapped for scope mounts. Open sights, rings, bases avail. from KDF.

Features: Three-lug, front-locking action with ultra-fast lock time. Imported from West Germany by KDF, Inc.
Price: Standard calibers $1,075.00
Price: Magnum calibers $1,125.00

Parker-Hale 81 Classic

PARKER-HALE MODEL 81 CLASSIC RIFLE
Caliber: 22-250, 243, 6mm Rem., 270, 6.5x55, 7x57, 7x64, 308, 30-06, 300 Win. Mag., 7mm Rem. Mag., 4-shot magazine.
Barrel: 24".
Weight: About 7¾ lbs. **Length:** 44½" over-all.
Stock: European walnut in classic style with oil finish, hand-cut checkering; palm swell pistol grip, rosewood grip cap.
Sights: Drilled and tapped for open sights and scope mounting. Scope bases included.
Features: Uses Mauser-style action; one-piece steel, Oberndorf-style trigger guard with hinged floorplate; rubber butt pad; quick-detachable sling swivels. Imported from England by Precision Sports, Inc. Introduced 1984.
Price: $799.95
Price: Optional set trigger $84.95

Parker-Hale Model 1100 Lightweight Rifle
Similar to the Model 81 Classic except has slim barrel profile, hollow bolt handle, alloy trigger guard/floorplate. The Monte Carlo stock has a Schnabel fore-end, hand-cut checkering, swivel studs, palm swell pistol grip. Comes with hooded ramp front sight, open Williams rear adjustable for windage and elevation. Same calibers as Model 81. Over-all length of 43", weight 6½ lbs., with 22" barrel. Imported from England by Precision Sports, Inc. Introduced 1984.
Price: $559.95
Price: Optional set trigger $84.95

CENTERFIRE RIFLES—BOLT ACTIONS

Parker-Hale 1200 Super

PARKER-HALE MODEL 1200 SUPER BOLT ACTION
Caliber: 22-250, 243, 6mm, 25-06, 270, 6.5x55, 7x57, 7x64, 308, 30-06, 8mm, 7mm Rem. Mag., 300 Win. Mag.
Barrel: 24".
Weight: About 7½ lbs. **Length:** 44½" over-all.
Stock: European walnut, rosewood grip and fore-end tips, hand-cut checkering; roll-over cheekpiece; palm swell pistol grip; ventilated recoil pad; wrap-around checkering.
Sights: Hooded post front, open rear.
Features: Uses Mauser-style action with claw extractor; gold plated adjustable trigger; silent side safety locks trigger, sear and bolt; aluminum trigger guard. Imported from England by Precision Sports, Inc. Introduced 1984.
Price: **$659.95**
Price: Optional set trigger **$84.95**

Parker-Hale Model 81 African Rifle
Similar to the Model 81 Classic except chambered only for 300 H&H, 308 Norma Mag., 375 H&H and 9.3x62. Has adjustable trigger, barrel band front swivel, African express rear sight, engraved receiver. Classic-style stock has a solid butt pad, checkered p.g. and fore-end. Introduced 1986.
Price: **$999.95**

Parker-Hale Model 1200 Super Clip Rifle
Same as the Model 1200 Super except has a detachable steel box magazine and steel trigger guard. Imported from England by Precision Sports, Inc. Introduced 1984.
Price: **$699.95**
Price: Optional set trigger **$84.95**

Parker-Hale Model 1100M African Magnum
Similar to the Model 1000 Standard except has 24" barrel, 46" over-all length, weighs 9½ lbs., and is chambered for 375 H&H Magnum, 404 Jeffery and 458 Win. Magnum. Has hooded post front sight, shallow V-notch rear, 180° flag safety (low 45° scope safety available). Specially lengthened steel magazine has hinged floorplate; heavily reinforced, glass bedded and weighted stock has a ventilated rubber recoil pad. Imported from England by Precision Sports, Inc. Introduced 1984.
Price: **$899.95**

PARKER-HALE MODEL 2100 MIDLAND RIFLE
Caliber: 22-250, 243, 6mm, 270, 6.5x55, 7x57, 7x64, 308, 30-06.
Barrel: 22".
Weight: About 7 lbs. **Length:** 43" over-all.
Stock: European walnut, cut-checkered pistol grip and fore-end; sling swivels.
Sights: Hooded post front, flip-up open rear.
Features: Mauser-type action has twin front locking lugs, rear safety lug, and claw extractor; hinged floorplate; adjustable single stage trigger; silent side safety. Imported from England by Precision Sports, Inc. Introduced 1984.
Price: **$369.95**

Parker-Hale Model 1000 Standard Rifle
Similar to the Model 1200 Super except has standard walnut Monte Carlo stock with satin finish, no rosewood grip/fore-end caps; fitted with checkered buttplate, standard sling swivels. Imported from England by Precision Sports, Inc. Introduced 1984.
Price: **$499.95**
Price: Optional set trigger **$84.95**

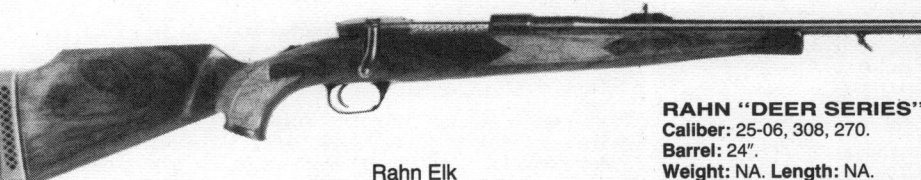
Rahn Elk

RAHN "DEER SERIES" BOLT ACTION RIFLE
Caliber: 25-06, 308, 270.
Barrel: 24".
Weight: NA. **Length:** NA.
Stock: Circassian walnut with rosewood fore-end and grip caps, Monte Carlo cheekpiece, semi-Schnabel fore-end; hand checkered.
Sights: Bead front, open adjustable rear. Drilled and tapped for scope mount.
Features: Free floating barrel; rubber recoil pad; one-piece trigger guard with hinged, engraved floorplate; 22 rimfire conversion insert available. Introduced 1986. From Rahn Gun Works, Inc.
Price: **$800.00**
Price: With custom stock made to customer specs **$850.00**

Rahn "Elk Series" Rifle
Similar to the "Deer Series" except chambered for 6mmx56, 30-06, 7mm Rem. Mag. and has elk head engraving on floorplate. Introduced 1986.
Price: **$850.00**
Price: With stock made to customer specs **$900.00**

Rahn "Safari Series" Rifle
Similar to the "Deer Series" except chambered for 308 Norma Mag., 300 Win. Mag., 8x68S, 9x64. Choice of Cape buffalo, rhino or elephant engraving. Gold oval nameplate with three initials. Introduced 1986.
Price: **$950.00**
Price: With stock made to customer specs **$1,000.00**

Rahn "Himalayan Series" Rifle
Similar to the "Deer Series" except chambered for 5.6x57 or 6.5x68S, short stock of walnut or fiberglass, and floorplate engravings of a yak with scroll border. Introduced 1986.
Price: **$850.00**
Price: With walnut stock made to customer specs **$900.00**

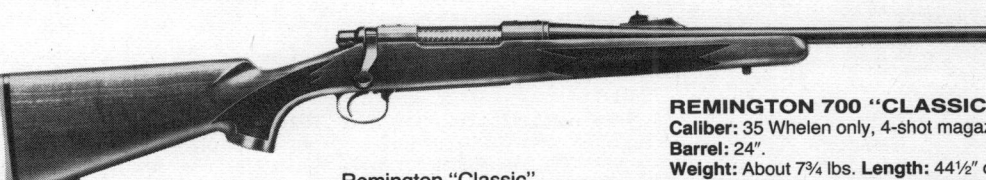
Remington "Classic"

REMINGTON 700 "CLASSIC" RIFLE
Caliber: 35 Whelen only, 4-shot magazine.
Barrel: 24".
Weight: About 7¾ lbs. **Length:** 44½" over-all.
Stock: American walnut, 20 l.p.i. checkering on p.g. and fore-end. Classic styling. Satin finish.
Sights: Hooded ramp front, step-adjustable rear. Receiver drilled and tapped for scope mounting.
Features: A "classic" version of the M700ADL with straight comb stock. Fitted with rubber recoil pad. Sling swivel studs installed. Limited production in 1987 only.
Price: About **$440.00**

CAUTION: PRICES CHANGE. CHECK AT GUNSHOP.

CENTERFIRE RIFLES—BOLT ACTIONS

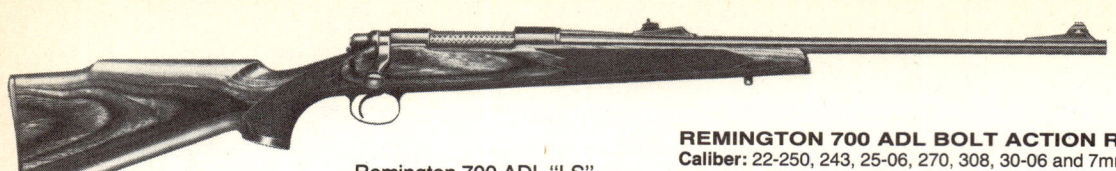

Remington 700 ADL "LS"

Remington Model 700 Gun Kit
Same as the Model 700 ADL except comes with a completely inletted walnut stock furnished in rough-shaped condition. Long or short 700 ADL action, blind magazine, factory sights, swivel studs, butt plate. Directions and three checkering templates are included. Available in 243, 308, 270, 30-06, 7mm Rem. Mag.
Price: $333.00
Price: 7mm Rem. Mag. $353.00

REMINGTON 700 ADL BOLT ACTION RIFLE
Caliber: 22-250, 243, 25-06, 270, 308, 30-06 and 7mm Rem. Mag.
Barrel: 22" or 24" round tapered.
Weight: 7 lbs. **Length:** 41½" to 43½" over-all.
Stock: Walnut. RKW finished p.g. stock with impressed checkering, Monte Carlo.
Sights: Gold bead ramp front; removable, step-adj. rear with windage screw.
Features: Side safety, receiver tapped for scope mounts.
Price: About $380.00
Price: 7mm Rem. Mag., about $400.00
Price: Model 700 ADL/LS (laminated stock, 30-06 only) $440.00

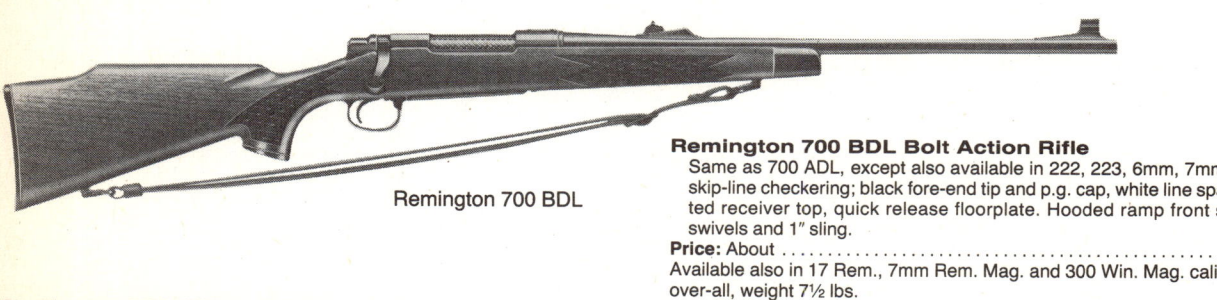

Remington 700 BDL

Remington 700 BDL Left Hand
Same as 700 BDL except mirror-image left-hand action, stock. Available in 243, 308, 270, 30-06 only.
Price: About $487.00
Price: 7mm Rem. Mag., about $507.00

Remington 700 BDL Bolt Action Rifle
Same as 700 ADL, except also available in 222, 223, 6mm, 7mm-08 Rem.; skip-line checkering; black fore-end tip and p.g. cap, white line spacers. Matted receiver top, quick release floorplate. Hooded ramp front sight. Q.D. swivels and 1" sling.
Price: About $447.00
Available also in 17 Rem., 7mm Rem. Mag. and 300 Win. Mag. calibers. 44½" over-all, weight 7½ lbs.
Price: About $467.00
Price: Custom Grade I, about $1,200.00
Price: Custom Grade II, about $2,133.00
Price: Custom Grade III, about $3,333.00
Price: Custom Grade IV, about $5,200.00

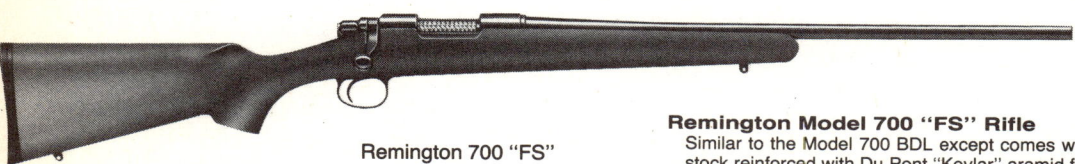

Remington 700 "FS"

Remington 700 BDL Varmint Special
Same as 700 BDL, except 24" heavy bbl., 43½" over-all, wgt. 9 lbs. Cals. 222, 223, 22-250, 243, 6mm Rem., 7mm-08 Rem. and 308. No sights.
Price: About $476.00

Remington 700 Safari
Similar to the 700 BDL except 8mm Rem. Mag., 375 H&H or 458 Win. Magnum calibers only with heavy barrel. Hand checkered, oil finished stock in classic or Monte Carlo style with recoil pad installed. Delivery time is about 5 months.
Price: About $827.00

Remington Model 700 "FS" Rifle
Similar to the Model 700 BDL except comes with a classic-style fiberglass stock reinforced with Du Pont "Kevlar" aramid fiber, black Old English style rubber recoil pad. Action has a blind magazine. Stock available in gray or camouflage. Right-hand actions available in 243, 308, 7mm Rem. Mag.; left-hand in 270, 30-06, 7mm Rem. Mag. Weight is 6⅝ lbs. (long action), 6½ lbs. (short action). Introduced 1987.
Price: $613.00
Price: 7mm Rem. Mag. $633.00

Remington Model 700 "Mountain Rifle"
Similar to the 700 BDL except weighs 6¾ lbs., has a 22" tapered barrel. Redesigned pistol grip, straight comb, contoured cheekpiece, satin stock finish, fine checkering, hinged floorplate and magazine follower, 2-position thumb safety. Chambered for 243, 270 Win., 7mm-08, 280 Rem., 30-06, 308, 4-shot magazine. Over-all length is 42½". Introduced 1986.
Price: About $447.00

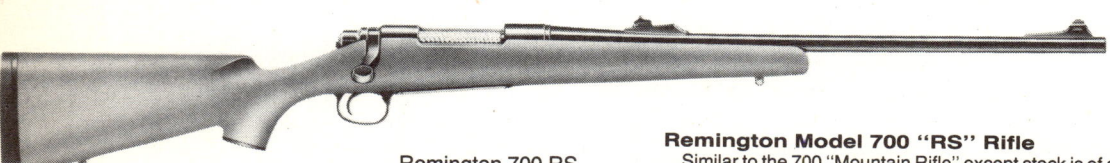

Remington 700 RS

Remington Model 700 Custom "KS" Mountain Rifle
Similar to the 700 "Mountain Rifle" except has Kevlar reinforced resin synthetic stock. Available in both left- and right-hand versions. Chambered for 270 Win., 280 Rem., 30-06, 7mm Rem. Mag., 300 Win. Mag., 338 Win. Mag., 8mm Rem. Mag., 375 H&H, all with 24" barrel only. Weight is 6 lbs., 6 oz. Introduced 1986.
Price: About $867.00

Remington Model 700 "RS" Rifle
Similar to the 700 "Mountain Rifle" except stock is of a Du Pont thermoplastic resin with glass reinforcement. Same style as the "Mountain Rifle," available in gray or camo with lightly textured finish (cheekpiece left smooth). Solid butt pad, grip cap with Remington logo. Right-hand, long action only with hinged floorplate in 270, 280 Rem., 30-06, 22" barrel, weight 6¾ lbs. Introduced 1987.
Price: $547.00

CENTERFIRE RIFLES—BOLT ACTIONS

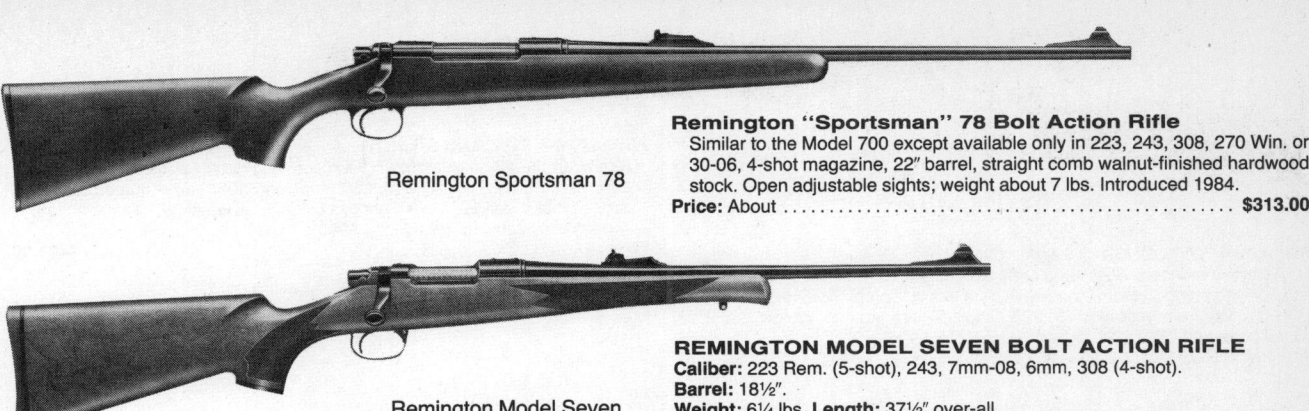

Remington Sportsman 78

Remington "Sportsman" 78 Bolt Action Rifle
Similar to the Model 700 except available only in 223, 243, 308, 270 Win. or 30-06, 4-shot magazine, 22" barrel, straight comb walnut-finished hardwood stock. Open adjustable sights; weight about 7 lbs. Introduced 1984.
Price: About $313.00

Remington Model Seven

REMINGTON MODEL SEVEN BOLT ACTION RIFLE
Caliber: 223 Rem. (5-shot), 243, 7mm-08, 6mm, 308 (4-shot).
Barrel: 18½".
Weight: 6¼ lbs. **Length:** 37½" over-all.
Stock: Walnut, with modified Schnabel fore-end. Cut checkering.
Sights: Ramp front, adjustable open rear.
Features: New short action design; silent side safety; free-floated barrel except for single pressure point at fore-end tip. Introduced 1983.
Price: About $440.00

Remington Model Seven "FS" Rifle
Similar to the standard Model Seven except has a fiberglass stock reinforced with Du Pont Kevlar aramid fiber. Classic style in gray or camo, rubber butt pad. Weight is 5½ lbs. Calibers 243, 7mm-08, 308. Introduced 1987.
Price: $600.00

Remington Model Seven Custom "KS"
Similar to the standard Model Seven except has a stock of lightweight Kevlar aramid fiber and chambered only for 35 Rem. and 350 Rem. Mag. Barrel length is 20", weight 5¾ lbs. Same stock features, design as the "FS" rifle. Comes with iron sights and is drilled and tapped for scope mounting. Special order through Remington Custom Shop. Introduced 1987.
Price: $867.00

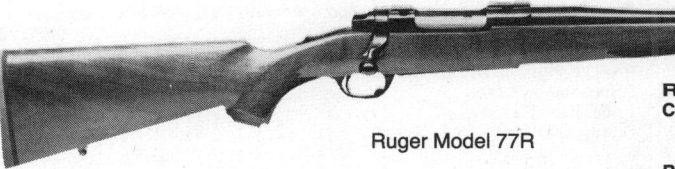

Ruger Model 77R

RUGER M-77R BOLT ACTION RIFLE
Caliber: 22-250, 6mm, 243, 308, 220 Swift (Short Stroke action); 270, 7x57, 257 Roberts, 280 Rem., 30-06, 25-06, 7mm Rem. Mag., 300 Win. Mag., 338 Win. Mag. (Magnum action).
Barrel: 22" round tapered (24" in 220 Swift and magnum action calibers).
Weight: 6¾ lbs. **Length:** 42" over-all (22" barrel).
Stock: Hand checkered American walnut, p.g. cap, sling swivel studs and recoil pad.
Sights: None supplied; comes with scope rings.
Features: Integral scope mount bases, diagonal bedding system, hinged floor plate, adj. trigger, tang safety.
Price: With Ruger steel scope rings, no sights (M-77R) $460.00

Ruger M-77RS Magnum Rifle
Similar to Ruger 77 except magnum-size action. Calibers 270, 7x57, 30-06, 243, 308, 25-06, 7mm Rem. Mag., 300 Win. Mag., 338 Win. Mag., with 24" barrel. Weight about 7 lbs. Integral-base receiver, Ruger 1" rings and open sights.
Price: $518.00

Ruger M-77RS Tropical Rifle
Similar to the Model 77RS Magnum except chambered only for 458 Win. Mag., 24" barrel, steel trigger guard and floorplate. Weight about 8¾ lbs. Comes with open sights and Ruger 1" scope rings.
Price: $600.00

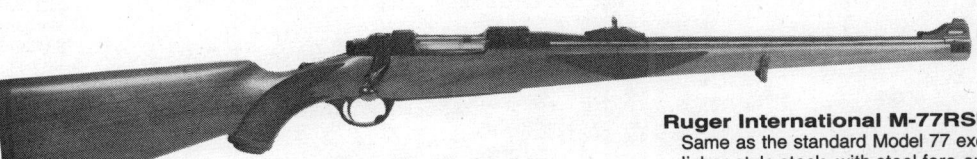

Ruger International 77

Ruger International M-77RSI Rifle
Same as the standard Model 77 except has 18½" barrel, full-length Mannlicher-style stock, with steel fore-end cap, loop-type sling swivel. Integral base receiver, open sights, Ruger 1" steel rings. Improved front sight. Available in 22-250, 250-3000, 243, 308, 270, 30-06. Weighs 7 lbs. Length over-all is 38⅜".
Price: $524.00

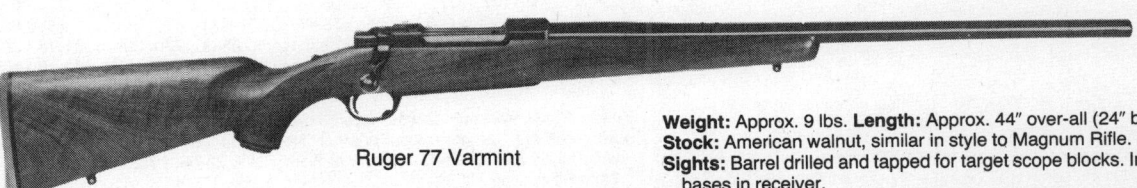

Ruger 77 Varmint

RUGER M-77V VARMINT
Caliber: 22-250, 220 Swift, 243, 25-06, 308.
Barrel: 24" heavy straight tapered, 24" in 220 swift.
Weight: Approx. 9 lbs. **Length:** Approx. 44" over-all (24" barrel).
Stock: American walnut, similar in style to Magnum Rifle.
Sights: Barrel drilled and tapped for target scope blocks. Integral scope mount bases in receiver.
Features: Ruger diagonal bedding system. Ruger steel 1" scope rings supplied. Fully adj. trigger. Barreled actions available in any of the standard calibers and barrel lengths.
Price: $482.00

CAUTION: PRICES CHANGE. CHECK AT GUNSHOP.

CENTERFIRE RIFLES—BOLT ACTIONS

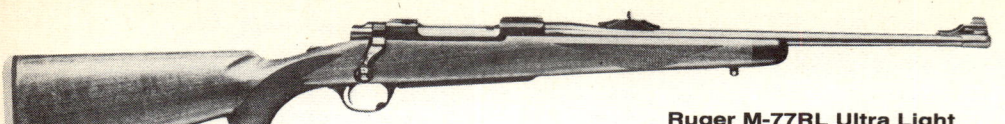

Ruger Ultra Light

Ruger M-77RL Ultra Light
Similar to the standard Model 77 except weighs only 6 lbs., chambered for 243, 270, 30-06, 257, 22-250, 250-3000 and 308; barrel tapped for target scope blocks; has 20" Ultra Light barrel. Over-all length 40". Ruger's steel 1" scope rings supplied. Introduced 1983.
Price: $498.00

Ruger M-77RLS Ultra Light Carbine
Similar to the Model 77RL Ultra Light except has 18½" barrel, Ruger Integral Scope Mounting System, iron sights, and hinged floorplate. Available in 270, 30-06 (Magnum action); 243, 308 (Short Stroke action). Weight is 6 lbs., over-all length 38⅞". Introduced 1987.
Price: M-77RLS $498.00

Sako Hunter

SAKO HUNTER RIFLE
Caliber: 17 Rem., 222, 223 (short action); 22-250, 243, 7mm-08, 308 (medium action); 25-06, 6.5x55, 270, 30-06, 7mm Rem. Mag., 7x64, 300 Win. Mag., 338 Win. Mag., 9.3x62, 375 H&H Mag., 300 Wea. Mag. (long action).
Barrel: 22" to 24" depending on caliber.
Weight: 5¾ lbs. (short); 6¼ lbs. (med.); 7¼ lbs. (long).
Stock: Hand-checkered European walnut.
Sights: None furnished. Scope mounts included.
Features: Adj. trigger, hinged floorplate. Imported from Finland by Stoeger.
Price: 17 Rem. $850.00
Price: 222, 223, 22-250, 243, 308, 7mm-08 . . . . $820.00
Price: Long action cals. (except magnums) $840.00
Price: Magnum cals. $850.00
Price: 375 H&H $860.00
Price: 300 Wea. $870.00

Sako Fiberclass Sporter
Similar to the Hunter except has a black fiberglass stock in the classic style, with wrinkle finish, rubber butt pad. Barrel length is 23", weight 7 lbs., 2 oz. Comes with scope mounts. Introduced 1985.
Price: 17 Rem. $1,160.00
Price: Short, medium, long action, std. cals. $1,130.00
Price: Magnum cals. $1,160.00

Sako Safari Grade Bolt Action
Similar to the Hunter except available in long action, calibers 300 Win. Mag., 338 Win. Mag. or 375 H&H Mag. only. Stocked in French walnut, checkered 20 l.p.i., solid rubber butt pad; grip cap and fore-end tip; quarter-rib "express" rear sight, hooded ramp front. Front sling swivel band-mounted on barrel.
Price: $2,115.00

Sako Hunter Left-Hand Rifle
Same gun as the Sako Hunter except has left-hand action, stock with dull finish. Available in long action and magnum calibers only. Introduced 1987.
Price: Standard calibers $950.00
Price: Magnum calibers $960.00
Price: 375 H&H $970.00

Sako Hunter LS

Sako Hunter LS Rifle
Same gun as the Sako Hunter except has laminated stock with dull finish. Chambered for same calibers. Introduced 1987.
Price: Short and medium action $925.00
Price: Long action $940.00
Price: Magnum cals. $945.00

Sako Carbine

Sako Carbine
Same 18½" barreled action and calibers as Sako Carbine but with conventional oil-finished stock of the Hunter model. Introduced 1986.
Price: 22-250, 243, 7mm-08, 308 Win. $820.00
Price: 25-06, 6.5x55, 270, 7x64, 30-06 . . . . $840.00
Price: 7mm Rem. Mag., 300 Win. Mag., 338 Win., 375 H&H. . . $850.00
Price: As Fiberclass with black fiberglass stock, 25-06, 270, 30-06 $1,130.00
Price: As above, 7mm Rem. Mag., 308 Mag., 338 Win., 375 H&H . $1,160.00

Sako Heavy Barrel
Same as std. Super Sporter except has beavertail fore-end; available in 222, 223 (short action), 22 PPC, 6mm PPC (single shot), 22-250, 243, 308 (medium action). Weight from 8¼ to 8½ lbs. 5-shot magazine capacity.
Price: 222, 223 (short action) $1,035.00
Price: 22-250, 243, 308 (medium action) $1,035.00
Price: 22 PPC, 6mm PPC (single shot) $925.00

Sako Mannlicher-Style Carbine
Same as the Carbine except has full "Mannlicher" style stock, 18½" barrel, weighs 7½ lbs., chambered for 222 Rem., 243, 25-06, 270, 308 and 30-06, 7mm Rem. Mag., 300 Win. Mag., 338 Win. Mag., 375 H&H. Introduced 1977. From Stoeger.
Price: $885.00
Price: Magnum cals. $915.00
Price: 375 H&H $935.00

CENTERFIRE RIFLES—BOLT ACTIONS

Sako Deluxe Sporter

Sako Super Deluxe Sporter
Similar to Deluxe Sporter except has select European walnut with high gloss finish and deep cut oak leaf carving. Metal has super high polish, deep blue finish.
Price: $2,115.00

Sako Deluxe Sporter
Same action as Hunter except has select wood, rosewood p.g. cap and fore-end tip. Fine checkering on top surfaces of integral dovetail bases, bolt sleeve, bolt handle root and bolt knob. Vent. recoil pad, skip-line checkering, mirror finish bluing.
Price: $1,065.00
Price: 7mm Rem. Mag., 300 Win. Mag., 338 Mag., 375 H&H $1,090.00

Sauer Model 200

SAUER 90 RIFLE
Caliber: 22-250, 243, 308 (Short, Stutzen) 25-06, 270, 30-06, (Medium, Stutzen); 7mm Rem. Mag., 300 Win., 300 Wea., 375 H&H (Magnum); 458 Win. Mag. (Safari).
Barrel: 20" (Stutzen), 24", 26".
Weight: 7 lbs., 6 oz. (Junior). **Length:** 42½" over-all.
Stock: European walnut with oil finish, recoil pad.
Sights: Post front on ramp, open rear adj. for w.
Features: Detachable 3-4 round box magazine; rear bolt locking lugs; 65° bolt throw; front sling swivel on barrel band. Introduced 1986. Imported from West Germany by Sigarms.
Price: About $1,175.00
Price: Safari, about $1,675.00

SAUER MODEL 200 RIFLE
Caliber: 243, 308, 25-06, 270, 30-06.
Barrel: 24", interchangeable.
Weight: 6⅔ lbs. (Alloy) to 7¾ lbs. (Steel). **Length:** 44" over-all.
Stock: European walnut with recoil pad; checkered p.g. and fore-end.
Sights: None furnished. Drilled and tapped for iron sights and scope mount.
Features: Easily interchangeable barrels, buttstock and fore-end; removable box magazine; steel and alloy versions; left-hand models available. Introduced 1986. Imported from West Germany by Sigarms.
Price: Standard Grade, about $875.00
Price: LUX Grade, about $1,075.00
Price: Carbon fiber, about $1,200.00
Price: Magnum (special order, 7mm Rem. Mag., 300 Win. Mag. $815.00

Savage Model 110E

Savage Model 110F Bolt Action Rifle
Similar to the Model 110E except chambered only for 270, 30-06, 7mm Rem. Mag., and has a black Du Pont Rynite® stock with black butt pad. Introduced 1988.
Price: $329.00

SAVAGE 110E BOLT ACTION RIFLE
Caliber: 223, 270, 30-06, 243, 5 shot; 7mm Rem. Mag., 4 shot.
Barrel: 22" round tapered, 24" for magnum.
Weight: 6¾ lbs. **Length:** 42⅜" (22" barrel).
Stock: Walnut finished hardwood with Monte Carlo; hard rubber buttplate.
Sights: Ramp front, step adj. rear.
Features: Top tang safety, receiver tapped for scope mount. Full floating barrel; adjustable trigger.
Price: $259.00
Price: Without sights $249.00

Savage Model 110B Bolt Action Rifle
Similar to the Model 110E except has brown laminated Monte Carlo stock with brown butt pad. Weighs 6¾ lbs. Introduced 1988.
Price: $329.00

Steyr-Mannlicher Professional

STEYR-MANNLICHER MODEL M
Caliber: 7x64, 7x57, 25-06, 270, 30-06. Left-hand action cals.—7x64, 25-06, 270, 30-06. Optional cals.—6.5x57, 8x57JS, 9.3x62, 6.5x55, 7.5x55.
Barrel: 20" (full-stock); 23.6" (half-stock).
Weight: 6.8 lbs. to 7.5 lbs. **Length:** 39" (full-stock); 43" (half-stock).

Stock: Hand checkered walnut. Full Mannlicher or std. half stock with M.C. and rubber recoil pad.
Sights: Ramp front, open U-notch rear.
Features: Choice of interchangeable single or double set triggers. Detachable 5-shot rotary magazine. Drilled and tapped for scope mounting. Available as "Professional" model with Parkerized finish and synthetic stock (right hand action only). Imported by Gun South, Inc.
Price: Full-stock (carbine) $1,939.00
Price: Half-stock (rifle) $1,812.00
Price: For left-hand action (full stock) add about $173.00
Price: Professional model (full stock) $1,532.00

CAUTION: PRICES CHANGE. CHECK AT GUNSHOP.

CENTERFIRE RIFLES—BOLT ACTIONS

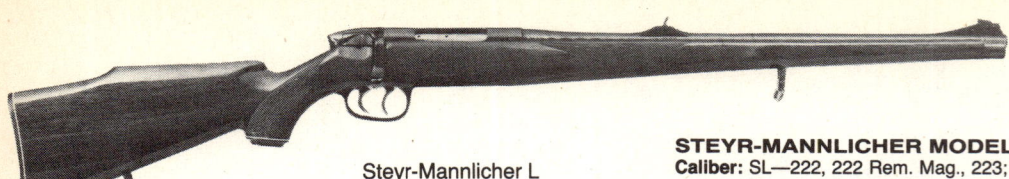

Steyr-Mannlicher L

Steyr-Mannlicher "Luxus"
Similar to Steyr-Mannlicher Models L and M except has single set trigger and detachable 3-shot steel magazine. Same calibers as L and M. Oil finish or high gloss lacquer on stock.
Price: Full-stock **$2,495.00**
Price: Half-stock **$2,364.00**

STEYR-MANNLICHER MODELS S & S/T
Caliber: Model S—300 Win. Mag., 338 Win. Mag., 7mm Rem. Mag., 300 H&H Mag., 375 H&H Mag. (6.5x68, 8x68S, 9.3x64 optional); S/T—375 H&H Mag., 458 Win. Mag. (9.3x64 optional).
Barrel: 25.6".
Weight: 8.4 lbs. (Model S). **Length:** 45" over-all.
Stock: Half-stock with M.C. and rubber recoil pad. Hand checkered walnut. Available with optional spare magazine inletted in butt.
Sights: Ramp front, U-notch rear.
Features: Choice of interchangeable single or double set triggers, detachable 4-shot magazine. Drilled and tapped for scope mounts. Imported by Gun South, Inc.
Price: Model S **$1,952.00**
Price: Model S/T 375 H&H, 458 Win. Mag. **$2,176.00**

STEYR-MANNLICHER MODELS SL & L
Caliber: SL—222, 222 Rem. Mag., 223; SL Varmint—222; L—22-250, 6mm, 243, 308 Win.; L Varmint—22-250, 243, 308 Win.
Barrel: 20" (full-stock); 23.6" (half-stock).
Weight: 6 lbs. (full-stock). **Length:** 38¼" (full-stock).
Stock: Hand checkered walnut. Full Mannlicher or standard half-stock with Monte Carlo.
Sights: Ramp front, open U-notch rear.
Features: Choice of interchangeable single or double set triggers. Five-shot detachable "Makrolon" rotary magazine, 6 rear locking lugs. Drilled and tapped for scope mounts. Imported by Gun South, Inc.
Price: Full-Stock **$1,939.00**
Price: Half-stock **$1,812.00**

Steyr-Mannlicher Varmint, Models SL and L
Similar to standard SL and L except chambered only for 222 Rem. (SL), 22-250, 243, 308. Has 26" heavy barrel, no sights (drilled and tapped for scope mounts). Choice of single or double set triggers. Five-shot detachable magazine.
Price: **$1,939.00**

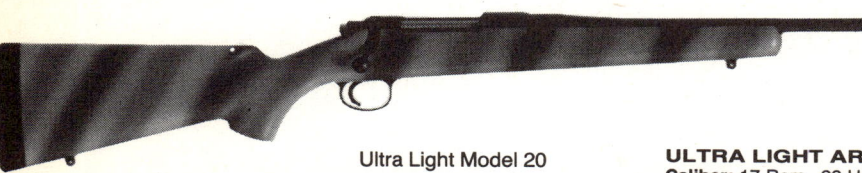

Ultra Light Model 20

Ultra Light Arms Model 20S Rifle
Similar to the Model 20 except uses short action chambered for 17 Rem., 222 Rem., 223 Rem., 22 Hornet. Has 22" Douglas Premium No. 1 contour barrel, weighs 4¾ lbs., 41" over-all length.
Price: **$1,800.00**
Price: Model 20S Left Hand (left-hand action and stock) **$1,900.00**

Ultra Light Arms Model 28 Rifle
Similar to the Model 20 except in 264, 7mm Rem. Mag., 300 Win. Mag., 338 Win. Mag. Uses 24" Douglas Premium No. 2 contour barrel. Weighs 5½ lbs., 45" over-all length. KDF or U.L.A. recoil arrestor built in. Any custom feature available on any U.L.A. product can be incorporated.
Price: Right hand **$2,350.00**
Price: Left hand **$2,450.00**

ULTRA LIGHT ARMS MODEL 20 RIFLE
Caliber: 17 Rem., 22 Hornet, 222 Rem., 222 Rem. Mag., 223 Rem., 22-250, 6mm Rem., 243, 250-3000, 257 Roberts, 257 Ackley, 7x57, 7x57 Ackley, 7mm-08, 284 Win., 300 Savage, 358 Win.
Barrel: 22" or 24" Douglas Premium No. 1 contour.
Weight: 4½ lbs. **Length:** 41½" over-all.
Stock: Composite Kevlar, graphite reinforced. Du Pont Imron paint colors — green, black, brown and camo options. Choice of length of pull.
Sights: None furnished. Scope mount included.
Features: Timney adj. trigger; two-position three-function safety. Benchrest quality action. Matte or bright stock and metal finish. 3" magazine length. Shipped in a hard case. From Ultra Light Arms, Inc.
Price: Right hand **$1,800.00**
Price: Model 20 Left Hand (left-hand action and stock) **$1,900.00**
Price: Model 24 (25-06, 270, 7mm Express Rem., 30-06, 3⅜" magazine length) **$1,875.00**
Price: Model 24 Left Hand (left-hand action and stock) **$1,975.00**

VOERE 2155, 2165 BOLT ACTION RIFLE
Caliber: 22-250, 270, 308, 243, 30-06, 7x64, 5.6x57, 6.5x55, 8x57 JRS, 7mm Rem. Mag., 300 Win. Mag., 8x68S, 9.3x62, 9.3x64, 6.5x68.
Stock: European walnut, hog-back style; checkered pistol grip and fore-end.
Sights: Ramp front, open adjustable rear.
Features: Mauser-type action with 5-shot detachable box magazine; double set or single trigger; drilled and tapped for scope mounting. Imported from Austria by L. Joseph Rahn. Introduced 1984.
Price: M2165, standard calibers, single trigger **$885.00**
Price: As above, double set triggers **$925.00**
Price: M2165, magnum calibers, single trigger **$915.00**
Price: As above, double set triggers **$955.00**
Price: M2165, full-stock, single trigger **$925.00**
Price: As above, double set triggers **$985.00**
Price: M2155 (as above, no jeweling, military safety, single trigger) . **$700.00**
Price: As above, double triggers **$750.00**

Voere Model 2165

> Consult our Directory pages for the location of firms mentioned.

CENTERFIRE RIFLES—BOLT ACTIONS

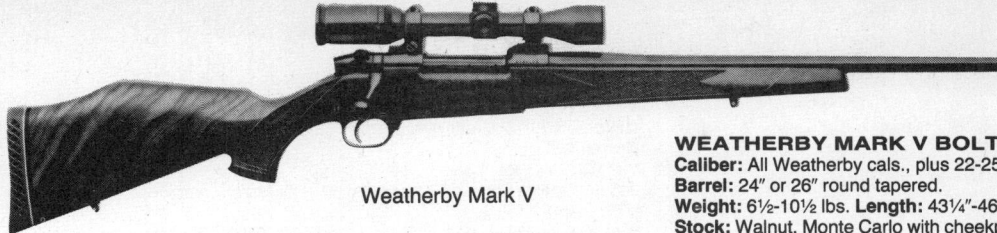
Weatherby Mark V

WEATHERBY MARK V BOLT ACTION RIFLE
Caliber: All Weatherby cals., plus 22-250 and 30-06.
Barrel: 24" or 26" round tapered.
Weight: 6½-10½ lbs. **Length:** 43¼"-46½" over-all.
Stock: Walnut, Monte Carlo with cheekpiece, high luster finish, checkered p.g. and fore-end, recoil pad.
Sights: Optional (extra).
Features: Cocking indicator, adj. trigger, hinged floorplate, thumb safety, quick detachable sling swivels.
Price: Cals. 224 and 22-250, std. bbl., right-hand only **$971.00**
Price: With 26" semi-target bbl., right-hand only **$987.00**
Price: Cals. 240, 257, 270, 7mm, 30-06 and 300 (24"bbl.) right- or left-hand **$991.00**
Price: With 26" No. 2 contour bbl., right-hand or 300 W.M. left only **$1,011.00**
Price: Cal. 340 (26" bbl.), right- or left-hand.................... **$1,011.00**
Price: Cal. 378 (26" bbl.), right- or left-hand.................... **$1,165.00**
Price: Cal. 460 (26" bbl.), right- or left-hand.................... **$1,305.00**

Weatherby Mark V Rifle Left Hand
Available in all Weatherby calibers, plus 30-06 with 24" barrel. Left hand 26" barrel available in 300 and 340 calibers. Not available in 224 WM and 22-250 Varmintmaster.

WEATHERBY EUROMARK BOLT ACTION RIFLE
Caliber: All Weatherby calibers except 224, 22-250.
Barrel: 24" or 26" round tapered.
Weight: 6½ to 10½ lbs. **Length:** 44¼" over-all (24" bbl.).
Stock: Walnut, Monte Carlo with extended tail, fine-line hand checkering, satin oil finish, ebony fore-end tip and grip cap with maple diamond, solid butt pad.
Sights: Optional (extra).
Features: Cocking indicator; adj. trigger; hinged floor plate; thumb safety; q.d. sling swivels. Introduced 1986.
Price: With 24" barrel (240, 257, 270, 7mm, 30-06, 300), right- or left-hand **$1,040.00**
Price: 26" No. 2 Contour barrel, right- or left-hand (300 only)...... **$1,060.00**
Price: 340 W.M., 26", right- or left-hand **$1,060.00**
Price: 378 W.M., 26", right or left-hand **$1,214.00**
Price: 460 W.M., 26", right or left-hand **$1,354.00**

Weatherby Vanguard VGX

WEATHERBY VANGUARD VGX, VGS RIFLES
Caliber: 22-250, 25-06, 243, 270, and 30-06 (5-shot); 7mm Rem. and 300 Win. Mag. (3-shot).
Barrel: 24" hammer forged.
Weight: 7⅞ lbs. **Length:** 44½" over-all.
Stock: American walnut, p.g. cap and fore-end tip, hand inletted and checkered. 13½" pull.
Sights: Optional, available at extra cost.
Features: Side safety, adj. trigger, hinged floorplate, receiver tapped for scope mounts. Imported from Japan by Weatherby.
Price: VGS **$467.00**
Price: VGX—deluxe wood, different checkering, ventilated recoil pad **$600.00**

Weatherby Vanguard Fiberguard Rifle
Uses the Vanguard barreled action and a forest green or black wrinkle-finished fiberglass stock. All metal is matte blue. Has a 20" barrel, weighs 6½ lbs., measures 40" in 223, 243, and 308; 40½" in 270, 7mm Rem. Mag., 30-06. Accepts same scope mount bases as Mark V action. Introduced 1985.
Price: Right-hand only... **$560.00**

Weatherby Vanguard VGL

Weatherby Vanguard VGL Rifle
Similar to the standard Vanguard except has a short action, chambered for 223, 243, 270, 30-06, 7mm Rem. Mag. with 20" barrel. Barrel and action have a non-glare blue finish. Guaranteed to shoot a 1½" 3-shot group at 100 yards. Stock has a non-glare satin finish, hand checkering and a black butt pad with black spacer. Introduced 1984.
Price: **$467.00**

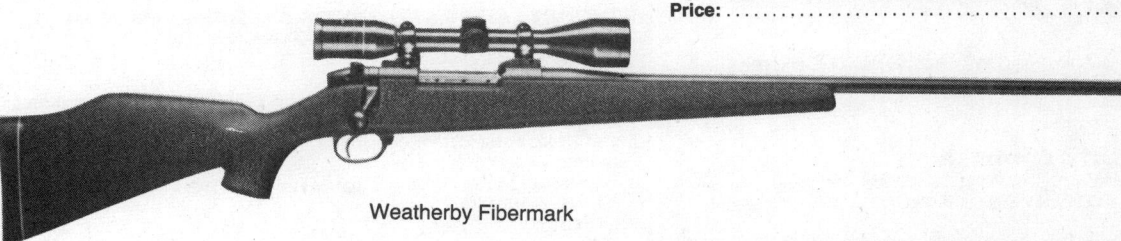
Weatherby Fibermark

Weatherby Fibermark Rifle
Same as the standard Mark V except the stock is of fiberglass; finished with a non-glare black wrinkle finish and black recoil pad; receiver and floorplate have low luster blue finish; fluted bolt has a satin finish. Available in left- or right-hand, 24" or 26" barrel, 240 Weatherby Mag. through 340 Weatherby Mag. calibers. Introduced 1983.
Price: 240 W.M. through 300 W.M., 24" bbl. **$1,123.00**
Price: 240 W.M. through 340 W.M., 26" bbl., right-hand or 300, 340 W.M. left-hand only **$1,143.00**

Weatherby Lazer Mark V Rifle
Same as standard Mark V except stock has extensive laser carving under cheekpiece on butt, p.g. and fore-end. Introduced 1981.
Price: 22-250, 224 Wea., 24" bbl., right-hand only **$1,085.00**
Price: As above, 26" bbl., right-hand only **$1,100.00**
Price: 240 Wea. thru 300 Wea., 24" bbl., right- or left-hand **$1,105.00**
Price: As above, 26" bbl., right-hand or 300 W.M. left-hand **$1,125.00**
Price: 340 Wea., right- or left-hand **$1,127.00**
Price: 378 Wea., right- or left-hand **$1,281.00**
Price: 460 Wea., right- or left-hand **$1,421.00**

CAUTION: PRICES CHANGE. CHECK AT GUNSHOP.

CENTERFIRE RIFLES—BOLT ACTIONS

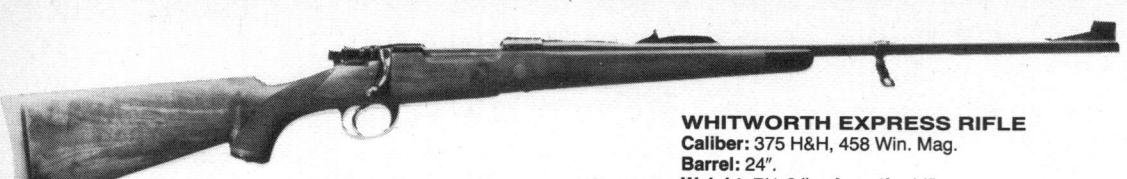
Whitworth Express Rifle

WHITWORTH EXPRESS RIFLE
Caliber: 375 H&H, 458 Win. Mag.
Barrel: 24".
Weight: 7½-8 lbs. **Length:** 44".
Stock: Classic English Express rifle design of hand checkered, select European walnut.
Sights: Three leaf open sight calibrated for 100, 200, 300 yards on ¼-rib, ramp front with removable hood.
Features: Solid rubber recoil pad, barrel-mounted sling swivel, adjustable trigger, hinged floor plate, solid steel recoil cross bolt.
Price: 375, 458, with express sights. $690.00

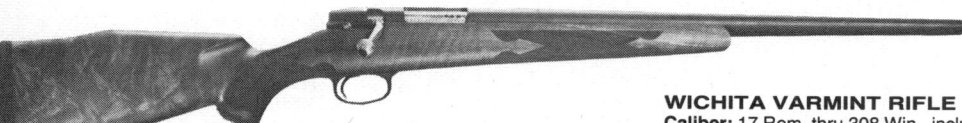
Wichita Varmint Rifle

WICHITA VARMINT RIFLE
Caliber: 17 Rem. thru 308 Win., including 22 and 6mm PPC.
Barrel: 20⅛".
Weight: 9lbs. **Length:** 40⅛" over-all.
Stock: AAA Fancy American walnut. Hand-rubbed finish, hand-checkered, 20 l.p.i. pattern. Hand-inletted, glass bedded, steel grip cap, Pachmayr rubber recoil pad.
Sights: None. Drilled and tapped for scope mounts.
Features: Right or left-hand Wichita action with three locking lugs. Available as a single shot or repeater with 3-shot magazine. Checkered bolt handle. Bolt is hand fitted, lapped and jeweled. Side thumb safety. Firing pin fall is ³⁄₁₆". Non-glare blue finish. From Wichita Arms.
Price: Single shot $1,975.00
Price: With blind box magazine $2,225.00

WICHITA CLASSIC RIFLE
Caliber: 17 Rem. thru 308 Win., including 22 and 6mm PPC.
Barrel: 21⅛".
Weight: 8 lbs. **Length:** 41" over-all.
Stock: AAA Fancy American walnut. Hand-rubbed and checkered (20 l.p.i.). Hand-inletted, glass bedded, steel grip cap. Pachmayr rubber recoil pad.
Sights: None. Drilled and tapped for scope mounting.
Features: Available as single shot or repeater. Octagonal barrel and Wichita action, right or left-hand. Checkered bolt handle. Bolt is hand-fitted, lapped and jewelled. Adjustable Canjar trigger is set at 2 lbs. Side thumb safety. Firing pin fall is ³⁄₁₆". Non-glare blue finish. From Wichita Arms.
Price: Single shot $2,950.00
Price: With blind box magazine $3,200.00

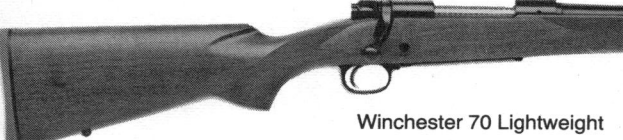
Winchester 70 Lightweight

WINCHESTER MODEL 70 LIGHTWEIGHT RIFLE
Caliber: 270, 30-06 (standard action); 22-250, 223, 243, 308 (short action), both 5-shot magazine, except 6-shot in 223.
Barrel: 22".
Weight: 6¼ lbs. **Length:** 40½" over-all (std.), 40" (short).
Stock: American walnut with satin finish, deep-cut checkering.
Sights: None furnished. Drilled and tapped for scope mounting.
Features: Three position safety; stainless steel magazine follower; hinged floorplate; sling swivel studs. Introduced 1984.
Price: With sights, about $399.00
Price: With Win-Tuff laminated stock $409.00
Price: With Win-Cam green-shaded laminated stock, 270, 30-06 only $476.00

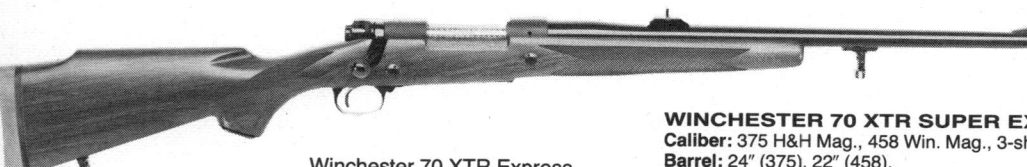
Winchester 70 XTR Express

WINCHESTER 70 XTR SUPER EXPRESS MAGNUM
Caliber: 375 H&H Mag., 458 Win. Mag., 3-shot magazine.
Barrel: 24" (375), 22" (458).
Weight: 8½ lbs.
Stock: American walnut with Monte Carlo cheekpiece. XTR wrap-around checkering and finish.
Sights: Hooded ramp front, open rear.
Features: Two steel crossbolts in stock for added strength. Front sling swivel mounted on barrel. Contoured rubber butt pad. Made under license by U.S. Repeating Arms Co.
Price: About $793.00

WINCHESTER 70 XTR SPORTER
Caliber: 22-250, 223, 243, 270, 270 Wea., 30-06, 264 Win. Mag., 7mm Rem. Mag., 300 Win. Mag., 300 Wea. Mag., 338 Win. Mag., 3-shot magazine.
Barrel: 24".
Weight: 7¾ lbs. **Length:** 44½" over-all.
Stock: American walnut with Monte Carlo cheekpiece. XTR checkering and satin finish.
Sights: None furnished; optional hooded ramp front, adjustable folding leaf rear.
Features: Three-position safety, detachable sling swivels, stainless steel magazine follower, rubber butt pad, epoxy bedded receiver recoil lug. Made under license by U.S. Repeating Arms Co.
Price: With sights, about $465.00
Price: Without sights, about $451.00
Price: 300 Wea. Mag., without sights, about $468.00

Winchester Model 70 Winlite Rifle
Similar to the Model 70 XTR Sporter except has McMillan black fiberglass stock. No sights are furnished but receiver is drilled and tapped for scope mounting. Available in 270, 280, 30-06 (22" barrel, 4-shot magazine), 7mm Rem. Mag., 300 Wea., 300 Win. Mag., 338 Win. Mag. (24" barrel, 3-shot magazine). Weight is 6¼-6½ lbs. for 270, 30-06, 6¾-7 lbs. for 7mm Mag., 338. Introduced 1986.
Price: About $636.00
Price: 300 Weatherby, about $654.00

CENTERFIRE RIFLES—BOLT ACTION

Winchester 70 Featherweight

Winchester Model 70 XTR Featherweight
Available with standard action in 270 Win., 280 Rem., 30-06, short action in 22-250, 223, 243, 308; 22" tapered Featherweight barrel; classic-style American walnut stock with Schnabel fore-end, wrap-around XTR checkering fashioned after early Model 70 custom rifle patterns. Red rubber butt pad with black spacer; sling swivel studs. Weighs 6¾ lbs. (standard action), 6½ lbs. (short action). Introduced 1984.
Price: About **$465.00**

Winchester Ranger

Winchester Ranger Rifle
Similar to Model 70 XTR Sporter except chambered only for 243, 270, 30-06, with 22" barrel. American hardwood stock, no checkering, composition butt plate. Metal has matte blue finish. Introduced 1985.
Price: About **$336.00**
Price: Ranger Youth, 243 only, scaled-down stock **$345.00**

CENTERFIRE RIFLES—SINGLE SHOTS

Classic and modern designs for sporting and competitive use.

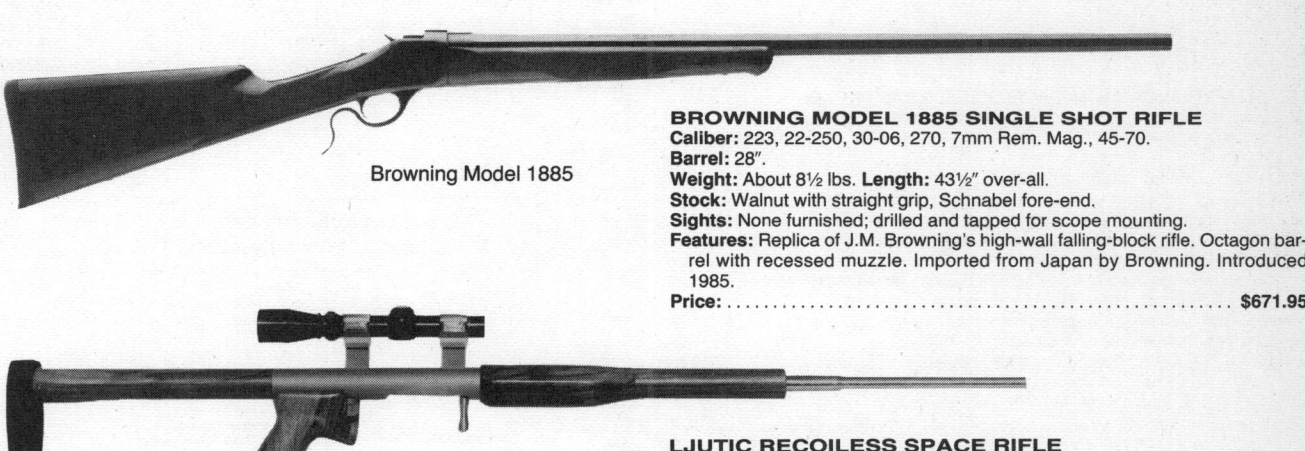

Browning Model 1885

BROWNING MODEL 1885 SINGLE SHOT RIFLE
Caliber: 223, 22-250, 30-06, 270, 7mm Rem. Mag., 45-70.
Barrel: 28".
Weight: About 8½ lbs. **Length:** 43½" over-all.
Stock: Walnut with straight grip, Schnabel fore-end.
Sights: None furnished; drilled and tapped for scope mounting.
Features: Replica of J.M. Browning's high-wall falling-block rifle. Octagon barrel with recessed muzzle. Imported from Japan by Browning. Introduced 1985.
Price: **$671.95**

Ljutic Space Rifle

LJUTIC RECOILESS SPACE RIFLE
Caliber: 22-250, 30-30, 30-06, 308, single-shot.
Barrel: 24".
Weight: 8¾ lbs. **Length:** 44" over-all.
Stock: Walnut stock, fore-end and grip.
Sights: Iron sights or scope mounts.
Features: Revolutionary design has anti-recoil mechanism. Twist-bolt action uses six moving parts. Scope and mounts extra. Introduced 1981. From Ljutic Industries.
Price: **$3,695.00**

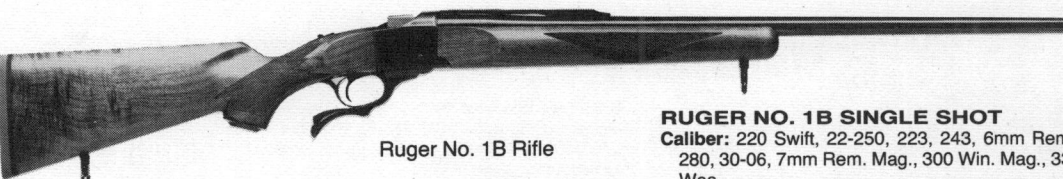

Ruger No. 1B Rifle

RUGER NO. 1B SINGLE SHOT
Caliber: 220 Swift, 22-250, 223, 243, 6mm Rem., 25-06, 257 Roberts, 270, 280, 30-06, 7mm Rem. Mag., 300 Win. Mag., 338 Win. Mag., 270 Wea., 300 Wea.
Barrel: 26" round tapered with quarter-rib; with Ruger 1" rings.
Weight: 8 lbs. **Length:** 43⅜" over-all.
Stock: Walnut, two-piece, checkered p.g. and semi-beavertail fore-end.
Sights: None, 1" scope rings supplied for integral mounts.
Features: Under lever, hammerless falling block design has auto ejector, top tang safety.
Price: **$575.00**
Price: Barreled action **$389.50**

Ruger No. 1S Medium Sporter
Similar to the No. 1B Standard Rifle except has Alexander Henry-style fore-end, adjustable folding leaf rear sight on quarter-rib, ramp front sight base and dovetail-type gold bead front sight. Calibers 7mm Rem. Mag., 338 Win. Mag., 300 Win. Mag. with 26" barrel, 45-70 with 22" barrel. Weight about 7½ lbs. in 45-70.
Price: No. 1S **$575.00**
Price: Barreled action **$389.50**

CAUTION: PRICES CHANGE. CHECK AT GUNSHOP.

CENTERFIRE RIFLES—SINGLE SHOTS

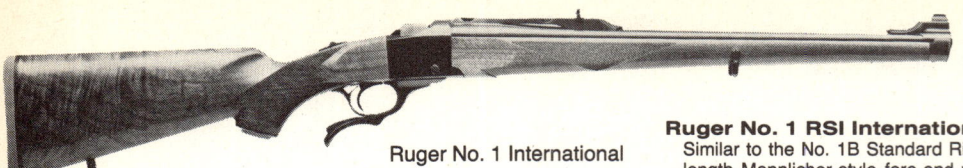

Ruger No. 1 International

Ruger No. 1 RSI International
Similar to the No. 1B Standard Rifle except has lightweight 20" barrel, full length Mannlicher-style fore-end with loop sling swivel, adjustable folding leaf rear sight on quarter rib, ramp front with gold bead. Calibers 243, 30-06, 270 and 7x57. Weight is about 7¼ lbs.
Price: No. 1RSI $595.00
Price: Barreled action $389.50

Ruger No. 1A Light Sporter
Similar to the No. 1B Standard Rifle except has lightweight 22" barrel, Alexander Henry-style fore-end, adjustable folding leaf rear sight on quarter-rib, dovetailed ramp front with gold bead. Calibers 243, 30-06, 270 and 7x57. Weight about 7¼ lbs.
Price: No. 1A $575.00
Price: Barreled action $389.50

Ruger No. 1H Tropical Rifle
Similar to the No. 1B Standard Rifle except has Alexander Henry fore-end, adjustable folding leaf rear sight on quarter-rib, ramp front with dovetail gold bead front, 24" heavy barrel. Calibers 375 H&H (weight about 8¼ lbs.) and 458 Win. Mag. (weight about 9 lbs.).
Price: No. 1H $575.00
Price: Barreled action $389.50

Ruger No. 1V Special Varminter
Similar to the No. 1B Standard Rifle except has 24" heavy barrel. Semi-beavertail fore-end, barrel tapped for target scope block, with 1" Ruger scope rings. Calibers 22-250, 220 Swift, 223, 25-06, 6mm. Weight about 9 lbs.
Price: No. 1V $575.00
Price: Barreled action $389.50

NAVY ARMS ROLLING BLOCK RIFLE
Caliber: 45-70.
Barrel: 30".
Stock: Walnut finished.
Sights: Fixed front, adj. rear.
Features: Reproduction of classic rolling block action. Available in Buffalo Rifle (octagonal bbl.) and Creedmoor (half-round, half-octagonal bbl.) models. From Navy Arms.
Price: 26", 30" full octagon barrel $489.00
Price: Creedmoor Model, 30" full octagon $521.00
Price: 30", half-round $489.00
Price: 26", half-round $489.00
Price: Half-round Creedmoor $521.00

C. SHARPS ARMS NEW MODEL 1875 RIFLE
Caliber: 22 LR Stevens, 32-40 & 38-55 Ballard, 40-90 3¼", 40-90 2⅝", 40-70 2¹⁰⁄₁₀", 40-70 2¼", 40-70 2½", 40-50 1¹¹⁄₁₆" 40-50 1⅞", 45-90 2⁴⁄₁₀" 45-70 2¹⁄₁₀".
Barrel: 24", 26", 30" (standard); 32", 34" optional.
Weight: 8-12 lbs.
Stock: Walnut, straight grip, shotgun butt with checkered steel buttplate.
Sights: Silver blade front, Rocky Mountain buckhorn rear.
Features: Recreation of the 1875 Sharps rifle. Production guns will have case colored receiver. Available in Custom Sporting and Target versions upon request. Announced 1986. From C. Sharps Arms Co.
Price: 1875 Carbine (24" tapered round bbl.) $575.00
Price: 1875 Saddle Rifle (26" tapered oct. bbl.) $650.00
Price: 1875 Sporting Rifle (30" tapered oct. bbl.) $650.00

Consult our directory pages for the location of firms mentioned.

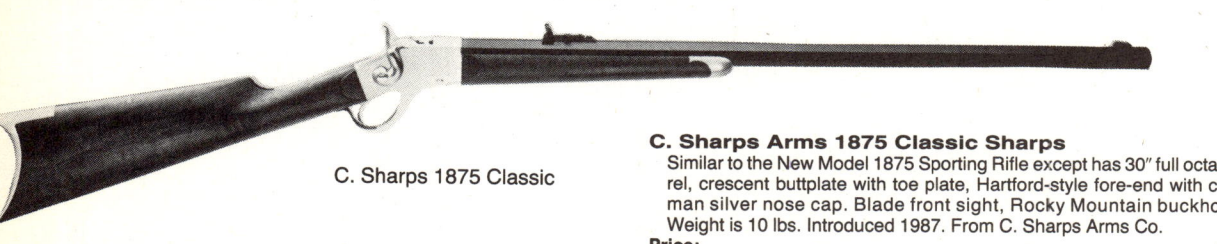

C. Sharps 1875 Classic

C. Sharps Arms 1875 Classic Sharps
Similar to the New Model 1875 Sporting Rifle except has 30" full octagon barrel, crescent buttplate with toe plate, Hartford-style fore-end with cast German silver nose cap. Blade front sight, Rocky Mountain buckhorn rear. Weight is 10 lbs. Introduced 1987. From C. Sharps Arms Co.
Price: $995.00

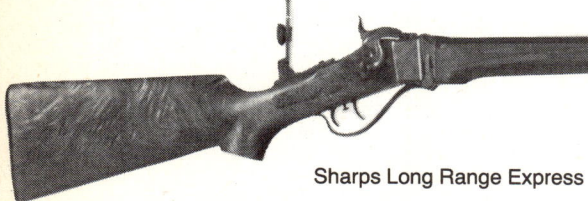

Sharps Long Range Express

SHILOH SHARPS 1874 LONG RANGE EXPRESS
Caliber: 40-50 BN, 40-70 BN, 40-90 BN, 45-70 ST, 45-90 ST, 45-110 ST, 50-70 ST, 50-90 ST, 50-110 ST, 32-40, 38-55, 40-70 ST, 40-90 ST.
Barrel: 34" tapered octagon.
Weight: 10½ lbs. Length: 51" over-all.
Stock: Oil-finished semi-fancy walnut with pistol grip, shotgun-style butt, traditional cheek rest and accent line. Schnabel fore-end.
Sights: Globe front, sporting tang rear.
Features: Recreation of the Model 1874 Sharps rifle. Double set triggers. Made in U.S. by Shiloh Rifle Mfg. Co.
Price: $795.00
Price: Sporting Rifle No. 1 (similar to above except with 30" bbl., blade front, buckhorn rear sight) $775.00
Price: Sporting Rifle No. 3 (similar to No. 1 except straight-grip stock, standard wood) $675.00

Shiloh Sharps "The Jaeger"
Similar to the Montana Roughrider except has half-octagon 26" lightweight barrel, calibers 30-40, 30-30, 307 Win., 45-70. Standard supreme black walnut.
Price: $750.00

CENTERFIRE RIFLES—SINGLE SHOTS

Sharps 1874 Military

Shiloh Sharps 1874 Military Rifle
Has 30" round barrel. Iron block front sight and Lawrence-style rear ladder sight. Military butt, buttplate with patchbox assembly, three barrel bands; single trigger (double set availble). Calibers 40-50x1 11/16" BN, 40-70x2 1/10" BN, 40-90 BN, 45-70x2 1/10" ST, 50-70 ST.
Price: $800.00

Shiloh Sharps 1874 Montana Roughrider
Similar to the No. 1 Sporting Rifle except available with half-octagon or full octagon barrel in 24", 26", 28", 30", 34" lengths; standard supreme or semi-fancy wood, shotgun, pistol grip or military-style butt. Weight about 8½ lbs. Calibers 30-40, 30-30, 40-50x1 11/16" BN, 40-70x2 1/10" BN, 45-70x2 1/10" ST. Globe front and tang sight optional.
Price: Standard supreme $725.00
Price: Semi-fancy $775.00

Shiloh Sharps 1874 Business Rifle
Similar to No. 3 Rifle except has 28" heavy round barrel, military-style buttstock and steel buttplate. Weight about 9½ lbs. Calibers 40-50 BN, 40-70 BN, 40-90 BN, 45-70 ST, 45-90 ST, 50-70 ST, 50-100 ST, 32-40, 38-55, 40-70 ST, 40-90 ST.
Price: $650.00
Price: 1874 Carbine (similar to above except 24" round bbl., single trigger—double set avail.) $650.00
Price: 1874 Saddle Rifle (similar to Carbine except has 26" octagon barrel, semi-fancy shotgun butt) $750.00

Thompson/Center Contender

THOMPSON/CENTER CONTENDER CARBINE
Caliber: 22 LR, 22 Hornet, 223 Rem., 7mm T.C.U., 7x30 Waters, 30-30 Win., 357 Rem. Maximum, 35 Rem., 44 Mag., 410, single shot.
Barrel: 21".

Weight: 5 lbs., 2 oz. **Length:** 35" over-all.
Stock: Checkered American walnut with rubber butt pad.
Sights: Blade front, open adj. rear.
Features: Uses the T/C Contender action. Eleven interchangeable barrels available, all with sights, drilled and tapped for scope mounting. Introduced 1985. Offered as a complete Carbine only.
Price: Rifle calibers $370.00
Price: Extra barrels, rifle calibers, each $160.00
Price: 410 shotgun $390.00
Price: Extra 410 barrel $180.00

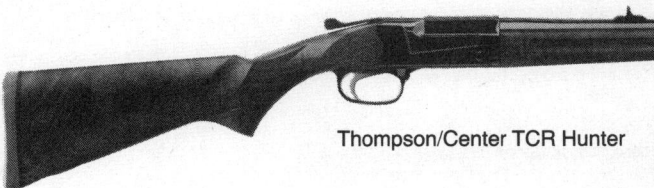

Thompson/Center TCR Hunter

UBERTI ROLLING BLOCK BABY CARBINE
Caliber: 22 LR, 22 WMR, 22 Hornet, 357 Mag., single shot.
Barrel: 22".
Weight: 4.8 lbs. **Length:** 35½" over-all.
Stock: Walnut stock and fore-end.
Sights: Blade front, fully adj. open rear.
Features: Resembles Remington New Model No. 4 carbine. Brass trigger guard and buttplate; color case-hardened frame, blued barrel. Imported by Benson Firearms, Uberti USA.
Price: $360.00

THOMPSON/CENTER TCR '87 SINGLE SHOT RIFLE
Caliber: 22 Hornet, 222 Rem., 223 Rem., 22-250, 243 Win., 270, 308, 7mm-08, 30-06, 32-40 Win., 12 ga. slug.
Barrel: 23" (standard), 25⅞" (heavy).
Weight: About 6¾ lbs. **Length:** 39½" over-all.
Stock: American black walnut, checkered p.g. and fore-end.
Sights: None furnished.
Features: Break-open design with interchangeable barrels. Single-stage trigger. Cross-bolt safety. Made in U.S. by T/C. Introduced 1983.
Price: With Medium Sporter barrel (223, 22-250, 7mm-08, 308, 32-40 Win.) $395.00
Price: With Light Sporter barrel (22 Hornet, 222, 223, 22-250, 243, 270, 308, 30-06) $395.00
Price: 12 ga. slug barrel $165.00
Price: Extra Medium or Light Sporter barrel $165.00

DRILLINGS, COMBINATION GUNS, DOUBLE RIFLES

Designs for sporting and utility purposes worldwide.

Armsport 2783 Combo

ARMSPORT 2782 O/U TURKEY GUN
Caliber/Gauge: 12 ga. (3") over 222 Rem., 270 Win.; 20 ga. over 222, 243, 270.
Barrel: 28" (Full).
Weight: 8 lbs.
Stock: European walnut.
Sights: Blade front, leaf rear.
Features: Ventilated top and middle ribs; flip-up rear sight; silvered receiver. Introduced 1986. Imported from Italy by Armsport.
Price: 12/222 .... $750.00
Price: All other listed calibers $1,350.00

CAUTION: PRICES CHANGE. CHECK AT GUNSHOP.

DRILLINGS, COMBINATION GUNS, DOUBLE RIFLES

BRNO SUPER EXPRESS O/U DOUBLE RIFLE
Caliber: 7x65R, 9.3x74R, 375 H&H, 458 Win. Mag.
Barrel: 23½".
Weight: 8½ to 9 lbs. **Length:** 40" over-all.
Stock: European walnut with raised cheekpiece, skip-line checkering.
Sights: Bead on ramp front, quarter-rib with open rear.
Features: Sidelock action with engraved sideplates; double set triggers; selective automatic ejectors; rubber recoil pad. Barrels regulated for 100 meters. Imported from Czechoslovakia by BRNO U.S.A., Inc.
Price: $3,900.00

BRNO ZH SERIES 300 COMBINATION GUN
Caliber/Gauge: 5.6x52R/12 ga., 5.6x50R Mag./12, 7x57R/12, 7x57R/16.
Barrel: 23½" (Full).
Weight: 7.9 lbs. **Length:** 40½" over-all.
Stock: Walnut.
Sights: Bead on blade front, folding leaf rear.
Features: Boxlock action; 8-barrel set for combination calibers and o/u shotgun barrels in 12 ga. (Field, Trap, Skeet) and 16 ga. (Field). Imported from Czechoslovakia by BRNO U.S.A., Inc.
Price: $3,500.00

BERETTA EXPRESS S689, SSO DOUBLE RIFLES
Caliber: 30-06, 9.3x74R, 375 H&H, 458 Win. Mag., 458 H&H.
Barrel: 23", 25.5".
Weight: 7.7 lbs.
Stock: European walnut, hand-checkered grip and fore-end.
Sights: Blade front on ramp, open V-notch rear.
Features: Boxlock action (689), sidelock action (SSO) with silvered, engraved receiver; ejectors; double triggers; recoil pad. Imported from Italy by Beretta U.S.A. Corp. Introduced 1984.
Price: S689, 30-06, 9.3x74R.................... $3,640.00 to $49,000.00
Price: SSO, 375 H&H, 458 Win. Mag........... $11,900.00 to $14,250.00

Churchill Regent Combo

CHURCHILL REGENT COMBINATION GUN
Caliber/Gauge: 12 (3") over 222, 223, 243, 270, 308, 30-06.
Barrel: 25" (Imp. Mod.)
Weight: 8 lbs. **Length:** 42" over-all.
Stock: Hand checkered European walnut, oil finish, Monte Carlo comb.
Sights: Blade on ramp front, open rear.
Features: Silvered, engraved receiver; double triggers; dovetail scope mount. Imported by Kassnar Imports, Inc. Introduced 1985.
Price: $739.00

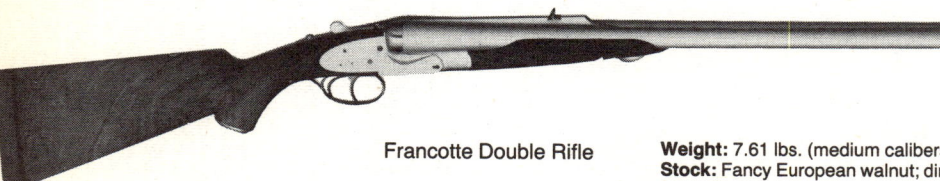

Francotte Double Rifle

AUGUSTE FRANCOTTE DOUBLE RIFLES
Caliber: 243, 7x57R, 7x65R, 8x57JRS, 270, 30-06, 308, 338, 300 Win. Mag., 9.3x74R, 375 H&H, 416 Rigby, 458 Win. Mag.; others on request.
Barrel: 23½" standard; other lengths on request.

Weight: 7.61 lbs. (medium calibers), 11.1 lbs. (mag. calibers).
Stock: Fancy European walnut; dimensions to customer specs. Straight or pistol grip style.
Sights: Bead on ramp front, leaf rear on quarter-rib; to customer specs.
Features: Chopper lump barrels; special extractor for rimmed cartridges; back-action sidelocks; double trigger with hinged front trigger. Automatic or free safety. Wide range of options available. Imported from Belgium by Armes de Chasse.
Price: .... NA

Heym 88B Safari

HEYM MODEL 88B SAFARI DOUBLE RIFLE
Caliber: 375 H&H, 458 Win. Mag., 470 Nitro Express.
Action: Boxlock with interceptor sear. Automatic ejectors with disengagement sear.
Barrel: 25".
Weight: About 10 lbs.
Stock: Best quality Circassian walnut; classic design with cheekpiece; oil finish, hand-checkering; Presentation butt pad; steel grip cap.
Sights: Large silver bead on ramp front, quarter-rib with three-leaf express rear.
Features: Double triggers; engraved, silvered frame. Introduced 1985. Imported from West Germany by Paul Jaeger, Inc.
Price: 375 and 458 .... $9,800.00
Price: 470 Nitro Express $9,800.00
Price: Trap door grip cap $350.00
Price: Best quality leather case $550.00

Consult our Directory pages for the location of firms mentioned.

DRILLINGS, COMBINATION GUNS, DOUBLE RIFLES

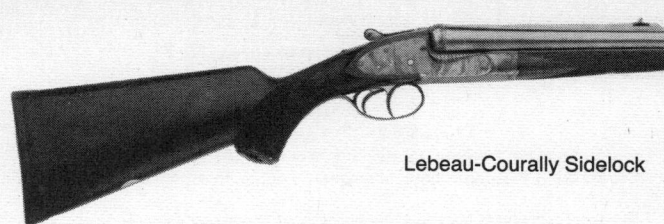

Lebeau-Courally Sidelock

LEBEAU-COURALLY SIDELOCK DOUBLE RIFLE
Caliber: 8x57 JRS, 9.3x74R, 375 H&H, 458 Win.
Barrel: 23½" to 26".
Weight: 7 lbs., 8 oz. to 9 lbs., 8 oz.
Stock: Dimensions to customer specs. Best quality French walnut selected for maximum strength, pistol grip with cheekpiece, splinter or beavertail fore-end; steel grip cap.
Sights: Bead on ramp front, express rear on ¼-rib.
Features: Holland & Holland pattern sidelock with ejectors, chopper lump barrels; reinforced action with classic pattern; choice of numerous engraving patterns; can be furnished with scope in fitted claw mounts. Imported from Belgium by Wm. Larkin Moore.
Price: From $25,000.00
Price: Box-lock, from $12,800.00

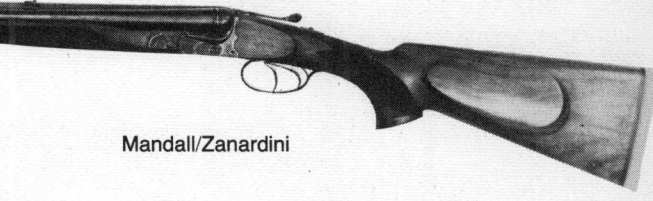

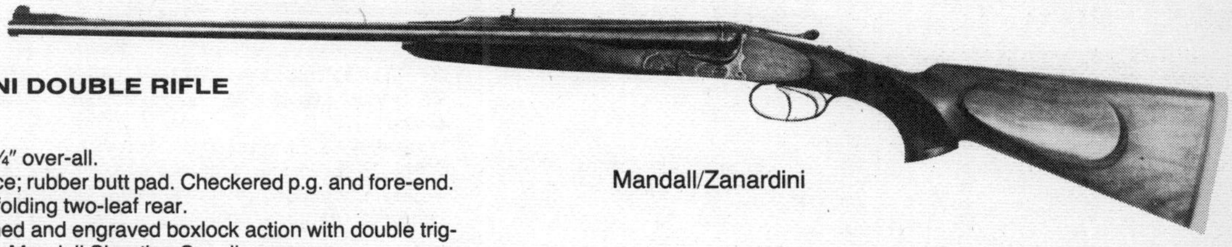

Mandall/Zanardini

MANDALL/ZANARDINI DOUBLE RIFLE
Caliber: 470 Nitro Express.
Barrel: 24".
Weight: 9¼ lbs. **Length:** 42¼" over-all.
Stock: Walnut with cheekpiece; rubber butt pad. Checkered p.g. and fore-end.
Sights: Bead on ramp front, folding two-leaf rear.
Features: Color case-hardened and engraved boxlock action with double triggers. Imported from Italy by Mandall Shooting Supplies.
Price: $8,995.00

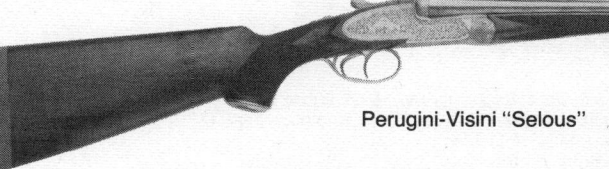

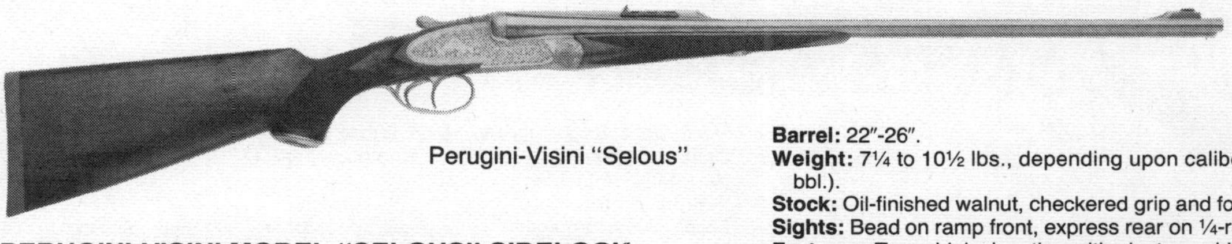

Perugini-Visini "Selous"

PERUGINI-VISINI MODEL "SELOUS" SIDELOCK DOUBLE RIFLE
Caliber: 30-06, 7mm Rem. Mag., 7x65R, 9.3x74R, 270 Win., 300 H&H, 338 Win., 375 H&H, 458 Win. Mag., 470 Nitro.
Barrel: 22"-26".
Weight: 7¼ to 10½ lbs., depending upon caliber. **Length:** 41" over-all (24" bbl.).
Stock: Oil-finished walnut, checkered grip and fore-end; cheekpiece.
Sights: Bead on ramp front, express rear on ¼-rib.
Features: True sidelock action with ejectors; sideplates are hand detachable; comes with leather trunk case. Introduced 1983. Imported from Italy by Wm. Larkin Moore.
Price: $21,800.00

Perugini-Visini Victoria-D

Perugini-Visini Victoria Double Rifles
A boxlock double rifle which shares many of the same features of the Selous model. Calibers 7x65R, 30-06, 9.3x74R, 375 H&H Mag., 458 Win. Mag., 470; double triggers; automatic ejectors. Many options available, including an extra 20-ga. barrel set.
Price: Victoria-M (7x65R, 30-06, 9.3x74R), from about $6,800.00
Price: Victoria-D (375, 458, 470), from about $12,500.00

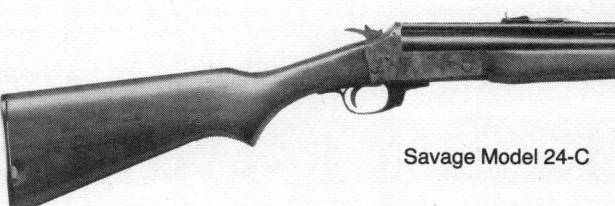

Savage Model 24-C

SAVAGE MODEL 24-C O/U
Caliber/Gauge: 22 S, L, LR over 20 ga.
Action: Take-down, low rebounding visible hammer. Single trigger, barrel selector spur on hammer.
Barrel: 20" separated barrels; Cyl. choke.
Weight: 5¾ lbs. **Length:** 36½" over-all (taken down 20").
Stock: Walnut finished hardwood.
Sights: Ramp front, rear open adj. for e. Grooved for tip-off scope mount.
Features: Trap door butt holds one shotshell and ten 22 cartridges, comes with special carrying case. Measures 7"x22" when in case.
Price: $199.00

Savage Model 24-V
Similar to Model 24-C except 222 Rem., 223 Rem. or 30-30 and 3" 20 ga.; 24" barrel; stronger receiver; color case-hardened frame; folding leaf rear sight; receiver tapped for scope.
Price: $249.00

SAVAGE MODEL 389 O/U COMBINATION
Caliber/Gauge: 12 ga. over 222 or 308.
Barrel: 25¾" separated barrels with floating front mount for windage, elevation adjustment. Has choke tubes.
Weight: NA. **Length:** NA.
Stock: Oil-finished walnut with recoil pad, cut-checkered grip and fore-end.
Sights: Blade front, folding leaf rear. Vent. rib milled for scope mount.
Features: Matte finish, extractors, double triggers, q.d. swivel studs. Introduced 1988.
Price: $759.00

SAVAGE MODEL 24 O/U COMBINATION GUN
Caliber/Gauge: 22 LR or 22 WMR over 20 ga. (3").
Barrel: 24"; separated with floating front mount.
Weight: 6½ lbs. **Length:** 40" over-all.
Stock: Walnut-finished hardwood with Monte Carlo.
Sights: Ramp front, adjustable sporting rear. Grooved for tip-off mount.
Features: Barrel selector in hammer; bottom opening lever.
Price: $179.00

CAUTION: PRICES CHANGE. CHECK AT GUNSHOP.

DRILLINGS, COMBINATION GUNS, DOUBLE RIFLES

Sile Valley Combo

SILE VALLEY COMBO GUN
Caliber/Gauge: 12 ga. over 222 Rem. or 308 Win., 3" chamber.
Barrel: 23½" (Cyl.).
Weight: 8¼ lbs. **Length:** 43" over-all.
Stock: Satin-finished walnut, checkered p.g. and fore-end; checkpiece; recoil pad.
Sights: Ramp front, folding rear. Accepts claw-type scope mount.
Features: Automatic safety; double triggers; engraved and silvered receiver. Imported by Sile.
Price: $679.95

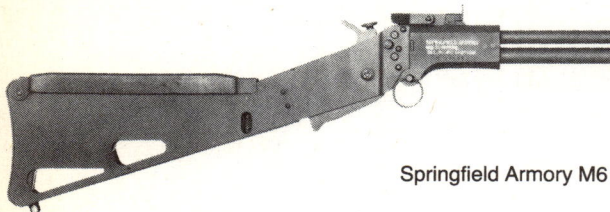

Springfield Armory M6

SPRINGFIELD ARMORY M6 SCOUT SURVIVAL RIFLE
Caliber: 22 LR, 22 WMR, 22 Hornet over 410 shotgun.
Barrel: 18".
Weight: 4 lbs. **Length:** 31½" over-all.
Stock: Steel, folding, with magazine for 15 22 LR, four 410 cartridges.
Sights: Blade front, military aperture for 22; V-notch for 410.
Features: All metal construction. Designed for quick disassembly and minimum maintenance. Folds for compact storage. Introduced 1982. Made in U.S. by Springfield Armory.
Price: About $122.00

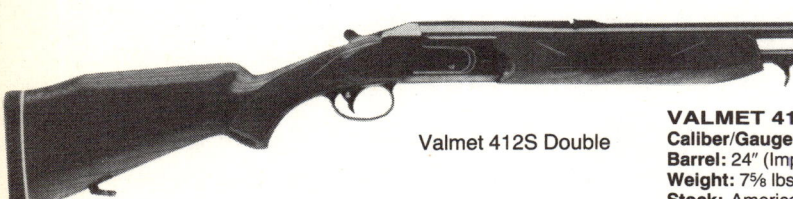

Valmet 412S Double

VALMET 412S COMBINATION GUN
Caliber/Gauge: 12 over 222, 308, 30-06, 9.3x74R.
Barrel: 24" (Imp. Mod.).
Weight: 7⅝ lbs.
Stock: American walnut, with recoil pad. Monte Carlo style. Standard measurements 14"x1⅜"x2"x2⅜".
Sights: Blade front, flip-up-type open rear.
Features: Barrel selector on trigger. Hand checkered stock and fore-end. Barrels are screw-adjustable to change bullet point of impact. Barrels are interchangeable. Introduced 1980. Imported from Finland by Valmet.
Price: $1,099.00
Price: Extra barrels, from $524.00

VALMET 412S DOUBLE RIFLE
Caliber: 30-06, 9.3x74R.
Barrel: 24".
Weight: 8⅝ lbs.
Stock: American walnut with Monte Carlo style.
Sights: Ramp front, adjustable open rear.
Features: Barrel selector mounted in trigger. Cocking indicators in tang. Recoil pad. Valmet scope mounts available. Interchangeable barrels. Introduced 1980. Imported from Finland by Valmet.
Price: Extractors, 30-06 .... $1,205.00
Price: With ejectors, 9.3x74R $1,315.00

A. ZOLI RIFLE-SHOTGUN O/U COMBO
Caliber/Gauge: 12 ga. over 222, 308 or 30-06.
Barrel: Combo—24", shotgun—28" (Mod. & Full).
Weight: About 8 lbs. **Length:** 41" over-all (24" bbl.)
Stock: European walnut.
Sights: Blade front, flip-up rear.
Features: Available with German claw scope mounts on rifle/shotgun barrels. Comes with set of 12/12 (Mod. & Full) barrels. Imported from Italy by Mandall Shooting Supplies.
Price: With two barrel sets $1,695.00

RIMFIRE RIFLES—AUTOLOADERS

Designs for hunting, utility and sporting purposes, including training for competition.

AMT Lightning 25/22

AMT Lightning Small-Game Hunting Rifle
Same as the Lightning 25/22 except has conventional stock of black fiberglass-filled nylon, checkered at the grip and fore-end, and fitted with Uncle Mike's swivel studs. Removable recoil pad provides storage for ammo, cleaning rod and survival knife. No iron sights—comes with 4x, 1" scope and mounts. Has a 22" target weight barrel, weighs 6¾ lbs., over-all length of 40½". Introduced 1987. From AMT.
Price: With scope $269.95

AMT LIGHTNING 25/22 RIFLE
Caliber: 22 LR, 25-shot magazine.
Barrel: 18", tapered or bull.
Weight: 6 lbs. **Length:** 26½" (folded), 37" (open).
Stock: Folding stainless steel.
Sights: Ramp front, rear adjustable for windage.
Features: Made of stainless steel with matte finish. Receiver dovetailed for scope mounting. Extended magazine release. Standard or "bull" barrel. Introduced 1984. From AMT.
Price: $269.95

RIMFIRE RIFLES—AUTOLOADERS

AP-74 Auto

AP-74 AUTO RIFLE
Caliber: 22 LR, 32 ACP, 15-shot magazine.
Barrel: 20″, including flash reducer.
Weight: 6½ lbs. **Length:** 38½″ over-all.
Stock: Black plastic.
Sights: Ramp front, adj. peep rear.
Features: Pivotal take-down, easy disassembly. AR-15 look-alike. Sling and sling swivels included. Imported by EMF.
Price: 22 LR $295.00
Price: 32 ACP $320.00

Anschutz Model 525

ANSCHUTZ DELUXE MODEL 525 AUTO
Caliber: 22 LR, 10-shot clip.
Barrel: 24″.
Weight: 6½ lbs. **Length:** 43″ over-all.
Stock: European hardwood; checkered pistol grip, Monte Carlo comb, beavertail fore-end.
Sights: Hooded ramp front, folding leaf rear.
Features: Rotary safety, empty shell deflector, single stage trigger. Receiver grooved for scope mounting. Introduced 1982. Imported from Germany by PSI.
Price: $409.00

ARMSCOR MODEL 20P AUTO RIFLE
Caliber: 22 LR, 15-shot magazine.
Barrel: 20¾″.
Weight: 5.5 lbs. **Length:** 39¾″ overall.
Stock: Walnut-finished mahogany.
Sights: Bead front, rear adjustable for e.
Features: Receiver grooved for scope mounting. Blued finish. Introduced 1987. Imported from the Philippines by Armscor.
Price: About $95.95
Price: Model 2000 (as above except has checkered stock, fully adj. sight), about $98.95

ARMSCOR MODEL 1600 AUTO RIFLE
Caliber: 22 LR, 15-shot magazine.
Barrel: 18″.
Weight: 5¼ lbs. **Length:** 38½″ over-all.
Stock: Black ebony wood.
Sights: Post front, aperture rear.
Features: Resembles Colt AR-15. Matte black finish. Introduced 1987. Imported from the Philippines by Armscor.
Price: About $121.95
Price: M1600R (as above except has retractable buttstock, ventilated fore-end), about $137.95

ARMSCOR AK22 AUTO RIFLE
Caliber: 22 LR, 15-shot magazine.
Barrel: 18½″.
Weight: 7 lbs. **Length:** 36″ over-all.
Stock: Plain mahogany.
Sights: Post front, open rear adjustable for w. and e.
Features: Resembles the AK-47. Matte black finish. Introduced 1987. Imported from the Philippines by Armscor.
Price: About $171.95

Auto-Ordnance 1927A-3

AUTO ORDNANCE MODEL 1927A-3
Caliber: 22 LR, 10, 30 or 50-shot magazine.
Barrel: 16″, finned.
Weight: About 7 lbs.
Stock: Walnut stock and fore-end.
Sights: Blade front, open rear adjustable for windage and elevation.
Features: Recreation of the Thompson Model 1927, only in 22 Long Rifle. Alloy receiver, finned barrel.
Price: $487.50

Bernardelli Carbine

BERNARDELLI SEMI-AUTO CARBINE
Caliber: 22 LR, 5-shot magazine.
Barrel: 21″.
Weight: 5 lbs., 3 oz. **Length:** 40″ over-all.
Stock: European hardwood.
Sights: Hooded post front, open adjustable rear.
Features: Blued barrel, painted receiver. Imported from Italy by Mandall Shooting Supplies.
Price: $299.50

CAUTION: PRICES CHANGE. CHECK AT GUNSHOP.

RIMFIRE RIFLES—AUTOLOADERS

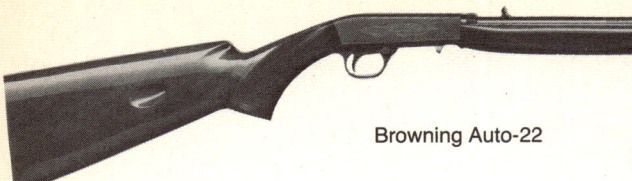
Browning Auto-22

BROWNING AUTO-22 RIFLE
Caliber: 22 LR, 11-shot.
Barrel: 19¼".
Weight: 4¾ lbs. **Length:** 37" over-all.
Stock: Checkered select walnut with p.g. and semibeavertail fore-end.
Sights: Gold bead front, folding leaf rear.
Features: Engraved receiver with polished blue finish; cross-bolt safety; tubular magazine in buttstock; easy take down for carrying or storage. Imported from Japan by Browning.
Price: Grade I $328.50

Browning Auto-22 Grade VI
Same as the Grade I Auto-22 except available with either grayed or blued receiver with extensive engraving with gold-plated animals: right side pictures a fox and squirrel in a woodland scene; left side shows a beagle chasing a rabbit. On top is a portrait of the beagle. Stock and fore-end are of high grade walnut with a double-bordered cut checkering design. Introduced 1987.
Price: Grade VI, blue or gray receiver........................... $674.95

CALICO MODEL 100 CARBINE
Caliber: 22 LR, 100-shot magazine.
Barrel: 16".
Weight: 5.7 lbs. (loaded). **Length:** 35.8" over-all (stock extended).
Stock: Folding steel.
Sights: Post front adjustable for e., notch rear adjustable for w.
Features: Uses alloy frame and helical-feed magazine; ambidextrous safety; removable barrel assembly; pistol grip compartment; flash suppressor; bolt stop. Made in U.S. From Calico.
Price: $299.95

Calico Model 100

Calico Model 100S Sporter
Similar to the Model 100 except has hand-rubbed wood buttstock and fore-end. Weight is 4¾ lbs. Introduced 1987.
Price: $318.95

Charter AR-7 Explorer

CHARTER AR-7 EXPLORER CARBINE
Caliber: 22 LR, 8-shot clip.
Barrel: 16" alloy (steel-lined).
Weight: 2½ lbs. **Length:** 34½"/16½" stowed.
Stock: Moulded black Cycloac, snap-on rubber butt pad.
Sights: Square blade front, aperture rear adj. for e.
Features: Take-down design stores bbl. and action in hollow stock. Light enough to float.
Price: Black, Silvertone or camouflage finish $115.00

Daisy Model 2213

DAISY MODEL 2213 AUTO RIFLE
Caliber: 22 LR, 7-shot clip.
Barrel: 19".
Weight: 6.5 lbs. **Length:** 34.75" over-all.
Stock: Walnut.
Sights: Blade on ramp front, fully adjustable, removable notch rear.
Features: Removable trigger assembly; adjustable trigger; receiver dovetailed for scope mounting. Introduced 1988.
Price: About $110.00

Daisy Model 2203 Auto Rifle
Similar to the Model 2213 except has a moulded copolymer stock that is adjustable for length of pull. Introduced 1988.
Price: About $80.00

F.I.E. Black Beauty

F.I.E. GR-8 BLACK BEAUTY AUTO RIFLE
Caliber: 22 LR, 14-shot tubular magazine.
Barrel: 19⅝".
Weight: 4 lbs. **Length:** 38½" over-all.
Stock: Moulded black nylon, checkered pistol grip and fore-end.
Sights: Blade on ramp front, adjustable open rear.
Features: Made mostly of moulded nylon; tube magazine housed in buttstock; top tang safety; receiver grooved for tip-off scope mounts. Imported from Brazil by F.I.E. Introduced 1984.
Price: $109.95

F.I.E./FRANCHI PARA CARBINE
Caliber: 22 LR, 11-shot magazine.
Barrel: 19".
Weight: 4 lbs., 12 oz. **Length:** 39¼" over-all.
Stock: Metal skeleton buttstock, walnut p.g. and fore-end.
Sights: Hooded front, open adj. rear.
Features: Take-down rifle comes in its own fitted carrying case. Receiver grooved for scope mounting. Tube magazine feeds through buttplate. Limited production. Introduced 1986. Imported from Italy by F.I.E. Corp.
Price: $234.95

RIMFIRE RIFLES—AUTOLOADERS

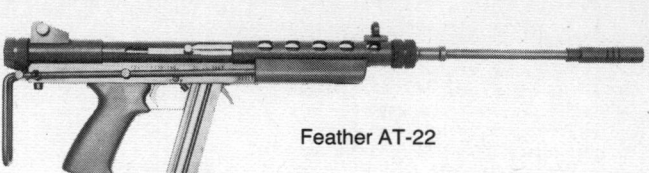
Feather AT-22

FEATHER AT-22 AUTO CARBINE
Caliber: 22 LR, 20-shot magazine.
Barrel: 17".
Weight: 3.25 lbs. **Length:** 34.75" over-all (stock extended).
Stock: Telescoping wire; composition pistol grip.
Sights: Protected post front, adjustable aperture rear.
Features: Removable barrel. Length when folded is 26". Matte black finish. Scope, mount, sling, barrel shroud shown are optional. From Feather Enterpirses. Introduced 1986.
Price: $239.95

Federal XC-220

FEDERAL MODEL XC-220 AUTO CARBINE
Caliber: 22 LR, 28-shot magazine.
Barrel: 16.5" (with flash hider).
Weight: 7½ lbs. **Length:** 34½" over-all.
Stock: Detachable tube steel.
Sights: Hooded post front, peep rear adjustable for w. and e. Receiver grooved for scope mounting.
Features: Parkerized finish; all heli-arc welded steel construction; quick takedown. From Federal Engineering Corp.
Price: $341.25

Heckler & Koch 300

HECKLER & KOCH MODEL 300 AUTO RIFLE
Caliber: 22 WMR, 5-shot box mag.
Barrel: 19¾".
Weight: 5¾ lbs. **Length:** 39½" over-all.
Stock: European walnut, Monte Carlo with cheek rest; checkered p.g. and Schnabel fore-end.
Sights: Post front adj. for elevation, V-notch rear adj. for windage.
Features: Polygonal rifling, comes with sling swivels; straight blow-back inertia bolt action; single-stage trigger (3½-lb. pull). Clamp scope mount with 1" rings available at extra cost. Limited quantity available. Imported from West Germany by Heckler & Koch, Inc.
Price: HK300 .... $598.00

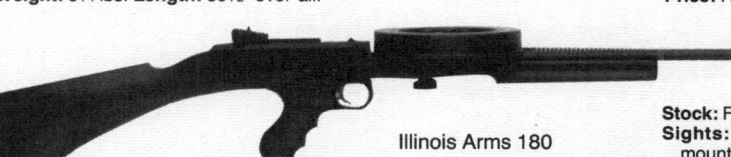
Illinois Arms 180

ILLINOIS ARMS CO. MODEL 180 AUTO
Caliber: 22 LR, 22 Short Magnum; 165-round magazine.
Barrel: 18".
Weight: 9 lbs. **Length:** 37" over-all.
Stock: Fiber-reinforced composition standard; walnut and retractable optional.
Sights: Protected post front, adjustable rear; receiver grooved for scope mounting or laser sight.
Features: Finned barrel; top-mounted 165-round magazine; matte blue-black finish. Parts interchage with the American 180. Made in U.S. Introduced 1988. From Illinois Arms Co.
Price: $798.00
Price: With walnut stock $918.00
Price: Optional retractable stock $105.00

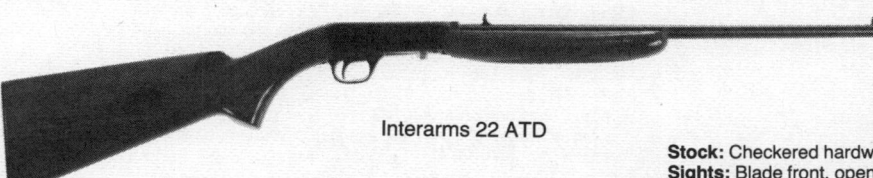
Interarms 22 ATD

INTERARMS MODEL 22 ATD RIFLE
Caliber: 22 LR, 11-shot magazine.
Barrel: 19.4".
Weight: 4.6 lbs. **Length:** 36.6." over-all.
Stock: Checkered hardwood.
Sights: Blade front, open adjustable rear.
Features: Browning-design takedown action for storage, transport. Cross-bolt safety. Tube magazine loads through buttplate. Blue finish with engraved receiver. Introduced 1987. Imported from China by Interarms.
Price: $179.00
Price: With camouflage case. $195.00

Iver Johnson 3112

IVER JOHNSON MODEL 3112 RIFLE
Caliber: 22 Long Rifle (15-shot magazine).
Barrel: 18".
Weight: 5.8 lbs. **Length:** 38" over-all.
Stock: Walnut-finished hardwood.
Sights: Blade front, peep rear adjustable for w. and e.
Features: Resembles the U.S. 30-cal. M-1 Carbine. Introduced 1985. From Iver Johnson.
Price: $166.50

CAUTION: PRICES CHANGE. CHECK AT GUNSHOP.

RIMFIRE RIFLES—AUTOLOADERS

Marlin Model 60

MARLIN 60 SEMI-AUTO RIFLE
Caliber: 22 LR, 17-shot tubular mag.
Barrel: 22" round tapered.
Weight: About 5½ lbs. **Length:** 40½" over-all.
Stock: Walnut finished Monte Carlo, full pistol grip; Mar-Shield® finish.
Sights: Ramp front, open adj. rear.
Features: Matted receiver is grooved for tip-off mounts. Manual bolt hold-open; automatic last-shot bolt hold-open.
Price: $124.95

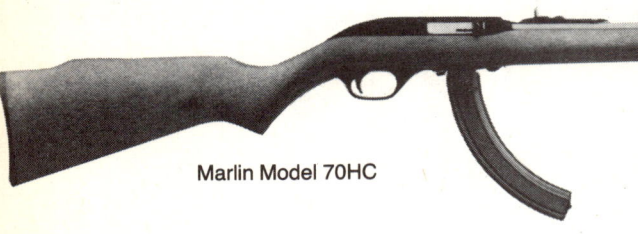

Marlin Model 70HC

MARLIN MODEL 70HC AUTO
Caliber: 22 LR, 25-shot clip magazine.
Barrel: 18" (16-groove rifling).
Weight: 5 lbs. **Length:** 36½" over-all.
Stock: Walnut-finished hardwood with Monte Carlo, full p.g. Mar-Shield® finish.
Sights: Ramp front, adj. open rear. Receiver grooved for scope mount.
Features: Receiver top has serrated, non-glare finish; cross-bolt safety; manual bolt hold-open.
Price: $130.95

Marlin 70P Papoose

Marlin Model 70P Papoose
Similar to the Model 70 except is a take-down model with easily removable barrel—no tools needed. Has 16¼" Micro-Groove® barrel, walnut-finished hardwood stock, ramp front, adjustable open rear sights, cross-bolt safety. Take-down feature allows removal of barrel without tools. Over-all length is 35¼", weight is 3¾ lbs. Receiver grooved for scope mounting. Comes with 4x scope, mounts and zippered case. Introduced 1986.
Price: With scope $153.95

MARLIN MODEL 995 SEMI-AUTO RIFLE
Caliber: 22 LR, 7-shot clip magazine
Barrel: 18" Micro-Groove®.
Weight: 5 lbs. **Length:** 36¾" over-all.
Stock: American black walnut, Monte Carlo-style, with full pistol grip. Checkered p.g. and fore-end; white buttplate spacer; Mar-Shield® finish.
Sights: Ramp bead front with Wide-Scan® hood; adjustable folding semi-buckhorn rear.
Features: Receiver grooved for tip-off scope mount; bolt hold-open device; cross-bolt safety. Introduced 1979.
Price: $156.95

MARLIN MODEL 75C SEMI-AUTO RIFLE
Caliber: 22 LR, 13-shot tubular magazine.
Barrel: 18".
Weight: 5 lbs. **Length:** 36½" over-all.
Stock: Walnut-finished hardwood; Monte Carlo with full p.g.
Sights: Ramp front, adj. open rear.
Features: Manual bolt hold-open; automatic last-shot bolt hold-open; cross-bolt safety; receiver grooved for scope mounting.
Price: $124.95

Mitchell AK-22

MITCHELL AK-22 SEMI-AUTO RIFLE
Caliber: 22 LR, 29-shot magazine; 22 WMR, 10-shot magazine.
Barrel: 16½".
Weight: 3.1 lbs. **Length:** 38" over-all.
Stock: European walnut.
Sights: Post front, open adj. rear.
Features: Replica of the AK-47 assult rifle. Wide magazine to maintain appearance. Imported from Italy by Mitchell Arms.
Price: 22 LR $275.00
Price: 22 WMR $285.00

Mitchell Galil/22

MITCHELL GALIL/22 AUTO RIFLE
Caliber: 22 LR, 29-shot magazine; 22 WMR, 10-shot magazine.
Barrel: 16.5".
Weight: 5.7 lbs. **Length:** 36" over-all.
Stock: European walnut butt, grip, fore-end.
Sights: Post front adjustable for elevation, rear adjustable for windage.
Features: Replica of the Israeli Galil rifle. Introduced 1987. Imported by Mitchell Arms, Inc.
Price: 22 LR $259.95
Price: 22 WMR $274.95

RIMFIRE RIFLES—AUTOLOADERS

Mitchell M-16/22

MITCHELL MAS/22 AUTO RIFLE
Caliber: 22 LR, 29-shot magazine; 22 WMR, 10-shot magazine.
Barrel: 16.5".
Weight: 4.7 lbs. **Length:** 28.5" over-all.
Stock: Walnut butt, grip and fore-end.
Sights: Adjustable post front, flip-type aperture rear.
Features: Bullpup design resembles French armed forces rifle. Top cocking lever, flash hider. Introduced 1987. Imported by Mitchell Arms, Inc.
Price: 22 LR $259.95
Price: 22 WMR $274.95

MITCHELL M-16/22 RIFLE
Caliber: 22 LR.
Barrel: 18.5".
Weight: 6.1 lbs. **Length:** 39" over-all.
Stock: Black composition.
Sights: Adjustable post front, adjustable aperture rear.
Features: Replica of the AR-15 rifle. Full width magazine. Comes with military-type sling. Introduced 1987. Imported by Mitchell Arms, Inc.
Price: 22 LR $259.95
Price: 22 WMR, 32 ACP $274.95

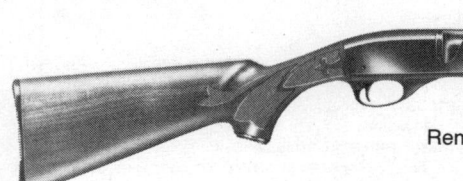

Remington 552 BDL

REMINGTON 552BDL AUTOLOADING RIFLE
Caliber: 22 S (20), L (17) or LR (15) tubular mag.
Barrel: 21" round tapered.
Weight: About 5¾ lbs. **Length:** 40" over-all.
Stock: Full-size, walnut. Checkered grip and fore-end.
Sights: Bead front, open rear adj. for w. & e.
Features: Positive cross-bolt safety, receiver grooved for tip-off mount.
Price: About $192.00

Ruger 10/22 RB

RUGER 10/22 AUTOLOADING CARBINE
Caliber: 22 LR, 10-shot rotary mag.
Barrel: 18½" round tapered.
Weight: 5 lbs. **Length:** 37¼" over-all.
Stock: American hardwood with p.g. and bbl. band.
Sights: Gold bead front, folding leaf rear adj. for e.
Features: Detachable rotary magazine fits flush into stock, cross-bolt safety, receiver tapped and grooved for scope blocks or tip-off mount. Scope base adapter furnished with each rifle.
Price: Model 10/22 RB (birch stock) $176.00
Price: Model 10/22 R (American walnut stock) $196.00

Ruger 10/22 Auto Sporter
Same as 10/22 Carbine except walnut stock with hand checkered p.g. and fore-end; straight buttplate, no bbl. band, has sling swivels.
Price: Model 10/22 DSP $222.00

VOERE MODEL 2115 AUTO RIFLE
Caliber: 22 LR, 8 or 15-shot magazine.
Barrel: 18.1".
Weight: 5.75 lbs. **Length:** 37.7" over-all.
Stock: Walnut-finished beechwood with cheekpiece; checkered pistol grip and fore-end.
Sights: Post front with hooded ramp, leaf rear.
Features: Clip-fed autoloader with single stage trigger, wing-type safety. Imported from Austria by L. Joseph Rahn. Introduced 1984.
Price: Model 2115 .... $325.00
Price: Model 2114S (as above except no cheekpiece, checkering or white line spacers at grip, buttplate) $330.00

TRADEWINDS MODEL 260-A AUTO RIFLE
Caliber: 22 LR, 5-shot (10-shot mag. avail.).
Barrel: 22½".
Weight: 5¾ lbs. **Length:** 41½".
Stock: Walnut, with hand checkered p.g. and fore-end.
Sights: Ramp front with hood, 3-leaf folding rear, receiver grooved for scope mount.
Features: Double extractors, sliding safety. Imported by Tradewinds.
Price: $250.00

Weatherby Mark XXII

WEATHERBY MARK XXII AUTO RIFLE, CLIP MODEL
Caliber: 22 LR only, 5- or 10-shot clip.
Barrel: 24" round contoured.
Weight: 6 lbs. **Length:** 42¼" over-all.
Stock: Walnut, Monte Carlo comb and cheekpiece, rosewood p.g. cap and fore-end tip. Skip-line checkering.
Sights: Gold bead ramp front, 3-leaf folding rear.
Features: Thumb operated tang safety. Single shot or semi-automatic side lever selector. Receiver grooved for tip-off scope mount. Single pin release for quick takedown.
Price: $454.00

Weatherby Mark XXII Tubular Model
Same as Mark XXII Clip Model except 15-shot tubular magazine.
Price: $454.00

CAUTION: PRICES CHANGE. CHECK AT GUNSHOP.

RIMFIRE RIFLES—LEVER & SLIDE ACTIONS

Classic and modern models for sport and utility, including training.

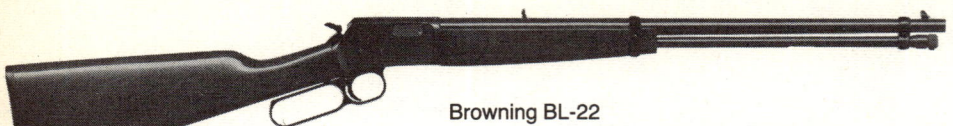
Browning BL-22

BROWNING BL-22 LEVER ACTION RIFLE
Caliber: 22 S(22), L(17) or LR(15). Tubular mag.
Barrel: 20" round tapered.
Weight: 5 lbs. **Length:** 36¾" over-all.
Stock: Walnut, 2-piece straight grip Western style.
Sights: Bead post front, folding-leaf rear.
Features: Short throw lever, half-cock safety, receiver grooved for tip-off scope mounts. Imported from Japan by Browning.
Price: Grade I $286.95
Price: Grade II (engraved receiver, checkered grip and fore-end) . . . $326.95

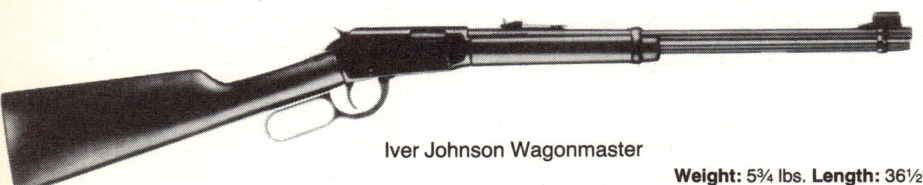
Iver Johnson Wagonmaster

IVER JOHNSON WAGONMASTER RIFLE
Caliber: 22 Long Rifle (21 Short, 17 Long, 15 Long Rifle), 22 WMR (12-shot magazine).
Barrel: 19".
Weight: 5¾ lbs. **Length:** 36½" over-all.
Stock: Walnut-finished hardwood.
Sights: Hooded ramp front, open adjustable rear.
Features: Polished blue finish. Receiver grooved for scope mounting. Introduced 1985. From Iver Johnson.
Price: 22 Long Rifle $166.50
Price: 22 WMR $187.50

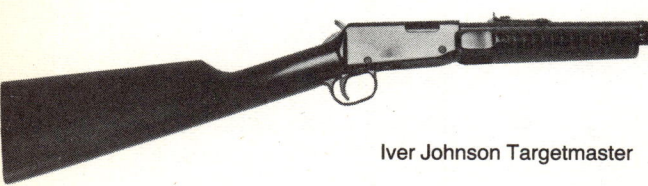
Iver Johnson Targetmaster

IVER JOHNSON TARGETMASTER RIFLE
Caliber: 22 Long Rifle (19 Short, 15 Long, 12 Long Rifle).
Barrel: 18".
Weight: 5¾ lbs. **Length:** 36½" over-all.
Stock: Walnut-finished hardwood.
Sights: Hooded ramp front, open adjustable rear.
Features: Polished blue finish. Receiver grooved for scope mounting. Introduced 1985. From Iver Johnson.
Price: Standard or Youth Model $166.50

Marlin 1894M

MARLIN MODEL 1894M CARBINE
Caliber: 22 WMR, 10-shot magazine.
Barrel: 20" Micro-Groove®.
Weight: 6¼ lbs. **Length:** 37½" over-all.
Stock: Straight grip stock of American black walnut, Mar-Shield® finish.
Sights: Ramp front with brass bead, adjustable semi-buckhorn folding rear.
Features: Has hammer block safety. Side-ejecting solid-top receiver tapped for scope mount or receiver sight; squared finger lever, reversible offset hammer spur for scope use. Scope shown is optional. Introduced 1983.
Price: $357.95

Marlin Golden 39AS

MARLIN GOLDEN 39AS LEVER ACTION RIFLE
Caliber: 22 S(26), L(21), LR(19), tubular magazine.
Barrel: 24" Micro-Groove®.
Weight: 6½ lbs. **Length:** 40" over-all.
Stock: American black walnut with white line spacers at p.g. cap and buttplate; Mar-Shield® finish. Swivel studs.
Sights: Bead ramp front with detachable Wide-Scan™ hood, folding rear semi-buckhorn adj. for w. and e.
Features: Hammer-block safety; rebounding hammer. Take-down action, receiver tapped for scope mount (supplied), offset hammer spur; gold plated steel trigger.
Price: $318.95

Consult our Directory pages for the location of firms mentioned.

RIMFIRE RIFLES—LEVER & SLIDE ACTIONS

Marlin 39TDS

MARLIN MODEL 39TDS CARBINE
Caliber: 22 S (16), 22 L (12), 22 LR (10).
Barrel: 16½" Micro-Groove®.
Weight: 5¼ lbs. **Length:** 32⅝" over-all.
Stock: American black walnut with straight grip; short fore-end with blued tip. Mar-Shield® finish.
Sights: Ramp front with Wide-Scan™ hood, adjustable semi-buckhorn rear.
Features: Take-down style, comes with carrying case. Hammer-block safety, rebounding hammer; blued metal, gold-plated steel trigger. Introduced 1988.
Price: With case $355.95

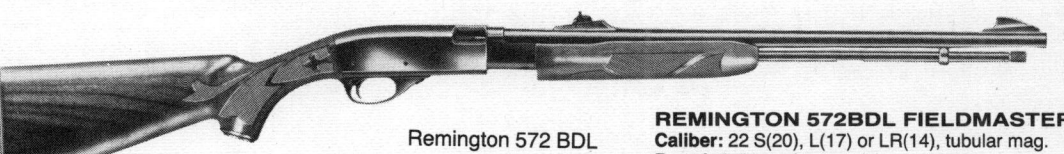

Remington 572 BDL

REMINGTON 572BDL FIELDMASTER PUMP RIFLE
Caliber: 22 S(20), L(17) or LR(14), tubular mag.
Barrel: 21" round tapered.
Weight: 5½ lbs. **Length:** 42" over-all.
Stock: Walnut with checkered p.g. and slide handle.
Sights: Blade ramp front; sliding ramp rear adj. for w. & e.
Features: Cross-bolt safety, removing inner mag. tube converts rifle to single shot; receiver grooved for tip-off scope mount.
Price: About $203.00

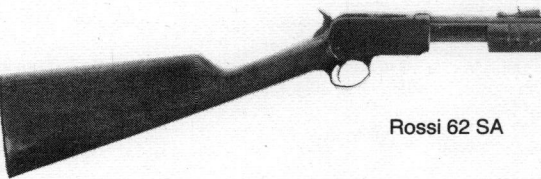

Rossi 62 SA

ROSSI 62 SA PUMP RIFLE
Caliber: 22 S, L or LR, 22 WMR.
Barrel: 23", round or octagon.
Weight: 5¾ lbs. **Length:** 39¼" over-all.
Stock: Walnut, straight grip, grooved fore-end.
Sights: Fixed front, adj. rear.
Features: Capacity 20 Short, 16 Long or 14 Long Rifle. Quick takedown. Imported from Brazil by Interarms.

Rossi 62 SAC Carbine
Same as standard model except has 16¼" barrel. Magazine holds slightly fewer cartridges.
Price: Blue. $192.00
Price: Nickel $207.00

Price: Blue. $192.00
Price: Nickel $207.00
Price: Blue, with octagon barrel. $217.00
Price: 22 WMR, as Model 59 . . . . $237.00

Winchester 9422

WINCHESTER 9422 XTR LEVER ACTION RIFLE
Caliber: 22 S(21), L(17), LR (15), tubular mag.
Barrel: 20½".
Weight: 6¼ lbs. **Length:** 37⅛" over-all.
Stock: American walnut, 2-piece, straight grip (no p.g.).
Sights: Hooded ramp front, adj. semi-buckhorn rear.
Features: Side ejection, receiver grooved for scope mounting, takedown action. Has XTR wood and metal finish. Made under license by U.S. Repeating Arms Co.
Price: About $324.00
Price: With Win-Tuff laminated stock, about $331.00

Winchester 9422M XTR Lever Action Rifle
Same as the 9422 except chambered for 22 WMR cartridge, has 11-round mag. capacity.
Price: About $324.00
Price: With Win-Cam stock, about $331.00
Price: With Win-Tuff laminated stock, about $331.00

Winchester 9422 Pistol Grip

Winchester 9422 XTR Pistol Grip
Similar to 9422 XTR except has uncheckered, satin-finished walnut stock with fluted comb, crescent steel buttplate, curved finger lever, and capped pistol grip. Over-all length is 39⅛", barrel length 22½", weight is 6½ lbs. In 22 Short, Long, Long Rifle and 22 WMR. Introduced 1985.
Price: About $324.00

CAUTION: PRICES CHANGE. CHECK AT GUNSHOP.

RIMFIRE RIFLES—BOLT ACTIONS & SINGLE SHOTS

Includes models for a variety of sports, utility and competitive shooting.

Anschutz 1416/1516

ANSCHUTZ DELUXE 1416/1516 RIFLES
Caliber: 22 LR (1416D), 5-shot clip; 22 WMR (1516D), 4-shot clip.
Barrel: 22½".
Weight: 6 lbs. **Length:** 41" over-all.
Stock: European walnut; Monte Carlo with cheekpiece, Schnabel fore-end, checkered pistol grip and fore-end.
Sights: Hooded ramp front, folding leaf rear.
Features: Uses Model 1403 target rifle action. Adjustable single stage trigger. Receiver grooved for scope mounting. Imported from Germany by PSI.
Price: 1416D, 22 LR **$552.00**
Price: 1516D, 22 WMR **$572.80**
Price: 1416D Classic left-hand **$630.00**

Anschutz 1418D/1518D Deluxe Rifles
Similar to the 1416D/1516D rifles except has full-length Mannlicher-style stock, shorter 19¾" barrel. Weighs 5½ lbs. Stock has buffalo horn Schnabel tip. Double set trigger available on special order. Model 1418D chambered for 22 LR, 1518D for 22 WMR Imported from Germany by PSI.
Price: 1418D **$750.00**
Price: 1518D **$788.00**

Anschutz 1422/1522

ANSCHUTZ 1422D/1522D CLASSIC RIFLES
Caliber: 22 LR (1422D), 5-shot clip; 22 WMR (1522D), 4-shot clip.
Barrel: 24".
Weight: 7¼ lbs. **Length:** 43" over-all.
Stock: Select European walnut; checkered pistol grip and fore-end.
Sights: Hooded ramp front, folding leaf rear.
Features: Uses Match 54 action. Adjustable single stage trigger. Receiver drilled and tapped for scope mounting. Introduced 1982. Imported from Germany by PSI.
Price: 1422D, 22LR **$873.00**
Price: 1522D, 22 WMR **$898.00**

Anschutz 1422D/1522D Custom Rifles
Similar to the Classic models except have roll-over Monte Carlo cheekpiece, slim fore-end with Schnabel tip, Wundhammer palm swell on pistol grip, rosewood grip cap with white diamond insert. Skip-line checkering on grip and fore-end. Introduced 1982. Imported from Germany by PSI.
Price: 1422D **$939.00**
Price: 1522D **$967.00**

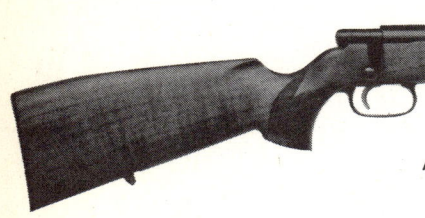

Anschutz Bavarian

ANSCHUTZ BAVARIAN BOLT ACTION RIFLE
Caliber: 22 LR, 22 WMR, 5-shot clip.
Barrel: 24".
Weight: 7¼ lbs. **Length:** 43" over-all.
Stock: European walnut with Bavarian cheek rest. Checkered p.g. and fore-end.
Sights: Hooded ramp front, folding leaf rear.
Features: Uses the improved 1700 Match 54 action with adjustable 5096 trigger. Drilled and tapped for scope mounting. Introduced in 1988. Imported from Germany by Precision Sales International.
Price: **$967.00**

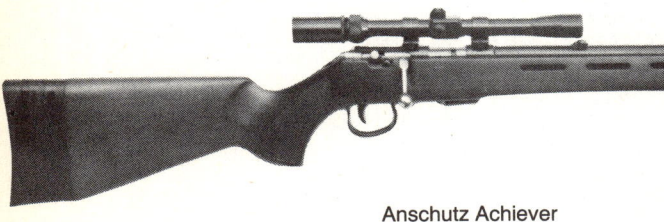

Anschutz Achiever

ANSCHUTZ ACHIEVER BOLT ACTION RIFLE
Caliber: 22 LR, 5-shot clip.
Barrel: 19½".
Weight: 5 lbs. **Length:** 35½" to 36⅔" over-all.
Stock: Walnut-finished hardwood with adjustable buttplate, vented fore-end, stippled pistol grip. Length of pull adjustable from 11⅞" to 13".
Sights: Hooded front, open rear adjustable for w. and e.
Features: Uses Mark 2000-type action with adjustable two-stage trigger. Receiver grooved for scope mounting. Designed for training in junior rifle clubs and for starting young shooters. Introduced 1987. Imported from West Germany by PSI.
Price: **$319.50**
Price: Sight Set #1 .... **$54.00**

ARMSCOR MODEL 14P BOLT ACTION RIFLE
Caliber: 22 LR, 5-shot magazine.
Barrel: 23".
Weight: 6 lbs. **Length:** 41.5" over-all.
Stock: Walnut-finished mahogany.
Sights: Bead front, rear adjustable for e.
Features: Receiver grooved for scope mounting. Blued finish. Introduced 1987. Imported from the Philippines by Armscor.
Price: About **$99.95**

Armscor Model 1500 Rifle
Similar to the Model 14P except chambered for 22 WMR. Has 21.5" barrel, double lug bolt, checkered stock, weighs 6.5 lbs. Introduced 1987.
Price: About **$156.95**

RIMFIRE RIFLES—BOLT ACTIONS & SINGLE SHOTS

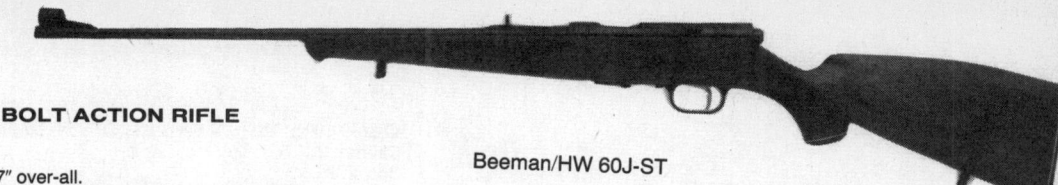
Beeman/HW 60J-ST

BEEMAN/HW 60J-ST BOLT ACTION RIFLE
Caliber: 22 LR.
Barrel: 22.8".
Weight: 6.5 lbs. **Length:** 41.7" over-all.
Stock: Walnut with cheekpiece, cut checkered p.g. and fore-end.
Sights: Hooded blade on ramp front, open rear.
Features: Polished blue finish; oil-finished walnut. Imported from West Germany by Beeman. Introduced 1988.
Price: $488.00

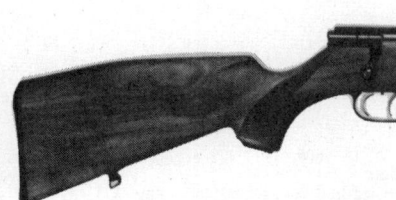
Beeman/Krico 320

BEEMAN/KRICO MODEL 320 BOLT ACTION RIFLE
Caliber: 22 LR, 5-shot magazine.
Barrel: 19.5".
Weight: 6 lbs. **Length:** 38½" over-all.
Stock: Select European walnut; full-length Mannlicher-style with curved European comb and cheekpiece; cut checkered grip and fore-end.
Sights: Blade front on ramp, open rear adjustable for windage.
Features: Single or double set trigger; blued steel fore-end cap; detachable box magazine. Imported from West Germany by Beeman.
Price: $1,100.00

BRNO ZKM 452 BOLT ACTION RIFLE
Caliber: 22 LR, 5- or 10-shot magazine.
Barrel: 25".
Weight: 6 lbs., 10 oz. **Length:** 43½" over-all.
Stock: Beechwood.
Sights: Hooded bead front, open rear adj. for e.
Features: Blue finish; oiled stock with checkered p.g. Imported from Czechoslovakia by BRNO U.S.A., Inc.
Price: $399.00

Browning A-Bolt 22

BROWNING A-BOLT 22 BOLT ACTION RIFLE
Caliber: 22 LR, 5- and 15-shot magazines standard.
Barrel: 22".
Weight: 5 lbs., 9 oz. **Length:** 40¼" over-all.
Stock: Walnut with cut checkering, rosewood grip cap and fore-end tip.
Sights: Offered with or without open sights. Open sight model has ramp front and adjustable folding leaf rear.
Features: Short 60-degree bolt throw. Top tang safety. Grooved for 22 scope mount. Drilled and tapped for full-size scope mounts. Detachable magazines. Gold-colored trigger preset at about 4 lbs. Imported from Japan by Browning. Introduced 1986.
Price: A-Bolt 22, no sights $319.95
Price: A-Bolt 22, with open sights $329.95

Browning A-Bolt Gold Medallion
Similar to the standard A-Bolt except stock is of high-grade walnut with brass spacers between stock and rubber recoil pad and between the rosewood grip cap and fore-end. Medallion-style engraving covers the receiver flats, and the words "Gold Medallion" are engraved and gold filled on the right side of the barrel. High gloss stock finish. Introduced 1988.
Price: $423.95

Cabanas Master

CABANAS MASTER BOLT ACTION RIFLE
Caliber: 177, round ball or pellet; single shot.
Barrel: 19½".
Weight: 8 lbs. **Length:** 45½" over-all.
Stock: Walnut target-type with Monte Carlo.
Sights: Blade front, fully adjustable rear.
Features: Fires round ball or pellet with 22-cal. blank cartridge. Bolt action. Imported from Mexico by Mandall Shooting Supplies. Introduced 1984.
Price: $150.00
Price: Varmint model (21½" barrel, 4½ lbs., 41" o.a.l. varmint-type stock) $109.95

Cabanas Leyre Bolt Action Rifle
Similar to Master model except 44" over-all, has sport/target stock.
Price: $134.95
Price: Model R83 (17" barrel, hardwood stock, 40" o.a.l.) $79.95
Price: Mini 82 Youth (16½" barrel, 33" o.a.l., 3½ lbs.) $69.95
Price: Pony Youth (16" barrel, 34" o.a.l., 3.2 lbs.) $79.95
Price: Safari $99.95

CABANAS LASER RIFLE
Caliber: 177.
Barrel: 19".
Weight: 6 lbs., 12 oz. **Length:** 42" over-all.
Stock: Target-type thumbhole.
Sights: Blade front, open fully adjustable rear.
Features: Fires round ball or pellets with 22 blank cartridge. Imported from Mexico by Mandall Shooting Supplies.
Price: $159.95

Cabanas Espronceda IV Bolt Action Rifle
Similar to the Leyre model except has full sporter stock, 18¾ barrel, 40" over-all length, weighs 5½ lbs.
Price: $119.95

CAUTION: PRICES CHANGE. CHECK AT GUNSHOP.

RIMFIRE RIFLES—BOLT ACTIONS & SINGLE SHOTS

Century Weekender

CENTURY WEEKENDER SPORTER RIFLE
Caliber: 22 LR, 5-shot magazine.
Barrel: 23.5".
Weight: NA. **Length:** 42" over-all.
Stock: European hardwood.
Sights: Hooded blade front, open adjustable rear.
Features: Blue finish; sling swivels. Introduced 1987. Imported by Century International Arms.
Price: $86.95

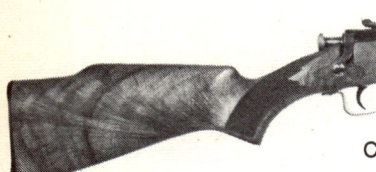

Chipmunk Rifle

CHIPMUNK SINGLE SHOT RIFLE
Caliber: 22, S, L, LR, single shot.
Barrel: 16 1/8".
Weight: About 2½ lbs. **Length:** 30" over-all.
Stock: American walnut, or camouflage.
Sights: Post on ramp front, peep rear adj. for windage and elevation.
Features: Drilled and tapped for scope mounting using special Chipmunk base ($9.95). Made in U.S.A. Introduced 1982. From Chipmunk Mfg.
Price: $129.95
Price: Deluxe Model with hand checkered fancy stock $179.95

Daisy Legacy 2202

DAISY LEGACY 2202 BOLT ACTION REPEATER
Caliber: 22 LR, 10-shot rotary magazine.
Barrel: 19". Octagonal barrel shroud.
Weight: 6.5 lbs. **Length:** 34.75" to 36.75" (variable).
Stock: Moulded lightweight copolymer.
Sights: Blade on ramp front, fully adjustable removeable rear.
Features: Adjustable buttstock length; removeable bolt and trigger assembly; adjustable trigger pull; barrel interchanges with smoothbore unit. Receiver dovetailed for scope mounting. Introduced 1988. Made in U.S. by Daisy.
Price: About $75.00

Daisy Legacy 2212 Bolt Action Repeater
Same as the Model 2202 except has walnut stock, fixed length of pull.
Price: About $99.00

Daisy Legacy 2222

Daisy Legacy 2222 Bolt Action Repeater
Same as the Model 2202 except comes with a smoothbore barrel with ventilated rib, bead front sight. Barrel interchanges with rifled unit.
Price: About $90.00

Daisy Legacy 2232 Bolt Action Repeater Combo
Same gun as the Model 2202 except comes with both rifled and smoothbore barrels, floatable nylon Cordura carrying case, takedown tool and cleaning kit.
Price: About $125.00
Price: As above with walnut stock, about $149.00

Daisy Legacy 2201

DAISY LEGACY 2201 BOLT ACTION SINGLE SHOT
Caliber: 22 L.R.
Barrel: 19". Octagonal barrel shroud.
Weight: 6.5 lbs. **Length:** 34.75" to 36.75" (variable)
Stock: Moulded copolymer.
Sights: Blade on ramp front, fully adjustable removeable notch rear.
Features: Adjustable buttstock length; removeable bolt and trigger assembly; adjustable trigger pull; barrel interchanges with smoothbore unit. Receiver dovetailed for scope mounting. Introduced 1988. Made in U.S. by Daisy.
Price: About $65.00

Daisy Legacy 2221 Single Shot Smoothbore
Similar to the Model 2201 except has smoothbore barrel with ventilated rib and bead front sight. Designed for shooting 22 RF shotshells. Weighs 6 lbs.
Price: About $80.00

Daisy Legacy 2231 Bolt Action Combo
Same as the Model 2201 except comes with both rifled and smoothbore barrels, waterproof, floatable nylon Cordura carrying case, takedown tool and cleaning kit.
Price: About $110.00

Daisy Legacy 2211 Bolt Action Single Shot
Same gun as the Model 2201 except comes with walnut stock, fixed length of pull.
Price: About $94.95

RIMFIRE RIFLES—BOLT ACTIONS & SINGLE SHOTS

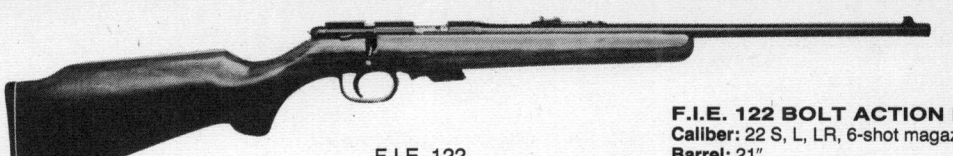

F.I.E. 122

F.I.E. 122 BOLT ACTION RIFLE
Caliber: 22 S, L, LR, 6-shot magazine.
Barrel: 21".
Weight: 5½ lbs. **Length:** 39" over-all.
Stock: Walnut-finished hardwood.
Sights: Blade front, open rear adj. for w. & e.
Features: Sliding wing-type safety lever, double extractors, red cocking indicator, receiver grooved for scope mounts. Imported from Brazil by F.I.E. Introduced 1986.
Price: **$109.95**

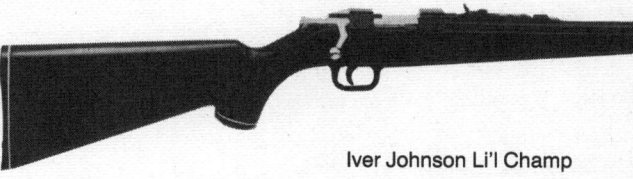

Iver Johnson Li'l Champ

IVER JOHNSON LI'L CHAMP RIFLE
Caliber: 22 S, L, LR, single shot.
Barrel: 16¼".
Weight: 3 lbs., 2 oz. **Length:** 32½" over-all.
Stock: Moulded composition.
Sights: Blade on ramp front, adj. rear.
Features: Sized for junior shooters. Nickel-plated bolt. Made in U.S.A. Introduced 1986. From Iver Johnson.
Price: **$91.50**

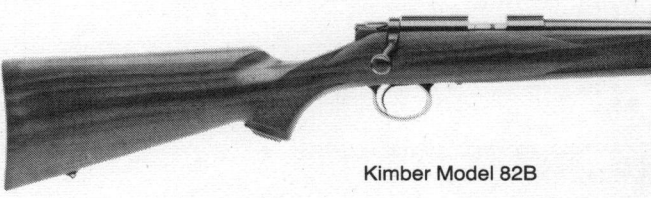

Kimber Model 82B

KIMBER MODEL 82B BOLT ACTION RIFLE
Caliber: 22 LR, 5-shot detachable magazine.
Barrel: 22"; 6-grooves; 1-in 16" twist; 24" varmint.
Weight: About 6¼ lbs. **Length:** 40½" over-all (Sporter).
Stock: Two styles available. "Classic" is Claro walnut with plain, straight comb; "Custom Classic" is of fancy select grade Claro walnut, ebony fore-end tip, Niedner-style buttplate; "Continental" has a full-length Mannlicher-style stock with steel nose cap and barrel band. All have 18 lpi hand cut, borderless checkering, steel grip cap, checkered steel buttplate. Fully inletted swivel studs.
Sights: Hooded ramp front with bead, folding leaf rear (optional).
Features: High quality, adult-sized, bolt action rifle. Barrel screwed into receiver; rocker-type silent safety; twin rear locking lugs. All steel construction. Fully adjustable trigger; receiver grooved for Kimber scope mounts. High polish blue. Barreled actions available. Also available in true left-hand version in selected models. Made in U.S.A. Introduced 1979. Contact Kimber for full details.

Kimber Model 82, 84 Super America
Super-grade version of the Models 82 and 84. Has the Classic stock only of specially selected, high-grade, California claro walnut, with Continental beaded cheekpiece and ebony fore-end tip; borderless, full-coverage 20 lpi checkering; Niedner-type checkered steel buttplate. Options include barrel quarter-rib with a folding leaf sight, skeleton grip cap, checkered bolt knob. Available in 22 Long Rifle, 17 Rem., 22 Hornet, 221 Fireball, 222 Rem., 223 Rem.
Price: Model 82 22 Long Rifle, less scope **$1,150.00**
Price: Model 82 22 Hornet, less scope **$1,195.00**
Price: Model 84, 223 .... **$1,285.00**

Price: 22 LR Classic stock, no sights, plain or heavy bbl. (left hand avail.) **$750.00**
Price: Continental **$850.00**
Price: As above, Custom Classic, plain or heavy bbl. (left hand avail.) **$995.00**
Price: Kimber scope mounts, from **$48.00**
Price: Optional open sights fitted **$55.00**

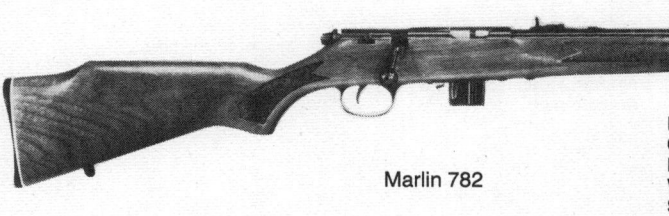

Marlin 782

MARLIN 780 BOLT ACTION RIFLE
Caliber: 22 S, L, or LR; 7-shot clip magazine.
Barrel: 22" Micro-Groove.
Weight: 5½ lbs. **Length:** 41".
Stock: Monte Carlo American black walnut with checkered p.g. and fore-end. White line spacer at buttplate. Mar-Shield® finish.
Sights: Wide-Scan® ramp front, folding semi-buckhorn rear adj. for w. & e.
Features: Receiver anti-glare serrated and grooved for tip-off scope mount.
Price: **$161.95**

Marlin 781 Bolt Action Rifle
Same as the Marlin 780 except tubular magazine holds 25 Shorts, 19 Longs or 17 Long Rifle cartridges. Weight 6 lbs.
Price: **$168.95**

Marlin 782 Bolt Action Rifle
Same as the Marlin 780 except 22 WMR cal. only, weight about 6 lbs. Comes with swivel studs.
Price: **$178.95**

Marlin 783 Bolt Action Rifle
Same as Marlin 782 except Tubular magazine holds 12 rounds of 22 WMR ammunition.
Price: **$185.95**

Marlin 25 Bolt Action Repeater
Similar to Marlin 780, except walnut finished p.g. stock, adjustable open rear sight, ramp front.
Price: **$125.95**

CAUTION: PRICES CHANGE. CHECK AT GUNSHOP.

RIMFIRE RIFLES—BOLT ACTIONS & SINGLE SHOTS

Marlin Midget Magnum

MARLIN 15Y "LITTLE BUCKAROO"
Caliber: 22, S, L, LR, single shot.
Barrel: 16¼" Micro-Groove®.
Weight: 4¼ lbs. **Length:** 33¼" over-all.
Stock: One-piece walnut-finished hardwood with Monte Carlo; Mar-Shield® finish.
Sights: Ramp front, adjustable open rear.
Features: Beginner's rifle with thumb safety, easy-load feed throat, red cocking indicator. Receiver grooved for scope mounting. Introduced 1984.
Price: $120.95

Marlin 25MB "Midget Magnum"
Similar to the Model 25M except has 16¼" Micro-groove® barrel, 35¼" over-all length and weighs 4¾ lbs. Has walnut-finish hardwood stock; receiver is grooved for tip-off scope mount and gun comes with both iron sights and 4x scope, zippered nylon case. Large thumbscrew allows easy take-down. Introduced 1987.
Price: $172.95

Marlin Model 25M Bolt Action Rifle
Similar to the Model 25 except chambered for 22 WMR. Has 7-shot clip magazine, 22" Micro-Groove® barrel, walnut-finished hardwood stock. Introduced 1983.
Price: $141.95

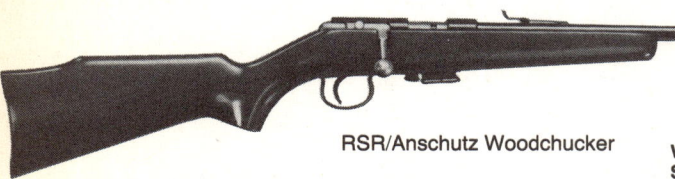
RSR/Anschutz Woodchucker

RSR/ANSCHUTZ WOODCHUCKER RIFLE
Caliber: 22 LR, 5-shot clip.
Barrel: 16¼".
Weight: 3 lbs., 10 oz. **Length:** 32¼" over-all.
Stock: Hardwood; 12" length of pull.
Sights: Bead front, U-notch rear with step elevator.
Features: Dual opposing extractors; receiver grooved for scope mounting. Made in Germany by Anschutz; imported by RSR Wholesale Guns, Inc.
Price: $175.95

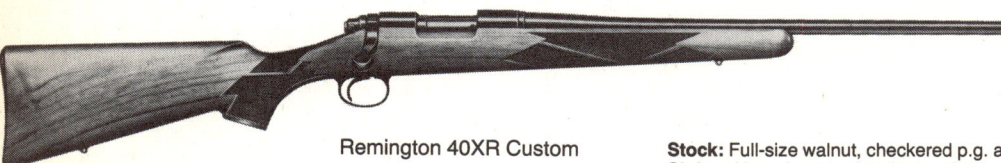
Remington 40XR Custom

REMINGTON 40XR RIMFIRE CUSTOM SPORTER
Caliber: 22 LR.
Barrel: 24".
Weight: 10 lbs. **Length:** 42½" over-all.
Stock: Full-size walnut, checkered p.g. and fore-end.
Sights: None furnished; drilled and tapped for scope mounting.
Features: Custom Shop gun. Duplicates Model 700 centerfire rifle.
Price: Grade I $1,200.00
Price: Grade II $2,133.00
Price: Grade III $3,333.00
Price: Grade IV $5,200.00

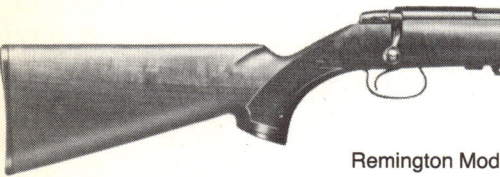
Remington Model 541-T

REMINGTON MODEL 581-S "SPORTSMAN" RIFLE
Caliber: 22 S, L or LR. 5-shot clip mag.
Barrel: 24" round.
Weight: 4¾ lbs. **Length:** 42⅜" over-all.
Stock: Walnut finished hardwood, Monte Carlo with p.g.
Sights: Bead post front, screw adj. open rear.
Features: Sliding side safety, wide trigger, receiver grooved for tip-off scope mounts. Comes with single-shot adapter. Reintroduced 1986.
Price: About $184.00

REMINGTON MODEL 541-T
Caliber: 22 S, L, LR, 5-shot clip.
Barrel: 24".
Weight: 5⅞ lbs. **Length:** 42½" over-all.
Stock: Walnut, cut-checkered p.g. and fore-end. Satin finish.
Sights: None. Drilled and tapped for scope mounts.
Features: Clip repeater. Thumb safety. Re-introduced 1986.
Price: About $333.00

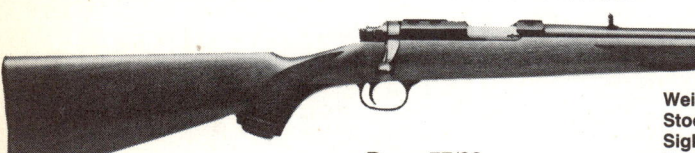
Ruger 77/22

RUGER 77/22 RIMFIRE BOLT ACTION RIFLE
Caliber: 22 Long Rifle, 10-shot magazine.
Barrel: 20".
Weight: About 5¾ lbs. **Length:** 39¾" over-all.
Stock: Straight-grained American walnut.
Sights: Gold bead front, adjustable folding leaf rear, or no sights.
Features: Mauser-type action uses Ruger's 10-shot rotary magazine; 3-position safety; simplified bolt stop; patented bolt locking system. Uses the dual-screw barrel attachment system of the 10/22 rifle. Integral scope mounting system with 1" Ruger rings. Introduced 1983.
Price: 77/22 R (plain barrel, no sights, with Ruger 1" rings) $364.50
Price: 77/22 S (gold bead front sight, folding leaf rear) $364.50
Price: 77/22 RS (scope rings and open sights) $384.50

RIMFIRE RIFLES—BOLT ACTIONS & SINGLE SHOTS

Varner Favorite

VARNER FAVORITE SINGLE SHOT RIFLE
Caliber: 22 LR.
Barrel: 21½"; half round, half octagon.
Weight: 5 lbs.
Stock: American walnut.
Sights: Blade front, open step-adjustable rear and peep.
Features: Recreation of the Stevens Favorite rifle with takedown barrel. Target grade barrel. Made in U.S. Introduced 1988. From Varner Sporting Arms, Inc.
Price: Field Grade $249.00
Price: Sporter Grade (finely figured walnut) $369.00
Price: Presentation Grade (AAA Fancy walnut, checkered grip and fore-end, includes hard custom takedown case) $495.00

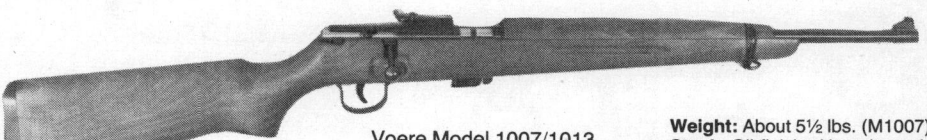
Voere Model 1007/1013

VOERE MODEL 1007/1013 BOLT ACTION RIFLE
Caliber: 22 LR (M1007 Biathlon), 22 WMR (M1013).
Barrel: 18".
Weight: About 5½ lbs. (M1007)
Stock: Oil-finished beechwood.
Sights: Hooded front, open adjustable rear.
Features: Single-stage trigger (M1013 available with double set). Military-look stock; sling swivels. Convertible to single shot. Imported from Austria by L. Joseph Rahn. Introduced 1984.
Price: 1007 Biathlon $310.00
Price: 1013, 22 WMR $350.00

COMPETITION RIFLES—CENTERFIRE & RIMFIRE

Includes models for classic American and ISU target competition and other sporting and competitive shooting.

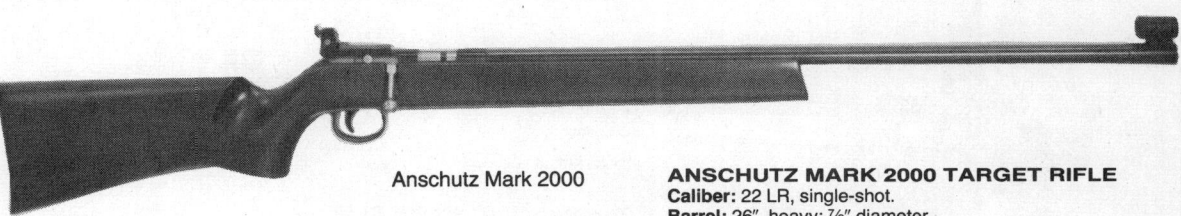
Anschutz Mark 2000

ANSCHUTZ MODEL 64-MS, 64-MS LEFT
Caliber: 22 LR, single shot.
Barrel: 21¾", medium heavy; ⅞" diameter.
Weight: 8 lbs. 1 oz. **Length:** 39½" over-all.
Stock: Walnut finished hardwood, silhouette-type.
Sights: None furnished. Receiver drilled and tapped for scope mounting.
Features: Designed for metallic silhouette competition. Stock has stippled checkering, contoured thumb groove with Wundhammer swell. Two-stage #5091 trigger. Slide safety locks sear and bolt. Introduced 1980. Imported from West Germany by PSI.
Price: Model 64-MS $663.00
Price: Model 64-MS Left $733.00
Price: 64-MS FWT (same as 64-MS except weighs about 6¼ lbs. ... $596.00

ANSCHUTZ MARK 2000 TARGET RIFLE
Caliber: 22 LR, single-shot.
Barrel: 26", heavy; ⅞" diameter.
Weight: 8 lbs. **Length:** 43" over-all.
Stock: Walnut finished hardwood.
Sights: Globe front (insert-type), micro-click peep rear.
Features: Has 3-lb. single-stage trigger; stock has thumb groove, Wundhammer swell, full length slide rail. Imported from West Germany by PSI.
Price: Without sights $399.50
Price: Sight set #2 .... $43.50

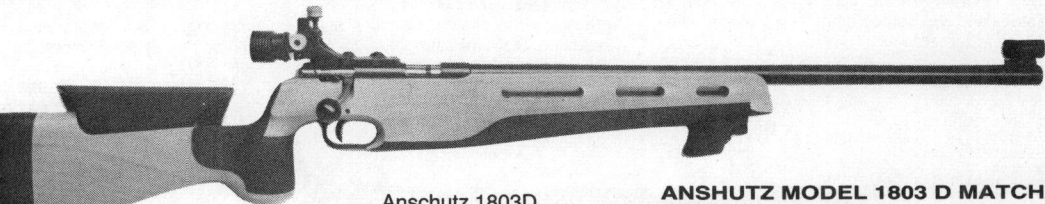
Anschutz 1803D

ANSHUTZ MODEL 1803 D MATCH RIFLE
Caliber: 22 LR, single shot.
Barrel: 25½", ¾" diameter.
Weight: 8.6 lbs. **Length:** 43¾" over-all.
Stock: Walnut-finished hardwood with adjustable cheekpiece; stippled grip and fore-end.
Sights: None furnished.
Features: Uses Anshultz Match 64 action and #5091 two-stage trigger. A medium weight rifle for intermediate and advanced Junior Match competition. Introduced 1987. Imported from West Germany by PSI.
Price: Right-hand $739.00
Price: Left-hand $842.50

CAUTION: PRICES CHANGE. CHECK AT GUNSHOP.

COMPETITION RIFLES—CENTERFIRE & RIMFIRE

ANSCHUTZ MODEL 1403D MATCH RIFLE
Caliber: 22 LR only, single shot.
Barrel: 26"; 11/16" dia.
Weight: 7¾ lbs. **Length:** 44" over-all.
Stock: Walnut finished hardwood, cheekpiece, checkered p.g., beavertail fore-end, adj. buttplate.
Sights: None furnished.
Features: Sliding side safety, adj. #5053 single stage trigger, receiver grooved for Anschutz sights. Imported from West Germany by PSI.
Price: Without sights $667.50
Price: M1403D left hand $724.50

ANSCHUTZ 1808ED SUPER RUNNING TARGET
Caliber: 22 LR, single shot.
Barrel: 23½"; ⅞" diameter.
Weight: 9¼ lbs. **Length:** 42" over-all.
Stock: European hardwood. Heavy beavertail fore-end, adjustable cheekpiece, buttplate, stippled pistol grip and fore-end.
Sights: None furnished. Receiver grooved for scope mounting.
Features: Uses Super Match 54 action. Adjustable trigger from 14 oz. to 3.5 lbs. Removable sectioned barrel weights. **Special Order Only.** Introduced 1982. Imported from Germany by PSI.
Price: Right hand $1,235.00
Price: Left hand, 1808EDL $1,359.00

Anschutz Model 1913

Anschutz 1913 Super Match Rifle
Same as the Model 1911 except European walnut International-type stock with adj. cheekpiece, adj. aluminum hook buttplate, adjustable hand stop, weight 15½ lbs., 46" over-all. Imported from West Germany by PSI.
Price: Right hand, no sights $2,067.00
Price: M1913-L (left-hand action and stock) $2,237.00

ANSCHUTZ 1911 MATCH RIFLE
Caliber: 22 LR, single shot.
Barrel: 27¼" round (1" dia.).
Weight: 11 lbs. **Length:** 46" over-all.
Stock: Walnut-finished European hardwood; American prone style with Monte Carlo, cast-off cheekpiece, checkered p.g., beavertail fore-end with swivel rail and adj. swivel, adj. rubber buttplate.
Sights: None. Receiver grooved for Anschutz sights (extra). Scope blocks.
Features: Two-stage #5018 trigger adjustable from 2.1 to 8.6 oz. Extremely fast lock time. Imported from West Germany by PSI.
Price: Right hand, no sights $1,444.00
Price: M1911-L (true left-hand action and stock) $1,570.00

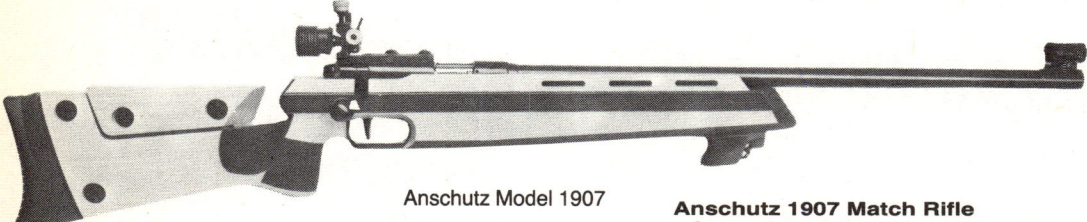

Anschutz Model 1907

Anschutz Model 1910 Super Match II
Similar to the Super Match 1913 rifle except has a stock of European hardwood with tapered fore-end and deep receiver area. Hand and palm rests not included. Uses Match 54 action. Adjustable hook buttplate and cheekpiece. Sights not included. Introduced 1982. Imported from Germany by PSI.
Price: Right hand $1,844.00
Price: Left hand $2,000.00

Anschutz 1907 Match Rifle
Same action as Model 1913 but with ⅞" diameter 26" barrel. Length is 44½" over-all, weight 10 lbs. Blond wood finish with vented fore-end. Designed for ISU requirements, suitable for NRA matches.
Price: Right hand, no sights $1,232.00
Price: M1907-L (true left-hand action and stock) $1,340.00

ANSCHUTZ 1827B BIATHLON RIFLE
Caliber: 22 LR, 5-shot magazine.
Barrel: 21½".
Weight: 9 lbs. with sights. **Length:** 42½" over-all.
Stock: Walnut-finished hardwood; cheekpiece, stippled pistol grip and fore-end.
Sights: Globe front specially designed for Biathlon shooting, micrometer rear with hinged snow cap.
Features: Uses Match 54 action and adjustable trigger; adjustable wooden buttplate, Biathlon butthook, adjustable hand-stop rail. **Special Order Only.** Introduced 1982. Imported from Germany by PSI.
Price: Right hand $1,598.00
Price: Left hand $1,801.00

Anschutz Model 54.18 MS Silhouette Rifle
Same basic features as Anschutz 1913 Super Match but with special metallic silhoutte European hardwood stock and two-stage trigger. Has 22" barrel; receiver drilled and tapped.
Price: $1,129.00
Price: Model 54.18 MSL (true left-hand version of above) $1,228.00

BEEMAN/HW 660 MATCH RIFLE
Caliber: 22 LR.
Barrel: 26".
Weight: 10.7 lbs. **Length:** 45.3" over-all.
Stock: Match-type walnut with adjustable cheekpiece and buttplate.
Sights: Globe front, match aperture rear.
Features: Adjustable match trigger; stippled p.g. and fore-end; fore-end accessory rail. Imported from West Germany by Beeman. Introduced 1988.
Price: $725.00

Beeman/HW 660

COMPETITION RIFLES—CENTERFIRE & RIMFIRE

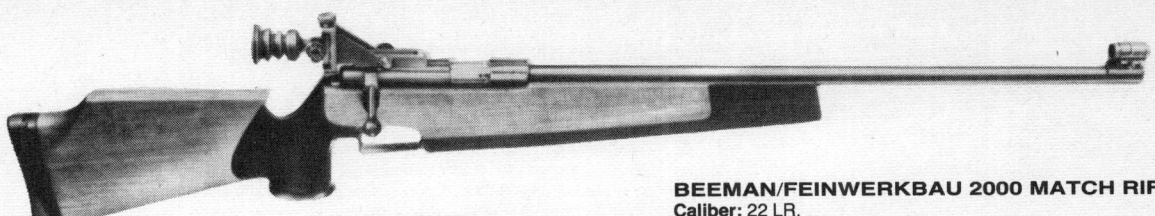
Beeman/FWB 2000

BEEMAN/FEINWERKBAU 2000 MATCH RIFLE
Caliber: 22 LR.
Barrel: 26¼"; 22" for Mini-Match.
Weight: 9 lbs. 12 oz. **Length:** 43¾" over-all (26¼" bbl.).
Stock: Standard match. Walnut with stippled p.g. and fore-end; walnut-stained birch for the Mini-Match.
Sights: Globe front with interchangeable inserts; micrometer match aperture rear.
Features: Meets ISU standard rifle specifications. Shortest lock time of any small bore rifle. Electronic or mechanical trigger, fully adjustable for weight, release point, length, lateral position, etc. Available in Standard and Mini-Match models. Introduced 1979. Imported from West Germany by Beeman.
Price: Model 2000 .... **$1,285.00 to $1,850.00**
Price: Mini-Match .... **$1,225.00 to $1,675.00**

BEEMAN/FEINWERKBAU 2600 TARGET RIFLE
Caliber: 22 LR, single shot.
Barrel: 26.3".
Weight: 10.6 lbs. **Length:** 43.7" over-all.
Stock: Laminated hardwood and hard rubber.
Sights: Globe front with interchangeable inserts; micrometer match aperture rear.
Features: Identical smallbore companion to the Beeman/FWB 600 air rifle. Free floating barrel. Match trigger has fingertip weight adjustment dial. Introduced 1986. Imported from West Germany by Beeman.
Price: Right hand **$1,375.00**
Price: Left hand **$1,550.00**

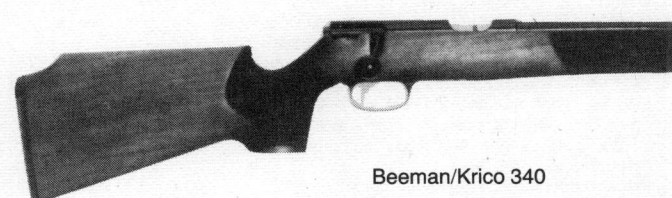
Beeman/Krico 340

BEEMAN/KRICO 340 SILHOUETTE RIFLE
Caliber: 22 Long Rifle, 5-shot clip.
Barrel: 21", match quality.
Weight: 7.5 lbs. **Length:** 39.5" over-all.
Stock: European walnut match-style designed for off-hand shooting. Suitable for right- or left-hand shooters. Stippled grip and fore-end.
Sights: None furnished. Receiver grooved for tip-off mounts.
Features: Free-floated heavy barrel; fully adjustable two-stage match trigger or double set trigger. Meets NRA official MS rules. Introduced 1983. Imported by Beeman.
Price: **$1,186.00**

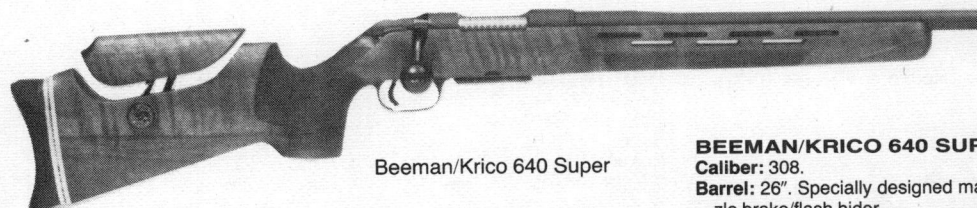
Beeman/Krico 640 Super

BEEMAN/KRICO 640 SUPER SNIPER
Caliber: 308.
Barrel: 26". Specially designed match bull barrel, matte blue finish, with muzzle brake/flash hider.
Weight: 9.6 lbs. **Length:** 44¾" over-all.
Stock: Select walnut with oil finish. Spring-loaded, adj. cheekpiece, adjustable recoil pad.
Sights: None furnished. Drilled and tapped for scope mounts.
Features: Match trigger with 10mm wide shoe; single standard or double set trigger available. All metal has matte blue finish. Bolt knob has 1¼" diameter. Scope mounts available for special night-sight devices. Imported from West Germany by Beeman.
Price: Without scope, mount **$2,363.00**

FINNISH LION STANDARD TARGET RIFLE
Caliber: 22 LR, single shot.
Barrel: 27⅝".
Weight: 10½ lbs. **Length:** 44 9/16" over-all.
Stock: French walnut, target style.
Sights: None furnished. Globe front, International micrometer rear available.
Features: Optional accessories: palm rest, hook buttplate, fore-end stop and swivel assembly, buttplate extension, 5 front sight aperture inserts, 3 rear sight apertures, Allen wrench. Adjustable trigger. Imported from Finland by Mandall Shooting Supplies.
Price: **$550.00**

HECKLER & KOCH PSG-1 MARKSMAN RIFLE
Caliber: 308, 5- and 20-shot magazines.
Barrel: 25.6", heavy.
Weight: 17.8 lbs. **Length:** 47.5" over-all.
Stock: Matte black high impact plastic, adj. for length, pivoting butt cap, vertically-adj. cheekpiece; target-type pistol grip with adj. palm shelf.
Sights: Hendsoldt 6x42 scope.
Features: Uses HK-91 action with low-noise bolt closing device; special fore-end with T-way rail for sling swivel or tripod. Gun comes in special foam-fitted metal transport case with tripod, two 20-shot and two-5-shot magazines, cleaning rod. Imported from West Germany by Heckler & Koch, Inc. Introduced 1986.
Price: **$8,599.00**

BEEMAN/WEIHRAUCH HW60 TARGET RIFLE
Caliber: 22 LR, single shot.
Barrel: 26.8".
Weight: 10.8 lbs. **Length:** 45.7" over-all.
Stock: Walnut with adjustable buttplate. Stippled p.g. and fore-end. Rail with adjustable swivel.
Sights: Hooded ramp front, match-type aperture rear.
Features: Adj. match trigger with push-button safety. Left-hand version also available. Introduced 1981. Imported from West Germany by Beeman.
Price: Right hand **$698.00**
Price: Left hand **$739.00**

CAUTION: PRICES CHANGE. CHECK AT GUNSHOP.

COMPETITION RIFLES—CENTERFIRE & RIMFIRE

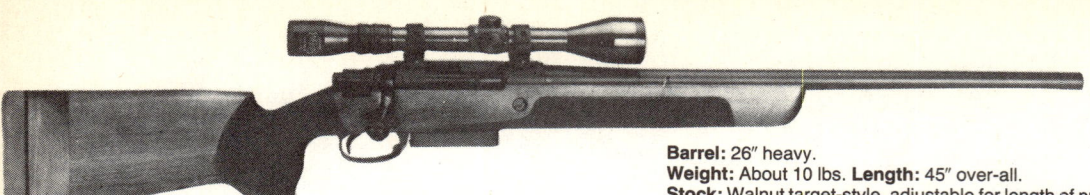

Parker-Hale M87

PARKER-HALE M87 TARGET RIFLE
Caliber: 308 Win., 243, 6.5x55, 30-06, 300 Win. Mag. (other calibers on request), 5-shot detachable box magazine.
Barrel: 26" heavy.
Weight: About 10 lbs. **Length:** 45" over-all.
Stock: Walnut target-style, adjustable for length of pull; solid buttpad; accessory rail with hand-stop. Deeply stippled grip and fore-end.
Sights: None furnished. Receiver dovetailed for Parker-Hale "Roll-Off" scope mounts.
Features: Mauser-style action with large bolt knob. Parkerized finish. Introduced 1987. Imported from England by Precision Sports.
Price: $1,175.00

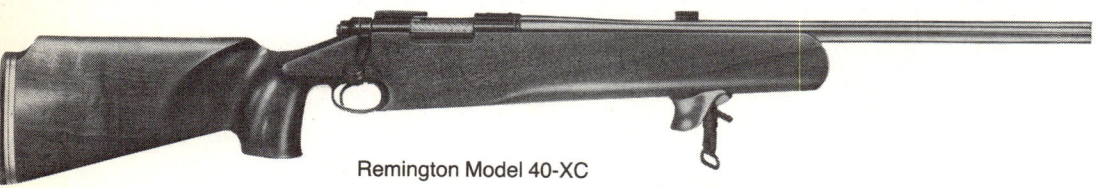

Remington Model 40-XC

REMINGTON MODEL 40XB-BR
Caliber: 22 BR Rem., 222 Rem., 223, 6mmx47, 6mm BR Rem., 7.62 NATO (308 Win.).
Barrel: 20" (light varmint class), 26" (heavy varmint class).
Weight: Light varmint class, 7¼ lbs.; heavy varmint class, 12 lbs. **Length:** 38" (20" bbl.), 44" (26" bbl.).
Stock: Select walnut.
Sights: None. Supplied with scope blocks.
Features: Unblued stainless steel barrel, trigger adj. from 1½ lbs. to 3½ lbs. Special 2/2-oz. trigger at extra cost. Scope and mounts extra.
Price: About $1,000.00
Price: Extra for 2-oz. trigger, about $133.00

REMINGTON 40-XC NAT'L MATCH COURSE RIFLE
Caliber: 7.62 NATO, 5-shot.
Barrel: 23¼", stainless steel.
Weight: 10 lbs. without sights. **Length:** 42½" over-all.
Stock: Walnut, position-style, with palm swell.
Sights: None furnished.
Features: Designed to meet the needs of competitive shooters firing the national match courses. Position-style stock, top loading clip slot magazine, anti-bind bolt and receiver, bright stainless steel barrel. Meets all I.S.U. Army Rifle specifications. Adjustable buttplate, adjustable trigger.
Price: About $1,000.00
Price: Model 40-XC KS (Kevlar stock) $1,133.00

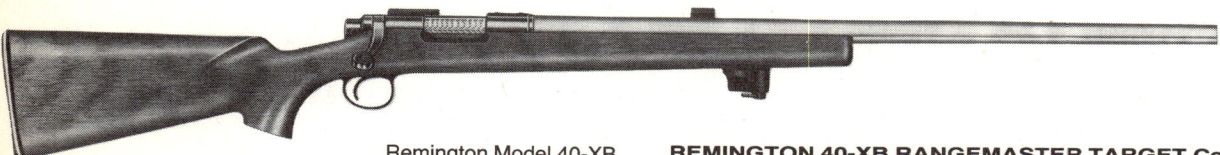

Remington Model 40-XB

Remington 40-XB KS Varmint Special
Similar to the standard Model 40-XB except has Du Pont Kevlar aramid fiber stock with straight comb, cheekpiece, palm-swell grip, black recoil pad. Swivel studs easily removable. Stock color is satin black with light texture. Single shot or repeater. Chamberings include 220 Swift. Introduced 1987. Custom Shop order.
Price: Single shot $1,067.00
Price: Repeater $1,147.00
Price: Extra for 2-oz. trigger $133.00

REMINGTON 40-XB RANGEMASTER TARGET Centerfire
Caliber: 222 Rem., 22-250, 6mm Rem., 243, 25-06, 7mm Rem. Mag., 30-338 (30-7mm Rem. Mag.), 300 Win. Mag., 7.62 NATO (308 Win.), 30-06, single shot.
Barrel: 27¼" round (Stand. dia.—¾", Hvy. dia.—⅞").
Weight: Std.—9¼ lbs., Hvy.—11¼ lbs. **Length:** 47" over-all.
Stock: American walnut with high comb and beavertail fore-end stop. Rubber non-slip buttplate.
Sights: None. Scope blocks installed.
Features: Adjustable trigger pull. Receiver drilled and tapped for sights.
Price: Standard s.s., stainless steel barrel, about $933.00
Price: Repeating model, about $1,013.00
Price: Extra for 2-oz. trigger, about $133.00

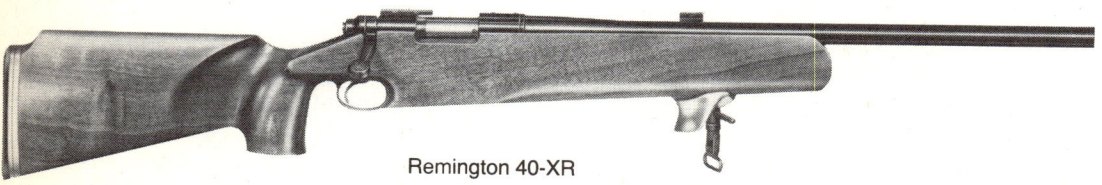

Remington 40-XR

Consult our Directory pages for the location of firms mentioned.

REMINGTON 40-XR RIMFIRE POSITION RIFLE
Caliber: 22 LR, single-shot.
Barrel: 24", heavy target.
Weight: 10 lbs. **Length:** 43" over-all.
Stock: Position-style with front swivel block on fore-end guide rail.
Sights: Drilled and tapped. Furnished with scope blocks.
Features: Meets all I.S.U. specifications. Deep fore-end, buttplate vertically adjustable, wide adjustable trigger.
Price: About $933.00
Price: Model 40-XR KS (Kevlar stock) $1,067.00

COMPETITION RIFLES—CENTERFIRE & RIMFIRE

Springfield M1A Match

SPRINGFIELD ARMORY M1A SUPER MATCH
Caliber: 308 Win.
Barrel: 22″, heavy Douglas Premium, or Hart stainless steel.
Weight: About 10 lbs. **Length:** 44½″ overall.
Stock: Heavy walnut competition stock with longer pistol grip, contoured area behind the rear sight, thicker butt and fore-end, glass bedded.
Sights: National Match front and rear.
Features: Has new figure-eight style operating rod guide, new stock design. Introduced 1987. From Springfield Armory, Inc.
Price: About $1,231.00

SPRINGFIELD ARMORY MODEL 700 BASR
Caliber: 308 Win., 5-shot magazine.
Barrel: 26″ heavy Douglas Premium, 1-11″ twist.
Weight: 13.5 lbs. (with bipod, scope, mount). **Length:** 46.25″ over-all.
Stock: Synthetic fiber with rubber recoil pad.
Sights: None furnished.
Features: Comes with leather military sling and Parker-Hale folding, adjustable bipod, Guaranteed to deliver MOA accuracy with Federal Match ammunition. Introduced 1987. From Springfield Armory.
Price: $1,994.00
Price: Model 24, with stainless barrel $2,288.00
Price: As above with adjustable stock $2,496.00

SPRINGFIELD ARMORY M-21 SNIPER RIFLE
Caliber: 308 Win.
Barrel: 22″, Douglas heavy, air-gauged.
Weight: 15.25 lbs. (with bipod, scope mount). **Length:** 44¼″ over-all.
Stock: Heavy walnut with adjustable comb, ventilated recoil pad. Glass bedded.
Sights: National Match front and rear.
Features: Refinement of the standard M1-A rifle. Has specially knurled shoulder for new figure-eight operating rod guide. New style folding and removable bipod. Guaranteed to deliver MOA accuracy. Comes with six 20-round magazines, leather military sling, cleaning kit. Introduced 1987. From Springfield Armory.
Price: $2,320.00

STEYR-MANNLICHER MATCH UIT RIFLE
Caliber: 243 Win. or 308 Win., 10-shot magazine.
Barrel: 25.5″.
Weight: 10.9 lbs. **Length:** 44.48″ over-all.
Stock: Walnut with stippled grip and fore-end. Special UIT Match design.
Sights: Walther globe front, Walther peep rear.
Features: Double-pull trigger adjustable for let-off point, slack, weight of first-stage pull, release force and length; buttplate adjustable for height and length. Meets UIT specifications. Introduced 1984. Imported from Austria by Gun South, Inc.
Price: $2,350.00

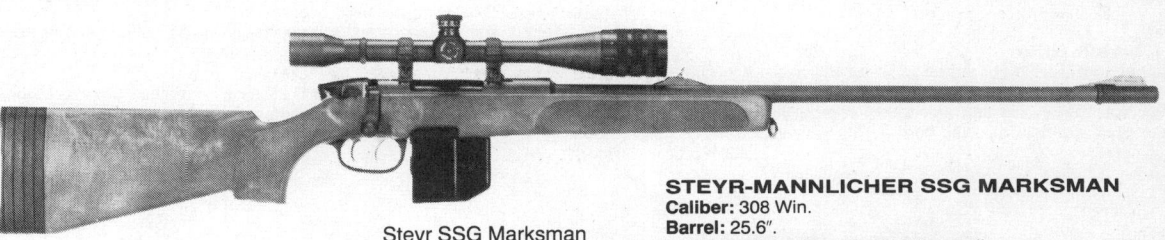
Steyr SSG Marksman

Steyr-Mannlicher SSG Match
Same as Model SSG Marksman except has heavy barrel, match bolt, Walther target peep sights and adj. rail in fore-end to adj. sling travel. Weight is 11 lbs.
Price: Synthetic half-stock $1,875.00
Price: Walnut half-stock $2,125.00

STEYR-MANNLICHER SSG MARKSMAN
Caliber: 308 Win.
Barrel: 25.6″.
Weight: 8.6 lbs. **Length:** 44.5″ over-all.
Stock: Choice of ABS "Cycolac" synthetic half-stock or walnut. Removable spacers in butt adjusts length of pull from 12¾″ to 14″.
Sights: Hooded blade front, folding leaf rear.
Features: Parkerized finish. Choice of interchangeable single or double set triggers. Detachable 5-shot rotary magazine (10-shot optional). Drilled and tapped for scope mounts. Imported from Austria by Gun South, Inc.
Price: Synthetic half-stock $1,592.00
Price: Walnut half-stock $1,995.00
Price: SSG PII (large bolt knob, heavy bbl., no sights, fore-end rail) . **$1,995.00**

Tanner Free Rifle

TANNER 300 METER FREE RIFLE
Caliber: 308 Win., 7.5 Swiss, single shot.
Barrel: 28.7″.
Weight: 15 lbs. **Length:** 45.3″ over-all.
Stock: Seasoned walnut, thumb-hole style, with accessory rail, palm rest, adjustable hook butt.
Sights: Globe front with interchangeable inserts, Tanner-design micrometer-diopter rear with adjustable aperture.
Features: Three-lug revolving-lock bolt design; adjustable set trigger; short firing pin travel; supplied with 300-meter test target. Imported from Switzerland by Osborne's Supplies. Introduced 1984.
Price: About $3,900.00

CAUTION: PRICES CHANGE. CHECK AT GUNSHOP.

COMPETITION RIFLES—CENTERFIRE & RIMFIRE

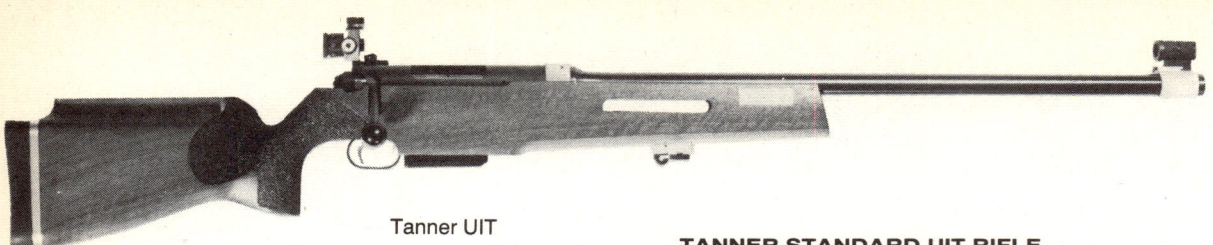

Tanner UIT

TANNER 50 METER FREE RIFLE
Caliber: 22 LR, single shot.
Barrel: 27.7".
Weight: 13.9 lbs. **Length:** 43.4" over-all.
Stock: Seasoned nutwood with palm rest, accessory rail, adjustable hook butt-plate.
Sights: Globe front with interchangeable inserts, Tanner micrometer-diopter rear with adjustable aperture.
Features: Bolt action with externally adjustable set trigger. Supplied with 50-meter test target. Imported from Switzerland by Osborne's Supplies. Introduced 1984.
Price: About $2,950.00

TANNER STANDARD UIT RIFLE
Caliber: 308, 7.5mm Swiss, 10-shot.
Barrel: 25.8".
Weight: 10.5 lbs. **Length:** 40.6" over-all.
Stock: Match style of seasoned nutwood with accessory rail; coarsely stippled pistol grip; high cheekpiece; vented fore-end.
Sights: Globe front with interchangeable inserts, Tanner micrometer-diopter rear with adjustable aperture.
Features: Two locking lug revolving bolt encloses case head. Trigger adjustable from ½ to 6½ lbs.; match trigger optional. Comes with 300-meter test target. Imported from Switzerland by Osborne's. Introduced 1984.
Price: About $3,700.00

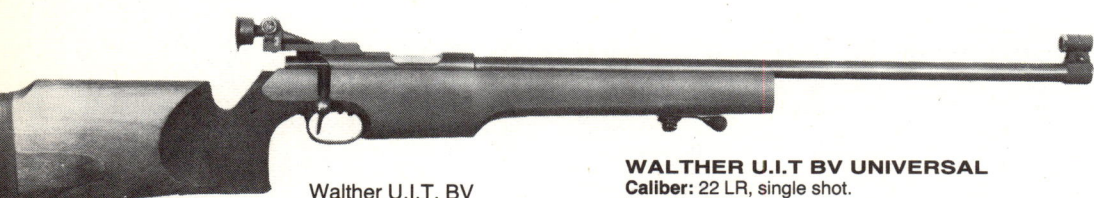

Walther U.I.T. BV

Walther GX-1 Match Rifle
Same general specs as U.I.T. except has 25½" barrel, over-all length of 44½", weight of 15½ lbs. Stock is designed to provide every conceivable adjustment for individual preference and anatomical compatibility. Left-hand stock available on special order. Imported from Germany by Interarms.
Price: $2,100.00

WALTHER U.I.T BV UNIVERSAL
Caliber: 22 LR, single shot.
Barrel: 25½".
Weight: 10 lbs., 3 oz. **Length:** 44¾" over-all.
Stock: Walnut, adj. for length and drop; fore-end guide rail for sling or palm rest.
Sights: Globe-type front, fully adj. aperture rear.
Features: Conforms to both NRA and U.I.T. requirements. Fully adj. trigger. Left-hand stock available on special order. Imported from Germany by Interarms.
Price: $1,625.00

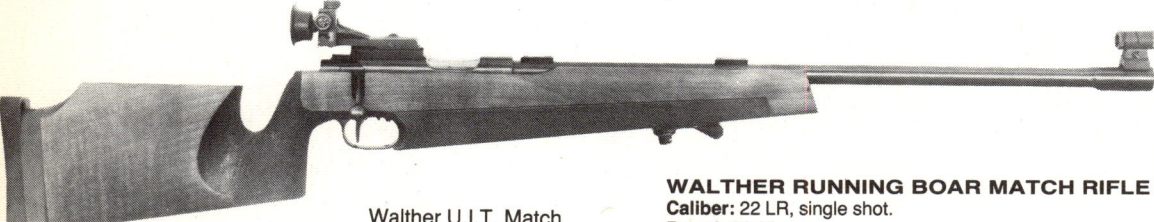

Walther U.I.T. Match

Walther U.I.T. Match
Same specifications and features as standard U.I.T. Super rifle but has scope mount bases. Fore-end has new tapered profile, fully stippled. Imported from Germany by Interarms.
Price: $1,500.00

WALTHER RUNNING BOAR MATCH RIFLE
Caliber: 22 LR, single shot.
Barrel: 23.6".
Weight: 8 lbs. 5 oz. **Length:** 42" over-all.
Stock: Walnut thumb-hole type. Fore-end and p.g. stippled.
Features: Especially designed for running boar competition. Receiver grooved to accept dovetail scope mounts. Adjustable cheekpiece and butt plate. 1.1 lb. trigger pull. Left-hand stock available on special order. Imported from Germany by Interarms.
Price: $1,200.00

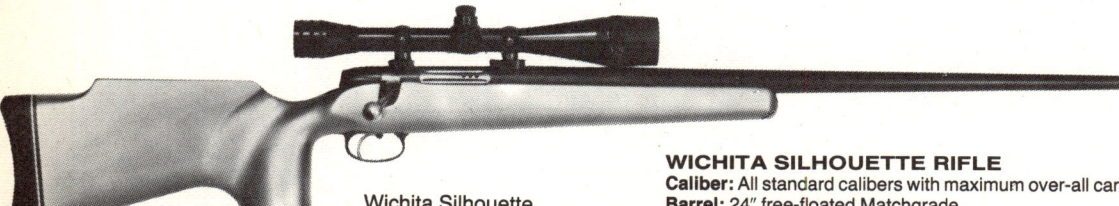

Wichita Silhouette

WICHITA SILHOUETTE RIFLE
Caliber: All standard calibers with maximum over-all cartridge length of 2.800".
Barrel: 24" free-floated Matchgrade.
Weight: About 9 lbs.
Stock: Metallic gray fiberthane with ventilated rubber recoil pad.
Sights: None furnished. Drilled and tapped for scope mounts.
Features: Legal for all NRA competitions. Single shot action. Fluted bolt, 2-oz. Canjar trigger; glass-bedded stock. Introduced 1983. From Wichita Arms.
Price: $2,150.00
Price: Left-hand $2,400.00

SHOTGUNS—AUTOLOADERS

Includes a wide variety of sporting guns and guns suitable for various competitions.

ARMSPORT 2751 GAS AUTO SHOTGUN
Gauge: 12, 3" chamber.
Barrel: 28" (Mod.), 30" (Full).
Weight: 7 lbs.
Stock: European walnut.
Features: Gas-operated action; blued receiver with light engraving. Introduced 1986. Imported from Italy by Armsport.
Price: With fixed choks $575.00
Price: Blue, choke tubes, 28" bbl. $650.00
Price: With silvered receiver $675.00

BENELLI M1 SUPER 90 FIELD AUTO SHOTGUN
Gauge: 12, 3" chamber.
Barrel: 28" (choke tubes).
Weight: 7 lbs., 4 oz.
Stock: High impact polymer.
Sights: Metal bead front.
Features: Sporting version of the military & police gun. Uses the rotating Montefeltro bolt system. Ventilated rib; blue finish. Imported from Italy by Heckler & Koch
Price: $655.00

Benelli Montefeltro

Benelli Montefeltro Super 90 Shotgun
Similar to the M1 Super 90 except has checkered walnut stock with high-gloss finish. Uses the Montefeltro rotating bolt system with a simple inertia recoil design. Has 28" barrel with Imp., Mod., full choke tubes. Weight is 6 lbs., 14 oz. Finish is matte black. Introduced 1987.
Price: Right hand $664.00
Price: Left hand $724.00

BERETTA A-303 AUTO SHOTGUN
Gauge: 12 or 20, 2¾" or 3" chamber.
Barrel: 12-ga.—22" (Slug), 26" (Imp. Cyl., Skeet or Mobilchoke), 28" (Mod. or Mobilchoke); 30 " (Full or Mobilchoke) 32" (Full or Mobilchoke); 20-ga—22" (Cyl./Slug) 24" (Youth); 26" (Mobilchoke or Skeet); 28" (Mobilchoke); 30" (Mobilchoke).
Weight: About 6½ lbs., 20 gauge; about 7½ lbs., 12 gauge.
Stock: American walnut; hand-checkered grip and fore-end.
Features: Gas-operated action, alloy receiver, magazine cut-off, push-button safety. Mobilchoke models come with three interchangeable flush-mounted screw-in choke tubes. Imported from Italy by Beretta U.S.A. Introduced 1983.
Price: 12 or 20 ga., standard chokes $506.00
Price: Mobilchoke, 12 ga. or 20 ga. $574.000
Price: 12 ga. trap with Monte Carlo stock $660.00
Price: 12 ga. trap with standard trap stock $606.00
Price: 12 or 20 ga. skeet $606.00
Price: Slug, 12 or 20 ga. $554.00
Price: A303 Youth Gun, 20 ga., 3" chamber, 24" barrel, Mobilchoke $574.00
Price: A303 Sporting clays $660.00

BERETTA 1200F and FP
Gauge: 12 ga., 2¾" chamber.
Barrel: 28" (Mod., Model 1200F); 20" (Cyl., Model 1200 FP).
Weight: 7.3 lbs.
Stock: Special strengthened technopolymer, matte black finish
Features: Resists abrasion and adverse effects of water, salt and other damaging materials associated with tough field conditions. Imported from Italy by Beretta U.S.A. Introduced 1988.
Price: 1200 F or 1200 FP $440.00

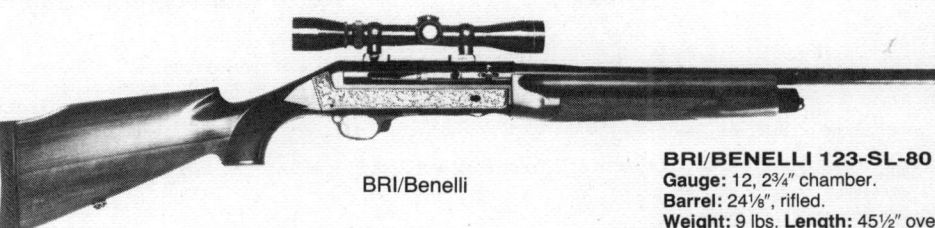

BRI/Benelli

BRI/BENELLI 123-SL-80 RIFLED SHOTGUN
Gauge: 12, 2¾" chamber.
Barrel: 24⅛", rifled.
Weight: 9 lbs. **Length:** 45½" over-all.
Stock: European walnut with checkered p.g. and fore-end.
Sights: None furnished. Drilled and tapped for scope mounting.
Features: Rifled bore. Quick interchangeable barrels; cross-bolt safety; engraved receiver; recoil pad. From Ballistic Research Industries.
Price: $895.00

Browning Sweet Sixteen

BROWNING AUTO-5 LIGHT 12 and 20, SWEET 16
Gauge: 12, 16, 20; 5-shot; 3-shot plug furnished; 2¾" or 3" chamber.
Action: Recoil operated autoloader; takedown.
Barrel: 26", 28", 30" Invector (choke tube) barrel; also available with Light 20 ga. 28" (Mod.) or 26" (Imp. Cyl.) barrel.
Weight: 12, 16 ga. 7¼ lbs., 20 ga. 6⅜ lbs.
Stock: French walnut, hand checkered half-p.g. and fore-end. 14¼" × 1⅝" × 2½".
Features: Receiver hand engraved with scroll designs and border. Double extractors, extra bbls. interchangeable without factory fitting; mag. cut-off; cross-bolt safety. Buck Special no longer inventoried, but can be ordered as a Buck Special extra barrel, plus an action only. Imported from Japan by Browning.
Price: Light 12, 20, Sweet 16, vent. rib., Invector $664.95
Price: Extra Invector barrel $230.95
Price: Extra fixed-choke barrel (Light 20 only) $194.95
Price: 12, 16, 20 Buck Special barrel $234.00

CAUTION: PRICES CHANGE. CHECK AT GUNSHOP.

SHOTGUNS—AUTOLOADERS

Browning Auto-5 Gold Classic
Same as the standard Auto-5 Light 12 with 28" (Mod.) barrel. Has engraved hunting and wildlife scenes with gold animals and portrait. Only 500 will be made, each numbered "1 of Five Hundred," etc. with "Browning Gold Classic." Select, figured walnut, special checkering with carved border, and the semi-pistol grip stock. Introduced 1984.
Price: Auto-5 Gold Classic $6,500.00

Browning Auto-5 Magnum 12
Same as standard Auto-5 except chambered for 3" magnum shells (also handles 2¾" magnum and 2¾" HV loads). 28" Mod., Full; 30" and 32" (Full) bbls. Comes with Invector choke tubes. 14"x1⅝"x2½" stock. Recoil pad. Wgt. 8¾ lbs.
Price: With Invector choke tubes............................. $685.95
Price: Extra Invector barrel.................................. $230.95

Browning Auto-5 Magnum 20
Same as Magnum 12 except 26" or 28" barrel with Invector choke tubes. With ventilated rib, 7½ lbs.
Price: Invector only $685.95
Price: Extra Invector barrel.................................. $230.95

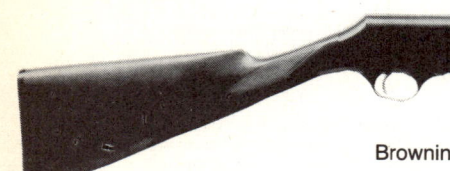
Browning B-80 Upland

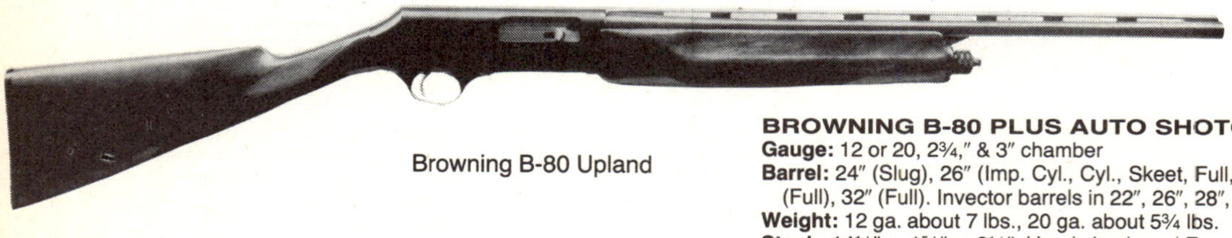

BROWNING B-80 PLUS AUTO SHOTGUN
Gauge: 12 or 20, 2¾", & 3" chamber.
Barrel: 24" (Slug), 26" (Imp. Cyl., Cyl., Skeet, Full, Mod.), 28" (Full, Mod.) 30" (Full), 32" (Full). Invector barrels in 22", 26", 28", 30", 12 or 20 ga.
Weight: 12 ga. about 7 lbs., 20 ga. about 5¾ lbs.
Stock: 14¼" × 1⅝" × 2½". Hand checkered French walnut. Solid black recoil pad.
Features: Shoots all popular factory 2¾" and 3" loads without adjustment. Vent. rib barrels have non-reflective rib; alloy receiver; cross-bolt safety; interchangeable barrels. Buck Special no longer inventoried, but can be ordered as a Buck Special extra barrel and action only. Introduced 1981. Imported from Belgium by Browning.
Price: Invector, vent. rib, 12 or 20 ga........................ $588.95
Price: Extra Invector barrels................................. $207.95
Price: Extra fixed-choke barrels, 20 ga. only.................. $131.25
Price: Extra Buck Special barrel $207.95

Browning B-80 Upland Special Auto Shotgun
Same as standard B-80 except has 22" Invector barrel. Straight grip stock with 14" length of pull; 12 and 20 gauge. Introduced 1986.
Price: $589.95

Browning A-500

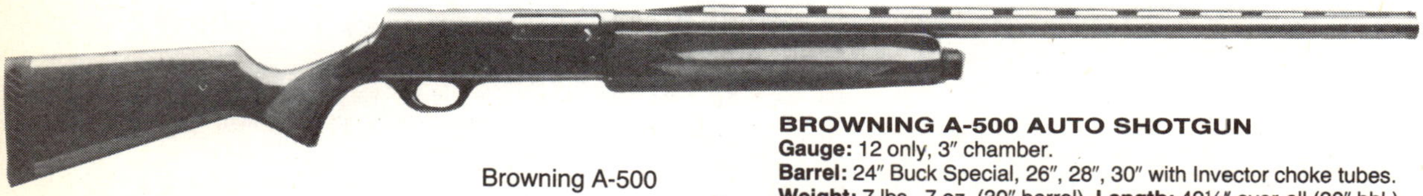

COSMI AUTOMATIC SHOTGUN
Gauge: 12 or 20, 2¾" or 3" chamber.
Barrel: 22" to 34". Choke (including choke tubes) and length to customer specs. Boehler steel.
Weight: About 6¼ lbs. (20 ga.).
Stock: Length and style to customer specs. Hand-checkered exhibition grade circassian walnut standard.
Features: Hand-made, essentially a custom gun. Recoil-operated auto with tip-up barrel. Made completely of stainless steel (lower receiver polished); magazine tube in buttstock holds 7 rounds. Double ejectors, double safety system. Comes with fitted leather case. Imported from Italy by Incor Inc.
Price: From $7,100.00

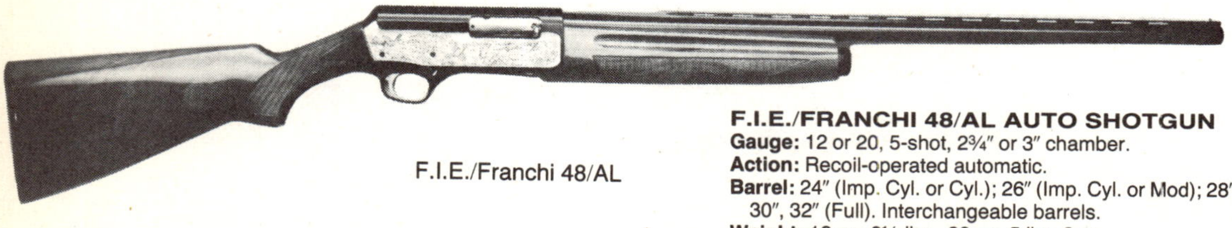

BROWNING A-500 AUTO SHOTGUN
Gauge: 12 only, 3" chamber.
Barrel: 24" Buck Special, 26", 28", 30" with Invector choke tubes.
Weight: 7 lbs., 7 oz. (30" barrel). **Length:** 49½" over-all (30" bbl.).
Stock: 14¼" x 1½" x 2½"; select walnut with gloss finish; checkered p.g. and fore-end; black vent. recoil pad.
Sights: Metal bead front.
Features: Uses a short-recoil action with four-lug rotary bolt and composite and coil spring buffering system. Shoots all loads without adjustment. Has a magazine cut-off, Invector chokes. Introduced 1987. Imported from Belgium by Browning.
Price: $559.95
Price: Extra Invector and Back Special barrels.................. $199.95

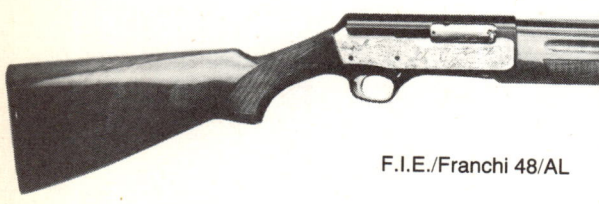
F.I.E./Franchi 48/AL

F.I.E./FRANCHI 48/AL AUTO SHOTGUN
Gauge: 12 or 20, 5-shot, 2¾" or 3" chamber.
Action: Recoil-operated automatic.
Barrel: 24" (Imp. Cyl. or Cyl.); 26" (Imp. Cyl. or Mod); 28" (Skeet, Mod. or Full); 30", 32" (Full). Interchangeable barrels.
Weight: 12 ga. 6¼ lbs., 20 ga. 5 lbs. 2 oz.
Stock: Epoxy-finished walnut, with cut-checkered pistol grip and fore-end.
Features: Chrome-lined bbl., easy takedown, 3-round plug provided. Ventilated rib barrel. Imported from Italy by F.I.E.
Price: Vent. rib 12, 20 .... $454.95
Price: Hunter model (engraved) $489.95
Price: 12 ga. Magnum...................................... $489.95
Price: Extra barrel $179.95

F.I.E./Franchi Slug Gun
Same as Standard automatic except 22" Cylinder bored plain barrel, adj. rifle-type sights.
Price: 12 or 20 ga., standard $454.95
Price: As above, Hunter grade $489.95
Price: Extra barrel $179.95

SHOTGUNS—AUTOLOADERS

F.I.E/Franchi PG-80

F.I.E./FRANCHI PRESTIGE, ELITE SHOTGUNS
Gauge: 12, 2¾", or 3" chamber.
Barrel: 24" (Slug), 26" (Imp. Cyl.), 26", 28" (Mod.), 28" (Full), 30", 32" (3" Full).
Weight: 7 lbs., 6 oz. **Length:** 50" over-all.
Stock: Checkered, oil finished European walnut.
Features: Gas-operated action. Prestige model has plain blued receiver, Elite has engraved receiver. Both models have 7mm-wide vent. rib. Gas piston is stainless steel. Introduced 1985. Imported from Italy by F.I.E. Corp.
Price: Prestige $489.95
Price: Elite $539.95
Price: Extra barrels $179.95

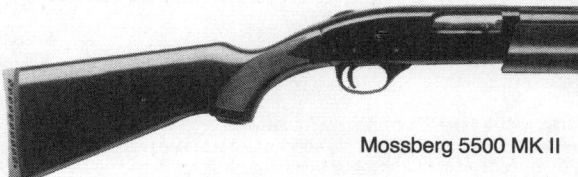
Mossberg 5500 MK II

MOSSBERG MODEL 5500 MKII AUTO SHOTGUN
Gauge: 12, 2¾" chamber.
Barrel: 28" (ACCU-CHOKE Full, Mod., Imp. Cyl. tubes).
Weight: 7½ lbs. **Length:** 48" over-all.
Stock: 14"x1½"x2½". Walnut-stained hardwood with checkered grip, fore-end; recoil pad.
Sights: White front bead, brass mid-bead.
Features: Twin extractors, ambidextrous thumb safety; interchangeable barrels accept choke tubes for steel shot. Extra 3" chamber ACCU-CHOKE barrels available. Announced 1988.
Price: About $294.95

Remington 11-87

REMINGTON MODEL 11-87 PREMIER SHOTGUN
Gauge: 12 ga., 3" chamber.
Barrel: 26", 28", 30" REM Choke tubes.
Weight: About 8¼ lbs. **Length:** 46" over-all (26" bbl.).
Stock: Walnut with satin finish; cut checkering; solid brown butt pad; no white spacers.
Sights: Bradley-type white-faced front, metal bead middle.
Features: Pressure compensating gas system allows shooting 2¾" or 3" loads interchangeably with no adjustments. Stainless magazine tube; redesigned feed latch, barrel support ring on operating bars; pinned fore-end. Introduced 1987.
Price: $527.00
Price: Left hand $573.00

Remington Model 11-87 Special Purpose Deer Gun
Similar to the 11-87 Special Purpose Magnum except has 21" barrel with rifle sights and fixed Imp. Cyl. slug choke. Gas system set to handle all 2¾" and 3" slug, buckshot, high velocity field and magnum loads. Not designed to function with light 2¾" field loads. Introduced 1987.
Price: $499.00

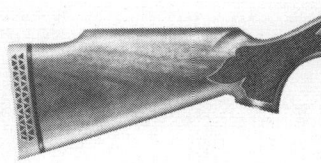
Remington 11-87 Trap

Remington Model 11-87 Premier Trap
Similar to 11-87 Premier except trap dimension stock with straight or Monte Carlo comb; select walnut with satin finish and Tournament-grade cut checkering; 30" barrel with Trap Full or REM Chokes (Trap Full, Trap Extra Full, Trap Super Full). Gas system set for 2¾" shells only. Introduced 1987.
Price: With straight stock, REM choke $580.00
Price: As above, Trap Full choke $567.00
Price: With Monte Carlo stock $593.00
Price: As above, Trap Full choke $580.00

Remington Model 11-87 Premier Skeet
Similar to 11-87 Premier except Skeet dimension stock with cut checkering, satin finish, two-piece buttplate; 26" barrel with Skeet or REM Chokes (Skeet, Imp. Skeet). Gas system set for 2¾" shells only. Introduced 1987.
Price: $573.00
Price: With Skeet choke $560.00

Remington Model 11-87 Special Purpose Magnum
Similar to the 11-87 Premier except has dull stock finish, Parkerized exposed metal surfaces. Bolt and carrier have dull blackened coloring. Comes with 26" or 30" barrel with Rem Chokes, padded Cordura nylon sling and q.d. swivels. Introduced 1987.
Price: $525.00

Remington Model 1100

REMINGTON MODEL 1100 AUTO
Gauge: 20, 28, 410.
Barrel: 25" (Full, Mod.), 26", 28", REM Chokes.
Weight: 7½ lbs.
Stock: 14"x1½"x2½" American walnut, checkered p.g. and fore-end.
Features: Quickly interchangeable barrels. Matted receiver top with scroll work on both sides of receiver. Cross-bolt safety.
Price: With REM chokes about $533.00

CAUTION: PRICES CHANGE. CHECK AT GUNSHOP.

SHOTGUNS—AUTOLOADERS

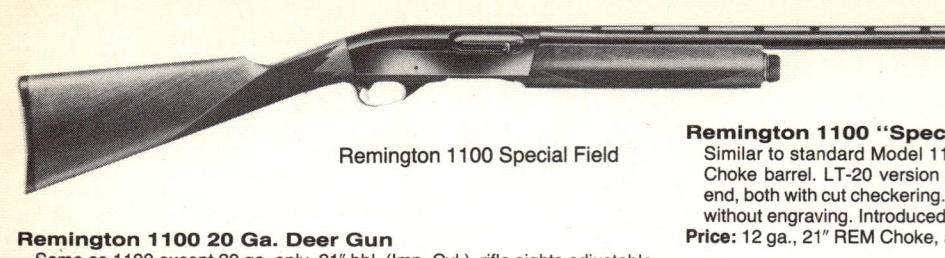
Remington 1100 Special Field

Remington 1100 20 Ga. Deer Gun
Same as 1100 except 20 ga. only, 21" bbl. (Imp. Cyl.), rifle sights adjustable for w. and e.; recoil pad with white spacer. Weight 7¼ lbs.
Price: About $480.00

Remington 1100D Tournament Auto
Same as 1100 Standard except vent. rib, better wood, more extensive engraving.
Price: About $2,291.00

Remington 1100F Premier Auto
Same as 1100D except select wood, better engraving.
Price: About $4,720.00
Price: With gold inlay, about $7,079.00

SKB MODEL 1300 AUTO SHOTGUN
Gauge: 12, 2¾" or 3", 20, 3".
Barrel: 22" (Slug), 26", 28" (Inter Choke tubes).
Weight: 6½ to 7¼ lbs. Length: 48¼" over-all (28" barrel).
Stock: 14½"x1½"x2½". Walnut, with hand checkered grip and fore-end.
Sights: Metal bead front.
Features: Gas operated with Universal Automatic System. Blued receiver. Magazine cut-off system. Introduced 1988. Imported from Japan by Ernie Simmons Ent.
Price: Field $495.00
Price: 1300 Slug $499.00

TRADEWINDS H-170 AUTO SHOTGUN
Gauge: 12 only, 2¾" chamber.
Action: Recoil-operated automatic.
Barrel: 26", 28" (Mod.) and 28" (Full), chrome lined.
Weight: 7 lbs.
Stock: Select European walnut stock, p.g. and fore-end hand checkered.
Features: Light alloy receiver, 5-shot tubular magazine, ventilated rib. Imported from Italy by Tradewinds.
Price: $395.00

Remington 1100 "Special Field"
Similar to standard Model 1100 except 12 ga. only, comes with 21" REM Choke barrel. LT-20 version 6½ lbs.; has straight-grip stock, shorter fore-end, both with cut checkering. Comes with vent rib only; matte finish receiver without engraving. Introduced 1983.
Price: 12 ga., 21" REM Choke, about $520.00

Remington 1100 LT-20 and Small Gauge
Same as 1100 except 20 and 28 ga. 2¾" (5-shot). 45½" over-all. Available in 25" bbl. (Full, Mod., or Imp. Cyl.) only.
Price: With vent rib, about $525.00
Price: 3" Magnum $533.00

Remington 1100 Tournament Skeet
Same as the 1100 except 26" bbl., special Skeet boring, vent. rib (high rib on LT-20), ivory bead front and metal bead middle sights. 14"×1½"×2½" stock. 20, 28, 410 ga. Wgt. 7½ lbs., cut checkering, walnut, new receiver scroll.
Price: Tournament Skeet (28, 410), about $589.00
Price: Tournament Skeet (20), about $589.00

SKB Model 1900 Auto Shotgun
Similar to the Model 1300 except has engraved bright-finish receiver, grip cap, gold plated trigger. Introduced 1988.
Price: Field $550.00
Price: Slug gun (22" barrel, rifle sights) $550.00
Price: Deluxe Trap (2¾" chamber, 30" barrel with Inter Choke tubes, Monte Carlo stock) $575.00

SKB Model 1900 Trap
Similar to the Model 1900 Field except in 12 gauge only (2¾" chamber), 30" barrel with Inter Choke tubes and 9.5mm wide rib. Introduced 1988.
Price: $575.00

SKB Model 3000 Auto Shotgun
Similar to the Model 1900 except has more elaborate engraving, initial plate in buttstock.
Price: Field $585.00
Price: Trap $595.00

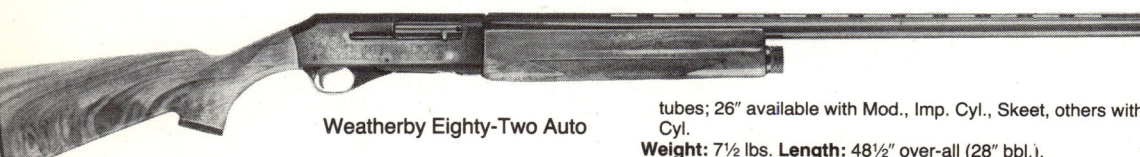
Weatherby Eighty-Two Auto

WEATHERBY EIGHTY-TWO AUTO
Gauge: 12 only, 2¾" and 3" chamber.
Barrel: 22" Slug (with sights), 26", 28", 30" with IMC (Integral Multi-Choke) tubes; 26" available with Mod., Imp. Cyl., Skeet, others with Full, Mod., Imp. Cyl.
Weight: 7½ lbs. Length: 48½" over-all (28" bbl.).
Stock: Walnut, handcheckered p.g. and fore-end, rubber recoil pad.
Features: Gas-operated autoloader with "Floating Piston." Cross-bolt safety, fluted bolt, gold plated trigger. Each gun comes with three flush fitting IMC choke tubes. Imported from Japan by Weatherby. Introduced 1982.
Price: $555.00
Price: Extra interchangeable barrel $229.00
Price: Extra IMC choke tubes $16.00

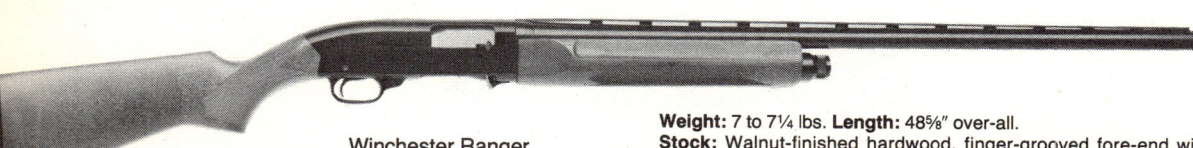
Winchester Ranger

WINCHESTER RANGER AUTO SHOTGUN
Gauge: 12 and 20, 2¾" chamber.
Barrel: 28" vent. rib with Winchoke tubes (Imp. Cyl., Mod., Full), or 28" plain barrel (Mod.).
Weight: 7 to 7¼ lbs. Length: 48⅝" over-all.
Stock: Walnut-finished hardwood, finger-grooved fore-end with deep cut checkering.
Sights: Metal bead front.
Features: Cross-bolt safety, front-locking rotating bolt, black serrated buttplate, gas-operated action. Made under license by U.S. Repeating Arms. Co.
Price: Vent. rib with Winchoke, about $291.00
Price: Deer barrel combo, about $331.00
Price: Deer gun, about $288.00

SHOTGUNS—SLIDE ACTIONS

Includes a wide variety of sporting guns and guns suitable for competitive shooting.

ARMSPORT 2755 PUMP SHOTGUN
Gauge: 12, 3" chamber.
Barrel: 28" (Mod.), 30" (Full).
Weight: 7 lbs.
Stock: European walnut.
Features: Ventilated rib; rubber recoil pad; polished blue finish. Introduced 1986. Imported from Italy by Armsport.
Price: Fixed chokes.. $395.00
Price: 28", 30", choke tubes... $465.00
Price: Police model with 20" (Imp. Cyl.), black receiver........... $375.00

ARMSCOR MODEL 30 PUMP SHOTGUN
Gauge: 12, 5-shot magazine.
Barrel: 28" (Mod.), 30" (Full).
Weight: 7.3 lbs. **Length:** 47" over-all. (28").
Stock: Plain mahogany.
Sights: Metal bead front.
Features: Double action bars; blue finish; grooved fore-end. Introduced 1987. Imported from the Philippines by Armscor.
Price: About... $199.95

Browning Model 12

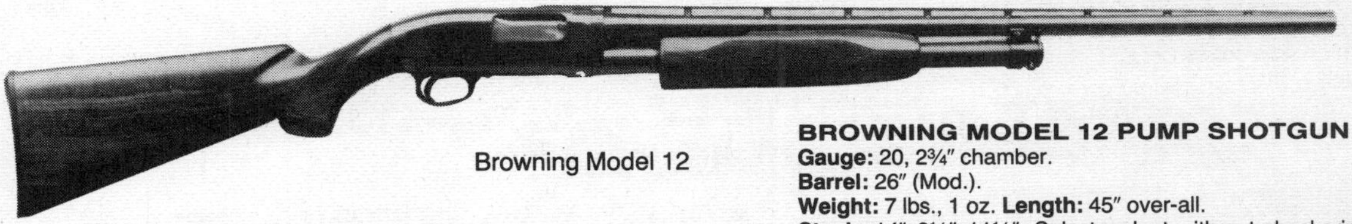

BRI "SPECIAL" RIFLED PUMP SHOTGUN
Gauge: 12, 3" chamber.
Barrel: 24" (Cyl.) rifled.
Weight: 7½ lbs. **Length:** 44" over-all.
Stock: Walnut with high straight comb. Rubber recoil pad.
Sights: None. Comes with scope mount on barrel.
Features: Uses Mossberg Model 500 Trophy Slugster action; double slide bars, twin extractors, dual shell latches; top receiver safety. From Ballistic Research Industries. Introduced 1988.
Price: About... $645.00

BROWNING MODEL 12 PUMP SHOTGUN
Gauge: 20, 2¾" chamber.
Barrel: 26" (Mod.).
Weight: 7 lbs., 1 oz. **Length:** 45" over-all.
Stock: 14"x2½"x1½". Select walnut with cut checkering, semi-gloss finish; Grade V has high-grade walnut.
Features: Reproduction of the Winchester Model 12. Has high post floating rib with grooved sighting plane; cross-bolt safety in trigger guard; polished blue finish. Limited to 8,500 Grade I and 4,000 Grade V guns. Introduced 1988. Imported from Japan by Browning.
Price: Grade I... $699.95
Price: Grade V.. $1,100.00

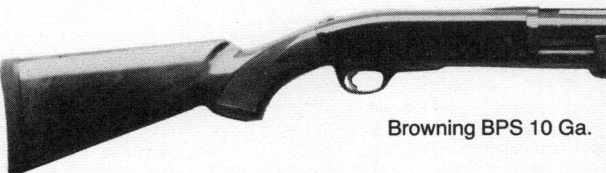
Browning BPS 10 Ga.

Browning BPS Pump Shotgun (Ladies and Youth Model)
Same as BPS Upland Special except 20 ga. only, 22" Invector barrel, stock has pistol grip with recoil pad. Length of pull is 13¼". Introduced 1986.
Price:.. $433.50

Browning BPS "Stalker" Pump Shotgun
Same gun as the standard BPS except all exposed metal parts have a matte blued finish and the stock has a durable black finish with a black recoil pad. Available in 12 ga. with 3" chamber, 22", 28", 30" barrel with Invector choke system. Introduced 1987.
Price:.. $433.50

BROWNING BPS PUMP SHOTGUN
Gauge: 10, 3½" chamber; 12 or 20 gauge, 3" chamber (2¾" in target guns), 5-shot magazine.
Barrel: 10 ga.—24" Buck Special, 28", 30", 32" Invector; 22", 24", 26", 28", 30", 32" (Imp. Cyl., Mod. or Full). Also available with Invector choke tubes, 12 or 20 ga.; Upland Special has 22" barrel with Invector tubes.
Weight: 7 lbs. 8 oz. (28" barrel). **Length:** 48¾" over-all (28" barrel).
Stock: 14¼"x1½"x2½". Select walnut, semi-beavertail fore-end, full p.g. stock.
Features: Bottom feeding and ejection, receiver top safety, high post vent. rib. Double action bars eliminate binding. Vent. rib barrels only. Introduced 1977. Imported from Japan by Browning.
Price: Grade I Hunting, Upland Special, Invector................. $433.50
Price: Extra Invector barrel...................................... $185.95
Price: Buck Special barrel with rifle sights....................... $191.95
Price: Grade I Hunting, 10 ga..................................... $508.50
Price: Extra 10 ga. Invector barrel................................ $218.95
Price: Extra Buck Special barrel................................. $224.95

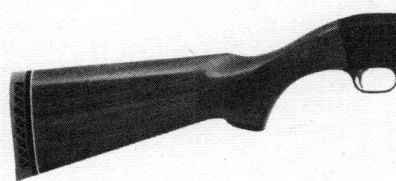
Ithaca 87 Supreme

ITHACA MODEL 87 DEERSLAYER SHOTGUN
Gauge: 12, 20, 3" chamber.
Barrel: 20", 25" (Special Bore).
Weight: 6 to 6¾ lbs.
Stock: 14"x1½"x2¼". American walnut. Checkered p.g. and slide handle.
Sights: Raybar blade front on ramp, rear adjustable for windage and elevation, and grooved for scope mounting.
Features: Bored for slug shooting. Bottom ejection, cross-bolt safety. Reintroduced 1988. From Ithaca Acquisition Corp.
Price:.. $377.00
Price: Ultralight Deerslayer (20 ga. only, 2¾", 5 lbs.)............ $412.00
Price: Deluxe Combo (12 and 20 ga. barrels)..................... $472.00

ITHACA MODEL 87 SUPREME PUMP SHOTGUN
Gauge: 12, 20, 3" chamber, 5-shot magazine.
Barrel: 26" (Imp. Cyl., Mod., Full), 28" (Mod.), 30" (Full). Vent. rib.
Weight: 6¾ to 7 lbs.
Stock: 14"x1½"x2¼". Full fancy-grade walnut, checkered p.g. and slide handle.
Sights: Raybar front.
Features: Bottom ejection, cross-bolt safety. Polished and blued engraved receiver. Reintroduced 1988. From Ithaca Acquisition Corp.
Price:.. $831.00
Price: M87 Camo Vent (28", Mod. choke tube, camouflage finish)... $472.00

Ithaca Deerslayer II Rifled Shotgun
Similar to the Deerslayer except has rifled 25" barrel and unchecked American walnut stock and fore-end. Monte Carlo comb. Solid frame construction. Introduced 1988.
Price:.. $472.00

CAUTION: PRICES CHANGE. CHECK AT GUNSHOP.

SHOTGUNS—SLIDE ACTIONS

Ithaca Model 87 Ultralight Pump Shotgun
Similar to the Model 87 Supreme except the receiver is made of aircraft-quality aluminum. Available in 12 ga., 2¾" chamber or 20 ga., 2¾" chamber, 25" (Mod.) with choke tube. Weight is 5 lbs. (20 ga.), 6 lbs. (12 ga.). Reintroduced 1988.
Price: **$430.00**

Ithaca Model 87 Deluxe Pump Shotgun
Similar to the Model 87 Supreme Vent Rib except comes with choke tubes in 25", 26", 28" (Mod.), 30" (Full). Standard-grade walnut.
Price: **$395.00**

Mossberg Model 835

Weight: 7¾ lbs. **Length:** 48½" over-all.
Stock: 14"x1½"x2½". Walnut-stained hardwood or camo synthetic; both have recoil pad.
Sights: White bead front, brass mid-bead.
Features: Backbored barrel to reduce recoil, improve patterns. Ambidextrous thumb safety, twin extractors, dual slide bars. Announced 1988.
Price: About **$399.95**

MOSSBERG MODEL 835 ULTI-MAG PUMP
Gauge: 12, 3½" chamber.
Barrel: 28", ACCU-MAG choke tubes.

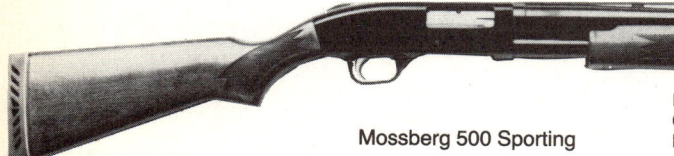
Mossberg 500 Sporting

MOSSBERG MODEL 500 SPORTING PUMP
Gauge: 12, 20, 410, 3" chamber.
Barrel: 18½" to 30" with ACCU-CHOKE tubes, plain or vent. rib; ACCU-STEEL tubes for steel shot.
Weight: 6¼ lbs. (410), 7¼ lbs. (12). **Length:** 48" over-all (28" barrel).
Stock: 14"x1½"x2½". Walnut-stained hardwood. Checkered grip and fore-end.
Sights: White bead front, brass mid-bead.
Features: Ambidextrous thumb safety, twin extractors, disconnecting safety, dual action bars. From Mossberg.
Price: From about **$247.95**
Price: Sporting Combos (field barrel and Slugster barrel), from **$278.95**

MOSSBERG MODEL 500 TROPHY SLUGSTER
Gauge: 12, 3" chamber.
Barrel: 24", smooth or rifled bore. Plain (no rib).
Weight: 7¼ lbs. **Length:** 44" overall.
Stock: 14" pull, 1⅜" drop at heel. Walnut-stained hardwood; high comb design with recoil pad and q.d. swivel studs.
Features: Ambidextrous thumb safety, twin extractors, dual slide bars. Comes with scope mount. Introduced 1988.
Price: Smoothbore, about **$289.95**
Price: Rifled bore, about **$307.95**

Mossberg Model 500 Camo Pump
Same as the Model 500 Sporting Pump except entire gun is covered with special camouflage finish. Available with synthetic field or Speedfeed stock. Receiver drilled and tapped for scope mounting. Comes with q.d. swivel studs, swivels, camouflage sling. In 12 ga. only.
Price: From about **$289.95**
Price: Camo Combo (as above with extra Slugster barrel), from about **$334.95**

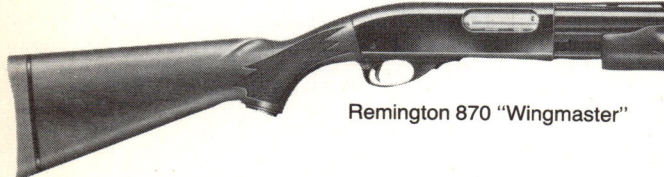
Remington 870 "Wingmaster"

REMINGTON MODEL 870 WINGMASTER
Gauge: 12, 3" chamber.
Barrel: 26", 28", 30" (REM Chokes).
Weight: 7¼ lbs. **Length:** 46½" over-all (26" bbl.).
Stock: 14"x2½"x1". American walnut with satin finish, cut checkered p.g. and fore-end. Rubber butt pad.
Sights: Ivory bead front, metal mid-bead.
Features: Double action bars; cross-bolt safety; blue finish. Available in right- or left-hand style. Introduced 1986.
Price: **$429.00**
Price: Left hand **$472.00**
Price: Brushmaster Deer Gun (rifle sights, 20" bbl., fixed choke) **$381.00**
Price: Deer Gun, left hand **$423.00**
Price: 20 ga., vent. rib, 26", 28" (REM Choke) **$427.00**
Price: As above, Youth Gun (21" REM Choke, 13" stock) **$417.00**

Remington Model 870 Brushmaster Deluxe
Carbine version of the M870 with 20" bbl. (Imp. Cyl.) for rifled slugs. 40½" over-all, wgt. 6½ lbs. Recoil pad. Adj. rear, ramp front sights, 12 or 20 ga. Deluxe.
Price: Brushmaster 12 ga., about **$381.00**
Price: As above, 20 ga. **$365.00**

Remington Model 870 Express
Similar to the 870 Wingmaster except has a walnut-toned, hardwood stock with solid, black recoil pad and pressed checkering on grip and fore-end. Outside metal surfaces have a black oxide finish. Comes only with 28" vent rib barrel with a Mod. REM Choke tube. Introduced 1987.
Price: **$223.00**
Price: Express Combo (with extra 20" Deer barrel) **$320.00**

Remington Model 11-87 Special Purpose Magnum
Similar to the 11-87 Premier except has dull stock finish, Parkerized exposed metal surfaces. Bolt and carrier have dull blackened coloring. Comes with 26" or 30" barrel with Rem Chokes, padded Cordura nylon sling and q.d. swivels. Introduced 1987.
Price: **$525.00**

Remington 870 High Grades
Same as 870 except better walnut, hand checkering. Engraved receiver and bbl. Vent. rib. Stock dimensions to order.
Price: 870D, about **$2,291.00**
Price: 870F, about **$4,720.00**
Price: 870F with gold inlay, about **$7,079.00**

Remington 870 Small Gauges
Exact copies of the large ga. Model 870, except that guns are offered in 28 and 410 ga. 25" barrel (Full, Mod., Imp. Cyl.). D and F grade prices same as large ga. M870 prices.
Price: With vent. rib barrel, about **$427.00**

SHOTGUNS—SLIDE ACTIONS

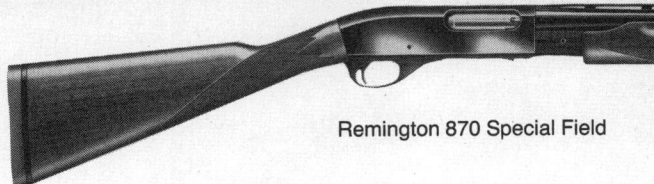
Remington 870 Special Field

Remington 870 "Special Purpose" Magnum
Similar to the Model 870 except chambered only for 12-ga., 3" shells, vent. rib. 26" or 30" REM Choke barrel. All exposed metal surfaces are finished in dull, non-reflective black. Wood has an oil finish. Comes with padded Cordura 2" wide sling, quick-detachable swivels. Chrome-lined bores. Dark recoil pad. Introduced 1985.
Price: About $420.00

Remington Model 870 "Special Field"
Similar to the standard Model 870 except comes with 21" barrel only, 3" chamber, choked Imp. Cyl., Mod., Full and REM Choke; 12 ga. weighs 6¾ lbs., Ltwt. 20 weighs 6 lbs.; has straight-grip stock, shorter fore-end, both with cut checkering. Vent. rib barrel only. Introduced 1984.
Price: 12 or 20 ga., REM Choke, about $429.00

Remington 870 TC Trap
Same as the M870 except 12 ga. only, 30" fixed Full or REM Choke, vent. rib bbl., ivory front and white metal middle beads. Special sear, hammer and trigger assy. 14⅜"×1½"×1⅞" stock with recoil pad. Hand fitted action and parts. Wgt. 8 lbs.
Price: Model 870TC Trap, REM choke, about $547.00
Price: As above, fixed choke $533.00
Price: TC Trap with Monte Carlo stock, about $560.00
Price: As above, fixed choke $547.00

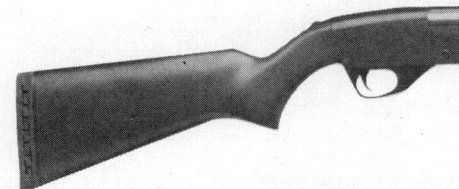
Stevens 67

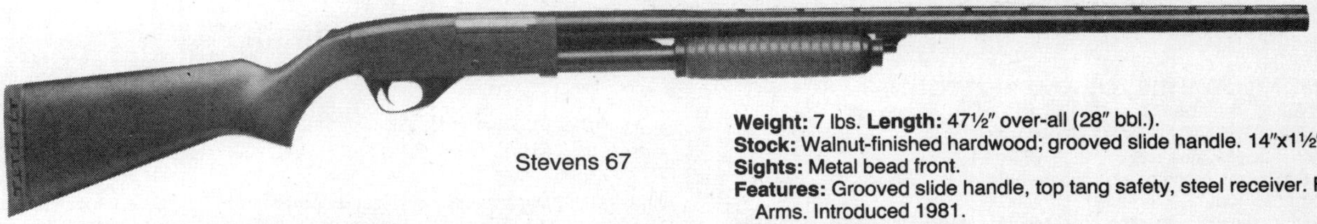

STEVENS MODEL 67 PUMP SHOTGUN
Gauge: 12, 20 (2¾" & 3").
Barrel: 28" (Mod.).
Weight: 7 lbs. **Length:** 47½" over-all (28" bbl.).
Stock: Walnut-finished hardwood; grooved slide handle. 14"x1½"x2½".
Sights: Metal bead front.
Features: Grooved slide handle, top tang safety, steel receiver. From Savage Arms. Introduced 1981.
Price: Model 67L Lobo $159.00
Price: Model 67 Slug Gun (21" barrel, rifle sights) $184.00
Price: Model 67-VRT (as above with vent. rib) $199.00

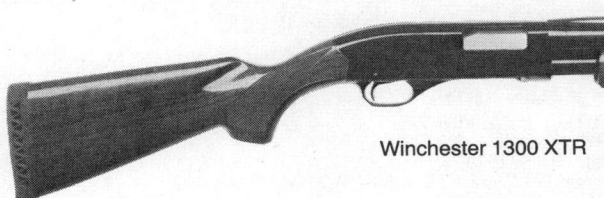
Winchester 1300 XTR

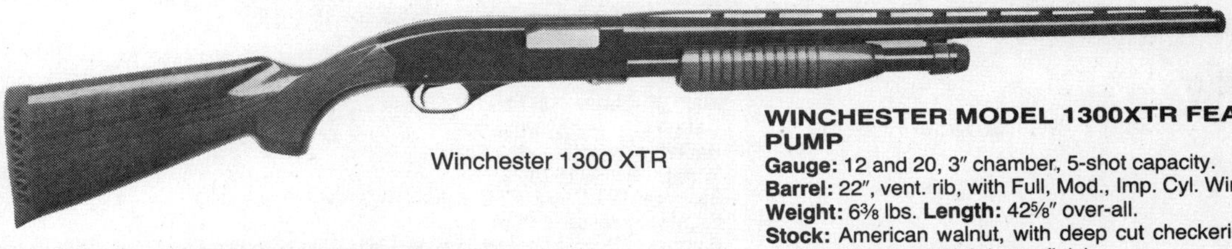

Winchester Model 1300 Rifled Deer Gun
Same as the Model 1300 except has rifled 22" barrel, Win-Tuff laminated stock or walnut, rifle-type sights. Introduced 1988.
Price: Walnut stock $367.00
Price: Laminated stock $378.00

Winchester Model 1300 Turkey
Similar to the standard Model 1300 Featherweight except 12 ga. only, 30" barrel with Mod., Full and Extra Full Winchoke tubes, matte finish wood and metal, and comes with recoil pad, Cordura sling and swivels.
Price: About $338.00
Price: With Win-Cam green-shaded laminated stock, about $349.00
Price: National Wild Turkey Federation edition $368.00

WINCHESTER RANGER PUMP GUN
Gauge: 12 or 20, 3" chamber, 4-shot magazine.
Barrel: 28" vent rib with Full, Mod., Imp. Cyl. Winchoke tubes.
Weight: 7 to 7¼ lbs. **Length:** 48⅝" to 50⅝" over-all.
Stock: Walnut finished hardwood with ribbed fore-end.
Sights: Metal bead front.
Features: Cross-bolt safety, black rubber butt pad, twin action slide bars, front-locking rotating bolt. Made under license by U.S. Repeating Arms Co.
Price: Vent. rib barrel, Winchoke, about $255.00

WINCHESTER MODEL 1300XTR FEATHERWEIGHT PUMP
Gauge: 12 and 20, 3" chamber, 5-shot capacity.
Barrel: 22", vent. rib, with Full, Mod., Imp. Cyl. Winchoke tubes.
Weight: 6⅜ lbs. **Length:** 42⅝" over-all.
Stock: American walnut, with deep cut checkering on pistol grip, traditional ribbed fore-end; high luster finish.
Sights: Metal bead front.
Features: Twin action slide bars; front-locking rotating bolt; roll-engraved receiver; blued, highly polished metal; cross-bolt safety with red indicator. Introduced 1984.
Price: About $324.00

Winchester 1300 Waterfowl Pump
Similar to the 1300 Featherweight except in 3" 12 ga. only, 30" vent. rib barrel with Winchoke system; stock and fore-end of walnut with low-luster finish. All metal surfaces have special non-glare matte finish. Introduced 1985.
Price: About $338.00
Price: With laminated stock $349.00
Price: Combo Pac with extra 22" barrel $425.00

Winchester Ranger Pump Gun Combination
Similar to the standard Ranger except comes with two barrels: 22" (Cyl.) deer barrel with rifle-type sights and an interchangeable 28" vent. rib Winchoke barrel with Full, Mod. and Imp. Cyl. choke tubes. Available in 12 and 20 gauge 3" only, with recoil pad. Introduced 1983.
Price: With two barrels, about $300.00

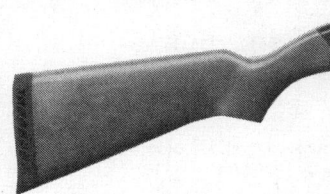
Winchester Ranger

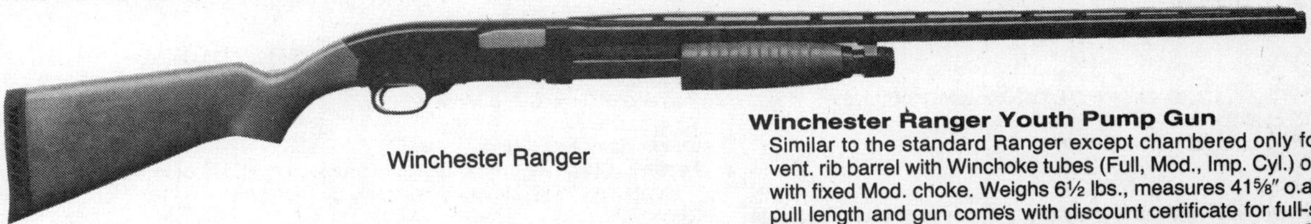

Winchester Ranger Youth Pump Gun
Similar to the standard Ranger except chambered only for 3" 20 ga., 22" vent. rib barrel with Winchoke tubes (Full, Mod., Imp. Cyl.) or 22" plain barrel with fixed Mod. choke. Weighs 6½ lbs., measures 41⅝" o.a.l. Stock has 13" pull length and gun comes with discount certificate for full-size stock. Introduced 1983. Made under license by U.S. Repeating Arms Co.
Price: Vent. rib barrel, Winchoke, about $268.00
Price: Plain barrel, Mod. choke, about $230.00

SHOTGUNS—OVER-UNDERS

Includes a variety of game guns and guns for competitive shooting.

American Arms Silver

AMERICAN ARMS SILVER I O/U
Gauge: 12, 20, 28, 410, 3" chamber (28 has 2¾")
Barrel: 26" (Imp. Cyl. & Mod., all gauges), 28" (Mod. & Full, 12, 20).
Weight: About 6¾ lbs.
Stock: 14⅛"x1⅜"x2⅜". Checkered walnut.
Sights: Metal bead front.
Features: Boxlock action with scroll engraving, silver finish. Chrome-lined barrels. Manual safety. Rubber recoil pad. Introduced 1987. Imported by American Arms, Inc.
Price: 12 or 20 gauge $459.00
Price: 28 or 410 . . . . $585.00

American Arms Silver II Shotgun
Similar to the Silver I except in 12 or 20 gauge only with 26" (12 and 20) or 28" (12 ga. only), choke tubes, automatic selective ejectors, single selective trigger. Weight is 6 lbs., 15 oz. for 12 gauge, 6 lbs., 10 oz. in 20 gauge.
Price: $620.00

American Arms Bristol

AMERICAN ARMS BRISTOL O/U SHOTGUN
Gauge: 12 or 20, 3" chamber.
Barrel: 26" (12 and 20), 28" (12 only). Choke tubes.
Weight: 7 lbs., 1 oz. (12 ga.), 6 lbs., 12 oz. (20 ga.).
Stock: 14⅛"x1⅜"x2⅜". Hand checkered walnut with oil finish.
Sights: Metal bead front.
Features: Boxlock action with dummy sideplates and silver finish, scroll engraving; single selective, gold-colored trigger; chrome-lined bores; manual safety; automatic selective ejectors. Imported from Italy by American Arms, Inc. Introduced 1987.
Price: $850.00

American Arms Waterfowl

AMERICAN ARMS WATERFOWL SPECIAL O/Us
Gauge: 10, 3½" chambers.
Barrel: 32": (steel Full & Full).
Weight: 9 lbs., 15 oz.
Stock: 14½"x1⅜"x2⅜". Checkered walnut with cull finish.
Sights: Metal bead front.
Features: Boxlock action with non-reflective sideplates and barrels; chrome-lined barrels; double triggers; extractors; sling swivels. Comes with camouflage sling. Introduced 1988. Imported by American Arms, Inc.
Price: $875.00
Price: 12-ga. Waterfowl Special (as above except in 12 ga., 3½" chamber, 28" with choke tubes, selective ejectors, single selective trigger) $650.00

American Arms Turkey Special
Similar to the Waterfowl Special 10-gauge gun except has 26" barrels with choke tubes. Double triggers, extractors.
Price: $940.00

Armsport 1225

ARMSPORT MODEL 2700 O/U GOOSE GUN
Gauge: 10 ga., 3½" chambers.
Barrel: 27" (Imp. & Mod.), 32" (Full & Full).
Weight: About 9.8 lbs.
Stock: European walnut.
Features: Boss-type action; double triggers; extractors. Introduced 1986. Imported from Italy by Armsport.
Price: $950.00

ARMSPORT 1225/1226 O/U FOLDING SHOTGUN
Gauge: 12, 20, 3" chambers.
Barrel: 26" (Imp. & Mod.), 28" (Mod. & Full).
Weight: 6 lbs.
Stock: European walnut.
Features: Top-break folding action; double triggers; extractors; silvered receiver with light engraving. Introduced 1986. Imported from Italy by Armsport.
Price: $375.00

ARMSPORT MODEL 2700 O/U
Gauge: 12 or 20 ga.
Barrel: 26" (Imp. Cyl. & Mod.); 28" (Mod. & Full); vent. rib.
Weight: 8 lbs.
Stock: European walnut, hand checkered p.g. and fore-end.
Features: Single selective trigger, automatic ejectors, engraved receiver. Imported by Armsport.
Price: M2733/2735 (Boss-type action, 12, 20, extractors) $590.00
Price: M2741/2743 (as above with ejectors) $650.00
Price: M2730/2731 (as above with single trigger, screw-in chokes) . $775.00
Price: M2705 (410 ga., 26" Imp. & Mod., double triggers) $595.00
Price: M2720 (as above with single trigger) $650.00

ARMSPORT 2900 TRI-BARREL SHOTGUN
Gauge: 12, 3" chambers.
Barrel: 28" (Imp. Cyl. & Mod. & Full).
Weight: 7¾ lbs.
Stock: European walnut.
Features: Top-tang barrel selector: double triggers; silvered, engraved frame. Introduced 1986. Imported from Italy by Armsport.
Price: $1,850.00

SHOTGUNS—OVER-UNDERS

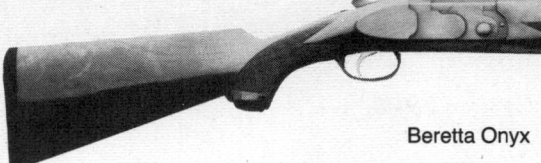

Beretta Onyx

BERETTA MODEL SO5, SO6 SHOTGUNS
Gauge: 12, 2¾" chambers
Barrel: To customer's specs.
Stock: To customer's specs.
Features: SO5—Trap, Skeet and Sporting Clays models available in standard SO5 and SO5 EELL; SO6— SO6 and SO6 EELL are field models made to customer specifications. SO6 has a case-hardened receiver with contour hand engraving. SO6 EELL has hand-engraved receiver in a fine floral or "fine English" pattern, with bas-relief chisel work and gold inlays. SO6 and SO6 EELL are available, at no extra charge, with sidelocks removable by hand. Imported from Italy by Beretta U.S.A.
Price: SO5 Trap, Skeet, Sporting $14,250.00
Price: SO5 EELL Trap, Skeet, Sporting $21,750.00
Price: SO6 Field, Custom Specs $16,125.00
Price: SO6 EELL Field, Custom Specs $24,975.00

BERETTA OVER/UNDER FIELD SHOTGUNS
Gauge: 12, 20, 28, 2¾" and 3" chambers.
Barrels: 26" and 28" (fixed chokes or Mobilchoke tubes).
Stock: Close-grained walnut.
Features: Highly-figured, American walnut stocks and fore-ends, and a unique, weather-resistant finish on barrels. Available in two grades: Golden Onyx has individual game game scenes of flushing pheasant and rising ducks on the receiver; the 686 Onyx bears a gold P. Beretta signature on each side of the receiver. Imported from Italy by Beretta U.S.A.
Price: 686 Onyx $1,035.00
Price: 686 two bbl. Set $1,600.00
Price: 686 Field $925.00
Price: 687L Field $1,300.00
Price: 687 Golden Onyx $1,665.00
Price: 687 EL .... $2,450.00 to $2,520.00
Price: 687 EELL .... $3,500.00 to $3,640.00

Beretta 682 Sporting

BERETTA SPORTING CLAYS SHOTGUNS
Gauge: 12 and 20, 2¾" chambers.
Barrel: 28", Mobilchoke.
Stock: Close-grained walnut.
Sights: Luminous front sight and center bead.
Features: Equipped with Beretta Mobilchoke flush-mounted screw-in choke tube system. Models vary according to grade, from field-grade Beretta 686 Sporting with its floral engraving pattern, to competition-grade Beretta 682 Sporting with its brushed satin finish and adjustable length of pull, to the 687 Sporting with intricately hand-engraved game scenes, fine line, deep-cut checkering. Imported from Italy by Beretta U.S.A. Corp.
Price: 686 Sporting $1,680.00
Price: 682 Sporting $2,100.00
Price: 687 Sporting $2,240.00
Price: 687 Sporting (20-gauge) $2,240.00

BRNO 500 OVER/UNDER SHOTGUN
Gauge: 12, 2¾" chambers.
Barrel: 27½" (Full & Mod.).
Weight: 7 lbs. **Length:** 44½" over-all.
Stock: Walnut, with raised cheekpiece.
Features: Boxlock action with ejectors; double triggers; acid-etched engraving. Imported from Czechoslovakia by Saki International.
Price: $899.00

BERETTA SERIES 682 OVER/UNDERS
Gauge: 12, 2¾" chambers.
Barrel: Skeet—26" and 28"; trap—30" and 32", Imp. Mod. & Full and Mobilchoke; trap mono shotguns—32" and 34" Mobilchoke; trap top single guns—32" and 34" Full and Mobilchoke; trap combo sets—from 30" o/u, 32" unsingle to 32" o/u, 34" top single.
Stock: Close-grained walnut, hand checkered.
Sights: Luminous front sight and center bead.
Features: Trap Monte Carlo stock has deluxe trap recoil pad. Various grades available; contact Beretta U.S.A. for details. Imported from Italy by Beretta U.S.A. Corp.
Price: 682 Skeet $2,030.00
Price: 682 Trap $2,030.00
Price: 682 Trap Mono Shotguns $1,890.00
Price: 682 Trap Top Single Shotguns $1,960.00 to $2,030.00
Price: 682 Trap Combo Sets .... $2,520.00 to $2,800.00

BABY BRETTON OVER/UNDER SHOTGUN
Gauge: 12 or 20, 2¾" chambers.
Barrel: 27½" (Cyl., Imp. Cyl., Mod., Full choke tubes).
Weight: About 5 lbs.
Stock: Walnut, checkered pistol grip and fore-end, oil finish.
Features: Receiver slides open on two guide rods, is locked by a large thumb lever on the right side. Extractors only. Light alloy barrels. Imported from France by Mandall Shooting Supplies.
Price: $895.00
Price: Deluxe (silvered, engraved receiver, double triggers, 12, 16, 20 ga.) $1,295.00

BRNO Super

BRNO SUPER OVER/UNDER SHOTGUN
Gauge: 12, 2¾" or 3" chambers.
Barrel: 27½" (Full & Mod.).
Weight: 7 lbs., 4 oz. (Field). **Length:** 44" over-all.
Stock: Walnut, with raised cheekpiece.
Features: Sidelock action with double safety interceptor sears; double triggers on Field model; automatic selective ejectors; engraved sideplates. Trap and Skeet models available. Imported from Czechoslovakia by Saki International.
Price: $899.00

BRNO CZ 581 OVER/UNDER SHOTGUN
Gauge: 12, 2¾" or 3" chambers.
Barrel: 28" (Full & Mod.).
Weight: 7 lbs., 6 oz. **Length:** 45½" over-all.
Stock: Turkish walnut with raised cheekpiece.
Features: Boxlock action; automatic selective ejectors; automatic safety; sling swivels; vent. rib; double triggers. Imported from Czechoslovakia by Saki International.
Price: $649.00

CAUTION: PRICES CHANGE. CHECK AT GUNSHOP.

SHOTGUNS—OVER-UNDERS

BRNO ZH 301

BRNO ZH 301 OVER/UNDER SHOTGUN
Gauge: 12, 2¾" or 3" chambers.
Barrel: 27½" (Full & Mod.).
Weight: 7 lbs. **Length:** 44½" over-all.
Stock: Walnut.
Features: Boxlock action with acid-etch engraving; double triggers. Imported from Czechoslovakia by Saki International.
Price: $599.00

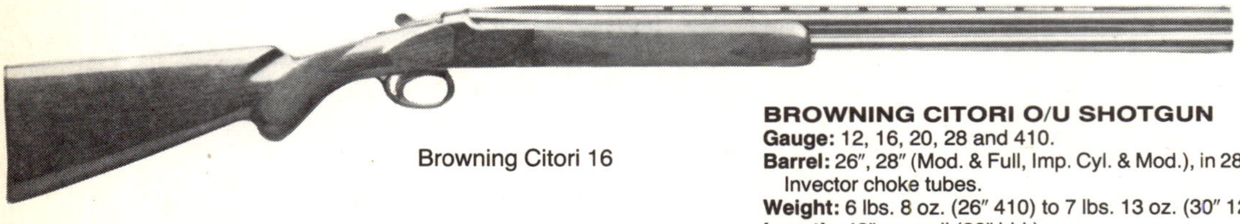

Browning Citori 16

Browning Citori O/U Skeet Models
Similar to standard Citori except 26", 28" (Skeet & Skeet) only; stock dimensions of 14⅜"×1½"×2", fitted with Skeet-style recoil pad; conventional target rib and high post target rib.
Price: Grade I Invector (high post rib)......................... $1,048.00
Price: Grade I, 12 & 20 (high post rib)......................... $1,014.00
Price: Grade I, 28 & 410 (high post rib)....................... $1,060.00
Price: Grade III, 12 and 20 (high post rib).................... $1,410.00
Price: Grade VI, 12 and 20 (high post rib).................... $1,990.00
Price: Four barrel Skeet set—12, 20, 28, 410 barrels, with case, Grade I only $3,397.00
Price: Grade III, four-barrel set (high post rib)............... $3,728.00
Price: Grade VI, four-barrel set (high post rib)............... $4,237.00
Price: Grade I, three-barrel set................................ $2,365.00
Price: Grade III, three-barrel set $2,625.00
Price: Grade VI, three-barrel set $3,255.00

Browning Citori O/U Trap Models
Similar to standard Citori except 12 gauge only; 30", 32" (Full & Full, Imp. Mod. & Full, Mod. & Full), 34" single barrel in Combo Set (Full, Imp. Mod., Mod.), or Invector model; Monte Carlo cheekpiece (14⅜"×1⅜"×1⅜"×2"); fitted with trap-style recoil pad; conventional target rib and high post target rib.
Price: Grade I, Invector high post target rib $1,060.00
Price: Grade III, Invector, high post target rib $1,410.00
Price: Grade VI, Invector, high post target rib $1,990.00

BROWNING CITORI O/U SHOTGUN
Gauge: 12, 16, 20, 28 and 410.
Barrel: 26", 28" (Mod. & Full, Imp. Cyl. & Mod.), in 28 and 410. Also offered with Invector choke tubes.
Weight: 6 lbs. 8 oz. (26" 410) to 7 lbs. 13 oz. (30" 12-ga.).
Length: 43" over-all (26" bbl.).
Stock: Dense walnut, hand checkered, full p.g., beavertail fore-end. Field-type recoil pad on 12 ga. field guns and trap and Skeet models.
Sights: Medium raised beads, German nickel silver.
Features: Barrel selector integral with safety, auto ejectors, three-piece takedown. Imported from Japan by Browning.
Price: Grade I Hunting, Invector $948.00
Price: Grade III, Invector, 12 and 20 .... $1,282.00
Price: Grade VI, Invector, 12 and 20 .... $1,880.00
Price: Grade I, 28 & 410, fixed chokes $937.00
Price: Grade III, 28 and 410, fixed chokes $1,410.00
Price: Grade VI, 28 and 410, high post rib, fixed chokes $1,990.00
Price: Grade I Lightning, Invector, 12, 16 20................ $958.00
Price: Grade III Lightning, Invector, 12, 16, 20 .... $1,292.00
Price: Grade VI Lightning, Invector, 12, 16, 20 .... $1,890.00

Consult our Directory pages for the location of firms mentioned.

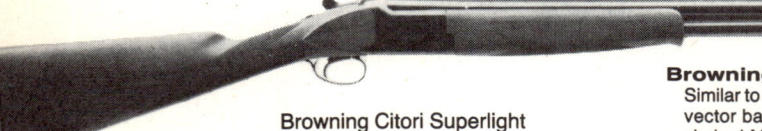

Browning Citori Superlight

Browning Superlight Citori Over/Under
Similar to the standard Citori except available in 12, 20 with 24", 26" or 28" Invector barrels, 28 or 410 with 26" barrels choked Imp. Cyl. & Mod. or 28" choked Mod. & Full. Has straight grip stock, Schnabel fore-end tip. Superlight 12 weighs 6 lbs. 9 oz. (26" barrels); Superlight 20, 5 lbs., 12 oz. (26" barrels). Introduced 1982.
Price: Grade I only, 28 or 410 .... $937.00
Price: Grade III, Invector, 12 or 20 .... $1,282.00
Price: Grade III, 28 or 410 .... $1,410.00
Price: Grade VI, Invector, 12 or 20 .... $1,880.00
Price: Grade VI, 28 or 410 .... $1,990.00
Price: Grade I Invector, 12 or 20............................. $974.00
Price: Grade I Invector, Upland Special (24" bbls.), 12 or 20 .... $974.00

BROWNING OVER/UNDER GOLD CLASSIC
Gauge: 20, 2¾" chambers.
Barrel: 26" (Imp. Cyl. & Mod.).
Weight: 6⅜ lbs.
Stock: 14¼"x1⅝"x2½". Select walnut with straight grip, schnabel fore-end.
Features: Receiver has upland setting of bird dogs, pheasant and quail in inlaid gold on satin gray finish. Stock has fine checkering and decorative carving with oil finish. Introduced 1984. Made in Belgium.
Price: $6,000.00

Browning Limited Edition Waterfowl Superposed
Same specs as the Superposed Gold Classic. Available in 12 ga. only, 28" (Mod. & Full). Limited to 500 guns, the edition number of each gun is inscribed in gold on the bottom of the receiver with "Black Duck" and its scientific name. Sides of receiver have two gold inlayed black ducks, bottom has two, and one on the trigger guard. Receiver is completely engraved and grayed. Stock and fore-end are highly figured dark French walnut with 24 lpi checkering, hand-oiled finish, checkered butt. Comes with form-fitted, velvet-lined, black walnut case. Introduced 1983.
Price: $8,000.00
Price: Similar treatment as above except for the Pintail Duck Issue $7,700.00

SHOTGUNS—OVER-UNDERS

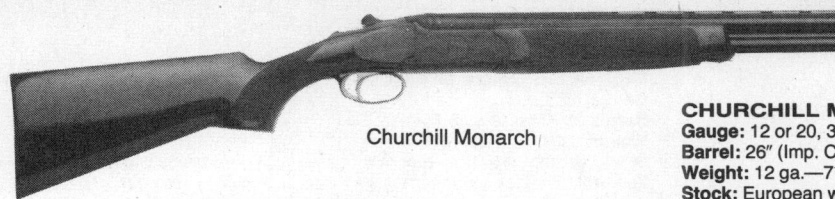
Churchill Monarch

CHURCHILL MONARCH OVER/UNDER SHOTGUNS
Gauge: 12 or 20, 3" chambers.
Barrel: 26" (Imp. Cyl. & Mod.), 28" (Mod. & Full). Chrome lined.
Weight: 12 ga.—7½ lbs, 20 ga.—6½ lbs.
Stock: European walnut with checkered p.g. and fore-end.
Features: Single selective trigger; blued, engraved receiver; vent. rib. Introduced 1986. Imported by Kassnar Imports, Inc.
Price: .... $419.00 to $449.00

Churchill Regent Over/Under Shotguns
Similar to the Windsor Grade except better wood with oil finish, better engraving; available only in 12 or 20 gauge (3" chambers), 27" barrels, with ICT interchangeable choke tubes (Imp. Cyl., Mod., Full). Regent VII has dummy sideplates. Introduced 1984.
Price: Regent VII, 12 or 20 ga. $889.00

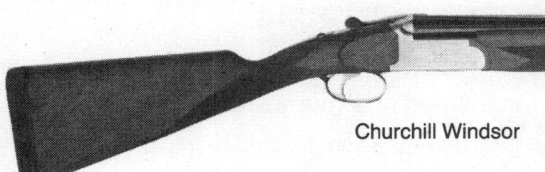
Churchill Windsor

CHURCHILL WINDSOR OVER/UNDER SHOTGUNS
Gauge: 12, 20, 28, 410, 3" chambers.
Barrel: 26" (Skeet & Skeet, Imp. Cyl. & Mod.), 28" (Mod. & Full), 30" (Mod. & Full, Full & Full), 12 ga.; 26" (Skeet & Skeet, Imp. Cyl. & Mod.), 28" (Mod. & Full) 20 ga.; 25", 26" (Imp. Cyl. & Mod), 28" (Mod. & Full), 28 ga.; 24", 26" (Full & Full), 410 ga.; or 27", 30" ICT choke tubes.
Stock: European walnut, checkered pistol grip, oil finish.
Features: Boxlock action with silvered, engraved finish; single selective trigger; automatic ejectors on Windsor IV, extractors only on Windsor III. Also available in Flyweight version with 23", 25" barrels, fixed or ICT chokes, straight-grip stock. Imported from Italy by Kassnar. Introduced 1984.
Price: Windsor III .... $549.00 to $649.00
Price: Windsor IV .... $619.00 to $719.00

Churchill Regent Trap & Skeet
Trap has ventilated side rib, Monte Carlo stock, Churchill recoil pad. Oil finished wood, fine checkering, chrome bores. Weight is 8 lbs. Regent Skeet available in 12 or 20 ga., 26" (Skeet & Skeet); oil finished stock measures 14½"x1½"x2⅜". Both guns have silvered and engraved receivers. Introduced 1984.
Price: Regent Trap (30" Imp. Mod. & Full)................. $869.00
Price: Regent Skeet, 12 or 20 ga. $809.00

CLASSIC MODEL 101 FIELD GRADE I
Gauge: 12 or 20, 3" chambers.
Action: Top lever, break open. Manual safety combined with bbl. selector at top of receiver tang.
Barrel: 25½", 28", interchangeable choke tubes.
Weight: 12 ga. 7 lbs. **Length:** 44⅞" over-all.
Stock: 14½" x 1½" x 2½". Checkered walnut p.g. and fore-end; fluted comb. Straight English or standard.
Features: Single selective adjustable trigger, auto ejectors. Hand engraved blued receiver. Suitable for steel shot. Chrome lined bores and chambers. Comes with hard gun case. Manufactured in and imported from Japan by Classic Doubles.
Price: $2,335.00

Classic 101 Field I

Classic Model 101 Waterfowler
Same as Model 101 Field Grade except in 12 ga. only, 3" chambers, 30" barrels. Comes with four choke tubes: Mod., Imp. Mod., Full, Extra-Full. Non-glare wood finish, matte blued receiver with hand etching and engraving. Introduced 1981. Manufactured in and imported from Japan by Classic Doubles.
Price: $1,865.00

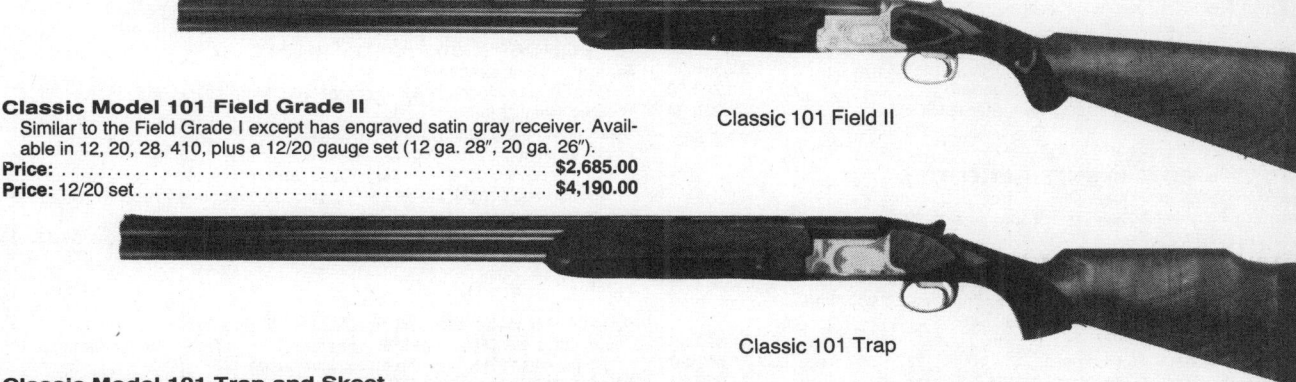
Classic 101 Field II

Classic 101 Trap

Classic Model 101 Field Grade II
Similar to the Field Grade I except has engraved satin gray receiver. Available in 12, 20, 28, 410, plus a 12/20 gauge set (12 ga. 28", 20 ga. 26").
Price: $2,685.00
Price: 12/20 set. $4,190.00

Classic Model 101 Trap and Skeet
Similar to the Model 101 Field Grades except designed for target competition. Barrels have high, tapered vent. rib; barrel vents for Skeet guns, barrel ports for trap guns; Skeet models have mechnical trigger, trap have inertia trigger. Stocks pre-drilled for recoil reducer, and are quick detachable. Standard or Monte Carlo stock. Trap available as o/u, single barrel or Combo.
Price: Trap, from... $2,535.00
Price: Skeet, 12 and 20 .... $2,335.00
Price: Skeet, 410 .... $5,840.00

Classic Model 101 Sporter O/U
Similar to the Field Grade II except designed for Sporting Clays and has different balance than a field gun. Available in 12 ga. only with 28" or 30" barrels with six choke tubes. Top of frame and top lever have matte finish. Frame has silvered finish, light engraving.
Price: $2,425.00
Price: Combo includes both barrel sets $3,610.00

CAUTION: PRICES CHANGE. CHECK AT GUNSHOP.

SHOTGUNS—OVER-UNDERS

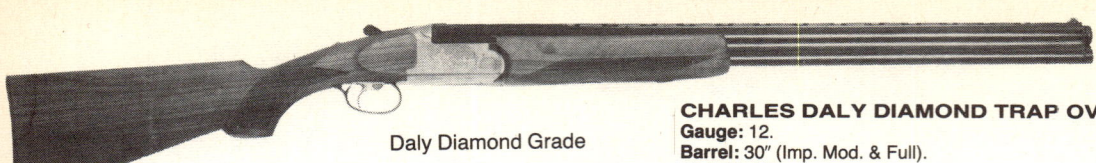

Daly Diamond Grade

CHARLES DALY DIAMOND TRAP OVER/UNDER
Gauge: 12.
Barrel: 30" (Imp. Mod. & Full).
Weight: 7 lbs.
Stock: Select extra-fancy European walnut, oil finish. Monte Carlo comb.
Features: Boxlock action with single selective competition trigger; silvered and engraved receiver; selective automatic ejectors; 22 lpi checkering on grip and fore-end. Imported from Italy by Outdoor Sports Headquarters. Introduced 1984.
Price: $1,050.00

Charles Daly Diamond Skeet Over/Under
Similar to the standard Diamond Trap except has oil-finished Skeet stock, competition vent. rib, target trigger. Available in 12 gauge only, 26" (Skeet & Skeet).
Price: $1,000.00

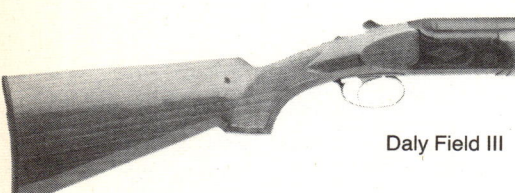

Daly Field III

CHARLES DALY FIELD III OVER/UNDER
Gauge: 12 or 20.
Barrel: 26" (Imp. Cyl. & Mod.), 28", 30" (Full & Mod.); vent. rib.
Weight: About 6¾ lbs.
Stock: Select European walnut, checkered pistol grip and fore-end.
Features: Single selective trigger; extractors only; blued and engraved frame; chrome lined bores. Imported from Italy by Outdoor Sports Headquarters. Introduced 1984.
Price: $450.00

Charles Daly Superior II Over/Under
Similar to the Field III model except single selective trigger; auto ejectors, better wood, silvered receiver, more and better engraving. Same barrel lengths and chokes.
Price: $875.00

F.I.E./MAROCCINI "PRITI" O/U SHOTGUN
Gauge: 12 or 20 ga., 3" chambers.
Barrel: 26" (Imp. Cyl. & Mod.), 28" (Mod. & Full); vent. top and middle ribs.
Weight: 7¾ lbs.
Stock: Walnut, hand checkered. Recoil pad; epoxy finish.
Features: Auto safety; extractors; double triggers; engraved antique silver receiver. Imported from Italy by F.I.E.
Price: $399.95

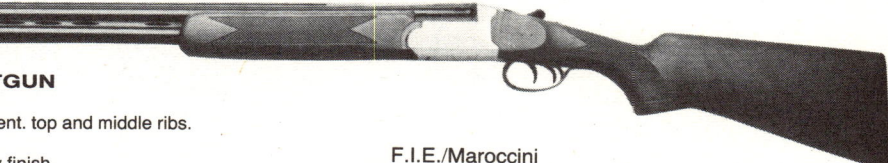

F.I.E./Maroccini

F.I.E./FRANCHI "ALCIONE S" OVER/UNDER
Gauge: 12 ga. only, 3" chambers.
Barrel: 26" (Imp. Cyl. & Mod.), 28" (Mod. & Full).
Weight: 6 lbs. 13 oz.
Stock: French walnut with cut checkered pistol grip and fore-end. Recoil pad; epoxy finish.
Features: Top tang safety, automatic ejectors, single selective trigger. Chrome plated bores. Decorative scroll on silvered receiver. Introduced 1982. Imported from Italy by F.I.E. Corp.
Price: Diamond Grade $724.95

KRIEGHOFF K-80 O/U TRAP SHOTGUN
Gauge: 12, 2¾" chambers.
Barrel: 30", 32" (Imp. Mod. & Full).
Weight: About 8½ lbs.
Stock: Four stock dimensions available; all have palm-swell grips. Checkered walnut.
Features: Satin nickel receiver. Selective mechnical trigger, adjustable for position. Ventilated step rib. Introduced 1980. Imported from West Germany by Krieghoff International, Inc.
Price: Standard grade $4,480.00
Price: K-80 Unsingle (32", 34", Full), Standard $5,350.00
Price: K-80 Top Single (34", Full), Standard $4,745.00
Price: K-80 Combo (two-barrel set), Standard $6,880.00

KRIEGHOFF K-80 PIGEON SHOTGUN
Gauge: 12, 2¾" chambers.
Barrel: 28", 30" standard, 29" optional (Imp. Mod. & Special Full).
Weight: About 8 lbs.
Stock: Four stock dimensions available. Checkered walnut.
Features: Choice of steel or Dural receiver, both with satin gray finish, engraving. Selective mechanical trigger adjustable for position. Ventilated step rib. Free-floating barrels. Comes with hard case. Introduced 1980. Imported from West Germany by Krieghoff International.
Price: Standard grade $4,480.00

KRIEGHOFF K-80 SKEET SHOTGUN
Gauge: 12, 2¾" chambers.
Barrel: 28" (Skeet & Skeet or optional Tula chokes).
Weight: About 7¾ lbs.
Stock: American Skeet or straight Skeet stocks, with palm-swell grips. Walnut.
Features: Satin gray receiver finish. Selective mechanical trigger adjustable for position. Standard 5/16" vent. rib. Introduced 1980. Imported from West Germany by Krieghoff International, Inc.
Price: Standard, Skeet chokes $4,390.00
Price: As above, Tula chokes $4,550.00
Price: Lightweight model (weighs 7 lbs.), Standard $4,250.00
Price: Two-Barrel Set (tube concept), 12 ga., standard $6,200.00

Krieghoff K-80 Sporting Clays Over/Under
Similar to the Pigeon model gun except has a Schnabel fore-end tip and comes with screw-in choke tubes. Introduced 1988.
Price: Standard grade $4,930.00

Krieghoff K-80 International Skeet
Similar to the Standard Skeet except has ½" ventilated Broadway-style rib, special Tula chokes with gas release holes at muzzle. International Skeet stock. Comes in fitted aluminum case.
Price: Standard grade $4,725.00

Krieghoff K-80 Four-Barrel Skeet Set
Similar to the Standard Skeet except comes with barrels for 12, 20, 28, 410 in 28" length with Tula choke system. Comes with fitted leather case with canvas cover.
Price: Standard grade $8,980.00

SHOTGUNS—OVER-UNDERS

Ljutic LM-6

Ljutic Four Barrel Skeet Set
LM-6 over/under 12-ga. frame with matched set of four 28" barrels in 12, 20, 28 and 410. Ljutic Paternator chokes and barrel are integral. Stock is to customer specs, of fine American or French walnut with EX (or Extra) Fancy checkering.
Price: Four barrel set.. $26,995.00

MERKEL OVER/UNDER SHOTGUNS
Gauge: 12, 16, 20, 28, 410, 2¾", 3" chambers.
Barrel: 26", 26¾", 28" (standard chokes).
Weight: 6 to 7 lbs.
Stock: European walnut. Straight English or pistol grip.
Features: Models 200E and 201E are boxlocks, 203E and 303E are sidelocks. All have auto. ejectors, articulated front triggers. Auto. safety, selective and non-selective triggers optional. Imported from East Germany by Armes de Chasse.
Price: 200E, about.. $2,400.00
Price: 201E, about.. $3,100.00
Price: 203E (sidelock), about................................ $6,400.00
Price: 303E (sidelock), about................................ $10,200.00

LJUTIC T.C. LM-6 DELUXE O/U
Gauge: 12 ga.
Barrel: 28" to 34", choked to customer specs for live birds, trap, International Trap.
Weight: To customers specs.
Stock: To customer specs. Oil finish, hand checkered.
Features: Custom-made gun. Hollow-milled rib, pull or release trigger, push-button opener in front of trigger guard. From Ljutic Industries.
Price: Super Deluxe LM-6 o/u............................... $9,984.00
Price: Over/under Combo (interchangeable single barrel, two trigger guards, one for single trigger, one for doubles)........... $14,995.00
Price: Extra over-under barrel sets, 29"–32".................. $4,995.00

> Consult our Directory pages for the location of firms mentioned.

Navy Bird Hunter

NAVY ARMS MODEL 410 O/U SHOTGUN
Gauge: 410, 3" chambers.
Barrel: 26" (Full & Full, Skeet & Skeet).
Weight: 6¼ lbs.
Stock: European walnut; checkered p.g. and fore-end.
Features: Chrome-lined barrels, hard chrome finished receiver with engraving, vent. rib. Single trigger. Imported from Italy by Navy Arms. Introduced 1986.
Price: $299.00

NAVY ARMS MODEL 83/93 BIRD HUNTER O/U
Gauge: 12, 20, 3" chambers.
Barrel: 28" (Imp. Cyl. & Mod., Mod. & Full).
Weight: About 7½ lbs.
Stock: European walnut, checkered grip and fore-end.
Sights: Metal bead front.
Features: Boxlock action with double triggers; extractors only; silvered, engraved receiver; vented top and middle ribs. Imported from Italy by Navy Arms. Introduced 1984.
Price: Model 83 (extractors)..................................... $482.00
Price: Model 93 (ejectors).. $559.00

Navy Arms Model 95/96
Same as the 83/93 Bird Hunter except comes with five interchangeable choke tubes. Model 96 has gold-plated single trigger and ejectors.
Price: Model 95 (extractors)..................................... $598.00
Price: Model 96 (ejectors).. $715.00

Omega Standard

Omega Deluxe Over/Under
Similar to the Standard model except does not fold. In 12 ga. only, 26" (Imp. Cyl. & Mod), 28" (Mod. & Full), 3" chambers. Weight about 7¼ lbs. Single non-selective trigger. Introduced 1988.
Price: $369.00

OMEGA STANDARD FOLDING O/U SHOTGUN
Gauge: 12, 20, 28, 410, 3" chambers.
Barrel: 12 ga.—26" (Imp. Cyl. & Mod.), 28" (Mod. & Full); 20 ga.—26" (Imp. Cyl. & Mod.), 28" (Mod. & Full); 28 ga.—26" (Imp. Cyl. & Mod., Mod. & Full); 410—26" (Full & Full).
Weight: About 6-7½ lbs.
Stock: Checkered European walnut.
Features: Single trigger; automatic safety; vent rib. Imported from Italy by Kassnar Imports, Inc. Introduced 1986.
Price: $319.00

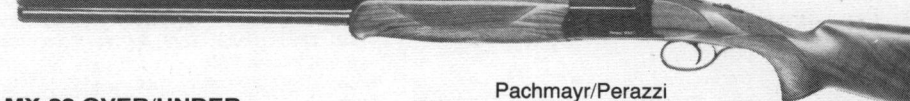
Pachmayr/Perazzi

PACHMAYR/PERAZZI MX-20 OVER/UNDER
Gauge: 20, 3" chambers.
Barrel: 26" (Cyl., Imp. Cyl., Mod., Imp. Mod., Full choke tubes). Fixed chokes available.
Weight: 6 lbs., 8 oz.
Stock: 14½"x1⅜"x2¼"x1½"; select European walnut with 26 l.p.i. checkering, checkered butt.
Sights: Nickel silver front bead.
Features: Boxlock action, uses special 20-gauge frame. Carved schnabel-type fore-end. Single selective trigger, automatic selective ejectors, manual safety. Comes with lockable fitted case. Introduced 1986. From Pachmayr, Ltd.
Price: $3,995.00

SHOTGUNS—OVER-UNDERS

PERAZZI MX8/MX8 SPECIAL TRAP, SKEET
Gauge: 12, 2¾" chambers.
Barrel: Trap–29½" (Imp. Mod. & Extra Full), 31½" (Full & Extra Full). Choke tubes optional. Skeet–27⅝" (Skeet & Skeet).
Weight: About 8½ lbs. (Trap); 7 lbs., 15 oz. (Skeet).
Stock: Interchangeable and custom made to customer specs.
Features: Has detachable and interchangeable trigger group with flat V springs. Flat 7/16" ventilated rib. Many options available. Imported from Italy by Perazzi U.S.A., Inc.
Price: From $4,700.00
Price: MX8 Special (adj. four-position trigger), from............. $4,900.00
Price: MX8 Special Single (32" or 34" single barrel, step rib), from. $4,600.00
Price: MX8 Special Combo (o/u and single barrel sets), from $7,100.00

Perazzi Grand American 88 Special
Similar to the MX8 except has tapered 7/16" x 5/16" high ramped rib. Choked Imp. Mod. & Full, 29½" barrels.
Price: From $7,100.00
Price: Special Single (32" or 34" single barrel), from $4,650.00

PERAZZI MIRAGE SPECIAL SPORTING O/U
Gauge: 12, 2¾" chambers.
Barrel: 27⅝", 28⅜" (Imp. Mod. & Extra Full).
Weight: 7 lbs, 12 oz.
Stock: To customer specs; interchangeable.
Features: Has adjustable four-position trigger; flat 7/16" x 5/16" vent. rib. Many options available. Imported from Italy by Perazzi U.S.A., Inc.
Price: $4,900.00

Perazzi Mirage Special Four Gauge Skeet
Similar to the Mirage Sporting model except has Skeet dimensions, interchangeable, adjustable four-position trigger assembly. Comes with four barrel sets in 12, 20, 28, 410, flat 5/16" x 5/16" rib.
Price: From $11,400.00
Price: MX3 Special Set, from $10,200.00

PERAZZI MX12 HUNTING OVER/UNDER
Gauge: 12, 2¾" chambers.
Barrel: 26", 27⅝" (Mod. & Full). choke tubes available (MX12C).
Weight: 7 lbs., 4 oz.
Stock: To customer specs; interchangeable.
Features: Single selective trigger; coil springs used in action; schnabel fore-end tip. Imported from Italy by Perazzi U.S.A., Inc.
Price: From $4,550.00
Price: MX12C (with choke tubes), from $4,850.00

Perazzi MX3 Special Single, Over/Under
Similar to the MX8 Special except has an adjustable four-position trigger, high 7/16" x 5/16" rib, weighs 8½ lbs. Choked Mod. & Full.
Price: From $4,400.00
Price: MX3 Special Single (32" or 34" single barrel), from $3,550.00
Price: MX3 Special Combo (o/u and single barrel sets), from $5,400.00

Perazzi MX4 Over/Under
Similar to the MX3 Special and has same locking system as the MX8, but with detachable, four-position trigger assembly for improved stock fit. Bottom barrel fires first. Has flat 7/16" x 7/16" rib; 29½" barrels only. Skeet version choked Skeet & Skeet, 27⅝" barrels, weighs 7 lbs., 15 oz. MX4C has choke tubes.
Price: .... NA

Perazzi Mirage Special Skeet Over/Under
Similar to the MX8 Skeet except has adjustable four-position trigger, Skeet stock dimensions.
Price: From $4,900.00

Perazzi MX1, MX1B Sporting Over/Under
Similar to the MX8 except has ramped, tapered rib, interchangeable trigger assembly with leaf hammer springs, 27⅝" barrels choked Imp. Mod. & Extra Full. Weight is 7 lbs., 12 oz.
Price: From $4,800.00
Price: MX1B (as above except has flat conventional rib), from $4,800.00

PERAZZI TM1 SPECIAL SINGLE TRAP
Gauge: 12, 2¾" chambers.
Barrel: 32" or 34" (Extra Full).
Weight: 8 lbs., 6 oz.
Stock: To customer specs; interchangeable.
Features: Tapered and stepped high rib; adjustable four-position trigger. Also available with choke tubes. Imported from Italy by Perazzi U.S.A., Inc.
Price: From $3,700.00
Price: TMX Special Single (as above except special high rib), from $3,700.00

Perazzi MX20 Hunting Over/Under
Similar to the MX12 except 20-ga. frame size. Available in 20, 28, 410 with 2¾" or 3" chambers, 26" only, and choked Mod. & Full. Weight is 6 lbs., 6 oz.
Price: From $8,000.00
Price: MX20C (as above, 20 ga. only, choke tubes), from $8,300.00

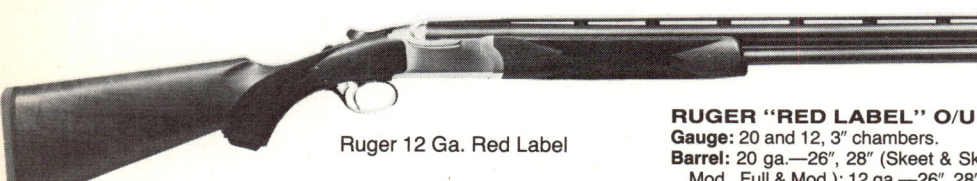

Ruger 12 Ga. Red Label

ROTTWEIL 72 AMERICAN SKEET
Gauge: 12, 2¾" chambers.
Barrel: 26¾" (Skeet & Skeet).
Weight: About 7½ lbs.
Stock: 14½" × 1⅜" × 1⅜" × ¼". Select French walnut with satin oil finish; hand checkered grip and fore-end; double ventilated recoil pad.
Sights: Plastic front in metal sleeve, center bead.
Features: Interchangeable trigger groups with coil springs; interchangeable buttstocks; special .433" ventilated rib; matte finish silvered receiver with light engraving. Introduced 1978. Imported from West Germany by Dynamit Nobel.
Price: $2,395.00

RUGER "RED LABEL" O/U SHOTGUN
Gauge: 20 and 12, 3" chambers.
Barrel: 20 ga.—26", 28" (Skeet & Skeet, Imp. Cyl. & Mod.), 28" (Imp. Cyl. & Mod., Full & Mod.); 12 ga.—26", 28" (Skeet & Skeet, Imp. Cyl. & Mod., Full & Mod.); 12 ga.—26", 28" (Skeet, Imp. Cyl., Mod., Full Screw-In choke tubes).
Weight: About 7 lbs. (20 ga.), 7½ lbs. (12 ga.). **Length:** 43" over-all (26" barrels).
Stock: 14"x1½"x2½". Straight gain American walnut. Checkered p.g. and fore-end, rubber recoil pad.
Features: Automatic safety/barrel selector, stainless steel trigger. Patented barrel side spacers may be removed if desired. 20 ga. available in blued steel only, 12 ga. available only with stainless receiver. 20 ga. introduced 1977; 12 ga. introduced 1982.
Price: 20 ga., blued $798.00
Price: 12 ga., stainless receiver $798.00
Price: As above, screw-In choke tubes $987.50

SHOTGUNS—OVER-UNDERS

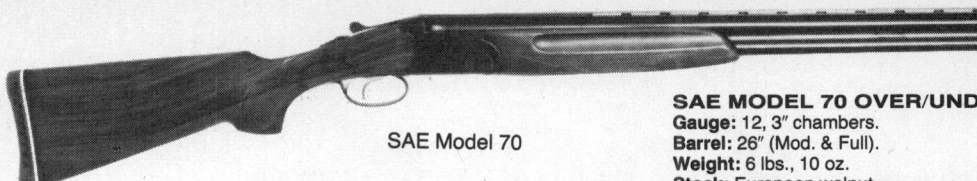
SAE Model 70

SAE Model 66C Over/Under
Similar to the Model 70 except has dummy sideplates, extensive engraving and gold inlays, oil-finished walnut with Monte Carlo. Available in 12 ga. only, 26" (Skeet & Skeet), 28" (Mod. & Full).
Price: $1,375.95

SAE MODEL 70 OVER/UNDER SHOTGUN
Gauge: 12, 3" chambers.
Barrel: 26" (Mod. & Full).
Weight: 6 lbs., 10 oz.
Stock: European walnut.
Features: Boxlock action with single mechanical trigger, automatic selective ejectors, automatic safety. Blued, engraved receiver. Introduced 1987. Imported from Spain by Spain America Ent.
Price: $475.80
Price: Model 70 Multichoke (12 ga. only, 27", choke tubes, silvered receiver) $525.70

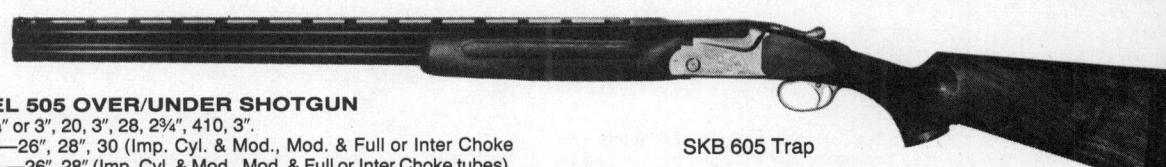
SKB 605 Trap

SKB MODEL 505 OVER/UNDER SHOTGUN
Gauge: 12, 2¾" or 3", 20, 3", 28, 2¾", 410, 3".
Barrel: 12 ga.—26", 28", 30 (Imp. Cyl. & Mod., Mod. & Full or Inter Choke tubes), 20 ga.—26", 28" (Imp. Cyl. & Mod., Mod. & Full or Inter Choke tubes), 28 and 410—26", 28" (Imp. Cyl. & Mod., Mod. & Full).
Weight: 6.6 to 7.4 lbs. **Length:** 45³⁄₁₆" over-all.
Stock: 14⅛"x1½"x2³⁄₁₆". Hand checkered walnut.
Sights: Metal bead front.
Features: Blued boxlock action; ejectors; single selective trigger. Introduced 1988. Imported from Japan by Ernie Simmons Enterprises.
Price: $795.00
Price: Two-barrel Field Set, 12 and 20, choke tubes $1,250.00
Price: As above, 28 and 410, fixed chokes $1,250.00
Price: Model 505 Trap, Skeet $825.00
Price: Model 505 Single Barrel Trap $825.00
Price: Skeet set, 20, 28, 410 .... $1,850.00

SKB Model 605 Over/Under Shotgun
Similar to the Model 505 except has silvered, engraved receiver.
Price: $975.00
Price: Two-barrel Field Set, 12 and 20 ga., choke tubes $1,450.00
Price: As above, 28 and 410, fixed chokes $1,450.00
Price: Model 605 Trap, Skeet $995.00
Price: Model 605 Single Barrel Trap $995.00
Price: Skeet Set, 20, 28, 410 .... $1,995.00

SKB Model 885 Over/Under Trap, Skeet
Similar to the Model 505 except has engraved sideplates, silvered receiver, standard or Monte Carlo stock; 2¾" chambers; Inter Choke tubes. Skeet in 12 or 20 ga.
Price: $1,495.00
Price: Skeet Set, 20, 28, 410 .... $2,650.00

SKB 885 Trap

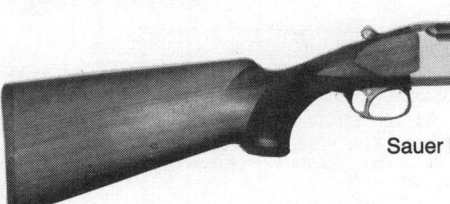
Sauer Franchi S

SAN MARCO WILDFOWLER O/U
Gauge: 10, 3½" chambers.
Barrel: 28", 32" (Full & Full).
Weight: 9 lbs, 3 oz. **Length:** 50" over-all (32" barrel).
Stock: 14¹⁄₁₆"x1½"x2". Walnut, checkered p.g. and fore-end.
Features: Boxlock action, extractors, or ejectors, non-selective double triggers. Matte finish on metal. Imported by Ballistic Products, Inc.
Price: With extractors $625.00
Price: With ejectors $725.00

SAUER-FRANCHI O/U SHOTGUNS
Gauge: 12, 2¾" chambers.
Barrel: 28" (Imp. Cyl. & Imp. Mod., Mod. & Full, Skeet 1 & Skeet 2); 29" (Special Trap).
Weight: 7½ lbs. **Length:** 45⅓" over-all.
Stock: European walnut.
Features: Blued frame on Standard model, others with silvered, engraved frames; single selective trigger; selective auto. ejectors; vent. rib. Introduced in U.S. 1986. Imported from West Germany by Sigarms.
Price: Standard, about $785.00
Price: Regent, about $825.00
Price: Favorit, about $875.00
Price: Diplomat, about $1,520.00
Price: Sporting S, Trap, Skeet models, about $1,375.00

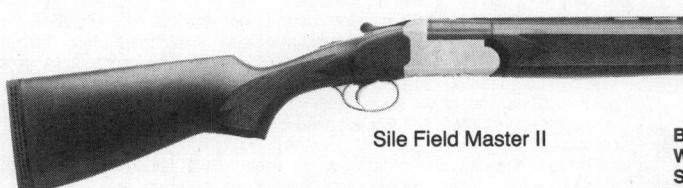
Sile Field Master II

SILE FIELD MASTER II O/U SHOTGUN
Gauge: 12, 3" chambers.
Barrel: 28" (Cyl., Imp. Cyl., Mod., Imp. Mod., Full choke tubes).
Weight: 7½ lbs. **Length:** 45¼" over-all.
Stock: Satin-finished walnut, cut-checkered p.g. and fore-end.
Features: Single selective trigger; extractors; automatic safety; engraved silvered receiver. Imported by Sile.
Price: $475.95
Price: Field Hunter I (similar to above except 26" (Imp. Cyl. & Mod.) or 28" (Mod. & Full) $335.95
Price: Field Hunter II (as above except with choke tubes) $391.95

CAUTION: PRICES CHANGE. CHECK AT GUNSHOP.

SHOTGUNS—OVER-UNDERS

Sile Trap King O/U Shotgun
Similar to the Field Master II except has 2¾" chambers, 30" barrels choked Mod. & Full or Full & Full. Walnut Monte Carlo stock with palm swell and recoil pad. Weight is 8½ lbs. Automatic ejectors.
Price: $559.95

Sile Field King Super Light, Field Hunter, Slug Master O/U
Similar to the Field Master II except in 12 ga. only with 28" barrels (Mod. & Full). Weighs 6¼ lbs. Imported by Sile.
Price: $489.95
Price: Field Hunter (similar to above, with 23½" Cyl. & Cyl. barrels, ramp front sight, folding rear) $391.95
Price: Slug Master $461.95

SIMSON/SUHL MODEL 85 EJ OVER/UNDER
Gauge: 12, 2¾" chambers.
Barrel: 28" (Imp. Cyl. & Mod.).
Weight: 6¾ lbs.
Stock: European walnut; pistol grip style.
Features: Anson & Deeley modified boxlock action with double triggers, manual safety. Cold hammer forged barrels, double locking lugs. Choking and patterning for steel shot (by importer). Auto safety, vent. rib optional. Imported from East Germany by Armes de Chasse.
Price: $1,000.00

Sile Field King, Skeet King O/U Shotgun
Similar to the Field Master II except 26", 28" (Imp. Cyl. & Mod.), 28" (Mod. & Full) for Field; Skeet has 26" (Skeet & Skeet); both fixed chokes. Single non-selective trigger.
Price: $391.95

SILE SKY STALKER OVER/UNDER
Gauge: 20, 28, 410, 3" chambers.
Barrel: 26", 28" (Imp. Cyl. & Mod., Mod. & Full, Full & Full, Skeet & Skeet).
Weight: About 6¾ lbs.
Stock: Walnut-finished hardwood, checkered p.g. and fore-end.
Features: Folds in half for storage or carry. Mechanical extractors; single non-selective trigger. Imported by Sile.
Price: $239.95

STOEGER/IGA OVER/UNDER SHOTGUN
Gauge: 12, 20, 3" chambers.
Barrel: 26" (Full & Full, Imp. Cyl. & Mod.), 28" (Mod. & Full).
Weight: 6¾ to 7 lbs.
Stock: 14½"x1½"x2½". Oil finished hardwood with checkered pistol grip and fore-end.
Features: Manual safety, single trigger, extractors only, ventilated top rib. Introduced 1983. Imported from Brazil by Stoeger Industries.
Price: $380.00

Techi-Mec SPL 640

TECHNI-MEC MODEL SR 692 EM OVER/UNDER
Gauge: 12, 16, 20, 2¾" or 3" chambers.
Barrel: 26", 28", 30" (Mod., Full, Imp. Cyl., Cyl.).
Weight: 6½ lbs.
Stock: 14½"x ½"x2½". European walnut with checkered grip and fore-end.
Features: Boxlock action with dummy sideplates, fine game scene engraving; single selective trigger; automatic ejectors available. Imported from Italy by L. Joseph Rahn. Introduced 1984.
Price: $725.00
Price: Slug gun $685.00

TECHNI-MEC MODEL SPL 640 FOLDING O/U
Gauge: 12, 16, 20, 28, 2¾" chambers; 410, 3" chambers.
Barrel: 26" (Mod. & Full).
Weight: 5½ lbs.
Stock: European walnut.
Features: Gun folds in half for storage, transportation. Chrome lined barrels; ventilated rib; photo-engraved silvered receiver. Imported from Italy by L. Joseph Rahn, Mandall. Introduced 1984.
Price: Double triggers $260.00
Price: Single trigger $275.00
Price: Model SPL 642, double triggers $275.00
Price: As above, single trigger $285.00

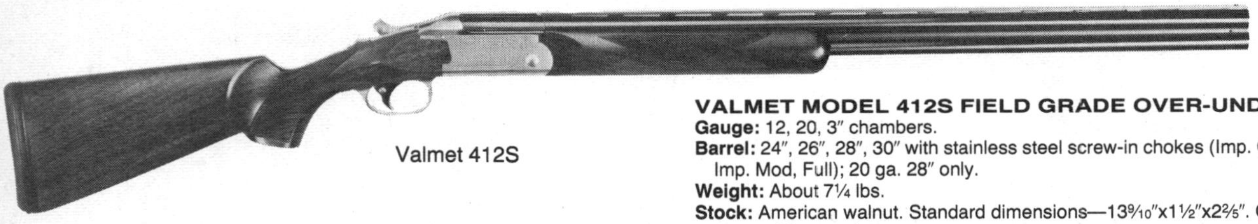

Valmet 412S

VALMET MODEL 412S FIELD GRADE OVER-UNDER
Gauge: 12, 20, 3" chambers.
Barrel: 24", 26", 28", 30" with stainless steel screw-in chokes (Imp. Cyl., Mod., Imp. Mod., Full); 20 ga. 28" only.
Weight: About 7¼ lbs.
Stock: American walnut. Standard dimensions—13⁹⁄₁₀"x1½"x2⅖". Checkered p.g. and fore-end.
Features: Free interchangeability of barrels, stocks and fore-ends into double rifle model, combination gun, etc. Barrel selector in trigger; auto. top tang safety; barrel cocking indicators. Introduced 1980. Imported from Finland by Valmet.
Price: Model 412S (ejectors) $959.00

WEATHERBY ORION O/U SHOTGUN
Gauge: 12 or 20 ga., 3" chambers; 2¾" on Trap gun.
Action: Boxlock (simulated side lock).
Barrel: Fixed choke, 12, 20 ga.—26", 28" (Skeet & Skeet); IMC Multi-Choke tubes; 12, 20, 410, Field models—26" (Skeet, Imp. Cyl., Mod.), 28" (Imp. Cyl., Mod., Full), 30" (12 ga. only. Full, Mod., Full); o/u Trap models—30", 32" (Mod., Imp. Mod., Full).
Weight: 7 lbs., 8 oz. (12 ga., 26").
Stock: American walnut, checkered p.g. and fore-end. Rubber recoil pad. Dimensions for field and Skeet models, 20 ga., 14"x1½"x2½".
Features: Selective auto ejectors, single selective mechanical trigger. Top tang safety, Greener cross-bolt. Introduced 1982. Imported from Japan by Weatherby.
Price: Skeet, fixed choke $1,011.00
Price: 12 or 20 ga. IMC Multi-Choke, Field $1,000.00
Price: IMC Multi-Choke, Trap $1,051.00
Price: Extra IMC choke tubes $16.00

Valmet 412 ST Trap and Skeet
Target versions of the 412S gun with hand-honed actions, mechanical single triggers, elongated forcing cones and stainless steel choke tubes. Target safety is locked in "Fire" position (removal of a screw converts it to automatic safety); automatic ejectors; cocking indicators. Walnut stocks with double palm swells are quickly interchangeable. Trap guns have high stepped rib, 30", 32" O-U and 32", 34" single barrels; Skeet guns in 12, 20 ga. with 28" barrels.
Grade II guns have semi-fancy wood, matte nickel finished receiver with matte blue locking bolt and lever, gold trigger, pre-drilled stock for insertion of a recoil reducer, more checkering at stock wrist. Introduced 1987.
Price: Grade I $1,149.00
Price: Grade II $1,449.00

SHOTGUNS—OVER-UNDERS

Weatherby Athena

WEATHERBY ATHENA O/U SHOTGUN
Gauge: 12, 20, 28, 410, 3" chambers; 2¾" on Trap gun.
Action: Boxlock (simulated side lock) top lever break-open. Selective auto ejectors, single selective trigger (selector inside trigger guard).
Barrel: Fixed choke, 12, 20 ga.—26", 28" (Skeet & Skeet); IMC Multi-Choke tubes 12, 20, 410, Field models—26" (Skeet, Imp. Cyl., Mod.), 28" (Imp. Cyl., Mod., Full), 30" (12 ga. only. Full, Mod., Full); o/u Trap models—30", 32" (Mod., Imp. Mod., Full).
Weight: 12 ga. 7⅜ lbs., 20 ga. 6⅞ lbs.
Stock: American walnut, checkered p.g. and fore-end (14¼"×1½"×2½").
Features: Mechanically operated trigger. Top tang safety, Greener cross-bolt, fully engraved receiver, recoil pad installed. IMC models furnished with three interchangeable flush-fitting choke tubes. Imported from Japan by Weatherby. Introduced 1982.
Price: Skeet, fixed choke $1,601.00
Price: 12 or 20 ga., IMC Multi-Choke, Field $1,590.95
Price: IMC Multi-Choke Trap $1,611.00
Price: Extra IMC Choke tubes $16.00
Price: Master Skeet Tube Set (12-ga. gun with six Briley tubes in 20, 28, 410) $3,200.00

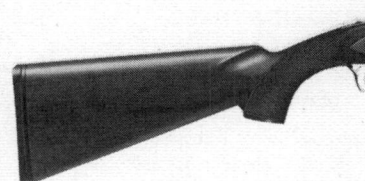

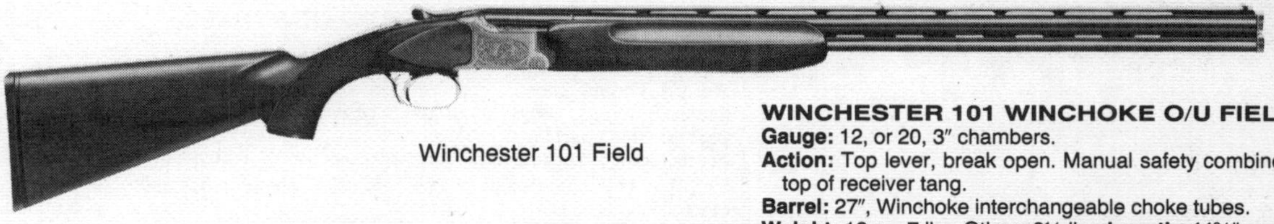

Winchester 101 Field

WINCHESTER 101 WINCHOKE O/U FIELD GUN
Gauge: 12, or 20, 3" chambers.
Action: Top lever, break open. Manual safety combined with bbl. selector at top of receiver tang.
Barrel: 27", Winchoke interchangeable choke tubes.
Weight: 12 ga. 7 lbs. Others 6½ lbs. **Length:** 44¾" over-all.
Stock: 14"×1½"×2½". Checkered walnut p.g. and fore-end; fluted comb.
Features: Single selective trigger, auto ejectors. Hand engraved satin gray receiver. Comes with hard gun case. Manufactured in and imported from Japan by Winchester Group, Olin Corp.
Price: $1,495.00
Price: Two Barrel Set (12 and 20) $2,330.00

Winchester Model 101 Waterfowl Winchoke
Same as Model 101 Field Grade except in 12 ga. only, 3" chambers, 30" barrels. Comes with four Winchoke tubes: Mod., Imp. Mod., Full, Extra-Full. Blued receiver with hand etching and engraving. Introduced 1981. Manufactured in and imported from Japan by Winchester Group, Olin Corp.
Price: $1,595.00

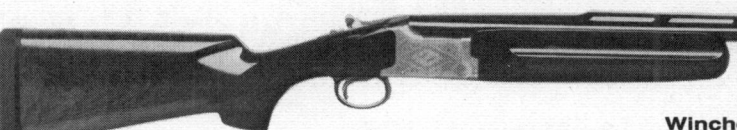

Winchester 101 Oversingle

Winchester Model 101 Pigeon Grade
Similar to the Model 101 Field except comes in two styles: Lightweight-Winchoke (12 or 20 ga., six choke tubes for 12 ga., four for 20, 28 ga., 27", 28"), Featherweight (12 or 20 ga., Imp. Cyl. & Mod., 25½"), all with 3" chambers. Vent. rib barrel with middle bead, fancy American walnut. Featherweight has English-style stock. Hard case included. Introduced 1983. Manufactured in and imported from Japan by Winchester Group, Olin Corp.
Price: Featherweight $1,580.00
Price: Lightweight-Winchoke $1,915.00

Winchester 101 Diamond Grade Target Guns
Similar to the Model 101 except designed for trap and Skeet competition, with tapered and elevated rib, anatomically contoured trigger and internationally-dimensioned stock. Receiver has deep-etched diamond-pattern engraving. Skeet guns available in 12, 20, 28 and 410 with ventilated muzzles to reduce recoil. Trap guns in 12 ga. only; over/under, combination and single-barrel configurations in a variety of barrel lengths with Winchoke system. Straight or Monte Carlo stocks available. Introduced 1982. Manufactured in and imported from Japan by Winchester Group, Olin Corp.
Price: Trap, o/u, standard and Monte Carlo, 30", 32" $1,860.00
Price: Trap, o/u-single bbl. combo sets, Unsingle $2,940.00
Price: Skeet, 12 and 20 .... $1,915.00
Price: Skeet, 28 and 410 .... $1,915.00
Price: Four barrel Skeet set (12, 20, 28, 410) $5,095.00
Price: Trap Oversingle, 34", Monte Carlo or std. stock $2,145.00
Price: As above, combo $3,495.00

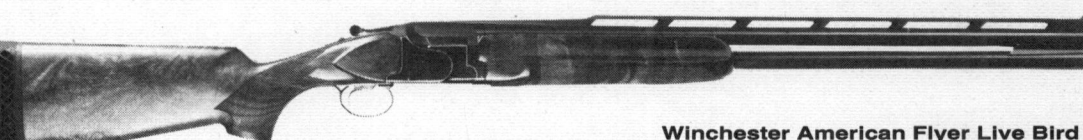

Winchester American Flyer

Winchester American Flyer Live Bird Gun, Combo Set
Similar to the Model 101 except 12 ga. only (2¾" chambers), 28" barrels with under barrel fitted with internal Winchoke system and four tubes; over barrel choked Extra Full. Combination Set includes an extra set of 29½" barrels with same choke specs. Back-bored barrels, matte finish on top of receiver, competition vent. rib. Full fancy American walnut reverse-tapered stock. Comes with luggage-type case. Blued receiver with gold wire border inlays, gold pigeon inlay. Introduced 1987.
Price: 28" or 29½" $2,870.00
Price: Combination Set, 28", 29½" $3,590.00

Consult our Directory pages for the location of firms mentioned.

Winchester Quail Special O/U Small Frame
Similar to the Model 101 except built with small frame for 28 and 410 gauge (3" chambers). 28 gauge has internal Winchoke system and four tubes with 25½" barrels; 410 has 25½" barrels choked Full & Mod. Silvered, engraved receiver. Introduced 1987.
Price: $2,200.00

CAUTION: PRICES CHANGE. CHECK AT GUNSHOP.

SHOTGUNS—OVER-UNDERS

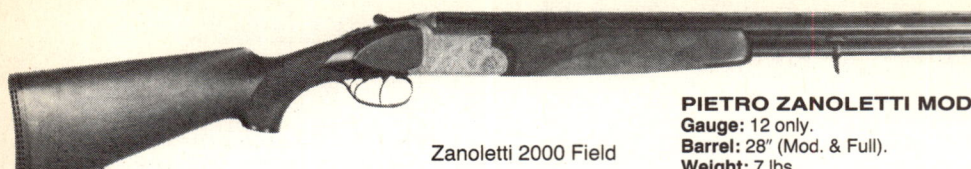

Zanoletti 2000 Field

PIETRO ZANOLETTI MODEL 2000 FIELD O/U
Gauge: 12 only.
Barrel: 28″ (Mod. & Full).
Weight: 7 lbs.
Stock: European walnut, checkered grip and fore-end.
Sights: Gold bead front.
Features: Boxlock action with auto ejectors, double triggers; engraved receiver. Imported from Italy by Mandall Shooting Supplies. Introduced 1984.
Price: $695.00

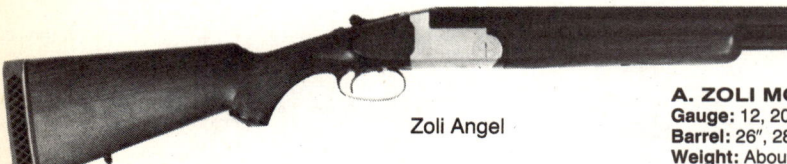

Zoli Angel

A. ZOLI MODEL ANGEL FIELD GRADE O/U
Gauge: 12, 20.
Barrel: 26″, 28″, 30″ (Mod. & Full).
Weight: About 7½ lbs.
Stock: Straight grained walnut with checkered grip and fore-end.
Sights: Gold bead front.
Features: Boxlock action with single selective trigger, auto ejectors; extra-wide vent. top rib. Imported from Italy by Mandall Shooting Supplies.
Price: $895.00
Price: Condor model $895.00

A. ZOLI DELFINO S.P. O/U
Gauge: 12 or 20, 3″ chambers.
Barrel: 28″ (Mod. & Full); vent. rib.
Weight: 5½ lbs.
Stock: Walnut. Hand checkered p.g. and fore-end; cheekpiece.
Features: Color case hardened receiver with light engraving; chrome lined barrels; automatic sliding safety; double triggers; ejectors. From Mandall Shooting Supplies.
Price: $895.00

SHOTGUNS—SIDE-BY-SIDES

Variety of models for utility and sporting use, including some competitive shooting.

American Arms York

AMERICAN ARMS YORK DOUBLE SHOTGUN
Gauge: 12, 20, 28, 410, 3″ chambers (except 28, 2¾″).
Barrel: 26″ (Imp. Cyl. & Mod., all gauges), 28″ (Mod. & Full, 12 and 20 gauges).
Weight: 6¼ to 6¾ lbs.
Stock: 14⅛″x1⅜″x2⅜″. Hand-checkered walnut with gloss finish.
Sights: Metal bead front.
Features: Boxlock action with English-style scroll engraving, silvered finish. Double triggers, extractors. Independent floating firing pins. Manual safety. Five year warranty. Introduced 1987. Imported from Spain by American Arms, Inc.
Price: 12 or 20 gauge $499.00
Price: 28 or 410 .... $530.00

American Arms Derby Side-by-Side
Similar to the York model except has sidelock action with English-style engraving on the silvered sideplates. Straight-grip walnut stock with splinter fore-end, hand rubbed oil finish. Double or single non-selective trigger, automatic selective ejectors. Same chokes, rib, barrel lengths as the York. Has 5-year warranty. From American Arms, Inc.
Price: 12 and 20, double trigger $830.00
Price: As above, single trigger............................... $875.00
Price: 28 and 410, double trigger $875.00
Price: As above, single trigger............................... $900.00
Price: Two-barrel set, 20/28 ga., double triggers $1,095.00
Price: As above, single trigger............................... $1,125.00

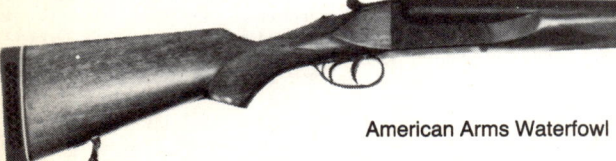

American Arms Waterfowl

AMERICAN ARMS WATERFOWL SPECIAL
Gauge: 10, 3½″ chambers.
Barrel: 32″ (Full & Full). Flat rib.
Weight: 10 lbs., 13 oz.
Stock: 14 5/16″x1⅜″x2⅜″. Hand checkered walnut with beavertail fore-end, full pistol grip, dull finish, rubber recoil pad.
Features: Boxlock action with double triggers. All metal has Parkerized finish. Comes with camouflaged sling, sling swivels, 5-year warranty. Introduced 1987. Imported from Italy by American Arms, Inc.
Price: $645.00

American Arms Turkey Special Side-by-Side
Similar to the Waterfowl Special except in 12 ga. with 3″ chambers, 26″ barrels with choke tubes. Comes with camouflage sling, swivels, 5-year warranty. From American Arms, Inc.
Price: $550.00
Price: As above, 10 ga....................................... $695.00

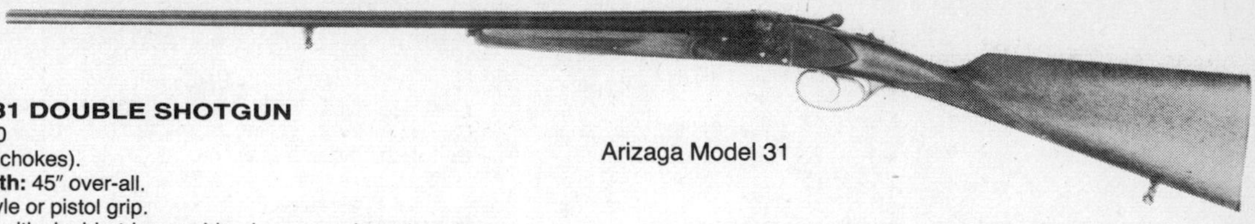

SHOTGUNS—SIDE-BY-SIDES

Arizaga Model 31

ARIZAGA MODEL 31 DOUBLE SHOTGUN
Gauge: 12, 16, 20, 28, 410
Barrel: 26", 28" (standard chokes).
Weight: 6 lbs., 9 oz. **Length:** 45" over-all.
Stock: Straight English style or pistol grip.
Features: Boxlock action with double triggers; blued, engraved receiver. Imported by Mandall Shooting Supplies.
Price: $399.95

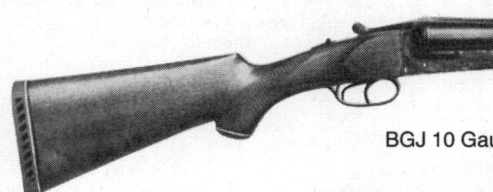
BGJ 10 Gauge

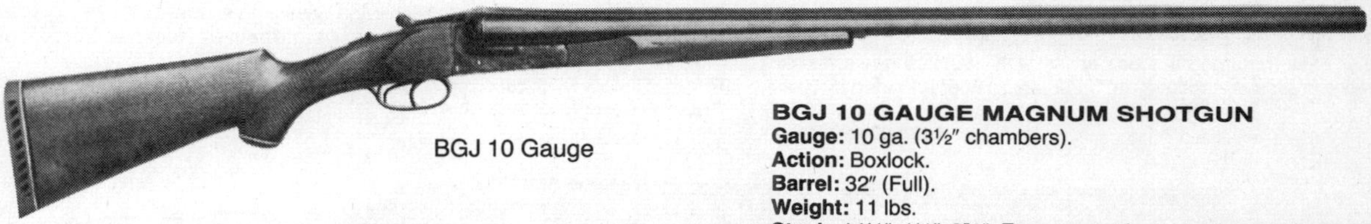

BGJ 10 GAUGE MAGNUM SHOTGUN
Gauge: 10 ga. (3½" chambers).
Action: Boxlock.
Barrel: 32" (Full).
Weight: 11 lbs.
Stock: 14½"x1½"x2⅝". European walnut, checkered at p.g. and fore-end.
Features: Double triggers; color hardened action, rest blued. Front and center metal beads on matted rib; ventilated rubber recoil pad. Fore-end release has positive Purdey-type mechanism. Imported from Spain by Mandall Shooting Supplies.
Price: $599.95

BERNARDELLI SERIES S. UBERTO DOUBLES
Gauge: 12, 16, 20, 28, 2¾" or 3" chambers.
Barrel: 25⅝", 26¾", 28", 29⅛" (Mod. & Full).
Weight: 6 to 6½ lbs.
Stock: 14³⁄₁₆"x2⅜"x1⁹⁄₁₆" standard dimensions. Select walnut with hand checkering.
Features: Anson & Deeley boxlock action with Purdey locks, choice of extractors or ejectors. Uberto 1 has color case-hardened receiver, Uberto 2 and F.S. silvered and differ in amount and quality of engraving. Custom options available. Prices vary with importer and are shown respectively. Imported from Italy by Armes De Chasse and Mandall Shooting Supplies.
Price: S. Uberto 1 .... $1,297.20 to $1,217.96
Price: As above with ejectors .... $1,428.00 to $1,373.52
Price: S. Uberto 2 .... $1,356.00 to $1,275.58
Price: As above with ejectors .... $1,486.80 to $1,430.16
Price: S. Uberto F.S. .... $1,560.00 to $1,492.46
Price: As above with ejectors .... $1,690.80 to $1,647.00

Bernardelli Series Roma Shotguns
Similar to the Series S. Uberto Models except with dummy sideplates to simulate sidelock action. In 12, 20, 28 gauge, 25½", 26¾", 28", 29" barrels. Straight English or pistol grip stock. Chrome-lined barrels, boxlock action, double triggers, ejectors, automatic safety. Checkered butt. Special choke combinations, barrel lengths optional.
Price: Roma 3, about $1,400.00
Price: Roma 4, about $1,600.00
Price: Roma 6, about $2,000.00

ARMSPORT 1050 SIDE-BY-SIDE SHOTGUNS
Gauge: 12, 20, 410, 3" chambers.
Barrel: 12 ga.—28" (Mod. & Full), 20 ga., 410—26" (Imp. Cyl. & Mod.).
Weight: 5¾-6 lbs.
Stock: European walnut
Features: Double triggers; extractors; silvered, engraved receiver. Introduced 1986. Imported from Italy by Armsport.
Price: 12, 20 ga. $595.00
Price: 28, 410 .... $595.00

Bernardelli System Holland H. Side-by-Side
True sidelock action. Available in 12 gauge only, reinforced breech, three round Purdey locks, automatic ejectors, folding right trigger. Model VB Liscio has color case-hardened receiver and sideplates with light engraving. VB and VB Tipo Lusso are silvered and engraved.
Price: VB Liscio .... $6,840.00 to $6,716.00
Price: VB .... $7,680.00 to $7,782.00
Price: VB Tipo Lusso .... $9,240.00 to $9,107.00

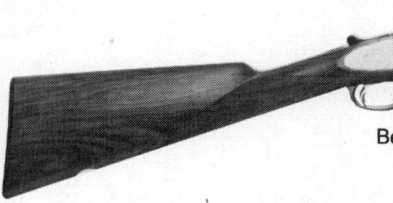
Beretta Model 627 EL

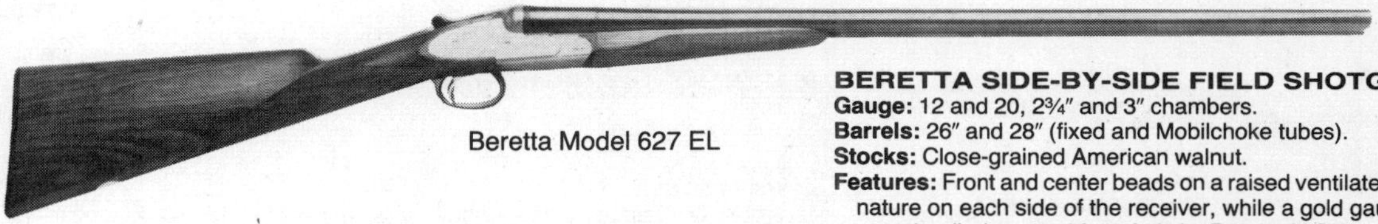

BERETTA SIDE-BY-SIDE FIELD SHOTGUNS
Gauge: 12 and 20, 2¾" and 3" chambers.
Barrels: 26" and 28" (fixed and Mobilchoke tubes).
Stocks: Close-grained American walnut.
Features: Front and center beads on a raised ventilated rib. Has P. Beretta signature on each side of the receiver, while a gold gauge marking is inscribed atop the rib. Imported from Italy by Beretta U.S.A.
Price: 626 Field $995.00
Price: 626 Onyx $1,265.00
Price: 627 EL $1,995.00
Price: 627 EELL (pistol grip or straight English stock) $3,500.00

BRNO ZP 149

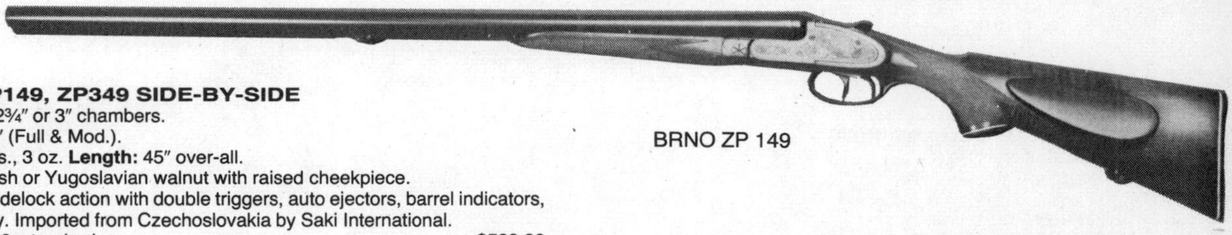

BRNO ZP149, ZP349 SIDE-BY-SIDE
Gauge: 12, 2¾" or 3" chambers.
Barrel: 28½" (Full & Mod.).
Weight: 7 lbs., 3 oz. **Length:** 45" over-all.
Stock: Turkish or Yugoslavian walnut with raised cheekpiece.
Features: Sidelock action with double triggers, auto ejectors, barrel indicators, auto safety. Imported from Czechoslovakia by Saki International.
Price: ZP 149, standard $589.00
Price: As above, engraved $609.00
Price: ZP 349, extractors, standard $629.00
Price: As above, engraved $649.00

CAUTION: PRICES CHANGE. CHECK AT GUNSHOP.

SHOTGUNS—SIDE-BY-SIDES

Churchill Windsor I

CHURCHILL ROYAL SIDE-BY-SIDE SHOTGUN
Gauge: 12 (3"), 16 (2¾"), 20, 28, 410 (3").
Barrel: 12 ga.—26" (Imp. Cyl. & Mod.), 28" (Mod. & Full); 16 ga.—28" (Mod. & Full); 20 ga.—28" (Imp. Cyl. & Mod., Mod. & Full); 410—26" (Full & Full).
Weight: 5¾ to 6½ lbs.
Stock: Straight-grip style of checkered European walnut.
Features: Color case-hardened boxlock action with double triggers, extractors; chromed barrels with concave rib. Introduced 1988. Imported by Kassnar.
Price: . . . . $559.00 to $589.00

CHURCHILL WINDSOR SIDE-BY-SIDE SHOTGUNS
Gauge: 10 (3½"), 12, 16, 20, 28, 410 (2¾" 16 ga., 3" others).
Barrel: 24" (Mod. & Full), 410 and 20 ga.; 26" (Imp. Cyl. & Mod., Mod. & Full); 28" (Mod. & Full, Skeet & Skeet—28 ga.); 30" (Full & Full, Mod. & Full); 32" (Full & Full—10 ga.).
Weight: About 7½ lbs. (12 ga.).
Stock: Hand checkered European walnut with rubber butt pad.
Features: Anson & Deeley boxlock action with silvered and engraved finish; automatic top tang safety; double triggers; beavertail fore-end. Windsor I with extractors only. Also available in Flyweight versions, 23", 25", fixed or ICT chokes, straight stock. Imported from Spain by Kassnar. Introduced 1984.
Price: Windsor I, 10 ga. . . . . $679.00 to $969.00
Price: Windsor I, 12 through 410 ga. . . . . $559.00 to $629.00

Classic Model 201

CLASSIC MODEL 201 DOUBLE
Gauge: 12, 20, 28/410.
Barrel: 26" (Imp. Cyl. & Mod); choke tubes available on 12 ga. model only; 28" (Imp. Cyl. & Mod., Mod. & Full) for 28/410 set.
Weight: About 7 lbs. **Length:** 43¼" over-all (26" barrel).
Stock: 14½" x 1½" x 2¼". Fancy grade American walnut. Straight English on 20 ga. only.
Features: Automatic selective ejectors; elongated forcing cones; top automatic tang safety. Suitable for steel shot. Blued frame. Imported from Japan by Classic Doubles.
Price: 12 ga. $2,685.00
Price: 20 ga. $2,830.00
Price: 28/410 set. $4,500.00

CRUCELEGUI HERMANOS MODEL 150 DOUBLE
Gauge: 12, 16 or 20, 2¾" chambers.
Action: Greener triple crossbolt.
Barrel: 20", 26", 28", 30", 32" (Cyl. & Cyl., Full & Full, Mod. & Full, Mod. & Imp. Cyl., Imp. Cyl. & Full, Mod. & Mod.).
Weight: 5 to 7¼ lbs.
Stock: Hand checkered walnut, beavertail fore-end.
Features: Exposed hammers; double triggers; color case-hardened receiver; sling swivels; chrome lined bores. Imported from Spain by Mandall Shooting Supplies.
Price: $399.95
Price: Model 225 (hammerless version) $399.95

Ferlib Model F VII

FERLIB MODEL F VII DOUBLE SHOTGUN
Gauge: 12, 20, 28, 410.
Barrel: 25" to 28".
Weight: 5½ lbs. (20 ga.).
Stock: Oil-finished walnut, checkered straight grip and fore-end.
Features: Boxlock action with fine scroll engraved, silvered receiver. Double triggers standard. Introduced 1983. Imported from Italy by Wm. Larkin Moore.
Price: 12 or 20 ga. $4,750.00
Price: 28 or 410 ga. $5,488.00
Price: Extra for single trigger $375.00

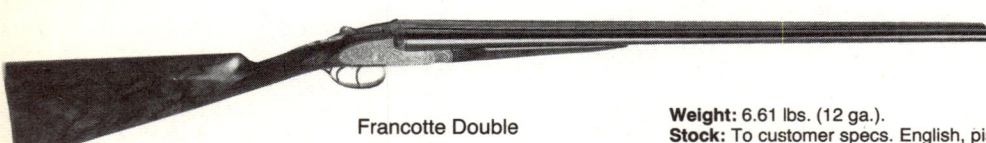

Francotte Double

AUGUSTE FRANCOTTE SIDE-BY-SIDE SHOTGUNS
Gauge: 12, 16, 20, 28, 410.
Barrel: 26" thru 30". To customer specs.
Weight: 6.61 lbs. (12 ga.).
Stock: To customer specs. English, pistol grip, half-pistol grip; European walnut.
Features: Chopper lump barrels; BAR action sidelocks or boxlock. Full selection of options available from the maker. Imported from Belgium by Armes de Chasse.
Price: . . . . NA

Garbi Model 51B

GARBI MODEL 51B SIDE-BY-SIDE
Gauge: 12, 16, 20, 2¾" chambers.
Barrel: 28" (Mod. & Full).
Weight: 5½ to 6½ lbs.
Stock: Walnut, to customer specs.
Features: Boxlock action; hand-engraved receiver; hand-checkered stock and fore-end; double triggers; extractors. Introduced 1980. Imported from Spain by L. Joseph Rahn, Inc.
Price: Model 51B, 12, 16, 20 ga., ejectors $1,100.00

SHOTGUNS—SIDE-BY-SIDES

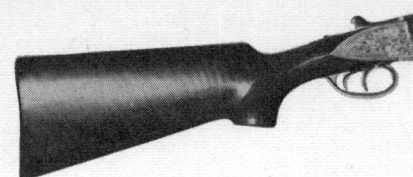
Garbi Model 60

GARBI MODEL 60 SIDE-BY-SIDE
Gauge: 12, 16, 20, 2¾" chambers.
Barrel: 26", 28", 30"; choked to customers specs.
Weight: 5½ to 6½ lbs.
Stock: Select walnut. Dimensions to customer specs.
Features: Sidelock action. Scroll engraving on receiver. Hand checkered stock. Double triggers. Extractors. Imported from Spain by L. Joseph Rahn, Inc.
Price: Model 60A, 12 ga. only $1,000.00
Price: With demi-bloc barrels and ejectors, 12, 16, 20 ga. $1,440.00

Garbi Model 62
Similar to Model 60 except choked Mod. & Full, plain receiver with engraved border, demi-bloc barrels, gas exhaust valves, jointed triggers, extractors. Imported from Spain by L. Joseph Rahn.
Price: Model 62A, 12 ga., only................................. $987.00
Price: Model 62B, 12, 16, 20 ga., ejectors $1,400.00

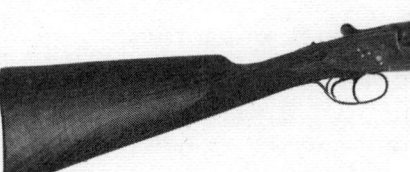
Garbi Model 71

GARBI MODEL 71 DOUBLE
Gauge: 12, 16, 20, 28.
Barrel: 26", 28" choked to customer specs.
Weight: 5 lbs., 15 oz. (20 ga.).
Stock: 14½"x2¼"x1½". European walnut. Straight grip, checkered butt, classic fore-end.
Features: Sidelock action, automatic ejectors, double triggers standard. Color case-hardened action, coin finish optional. Five other models are available. Imported from Spain by L. Joseph Rahn and Wm. Larkin Moore.
Price: Model 71 .... $2,200.00 to $2,600.00

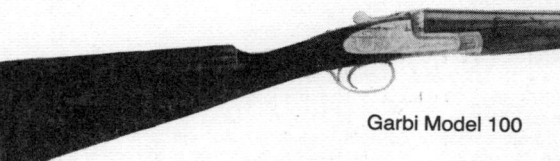
Garbi Model 100

GARBI MODEL 100 DOUBLE
Gauge: 12, 16, 20, 28.
Barrel: 26", 28", choked to customer specs.
Weight: 5½ to 7½ lbs.
Stock: 14½"x2¼"x1½". European walnut. Straight grip, checkered butt, classic fore-end.
Features: Sidelock action, automatic ejectors, double triggers standard. Color case-hardened action, coin finish optional. Single trigger; beavertail fore-end, etc. optional. Five other models are available. Imported from Spain by Wm. Larkin Moore and L. Joseph Rahn.
Price: From.. $2,450.00 to $3,000.00

Garbi Model 101 Side-by-Side
Similar to the Garbi Model 100 except is available with optional level, file-cut, Churchill or ventilated top rib, and in a 12-ga. pigeon or wildfowl gun. Has Continental-style floral and scroll engraving, select walnut stock. Better overall quality than the Model 100. Imported from Spain by L. Joseph Rahn and Wm. Larkin Moore.
Price: .... $3,700.00 to $4,500.00

GARBI MODEL 102 SHOTGUN
Gauge: 12, 16, 20.
Barrel: 12 ga.—25" to 30", 16 & 20 ga.—25" to 28". Chokes as specified.
Weight: 20 ga.—5 lbs., 15 oz. to 6 lbs., 4 oz.
Stock: 14½"x2¼"x1½"; select walnut.
Features: Holland pattern sidelock ejector with chopper lump barrels, Holland-type large scroll engraving. Double triggers (hinged front) std., non-selective single trigger available. Many options available. Imported from Spain by L. Joseph Rahn and Wm. Larkin Moore.
Price: From.. $3,700.00 to $4,500.00

Garbi Model 103A, B Side-by-Side
Similar to the Garbi Model 101 except has Purdey-type fine scroll and rosette engraving. Better over-all quality than the Model 101. Model 103B has nickel-chrome steel barrels, H&H-type easy opening mechanism; other mechanical details remain the same. Imported from Spain by Wm. Larkin Moore and L. Joseph Rahn, Inc.
Price: Model 103A, from .... $3,700.00 to $4,500.00
Price: Model 103B, from .... $5,244.00 to $6,000.00

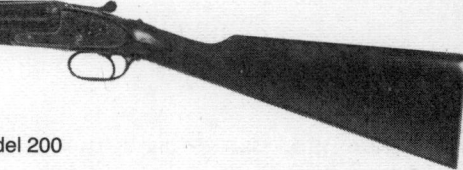
Garbi Model 200

Garbi Model 200 Side-by-Side
Similar to the Garbi Model 100 except has barrels of nickel-chrome steel, heavy-duty locks, magnum proofed. Very fine continental-style floral and scroll engraving, well figured walnut stock. Other mechanical features remain the same. Imported from Spain by L. Joseph Rahn and Wm. Larkin Moore.
Price: .... $5,300.00 to $6,250.00

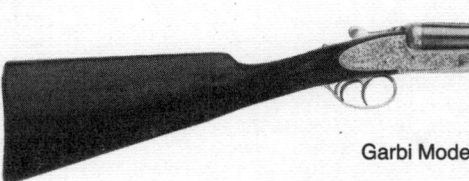
Garbi Model Special

Garbi Model Special Side-by-Side
Similar to the Garbi Model 100 except has best quality wood and metal work. Special game scene engraving with or without gold inlays, fancy figured walnut stock. Imported from Spain by Wm. Larkin Moore.
Price: From $6,250.00

CAUTION: PRICES CHANGE. CHECK AT GUNSHOP.

SHOTGUNS—SIDE-BY-SIDES

HATFIELD UPLANDER SHOTGUN
Gauge: 20, 3" chambers.
Barrel: 26" (Imp. Cyl. & Mod.).
Weight: 5¾ lbs.
Stock: Straight English style, special select XXX fancy walnut. Hand rubber oil finish. Splinter fore-end.
Features: Double locking under lug boxlock action; color case-hardened frame; single non-selective trigger. Introduced 1988. From Hatfield.
Price: Grade 1 .... $995.00
Price: Grade 2 .... $1,495.00
Price: Grade 3 .... $2,495.00
Price: Grade 4 .... $3,995.00
Price: Grade 5 .... $5,595.00

LEBEAU-COURALLY BOXLOCK SHOTGUN
Gauge: 12, 16, 20, 28.
Barrel: 26" to 30", choked to customer specs.
Weight: 6 lbs., 6 oz. to 8 lbs., 4 oz. (12 ga.)
Stock: Dimensions to customer specs. Select French walnut with hand rubbed oil finish, straight grip (p.g. optional), splinter fore-end (beavertail optional).
Features: Anson & Deeley boxlock with ejectors, Purdey-type fastener; choice of rounded action, with or without sideplates; choice of level rib, file cut or smooth; choice of numerous engraving patterns. Imported from Belguim by Wm. Larkin Moore.
Price: $11,300.00

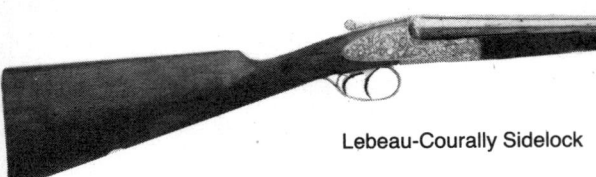
Lebeau-Courally Sidelock

LEBEAU-COURALLY SIDELOCK SHOTGUN
Gauge: 12, 16, 20 (standard), 28 (optional).
Barrel: 26" to 30", choked to customer specs.
Weight: 6 lbs., 6 oz. to 8 lbs., 4 oz. (12 ga.)
Stock: Dimensions to customer specs. Best quality French walnut with hand rubbed oil finish, straight grip stock and checkered butt (std.), classic splinter fore-end.
Features: Holland & Holland pattern sidelock ejector double with chopper lump barrels; choice of classic or rounded action; concave or level rib, file cut or smooth; choice of numerous engraving patterns. Can be furnished with H&H type self-opening mechanism. Imported from Belguim by Wm. Larkin Moore.
Price: From $22,700.00
Price: Boxlock, from $11,300.00

MERCURY MODEL G1032 DOUBLE BARREL SHOTGUN
Gauge: 10, 3½" chambers.
Action: Triple-lock Anson & Deeley type.
Barrel: 32" (Full & Full).
Weight: 10⅛ lbs.
Stock: 14"x1⅝"x2¼" walnut, checkered p.g. stock and beavertail fore-end, recoil pad.
Features: Double triggers, front hinged, auto safety, extractors; safety gas ports, engraved frame. Imported from Spain by Tradewinds.
Price: $480.00

MERKEL SIDE-BY-SIDE SHOTGUNS
Gauge: 12, 16, 20, 2¾" or 3" chambers
Barrel: 26", 26¾", 28" (standard chokes).
Weight: 6 to 7 lbs.
Stock: European walnut. Straight English or pistol grip.
Features: Models 47E, 147E, 122 are boxlocks; others are sidelocks. All have double triggers, double lugs and Greener cross-bolt locking and automatic ejectors. Choking and patterning for steel shot (by importer). Upgraded wood, engraving, etc. optional. Imported from East Germany by Armes de Chasse.
Price: Model 47E, about $950.00
Price: Model 147E, about $1,500.00
Price: Model 47S, about $2,600.00
Price: Model 147S, about $3,300.00
Price: Model 247S, about $3,300.00
Price: Model 347S, about $3,700.00
Price: Model 447S, about $4,200.00

OMEGA FOLDING SIDE-BY-SIDE SHOTGUNS
Gauge: 20, 28, 410, 3" chambers.
Barrel: 20 ga.—26" (Imp. Cyl. & Mod.); 28 ga.—26" (Mod. & Full); 410—26" (Full & Full).
Weight: 5½ lbs.
Stock: Standard has checkered beechwood, Deluxe has walnut; Standard has semi-pistol grip.
Features: Blued barrels and receiver; top tang safety. Imported from Italy by Kassnar. Introduced 1984.
Price: Standard .... $229.00 to $269.00
Price: Deluxe $250.00

Parker-Hale 645E

PARKER-HALE MODEL "600" SERIES DOUBLES
Gauge: 12, 16, 20, 2¾" chambers; 28, 410, 3" chambers.
Barrel: 25", 26", 27", 28" (Imp. Cyl. & Mod., Mod. & Full).
Weight: 12 ga., 6¾-7 lbs.; 20 ga., 5¾-6 lbs.
Stock: 14½"×1½"×2½". Hand checkered walnut with oil finish. "E" (English) models have straight grip, splinter fore-end, checkered butt. "A" (American) models have p.g. stock, beaver-tail fore-end, buttplate.
Features: Boxlock action; silvered, engraved action; auto safety; ejectors or extractors. E-models have double triggers, concave rib (XXV models have Churchill-type rib); A-models have single, non-selective trigger, raised matted rib. Made in Spain by Ugartechea. Imported by Precision Sports. Introduced 1986.
Price: 640E (12, 16, 20; 26", 28"), extractors $529.95
Price: 640E (28, 410; 27" only), extractors $599.95
Price: 640A (12, 16, 20; 26", 28"), extractors $629.95
Price: 640A (28, 410, 27" only), extractors $699.95
Price: 645E (12, 16, 20; 26", 28"), with ejectors $679.95
Price: 645E (28, 410; 27"), with ejectors $749.95
Price: 645A (12, 16, 20; 26", 28") with ejectors $779.95
Price: 645A (28, 410, 27" only), ejectors $849.95
Price: 645E-XXV (12, 16, 20; 25"), with ejectors $699.95
Price: 645E-XXV (28, 410, 27"), with ejectors $779.95
Price: 645E Bi-Gauge (20/28 or 28/410), ejectors $1,199.95
Price: 645A Bi-Gauge (20/28 or 28/410), ejectors $1,295.95
Price: 670E (12, 16, 20, 26", 28") sidelock, with ejectors $2,900.00
Price: 670E (28, 410; 27") sidelock, with ejectors $3,100.00
Price: 680E-XXV (12, 16, 20; 25") sidelock, ejectors, case-color action $2,700.00
Price: 680E-XXV (28, 410; 25") sidelock, ejectors, case-color action $2,900.00

PERUGINI-VISINI CLASSIC DOUBLE SHOTGUN
Gauge: 12, 20, 2¾" or 3".
Barrel: NA.
Weight: NA. **Length:** NA.
Stock: Straight English type of high grade European briar walnut; oil finish.
Features: H&H-type hand-detachable sidelocks internally gold plated; single or double triggers; automatic ejectors. Many options available. Imported from Italy by Wm. Larkin Moore.
Price: From about $12,000.00

Perugini-Visini Liberty Double Shotgun
A boxlock gun that shares many of the same features of the Classic model. Available in 12, 20, 28, 410, 2¾" or 3" chambers. Many options available and can be had as a matched pair.
Price: From about $5,900.00

SHOTGUNS—SIDE-BY-SIDES

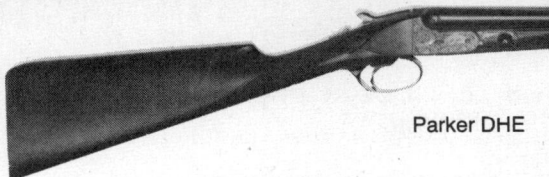

Parker DHE

PARKER DHE SIDE-BY-SIDE SHOTGUN
Gauge: 12, 20, 28, 2¾" or 3" chambers.
Barrel: 26" (Imp. Cyl. & Mod., 2¾" chambers), Skeet & Skeet available, 28" (Mod. & Full, 3" chambers only).

Weight: About 6¾ lbs. (12 ga.), 6½ lbs. (20 ga.), 5½ lbs. (28 ga.), 5 lbs. (410).
Stock: Fancy American walnut, checkered grip and fore-end. Straight stock or pistol grip, splinter or beavertail fore-end; 28 l.p.i. checkering.
Features: Reproduction of the original Parker—most parts interchangeable with original. Double or single selective trigger; checkered skeleton buttplate; selective ejectors; bores hard chromed, excluding choke area. Two-barrel sets available. Hand engraved scroll and scenes on case-hardened frame. Fitted leather trunk included. Limited production. Introduced 1984. Made by Winchester in Japan. Imported by Parker Div. of Reagent Chemical.
Price: D Grade, one barrel set $2,970.00
Price: B Grade $3,970.00
Price: A-1 Special... $8,740.00

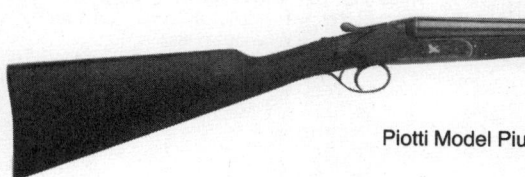

Piotti Model Piuma

PIOTTI MODEL PIUMA SIDE-BY-SIDE
Gauge: 12, 16, 20, 28, 410.
Barrel: 25" to 30" (12 ga.), 25" to 28" (16, 20, 28, 410).

Weight: 5½ to 6¼ lbs. (20 ga.).
Stock: Dimensions to customer specs. Straight grip stock with checkered butt, classic splinter fore-end, hand rubbed oil finish are standard; pistol grip, beavertail fore-end, satin luster finish optional.
Features: Anson & Deeley boxlock ejector double with chopper lump barrels. Level, file-cut rib, light scroll and rosette engraving, scalloped frame. Double triggers with hinged front standard, single non-selective optional. Coin finish standard, color case-hardened optional. Imported from Italy by Wm. Larkin Moore.
Price: $5,700.00

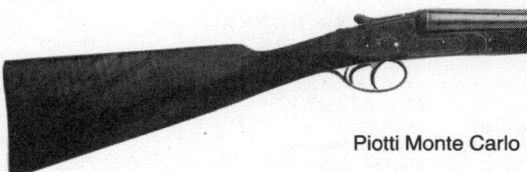

Piotti Monte Carlo

Piotti Model Monte Carlo Side-by-Side
Similar to the Piotti King No. 1 except has Purdey-style scroll and rosette engraving, no gold inlays, over-all workmanship not as finely detailed. Other mechanical specifications remain the same. Imported from Italy by Wm. Larkin Moore.
Price: $10,200.00

PIOTTI KING NO. 1 SIDE-BY-SIDE
Gauge: 12, 16, 20, 28, 410.
Barrel: 25" to 30" (12 ga.), 25" to 28". (16, 20, 28 410). To customer specs. Chokes as specified.
Weight: 6½ lbs. to 8 lbs. (12 ga., to customer specs.)
Stock: Dimensions to customer specs. Finely figured walnut; straight grip with checkered butt with classic splinter fore-end and hand-rubbed oil finish standard. Pistol grip, beavertail fore-end, satin luster finish optional.
Features: Holland & Holland pattern sidelock action, auto ejectors. Double trigger with front trigger hinged standard; non-selective single trigger optional. Coin finish standard; color case-hardened optional. Top rib: level, file cut standard; concave, ventilated optional. Very fine, full coverage scroll engraving with small floral bouquets, gold crown in top lever, name in gold, and gold crest in fore-end. Imported from Italy by Wm. Larkin Moore.
Price: $12,500.00

Piotti Model King Extra Side-by-Side
Similar to the Piotti King No. 1 except highest quality wood and metal work. Choice of either bulino game scene engraving or game scene engraving with gold inlays. Engraved and signed by a master engraver. Exhibition grade wood. Other mechanical specifications remain the same. Imported from Italy by Wm. Larkin Moore.
Price: $18,000.00

Piotti Model Lunik Side-by-Side
Similar to the Piotti King No. 1 except better over-all quality. Has Renaissance-style large scroll engraving in relief, gold crown in top lever, gold name, and gold crest in fore-end. Best quality Holland & Holland-pattern sidelock ejector double with chopper lump (demi-bloc) barrels. Other mechanical specifications remain the same. Imported from Italy by Wm. Larkin Moore.
Price: $13,400.00

Remington Parker

REMINGTON PARKER AHE SIDE-BY-SIDE
Gauge: 20, 2¾" chambers.
Barrel: 28" (any combination of Skeet, Imp. Cyl., Mod., Full chokes).
Weight: About 6½ lbs.
Stock: Circassian or American walnut; straight or pistol grip; beavertail or splinter fore-end; rubber recoil pad, Parker buttplate or engraved skeleton steel buttplate. Checkered 28 lpi.
Features: Custom-made gun. Single selective trigger, automatic ejectors; scroll-engraved color case-hardened receiver. Automatic ejectors. Limited production. Reintroduced 1988. From Remington.
Price: From $11,700.00

RIZZINI BOXLOCK SIDE-BY-SIDE
Gauge: 12, 20, 28, 410.
Barrel: 25" to 30" (12 ga.), 25" to 28" (20, 28, 410).
Weight: 5½ to 6¼ lbs. (20 ga.).
Stock: Dimensions to customer specs. Straight grip stock with checkered butt, classic splinter fore-end, hand rubbed oil finish are standard; pistol grip, beavertail fore-end, satin luster finish optional.
Features: Anson & Deeley boxlock ejector double with chopper lump barrels. Level, file-cut rib, light scroll and rosette engraving, scalloped frame. Double triggers with hinged front standard, single non-selective optional. Coin finish standard, color case-hardened optional. Imported from Italy by Wm. Larkin Moore.
Price: 12, 20 ga., from...................................... $9,700.00
Price: 28, 410 ga., from...................................... $12,400.00

CAUTION: PRICES CHANGE. CHECK AT GUNSHOP.

SHOTGUNS—SIDE-BY-SIDES

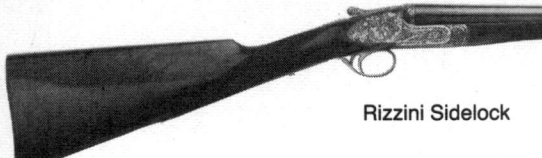
Rizzini Sidelock

ROSSI "SQUIRE" DOUBLE BARREL
Gauge: 12, 20, 410, 3" chambers.
Barrel: 12—28" (Mod. & Full); 20 ga.—26" (Imp. Cyl. & Mod.), 28" (Mod. & Full); 410—26" (Full & Full).
Weight: About 7½ lbs.
Stock: Walnut-finished hardwood.
Features: Double triggers, raised matted rib, beavertail fore-end. Massive twin underlugs mesh with synchronized sliding bolts. Introduced 1978. Imported by Interarms.
Price: 12 or 20 ga. $352.00
Price: 410 .... $357.00

RIZZINI SIDELOCK SIDE-BY-SIDE
Gauge: 12, 20, 28, 410.
Barrel: 25" to 30" (12 ga.), 25" to 28" (20, 28, 410). To customer specs. Chokes as specified.
Weight: 6½ lbs. to 8 lbs. (12 ga., to customer specs.)
Stock: Dimensions to customer specs. Finely figured walnut; straight grip with checkered butt with classic splinter fore-end and hand-rubbed oil finish standard. Pistol grip, beavertail fore-end, satin luster finish optional.
Features: Holland & Holland pattern sidelock action, auto ejectors. Double trigger with front trigger hinged standard; non-selective single trigger optional. Coin finish standard; color case-hardened optional. Top rib level, file cut standard; concave, ventilated optional. Very fine, full coverage scroll engraving with small floral bouquets, gold crown in top lever, name in gold, and gold crest in fore-end. Imported from Italy by Wm. Larkin Moore.
Price: 12, 20 ga., from $17,500.00
Price: 28, 410 ga., from $21,600.00

Rossi Overland

ROSSI OVERLAND DOUBLE BARREL
Gauge: 12, 20, 410, 3" chambers
Action: Sidelock with external hammers; Greener crossbolt.
Barrel: 12 ga., 20" (Imp. Cyl. & Mod.), 28" (Mod. & Full), 20 ga., 20", 26" (Imp. Cyl. & Mod.), 410 ga., 26" (Full & Full).
Weight: 6½ to 7 lbs.
Stock: Walnut p.g. with beavertail fore-end.
Features: Solid raised matted rib. Exposed hammers. Imported by Interarms.
Price: 12 or 20 .... $332.00
Price: 410 .... $337.00

S.A.B. RENATO GAMBA DOUBLE SHOTGUNS
Gauge: 12, 20, 28.
Barrel: 26¾", 28" (standard chokes).
Weight: 6¾ to 7 lbs.
Stock: European walnut. Straight English or pistol grip.
Features: Boxlock action, double triggers, chrome-lined barrels. Ejectors and automatic safety optional. Imported by Armes de Chasse.
Price: Principessa (boxlock), about $1,500.00
Price: Oxford (boxlock), about $1,800.00
Price: London (sidelock), about $5,000.00

SAE Model 209E Double
Similar to the Model 340X except has coin-finish engraved receiver, available in 12, 20, 410 (2¾"). Fancy, oil-finished walnut.
Price: $884.00

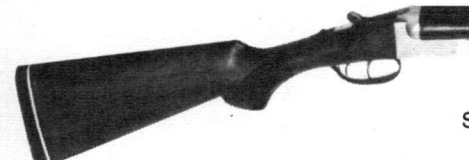
SAE 210S

SAE MODEL 210S DOUBLE
Gauge: 12, 20, 410, 3" chambers.
Barrel: 26" (Mod. & Full), 28" (Mod. & Imp. Cyl.).
Weight: 7 lbs.
Stock: European walnut with p.g., splinter fore-end.
Features: Boxlock action with double triggers, automatic safety, extractors. Introduced 1987. Imported from Spain America Ent.
Price: $427.70

SAE Model 340X Double
Similar to the Model 210S except is true sidelock. Available in 12 or 20 ga. (2¾"), 26" (Mod. & Full), 28" (Mod. & Imp. Cyl.). Color case-hardened receiver with engraving. Weight is 6.9 lbs. Selective ejectors, double triggers.
Price: $648.70

SKB Model 200

SKB MODEL 200 DOUBLE SHOTGUN
Gauge: 12, 20, 3" chambers.
Barrel: 25", 26" (Inter Choke tubes).
Weight: 6 lbs., 10 oz. (12 ga.). **Length:** 42⅛" over-all (26" barrels).
Stock: 14" x 1½" x 2⅝". Walnut with checkered grip and fore-end, recoil pad.
Sights: Metal bead front.
Features: Engraved boxlock action with silvered finish. Gold-plated trigger. Introduced 1988. Imported from Japan by Ernie Simmons Enterprises.
Price: $895.00
Price: Model 200E with straight English-style stock. $895.00

SKB Model 400 Double Shotgun
Similar to the Model 200 except has engraved and silvered sideplates. Standard or straight English-style stock.
Price: $1,195.00

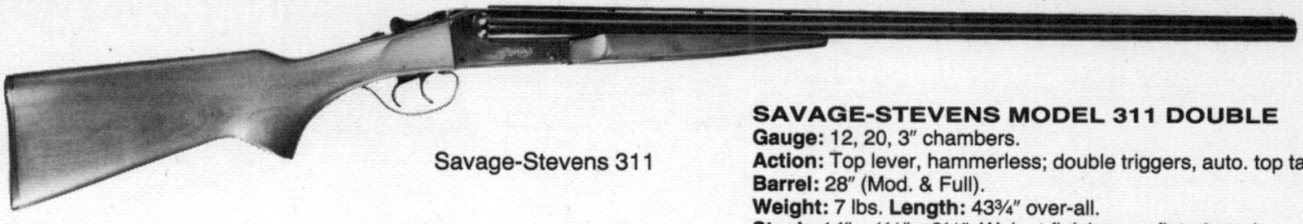

SHOTGUNS—SIDE-BY-SIDES

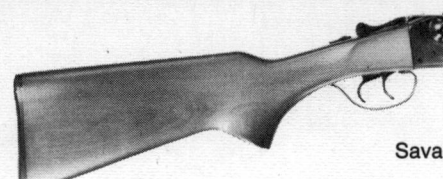
Savage-Stevens 311

SAVAGE-STEVENS MODEL 311 DOUBLE
Gauge: 12, 20, 3" chambers.
Action: Top lever, hammerless; double triggers, auto. top tang safety.
Barrel: 28" (Mod. & Full).
Weight: 7 lbs. **Length:** 43¾" over-all.
Stock: 14" x 1½" x 2½". Walnut finish, p.g., fluted comb.
Features: Automatic top tang safety. Extractors; double triggers.
Price: $249.00

Savage Model 311 "Waterfowler" Double
Similar to the Model 311 except in 12 ga. only (3" chambers) with 28" barrels choked for Full steel shot pattern; has low gloss finish. Introduced 1988.
Price: $339.00

W&C Scott Bowood DeLuxe Game Gun
Similar to the Chatsworth Grande Luxe except less ornate metal and wood work; checkered 24 l.p.i. at fore-end and pistol grip. Imported from England by L. Joseph Rahn.
Price: 12 or 16 ga. $8,000.00
Price: 20 or 28 ga. $8,400.00

W&C SCOTT CHATSWORTH GRANDE LUXE DOUBLE
Gauge: 12, 16, 20, 28.
Barrel: 25", 26", 27", 28", 30" (chokes to order); concave rib standard, Churchill or flat rib optional.
Weight: About 6½ lbs. (12 ga.).
Stock: 14¾"x1½"x2¼", or made to customer specs. French walnut with 32 l.p.i. checkering.
Features: Entirely hand fitted; boxlock action (sideplates optional); English scroll engraving; gold name plate shield in stock. Imported from England by L. Joseph Rahn.
Price: 12 or 16 ga. $9,000.00
Price: 20 or 28 ga. $9,500.00

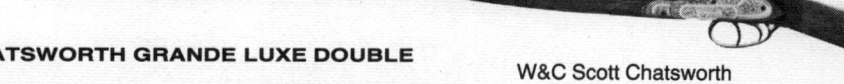
W&C Scott Chatsworth

W&C Scott Kinmount Game Gun
Similar to the Bowood DeLuxe Game Gun except less ornate engraving and wood work; checkered 20 l.p.i.; other details essentially the same. Imported from England by L. Joseph Rahn.
Price: 12 or 16 ga. $7,000.00
Price: 20 or 28 ga. $7,300.00

IGA Side-by-Side

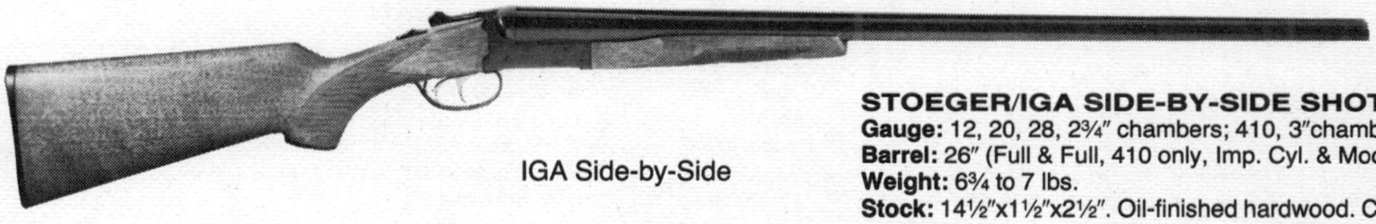

STOEGER/IGA SIDE-BY-SIDE SHOTGUN
Gauge: 12, 20, 28, 2¾" chambers; 410, 3" chambers.
Barrel: 26" (Full & Full, 410 only, Imp. Cyl. & Mod.), 28" (Mod. & Full).
Weight: 6¾ to 7 lbs.
Stock: 14½"x1½"x2½". Oil-finished hardwood. Checkered pistol grip and fore-end.
Features: Automatic safety, extractors only, solid matted barrel rib. Double triggers only. Introduced 1983. Imported from Brazil by Stoeger Industries.
Price: $265.00
Price: Coach Gun, 12 or 20 ga., 20" bbls. $260.00

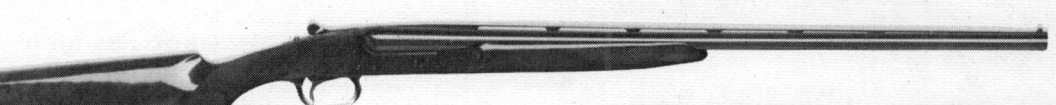
Winchester 23 Classic

WINCHESTER MODEL 23 CLASSIC SHOTGUN
Gauge: 12, 20, 28, 410.
Barrel: 26" (Imp. Cyl. & Mod., except 410 Mod. & Full).
Weight: 5⅞ to 7 lbs. **Length:** 43¼" over-all.
Stock: 14½"x1½"x2⅜". Fancy grade American walnut with pistol grip.
Features: Blued receiver with scroll engraving; gold inlay on bottom: pheasant on 12, 20, quail on 28, 410. Ebony inlay in fore-end, gold initial plate in stock. Single selective trigger, automatic safety, selective ejectors. Introduced 1986. Imported from Japan by Winchester Group, Olin Corp.
Price: 12 and 20 gauge. $1,975.00
Price: 28 and 410 gauge. $2,080.00

Winchester Model 23 Light Duck
Same basic features as the standard Model 23 Pigeon Grade except has plain, blued frame, 28" barrels choked Full and Full; 20 ga.; 3" chambers. Comes with hard case. Matching serial numbers to previously issued Heavy Duck. Introduced 1983.
Price: $1,095.00
Price: Golden Quail (12 ga., 25½", Imp. Cyl. & Mod.) $2,000.00
Price: Golden Quail 410 .... $2,190.00
Price: Custom Two Barrel Set (20, 28 ga. bbls., full fancy walnut, leather luggage-style case) $4,735.00

Consult our Directory pages for the location of firms mentioned.

Winchester Custom Model 23 Shotgun
Same as the Model 23 Classic except has plain blued receiver with no engraving, internal Winchoke system with six tubes (Extra Full, Full, Mod., Imp. Mod., Imp. Cyl., Skeet). Chrome-lined bores and chambers suitable for steel shot. Comes with luggage-style case. Introduced 1987.
Price: $1,715.00

CAUTION: PRICES CHANGE. CHECK AT GUNSHOP.

SHOTGUNS—BOLT ACTIONS & SINGLE SHOTS

Variety of designs for utility and sporting purposes, as well as for competitive shooting.

American Arms Single

AMERICAN ARMS SINGLE BARREL SHOTGUN
Gauge: 12, 20, 410, 3" chamber.
Barrel: 26" (Full, 410 ga.), 28" (Mod., Full).
Weight: About 6½ lbs.
Stock: Walnut-finished hardwood with checkered grip, fore-end.
Sights: Bead front.
Features: Manual thumb safety; chrome-lined barrel. Imported from Italy by American Arms, Inc. Introduced 1988.
Price: $108.00

American Arms Waterfowl Special
Similar to the Single Barrel model except chambered for 10 ga. 3½", has 30" (Full) barrel. Matte finish.
Price: $160.00

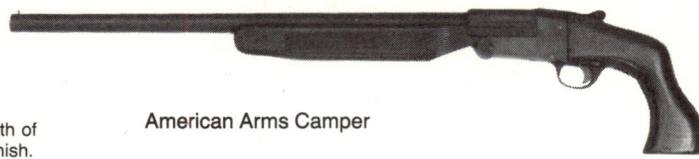

American Arms Camper

American Arms Camper Special
Similar to the Single Barrel except has 21" barrel (Mod.), over-all length of 27", pistol grip instead of buttstock. Gun folds for storage, carry. Matte finish.
Price: $108.00

American Arms Turkey Special
Similar to the Single Barrel except chambered for 10 ga. 3½", has 26" barrel with choke tube. Matte finish.
Price: $189.00

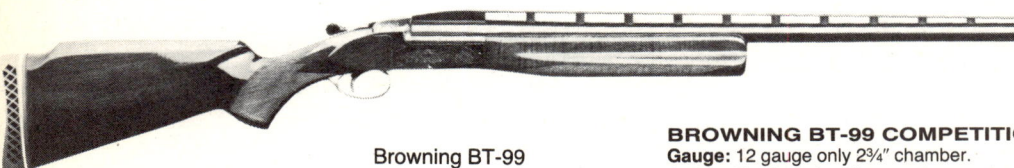

Browning BT-99

BROWNING BT-99 COMPETITION TRAP SPECIAL
Gauge: 12 gauge only 2¾" chamber.
Action: Top lever break-open, hammerless.
Barrel: 32" or 34" with 11/32" wide high post floating vent. rib. Comes with Invector choke tubes or fixed Full, Imp. Mod.
Weight: 8 lbs. (32" bbl.).
Stock: French walnut; hand checkered, full pistol grip, full beavertail fore-end; recoil pad. Trap dimensions with M.C. 14⅜" × 1⅜" × 1⅜" × 2".
Sights: Ivory front and middle beads.
Features: Gold-plated trigger with 3½-lb. pull, deluxe trap-style recoil pad, auto ejector, no safety. Available with either Monte Carlo or standard stock. Imported from Japan by Browning.
Price: Grade I Invector $1,005.00
Price: As above, non-Invector $981.00

F.I.E. "S.S.S." SINGLE BARREL
Gauge: 12, 20, 410, 3" chamber.
Action: Button-break on trigger guard.
Barrel: 18½" (Cyl.).
Weight: 6½ lbs.
Stock: Walnut finished hardwood, full beavertail fore-end.
Features: Exposed hammer. Automatic ejector. Imported from Brazil by F.I.E. Corp.
Price: $129.95

FIE Hamilton & Hunter

F.I.E. "HAMILTON & HUNTER" SINGLE BARREL
Gauge: 12, 20, 410, 3" chamber.
Barrel: 12, 20 ga. 28" (Full); 410 ga. (Full).
Weight: 6½ lbs.
Stock: Walnut stained hardwood, beavertail fore-end.
Sights: Metal bead front.
Features: Trigger guard button is pushed to open action. Exposed hammer, auto ejector, three-piece takedown. Imported from Brazil by F.I.E. Corp.
Price: $98.95
Price: Youth model $98.95

Ithaca Custom Trap

ITHACA 5E CUSTOM TRAP SINGLE BARREL
Gauge: 12, 2¾" chamber.
Barrel: 32", 34" (Full).
Weight: 8½ lbs.
Stock: 14⅜" x 1⅜" x 1⅜". AA Fancy American walnut.
Sights: White bead front, brass middle bead.
Features: Frame, top lever, trigger guard extensively engraved and gold inlaid. Reintroduced 1988. From Ithaca Acquisition Corp.
Price: $7,176.00
Price: 5E Dollar Trap $10,000.00

SHOTGUNS—BOLT ACTIONS & SINGLE SHOTS

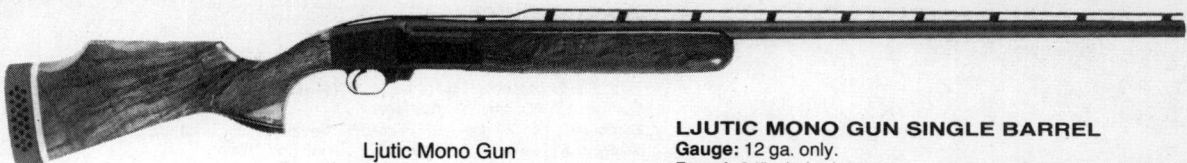
Ljutic Mono Gun

LJUTIC MONO GUN SINGLE BARREL
Gauge: 12 ga. only.
Barrel: 34", choked to customer specs; hollow-milled rib, 35½" sight plane.
Weight: Approx. 9 lbs.
Stock: To customer specs. Oil finish, hand checkered.
Features: Totally custom made. Pull or release trigger; removable trigger guard contains trigger and hammer mechanism; Ljutic pushbutton opener on front of trigger guard. From Ljutic Industries.
Price: $3,695.00
Price: With standard, medium or Olympic rib, custom 32"-34" bbls. $3,795.00
Price: As above with screw-in choke barrel $3,995.00

KRIEGHOFF KS-5 TRAP GUN
Gauge: 12, 2¾" chamber.
Barrel: 32", 34"; Full choke or choke tubes.
Weight: About 8½ lbs.
Stock: 14⅜" x 1⅞" x 1⅜" x 1⅜" or 14⅜" x 2" x 1½" x 1½". Walnut.
Features: Ventilated tapered step rib. Adjustable trigger or release trigger. Receiver finished with electroless nickel. Available with adjustable comb stock. Introduced 1988. Imported from West Germany by Krieghoff International, Inc.
Price: Fixed choke, cased................................. $2,395.00

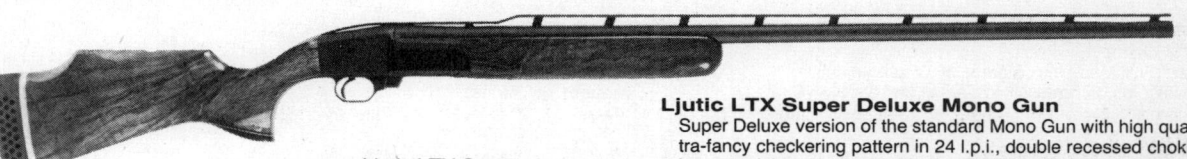
Ljutic LTX Super

Ljutic LTX Super Deluxe Mono Gun
Super Deluxe version of the standard Mono Gun with high quality wood, extra-fancy checkering pattern in 24 l.p.i., double recessed choking. Available in two weights: 8¼ lbs. or 8¾ lbs. Extra light 33" barrel; medium-height rib. Introduced 1984. From Ljutic Industries.
Price: $4,995.00
Price: With three screw-in choke tubes $5,595.00

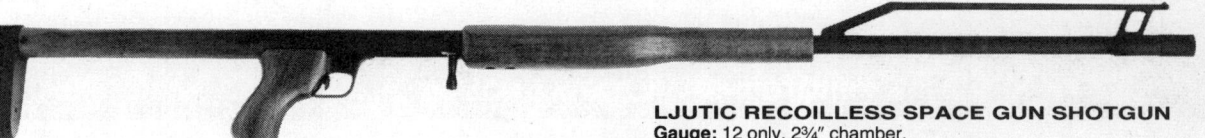
Ljutic Space Shotgun

LJUTIC RECOILLESS SPACE GUN SHOTGUN
Gauge: 12 only, 2¾" chamber.
Barrel: 30" (Full). Screw-in or fixed-choke barrel.
Weight: 8½ lbs.
Stock: 14½" to 15" pull length; universal comb; medium or large p.g.
Sights: Vent. rib.
Features: Pull trigger standard, release trigger available; anti-recoil mechanism. Revolutionary new design. Introduced 1981. From Ljutic Industries.
Price: From $3,695.00

Marlin Model 55

MARLIN MODEL 55 GOOSE GUN BOLT ACTION
Gauge: 12 only, 2¾" or 3" chamber.
Action: Bolt action, thumb safety, detachable 2-shot clip. Red cocking indicator.
Barrel: 36" (Full).
Weight: 8 lbs. **Length:** 56¾" over-all.
Stock: Walnut-finished hardwood, p.g., ventilated recoil pad. Swivel studs. Mar-Shield® finish.
Features: Brass bead front sight, U-groove rear sight.
Price: $213.95

NAVY ARMS MODEL 105 FOLDING SHOTGUN
Gauge: 12, 20, 410, 3" chamber.
Barrel: 28" (Full); 26" (Full) in 410 ga.
Stock: Walnut-stained hardwood. Checkered p.g. and fore-end. Metal bead front.
Features: Folding, hammerless, top-lever action with cross-bar action. Chrome-lined barrel, blued receiver. Deluxe has vent. rib, engraved hard-chrome receiver. Introduced 1987. From Navy Arms.
Price: Model 105S Standard $144.50
Price: Model 105L Deluxe $158.00

NEW ENGLAND FIREARMS "PARDNER" SHOTGUN
Gauge: 12, 20, 410, 3" chamber.
Barrel: 12 ga.—28" (Full, Mod.); 20 ga.—26" (Full, Mod.); 410—26" (Full).
Weight: About 5½ lbs. **Length:** 43" over-all (28" barrel).
Stock: Walnut-finished hardwood; 13¾" pull length (12½" youth).
Features: Transfer-bar ignition; side lever action release. Color case-hardened receiver, blued barrel. Introduced 1987. From New England Firearms Co.
Price: .... NA

NEW ENGLAND FIREARMS "HANDI-GUN"
Caliber/Gauge: 22 Hornet or 30-30; 20 ga., 3" chamber.
Barrel: 22", interchangeable.
Weight: 6½ lbs. **Length:** 37" over-all.
Stock: American hardwood.
Sights: Rifle—ramp front, open adjustable rear; shotgun barrel has front bead.
Features: Break-open single shot with interchangeable barrels. Matte electroless nickel finish. Introduced 1987. From New England Firearms Co.
Price: Two-barrel system, with carrying case .... NA

New England Firearms 10 Gauge Shotgun
Similar ot the 12 ga. "Pardner" except chambered for 3½" 10 ga. shell, has 32" (Full) barrel, giving 47" o.a.l. Introduced 1987.
Price: .... NA

CAUTION: PRICES CHANGE. CHECK AT GUNSHOP.

SHOTGUNS—BOLT ACTIONS & SINGLE SHOTS

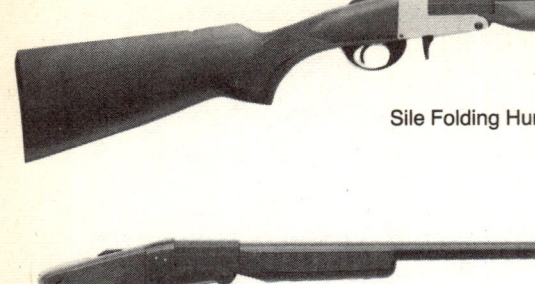

Sile Folding Hunter

Sile Protector

SILE FOLDING HUNTER SINGLE BARREL
Gauge: 12, 20, 410, 3" chamber.
Barrel: 12 and 20 ga.—28" (Mod.); 410—26" (Full). Vent. rib or plain barrel.
Weight: 5¼ to 6 lbs. **Length:** 45" over-all (28" barrel).
Stock: Walnut, checkered p.g. and fore-end.
Features: Folds in half for storage or carry. Manual safety. Engraved, chromed receiver. Imported by Sile.
Price: Vent. Rib $139.95
Price: Plain barrel $125.95

Sile Protector Single Barrel Shotgun
Similar to the Folding Hunter except has grooved walnut pistol grip (no buttstock), fore-end; 19¾" barrel; weighs 4.1 lbs., 27" over-all. In 12, 20, 410 ga. Extractor only. Folds for carry or storage. From Sile.
Price: $111.95

WEATHERBY ATHENA SINGLE BARREL TRAP
Gauge: 12, 2¾" chamber.
Barrel: 32", 34" (Full, Mod., Imp. Mod. Multi-Choke tubes).
Weight: About 8½ lbs. **Length:** 49½" over-all with 32" barrel.
Stock: 14⅜" x 1⅜" x 2⅛" x 1¾". American walnut with checkered p.g. and fore-end.
Sights: White front, brass middle bead.
Features: Engraved, silvered sideplate receiver; ventilated rubber recoil pad. Can be ordered with an extra over-under barrel set. Introduced 1988. Imported from Japan by Weatherby.
Price: $1,611.00
Price: Combo $2,100.00

STOEGER/IGA SINGLE BARREL SHOTGUN
Gauge: 12, 2¾", 20, 410, 3".
Barrel: 12, 20 ga.—26", 28" (Imp. Cyl., Mod., Full), 410—28" (Imp. Cyl., Mod., Full).
Weight: 5¼ lbs.
Stock: 14" x 1½" x 2½". Brazilian hardwood.
Sights: Metal bead front.
Features: Exposed hammer with half-cock safety; extractor; blue finish. Introduced 1987. Imported from Brazil by Stoeger Industries.
Price: $95.00

SHOTGUNS—MILITARY & POLICE

Designs for utility, suitable for and adaptable to competitions and other sporting purposes.

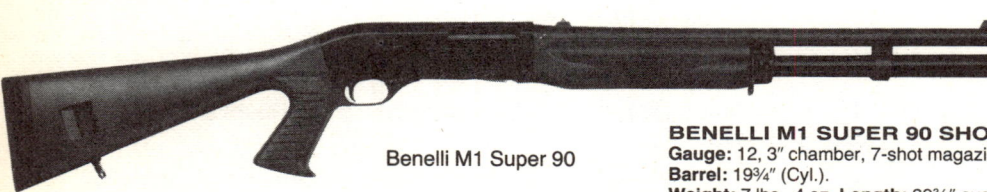

Benelli M1 Super 90

BENELLI M1 SUPER 90 SHOTGUN
Gauge: 12, 3" chamber, 7-shot magazine.
Barrel: 19¾" (Cyl.).
Weight: 7 lbs., 4 oz. **Length:** 39¾" over-all.
Stock: High-impact polymer with sling loop in side of butt; rubberized pistol grip on optional SWAT stock.
Sights: Post front, buckhorn rear adj. for w.
Features: Alloy receiver with rotating locking lug bolt; matte finish; automatic shell release lever. Comes with carrier for speed loading and magazine reducer plug. Optional vent. rib and interchangeable barrels available. Introduced 1986. Imported by Heckler & Koch, Inc.
Price: $613.00
Price: With pistol grip stock $649.50

ARMSCOR MODEL 30R RIOT GUN
Gauge: 12, 6- or 8-shot capacity.
Barrel: 20" (Cyl.).
Weight: 6¾ lbs. **Length:** 39" over-all.
Stock: Plain mahogany.
Sights: Metal bead front.
Features: Double action bars; blue finish; grooved fore-end. Introduced 1987. Imported from the Philippines by Armscor.
Price: About $202.95

Beretta 1200FP

BERETTA MODEL 1200FP AUTO SHOTGUN
Gauge: 12, 2¾" chamber.
Barrel: 20" (Cyl.).
Weight: 7.3 lbs. **Length:** NA
Stock: Special strengthened technopolymer, matte black finish.
Sights: Fixed rifle type.
Features: Has 6-shot magazine. Introduced 1988. Imported from Italy by Beretta U.S.A.
Price: $440.00

Consult our Directory pages for the location of firms mentioned.

SHOTGUNS—MILITARY & POLICE

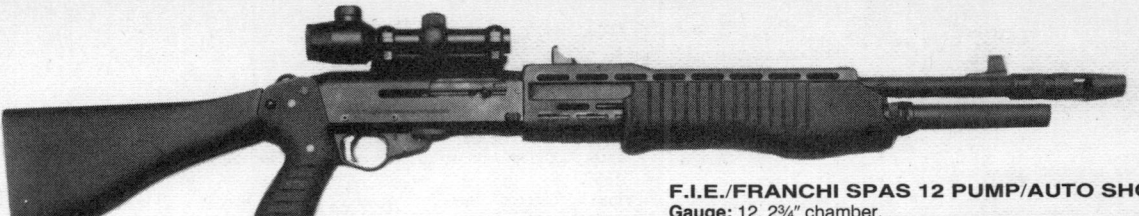

F.I.E./Franchi SPAS 12

F.I.E./FRANCHI SPAS 12 PUMP/AUTO SHOTGUN
Gauge: 12, 2¾" chamber.
Barrel: 21½". Barrel threaded for SPAS accessories.
Weight: 9.6 lbs. **Length:** 31¾" (stock folded).
Stock: Folding metal or optional fixed composition.
Sights: Blade front, aperture rear.
Features: Functions as pump and/or gas-operated auto. Has 8-shot magazine. Parkerized alloy receiver, chrome lined bore, resin pistol grip and pump handle. Made in Italy by Franchi. Introduced 1983. Imported by F.I.E. Corp.
Price: $599.95
Price: Mod. or Full choke tube $39.95
Price: Optional fixed stock $74.95

F.I.E/Franchi LAW 12 Auto Shotgun
A semi-automatic-only lightweight variation of the SPAS 12 pump/auto. Has a 21½" barrel, 8-shot magazine, matte black finish. Over-all length is 41½", weight about 7½ lbs. Stock and pistol grip of nylon resin is detachable. Accessories include shot diverter tube, Full or Modified choke tubes, scope mount, olive drab sling, take-down tool, carry handle. Introduced 1987. Imported from Italy by F.I.E.
Price: $559.95

F.I.E./Franchi SAS 12

F.I.E./Franchi SAS 12 Pump Shotgun
A slide-action-only, lightweight variation of the SPAS 12 pump/auto shotgun, with the same specifications as the LAW 12. Introduced 1987. Imported from Italy by F.I.E.
Price: $359.95

Holmes Model 88

HOLMES MODEL 88 PUMP SHOTGUN
Gauge: 12, 2¾" chamber, 5- or 10-shot magazine.
Barrel: 18¼" (Cyl.); 20" (choke tubes).
Weight: 9 lbs. **Length:** 38¼" over-all (18¼" barrel).
Stock: Synthetic.
Sights: Post front, fixed rear.
Features: Double action bars; matte blue finish. Announced 1988. From Holmes Firearms.
Price: With one magazine $495.00
Price: Extra magazines, each $40.00

ITHACA MODEL 87 M&P DSPS SHOTGUNS
Gauge: 12, 3" chamber, 5 or 8-shot magazine.
Barrel: 20" (Cyl.).
Weight: 7 lbs.
Stock: Walnut.
Sights: Bead front on 5-shot, rifle sights on 8-shot.
Features: Parkerized finish; bottom ejection; cross-bolt safety. Reintroduced 1988. From Ithaca Acquisition Corp.
Price: M&P, 5-shot. $338.00
Price: DSPS, 8-shot $338.00

Ithaca Model 87 Hand Grip Shotgun
Similar to the Model 87 M&P except has black polymer pistol grip and slide handle with nylon sling. In 12 or 20 gauge, 18½" barrel (Cyl.), 5-shot magazine. Reintroduced 1988.
Price: $355.00

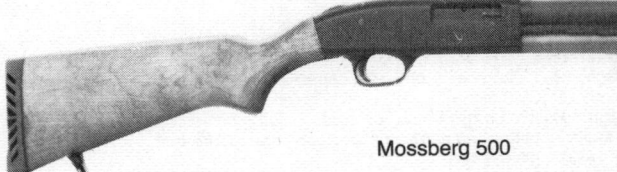

Mossberg 500

MOSSBERG MODEL 500 SECURITY SHOTGUNS
Gauge: 12, 2¾" chamber.
Barrel: 18½", 20" (Cyl.).
Weight: 7 lbs.
Stock: Walnut-finished hardwood; synthetic field or Speedfeed.
Sights: Metal bead front.
Features: Available in 6- or 8-shot models. Top-mounted safety, double action slide bars, swivel studs, rubber recoil pad. Blue, Parkerized or electroless nickel finishes. Price list not complete—contact Mossberg for full list.
Price: From about $251.95
Price: Mini Combo (as above except also comes with a handguard and pistol grip kit), from about $258.95
Price: Maxi Combo (as above except also comes with an extra field barrel), from about $279.95

Mossberg Model 500 Mariner Pump
Similar to the Model 500 Security except all metal parts finished with MARINECOAT, a Teflon and metal coating to resist rust and corrosion. Choice of synthetic field or Speedfeed stocks or pistol grip.
Price: From about $349.95
Price: Mini Combo (as above except includes handguard and pistol grip kit), about $389.95

CAUTION: PRICES CHANGE. CHECK AT GUNSHOP.

SHOTGUNS—MILITARY & POLICE

Mossberg 590

Mossberg Bullpup

MOSSBERG 500 BULLPUP
Gauge: 12, 2¾" chamber; 6- or 8-shot.
Barrel: 18½", 20" (Cyl.).

Mossberg Model 590 Military Shotgun
Similar to the Model 500 Security except has 20" barrel only, 9-shot magazine. Available with wood stock, synthetic field, Speedfeed stock. Introduced 1987.
Price: Wood stock, blue $328.95
Price: Speedfeed stock, Parkerized $402.95
Price: Synthetic stock, Parkerized $369.95

Weight: 9½ lbs. (6 shot). **Length:** 28½" over-all (18½" bbl.).
Stock: Bullpup design of high-impact plastics.
Sights: Fixed, mounted in carrying handle.
Features: Uses the M500 pump shotgun action. Cross-bolt and grip safeties. Introduced 1986.
Price: 6 shot $394.95
Price: 8 shot $409.95

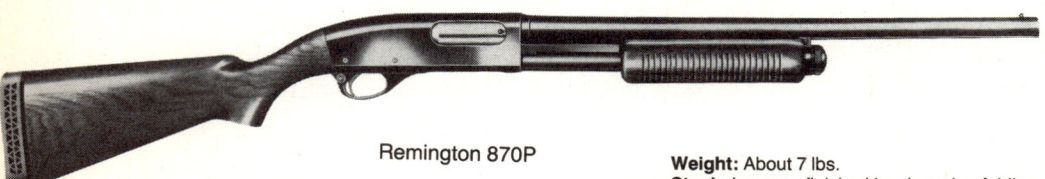

Remington 870P

REMINGTON MODEL 870P POLICE SHOTGUN
Gauge: 12, 3" chamber.
Barrel: 18", 20" (Police Cyl.), 20" (Imp. Cyl.).

Weight: About 7 lbs.
Stock: Lacquer-finished hardwood or folding stock.
Sights: Meal bead front or rifle sights.
Features: Solid steel receiver, double-action slide bars.
Price: Wood stock, 18" or 20", bead sight, about $312.00
Price: Wood stock, 20", rifle sights, about $333.00

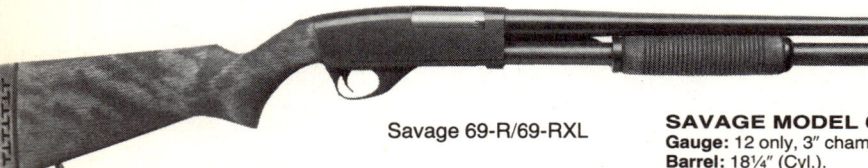

Savage 69-R/69-RXL

Savage Model 69-RXG Pump Shotgun
Similar to the Model 69-RXL except has pistol grip and grooved slide handle of DuPont Rynite® composition. Introduced 1988.
Price: $189.00

SAVAGE MODEL 69-RXL PUMP SHOTGUN
Gauge: 12 only, 3" chamber.
Barrel: 18¼" (Cyl.).
Weight: 6½ lbs. **Length:** 38" over-all.
Stock: Walnut-finished hardwood.
Sights: Bead front.
Features: Top tang safety, 7-shot magazine. Stock has fluted comb and full pistol grip, ventilated rubber pad. QD swivel studs. Introduced 1982.
Price: $179.00

STEVENS MODEL 311-R GUARD GUN DOUBLE
Gauge: 12 ga., 3" chambers.
Barrel: 18¼" (Cyl. & Cyl.).
Weight: 6¾ lbs. **Length:** 34" over-all.
Stock: Walnut-finished hardwood.
Sights: Bead front.
Features: Top tang safety, double triggers, color case-hardened frame, blue barrels. Ventilated rubber recoil pad. Introduced 1982.
Price: $249.00

USAS-12 AUTO SHOTGUN
Gauge: 12, 2¾"; 10- or 20-shot drum magazine.
Barrel: 18¼" (Cyl.).
Weight: 10 lbs. **Length:** 38" over-all.
Stock: Composition butt, pistol grip, fore-end.
Sights: Fixed.
Features: Gas-operated action; Parkerized finish. From Gilbert Equipment Co.
Price: $700.00

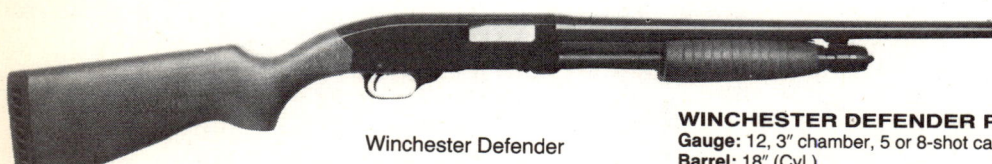

Winchester Defender

Winchester Pistol Grip Pump Security Shotguns
Same as regular Security Series but with pistol grip and fore-end of high-impact resistant ABS plastic with non-glare black finish. Introduced 1984.
Price: Pistol Grip Defender, about $233.00

Winchester "Stainless Marine" Pump Gun
Same as the Defender except has bright chrome finish, stainless-steel barrel, rifle-type sights only. Has special fore-end cap for easy cleaning and inspection.
Price: About $387.00

WINCHESTER DEFENDER PUMP GUN
Gauge: 12, 3" chamber, 5 or 8-shot capacity.
Barrel: 18" (Cyl.).
Weight: 6¾ lbs. **Length:** 38⅝" over-all.
Stock: Walnut finished hardwood stock and ribbed fore-end.
Sights: Metal bead front.
Features: Cross-bolt safety, front-locking rotating bolt, twin action slide bars. Black rubber butt pad. Made under license by U.S. Repeating Arms Co.
Price: 8-shot, about $233.00
Price: 5-shot, about $224.00
Price: As above with rifle sights, about $240.00
Price: Defender Combo (with p.g. and extra 28" bbl.) $261.00
Price: As above with extra vent. rib bbl. $280.00

BLACK POWDER GUNS

The following pages catalog the black powder arms currently available to U.S. shooters. These range from quite precise replicas of historically significant arms to toally new designs created expressly to give the black powder shooter the benefits of modern technology.

Most of the replicas are imported, and many are available from more than one source. Thus, examples of a given model such as the 1860 Army revolver or Zouave rifle purchased from different importers may vary in price, finish and fitting. Most of them bear proof marks, indicating that they have been test fired in the proof house of their country of origin.

A list of the importers and the retail price range are included with the description for each model. Many local dealers handle more than one importer's products, giving the prospective buyer an opportunity to make his own judgment in selecting a black powder gun. Most importers have catalogs available free or at nominal cost, and some are well worth having for the useful information on black powder shooting they provide in addition to their detailed descriptions and specifications of the guns.

A number of special accessories are also available for the black powder shooter. These include replica powder flasks, bullet moulds, cappers and tools, as well as more modern devices to facilitate black powder cleaning and maintenance. Ornate presentation cases and even detachable shoulder stocks are also available for some black powder pistols from their importers. Again, dealers or the importers will have catalogs.

The black powder guns are arranged in four sections: Single Shot Pistols, Revolvers, Muskets & Rifles, and Shotguns. The guns within each section are arranged roughly by date of the original, with the oldest first. Thus the 1836 Paterson replica leads off the revolver section, and flintlocks precede percussion arms in the other sections.

BLACK POWDER SINGLE SHOT PISTOLS—FLINT & PERCUSSION

Scottish Black Watch

BLACK WATCH SCOTCH PISTOL
Caliber: 577 (.550″ round ball).
Barrel: 7″, smoothbore.
Weight: 1½ lbs. **Length:** 12″ over-all.
Stock: Brass.
Sights: None.
Features: Faithful reproduction of this military flintlock. From Dixie.
Price: $135.00

CHARLEVILLE FLINTLOCK PISTOL
Caliber: 69 (.680″ round ball).
Barrel: 7½″.
Weight: 48 oz. **Length:** 13½″ over-all.
Stock: Walnut.
Sights: None.
Features: Brass frame, polished steel barrel, iron belt hook, brass buttcap and backstrap. Replica of original 1777 pistol. Imported by Dixie.
Price: $140.00

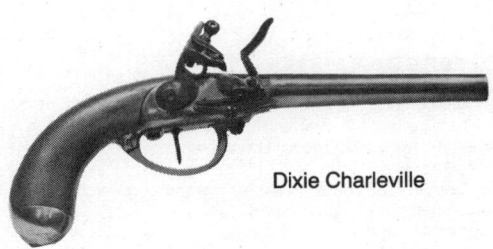
Dixie Charleville

DIXIE QUEEN ANNE FLINTLOCK PISTOL
Caliber: 50 (.490″ round ball).
Barrel: 7½″, smoothbore.
Stock: Walnut.
Sights: None.
Features: Browned steel barrel, fluted brass trigger guard, brass mask on butt. Lockplate left in the white. Made by Pedersoli in Italy. Introduced 1983. Imported by Dixie Gun Works.
Price: $131.00
Price: Kit $115.00

Dixie Queen Anne

LYMAN PLAINS PISTOL
Caliber: 50 or 54.
Barrel: 8″, 1-in-30″ twist, both calibers.
Weight: 50 oz. **Length:** 15″ over-all.
Stock: Walnut half-stock.
Sights: Blade front, square notch rear adj. for windage.
Features: Polished brass trigger guard and ramrod tip, color case-hardened coil spring lock, spring-loaded trigger, stainless steel nipple, blackened iron furniture. Hooked patent breech, detachable belt hook. Introduced 1981. From Lyman Products.
Price: Finished $159.95
Price: Kit $129.00

Lyman Plains Pistol

DIXIE PENNSYLVANIA PISTOL
Caliber: 44 (.430″ round ball).
Barrel: 10″ (⅞″ octagon).
Weight: 2½ lbs.
Stock: Walnut-stained hardwood.
Sights: Blade front, open rear drift-adj. for windage; brass.
Features: Available in flint only. Brass trigger guard, thimbles, nosecap, wedgeplates; high-luster blue barrel. Imported from Italy by Dixie Gun Works.
Price: Finished $119.95
Price: Kit $88.75

CAUTION: PRICES CHANGE. CHECK AT GUNSHOP.

BLACK POWDER SINGLE SHOT PISTOLS—FLINT & PERCUSSION

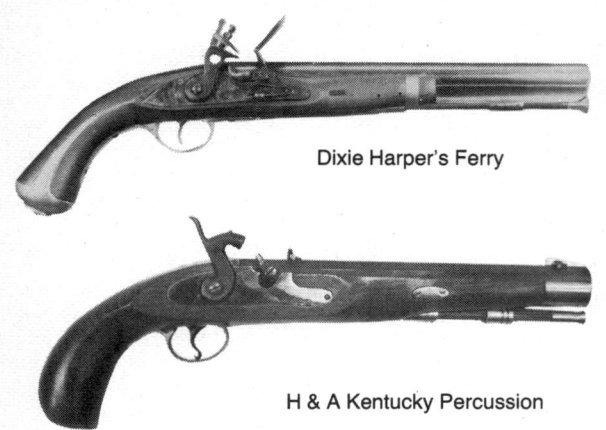

Dixie Harper's Ferry

H & A Kentucky Percussion

HARPER'S FERRY 1806 PISTOL
Caliber: 58 (.570" round ball).
Barrel: 10".
Weight: 40 oz. **Length:** 16" over-all.
Stock: Walnut.
Sights: Fixed.
Features: Case-hardened lock, brass mounted browned bbl. Replica of the first U.S. Gov't.-made flintlock pistol. Imported by Navy Arms, Dixie, EMF.
Price: .... $$165.00 to 270.00
Price: Kit (Dixie) $135.00

KENTUCKY FLINTLOCK PISTOL
Caliber: 44, 45.
Barrel: 10 1/8".
Weight: 32 oz. **Length:** 15 1/2" over-all.
Stock: Walnut.
Sights: Fixed.
Features: Specifications, including caliber, weight and length may vary with importer. Case-hardened lock, blued bbl.; available also as brass bbl. flint Model 1821. Imported by Armsport, Navy Arms (44 only), The Armoury, EMF.
Price: .... $40.95 to $207.00
Price: In kit form, from .... $90.00 to $112.00
Price: Single cased set (Navy Arms) $235.00
Price: Double cased set (Navy Arms) $389.00

Kentucky Percussion Pistol
Similar to flint version but percussion lock. Imported by The Armoury, Navy Arms, CVA, Armsport, Hopkins & Allen, Muzzle Loaders, Inc., Traditions.
Price: .... $97.50 to $139.00
Price: In kit form (Traditions, Armoury)................. $35.95 to $102.00
Price: Single cased set (Navy Arms) $230.00
Price: Double cased set (Navy Arms) $360.00

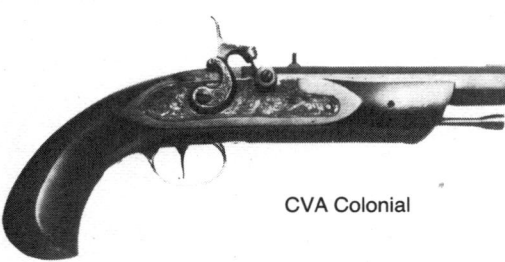

CVA Colonial

CVA COLONIAL PISTOL
Caliber: 45.
Barrel: 6 3/4", octagonal, rifled.
Length: 12 3/4" over-all.
Stock: Selected hardwood.
Features: Case-hardened lock, brass furniture, fixed sights. Steel ramrod. Available in percussion only. Imported by CVA.
Price: Finished $86.95
Price: Kit $57.95

DIXIE OVERCOAT PISTOL
Caliber: 39.
Barrel: 4" smoothbore.
Weight: 13 oz. **Length:** 8" over-all.
Stock: Walnut-finished hardwood. Checkered p.g.
Sights: Bead front.
Features: Shoots .380" balls. Breech plug and engraved lock are burnished steel finish; barrel and trigger guard blued.
Price: Engraved model $34.50

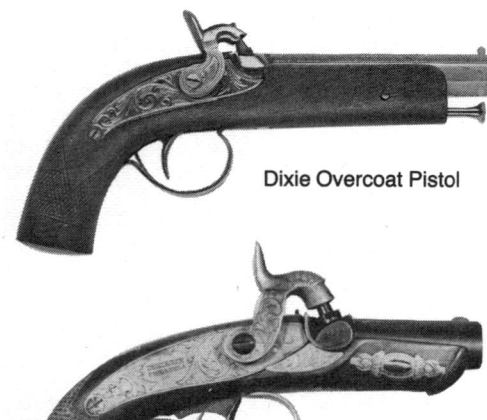

Dixie Overcoat Pistol

Dixie Lincoln Derringer

DIXIE W. PARKER FLINTLOCK PISTOL
Caliber: 45.
Barrel: 11", rifled.
Weight: 40 oz. **Length:** 16 1/2" over-all.
Stock: Walnut.
Sights: Blade front, notch rear.
Features: Browned barrel, silver plated trigger guard, finger rest, polished and engraved lock. Double set triggers. Imported by Dixie Gun Works.
Price: $270.00

DIXIE LINCOLN DERRINGER
Caliber: 41.
Barrel: 2", 8 lands, 8 grooves.
Weight: 7 oz. **Length:** 5 1/2" over-all.
Stock: Walnut finish, checkered.
Sights: Fixed.
Features: Authentic copy of the "Lincoln Derringer." Shoots .400" patched ball. German silver furniture includes trigger guard with pineapple finial, wedge plates, nose, wrist, side and teardrop inlays. All furniture, lockplate, hammer, and breech plug engraved. Imported from Italy by Dixie Gun Works.
Price: With wooden case $285.95
Price: Kit (not engraved) $89.95

PHILADELPHIA DERRINGER PERCUSSION PISTOL
Caliber: 45.
Barrel: 3 1/8".
Weight: 16 oz. **Length:** 7" over-all.
Stock: Select hardwood.
Sights: Fixed.
Features: Engraved wedge holder and bbl. Imported by CVA.
Price: $74.95
Price: Kit form $41.95

BLACK POWDER SINGLE SHOT PISTOLS—FLINT & PERCUSSION

Dixie Philadelphia

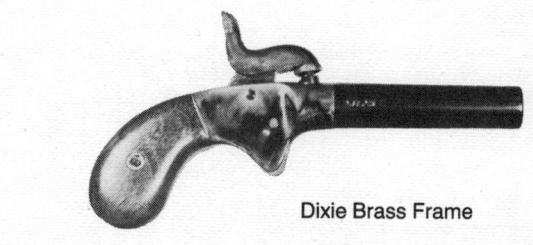

Dixie Brass Frame

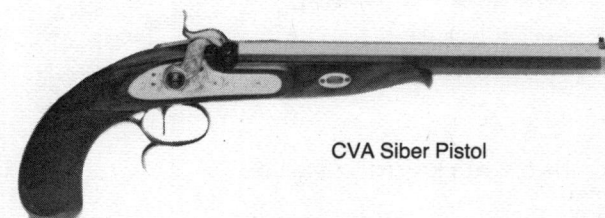

CVA Siber Pistol

DIXIE PHILADELPHIA DERRINGER
Caliber: 41.
Barrel: 3½", octagon.
Weight: 8 oz. **Length:** 5½" over-all.
Stock: Walnut, checkered p.g.
Sights: Fixed.
Features: Barrel and lock are blued; brass furniture. From Dixie Gun Works.
Price: **$45.00**

DIXIE BRASS FRAME DERRINGER
Caliber: 41.
Barrel: 2½".
Weight: 7 oz. **Length:** 5½" over-all.
Stocks: Walnut.
Features: Brass frame, color case-hardened hammer and trigger. Shoots .395" round ball. Engraved model available. From Dixie Gun Works.
Price: Plain model **$49.95**
Price: Engraved model **$74.95**
Price: Kit form, plain model **$42.50**

DIXIE ABILENE DERRINGER
Caliber: 41.
Barrel: 2½", 6-groove rifling.
Weight: 8 oz. **Length:** 6½" over-all.
Stock: Walnut.
Features: All steel version of Dixie's brass-framed derringers. Blued barrel, color case-hardened frame and hammer. Shoots .395" patched ball. Comes with wood presentation case.
Price: **$69.95**
Price: Kit form **$51.95**

CVA SIBER PISTOL
Caliber: 45.
Barrel: 10½".
Weight: 34 oz. **Length:** 15½" over-all.
Stock: High-grade French walnut, checkered grip.
Sights: Barleycorn front, micro adjustable rear.
Features: Reproduction of pistol made by Swiss watchmaker Jean Siber in the 1800s. Precise lock and set trigger give fast lock time. Has engraving, blackened stainless barrel, trigger guard. Imported by CVA.
Price: **$314.95**

FRENCH-STYLE DUELING PISTOL
Caliber: 44.
Barrel: 10".
Weight: 35 ozs. **Length:** 15¾" over-all.
Stock: Carved walnut.
Sights: Fixed.
Features: Comes with velvet-lined case and accessories. Imported by Mandall Shooting Supplies.
Price: **$295.00**

MOORE & PATRICK FLINT DUELING PISTOL
Caliber: 45.
Barrel: 10", rifled.
Weight: 32 oz. **Length:** 14½" over-all.
Stock: European walnut, checkered.
Sights: Fixed.
Features: Engraved, silvered lock plate, blue barrel. German silver furniture. Imported from Italy by Hopkins & Allen, Dixie.
Price: **$285.00**

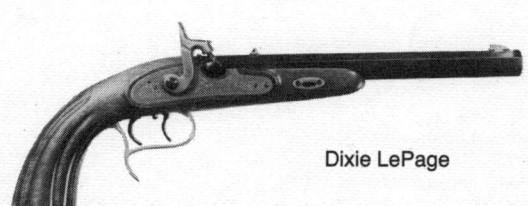

Dixie LePage

DIXIE LE PAGE PERCUSSION DUELING PISTOL
Caliber: 45.
Barrel: 10", rifled.
Weight: 40 oz. **Length:** 16" over-all.
Stock: Walnut, fluted butt.
Sights: Blade front, notch rear.
Features: Double set triggers. Blued barrel; trigger guard and butt cap are polished silver. Imported by Dixie Gun Works.
Price: **$225.00**

NAVY ARMS LE PAGE DUELING PISTOL
Caliber: 45.
Barrel: 9", octagon, rifled.
Weight: 34 oz. **Length:** 15" over-all.
Stock: European walnut.
Sights: Adjustable rear.
Features: Single set trigger. Polished metal finish. From Navy Arms.
Price: Percussion **$312.00**
Price: Single cased set, percussion **$560.00**
Price: Double cased set, percussion **$900.00**
Price: Flintlock, rifled **$340.00**
Price: Flintlock, smoothbore **$340.00**
Price: Flintlock, single cased set **$659.00**
Price: Flintlock, double cased set **$1,100.00**

DIXIE SCREW BARREL PISTOL
Caliber: .445".
Barrel: 2½".
Weight: 8 oz. **Length:** 6½" over-all.
Stock: Walnut.
Features: Trigger folds down when hammer is cocked. Close copy of the originals once made in Belgium. Uses No. 11 percussion caps.
Price: **$89.00**
Price: Kit **$53.00**

CAUTION: PRICES CHANGE. CHECK AT GUNSHOP.

BLACK POWDER SINGLE SHOT PISTOLS—FLINT & PERCUSSION

ELGIN CUTLASS PISTOL
Caliber: 44 (.440″).
Barrel: 4¼″.
Weight: 21 oz. **Length:** 12″ over-all.
Stock: Walnut.
Sights: None.
Features: Replica of the pistol used by the U.S. Navy as a boarding weapon. Smoothbore barrel. Available as a kit or finished. Made in U.S. by Navy Arms.
Price: Kit $78.50
Price: Finished $104.95

NAVY ARMS SNAKE EYES
Caliber: 36.
Barrel: 2⅝″, double barrel.
Weight: 24 ozs. **Length:** 6¾″ over-all.
Stocks: Composition pearl.
Sights: None.
Features: Solid brass barrels and receiver. Also comes in kit form, 90% complete with only 14 pieces. From Navy Arms.
Price: Complete $74.95
Price: Kit $54.00

ETHAN ALLEN PEPPERBOX
Caliber: 36.
Barrel: 3⅛″, four smoothbore barrels.
Weight: 38 oz. **Length:** 9″ over-all.
Stock: Walnut.
Sights: None.
Features: Steel barrels, brass receiver. Also comes in kit form, 90% completed. From Navy Arms.
Price: Complete $79.95
Price: Kit $59.25

NEW ORLEANS ACE
Caliber: 44.
Barrel: 3½″, rifled or smoothbore.
Weight: 16 oz. **Length:** 9″ over-all.
Stock: Walnut.
Sights: None.
Features: Solid brass frame (receiver). Available complete or in kit form. Kit is 90% complete, no drilling or tapping, fully inletted. From Navy Arms.
Price: Complete (smoothbore)............................. $58.50
Price: Kit (smoothbore) $43.25

Elgin Cutlass Pistol

NAVY ARMS DUCKFOOT
Caliber: 36.
Barrel: 2⅞″, three barrels.
Weight: 32 oz. **Length:** 10½″ over-all.
Stock: Walnut.
Sights: None.
Features: Steel barrels and receiver, brass frame. Also comes in kit form, 90% completed, no drilling or tapping. From Navy Arms.
Price: Complete $69.95
Price: Kit $48.95

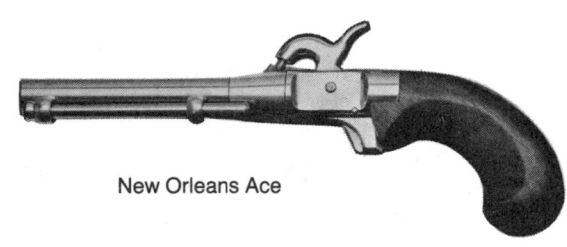
New Orleans Ace

HOPKINS & ALLEN BOOT PISTOL
Caliber: 45.
Barrel: 6″.
Weight: 42 oz. **Length:** 13″ over-all.
Stock: Walnut.
Sights: Silver blade front, rear adj. for e.
Features: Under-hammer design. From Hopkins & Allen.
Price: Kit form $78.65
Price: Target version with wood fore-end, ramrod, hood front sight, elevator rear $98.80

H & A Target Boot

CVA VEST POCKET DERRINGER
Caliber: 44.
Barrel: 2½″, brass.
Weight: 7 oz.
Stock: Two-piece walnut.
Features: All brass frame with brass ramrod. A muzzle-loading version of the Colt No. 3 derringer.
Price: Finished $43.95
Price: Kit $37.95

TRADITIONS TRAPPER PISTOL
Caliber: 45, 50.
Barrel: 10¾″, ⅞″ flats.
Weight: 1¾ lbs. **Length:** 16⅝″ over-all.
Stock: Beech.
Sights: Blade front, adjustable rear.
Features: Double set triggers; brass butt cap, trigger guard, wedge plate, fore-end tip, thimble. From Traditions Inc.
Price: $108.00
Price: Kit $85.00

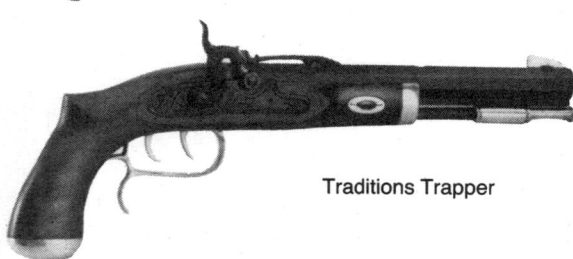
Traditions Trapper

DIXIE TORNADO TARGET PISTOL
Caliber: 44 (.430″ round ball).
Barrel: 10″, octagonal, 1-in-22″ twist.
Stock: Walnut, target-style. Left unfinished for custom fitting. Walnut fore-end.
Sights: Blade on ramp front, micro-type open rear adjustable for windage and elevation.
Features: Grip frame style of 1860 Colt revolver. Improved model of the Tingle and B.W. Southgate pistol. Trigger adjustable for pull. Frame, barrel, hammer and sights in the white, brass trigger guard. Comes with solid brass, walnut-handled cleaning rod with jag and nylon muzzle protector. Introduced 1983. From Dixie Gun Works.
Price: $151.95

Dixie Tornado Pistol

BLACK POWDER REVOLVERS

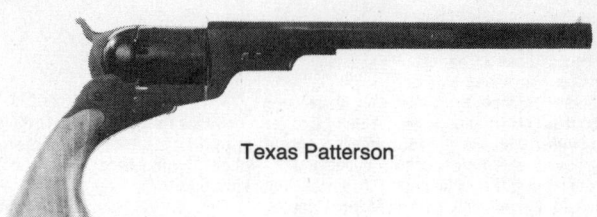
Texas Patterson

TEXAS PATERSON 1836 REVOLVER
Caliber: 36 (.376" round ball).
Barrel: 7½".
Weight: 42 oz.
Stocks: One-piece walnut.
Sights: Fixed.
Features: Copy of Sam Colt's first commercially-made revolving pistol. Has no loading lever but comes with loading tool. From Dixie Gun Works, Navy Arms.
Price: .... $310.00 to $320.00

WALKER 1847 PERCUSSION REVOLVER
Caliber: 44, 6-shot.
Barrel: 9".
Weight: 84 oz. **Length:** 15½" over-all.
Stocks: Walnut.
Sights: Fixed.
Features: Case-hardened frame, loading lever and hammer; iron backstrap; brass trigger guard; engraved cylinder. Imported by CVA, Muzzleloaders, Inc., Navy Arms, Dixie, Armsport, Benson Firearms.
Price: About .... $185.00 to $295.00
Price: Single cased set (Navy Arms) $350.00
Price: Preassembled kit (CVA) $166.95

Walker 1847

UBERTI 1st MODEL DRAGOON
Caliber: 44.
Barrel: 7½", part round, part octagon.
Weight: 64 oz.
Stocks: One piece walnut.
Sights: German silver blade front, hammer notch rear.
Features: First model has oval bolt cuts in cylinder, square-back flared trigger guard, V-type mainspring, short trigger. Ranger and Indian scene roll-engraved on cylinder. Color case-hardened frame, loading lever, plunger and hammer; blue barrel, cylinder, trigger and wedge. Available with old-time charcoal blue or standard blue-black finish. Polished brass backstrap and trigger guard. From Benson Firearms, Uberti USA.
Price: $240.00

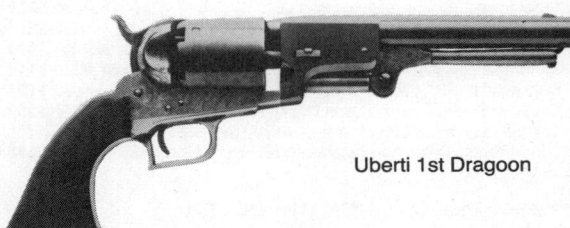
Uberti 1st Dragoon

Uberti 2nd Model Dragoon Revolver
Similar to the 1st Model except this model is distinguished by its rectangular bolt cuts in the cylinder.
Price: $240.00
Price: As Confederate Tucker & Sherrard, with 3rd Model loading lever and special cylinder engraving. $240.00

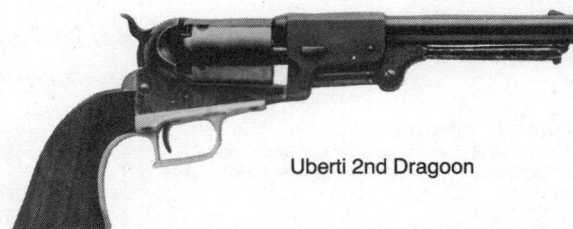
Uberti 2nd Dragoon

Uberti 3rd Model Dragoon Revolver
Similar to the 2nd Model except for oval trigger guard, long trigger, modifications to the loading lever and latch. Imported by Benson Firearms, Uberti USA.
Price: Military (frame cut for shoulder stock, steel backstrap) $269.00
Price: Civilian (brass backstrap, trigger guard) $240.00
Price: Western (silver-plated backstrap, trigger guard) $269.00
Price: Shoulder stock $139.00

Dixie Third Dragoon

DIXIE THIRD MODEL DRAGOON
Caliber: 44 (.454" round ball).
Barrel: 7⅜".
Weight: 4 lbs., 2½ oz.
Stocks: One-piece walnut.
Sights: Brass pin front, hammer notch rear, or adjustable folding leaf rear.
Features: Cylinder engraved with Indian fight scene. This is the only Dragoon replica with folding leaf sight. Brass backstrap and trigger guard; color case-hardened steel frame, blue-black barrel. Imported by Dixie Gun Works.
Price: $185.00

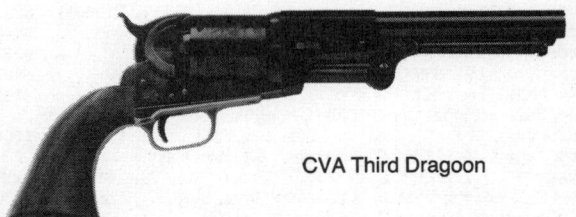
CVA Third Dragoon

CVA Third Model Colt Dragoon
Similar to the Dixie Third Dragoon except has 7½" barrel, weighs 4 lbs., 6 ozs., blade front sight. Over-all length of 14". 44 caliber, 6-shot.
Price: $182.95

CAUTION: PRICES CHANGE. CHECK AT GUNSHOP.

BLACK POWDER REVOLVERS

Dixie 1848

Dixie 1851 Navy

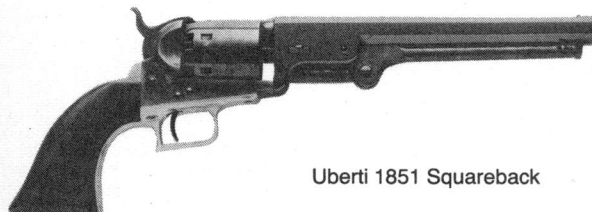
Uberti 1851 Squareback

1848 BABY DRAGOON, 1849 POCKET, WELLS FARGO REVOLVERS
Caliber: 31.
Barrel: 3", 4", 5"; 7 groove, RH twist.
Weight: About 21 oz.
Stocks: Varnished walnut.
Sights: Brass pin front, hammer notch rear.
Features: No loading lever on Baby Dragoon or Wells Fargo models. Unfluted cylinder with stagecoach holdup scene; cupped cylinder pin; no grease grooves; one safety pin on cylinder and slot in hammer face; straight (flat) mainspring. From Benson Firearms, Dixie, Uberti USA.
Price: 6" barrel, with loading lever (Dixie) $150.00
Price: Brass backstrap, trigger guard (Benson, Uberti USA) $229.00
Price: As above, silver plated (Benson, Uberti USA) $240.00

NAVY MODEL 1851 PERCUSSION REVOLVER
Caliber: 36, 44, 6-shot.
Barrel: 7½".
Weight: 44 oz. **Length:** 13" over-all.
Stocks: Walnut finish.
Sights: Post front, hammer notch rear.
Features: Brass backstrap and trigger guard; some have 1st Model squareback trigger guard, engraved cylinder with navy battle scene; case-hardened frame, hammer, loading lever. Imported by The Armoury, Navy Arms, Benson Firearms, Muzzleloaders Inc., E.M.F., Dixie, Euroarms of America, Armsport, Hopkins & Allen, CVA., Sile, Uberti USA.
Price: Brass frame .... $90.00 to $229.00
Price: Steel frame .... $125.00 to $229.00
Price: Stainless (Benson, Uberti USA) $295.00
Price: Sillver-plated backstrap, trigger guard (Benson, Uberti USA) . $249.00
Price: Kit form .... $87.95 to $119.95
Price: Engraved model (Dixie) $135.00
Price: Single cased set, steel frame (Navy Arms) $250.00
Price: Double cased set, steel frame (Navy Arms) $414.00
Price: London Model with iron backstrap (Benson, Uberti USA) $245.00

1851 SHERIFF MODEL PERCUSSION REVOLVER
Caliber: 36, 44, 6-shot.
Barrel: 5".
Weight: 40 oz. **Length:** 10½" over-all.
Stocks: Walnut.
Sights: Fixed.
Features: Brass backstrap and trigger guard; engraved navy scene; case-hardened frame, hammer, loading lever. Imported by E.M.F, Sile.
Price: Steel frame $170.00
Price: Brass frame .... $90.95 to $125.00
Price: Kit, brass or steel frame .... $114.00 to $160.00

ARMY 1851 PERCUSSION REVOLVER
Caliber: 44, 6-shot.
Barrel: 7½".
Weight: 45 oz. **Length:** 13" over-all.
Stocks: Walnut finish.
Sights: Fixed.
Features: 44 caliber version of the 1851 Navy. Imported by The Armoury, E.M.F.
Price: .... $95.00 to $140.00

1851 NAVY-SHERIFF
Same as 1851 Sheriff model except has 4" barrel. Imported by Benson, CVA, (5½" bbl.), E.M.F., Euroarms of America, Uberti USA.
Price: .... $80.00 to $229.00
Price: Kit (CVA) $91.95
Price: Engraved, brass and nickel plated (CVA), with flask $200.00
Price: Stainless steel (Benson, Uberti USA) $295.00

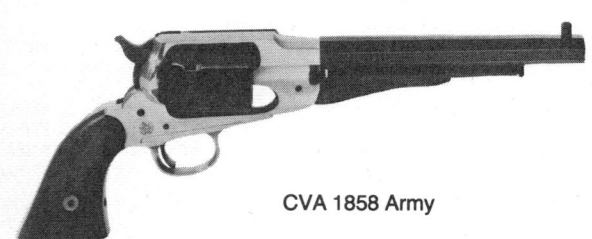
CVA 1858 Army

NEW MODEL 1858 ARMY PERCUSSION REVOLVER
Caliber: 36 or 44, 6-shot.
Barrel: 6½" or 8".
Weight: 40 oz. **Length:** 13½" over-all.
Stocks: Walnut.
Sights: Blade front, groove-in-frame rear.
Features: Replica of Remington Model 1858. Also available from some importers as Army Model Belt Revolver in 36 cal., shortened and lightened version of the 44. Target Model (Benson, Uberti USA, Navy) has fully adj. target rear sight, target front, 36 or 44. Imported by CVA (as 1858 Remington Army), Dixie, Navy Arms, Hopkins & Allen, The Armoury, E.M.F., Euroarms of America (engraved, stainless and plain), Armsport, Benson Firearms, Muzzle Loaders, Inc., Uberti USA.
Price: Steel frame .... $135.00 to $229.00
Price: Steel frame kit (Euroarms) $143.00
Price: Single cased set (Navy Arms) $277.00
Price: Double cased set (Navy Arms) $467.00
Price: Nickel finish (E.M.F.) $152.75
Price: Stainless steel Model 1858 (Euroarms, Uberti, Sile, Navy Arms, Benson) .... $140.00 to $299.00
Price: Target Model 1858 (Euroarms, Uberti, Sile, Navy, E.M.F., Benson) .... $95.95 to $239.00
Price: Brass frame, finished (CVA, Navy Arms, Sile) ...... $97.95 to $134.95
Price: As above, kit (CVA, Dixie, Navy Arms) .... $94.75 to $132.00

Uberti 1861 Navy Percussion Revolver
Similar to 1851 Navy except has round 7½" barrel, rounded trigger guard, German silver blade front sight, "creeping" loading lever. Available with fluted or round cylinder. Imported by Benson Firearms, Uberti USA.
Price: Steel backstrap, trigger guard, cut for stock $245.00
Price: Brass backstrap, trigger guard $229.00
Price: Silver plated backstrap, trigger guard $249.00
Price: Stainless steel $305.00

CVA 1858 Remington Target
Similar to the New Model 1858 Remington except has ramped blade front sight, adjustable rear.
Price: $182.95

BLACK POWDER REVOLVERS

Navy 1858 Remington-Style

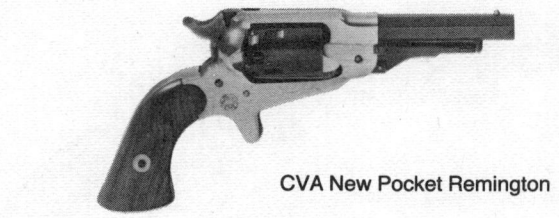
CVA New Pocket Remington

Dixie 1860 Army

Uberti 1862 Pocket Navy

NAVY ARMS 1858 REMINGTON-STYLE REVOLVER
Caliber: 44.
Barrel: 8".
Weight: 2 lbs., 13 ozs.
Stocks: Smooth walnut.
Sights: Dovetailed blade front.
Features: First exact reproduction—correct in size and weight to the original, with progressive rifling; highly polished with blue finish, silver-plated trigger guard. From Navy Arms.
Price: Deluxe model $315.00

CVA NEW MODEL POCKET REMINGTON
Caliber: 31.
Barrel: 4", octagonal.
Weight: 15½ oz. **Length:** 7½" over-all.
Stocks: Two-piece walnut.
Sights: Post front, grooved top-strap rear.
Features: Spur trigger, brass frame with blued barrel and cylinder. Available finished or in kit form. Introduced 1984.
Price: Finished $91.95
Price: Kit $76.95

1860 ARMY PERCUSSION REVOLVER
Caliber: 44, 6-shot.
Barrel: 8".
Weight: 40 oz. **Length:** 13⅝" over-all.
Stocks: Walnut.
Sights: Fixed.
Features: Engraved navy scene on cylinder; brass trigger guard; case-hardened frame, loading lever and hammer. Some importers supply pistol cut for shoulder detachable shoulder stock, have accessory stock available. Imported by E.M.F., CVA, Navy Arms, The Armoury, Dixie (half-fluted cylinder, not roll engraved), Euroarms of America (brass or steel model), Armsport, Hopkins & Allen, Benson Firearms, Muzzleloaders, Inc., Sile, Uberti USA.
Price: About .... $132.95 to 235.00
Price: Single cased set (Navy Arms,) $274.00
Price: Double cased set (Navy Arms) $460.00
Price: 1861 Navy: Same as Army except 36 cal., 7½" bbl., wt. 41 oz., cut for shoulder stock; round cylinder (fluted avail.), from E.M.F., CVA (brass frame) .... $229.00 to $249.00
Price: Steel frame kit (E.M.F., Euroarms) $140.00
Price: Stainless steel (Benson, Uberti USA) $305.00

GRISWOLD & GUNNISON PERCUSSION REVOLVER
Caliber: 36 or 44, 6-shot.
Barrel: 7½".
Weight: 44 oz. (36 cal.). **Length:** 13" over-all.
Stocks: Walnut.
Sights: Fixed.
Features: Replica of famous Confederate pistol. Brass frame, backstrap and trigger guard; case-hardened loading lever; rebated cylinder (44 cal. only). Rounded Dragoon-type barrel. Imported by Navy Arms, (as Reb Model 1860), Benson, E.M.F., Uberti USA.
Price: About $229.00
Price: Kit (E.M.F.) $73.50
Price: Single cased set (Navy Arms) $230.00
Price: Double cased set (Navy Arms) $370.00
Price: Reb 1860 (Navy Arms) $119.50

1862 POCKET POLICE PERCUSSION REVOLVER
Caliber: 36, 5-shot.
Barrel: 4½", 5½", 6½", 7½".
Weight: 26 oz. **Length:** 12" over-all (6½" bbl.).
Stocks: Walnut.
Sights: Fixed.
Features: Round tapered barrel; half-fluted and rebated cylinder; case-hardened frame, loading lever and hammer; silver or brass trigger guard and backstrap. Imported by CVA, Navy Arms (5½" only), Benson Firearms, Uberti USA.
Price: About $229.00
Price: Single cased set with accessories (Navy Arms) $300.00
Price: Stainless steel (Benson, Uberti USA) 4½", 5½" $289.00
Price: Kit (CVA) $81.95
Price: With silver-plated backstrap, trigger guard (Benson, Uberti USA) $245.00

UBERTI 1862 POCKET NAVY PERCUSSION REVOLVER
Caliber: 36, 5-shot.
Barrel: 4½", 5½", 6½", octagonal, 7-groove, LH twist.
Weight: 27 oz. (5½" barrel). **Length:** 10½" over-all (5½" bbl.).
Stocks: One piece varnished walnut.
Sights: Brass pin front, hammer notch rear.
Features: Rebated cylinder, hinged loading lever, brass or silver-plated backstrap and trigger guard, color cased frame, hammer, loading lever, plunger and latch, rest blued. Has original-type markings. From Benson Firearms, Inc., Uberti USA..
Price: With brass backstrap, trigger guard $229.00
Price: With silver-plated backstrap, trigger guard $245.00
Price: Stainless steel (4½", 5½" only) $289.00

ROGERS & SPENCER PERCUSSION REVOLVER
Caliber: 44.
Barrel: 7½".
Weight: 47 oz. **Length:** 13¾" over-all.
Stocks: Walnut.
Sights: Cone front, integral groove in frame for rear.
Features: Accurate reproduction of a Civil War design. Solid frame; extra large nipple cut-out on rear of cylinder; loading lever and cylinder easily removed for cleaning. From Euroarms of America (standard blue, engraved, burnished, target models), Muzzle Loaders, Inc., Navy Arms.
Price: .... $120.00 to $240.00
Price: Nickel plated $120.00
Price: Engraved (Euroarms) $236.00
Price: Kit version $95.00
Price: Target version $234.00
Price: Brushed satin chrome (Navy Arms) $259.00
Price: Burnished London Gray (Euroarms) $239.00

CAUTION: PRICES CHANGE. CHECK AT GUNSHOP.

BLACK POWDER REVOLVERS

LE MAT CAVALRY MODEL REVOLVER
Caliber: 44/65.
Barrel: 6¾" (revolver); 4⅞" (single shot).
Weight: NA.
Stocks: Hand-checkered walnut.
Sights: Post front, hammer-notch rear.
Features: Exact reproduction with all-steel construction; 44-cal. 9-shot cylinder, 65-cal. single barrel; color case-hardened hammer with selector; spur trigger guard; ring at butt; lever-type barrel release. From Navy Arms.
Price: Cavalry model (lanyard ring, spur trigger guard) $500.00
Price: Army model (round trigger guard, pin-type barrel release) $500.00
Price: Naval-style (thumb selector on hammer) $500.00

SPILLER & BURR REVOLVER
Caliber: 36 (.375" round ball).
Barrel: 7", octagon.
Weight: 2½ lbs. **Length:** 12½" over-all.
Stocks: Two-piece walnut.
Sights: Fixed.
Features: Reproduction of the C.S.A. revolver. Brass frame and trigger guard. Also available as a kit. From Dixie, Navy Arms.
Price: . . . . $125.00 to $142.00
Price: Kit form $65.00
Price: Single cased set (Navy Arms) $252.00
Price: Double cased set (Navy Arms) $417.00

Freedom Mini Percussion

Le Mat Cavalry Model

DIXIE "WYATT EARP" REVOLVER
Caliber: 44.
Barrel: 12" octagon.
Weight: 46 oz. **Length:** 18" over-all.
Stocks: Two piece walnut.
Sights: Fixed.
Features: Highly polished brass frame, backstrap and trigger guard; blued barrel and cylinder; case-hardened hammer, trigger and loading lever. Navy-size shoulder stock ($45.00) will fit with minor fitting. From Dixie Gun Works.
Price: $130.00

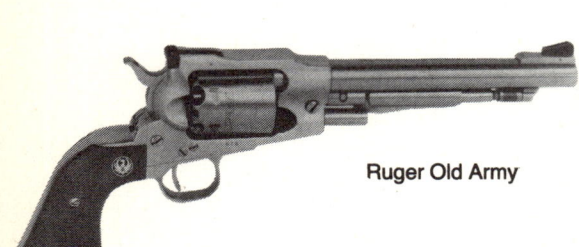

Ruger Old Army

RUGER 44 OLD ARMY PERCUSSION REVOLVER
Caliber: 44, 6-shot. Uses .457" dia. lead bullets.
Barrel: 7½" (6-groove, 16" twist).
Weight: 46 oz. **Length:** 13¾" over-all.
Stocks: Smooth walnut.
Sights: Ramp front, rear adj. for w. and e.
Features: Stainless steel standard size nipples, chrome-moly steel cylinder and frame, same lockwork as in original Super Blackhawk. Also available in stainless steel in very limited quantities. Made in USA. From Sturm, Ruger & Co.
Price: Stainless steel (Model KBP-7) $356.31
Price: Blued steel (Model BP-7) $279.17

FREEDOM ARMS PERCUSSION MINI REVOLVER
Caliber: 22, 5-shot.
Barrel: 1", 1¾", 3".
Weight: 4¾ oz. (1" bbl.).
Stocks: Simulated ebony.
Sights: Fixed.
Features: Percussion version of the 22 RF gun. All stainless steel; spur trigger. Gun comes with leather carrying pouch, bullet seating tool, powder measure, 20 29-gr. bullets. Introduced 1983. From Freedom Arms.
Price: 1" barrel $184.50

BLACK POWDER MUSKETS & RIFLES

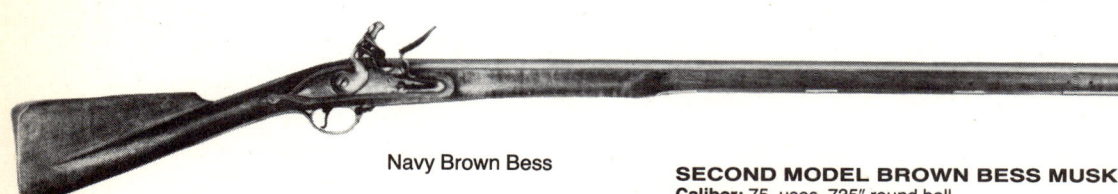

Navy Brown Bess

SECOND MODEL BROWN BESS MUSKET
Caliber: 75, uses .735" round ball.
Barrel: 42", smoothbore.
Weight: 9½ lbs. **Length:** 59" over-all.
Stock: Walnut (Navy); walnut-stained hardwood (Dixie).
Sights: Fixed.
Features: Polished barrel and lock with brass trigger guard and buttplate. Bayonet and scabbard available. From Navy Arms, Dixie, E.M.F.
Price: Finished . . . . $399.00 to $750.00
Price: Kit (Dixie, Navy) . . . . $375.00 to $430.00

NAVY ARMS CHARLEVILLE MUSKET
Caliber: 69.
Barrel: 44⅝".
Weight: 8¾ lbs. **Length:** 59⅜" over-all.
Stock: Walnut.
Sights: Blade front.
Features: Replica of Revolutionary War 1763 musket. Bright metal, walnut stock. From Navy Arms.
Price: Finished $550.00
Price: Kit $450.00

BLACK POWDER MUSKETS & RIFLES

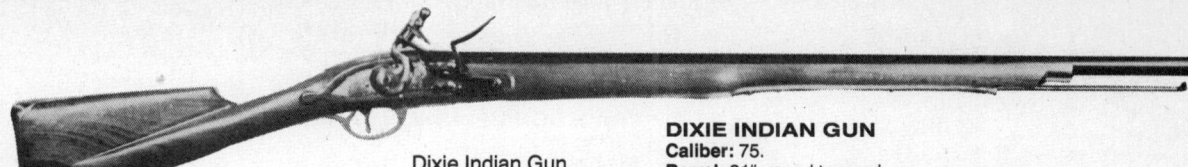

Dixie Indian Gun

DIXIE INDIAN GUN
Caliber: 75.
Barrel: 31", round tapered.
Weight: About 9 lbs. **Length:** 47" over-all.
Stock: Hardwood.
Sights: Blade front.
Features: Modified Brown Bess musket; brass furniture, browned lock and barrel. Lock is marked "GRICE 1762" with crown over "GR." Serpent-style sideplate. Introduced 1983.
Price: Complete $375.00
Price: As above, in kit form $360.00

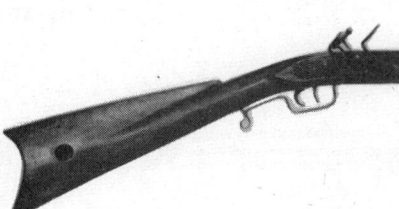

Dixie Tennessee Rifle

DIXIE TENNESSEE MOUNTAIN RIFLE
Caliber: 32 or 50.
Barrel: 41½", 6-groove rifling, brown finish.
Length: 56" over-all.
Stock: Walnut, oil finish; Kentucky-style.
Sights: Silver blade front, open buckhorn rear.
Features: Recreation of the original mountain rifles. Early Schultz lock, interchangeable flint or percussion with vent plug or drum and nipple. Tumbler has fly. Double-set triggers. All metal parts browned. From Dixie.
Price: Flint or percussion, finished rifle, 50 cal. $335.00
Price: Kit, 50 cal. $275.00
Price: Left-hand model, flint or perc. $335.00
Price: Left-hand kit, flint or perc., 50 cal. $275.00
Price: Squirrel Rifle (as above except in 32 cal. with ¹³⁄₁₆" barrel), flint or percussion $335.00
Price: Kit, 32 cal., flint or percussion $275.00

KENTUCKY FLINTLOCK RIFLE
Caliber: 44, 45 or 50.
Barrel: 35".
Weight: 7 lbs. **Length:** 50" over-all.
Stock: Walnut stained, brass fittings.
Sights: Fixed.
Features: Available in Carbine model also, 28" bbl. Some variations in detail, finish. Kits also available from some importers. Imported by Navy Arms, The Armoury, CVA (45-cal. only), Armsport, Muzzleloaders, Inc.
Price: About .... $217.95 to 324.00
Price: Kit form (CVA, percussion) .... $127.95 to $148.95
Price: Deluxe model, flint or percussion, 50-cal. (Navy Arms) $275.00

Kentucky Percussion Rifle
Similar to flintlock except percussion lock. Finish and features vary with importer. Imported by Navy Arms (45 cal.), The Armoury, CVA, Armsport (rifle-shotgun combo), Muzzle Loaders, Inc.
Price: About $299.00
Price: Armsport combo $235.00
Price: 50 cal. (Navy Arms) $299.00
Price: Kit, 45 cal. (CVA) $134.95

KENTUCKIAN RIFLE & CARBINE
Caliber: 44.
Barrel: 35" (Rifle), 27½" (Carbine).
Weight: 7 lbs. (Rifle), 5½ lbs. (Carbine). **Length:** 51" (Rifle) over-all, Carbine 43".
Stock: Walnut stain.
Sights: Brass blade front, steel V-ramp rear.
Features: Octagon bbl., case-hardened and engraved lock plate. Brass furniture. Imported by Dixie, Armsport.
Price: Rifle or carbine, flint $225.00
Price: As above, percussion $210.00

Hatfield Squirrel Rifle

HATFIELD SQUIRREL RIFLE
Caliber: 36, 45, 50.
Barrel: 39½", octagon, 32" on half-stock.
Weight: 8 lbs. (32 cal.).
Stock: American fancy maple fullstock.
Sights: Silver blade front, buckhorn rear.
Features: Recreation of the traditional squirrel rifle. Available in flint or percussion with brass trigger guard and buttplate. From Hatfield Rifle Works. Introduced 1983.
Price: Full stock, flint or percussion Grade I $399.95
Price: As above, Grade II $465.95
Price: As above, Grade III $565.95

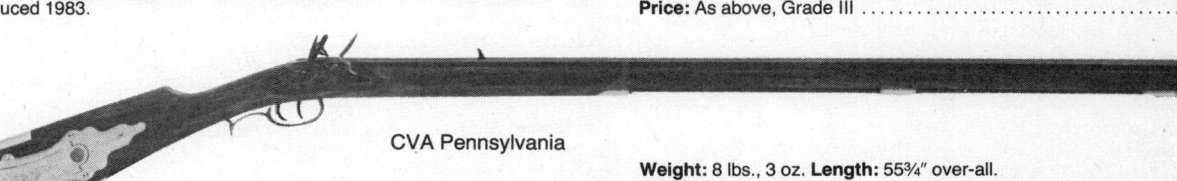

CVA Pennsylvania

CVA PENNSYLVANIA LONG RIFLE
Caliber: 50.
Barrel: 40", octagonal; ⅞" flats.
Weight: 8 lbs., 3 oz. **Length:** 55¾" over-all.
Stock: Select walnut.
Sights: Brass blade front, fixed semi-buckhorn rear.
Features: Color case-hardened lock plate, brass buttplate, toe plate, patchbox, trigger guard, thimbles, nosecap; blued barrel, double-set triggers; authentic V-type mainspring. Introduced 1983. From CVA.
Price: Finished, percussion $331.95
Price: Finished, flintlock $322.95

CAUTION: PRICES CHANGE. CHECK AT GUNSHOP.

BLACK POWDER MUSKETS & RIFLES

Traditions Pennsylvania

TRADITIONS PENNSYLVANIA RIFLE
Caliber: 45, 50.
Barrel: 41 3/8", 7/8" flats.
Weight: 9 lbs. **Length:** 56 5/8" over-all.
Stock: Walnut.
Sights: Blade front, adjustable rear.
Features: Brass patch box and ornamentation. Double set triggers. From Traditions Inc.
Price: Flintlock $300.00
Price: Percussion $290.00
Price: Shenandoah rifle, flint $196.00
Price: As above, percussion $186.00

THOMPSON/CENTER PENNSYLVANIA HUNTER RIFLE
Caliber: 50.
Barrel: 31", half octagon, half round.
Weight: About 7 1/2 lbs. **Length:** 48" over-all.
Stock: Black walnut.
Sights: Open, adjustable.
Features: Rifled 1:66" for round ball shooting. Available in flintlock or percussion.
Price: Percussion $265.00
Price: Flintlock $280.00

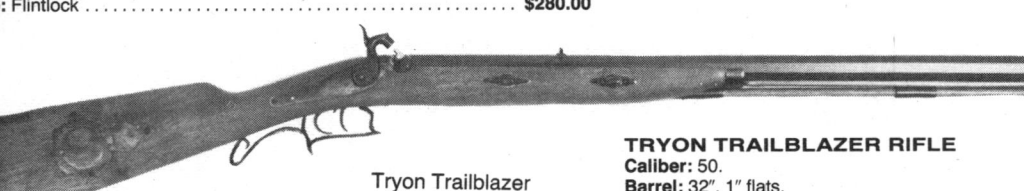

Tryon Trailblazer

TRYON TRAILBLAZER RIFLE
Caliber: 50.
Barrel: 32", 1" flats.
Weight: 9 lbs. **Length:** 48" over-all.
Stock: European walnut with cheekpiece.
Sights: Blade front, semi-buckhorn rear.
Features: Reproduction of a rifle made by George Tyron about 1820. Double-set triggers, back action lock, hooked breech with long tang. From Armsport.
Price: $445.00

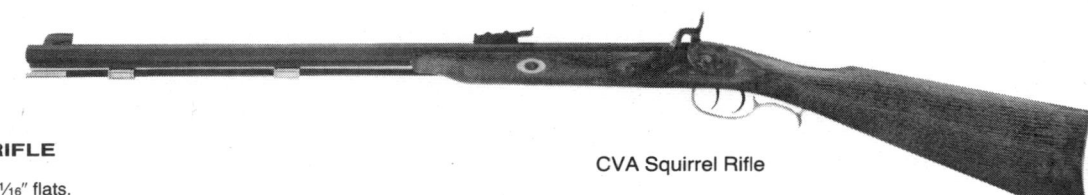

CVA Squirrel Rifle

CVA SQUIRREL RIFLE
Caliber: 32.
Barrel: 25", octagonal; 11/16" flats.
Weight: 5 lbs., 12 oz. **Length:** 40 3/4" over-all.
Stock: Hardwood.
Sights: Beaded blade front, fully adjustable hunting-style rear.
Features: Available in right- or left-hand versions. Color case-hardened lock plate, brass buttplate, trigger guard, wedge plates, thimbles; double set triggers; hooked breech; authentic V-type mainspring. Introduced 1983. From CVA.
Price: Finished, percussion, right-hand $182.95
Price: Finished, left-hand $191.95
Price: Kit, percussion, right-hand $126.95
Price: As above, left hand $134.95
Price: As above, right hand with 32 or 45 cal. barrel ... $142.95

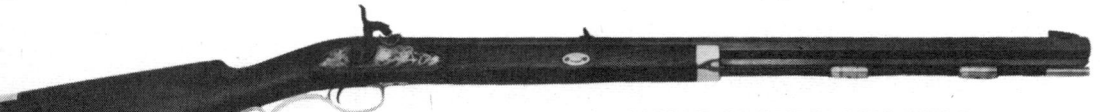

Lyman Great Plains

LYMAN GREAT PLAINS RIFLE
Caliber: 50 or 54 cal.
Barrel: 32", 1-66" twist.
Weight: 9 lbs.
Stock: Walnut.
Sights: Steel blade front, buckhorn rear adj. for w. & e. and fixed notch primitive sight included.
Features: Blued steel furniture. Stainless steel nipple. Coil spring lock, Hawken-style trigger guard and double set triggers. Round thimbles recessed and sweated into rib. Steel wedge plates and toe plate. Introduced 1979. From Lyman.
Price: Percussion $314.95
Price: Flintlock $334.95
Price: Percussion kit $244.95

Consult our Directory pages for the location of firms mentioned.

CHENEY PLAINS RIFLE
Caliber: 50, 54.
Barrel: 30"; 1" flats; 1-in-70" twist.
Weight: 8 1/2 to 9 lbs. **Length:** 47 1/4" over-all.
Stock: Full- or half-stock; birdseye northern maple.
Sights: Blade front, drift-adjustable buckhorn rear.
Features: Hot browned steel, polished brass or browned furniture, hand-rubbed oil on wood; single set trigger; custom fit cleaning jag supplied. From Cheney Firearms Co.
Price: Percussion or flintlock $449.00

PENNSYLVANIA FULL STOCK RIFLE
Caliber: 45 or 50.
Barrel: 32" rifled, 15/16" dia.
Weight: 8 1/2 lbs.
Stock: Walnut.
Sights: Fixed.
Features: Available in flint or percussion. Blued lock and barrel, brass furniture. Offered complete or in kit form. From The Armoury.
Price: Flint $250.00
Price: Percussion $225.00

BLACK POWDER MUSKETS & RIFLES

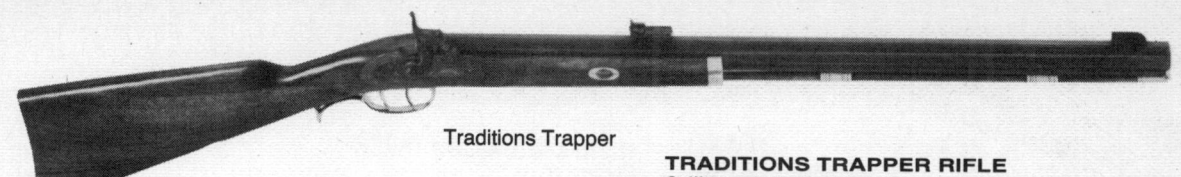

Traditions Trapper

TRADITIONS TRAPPER RIFLE
Caliber: 36, 45, 50.
Barrel: 25″, ⅞″ flats.
Weight: 5 lbs. **Length:** 40½″ over-all.
Stock: Beech.
Sights: Beaded blade front, adjustable rear.
Features: Metal ramrod, brass furniture. From Traditions Inc.
Price: $178.00
Price: Frontier Scout (similar to above except shorter length of pull, weighs 4¾ lbs., 27″ bbl., 45 or 50 cal.) $156.00

CVA KENTUCKY RIFLE
Caliber: 45 (.451″ bore).
Barrel: 33½″, rifled, octagon (⅞″ flats).
Length: 48″ over-all.
Stock: Select hardwood.
Sights: Brass Kentucky blade-type front, fixed open rear.
Features: Available in either flint or percussion. Stainless steel nipple included. From CVA.
Price: Percussion $229.95
Price: Percussion kit $134.95

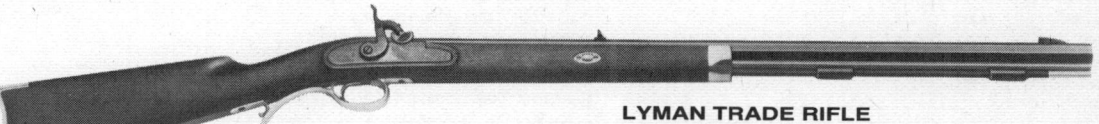

Lyman Trade Rifle

LYMAN TRADE RIFLE
Caliber: 50 or 54.
Barrel: 28″ octagon, 1-48″ twist.
Weight: 8¾ lbs. **Length:** 45″ over-all.
Stock: European walnut.
Sights: Blade front, open rear adj. for w. or optional fixed sights.
Features: Fast twist rifling for conical bullets. Polished brass furniture with blue steel parts, stainless steel nipple. Hook breech, single trigger, coil spring percussion lock. Steel barrel rib and ramrod ferrules. Introduced 1980. From Lyman.
Price: Percussion $229.95
Price: Kit, percussion $179.95
Price: Flintlock $254.95

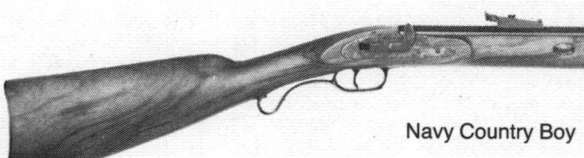

Navy Country Boy

NAVY ARMS COUNTRY BOY RIFLE
Caliber: 32, 36, 45, 50.
Barrel: 26″.
Weight: 6 lbs.
Stock: Walnut.
Sights: Blade front, adjustable rear.
Features: Octagonal rifled barrel; blue finish; hooked breech; Mule Ear lock for fast ignition. From Navy Arms.
Price: $250.00
Price: Kit $192.00

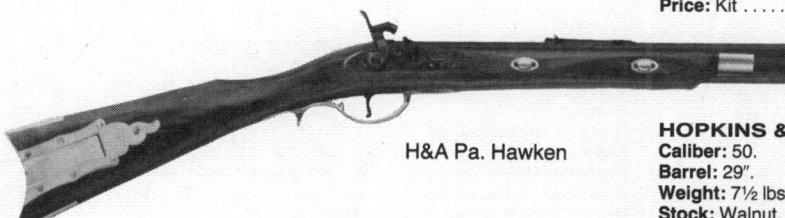

H&A Pa. Hawken

HOPKINS & ALLEN PA. HAWKEN RIFLE
Caliber: 50.
Barrel: 29″.
Weight: 7½ lbs. **Length:** 44″ over-all.
Stock: Walnut.
Sights: Blade front, open rear adjustable for elevation.
Features: Single trigger, dual barrel wedges. Convertible ignition system. Brass patch box.
Price: With percussion lock $250.00
Price: Conversion kit (percussion to flint) $45.95

Uberti Santa Fe

UBERTI SANTA FE HAWKEN RIFLE
Caliber: 50 or 54.
Barrel: 32″, octagonal.
Weight: 9.8 lbs. **Length:** 50″ over-all.
Stock: Walnut, with beavertail cheekpiece.
Sights: German silver blade front, buckhorn rear.
Features: Browned finish, color case-hardened lock, double triggers, German silver ferrule, wedge plates. Imported by Benson Firearms, Uberti USA.
Price: $385.00
Price: Kit $339.00

CAUTION: PRICES CHANGE. CHECK AT GUNSHOP.

BLACK POWDER MUSKETS & RIFLES

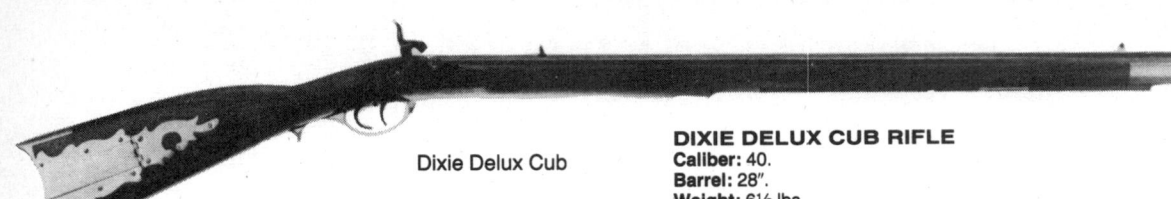

Dixie Delux Cub

DIXIE DELUX CUB RIFLE
Caliber: 40.
Barrel: 28".
Weight: 6½ lbs.
Stock: Walnut.
Sights: Fixed.
Features: Short rifle for small game and beginning shooters. Brass patchbox and furniture. Flint or percussion.
Price: Finished $250.00
Price: Kit $205.00

HOPKINS & ALLEN BRUSH RIFLE
Caliber: 36 or 45.
Barrel: 25", octagon, 15/16" flats.
Weight: 7 lbs.
Stock: Hardwood.
Sights: Silver blade front, notch rear.
Features: Convertible ignition system. Brass furniture. Introduced 1983.
Price: Percussion $227.90
Price: Pre-assembled kit, percussion $159.90
Price: Kit, percussion $119.45

TRYON RIFLE
Caliber: 50, 54.
Barrel: 34", octagon; 1-63" twist.
Weight: 9 lbs. **Length:** 49" over-all.
Stock: European walnut with steel furniture.
Sights: Blade front, fixed rear.
Features: Reproduction of an American plains rifle with double set triggers and back-action lock. Imported from Italy by Dixie.
Price: $299.00
Price: Kit $249.00

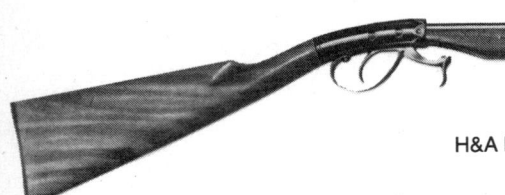

H&A Heritage

HOPKINS & ALLEN UNDERHAMMER RIFLES
Caliber: 31, 36, 45, 50, 58.
Barrel: 20", 25" 32", 42", octagonal.
Weight: 6½ lbs. **Length:** 37" over-all.
Stock: American walnut.
Features: Blued barrel and receiver, black buttplate. All models available with straight or pistol grip stock. Offered as kits, pre-assembled kits ("white" barrel, unfinished stock), or factory finished. Prices shown are for factory finished guns.
Price: Buggy, cals. 31, 36, 45, 20" or 25" bbl. × 15/16" $247.75
Price: Heritage, 36, 45, 50-cal., 32" bbl. × 15/16" $261.65
Price: Deerstalker, 58-cal., 28" bbl. × 1⅛" $270.25
Price: Target, 45-cal, 42" bbl. × 1⅛" $284.10

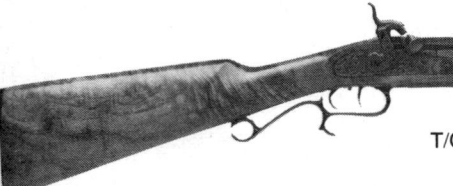

T/C Renegade

THOMPSON/CENTER RENEGADE RIFLE
Caliber: 50 and 54 plus 56 cal., smoothbore.
Barrel: 26", 1" across the flats.
Weight: 8 lbs.
Stock: American walnut.
Sights: Open hunting (Partridge) style, fully adjustable for w. and e.
Features: Coil spring lock, double set triggers, blued steel trim.
Price: Percussion model $275.00
Price: Flintlock model, 50 cal. only $285.00
Price: Percussion kit $200.00
Price: Flintlock kit $210.00
Price: Left-hand precussion, 50 or 54 cal. $285.00

Thompson/Center Renegade Hunter
Similar to standard Renegade except has single trigger in a large-bow shotgun-style trigger guard, no brass trim. Available im 50 caliber only. Color case-hardened lock, rest blued. Introduced 1987. From Thompson/Center.
Price: $255.00

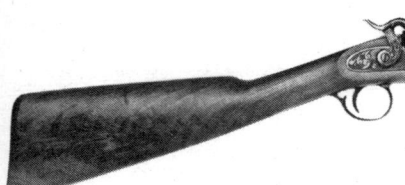

T/C New Englander

THOMPSON/CENTER NEW ENGLANDER RIFLE
Caliber: 50, 54.
Barrel: 26", round.
Weight: 7 lbs., 15 oz.
Stock: American walnut.
Sights: Open, adjustable.
Features: Color case-hardened percussion lock with engraving, rest blued. Also accepts 12-ga. shotgun barrel. Introduced 1987. From Thompson/Center.
Price: Right or left-hand model $225.00
Price: Accessory 12 ga. barrel, right hand $97.50
Price: As above, left hand $105.00

BLACK POWDER MUSKETS & RIFLES

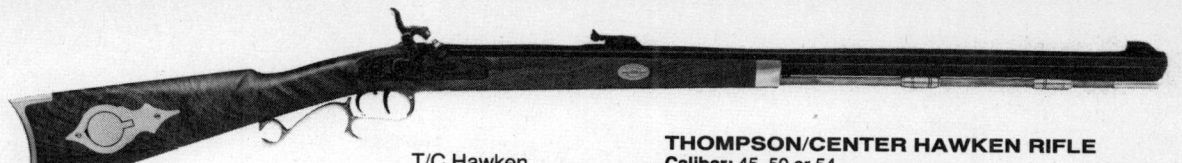

T/C Hawken

THOMPSON/CENTER CHEROKEE RIFLE
Caliber: 32, 45.
Barrel: 24", 13/16" across flats.
Weight: About 6 lbs.
Stock: American walnut.
Sights: Open hunting style; round notch rear fully adjustable for w. and e.
Features: Single trigger only. Interchangeable barrels. Brass buttplate, trigger guard, fore-end escutcheons and lock plate screw bushing. Introduced 1984.
Price: 32, 45 caliber... $265.00
Price: Interchangeable 32, 45-cal. barrel... $115.00
Price: Kit, percussion, 32, 45... $200.00
Price: Kit barrels... $80.00

THOMPSON/CENTER HAWKEN RIFLE
Caliber: 45, 50 or 54.
Barrel: 28" octagon, hooked breech.
Stock: American walnut.
Sights: Blade front, rear adj. for w. & e.
Features: Solid brass furniture, double set triggers, button rifled barrel, coil-type main spring. From Thompson/Center Arms.
Price: Percussion Model (45, 50 or 54 cal.)... $325.00
Price: Flintlock model (50 cal.)... $340.00
Price: Percussion kit... $230.00
Price: Flintlock kit... $245.00

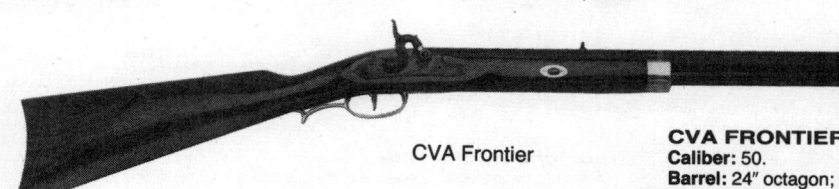

CVA Frontier

CVA MOUNTAIN RIFLE
Caliber: 50, 54.
Barrel: 32" octagon, 15/16" flats.
Weight: 9 lbs. **Length:** 48" over-all.
Stock: European walnut with cheekpiece.
Sights: German silver blade front, adjustable open rear.
Features: Color case-hardened and engraved lockplate; bridle, fly, screw-adjustable sear engagement. Double set triggers. Pewter nose cap, trigger guard, buttplate. From CVA.
Price: Either caliber... $307.95

CVA FRONTIER RIFLE
Caliber: 50.
Barrel: 24" octagon; 15/16" flats.
Weight: 6½ lbs. **Length:** 40" over-all.
Stock: Select hardwood.
Sights: Brass blade front, fixed open rear.
Features: Color case-hardened lockplate, screw-adjustable sear engagement, V-type mainspring. Early style brass trigger with tension spring. Brass buttplate, trigger guard, wedge plate, nose cap, thimble. From CVA.
Price:... $167.95
Price: Kit... $119.95

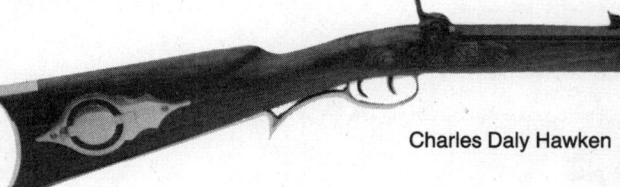

Charles Daly Hawken

ARMOURY R140 HAWKIN RIFLE
Caliber: 45, 50 or 54,.
Barrel: 29"
Weight: 8¾ to 9 lbs. **Length:** 45¾" over-all.
Stock: Walnut, with cheekpiece.
Sights: Dovetail front, fully adjustable rear.
Features: Octagon barrel, removable breech plug; double set triggers; blued barrel, brass stock fittings, color case-hardened percussion lock. From Armsport, The Armoury.
Price:... $225.00 to $280.00

CVA Missouri Ranger Rifle
Similar to the St. Louis Hawken except has blackened nose cap, trigger guard, thimbles and wedge plates and black rubber buttplate. Has brass blade front sight, fixed semi-buckhorn rear; adjustable double set trigger. Weight 7 lbs., 8 oz. From CVA.
Price: Finished, right-hand... $174.95
Price: Finished, left-hand... $182.95
Price: Kit (right-hand only)... $129.95

CHARLES DALY HAWKEN RIFLE
Caliber: 45, 50, 54.
Barrel: 28" octagonal, 7/8" flats.
Weight: 7½ lbs. **Length:** 45½" over-all.
Stock: European hardwood.
Sights: Blade front, open fully adjustable rear.
Features: Color case-hardened lock uses coil springs; trigger guard, buttplate, fore-end cap, ferrules and ramrod fittings are polished brass. Left-hand model available in 50-cal. only. Imported by Outdoor Sports Headquarters. Introduced 1984.
Price: Right-hand, percussion... $259.95
Price: Left-hand, percussion (50-cal. only)... $289.00
Price: Right-hand, flintlock... $299.00
Price: Left-hand, flintlock (50-cal. only)... $319.00
Price: Wilderness Hawken (50 cal. only)... $189.95

CVA HAWKEN RIFLE
Caliber: 50.
Barrel: 28", octagon; 1" across flats; 1-66" twist.
Weight: 8 lbs. **Length:** 44" over-all.
Stock: Select walnut.
Sights: Beaded blade front, fully adj. open rear.
Features: Fully adj. double set triggers; brass patch box, wedge plates, nose-cap, thimbles; trigger guard and buttplate; blued barrel; color case-hardened, engraved lockplate. Percussion only. Hooked breech, chrome bore. Introduced 1981.
Price: Finished rifle percussion... $322.95
Price: Presentation Grade (checkered walnut stock, engraved lock plate)... $585.95
Price: St. Louis Hawken (as above, except does not have chrome bore; hardwood stock) finished... $199.95
Price: As above, kit... $151.95
Price: As above, combo kit (50, 54-cal. bbls.)... $167.95

CAUTION: PRICES CHANGE. CHECK AT GUNSHOP.

BLACK POWDER MUSKETS & RIFLES

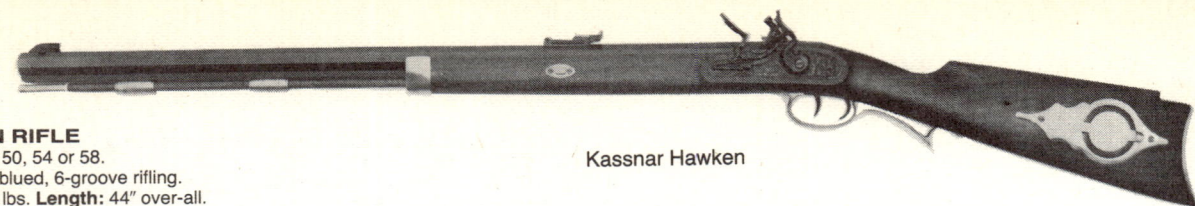

Kassnar Hawken

HAWKEN RIFLE
Caliber: 45, 50, 54 or 58.
Barrel: 28", blued, 6-groove rifling.
Weight: 8¾ lbs. **Length:** 44" over-all.
Stock: Walnut with cheekpiece.
Sights: Blade front, fully adj. rear.
Features: Coil mainspring, double set triggers, polished brass furniture. Introduced 1977. From Kassnar (flint or percussion, right- or left-hand), Muzzle Loaders, Inc., Armsport, Hopkins & Allen, 50-cal. only, Traditions, Sile.
Price: .... $245.00 to $275.00
Price: True left-hand rifle, percussion (Kassnar) $279.00
Price: As above, flintlock (Kassnar) $309.00
Price: Right-hand percussion, Carbine (Kassnar) $249.00
Price: St. Louis Hawken with steel furniture (Muzzle Loaders, Inc.) . $193.00
Price: Hawken Deluxe rifle or carbine with hard chrome bore (Sile) . $219.95
Price: Hawken Hunter, as above except has black-finished furniture (Sile) $244.95
Price: Hawken Deluxe Prefinished Kit (Sile) $195.00

ITHACA-NAVY HAWKEN RIFLE
Caliber: 50 and 54.
Barrel: 32" octagonal, 1-inch dia.
Weight: About 9 lbs.
Stock: Walnut.
Sights: Blade front, rear adj. for w.
Features: Hooked breech, 1⅞" throw percussion lock. Attached twin thimbles and under-rib. German silver barrel key inlays, Hawken-style toe and buttplates, lock bolt inlays, barrel wedges, entry thimble, trigger guard, ramrod and cleaning jag, nipple and nipple wrench. Introduced 1977. From Navy Arms
Price: Complete, percussion $480.00
Price: Kit, percussion $374.00

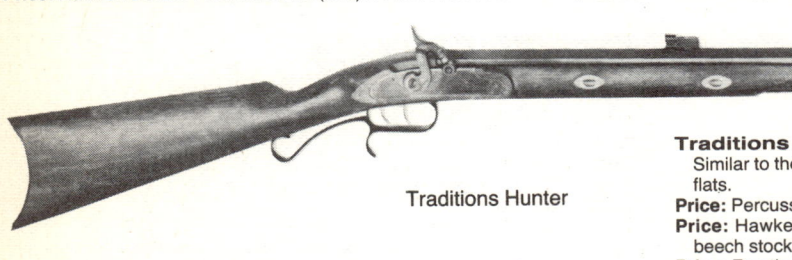

Traditions Hunter

Traditions Hunter Rifle
Similar to the Hawken except has blackened furniture. Has 29" barrel with 1" flats.
Price: Percussion only, 50 or 54 cal. $259.00
Price: Hawken Woodsman (similar to above, brass furniture, 50 cal. only, beech stock) $200.00
Price: Frontier (beech stock, 45 cal., flintlock) $185.00
Price: As above, 50 cal. percussion only $175.00
Price: Frontier Carbine (25⅛" bbl., 45, 50 cal., percussion) ... $175.00

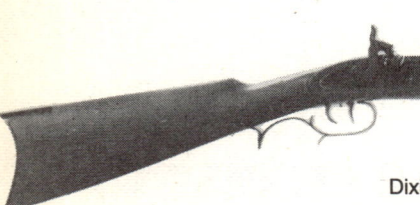

Dixie Hawken

DIXIE HAWKEN RIFLE
Caliber: 45, 50, 54.
Barrel: 30".
Weight: 8 lbs. **Length:** 46½" over-all.
Stock: Walnut.
Sights: Blade front, adjustable rear.
Features: Blued barrel, double set triggers, steel crescent buttplate. Imported by Dixie.
Price: Finished $225.00
Price: Kit $185.00

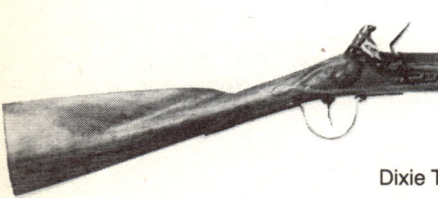

Dixie Trade Gun

DIXIE NORTHWEST TRADE GUN
Caliber/Gauge: 20 (.600 round ball or 1 oz.#6 shot).
Barrel: 36", smoothbore.
Weight: 7½ lbs. **Length:** 53½" over-all.
Stock: Walnut, 13½" pull.
Sights: Brass blade front only.
Features: Flintlock. Brass buttplate, serpentine sideplate; browned barrel, Wheeler flint lock, trigger guard; hickory ramrod with brass tip. From Dixie Gun Works.
Price: Finished $495.00
Price: Kit $350.00

Dixie Wesson Rifle

DIXIE PERCUSSION WESSON RIFLE
Caliber: 50.
Barrel: 28"; 1⅛" octagon, with false muzzle.
Length: 45" over-all.
Sights: Hand checkered walnut.
Stock: Blade front, rear adj. for e.
Features: Adjustable double set triggers, color case-hardened frame. Comes with loading rod and loading accessories. From Dixie Gun Works.
Price: With false muzzle $395.00

BLACK POWDER MUSKETS & RIFLES

Parker-Hale 1853

PARKER-HALE ENFIELD 1853 MUSKET
Caliber: .577".
Barrel: 39", 3-groove cold-forged rifling.
Weight: About 9 lbs. **Length:** 55" over-all.
Stock: Seasoned walnut.
Sights: Fixed front, rear step adj. for elevation.
Features: Three band musket made to original specs from original gauges. Solid brass stock furniture, color hardened lockplate, hammer; blued barrel, trigger. Imported from England by Navy Arms.
Price: $475.00

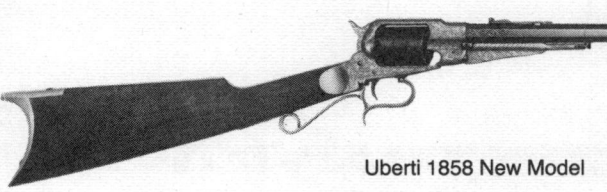

Uberti 1858 New Model

UBERTI 1858 NEW ARMY REVOLVING CARBINE
Caliber: 44.
Barrel: 18".
Weight: 4.6 lbs. **Length:** 37" over-all.
Stock: Walnut.
Sights: Ramp front, rear adjustable for e.
Features: Carbine version of the 1858 New Army revolver. Brass trigger guard and buttplate; blued, tapered octagonal barrel. Imported from Italy by Benson Firearms, Uberti USA.
Price: $385.00

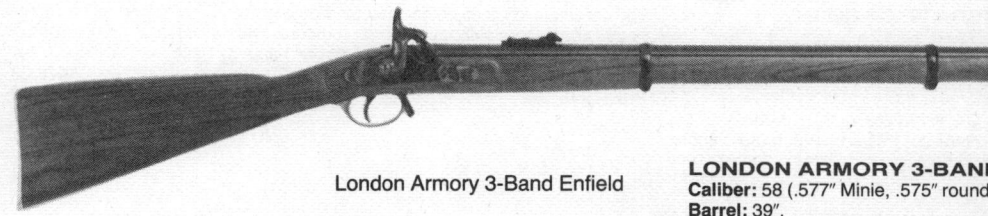

London Armory 3-Band Enfield

LONDON ARMORY 3-BAND 1853 ENFIELD
Caliber: 58 (.577" Minie, .575" round ball, .580" maxi ball).
Barrel: 39".
Weight: 9½ lbs. **Length:** 54" over-all.
Stock: European walnut.
Sights: Inverted "V" front, traditional Enfield folding ladder rear.
Features: Recreation of the famed London Armory Company Pattern 1862 Enfield Musket. One-piece walnut stock, brass buttplate, trigger guard and nosecap. Lockplate marked "London Armoury Co." and with a British crown. Blued Baddeley barrel bands. From Dixie, Euroarms of America, Navy Arms, Muzzle Loaders, Inc.
Price: About .... $395.00 to $427.00
Price: Assembled kit (Euroarms). $380.00

LONDON ARMORY 2-BAND ENFIELD 1858
Caliber: .577" Minie, .575" round ball.
Barrel: 33".
Weight: 10 lbs. **Length:** 49" over-all.
Stock: Walnut.
Sights: Folding leaf rear adjustable for elevation.
Features: Blued barrel, color case-hardened lock and hammer, polished brass buttplate, trigger guard, nose cap. From Navy Arms, Euroarms of America, Dixie.
Price: .... $325.00 to $450.00
Price: Assembled kit (Euroarms). $365.00

LONDON ARMORY ENFIELD MUSKETOON
Caliber: 58, Minie ball.
Barrel: 24", round.
Weight: 7-7½ lbs. **Length:** 40½" over-all.
Stock: Walnut, with sling swivels.
Sights: Blade front, graduated military-leaf rear.
Features: Brass trigger guard, nose cap, buttplate; blued barrel, bands, lockplate, swivels. Imported by Euroarms of America.
Price: Kit (fully assembled). $322.00

PARKER-HALE ENFIELD PATTERN 1858 NAVAL RIFLE
Caliber: 577".
Barrel: 33".
Weight: 8½ lbs. **Length:** 48½" over-all.
Stock: European walnut.
Sights: Blade front, step adj. rear.
Features: Two-band Enfield percussion rifle with heavy barrel. 5-groove progressive depth rifling, solid brass furniture. All parts made exactly to original patterns. Imported from England by Navy Arms.
Price: $500.00

Parker-Hale 1861

PARKER-HALE ENFIELD 1861 MUSKETOON
Caliber: 58.
Barrel: 24".
Weight: 7 lbs. **Length:** 40½" over-all.
Stock: Walnut.
Sights: Fixed front, adj. rear.
Features: Percussion muzzleloader, made to original 1861 English patterns. Imported from England by Navy Arms.
Price: $400.00

CAUTION: PRICES CHANGE. CHECK AT GUNSHOP.

BLACK POWDER MUSKETS & RIFLES

Parker-Hale Whitworth

PARKER-HALE VOLUNTEER RIFLE
Caliber: .451".
Barrel: 32".
Weight: 9½ lbs. **Length:** 49" over-all.
Stock: Walnut, checkered wrist and fore-end.
Sights: Globe front, adjustable ladder-type rear.
Features: Recreation of the type of gun issued to volunteer regiments during the 1860s. Rigby-pattern rifling, patent breech, detented lock. Stock is glass bedded for accuracy. Comes with comprehensive accessory/shooting kit. From Navy Arms.
Price: $725.00

PARKER-HALE WHITWORTH MILITARY TARGET RIFLE
Caliber: 45.
Barrel: 36".
Weight: 9¼ lbs. **Length:** 52½" over-all.
Stock: Walnut. Checkered at wrist and fore-end.
Sights: Hooded post front, open step-adjustable rear.
Features: Faithful reproduction of the Whitworth rifle, only bored for 45-cal. Trigger has a detented lock, capable of being adjusted very finely without risk of the sear nose catching on the half-cock bent and damaging both parts. Introduced 1978. Imported from England by Navy Arms.
Price: $750.00

Dixie Springfield

COOK & BROTHER CONFEDERATE CARBINE
Caliber: 58.
Barrel: 24".
Weight: 7½ lbs. **Length:** 40½" over-all.
Stock: Select walnut.
Features: Recreation of the 1861 New Orleans-made artillery carbine. Color case-hardened lock, browned barrel. Buttplate, trigger guard, barrel bands, sling swivels and nosecap of polished brass. From Euroarms of America.
Price: $365.00

DIXIE 1863 SPRINGFIELD MUSKET
Caliber: 58 (.570" patched ball or .575" Minie).
Barrel: 50", rifled.
Stock: Walnut stained.
Sights: Blade front, adjustable ladder-type rear.
Features: Bright-finish lock, barrel, furniture. Reproduction of the last of the regulation muzzleloaders. Imported from Japan by Dixie Gun Works.
Price: Finished $475.00
Price: Kit $330.00

Navy 1863 Springfield

NAVY ARMS 1863 SPRINGFIELD
Caliber: 58, uses .575" mini-ball.
Barrel: 40", rifled.
Weight: 9½ lbs. **Length:** 56" over-all.
Stock: Walnut.
Sights: Open rear adj. for elevation.
Features: Full-size 3-band musket. Polished bright metal, including lock. From Navy Arms.
Price: Finished rifle $500.00
Price: Kit $400.00

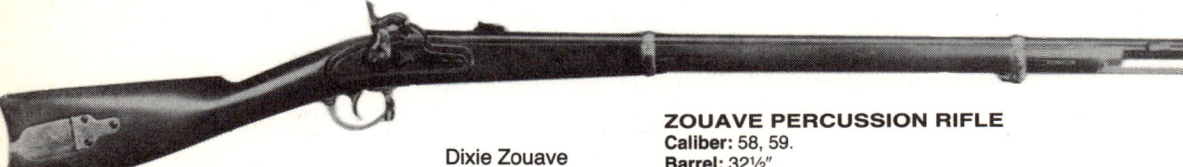

Dixie Zouave

Mississippi Model 1841 Percussion Rifle
Similar to Zouave rifle but patterned after U.S. Model 1841. Imported by Dixie.
Price: $430.00

ZOUAVE PERCUSSION RIFLE
Caliber: 58, 59.
Barrel: 32½".
Weight: 9½ lbs. **Length:** 48½" over-all.
Stock: Walnut finish, brass patch box and buttplate.
Sights: Fixed front, rear adj. for e.
Features: Color case-hardened lock plate, blued barrel. from Dixie, Euroarms (M1863).
Price: About $275.00
Price: Kit (Euroarms) $263.00

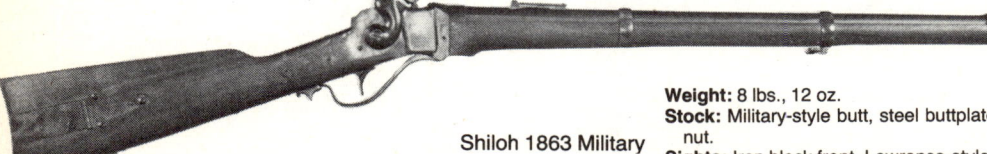

Shiloh 1863 Military

SHILOH SHARPS 1863 MILITARY RIFLE
Caliber: 54.
Barrel: 30", round.
Weight: 8 lbs., 12 oz.
Stock: Military-style butt, steel buttplate and patch box. Standard-grade walnut.
Sights: Iron block front, Lawrence-style ladder rear.
Features: Recreation of the 1863 percussion rifle. Made in U.S. by Shiloh Rifle Mfg. Co.
Price: $800.00
Price: 1863 Military Carbine (as above except has 22" round bbl. band on military-style fore-end, saddle bar and ring) $650.00

BLACK POWDER MUSKETS & RIFLES

Shiloh 1863 Sporting

Shiloh Sharps Model 1863 Sporting Rifle
Similar to the Military Carbine except has 30″ octagon barrel, blade front and sporting rear sights, shotgun butt available, steel buttplate, schnabel fore-end. Standard-grade wood (semi-fancy available).
Price: $695.00

Shiloh Sharps 1862 Confederate Robinson
Recreation of the 54-cal. 1862 Confederate Robinson carbine with 21½″ round barrel; iron block front, fixed V-notch rear sights; brass buttplate and barrel band; sling swivel on buttstock. Weight is about 7½ lbs.
Price: $750.00

Santfl Schuetzen

SANFTL SCHUETZEN PERCUSSION TARGET RIFLE
Caliber: 45 (.445″ round ball).
Barrel: 29″, ⅞″ octagon.
Weight: 9 lbs. Length: 43″ over-all.
Stock: Walnut, schuetzen-style.
Sights: Open tunnel front post, peep rear adjustable for windage & elevation.
Features: True back-action lock with "backward" hammer; screw-in breech plug; buttplate, trigger guard and stock inlays are polished brass. Imported from Italy by Dixie Gun Works.
Price: $595.00

Rigby-style Target

RIGBY-STYLE TARGET RIFLE
Caliber: .451.
Barrel: 32½″.
Weight: 7¾ lbs.
Stock: Walnut; hand-checkered pistol grip, fore-end.
Sights: Target front with micrometer adjustment; adjustable Vernier peep rear.
Features: Comes cased with loading accessories—bullet starter, bullet sizer, special ramrod. Introduced 1985. From Navy Arms.
Price: $550.00

CVA EXPRESS RIFLE
Caliber: 50 (.490″ ball).
Barrel: 28″, round.
Weight: 9 lbs.
Stock: Walnut-stained hardwood.
Sights: Bead and post front, adjustable rear.
Features: Double rifle with twin percussion locks and triggers. Hooked breech. Introduced 1985. From CVA.
Price: Finished $362.95
Price: Kit $301.95
Price: Presentation Express (hand-checkered stock, engraved and polished locks, hammers, tang) $742.95

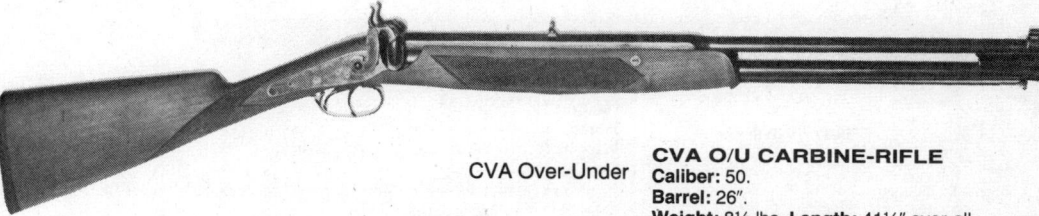

CVA Over-Under

CVA O/U CARBINE-RIFLE
Caliber: 50.
Barrel: 26″.
Weight: 8½ lbs. Length: 41¼″ over-all.
Stock: Checkered walnut.
Sights: Blade front with gold bead, folding rear adjustable for w. and e.
Features: Two-shot over/under with two hammers, two triggers. Polished blue finish. From CVA.
Price: $441.95

KODIAK DOUBLE RIFLE
Caliber: 54x54, 58x58, 50x50 and 58-cal./12 ga. optional.
Barrel: 28″, 5 grooves, 1-in-48″ twist.
Weight: 9½ lbs. Length: 43¼″ over-all.
Stock: Czechoslovakian walnut, hand checkered.
Sights: Adjustable bead front, adjustable open rear.
Features: Hooked breech allows interchangeability of barrels. Comes with sling and swivels, adjustable powder measure, bullet mould and bullet starter. Engraved lockplates, top tang and trigger guard. Locks and top tang polished, rest blued. Introduced 1976. Imported from Italy by Trail Guns Armory, Inc.
Price: 50, 54, 58 cal. SxS $549.50
Price: 50 cal. x 12 ga., 58x12 .... $549.50
Price: Spare barrels, all calibers $294.25
Price: Spare barrels, 12 ga. x 12 ga. $195.00

Consult our Directory pages for the location of firms mentioned.

BLACK POWDER SHOTGUNS

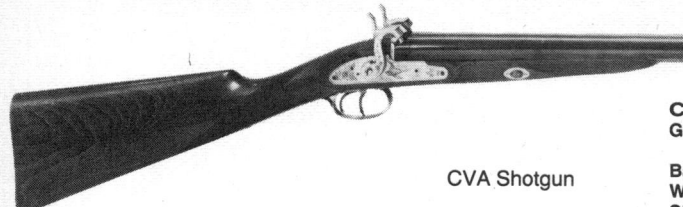
CVA Shotgun

CVA TRAPPER PERCUSSION
Gauge: 12.
Barrel: 28". Choke tubes (Mod., Imp., Full).
Weight: NA. **Length:** 46" over-all.
Stock: English-style straight grip of walnut-finished hardwood.
Sights: Brass bead front.
Features: Single blued barrel; color case-hardened lockplate and hammer; screw adjustable sear engagements, V-type mainspring; brass wedge plates; black trigger guard and tang. From CVA.
Price: Finished $227.95
Price: Kit $189.95

CVA BRITTANY II 410 PERCUSSION SHOTGUN
Gauge: 410.
Barrel: 24".
Weight: 6 lbs., 4 oz. **Length:** 38" over-all.
Stock: Hardwood with pistol grip, M.C. comb.
Sights: Brass bead front.
Features: Color case-hardened lockplates; double triggers (front is hinged); brass wedge plates; stainless nipple. Introduced 1986. From CVA.
Price: Finished $167.95
Price: Kit $120.95

HOPKINS & ALLEN PERCUSSION SHOTGUN
Gauge: 12.
Barrel: 28".
Weight: 6 lbs.
Stock: Walnut. Checkered wrist and fore-end.
Features: Hooked breech design for easy take down. Engraved lockplates. Imported by Hopkins & Allen.
Price: $260.00

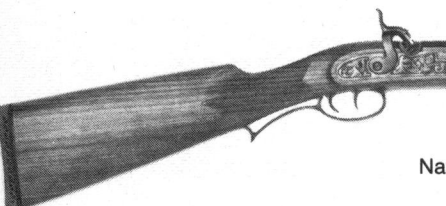
Navy Hunter

NAVY ARMS HUNTER SHOTGUN
Gauge: 20.
Barrel: 28½", interchangeable choke tubes (Full, Mod.).
Stock: Walnut, Hawken-style, checkered p.g. and fore-end.
Sights: Bead front.
Features: Chrome-lined barrel; rubber butt pad; color case-hardened lock; double set triggers; blued furniture. Comes with two flush-mounting choke tubes. Introduced 1986. From Navy Arms.
Price: $315.00

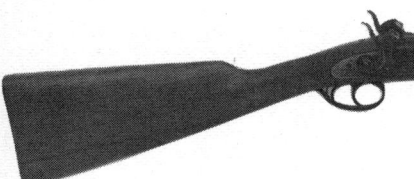
Navy T&T Shotgun

NAVY ARMS T&T SHOTGUN
Gauge: 12.
Barrel: 28" (Full & Full).
Weight: 7½ lbs.
Stock: Walnut.
Sights: Bead front.
Features: Color case-hardened locks, blued steel furniture. From Navy Arms.
Price: $432.00

Navy Fowler

NAVY ARMS FOWLER SHOTGUN
Gauge: 12.
Barrel: 28".
Weight: 7 lbs., 12 oz. **Length:** 45" over-all.
Stock: Walnut.
Features: Color case-hardened lockplates and hammers; checkered stock. Imported by Navy Arms.
Price: Fowler model, 12 ga. only $332.00
Price: Fowler kit, 12 ga. only $249.00

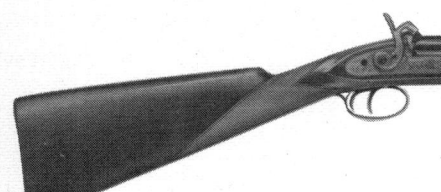
Dixie Double Barrel

DIXIE MAGNUM PERCUSSION SHOTGUN
Gauge: 10, 12.
Barrel: 30" (Imp. Cyl. & Mod.) in 10 ga.; 28" in 12 ga.
Weight: 6¼ lbs. **Length:** 45" over-all.
Stock: Hand checkered walnut, 14" pull.
Features: Double triggers, light hand engraving. Case-hardened locks in 12 ga.; polished steel in 10 ga. with sling swivels. From Dixie.
Price: Upland $325.00
Price: 12 ga. kit $305.00
Price: 10 ga. $365.00
Price: 10 ga. kit $305.00

BLACK POWDER SHOTGUNS

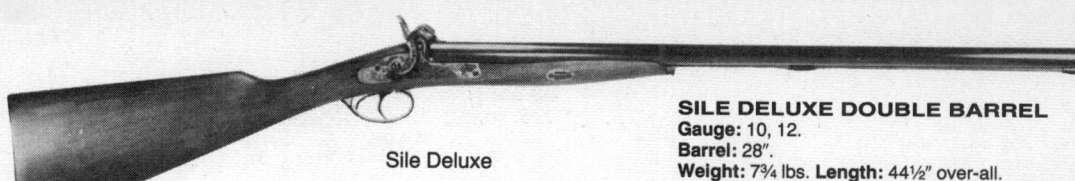
Sile Deluxe

SILE DELUXE DOUBLE BARREL
Gauge: 10, 12.
Barrel: 28".
Weight: 7¾ lbs. **Length:** 44½" over-all.
Stock: Walnut; straight English style; checkered p.g. and fore-end.
Features: Percussion locks with double triggers; chrome-lined bores; engraved color case-hardened lockplates and hammers. Imported by Sile.
Price: $325.00
Price: Confederate Cavalry Model (as above except 14" barrels, weighs 6½ lbs., over-all length of 30½") $325.00

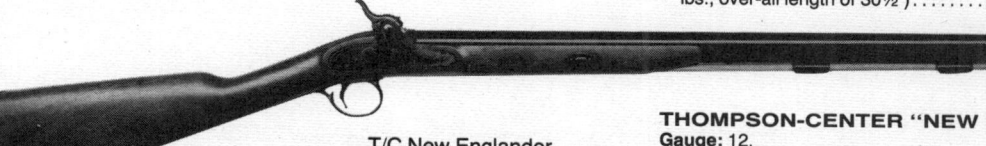
T/C New Englander

THOMPSON-CENTER "NEW ENGLANDER" SHOTGUN
Gauge: 12.
Barrel: 28" (Imp. Cyl.), round.
Weight: 5 lbs, 2 oz.
Stock: Select American black walnut with straight grip.
Features: Percussion lock is color case-hardened, rest blued. Also accepts 26" round 50- and 54-cal. rifle barrel. Introduced 1986.
Price: Right hand $210.00
Price: Left hand $225.00
Price: Accessory rifle barrel, right hand, 50 or 54 .... $97.50
Price: As above, left hand $105.00

TRAIL GUNS KODIAK 10 GAUGE DOUBLE
Gauge: 10.
Barrel: 20", 30¾" (Cyl. bore).
Weight: About 9 lbs. **Length:** 47⅛" over-all.
Stock: Walnut, with cheek rest. Checkered wrist and fore-end.
Features: Chrome-plated bores; engraved lockplates, brass bead front and middle sights; sling swivels. Introduced 1980. Imported form Italy by Trail Guns Armory.
Price: $350.00

AIR GUNS—HANDGUNS

AIR MATCH MODEL 600 PISTOL
Caliber: 177, single shot.
Barrel: 8.8".
Weight: 32 oz. **Length:** 13.19" over-all.
Power: Single stroke pneumatic.
Stocks: Match-style with adjustable palm shelf.
Sights: Interchangeable post front, fully adjustable match rear with interchangeable blades.
Features: Velocity of 420 fps. Adjustable trigger with dry-fire option. Available with three different grip styles, barrel weight, sight extension. Add $5.00 for left-hand models. Introduced 1984. Imported from Italy by Great Lakes Airguns.
Price: With adjustable or fixed grip $529.50

Air Match 600

AIR SHOT BSA SCORPION PISTOL
Caliber: 177 or 22, single shot.
Barrel: 7⅞", rifled steel.
Weight: 54 oz. **Length:** 15 ¾" over-all.
Power: Spring-piston, single-stroke pneumatic.
Stocks: Contoured moulded plastic with thumb-rest, checkering.
Sights: Hooded adjustable front post or bead, fully adjustable match rear.
Features: Velocity of 510 fps (177), 380 fps (22). Adjustable trigger; automatic safety; receiver grooved for scope mounting. Imported from England by Air-Shot Corp.
Price: $94.95

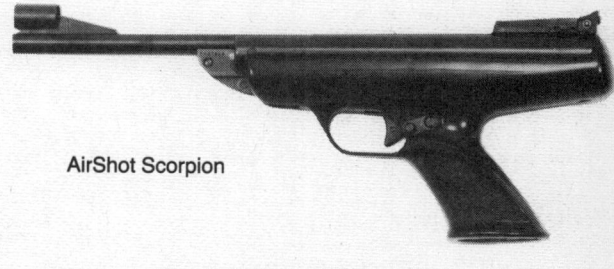
AirShot Scorpion

BEEMAN P1 MAGNUM AIR PISTOL
Caliber: 177, 20, 22, single shot.
Barrel: 8.4".
Weight: 2.5 lbs. **Length:** 11" over-all.
Power: Top lever cocking; spring piston.
Stocks: Checkered walnut.
Sights: Blade front, square notch rear with click micrometer adjustments for w. and e. Grooved for scope mounting.
Features: Dual power for 177 and 20 cal: low setting gives 350-400 fps; high setting 500-600 fps. Rearward expanding mainspring simulates firearm recoil. All Colt 45 auto grips fit gun. Dry firing feature for practice. Optional wooden shoulder stock. Introduced 1985. Imported by Beeman.
Price: 177, 22 cal. $288.00
Price: 20 cal. $295.00

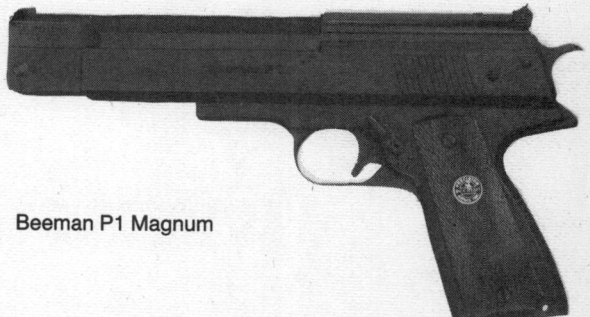
Beeman P1 Magnum

AIR GUNS—HANDGUNS

BEEMAN/FEINWERKBAU MODEL 2 CO₂ PISTOL
Caliber: 177, single shot.
Barrel: 8.9" or 10.1".
Weight: 2.5 lbs. **Length:** 16.1" or 14.8" over-all.
Power: Special CO₂ cylinder.
Stocks: Stippled walnut with adjustable palm shelf.
Sights: Blade front with interchangeable inserts; open micro. click rear with adjustable notch width.
Features: Power adjustable from 360 fps to 525 fps. Fully adjustable trigger; three weights for balance and weight adjustments. Short-barrel Mini-2 model also available. Introduced 1983. Imported by Beeman.
Price: Right-hand $780.00
Price: Left-hand $840.00
Price: Mini-2, right hand $790.00
Price: Mini-2, left hand $860.00

FWB Mini-2

BEEMAN/WEBLEY HURRICANE PISTOL
Caliber: 177 or 22, single shot.
Barrel: 8", rifled.
Weight: 2.4 lbs. **Length:** 11½" over-all.
Power: Spring piston.
Stocks: Thumbrest, checkered high-impact synthetic.
Sights: Hooded front; micro-click rear adj. for w. and e.
Features: Velocity of 470 fps (177-cal.). Single stroke cocking, adjustable trigger pull, manual safety. Rearward recoil like a firearm pistol. Steel piston and cylinder. Scope base included; 1.5x scope **$49.95** up extra. Shoulder stock available. Introduced 1977. Imported from England by Beeman.
Price: $149.95

Beeman/Webley Hurricane

BEEMAN/WEBLEY TEMPEST AIR PISTOL
Caliber: 177 or 22, single shot.
Barrel: 6.75", rifled ordnance steel.
Weight: 32 oz. **Length:** 9" over-all.
Power: Spring piston.
Stocks: Checkered black epoxy with thumbrest.
Sights: Post front; rear has sliding leaf adjustable for w. and e.
Features: Adjustable trigger pull, manual safety. Velocity 470 fps (177 cal.). Steel piston in steel liner for maximum performance and durability. Unique rearward spring simulates firearm recoil. Shoulder stock available. Introduced 1979. Imported from England by Beeman.
Price: $129.95

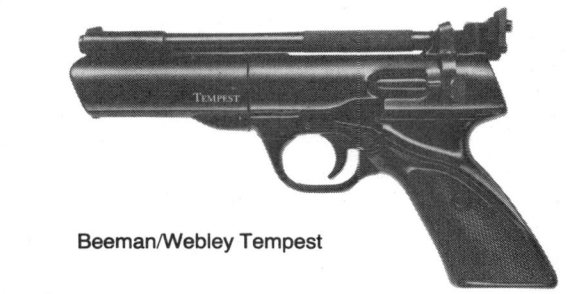
Beeman/Webley Tempest

BEEMAN/FEINWERKBAU FWB-65 MKII AIR PISTOL
Caliber: 177, single shot.
Barrel: 6.1" or 7.5", removeable bbl. wgt. avail.
Weight: 42 oz. **Length:** 13.3" or 14.1" over-all.
Power: Spring, sidelever cocking.
Stocks: Walnut, stippled thumbrest; adjustable or fixed.
Sights: Front, interchangeable post element system, open rear, click adj. for w. & e. and for sighting notch width. Scope mount avail.
Features: New shorter barrel for better balance and control. Cocking effort 9 lbs. 2-stage trigger, 4 adjustments. Quiet firing, 525 fps. Programs instantly for recoil or recoilless operation. Permanently lubricated. Steel piston ring. Special switch converts trigger from 17.6 oz. pull to 42 oz. let-off. Imported by Beeman.
Price: Right-hand.................................. $775.00 to $795.00
Price: Left-hand, 6.1" barrel................................. $825.00
Price: Model 65 Mk.I (7.5" bbl.) .... $725.00 to $779.00

FWB 65 Mk. II

Beeman/Weihrauch HW-70

BEEMAN/WEIHRAUCH HW-70 AIR PISTOL
Caliber: 177; single shot.
Barrel: 6¼", rifled.
Weight: 38 oz. **Length:** 12¾" over-all.
Power: Spring, barrel cocking.
Stocks: Plastic, with thumbrest.
Sights: Hooded post front, square notch rear adj. for w. and e.
Features: Adj. trigger. 24-lb. cocking effort, 410 fps MV; automatic barrel safety. Imported by Beeman.
Price: From Beeman..................................... $147.50

AIR GUNS—HANDGUNS

Benjamin 242/247

Crosman 357

Crosman Model 3357 Spot Marker
Same specs as 8" Model 357 but shoots 50-cal. paint balls. Has break-open action for quick loading 6-shot clip of paint balls. CO_2 power allows repeater firing; hammer block safety; adjustable rear sight, blade front.
Price: About $89.00

CROSMAN MODEL 1322 AIR PISTOL
Caliber: 22, single shot.
Barrel: 8", button rifled.
Weight: 37 oz. **Length:** 13⅝".
Power: Hand pumped.
Sights: Blade front, rear adj. for w. and e.
Features: Moulded plastic grip, hand size pump forearm. Cross-bolt safety. Also available in 177/BB cal. as **Model 1377**.
Price: About $50.00
Price: 1377, about $50.00

CROSMAN/BLASER CONVERSION KIT
Caliber: 177, single shot.
Barrel: 5½", rifled steel.
Weight: 16 oz.
Power: CO_2 Powerlet.
Sights: Blade front, open adj. rear.
Features: Velocity about 400 fps. Converts Colt 45 auto (Series 70 and earlier) into an airgun—replaces slide and magazine and gives same weight and balance, trigger pull, sights as the Colt. About 60 shots per Powerlet.
Price: About $130.00

CROSMAN/SKANAKER MATCH AIR PISTOL
Caliber: 177.
Barrel: 9.94".
Weight: 37 oz. **Length:** 16.38" over-all.
Power: Refillable CO_2 cylinders.
Stocks: Stippled hardwood adjustable for thickness; adjustable palm shelf.
Sights: Three-way adjustable post front, open rear with three interchangeable leaves.
Features: Velocity of 550 fps. Angled, adjustable match trigger can be aligned to fit the natural position of the trigger finger. Barrel is hinged near the muzzle for loading. Introduced 1987.
Price: About $600.00

BEEMAN/FEINWERKBAU MODEL 90 PISTOL
Caliber: 177, single shot.
Barrel: 7.5", 12-groove rifling.
Weight: 3.0 lbs. **Length:** 16.4" over-all.
Power: Spring piston, single stroke sidelever cocking.
Stocks: Stippled walnut with adjustable palm shelf.
Sights: Interchangeable blade front, fully adjustable open notch rear.
Features: Velocity of 475 to 525 fps. Has new adjustable electronic trigger. Recoilless action, metal piston ring and dual mainsprings. Cocking effort is 12 lbs. Introduced 1983. Imported by Beeman.
Price: . . . . $880.00 to $955.00

BENJAMIN 242/247 SINGLE SHOT PISTOLS
Caliber: 177 and 22.
Weight: 32 oz. **Length:** 11¾" over-all.
Power: Hand pumped.
Stocks: Walnut pump handle, optional walnut grips.
Sights: Blade front, open adjustable rear.
Features: Bolt action; fingertip safety; adjustable power.
Price: Model 242 (22 cal.) $86.95
Price: Model 247 (177 cal.) $86.95

CROSMAN MODEL 357 AIR PISTOL
Caliber: 177, 6- or 10-shot.
Barrel: 4" (Model 357 Four), 6" (Model 357 Six), 8" (Model 357 Eight); rifled steel.
Weight: 32 oz. (6") **Length:** 11⅜" over-all.
Power: CO_2 Powerlet.
Stocks: Checkered wood-grain plastic.
Sights: Ramp front, fully adjustable rear.
Features: Average 430 fps (Model 357 Six). Break-open barrel for easy loading. Single or double action. Vent rib barrel. Wide, smooth trigger. Two speed loaders come with each gun.
Price: 4" or 6", about $55.00
Price: 8", about $60.00
Price: Model 1357 (as above, except shoots BBs, 6-shot clip), about $55.00

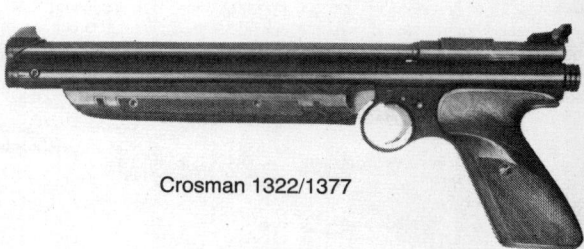
Crosman 1322/1377

Crosman/Blaser

CROSMAN 338 AUTO PISTOL
Caliber: BB, 20-shot magazine.
Barrel: 5", steel.
Weight: 24 oz. **Length:** 8½" over-all.
Power: CO_2 Powerlet.
Stocks: Checkered plastic.
Sights: Patridge front, adjustable rear.
Features: Velocity about 370 fps. Replica of the Walther P-38 pistol. Semi-automatic repeater; thumb-operated lever safety. Introduced 1986.
Price: About $42.00

CAUTION: PRICES CHANGE. CHECK AT GUNSHOP.

AIR GUNS—HANDGUNS

DAISY POWER LINE MODEL 44 REVOLVER
Caliber: 177 pellets, 6-shot.
Barrel: 6", rifled steel; interchangeable 4" and 8".
Weight: 2.7 lbs.
Power: CO_2.
Stocks: Moulded plastic with checkering.
Sights: Blade on ramp front, fully adjustable notch rear.
Features: Velocity up to 400 fps. Replica of 44 Magnum revolver. Has swing-out cylinder and interchangeable barrels. Introduced 1987. From Daisy.
Price: $56.00

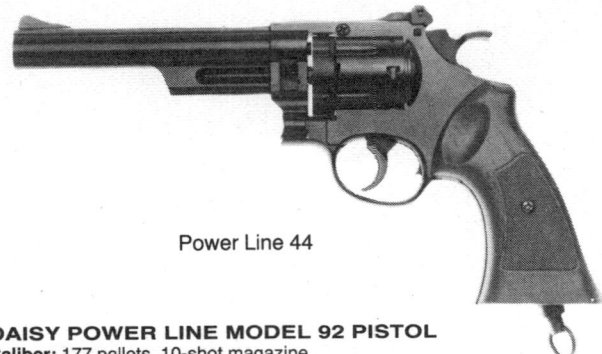
Power Line 44

Daisy Power Line 92

DAISY POWER LINE MODEL 92 PISTOL
Caliber: 177 pellets, 10-shot magazine.
Barrel: Rifled steel.
Weight: 2.15 lbs. **Length:** 8.5" over-all.
Power: CO_2.
Stocks: Cast checkered metal.
Sights: Blade front, adjustable V-slot rear.
Features: Semi-automatic action; 400 fps. Replica of the official 9mm sidearm of the United States armed forces.
Price: About $57.00

DAISY MODEL 188 BB PISTOL
Caliber: BB.
Barrel: 9.9", steel smoothbore.
Weight: 1.67 lbs. **Length:** 11.7" over-all.
Stocks: Die-cast metal; checkered with thumbrest.
Sights: Blade and ramp front, open fixed rear.
Features: 24-shot repeater. Spring action with under-barrel cocking lever. Grip and receiver of die-cast metal. Introduced 1979.
Price: About $21.00

Daisy Model 188

DAISY/YOUTH LINE MODEL 1500 PISTOL
Caliber: BB, 60-shot reservoir.
Barrel: 1.5", smooth bore.
Weight: 22 oz. **Length:** 11.1" over-all.
Power: Daisy CO_2 cylinder
Stocks: Moulded wood-grain plastic with checkering.
Sights: Blade on ramp front, fully adjustable notch rear.
Features: Velocity of 340 fps. Gravity feed magazine. Cross-bolt safety.
Price: About $32.00

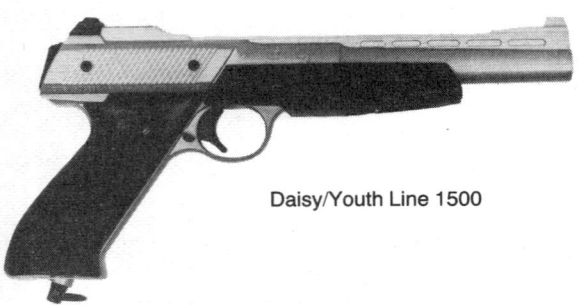
Daisy/Youth Line 1500

Power Line 777

DAISY/POWER LINE MATCH 777 PELLET PISTOL
Caliber: 177, single shot.
Barrel: 9.61" rifled steel by Lothar Walther.
Weight: 32 oz. **Length:** 13½" over-all.
Power: Sidelever, single pump pneumatic.
Stocks: Smooth hardwood, fully contoured with palm and thumb rest.
Sights: Blade and ramp front, match-grade open rear with adj. width notch, micro. click adjustments.
Features: Adjustable trigger; manual cross-bolt safety. MV of 385 fps. Comes with cleaning kit, adjustment tool and pellets. From Daisy.
Price: About $199.50

Daisy/Power Line 747 Pistol
Similar to the 717 pistol except has a 12-groove rifled steel barrel by Lothar Walther. Velocity of 360 fps. Manual cross-bolt safety.
Price: About $85.00

DAISY/POWER LINE 717 PELLET PISTOL
Caliber: 177, single shot.
Barrel: 9.61".
Weight: 2.8 lbs. **Length:** 13½" over-all.
Stocks: Moulded wood-grain plastic, with thumbrest.
Sights: Blade and ramp front, micro, adjustable notch rear.
Features: Single pump pneumatic pistol. Rifled steel barrel. Cross-bolt trigger block. Muzzle velocity 385 fps. From Daisy. Introduced 1979.
Price: About $56.00

DAISY/POWER LINE CO_2 1200 PISTOL
Caliber: BB, 177.
Barrel: 10½", smooth.
Weight: 1.6 lbs. **Length:** 11.1" over-all.
Power: Daisy CO_2 cylinder.
Stocks: Contoured, checkered moulded wood-grain plastic.
Sights: Blade ramp front, fully adj. square notch rear.
Features: 60-shot BB reservoir, gravity feed. Cross-bolt safety. Velocity of 420-450 fps for more than 100 shots. From Daisy.
Price: About $32.00

AIR GUNS—HANDGUNS

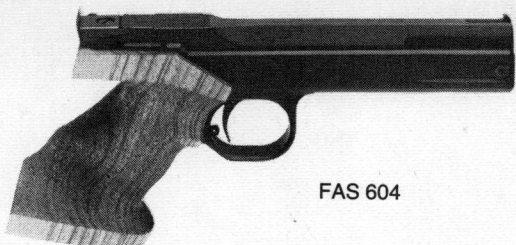
FAS 604

FAS MODEL 604 AIR PISTOL
Caliber: 177, single shot.
Barrel: 7.4", 10-groove rifled steel.
Weight: 2.3 lbs. **Length:** 11.3" over-all.
Power: Single stroke pneumatic.
Stocks: Anatomically shaped stippled walnut; small, medium, large sizes.
Sights: Adjustable.
Features: Top of receiver is cocking arm, requires 13 lbs. effort. Adjustable trigger may be dry-fired without fully cocking pistol. Imported from Italy by Osborne's. Introduced 1984.
Price: $395.00

FAS MODEL AP 604 AIR PISTOL
Caliber: 177, single shot.
Barrel: 7.5", 10-groove rifled steel.
Weight: 2.3 lbs. **Length:** 11.3" over-all.
Power: Single stroke pneumatic.
Stocks: Anatomically shaped stippled hardwood.
Sights: Post front, fully adjustable rear.
Features: Velocity of 370 fps. Top of receiver is cocking arm, requires 13 lbs. effort. Adjustable trigger may be dry-fired without fully cocking pistol. Imported from Italy by Great Lakes Airguns.
Price: $479.50

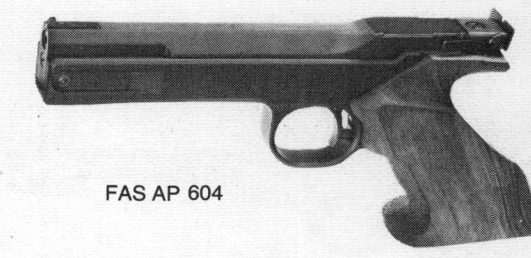
FAS AP 604

"GAT" AIR PISTOL
Caliber: 177, single shot.
Barrel: 7½" cocked, 9½" extended.
Weight: 22 oz.
Power: Spring piston.
Stocks: Composition.
Sights: Fixed.
Features: Shoots pellets or darts. Matte black finish. Imported by Stone Enterprises, Inc.
Price: $19.95

MARKSMAN 17 AIR PISTOL
Caliber: 177, single shot.
Barrel: 7.5".
Weight: 46 oz. **Length:** 14.5" over-all.
Power: Spring air, barrel-cocking.
Stocks: Checkered composition with right-hand thumb rest.
Sights: Tunnel front, fully adj. rear.
Features: Velocity of 330-360 fps. Introduced 1986. Imported from Spain by Marksman Products.
Price: $86.95

Marksman Model 17

MARKSMAN PLAINSMAN 1049 CO_2 PISTOL
Caliber: BB, 100-shot repeater.
Barrel: 5⅞", smooth.
Weight: 28 oz. **Length:** 9½" over-all.
Stocks: Simulated walnut with thumbrest.
Power: 8.5 or 12.5 gram CO_2 cylinders.
Features: Velocity of 400 fps. Three-position power switch. Auto. ammunition feed. Positive safety.
Price: $37.50

MARKSMAN #1010 REPEATER PISTOL
Caliber: 177, 20-shot repeater.
Barrel: 2½", smoothbore.
Weight: 24 oz. **Length:** 8¼" over-all.
Power: Spring.
Features: Thumb safety. Black finish. Uses BBs, darts or pellets. Repeats with BBs only.
Price: Matte black finish $20.50
Price: Model 1010X (as above except nickel plated) $28.00

Marksman 1010

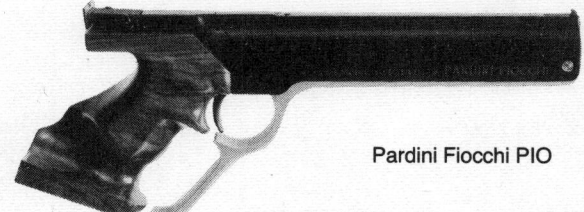
Pardini Fiocchi PIO

PARDINI FIOCCHI PIO MATCH AIR PISTOL
Caliber: 177.
Barrel: 7.7".
Weight: 37 ozs. **Length:** 14" over-all.
Power: Single stroke pneumatic.
Stocks: Stippled walnut with palm shelf.
Sights: Post front, fully adjustable open rear.
Features: Muzzle velocity of 425 fps. Cocking lever forms trigger guard. Imported from Italy by Fiocchi of America.
Price: $375.00

RWS/DIANA MODEL 6M MATCH AIR PISTOL
Caliber: 177, single shot.
Barrel: 7".
Weight: 3 lbs. **Length:** 16" over-all.
Power: Spring air, barrel cocking.
Stocks: Walnut-finished hardwood with thumbrest.
Sights: Adjustable front, micro. click open rear.
Features: Velocity of 410 fps. Recoilless double piston system, moveable barrel shroud to protect front sight during cocking. Imported from West Germany by Dynamit Nobel-RWS, Inc.
Price: Right hand $335.00
Price: Left hand $350.00

CAUTION: PRICES CHANGE. CHECK AT GUNSHOP.

AIR GUNS—HANDGUNS

RWS/DIANA MODEL 5G AIR PISTOL
Caliber: 177, single shot.
Barrel: 7″.
Weight: 2¾ lbs. **Length:** 16″ over-all.
Power: Spring air, barrel cocking.
Stocks: Plastic, thumbrest design.
Sights: Tunnel front, micro click open rear.
Features: Velocity of 410 fps. Two-stage trigger with automatic safety. Imported from West Germany by Dynamit Nobel-RWS, Inc.
Price: $150.00

RWS/Diana MODEL 5GS Air Pistol
Same as the Model 5G except comes with 1.5x15 pistol scope with ramp-style mount, muzzle brake/weight. No open sights supplied. Introduced 1983.
Price: $210.00

RWS Model 5G

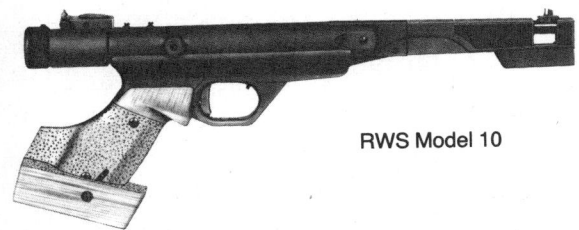
RWS Model 10

RECORD "JUMBO" DELUXE AIR PISTOL
Caliber: 177, single shot.
Barrel: 6″, rifled.
Weight: 1.9 lbs. **Length:** 7.25″ over-all.
Power: Spring air, lever cocking.
Stocks: Smooth walnut.
Sights: Post front, fully adjustable open rear.
Features: Velocity of 322 fps. Thumb safety. Grip magazine compartment for extra pellet storage. Introduced 1983. Imported from West Germany by Great Lakes Airguns.
Price: $79.95

RECORD CHAMPION AIR PISTOL
Caliber: 177, 12-shot repeater.
Barrel: 7.6″, rifled.
Weight: 2.8 lbs. **Length:** 10.2″ over-all.
Power: Spring air, sidelever cocking.
Stocks: Smooth hardwood. Contoured target style available.
Sights: Post front, fully adjustable rear.
Features: Velocity of 420 fps. Magazine loads into bottom of grip. Ambidextrous grips. Introduced 1987. Imported from West Germany by Great Lakes Airguns.
Price: $136.54

RWS/Diana Model 10 Match Air Pistol
Refined version of the Model 6M. Has special adjustable match trigger, oil finished and stippled match grips, barrel weight. Also available in left-hand version, and with fitted case.
Price: Model 10 .... $595.00
Price: Model 10, left-hand $640.00
Price: Model 10, with case $625.00
Price: Model 10, left-hand, with case $670.00

Record Champion

Sharp "U-FP"

SHARP MODEL "U-FP" CO₂ PISTOL
Caliber: 177, single shot.
Barrel: 8″, rifled steel.
Weight: 2.4 lbs. **Length:** 11.6″ over-all.
Power: 12 gram CO_2 cylinder.
Stocks: Smooth hardwood. Walnut target stocks available.
Sights: Post front, fully adjustable target rear.
Features: Variable power adjustment up to 545 fps. Adjustable trigger. Also available with adjustable field sight. Imported from Japan by Great Lakes Airguns.
Price: With target sights $199.50
Price: With field sights $179.50

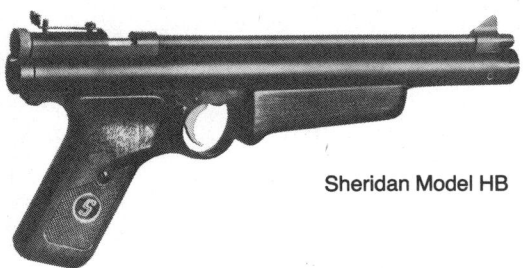
Sheridan Model HB

SHERIDAN MODEL HB PNEUMATIC PISTOL
Caliber: 5mm, single shot.
Barrel: 9⅜″, rifled.
Weight: 36 oz. **Length:** 12″ over-all.
Power: Underlever pneumatic pump.
Stocks: Checkered simulated walnut; fore-end is walnut.
Sights: Blade front, fully adjustable rear.
Features: "Controller-Power" feature allows velocity and range control by varying the number of pumps—3 to 10. Maximum velocity of 400 fps. Introduced 1982. From Sheridan Products.
Price: $86.95

WALTHER CP CO₂ AIR PISTOL
Caliber: 177, single shot.
Barrel: 9″.
Weight: 40 oz. **Length:** 14¾″ over-all.
Power: CO_2.
Stocks: Full target type stippled wood with adjustable hand-shelf.
Sights: Target post front, fully adjustable rear.
Features: Velocity of 520 fps. CO_2 powered; target-quality trigger; comes with adaptor for charging with standard CO_2 air tanks, case, and accessories. Introduced 1983. Imported from West Germany by Interarms.
Price: $825.00
Price: Junior Model (modified grip, shorter gas cylinder) $825.00

AIR GUNS—AIR SOFT HANDGUNS

Gas Auto Mag

COMMAND POST GAS AUTO MAG PISTOL
Caliber: 25-cal. plastic shot.
Barrel: NA
Weight: 2 lbs. **Length:** 10″ over-all.
Power: Liquid charge Flon-12 gas system.
Stocks: Checkered black plastic.
Sights: Ramp front, adjustable rear.
Features: Nickel finish. Replica of the Auto Mag pistol. Available from The Command Post, Inc.
Price: $79.98

Model 645

COMMAND POST MODEL 645 PISTOL
Caliber: 25-cal. plastic shot.
Barrel: NA
Weight: 12 oz. **Length:** 9″ over-all.
Power: Spring-air, slide cocking.
Stocks: Checkered black plastic.
Sights: Ramp front, notch rear.
Features: Replica of the Model 645 auto pistol. Stainless finish.
Price: $29.98

COMMAND POST M-11 GAS PISTOL
Caliber: 25-cal. plastic shot.
Barrel: NA
Weight: 3 lbs. **Length:** 15″ over-all.
Power: Direct gas power.
Stocks: Moulded plastic.
Sights: Post front, aperture rear.
Features: Full-size replica of the MAC-11. Removeable fake suppressor. Front hand strap. Semiauto fire. Available from The Command Post, Inc.
Price: $64.98

Airsoft 04

M-11 Gas Pistol

COMMAND POST AIRSOFT 04
Caliber: 25-cal. plastic pellets.
Barrel: Smoothbore.
Weight: 1.1 lbs. **Length:** 10.5″ over-all.
Power: Spring.
Stocks: Woodgrain moulded grip with checkering.
Sights: Blade and ramp front, notched rear.
Features: Fully detailed replica of a classic 44 Magnum, six-shot revolver with swing-out cylinder for easy loading.
Price: About $33.00

Consult our Directory pages for the location of firms mentioned.

COMMAND POST AIRSOFT 09
Caliber: 25-cal. plastic shot.
Barrel: Smoothbore.
Weight: 12 oz. **Length:** 9.5″ over-all.
Power: Slide action, spring air.
Stocks: Moulded grip with checkering.
Sights: Blade front, notched rear.
Features: Detailed replica of the official 9mm sidearm recently adopted by the U.S. Armed Forces, the Beretta 9mm. Takes seven-shot clip, ejects spent shells.
Price: About $24.98

Airsoft 09

COMMAND POST AIRSOFT 13
Caliber: 25-cal. plastic shot.
Barrel: Smoothbore.
Weight: 2.6 lbs. **Length:** 15.5″ over-all.
Power: Bolt action, spring air.
Stocks: Moulded grip and receiver.
Sights: Post front, notched rear.
Features: Replica of the world-famous Israeli semi-automatic assault pistol; loads with 22-shot clip.
Price: About $39.98

CAUTION: PRICES CHANGE. CHECK AT GUNSHOP.

AIR GUNS—AIR SOFT HANDGUNS

Airsoft 57

COMMAND POST AIRSOFT 57 REVOLVER
Caliber: 25 (6mm) plastic pellets; 6-shot.
Barrel: Smoothbore.
Weight: NA. **Length:** 10½" over-all.
Stocks: Moulded woodgrain with checkering.
Sights: Blade and ramp front, notch rear.
Features: Fires spring-activated 25-cal. plastic pellets loaded into plastic cartridges. Cylinder swings out for loading. Introduced 1985.
Price: About $24.98

COMMAND POST AIRSOFT 45
Caliber: 25-cal. plastic shot.
Barrel: Smoothbore.
Weight: 12 oz. **Length:** 8.5" over-all.
Power: Slide cocking, spring air.
Stocks: Moulded grip with checkering.
Sights: Ramp front, notched rear.
Features: Detailed replica of the 45 auto pistol. Holds seven-shot clip, ejects spent shells.
Price: About $24.98

COMMAND POST AIRSOFT 59 PISTOL
Caliber: 25 (6mm) plastic pellets; 10-shot clip.
Barrel: Smoothbore.
Weight: NA. **Length:** 9" over-all.
Stocks: Moulded with checkering.
Sights: Blade and ramp front, notch rear.
Features: Fires 25-cal. plastic pellets loaded into plastic cartridges. Clip fed, semi-auto action ejects spent shells. Introduced 1985.
Price: About $24.98

COMMAND POST TRACER SCORPION
Caliber: 25-cal. plastic glow shot.
Barrel: NA.
Weight: 2½ lbs. **Length:** 24" over-all (stock extended).
Power: Spring piston, bolt action.
Stock: Moulded woodgrain composition; folding wire butt.
Sights: Post front, notch rear.
Features: Shoots "glow BBs" for tracer effect. Available from The Command Post, Inc.
Price: $89.98

Tracer Scorpion

AIR GUNS—LONG GUNS

Air Arms Firepower

AIR ARMS FIREPOWER AIR RIFLE
Caliber: 22, 35-shot Auto-Load system.
Barrel: 14¾", Walther with 12 grooves.
Weight: 7 lbs., 8 oz. **Length:** 40½" over-all.
Power: Spring-air, sidelever.
Stock: Synthetic, military-style.
Sights: Blade on ramp front, adjustable aperture rear.
Features: Velocity of 700+ fps. Adjustable trigger; removeable sights; receiver grooved for scope mounting. High polish blue finish; sling swivels. Introduced 1987. Imported from England by Great Lakes Airguns.
Price: $277.00

Air Arms Khamsin

AIR ARMS MODEL KHAMSIN
Caliber: 177, 22; single shot.
Barrel: 15", rifled.
Weight: 8 lbs., 2 oz. **Length:** 39¾" over-all.
Power: Spring-air, side-lever cocking.
Stock: Oil-finished French walnut thumbhole-style, with cut checkering on p.g. and fore-end. Ventilated rubber buttplate and sling swivels.
Sights: None furnished. Comes with scope anti-slip block.
Features: Velocity up to 852 fps (177 cal.). Polished brass trigger and trigger guard. Introduced 1987. Imported from England by Great Lakes Airguns.
Price: Either caliber $486.58
Price: With AutoLoad 34-pellet magazine $527.93

Air Arms Model Bora
Similar to the Mistral model except has 11" barrel, weighs 7.7 lbs. and has 35.8" over-all length. Velocity up to 872 fps (177 cal.). Imported from England by Great Lakes Airguns.
Price: 177 or 22 .... $277.00
Price: With AutoLoad 34-pellet magazine $294.21

AIR GUNS—LONG GUNS

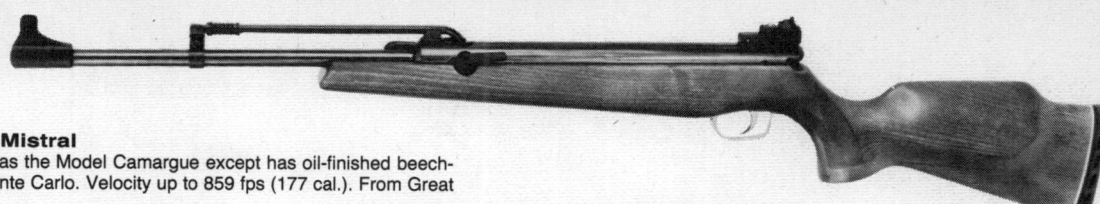
Air Arms Mistral

Air Arms Model Mistral
Basically the same as the Model Camargue except has oil-finished beechwood stock with Monte Carlo. Velocity up to 859 fps (177 cal.). From Great Lakes Airguns.
Price: Either 177 or 22 caliber **$277.00**
Price: With AutoLoad 34-pellet magazine **$294.21**

Air Arms Model Camargue
Basically the same as the Khamsin model except has a Tyrolean-style stock, post front sight with protective ears, micrometer-adjustable aperture rear. Velocity up to 871 fps (177 cal.). From Great Lakes Airguns.
Price: Either caliber **$363.91**
Price: With AutoLoad 34-pellet magazine **$433.26**

BSA Airsporter-S

AIR SHOT BSA AIRSPORTER-S RIFLES
Caliber: 177 or 22, single shot.
Barrel: 14.3" (Carbine), 19.5" (Rifle).
Weight: 7.4 lbs. (Carbine), 8 lbs. (Rifle) **Length:** 39.5" over-all (Carbine).
Power: Spring-piston, single-stroke pneumatic; under lever cocking.
Stock: Walnut-stained hardwood with Monte Carlo comb, checkered p.g., fore-end; vent. recoil pad.
Sights: Hooded adjustable front bead/blade, fully adjustable match rear.
Features: Velocity of 825 fps (177), 600 fps (22). "Maxigrip" scope mounting system; two-stage adjustable match trigger. Fixed heavy barrel with loading plug. Imported from England by AirShot Corp.
Price: **$246.95**

Air Shot BSA Airsporter Stutzen
Similar to the Airsporter-S except has full-length Mannlicher-style stock with Monte Carlo comb, cheekpiece, 14" barrel, over-all length of 39", weight of 7.8 lbs., low-profile rear sight.
Price: **$286.95**

BSA Mercury

AIR SHOT BSA MERCURY AIR RIFLE
Caliber: 177 or 22, single shot.
Barrel: 18.5", rifled steel.
Weight: 7 lbs. **Length:** 43.5" over-all.
Power: Spring-piston, single-stroke pneumatic, barrel cocking.
Stock: Walnut-stained hardwood with Monte Carlo comb, checkered p.g., vent. recoil pad.
Sights: Hooded adjustable front, fully adjustable rear.
Features: Velocity of 700 fps (177), 550 fps (22). Two-stage adjustable trigger. Receiver grooved for scope mounting. Imported from England by AirShot Corp.
Price: **$156.95**

BSA Mercury Super

AIR SHOT BSA MERCURY SUPER RIFLES
Caliber: 177 or 22, single shot.
Barrel: 14" (Carbine), 19.4" (Rifle).
Weight: 6.8 lbs. (Carbine), 7.4 lbs. (Rifle). **Length:** 39" over-all (Carbine).
Power: Spring-piston, single-stroke pneumatic, barrel cocking.
Stock: Walnut-stained hardwood with Monte Carlo comb, checkered p.g. and fore-end, vent. recoil pad.
Sights: Hooded adjustable front bead/blade, fully adjustable match rear.
Features: Velocity of 850 fps (177), 625 fps (22). "Maxigrip" scope mounting system with arrestor block. Two-stage adjustable match trigger. Imported from England by AirShot Corp.
Price: **$194.95**

BSA Meteor Super

AIR SHOT BSA METEOR SUPER AIR RIFLE
Caliber: 177 or 22, single shot.
Barrel: 18.5", rifled steel.
Weight: 6 lbs. **Length:** 42" over-all.
Power: Spring-piston, single-stroke pneumatic, barrel cocking.
Stock: Walnut-stained hardwood with Monte Carlo comb, vent. recoil pad.
Sights: Hooded adjustable front, fully adjustable rear.
Features: Velocity of 800 fps (177), 585 fps (22). Adjustable trigger. Receiver grooved for scope mounting. Imported from England by AirShot Corp.
Price: **$115.95**

Air Shot Meteor Air Rifle
Similar to the Meteor Super except has straight-comb stock. Comes with extra aperture rear sight.
Price: **$97.95**

CAUTION: PRICES CHANGE. CHECK AT GUNSHOP.

AIR GUNS—LONG GUNS

BSA Supersport Standard

Air Shot BSA Supersport Custom
Similar to the Standard except has checkered Monte Carlo stock, "Maxigrip" scope mounting system with arrestor block.
Price: $286.95

AIR SHOT BSA SUPERSPORT STANDARD RIFLE
Caliber: 177 or 22, single shot.
Barrel: 18.5".
Weight: 6 lbs., 6 oz. **Length:** 42" over-all.
Power: Spring-piston, single-stroke pneumatic.
Stock: Walnut-stained hardwood with ventilated rubber recoil pad.
Sights: Hooded adjustable front bead/blade, fully adjustable match rear.
Features: Velocity of 950 fps (177), 700 fps (22). Single-stage adjustable trigger, silent safety. Receiver grooved for scope mounting. Imported from England by AirShot Corp.
Price: $179.95

Air Shot Survival

AIR SHOT SURVIVAL CARBINE
Caliber: 177, 25-shot feed tube.
Barrel: 12", rifled steel.
Weight: 5 lbs., 10 oz. **Length:** 32" over-all.
Power: Spring-piston, single-stroke pneumatic.
Stock: Moulded composition, folding skeleton butt.
Sights: Hooded ramp front, fully adjustable match rear.
Features: Velocity of 625 fps. Automatic safety. Receiver grooved for scope mounting. Comes with web sling. Imported from Brazil by AirShot Corp.
Price: $71.95

Anschutz 2001

ANSCHUTZ 2001 MATCH AIR RIFLE
Caliber: 177, single shot.
Barrel: 26".
Weight: 10½ lbs. **Length:** 44½" over-all.
Stock: European hardwood; stippled grip and fore-end.
Sights: Globe front, #6824 Micro Peep rear.
Features: Balance, weight match the 1907 ISU smallbore rifle. Uses #5019 match trigger. Recoil and vibration free. Fully adjustable cheekpiece and buttplate. Introduced 1988. Imported from Germany by Precision Sales International.
Price: Right hand $1,290.00
Price: Left hand $1,355.00

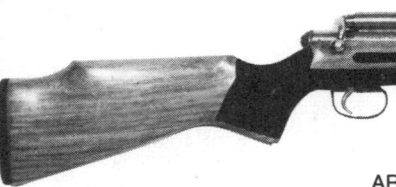
ARS/Farco Shotgun

ARS/FARCO CO_2 AIR SHOTGUN
Caliber: 51 (28 gauge).
Barrel: 30".
Weight: 7 lbs. **Length:** 48½" over-all.
Power: 10-oz. refillable CO_2 tank.
Stock: Hardwood.
Sights: Bead front, fixed dovetail rear.
Features: Gives over 100 ft. lbs. energy for taking small game. Imported by Air Rifle Specialists.
Price: $400.00

Beeman/FWB 124

BEEMAN/FEINWERKBAU 124/127 MAGNUM
Caliber: 177 (FWB-124); 22 (FWB-127); single shot.
Barrel: 18.3", 12-groove rifling.
Weight: 6.8 lbs. **Length:** 43½" over-all.
Power: Spring piston air; single stroke barrel cocking.
Stock: Walnut finished hardwood.
Sights: Tunnel front; click-adj. rear for w., slide-adj. for e.
Features: Velocity 680-820 fps, cocking effort of 18 lbs. Forged steel receiver; nylon non-drying piston and breech seals. Auto. safety, adj. trigger. Hand-checkered p.g. and fore-end, high comb cheekpiece, and buttplate with white spacer. Imported by Beeman.
Price: Deluxe model, right hand $399.98
Price: As above, left hand $439.98

AIR GUNS—LONG GUNS

BEEMAN/FEINWERKBAU 300-S SERIES MATCH RIFLE
Caliber: 177, single shot.
Barrel: 19.9", fixed solid with receiver.
Weight: Approx. 10 lbs. with optional bbl. sleeve. **Length:** 42.8" over-all.
Power: Single stroke sidelever, spring piston.
Stock: Match model—walnut, deep fore-end, adj. buttplate.
Sights: Globe front with interchangeable inserts. Click micro. adj. match aperture rear. Front and rear sights move as a single unit.
Features: Recoilless, vibration free. Five-way adjustable match trigger. Grooved for scope mounts. Permanent lubrication, steel piston ring. Cocking effort 9 lbs. Optional 10 oz. bbl. sleeve. Available from Beeman.
Price: Right-hand $859.00
Price: Left-hand $930.00

BEEMAN BETA AIR RIFLE
Caliber: 177 or 22.
Barrel: 18.8".
Weight: 8.4 lbs. **Length:** 44.5" over-all.
Power: Spring-piston, barrel cocking.
Stock: Stained beech; Monte Carlo comb and cheekpiece; cut-checkered p.g.; rubber butt pad.
Sights: Blade on ramp front, open adjustable rear.
Features: Anti-vibration mechanism. Imported by Beeman.
Price: . . . . NA

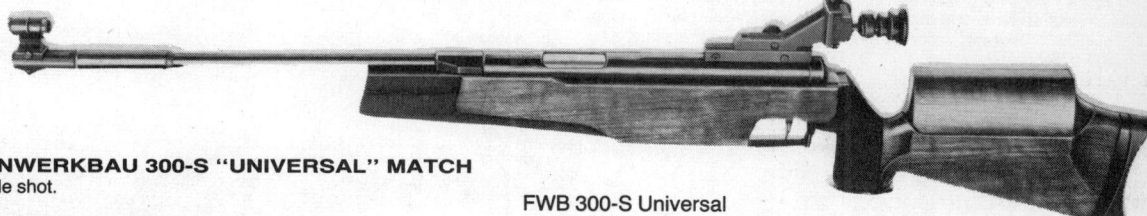
FWB 300-S Universal

BEEMAN/FEINWERKBAU 300-S "UNIVERSAL" MATCH
Caliber: 177, single shot.
Barrel: 19.9".
Weight: 10.2 lbs. (without barrel sleeve). **Length:** 43.3" over-all.
Power: Spring piston, single stroke sidelever.
Stock: Walnut, stippled p.g. and fore-end. Detachable cheekpieces (one std., high for scope use.) Adjustable buttplate, accessory rail. Buttplate and grip cap spacers included.
Sights: Two globe fronts with interchangeable inserts. Rear is match aperture with rubber eyecup and sight viser. Front and rear sights move as a single unit.
Features: Recoilless, vibration free. Grooved for scope mounts. Steel piston ring. Cocking effort about 9½ lbs. Barrel sleeve optional. Left-hand model available. Introduced 1978. Imported by Beeman.
Price: Right-hand $998.00
Price: Left-hand $1,075.00

BEEMAN/FEINWERKBAU 300-S MINI-MATCH
Caliber: 177, single shot.
Barrel: 17⅛".
Weight: 8.8 lbs. **Length:** 40" over-all.
Power: Spring piston, single stroke sidelever cocking.
Stock: Walnut. Stippled grip, adjustable buttplate. Scaled-down for youthful or slightly built shooters.
Sights: Globe front with interchangeable inserts, micro. adjustable rear. Front and rear sights move as a single unit.
Features: Recoilless, vibration free. Grooved for scope mounts. Steel piston ring. Cocking effort about 9½ lbs. Barrel sleeve optional. Left-hand model available. Introduced 1978. Imported by Beeman.
Price: Right-hand $870.00
Price: Left-hand $879.00

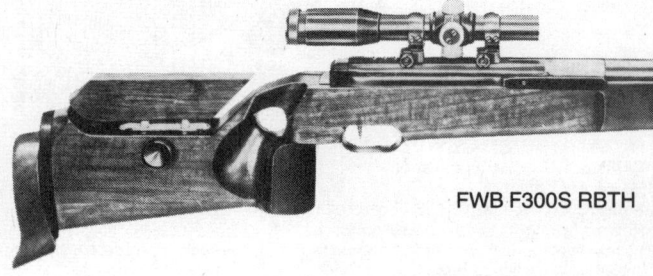
FWB F300S RBTH

BEEMAN/FEINWERKBAU F300-S RUNNING BOAR (TH)
Caliber: 177, single shot.
Barrel: 19.9", rifled.
Weight: 10.9 lbs. **Length:** 43" over-all.
Power: Single stroke sidelever, spring piston.
Stock: Walnut with adjustable buttplate, grip cap and comb. Designed for fixed and moving target use.
Sights: None furnished; grooved for optional scope.
Features: Recoilless, vibration free. Permanent lubrication and seals. Barrel stabilizer weight included. Crisp single-stage trigger. Available from Beeman.
Price: Right-hand $910.00
Price: Left-hand $998.00

Beeman/FWB 601 Running Target
Similar to the standard Model 600. Has 16.9" barrel (33.7" with barrel sleeve); special match trigger, short loading gate which allows scope mounting. No sights—built for scope use only. Introduced 1987.
Price: Right hand $1,125.00
Price: Left hand $1,255.00
Price: Running target scope mounts $139.95

BEEMAN/FEINWERKBAU MODEL 601 AIR RIFLE
Caliber: 177, single shot.
Barrel: 16.6".
Weight: 10.8 lbs. **Length:** 43" over-all.
Power: Single stroke pneumatic.
Stock: Special laminated hardwoods and hard rubber for stability.
Sights: Tunnel front with interchangeable inserts, click micrometer match aperture rear.
Features: Recoilless action; double supported barrel; special, short rifled area frees pellet from barrel faster so shooter's motion has minimum effect on accuracy. Fully adjustable match trigger. Trigger and sights blocked when loading latch is open. Imported by Beeman. Introduced 1984.
Price: Right-hand $1,175.00
Price: Left-hand $1,295.00

BEEMAN/FWB C60 CO$_2$ RIFLE
Caliber: 177.
Barrel: 16.9". With barrel sleeve, 25.4".
Weight: 10 lbs. **Length:** 42.6" over-all.
Stock: Laminated hardwood and hard rubber.
Sights: Tunnel front with interchangeable inserts, quick release micro. click match aperture rear.
Features: Similar features, performance as Beeman/FWB 600. Virtually no cocking effort. Right or left hand. Running target version available. Introduced 1987. Imported from Germany by Beeman.
Price: Right-hand $1,085.00
Price: Left-hand $1,185.00

BEEMAN/HARPER AIRCANE
Caliber: 22 and 25, single shot.
Barrel: 31½", rifled.
Weight: 1 lb. **Length:** 34" over-all.
Features: Walking cane also acts as an airgun. Solid walnut handle with polished brass ferrule. Available in various hand-carved models. Intricate deep engraving on the ferrule. Uses rechargeable air "cartridges" loaded with pellets. Kit includes separate pump, extra cartridges and fitted case. Introduced 1987. Imported by Beeman.
Price: Basic set $495.95
Price: Goose, Labrador, Spaniel sets $555.00

CAUTION: PRICES CHANGE. CHECK AT GUNSHOP.

AIR GUNS—LONG GUNS

Beeman HW77

BEEMAN/HW77 AIR RIFLE & CARBINE
Caliber: 177 or 22, single shot.
Barrel: 14.5" or 18.5", 12-groove rifling.
Weight: 8.9 lbs. **Length:** 39.7" or 43.7" over-all.
Power: Spring-piston; underlever cocking.
Stock: Walnut-stained beech; rubber buttplate, cut checkering on grip; cheekpiece.
Sights: Blade front, open adjustable rear.
Features: Velocity 830 fps. Fixed-barrel with fully opening, direct loading breech. Extended underlever gives good cocking leverage. Adjustable trigger. Grooved for scope mounting. Carbine has 14.5" barrel, weighs 8.7 lbs., and is 39.7" over-all. Imported by Beeman.
Price: Right-hand $399.98
Price: Left-hand $439.98

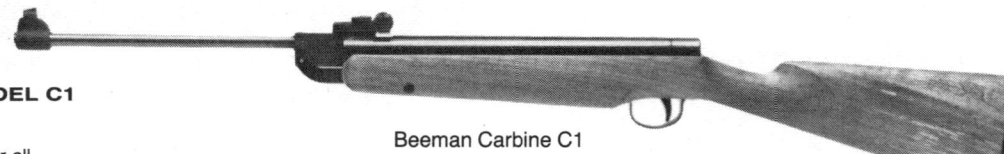
Beeman Carbine C1

BEEMAN CARBINE MODEL C1
Caliber: 177, single shot.
Barrel: 14", 12-groove rifling.
Weight: 6¼ lbs. **Length:** 38" over-all.
Power: Spring-piston, barrel cocking.
Stock: Walnut-stained beechwood with rubber butt pad.
Sights: Blade front, rear click-adjustable for windage and elevation.
Features: Velocity 830 fps. Adjustable trigger. Receiver grooved for scope mounting. Imported by Beeman.
Price: $199.95

Beeman/Webley Omega

BEEMAN/WEBLEY OMEGA AIR RIFLE
Caliber: 177.
Barrel: 19¼", rifled.
Weight: 7.8 lbs. **Length:** 43½" over-all.
Power: Spring-piston air; barrel cocking.
Stock: Walnut-stained beech with cut-checkered grip; cheekpiece; rubber butt-pad.
Features: Special quick-snap barrel latch; self-lubricating piston seal; receiver grooved for scope mounting. Introduced 1985. Imported from England by Beeman.
Price: $349.50

BEEMAN HW 35L/35EB SPORTER RIFLES
Caliber: 177 (35L), 177 or 22 (35EB), single shot.
Barrel: 19½".
Weight: 8 lbs. **Length:** 43½" over-all (35L).
Power: Spring, barrel cocking.
Stock: Walnut finish with high comb, full pistol grip.
Sights: Globe front with five inserts, target micrometer rear with rubber eyecup.
Features: Fully adjustable trigger, manual safety. Thumb-release barrel latch. Model 35L has Bavarian cheekpiece stock, 35EB has walnut, American-style stock with cheekpiece, sling swivels, white spacers. Imported by Beeman.
Price: Model 35L $317.50
Price: Model 35EB $337.50

BEEMAN/HW 55 TARGET RIFLES

Model:	55SM	55MM	55T
Caliber:	177	177	177
Barrel:	18½"	18½"	18½"
Length:	43½"	43½"	43½"
Wgt. lbs.:	7.8	7.8	7.8
Rear sight:	All aperture		
Front sight:	All with globe and 4 interchangeable inserts.		
Power:	All spring (barrel cocking). 660-700 fps.		
Price:	$389.50	$489.50	$539.50

Features: Trigger fully adj. and removable. Micrometer rear sight adj. for w. and e. in all. Pistol grip high comb stock with beavertail fore-end, walnut finish stock on 55SM. Walnut stock on 55MM, Tyrolean stock on 55T. Imported by Beeman.

BEEMAN/WEBLEY VULCAN II DELUXE
Caliber: 177 or 22, single shot.
Barrel: 17", rifled.
Weight: 7.6 lbs. **Length:** 43.7" over-all.
Power: Spring-piston air, barrel cocking.
Stock: Walnut. Cut checkering, rubber butt pad, cheekpiece. Standard version has walnut-stained beech.
Sights: Hooded front, micrometer rear.
Features: Velocity of 830 fps (177), 675 fps (22). Single stage adjustable trigger; receiver grooved for scope mounting. Self-lubricating piston seal. Introduced 1983. Imported by Beeman.
Price: Standard $199.95
Price: Deluxe $269.95

BEEMAN R1 LASER AIR RIFLE
Caliber: 177, 20, 22, 25, single shot.
Barrel: 16.1" or 19.6".
Weight: 8.4 lbs. **Length:** 41.7" over-all (16.1" barrel).
Power: Spring-piston, barrel cocking.
Stock: Laminated wood with Monte Carlo comb and cheekpiece; checkered p.g. and fore-end; rubber butt pad.
Sights: Tunnel front with interchangeable inserts, open adjustable rear.
Features: Velocity up to 1,050 fps (177). Receiver grooved for scope mounting. Imported by Beeman.
Price: 177 or 22 cal. $750.00
Price: 20 cal. $760.00
Price: 25 cal. .... NA

Beeman R7 Air Rifle
Similar to the R8 model except has lighter ambidextrous stock, match grade trigger block; velocity of 680-700 fps; barrel length 17"; weight 5.8 lbs. Milled steel safety. Imported by Beeman.
Price: $219.98

AIR GUNS—LONG GUNS

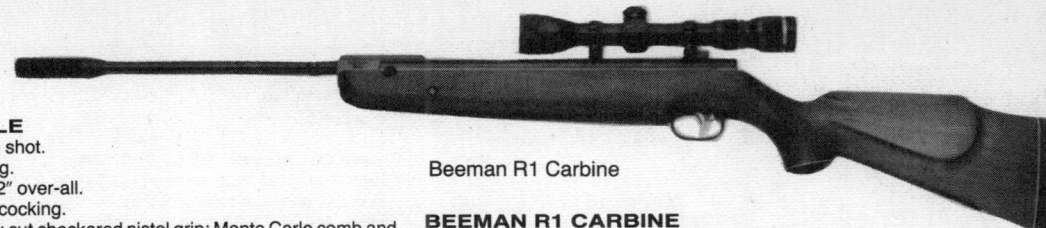

BEEMAN R1 AIR RIFLE
Caliber: 177, 20 or 22, single shot.
Barrel: 19.6", 12-groove rifling.
Weight: 8.5 lbs. **Length:** 45.2" over-all.
Power: Spring-piston, barrel cocking.
Stock: Walnut-stained beech; cut checkered pistol grip; Monte Carlo comb and cheekpiece; rubber buttpad.
Sights: Tunnel front with interchangeable inserts, open rear click adjustable for windage and elevation. Grooved for scope mounting.
Features: Velocity of 940-1050 fps (177), 860 fps (20), 800 fps (22). Non-drying nylon piston and breech seals. Adjustable metal trigger. Milled steel safety. Right- or left-hand stock. Custom and Super Laser versions available. Imported by Beeman.
Price: Right-hand $379.95
Price: Left-hand $419.95

BEEMAN R1 CARBINE
Caliber: 177, 20, 22, 25, single shot.
Barrel: 16.1".
Weight: 8.6 lbs. **Length:** 41.7" over-all.
Power: Spring-piston, barrel cocking.
Stock: Stained beech; Monte Carlo comb and checkpiece; cut-checkered p.g.; rubber butt pad.
Sights: Tunnel front with interchangeable inserts, open adjustable rear; receiver grooved for scope mounting.
Features: Velocity up to 1,000 fps (177). Non-drying nylon piston and breech seals. Adjustable metal trigger. Right- or left-hand stock. Imported by Beeman.
Price: 177 or 22, right hand $379.95
Price: 20 cal., right hand $389.95
Price: 25 cal., right hand $384.95

BEEMAN R10 AIR RIFLES
Caliber: 177, 20, 22, single shot.
Barrel: 16.1" and 19.7"; 12-groove rifling.
Weight: 7.9 lbs. **Length:** 46" over-all.
Power: Spring-piston, barrel cocking.
Stock: Standard—walnut finished hardwood with M.C. comb, rubber buttplate; Deluxe has white spacers at grip cap, buttplate, checkered grip, cheekpiece, rubber buttplate.
Sights: Tunnel front with interchangeable inserts, open rear click adj. for w. and e. Receiver grooved for scope mounting.
Features: Over 1000 fps. in 177 cal. only; 26 lb. cocking effort; milled steel safety and body tube. Right- and left-hand models, Custom and Super Laser versions available. Introduced 1986. Imported by Beeman.
Price: .... $299.98 to $409.98

BEEMAN R8 AIR RIFLE
Caliber: 177, single shot.
Barrel: 18.3".
Weight: 7.2 lbs. **Length:** 43.1" over-all.
Power: Barrel cocking, spring-piston.
Stock: Walnut with Monte Carlo cheekpiece; checkered pistol grip.
Sights: Globe front, fully adjustable rear; interchangeable inserts.
Features: Velocity of 735 fps. Similar to the R1. Nylon piston and breech seals. Adjustable match-grade, two-stage, grooved metal trigger. Milled steel safety. Rubber buttpad. Imported by Beeman.
Price: $299.98

BENJAMIN 342/347 AIR RIFLES
Caliber: 22 or 177, pellets or BB; single shot.
Barrel: 23", rifled.
Weight: 6 lbs. **Length:** 35" over-all.
Power: Hand pumped.
Features: Bolt action, walnut Monte Carlo stock and pump handle. Ramp-type front sight, adj. stepped leaf type rear. Push-pull safety.
Price: M342, 22 .... $104.05
Price: M347, 177 .... $104.05

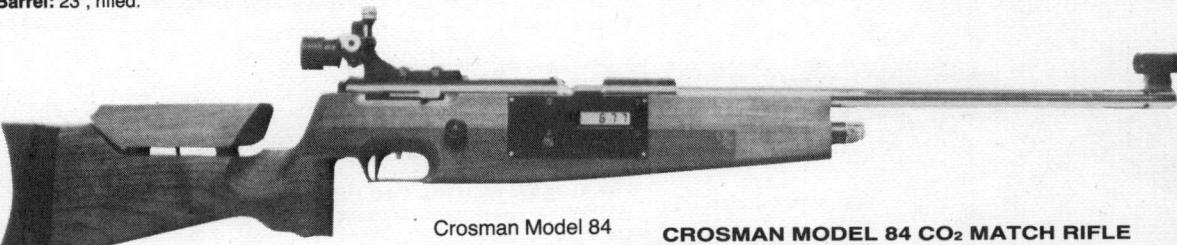

CROSMAN MODEL 66 POWERMASTER
Caliber: 177 (single shot) or BB
Barrel: 20", rifled, solid steel.
Weight: 3 lbs., 14 oz. **Length:** 38½" over-all.
Stock: Wood-grained plastic; checkered p.g. and fore-end.
Sights: Ramp front, fully adjustable open rear.
Features: Velocity about 675 fps. bolt action, cross-bolt safety. Introduced 1983.
Price: About $42.00
Price: Model 664X (as above, with 4x scope) $45.00

CROSMAN MODEL 84 CO_2 MATCH RIFLE
Caliber: 177, single shot.
Barrel: 21". Barrel has a chrome shroud to give extra sight radius.
Weight: 9 lbs., 9 oz. **Length:** 45.5" over-all.
Power: Refillable CO_2 cylinders.
Stock: Walnut; Olympic match design with stippled pistol grip and fore-end, adjustable buttplate and comb.
Sights: Match sights—globe front, micrometer adjustable rear.
Features: A CO_2 pressure regulated rifle with adjustable velocity up to 720 fps. Each CO_2 cylinder has more than enough power to complete a 60-shot Olympic match course. Electric trigger adjustable from ½-oz. to 3 lbs. Each gun can be custom fitted to the shooter. Made in U.S.A. Introduced 1984.
Price: About $1,379.00

CAUTION: PRICES CHANGE. CHECK AT GUNSHOP.

AIR GUNS—LONG GUNS

Crosman Anschutz 380

CROSMAN ANSCHUTZ MODEL 380 AIR RIFLE
Caliber: 177, single shot.
Barrel: 20¼".
Weight: 10.8 lbs. **Length:** 42⅛" over-all.
Power: Spring piston, sidelever cocking.
Stock: European hardwood match design with stippled grip and fore-end. Adjustable cheekpiece and buttplate.
Sights: Match. Hooded front, micrometer adjustable rear.
Features: Velocity about 600 fps. Recoiless and vibration free; two-stage match trigger adjustable from 2.1-oz. to 8.6-oz. pull. Available in left-hand model. Imported from West Germany by Crosman.
Price: Right-hand, about $950.00
Price: Left-hand, about $987.00

Crosman A*I*R* 17

CROSMAN A*I*R* 17
Caliber: BB and 177, 200-shot reservoir.
Barrel: 19½", steel.
Weight: 3 lbs., 1 oz. **Length:** 36¾" over-all.
Power: Pneumatic.
Stock: Black textured ABS plastic.
Features: Velocity of 450 fps (BB), 400 fps (pellet). Single-pump replica of the M-16 rifle. Comes with four-shot pellet clip. Storage compartment in stock. Introduced 1986.
Price: About $39.00

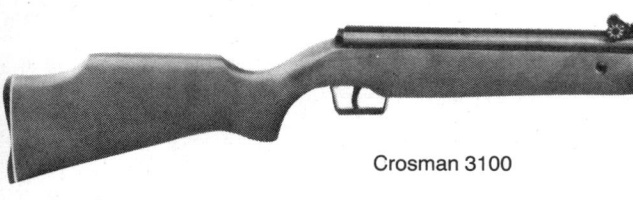

Crosman 3100

CROSMAN MODEL 3100 RIFLE
Caliber: 177, single shot.
Barrel: 16⁷⁄₁₆".
Weight: 6 lbs. **Length:** 39¾" over-all.
Power: Spring-air, barrel cocking.
Stock: Hardwood with Monte Carlo.
Sights: Hooded front with three apertures, micro. adj. rear.
Features: Velocity of 600 fps. Single-stroke cocking; adjustable trigger; thumb safety; rubber buttplate. Introduced 1986. Imported by Crosman.
Price: About $59.00

Crosman Z-77

CROSMAN Z-77 CARBINE
Caliber: BB, 20-shot magazine.
Barrel: 7", steel.
Weight: 35 oz. **Length:** 16½" over-all (closed), 25" (open).
Power: CO_2 Powerlet.
Stock: Folding shoulder stock.
Sights: Post front, open rear.
Features: Velocity about 400 fps. Replica of the UZI. Semi-automatic action. Gives about 80 shots per Powerlet. Comes with sling. Introduced 1987.
Price: About $49.00

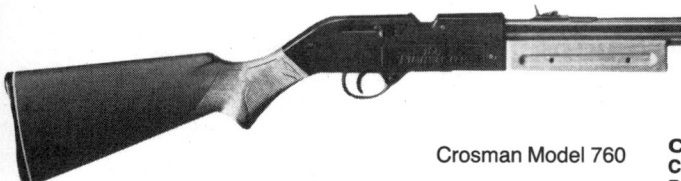

Crosman Model 760

CROSMAN MODEL 760 PUMPMASTER
Caliber: 177 pellets or BB, 200-shot.
Barrel: 19½", steel.
Weight: 3 lbs., 1 oz. **Length:** 36" over-all.
Power: Pneumatic, hand pump.
Features: Short stroke, power determined by number of strokes. Walnut finished plastic checkered stock and fore-end. Post front sight and adjustable rear sight. Cross-bolt safety. Introduced 1983.
Price: About $30.00

CROSMAN MODEL 781 SINGLE PUMP
Caliber: 177, BB, 4-shot pellet clip, 195-shot BB magazine.
Barrel: 19½".
Weight: 2 lbs., 14 oz. **Length:** 34¾" over-all.
Power: Pneumatic, single pump.
Stock: Wood-grained plastic; checkered p.g. and fore-end.
Sights: Blade front, open adjustable rear.
Features: Velocity of 350-400 fps (pellets). Uses only one pump. Hidden BB reservoir holds 195 shots; pellets loaded via 4-shot clip. Introduced 1984.
Price: About $29.00

AIR GUNS—LONG GUNS

CROSMAN MODEL 2200 MAGNUM AIR RIFLE
Caliber: 22, single shot.
Barrel: 19", rifled steel.
Weight: 4 lbs., 12 oz. **Length:** 39" over-all.
Stock: Full-size, wood-grained plastic with checkered p.g. and fore-end.
Sights: Ramp front, open step-adjustable rear.
Features: Variable pump power—3 pumps give 395 fps, 6 pumps 530 fps, 10 pumps 620 fps (average). Full-size adult air rifle. Has white line spacers at pistol grip and buttplate. Introduced 1978.
Price: About $54.00

CROSMAN MODEL 2100 CLASSIC AIR RIFLE
Caliber: 177 pellets or BBs, 200-shot BB magazine.
Barrel: 21", rifled.
Weight: 4 lbs., 13 oz. **Length:** 39¾" over-all.
Power: Pump-up, pneumatic.
Stock: Wood-grained checkered ABS plastic.
Features: Three pumps give about 450 fps, 10 pumps about 795 fps. Crossbolt safety; concealed reservoir holds over 180 BBs.
Price: About $54.00

CROSMAN MODEL 6300 CHALLENGER AIR RIFLE
Caliber: 177, single shot.
Power: Spring-air, barrel-cocking.
Stock: Stained hardwood.
Sights: Hooded front, micrometer adjustable rear.
Features: Velocity of 690 to 720 fps. Adjustable trigger; automatic safety; comes with mount base for peep sight or scope. Introduced 1985.
Price: About $126.00

CROSMAN MODEL 788 BB SCOUT RIFLE
Caliber: BB only.
Barrel: 14", steel.
Weight: 2 lbs. 7 oz. **Length:** 31½" over-all.
Stock: Wood-grained ABS plastic.
Sights: Blade on ramp front, open adj. rear.
Features: Variable pump power—3 pumps give MV of 330 fps, 6 pumps 437 fps, 10 pumps 500 fps (BBs, average). Steel barrel, cross-bolt safety. Introduced 1978.
Price: About $26.00

CROSMAN MODEL 6100 CHALLENGER RIFLE
Caliber: 177, single shot.
Weight: 7 lbs., 12 oz. **Length:** 46" over-all.
Power: Spring air, barrel cocking.
Stock: Stained hardwood with checkered pistol grip, rubber recoil pad.
Sights: Hooded front, micro.-adj. rear.
Features: Average velocity 820 fps. Automatic safety, two-stage adjustable trigger. Receiver grooved for scope mounting. Introduced 1982. Imported from West Germany by Crosman Air Guns.
Price: About $200.00

Crosman Model 6500 Challenger Air Rifle
Similar to the Model 6300 except has tunnel front sight with interchangeable bead for post or aperture inserts; positive barrel locking mechanism; automatic safety; rubber butt pad. Introduced 1985.
Price: About $140.00

Daisy Model 95

DAISY YOUTHLINE RIFLES
Model:	95	111	105
Caliber:	BB	BB	BB
Barrel:	18"	18"	13½"
Length:	35.2"	34.3"	29.8"
Power:	Spring	Spring	Spring
Capacity:	700	650	400
Price: About	$30.00	$26.00	$20.00

Features: Model 95 stock and fore-end are wood; 105 and 111 have plastic stocks.

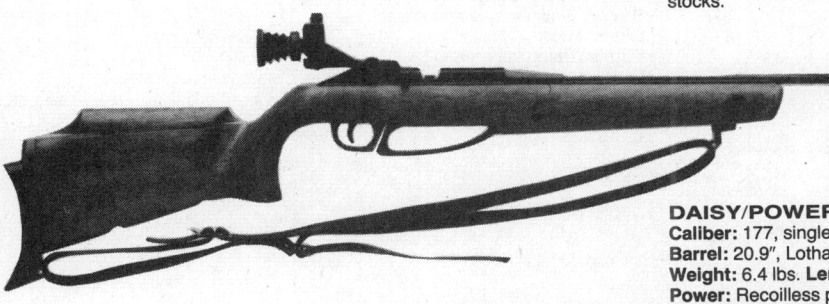
Daisy 753

DAISY/POWER LINE MODEL 753 TARGET RIFLE
Caliber: 177, single shot.
Barrel: 20.9", Lothar Walther.
Weight: 6.4 lbs. **Length:** 39.75" over-all.
Power: Recoilless pneumatic, single pump.
Stock: Walnut with adjustable cheekpiece and buttplate.
Sights: Globe front with interchangeable inserts, diopter rear with micro. click adjustments.
Features: Includes front sight reticle assortment, web shooting sling.
Price: About $235.00

Daisy Model 840

DAISY MODEL 840
Caliber: 177 pellet (single-shot) or BB (350-shot).
Barrel: 19", smoothbore, steel.
Weight: 2.7 lbs. **Length:** 36.8" over-all.
Stock: Moulded wood-grain stock and fore-end.
Sights: Ramp front, open, adj. rear.
Features: Single pump pneumatic rifle. Muzzle velocity 335 fps (BB), 300 fps (pellet). Steel buttplate; straight pull bolt action; cross-bolt safety. Fore-end forms pump lever. Introduced 1978.
Price: About $33.00

CAUTION: PRICES CHANGE. CHECK AT GUNSHOP.

AIR GUNS—LONG GUNS

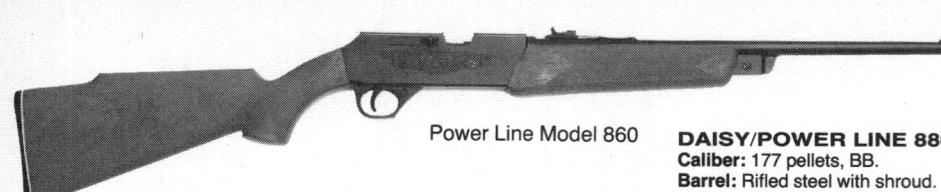
Power Line Model 860

DAISY/POWER LINE 856 PUMP-UP AIR GUN
Caliber: 177 (pellets), BB, 100-shot BB magazine.
Barrel: Rifled steel with shroud.
Weight: 2¾ lbs. **Length:** 37.4″ over-all.
Power: Pneumatic pump-up.
Stock: Moulded wood-grain plastic.
Sights: Ramp and blade front, open rear adjustable for e.
Features: Velocity from 315 fps (two pumps) to 650 fps (10 pumps). Finger grooved fore-end. Cross-bolt trigger-block safety. Introduced 1985. From Daisy.
Price: About $37.00

DAISY/POWER LINE 900 PELLET REPEATER
Caliber: 177 pellets, 5-shot clip.
Barrel: Rifled steel.
Weight: 4.3 lbs. **Length:** 38.4″ over-all.
Power: Spring air.
Stock: Full-length moulded stock with checkering, cheekpiece, white spacers.
Sights: Blade and ramp front, V-slot rear fully adjustable for w. & e.
Features: Easy loading, automatic indexing five-shot clip. Heavy die-cast metal receiver, dovetail mount for scope, heavy die-cast pump lever. Single pump for 545 fps muzzle velocity.
Price: About $67.00

DAISY/POWER LINE 880 PUMP-UP AIR GUN
Caliber: 177 pellets, BB.
Barrel: Rifled steel with shroud.
Weight: 4.5 lbs. **Length:** 37¾″ over-all.
Power: Pneumatic pump-up.
Stock: Wood-grain moulded plastic with Monte Carlo cheekpiece.
Sights: Ramp front, open rear adj. for e.
Features: Crafted by Daisy. Variable power (velocity and range) increase with pump strokes. 10 strokes for maximum power. 100-shot BB magazine. Cross-bolt trigger safety. Positive cocking valve.
Price: About $51.00

DAISY/POWER LINE 860 PUMP-UP AIR GUN
Caliber: 177 (pellets), BB, 100-shot BB magazine.
Barrel: Rifled steel with shroud.
Weight: 4.18 lbs. **Length:** 37.4″ over-all.
Power: Pneumatic pump-up.
Stock: Moulded wood-grain with Monte Carlo cheekpiece.
Sights: Ramp and blade front, open rear adjustable for e.
Features: Velocity from 315 fps (two pumps) to 650 fps (10 pumps). Shoots BBs or pellets. Heavy die-cast metal receiver. Cross-bolt trigger-block safety. Introduced 1984. From Daisy.
Price: About $45.00

Daisy/Power Line Model 814
Similar to the Model 914 except has a detachable wire stock and pistol grip. Weight is 2.8 lbs.
Price: About $44.00

Daisy Model 914

DAISY/POWER LINE MODEL 914
Caliber: BB or 177.
Barrel: 19″, smoothbore.
Weight: 6 lbs. **Length:** 38.2″ over-all.
Power: Single-stroke pneumatic.
Stock: Moulded plastic.
Sights: Ramp front, peep rear.
Features: Velocity of 335 fps. Resembles a famous sporter rifle.
Price: About $42.50

Power Line Model 922

DAISY/POWER LINE MODEL 922
Caliber: 22, 5-shot clip.
Barrel: Rifled steel with shroud.
Weight: 4.5 lbs. **Length:** 37¾″ over-all.
Stock: Moulded wood-grained plastic with checkered p.g. and fore-end, Monte Carlo cheekpiece.
Sights: Ramp front, fully adj. open rear.
Features: Muzzle velocity from 270 fps (two pumps) to 530 fps (10 pumps). Straight pull bolt action. Separate buttplate and grip cap with white spacers. Introduced 1978.

Price: About $61.00
Price: Models 970/920 (as above with hardwood stock and fore-end), about $100.00

Daisy Model 953

DAISY/POWER LINE 953
Caliber: 177 pellets.
Barrel: 20.9″; 12-groove rifling, high-grade solid steel by Lothar Walther®, precision crowned; bore sized for precision match pellets.
Weight: 5.08 lbs. **Length:** 38.9″ over-all.
Power: Single-pump pneumatic.
Stock: Full-length, select American hardwood, stained and finished; black buttplate with white spacers.
Sights: Globe front with four aperture inserts; precision micrometer adjustable rear peep sight mounted on a standard ⅜″ dovetail receiver mount.
Features: Single-shot.
Price: About $149.50

AIR GUNS—LONG GUNS

Daisy Red Ryder

DAISY 1938 RED RYDER COMMEMORATIVE
Caliber: BB, 650-shot repeating action.
Barrel: Smoothbore steel with shroud.
Weight: 2.2 lbs. **Length:** 35.4" over-all.
Stock: Wood stock burned with Red Ryder lariat signature.
Sights: Post front, adjustable V-slot rear.
Features: Wood fore-end. Saddle ring with leather thong. Lever cocking. Gravity feed. Controlled velocity. Commemorates one of Daisy's most popular guns, the Red Ryder of the 1940s and 1950s.
Price: About $41.00

El Gamo 128

EL GAMO MODEL 128 MATCH RIFLE
Caliber: 177, single shot.
Barrel: 17.5"; Lothar Walther with 12 lands and grooves; sized for match pellets.
Weight: 10.6 lbs. **Length:** 43.3" over-all.
Power: Recoilless pneumatic, single pump.
Stock: Match-style hardwood with sling rail and adjustable rubber buttplate.
Sights: Anschutz front and rear; globe front, diopter rear.
Features: Adjustable trigger. Imported from Spain by Daisy.
Price: About $800.00

EL GAMO 126 SUPER MATCH TARGET RIFLE
Caliber: 177, single shot.
Barrel: Match grade, precision rifled.
Weight: 10.6 lbs. **Length:** 43.8" over-all.
Power: Single pump pneumatic.
Stock: Match-style, hardwood, with stippled grip and fore-end.
Sights: Hooded front with interchangeable elements, fully adjustable match rear.
Features: Velocity of 590 fps. Adjustable trigger; easy loading pellet port; adjustable buttpad. Introduced 1984. Imported from Spain by Daisy.
Price: About $329.50

FX-2 Air Rifle
Similar to the FX-1 except weighs 5.8 lbs., 41" over-all; front sight is hooded post on ramp, rear sight has two-way click adjustments. Adjustable trigger. Imported by Beeman.
Price: $79.50

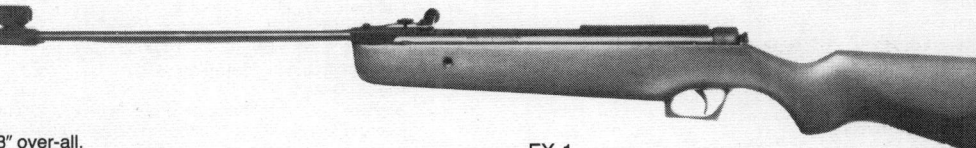
FX-1

FX-1 AIR RIFLE
Caliber: 177, single shot.
Barrel: 18", rifled.
Weight: 6.6 lbs. **Length:** 43" over-all.
Power: Spring-piston, barrel cocking.
Stock: Walnut-stained hardwood.
Sights: Tunnel front with interchangeable inserts; rear with rotating disc to give four sighting notches.
Features: Velocity 680 fps. Match-type adjustable trigger. Receiver grooved for scope mounting. Imported by Beeman.
Price: $99.50

> Consult our Directory pages for the location of firms mentioned.

FAMAS Air Rifle

FAMAS SEMI-AUTO AIR RIFLE
Caliber: 177, 10-shot magazine.
Barrel: 19.2".
Weight: About 8 lbs. **Length:** 29.8" over-all.
Power: 12 gram CO_2.
Stock: Synthetic bullpup design.
Sights: Adjustable front, aperture rear.
Features: Velocity of 425 fps. Duplicates size, weight and feel of the centerfire MAS French military rifle in caliber 223. Introduced 1988. Imported from France by Century International Arms.
Price: $395.00

"GAT" AIR RIFLE
Caliber: 177, single shot.
Barrel: 17¼" cocked, 23¼" extended.
Weight: 3 lbs.
Power: Spring piston.
Stock: Composition.
Sights: Fixed.
Features: Velocity about 450 fps. Shoots pellets, darts, corks. Imported by Stone Enterprises, Inc.
Price: $39.95

MARKSMAN 29 AIR RIFLE
Caliber: 177 or 22, single shot.
Barrel: 18.5".
Weight: 6 lbs. **Length:** 41.5" over-all.
Power: Spring air, barrel cocking.
Stock: Stained hardwood.
Sights: Blade front, open adj. rear.
Features: Velocity of 790-830 fps (177), 610-640 fps (22). Introduced 1986. Imported from England by Marksman Products.
Price: Either caliber $183.95

CAUTION: PRICES CHANGE. CHECK AT GUNSHOP.

AIR GUNS—LONG GUNS

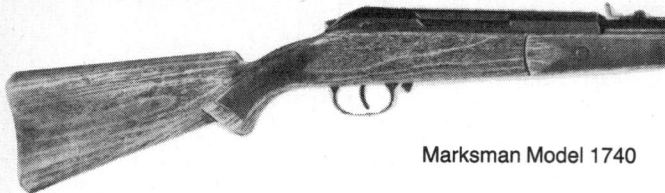

Marksman Model 1740

MARKSMAN 70 AIR RIFLE
Caliber: 177 or 22, single shot.
Barrel: 19.75".
Weight: 8 lbs. **Length:** 45.5" over-all.
Power: Spring air, barrel cocking.
Stock: Stained hardwood with M.C. cheekpiece, rubber butt-pad, cut checkered p.g.
Sights: Hooded front, open fully adj. rear.
Features: Velocity of 910-940 fps (177), 740-780 fps (22); two-stage adj. trigger. Introduced 1986. Imported from West Germany by Marksman Products.
Price: 177 or 22 .... $258.95

MARKSMAN 1740 AIR RIFLE
Caliber: 177 or 100-shot BB repeater.
Barrel: 15½", smoothbore.
Weight: 5 lbs., 1 oz. **Length:** 36½" over-all.
Power: Spring, barrel cocking.
Stock: Moulded high-impact ABS plastic.
Sights: Ramp front, open rear adj. for e.
Features: Automatic safety; fixed front, adj. rear sight; shoots 177 cal. BB's, pellets and darts. Velocity about 475-500 fps.
Price: $40.00
Price: Model 1780 (shoots only pellets) $45.00

Marksman 55 Air Rifle
Similar to the Model 70 except has unchecked hardwood stock, no cheekpiece, plastic butt-plate. Over-all length is 45.25", weight is 7½ lbs. Available in 177 caliber only.
Price: $217.00

MAUSER MODEL 300 SL AIR RIFLE
Caliber: 177, single shot.
Barrel: 18.9".
Weight: 8 lbs., 8 oz. **Length:** 43.7" over-all.
Power: Spring air, under-lever cocking.
Stock: Match style, hardwood, with stippled p.g., rubber buttpad.
Sights: Tunnel front, match aperture rear.
Features: Velocity of 550-600 fps. Dovetail mount for diopter or scope. Automatic safety. Imported from West Germany by Marksman Products.
Price: $291.95

Mauser 300 SL

RWS/DIANA MODEL 24 AIR RIFLE
Caliber: 177, 22; single shot.
Barrel: 17", rifled.
Weight: 6 lbs. **Length:** 42" over-all.
Power: Spring air, barrel cocking.
Stock: Beech.
Sights: Hooded front, adjustable rear.
Features: Velocity of 700 fps (177). Easy cocking effort; blue finish. Imported from West Germany by Dynamit Nobel-RWS, Inc.
Price: $140.00
Price: Model 34 (as above, except 19" bbl., 7½ lbs., adj. trigger, synthetic seals) $210.00

RWS/DIANA MODEL 36 AIR RIFLE
Caliber: 177, 22; single shot.
Barrel: 19", rifled.
Weight: 8 lbs. **Length:** 45" over-all.
Power: Spring air, barrel cocking.
Stock: Beech.
Sights: Hood front (interchangeable inserts avail.), adjustable rear.
Features: Velocity of 1000 fps (177-cal.). Comes with scope mount; two-stage adjustable trigger. Imported from West Germany by Dynamit Nobel-RWS, Inc.
Price: $250.00
Price: Model 38 (as above, walnut stock) $280.00

RWS/DIANA MODEL 52 AIR RIFLE
Caliber: 177, 22; single shot.
Barrel: 17", rifled.
Weight: 8½ lbs. **Length:** 43" over-all.
Power: Spring air, side-lever cocking.
Stock: Beech.
Sights: Ramp front, adjustable rear.
Features: Velocity of 1100 fps (177). Blue finish. Solid rubber buttpad. Imported from West Germany by Dynamit Nobel-RWS, Inc.
Price: $325.00

RWS/DIANA MODEL 45 AIR RIFLE
Caliber: 177, single shot.
Weight: 7¾ lbs. **Length:** 46" over-all.
Power: Spring air, barrel cocking.
Stock: Walnut-finished hardwood with rubber recoil pad.
Sights: Globe front with interchangeable inserts, micro. click open rear with four-way blade.
Features: Velocity of 820 fps. Dovetail base for either micrometer peep sight or scope mounting. Automatic safety. Imported from West Germany by Dynamit Nobel-RWS, Inc.
Price: 177 .... $225.00

RWS/DIANA MODEL 75T 01 MATCH AIR RIFLE
Caliber: 177, single shot.
Barrel: 19".
Weight: 11 lbs. **Length:** 43.7" over-all.
Power: Spring air, side-lever cocking.
Stock: Oil finished walnut with stippled grip, adjustable buttplate, accessory rail. Conforms to I.S.U. rules.
Sights: Globe front with 5 inserts, fully adjustable match peep rear.
Features: Velocity of 574 fps. Fully adjustable trigger. Model 75 HV has stippled fore-end, adjustable cheekpiece. Uses double opposing piston system for recoilless operation. Imported from West Germany by Dynamit Nobel-RWS, Inc.
Price: Model 75T 01 .... $770.00
Price: Model 75 HVT 01 .... $860.00
Price: Model 75T 01 left-hand $800.00
Price: Model 75 HVT 01 left-hand $900.00
Price: Model 75 UT 01 (adj. cheekpiece, buttplate, M82 sight) $920.00

RWS/Diana Model 75KT 01 Running Boar Air Rifle
Similar to the Model 75 Match except has adjustable cheekpiece and buttplate, different stock, sandblasted barrel sleeve, detachable barrel weight, elevated-grip cocking lever, and a 240mm scope mount. Introduced 1983.
Price: $880.00

SAE MODEL 92 AIR RIFLE
Caliber: 177, single shot.
Barrel: NA.
Weight: 7.2 lbs. **Length:** NA.
Power: Spring-air, side-lever cocking.
Stock: European hardwood.
Sights: Tunnel front, open rear adj. for w. and e.
Features: Velocity of 650 fps. Adjustable trigger. Cocking effort of 19 lbs. Imported from Spain by Spain America Ent.
Price: $185.00
Price: Model 47 (as above, with vertical p.g.) $185.00

AIR GUNS—LONG GUNS

SAE Jet 900

SAE MODEL JET 900 AIR RIFLE
Caliber: 177, single shot.
Barrel: NA.
Weight: 7.5 lbs. **Length:** 46″ over-all.
Power: Spring-air, barrel cocking.
Stock: Hardwood.
Sights: Hooded post front, open fully adjustable rear.
Features: Velocity of 900 FPS. Two-stage adjustable trigger, automatic safety. Imported from Spain by Spain America Ent.
Price: $225.00

SAE MODEL 73 AIR RIFLE
Caliber: 177, single shot.
Barrel: 21″.
Weight: 6.7 lbs. **Length:** 43″ over-all.
Power: Spring-air, barrel cocking.
Stock: Hardwood.
Sights: Tunnel front, open rear adj. for w. and e.
Features: Velocity of 650 fps. cocking effort about 8 lbs. Imported from Spain by Spain America Ent.
Price: $150.00
Price: Model 61C (as above, 16″ bbl.) $135.00
Price: Model 15 (as above, 17″ bbl.) $105.00
Price: Model Norica Young (M61C with colored, painted wood) $125.00

SAE Commando

SAE COMMANDO AIR CARBINE
Caliber: 177, single shot.
Barrel: 16″.
Weight: 5.1 lbs. **Length:** 27″ over-all.
Power: Spring-air, barrel cocking.
Stock: Retractable steel, camouflage painted fore-end.
Sights: Hooded post front, open rear adj. for w. and e.
Features: Velocity of 500 fps. Blue finish. Imported from Spain by Spain America Ent.
Price: $135.00

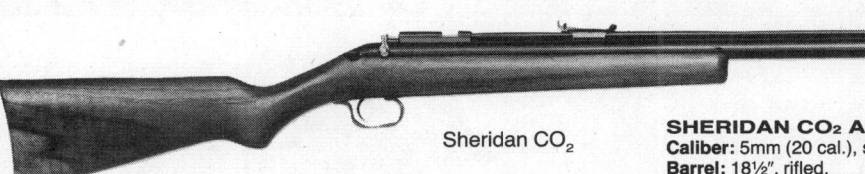

Sheridan CO_2

SHERIDAN BLUE AND SILVER STREAK RIFLES
Caliber: 5mm (20 cal.), single shot.
Barrel: 18½″, rifled.
Weight: 5 lbs. **Length:** 37″ over-all.
Power: Hand pumped (swinging fore-end).
Features: Rustproof barrel and piston tube. Takedown. Thumb safety. Mannlicher-type walnut stock.
Price: Blue Streak $109.85
Price: Silver Streak $113.95

SHERIDAN CO_2 AIR RIFLES
Caliber: 5mm (20 cal.), single shot.
Barrel: 18½″, rifled.
Weight: 6 lbs. **Length:** 37″ over-all.
Power: Standard 12 gram CO_2 cylinder.
Stock: Walnut sporter.
Sights: Open, adj. for w. and e. Optional Sheridan-Williams 5D-SH receiver sight or Weaver D4 scope.
Features: Bolt action single-shot, CO_2 powered. Velocity approx. 514 fps, manual thumb safety. Blue or Silver finish.
Price: CO_2 Blue Streak $96.20
Price: CO_2 Silver Streak $100.55
Price: CO_2 Blue Streak with receiver sight $114.40
Price: CO_2 Blue Streak with scope $131.90

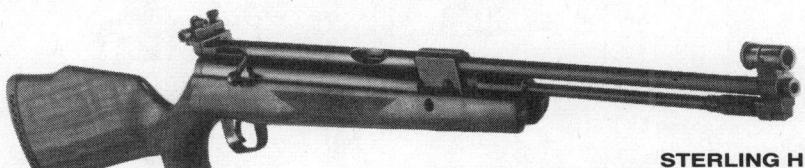

Sterling HR-83

THEOBEN SIROCCO CLASSIC AIR RIFLE
Caliber: 177 or 22.
Barrel: 15½″, Anschutz.
Weight: 7¾ lbs. **Length:** 44″ over-all.
Power: Gas-ram piston. Variable power.
Stock: Hand-checkered walnut.
Sights: None supplied. Comes with scope mount.
Features: Velocity 1,100 fps (177), 900 fps (22). Adjustable recoil pad, barrel weight. Choked or unchoked barrel. Imported from England by Air Rifle Specialists.
Price: $860.00
Price: Grand Prix model (as above except thumbhole stock) $940.00

STERLING HR-81/HR-83 AIR RIFLE
Caliber: 177 or 22, single shot.
Barrel: 18½″.
Weight: 8½ lbs. **Length:** 42½″ over-all.
Power: Spring air (barrel cocking).
Stock: Stained hardwood, with cheekpiece, checkered pistol grip.
Sights: Tunnel-type front with four interchangeable elements, open adjustable V-type rear.
Features: Velocity of 700 fps (177), 600 fps (22). Bolt action with easily accessible loading port; adjustable single-stage match trigger; rubber recoil pad. Integral scope mount rails. Scope and mount optional. Introduced 1983. Made in U.S.A. by Benjamin Air Rifle Co.
Price: HR 81-7 (177 cal., standard walnut stock) $259.44
Price: HR 81-2 (as above, 22 cal.) $269.67
Price: HR 83-7 (177 cal., deluxe walnut stock) $368.23
Price: HR 83-2 (as above, 22 cal.) $372.74
Price: For 4x40 wide angle scope, add $82.35

CAUTION: PRICES CHANGE. CHECK AT GUNSHOP.

AIR GUNS—LONG GUNS

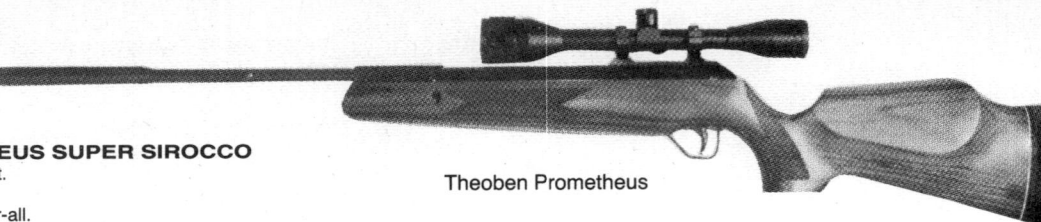
Theoben Prometheus

THEOBEN-PROMETHEUS SUPER SIROCCO
Caliber: 177 or 22; single shot.
Barrel: 15¾".
Weight: NA. **Length:** 44" over-all.
Power: Gas-ram piston.
Stock: English walnut, checkered p.g. and fore-end.
Sights: None furnished; scope base and rings provided.
Features: Velocity 950-1200 fps. One-stroke cocking mechanism with captive gas-ram piston. Designed to shoot Prometheus and Titan Black pellets. Imported from England by Fisher Enterprises.
Price: Deluxe Super Sirocco $870.00
Price: Grand Prix $925.00
Price: Eliminator (thumbhole stock) $1,475.00

WALTHER LGR UNIVERSAL MATCH AIR RIFLE
Caliber: 177, single shot.
Barrel: 25.5".
Weight: 13 lbs. **Length:** 44¾" over-all.
Power: Spring air, barrel cocking.
Stock: Walnut match design with stippled grip and fore-end, adjustable cheekpiece, rubber butt pad.
Features: Has the same weight and contours as the Walther U.I.T. rimfire target rifle. Comes complete with sights, accessories and muzzle weight. Imported from West Germany by Interarms.
Price: $1,100.00

Theoben Sirocco Eliminator Air Rifle
Similar to the Sirocco Grand Prix except more powerful. Gives 1,400 fps in 177 cal., 1,100 fps in 22. Walnut thumbhole stock, adjustable recoil pad, scope mount. Variable power. Barrel weight, leather cobra sling, swivels. Choked barrel only.
Price: $1,450.00

Walther LGR Running Boar Air Rifle
Same basic specifications as standard LGR except has a high comb thumbhole stock. Has adjustable cheekpiece and buttplate, no sights. Introduced 1977.
Price: $975.00

AIR GUNS—AIR SOFT LONG GUNS

COMMAND POST UZI PUMP
Caliber: 25-cal. plastic shot.
Barrel: NA.
Weight: 4 lbs. **Length:** 25" over-all (stock extended).
Power: Spring-air, pump action.
Stock: Black plastic.
Sights: Post front, aperture rear.
Features: Full-size replica of the Uzi submachine gun. Available from The Command Post, Inc.
Price: $109.98

Uzi Pump

MP5 A-3

COMMAND POST M-60 A1
Caliber: 25-cal. plastic shot.
Barrel: NA.
Weight: 14 lbs. **Length:** 42" over-all.
Power: Gas powered.
Stock: Moulded plastic.
Sights: Tangent rear, high-post front.
Features: Full-size, full-auto replica of the U.S. M-60 machinegun. Available from The Command Post, Inc.
Price: $1,398.98

COMMAND POST MP5-A3 CARBINE
Caliber: 25 (6mm) plastic BB, 42-shot magazine.
Barrel: Smoothbore.
Weight: 2 lbs., 14 oz. **Length:** 25" over-all (stock extended).
Power: Air piston; bolt action.
Stock: Metal and plastic.
Sights: Protected post front, aperture rear.
Features: Accuracy range of 50-70 feet. Telescoping stock version of the famous German submachine gun. Comes with 100 BBs. Available from The Command Post, Inc.
Price: $89.98
Price: Model G-3A4 .... $169.98

COMMAND POST AIRSOFT 12
Caliber: 25-cal. plastic shot.
Barrel: Smoothbore.
Weight: 3.25 lbs. **Length:** 18.5" over-all.
Power: Pump or bolt action, spring air.
Stock: Moulded grip.
Sights: Blade front, notched rear.
Features: Detailed replica of a famous American-made semi-automatic firearm; takes 30-shot clip.
Price: About $62.00

AIR GUNS—AIR SOFT LONG GUNS

Command Post Grease Gun

COMMAND POST GREASE GUN
Caliber: 25 (6mm) plastic BB, 30-shot magazine.
Barrel: Smoothbore.
Weight: 4 lbs. **Length:** 22½" over-all (stock folded).
Power: Air piston; bolt action.
Stock: Moulded plastic; telescoping wire butt.
Sights: Blade front, aperature rear.
Features: Accuracy range of 25-35 feet. Realistic copy of the WWII submachine gun. Cartridges are automatically ejected and fed upon cocking. Available from The Command Post, Inc.
Price: $159.98

Airsoft 15

COMMAND POST AIRSOFT 15
Caliber: 25-cal. plastic shot.
Barrel: Smoothbore.
Weight: 2.5 lbs. **Length:** 15.5" over-all.
Power: Pump action, spring air.
Stock: Moulded receiver and grip.
Sights: Post front, 4-way adjustable rear.
Features: Detailed replica of the famous German-made police weapon. 12-shot banana clip, automatically ejects spent shells.
Price: About $62.00

COMMAND POST AIRSOFT 14
Caliber: 25-cal. plastic shot.
Barrel: Smoothbore.
Weight: 2.9 lbs. **Length:** 26" over-all.
Power: Pump or bolt action, spring air.
Stock: Hardwood stock with moulded pistol and pump grips.
Sights: Blade front, adjustable rear peep sight.
Features: Fully-detailed replica of a famous semi-automatic rifle; takes 10-shot clip.
Price: About $49.98

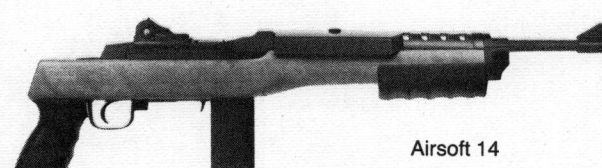

Airsoft 14

Command Post XM-177E2

COMMAND POST XM-177E2 CARBINE
Caliber: 25 (6mm) plastic BB, 13-shot.
Barrel: Smoothbore.
Weight: 4 lbs. **Length:** 32½" over-all.
Power: Air piston; bolt action or semi-auto with blowback assist.
Stock: Moulded plastic; collapsible.
Sights: Post front, aperture rear.
Features: Accuracy range of 40-50 feet. Exact replica of the popular assault rifle. Comes with 40 BBs, two blowback assist cartridges, 60 blowback caps, takedown wrenches, blowback cartridge tools, sling. Available from The Command Post, Inc.
Price: $98.98
Price: As above except M-16 replica $98.98

Airsoft 870

COMMAND POST AIRSOFT 870
Caliber: 25-cal. plastic shot.
Barrel: Smoothbore.
Weight: 3.6 lbs. **Length:** 40" over-all.
Power: Slide action, spring air.
Stock: Moulded, with checkering.
Sights: Bead front.
Features: Detailed replica of Remington 870 Wingmaster; authentic working action, five-shot magazine, ejects spent shells.
Price: About $66.00

CAUTION: PRICES CHANGE. CHECK AT GUNSHOP.

AIR GUNS—PAINT BALL HANDGUNS

007 PUMP ACTION PAINT BALL PISTOL
Caliber: 68, 16-shot magazine.
Barrel: 4½".
Weight: 2 lbs., 10 oz. **Length:** 10¼" over-all.
Power: 12-gram CO_2.
Stocks: Checkered plastic.
Sights: Blade front, notch rear.
Features: Velocity of 205 fps, muzzle energy of 4.5 ft. lbs. Gives 20+ shots per CO_2. Rapid loading. Introduced 1987. From The Command Post, Inc.
Price: $119.98

007 Sport Paint Ball Pistol
Similar to the 007 Pump except has 25-shot magazine, 6" barrel, wire stock, combat pump handle. Custom built by The Command Post, Inc.
Price: $179.98

007 Tournament Paint Ball Pistol
Similar to the 007 Pump except has 25-shot gravity magazine, 2" barrel extension. Custom built by The Command Post, Inc.
Price: $199.98

3357 D/A PAINT BALL REVOLVER
Caliber: 50, 6-shot cylinder.
Barrel: 6".
Weight: 2 lbs., 12 oz. **Length:** 12½" over-all.
Power: 12-gram CO_2.
Stocks: Checkered plastic.
Sights: Ramped blade front, adjustable notch rear.
Features: Velocity of 230 fps, muzzle energy of 2.1 ft. lbs. Gives 30-70 shots per CO_2; metal construction; single or double action. Introduced 1987. From The Command Post, Inc.
Price: $89.98

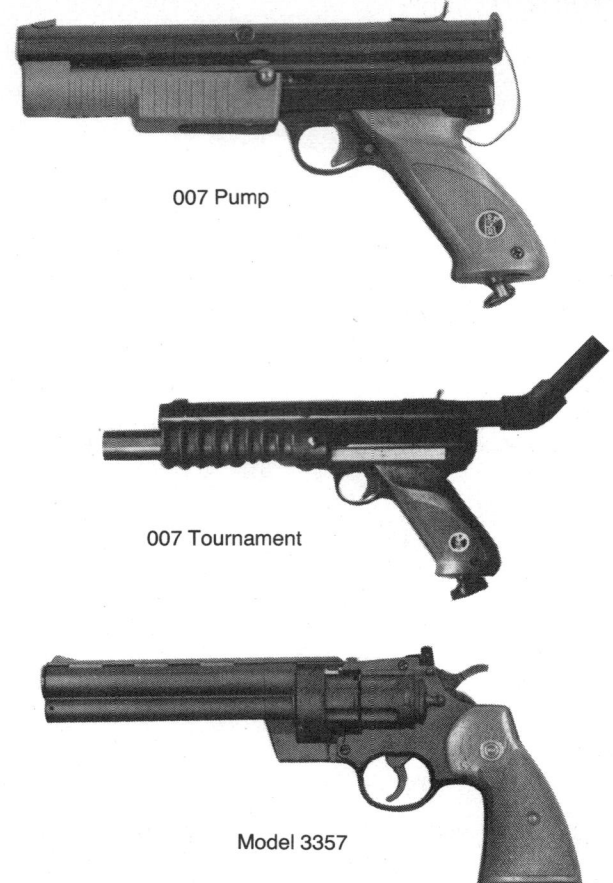

007 Pump

007 Tournament

Model 3357

Model 85

PURSUIT RAPID FIRE PAINT PISTOL
Caliber: 68 (paint balls), 10-shot magazine.
Barrel: 6½".
Weight: 36 oz. **Length:** 9" over-all.
Power: 12-gram CO_2.
Stocks: Smooth wood with thumbrest.
Sights: Bead front, adjustable rear.
Features: Shoots 68-cal. paint balls; uses gravity-feed magazine. Comes with Rapid Fire Pump Kit. From Pursuit Marketing, Inc.
Price: $135.00

PURSUIT PMI I PAINT PISTOL
Caliber: 68 (paint balls), 10-shot magazine.
Barrel: 10¼".
Weight: 36 oz. **Length:** 14⅜" over-all.
Power: 12-gram CO_2.
Stocks: Checkered, with thumbrest.
Sights: Bead front, open rear.
Features: Rapid-fire, pump-action long-barrel pistol uses factory centerfire bolt. Uses gravity or direct-feed magazine. Introduced 1988. From Pursuit Marketing, Inc.
Price: $169.00

MODEL 85 PAINT BALL MACHINE PISTOL
Caliber: 9.5 mm, 24-shot removeable magazine.
Barrel: 5", rifled.
Weight: 25 oz. **Length:** 9⅜" over-all.
Stocks: Resin.
Sights: Blade front, notch rear.
Features: Velocity of 440 fps, muzzle energy of 3.4 ft. lbs. Stainless steel impregnated in fiber-filled resin construction. Has a cyclic rate of 1,200 rounds per minute; fires from open bolt; reloadable cartridges. Not a firearm by B.A.T.F. standards. Introduced 1987. Made in Canada. From Para-Ordnance, Inc.
Price: $299.95

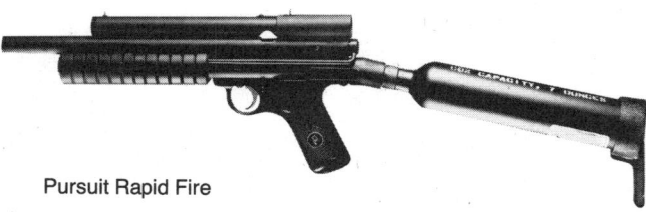

Pursuit Rapid Fire

Pursuit PMI II Paint Pistol
Similar to the PMI I pistol except comes only with 7-oz. Constant Air system, new factory 6-inch aluminum pump handle. Weight, including air tank, is 3¾ lbs. Introduced 1988.
Price: $280.00
Price: Pursuit 68 Magnum (as above with direct feed loading) $325.00

AIR GUNS—PAINT BALL HANDGUNS

SPLATMASTER® 102 MARKING PISTOL
Caliber: 68 (paint balls), 12-shot magazine.
Barrel: 5¾".
Weight: 1.8 lbs. **Length:** 12¼" over-all.
Power: 12.5 gram CO_2 cylinder.
Stocks: Checkered fiber reinforced plastic.
Sights: Open, fixed.
Features: Velocity at about 260 fps. Shoots 68-cal. paint-balls. Made of fiber reinforced plastic with an aluminum valve system. Moulded in a camouflage pattern. Gives about 30 shots per CO_2 cylinder. Introduced 1987. From National Survival Game, Inc.
Price: $89.95

Splatmaster

Uzi Mk. I

UZI MKI PUMP ACTION PAINT BALL GUN
Caliber: 68, 38-shot magazine.
Barrel: 7".
Weight: 2 lbs., 8 oz. **Length:** 16" over-all.
Power: 12-gram CO_2.
Stocks: Grooved plastic.
Sights: Blade front, notch rear.
Features: Velocity of 210 fps, muzzle energy of 4.7 ft. lbs. Gives 30+ shots per CO_2; rapid-load magazine. Introduced 1987. Imported from Canada by The Command Post, Inc.
Price: $119.98

AIR GUNS—PAINT BALL LONG GUNS

Black Widow

BLACK WIDOW PAINT BALL GUN
Caliber: 68, 25-shot magazine.
Barrel: NA.
Weight: 12 lbs. **Length:** 34" over-all.
Power: 7-oz. bulk CO_2.
Stock: Black-painted wood.
Sights: Optic Point sighting device.
Features: Combat-grip pump. Matte finish on entire gun. From The Command Post, Inc.
Price: $429.98

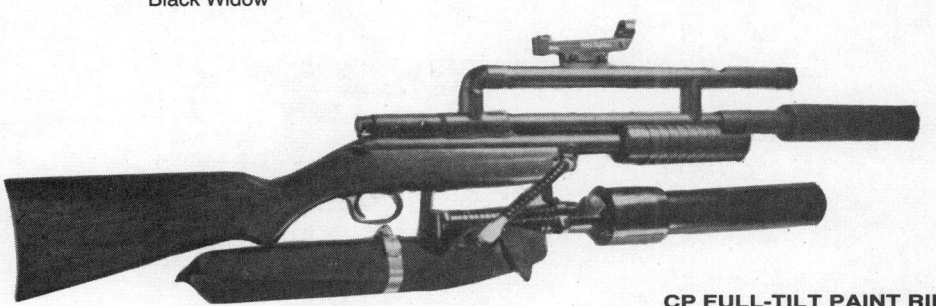
CP Full-Tilt

CP FULL-TILT PAINT RIFLE
Caliber: 68, 20-shot Posi-Feed magazine.
Barrel: NA.
Weight: 12 lbs. **Length:** 29" over-all.
Power: 10-oz. bulk CO_2.
Stock: Wood
Sights: Optic Point sighting device.
Features: Noise suppressor, combat pump. "M-79" paint Grenade Launcher installed. Spring-fed magazine. Custom built by The Command Post, Inc.
Price: $798.78

Consult our Directory pages for the location of firms mentioned.

CUSTOM GRAVITY-FEED PAINT RIFLE
Caliber: 68, 25-shot magazine.
Barrel: NA.
Weight: 7 lbs. **Length:** 28" over-all.
Power: 12-gram CO_2.
Stock: Wood.
Sights: Optic Point sighting device.
Features: Gravity feed; over-size Delron pump. Custom built by The Command Post, Inc.
Price: $259.98

NINJA PAINT BALL GUN
Caliber: 68, 20-shot magazine.
Barrel: 11".
Weight: 9 lbs. **Length:** 28" over-all.
Power: 10-oz. bulk CO_2 system.
Stock: Moulded composition.
Sights: 1.5x scope.
Features: Velocity about 225 fps. Gives up to 500 shots per charge. Converts to pistol. Gravity-feed magazine. Available from The Command Post, Inc.
Price: $379.98

CAUTION: PRICES CHANGE. CHECK AT GUNSHOP.

AIR GUNS—PAINT BALL LONG GUNS

007 Assault

007 ASSAULT PUMP PAINT BALL GUN
Caliber: 68, 15-shot magazine.
Barrel: 16".
Weight: 6 lbs., 5 oz. **Length:** 35" over-all (stock extended).
Power: 12-gram CO_2 or 10-oz. bulk CO_2 tank.
Stock: Folding, plastic and hard rubber over steel.
Sights: Adjustable Optic Point Site.
Features: Velocity of 240 fps, muzzle energy of 6.1 ft. lbs. Convertible power source—20 shots per CO_2 or 500+ shots from remotely mounted bulk tank. Steel construction. Introduced 1987. Custom built by The Command Post, Inc.
Price: $359.98

PMI CUSTOM PAINT BALL GUN
Caliber: 68, 20-shot magazine.
Barrel: NA.
Weight: 6 lbs. **Length:** 26" over-all.
Power: 10-oz. bulk CO_2.
Stock: Moulded black plastic.
Sights: Post front, notch rear.
Features: Velocity about 290 fps. Easily converted to 12-gram CO_2. Custom built by The Command Post, Inc.
Price: $289.98

PMI Custom

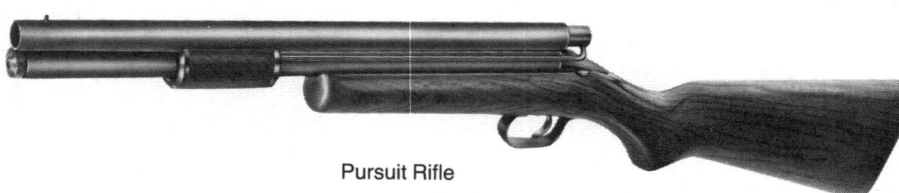
Pursuit Rifle

PURSUIT PAINT RIFLE
Caliber: 68 (paint balls), 15-shot magazine.
Barrel: 12".
Weight: 5 lbs. **Length:** 31" over-all.
Power: 12-gram CO_2.
Stock: Smooth maple.
Sights: Bead front.
Features: Shoots 68-cal. paint balls; gravity-feed magazine. Comes with Rapid Fire Pump Kit. From Pursuit Marketing, Inc.
Price: $170.00

SAMURAI PAINT BALL GUN
Caliber: 68, 20-shot gravity magazine.
Barrel: NA.
Weight: 9½ lbs. **Length:** 26" over-all.
Power: 10-oz. bulk CO_2.
Stock: Moulded black plastic.
Sights: Post front, notch rear.
Features: Fast pump action. Easily converts to 12-gram CO_2. Custom built by The Command Post, Inc.
Price: $299.98

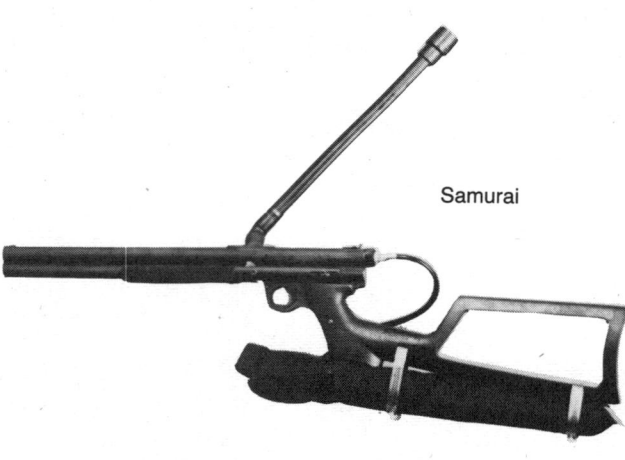
Samurai

SNIPER PUMP MK II PAINT BALL GUN
Caliber: 68, 25-shot magazine.
Barrel: NA.
Weight: 6 lbs. **Length:** 26" over-all.
Power: 12-gram CO_2 or 7-oz. bulk CO_2 tank.
Stock: Wire.
Sights: 1.5x scope.
Features: Velocity of about 240 fps. Up to 350 shots per tank. Custom built by The Command Post, Inc.
Price: $299.98

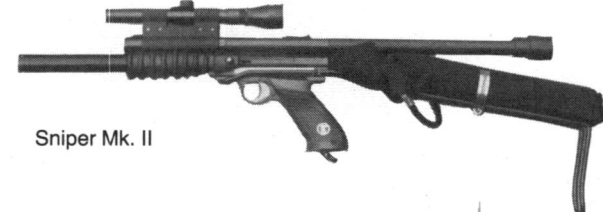
Sniper Mk. II

Tippmann SMG-60

TIPPMANN SMG-60 AUTOMATIC
Caliber: 60 (paint balls), 15-shot magazine.
Barrel: 11".
Weight: 5 lbs. **Length:** 29" over-all.
Power: CO_2 cylinder.
Stock: 8-oz. CO_2 cylinder forms stock.
Sights: Fixed.
Features: Velocity of 290-300 fps. Selective-fire paint-ball gun (semi- or full-auto). Full-auto rate of fire is 600 r.p.m. Open bolt, blowback action. Introduced 1987. From Tippmann Arms Co.
Price: $349.00

AVERAGE CENTERFIRE RIFLE CARTRIDGE BALLISTICS AND PRICES

Caliber	Bullet Wgt. Grs.	— VELOCITY (fps) — Muzzle	100 yds.	200 yds.	300 yds.	400 yds.	— ENERGY (ft. lbs.) — Muzzle	100 yds.	200 yds.	300 yds.	400 yds.	— TRAJ. (in.) — 100 yds.	200 yds.	300 yds.	400 yds.	Approx. Price per box
17 Rem.	25	4040	3284	2644	2086	1606	906	599	388	242	143	+2.0	+1.7	−3.7	−17.4	**NA**
22 Hornet	45	2690	2042	1502	1128	948	723	417	225	127	90	+1.0	−5.3	+27.6	—	**$21.99***
218 Bee	46	2760	2102	1550	1155	961	778	451	245	136	94	+1.0	−5.2	−26.3	—	**36.85***
222 Rem.	50	3140	2602	2123	1700	1350	1094	752	500	321	202	+2.0	−0.4	−10.6	−33.1	**9.38**
222 Rem.	55	3020	2562	2147	1773	1451	1114	801	563	384	257	+2.0	+0.4	−10.5	−31.8	**9.38**
222 Rem. Mag.	55	3240	2748	2305	1906	1556	1282	922	649	444	296	+2.0	+0.2	−8.2	−26.3	**NA**
223 Rem.	40	3650	3010	2450	1950	1530	1185	805	535	340	205	+2.0	+1.0	−5.9	−22.0	**11.04**
223 Rem.	55	3240	2747	2305	1906	1556	1282	922	649	444	296	+2.0	+0.2	−8.2	−26.3	**10.29**
224 Wea. Mag.[2]	55	3650	3192	2780	2403	2056	1627	1244	943	705	516	+2.0	+2.0	−2.4	−12.2	**NA**
22-250 Rem.	40	4000	3320	2720	2200	1740	1420	980	660	430	265	+2.0	+1.8	−3.2	−15.5	**11.46**
22-250 Rem.	55	3680	3137	2656	2222	1832	1654	1201	861	603	410	+2.0	+1.3	−4.3	−17.1	**10.71**
220 Swift	50	4110	3610	3135	2680	NA	1875	1450	1090	800	NA	+2.0	+2.8	+	−6.9	**21.43**
22 Savage Hi-Power	71	2790	2295	1885	1560	NA	1225	830	560	383	NA	+2.0	+0.8	−12.6	—	**22.71**
243 Win.	80	3350	2955	2593	2259	1951	1993	1551	1194	906	676	+2.0	+0.9	−5.4	−18.6	**12.86**
243 Win.	85	3320	3070	2830	2600	2380	2080	1770	1510	1280	1070	+2.0	+1.2	−4.5	−14.2	**14.28+**
243 Win.	100	2960	2697	2449	2215	1993	1945	1615	1332	1089	882	+2.0	+0.2	−7.5	−22.2	**12.86+**
6mm Rem.	80	3470	3064	2694	2352	2036	2139	1667	1289	982	736	+2.0	+1.1	−4.5	−16.5	**12.86**
6mm Rem.	100	3100	2829	2573	2332	2104	2133	1777	1470	1207	983	+2.0	+0.6	−6.1	−19.2	**12.86**
240 Wea. Mag.[2]	87	3500	3202	2924	2663	2416	2366	1980	1651	1370	1127	+2.0	+2.2	−1.8	−10.6	**NA**
240 Wea. Mag.[2]	100	3395	3106	2835	2581	2339	2559	2142	1785	1478	1215	+2.0	+1.6	−3.0	−12.8	**NA**
25-20 Win.	86	1460	1194	1030	931	858	407	272	203	165	141	+	−8.2	−23.5	—	**24.98***
25-35 Win.	117	2230	1866	1545	1282	1097	1292	904	620	427	313	+2.0	−5.3	−27.4	—	**16.17**
250-3000 Savage	100	2820	2504	2210	1936	1684	1765	1392	1084	832	630	+2.0	−0.6	−10.4	−29.5	**13.70**
257 Roberts	100	3000	2633	2295	1982	1697	1998	1539	1169	872	639	+2.0	−0.4	−9.4	−27.2	**15.13**
257 Roberts	117	2650	2291	1961	1663	1404	1824	1363	999	718	512	+2.0	−1.0	−15.0	—	**14.36**
25-06 Rem.	87	3440	2995	2591	2222	1884	2286	1733	1297	954	686	+2.0	+1.1	−5.1	−18.4	**13.94**
25-06 Rem.	90	3440	3043	2680	2340	2034	2364	1850	1435	1098	827	+2.0	+1.2	−4.2	−16.6	**13.94**
25-06 Rem.	100	3230	2893	2580	2287	2014	2316	1858	1478	1161	901	+2.0	+0.8	−5.7	−18.9	**13.95**
25-06 Rem.	120	2990	2730	2484	2252	2032	2382	1985	1644	1351	1100	+2.0	+	−7.5	−22.0	**13.94**
257 Wea. Mag.[2]	87	3825	3456	3118	2805	2513	2826	2308	1878	1520	1220	+2.0	+2.7	−0.3	−7.7	**NA**
257 Wea. Mag.[2]	100	3555	3237	2941	2665	2404	2806	2326	1920	1556	1283	+2.0	+2.1	−1.8	−10.5	**NA**
257 Wea. Mag.[2]	117	3300	2882	2502	2152	1830	2829	2158	1626	1203	870	+2.0	+1.2	−5.1	−18.9	**NA**
6.5x50 Jap.	139	2360	2185	2035	1900	NA	1720	1475	1243	1083	NA	+2.0	−1.6	−13.4	NA	**22.71**
6.5x50 Jap.	156	2065	1870	1690	1530	NA	1480	1215	990	810	NA	+2.0	−4.6	−23.3	NA	**22.71**
6.5x52 Carcano	156	2430	2210	2000	1800	NA	2045	1690	1385	1125	NA	+2.0	−2.0	−14.7	NA	**22.71**
6.5x55 Swedish	140	2855	2665	2500	2350	NA	2350	2210	1930	1677	NA	+2.0	0.6	−6.7	NA	**22.71**
6.5x55 Swedish	156	2645	2415	2205	2010	NA	2425	2015	1701	1414	NA	+2.0	−1.0	−12.1	NA	**22.71**
6.5 Rem. Mag.	120	3210	2905	2621	2353	2102	2745	2248	1830	1475	1177	+2.0	+0.7	−5.6	−19.3	**NA**
264 Win.	140	3030	2782	2548	2326	2114	2854	2406	2018	1682	1389	+2.0	+0.4	−6.6	−18.4	**18.93**
270 Win.	100	3430	3021	2649	2305	1988	2612	2027	1557	1179	877	+2.0	−1.0	−4.9	−17.5	**13.95**
270 Win.	130	3060	2776	2510	2259	2022	2702	2225	1818	1472	1180	+2.0	−0.4	−6.8	−20.8	**13.94**
270 Win.	150	2850	2585	2336	2100	1879	2705	2226	1817	1468	1175	+2.0	−0.4	−9.2	−25.8	**13.94**
270 Wea.Mag.[2]	100	3760	3380	3033	2712	2412	3139	2537	2042	1633	1292	+2.0	−2.4	−0.9	−8.9	**NA**
270 Wea.Mag.[2]	130	3375	3100	2842	2598	2366	3287	2773	2330	1948	1616	+2.0	+1.9	−2.4	−11.6	**NA**
270 Wea.Mag.[2]	150	3245	3019	2803	2598	2402	3507	3034	2617	2248	1922	+2.0	+1.8	−3.0	−12.8	**NA**
7x30 Waters	120	2700	2300	1930	1600	1330	1940	1405	990	685	470	+2.0	2.0	−11.0	−20.0	**13.94**
7mm-08 Rem.	140	2860	2625	2402	2189	1988	2542	2142	1793	1490	1228	+2.0	0.2	−8.4	−23.9	**NA**
7mm Mauser	140	2660	2435	2221	2018	1827	2199	1843	1533	1266	1037	+2.0	1.0	−11.1	−29.7	**14.18**
7mm Mauser	150	2755	2540	2330	2135	NA	2530	2150	1810	1515	NA	+2.0	+	−8.4	NA	**14.18**
7mm Mauser	175	2440	2137	1857	1603	1382	2313	1774	1340	998	742	+2.0	−2.7	−17.6	—	**14.18**
7x57R	150	2690	2475	2285	2080	NA	2410	2040	1830	1515	NA	+2.0	+	−8.4	NA	**23.81**
280 Rem.	140	3000	2758	2528	2309	2102	2797	2363	1986	1657	1373	—	—	—	—	**19.07+**
280 Rem.	150	2970	2699	2444	2203	1975	2937	2426	1989	1616	1299	+2.0	+0.2	−7.5	−22.4	**19.91**
280 Rem.	165	2820	2510	2220	1950	1701	2913	2308	1805	1393	1060	+2.0	0.6	−10.3	−29.3	**19.91**
7x64 Brenneke	150	2890	2600	2330	2115	NA	2780	2250	1810	1490	NA	+2.0	+0.6	−8.4	NA	**23.81**
284 Win.	150	2860	2595	2344	2108	1886	2724	2243	1830	1480	1185	+2.0	−0.2	−8.8	−25.2	**18.28**
7mm Rem. Mag.	150	3110	2830	2568	2320	2085	3221	2667	2196	1792	1448	+2.0	+0.6	−6.1	−19.3	**17.26**
7mm Rem. Mag.	160	2950	2730	2520	2320	2120	3090	2650	2250	1910	1600	+2.0	+0.4	−7.1	−21.6	**19.07+**
7mm Rem. Mag.	175	2860	2645	2440	2244	2057	3178	2718	2313	1956	1644	+2.0	+	−7.9	−22.7	**17.26**
7mm Wea. Mag.[2]	139	3400	3138	2892	2659	2437	3567	3039	2580	2181	1832	+2.0	+2.1	−2.1	−11.1	**NA**
7mm Wea. Mag.[2]	160	3200	3004	2816	2637	2464	3637	3205	2817	2469	2156	+2.0	+1.7	−3.0	−12.6	**NA**
30 Carbine[1]	110	1990	1567	1236	1035	923	967	600	373	262	208	+1.0	−11.5	—	—	**8.93**
30 Rem.	170	2120	1822	1555	1328	1153	1696	1253	913	666	502	+2.0	5.7	−27.8	—	**NA**
30-30 Win.	55	3400	2693	2085	1570	1187	1412	886	521	301	172	+2.0	+	−10.2	−35.0	**NA**
30-30 Win.	125	2570	2090	1660	1320	1080	1830	1210	770	480	320	+2.0	−2.4	−19.4	—	**10.95**
30-30 Win.	150	2390	1973	1605	1303	1095	1902	1296	858	565	399	+2.0	−4.2	−25.6	—	**10.95**
30-30 Win.	170	2200	1895	1619	1381	1191	1827	1355	989	720	535	+2.0	−4.8	−25.1	—	**10.95**
300 Savage	150	2630	2311	2015	1743	1500	2303	1779	1352	1012	749	+2.0	−1.6	−13.9	−36.6	**14.10**
300 Savage	180	2350	2137	1935	1745	1570	2207	1825	1496	1217	985	+2.0	−2.6	−19.7	—	**14.10**
303 Savage	190	1890	1612	1372	1183	1055	1507	1096	794	591	469	+2.0	−8.8	−38.1	—	**18.74**
30-40 Krag	180	2430	2213	2207	1813	1632	2360	1957	1610	1314	1064	+2.0	−2.2	−15.0	−38.5	**14.68**
307 Win.	150	2760	2321	1924	1575	1289	2538	1795	1233	826	554	+2.0	−1.4	−15.4	—	**14.10**
308 Win.	55	3770	3215	2726	2286	1888	1735	1262	907	638	435	+2.0	+1.4	−4.2	−15.8	**NA**
308 Win.	150	2820	2533	2263	2009	1774	2648	2137	1705	1344	1048	+2.0	−0.6	10.0	−28.1	**13.94**
308 Win.	165	2700	2520	2330	2160	1990	2670	2310	1990	1700	1450	+2.0	+	−8.4	−24.3	**13.94**
308 Win.	180	2620	2393	2178	1974	1782	2743	2288	1896	1557	1269	2.0	−1.2	−11.7	−31.3	**13.94**
30-06 Spring.	55	4080	3485	2965	2502	2083	2033	1483	1074	764	530	+2.0	+1.9	−2.1	−11.7	**NA**
30-06 Spring.	150	2910	2617	2342	2083	1843	2820	2281	1827	1445	1131	+2.0	−0.2	−8.5	−24.6	**13.94**
30-06 Spring.	165	2800	2534	2283	2047	1825	2872	2352	1909	1534	1220	+2.0	−0.6	−9.9	−27.5	**14.54**
30-06 Spring.	180	2700	2469	2250	2042	1846	2913	2436	2023	1666	1362	+2.0	−0.8	−10.5	−28.6	**13.94**
30-06 Spring.	220	2410	2130	1870	1632	1422	2837	2216	1708	1301	758	+2.0	−2.7	−20.5	NA	**13.94**
7.5x55 Swiss	180	2650	2460	2250	2060	NA	2800	2380	2020	1690	NA	+2.0	−0.2	−9.2	NA	**23.81**
7.62x54R Russ.	180	2575	2360	2165	1975	NA	2650	2270	1875	1560	NA	+2.0	−0.6	−10.4	NA	**24.06**
308 Norma Mag.	180	3020	2780	2580	2385	NA	3645	3095	2670	2270	NA	+2.0	+1.4	−5.9	NA	**28.76**
300 H&H Mag.	180	2880	2640	2412	2196	1990	3315	2785	2325	1927	1583	+2.0	−0.2	−8.3	−23.7	**19.12**
300 Win. Mag.	150	3290	2951	2636	2342	2068	3605	2900	2314	1827	1424	+2.0	+0.9	−5.3	−17.8	**18.18**
300 Win. Mag.	180	2960	2745	2540	2344	2157	3501	3011	2578	2196	1859	+2.0	+	−7.3	−20.9	**18.17**
300 Win. Mag.	200	2830	2680	2530	2380	2240	3560	3180	2830	2520	2230	+2.0	+0.6	−6.2	−19.1	**20.02+**
300 Win. Mag.	220	2680	2448	2228	2020	1823	3508	2927	2424	1993	1623	+2.0	−1.0	−11.0	−29.5	**19.12**
300 Wea. Mag.[2]	110	3900	3441	3028	2652	2305	3714	2891	2239	1717	1297	+2.0	+2.6	−0.6	−9.2	**NA**
300 Wea. Mag.[2]	150	3600	3297	3015	2751	2502	4316	3621	3028	2520	1709	+2.0	+2.3	−1.2	−9.2	**NA**
300 Wea. Mag.[2]	180	3300	3077	2865	2663	2470	4352	3784	3280	2834	2438	+2.0	−2.6	−3.0	−12.4	**NA**
300 Wea. Mag.[2]	220	2905	2498	2126	1787	1490	4122	3047	2207	1560	1085	+2.0	−0.1	−9.9	−22.3	**NA**
7.7x58 Jap.	130	2950	2635	2340	2065	NA	2513	2005	1581	1230	NA	+2.0	+0.2	−7.9	NA	**24.07**
7.7x58 Jap.	180	2495	2290	2100	1920	NA	2485	2100	1765	1475	NA	+2.0	+1.2	−12.2	NA	**24.07**
7.65x53 Argen.	150	2660	2390	2120	1870	NA	2355	1895	1573	1224	NA	+2.0	−0.2	−9.1	NA	**22.71**
303 British	180	2460	2124	1817	1542	1311	2418	1803	1319	950	687	+2.0	−2.8	−21.3	—	**17.77**
8mm Rem. Mag.	185	3080	2761	2464	2186	1927	3896	3131	2494	1963	1525	+2.0	+0.4	−7.0	−21.7	**NA**
8mm Rem. Mag.	220	2830	2581	2346	2123	1913	3912	3254	2688	2201	1787	+2.0	−0.4	−9.1	−25.5	**NA**
8mm Mauser	170	2360	1969	1622	1333	1123	2102	1463	993	651	476	+2.0	−4.1	−24.9	—	**14.36**

CAUTION: PRICES CHANGE. CHECK AT GUNSHOP.

AVERAGE CENTERFIRE RIFLE CARTRIDGE BALLISTICS AND PRICES

Caliber	Bullet Wgt. Grs.	Muzzle	VELOCITY (fps) 100 yds.	200 yds.	300 yds.	400 yds.	Muzzle	ENERGY (ft. lbs.) 100 yds.	200 yds.	300 yds.	400 yds.	TRAJ. (in.) 100 yds.	200 yds.	300 yds.	400 yds.	Approx. Price per box
8x57 JS Mauser	165	2855	2525	2225	1955	NA	2985	2335	1733	1338	NA	+2.0	+	− 8.0	NA	22.71
8x57 JS Mauser	196	2525	2195	1895	1625	NA	2780	2100	1560	1150	NA	+2.0	− 2.0	−15.7	NA	22.71
32-20 Win.	100	1210	1021	913	834	769	325	231	185	154	131	+	−32.3	—	—	17.84
32 Win. Spl.	170	2250	1921	1626	1372	1175	1911	1393	998	710	521	+2.0	− 4.7	−24.7	—	11.62
338 Win. Mag.	200	2960	2658	2375	2110	1862	3890	3137	2505	1977	1539	+2.0	+	− 8.2	−24.3	21.91
338 Win. Mag.	210	2830	2590	2370	2150	1940	3735	3130	2610	2155	1760	+2.0	− 0.2	− 8.7	−24.7	24.21
338 Win. Mag.	225	2780	2572	2374	2184	2003	3862	3306	2816	2384	2005	+2.0	− 1.4	−11.1	−27.8	21.91
338 Win. Mag.	250	2660	2456	2261	2075	1898	3927	3348	2837	2389	1999	+2.0	− 0.8	−10.5	−28.2	24.42+
340 Wea. Mag.[2]	200	3260	3011	2775	2552	2339	4719	4025	3420	2892	2429	+2.0	+ 1.6	− 3.3	−13.5	NA
340 Wea. Mag.[2]	210	3250	2991	2746	2515	2295	4924	4170	3516	2948	2455	+2.0	+ 1.7	− 3.3	−13.8	NA
340 Wea. Mag.[2]	250	3000	2806	2621	2443	2272	4995	4371	3812	3311	2864	+2.0	+	− 5.0	−16.8	NA
351 Win. S.L.	180	1850	1556	1310	1128	1012	1368	968	686	508	409	+	−13.6	—	—	40.41
35 Rem.	150	2300	1874	1506	1218	1039	1762	1169	755	494	359	+2.0	− 5.1	−27.8	—	12.86
35 Rem.	200	2080	1698	1376	1140	1001	1921	1280	841	577	445	+2.0	− 5.3	−32.1	—	12.86
356 Win.	200	2460	2114	1797	1517	1284	2688	1985	1434	1022	732	+2.0	− 3.0	−18.9	—	21.87
358 Win.	200	2490	2171	1876	1610	1379	2753	2093	1563	1151	844	+2.0	− 2.6	−17.5	—	23.02
357 Magnum	180	1550	1160	980	860	770	960	535	383	295	235	+	−23.4	—	—	20.41
350 Rem. Mag.	200	2710	2410	2130	1870	1631	3261	2579	2014	1553	1181	+2.0	− 1.2	−12.1	−32.9	NA
9.3x57 Mauser	286	2065	1820	1580	1400	NA	2715	2100	1622	1274	NA	+2.0	− 2.8	−25.9	—	27.54
9.3x62 Mauser	286	2360	2090	1830	1580	NA	3545	2770	2177	1622	NA	+2.0	− 2.0	−23.2	—	27.54
375 Win.	200	2200	1841	1526	1268	1089	2150	1506	1034	714	527	+2.0	− 5.2	−27.4	—	18.82
375 Win.	250	1900	1647	1424	1239	1103	2005	1506	1126	852	676	+2.0	− 7.9	−34.8	—	18.82
375 H&H Mag.	270	2690	2420	2166	1928	1707	4337	3510	2812	2228	1747	+2.0	− 1.0	−11.5	−31.4	22.74
375 H&H Mag.	300	2530	2171	1843	1551	1307	4263	3139	2262	1602	1138	+2.0	− 2.6	−17.1	—	23.95
378 Wea. Mag.[2]	270	3180	2976	2781	2594	2415	6062	5308	4635	4034	3495	+2.0	+ 1.6	− 3.4	−13.2	NA
378 Wea. Mag.[2]	300	2925	2576	2252	1952	1680	5698	4419	3379	2538	1881	+2.0	+	− 8.7	−26.9	NA
38-40 Win.	180	1160	999	901	827	764	538	399	324	273	233	+	−23.4	—	—	30.12*
38-55 Win.	255	1320	1190	1091	1018	963	987	802	674	587	525	+	−18.1	—	—	17.51
44-40 Win.	200	1190	1006	900	822	756	629	449	360	300	254	+	−33.3	—	—	28.06*
44 Rem. Mag.	240	1760	1380	1114	970	878	1650	1015	661	501	411	+	−17.6	—	—	10.85
444 Marlin	240	2350	1815	1377	1087	941	2942	1755	1010	630	472	+2.0	− 5.8	−32.7	—	NA
444 Marlin	265	2120	1733	1405	1160	1012	2644	1768	1162	791	603	+2.0	− 6.8	−33.4	—	NA
45-70 Gov.	300	1880	1650	1425	1235	1105	2355	1815	1355	1015	810	+	−12.8	—	—	16.67
45-70 Gov.	405	1330	1168	1055	977	918	1590	1227	1001	858	758	+	−24.6	—	—	16.68
458 Win. Mag.	500	2040	1823	1623	1442	1237	4620	3689	2924	1839	1469	+2.0	− 5.6	−26.4	—	29.21
458 Win. Mag.	510	2040	1770	1527	1319	1157	4712	3547	2540	1970	1239	+2.0	− 6.4	−27.3	—	29.21
460 Wea. Mag.[2]	500	2700	2404	2128	1869	1635	8092	6416	5026	3878	2969	+2.0	− 0.6	−10.7	−31.3	NA

From 24" barrel except as noted (1 = 20" bbl.; 2 = 26" bbl.). Energies and velocities based on most commonly used bullet profile. Variations can and will occur with different bullet profiles and/or different lots of ammunition as well as individual barrels. Trajectory based on scope reticle 1.5" above center of bore line. + indicates bullet strikes point of aim.

NOTES: * = 50 cartridges to a box pricing (all others 20 cartridges to a box pricing)
NA = Information not available from the manufacturer.
— = Trajectory falls more than 40 inches below line of sight.
+ = Premium priced ammunition.

Please note that the actual ballistics obtained in your gun can vary considerably from the advertised ballistics. Also, ballistics can vary from lot to lot, even within the same brand. All prices were correct at the time this table was prepared. All prices are subject to change without notice.

CENTERFIRE HANDGUN CARTRIDGES—BALLISTICS AND PRICES

Caliber	Gr.	Bullet Style	Velocity (fps) Muzzle	50 yds.	Energy (ft. lbs.) Muzzle	50 yds.	Barrel Length In Inches	Approx. price/box
22 Rem. Jet	40	JSP	2100	1790	390	285	8 3/8	$ NA
221 Rem. Fireball	50	JSP	2650	2380	780	630	10 1/2	NA
25 Auto	45	LE	815	729	66	53	2	14.72
25 Auto	50	FMC	760	707	64	56	2	13.78
30 Luger	93	FMC	1220	1110	305	253	4 1/2	24.74
30 Carbine	110	JHP, FMC	1740	1552	740	588	10	8.93*
32 S&W	85, 88	LRN	680	645	90	81	3	13.12
32 S&W Long	98	LRN, LWC	705	670	115	98	4	13.85
32 H&R Mag.	85	JHP	1100	1020	230	195	4 1/2	17.30
32 H&R Mag.	95	LSWC	1030	940	225	190	4 1/2	15.30
32 Short Colt	80	LRN	745	665	100	79	4	13.02
32 Long Colt	82	LRN	755	715	100	93	4	13.61
32 Auto	60	STHP	970	895	125	107	4	18.12
32 Auto	71	FMC	905	855	129	115	4	15.60
380 Auto	85, 88	JHP	1000	921	189	160	3 3/4	15.92
380 Auto	95	FMC	955	865	190	160	3 3/4	15.92
38 Auto	130	FMC	1040	980	310	275	4 1/2	16.85
38 Super Auto + P	115	JHP	1300	1147	431	336	5	NA
38 Super Auto + P	125	STHP	1240	1130	427	354	5	20.65
38 Super Auto + P	130	FMC	1215	1099	426	348	5	16.85
9mm Luger	115	JHP	1160	1060	345	285	4	19.34
9mm Luger	115	STHP	1225	1095	383	306	4	22.43
9mm Luger	123, 124	FMC	1110	1030	339	292	4	19.34
38 S&W	146	LRN	685	650	150	135	4	14.60
38 Short Colt	125	LRN	730	685	150	130	4	NA
38 Special	148	LWC	710	634	166	132	4V	15.27
38 Special	110	STHP	945	894	218	195	4V	21.55
38 Special	158	LRN, LSWC	753	721	200	132	4V	15.27
38 Special	95	JHP	1175	1044	291	230	4V	21.55
38 Special + P	110	JHP	995	926	242	210	4V	18.59
38 Special + P	125	JSP, JHP	945	898	248	224	4V	18.59
38 Special + P	158	LSWC, LHP	890	855	278	257	4V	16.26
357 Magnum	110	JHP	1295	1094	410	292	4V	20.41
357 Magnum	125	JHP, JSP	1450	1240	583	427	4V	20.41
357 Magnum	145	STHP	1290	1155	535	428	4V	22.20
357 Magnum	158	JSP, LSWC, JHP	1235	1104	535	428	4V	20.41
357 Magnum	180	JHP	1090	980	475	385	4V	20.41
357 MAXIMUM	158	JHP	1825	1588	1168	885	10 1/2	NA
357 MAXIMUM	180	JHP	1555	1328	966	705	10 1/2	NA
10mm Auto	165	JHP	1400	NA	719	NA	NA	NA
10mm Auto	200	FMC	1200	NA	635	NA	NA	NA
41 Rem. Mag.	175	STHP	1250	1120	607	488	4V	31.13
41 Rem. Mag.	210	LSWC	965	898	434	376	4V	22.90
41 Rem. Mag.	210	JHP, JSP	1300	1162	788	630	4V	10.92*
44 Special	200	LSWC HP, STHP	900	830	360	305	6 1/2	20.58
44 Special	246	LRN	755	725	310	285	6 1/2	20.59
44 Rem. Mag.	180	JHP	1610	1365	1036	745	4V	11.04*
44 Rem. Mag.	210	STHP	1250	1106	729	570	4V	12.58
44 Rem. Mag.	220	FMC	1390	1260	945	775	6 1/2V	28.56
44 Rem. Mag.	240	LSWC	1000	947	533	477	6 1/2V	22.45
44 Rem. Mag.	240	LSWC/GC	1350	1186	971	749	4V	26.42
44 Rem. Mag.	240	JHP, JSP	1180	1081	741	623	4V	10.85*
45 Auto	185	JWC	770	707	244	205	5	22.40
45 Auto	185	JHP	940	890	363	325	5	22.40
45 Auto	230	FMC	810	776	335	308	5	21.57
45 Auto Rim.	230	LRN	810	770	335	305	5 1/2	NA
45 Win. Mag.	230	FMC	1400	1232	1001	775	5	25.85
45 Colt	225	JHP, LHP	900	860	405	369	5 1/2	20.90
45 Colt	250, 255	LRN	860	820	420	380	5 1/2	8.49*

Notes: Blanks are available in 32 S&W, 38 S&W and 38 Special. V after barrel length indicates test barrel was vented and produced results approximating a revolver with its cylinder to barrel gap.

Abbreviations: JSP (jacketed soft point); LE (lead expanding); FMC (full metal case); JHP (jacketed vertip hollow point); LHP (lead hollow point); LSWCHP (lead semi-wadcutter hollow point); STHP (silvertip hollow point); LHP (lead hollow point); LSWCHP (lead semi-wadcutter hollow point); LSWC/GC (lead semi-wadcutter with gas check); JWC (jacketed wadcutter)

*20 rounds per box; all others 50 rounds per box

RIMFIRE AMMUNITION—BALLISTICS AND PRICES

Cartridge Type	Bullet Wt. Grs.	Bullet Type	Velocity (fsp) 22½" Barrel Muzzle	50 yds.	100 Yds.	Energy (ft. lbs.) 22½" Barrel Muzzle	50 Yds.	100 Yds.	Velocity (fps) 6" Barrel Muzzle	50 Yds.	Energy (ft. lbs.) 6" Barrel Muzzle	50 Yds.	Approx. Price Per Box 50 Rds.	100 Rds.
22 CB Short (CCI & Win.)	29	solid	727	667	610	34	29	24	706	—	32	—	**NA**	**$3.83**
22 CB Long (CCI only)	29	solid	727	667	610	34	29	24	706	—	32	—	**NA**	**3.83**
22 Short Match (CCI only)	29	solid	830	752	695	44	36	31	786	—	39	—	**NA**	**3.83**
22 Short Std. Vel. (Rem. only)	29	solid	1045	—	810	70	—	42	865	—	48	—	**1.80**	**NA**
22 Short H. Vel. (Fed., Rem., Win.)	29	solid	1095	—	903	77	—	53	—	—	—	—	**1.80**	**NA**
22 Short H. Vel. (CCI only)	29	solid	1132	1104	920	83	65	55	1065	—	73	—	**NA**	**2.94**
22 Short H. Vel. HP (Rem. only)	27	HP	1120	—	904	75	—	49	—	—	—	—	**1.91**	**NA**
22 Short H. Vel. HP (CCI only)	27	HP	1164	1013	920	81	62	51	1077	—	69	—	**NA**	**3.13**
22 Long Std. Vel. (CCI only)	29	solid	1180	1038	946	90	69	58	1031	—	68	—	**NA**	**2.79**
22 Long H. Vel. (Fed., Rem.)	29	solid	1240	—	962	99	—	60	—	—	—	—	**1.91**	**NA**
22 LR Pistol Match (Win. only)	40	solid	—	—	—	—	—	—	1060	950	100	80	**5.10**	**NA**
22 LR Match (Rifle) (CCI only)	40	solid	1138	1047	975	116	97	84	1027	925	93	76	**4.28**	**2.79**
22 LR Std. Vel.	40	solid	1138	1046	975	115	97	84	1027	925	93	76	**1.72**	**3.59**
22 LR H. Vel.	40	solid	1255	1110	1017	140	109	92	1060	—	100	—	**1.72**	**3.59**
22 LR H. Vel. HP	36-38	HP	1280	1126	1010	131	101	82	1089	—	95	—	**1.99**	**4.15**
22 LR-Hyper Vel. (Fed., Rem., Win.,(2))	33-34	HP	1500	1240	1075	165	110	85	—	—	—	—	**1.99**	**NA**
22 LR-Hyper Vel.	36	solid	1410	1187	1056	159	113	89	—	—	—	—	**1.75**	**NA**
22 Stinger (CCI only)	32	HP	1640	1277	1132	191	115	91	1395	1060	138	80	**3.52**	**NA**
22 Win. Mag. Rimfire	40	FMC or HP	1910	1490	1326	324	197	156	1428	—	181	—	**6.07**	**NA**
22 LR Shot (CCI, Fed., Win.)	—	#11 or #12 shot	1047	—	—	—	—	—	950	—	—	—	**4.58**	**NA**
22 Win. Mag. Rimfire Shot (CCI only)	—	#11 shot	1126	—	—	—	—	—	1000	—	—	—	**4.24**	**NA**
22 Win. Mag. Rimfire	50	JHP	1650	—	1280	300	—	180	—	—	—	—	**Unk**	**NA**

Please Note: The actual ballistics obtained from your gun can vary considerably from the advertised ballistics. Also, ballistics can vary from lot to lot even with the same brand. All prices were correct at the time this chart was prepared. All prices are subject to change without notice.

(1) per 250 rounds. (2) also packaged 250 rounds per box.

SHOTSHELL LOADS AND PRICES

Winchester-Western, Remington-Peters, Federal

Dram Equivalent	Shot Ozs.	Load Style	Shot Sizes	Brands	Average Price Per Box	Nominal Velocity (fps)
10 Gauge 3½" Magnum						
4½	2¼	Premium(1)	BB, 2, 4, 6	Fed., Win.	$26.47	1205
4¼	2	H.V.	BB, 2, 4, 5, 6	Fed.	24.87	1210
Max	1¾	Slug, rifled	Slug	Fed.	6.06	1280
Max	54 pellets	Buck, Premium(1)	4 (Buck)	Fed., Win.	6.03	1100
Max	18 pellets	Buck, Premium(1)	00 Buck	Fed., Win.	6.03	1100
Max	1¾	Steel shot	BB, 2	Win.	22.39	1260
4¼	1⅝	Steel shot	BB, 2	Fed.	22.38	1285
12 Gauge 3" Magnum						
4	1⅞	DuPlex Premium	BBx4-2x6	Rem.	NA	1210
4	1⅞	Premium(1)	BB, 2, 4, 6	Fed., Rem., Win.	16.27	1210
4	1⅝	Premium(1)	2, 4, 5, 6	Fed., Rem., Win.	15.46	1280
4	1⅞	H.V.	BB, 2, 4	Fed., Rem.	15.56	1210
4	1⅝	H.V.	2, 4, 6	Fed., Rem.	14.39	1280
4	Variable	Buck, Premium(1)	000, 00, 1, 4	Fed., Rem., Win.	3.05	1210 to 1225
3½	1¼	DuPlex Premium	BBx2-BBx4-2x6	Rem.	NA	1375
3½	1⅜	Steel Shot	BB, 1, 2, 4	Fed.	15.65	1245
3½	1¼	Steel Shot	F, T, BBB, BB 1, 2, 4	Rem., Win.	14.38	1375
4	2	Premium(1)	BB, 2, 4, 6	Fed.	18.27	1175
Max	1	Slug, rifled	Slug	Rem.	4.77	1760
12 Gauge 2¾" Hunting & Target						
3¾	1½	DuPlex Premium	BBx4-2x6	Rem.	NA	1260
3¾	1½	Premium(1), Mag.	BB, 2, 4, 5, 6	Fed., Rem., Win.	14.57	1260
3¾	1½	H.V., Mag.	BB, 2, 4, 5, 6	Fed., Rem.	12.94	—
3¾	1¼	H.V., Premium(1)	2, 4, 6, 7½	Fed., Rem.	11.50	1330
3¾	1¼	H.V., Promo	BB, 2, 4, 5, 6 7½, 8, 9	Fed., Rem., Win.	8.78	1330
3¼	1¼	Std. Vel., Premium(1)	7½, 8	Fed., Rem.	10.07	1220
3¼	1⅛	Std. Vel., Premium(1)	7½, 8	Fed., Rem.	9.73	1255
3¼	1¼	Std. Vel.	6, 7½, 8, 9	Fed., Rem., Win.	8.89	1220
3¼	1⅛	Std. Vel.	4, 5, 6, 7½, 8, 9	Fed., Rem., Win.	8.12	1255
3¼	1	Std. Vel., Promo	6, 7½, 8	Fed., Rem., Win.	5.87	1290
Max.	1¼	Slug, rifled, Mag.	Slug	Fed.	4.28	1490
Max.	1	Slug, rifled	Slug	Fed., Rem., Win.	3.46	1560
Max.	1	Slug, rifled, hi-vel.	Slug	Rem.	NA	1680
4	Variable	Buck, Mag., Premium(1)	00, 1, 4 (Buck)	Fed., Rem., Win.	8.28	1075 to 1290
3¾	Variable	Buck, Premium(1)	000, 00, 0, 1, 4 (Buck)	Fed., Rem., Win.	7.58	1250 to 1325
3¾	1⅜	H.V.	2, 4, 6	Fed.	12.14	1295
3¼	1¼	Pigeon	6, 7½, 8	Fed., Win.	9.09	1220
3	1⅛	Trap & Skeet	7½, 8, 9	Fed., Rem., Win.	8.18	1200

Dram Equivalent	Shot Ozs.	Load Style	Shot Sizes	Brands	Average Price Per Box	Nominal Velocity (fps)
2¾	1⅛	Trap & Skeet	7½, 8, 8½, 9	Fed., Rem., Win.	8.18	1145
2¾	1	Trap & Skeet	7½, 8, 8½	Fed., Rem., Win.	8.01	1180
3¾	1¼	Steel Shot	BB, 1, 2, 4, 6	Fed., Win.	14.38	1275
3¾	1⅛	Steel Shot	1, 2, 4, 6	Fed., Rem., Win.	13.19	1365
3¾	1⅛	DuPlex Premium	BBx2-BBx4, 2x6	Rem.	NA	1365
16 Gauge 2¾"						
3¼	1¼	H.V., Mag., Premium(1)	2, 4, 6	Fed., Win.	12.76	1260
3¼	1⅛	H.V., Promo.	4, 5, 6, 7½, 9	Fed., Rem., Win.	8.62	1295
2¾	1⅛	Std. Vel.	4, 6, 7½, 8, 9	Fed., Rem., Win.	8.12	1185
2½	1	Std. Vel., Promo.	6, 7½, 8	Fed., Win.	5.87	1165
Max.	⅘	Slug, rifled	Slug	Fed., Rem., Win.	3.46	1570
Max.	12 pellets	Buck	1 (Buck)	Fed., Rem., Win.	3.05	1225
20 Gauge 3" Magnum						
3	1¼	Premium(1)	2, 4, 6	Fed., Rem., Win.	12.91	1185
3	1¼	H.V.	2, 4, 6, 7½	Fed., Rem.	12.01	1185
Max.	18 pellets	Buck	2 (Buck)	Fed.	3.72	1200
Max.	1	Steel Shot	2, 4, 6	Fed., Rem., Win.	12.60	1330
20 Gauge 2¾" Hunting & Target						
2¾	1⅛	Premium(1), Mag.	4, 6, 7½	Fed., Rem., Win.	11.42	1175
2¾	1⅛	H.V., Mag.	4, 6, 7½	Fed., Rem.	10.67	1175
2¾	1	H.V., Premium(1)	4, 6	Fed., Rem.	9.97	1220
2¾	1	H.V., Promo.	4, 5, 6, 7½, 8, 9	Fed., Rem., Win.	8.30	1220
2½	1	Std. Vel., Premium(1)	7½, 8	Fed., Rem.	8.79	1165
2½	1	Std. Vel.	4, 5, 6, 7½, 8, 9	Fed., Rem., Win.	7.61	1165
2¼	⅞	Promo	6, 7½, 8	Fed., Rem., Win.	5.87	1210
Max.	¾	Slug, rifled	Slug	Fed., Rem., Win.	3.21	1570
Max.	20 pellets	Buck	3 (Buck)	Fed., Rem., Win.	3.03	1200
2½	⅞	Skeet	8, 9	Fed., Rem., Win.	7.66	1200
2¾	¾	Steel Shot	4, 6	Fed., Win.	11.90	1425
28 Gauge 2¾" Hunting & Target						
2¼	¾	H.V., Premium(1)	6, 7½	Fed., Rem., Win.	10.13	1295
2	¾	Skeet	9	Fed., Rem., Win.	9.06	1200
410 Bore Hunting & Target						
Max.	11/16	3" H.V.	4, 5, 6, 7½, 8	Fed., Rem., Win.	8.66	1135
Max.	½	2½" H.V.	4, 6, 7½	Fed., Rem., Win.	7.36	1135
Max.	½	2½" Target	9	Fed., Rem., Win.	7.50	1200
Max.	⅕	Slug, rifled	Slug	Fed., Rem., Win.	3.05	1815

(1) Premium shells usually incorporate high antimony extra hard shot and a granulated polyethelene buffer to increase pattern density at long ranges. In general, prices are per 25-round box. Rifled slugs and buckshot prices are per 5-round pack. Premium buckshot prices per 10-round pack. Not every brand is available in every shot size. Price of Skeet and trap loads may vary widely.

Exterior Ballistic Data for British Centerfire Rifle Cartridges

Cartridge	Case length inches	Bullet weight (grs.)	Powder weight (grs.)	Velocity (ft./sec.) Muzzle	Velocity 100 yd.	Velocity 200 yd.	Energy (ft./lb.) Muzzle	Energy 100 yd.	Energy 200 yd.	Drop (in.)† 100 yd.	Drop (in.)† 200 yd.
* 297/230 (Morris) Short	9/16	37L	1¾ RN	875	720		63	43		15.0	
* 297/230 (Morris) Long	¾	37L	2¾ CN	1200	920	760	120	70	48	15.0	71.0
*p 240 H&H Apex Flanged	2½	100CP	38½ NC	2800	2570	2355	1740	1470	1230	2.3	10.0
240 Belted Rimless	2½	100CP	40½ NC	2900	2665	2445	1870	1580	1330	2.2	9.2
* 242 Rimless Nitro Exp.	2⅜	100CP	42 NC	3000	2740	2490	1970	1635	1355	2.0	8.6
244 H&H Magnum (Belted)	2¾	100CP		3500	3230	2970	2725	2320	1980	1.6	5.1
297/250 Rook Rifle	13/16	56L	3 CN	1150	940	805	165	110	80	15.5	70.0
256 (6.5mm) Mannlicher	2⅛	160SN	36 NC	2350	2045	1765	1960	1490	1110	3.4	15.5
6.5mm Mann.-Schon.	2⅛	160SN	36 NC	2300	2000	1725	1880	1420	1060	3.6	16.0
275 H&H Magnum (Belted)	2½	160CP	52 NC	2700	2505	2320	2600	2230	1920	2.5	10.5
275 High Velocity (7mm)	2¼	140CP	48 NC	2900	2705	2515	2620	2280	1970	2.2	9.0
276 (7mm) Mauser	2¼	173SN	38 NC	2300	2015	1765	2040	1560	1200	3.9	16.0
p 7mm H&H Magnum Flanged	2½	140CP		2650	2450		2184	1867			
* 280 Flanged Nitro Exp.	2⅝	140CP	52 NC	2800	2570	2355	2440	2060	1730	2.3	10.0
* 280 Flanged Nitro Exp.	2⅝	160HP	52 NC	2600	2300	2020	2400	1880	1450	2.8	12.0
280 Ross Rimless Nitro	2⅝	140CP	54 NC	2900	2665	2445	2620	2210	1860	2.2	9.0
280 Ross Rimless Nitro		160HP	54 NC	2700	2395	2110	2600	2040	1580	2.6	11.5
* 280 Jeffery Rimless	2½	140CP	57 NC	3000	2870	2735	2800	2555	2390	2.1	10.0
300 (.295) Rook Rifle	1⅛	80L	4½ CN	1100	915	785	215	150	110	16.5	75.0
300 Sherwood	1½	140L	8½ CN	1400	1195	1060	610	445	350	9.9	44.0
300 H&H Magnum Belted	2¾	150SN	58 C	3000	2660	2350	3000	2360	1835	2.2	9.8
or (30 Super Magnum)		180SN	55 C	2750	2430	2130	3020	2360	1815	2.8	12.5
or (30 Super Magnum)		220SN	49 C	2300	2045	1810	2115	1675	1305	3.9	17.0
p 30 Super Flanged H&H	2¾	150SN	55 C	2875	2581		2755	2225			
p 30 Super Flanged H&H		180SN	50 C	2575	2309		2653	2131			
p 30 Super Flanged H&H		220SN	46 C	2250	2045		2475	2045			
* 30 Purdey Flanged Nitro	2⅜	150SN		2700	2385	2090	2430	1900	1460	2.6	11.5
303 British (Mark 6)	2¼	215S	31 C	2050	1855	1670	2010	1650	1330	4.4	19.0
303 British (Mark 7)	2¼	174S	37 C	2450	2250	2055	2320	1960	1640	3.0	13.0
303 British	2¼	150CP	38 C	2700	2465	2240	2440	2030	1680	2.5	11.0
303 British	2¼	174SN	41 NC	2450	2195	1955	2315	1870	1480	3.1	13.5
303 British	2¼	215SN	31 C	2050	1790	1555	2010	1530	1160	4.6	20.0
310 Cadet	1⅛	120L	6 CN	1200	1010	890	385	270	210	14.0	62.0
318 Rimless Nitro Exp.	2⅜	180CP	55 NC	2700	2395	2110	2920	2300	1780	2.6	11.5
318 Rimless Nitro Exp.		250SN	52 NC	2400	2040	1715	3200	2320	1640	3.3	15.0
333 Rimless Nitro Exp.	2⅜	300SN	65 NC	2200	1950	1720	3230	2540	1980	3.9	17.0
* 400/350 Nitro Exp.	2¾	310SN	43 NC	2000	1795	1610	2760	2220	1790	4.7	20.0
350 Rigby Magnum Rimless	2¾	225SN	65 NC	2625	2307		3440	2657			
350 No. 2 Rigby Flanged	2¾	225SN		2600			3400				
* 360 Nitro Exp. Flanged	2¼	300SN	30 C	1650	1490	1355	1820	1480	1210	6.9	29.0
* 360 Nitro for Black Powd.	2¼	190CT	22 C	1650	1285	1070	1150	700	485	7.6	36.0
o 400/360 Purdey Flanged	2¾	300SN	40 C	1950	1776		2537	2102			
o 400/360 Westley Richards	2¾	314SN	41 C	1900	1724		2520	2072			
o 360 No. 2 Nitro Exp.	3	320SN	55 C	2200	1999		3442	2845			
o 369 Purdey Nitro Exp.	2⅝	270SN	64½ NC	2500	2135	1800	3760	2740	1950	3.1	14.0
375 Flanged Nitro Exp.	2½	270SN	40 C	2000	1735	1405	2400	1810	1190	4.9	22.0
o 375 Rimless W.R. Nitro	2¼	270SN	43 C	2100	1870		2640	2100			
375 Flanged Magnum Nitro	2⅞	270SN	59 C	2600	2280	1980	4060	3120	2360	2.8	12.5
375 Flanged Magnum Nitro		300SN	56 C	2400	2105	1825	3850	2960	2220	3.3	14.5
375 Belted H&H Magnum	2⅞	235CP	62 C	2800	2495	2215	4100	3260	2560	2.4	10.5
375 Belted H&H Magnum		270SN	61 C	2650	2325	2020	4220	3250	2450	2.9	12.0
375 Belted H&H Magnum		300SN	58 C	2500	2200	1915	4170	3230	2450	3.0	13.5
450/400 Nitro Exp.	3	400SN	60 C	2100	1845	1610	3920	3030	2310	4.3	19.0
450/400 Magnum Nitro Exp.	3¼	400SN	60 C	2150	1890	1650	4110	3180	2420	4.1	18.0
404 Jeffery Rimless	2⅞	400SN	60 C	2125	1885	1670	4020	3160	2480	4.2	18.0
p 416 Rigby Magnum	2⅞	410SN	71 C	2371	2110		5100				
p 425 Westley Richards	2⅝	410SN		2350			5010				
o 450 Nitro Exp.	3¼	480SN	70 C	2150	1900	1665	4930	3860	2960	4.1	18.0
* 500/450 Magnum Nitro Exp.	3¼	480SN	75 C	2175	1987		5050	4220			
o 450 No. 2 Nitro Exp.	3½	480SN	80 C	2175	1904		5050	3900			
o 450 Black Powder Exp.	3¼	310L	120 Blk	1800	1510		2240	1570			
o 450 Nitro for B.P. Exp.	3¼	365CT	52 C	2100	1809		3578	2655			
577/450 Martini-Henry	2¼	480L	38½ C	1350	1210	1110	1950	1560	1320	10.0	44.0
577/450 Martini-Henry B.P.	2¼	480L	85 Blk	1350	1210	1110	1950	1560	1320	10.0	44.0
465 H&H Nitro Exp.	3¼	480SN	73 C	2150	1830	1620	4930	3580	2800	4.1	18.5
470 Nitro Exp.	3¼	500SN	75 C	2150	1890	1650	5140	3980	3030	4.1	18.0
* 475 Nitro Exp.	3¼	480SN	75 C	2175	2000	1830	5040	4260	3580	4.2	18.0
r 475 No. 2 Nitro Exp.	3½	480SN	85 C	2200	1925	1680	5170	3960	3020	3.9	17.0
o 475 No. 2 Jeffery	3½	500SN	85 C	2150	1880	1635	5140	3930	2970	4.1	18.0
o 476 Nitro Exp.	3	520SN	75 C	2100	1925	1760	5085	4295	3585	4.6	20.0
500 Nitro Exp.	3	570SN	80 C	2150	1890	1650	5850	4530	3450	4.1	18.0
* 500 Nitro for B.P. Exp.	3	440CT	55 C	1900	1570	1290	3530	2410	1630	5.5	25.0
o 500 Black Powder Exp.	3	340CT	136 Blk	1925	1585		2800	1900			
p 500 Jeffery Rimless		535SN	95 C	2400			6800				
p 505 Gibbs Rimless Magnum		525SN	90 C	2300			6180				
577 Solid Snider	1⅞	480L	70 Blk	1250	1055	940	1670	1190	940	13.0	57.0
r 577 Nitro Exp.	3	750SN	100 C	2050	1795	1570	7010	5380	4110	4.5	20.0
o 600 Nitro Exp.	3	900S	110 C	1950	1650	1390	7600	5450	3870	5.1	23.0

ABBREVIATIONS

BP or Blk—Black Powder
C—Cordite
NC—Nitro-Cellulose
CN—Cadet Neonite
RN—Revolver Neonite

*Discontinued

SN—Soft Nose
CP—Copper Point
CT—Copper Tube
L—Lead
S—Solid (Jacketed)

†—Drop is computed from horizontal line of departure for the bullet.
*—Available while stocks last; will then become obsolete.
o—Obsolete; no longer available.
r—Re-introduced and again available.
p—Proprietary Cartridge; available only from specific maker.

Chokes & Brakes

Briley Screw-In Chokes
Installation of these choke tubes requires that all traces of the original choking be removed, the barrel threaded internally with square threads and then the tubes are custom fitted to the specific barrel diameter. The tubes are thin and, therefore, made of stainless steel. Cost of installation for single-barrel guns (pumps, autos) runs **$75.00**; un-single target guns run **$150.00**; over-unders and side-by-sides cost **$150.00** per barrel. Steel shot, add **$10.00**. Prices include one choke tube and a wrench for disassembly. Extra tubes are **$40.00** each.

Cellini Stabilizer System
Designed for handgun, rifle and shotgun applications, the Cellini Stabilizer System is available as a removable factory-installed accessory. Over-all length is 2½", weight is 3.5 ounces, and the unit must be installed by the maker. It is said to reduce muzzle jump to nearly zero, even for automatic weapons. Cost starts at **$89.00**. Contact Cellini for full details.

Cutts Compensator
The Cutts compensator is one of the oldest variable choke devices available. Manufactured by Lyman Gunsight Corporation, it is available with a steel body. A series of vents allows gas to escape upward and downward. For the 12-ga. Comp body, six fixed-choke tubes are available: the Spreader—popular with skeet shooters; Improved Cylinder; Modified; Full; Superfull, and Magnum Full. Full, Modified and Spreader tubes are available for 12, or 20, and an Adjustable Tube, giving Full through Improved Cylinder chokes, is offered in 12, or 20 gauges. Cutts Compensator, complete with wrench, adaptor and any single tube **$68.80**; with adjustable tube **$89.80**. All single choke tubes **$18.95** each. No factory installation available.

Emsco Choke
E.M. Schacht of Waseca, Minn., offers the Emsco, a small diameter choke which features a precision curve rather than a taper behind the 1½" choking area. 9 settings are available in this 5 oz. attachment. Its removable recoil sleeve can be furnished in dural if desired. Choice of three sight heights. For 12, 16 or 20 gauge. Price installed, **$32.50, plus postage.** Not installed, **$24.50.**

Gentry Quiet Muzzle Brake
Developed by gunmaker David Gentry, the "Quiet Muzzle Brake" is said to reduce recoil by 65 to 80 percent with no loss of accuracy or velocity. There is no increase in noise level because the noise and gasses are directed away from the shooter. The barrel is threaded for installation and the unit is blued to match the barrel finish. Price, installed, is **$150.00.**

KDF Recoil Arrestor
This threaded muzzle brake has 24 pressure ports that direct combustion gases in all directions to reduce felt recoil up to a claimed 80% without affecting accuracy or ballistics. It is said to reduce felt recoil of a 30-06 to that of a 243. Price is about **$150.00** installed. From KDF Inc.

Lyman CHOKE
The Lyman CHOKE is similar to the Cutts Comp in that it comes with fixed-choke tubes or an adjustable tube, with or without recoil chamber. The adjustable tube version sells for **$39.95** with recoil chamber, in 12 or 20 gauge. Lyman also offers Single-Choke tubes at **$18.95**. This device may be used with or without a recoil-reduction chamber; cost of the latter is **$8.95** extra. Available in 12 or 20 gauge only. No factory installation offered.

Mag-Na-Port
Electrical Discharge Machining works on any firearm except those having non-conductive shrouded barrels. EDM is a metal erosion technique using carbon electrodes that control the area to be processed. The Mag-na-port venting process utilizes small trapezoidal openings to direct powder gases upward and outward to reduce recoil.

No effect is had on bluing or nickeling outside the Magna-port area so no refinishing is needed. Cost for the Mag-na-port treatment is **$59.00** for revolvers, **$80.00** for auto pistols, **$75.00** for rifles, plus transportation both ways, and **$2.50** for handling.

Poly-Choke
Marble Arms Corp., manufacturer of the Poly-Choke adjustable shotgun choke, now offers two models in 12, 16, 20, and 28 gauge—the Ventilated and Standard style chokes. Each provides nine choke settings including Xtra-Full and Slug. The Ventilated model reduces 20% of a shotgun's recoil, the company claims, and is priced at **$71.00**. The Standard Model is **$63.00**. Postage not included. Contact Marble Arms for more data.

Reed-Choke
Reed-Choke is a system of interchangeable choke tubes that can be installed in any single or double-barreled shotgun, including over-unders. The existing chokes are bored out, the muzzles over-bored and threaded for use. A choice of three Reed-Choke tubes are supplied—Skeet, Imp. Cyl., Mod., Imp. Mod., or Full. Flush fitting, no notches exposed. Designed for thin-walled barrels. Made from 174 stainless steel. Cost of the installation is **$179.95** for single-barrel guns, **$229.95** for doubles. Extra tubes cost **$40** each. Postage and handling charges are **$8.50**.

Pro-Port
A compound ellipsoid muzzle venting process similar to Mag-na-porting, only exclusively applied to shotguns. Like Mag-na-porting, this system reduces felt recoil, muzzle jump, and shooter fatigue. Very helpful for Trap doubles shooters. Pro-Port is a patented process and installation is available in both the U.S. and Canada. Cost for the Pro-Port process is **$110.00** for over-unders (both barrels); **$80.00** for only the bottom barrel; and **$69.00** for single barrel shotguns. Prices do not include shipping and handling.

Techni-Port
The Techni-Port recoil compensation system is intended for revolvers, single-shot pistols and rifles. This is a machined process which involves back-boring the muzzle (with a 30° internal crown) and cutting an oval port on each side of the barrel. The process is said to reduce muzzle jump up to 60% and felt recoil up to 50%, with no reduction in velocity or accuracy. Cost of the Techni-Port process is **$99.95**, plus **$6.00** for return freight and insurance. Available from Delta Vectors, Inc.

Walker Choke Tubes
This interchangeable choke tube system uses an adaptor fitted to the barrel without swaging. Therefore, it can be fitted to any single-barreled gun. The choke tubes use the conical-parallel system as used on all factory-choked barrels. These tubes can be used in Winchester, Mossberg, Smith & Wesson, Weatherby, or similar barrels made for the standard screw-in choke system. Available for 10 gauge, 12, 16 and 20. Factory installation (single barrel) with choice of Standard Walker Choke tube is **$95.00, $190.00** for double barrels with two choke tubes. A full range of constriction is available. Contact Walker Arms for more data.

Walker Full Thread Choke Tubes
An interchangeable choke tube system using fully threaded inserts. Designed specifically for over-under or side-by-side shotgun barrels, but can be installed in single barrels, and is nearly invisible. No swaging, adaptor or change in barrel exterior dimensions. Available in 12 or 20 gauge. Factory installation cost: **$100.00,** single barrel with one choke tube; **$200.00** for double barrels with two choke tubes. Contact Walker Arms Co. for more data.

CAUTION: PRICES CHANGE. CHECK AT GUNSHOP.

Sporting Leaf and Open Sights

BURRIS SPORTING REAR SIGHT
Made of spring steel, supplied with multi-step elevator for coarse adjustments and notch plate with lock screw for finer adjustments. Price **14.49**

LYMAN No. 16
Middle sight for barrel dovetail slot mounting. Folds flat when scope or peep sight is used. Sight notch plate adjustable for e. White triangle for quick aiming. 3 heights: A—.400″ to .500″, B—.345″ to .445″, C—.500″ to .600″.
Price **$10.95**

MARBLE FALSE BASE #72, #73, #74
New screw-on base for most rifles replaces factory base. ⅜″ dovetail slot permits installation of any folding rear sight. Can be had in sweat-on models also. Price **$5.50**

MARBLE CONTOUR RAMP #14R
For late model Rem. 725, 740, 760, 742 rear sight mounting. ⁹⁄₁₆″ between mounting screws. Accepts all sporting rear sights. Price ... **$12.25**

MARBLE FOLDING LEAF
Flat-top or semi-buckhorn style. Folds down when scope or peep sights are used. Reversible plate gives choice of "U" or "V" notch. Adjustable for elevation. Price **$10.95**
Also available with both w. and e. adjustment **$12.75**

MARBLE SPORTING REAR
With white enamel diamond, gives choice of two "U" and two "V" notches of different sizes. Adjustment in height by means of double step elevator and sliding notch piece. For all rifles; screw or dovetail installation.
Price: .... **$11.25-$12.75**

Marble #20.

MARBLE #20 UNIVERSAL
New screw or sweat-on base. Both have .100″ elevation adjustment. In five base sizes. Three styles of U-notch, square notch, peep. Adjustable for w. and e.
Price: Screw-on **$18.50**
Price: Sweat-on **$17.00**

MILLETT RIFLE SIGHT
Open, fully adjustable rear sight fits standard ⅜″ dovetail cut in barrel. Choice of white outline or target rear blades, .360″. Front with white or orange bar, .343″, .400″, .430″, .460″, .500″, .540″.
Price: Rear sight **$47.29**
Price: Front sight **$10.49**

MILLETT SCOPE-SITE
Open, adjustable or fixed rear sights dovetail into a base integral with the top scope-mount ring. Blaze orange front ramp sight is integral with the front ring half. Rear sights have white outline aperture. Provides fast, short radius, Patridge-type open sights on top of the scope. Can be used with all Millett rings.
Price: Scope-Site ring set, adjustable **$69.95**
Price: As above, fixed **$39.95**
Price: Convertible Top Cap set, adjustable **$56.95**
Price: As above, fixed **$26.95**

WICHITA MULTI RANGE SIGHT SYSTEM
Designed for silhouette shooting. System allows you to adjust the rear sight to four repeatable range settings, once it is pre-set. Sight clicks to any of the settings by turning a serrated wheel. Front sight is adjustable for weather and light conditions with one adjustment. Specify gun when ordering.
Price: Rear sight **$77.00**
Price: Front sight **$44.00**

WILLIAMS DOVETAIL OPEN SIGHT
Open rear sight with w. and e. adjustment. Furnished with "U" notch or choice of blades. Slips into dovetail and locks with gib lock. Heights from .281″ to .531″. Price with blade **$13.00**
Price: Less Blade **$8.55**

WILLIAMS GUIDE OPEN SIGHT
Open rear sight with w. and e. adjustment. Bases to fit most military and commercial barrels. Choice of square "U" or "V" notch blade, ³⁄₁₆″, ¼″, ⁵⁄₁₆″, or ⅜″ high. Price with blade **$15.70**
Price: Extra blades, each **$4.45**
Price: Less blade **$11.25**

Micrometer Receiver Sights

BEEMAN/WEIHRAUCH MATCH APERTURE SIGHT
Micrometer ¼-minute click adjustment knobs with settings indicated on scales. Price **$79.95**

BEEMAN/FEINWERKBAU MATCH APERTURE SIGHTS
Locks into one of four eye-relief positions. Micrometer ¼-minute click adjustments; may be set to zero at any range. Extra windage scale visible beside eyeshade. Primarily for use at 5 to 20 meters. Price **$159.95**

BEEMAN SPORT APERTURE SIGHT
Positive click micrometer adjustments. Standard units with flush surface screwdriver adjustments. Deluxe version has target knobs.
Price: Standard **$34.98**
Price: Deluxe **$39.98**

FREELAND TUBE SIGHT
Uses Unertl 1″ micrometer mounts. For 22-cal. target rifles, inc. 52 Win., 37, 40X Rem. and BSA Martini. Price **$150.00**

LYMAN No. 57
¼-min. clicks. Stayset knobs. Quick release slide, adjustable zero scales. Made for almost all modern rifles. Price **$54.95**

LYMAN No. 66
Fits close to the rear of flat-sided receivers, furnished with Stayset knobs. Quick release slide, ¼-min. adj. For most lever or slide action or flat-sided automatic rifles. Price **$54.95**

LYMAN No. 66U
Light-weight, designed for most modern shotguns with a flat-sided, round-top receiver. ¼-minute clicks. Requires drilling, taping. Not for Browning A-5, Rem. M11. Price **$54.95**

MILLETT ASSAULT RIFLE SIGHTS
Fully adjustable, heat-treated nickel steel peep aperture receiver sights for AR-15, Mini-14. AR-15 rear sight has w. & e. adjustments; non-glare replacement ramp-style front also available. Mini-14 sight has fine w. & e. adjustments; replaces original.
Price: Rear sight for above three guns **$45.95**
Price: Front and rear combo for AR-15 .... **$55.95**
Price: Front sight for AR-15 .... **$10.95**
Price: Front and rear combo for Mini-14 .... **$60.95**
Price: Front sight for Mini-14 .... **$15.95**

WILLIAMS FP
Internal click adjustments. Positive locks. For virtually all rifles, T/C Contender, Heckler & Koch HK-91, Ruger Mini-14, plus Win., Rem. and Ithaca shotguns. Price, from **$45.50**
With Twilight Aperture **$46.90**
With Target Knobs **$54.05**
With Target Knobs & Twilight Aperture **$55.45**
With Square Notched Blade **$47.90**
With Target Knobs & Square Notched Blade **$56.55**
FP-GR (for dovetail-grooved receivers, 22s and air guns) **$45.50**

WILLIAMS 5-D SIGHT
Low cost sight for shotguns, 22's and the more popular big game rifles. Adjustment for w. and e. Fits most guns without drilling or tapping. Also for Br. SMLE. Price **$25.80**
With Twilight Aperture **$27.20**
With Shotgun Aperture **$25.80**

WILLIAMS GUIDE
Receiver sight for .30 M1 Car., M1903A3 Springfield, Savage 24's, Savage-Anschutz rifles and Wby. XXII. Utilizes military dovetail; no drilling. Double-dovetail W. adj., sliding dovetail adj. for e. Price **$24.50**
With Twilight Aperture **$25.90**
With Open Sight Blade **$22.50**

Front Sights

LYMAN HUNTING SIGHTS
Made with gold or white beads ¹⁄₁₆″ to ³⁄₃₂″ wide and in varying heights for most military and commercial rifles. Dovetail bases. Price ... **$7.50**

MARBLE STANDARD
Ivory, red, or gold bead. For all American made rifles, ¹⁄₁₆″ wide bead with semi-flat face which does not reflect light. Specify type of rifle when ordering. Price **$6.75**

MARBLE-SHEARD "GOLD"
Shows up well even in darkest timber. Shows same color on different colored objects; sturdily built. Medium bead. Various models for different makes of rifles so specify type of rifle when ordering. Price **$8.50**

MARBLE CONTOURED
Same contour and shape as Marble-Sheard but uses standard ¹⁄₁₆″ or ³⁄₃₂″ bead, ivory, red or gold. Specify rifle type. Price **$7.75**

MARBLE PATRIDGE
Gold-faced Patridge front sight is available in .250" or .34" widths and heights from .260" to .538". Price **$8.50**

POLY-CHOKE
Rifle front sights available in six heights and two widths. Model A designed to be inserted into the barrel dovetail; Model B is for use with standard .350 ramp; both have standard ⅜" dovetails. Gold or ivory color 1/16" bead. Price **$4.95**

Globe Target Front Sights

FREELAND SUPERIOR
Furnished with six 1" plastic apertures. Available in 4½"-6½" lengths. Made for any target rifle. Price **$46.00**
Price: With 6 metal insert apertures **$49.00**
Price: Front base **$12.50**

FREELAND TWIN SET
Two Freeland Superior Front Sights, long or short, allow switching from 50 yd. to 100 yd. ranges and back again without changing rear sight adjustment. Sight adjustment compensation is built into the set; just interchange and you're "on" at either range. Set includes 6 plastic apertures. Price **$67.00**

FREELAND MILITARY
Short model for use with high-powered rifles where sight must not extend beyond muzzle. Screw-on base; six plastic apertures. Price .. **$46.00**
Price: With 6 metal apertures **$49.00**
Price: Front base **$12.50**

LYMAN No. 17A TARGET
Includes 7 interchangeable inserts; 4 apertures, one transparent amber and two posts .50" and .100" in width. Price **$22.95**

Ramp Sights

LYMAN SCREW-ON RAMP
Used with 8-40 screws but may also be brazed on. Heights from .10" to .350". Ramp without sight **$13.50**

MARBLE FRONT RAMPS
Available in either screw-on or sweat-on style. 5 heights; 3/16", 5/16", 3/8", 7/16", 9/16". Standard ⅜" dovetail slot. Price **$13.75**
Hoods for above ramps **$3.00**

WILLIAMS SHORTY RAMP
Companion to "Streamlined" ramp, about ½" shorter. Screw-on or sweat-on. It is furnished in ⅛", 3/16", 9/32", and ⅜" heights without hood only.
Price: **$9.95**

WILLIAMS STREAMLINED RAMP
Hooded style in screw-on or sweat-on models. Furnished in 9/16", 7/16", ⅜", 5/16", 3/16" heights. Price with hood **$17.80**
Price: Without hood **$14.70**

Handgun Sights

BO-MAR DE LUXE BMCS
Gives ⅜" w. and e. adjustment at 50 yards on Colt Gov't 45, sight radius under 7". For GM and Commander models only. Uses existing dovetail slot. Has shield-type rear blade. Price **$54.75**

BO-MAR LOW PROFILE RIB & ACCURACY TUNER
Streamlined rib with front and rear sights; 7⅛" sight radius. Brings sight line closer to the bore than standard or extended sight and ramp. Weighs 5 oz. Made for Colt Gov't 45, Super 38, and Gold Cup 45 and 38. Price **$89.00**

BO-MAR COMBAT RIB
For S&W Model 19 revolver with 4" barrel. Sight radius 5¾"; weight 5½ oz. Price **$79.00**

BO-MAR FAST DRAW RIB
Streamlined full length rib with integral Bo-Mar micrometer sight and serrated fast draw sight. For Browning 9mm, S&W 39, Colt Commander 45, Super Auto and 9mm. Price **$79.00**

BO-MAR WINGED RIB
For S&W 4" and 6" length barrels—K-38, M10, HB 14 and 19. Weight for the 6" model is about 7¼ oz. Price **$89.00**

BO-MAR COVER-UP RIB
Adj. rear sight, winged front guards. Fits right over revolver's original front sight. For S&W 4" M-10HB, M-13, M-58, M-64 & 65, Ruger 4" models SDA-34, SDA-84, SS-34, SS-84, GF-34, GF-84. Price **$85.00**

C-MORE SIGHTS
Replacement front sight blades offered in two types and five styles. Made of DuPont Acetal, they come in a set of five high-contrast colors: blue, green, pink, red and yellow. Easy to install. Patridge style for Colt Python (all barrels), Ruger Super Blackhawk (7½"), Ruger Blackhawk (4⅝"); Ramp style for Python (all barrels), Blackhawk (4⅝"), Super Blackhawk (7½" and 10½"). From Mag-num Sales Ltd., Inc. Price, per set **$14.95**

MMC MODEL 84 SIGHT SYSTEM
Available with either service or target leaf for Colt 1911 type pistols, as well as Browning's P-35. Sleek, sculptured styling, blends smoothly with the lines of the pistol. High visibility white outline or 2-dot rear sight blades (3-dot system) give instant-aim sighting for low-light conditions.
Price: Rear sight **$50.70**
Price: Front sight (depending on style), from **$10.40**

MMC COMBAT FIXED REAR SIGHT (Colt 1911-Type Pistols)
This veteran MMC sight is well known to those who prefer a true combat sight for "carry" guns. Steel construction for long service. Choose from a wide variety of front sights.
Price: Combat Fixed Rear, plain **$17.55**
Price: As above, white outline **$22.50**
Price: Combat Front Sight for above, six styles, from..... **$4.90**

MMC M/85 ADJUSTABLE REAR SIGHT
Designed to be compatible with the Ruger P-85 front sight. Fully adjustable for windage and elevation.
Price: M/85 Adjustable Rear Sight, plain **$49.95**
Price: As above, white outline **$54.95**

MMC M/85.

MMC STANDARD ADJUSTABLE REAR SIGHT
Available for Colt 1911 type, Ruger Standard Auto, and now for S&W 469, and 659 pistols. No front sight change is necessary, as this sight will work with the original factory front sight.
Price: Standard Adjustable Rear Sight, plain leaf **$43.90**
Price: Standard Adjustable Rear Sight, white outline **$48.70**

MMC MINI-SIGHT
Miniature size for carrying, fully adjustable, for maximum accuracy with your pocket auto. MMC's Mini-Sight will work with the factory front sight. No machining is necessary, easy installation. Available for Walther PP, PPK, and PPK/S pistols. Will also fit fixed sight Browning High Power (P-35).
Price: Mini-Sight, plain **$55.65**
Price: Mini-Sight, white bar **$60.45**

MILLETT SERIES 100 ADJUSTABLE SIGHTS
Replacement sights for revolvers and auto pistols. Positive click adjustments for windage and elevation. Designed for accuracy and ruggedness. Made to fit S&W, Colt, Beretta, SIG Sauer P220, P225, P226, Ruger P-85, Ruger GP-100 (and others), Glock 17, CZ-75, TZ-75, Dan Wesson, Browning, AMT Hardballer. Rear blades are available in white outline or positive black target. All steel construction and easy to install.
Price: .... **$41.95** to **$67.29**

MILLETT MARK SERIES PISTOL SIGHTS
Mark I and Mark II replacement combat sights for government-type auto pistols, including H&K P7. Mark I is high profile, Mark II low profile. Both have horizontal light deflectors.
Price: Mark I, front and rear **$29.39**
Price: Mark II, front and rear **$41.95**
Price: For H&K P7 .... **$41.95**

MILLETT REVOLVER FRONT SIGHTS
All-steel replacement front sights with either white or orange bar. Easy to install. For Ruger GP-100, Redhawk, Security-Six, Police-Six, Speed-Six, Colt Trooper, Diamondback, King Cobra, Peacemaker, Python, Dan Wesson 22 and 15-2. Price .... **$11.59** to **$13.59**

MILLETT DUAL-CRIMP FRONT SIGHT
Replacement front sight for automatic pistols. Dual-Crimp uses an all-steel two-point hollow rivet system. Available in nine heights and four styles. Has a skirted base that covers the front sight pad. Easily installed with the Millett Installation Tool Set. Available in Blaze Orange Bar, White Bar, Serrated Ramp, Plain Post. Price **$13.59**

MILLETT STAKE-ON FRONT SIGHT
Replacement front sight for automatic pistols. Stake-On sights have skirted base that covers the front sight pad. Easily installed with the Millett Installation Tool Set. Available in seven heights and four styles—Blaze Orange Bar, White Bar, Serrated Ramp, Plain Post. Price **$13.59**

OMEGA OUTLINE SIGHT BLADES
Replacement rear sight blades for Colt and Ruger single action guns and the Interarms Virginian Dragoon. Standard Outline available in gold or white notch outline on blue metal. From Omega Sales. Price **$7.95**

OMEGA MAVERICK SIGHT BLADES
Replacement "peep-sight" blades for Colt, Ruger SAs, Virginian Dragoon. Three models available—No. 1, Plain, No. 2, Single Bar, No. 3 Double Bar Rangefinder. From Omega Sales. Price, each **$6.95**

TRIJICON SELF-LUMINOUS SIGHTS
Three-dot sighting system uses self-luminous inserts in the sight blade and leaf. Tritium "lamps" are mounted in a metal cylinder and protected by a polished crystal sapphire. For most popular handguns, fixed or adjustable sights, and some rifles. From Armson, Inc.
Price: .... **$25.95 to $189.90**

THOMPSON/CENTER "ULTIMATE" SIGHTS
Replacement front and rear sights for the T/C Contender. Front sight has four interchangeable blades (.060", .080", .100", .120"), rear sight has four notch widths of the same measurements for a possible 16 combinations. Rear sight can be used with existing soldered front sights.
Price: Front sight **$25.00**
Price: Rear sight **$65.00**

WICHITA SIGHT SYSTEMS
For 45 auto pistols. Target and Combat styles available. Designed by Ron Power. All-steel construction, click adjustable. Each sight has two traverse pins, a large hinge pin and two elevation return springs. Sight blade is serrated and mounted on an angle to deflect light. Patridge front for target, ramp front for combat. Both are legal for ISPC and NRA competitons.
Rear sight, target or combat **$54.50**
Front sight, patridge or ramp **$9.85**

WICHITA GRAND MASTER DELUXE RIBS
Ventilated rib has wings machined into it for better sight acquisition. Made of stainless steel, sights blued. Uses Wichita Multi-Range rear sight, adjustable front sight. Made for revolvers with 6" barrel.
Price: Model 301 (adj. sight K-frames with custom bbl. of 1.000"-1.032" dia., L and N frames with 1.062"-1.100" bbl.) **$143.00**
Price: Model 302 (fixed-sight K-frames; M10, 65, 13 with 1.000" bbl. N-frame with 1.062" bbl.) **$143.00**
Price: Model 303 (Model 29, 629 with factory bbl., adj. sight K, L, N frames) **$143.00**

WICHITA DOUBLE MASTER RIB
Ventilated rib has wings machined on either side of fixed front post sight for better acquisition and is relieved for Mag-na-ports. Milled to accept Weaver See-Thru-style rings. Made of blued steel. Has Wichita Multi-Range rear sight system. Made for Model 29/629 with factory barrel, and all adjustable-sight K, L and N frames.
Price: Model 403 .... **$128.95**

Shotgun Sights

ACCURA-SITE
For shooting shotgun slugs. Three models to fit most shotguns—"A" for vent. rib barrels, "B" for solid ribs, "C" for plain barrels. Rear sight has windage and elevation provisions. Easily removed and replaced. Includes front and rear sights. Price .... **$25.95 to $27.95**

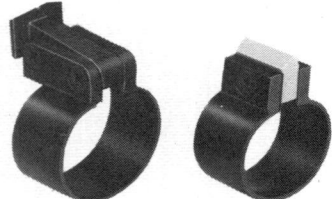

Slug Sights

LYMAN
Three sights of over-sized ivory beads. No. 10 Front (press fit) for double barrel or ribbed single barrel guns . . . **$3.50**; No. 10D Front (screw fit) for non-ribbed single barrel guns (comes with wrench) . . . **$4.50**; No. 11 Middle (press fit) for double and ribbed single barrel guns **$3.50**

MMC M&P COMBAT SHOTGUN SIGHT SET
A durable, protected ghost ring aperture, combat sight made of steel. Fully adjustable for windage and elevation.
Price: M&P Sight Set (front and rear) **$69.95**
Price: As above, installed **$79.95**

MARBLE
FOR DOUBLE BARREL SHOTGUNS (PRESS FIT)
Marble 214—Ivory front bead, 11/64" . . . **$3.55**; **215**—same with .080" rear bead and reamers . . . **$11.70. Marble 220**—Bi-color (gold and ivory) front bead, 11/64" and .080" rear bead, with reamers . . . **$13.50; Marble 221**—front bead only . . . **$5.15. Marble 223**—Ivory rear .080" . . . **$3.35. Marble 224**—Front sight reamer for 214-221 beads . . . **$2.55; Marble 226**—Rear sight reamer for 223. Price **$2.55**

MARBLE
FOR SINGLE OR DB SHOTGUNS (SCREW-ON FIT)
Marble 217—Ivory front bead 11/64" . . . **$3.90**; Marble 216 . . . **$8.00**; **Marble 218**—Bi-color front, 11/64" . . . **$5.60; Marble 219** . . . **$9.80; Marble 223T**—Ivory rear .080" Price **$5.30**
Marble Bradley type sights 223BT—1/8", 5/64" and 11/64" long. Gold, Ivory or Red bead **$3.15**

MILLETT SHURSHOT SHOTGUN SIGHT
A sight system for shotguns with a ventilated rib. Rear sight attaches to the rib, front sight replaces the front bead. Front has an orange face, rear has two orange bars. For 870, 1100, or other models.
Price: Front and rear **$15.95**
Price: Adjustable front and rear **$21.95**

POLY-CHOKE
Replacement front sights in four styles—Xpert, Poly Bead, Xpert Mid Rib sights, and Bev-L-Block. Xpert Front available in 3x56, 6x48 thread, 3/32" or 5/32" shank length, gold, ivory (**$4.35**); or Sun Spot orange bead (**$4.35**); Poly Bead is standard replacement 1/8" bead, 6x48 (**$2.20**); Xpert Mid Rib in tapered carrier (ivory only) or 3x56 threaded shank (gold only), **$3.35**; Hi and Lo Blok sights with 6x48 thread, gold or ivory (**$3.35**) or Sun Spot Orange (**$4.35**). From Marble Arms.

SLUG SIGHTS
Made of non-marring black nylon, front and rear sights stretch over and lock onto the barrel. Sights are low profile with blaze orange front blade. Adjustable for windage and elevation. For plain-barrel (non-ribbed) guns in 12, 16 and 20 gauge. From Innovision Ent.
Price: **$9.95**

WILLIAMS GUIDE BEAD SIGHT
Fits all shotguns, 1/8" ivory, red or gold bead. Screws into existing sight hole. Various thread sizes and shank lengths. Price **$4.50**

WILLIAMS SHOTGUN RAMP
Designed to elevate the front bead for slug shooting or for guns that shoot high. Diameters to fit most 12, 16, 20 ga. guns. Fastens by screw-clamp, no drilling required. Price, with Williams gold bead **$11.20**
Price: Without bead **$8.20**
Price: With Guide Bead **$12.70**

Sight Attachments

FREELAND LENS ADAPTER
Fits 1 1/8" O.D. prescription ground lens to all standard tube and receiver sights for shooting without glasses. Price without lens **$66.50**
Clear lens ground to prescription **$24.00**
Yellow or green prescription lens **$24.00**

MERIT IRIS SHUTTER DISC
Eleven clicks gives 12 different apertures. No. 3 Disc (**$50.00**) and Master, primarily target types, 0.22" to .125"; No. 4, 1/2" dia. hunting type, .025" to .155". Available for all popular sights. The Master Disc, with flexible rubber light shield, is particularly adapted to extension, scope height, and tang sights. All Merit Deluxe models have internal click springs; are hand fitted to minimum tolerance.
Master Deluxe **$60.00**
No. 4 Hunting Disc **$40.00**

MERIT LENS DISC
Similar to Merit Iris Shutter (Model 3 or Master) but incorporates provision for mounting prescription lens integrally. Lens may be obtained locally from your optician. Sight disc is 7/16" wide (Mod. 3), or 3/4" wide (Master). Model 3 Deluxe. Price **$63.00**
Master Deluxe **$74.00**

MERIT OPTICAL ATTACHMENT
For revolver and pistol shooters, instantly attached by rubber suction cup to regular or shooting glasses. Any aperture .020" to .156". Price, Deluxe (swings aside) **$60.00**

WILLIAMS APERTURES
Standard thread, fits most sights. Regular series 3/8" to 1/2" O.D., .050" to .125" hole. "Twilight" series has white reflector ring. .093" to .125" inner hole. Price, regular series . . . **$3.85**. Twilight series **$5.25**
Wide open 5/16" aperture for shotguns fits 5-D and Foolproof sights. Price **$6.80**

SCOPES & MOUNTS
HUNTING, TARGET ■ & VARMINT ■ SCOPES

Maker and Model	Magn.	Field at 100 Yds (feet)	Relative Brightness	Eye Relief (in.)	Length (in.)	Tube Diam. (in.)	W&E Adjustments	Weight (ozs.)	Price	Other Data
Action Arms										
Pro V[1]	0	—	—	—	5⅛	1	Int.	5.5	$195.00	Variable intensity LED red aiming dot. Average battery life up to 500 hours. Waterproof, nitrogen filled aluminum tube. Fits most standard 1″ rings. [1]Also available in Pro V 45° for left or right-side positioning of battery pack. Same price.
Inter Aims										
Mark V	0	—	—	—	5	1	Int.	6	189.00	Mark V for rifles, handguns, shotguns. Projects red dot aiming point. Dot size 1½″ @ 100 yds. Pro V intended for handguns. Dot size less than 1½″ @ 100 yds. Both waterproof. Battery life 50-10,000 hours. Imported by ADCO Int'l.
Pro V	0	—	—	—	4.5	1	Int.	3.9	229.00	
Aimpoint										
AP 1000[1]	0	—	—	—	6	—	Int.	7.8	159.95	Illuminates red dot in field of view. No parallax (dot does not need to be centered). Unlimited field of view and eye relief. On/off, adj. intensity. Dot covers 3″ @ 100 yds. Mounts avail. for all sights and scopes. [1]Clamps to Weaver-type bases. Available in blue (AP1000-B) or stainless (AP1000-S) finish. 3x scope attachment (for rifles only), $94.95. [2]Requires 1″ rings. Black or stainless finish. 3x scope attachment (for rifles only). $99.95. From Aimport. Made in Sweden.
Series 2000 Short[2]	0	—	—	—	5	1	Int.	5.3	209.95	
Series 2000 Long[2]	0	—	—	—	7.25	1	Int.	6	229.95	
Armson										
O.E.G.	0	—	—	—	5⅛	1	Int.	4.3	151.90	Shows red dot aiming point. No batteries needed. Standard model fits 1″ ring mounts (not incl.). Other models available for many popular shotguns, para-military rifles and carbines. Also available is a smaller model for rimfire rifles, with dovetail mount.
Armsport										
415	4	19	13.7	3.5	11.5	¾	Int.	6	22.00	[1]Duplex reticle. Crosshair reticle, $90. 4x20, $79, 4x32, $82 (Duplex). [2]Parallax adjustment. [3]For black powder rifles. Polished brass tube with mounts. 4x32 W.A., 4x40 W.A., 6x40 W.A. also avail. Contact Armsport for full details.
3720	3-7	22.5-9.5	43.5-8.1	2.4	11	¾	Int.	8.4	56.00	
2½x32	2.5	32	163.8	3.7	12	1	Int.	9.3	86.00	
4x40[1]	4	29	100	3.5	12.5	1	Int.	9	97.00	
6x32	6	17.8	28	3.2	12	1	Int.	9	86.00	
1.5-4.5x32	1.5-4.5	55.1-20.4	707.6-64	4-3.1	11.8	1	Int.	14.1	124.00	
2-7x32	2-7	50-19	81-22	3.1-2.9	12.2	1	Int.	13.8	124.00	
3-9x40	3-9	35.8-12.7	176.9-19.4	3.1-2.9	12.8	1	Int.	15.2	131.00	
4-12x40 WA[2]	4-12	31-11	36-10.9	2.9-2.8	14.7	1	Int.	16.4	245.00	
4x15 BP-1[3]	4	19	13	3.5	32	¾	Int.	44	110.00	
Bausch & Lomb										
2x Handgun	2	22.5	—	10-24	8.4	1	Int.	6.7	269.95	All except Target scopes have ¼-minute click adjustments; Target scopes have ⅛-minute adjustments with standard turrets and expanded turret knobs. Target scopes come with sunshades, screw-onlens caps. Contact Bushnell for details.
4x Handgun	4	25	—	10-20	8.4	1	Int.	7.0	289.95	
4x Balfor Compact	4	25	—	3.3	10.0	1	Int.	10.0	319.95	
1.5-6x	1.5-6	75-18	294-18.4	3.3	10.6	1	Int.	10.5	399.95	
2-8x Balvar Compact	2-8	51-13	—	3.5	10.0	1	Int.	11.5	419.95	
3-9x40	3-9	36-12	—	3.2	13.0	1	Int.	16.2	409.95	
2.5-10x Balvar	2.5-10	43.5-11	—	3.3	13.8	1	Int.	13	459.95	
6-24x Varmint	6-24	18-4.5	66.1-4.2	3.1	16.6	1	Int.	20.1	509.95	
■ 6x-24x Target	6-24	18-4.5	—	3.3	16.9	1	Int.	20.1	599.95	
■ 24x Target	24	4.7	—	3.2	15.2	1	Int.	15.7	599.95	
■ 36x Target	36	3.5	—	3.2	15.2	1	Int.	15.7	599.95	
Beeman										
Blue Ring 20[1]	1.5	14	150	11-16	8.3	¾	Int.	3.6	49.95	All scopes have 5-pt. reticle, all glass, fully coated lenses. [1]Pistol scope; cast mounts included. [2]Pistol scope; silhouette knobs. [3]Rubber armor coating; built-in double adj. mount, parallax-free setting. [4]Objective focus; built-in double-adj. mount; matte finish. [5]Objective focus. [6]Has 8 lenses; objective focus; milled mounts included. [7]Includes cast mounts. [8]Objective focus; silhouette knobs; matte finish. [9]Has 9 lenses. [10]Also in "L" models with reticle lighted by ambient light or tiny add-on illuminator. Lighted models slightly higher priced. Imported by Beeman.
Blue Ribbon 25[2]	2	19	150	10-24	9¹/₁₆	1	Int.	7.4	129.95	
SS-1[3]	2.5	30	61	3.25	5½	1	Int.	7	179.95	
SS-2[4,10]	3	34.5	74	3.5	6.8	1.38	Int.	13.6	225.00	
Blue Ribbon 50R[5]	2.5	33	245	3.5	12	1	Int.	11.8	169.98	
Blue Ring 35R[6]	3	25	67	2.5	11¼	¾	Int.	5.1	69.98	
30A[7]	4	21	21	2	10.2	¾	Int.	4.5	36.95	
Blue Ribbon 66R[8]	2-7	62-16	384-31	3	11.4	1	Int.	14.9	239.95	
Blue Ring 45R[9]	3-7	26-12	67-9	2.5	10⅝	¾	Int.	6	99.95	
Blue Ring 49R[5]	4	30	64	3	11.8	1	Int.	11.3	69.95	
MS-1	4	23	49	3.5	7.5	1	Int.	8	199.95	
SS-3[4]	1.5-4	44.6-24.6	172-24	3	5.75	⅞	Int.	8.5	250.00	
Blue Ribbon 67R[8]	3-9	435-15	265-29	3	14.4	1	Int.	15.2	349.00	
Blue Ribbon 68R[8]	4-12	30.5-11	150-13.5	3	14.4	1	Int.	15.2	379.95	
Blue Ribbon 54R[5]	4	29	96	3.5	12	1	Int.	12.3	169.98	
SS-2[4,10]	4	24.6	41	5	7	1.38	Int.	13.7	250.00	
29	4	21	21	2	10.2	¾	Int.	4.5	19.95	
Burris										
Fullfield										All scopes avail. in Plex reticle except Micro which has fine cross hair only. Steel-on-steel click adjustments. [1]Dot reticle $13 extra. [2]Post crosshair reticle $13 extra. [3]Matte satin finish $11 extra. [4]Available with parallax adjustment $28 extra (standard on 10x, 12x, 4-12x, 6-18x). [5]Silver Safari finish $20 extra. [6]Target knobs $20 extra. [7]Sunshade avail. [8]Avail. with Fine Plex reticle. LER = Long Eye Relief; IER = Intermediate Eye Relief; XER = Extra Eye Relief. From Burris.
1½x	1.6	62	—	3¼	10¼	1	Int.	9.0	178.95	
2½x	2.5	55	—	3¼	10¼	1	Int.	9.0	188.95	
4x[1,2,3]	3.75	36	—	3¼	11¼	1	Int.	11.5	198.95	
6x[1,3]	5.8	23	—	3¼	13	1	Int.	12.0	214.95	
10x[1,4,6,7,8]	9.8	12	—	3¼	15	1	Int.	15	262.95	
12x[1,4,6,7,8]	11.8	10.5	—	3¼	15	1	Int.	15	269.95	
1¾-5x[1,2]	1.7-4.6	66-25	—	3¼	10⅞	1	Int.	13	238.95	
2-7x[1,2,3]	2.5-6.8	47-18	—	3¼	12	1	Int.	14	263.95	
3-9x[1,2,3]	3.3-8.7	38-15	—	3¼	12⅝	1	Int.	15	278.95	
4-12x[1,4,8]	4.4-11.8	27-10	—	3¼	15	1	Int.	18	326.95	
6-18x[1,4,6,7,8]	6.5-17.6	16-7	—	3¼	15.8	1	Int.	18.5	338.95	
Mini Scopes										
4x[4,5]	3.6	24	—	3¾-5	8¼	1	Int.	7.8	156.95	

CAUTION: PRICES CHANGE. CHECK AT GUNSHOP.

HUNTING, TARGET ■ & VARMINT ■ SCOPES

Maker and Model	Magn.	Field at 100 Yds (feet)	Relative Brightness	Eye Relief (in.)	Length (in.)	Tube Diam. (in.)	W&E Adjustments	Weight (ozs.)	Price	Other Data
Burris (cont'd.)										
6x[1,4]	5.5	17	—	3¾-5	9	1	Int.	8.2	171.95	
2-7x	2.5-6.9	32-14	—	3¾-5	12	1	Int.	10.5	212.95	
3-9x[5]	3.6-8.8	25-11	—	3¾-5	12⅝	1	Int.	11.5	218.95	
4-12x[4]	4.5-11.6	19-8	—	3¾-4	15	1	Int.	15	289.95	
Handgun										
1½-4x LER[1,5]	1.6-3.8	16-11	—	11-25	10¼	1	Int.	11	253.95	
2½-7x LER[4,5]	2.7-6.7	12-7.5	—	11-28	12	1	Int.	12.5	262.95	
1x LER[1]	1.1	27	—	10-24	8¾	1	Int.	6.8	149.95	
2xLER[4,5,6]	1.7	21	—	10-24	8¾	1	Int.	6.8	155.95	
3x LER[4,6]	2.7	17	—	10-20	8⅞	1	Int.	6.8	168.95	
4x LER[1,4,5,6]	3.7	11	—	10-22	9⅝	1	Int.	9.0	175.95	
5x LER[1,4,6]	4.5	8.7	—	12-22	10⅞	1	Int.	9.2	189.95	
7x IER[1,4,5,6]	6.5	6.5	—	10-16	11¼	1	Int.	10	203.95	
10x IER[1,4,6]	9.5	4	—	8-12	13½	1	Int.	14	252.95	
2x Micro	1.7	15	—	7-24	9⅛	1	Int.	4	142.95	
3x Micro	2.7	17	—	8-22	9⅛	1	Int.	4	142.95	
Scout Scope										
1½x XER[3]	1.5	22	—	7-18	9	1	Int.	7.3	157.95	
2¾x XER[3]	2.7	15	—	7-14	9⅜	1	Int.	7.5	162.95	
Bushnell										
Armorlite 3-9x40	3-9	39-13	—	3.3	12	1	Int.	12.5	349.95	All ScopeChief, Banner and Custom models come with Multi-X reticle, with or without BDC (bullet drop compensator) that eliminates holdover. Prismatic Rangefinder (PRF) on some models. Contact Bushnell for data on full line. Prices include BDC—deduct $5 if not wanted. Add $30 for PRF. BDC feature available in all Banner models, except 2.5x. [1]4-times zoom ratio. [4]Has battery powered lighted reticle. Contact Bushnell for complete details.
Scope Chief VI	4	29	96	3½	12	1	Int.	9.3	153.95	
Scope Chief VI	3-9	35-12.6	267-30	3.3	12.6	1	Int.	14.3	241.95	
Scope Chief VI	3-9	39-13	241-26.5	3.3	12.1	1	Int.	13	301.95	
Scope Chief VI	2½-8	45-14	247-96	3.3	11.2	1	Int.	12.1	215.95	
Scope Chief VI	1½-4½	73.7-24.5	267-30	3.5-3.5	9.6	1	Int.	9.5	211.95	
Scope Chief VI	4-12	29-10	150-17	3.2	13.5	1	Int.	17	297.95	
Sportview Rangemaster 3-9x	3-9	38-12	—	3.5	11.75	1	Int.	10	111.95	
■ Sportview Rangemaster 4-12x	4-12	27-9	—	3.2	13.5	1	Int.	14	128.95	
Sportview Standard 4x	4	28	—	4	11.75	1	Int.	9.5	60.95	
Sportview Standard 3-9x	3-9	38-12	—	3.5	11.75	1	Int.	10	81.95	
Banner 22 Rimfire 4x	4	28	—	3	11.9	1	Int.	8	59.95	
Banner 22 Rimfire 3-7x	3-7	29-13	—	2.5	10	¾	Int.	6.5	67.95	
Banner 3-9x56	3-9	39-12.5	—	3.5	14.4	1	Int.	18.4	247.95	
Banner Lite-Site 1.5-6x	1.5-6	60-15	—	3.2	9.8	1	Int.	12.4	269.95	
Banner Lite-Site 3-9x	3-9	36-12	—	3.3	13.6	1	Int.	14	269.95	
Banner Trophy WA 1.75-5x	1.75-5	68.5-24.5	—	3.2	10.4	1	Int.	10.2	134.95	
Banner Trophy WA 4x	4	34.2	—	3.4	12.4	1	Int.	11.9	121.95	
Banner Trophy WA 3-9x	3-9	39-13	—	3.3	11.8	1	Int.	12.9	139.95	
Banner Shotgun 2.5x	2.5	45	—	3.5	10.9	1	Int.	8	79.95	
Banner Standard 4x	4	29	—	3.5	12	1	Int.	10	115.95	
Banner Standard 6x	6	19.5	—	3	13.5	1	Int.	11.5	143.95	
Banner Standard 3-9x	3-9	43-14	—	3	12.1	1	Int.	14	135.95	
Banner Standard 4-12x	4-12	29-10	—	3.2	13.5	1	Int.	15.5	209.95	
Charles Daly										
4x32	4	28	—	3.25	11.75	1	Int.	9.5	65.00	[1]For shotgun use. [2]Pistol scopes. From Outdoor Sports Headquarters.
4x40 WA	4	36	—	3.25	13	1	Int.	11.5	95.00	
6x40 WA	6	23	—	3	12.75	1	Int.	15	100.00	
2.5x32	2.5	47	—	3	12.25	1	Int.	10	75.00	
2-7x32 WA	2-7	56-17	—	3	11.5	1	Int.	12	119.00	
3-9x40	3-9	35-14	—	3	12.5	1	Int.	11.25	77.00	
3-9x40 WA	3-9	36-13	—	3	12.75	1	Int.	12.5	115.00	
4-16x40	4-16	25-7	—	3	14.25	1	Int.	16.75	130.00	
1-3.5x20[1]	1-3.5	91-31	—	3	9.75	1	Int.	16.25	158.00	
2x20[2]	2	16	—	16-25	8.75	1	Int.	6.5	105.00	
4x28[2]	4	6.5	—	16-25	9.3	1	Int.	8	105.00	
aus Jena										
ZF4x32-M	4	32	—	3.5	10.8	26mm	Int.	10	320.00	Fixed power scopes have 26mm alloy tubes, variables, 30mm alloy; rings avail. from importer. Also avail. with rail mount. Multi-coated lenses. Waterproof and fogproof. ⅓-min. clicks. Choice of nine reticles. Imported from W. Germany by Europtik, Ltd.
ZF6x42-M	6	22	—	3.5	12.6	26mm	Int.	13	355.00	
ZF8x56-M	8	17	—	3.5	14	26mm	Int.	17	415.00	
YZF1.5-6x42-M	1.5-6	67.8-22	—	3.5	12.6	30mm	Int.	14	535.00	
VZF3-12x56-M	3-12	30-11	—	3.5	15	30mm	Int.	18	595.00	
Kahles										
2.5 x 20[1]	2.5	61	—	3.25	9.6	1	Int.	12.7	450.00	[1]Steel only. [2]Lightweight model weighs 11 oz. [3]Aluminum only. [4]Lightweight model weighs 16 oz. [5]Lightweight model weighs 12.7 oz. [6]Lightweight model weighs 16 oz. [7]Lightweight model weighs 15.5 oz. [8]Lightweight model weighs 18 oz. Lightweight models priced slightly higher. Imported by Swarovski America, Ltd.
4 x 32[2]	4	33	—	3.25	11.3	1	Int.	15	465.00	
7 x 56[3]	7	20	—	3.25	14.4	1	Int.	16	610.00	
8 x 56[4]	8	17.1	—	3.25	14.4	1	Int.	23	595.00	
1.4-4.5 x 20[5]	1.1-4.5	79-29.5	—	3.25	10.5	30mm	Int.	15	560.00	
1.5-6 x 42[6]	1.5-6	61-21	—	3.25	12.6	30mm	Int.	20	625.00	
2.2-9 x 42[7]	2.2-9	39.5-15	—	3.25	13.3	30mm	Int.	20.4	765.00	
3-12 x 56[8]	3-12	30-11	—	3.25	15.25	30mm	Int.	25	835.00	
K-ZF84 (6x42)	6	23	—	3.25	15.5	1	Int.	17.5	860.00	
Kilham										
Hutson Handgunner II	1.7	8	—	—	5½	⅞	Int.	5.1	119.95	Unlimited eye relief; internal click adjustments; crosshair reticle. Fits Thompson/Center rail mounts, for S&W K, N, Ruger Blackhawk, Super, Super Single-Six, Contender
Hutson Handgunner	3	8	—	10-12	6	⅞	Int.	5.3	119.95	

HUNTING, TARGET & VARMINT SCOPES

Maker and Model	Magn.	Field at 100 Yds (feet)	Relative Brightness	Eye Relief (in.)	Length (in.)	Tube Diam. (in.)	W&E Adjustments	Weight (ozs.)	Price	Other Data
Laserscope										
FA-6	—	—	—	—	6.2	—	Int.	11	399.00	Projects high intensity beam of laser light onto target as an aiming point. Adj. for w. & e. FA-6 uses two 9V, others use eight AA batteries. Come with rings, switch, fastener. From Laser Devices, Inc.
FA-9	—	—	—	—	12	—	Int.	16	449.00	
FA-9P	—	—	—	—	9	—	Int.	14	449.00	
Lasersight										
LS45	0	—	—	—	7.5	—	Int.	8.5	459.95	Projects a highly visible beam of concentrated laser light onto the target. Adjustable for w. & e. Visible up to 500 yds. at night. For handguns, rifles, shotguns. Uses two standard 9V batteries. From Imatronic Lasersight.
Leatherwood										
ART II	3.0-8.8	31-12	—	3.5	13.9	1	Int.	42	750.00	Compensates for bullet drop via external circular cam. Matte gray finish. Designed specifically for the M1A/M-14 rifle. Quick Detachable model for rifles with Weaver-type bases. From North American Specialties.
Leupold										
M8-2X EER[1]	1.8	22.0	—	12-24	8.1	1	Int.	6.8	184.80	Constantly centered reticles, choice of Duplex, tapered CPC, Leupold Dot, Crosshair and Dot. CPC and Dot reticles extra. [1]2x and 4x scope have from 12"-24" of eye relief and are suitable for handguns, top ejection arms and muzzleloaders. [2]3x9 Compact, 6x Compact, 12x, 3x9, 3.5x10 and 6.5x20 come with Adjustable Objective. [3]Target scopes have 1-min divisions with ¼ min clicks, and Adjustable Objectives. 50-ft. Focus Adaptor available for indoor target ranges, **$44.80**. Sunshade available for all Adjustable Objective scopes, **$13.05**. [4]Also available in matte finish for about **$20.00** extra. [5]Dot or Duplex; focused at 300 yds. with A.O. **$368.40**.
M8-2X EER Silver[1]	1.8	22.0	—	12-24	8.1	1	Int.	6.8	202.70	
M8-4X EER[1]	3.5	9.5	—	12-24	8.4	1	Int.	7.6	225.65	
M8-4X EER Silver[1]	3.5	9.5	—	12-24	8.4	1	Int.	8.5	243.50	
M8-2.5X Compact	2.3	42	—	4.3	8.5	1	Int.	7.4	203.50	
M8-4X Compact	3.6	26.5	—	4.1	10.3	1	Int.	8.5	232.40	
2-7x Compact	2.5-6.6	41.7-16.5	—	3.8-3.0	9.9	1	Int.	8.5	293.15	
6x Compact & A.O.	5.7	16	—	3.9	10.7	1	Int.	8.5	276.95	
3-9x Compact & A.O.	3.2-8.5	34.5-13.5	—	3.8-3.1	11	1	Int.	9.5	355.90	
M8-4X[4]	3.6	28	—	4.4	11.4	1	Int.	8.8	253.40	
M8-6X	5.9	18.0	—	4.3	11.4	1	Int.	9.9	248.15	
M8-8X[2]	7.8	14.5	—	4.0	12.5	1	Int.	13.0	330.90	
M8-8x36[5]	7.7	14	—	3.7	11.8	1	Int.	10	330.90	
M8-12X[2]	11.6	9.2	—	4.2	13.0	1	Int.	13.5	335.30	
6.5 x 20 Target AO	6.5-19.2	14.8-5.7	—	5.3-3.7	14.2	1	Int.	16	542.95	
M8-12X Target[3]	11.6	9.2	—	4.2	13.0	1	Int.	14.5	408.85	
M8-24X[3]	24.0	4.7	—	3.2	13.6	1	Int.	14.5	542.95	
M8-36X[3]	36.0	3.2	—	3.4	13.9	1	Int.	15.5	542.95	
Vari-X-II 1X4	1.5-3.9	70.5-29.5	—	5.5	9.1	1	Int.	8.5	250.80	
Vari-X-II 2X7	2.5-6.6	44.0-19.0	—	4.1-3.7	10.7	1	Int.	10.4	301.90	
Vari-X-II 3X9[1,4]	3.5-9.0	32.0-13.5	—	4.1-3.7	12.3	1	Int.	14.5	324.30	
Vari-X-III 1.5X5	1.5-4.6	66.0-24.0	—	4.7-3.5	9.4	1	Int.	9.3	344.20	
Vari-X-III 2.5X8[4]	2.7-7.9	38.0-14.0	—	4.2-3.4	11.3	1	Int.	11.0	388.20	
Vari-X-III 3.5X10	3.4-9.9	29.5-10.5	—	4.6-3.6	12.4	1	Int.	13.0	406.10	
Vari-X-III 3.5X10[2]	3.4-9.9	29.5-10.5	—	4.6-3.6	12.4	1	Int.	14.4	443.60	
Vari-X-III 6.5X20[2]	6.5-19.2	14.8- 5.7	—	5.3-3.7	14.2	1	Int.	16	481.00	
Mirador										
RXW 4x40[1]	4	37	—	3.8	12.4	1	Int.	12	161.95	[1]Wide Angle scope. Multi-coated objective lens. Nitrogen filled; waterproof; shockproof. From Mirador Optical Corp.
RXW 1.5-5x20[1]	1.5-5	46-17.4	—	4.3	11.1	1	Int.	10	170.95	
RXW 3-9x40	3-9	43-14.5	—	3.1	12.9	1	Int.	13.4	224.95	
Nikon										
4x40	4	26	—	3.4	11.6	1	Int.	13.5	234.00	Multi-coated lenses; ¼-minute windage and elevation adjustments; nitrogen filled; waterproof. From Nikon Inc.
1.5-4.5x20	1.5-4.5	67.5-22.5	—	3.7	10	1	Int.	11.8	300.00	
2-7x32	2-7	43-12	—	4.1	11.4	1	Int.	12.3	343.00	
3-9x40	3-9	34.5-11.5	—	3.5-3.4	12.3	1	Int.	16	377.00	
Pentax										
4x	4	35	—	3¼	11.6	1	Int.	12.2	220.00	Multi-coated lenses, fog-proof, water-proof, nitrogen filled. Penta-Plex reticle. Click ¼-m.o.a. adjustments. Matte finish $5.00 extra. Imported by Pentax Corp.
6x	6	20	—	3¼	13.4	1	Int.	13.5	250.00	
2-7x	2-7	42.5-17	—	3-3¼	12	1	Int.	14	300.00	
3-9x	3-9	33-13.5	—	3-3¼	13	1	Int.	15	320.00	
3-9x Mini	3-9	26.5-10.5	—	3¾	10.4	1	Int.	13	270.00	
RWS										
100S	4	—	—	8	10½	¾		7	47.00	Air gun scopes. All have Dyna-Plex reticle. Imported from Japan by Dynamit Nobel of America.
150S	3-7	—	—	8	10½	¾		8	60.00	
200S	4	—	—	8	11¾	⅞		11½	70.00	
250S	3-7	—	—	8	11¾	⅞		12	80.00	
300	4	—	—	8	12¾	1		11	110.00	
350	4	—	—	8	10	1		10	95.00	
400	2-7	—	—	8	12¾	1		12	150.00	
800	1.5	—	—	28	8¾	1		6	100.00	
CS-10	2.5	—	—	8	5¾	1		7	100.00	
Redfield										
Ultimate Illuminator 3-12x[6]	2.9-11.7	27-10.5	—	3-3½	15.4	30mm	Int.	23	714.95	*Accutrac feature avail. on these scopes at extra cost. Traditionals have round lenses. 4-Plex reticle is standard. [1]"Magnum Proof." Specially designed for magnum and auto pistols. Uses "Double Dovetail" mounts. Also in brushed aluminum finish, 2½x **$211.95**, 4x **$222.95**. [2]With matte finish **$468.95**. [3]Also available with matte finish at extra cost. [4]All Golden Five Star scopes come with Butler Creek flip-up lens covers. [5]Black anodized finish. [6]56mm adj. objective; European #4 reticle; comes with 30mm steel rings with Rotary Dovetail System, hardwood box. ¼-min. click adj.
Illuminator Trad. 3-9x	2.9-8.7	33-11	—	3½	12¾	1	Int.	17	414.95	
Illuminator Widefield 3-9x[*2]	2.9-8.7	38-13	—	3½	12¾	1	Int.	17	459.95	
Tracker 4x[3]	3.9	28.9	—	3½	11.02	1	Int.	9.8	134.95	
Tracker 2-7x[3]	2.3-6.9	36.6-12.2	—	3½	12.20	1	Int.	11.6	172.95	
Tracker 3-9x[3]	3.0-9.0	34.4-11.3	—	3½	14.96	1	Int.	13.4	192.95	
Traditional 4x¾"	4	24½	27	3½	9⅜	¾	Int.	—	125.95	
Traditional 2½x	2½	43	64	3½	10¼	1	Int.	8½	161.95	
Golden Five Star 4x[4]	4	28.5	58	3.75	11.3	1	Int.	9.75	187.95	
Golden Five Star 6x[4]	6	18	40	3.75	12.2	1	Int.	11.5	206.95	
Golden Five Star 2-7x[4]	2.4-7.4	42-14	207-23	3-3.75	11.25	1	Int.	12	244.95	
Golden Five Star 3-9x[4]	3.0-9.1	34-11	163-18	3-3.75	12.50	1	Int.	13	262.95	
Golden Five Star 4-12xA.O.*[4]	3.9-11.4	27-9	112-14	3-3.75	13.8	1	Int.	16	337.95	

CAUTION: PRICES CHANGE. CHECK AT GUNSHOP.

HUNTING, TARGET & VARMINT SCOPES

Maker and Model	Magn.	Field at 100 Yds (feet)	Relative Brightness	Eye Relief (in.)	Length (in.)	Tube Diam. (in.)	W&E Adjustments	Weight (ozs.)	Price	Other Data
Redfield, (cont'd.)										
Golden Five Star 6-18xA.O.*[4]	6.1-18.1	18.6	50-6	3-3.75	14.3	1	Int.	18	357.95	
Compact Scopes										
Golden Five Star Compact 4x	3.8	28	—	3.5	9.75	1	Int.	8.8	184.95	
Golden Five Star Compact 6x	6.3	17.6	—	3.5	10.70	1	Int.	9.5	204.95	
Golden Five Star Compact 2-7x	2.4-7.1	40-16	—	3-3.5	9.75	1	Int.	9.8	241.95	
Golden Five Star Compact 3-9x	3.3-9.1	32-11.25	—	3-3.5	10.7	1	Int.	10.5	258.95	
Golden Five Star Compact 4-12x	4.1-12.4	22.4-8.3	—	3-3.5	12	1	Int.	13	326.95	
Pistol Scopes										
2½xMP[1]	2.5	9	64	14-19	9.8	1	Int.	10.5	192.95	
4xMP[1]	3.6	9	—	12-22	9¹¹⁄₁₆	1	Int.	11.1	205.95	
Golden Five Star 1-4x	1.3-4.0	80-26	—	3-3.75	9.50	1	Int.	10.25	234.95	
2-6x[5]	2-5.5	25-7	—	10-18	10.4	1	Int.	11	250.95	
Widefield Low Profile Compact										
Widefield 4xLP Compact	3.7	33	—	3.5	9.35	1	Int.	10	227.95	
Widefield 3-9x LP Compact	3.3-9	37.0-13.7	—	3-3.5	10.20	1	Int.	13	291.95	
Low Profile Scopes										
Widefield 2¾xLP	2¾	55½	69	3½	10½	1	Int.	8	214.95	
Widefield 4xLP	3.6	37½	84	3½	11½	1	Int.	10	239.95	
Widefield 6xLP	5.5	23	—	3½	12¾	1	Int.	11	261.95	
Widefield 1¾x5xLP	1¾-5	70-27	136-21	3½	10¾	1	Int.	11½	294.95	
Widefield 2x7xLP*	2-7	49-19	144-21	3½	11¾	1	Int.	13	304.95	
Widefield 3x-9xLP*	3-9	39-15	112-18	3½	12½	1	Int.	14	335.95	
Schmidt & Bender										[1]All steel. [2]Black chrome finish. [3]For silhouette and varmint shooting. Choice of nine reticles. 30-year warranty. All have ⅓-min. click adjustments, centered reticles, nitrogen filling. Most models avail. in aluminum with mounting rail. Imported from West Germany by Paul Jaeger, Inc.
Vari-M 1¼-4x20[1]	1¼-4	96-16	—	3¼	10.4	30mm	Int.	12.3	525.00	
Vari-M 1½-6x42	1½-6	60-19.5	—	3¼	12.2	30mm	Int.	17.5	550.00	
Vari-M 2½-10x56	2½-10	37.5-12	—	3¼	14.6	30mm	Int.	21.9	675.00	
All Steel 1½x15[2]	1½	90	—	3¼	10	1	Int.	11.8	399.00	
All Steel 4x36[2]	4	30	—	3¼	11.4	1	Int.	14	429.00	
All Steel 6x42[2]	6	21	—	3¼	13.2	1	Int.	17.3	429.00	
All Steel 8x56[2]	8	16.5	—	3¼	14.8	1	Int.	21.9	499.00	
■ All Steel 12x42[3]	12	16.5	—	3¼	13	1	Int.	17.9	429.00	
Shepherd										[1]Also avail. as 310-MOA, 310-1, 310-E ($376.00) with ultra fine crosshair. [2]Also avail. as Model 27-4 for rimfires ($345.00). Reticle patterns set for shooter's choice of ballistics. Dual reticle system with instant range finder, bullet drop compensator. Waterproof, nitrogen filled, shock-proof. From Shepherd Scope Ltd.
3940-E	3-9	43.5-15	178-20	3.3	13	1	Int.	17	444.00	
310-2[1]	3-10	35.3-11.6	178-16	3-3.75	12.8	1	Int.	18	376.00	
27-2[2]	2.5-7.5	42-14	164-18	2.5-3	11.6	1	Int.	16.3	349.00	
Simmons										[1]With ring mount. [2]With ring mount. [3]With rings. [4]3-9x32; also avail. 3-9x40 as #1038. [5]Avail. in brushed aluminum finish as #1052. [6]Avail. with silhouette knobs as #1085, in brushed aluminum as #1088. [7]½-min. dot or Truplex; Truplex reticle also avail. with dot. Sunshade, screw-in lens covers. Parallax adj.; Silhouette knobs; graduated drums. [8]"Simcoat" multi-coating on all lenses, 44mm obj. lens, high-gloss finish, parallax adj., polarized and yellow screw-in filters, ¼-min. click adj., leather lens covers incl. M1045—Presidential Ranger Gold Medal also avail. in 4-12x ($348.75), 6.5-20x ($390.00). M1044 has 44mm obj., Simcoat. M1086 Silver Medal pistol scope. Also in 2-6x, 2x20, 4x32. M1013 Silver Series "Quad." Also avail. 3-12x, 4-16x, 6-24x. Truplex reticle in all models. All scopes sealed, fog-proof, with constantly centered reticles. Imported from Japan by Simmons Outdoor Corp. **Partial listing.** Contact Simmons for complete details. Prices are approximate.
1002 Rimfire[1]	4	23	—	3	11.5	¾	Int.	6	9.95	
1004 Rimfire[2]	3-7	22.5-9.5	—	3	11	¾	Int.	8.4	31.50	
1007 Rimfire[3]	4	25	—	3	10	1	Int.	9	84.75	
1005 Waterproof	2½	46	—	3	11.5	1	Int.	9.3	72.00	
1013	1-4	63.1-15.7	—	3.5	9.8	1	Int.	8.8	119.25	
1025 W.A.	6	24.5	—	3	12.4	1	Int.	12	111.25	
1026 W.A.	1½-4½	86-28.9	—	3-3¼	10.6	1	Int.	13.2	123.75	
1027 W.A.	2-7	54.6-18.3	—	3-3¼	12	1	Int.	12.8	123.75	
1044 WA	3-10	36.2-10.5	—	3.9-3.3	13.1	1	Int.	16.3	198.75	
1036 Mono Tube[4]	3-9	42-14	—	3-3¼	13.3	1	Int.	13	191.25	
1040 Mono Tube	2-7	54-18	—	3-3¼	13.1	1	Int.	12.9	187.50	
1045	3-9	42-14	—	4-3.3	13.0	1	Int.	16.3	348.75	
1050 Compact[5]	4	22	—	3	9	1	Int.	9.1	150.00	
1054 Compact	3-9	40-14	—	3-3¼	10.5	1	Int.	10.5	195.00	
1074	6½-20	18-6	—	3	15	1	Int.	16	247.50	
1075	6½-10	22-12	—	3	15	1	Int.	16	247.50	
1076[7]	15	8	—	3	15	1	Int.	16	195.00	
1078[7]	24	6	—	3	15	1	Int.	16	202.50	
1073 Sil. Airgun	2-7	54.6-18.3	—	3-3¼	12.1	1	Int.	15.7	165.00	
1080 Handgun	2	18	—	10-20	7.1	1	Int.	8.1	105.00	
1084 Handgun[6]	4	9	—	10-20	8.7	1	Int.	9.5	150.00	
1086 Handgun	1-3	37.2-12.1	—	13-27	10.7	1	Int.	10.5	240.00	
1087 Handgun	2-6	16-6	—	13-27	11	1	Int.	10.8	281.25	
1090 Shotgun	1.5	49.9	—	5	6.8	1	Int.	7.0	117.00	
21005 Shotgun	2.5	29	—	4.6	7.1	1	Int.	7.1	52.50	
Gold Medal Series										
1067[8]	3-9	42-14	216-54	3.3	13	1	Int.	16.2	330.00	
1068[8]	4-12	31-11	121-14	3.9-3.2	14.2	1	Int.	19.1	337.00	
Swarovski Habicht										All models offered in either steel or lightweight alloy tubes except 1.5x20, ZFM 6x42 and Cobras. Weights shown are for lightweight versions. Choice of nine constantly centered reticles. Eyepiece recoil mechanism and rubber ring shield to protect face. Cobra and ZFM also available in NATO Stanag 2324 mounts. Imported by Swarovski America Ltd.
Nova 1.5x20	1.5	61	—	3¼	9.6	1	Int.	12.7	470.00	
Nova 4x32	4	33	—	3¼	11.3	1	Int.	15	500.00	
Nova 6x42	6	23	—	3¼	12.6	1	Int.	17.9	540.00	
Nova 8x56	8	17	—	3¼	14.4	1	Int.	23	635.00	
Nova 1.5 6x42	1.5-6	61-21	—	3¼	12.6	1	Int.	16	685.00	
Nova 2.2-9x42	2.2-9	39.5-15	—	3¼	13.3	1	Int.	15.5	835.00	
Nova 3-12x56	3-12	30-11	—	3¼	15.25	1	Int.	18	910.00	

CAUTION: PRICES CHANGE. CHECK AT GUNSHOP.

HUNTING, TARGET ■ & VARMINT ■ SCOPES

Maker and Model	Magn.	Field at 100 Yds (feet)	Relative Bright-ness	Eye Relief (in.)	Length (in.)	Tube Diam. (in.)	W&E Adjust-ments	Weight (ozs.)	Price	Other Data
Swarovski, (cont'd.)										
ZFM 6x42	6	23	—	3¼	12.5	1	Int.	18	**710.00**	
Cobra 1.5-14	1.5	50	—	3.9	7.87	1	Int.	10	**550.00**	
A-Line Scopes										
4x32A	4	30	—	3.2	11.5	1	Int.	10.8	**450.00**	
6x36A	6	21	—	3.2	11.9	1	Int.	11.5	**500.00**	
3-9x36A	3-9	39-13.5	—	3.3	11.9	1	Int.	13	**655.00**	
Swift										
600 4x15	4	16.2	—	2.4	11	¾	Int.	4.7	**14.00**	All Swift Mark I scopes, with the exception of the 4x15, have Quadraplex reticles and are fog-proof and waterproof. The 4x15 has crosshair reticle and is non-waterproof.
650 4x32	4	29	—	3½	12	1	Int.	9	**53.50**	
653 4x40 WA	4	35½	—	3¾	12¼	1	Int.	12	**63.00**	
654 3-9x32	3-9	35¾-12¾	—	3	12¾	1	Int.	13¾	**64.00**	
656 3-9x40 WA	3-9	42½-13½	—	2¾	12¾	1	Int.	14	**78.00**	
657 6x40	6	18	—	3¾	13	1	Int.	10	**72.00**	
Tasco										
WA 1x20 Wide Angle[1,3]	1	97	400.0	3	9¾	1	Int.	9.5	**199.95**	[1]Water, fog & shockproof; fully coated optics; ¼-min. click stops; haze filter caps; lifetime warranty. [2]30/30 range finding reticle. [3]World Class Wide Angle; Supercon multi-coated optics; Opti-Centered[R] 30/30 rangefinding reticle; lifetime warranty. [4]Shock-absorbing 30mm tubes; 44 and 52mm objective lenses; Opti-Centered[R] 30/30 rangefinding reticle. [5]Selective Bi-reticle display—converts from 30/30 to lighted post reticle. [6]Illuminated Opti-Centered Post Reticle. [7]⅓ greater zoom range. [8]Trajectory compensating scopes, Opti-Centered stadia reticle. [9]Anodized finish. [10]True one-power scope. [11]Coated optics; cross hair reticle; ring mounts included to fit most 22, 10mm receivers. [12]Fits Remington 870, 1100.
WA 1-3.5x20 Wide Angle[1,3,10]	1-3½	115-31	400.0-32.4	3½	9¾	1	Int.	10.2	**219.95**	
WA 4x40 Wide Angle[1,3]	4	36	100.0	3¼	13	1	Int.	11.5	**129.85**	
WA 3-9x40 Wide Angle[1,3]	3-9	43½-15	176.8-19.3	3⅛	12¾	1	Int.	12.5	**159.85**	
WA 2.5x32 Wide Angle[1,3]	2½	47	163.8	3	12⅛	1	Int.	10	**159.95**	
WA 2-7x32 Wide Angle[1,3]	2-7	56-17	256.0-20.2	3¼	11½	1	Int.	12	**159.95**	
WA 1.75-5x20 Wide Angle[1,3]	1¾-5	72-24	129.9-16.0	3	10⅝	1	Int.	9.8	**199.95**	
EU 4x44[1,2,4]	4	29	121.0	3	12⅜	30mm	Int.	16	**299.95**	
EU 6x44[1,2,4]	6	20	53.2	3	12⅜	30mm	Int.	16	**299.95**	
EU 39x44[1,2,4]	3-9	37½-14	213.1-23.0	3	12⅛	30mm	Int.	18.5	**319.95**	
EUI 39x44 (SBD)[1,4,5]	3-9	37½-13	213.1-23.0	3¼	12⅝	30mm	Int.	18.5	**599.95**	
EU 3-12x52[1,2,4]	3-12	33-8½	299.2-18.4	3	12¼	30mm	Int.	18.5	**349.95**	
IR 3-9x40 WA[1,3,6]	3-9	40-15	176.8-19.3	3	12¾	1	Int.	14.8	**399.95**	
W 3-12x40 MAG-IV[1,2,7]	3-12	33-11	176.8-10.8	3	12⅛	1	Int.	12	**129.95**	
W 4-16x40 MAG-IV[1,2,7]	4-16	25½-7	100.0-6.2	3	14¼	1	Int.	16.75	**169.95**	
TR 3-12x32[1,2]	3-12	34-9	112.3-6.7	3	12¾	1	Int.	12	**179.95**	
TR 4-16x40[1,2]	4-16	25½-7	100.0-6.2	3	14¼	1	Int.	16.75	**249.95**	
W 4x32[1,2,9]	4	28	64.0	3	11¾	1	Int.	9.5	**59.95**	
SW 4x32[1,2,9]	4	24½	256.0	4	9⅞	1	Int.	9.1	**119.95**	
W 3-9x32[1,2,9]	3-9	35-14	112.3-12.2	3¼	12¾	1	Int.	12.3	**79.95**	
P1x22	1	65-24	—	8-28	7¾	1	Int.	8	**199.95**	
P2x22	2	26-18	—	10-24	7¾	1	Int.	7.6	**199.95**	
P4x30	4	7-6	—	12-24	9¾	1	Int.	12.1	**259.95**	
P6x40	6	5-5½	—	12-23	11	1	Int.	14.2	**349.95**	
RF 4x15[11]	4	21	13.6	2½	11	¾	Int.	4	**14.95**	
RF 4x20DS[11]	4	20	25.0	2½	10½	¾	Int.	3.8	**23.95**	
SG 2.5x32 with Shotgun Mount[1,12]	2½	42	163.8	3¼	11¾	1	Int.	15.7	**129.95**	
Thompson/Center										
Lobo 1½ x[1]	1.5	16	127	11-20	7¾	⅞	Int.	5	**115.00**	[1]May be used on light to medium recoil guns, including muzzleloaders. Coated lenses, nitrogen filled, lifetime warranty. [2]For heavy recoil guns. Nitrogen filled. Duplex reticle only. Target turrets avail. on 1½x, 3x models. Electra Dot illuminated reticle available in RP 2½x ($40 extra) and RP 3x ($45 extra). [3] Rifle scopes have Electra Dot reticle. [4]Rail model for grooved receivers also available—**$195.00.** With Electra Dot reticle. Silver finish 3x RP Electra Dot **$205.00.**
Lobo 3x[1]	3	9	49	11-20	9	⅞	Int.	6.3	**120.00**	
RP 1½ x[2]	1.5	28	177	11-20	7½	1	Int.	5.1	**150.00**	
RP 2½x[2]	2.5	15	64	11-20	8½	1	Int.	6.5	**150.00**	
RP 3x[2]	3	13	44	11-20	8¾	1	Int.	5.4	**150.00**	
RP 4x[2]	4	10	71	12-20	9¼	1	Int.	10.4	**170.00**	
TC 4x Rifle[3]	4	29	64	3.3	12⅞	1	Int.	12.3	**200.00**	
TC 3/9V Rifle[3]	3-9	35.3-13.2	177-19	3.3	12⅞	1	Int.	15.5	**275.00**	
Short Tube 8630[4]	4	29	20	3	7¾	1	Int.	10.1	**190.00**	
Trijicon Spectrum										
4x40[1]	4	38	—	3.0	12.2	1	Int.	15.0	**289.00**	[1]Self-luminous low-light reticle glows in poor light; allows choice of red, amber or green via a selector ring on objective end. [2]Advanced Combat Optical Gunsight for AR-15, M-16, with integral mount. [3]Reticle glows only red in poor light. From Armson, Inc.
6x56[1]	6	24	—	3.0	14.1	1	Int.	20.3	**389.00**	
1-3x20[1]	1-3	94-33	—	3.7-4.9	9.6	1	Int.	13.2	**354.00**	
3-9x40[1]	3-9	35-14	—	3.3-3.0	13.1	1	Int.	16.0	**364.00**	
3-9x56[1]	3-9	35-14	—	3.3-3.0	14.2	1	Int.	21.5	**464.00**	
ACOG[2]	4	37	—	1.5	5.8	—	Int.	9.7	**595.00**	
4x32 Red[3]	4	29	—	3.3	11.6	1	Int.	10.2	**198.00**	
Unertl										
■ 1″ Target	6,8,10	16-10	17.6-6.25	2	21½	¾	Ext.	21	**181.00**	[1]Dural ¼ MOA click mounts. Hard coated lenses. Non-rotating objective lens focusing. [2]¼ MOA click mounts. [3]With target mounts. [4]With calibrated head. [5]Same as 1″ Target but without objective lens focusing. [6]Price with ¼ MOA click mounts. [7]With new Posa mounts. [8]Range focus until near rear of tube. Price is with Posa mounts. Magnum clamp. With standard mounts and clamp ring **$332.00.**
■ 1¼″ Target[1]	8,10,12,14	12-16	15.2-5	2	25	¾	Ext.	21	**244.00**	
■ 1½″ Target	8,10,12,14 16,18,20	11.5-3.2	—	2¼	25½	¾	Ext.	31	**275.00**	
■ 2″ Target[2]	8,10,12, 14,16,18, 24,30,36	8	22.6-2.5	2¼	26¼	1	Ext.	44	**375.00**	
■ Varmint, 1¼∞[3]	6,8,10,12	1-7	28-7.1	2½	19½	⅞	Ext.	26	**242.00**	
■ Ultra Varmint, 2″[4]	8,10 12,15	12.6-7	39.7-11	2½	24	1	Ext.	34	**351.00**	
Unertl										
■ Small Game[5]	4,6	25-17	19.4-8.4	2¼	18	¾	Ext.	16	**138.00**	
■ Vulture[6]	8 10	11.2 10.9	29 18½	3-4 —	15⅝ 16⅛	1	Ext.	15½	**270.00**	
■ Programmer 200[7]	8,10,12 14,16,18, 20,24,30,36	11.3-4	39-1.9	—	26½	1	Ext.	45	**465.00**	
■ BV-20[8]	20	8	4.4	4.4	17⅞	1	Ext.	21¼	**332.00**	

CAUTION: PRICES CHANGE. CHECK AT GUNSHOP.

HUNTING, TARGET ■ & VARMINT ■ SCOPES

Maker and Model	Magn.	Field at 100 Yds (feet)	Relative Brightness	Eye Relief (in.)	Length (in.)	Tube Diam. (in.)	W&E Adjustments	Weight (ozs.)	Price	Other Data
Weatherby										
Mark XXII	4	25	50	2.5-3.5	11¾	⅞	Int.	9.25	105.00	Lumiplex reticle in all models. Blue-black, non-glare finish.
Supreme 1¾-5x20	1.7-5	66.6-21.4	—	3.4	10.7	1	Int.	11	260.00	
Supreme 2-7x34	2.1-6.8	59-16	—	3.4	11¼	1	Int.	10.4	270.00	
Supreme 4x44	3.9	32	—	3	12½	1	Int.	11.6	270.00	
Supreme 3-9x44	3.1-8.9	36-13	—	3.5	12.7	1	Int.	11.6	320.00	
Weaver										
K2.5	2.5	35	—	3.7	10.2	1	Int.	8.5	144.44	Micro-Trac adjustment system with ¼-min. clicks on K2.5, K4, V3, V9, V10, RK4, RV7; ⅛-min. clicks on K6, KT15. All have Dual-X reticle. One-piece aluminum tube, gloss finish, nitrogen filled, multi-coated lenses, waterproof. From Weaver.
K4	4	30	—	3.3	11.8	1	Int.	10.8	177.78	
K6	6	20	—	3.6	13	1	Int.	11.2	188.89	
V3	1-3	95-35	—	3.9-3.7	9.5	1	Int.	9.5	200.00	
V9	2.9-8.7	37-13	—	3.5-3.4	13	1	Int.	11.2	222.22	
V10	1.9-9.3	46-11	—	3.3	12.6	1	Int.	12.8	277.78	
KT15	14.6	7.5	—	3.2	15.8	1	Int.	16.1	266.67	
RK4	3.8	25	—	3	10.8	⅞	Int.	7.7	122.22	
RV7	2.2-6.5	43-15	—	2.9-2.6	11.5	⅞	Int.	8.5	151.11	
Williams										
Twilight Crosshair	1½-5	57¾-21	177-16	3½	10¾	1	Int.	10	186.50	TNT models
Twilight Crosshair	2½	32	64	3¾	11¼	1	Int.	8½	132.00	
Twilight Crosshair	4	29	64	3½	11¾	1	Int.	9½	138.00	
Twilight Crosshair	2-6	45-17	256-28	3	11½	1	Int.	11½	186.50	
Twilight Crosshair	3-9	36-13	161-18	3	12¾	1	Int.	13½	196.00	
Pistol Scopes										
Twilight 1.5x	1.5	19	177	18-25	8.2	1	Int.	6.4	136.50	
Twilight 2x	2	17.5	100	18-25	8.5	1	Int.	6.4	138.50	
Zeiss										
Diatal C 4x32	4	30	—	3.5	10.6	1	Int.	11.3	525.00	All scopes have ¼-minute click-stop adjustments. Choice of Z-Plex or fine crosshair reticles. Rubber armored objective bell, rubber eyepiece ring. Lenses have T-Star coating for highest light transmission. Z-Series scopes offered in non-rail tubes with duplex reticles only. Imported from West Germany by Zeiss Optical, Inc.
Diatal C 6x32	6	20	—	3.5	10.6	1	Int.	11.3	565.00	
Diatal C 10x36	10	12	—	3.5	12.7	1	Int.	14.1	675.00	
Diatal ZA 4x32	4	34.5	—	3.5	10.8	1.02 (26mm)	Int.	10.6	525.00	
Diatal ZA 6x42	6	22.9	—	3.5	12.7	1.02 (26mm)	Int.	13.4	620.00	
Diatal ZA 8x56	8	18	—	3.5	13.8	1.02 (26mm)	Int.	17.6	710.00	
Diavari C 1.5-4.5	1.5-4.5	72-27	—	3.5	11.8	1	Int.	13.4	790.00	
Diavari C 3-9x36	3-9	36-13	—	3.5	11.2	1	Int.	15.2	915.00	
Diavari ZA 1.5-6	1.5-6	65.5-22.9	—	3.5	12.4	1.18 (30mm)	Int.	18.5	870.00	
Diavari ZA 2.5-10	2.5-10	41-13.7	—	3.5	14.4	1.18 (30mm)	Int.	22.8	1,030.00	

■ Signifies target and/or varmint scope. Hunting scopes in general are furnished with a choice of reticle—crosshairs, post with crosshairs, tapered or blunt post, or dot crosshairs, etc. The great majority of target and varmint scopes have medium or fine crosshairs but post or dot reticles may be ordered. W—Windage   E—Elevation   MOA—Minute of angle or 1" (approx.) at 100 yards, etc.

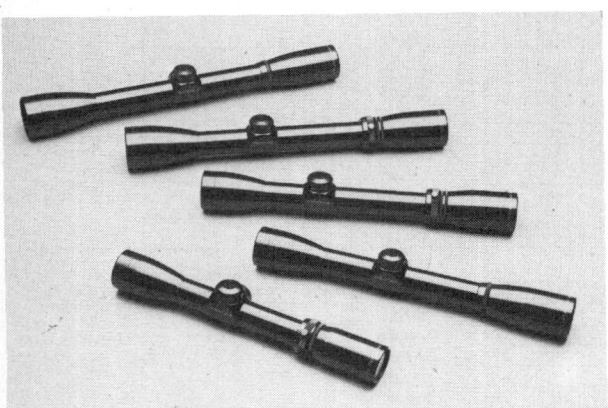

Pentax 4x, 2-7x, 3-9x, 6x, 3-9x Mini.

Interaims Mark V.

Burris Scout 2¾x.

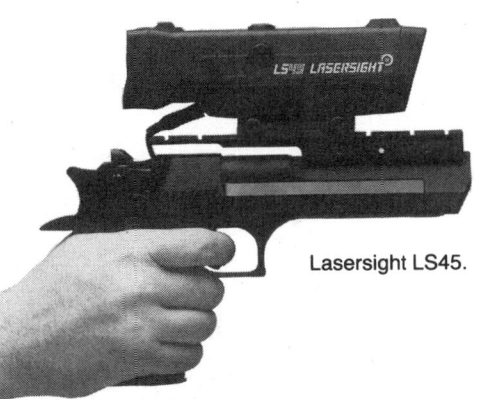

Lasersight LS45.

SCOPE MOUNTS

Maker, Model, Type	Adjust.	Scopes	Price	Suitable for
Action Arms	No	1" split rings.	$32.00	For UZI, Ruger Mk. II, Mini-14, Win. 94, AR-15, Rem. 870, Ithaca 37, and many other popular rifles, handguns. From Action Arms.
Aimpoint	No	1"	34.95-79.95	For many popular revolvers, auto pistols, shotguns, military-style rifles/carbines, sporting rifles. Most require no gunsmithing. Contact Aimpoint for details.
Aimtech	No	One piece base	59.95	Mounts scopes, electronics, lasers using a Weaver-type base. For S&W K, L and N frames. No gunsmithing, sight removal. Attaches to side of frame. In satin black or "stainless" finish. From L&S Technologies, Inc.
A.R.M.S.				
Swan G-3	No	Weaver-type	145.00	[1]See through mount. [2]Also FNC—$89.00. From A.R.M.S., Inc.
M16A1A2/AR-15[1]	No	Weaver-type rail	37.90	
FN FAL LAR	No	Weaver-type rail	95.00	
FN FAL LAR Para.[2]	No	—	120.00	
Beretta AR-70	No	—	59.00	
Armson				
AR-15[1]	No	O.E.G.	28.95	[1]Fastens with one nut. [2]Models 181, 182, 183, 184, etc. [3]Claw mount. [4]Claw mount, bolt cover still easily removable. From Armson, Inc.
Mini-14[2]	No	O.E.G.	39.95	
H&K[3]	No	O.E.G.	54.95	
UZI[4]	No	O.E.G.	54.95	
Armsport				
100 Series[1]	No	1" rings. Low, med., high	10.50	[1]Weaver-type rings. [2]Weaver-type base; most popular rifles. Made in U.S. From Armsport.
104 22-cal.	No	1".	10.50	
201 See-Thru	No	1"	13.50	
1-Piece Base[2]	No		5.00	
2-Piece Base[2]	No		2.50	
B-Square				
Pistols				
Beretta/Taurus 92/99	—	1"	69.95	[1]Clamp-on, blue finish. Stainless finish $59.95. [2]For Bushnell Phantom only. [3]Blue finish; stainless finish $59.95. [4]Clamp-on, for Bushnell Phantom only; stainless finish $49.95. [5]Requires drilling & tapping. [6]No gunsmithing, no sight removal; blue; stainless finish $59.95. [7]Weaver-style rings. Rings not included with Weaver-type bases. Partial listing of mounts shown here. Contact B-Square for more data. B-Square makes mounts for the following military rifles: AK47/AKS, Egyptian Hakim, French MAS 1936, M91 Argentine Mauser, Model 98 Brazilian and German Mausers, Model 93 Spanish Mauser (long and short), Model 1916 Mauser, Model 38 and 96 Swedish Mausers, Model 91 Russian (round and octagon receivers), Chinese SKS 56, SMLE No. 1, Mk. III, 1903 Springfield, U.S. 30-Cal. Carbine. All use long eye relief scopes, all priced at $39.95. Those following replace gun's rear sight: AK47/AKS, P14/1917 Enfield, FN49, M1 Garand, M1-A/M14 (no sight removal), SMLE No. 1, MK III/No. 4 & 5, MK I, 1903/1903-A3 Springfield, Beretta AR 70 (no sight removal), Japanese 7.7 Arisaka.
Browning Buck Mark	No	1"	29.95	
Colt 45 Auto	E only	1"	69.95	
Colt Python[1]	E	1"	49.95	
Daisy 717/722 Champion[2]	No	1"	19.95	
Daisy 44 Mono-Mount	—	1"	9.95	
Dan Wesson Clamp-On[3,7]	E	1"	49.95	
Hi-Standard Victor	W&E	1"	49.95	
Ruger 22 Auto Mono-Mount[4]	No	1"	39.95	
Ruger Single-Six[5]	No	1"	39.95	
S&W K, L, N frame	No	1"	49.95	
T-C Contender	W&E	1"	49.95	
Rifles				
Mini-14[6]	W&E	1"	49.95	
M-94 Side Mount	W&E	1"	49.95	
Ruger 77	W&E	1"	49.95	
Ruger Ranch/Mini-30	W&E	1"	49.95	
SMLE Side Mount	W&E	1"	49.95	
Rem. Model Seven, 600, 660, etc.[7]	No	1" One piece base	9.95	
Military				
M1-A	W&E	1"	59.95	
AR-15/16	W&E	1"	49.95	
FN-LAR/FAL[7]	E only	1"	99.50	
HK-91/93/94[7]	E only	1"	69.95	
Shotguns				
Benelli Super 90	No	1"	49.95	
Browning A-5	No	1"	49.95	
Franchi 48/AL	No	1"	49.95	
Franchi Elite, Prestige, SPAS	No	1"	49.95	
Ithaca 37, Mag 10	No	1"	39.95	
Mossberg 500, 712, 5500	No	1"	39.95	
Rem. 870/1100	No	1"	39.95	
Remington 870, 1100 (and L.H.)	No	1"	39.95	
S&W 1000P	No	1"	39.95	
Beeman				
Double Adjustable	W&E	1"	29.98	All grooved receivers and scope bases on all known air rifles and 22-cal. rimfire rifles (½" to ⅝"—6mm to 15mm). [1]Centerfire rifles. Scope detaches easily, returns to zero. [2]Designed specifically for Krico rifles.
Deluxe Ring Mounts	No	1"	28.98	
Professional Mounts	W&E	1"	98.95	
Professional Pivot[1]	W	1"	269.50	
Buehler[2]	W	1"	59.98	
Buehler				
One Piece (T)[1]	W only	1" split rings, 3 heights. 1" split rings, engraved 26mm split rings, 2 heights 30mm split rings, 1 height	Complete—71.50 Rings only—98.75 Rings only—52.00 Rings only—62.50	[1]Most popular models. [2]Sako dovetail receivers. [3]15 models. [4]No drilling & tapping. [5]Aircraft alloy, dyed blue or to match stainless; for Colt Diamondback, Python, Trooper, Ruger Blackhawk, Single-Six, Security-Six, S&W K-frame, Dan Wesson.
One Piece Micro Dial (T)[1]	W&E	1" split rings.	Complete—91.50	
Two Piece (T)[1]	W only	1" split rings.	Complete—71.50	
Two Piece Dovetail (T)[2]	W only	1" split rings.	Complete—88.00	
One Piece Pistol (T)[3]	W only	1" split rings.	Complete—71.50	
One Piece Pistol Stainless (T)[1]	W only	1" stainless rings.	Complete—93.00	
One Piece Ruger Mini-14 (T)[4]	W only	1" split rings.	Complete—88.00	
One Piece Pistol M83 Blue[4,5]	W only	1" split rings.	Complete—81.50	
One Piece Pistol M83 Silver[4,5]	W only	1" stainless rings.	Complete—95.00	

CAUTION: PRICES CHANGE. CHECK AT GUNSHOP.

SCOPE MOUNTS

Maker, Model, Type	Adjust.	Scopes	Price	Suitable for
Burris				
Supreme One Piece (T)[1]	W only	1" split rings, 3 heights.	1 piece-base—23.95	[1]Most popular rifles. Universal, rings, mounts fit Burris. Universal, Redfield, Leupold and Browning bases. Comparable prices. [2]Browning Standard 22 Auto rifle. [3]Grooved receivers. [4]Universal dovetail; accept Burris, Universal, Redfield, Leupold rings. For Dan Wesson, S&W, Virginian, Ruger Blackhawk, Win. 94. [5]Medium standard front, extension rear, per pair. Low standard front, extension rear, per pair. [6]Mini scopes, scopes with 2" bell, for M77R. Selected rings and bases available with matte Safari finish.
Trumount Two Piece (T)	W only	1" split rings, 3 heights.	2 piece base—21.95	
Browning Auto Mount[2]	No	¾", 1" split rings.	18.49	
Rings Mounts[3]	No	¾", 1" split rings.	1" rings—18.95	
L.E.R. Mount Bases[4]	No	1" split rings.	21.95	
Extension Rings[5]	No	1" scopes.	37.95	
Ruger Ring Mount[6]	W only	1" split rings	42.95	
Std. 1" Rings	—	Low, medium, high heights	30.95	
Zee Rings	—	Fit Weaver bases; medium and high heights	25.95	
Bushnell				
Detachable (T) mounts only[1]	W only	1" split rings, uses Weaver base.	Rings—16.95	[1]Most popular rifles. Includes windage adj.
22 mount	No	1" only.	Rings— 7.95	
Clearview				
Universal Rings (T)[1]	No	1" split rings.	19.95	[1]All popular rifles including Sav. 99. Uses Weaver bases. [2]Allows use of open sights. [3]For 22 rimfire rifles, with grooved receivers or bases. [4]Fits 13 models. Broadest view area of the type. [5]Side mount for both M94 and M94-375 Big Bore.
Mod 101, & 336[2]	No	1" split rings.	19.95	
Broad-View[4]	No	1"	19.95	
Model 22[3]	No	¾", ⅞", 1"	11.95	
94 Winchester[5]	No	1"	19.95	
Conetrol				
Huntur[1]	W only	1", 26mm, 26.5mm solid or split rings, 3 heights.	59.91	[1]All popular rifles, including metric-drilled foreign guns. Price shown for base, two rings. Matte finish. [2]Gunnur grade has mirror-finished rings, satin-finish base. Price shown for base, two rings. [3]Custum grade has mirror-finished rings and mirror-finished, streamlined base. Price shown for base, 2 rings. [4]Win. 94, Krag, older split-bridge Mannlicher-Schoenauer, Mini-14, M-1 Garand, etc. Prices same as above. [5]For all popular guns with integral mounting provision, including Sako, BSA, Ithacagun, Ruger, H&K and many others. Also for grooved-receiver rimfires and air rifles. Prices same as above. [6]For XP-100, T/C Contender, Colt SAA, Ruger Blackhawk, S&W. [7]Sculptured 2-piece bases as found on fine custom rifles. Price shown is for base alone. Also available unfinished—$74.91. [8]Replaces Ruger rib, positions scope farther back. [9]30mm rings made in projectionless style, medium height only. Three-ring mount available for T/.C Contender pistol, in Conetrol's three grades.
Gunnur[2]	W only	1", 26mm, 26.5mm solid or split rings, 3 heights.	74.91	
Custum[3]	W only	1", 26mm, 26.5mm solid or split rings, 3 heights.	89.91	
One Piece Side Mount Base[4]	W only	1", 26mm, 26.5mm solid or split rings, 3 heights.		
Daptar Bases[5]	W only	1", 26mm, 26.5mm solid or split rings, 3 heights.		
Pistol Bases, 2 or 3-ring[6]	W only	1" scopes.		
Fluted Bases[7]	W only	Standard Conetrol rings	99.99	
Ruger No. 1 Base[8]	W only	1", 26mm, 26.5mm solid or split rings.	NA	
30mm Rings[9]	W only	30mm	49.98-69.96	
EAW				
Quick Detachable Top Mount[1]	W&E	1"/26mm	175.00-185.00	[1]Also 30mm rings to fit Redfield or Leupold-type bases, low and high, $75. Most popular rifles. Elevation adjusted with variable-height sub-bases for rear ring. Imported by Del Sports, Inc., Paul Jaeger, Inc.
	W&E	1"/26mm with front extension ring.	175.00-199.00	
	W&E	30mm	175.00-199.00	
	W&E	30mm with front extension ring.	175.00-199.00	
Griffin & Howe				
Standard Double Lever (S).	No	1" or 26mm split rings.	180.00	All popular models (Garand $215). All rings $75. Top ejection rings available.
Holden				
Wide Ironsighter®	No	1" Split rings.	23.95	[1]Most popular rifles including Ruger Mini-14, H&R M700, and muzzleloaders. Rings have oval holes to permit use of iron sights. [2]For 1" dia. scopes. [3]For ¾" or ⅞" dia. scopes. [4]For 1" dia. extended eye relief scopes. [5]702—Browning A-Bolt; 709—Marlin 39A. [6]732—Ruger 77/22 R&RS, No. 1 Ranch Rifle; 777 fits Ruger 77R, RS. Both 732, 777 fit Ruger integral bases.
Ironsighter Center Fire[1]	No	1" Split rings.	23.95	
Ironsighter S-94	No	1" split rings	29.95	
Ironsighter 22 cal. rimfire				
Model #500[2]	No	1" Split rings.	12.95	
Model #600[3]	No	⅞" Split rings also fits ¾".	12.95	
Series #700[5]	No	1", split rings.	23.95	
Model 732, 777[6]	No	1", split scope	54.95	
Ironsighter Handguns[4]	No	1" Split rings.	29.95	
Jaeger				
QD, with windage (S)	W only	1", 3 heights.	250.00	All popular models. From Paul Jaeger, Inc.
Kimber				
Standard[1]	No	1", split rings	48.00	[1]High rings; low rings—$45.00; both only for Kimber rifles. [2]For Kimber rifles only. Also avail. for Mauser (FN,98) Rem. 700, 721, 722, 725, Win. M70, Mark X. [3]Vertically split rings; for Kimber and other popular CF rifles.
Double Lever[2]	No	1", split rings	82.50	
Non-Detachable[3]	No	1", split rings	48.00	
Kris Mounts				
Side-Saddle[1]	No	1", 26mm split rings.	11.98	[1]One-piece mount for Win. 94. [2]Most popular rifles and Ruger. [3]Blackhawk revolver. Mounts have oval hole to permit use of iron sights.
Two Piece (T)[2]	No	1", 26mm split rings.	7.98	
One Piece (T)[3]	No	1", 26mm split rings.	11.98	
KWIK MOUNT				
Shotgun Mount	No	1"	39.95	Wrap-around design; no gunsmithing required. Models for Browning A-5 12 ga., Rem. 870/1100, S&W 916, Savage 67 12 ga., Mossberg 500, Ithaca 37 & 51 12 ga., S&W 1000/3000, Win. 1400. From KenPatable Ent.
Kwik-Site				
KS-See-Thru[1]	No	1"	21.95	[1]Most rifles. Allows use of iron sights. [2]22-cal. rifles with grooved receivers. Allows use of iron sights. [3]Model 94, 94 Big Bore. No drilling or tapping. Also in non-adjustable model $30.95. [4]One-piece solid construction. Use on Weaver bases. 32mm obj. lens or larger. [5]Non-see-through model; for grooved receivers. [6]Allows Mag Lite or C or D, Mini Mag Lites to be mounted atop See-Thru mounts. [7]Fits any Redfield, Tasco, Weaver or universal-style dovetail base. Bright blue, black matte or satin finish. Standard, high heights.
KS-22 See-Thru[2]	No	1"	18.95	
KS-W94[3]	Yes	1"	39.95	
KSM Bench Rest[4]	No	1"	30.95	
KS-WEV	No	1"	21.95	
KS-WEV-HIGH	No	1"	21.95	
KS-T22 1"[5]	No	1"	18.95	
KS-FLM Flashlite[6]	No	Mini or C cell flashlight	49.95	
KS-T88[7]	No	1", 30mm	9.75	
Laserscope	No	Laserscope	37.95 to 69.95	Mounts Laserscope above or below barrel. For most popular military-type rifles, UZI & H&K submachine guns, Desert Eagle pistols. From Laser Devices, Inc.

SCOPE MOUNTS

Maker, Model, Type	Adjust.	Scopes	Price	Suitable for
Lasersight	No	LS45 only	34.95 to 149.00	For the LS45 Lasersight. Allows LS45 to be mounted alongside any 1″ scope. Universal adapter attaches to any full-length Weaver-type base. For most popular military-type rifles, Mossberg. Rem. Shotguns, Python, Desert Eagle, S&W N frame, Colt 45ACP. From Imatronic Lasersight.
Leupold				
STD Bases[1]	W only	One- or two-piece bases	21.50	[1]Rev. front and rear combinations. [2]Avail. polished, matte finish. [3]Base and two rings; Ruger, S&W, T/C; add $5.00 for silver finish. [4]Rem. 700, Win. 70-type actions. [5]For Ruger No. 1, 77/22; interchangeable with Ruger units. [6]For dovetailed rimfire rifles. [6]Sako; medium, low. [8]Must be drilled, tapped for each action. [9]Unfinished bottom, top completed; sold singly.
STD Rings[2]		1″ Super low, low, medium, high	31.10	
STD Handgun mounts[3]	No		54.80	
Dual Dovetail Bases[1,4]	No		21.50	
Dual Dovetail Rings	—	1″, Super low, low	31.10	
Ring Mounts[5,6,7]	No	1″	78.70	
Gunmaker Base[8]	W only	1″	14.20	
Gunmaker Ring Blanks[9]		1″	20.50	
Leatherwood				
Bridge Bases[1]	No	ART II	15.00	[1]Many popular bolt actions. From North American Specialties.
M1A/M-14 Q.D.	No	ART II	100.00	
AR-15/M-16 Base	No	ART II	18.00	
FN-FAL Base	No	ART II	95.00	
FN Para. Base	No	ART II	105.00	
Steyr SSG Base	No	ART II	55.00	
Marlin				
One Piece QD (T)	No	1″ split rings.	14.95	Most Marlin lever actions.
Millett				
Black Onyx Smooth		1″ Low, medium, high	26.95	Rem. 40X, 700, 722, 725, Ruger 77 (round top) Weatherby, etc. FN Mauser, FN Brownings, Colt 57, Interarms MkX, Parker-Hale, Sako (round receiver), many others. [1]Fits Win. M70, 70XTR, 670, Browning BBR, BAR, BLR, A-Bolt, Rem. 7400/7600, Four, Six, Marlin 336, Win. 94 A.E., Sav. 110. [2]To fit Weaver-type bases. Also for Colt, Dan Wesson, Ruger handguns—$39.95-$87.45. Avail. for Scope-Site (fixed, $39.95 or adjustable, $69.95; Onyx Smooth, $26.95, Chaparral Engraved, $39.95. Universal Bases also for Browning BAR, BLR, A-Bolt, Rem. 7400, 7600, Marlin 336, Win. 94 AE, Savage 110. [3]Engraved. Smooth **$26.95**. [4]For Rem. 870, 1100; smooth. [5]Two and three-ring sets for Colt Python, Trooper, Diamondback, Peacekeeper, Dan Wesson, Ruger Redhawk, Super Redhawk.
Chaparral Engraved		Engraved	39.95	
Universal Two Piece Bases				
700 Series	W only	Two-piece bases	20.95	
FN Series	W only	Two-piece bases	20.95	
70 Series[1]	W only	1″, two-piece bases	20.95	
Angle-Loc[2] Rings	W only	1″, low, medium, high	39.95	
Ruger 77 Rings[3]	—	1″	39.95	
Shotgun Rings[4]	—	1″	26.95	
Handgun Bases, Rings[5]	—	1″	29.95-44.85	
Redfield				
JR-SR(T)[1]	W only	¾″, 1″, 26mm, 30mm	JR—19.95-50.95 SR—25.95-39.95	[1]Low, med. & high, split rings. Reversible extension front rings for 1″. 2-piece bases for Sako. Colt Sauer bases $39.85. [2]Split rings for grooved 22's. See-thru mounts $16.15. [3]Used with MP scopes for S&W K or N frame. XP-100, Colt J or I frame. T/C Contender, Colt autos, black powder rifles. [4]One- and two-piece aluminum base; three ring heights. [5]For compact scopes on Browning A-Bolt long action, Remington 700, Winchester 70A.
Ring (T)[2]	No	¾″ and 1″.	58.95	
Double Dovetail MP[3]	No	1″, split rings.	58.95	
Midline Base & Rings[4]	No	1″.	11.95	
Widefield See-Thru Mounts[4]	No	1″.	19.95	
Compact[5]	W only	1″.	49.95	
S&K				
Insta-Mount (T) base only[1]	W only	Use S&K rings only.	20.00-73.00	[1]1903, A3, M1 Carbine, Lee Enfield #1, MK. III, #4, #5, M1917, M98 Mauser, FN Auto, AR-15, AR-180, M-14, M-1, Ger. K-43, Mini-14, M1-A, Krag, AKM, AK-47, Win. 94. [2]Most popular rifles already drilled and tapped. Horizontally and vertically split rings, matte or high gloss.
Conventional rings and bases[2]	W only	1″ split rings.	50.00	
SKulptured Bases, Rings[2]	W only	1″, 26mm, 30mm	From 50.00	
SSK Industries				
T'SOB	No	1″.	45.00-145.00	Custom installation using from two to four rings (included). For T/C Contender, most 22 auto pistols. Ruger and other S.A. revolvers, Ruger, Dan Wesson, S&W, Colt D.A. revolvers. Black or white finish.
Sako				
QD Dovetail	W only	1″ only.	99.95	Sako, or any rifle using Sako action, 3 heights available, Stoeger, importer.
Simmons				
1401	No	1″	8.50	Weaver-type bases. #1401 (low) also in high style (#1403). #1406, 1408 for grooved receiver 22s. Bases avail. for most popular rifles; one- and two-piece styles. Most popular rifles; 1-piece bridge mount. Ring sets—$39.00. [1]For 22 RF rifles.
1406	No	1″	8.50	
1408	No	1″	17.50	
Tasco				
791 and 793 series[1]	No	1″, regular or high.	11.95	[1]Many popular rifles. [2]For 22s with grooved receivers. [3]Most popular rifles. [4]"Quick Peep" 1″ ring mount; fits all 22-cal. rifles with grooved receivers. [5]For Ruger Mini-14; also in brushed aluminum. [6]Side mount for Win. 94. [7]Side mount rings and base for Win. 94 in 30-30, 375 Win. [8]Avail. for most rifles. Steel or aluminum rings.
797[2]	No	Split rings.	11.95	
799[4]	No	1″ only	11.95	
885 BK[7]	No	1″ only	23.95	
895[6]	No	1″ only	5.95	
896[5]	No	1″ only	39.95	
800L Series (with base)[3]	No	1″ only. Rings and base.	15.95	
World Class[8]				
Steel Bases	Yes	1″, 26mm, 30mm	29.95	
Steel Rings	Yes	1″, 26mm	39.95	
Steel 30mm Rings	Yes	30mm	79.95	
Thompson/Center				
Contender 9746[1]	No	T/C Lobo	13.50	[1]All Contenders except vent. rib. [2]T/C rail mount scopes; all Contenders except vent. rib. [3]All S&W K and Combat Masterpiece, Hi-Way Patrolman, Outdoorsman, 22 Jet, 45 Target 1955. Requires drilling, tapping. [4]Blackhawk, Super Blackhawk, Super Sin-
Contender 9741[2]	No	2½, 4 RP	13.50	
Contender 7410	No	Bushnell Phantom 1.3, 2.5x	13.50	
S&W 9747[3]	No	Lobo or RP	13.50	

CAUTION: PRICES CHANGE. CHECK AT GUNSHOP.

SCOPE MOUNTS

Maker, Model, Type	Adjust.	Scopes	Price	Suitable for
Thompson/Center (cont'd.)				gle-Six. Requires drilling, tapping. [5]45 or 50 cal.; replaces rear sight. [6]Rail mount scopes; 54-cal. Hawken, 50, 54, 56-cal. Renegade. Replaces rear sight. [7]Cherokee 32 or 45 cal., Seneca 36 or 45 cal. Replaces rear sight. Carbine mount #9743 for Short Tube scope #8640, $10.50.
Ruger 9748[4]	No	Lobo or RP	13.50	
Hawken 9749[5]	No	Lobo or RP	13.50	
Hawken/Renegade 9754[6]	No	Lobo or RP	13.50	
Cherokee/Seneca[7]	No	Lobo or RP	13.50	
New Englander 9757	No	Lobo or RP	13.50	
Unertl				[1]Unertl target or varmint scopes. [2]Any with regular dovetail scope bases.
Posa (T)[1]	Yes	¾", 1" scopes.	Per set 70.00	
¼ Click (T)[2]	Yes	¾", 1" target scopes.	Per set 100.00	
Weaver				[1]Nearly all modern rifles. Low, med., high. 1" extension $27. 1" med. stainless steel $35.33. [2]Nearly all modern rifles, shotguns. [3]Most modern big-bore rifles; std., high. [4]22s with ⅜" grooved receivers. [5]Nearly all modern rifles. 1" See-Thru extension $27. [6]Most modern big bore rifles. [7]No drilling, tapping. For Colt Python, Trooper, 357, Officer's Model, Ruger Blackhawk & Super, Mini-14, Security-Six, 22 auto pistols, Redhawk, Blackhawk SRM 357, S&W current K, L with adj. sights. [8]For Rem. 870/1100, Mossberg 500. No gunsmithing. [9]For some popular sporting rifles. [10]Dovetail design mount for Rem. 700, Win. 70, FN Mauser, low, med., high rings; std., extension bases. From Weaver
Detachable Mounts				
Top Mount[1]	No	1"	23.11	
		⅞"	22.22	
Side Mount[2]	No	1"	24.44	
		1" Long	28.89	
Pivot Mount[3]	No	1"	31.33	
Tip-Off Mount[4]	No	⅞"	17.78	
		1"	22.67	
See-Thru Mount				
Tip-Off[4]	No	⅞"	16.67	
		1"	23.11	
Detachable[5]	No	1"	23.11	
Integral[6]	No	1"	17.22	
Mount Base System[7]				
Blue Finish	No	1"	60.11	
Stainless Finish	No	1"	84.11	
Shotgun Mount System[8]	No	1"	60.11	
Rifle Mount System[9]	No	1"	26.67	
Imperial Mount Systems[10]				
Bases, pair	Yes	1"	22.33	
Rings, pair	No	1"	32.22	
Wideview				Models for many popular rifles—$18.95. Low ring, high ring and grooved receiver types—$7.95. From Wideview Scope Mount Corp.
WSM-22	No	1".	14.95	
WSM-94	No	1".	20.95	
WSM-94AE	No	1".	22.95	
Williams				[1]Most rifles, Br. S.M.L.E. (round rec) $3.85 extra. [2]Same. [3]Most rifles including Win. 94 Big Bore. [4]Many modern rifles. [5]Most popular rifles.
Offset (S)[1]	No	⅞", 1", 26mm solid, split or extension rings.	59.30	
QC (T)[2]	No	Same.	43.90	
QC (S)[3]	No	Same.	48.55	
Sight-Thru[4]	No	1", ⅞" sleeves $3.20.	21.00	
Streamline[5]	No	1" (bases form rings).	21.00	

(S)—Side Mount (T)Top Mount   22mm—.866"   25.4mm = 1"1.024"   26.5mm = 1.045"   30mm = 1.81"

Aimtech S&W mount.

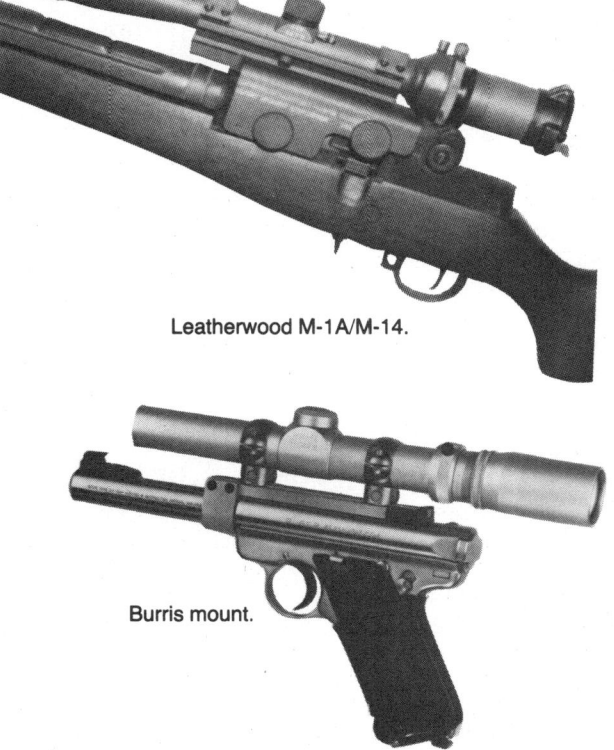

Leatherwood M-1A/M-14.

SSK T'SOB mount.

Burris mount.

SPOTTING SCOPES

Weatherby Sightmaster

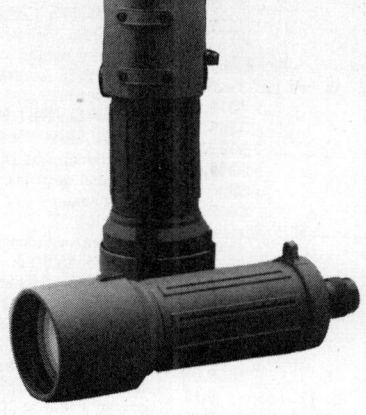

Mirador TTB Draw-Tube

Mirador SIB Scopes

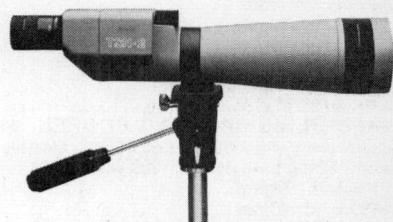

Kowa TSN-2

BAUSCH & LOMB DISCOVERER—15x to 60x zoom, 60mm objective. Constant focus throughout range. Field at 1000 yds. 40 ft (60x), 156 ft. (15x). Comes with lens caps. Length 17½", wgt. 47¼ oz.
   Price: $379.95
BUSHNELL SPACEMASTER II—70mm objective. Field at 1000 yds., 158' to 37'. Relative brightness, 5.76. Wgt., 50 oz. Length closed, 13"; prism focusing.
   Price: Without eyepiece $259.95
   15x, 20x, 40x and 60x eyepieces, each $55.95
   22x wide angle eyepiece $69.95

BUSHNELL ZOOM SPACEMASTER II—15x-45x zoom. 70mm objective. Field at 1000 yards 130'-65'. Relative brightness 9-1.7. Wgt. 53 oz., length 14". Shooter's stand tripod, carrying case.
   Price: $439.95
BUSHNELL COMPETITOR—40mm objective, 20x. Prismatic. Field at 1000 yards 140'. Minimum focus 33'. Length 10", weight 14.5 oz.
   Price: With tripod $113.95
BUSHNELL TROPHY—15x-45x zoom. Rubber armored, prismatic. 60mm objective. Field at 1000 yards 110' to 65'. Minimum focus 20'. Length with caps 11.6", weight 36 oz.
   Price: With tripod and carrying case $399.95
   Interchangeable eyepieces—15x, 20x, 22x, 25x, 60x, each $53.95
   15-36x zoom eyepiece $135.95

KOWA TSN-1-45°—Off-set-type. 77mm objective, 25x, fixed and zoom eyepieces; field at 1000 yds. 94'; relative brightness 9.6; length 15.4"; wgt. 48.8 oz. Lens shade and caps. Straight-type (TSN-2) also available with similar specs and prices.
   Price: $539.95
   Price: 20x-60x zoom eyepiece $179.95
   Price: 20x eyepiece (wide angle) $134.95
   Price: 25x, 40x eyepiece $84.95, $99.95
   Price: 25x LER eyepiece $134.95
KOWA TS-6—Compact straight-type. 60mm objective, 25x fixed power eyepiece; field at 1000 yards 93'; relative brightness 5.8; length 12.5"; weight 25 oz. Lens shade and caps included. Off-set type also available (TS-7).
   Price: $355.90
   Price: 25x eyepiece $58.95
   Price: 20x eyepiece (wide angle) $71.95
   Price: 40x eyepiece $35.95
   Price: 25x LER eyepiece $119.95

KOWA TS-601—45° off-set type. 60mm multi-coated objective, 25x fixed and zoom eyepieces; field at 1000 yards 93'; relative brightness 5.8; length 14.8"; weight 37 oz. Comes with lens shade and caps. Straight-type also available (TS-602).
   Price: $473.90
   Price: 25x eyepiece $83.95
   Price: 20x eyepiece (wide angle) $97.95
   Price: 40x eyepiece $87.95
   Price: 20x-60x zoom eyepiece $179.95
   Price: 25x LER eyepiece $134.95

KOWA TS-9C—Straight-type. 50mm objective, 20x compact model; fixed power eyepieces; objective focusing down to 17 ft.; field at 1000 yds. 157'; relative brightness 6.3; length 9.65"; wgt. 22.9 oz. Lens caps.
   Price: $140.95
   Price: 15x, 20x eyepieces, each $25.95
   Price: 11x-33x zoom eyepiece $79.95
   Price: As above, rubber armored (TS-9R) $154.95
LEUPOLD 20x50 COMPACT—50mm objective, 20x. Field at 100 yards 11.5 ft.; eye relief 1"; length 9.4"; weight 17.5 oz. Comes with Cordura nylon case.
   Price: $450.00
   Price: Armored model $476.80
   Price: Tripod $68.05
LEUPOLD 25x50 COMPACT—50mm objective, 25x. Field at 100 yds. 8.3 ft.; eye relief 1"; length over-all 9.4"; weight 17.5 oz. Comes with Cordura nylon case.
   Price: $476.80
   Price: Armored model $503.55
   Price: Armored, with reticle $530.55
   Price: Tripod $68.05
LEUPOLD 20x60 SPOTTING SCOPE—60mm objective, 20x. Field at 100 yards 11.5 ft., eye relief 1"; length 12.9", weight 21 oz. Comes with Cordura nylon case.
   Price: $476.80
   Price: Tripod $68.05
LEUPOLD 30x60 SPOTTING SCOPE—60mm objective, 30x. Field at 100 yds. 6.4 ft.; eye relief 1"; length over-all 12.9"; weight 21 oz. Comes with Cordura case.
   Price: $503.55
   Price: Armored model $530.55
   Price: Tripod $68.05
MIRADOR TTB SERIES—Draw tube armored spotting scopes. Available with 75mm or 80mm objective. Zoom model (28x-62x, 80mm) is 11⅞" (closed), weighs 50 ozs. Field at 1000 yds. 70-42 ft. Comes with lens covers.
   Price: 28-62x80mm $782.95
   Price: 32x80mm $665.95
   Price: 26-58x75mm $692.95
   Price: 30x75mm $575.95
MIRADOR SSD SPOTTING SCOPES—60mm objective, 15x, 20x, 22x, 25x, 40x, 60x, 20-60x; field at 1000 yds. 37 ft.; length 10¼"; weight 33 ozs.
   Price: 15x, 20x, 25x, 40x, 60x $422.95
   Price: 22x Wide Angle $431.95
   Price: 20-60x Zoom $539.95
   Price: As above, with tripod, case $719.95
MIRADOR SIA SPOTTING SCOPES—Similar to the SSD scopes except with 45° eyepiece. Length of 12¼", weight 39 ozs.
   Price: 15x, 20x, 25x, 40x, 60x $530.95
   Price: 22x Wide Angle $539.95
   Price: 20-60x Zoom $647.95
MIRADOR SSA SPOTTING SCOPES—Lightweight, slender version of the SSD series with 50mm objective. Length 11⅛", weight 28 ozs.
   Price: 12x, 16x, 20x, 32, 48x $305.95
   Price: 18x Wide Angle $314.95
   Price: 16-48x Zoom $422.95

CAUTION: PRICES CHANGE. CHECK AT GUNSHOP.

MIRADOR SSR SPOTTING SCOPES—50mm objective. Similar to SSD except rubber armored in black or camouflage. Length 11⅛", weight 31 ozs.
    Price: Black, 12x, 16x, 20x, 32x, 48x $359.95
    Price: Black, 18x Wide Angle $368.95
    Price: Black, 16-48x Zoom $476.95
    Price: Camouflage, 12x, 16x, 20x, 32x, 48x $368.95
    Price: Camouflage, 18x Wide Angle $377.95
    Price: Camouflage, 16-48x Zoom $485.95
MIRADOR SSF FIELD SCOPES—Fixed or variable power, choice of 50mm, 60mm, 75mm objective lens. Length 9¾", weight 20 ozs. (15-32x50).
    Price: 20x50mm $215.95
    Price: 25x60mm $269.95
    Price: 30x75mm $323.95
    Price: 15-32x50mm Zoom $341.95
    Price: 18-40x60mm Zoom $395.95
    Price: 22-47x75mm Zoom $449.95
MIRADOR SRA MULTI ANGLE SCOPES—Similar to SSF Series except eyepiece head rotates for viewing from any angle.
    Price: 20x50mm $350.95
    Price: 25x60mm $395.95
    Price: 30x75mm $440.95
    Price: 15-32x50mm Zoom $476.95
    Price: 18-40x60mm Zoom $521.95
    Price: 22-47x75mm Zoom $566.95
MIRADOR SIB SPOTTING SCOPES—Short-tube, 45° scopes with porro-prism design. 50mm and 60mm objective. Length 10¼", weight 18.5 ozs. (15-32x50mm); field at 1000 yds. 129-81 ft.
    Price: 20x50mm $287.95
    Price: 25x60mm $332.95
    Price: 15-32x50mm Zoom $413.95
    Price: 18-40x60mm Zoom $485.95
PENTAX MODEL 300—Catadioptric 20x spotting scope has 68mm objective, interchangeable 24x, 33x eyepieces. Field of view 45 ft. at 1000 feet. Length over-all is 5.9", weight is 26.5 oz. Comes with table top tripod, hood and case.
    Price: $390.00
    Price: With Rubber Armor (300R) $490.00
    Price: 24x, 33x eyepiece $56.00
PENTAX MODEL 500—Similar to the Model 300 except is 25x, has field of view of 31 ft. at 1000 ft. Interchangeable 40x, 55x eyepieces. Over-all length of 7.8", weight 31.7 oz. Comes with table top tripod, hood and case.
    Price: $450.00
    Price: With Rubber Armor (500R) $550.00
    Price: 40x, 55x eyepiece $56.00
REDFIELD 30x CAT SPOTTER—60mm objective, 30x. Field of view 9.5 ft. at 100 yds. Uses catadioptric lens system. Length over-all is 7.5", weight is 11.5 oz. Eye relief 0.5". Also comes in camo armor coating.
    Price: $452.95
    Price: With Armor Camouflage $466.95
REDFIELD REGAL II & III—Regal II has 60mm objective, interchangeable 25x and 18x-40x zoom eyepieces. Regal III has 50mm objective, interchangeable 20x and 15x-32x zoom eyepieces, and is shorter and lighter. Field at 1000 yds.—Regal II, 125 ft. @ 25x; Regal III, 157 ft. @ 20x. Both have dual rotation of eyepiece and scope body. With aluminum carrying case, tripod.
    Price: Regal II $659.95
    Price: Regal III $621.95
REDFIELD REGAL IV & V—Conventional straight thru viewing. Regal IV has 60mm objective and interchangeable 25x and 20x-60x zoom eyepieces. Regal V has 50mm objective and 20x and 16x-48x zoom eyepieces and is shorter and lighter. Field at 1000 yds.—Regal IV, 94 ft. @ 25x; Regal V, 118 ft. @ 20x. Both come with tripod and aluminum carrying case.
    Price: Regal IV $678.95
    Price: As above with black rubber Armorcoat $697.95
REDFIELD REGAL VI—60mm objective, 25x fixed and 20x-60x interchangeable eyepieces. Has 45° angled eyepiece, front-mounted focus ring, 180° tube rotation. Field at 1000 yds., 94 ft. @ 25x; length, 12¼"; weight, 40 oz. Comes with tripod, aluminum carrying case.
    Price: Regal VI $734.95
SIMMONS 1209 COMPACT—50mm objective, 25x. Camouflage finish. Length is 9", weight 30 oz. Comes with tripod.
    Price: $115.50
SIMMONS 1210—50mm objective, 25x standard, 16, 20, 40, 48, 16-36x zoom eyepieces available. Field at 1000 yds. 22 ft. Length 12.2", weight 32 oz. Comes with tripod, 3x finder scope with crosshair.
    Price: About $187.00
    Price: Fixed eyepieces $57.00
    Price: Zoom eyepiece $150.00
SIMMONS 1215—50mm objective, 25x standard, 16, 20, 40, 48, 16-36x zoom eyepieces available. Field at 1000 yds. 22 ft. Length 12.2", weight 48 oz. Comes with tripod, 3x finder scope with crosshair. Green camo rubber.
    Price: About $292.00
    Price: Fixed eyepieces $57.00
    Price: Zoom eyepiece $150.00

SIMMONS 1220—60mm objective, 25x standard, 16, 20, 40, 48, 16-36x zoom eyepieces available. Field at 1000 yds. 22 ft. Length 13.8", weight 44 oz. with tripod (included). Has 3x finder scope with crosshairs.
    Price: About $345.00
    Price: Fixed eyepieces $57.00
    Price: Zoom eyepiece $150.00
SIMMONS 1299 15-60x ZOOM—60mm objective, 15-60x zoom. Field at 1000 yds. 156-40 ft. Slide-out sunshade. Has 3x finder scope. Photo adaptable and comes with a photo adapter tube for T-mount cameras. Black finish. Tripod not included.
    Price: $375.00
SWAROVSKI HABICHT HAWK 30x75S TELESCOPE—75mm objective, 30x. Field at 1,000 yds. 90ft. Minimum, focusing distance 90 ft. Length: closed 13 in., extended 20½". Weight: 47 oz. Precise recognition of smallest details even at dusk. Leather or rubber covered, with caps and carrying case.
    Price: $685.00
    Same as above with short range supplement. Minimum focusing distance 24 to 30 ft. $870.00
SWAROVSKI 25-40x75 TELESCOPE—75mm objective, variable power from 25x to 40x with a field of 98 ft. (25x) and 72 ft. (40x). Minimum focusing distance 66 ft. Length closed is 11.3", extended 15.6"; weight 46.8 oz. Rubber covered.
    Price: Standard $980.00
SWIFT TELEMASTER M841—60mm objective. 15x to 60x variable power. Field at 1000 yards 160 feet (15x) to 40 feet (60x). Wgt. 3.4 lbs. 17.6" over-all.
    Price: $385.00
SWIFT M700 SCOUT—9x-30x, 30mm spotting scope. Length 15½", weighs 2.1 lbs. Field of 204 ft. (9x), 60 ft. (30x).
    Price: $140.00
SWIFT SEARCHER M839—60mm objective, 20x, 40x. Field at 1000 yds. 118 ft. (30x), 59 ft. (40x). Length 12.6", weight 3 lbs. Rotating eyepiece head for straight or 45-degree viewing.
    Price: $380.00
    Price: 30x, 50x eyepieces, each $45.00
    Price: Tripod $36.00
TASCO 17ET SPOTTING SCOPE—60mm objective lens, 20-60x zoom with black metal tripod, micro-adjustable elevation control.
    Price: $199.95
TASCO 20E SPOTTING SCOPE—50mm objective, 15-45x zoom. Field at 1,000 yds. 95-42 ft.; includes tripod with pan-head lever.
    Price: $119.95
TASCO 25TPC WORLD CLASS CAMO RUBBER COVERED—60mm objective lens, 25x, BAK-4 prism. Accepts available 15x, 20x, 40x, 60x, & 20-60x eyepieces and photo-adaptor tube. Field at 1,000 yds. 105'. Matching olive drab tripod, Weight 38.3 oz., length 11⅞".
    Price: $849.95
TASCO 25TPCZ WORLD CLASS CAMO ARMORED ZOOM—Same as above, but with 20-60x eyepiece. Field at 1,000 yds. 97 ft. @ 20x.
    Price: $1,049.95
TASCO 34TZ RUBBER COVERED—50mm objective lens, 15-40x zoom. Field at 1,000 yards 136 ft. With tripod, weight 29.9 oz., length 13¾".
    Price: $329.95
TASCO 9000T WORLD CLASS SPOTTING SCOPE—60mm objective lens, 15-60x zoom. Field at 1,000 yds. 160 ft. @ 15x. Fully multi-coated optics, includes camera adaptor and camera case.
    Price: $459.95
    Price: 9002T (same as 9000T but includes a tripod with pan-head lever) $519.95
UNERTL "FORTY-FIVE"—54mm objective. 20x (single fixed power). Field at 100 yds. 10'10"; eye relief 1"; focusing range infinity to 33 ft. Wgt. about 32 oz.; over-all length 15¾". With lens covers.
    Price: With multi-layer lens coating $348.00
    Price: With mono-layer magnesium coating $270.00
UNERTL RIGHT ANGLE—63.5mm objective, 24x. Field at 100 yds., 7 ft. Relative brightness, 6.96. Eye relief, ½". Wgt. 41 oz. Length closed., 19". Push-pull and screw-focus eyepiece. 16x and 32x eyepieces $50.00 each.
    Price: $306.00
UNERTL STRAIGHT PRISMATIC—Same as Unertl Right Angle except: straight eyepiece and wgt. of 40 oz.
    Price: $262.00
UNERTL 20x STRAIGHT PRISMATIC—54mm objective. 20x. Field at 100 yds., 8.5 ft. Relative brightness, 6.1. Eye relief, ½". Wgt. 36 oz. Length closed, 13½". Complete with lens covers.
    Price: $220.00
UNERTL TEAM SCOPE—100mm objective. 15x, 24x, 32x eyepieces. Field at 100 yds. 13 to 7.5 ft. Relative brightness, 39.06 to 9.79. Eye relief, 2" to 1½". Weight 13 lbs. 29⅞" overall. Metal tripod, yoke and wood carrying case furnished (total weight, 80 lbs.)
    Price: $1,200.00
WEATHERBY—60mm objective, 20x-60x zoom
    Price: Scope only $329.95
    Price: Scope and tripod $397.00
    Price: Tripod for above $76.00

Directory of the Arms Trade

INDEX TO THE DIRECTORY

AMMUNITION (Commercial) 297	GUNSMITHS, HANDGUN (see Pistolsmiths) 315
AMMUNITION (Custom) 297	GUNSMITH SCHOOLS 309
AMMUNITION (Foreign) 298	GUNSMITH SUPPLIES, TOOLS, SERVICES 309
AMMUNITION COMPONENTS—BULLETS, POWDER, PRIMERS 298	HANDGUN ACCESSORIES 310
ANTIQUE ARMS DEALERS 299	HANDGUN GRIPS 311
APPRAISERS, GUNS, ETC. 299	HEARING PROTECTORS 311
AUCTIONEERS, GUNS, ETC. 300	HOLSTERS & LEATHER GOODS 311
BOOKS (ARMS), Publishers and Dealers 300	HUNTING AND CAMP GEAR, CLOTHING, ETC. 312
BULLET & CASE LUBRICANTS 300	KNIVES AND KNIFEMAKERS'S SUPPLIES— FACTORY and MAIL ORDER 312
BULLET SWAGE DIES AND TOOLS 300	LABELS, BOXES, CARTRIDGE HOLDERS 313
CARTRIDGES FOR COLLECTORS 300	LOAD TESTING and PRODUCT TESTING (CHRONOGRAPHING, BALLISTIC STUDIES) 313
CASES, CABINETS AND RACKS—GUN 301	MISCELLANEOUS 313
CHOKE DEVICES, RECOIL ABSORBERS & RECOIL PADS . 301	MUZZLE-LOADING GUNS, BARRELS or EQUIPMENT 314
CHRONOGRAPHS AND PRESSURE TOOLS 301	PISTOLSMITHS 315
CLEANING & REFINISHING SUPPLIES 301	REBORING AND RERIFLING 316
CUSTOM GUNSMITHS 302	RELOADING TOOLS AND ACCESSORIES 316
CUSTOM METALSMITHS 305	RESTS—BENCH, PORTABLE, ETC. 317
DECOYS 305	RIFLE BARREL MAKERS 317
ENGRAVERS, ENGRAVING TOOLS 305	SCOPES, MOUNTS, ACCESSORIES, OPTICAL EQUIPMENT 317
GAME CALLS 306	
GUN PARTS, U.S. AND FOREIGN 306	SIGHTS, METALLIC 318
GUNS (Air) 309	STOCKS (Commercial and Custom) 319
GUNS (Foreign) 308	TARGETS, BULLET & CLAYBIRD TRAPS 320
GUNS (U.S.-made) 307	TAXIDERMY 320
GUNS & GUN PARTS, REPLICA AND ANTIQUE 309	TRAP & SKEET SHOOTERS' EQUIPMENT 320
GUNS, SURPLUS—PARTS AND AMMUNITION 309	TRIGGERS, RELATED EQUIPMENT 320
GUNSMITHS, CUSTOM (see Custom Gunsmiths) 302	

AMMUNITION (Commercial)

Activ Industries, Inc., P.O. Box F, 100 Zigor Rd., Kearneysville, WV 25430/304-725-0451 (shotshells only)
Alberts Corp., 519 East 19th St., Paterson, NJ 07514/201-684-1676
Brass Extrusion Laboratories, Ltd., 800 W. Maple Lane, Bensenville, IL 60106/312-595-2792
Cascade Cartridge Inc., (See Omark)
Dynamit Nobel-RWS Inc., 105 Stonehurst Court, Northvale, NJ 07647/201-767-1995(RWS)
Eley-Kynoch, ICI-America, Wilmington, DE 19897/302-575-3000
Elite Ammunition, P.O. Box 3251, Hinsdale, IL 60522/312-366-9006
Estate Cartridge Inc., P.O. Box 3702, Conroe, TX 77305 (shotshell)
Federal Cartridge Co., 900 Ehlen Dr., Anoka, MN 55303/612-422-2840
Fisher Enterprises, 655 Main St. #305, Edmonds, WA 98020/206-776-4365 (Prometheus airgun pellets)
Freedom Arms Co., P.O. Box 1776, Freedom, WY 83120/307-883-2468
Frontier Cartridge Division-Hornady Mfg. Co., Box 1848, Grand Island, NE 68801/308-382-1390
Hansen Cartridge Co., 244 Old Post Rd., Southport, CT 06490/203-259-5424
ICI-America, Wilmington, DE 19897/302-575-3000(Eley-Kynoch)
Liquid Assets Inc., P.O. Box 4005, Key West, FL 33040 (P.E.A.C.E.)
Mitchell Arms, Inc., 3411 Lake Center Dr., Santa Ana, CA 92704/714-957-5711
Omark Industries, P.O. Box 856, Lewiston, ID 83501/208-746-2351
P.P.C. Corp., 625 E. 24th St., Paterson, NJ 07514
Palcher Ammunition, Techstar Engineering, Inc., 2239 S. Huron Ave., Santa Ana, CA 92705/714-556-7384
Precision Prods. of Wash., Inc., N. 311 Walnut Rd., Spokane, WA 99206/509-928-0604 (Exammo)
Prometheus/Titan Black (See Fisher Enterprises)
RWS (See Dynamit Nobel)
Remington Arms Co., 1077 Market St., Wilmington, DE 19898
Southern Ammunition Co, Inc., Rte. 1, Box 6B, Latta, SC 29565/803-752-7751
3-D Inv., Inc., Box J, Main St., Doniphan, NE 68832/402-845-2285
United States Ammunition Co. (USAC), Inc., 45500 - 15th St. East, Tacoma, WA 98424/206-922-7589
Weatherby's, 2781 E. Firestone Blvd., South Gate, CA 90280
Winchester, 427 N. Shamrock St., East Alton, IL 62024/618-258-2000

AMMUNITION (Custom)

A Square Co., Inc., Rt. 4, Simmons Rd., Madison, IN 47250/812-273-3633
Accuracy Systems Inc., 15205 N. Cave Creek Rd., Phoenix, AZ 85032/602-971-1991
Allred Bullet Co., 932 Evergreen Dr., Logan, UT 84321/801-752-6983
Beal's Bullets, 170 W. Marshall Rd., Lansdowne, PA 19050/215-259-1220 (Auto Mag Specialists)
Black Mountain Bullets, Rte. 3, Box 297, Warrenton, VA 22186/703-347-1199
Brass Extrusion Labs. Ltd., (B.E.L.L.) 800 W. Maple Lane, Bensenville, IL 60106/312-595-2792
Russell Campbell Custom Loaded Ammo, 219 Leisure Dr., San Antonio, TX 78201/512-735-1183
Cartridges Unlimited, Rt. 1, Box 50, South Kent, CT 06785/203-927-3053 (British Express; metric; U.S.)
Cor-Bon Bullet Co., P.O. Box 10126, Detroit, MI 48210/313-894-2373
Cumberland Arms, Rt. 1, Box 1150, Shafer Rd., Blantons Chapel, Manchester, TN 37355
Custom Tackle & Ammo, P.O. Box 1886, Farmington, NM 87499/505-632-3539
Elko Arms, 28 rue Ecole Moderne, 7400 Soignies, Belgium/32-67.33.29.34
E.W. Ellis Sport Shop, RFD 1, Box 315, Corinth, NY 12822
Ellwood Epps Northern Ltd., 210 Worthington St. W., North Bay, Ont. P1B 3B4, Canada
Estate Cartridge Inc., P.O. Box 3702, Conroe, TX 77305/409-539-9144 (shotshell)
Jack First Distributors, Inc., 44633 Sierra Hwy., Lancaster, CA 93534/805-945-6981
Ramon B. Gonzalez, P.O. Box 370, Monticello, NY 12701/914-794-4515
"Gramps" Antique Cartridges, Ellwood Epps, Box 341, Washago, Ont. L0K 2B0 Canada/705-689-5348
Hardin Specialty Distributors, P.O. Box 338, Radcliff, KY 40160/502-351-6649
R.H. Keeler, 817 "N" St., Port Angeles, WA 98362/206-457-4702
K.K. Arms Co., Star Route Box 671, Kerrville, TX 78028/512-257-4718
KTW Inc., 710 Foster Park Rd., Lorain, OH 44053/216-233-6919
Lindsley Arms Cartridge Co., Inc., P.O. Box 757, 20 Crescent St., Henniker, NH 03242/603-428-3127 (inq. S.A.S.E.)
Lomont Precision Bullets, 4236 West 700 South, Poneto, IN 46781/219-694-

AMMUNITION (Custom) — cont'd.

6792 (custom cast bullets only)
McConnellstown Reloading & Cast Bullets, Inc., R.D. 3, Box 40, Huntingdon, PA 16652/814-627-5402
Mack's Sport Shop, Box 1155, Kodiak, AK 99615/907-486-4276
MagSafe Ammo, P.O. Box 5692, Olympia, WA 98503/206-456-4623
North American Arms, 1800 North 300 West, Spanish Fork, UT 84660/801-798-7401
Numrich Arms Corp., 203 Broadway, W. Hurley, NY 12491
Patriot Mfg. & Sales, Banyan Plaza, Suite 334, Box 9000, Sebring, FL 33870/813-655-1798
Precision Ammo Co., P.O. Box 63, Garnerville, NY 10923/914-947-2720
Precision Prods. of Wash., Inc., N. 311 Walnut Rd., Spokane, WA 99206/509-928-0604 (Exammo)
Anthony F. Sailer-Ammunition (AFSCO), 731 W. Third St., Owen, WI 54760/715-229-2516
Sanders Cust. Gun Serv., 2358 Tyler Lane, Louisville, KY 40205
George W. Spence, 115 Locust St., Steele, MO 63877/314-695-4926 (boxer-primed cartridges)
The 3-D Company, Box J, Main St., Doniphan, NE 68832/402-845-2285 (reloaded police ammo)
R. A. Wardrop, P.O. Box 245, Mechanicsburg, PA 17055/717-766-9663
Zero Ammunition Co., Inc., P.O. Box 1188, Cullman, AL 35056/205-739-1606

AMMUNITION (Foreign)

Action Arms Ltd., P. O. Box 9573, Philadelphia, PA 19124/215-744-0100
Beeman Inc., 3440-GD Airway Dr., Santa Rosa, CA 95403/707-578-7900
Dan/Arms, RD 6, Box 674F, Ruppsville, Allentown, PA 18106/215-391-1966
Dynamit Nobel-RWS, Inc., 105 Stonehurst Ave., Northvale, NJ 07647/210-767-1995(RWS, Geco, Rottweil)
Fiocchi of America, Inc., Rt. 2, Box 90-8, Ozark, MO 65721/417-725-4118
Gun South, Inc., P.O. Box 129, 108 Morrow Ave. Trussville, AL 35173/205-655-8299
Hansen Cartridge Co., 244 Old Post Rd., Southport, CT 06490/203-259-5424
Hirtenberger Patronen-, Zundhutchen- & Metallwarenfabrik, A.G., Leobersdorfer Str. 33, A2552 Hirtenberg, Austria
Hunters Specialty, Inc., 130 Orchard Dr., Pittsburgh, PA 15235/412-795-8885 (Hirtenberger)
Paul Jaeger, Inc., P.O. Box 449, 1 Madison Ave., Grand Junction, TN 38039/901-764-6909 (RWS centerfire ammo)
Kendall International Arms, 418 Fithian Ave., Paris, KY 40361/606-987-6946 (Lapua)
Lapua (See Kendall International)
PMC Ammunition, 4890 So. Alameda, Vernon, CA 90058/213-587-7100
RWS (Rheinische-Westfälische Sprengstoff) See Dynamit Nobel; Paul Jaeger, Inc.
Sports Emporium, 1414 Willow Ave., Philadelphia, PA 19126 (Danarms shotshells)

AMMUNITION COMPONENTS—BULLETS, POWDER, PRIMERS

A Square Co., Inc., Rt. 4, Simmons Rd., Madison, IN 47250/812-273-3633 (cust. bull.; brass)
Accurate Arms Co., Inc., (Propellents Div.), Rt. 1, Box 167, McEwen, TN, 37101/615-729-4207/4208 (powders)
Acme Custom Bullets, 5708 Evers Rd., San Antonio, TX 78238/512-680-4828
Alaska Bullet Works, P.O. Box 54, Douglas, AK 99824/907-789-1576 (Alaska copper-bond cust. bull.; Kodiak bonded core bullets)
Alberts Corp., 519 E. 19th St., Paterson, NJ 07514/201-684-1676 (swaged bullets)
Allred Bullet Co., 932 Evergreen Dr., Logan, UT 84321/801-752-6983 (custom bullets)
American Bullets, P.O. Box 15313, Atlanta, GA 30333/404-482-4253
American Products Co., 14729 Spring Valley Rd., Morrison, IL 61270/815-772-3336 (12-ga. shot wad)
Ammo-O-Mart Ltd., P.O. Box 125, Hawkesbury, Ont., Canada K6A 2R8/613-632-9300 (Nobel powder)
Ballistic Prods., Inc., Box 408, 2105 Daniels St., Long Lake, MN 55356/612-473-1550 (shotgun powders, primers)
Ballistic Research Industries (BRI), 2825 S. Rodeo Gulch Rd. #8, Soquel, CA 95073/408-476-7981 (Sabo shotgun slug; Gualandislug)
Barnes Bullets, Inc., P.O. Box 215, American Fork, UT 84003/801-756-4222
Bell's Gun & Sport Shop, 3309-19 Mannheim Rd., Franklin Pk., IL 60131/312-678-1900
Berger Bullets, 4234 N. 63rd Ave., Phoenix, AZ 85033/602-846-5791 (cust. 22, 6mm benchrest bull.)
Bergman and Williams, 2450 Losee Rd., Suite F, No. Las Vegas, NV 89030/702-642-1091 (copper tube 308 cust. bull.; lead wire i. all sizes)
Bitterroot Bullet Co., Box 412, Lewiston, ID 83501/208-743-5635 (Broch.:USA, Can. & Mexico $1 plus legal size env., intl. $2; lit. pkg.: USA, Can. & Mexico $7.50, intl. $10.50
Black Mountain Bullets, Rte. 3, Box 297, Warrenton, VA 22186/703-347-1199 (custom Fluid King match bullets)

B.E.L.L., Brass Extrusion Laboratories, Ltd., 800 W. Maple Lane, Bensenville, IL 60106 312/595-2792
Bruno Bullets, 10 Fifth St. Kelayres, PA 18231/717-929-1791 (22, 6mm benchrest bull.)
Buffalo Rock Shooters Supply, R. Rt. 1, Ottawa, IL 61350/815-433-2471
Bullet Swaging Supply, Inc., P.O. Box 1056, 303 McMillan Rd., West Monroe, LA 71219/318-387-7257
CCI, (See: Omark Industries)
CheVron Bullets, R.R. 1, Ottawa, IL 61350/815-433-2471
Colorado Sutlers Arsenal, Box 991, Granby, CO 80446/303-887-2813
Competition Bullets Inc., 9996-29 Ave., Edmonton, Alb. T6N 1A2, Canada/403-463-2817
Cooper-Woodward, 8073 Canyon Ferry Rd., Helena, MT 59601/406-475-3321
Corbin Mfg. & Supply, Inc., 600 Industrial Circle, P.O. Box 2659, White City, OR 97503/503-826-5211 (bullets)
Cor-Bon Custom Bullets, P.O. Box 10126, Detroit, MI 48210/313-894-2373 (375, 44, 45 solid brass partition bull.)
DuPont, (See IMR Powder Co.)
Dynamit Nobel-RWS Inc., 105 Stonehurst Court, Northvale, NJ 07647/201-767-1995 (RWS percussion caps)
Eagle Bullet Works, P.O. Box 2104, White City, OR 97503/503-826-7143 (Div-Cor 375, 224, 257 cust. bull.)
Excaliber Wax, Inc., P.O. Box 432, Kenton, OH 43326/419-673-0512 (wax bullets)
Federal Cartridge Co., 900 Ehlen Dr., Anoka, MN 55303/612-422-2840 (primers)
Fisher Enterprises, 655 Main St. #305, Edmonds, WA 98020/206-776-4365
Forty Five Ranch Enterprises, 119 S. Main, Miami, OK 74354/918-542-9307
Fowler Bullets, 3731 McKelvey St., Charlotte, NC 28215/704-568-7661 (benchrest bullets)
Glaser Safety Slug, P.O. Box 8223, Foster City, CA 94404/415-345-7677
GOEX, Inc., Belin Plant, 1002 Springbrook Ave., Moosic, PA 18507/717-457-6724 (blackpowder)
Golden Powder International Sales, Inc., 8444 Wilshire Blvd., Suite 201, Beverly Hills, CA 90211/213-653-1301 (Golden Powder/blackpowder)
Green Bay Bullets, P.O. Box 10446, 1486 Servais St., Green Bay, WI 54307-54304/414-497-2949 (cast lead bullets)
Grills-Hanna Bulletsmith Co., Lt., Box 655, Black Diamond, Alb. TOL OHO Canada/403-652-4393 (38, 9mm, 12-ga.)
Grizzly Bullets, 2137 Hwy. 200, Trout Creek, MT 59874/406-847-2627 (cust.)
GTM Co., George T. Mahaney, 15915B E. Main St., La Puente, CA 91744 (all brass shotshells)
Gun City, 212 West Main Ave., Bismarck, ND 58501/701-223-2304
Hansen Custom Bullets, 3221 Shelley St., Mohegan, NY 10547
Hardin Specialty Distr., P. O. Box 338, Radcliff, KY 40160/502-351-6649 (empty, primed cases)
Harrison Bullet Works, 6437 E. Hobart St., Mesa, AZ 85205/602-985-7844 (cust. swaged .41 Mag. bullets)
Robert W. Hart & Son, Inc. 401 Montgomery St., Nescopeck, PA 18635/717-752-3655
Hercules Inc., Hercules Plaza, Wilmington, DE 19894 (smokeless powder)
Hodgdon Powder Co. Inc., P.O. Box 2932, Shawnee Mission, KS 66201/913-362-9455 (smokeless, Pyrodex and black powder)
Hoffman New Ideas, Inc., 821 Northmoor Rd., Lake Forest, IL 60045/312-234-4075 (practice sub.vel. bullets)
Hornady Mfg. Co., P.O. Drawer 1848, Grand Island, NE 68802/308-382-1390
Hunters Specialty, Inc., 130 Orchard Dr., Pittsburgh, PA 15235/412-795-8885 (Hirtenberger bullets)
Huntington's, 601 Oro Dam Blvd., Oroville, CA 95965/916-534-1210
IMR Powder Co., Rt. 5 Box 247E, Plattsburgh, NY 12901/518-561-9530
Jaro Manuf., P.O. Box 6125, 206 E. Shaw, Pasadena, TX 77506/713-472-0417 (bullets)
Ka Pu Kapili, P.O. Box 745, Honokaa, HI 96272 (Hawaiian Special cust. bullets)
Kendall International Arms, 418 Fithian Ave., Paris, KY 40361/606-987-6946 (Lapua bull.)
Kodiak Custom Bullets, 8261 Henry Circle, Anchorage, AK 99507/907-349-2282
L.L.F. Die Shop, 1281 Highway 99 North, Eugene, OR 97402/503-688-5753
Lage Uniwad Co., 1814 21st St., Eldora, IA 50627/515-858-2634
Lapua (See Kendall International Arms)
Ljutic Ind., Inc., Box 2117, Yakima, WA 98907/509-248-0476 (Mono-wads)
Lomont Precision Bullets, 4236 West 700 South, Poneto, IN 46781/219-694-6792 (custom cast bullets)
Paul E. Low Jr., R.R. 1, Dunlap, IL 61525/309-685-1392 (jacketed 44- & 45-cal. bullets)
Lyman Products Corp., Rte. 147, Middlefield, CT 06455
McConnellstown Reloading & Cast Bullets, Inc., R.D. 3, Box 40, Huntingdon, PA 16652/814-627-5402
Mack's Sport Shop, Box 1155, Kodiak, AK 99615/907-486-4276 (cust. bull.)
Magnus Bullet Co., Inc., P.O. Box 2225, Birmingham, AL 35201/205-785-3357
Marshall Enterprises, 792 Canyon Rd., Redwood City, CA 94062/415-356-1230
Metallic Casting & Copper Corp. (MCC), 214 E. Third St., Mt. Vernon, NY 10550/914-1311 (cast bullets)
Michael's Antiques, Box 591, Waldoboro, ME 04572 (Balle Blondeau)
Miller Trading Co., 20 S. Front St., Wilmington, NC 28401/919-762-7107 (bullets)
Non-Toxic Components, Inc., P.O. Box 4202, Portland, OR 97208/503-226-7110 (steel shot kits)
NORMA (See Federal Cartridge Co.)
Nosler Bullets Inc., 107 S.W. Columbia, Bend, OR 97702/503-382-5108
Old Western Scrounger, 12924 Hwy A-12, Montague, CA 96064/916-459-5445
Omark Industries, P.O. Box 856, Lewiston, ID 83501/208-746-2351
Oro-Tech Industries, Inc., 1701 W. Charleston Blvd., Suite 510, Las Vegas, NV 89102/702-382-8109 (Golden Powder)
PMC Ammunition, 4890 So. Alameda, Vernon, CA 90058/213-587-7100
Patriotic Manufacturing & Sales, Banyan Plaza, Suite 334, Box 9000, Sebring,

AMMUNITION COMPONENTS — cont'd.

FL 33870/813-655-1798 (cust. bullets)
Pepperbox Gun Shop, P.O. Box 922, East Moline, IL 61244/309-796-0616 (257, 224 rifle cal. custom swaged bullets)
Polywad, Inc., P.O. Box 7916, Macon, GA 31209 (Spred-Rs for shotshells)
Pyrodex, See: Hodgdon Powder Co., Inc. (black powder substitute)
Robert Pomeroy, Morison Ave., East Corinth, ME 04427/207-285-7721 (formed cases, bullets)
Power Plus Enterprises, Inc., P.O. Box 6070, Columbus, GA 31907/404-561-1717 (12-ga. shotguns slugs; 308, 45 ACP, 357 cust. bull.)
Precision Ammo Co., P.O. Drawer 86, Valley Cottage, NY 10989/914-947-2710
Precision Swaged Bullets, Rte. 1, Box 93H, Ronan, MT 59864/406-676-5135 (silhouette; out-of-prods. Sharps)
Professional Hunter Supplies, P.O. Box 608; 444½ Main St., Ferndale, CA 95536/707-786-9460 (408, 375, 308, 510 cust. bull.)
Prometheus/Titan Black (See Fisher Enterprises)
Reardon Products, P.O. Box 126, Morrison, IL 61270/815-772-3155 (dry-lube powder)
Redwood Bullet Works, 3559 Bay Rd., Redwood City, CA 94063/415-367-6741 (cust. bullets)
Remington-Peters, 1007 Market St., Wilmington, DE 19898
Rubright Bullets, 1008 S. Quince Rd., Walnutport, PA 18088/215-767-1239 (cust. 22 & 6mm benchrest bullets)
S&S Precision Bullets, 22963 La Cadena, Laguna Hills, CA 92653/714-768-6836 (linotype cast bull.)
Sansom Bullets, 2506 Rolling Hills, Dr., Greenville, TX 75401 (custom)
Sierra Bullets Inc., 10532 So. Painter Ave., Santa Fe Springs, CA 90670
Southern Ammunition Co., Inc., Rt. 1, Box 6B, Latta, SC 29565/803-752-7751
Speer Products, Box 856, Lewiston, ID 83501
Sport Flite, P.O. Box 1082, Bloomfield Hills, MI 48308/313-647-3747 (zinc bases, gas checks)
Supreme Products Co., 1830 S. California Ave., Monrovia, CA 91016/800-423-7159/818-357-5395 (rubber bullets)
Swift Bullet Co., RR. 1, Box 140A, Quinter, KS 67752/913-754-3959 (375 big game, 224 cust.)
Tallon Bullets, 1194 Tidewood Dr., Bethel Park, PA 15102/412-471-4494 (dual. diam. 308 cust.)
Taracorp Industries, 16th & Cleveland Blvd., Granite City, IL 62040/618-451-4400 (Lawrence Brand lead shot)
Thunderbird Cartridge Co., P.O. Box 302, Phoenix, AZ 85001/602-237-3823 (powder)
Traft Gunshop, P.O. Box 1078, Buena Vista, CO 81211/303-395-6034 (cust. bull.)
Trophy Bonded Bullets, P.O. Box 262348, Houston, TX 77207/713-645-4499 (big game 458, 308, 375 bonded cust. bullets only)
Vitt/Boos, 2178 Nichols Ave., Stratford, CT 06497/203-375-6859 (Aerodynamic shotgun slug, 12-ga. only)
Ed Watson, Trophy Match Bullets, 2404 Wade Hampton Blvd., Greenville, SC 29615/803-244-7948 (22, 6mm cust. benchrest bull.)
Winchester/Olin, 427 N. Shamrock St., East Alton, IL 62024/618-258-2000
Worthy Products, Inc., Box 88 Main St., Chippewa Bay, NY 13623/315-324-5450 (slug loads)
Zero Bullet Co. Inc., P.O. Box 1188, Cullman, AL 35056/205-739-1606

ANTIQUE ARMS DEALERS

AD Hominem, R.R. 3, Orillia, Ont., L3V 6H3, Canada/705-689-5303
Antique Arms Co., David F. Saunders, 1110 Cleveland, Monett, MO 65708/417-235-6501
Antique Gun Parts, Inc., 1118 S. Braddock Ave., Pittsburgh, PA 15218/412-241-1811
Beeman Precision Arms, Inc., 3440-GD Airway Dr., Santa Rosa, CA 95403/707-578-7900 (airguns only)
Wm. Boggs, 1243 Grandview Ave., Columbus, OH 43212
Can Am Enterprises, 350 Jones Rd., Fruitland, ON L0R 1L0, Canada/416-643-4357 (catalog $2)
Century Intl. Arms, Inc., 5 Federal St., St. Albans, VT 05478/802-527-1252
Chas. Clements, Handicrafts Unltd., 1741 Dallas St., Aurora, CO 80010/303-364-0403
David Condon, Inc., P.O. Box 312, 14502-G Lee Rd., Chantilly, VA 22021/703-631-7748
Continental Kite & Key Co. (CONKKO), P.O. Box 40, Broomall, PA 19008/215-356-0711
John Corry, 628 Martin Lane, Deerfield, IL 60015/312-541-6250 (English guns)
Dixie Gun Works, Inc., P.O. Box 130, Gun Powder Lane, Union City, TN 38261/901-885-0561
Peter Dyson Ltd., 29-31 Church St., Honley, Huddersfield, W. Yorksh. HD7 2AH, England/0484-661062 (acc. f. ant. gun coll.; custom-and machine-made)
Ed's Gun House, Box 62, Rte. 1, Minnesota City, MN 55959/507-689-2925
Ellwood Epps Northern Ltd., 210 Worthington St. W., North Bay, Ont. PIB 3B4 Canada
William Fagan, Box 26100, Fraser, MI 48026/313-465-4637
Jack First Distributors, Inc., 44633 Sierra Hwy., Lancaster, CA 93534/805-945-6981
N. Flayderman & Co., P.O. Box 2446, Ft. Lauderdale, FL 33303/305-761-8855
The Flintlock Muzzle Loading Gun Shop, 1238 "G" So. Beach Blvd., Anaheim, CA 92804/714-821-6655
Chet Fulmer, P.O. Box 792, Rt. 2, Buffalo Lake, Detroit Lakes, MN 56501/218-847-7712
Robert S. Frielich, 396 Broome St., New York, NY 10013/212-254-3045
Garcia National Gun Traders, Inc., 225 S.W. 22nd Ave., Miami, FL 33135
Herb Glass, P.O. Box 25, Bullville, NY 10915/914-361-3021
James Goergen, Rte. 2, Box 182BB, Austin, MN 55912/507-433-9280
Griffin's Guns & Antiques, R.R. 4, Peterboro, Ont., Canada K9J 6X5/705-745-7022
Guncraft Sports, Inc., 125 E. Tyrone Rd., Oak Ridge, TN 37830/615-483-4024
Hansen & Company, 244 Old Post Rd., Southport, CT 06490/203-259-6222
Kelley's Harold Kelley, Box 125, Woburn, MA 01801/617-935-3389
Krider's Gun Shop, 114 W. Eagle Rd., Havertown, PA 19083/215-789-7828
Lever Arms Serv. Ltd., 2131 Burrard St. Vancouver, B.C., Canada V6J 3H8/604-736-0004
Liberty Antique Gunworks, 19 Key St., P.O. Box 183GD, Eastport, ME 04631/207-853-2327
Log Cabin Sport Shop, 8010 Lafayette Rd., Lodi, OH 44254/216-948-1082
Lone Pine Trading Post, Jct. Highways 61 and 248, Minnesota City, MN 55959/507-689-2925
Arthur McKee, 121 Eaton's Neck Rd., Northport, L.I., NY 11768/516-757-8850 (Rem. double shotguns)
Michael's Antiques, Box 591, Waldoboro, ME 04572
Charles W. Moore, R.D. #1, Box 276, Schenevus, NY 12155/607-278-5721
Museum of Historical Arms, 1038 Alton Rd., Miami Beach, FL 33139/305-672-7480 (ctlg $5)
Muzzleloaders Etc. Inc., 9901 Lyndale Ave. So., Bloomington, MN 55420/612-884-1161
New Orleans Arms Co., 5001 Treasure St., New Orleans, LA 70186/504-944-3371
Old Western Scrounger, 12924 Hwy A-12, Montague, CA 96064/916-459-5445 (write for list; $2)
Pioneer Guns, 5228 Montgomery, (Cincinnati) Norwood, OH 45212/513-631-4871
Pony Express Sport Shop, Inc., 16606 Schoenborn St., Sepulveda, CA 91343/818-895-1231
Martin B. Retting, Inc., 11029 Washington, Culver City, CA 90232/213-837-2412
Rutgers Gun & Boat Center, 127 Raritan Ave. Highland Park, NJ 08904/201-545-4344
San Francisco Gun Exch., 124 Second St., San Francisco, CA 94105/415-982-6097
Charles Semmer, 7885 Cyd Dr., Denver, CO 80221/303-429-6947
Don L. Shrum's Cape Outfitters, Rt. 2 Box 437-C, Cape Girardeau, MO 63701/314-335-4103
S&S Firearms, 74-11 Myrtle Ave., Glendale, NY 11385/718-497-1100
Steves House of Guns, Rte. 1, Minnesota City, MN 55959/507-689-2925
Stott's Creek Armory Inc., R 1 Box 70, Morgantown, IN 46160/317-878-5489
James Wayne, 308 Leisure Lane, Victoria, TX 77904/512-578-1258
Ward & Van Valkenburg, 114-32nd Ave. N., Fargo, ND 58102
M.C. Wiest, 125 E. Tyrone Rd., Oak Ridge, TN 37830/615-483-4024
Lewis Yearout, 308 Riverview Dr. E., Great Falls, MT 59404

APPRAISERS, GUNS, ETC.

Ad Hominem, R.R. 3, Orillia, ON L3V 6H3, Canada/705-689-5303
Antique Gun Parts, Inc., 1118 So. Braddock Ave., Pittsburgh, PA 15218/412-241-1811
Ahlman's, Rt. 1, Box 20, Morristown, MN 55052/507-685-4244
The Armoury Inc., Route 202, New Preston, CT 06777/203-868-0001
Beeman Precision Arms, Inc., 3440-GD Airway Dr., Santa Rosa, CA 95403/707-578-7900 (airguns only)
Christie's-East, 219 E. 67th St., New York, NY 10021/212-606-0400
E. Christopher Firearms Co., Inc., Route 128 & Ferry St., Miamitown, OH 45041/513-353-1321
Chas. Clements, Handicrafts Unltd., 1741 Dallas St., Aurora, CO 80010/303-364-0403
David Condon, Inc., P.O. Box 312, 14502-G Lee Rd., Chantilly, VA 22021/703-631-7748
John Corry, 628 Martin Lane, Deerfield, IL 60015/312-541-6250 (English guns)
Custom Tackle & Ammo, P.O. Box 1886, Farmington, NM 87499/505-632-3539
D.O.C. Specialists (Doc & Bud Ulrich), 2209 So. Central Ave., Cicero, IL 60650/312-652-3606
Ed's Gun House, Ed Kukowski, Route 1, Box 62, Minnesota City, MN 55952/507-689-2925
Ellwood Epps (Orillia) Ltd., R.R. 3, Hwy. 11 No., Orillia, Ont. L3V 6H3, Canada/705-699-5333
N. Flayderman & Co., Inc., P.O. Box 2446, Ft. Lauderdale, FL 33303/305-761-8855
Richard Geer, P.O. Box 1303, St. Charles, IL 60174/312-377-4625
James Goergen Rte. 2, Box 182BB, Austin, MN 55912/507-433-9280
"Gramps" Antique Cartridges, Ellwood Epps, Box 341, Washago, Ont. L0K 2B0 Canada/705-689-5348
Leon E. "Bud" Greenwald, 2553 S. Quitman St., Denver, CO 80219/303-935-3850
Griffin & Howe, 36 West 44th St., Suite 1011, New York, NY 10036/212-921-0980
Griffin & Howe, 33 Claremont Rd., Bernardsville, NJ 07924/201-766-2287
Guncraft Sports, Inc., 125 E. Tyrone Rd., Oak Ridge, TN 37830/615-483-4024
Hansen and Company, 244-246 Old Post Rd., Southport, CT 06490/203-259-6222

APPRAISERS, GUNS, ETC. — cont'd.

Lew Horton Sports Shop, 450 Waverly St., Framingham, MA 01772/617-485-3060
Kelley's, Harold Kelley, Box 125, Woburn, MA 01801/617-935-3389
Kenneth Kogan, P.O. Box 130, Lafayette Hills, PA 19444/215-233-4509
Liberty Antique Gunworks, 19 Key St., P.O. Box 183GD, Eastport, ME 04631/207-853-2327
Lone Pine Trading Post, Jct. Highways 248 & 61, Minnesota City, MN 55959/507-689-2925
Elwyn H. Martin, 937 So. Sheridan Blvd., Lakewood, CO 80226/303-922-2184
Miller Trading Co., 20 So. Front St., Wilmington, NC 28401/919-762-7107
The Museum of Historical Arms, Inc., 1038 Alton Rd., Miami Beach, FL 33139/305-672-7480
New England Arms Co., Lawrence Lane, Kittery Point, ME 03905/207-439-0593
Orvis Co. Inc., 10 River Rd., Manchester, VT 05254/802-362-3622
PM Airservices Ltd., P.O. Box 1573, Costa Mesa, CA 92628/714-968-2689
Pioneer Guns, 5228 Montgomery Rd., Norwood, OH 45212/513-631-4871
Pony Express Sport Shop, Inc., 16606 Schoenborn St., Sepulveda, CA 91343/818-895-1231
John Richards, Rte. 2, Box 325, Bedford, KY 40006/502-255-7222
Steel City Arms, Inc., P.O. Box 81926, Pittsburgh, PA 15217/412-461-3100
Dale A. Storey, DGS, Inc., 305 N. Jefferson, Casper, WY 82601/307-237-2414
James C. Tillinghast, P.O. Box 405GD, Hancock, NH 03449/603-525-66151
M. C. Wiest, 125 E. Tyrone Rd., Oak Ridge, TN 37830/615-483-4024
Lewis Yearout, 308 Riverview Dr. East, Great Falls, MT 59404/406-761-0589

AUCTIONEERS, GUNS, ETC.

Alberts Corp., 519 East 19th St., Paterson, NJ 07514/201-684-1676
Richard A. Bourne & Co. Inc., Box 141, Hyannis Port, MA 02647/617-775-0797
Christie's-East, 219 E. 67th St., New York, NY 10021/212-606-0400
Tom Keilman, 12316 Indian Mount, Austin, TX 78758
Kelley's, Harold Kelley, Box 125, Woburn, MA 01801/617-935-3389
"Little John's" Antique Arms, 777 S. Main St., Orange, CA 92668
Wayne Mock, Inc., Box 37, Tamworth, NH 03886/603-323-8749
Parke-Bernet (see Sotheby's)
Sotheby's, 1334 York Ave. at 72nd St., New York, NY 10021
James C. Tillinghast, Box 405GD, Hancock, NH 03449/603-525-6615

BOOKS (ARMS), Publishers and Dealers

Armory Publications, P.O. Box 44372, Tacoma, WA 98444/206-531-4632
Arms & Armour Press, Cassell TLC, Artillery House, Artillery Row, London SW1P 1RT England
Beeman Precision Arms Inc., 3440GD Airway Dr., Santa Rosa, CA 95403/707-578-7900 (airguns only)
Blacksmith Corp., P.O. Box 424, Southport, CT 06490/203-367-4041
Blacktail Mountain Books, 42 First Ave. West, Kalispell, MT 59901/406-257-5573
DBI Books, Inc., 4092 Commercial Ave., Northbrook IL 60062/312-272-6310
Dove Press, P.O. Box 3882, Enid, OK 73702/405-234-4347
Fortress Publications Inc., P.O. Box 9241, Stoney Creek, Ont. L8G 3X9, Canada/416-662-3505
Guncraft Books, Div. of Ridge Guncraft Sports, Inc., 125 E. Tyrone Rd., Oak Ridge, TN 37830/615-483-4024
The Gun Room Press, 127 Raritan Ave., Highland Park, NJ 08904/201-545-4344
Gunnerman Books, P.O. Box 4292, Auburn Hills, MI 48057/313-879-2779
Handgun Press, Box 406, Glenview, IL 60025/312-724-8816
Kopp Publishing Co., Box 224E, Hwy 13 South, Rte. 1, Lexington, MO 64067/816-259-2636
Lyman, Route 147, Middlefield, CT 06455
The Outdoorsman's Bookstore, Llangorse, Brecon, County Powys LD3 7UE, England
Paladin Press, P.O. Box 1307, Boulder, CO 80306/303-443-7250
Petersen Publishing Co., 84990 Sunset Blvd., Los Angeles, CA 90069
Gerald Pettinger Arms Books, Route 2, Russell, IA 50238/515-535-2239
Ray Riling Arms Books Co., 6844 Gorsten St., P.O. Box 18925, Philadelphia, PA 19119/215-438-2456
Rutgers Book Center, Mark Aziz, 127 Raritan Ave., Highland Park, NJ 08904/201-545-4344
Stackpole Books, Cameron & Kelker Sts., Telegraph Press Bldg., Harrisburg, PA 17105
Stoeger Publishing Co., 55 Ruta Court, South Hackensack, NJ 07606
Tara Press, P.O. Box 17211, Tucson, AZ 85731/602-296-5333
Ken Trotman Ltd., 135 Ditton Walk, Unit 11, Cambridge CB5 8QD, England
Paul Wahl Corp., P.O. Box 500, Bogota, NJ 07603-0500/201-261-9245
Winchester Press, 220 Old New Brunswick Rd., Piscataway, NJ 08854/201-981-0820
Wolfe Publishing Co., Inc., 6471 Air Park Dr., Prescott, AZ 86301/602-445-7810

BULLET & CASE LUBRICANTS

C-H Tool & Die Corp., 106 N. Harding St., Owen, WI 54460/715-229-2146
Clenzoil Corp., P.O. Box 1226, Sta. C, Canton, OH 44708/216-833-9758
Cooper-Woodward, 8073 Canyon Ferry Rd., Helena, MT 59601/406-475-3321 (Perfect Lube)
Corbin Mfg. & Supply Inc., 600 Industrial Circle, P.O. Box 2659, White City, OR 97503/503-826-5211
Dillon Precision Prods., Inc., 7442 E. Butherus Dr., Scottsdale, AZ 85260/602-948-8009
Green Bay Bullets, 1486 Servais St., Green Bay, WI 54304/414-497-2949 (EZE-Size case lube)
Javelina Products, P.O. Box 337, San Bernardino, CA 92402/714-882-5847 (Alox beeswax)
Jet-Aer Corp., 100 Sixth Ave., Paterson, NJ 07524
LeClear Industries, 1126 Donald Ave., P.O. Box 484, Royal Oak, MI 48068/313-588-1025
Lee Precision, Inc., 4275 Hwy. U, Hartford, WI 53027/414-673-3075
M&M Engineering, 10642 Arminta St., Sun Valley, CA 91352/818-842-8376 (case lubes)
Lyman Products Corp., Rte. 147, Middlefield, CT 06455 (Size-Ezy)
Micro-Lube, P.O. Box 117, Mesilla Park, NM 88047/505-524-4215
M&N Bullet Lube, P.O. Box 495, 151 N.E. Jefferson St., Madras, OR 97741/503-475-2992
Northeast Industrial, Inc., P.O. Box 249, 405 N. Canyon Blvd., Canyon City, OR 97820/503-575-2513 (Ten X-Lube; NEI mold prep)
Pacific Tool Co., P.O. Box 2048, Ordnance Plant Rd., Grand Island, NE 68801/308-384-2308
Ponsness-Warren, P.O. Box 8, Rathdrum, ID 83858/208-687-2231 (case lubes)
Radix Research & Marketing, Box 247, Woodland Park, CO 80866/303-687-3182 (Magnum Dri-Lube)
Redding Inc., 1089 Starr Rd., Cortland, NY 13045/607-753-3331
Rooster Laboratories, P.O. Box 412514, Kansas City, MO 64141/816-474-9711
SAECO (See Redding)
Sandia Die & Cartridge Co., Route 5, Box 5400, Albuquerque, NM 87123/505-298-5729
Shooters Accessory Supply (SAS) (See Corbin Mfg. & Supply)
Tamarack Prods. Inc., P.O. Box 625, Wauconda, IL 60084/312-526-9333 (Bullet lube)

BULLET SWAGE DIES AND TOOLS

Bullet Swaging Supply, Inc., P.O. Box 1056, 303 McMillan Rd., West Monroe, LA 71291/318-387-7257
C-H Tool & Die Corp., 106 N. Harding St., Owen, WI 54460/715-229-2146
Mrs. Lester Coats, 416 Simpson Ave., North Bend, OR 97459/503-756-6995 (lead wire core cutter)
Corbin Mfg. & Supply Inc., 600 Industrial Circle, P.O. Box 2659, White City, OR 97503/503-826-5211
Hollywood Loading Tools (See M&M Engineering)
Huntington Die Specialties, 601 Oro Dam Blvd., Oroville, CA 95965/916-534-1210
L.L.F. Die Shop, 1281 Highway 99 North, Eugene, OR 97402/503-688-5753
M&M Engineering, 10642 Arminta St., Sun Valley, CA 91352/818-842-8376
Rorschach Precision Products, P.O. Box 151613, Irving, TX 75015/214-790-3487
SAS Dies, (See Corbin Mfg. & Supply)
Seneca Run Iron Works Inc., dba "Swagease", P.O. Box 3032, Greeley, CO 80633/303-352-1452 (muzzle-loading round ball)
Sport Flite Mfg., Inc., 2520 Industrial Row, Troy, MI 48084/313-280-0648

CARTRIDGES FOR COLLECTORS

AD Hominem, R.R. 3, Orillia, Ont., Canada L3V 6H3/705-689-5303
Ammo-Mart Ltd., P.O. Box 125, Hawkesbury, ON, K6A 2R8 Canada/613-632-9300
Ida I. Burgess, Sam's Gun Shop, 25 Squam Rd., Rockport, MA 01966/617-546-6839
Cameron's, 16690 W. 11th Ave., Golden CO 80401/303-279-7365
Cartridges Unlimited, R. 1, Box 50, South Kent, CT 06785/203-927-3053
Creative Cartridge Co., 56 Morgan Rd., Canton, CT 06019/203-693-2529
Chas. E. Duffy, Williams Lane, West Hurley, NY 12419/914-679-2997
Tom M. Dunn, 1342 So. Poplar, Casper, WY 82601/307-237-3207
Ellwood Epps (Orillia) Ltd., Hwy. 11 North, Orillia, Ont. L3V 6H3, Canada/705-689-5333
Excaliber Wax, Inc., P.O. Box 432, Kenton, OH 43326/419-673-0512
Jack First Distributors, Inc., 44633 Sierra Hwy., Lancaster, CA 93534/805-945-6981
GTM Co., Geo. T. Mahaney, 15915B East Main St., La Puente, CA 91744/818-768-5806
Richard Geer, P.O. Box 1303, St. Charles, IL 60174/312-377-4625
Glaser Safety Slug, Inc., P.O. Box 8223, Foster City, CA 94404/415-345-7677
"Gramps" Antique Cartridges, Ellwood Epps, Box 341, Washago, Ont., Canada L0K 2B0
Griffin's Guns & Antiques, R.R. #4, Peterboro, Ont. K9J 6X5, Canada/705-745-7022
Gun Parts Corp., Box 2, West Hurley, NY 12491/914-679-2417
Hansen and Company, 244-246 Old Post Rd., Southport, CT 06490/203-259-6222
Idaho Ammunition Service, 410 21st Ave., Lewiston, ID 83501
Kelley's, Harold Kelley, Box 125, Woburn, MA 01801/617-935-3389
Metallic Casting & Copper Corp. (MCC), 214 E. Third St., Mt. Vernon, NY

CARTRIDGES FOR COLLECTORS — cont'd.

10550/914-664-1311
Old Western Scrounger, 12924 Hwy. A-12, Montague, CA 96064/916-459-5445
Jesse Ramos, P.O. Box 7105, La Puente, CA 91744/818-369-6384
San Francisco Gun Exchange, Inc., 124 Second St., San Francisco, CA 94105/415-982-6097
James C. Tillinghast, Box 405GD, Hancock, NH 03449/603-525-6615 (list $1)
Ward & VanValkenburg, 114-32nd Ave. No., Fargo, ND 58102/701-232-2351
Lewis Yearout, 308 Riverview Dr. E., Great Falls, MT 59404

CASES, CABINETS AND RACKS—GUN

API Outdoors Inc., 602 Kimbrough Dr., Tallulah, LA 71282/318-574-4903 (racks)
Alco Carrying Cases, 601 W. 26th St., New York, NY 10001/212-675-5820 (aluminum)
Bob Allen Co., 214 S.W. Jackson, Des Moines, IA 50315/515-283-2191/800-247-8048 (carrying)
The American Import Co., 1453 Mission St., San Francisco, CA 94103/415-863-1506
Armes de Chasse, P.O. Box 827, Chadsford, PA 19317/215-388-1146
Art Jewel Ltd., Eagle Business Ctr., 460 Randy Rd., Carol Stream, IL 60188/312-260-0040 (cases)
Beeman Precision Arms, Inc., 3440-GDD Airway Dr., Santa Rosa, CA 95403/707-578-7900
Bore Stores, Rt. 66, Box 430, Yellville, AR 72687 (synthetic cases)
Boyt Co., Div. of Welsh Sportg. Gds., P.O. Drawer 668, Iowa Falls, IA 50126/515-648-4626
Browning, Rt. 4, Box 624-B, Arnold, MO 63010
China IM/EX, P.O. Box 27573, San Francisco, CA 94127/415-661-2212 (soft-type cases)
Chipmunk Mfg. Co., 114 E. Jackson, P.O. Box 1104, Medford, OR 97501/503-664-5585 (cases)
Dara-Nes Inc., see: Nesci
Dart Mfg. Co., 4012 Bronze Way, Dallas, TX 75237/214-333-4221
Detroit-Armor Corp., 2233 No. Palmer Dr., Schaumburg, IL 60103/312-397-4070 (Saf-Gard steel gun safe)
Doskocil Mfg. Co., Inc., P.O. Box 1246, Arlington, TX 75010/817-467-5116 (Gun Guard carrying)
Ellwood Epps (Orillia) Ltd., R.R. 3, Hwy. 11 North, Orillia, Ont. L3V 6H3, Canada/705-689-5333 (custom gun cases)
Flambeau Plastics Corp., 801 Lynn, Baraboo, WI 53913
Fort Knox Security Products, 1051 N. Industrial Park Rd., Orem, UT 84057/801-224-7233 (safes)
Gun Parts Corp., Box 2, West Hurley, NY 12491/914-679-2417 (cases)
Hansen and Hansen, 244 Old Post Rd., Southport, CT 06490/203-259-7337
Marvin Huey Gun Cases, P.O. Box 22456, Kansas City, MO 64113/816-444-1637 (handbuilt leather cases)
Jumbo Sports Prods., P.O. Box 280-Airport Rd., Frederick, MD 21701
Kalispel Metal Prods. (KMP), P.O. Box 267, Cusick, WA 99119/509-445-1121 (aluminum boxes)
Kane Products Inc., 5572 Brecksville Rd., Cleveland, OH 44131/216-524-9962
Kolpin Mfg., Inc., Box 231, Berlin, WI 54923/414-361-0400
Marble Arms Corp., 420 Industrial Park, Gladstone, MI 49837/906-428-3710
Bill McGuire, 1600 No. Eastmont Ave., East Wenatchee, WA 98801
Nesci Enterprises, Inc., P.O. Box 119, Summit St., East Hampton, CT 06424/203-267-2588 (firearms security chests)
Paul-Reed, Inc., P.O. Box 227, Charlevoix, MI 49720
Penguin Industries, Inc., Airport Industrial Mall, Coatesville, PA 19320/215-384-6000
Proofmark, Ltd., P.O. Box 183, Alton, IL 62002/618-463-0120 (Italian Emmebi leather cases)
Protecto Plastics, Div. of Penguin Ind., Airport Industrial Mall, Coatesville, PA 19320/215-384-6000 (carrying cases)
Quality Arms, Inc., P.O. Box 19477, Houston, TX 77224/713-870-8377
Rahn Gun Works, Inc., 470 Market S.W., Box 33, Grand Rapids, MI 49503/616-235-6469 (leather trunk cases)
Red Head Brand Corp., 4949 Joseph Hardin Dr., Dallas, TX 75236/214-333-4141
Saf-T-Case Mfg. Co., 6327 Town Hill, Dallas, TX 75214
San Angelo Co., 1841 Industrial Ave., San Angelo, TX 76904/915-655-7126
Schulz Industries, 16247 Minnesota Ave., Paramount, CA 90723/213-439-5903 (carrying cases)
Security Gun Chest, (See Tread Corp.)
Sweet Home Inc., Subs, of Will-Burt Co., P.O. Box 250, Sweet Home, OR 97386/503-367-5185 (gun safes)
Tread Corp., P.O. Box 13207, Roanoke, VA 24032/703-982-6881 (security gun chest)
WAMCO, Inc., Mingo Loop, P.O. Box 337, Oquossoc, ME 04964-0337/800-227-1415 (wooden display cases)
Weather Shield Sports Equipm. Inc., Rte. #3, Petoskey Rd., Charlevoix, MI 49720
Wilson Case Co., 906 Juniata Ave., Juniata, NE 68955/402-751-2145 (cases)

CHOKE DEVICES, RECOIL ABSORBERS & RECOIL PADS

Action Products Inc., 22 N. Mulberry St., Hagerstown, MD 21740/800-228-7763 (rec. shock eliminator)
Arms Ingenuity Co., Box 1; 51 Canal St., Weatogue, CT 06089/203-658-5624 (Jet-Away)
Armsport, Inc., 3590 N.W. 49th St., Miami, FL 33142/305-635-7850 (choke devices)
Baer Custom Guns, 1725 Minesite Rd., Allentown, PA 18103/215-398-2362 (compensator syst. f. 45 autos)
Briley Mfg. Co., 1085-B Gessner, Houston, TX 77055/713-932-6995 (choke tubes)
C&H Research, 115 Sunnyside Dr., Lewis, KS 67552/316-324-5445 (Mercury recoil suppressor)
Vito Cellini, Francesca Inc., 3115 Old Ranch Rd., San Antonio, TX 78217/512-826-2584 (recoil reducer; muzzle brake)
Clinton River Gun Serv. Inc., 30016 S. River Rd., Mt. Clemens, MI 48045 (Reed Choke)
Reggie Cubriel, 15610 Purple Sage, San Antonio, TX 78255/512-695-3364 (leather recoil pads)
Delta Vectors, Inc., 7119 W. 79th St., Overland Park, KS 66204/913-642-0307 (Techni-Port recoil compensation)
Edwards Recoil Reducer, 269 Herbert St., Alton, IL 62002/618-462-3257
Emsco Variable Shotgun Chokes, 101 Second Ave., S.E., Waseca, MN 56093/507-835-1779
Fabian Bros. Sptg. Goods, Inc., 1510 Morena Blvd., Suite "I", San Diego, CA 92110/619-223-3955 (DTA Muzzle Mizer rec. abs.; MIL/brake)
Freshour Mfg., 1914-15th Ave. North, Texas City, TX 77590/713-945-7726 (muzzle brakes)
David Gentry Custom Gunmaker, 314 N. Hoffman, P.O. Box 1440, Belgrade, MT 59714/406-388-4867 (muzzle brakes)
Griggs Products, P.O. Box 789; 270 So. Main St., Suite 103, Bountiful, UT 84010/801-295-9696 (recoil director)
Gun Parts Corp., Box 2, West Hurley, NY 12491/914-679-2417
William E. Harper, The Great 870 Co., P.O. Box 6309, El Monte, CA 91734/213-579-3077
I.N.C., Inc., 1133 Kresky #4, Centralia, WA 98531/206-330-2042 (Sorbothane Kick-Eez recoil pad)
KDF, Inc., 2485 Hwy. 46 N., Seguin, TX 78155/512-379-8141 (muzzle brake)
La Paloma Marketing, 4210 E. La Paloma Dr., Tucson, AZ 85718/602-881-4750 (Action rec. shock eliminator)
Lyman Products Corp., Rte. 147, Middlefield, CT. 06455 (Cutts Comp.)
Mag-na-port International, Inc., 41302 Executive Drive, Mt. Clemens, MI 48045/313-469-6727 (muzzle-brake system)
Mag-Na-Port of Canada, 1861 Burrows Ave., Winnipeg, Manitoba R2X 2V6, Canada
Marble Arms Corp., 420 Industrial Park, Box 111, Gladstone, MI 49837/906-428-3710 (Poly-Choke)
Pachmayr Ltd., 1875 So. Mountain Ave., Monrovia, CA 91016/818-423-9704 (recoil pads)
P.A.S.T. Corp., 210 Park Ave., Columbia, MO 65205/314-449-7278 (recoil reducer shield)
Poly-Choke (See Marble Arms)
Pro-Port Ltd., 41302 Executive Dr., Mt. Clemens, MI 48045/313-469-7323
Protektor Model, 7 Ash St., Galeton, PA 16922/814-435-2442 (shoulder recoil pad)
Reed Choke (See Clinton River Gun Svc.)
Shogun Mfg. Inc., 304 So. Main St., P.O. Box 306, Kirksville, MO 63501/816-627-0500
Supreme Products Co., 1830 S. California Ave., Monrovia, CA 91016/800-423-7159/818-357-5395 (recoil pads)
Upper Missouri Trading Co., 304 Harold St., Crofton, NE 68730/402-388-4844
Walker Arms Co., Inc., Rte. 2, Box 73, Highway 80 West, Selma, AL 36701/205-872-6231

CHRONOGRAPHS AND PRESSURE TOOLS

Competition Electronics, Inc., 2542 Point O' Woods Dr., Rockford, IL 61111/815-877-3322
Custom Chronograph Inc., 5305 Reese Hill Rd., Sumas, WA 98295/206-988-7801
D&H Precision Tooling, 7522 Barnard Mill Rd., Ringwood, IL 60072/815-653-9611 (Pressure Testing Receiver)
H-S Precision, Inc., 112 N. Summit St., Prescott, AZ 86302/602-445-0607 (press. barrels)
Paul Jaeger, Inc., P.O. Box 449, 1 Madison Ave., Grand Junction, TN 38039
Oehler Research, Inc., P.O. Box 9135, Austin, TX 78766/512-327-6900
P.A.C.T., Inc., P.O. Box 531525, Grand Prairie, TX 75053/214-641-0049 (Precision chronogr.)
Quartz-Lok, 13137 N. 21st Lane, Phoenix, AZ 85029/602-863-2729
Tepeco, P.O. Box 342, Friendswood, TX 77546/713-482-2702 (Tepeco Speed-Meter)

CLEANING & REFINISHING SUPPLIES

American Gas & Chemical Co., Ltd., 220 Pegasus Ave., Northvale, NJ 07647/201-767-7300 (TSI gun lube)
Anderson Mfg. Co., P.O. Box 536, 6813 S. 220th St., Kent, WA 98032/206-872-7602 (stock finishes)
Armite Labs., 1845 Randolph St., Los Angeles, CA 90001/213-587-7744 (pen oiler)
Beeman Precision Arms, Inc., 3440-GD Airway Dr., Santa Rosa, CA 95403/707-578-7900 (airguns only)
Belltown, Ltd., RR2, Box 69, Kent, CT 06757/203-354-5750 (gun cleaning cloth kit)
Birchwood-Casey, 7900 Fuller Rd., Eden Prairie, MN 55344/612-927-7933
Blacksmith Corp., P.O. Box 424, Southport, CT 06490/800-531-2665 (Arctic Friction Free gun clg. equip.)
Blue and Gray Prods., Inc., R.D. #6, Box 362, Wellsboro, PA 16901/717-724-1383
Break-Free Corp., P.O. Box 25020, Santa Ana, CA 92799/714-953-1900 (lubricants)

CLEANING & REFINISHING SUPPLIES — cont'd.

Jim Brobst, 299 Poplar St., Hamburg, PA 19526/215-562-2103 (J-B Bore Cleaning Compound)
Brownells, Inc., 222 W. Liberty, Montezuma, IA 50171/515-623-5401
Browning Arms, Rt. 4, Box 624-B, Arnold, MO 63010
Chopie Mfg. Inc., 700 Copeland Ave., La Crosse, WI 54601/608-784-0926 (Black-Solve gun cleaner)
Clenzoil Corp., Box 1226, Sta. C, Canton, OH 44708/216-833-9758
Crouse's Country Cover, P.O. Box 160, Storrs, CT 06268/203-429-3710 (Masking Gun Oil)
J. Dewey Mfg. Co., 186 Skyview Dr., Southbury, CT 06488/203-264-3064 (one-piece gun clg. rod)
Dri-Slide, Inc., 411 N. Darling, Fremont, MI 49412/616-924-3950
The Dutchman's Firearms Inc., 4143 Taylor Blvd., Louisville, KY 40215/502-366-0555
Forster Products, 82 E. Lanark Ave., Lanark, IL 61046/815-493-6360
Fountain Prods., 492 Prospect Ave., W. Springfield, MA 01089/413-781-4551
Forty-Five Ranch Enterpr., 119 S. Main St., Miami, OK 74354/918-542-9307
Gun Parts Corp. (Successors to Numrich Arms Parts Div.), Box 2, West Hurley, NY 12491/914-679-2417 (gun blue)
Heller & Levin Associates, Inc., 88 Marlborough Court, Rockville Center, NY 11570/516-764-9349
Frank C. Hoppe Division, Penguin Ind., Inc., Airport Industrial Mall, Coatesville, PA 19320/215-384-6000
Hydrosorbent Products, Box 675D, Rye, NE 10580 (silica gel dehumidifier)
J-B Bore Cleaner, 299 Poplar St., Hamburg, PA 19526/215-562-2103
Ken Jantz Supply, 222 E. Main, Davis, OK 73030/405-369-2316
Jet-Aer Corp., 100 Sixth Ave., Paterson, NJ 07524 (blues & oils)
Kellog's Professional Prods., Inc., 325 Pearl St., Sandusky, OH 44870/419-625-6551
K.W. Kleinendorst, R.D. #1, Box 113B, Hop Bottom, PA 18824/717-289-4687 (rifle clg. cables)
Terry K. Kopp, Highway 13 South, Lexington, MO 64067/816-259-2636 (stock rubbing compound; rust preventative grease)
LPS Chemical Prods., Holt Lloyd Corp., 4647 Hugh Howell Rd., Box 3050, Tucker, GA 30084/404-934-7800
Mark Lee, P.O. Box 20379, Minneapolis, MN 55420/612-431-1727 (rust blue solution)
LEM Gun Specialties, P.O. Box 87031, College Park, GA 30337 (Lewis Lead Remover)
Lynx Line Gun Prods. Div., Protective Coatings, Inc., 773 Harkness Dr., Adrian, MI 49221/517-263-7800
MJL Industries, Inc., P.O. Box 122, McHenry, IL 60050/815-344-1040 (Rust Free)
Marble Arms Co., 420 Industrial Park, Gladstone, MI 49837/906-428-3710
Mike Marsh, Croft Cottage, Main St., Elton, Derbyshire DE4 2BY, ENGLAND/062-988-669 (gun accessories)
Micro Sight Co., 242 Harbor Blvd., Belmont, CA 94002/415-591-0769 (bedding compound)
Mount Labs, Inc. (See: LaPaloma Marketing, Inc.)
Nesci Enterprises, Inc., P.O. Box 119, Summit St., East Hampton, CT 06424/203-267-2588
Old World Oil Products, 3827 Queen Ave. No., Minneapolis, MN 55412/612-522-5037 (gun stock finish)
Omark Industries, P.O. Box 856, Lewiston, ID 83501/208-746-2351
Original Mink Oil, Inc., P.O. Box 20191, 11021 N.E. Beech St., Portland, OR 97220/503-255-2814
Outers Laboratories, Div. of Omark Industries, Route 2, Onalaska, WI 54650/608-781-5800
Ox-Yoke Originals, Inc., 34 W. Main St., Milo, ME 04463/800-231-8313 (dry lubrication patches)
Parker-Hale/Precision Sports, P.O. Box 708, Cortland, NY 13045
Bob Pease Accuracy, P.O. Box 787, Zipp Rd., New Braunfels, TX 78131/512-625-1342
A. E. Pennebaker Co., Inc., P.O. Box 1386, Greenville, SC 29602/803-235-8016 (Pyro Lux)
Precision Sports, P.O. Box 708, 3736 Kellogg Rd., Cortland, NY 13045/607-756-2851 (Parker-Hale)
R&S Industries Corp., 1312 Washington Ave., St. Louis, MO 63103/314-241-8464 (Miracle All Purpose polishing cloth)
RTI Research Ltd., P.O. Box 48300, Bental Three Tower, Vancouver, B.C. V7X 1A1, Canada/604-588-5141 (Accubore chemical bore cleaner)
Reardon Prod., P.O. Box 126, Morrison, IL 61270/815-772-3155 (Dry-Lube)
Rice Protective Gun Coatings, 235-30th St., West Palm Beach, FL 33407/305-848-7771
Richards Classic Oil Finish, John Richards, Rt. 2, Box 325, Bedford, KY 40006/502-255-7222 (gunstock oils, wax)
Rig Products, 87 Coney Island Dr., Sparks, NV 89431/703-331-5666
Rusteprufe Labs., Rte. 5, Sparta, WI 54656/608-269-4144
Rust Guardit, see: Schwab Industries
Schwab Industries, Inc., P.O. Box 1269, Sequim, WA 98382/206-683-2944
Tyler Scott, Inc., 8170 Corporate Park Dr., Cincinnati, OH 45242, Suite 141/513-489-2202 (ML black solvent; patch lube)
Seacliff Inc., 2210 Santa Anita, So. El Monte, CA 91733/818-350-0515 (portable parts washer)
Secoa Technologies, Inc., 3915 U.S. Hwy. 98 So., Lakeland, FL 33801/813-665-1734 (Teflon coatings)
Shooter's Choice (See Venco Industries)
TDP Industries, Inc., 603 Airport Blvd., Doylestown, PA 18901/215-345-8687
Taylor & Robbins, Box 164, Rixford, PA 16745 (Throat Saver)
Texas Platers Supply Co., 2453 W. Five Mile Parkway, Dallas, TX 75233
Totally Dependable Products; See: TDP
Treso, P.O. Box 4640, Pagosa Springs, CO 81157/303-731-2295 (mfg. Durango Gun Rod)
C. S. Van Gorden, 1815 Main St., Bloomer, WI 54724/715-568-2612 (Van's Instant Blue)
United States Products Co., 518 Melwood Ave., Pittsburgh, PA 15213/412-621-2130 (Gold Medallion bore cleaner/conditioner)
Venco Industries, Inc., 16770 Hilltop Park Pl., Chagrin Falls, OH 44022/216-543-8808 (Shooter's Choice bore cleaner & conditioner)
WD-40 Co., P.O. Box 80607, San Diego, CA 92138-9021/619-275-1400
J. C. Whitney & Co., 1917 Archer Ave., Chicago, IL 60680 (gunstock finish)
Williams Gun Sight, 7389 Lapeer Rd., Davison, MI 48423 (finish kit)
Wisconsin Platers Supply Co., (See Texas Platers Supply Co.)
Zip Aerosol Prods., See Rig

CUSTOM GUNSMITHS

Accuracy Gun Shop, Lance Martini, 3651 University Ave., San Diego, CA 92104/619-282-8500
Accuracy Systems Inc., 15203 N. Cave Creek Rd., Phoenix, AZ 85032/602-971-1991
Accuracy Unlimited, 16036 N. 49 Ave., Glendale, AZ 85306/602-978-9089
Ahlman's Inc., R.R. 1, Box 20, Morristown, MN 55052/507-685-4244
Don Allen Inc., HC55, Box 326, Sturgis, SD 57785/605-347-5227
American Custom Gunmakers Guild, c/o Jan Melchert, Exec. Scy., 220 Division St., Northfield, MN 55057/507-645-8811
Amrine's Gun Shop, 937 Luna Ave., Ojai, CA 93023
Ann Arbor Rod and Gun Co., 1946 Packard Rd., Ann Arbor, MI 48104/313-769-7866
Armament Gunsmithing Co., Inc., 525 Route 22, Hillside, NJ 07205/201-686-0960
Arms Services Corp., 330 Lockhouse Rd., Westfield, MA 01085/413-562-4196
Armurier Hiptmayer, P.O. Box 136, Eastman, Que. JOE 1P0, Canada/514-297-2492
Ed von Atzigen, The Custom Shop, 890 Cochrane Crescent, Peterborough, Ont., K9H 5N3 Canada/705-742-6693
Richard W. Baber, Alpine Gun Mill, 1507 W. Colorado Ave., Colorado Springs, CO 80904/303-634-4867
Bain & Davis Sptg. Gds., 307 E. Valley Blvd., San Gabriel, CA 91776/213-283-7449
Baer Custom Guns, 1725 Minesite Rd., Allentown, PA 18103/215-398-2362 (rifles)
Joe J. Balickie, Rte. 2, Box 56-G, Apex, NC 27502/919-362-5185
Barnes Custom Shop, dba Barnes Bullets Inc., P.O. Box 215, American Fork, UT 84003
Barta's Gunsmithing, 10231 US Hwy., #10, Cato, WI 54206/414-732-4472
Donald Bartlett, 31829-32nd Pl. S.W., Federal Way, WA 98023/206-927-0726
R. J. Beal, Jr., 170 W. Marshall Rd., Lansdowne, PA 19050/215-259-1220
Behlert Precision, RD 2 Box 63, Route 611 North, Pipersville, PA 18947/215-766-8681 (custom)
George Beitzinger, 116-20 Atlantic Ave., Richmond Hill, NY 11419/718-847-7661
Bell's Custom Shop, 3309 Mannheim Rd., Franklin Park, IL 60131/312-678-1900 (handguns)
Dennis M. Bellm Gunsmithing, Inc., 2376 So. Redwood Rd., Salt Lake City, UT 84119/801-974-0697
Bennett Gun Works, 561 Delaware Ave., Delmar, NY 12054/518-439-1862
Bergmann & Williams, 2450 Losee Rd., Suite F, No. Las Vegas, NV 89030/702-642-1091
Gordon Bess, 708 Royal Gorge Blvd., Canon City, CO 81212/303-275-1073
Al Biesen, 5021 Rosewood, Spokane, WA 99208/509-328-9340
Roger Biesen, W. 2039 Sinto Ave., Spokane, WA 99201
Stephen L. Billeb, Box 1176, Big Piney, WY 83113/307-276-5627
E.C. Bishop & Son Inc., 119 Main St., P.O. Box 7, Warsaw, MO 65355/816-438-5121
Duane Bolden, 1295 Lassen Dr., Hanford, CA 93230/209-582-6937 (rust bluing)
Charles Boswell (Gunmakers), Div. of Saxon Arms Ltd., 615 Jasmine Ave. No., Unit J,Tarpon Springs, FL 34689/813-938-4882
Kent Bowerly, Metolious Meadows Dr., H.C.R. Box 1903, Camp Sherman, OR 97730/503-595-6028
Larry D. Brace, 771 Blackfoot Ave., Eugene, OR 97404/503-688-1278
Brazos Arms Co., 7314 Skybright Lane, Houston, TX 77095/713-463-0826 (gunsmithing)
A. Briganti, 475 Rt. 32, Highland Mills, NY 10930/914-692-4409
Brown Precision Inc., P.O. Box 270GD, 7786 Molinos Ave., Los Molinos, CA 96055/800-543-2506/916-384-2506 (rifles)
Brown's Gun Shop, Ed Brown, Rte. 2 Box 2922, Perry, MO 63462/314-565-3261
David Budin, Main St., Margaretville, NY 12455/914-568-4103
Ida I. Burgess, Sam's Gun Shop, 25 Squam Rd., Rockport, MA 01966/617-546-6839 (bluing repairs)
Leo Bustani, P.O. Box 8125, W. Palm Beach, FL 33407/305-622-2710
Cache La Poudre Rifleworks, 140 No. College Ave., Ft. Collins, CO 80524/303-482-6913 (cust. ML)
Cameron's Guns, 16690 W. 11th Ave., Golden, CO 80401
Lou Camilli, 4700 Oahu Dr. N.E., Albuquerque, NM 87111/505-293-5259 (ML)
Dick Campbell, 20000 Silver Ranch Rd., Conifer, CO 80433/303-697-9150
Ralph L. Carter, Carter's Gun Shop, 225 G St., Penrose, CO 81240/303-372-6240
Larry T. Caudill, 1025A Palomas Dr. S.E., Albuquerque, NM 87108/505-255-2515
Shane Caywood, P.O. Box 321, Minocqua, WI 54548/715-356-5414
R. MacDonald Champlin, P.O. Box 693, Manchester, NH 03105/603-483-8559 (ML rifles and pistols)
F. Bob Chow's Gun Shop, Inc., 3185 Mission St., San Francisco, CA 94110/415-282-8358
E. Christopher Firearms Co., Inc., Route 128 & Ferry St., Miamitown, OH 45041/513-353-1321
Classic Arms Corp., P.O. Box 8, Palo Alto, CA 94302/415-321-7243
Clinton River Gun Serv. Inc., 30016 S. River Rd., Mt. Clemens, MI 48045/313-468-1090
Charles H. Coffin, 3719 Scarlet Ave., Odessa, TX 79762/915-366-4729

CUSTOM GUNSMITHS — cont'd.

Jim Coffin, 250 Country Club Lane, Albany, OR 97321/503-928-4391
David Costa, 94 Orient Ave., Arlington, MA 02174/617-643-9571
C. Ed Cox, 166 W. Wylie Ave., Washington, PA 15301/412-228-2932
Crocker, 1510 - 42nd St., Los Alamos, NM 87544 (rifles)
J. Lynn Crook, Rt. 6, Box 295-A, Lebanon, TN 37087/615-449-1930
Cumberland Arms, Rt. 1, Box 1150, Shafer Rd., Blantons Chapel, Manchester, TN 37355
Cumberland Knife & Gun Works, 5661 Bragg Blvd., Fayetteville, NC 28303/919-867-0009 (ML)
Custom Gun Guild, 2646 Church Dr. Doraville, GA 30340/404-455-0346
D&D Gun Shop, 363 Elmwood, Troy, MI 48083/313-583-1512
Dakota Arms, Inc., HC 55 Box 326, Sturgis, SD 57785/605-347-4686
Homer L. Dangler, Box 254, Addison, MI 49220/517-547-6745 (Kentucky rifles; brochure $3)
Sterling Davenport, 9611 E. Walnut Tree Dr., Tucson, AZ 85715/602-749-5590
Davis Co., 2793 Del Monte St., West Sacramento, CA 95691/916-372-6789
Ed Delorge, 2231 Hwy. 308, Thibodaux, LA 70301/504-447-1633
Jack Dever, 8520 N.W. 90, Oklahoma City, OK 73132/405-721-6393
R. H. Devereaux, D. D. Custom Rifles, 5240 Mule Deer Dr., Colorado Springs, CO 80919/719-548-8468
Dilliott Gunsmithing, Inc., Rt. 3, Box 340, Scarlett Rd., Dandridge, TN 37725/615-397-9204
Dominic DiStefano, 4303 Friar Lane, Colorado Springs, CO 80907
William Dixon, Buckhorn Gun Works, Rt. 4 Box 1230, Rapid City, SD 57702/605-787-6289
C. P. Donnelly-Siskiyou Gun Works, 405 Kubli Rd., Grants Pass, OR 97527/503-846-6604
Dowtin Gunworks (DGW), Rt. 4 Box 930A, Flagstaff, AZ 86001/602-779-1898
Charles E. Duffy, Williams Lane, West Hurley, NY 12491/914-679-2997
Duncan's Gunworks Inc., 1619 Grand Ave., San Marcos, CA 92069/619-727-0515
Jere Eggleston, P.O. Box 50238, Columbia, SC 29250/803-799-3402
Elko Arms, Dr. L. Kortz, 28 rue Ecole Moderne, B-7400 Soignies, H.T., Belgium
Bob Emmons, 238 Robson Rd., Grafton, OH 44044/216-458-5890
Englishtown Sporting Goods, Inc., David J. Maxham, 38 Main St., Englishtown, NJ 07726/201-446-7717
Dennis Erhardt, P.O. Box 502, Canyon Creek, MT 59633/406-368-2298
Ken Eyster, Heritage Gunsmiths Inc., 6441 Bishop Rd., Centerburg, OH 43011/614-625-6131
Andy Fautheree, P.O. Box 4607, Pagosa Springs, CO 81157/303-731-5003 (cust ML; send SASE)
Ted Fellowes, Beaver Lodge, 9245-16th Ave., S.W., Seattle, WA 98106/206-763-1698 (muzzleloaders)
Ferris Firearms, 1827 W. Hildebrand, San Antonio, TX 78201/512-734-0304
Fiberpro Inc., Robert Culbertson, 3636 California St., San Diego, CA 92101/619-295-7703 (rifles)
Jack First Distributors Inc., 44633 Sierra Highway, Lancaster, CA 93534/805-945-6981
Marshall F. Fish, Rt. 22 North, Box 2439, Westport, NY 12993/518-962-4897
Jerry A. Fisher, 1244-4th Ave. West, Kalispell, MT 59901/406-755-7093
Flaig's Inc., 2200 Evergreen Rd., Millvale, PA 15209/412-821-1717
Flint Creek Arms Co., P.O. Box 205, 136 Spring St., Philipsburg, MT 59858 (bluing, repairs)
Flynn's Cust. Guns, P.O. Box 7461, Alexandria, LA 71306/318-445-7130
James W. Fogle, RR 2, Box 258, Herrin, IL 62948/618-988-1795
Larry L. Forster, Box 212, 220-1st St. N.E., Gwinner, ND 58040/701-678-2475
Pete Forthofer's Gunsmithing, 711 Spokane Ave., Whitefish, MT 59937/406-862-2674
Fountain Products, 492 Prospect Ave., West Springfield, MA 01089/413-781-4651
Frank's Custom Rifles, 7521 E. Fairmount Pl., Tucson, AZ 85715/602-885-3901
Freeland's Scope Stands, 3737—14th Ave., Rock Island, IL 61201/309-788-7449
Fredrick Gun Shop, 10 Elson Drive, Riverside, RI 02915/401-433-2805
Frontier Shop & Gallery, Depot 1st & Main, Riverton, WY 82501/307-856-4498
Fuller Gunshop, Cooper Landing, AK 99572
Karl J. Furr, 76 East 350 No., Orem, UT 84057/801-225-2603
Gander Mountain, Inc., P.O. Box 128, Wilmot, WI 53192/414-862-2344
Garcia Natl. Gun Traders, Inc., 225 S.W. 22nd Ave., Miami, FL 33135
Gator Guns & Repair, 6255 Spur Hwy., Kenai, AK 99611/907-283-7947
David Gentry Custom Gunmaker, P.O. Box 1440, Belgrade, MT 59714/406-388-4867 (cust. Montana Mtn. Rifle)
Edwin Gillman, 33 Valley View Dr., Hanover, PA 17331/717-632-1662
Gilman-Mayfield, 1552 N. 1st, Fresno, CA 93703/209-237-2500
Dale Goens, Box 224, Cedar Crest, NM 87008
A. R. Goode, 4125 N.E. 28th Terr., Ocala, FL 32670/904-622-9575
Goodling's Gunsmithing, R.D. #1, Box 1097, Spring Grove, PA 17362/717-225-3350
Gordie's Gun Shop, Gordon Mulholland, 1401 Fulton St., Streator, IL 61364/815-672-7202
Charles E. Grace, 10144 Elk Lake Rd., Williamsburg, MI 49690/616-264-9483
Roger M. Green & J. Earl Bridges, P.O. Box 984, 435 East Birch, Glenrock, WY 82637/307-436-9804
Griffin & Howe, 36 W. 44th St., Suite 1011, New York, NY 10036/212-921-0980
Griffin & Howe, 33 Claremont Rd., Bernardsville, NJ 07924/201-766-2287
Guncraft, 117 W. Pipeline, Hurst, TX 76053/817-282-1464
Guncraft Sports, Inc., 125 E. Tyrone Rd., Oak Ridge, TN 37830/615-483-4024
Gunsite Gunsmithy, Box 451, Paulden, AZ 86334/602-636-4104
The Gun Works, Joe Williams, 236 Main St., Springfield, OR 97477/503-741-4118 (ML)
H-S Precision, Inc., 112 N. Summit, Prescott, AZ 86302/602-445-0607
Hagn Rifles & Actions, Martin Hagn, Box 444, Cranbrook, B.C. V1C 4H9, Canada/604-489-4861 (s.s. actions & rifles)
Fritz Hallberg, Silver Shields Inc., 7544 Lemhi #9; P.O. Box 7601, Boise, ID 83707/208-323-8991
Charles E. Hammans, P.O. Box 788, 2022 McCracken, Stuttgart, AR 72160/501-673-1388
Hammond Custom Guns, 619 S. Pandora, Gilbert, AZ 85234/602-892-3437
Dick Hanson, Hanson's Gun Center, 521 So. Circle Dr., Colorado Springs, CO 80910/303-634-4220
Harkrader's Cust. Gun Shop, 825 Radford St., Christiansburg, VA 24073
Rob't W. Hart & Son Inc., 401 Montgomery St., Nescopeck, PA 18635/717-752-3655 (actions, stocks)
Hartmann & Weiss KG, Rahlstedter Bahnhofstr. 47, 2000 Hamburg 73, W. Germany/040-677-55-85
Hubert J. Hecht, Waffen-Hecht, P.O. Box 2635, Fair Oaks, CA 95628/916-966-1020
Stephen Heilmann, P.O. Box 657, Grass Valley, CA 95945/916-272-8758
Iver Henriksen, 1211 So. 2nd St. W, Missoula, MT 59801 (Rifles)
Darwin Hensley, P.O. Box 179, Brightwood, OR 97011/503-622-5411
Heppler's Gun Shop, 6000 B Soquel Ave., Santa Cruz, CA 95062/408-475-1235
Klaus Hiptmayer, P.O. Box 136, Eastman, PQ J0E 1P0, Canada/514-297-2492
Wm. Hobaugh, The Rifle Shop, Box M, Philipsburg, MT 59858/406-859-3515
Duane A. Hobbie Gunsmithing, 2412 Pattie Ave., Wichita, KS 67216/316-264-8266
Richard Hodgson, 9081 Tahoe Lane, Boulder, CO 80301
Hoenig and Rodman, 6521 Morton Dr., Boise, ID 83705/208-375-1116
Peter Hofer, F. Lang-Str. 13, A-9170 Ferlach, Austria/0-42-27-3683 (cust.)
Dick Holland, 422 N.E. 6th St., Newport, OR 97365/503-265-7556
Hollis Gun Shop, 917 Rex St., Carlsbad, NM 88220/505-835-3782
Bill Holmes, Rt. 2, Box 242, Fayetteville, AR 72701/501-521-8958
Alan K. Horst, P.O. Box 68, 402 E. St., Albion, WA 99102/509-332-7109 (cust.)
Corey O. Huebner, 3604 S. 3rd W., Missoula, MT 59801/406-721-9647
Steven Dodd Hughes, P.O. Box 11455, Eugene, OR 97440/503-485-8869 (ML; ctlg. $3)
Al Hunkeler, Buckskin Machine Works, 3235 So. 358th St., Auburn, WA 98001/206-927-5412 (ML)
Hyper-Single Precision SS Rifles, 520 E. Beaver, Jenks, OK 74037/918-299-2391
Campbell H. Irwin, Hartland Blvd. (Rt. 20), East Hartland, CT 06027/203-653-3901
Jackalope Gun Shop, 1048 S. 5th St., Douglas, WY 82633/307-358-3854
Paul Jaeger, Inc. P.O. Box 449, 1 Madison Ave., Grand Junction, TN 38039/901-764-6909
R. L. Jamison, Jr., Route 4, Box 200, Moses Lake, WA 98837/509-762-2659
Jarrett Rifles, Inc., Rt. 1 Box 411, Jackson, SC 29831/803-471-3616 (rifles)
Jenkins Enterprises, Inc., 12317 Locksley Lane, Auburn, CA 95603/916-823-9652
Jerry's Gun Shop, 9220 Ogden Ave., Brookfield, IL 60513/312-485-5200
Jim's Gun Shop, James R. Spradlin, 113 Arthur, Pueblo, CO 81004/719-543-9462
Neal G. Johnson, Gunsmithing, Inc., 111 Marvin Dr., Hampton, VA 23666/804-838-8091
Peter S. Johnson, The Orvis Co., Inc., 10 River Rd., Manchester, VT 05254/802-362-3622
L. E. Jurras & Assoc., Box 680, Washington, IN 47501/812-254-7698
Ken's Gun Specialties, K. Hunnell, Rt. 1 Box 147, Lakeview, AR 72642/501-431-5606
Kesselring Gun Shop, 400 Pacific Hiway No., Burlington, WA 98233/206-724-3113
Benjamin Kilham, Kilham & Co., Main St., Box 37, Lyme, NH 03768/603-795-4112
Don Klein Custom Guns, Rt. 2, P.O. Box 277, Camp Douglas, WI 54618/608-427-6948
K. W. Kleinendorst, R.D. #1, Box 113B, Hop Bottom, PA 18824/717-289-4687
Terry K. Kopp, Highway 13 South, Lexington, MO 64067/816-259-2636
J. Korzinek, R.D. #2, Box 73, Canton, PA 17724/717-673-8512 (riflesmith) (broch. $2)
Krider's Gun Shop, 114 W. Eagle Rd., Havertown, PA 19083/215-789-7828
Lee Kuhns, 652 Northeast Palson Rd., Paulsbo, WA 98370/206-692-5790
Sam Lair, 520 E. Beaver, Jenks, OK 74037/918-299-2391 (single shots)
Maynard Lambert, Kamas, UT 84036
Ron Lampert, Rt. 1, Box 177, Guthrie, MN 56461/218-854-7345
Harry Lawson Co., 3328 N. Richey Blvd., Tucson, AZ 85716/602-326-1117
John G. Lawson, (The Sight Shop), 1802 E. Columbia, Tacoma, WA 98404/206-474-5465
Mark Lee, P.O. Box 20379, Minneapolis, MN 55420/612-431-1727
Frank LeFever & Sons, Inc., R.D. #1, Box 31, Lee Center, NY 13363/315-337-6722
Liberty Antique Gunworks, 19 Key St., P.O. Box 183GD, Eastport, ME 04631/207-853-2327
Lilja Precision Rifle Barrels, Inc., 245 Compass Creek Rd., P.O. Box 372, Plains, MT 59859/406-826-3084
Al Lind, 7821—76th Ave. S.W., Tacoma, WA 98498/206-584-6363
Ljutic Ind., Box 2117, Yakima, WA 98904 (shotguns)
James W. Lofland, 2275 Larkin Rd., Boothwyn, PA 19061/215-485-0391 (SS rifles)
London Guns Ltd., P.O. Box 3750, Santa Barbara, CA 93130/805-683-4141
Longbranch Gun Bluing Co., 2455 Jacaranda Lane, Los Osos, CA 93402/805-528-1792
McCann's Muzzle-Gun Works, Tom McCann, 200 Federal City Rd., Pennington, NJ 08534/609-737-1707 (ML)
McCormick's Gun Bluing, 609 N.E. 104th Ave., Vancouver, WA 98664/206-256-0579
Dennis McDonald, 8359 Brady St., Peosta, IA 52068/319-556-7940
Stan McFarland, 2221 Idella Ct., Grand Junction, CO 81506/303-243-4704 (cust. rifles)
Bill McGuire, 1600 N. Eastmont Ave., East Wenatchee, WA 98801
MPI Stocks, 7011 N. Reno Ave., Portland, OR 97203/503-289-8025 (rifles)
Darrell Madis, 2453 Five-Mile Pkwy. Dallas, TX 75233/214-330-7168

CUSTOM GUNSMITHS — cont'd.

Mag-na-port International, Inc., 41302 Executive Dr., Mt. Clemens, MI 48045/313-469-6727
Nick Makinson, R.R. #3, Komoka, Ont. N0L 1R0 Canada/519-471-5462 (English guns; repairs & renovations)
Monte Mandarino, 136 Fifth Ave. West, Kalispell, MT 59901/406-257-6208 (Penn. rifles)
Lowell Manley Shooting Supplies, 3684 Pine St., Deckerville, MI 48427/313-376-3665
Marquart Precision Co., P.O. Box 1740, Prescott, AZ 86302/602-445-5646
Elwyn H. Martin, Martin's Gun Shop, 937 S. Sheridan Blvd., Lakewood, CO 80226/303-922-2184
Maryland Gun Works, Ltd., TEC Bldg., 10097 Tyler Pl. #8, Ijamsville, MD 21754/301-831-8456
Mashburn Arms & Sporting Goods Co., Inc., 1218 N. Pennsylvania, Oklahoma City, OK 73107/405-236-5151
Seely Masker, Custom Rifles, 261 Washington Ave., Pleasantville, NY 10570/914-769-2627
Geo. E. Matthews & Son Inc., 10224 S. Paramount Blvd., Downey, CA 90241
Maurer Arms, 2154-16th St., Akron, OH 44314/216-745-6864 (muzzleloaders)
John E. Maxson, 3507 Red Oak Lane, Plainview, TX 79072/806-293-9042 (high grade rifles)
R. M. Mercer, 216 S. Whitewater Ave., Jefferson, WI 53549/414-674-3839
Miller Arms, Inc., Dean E. Miller, P.O. Box 260, St. Onge, SD 57779/605-578-1790
Miller Gun Works, S. A. Miller, P.O. Box 1053, 1440 Peltier Dr., Point Roberts, WA 98281/206-945-7014
Tom Miller, c/o Huntington's Sportsman's Store, 601 Oro Dam Blvd., Oroville, CA 95965/916-534-1210
Earl Milliron, 1249 N.E. 166th Ave., Portland, OR 97230/503-252-3725
Hugh B. Mills, Jr., 3615 Canterbury Rd., New Bern, NC 28560/919-637-4631
Monell Custom Guns, Red Mill Road, RD #2, Box 96, Pine Bush, NY 12566/914-744-3021
Wm. Larkin Moore & Co., 31360 Via Colinas, Suite 109, Westlake Village, CA 91361/818-889-4160
J. W. Morrison Custom Rifles, 4015 W. Sharon, Phoenix, AZ 85029/602-978-3754
Mitch Moschetti, P.O. Box 27065, Cromwell, CT 06416/203-632-2308
Mountain Bear Rifle Works, Inc., Wm. Scott Bickett, 100-B Ruritan Rd., Sterling, VA 22170/703-430-0420
Larry Mrock, R.F.D. 3, Box 207, Woodhill-Hooksett Rd., Bow, NH 03301/603-224-4096 (broch. $3)
William Neighbor, Bill's Gun Repair, 1007 Burlington St., Mendota, IL 61342/815-539-5786
Bruce A. Nettestad, R.R. 1, Box 140, Pelican Rapids, MN 56572/218-863-4301
New England Arms Co., Lawrence Lane, Kittery Point, ME 03905/207-439-0593
Newman Gunshop, 119 Miller Rd., Agency, IA 52530/515-937-5775 (ML)
Paul R. Nickels, P.O. Box 71043, Las Vegas, NV 89170/702-798-7533
Ted Nicklas, 5504 Hegel Rd., Goodrich, MI 48438/313-797-4493
William J. Nittler, 290 More Dr., Boulder Creek, CA 95006/408-338-3376 or 408-438-7331 (shotgun bbls. & actions;repairs)
Jim Norman, Custom Gunstocks, 14281 Cane Rd., Valley Center, CA92082/619-749-6252
Nu-Line Guns, 1053 Caulks Hill Rd., Harvester, MO 63303/314-441-4500
Eric Olson, 12721 E. 11th Ave., Spokane, WA 99216
Vic Olson, 5002 Countryside Dr., Imperial, MO 63052/314-296-8086
Oregon Trail Riflesmiths, Inc., P.O. Box 51, Mackay, ID 83251/208-588-2527
The Orvis Co., Inc., Peter S. Johnson, Rt. 7A, Manchester, VT 05254/802-362-3622
Maurice Ottmar, Box 657, 113 East Fir, Coulee City, WA 99115/509-632-5717
Pachmayr Ltd., 1875 So. Mountain Ave., Monrovia, CA 91016/818-357-7771
Jay A. Pagel, 1407 4th St. NW, Grand Rapids, MN 55744/218-326-3003 (cust. gunmaking & refinishing)
Pasadena Gun Center, 206 E. Shaw, Pasadena, TX 77506/713-472-0417
Paterson Gunsmithing, 438 Main St., Paterson, NJ 07502/201-345-4100
John Pell, 410 College Ave., Trinidad, CO 81082/719-846-9406
Penrod Precision, 126 E. Main St., P.O. Box 307, No. Manchester, IN 46962/219-981-8385
A. W. Peterson Gun Shop, 1693 Old Hwy. 441, Mt. Dora, FL 32757 (ML)
Eugene T. Plante, Gene's Custom Guns, 3890 Hill Ave., White Bear Lake, MN 55110/612-429-5105
Professional Gunsmiths of America, Hwy 13 South, Box 224E, Lexington, MO 64067/816-259-2636
Rifle Shop, Box M, Philipsburg, MT 59858
J. J. Roberts, 166 Manassas Dr., Manassas Park, VA 22111/703-330-0448
Wm. A. Roberts Jr., Rte. 4, Box 75, Athens, AL 35611/205-232-7027 (ML)
Don Robinson, Pennsylvania Hse., 36 Fairfaix Crescent, Southowram, Halifax, W. Yorkshire HX3 9SQ, England (airifle stocks)
Rocky Mountain Rifle Works, Ltd., 1707 14th St., Boulder, CO 80302/303-443-9189
Bob Rogers Guns, P.O. Box 305, 344 S. Walnut St., Franklin Grove, IL 61031/815-456-2685
Royal Arms, 1210 Bert Acosta, El Cajon, CA 92020/619-448-5466
R.P.S. Gunshop, 11 So. Haskell, Central Point, OR 97502/503-664-5010
Russell's Rifle Shop, Route 5, Box 92, Georgetown, TX 78626/512-778-5338
SSK Industries, Rt. 1, Della Dr., Bloomingdale, OH 43910/614-264-0176
Sanders Custom Gun Serv., 2358 Tyler Lane, Louisville, KY 40205
Sandy's Custom Gunshop, Rte. #1, Box 4, Rockport, IL 62370/217-437-4241
Roy V. Schaefer, 965 W. Hilliard Lane, Eugene, OR 97404/503-688-4333
Schumaker's Gun Shop, Rte. 4, Box 500, Colville, WA 99114/509-684-4848
Schwartz Custom Guns, 9621 Coleman Rd., Haslett, MI 48840/517-339-8939
David W. Schwartz Custom Guns, 2505 Waller St., Eau Claire, WI 54701/715-832-1735
Thad Scott Fine Guns Inc., P.O. Box 412, Indianola, MS 38751/601-887-5929
Butch Searcy Co., 15 RD3804, Farmington, NM 87401/505-327-3419
Shane's Gunsmithing, P.O. Box 321, Hwy. 51 So., Minocqua, WI 54548/715-356-7675
Shaw's, Finest in Guns, 9447 W. Lilac Rd., Escondido, CA 92026/619-728-7070
E. R. Shaw Inc., Small Arms Mfg. Co., Thoms Run Rd. & Prestley, Bridgeville, PA 15017/412-221-4343
Shell Shack, 113 E. Main, Laurel, MT 59044/406-628-8986 (ML)
Dan A. Sherk, 9701-17th St. Dawson Creek, B.C. V1G 4H7 Canada/604-782-5630
Shilen Rifles, Inc., 205 Metro Park Blvd., Ennis, TX 75119/214-875-5318
Shiloh Rifle Mfg. Co., Inc., P.O. Box 279; 20 Centennial Dr., Big Timber, MT 59011/406-932-4454
Harold H. Shockley, 204 E. Farmington Rd., Hanna City, IL 61536/309-565-4524 (hot bluing & plating)
Shootin' Shack, 1065 Silverbeach Rd. #1, Riviera Beach, FL 33403/305-842-0990 ('smithing services)
Shootist Supply, John Cook, 622 5th Ave., Belle Fourche, SD 57717/605-892-2811
Simmons Gun Spec., 700 So. Rogers Rd., Olathe, KS 66062/913-782-3131
John R. Skinner, c/o Orvis Co., 10 River Rd., Manchester, VT 05254
Steve Sklany, 566 Birch Grove Dr., Kalispell, MT 59901/406-755-4527 (Ferguson rifle)
Jerome F. Slezak, 1290 Marlowe, Lakewood (Cleveland), OH 44107/216-221-1668
Art Smith, 4124 Thrushwood Lane, Minnetonka, MN 55345/612-935-7829
John Smith, 912 Lincoln, Carpentersville, IL 60110
Jordan T. Smith, c/o Orvis Co., 10 River Rd., Manchester, VT 05254
Snapp's Gunshop, 6911 E. Washington Rd., Clare, MI 48617/517-386-9226
Fred D. Speiser, 2229 Dearborn, Missoula, MT 59801/406-549-8133
Spencer Reblue Service, 1820 Tupelo Trail, Holt, MI 48842/517-694-7474 (electroless nickel plating)
Sportsmen's Equip. Co., 915 W. Washington, San Diego, CA 92103/619-296-1501
Sportsmen's Exchange & Western Gun Traders, Inc., P.O. Box 111, 560 S. "C" St., Oxnard, CA 93030/805-483-1917
Ken Starnes, Rt. 1, Box 269, Scroggins, TX 75480/214-365-2312
Steelman's Gun Shop, 10465 Beers Rd., Swartz Creek, MI 48473/313-753-4884
Keith Stegall, Box 696, Gunnison, CO 81230
Date Storey, 1764 S. Wilson, Casper, WY 82601/307-237-2414
Stott's Creek Armory Inc., R 1 Box 70, Morgantown, IN 46160/317-878-5489 (antique only)
Victor W. Strawbridge, 6 Pineview Dr., Dover Point, Dover, NH 03820/603-742-0013
W. C. Strutz, Rifle Barrels, Inc., P.O. Box 611, Eagle River. WI 54521/715-479-4766
Suter's House of Guns, 332 N. Tejon, Colorado Springs, CO 80902/303-635-1475
A. D. Swenson's 45 Shop, P.O. Box 606, Fallbrook, CA 92028
Talmage Enterprises, 451 Phantom Creek Lane, P.O. Box 512, Meadview, AZ 86444/602-564-2380
Target Airgun Supply, P.O. Box 428, South Gate, CA 90280/213-569-3417
Taylor & Robbins, Box 164, Rixford, PA 16745
James A. Tertin, c/o Gander Mountain, P.O. Box 128 - Hwy. W, Wilmot, WI 53192/414-862-2344
Larry R. Thompson, Larry's Gun Shop, 521 E. Lake Ave., Watsonville, CA 95076/408-724-5328
Daniel Titus, 872 Penn St., Bryn Mawr, PA 19010/215-525-8829
Tom's Gunshop, Tom Gillman, 4435 Central, Hot Springs, AR 71913/501-624-3856
Trader Perry's Discount Guns & Repair, 649 Mercedes Ave., Manteca, CA 95336/209-823-7363
David Trevallion, R. 1, Box 39, Kittery Point, ME 03905/207-439-6822
Trinko's Gun Serv., 1406 E. Main, Watertown, WI 53094
James C. Tucker, 205 Trinity St., Woodland, CA 95695/916-662-3109
Dennis A. "Doc" & Bud Ulrich, D.O.C. Specialists, Inc., 2209 S. Central Ave., Cicero, IL 60650/312-652-3606
Upper Missouri Trading Co., Box 181, Crofton, MO 68730
Milton Van Epps, Rt. 69-A, Parish, NY 13131/313-625-7251
Gil Van Horn, P.O. Box 207, Llano, CA 93544
John Vest, P.O. Box 1552, Susanville, CA 96130/916-257-7228
Vic's Gun Refinishing, 6 Pineview Dr., Dover, NH 03820/603-742-0013
Walker Arms Co., Inc., Rt. 2, Box 73, Hiwy 80 West, Selma, AL 36701/205-872-6231
R. D. Wallace, Star Rt. 1 Box 76, Grandin, MO 63943/314-593-4773
R. A. Wardrop, Box 245, 409 E. Marble St., Mechanicsburg, PA 17055
Weatherby's, 2781 Firestone Blvd., South Gate, CA 90280/213-569-7186
Weaver Arms Co., P.O. Box 8, Dexter, MO 63841/314-568-3800 (ambidextrous bolt action)
Cecil Weems, P.O. Box 657, Mineral Wells, TX 76067/817-325-1462
Wells Sport Store, Fred Wells, 110 N. Summit St., Prescott, AZ 86301/602-445-3655
R. A. Wells Ltd., 3452 N. 1st Ave., Racine, WI 53402/414-639-5223
Robert G. West, 3973 Pam St., Eugene, OR 97402/503-689-6610
Terry Werth, 1203 Woodlawn Rd., Lincoln, IL 62656/217-732-1300
Western Gunstocks Mfg. Co., 550 Valencia School Rd., Aptos, CA 95003
Duane Wiebe, P.O. Box 497, Lotus, CA 95651/916-626-6240
David W. Wills, 2776 Brevard Ave., Montgomery, AL 36109/205-272-8446
Williams Gun Sight Co., 7389 Lapeer Rd., Davison, MI 48423
Williamson-Pate Gunsmith Service, 117 W. Pipeline, Hurst, TX 76053/817-282-1464
Wilson's Gun Shop, P.O. Box 578, Rt. 3, Box 211-D, Berryville, AR 72616/501-545-3616
Robert M. Winter, R.R. 2, Box 484, Menno, SD 57045/605-387-5322
Wisner's Gun Shop, Inc., P.O. Box 58; Hiway 6, Adna, WA 98552/206-748-8942
Lester Womack, 512 Westwood Dr., Prescott, AZ 86301/602-778-9624
Mike Yee, 29927-56 Pl. S., Auburn, WA 98001/206-839-3991
Russ Zeeryp, 1601 Foard Dr., Lynn Ross Manor. Morristown, TN 37814

CUSTOM METALSMITHS

Alley Supply Co., P.O. Box 848, Gardnerville, NV 89410/702-782-3800
Armament Gunsmithing Co., Inc., 525 Route 22, Hillside, NJ 07205/201-686-0960
Baer Custom Guns, 1725 Minesite Rd., Allentown, PA 18103/215-398-2362
Barta's Gunsmithing, 10231 US Hwy 10, Cato, WI 54206/414-732-4472
George Beitzinger, 116-20 Atlantic Ave., Richmond Hill, NY 11419/718-847-7661
Al Biesen & Assoc., West 2039 Sinto Ave., Spokane, WA 99201/509-328-6818
Ross Billingsley & Brownell, Box 25, Dayton, WY 82836/307-655-9344
E.C. Bishop & Son Inc., 119 Main St., P.O. Box 7, Warsaw, MO 65355/816-438-5121
Gregg Boeke, Rte. 2, Box 149, Cresco, IA 52136/319-547-3746
Larry D. Brace, 771 Blackfoot Ave., Eugene, OR 97404/503,688-1278
A. Briganti, 475 Rt. 32, Highland Mills, NY 10930/914-692-4409
Leo Bustani, P.O. 8125, W. Palm Beach, FL 33407/305-622-2710
C&G Precision, 10152 Trinidad, El Paso, TX 79925/915-592-5496
Ralph L. Carter, 225 G St., Penrose, CO 81240/303-372-6240
Clinton River Gun Serv. Inc., 30016 S. River Rd., Mt. Clemens, MI 48045/313-468-1090
Dave Cook, 5831-26th Lane, Brampton, MI 49837/906-428-1235
David Costa, 94 Orient Ave., Arlington, MA 02174/617-643-9571
Crandall Tool & Machine Co., 1545 N. Mitchell St., Cadillac, MI 49601/616-775-5562
Gordon D. Crocker, 1510 - 42nd St., Los Alamos, NM 87544/505-667-9117
Daniel Cullity Restorations, 209 Old County Rd., East Sandwich, MA 02537/508-888-1147
Custom Gun Guild, Frank Wood, 2646 Church Dr., Doraville, GA 30340/404-455-0346
D&D Gun Shop, 363 Elmwood, Troy, MI 48083/313-583-1512
D&H Precision Tooling, 7522 Barnard Mill Rd., Ringwood, IL 60072/815-653-9611
Jack Dever, 8520 N.W. 90th, Oklahoma City, OK 73132/405-721-6393
Dilliott Gunsmithing, Inc., Rte. 3 Box 340, Scarlett Rd., Dandridge, TN 37725/615-397-9204
Dominic DiStefano, 4303 Friar Lane, Colorado Springs, CO 80907/303-599-3366
Ken Eyster Heritage Gunsmiths Inc., 6441 Bishop Rd., Centerburg, OH 43011/614-625-43031
Flaig's Inc., 2200 Evergreen Rd., Millvale, PA 15209/412-821-1717
Fountain Prods., 492 Prospect Ave., W. Springfield, MA 01089/413-781-4651
Frank's Custom Rifles, 7521 E. Fairmount Pl., Tucson, AZ 85715/602-885-3901
Fredrick Gun Shop, 10 Elson Dr., Riverside, RI 02915/401-433-2805 (engine turning)
Geo. M. Fullmer, 2499 Mavis St., Oakland, CA 94601/415-533-4193 (precise chambering—300 cals.)
K. Genecco Gun Works, 10512 Lower Sacramento Rd., Stockton, CA 95210/209-951-0706
David Gentry Custom Gunmaker, P.O. Box 1440, Belgrade, MT 59714/406-388-4867
Roger M. Green & J. Earl Bridges, P.O. Box 984, 435 East Birch, Glenrock, WY 82637/307-436-9804
Griffin & Howe, 36 West 44th St., Suite 1011, New York, NY 10036/212-921-0980
Griffin & Howe, 33 Claremont Rd., Bernardsville, NJ 07924/201-766-2287
Hagn Rifles & Actions, Martin Hagn, Box 444, Carnbrook, B.C. VIC 4H9, Canada/604-489-4861
Hammond Custom Guns, 619 S. Pandora, Gilbert, AZ 85234/602-892-3437
Harkrader's Custom Gun Shop, 825 Radford St., Christiansburg, VA 24073
Robert W. Hart & Son, Inc., 401 Montgomery St., Nescopeck, PA 18635/717-752-3655
Hubert J. Hecht, Waffen-Hecht, P.O. Box 2635, Fair Oaks, CA 95628/916-966-1020
Stephen Heilmann, P.O. Box 657, Grass Valley, CA 95945/916-272-8758
Heppler's Gun Shop, 6000 B Soquel Ave., Santa Cruz, CA 95062/408-475-1235
Klaus Hiptmayer, P.O. Box 136, R.R. 112 #750, Eastman, Que. J0E1P0, Canada/514-297-2492
Wm. H. Hobaugh, Box M, Philipsburg, MT 59858/406-859-3515
Hollis Gun Shop, 917 Rex St., Carlsbad, NM 88220/505-885-3782
Paul Jaeger, Inc., P.O. Box 449, 1 Madison St., Grand Junction, TN 38039/901-764-6909
R. L. Jamison, Jr., Rt. 4, Box 200, Moses Lake, WA 98837/509-762-2659
Ken Jantz, 222 E. Main, Davis, OK 73030/405-369-2316
Jenkins Enterprises, Inc., 12317 Locksley Lane, Auburn, CA 95603/916-823-9652
Neil A. Jones, RD #1, Box 483A, Saegertown, PA 16433/814-763-2769
L. E. Jurras & Assoc., Box 680, Washington, IN 47501/812-254-7698
Kennons Custom Rifles, 5408 Biffle Rd., Stone Mountain, GA 30088/404-469-9339
Benjamin Kilham, Kilham & Co., Main St., Box 37, Lyme, NH 03768/603-795-4112
Terry K. Kopp, Highway 13 South, Lexington, MO 64067/816-259-2636
Ron Lampert, Rt. 1, Box 177, Guthrie, MN 56461/218-854-7345
Mark Lee, P.O. Box 20379, Minneapolis, MN 55420/612-431-1727
Lilja Precision Rifle Barrels, Inc., 245 Compass Creek Rd., P.O. Box 372, Plains, MT 59859/406-826-3084
Stan McFarland, 2221 Idealla Ct., Grand Junction, CO 81505/303-243-4704
McIntyre Tools & Guns, P.O. Box 491, State Rd. #1144, Troy, NC 27371/919-572-2603
Miller Arms, Inc., P.O. Box 260, St. Onge, SD 57779/605-578-1790
J. W. Morrison Custom Rifles, 4015 W. Sharon, Phoenix, AZ 85029/602-978-3754
Mullis Guncraft, 3518 Lawyers Road East, Monroe, NC 28110/704-283-8789
Bruce A. Nettestad, Rt. 1, Box 140, Pelican Rapids, MN 56572/218-863-4301
Vic Olson, 5002 Countryside Dr., Imperial, MO 63052/314-296-8086
Pasadena Gun Center, 206 E. Shaw, Pasadena, TX 77506/713-472-0417
James Pearson, The Straight Shooter Gun Shop, 8132 County LS Rt. 2, Newton, WI 53063/414-726-4676
Penrod Precision, 126 E. Main St., P.O. Box 307, No. Manchester, IN 46962/219-982-8385
Precise Chambering Co., 2499 Mavis St., Oakland, CA 94601/415-533-4193
Precise Metalsmithing Enterprises, James L. Wisner, 146 Curtis Hill Rd., Chehalis, WA 98532/206-748-3743
Bob Rogers Gunsmithing, P.O. Box 305; 344 S. Walnut St., Franklin Grove, IL 61031/815-456-2685
Butch Searcy Co., 15 RD 3804, Farmington, NM 87401/505-327-3419
Harold H. Shockley, 203 E. Farmington Rd., Hanna City, IL 61536/309-565-4524
Snapp's Gunshop, 6911 E. Washington Rd., Clare, MI 48617/517-386-9226
Dale A. Storey, DGS, Inc., 305 N. Jefferson, Casper, WY 82601/307-237-2414
Dave Talley, P.O. Box 821, Glenrock, WY 82637/307-436-8724
J. W. Van Patten, P.O. Box 145, Foster Hill, Milford, PA 18337/717-296-7069
Vic's Gun Refinishing, 6 Pineview Dr., Dover, NH 03820/603-742-0013
Herman Waldron, Box 475, Pomeroy, WA 99347/509-843-1404
R. D. Wallace, Star Rt. 1 Box 76, Grandin, MO 63943/314-593-4773
Fred Wells, Wells Sport Store, 110 N. Summit St., Prescott, AZ 86301/602-445-3655
Terry Werth, 1203 Woodlawn Rd., Lincoln, IL 62656/217-732-3870
Robert G. West, 3973 Pam St., Eugene, OR 97402/503-689-6610
John Westrom, Precise Firearm Finishing, 25 N.W. 44th Ave., Des Moines, IA 50313/515-288-8680

DECOYS

Advance Scouts, Inc. 2741 Patton Rd., Roseville, MN 55113/612-639-1326 (goose getters)
Carry-Lite, Inc., 5203 W. Clinton Ave., Milwaukee, WI 53223/414-355-3520
Deer Me Products Co., Box 34, 1208 Park St., Anoka, MN 55303/612-421-8971 (Anchors)
Flambeau Prods. Corp., 15981 Valplast Rd., Middlefield, OH 44062/216-632-1631
Kenneth J. Klingler, P.O. Box 141; Thistle Hill, Cabot, VT 05647/802-426-3811
Penn's Woods Products, Inc., 19 W. Pittsburgh St., Delmont, PA 15626/412-468-8311
Royal Arms, 1210 Bert Acosta, El Cajon, CA 92020/619-448-5466 (wooden, duck)
Ron E. Skaggs, P.O. Box 34; 114 Miles Ct., Princeton, IL 61356/815-875-8207

ENGRAVERS, ENGRAVING TOOLS

John J. Adams, P.O. Box 167, Corinth, VT 05039/802-439-5904
Gary Allard, Creek Side Metal & Woodcrafters, Fishers Hill, VA 22626/703-465-3903
Robert L. Barnard, Rt. 2 Box 327, Fordyce, AR 71742/501-352-5861
Billy R. Bates, 2905 Lynnwood Circle S.W., Decatur, AL 35603/205-355-3690
Sid Bell Originals Inc., R.D. 2, Box 219, Tully, NY 13159/607-842-6431
Jim Bina, P.O. Box 6532, Evanston, IL 60204/312-475-6377
Weldon Bledsoe, 6812 Park Place Dr., Fort Worth, TX 76118/817-589-1704
C. Roger Bleile, 5040 Ralph Ave., Cincinnati, OH 45238/513-251-0249
Rudolph V. Bochenski, 1410 Harlem Rd., Cheektowaga, NY 14206/716-896-3619
Erich Boessler, Gun Engraving Intl., Am Vogeltal 3, 8732 Munnerstadt, W. Germany/9733-9443
Ralph P. Bone, 718 N. Atlanta, Owasso, OK 74055/918-272-9745
Henry "Hank" Bonham, 218 Franklin Ave., Seaside Heights, NJ 08751/201-793-8309
Dan Bratcher, 311 Belle Air Pl., Carthage, MO 64836/417-358-1518
Frank Brgoch, 1580 So. 1500 East, Bountiful, UT 84010/801-295-1885
Dennis B. Brooker, 502 Hwy 92, Prole, IA 50229/515-961-8200
Brownells, Inc., 222 W. Liberty, Montezuma, IA 50171/515-623-5401 (engraving tools)
Byron Burgess, 710 Bella Vista Dr., Morro Bay, CA 93442/805-772-3974
E. Christopher Firearms Co., Inc., Route 128 & Ferry St., Miamitown, OH 45041/513-353-1321
Winston Churchill, Twenty Mile Stream Rd., RFD Box 29B, Proctorsville, VT 05153/802-226-7772
Clark Engravings, P.O. Box 80746, San Marino, CA 91108/818-287-1652
Frank Clark, 3714-27th St., Lubbock, TX 79410/806-799-1187
Crocker Engraving, 1510 - 42nd St., Los Alamos, NM 87544
Daniel Cullity, 209 Old County Rd., East Sandwich, MA 02537/508-888-1147
Custom Gun Guild, 2646 Church Dr., Doraville, GA 30340/404-455-0346
Ed Delorge, 2231 Hwy. 308, Thibodaux, LA 70301/504-447-1633
James R. DeMunck, P.O. Box 16523, Rochester, NY 14616/716-225-0626 (SASE)
W. R. Dilling Engravers, Rod Dilling, 105 N. Ridgewood Dr., Sebring, FL 33870/813-385-0647
Mark Drain, S.E. 3211 Kamilche Point Rd., Shelton, WA 98584/206-426-5452
Michael W. Dubber, 5325 W. Mill Rd., Evansville, IN 47712/812-963-6156
Robert Evans, 332 Vine St., Oregon City, OR 97045/503-656-5693
Ken Eyster, Heritage Gunsmiths Inc., 6441 Bishop Rd., Centerburg, OH 43011/614-625-6131
John Fanzoi, P.O. Box 25, Ferlach, Austria 9170
Jacqueline Favre, 3111 So. Valley View Blvd., Suite B-214, Las Vegas, NV 89102/702-876-6278

ENGRAVERS, ENGRAVING TOOLS — cont'd.

Armi FERLIB, 46 Via Costa, 25063 Gardone V.T. (Brescia), Italy
Firearms Engravers Guild of America, Robert Evans, Secy., 332 Vine St., Oregon City, OR 97045/503-656-5693
Jeff W. Flannery Engraving Co., 11034 Riddles Run Rd., Union, KY 41091/606-384-3127 (color ctlg. $5)
James W. Fogle. RR 2, Box 258, Herrin, IL 62948/618-988-1795
Fountain Prods., 492 Prospect Ave., W. Springfield, MA 01089/413-781-4651
Henry Frank, Box 984, Whitefish, MT 59937/406-862-2681
Leonard Francolini, 56 Morgan Rd., Canton, CT 06019/203-693-2529
GRS Corp., P.O. Box 748, 900 Overland St., Emporia, KS 66801/316-343-1084 (Gravermeister tool)
Jerome C. Glimm, 19 S. Maryland, Conrad, MT 59425/406-278-3574
Howard V. Grant, Hiawatha 153, Woodruff, WI 54568/715-356-7146
Griffin & Howe, 36 West 44th St., Suite 1011, New York, NY 10036/212-921-0980
Griffin & Howe, 33 Claremont Rd., Bernardsville, NJ 07924/201-766-2287
Gurney Engraving Method, #513-620 View St., Victoria, B.C. V8W 1J6 Canada/604-383-5243
John K. Gwilliam, 218 E. Geneva Dr., Tempe, AZ 85282/602-894-1739
Bryson J. Gwinnell, P.O. Box 998, Southwick, MA 01077
Hand Engravers Supply Co., 4348 Newberry Ct., Dayton, OH 45432/513-426-6762
Paul R. Harris Hand Engraving, 10630 Janet Lee, San Antonio, TX 78230/512-341-5121
Jack O. Harwood, 1191 S. Pendlebury Lane, Blackfoot, ID 83221/208-785-5368
Frank E. Hendricks, Master Engravers, Inc., Star Rt. 1A, Box 334, Dripping Springs, TX 78620/512-858-7828
Heidemarie Hiptmayer, R.R. 112, #750, P.O. Box 136, Eastman, Que. J0E 1P0, Canada/514-297-2492
Alan K. Horst, P.O. Box 68, 402 E. St., Albion, WA 99102/509-332-7109
Ken Hurst, P.O. Box 116, Estill, SC 29918/803-625-3070
Ralph W. Ingle, Master Engraver, #4 Missing Link, Rossville, GA 30741/404-866-5589 (color broch. $5)
Paul Jaeger, Inc., P.O. Box 449, 1 Madison Ave., Grand Junction, TN 38039/901-764-6909
Ken Jantz Supply, 222 E. Main, Davis, OK 73030/405-369-2316 (tools)
Bill Johns, 1113 Nightingale, McAllen, TX 78501/512-682-2971
Steven Kamyk, 9 Grandview Dr., Westfield, MA 01085/413-568-0457
T. J. Kaye, Rt. 2 Box 139A, Yoakum, TX 77995
Lance Kelly, 1824 Royal Palm Dr., Edgewater, FL 32032/904-423-4933
Jim Kelso, Rt. 1, Box 5300, Worcester, VT 05682/802-229-4254
E. J. Koevenig Engraving Service, P.O. Box 55, Rabbit Gulch, Hill City, SD 57745/605-574-2239
John Kudlas, 622-14th St. S.E., Rochester, MN 55904/507-288-5579
Nelson H. Largent, Silver Shield's Inc., 7614 Lemhi #1, Boise, ID 83709/208-323-8991
Leonard Leibowitz, 1202 Palto Alto St., Pittsburgh, PA 15212/412-231-5388 (etcher)
Franz Letschnig, Master-Engraver, 620 Cathcart, Rm. 422, Montreal, Queb. H3B 1M1, Canada/514-875-4989
Steve Lindsay, R.R.2 Cedar Hills, Kearney, NE 68847/308-236-7885
London Guns Ltd., P.O. Box 3750, Santa Barbara, CA 93130/805-683-4141
Dennis McDonald, 8359 Brady St., Peosta, IA 52068/319-556-7940
Lynton S.M. McKenzie, 6940 N. Alvernon Way, Tucson, AZ 85718/602-299-5090
Wm. H. Mains, 3111 S. Valley View Blvd., Suite B-214, Las Vegas, NV 89102/702-876-6278
Robert E. Maki, School of Firearms Engraving, P.O. Box 947, Northbrook, IL 60065/312-724-8238
Laura Mandarino, 136 5th Ave. West, Kalispell, MT 59901/406-257-6208
George Marek, P.O. Box 213, Westfield, MA 01086/413-568-9816
Frank Mele, Longdale Rd., Mahopac, NY 10541/914-225-8872
S. A. Miller, Miller Gun Works, P.O. Box 1053, 1440 Peltier Dr., Point Roberts, WA 98281/206-945-7014
Frank Mittermeier, 3577 E. Tremont Ave., New York, NY 10465/212-828-3843 (tool)
Mitch Moschetti, P.O. Box 27065, Denver, CO 80227/303-936-1184
Gary K. Nelson, 975 Terrace Dr., Oakdale, CA 95361/209-847-4590
NgraveR Co., 879 Raymond Hill Rd., Oakdale, CT 06370/203-848-8031 (tool)
New Orleans Arms Co., P.O. Box 26087, New Orleans, LA 70186/504-944-3371
New Orleans Jewelers Supply, 206 Chartres St., New Orleans, LA 70130/504-523-3839 (engr. tool)
Oker's Engraving, 365 Bell Rd., Bellford Mtn. Hts., P.O. Box 126, Shawnee, CO 80475/303-838-6042
Pachmayr Ltd., 1875 So. Mountain Ave., Monrovia, CA 91016/818-357-7771
C. R. Pedersen & Son, 2717 S. Pere Marquette, Ludington, MI 49431/616-843-2061
E. Larry Peters, c/o Kimber, 9039 SE Janssen Rd., Clackamas, OR 97015/503-656-6016
Scott Pilkington, P.O. Box 125, Dunlap, TN 37237/615-592-3786
Paul R. Piquette, 80 Bradford Dr., Feeding Hills, MA 01030/413-786-5811
Eugene T. Plante, Gene's Custom Guns, 3890 Hill Ave., P.O. Box 10534, White Bear Lake, MN 55110/612-429-5105
Jeremy W. Potts, 1680 So. Granby, Aurora, CO 80012/303-752-2528
Wayne E. Potts, 912 Poplar St., Denver, CO 80220/303-355-5462
Ed Pranger, 1414-7th St., Anacortes, WA 98221/206-293-3488
Proofmark, Ltd., P.O. Box 183, Alton, IL 62002/618-463-0120 (Italian Bottega Incisioni)
E. C. Prudhomme, #426 Lane Building, 610 Marshall St., Shreveport, LA 71101/318-425-8421
Leonard Puccinelli Design, P.O. Box 3494, Fairfield, CA 94533/707-422-3122
Martin Rabeno, Spook Hollow Trading Co., Box 37F, RD #1, Ellenville, NY 12428/914-647-4567
Jim Riggs, 206 Azalea, Boerne, TX 78006/512-249-8567 (handguns)
J. J. Roberts, 166 Manassas Dr., Manassas Park, VA 22111/703-330-0448
John R. and Hans Rohner, 710 Sunshine Canyon, Boulder, CO 80302/303-444-3841
Bob Rosser, 142 Ramsey Dr., Albertville, AL 35950/205-878-5388
Joe Rundell, 6198 Frances Rd., Clio, MI 48420/313-687-0559
Robert P. Runge, 94 Grove St., Ilion, NY 13357/315-894-3036
Shaw's "Finest In Guns," 9447 W. Lilac Rd., Escondido, CA 92026/619-728-7070
George Sherwood, Box 735, Winchester, OR 97495/503-672-3159
Ben Shostle, The Gun Room, 1201 Burlington Dr., Muncie, IN 47302/317-282-9073
W. P. Sinclair, 46 Westbury Rd., Edington, Wiltshire BA13 4PG, England
Ron Skaggs, P.O. Box 34, 114 Miles Ct., Princeton, IL 61356/815-875-8207
Mark A. Smith, 200 N. 9th, Sinclair, WY 82334/307-324-7929
Ron Smith, 3601 West 7th St., Ft. Worth, TX 76107/817-732-4623
Terry Theis, P.O. Box 252, Harper, TX 78631/512-864-4384
George W. Thiewes, 1846 Allen Lane, St. Charles, IL 60174/312-584-1383
Denise Thirion, Box 408, Graton, CA 95444/707-829-1876
Robert B. Valade, 931-3rd. Ave., Seaside, OR 97138/503-738-7672
John Vest, P.O. Box 1552, Susanville, CA 96130/916-257-7228
Ray Viramontez, 4348 Newberry Ct., Dayton, OH 45432/513-426-6762
Vernon G. Wagoner, 2325 E. Encanto, Mesa, AZ 85203/602-835-1307
R. D. Wallace, Star Rt. 1 Box 76, Grandin, MO 63943
Terry Wallace, 385 San Marino, Vallejo, CA 94590
Floyd E. Warren, 1273 State Rt. 305 N.E., Cortland, OH 44410/216-638-4219
Kenneth W. Warren, Mountain States Engraving, P.O. Box 4631, Scottsdale, AZ 85261/602-991-5035
Rachel Wells, 110 N. Summit St., Prescott, AZ 86301/602-445-3655
Sam Welch, CVSR Box 2110, Moab, UT 84532/801-259-7620
Claus Willig, Siedlerweg 17, 8720 Schweinfurt, West Germany/09721-41446
Bernie Wolfe, 900 Tony Lama, El Paso, TX 79915 (engraving, plating, scrimshawing)
Mel Wood, P.O. Box 1255, Sierra Vista, AZ 85636/602-455-5541

GAME CALLS

Burnham Bros., Box 669, 912 Main St., Marble Falls, TX 78654/512-693-3112
Joe Hall's Shooting Products, Inc., 443 Wells Rd., Doylestown, PA 18901/215-345-6354
Lohman Mfg. Co., P.O. Box 220, Neosho, MO 64850/417-451-4438
Mallardtone Game Calls, 2901 16th St., Moline, IL 61265/309-762-8089
Phil. S. Olt Co., Box 550, Pekin, IL 61554/309-348-3633
Quaker Boy Inc., 6426 West Quaker St., Orchard Parks, NY 14127/716-662-3979
Penn's Woods Products, Inc., 19 W. Pittsburgh St., Delmont, PA 15626
Pete Rickard, Inc., Box 209B, Cobleskill, NY 12043/518-234-2731
Scotch Game Call Co., Inc., 6619 Oak Orchard Rd., Elba, NY 14058/716-757-9958
Johnny Stewart Game Calls, Inc., Box 7954, 5100 Fort Ave., Waco, TX 76714/817-772-3261
Tink's Safariland Hunting Corp., P.O. Box NN, McLean, VA 22101/703-356-0622

GUN PARTS, U.S. AND FOREIGN

Armes de Chasse, P.O. Box 827, Chadds Ford, PA 19317/215-388-1146
Armsport, Inc., 3590 N.W. 49th St., Miami, FL 33142/305-635-7850
Badger Shooter's Supply, 106 So. Harding, Owen, WI 54460/715-229-2101
Behlert Custom Guns, Inc., RD 2, Box 36C, Route 611 North, Pipersville, PA 18947/215-766-8681 (handgun parts)
Can Am Enterprises, 350 Jones Rd., Fruitland, ON L0R 1L0, Canada/416-643-4357 (catalog $2)
Caspian Arms, 14 No. Main St., Hardwick, VT 05843/802-472-6454
Cherokee Gun Accessories, 4127 Bay St. Suite 226, Fremont, CA 94538/415-471-5770
D&E Magazines Mfg., P.O. Box 4876-D, Sylmar, CA 91342
Charles E. Duffy, Williams Lane, West Hurley, NY 12491
Essex Arms, Box 345, Island Pond, VT 05846/802-723-4313 (.45 1911A1 frames & slides)
Falcon Firearms Mfg. Corp., P.O. Box 3748, Granada Hills, CA 91344/818-885-0900 (barrels; magazines)
Federal Ordnance Inc., 1443 Potrero Ave., So. El Monte, CA 91733/213-350-4161
Jack First Distributors Inc., 44633 Sierra Highway, Lancaster, CA 93534/805-945-6981
Gun Parts Corp., Box 2, West Hurley, NY 12491/914-679-2417
Gun-Tec, P.O. Box 8125, W. Palm Beach, FL 33407 (Win. mag. tubing; Win. 92 conversion parts; SASE f. reply)
Hansen and Hansen, 244 Old Post Rd., Southport, CT 06490/203-259-7337
Hastings, Box 224, 822-6th St., Clay Center, KS 67432/913-632-3169
Heller & Levin Associates, Inc., 88 Marlborough Court, Rockville Center, NY 11570/516-764-9349
Liberty Antique Gunworks, 19 Key St., P.O. Box 183GD, Eastport, ME 04631/207-853-2327 (S&W only; ctlg. $5)
Walter H. Lodewick, 2816 N.E. Halsey, Portland, OR 97232/503-284-2554 (Winchester parts)
Arthur McKee, 121 Eaton's Neck Rd., Northport, L.I., NY 11768/516-757-8850 (micrometer rec. sights)
John V. Martz, 8060 Lakeview Lane, Lincoln, CA 95648/916-645-2250 (parts for Luger and P-38s)
Olympic Arms Inc. dba SGW, 624 Old Pacific Hwy. S.E., Olympia, WA 98503/206-456-3471
Pacific Intl. Merch. Corp., 2215 "J" St., Sacramento, CA 95816/916-446-2737 (Vega 45 Colt mag.)
Pre-64 Winchester Parts Co., P.O. Box 8125, W. Palm Beach, FL 33407 (send stamped env. w. requ. list)
Quality Parts Co., 101 Hanover St., Portland, ME 04101/800-556-SWAT

GUN PARTS, U.S. AND FOREIGN — cont'd.

Martin B. Retting, Inc., 11029 Washington Blvd., Culver City, CA 90232/213-837-2412
Royal Ordnance Works Ltd., P.O. Box 3245, Wilson, NC 27893/919-237-0515
Sarco, Inc., 323 Union St., Stirling, NJ 07980/201-647-3800
Sherwood Intl. Export Corp., 18714 Parthenia St., Northridge, CA 91324
Clifford L. Smires, R.D. 1, Box 100, Columbus, NJ 08022/609-298-3158 (Mauser rifle parts)
Springfield Sporters Inc., R.D. 1, Penn Run, PA 15765/412-254-2626
Triple-K Mfg. Co., 2222 Commercial St. San Diego, CA 92113/619-232-2066 (magazines, gun parts)
U.S.F.S. (United States Frame Specialists), P.O. Box 7762, Milwaukee, WI 53207/414-643-6387 (SA frames; back straps)

GUNS (U.S.-made)

AMAC (See Iver Johnson)
AMT (Arcadia Machine & Tool), 536 N. Vincent Ave., Covina, CA 91722/818-915-7803
Accuracy Systems, Inc., 15205 N. Cave Creek Rd., Phoenix, AZ 85032/602-971-1991
American Arms, Inc., P.O. Box 27163, Salt Lake City, UT 84127/801-971-5006
American Derringer Corp., 127 N. Lacy Dr., Waco, TX 76705/817-799-9111
American Industries, 8700 Brookpark Rd., Cleveland, OH 44129/216-398-8300
Arminex Ltd., 10231 N. Scottsdale Rd., #B13, Scottsdale, AZ 85253/602-998-6616
Armitage International, Ltd., 1635-A Blue Ridge Blvd., Seneca, SC 29678/803-882-5900 (Scarab Skorpion 9mm pistol)
Armes de Chasse, 3000 Valley Forge Circle, King of Prussia, PA 19406/215-783-6133
A Square Co., Inc., Rt. 4, Simmons, Rd., Madison, IN 47250/812-273-3633
Auto-Ordnance Corp., Williams Lane, West Hurley, NY 12491/914-679-7225
BF Arms, 1123 So. Locust, Grand Island, NE 68801/308-382-1121 (single shot pistol)
BJT, 445 Putman Ave., Hamden, CT 06517 (stainless double derringer)
Barrett Firearms Mfg., Inc., P.O. Box 1077, Murfreesboro, TN 37133/615-896-2938 (Light Fifty)
Beretta U.S.A., 17601 Beretta Dr., Accokeek, MD 20607/301-283-2191
Browning (Gen. Offices), Rt. 1, Morgan, UT 84050/801-876-2711
Browning (Parts & Service), Rt. 4, Box 624-B, Arnold, MO 63010/314-287-6800
Bryco Arms (Distributed by Jennings Firearms)
Bushmaster Firearms Co., 999 Roosevelt Trail, Bldg. #3, Windham, ME 04062 (police handgun)
Calico (California Instrument Co.), 405 E. 19th St., Bakersfield, CA 93305/805-323-1327
Caspian Arms, 14 No. Main St., Hardwick, VT 05843/802-472-6454
Century Gun Dist., Inc., 1467 Jason Rd., Greenfield, IN 46140/317-462-4524 (Century Model 100 SA rev.)
Champlin Firearms, Inc., Box 3191, Enid, OK 73702/405-237-7388
Charter Arms Corp., 430 Sniffens Ln., Stratford, CT 06497/203-377-8080
Chipmunk Manufacturing Inc., 114 E. Jackson, P.O. Box 1104, Medford, OR 97501/503-664-5585 (22 S.S. rifle)
Colt Firearms, P.O. Box 1868, Hartford, CT 06101/203-236-6311
Commando Arms (See Gibbs Guns, Inc.)
Competition Arms, Inc., 1010 S. Plumer, Tucson, AZ 85719/602-792-1075
Coonan Arms, Inc., 830 Hampden Ave., St. Paul, MN 55114/612-646-6672 (357 Mag. Autom.)
Dakota Arms, Inc., HC 55 Box 326, Sturgis, SD 57785/605-347-4686 (B.A. rifles)
Davis Industries, 15150 Sierra Bonita Lane, Chino, CA 91710/714-591-4726 (derringers; 32 auto pistol)
Detonics Mfg. Corp., 13456 S.E. 27th Pl., Bellevue, WA 98005/206-747-2100 (auto pistol)
DuBiel Arms Co., 1724 Baker Rd., Sherman, TX 75090/214-893-7313
E.M.F. Co. Inc., 1900 East Warner Ave. 1-D, Santa Ana, CA 92705/714-261-6611
Encom America, Inc., P.O. Box 5314, Atlanta, GA 30307/404-525-2801
Excalibur (See Arminex)
Excam, Inc., 4480 East 11th Ave., Hialeah, FL 33013/305-681-4661
F.I.E. Corp. (See Firearms Import & Export Corp.)
Falcon Firearms Mfg. Corp., P.O. Box 3748, Granada Hills, CA 91344/818-885-0900 (handguns)
Falling Block Works, P.O. Box 3087, Fairfax, VA 22038/703-476-0043
Feather Enterprises, 2500 Central Ave., Boulder, CO 80301/303-442-7021
Federal Eng. Corp., 2335 So. Michigan Ave., Chicago, IL 60616/312-842-1063
Firearms Imp. & Exp. Corp., P.O. Box 4866, Hialeah Lakes, Hialeah, FL 33014/305-685-5966 (FIE)
Freedom Arms Co., P.O. Box 1776, Freedom, WY 83120 (mini revolver, Casull rev.)
Freedom Arms Marketing (See: L.A.R. Mfg. Co.)
Frontier Shop & Gallery, Depot 1st & Main, Riverton, WY 82501/307-856-4498
Gibbs Guns, Inc., Rt. 2, Greenback, TN 37742/615-856-2813 (Commando Arms)
Gilbert Equipment Co., Inc., P.O. Box 9846, Mobile, AL 36609
Göncz Co., 11526 Burbank Blvd., #18, No. Hollywood, CA 91601/818-505-0408
Grendel, Inc., P.O. Box 908, Rockledge, FL 32955/305-636-1211
Hatfield Rifle Works, 2020 Calhoun, St. Joseph, MO 64501/816-279-8688 (squirrel rifle)
Holmes Firearms Corp., Rte. 6, Box 242, Fayetteville, AR 72703
Hopkins & Allen Arms, 3 Ethel Ave., P.O. Box 217, Hawthorne, NJ 07507/201-427-1165 (ML)
Lew Horton Dist. Co. Inc., 175 Boston Rd., Southboro, MA 01772/617-485-3060
Hyper-Single Precision SS Rifles, 520 E. Beaver, Jenks, OK 74037
Illinois Arms Co., Inc., 1401 Ardmore, Itasca, IL 60143/312-773-0303
Interarms Ltd., 10 Prince St., Alexandria, VA 22323/703-548-1400
Intratec, 12405 S.W. 130th St., Miami, FL 33186/305-232-1821
Ithaca Gun, 123 Lake St., Ithaca, NY 14850/607-273-0200
Jennings Firearms Inc., 3680 Research Way, Carson City, NV 89706/702-588-6884
Jennings-Hawken, 326½-4th St. N.W., Winter Haven, FL 33880 (ML)
Iver Johnson, 2202 Redmond Rd., Jacksonville, AR 72076/501-982-9491
KK Arms Co., Karl Kash, Star Route, Box 671, Kerrville, TX 78028/512-257-4718 (handgun)
Kimber of Oregon, Inc., 9039 S.E. Jannsen Rd., Clackamas, OR 97015/503-656-1704
Kimel Industries, Box 335, Matthews, NC 28105/704-821-7663
L.A.R. Manufacturing Co., 4133 West Farm Rd., West Jordan, UT 84084/801-255-7106 (Grizzly Win Mag pistol)
Law Enforcement Ordnance Corp., Box 649, Middletown, PA 17057/717-944-5500 (Striker-12 shotgun)
Ljutic Ind., Inc., P.O. Box 2117, 732 N 16th Ave., Yakima, WA 98907/509-248-0476 (Mono-Gun)
Loven-Pierson, Inc., 4 W. Main, P.O. Box 377, Apalachin, NY 13732/607-625-2303 (ML)
Magnum Sales, Div. of Mag-na-port, 41302 Executive Drive, Mt. Clemens, MI 48045/313-469-7534 (Ltd. editions & customized guns for handgun hunting)
Marlin Firearms Co., 100 Kenna Drive, New Haven, CT 06473
Merrill Pistol (See RPM)
Michigan Arms Corp., 363 Elmwood, Troy, MI 48083/313-583-1518 (ML)
M.O.A. Corp., 7996 Brookville-Salem Rd., Brookville, OH 45309/513-833-5559 (Maximum pistol)
O.F. Mossberg & Sons, Inc., 7 Grasso St., No. Haven, CT 06473
Navy Arms Co., 689 Bergen Blvd., Ridgefield, NJ 07657
New England Firearms Co., Inc., Industrial Rowe, Gardner, MA 01440/617-632-9393
North American Arms, 1800 North 300 West, Spanish Fork, UT 84660/801-798-7401
Olympic Arms Inc. dba SGW, 624 Old Pacific Hwy. S.E., Olympia, WA 98503/206-456-3471 (Safari Arms)
Oregon Trail Riflesmiths, Inc., P.O. Box 51, Mackay, ID 83251/208-588-2527 (ML)
Pachmayr, Ltd., 1875 So. Mountain Ave., Monrovia, CA 91016/818-357-7771
Patriot Distribution Co., 2872 So. Wentworth Ave., Milwaukee, WI 53207/414-769-0760 (Partisan Adventure assault pistol)
Pennsylvania Arms Co., Box 128, Duryea, PA 18642/717-457-4014
E. F. Phelps Mfg., Inc., 700 W. Franklin St., Evansville, IN 47710/812-423-2599 (Heritage I in 45-70)
Phillips & Bailey, Inc., 815A Yorkshire St., Houston, TX 77022/713-699-4288 (357/9 Ultra, rev. conv.)
Precision Small Parts, 155 Carlton Rd., Charlottesville, VA 22901
RPM (R&R Sporting Arms, Inc.), 150 Viking Ave., Brea, CA 92621/714-990-2444 (XL pistol; formerly Merrill)
Rahn Gun Works, Inc., 470 Market SW, Box 33, Grand Rapids, MI 49503/616-235-0634
Raven Arms, 1300 Bixby Dr., Industry, CA 91745/818-961-2511 (P-25 pistols)
Remington Arms Co., 1007 Market St., Wilmington, DE 19898
Ruger (See Sturm, Ruger & Co.)
Savage Industries, Inc., Springdale Rd., Westfield, MA 01085/413-562-2361
L.W. Seecamp Co., Inc., P.O. Box 255, New Haven, CT 06502/203-877-3429
C. Sharps Arms Co., Inc., P.O. Box 885, Big Timber, MT 59011/406-932-4353
Shiloh Rifle Mfg. Co., Inc., P.O. Box 279; 201 Centennial Dr., Big Timber, MT 59011/406-932-4454
Smith & Wesson, Inc., 2100 Roosevelt Ave., Springfield, MA 01101
Sokolovsky Corp., P.O. Box 70113, Sunnyvale, CA 94086/408-245-9268 (45 Automaster pistol)
Springfield Armory, Inc., 420 W. Main St., Geneseo, IL 61254/309-944-5631
SSK Industries, Rt. 1, Della Dr., Bloomingdale, OH 43910/614-264-0176
Steel City Arms, Inc., P.O. Box 81926, Pittsburgh, PA 15217/412-461-3100 (d.a. "Double Deuce" pistol)
Sturm, Ruger & Co., Inc., Lacey Place, Southport, CT 06490/203-259-7843
Super Six Limited, P.O. Box 266, Elkhorn, WI 53121/414-723-5058
Texas Longhorn Arms, Inc., P. O. Box 703, Richmond, TX 77469/713-341-0775 (S.A. sixgun)
Thompson/Center Arms, Farmington Rd., P.O. Box 5002, Rochester, NH 03867/603-332-2394
Tippmann Arms Co., 4402 New Haven Ave., Ft. Wayne, IN 46803/219-422-6448
Trail Guns Armoury, 1422 E. Main St., League City, TX 77573/713-332-5833 (muzzleloaders)
Trapper Gun, Inc., 18717 E. 14 Mile Rd., Fraser, MI 48026/313-792-0133 (handguns)
The Ultimate Game Inc., P.O. Box 1856, Ormond Beach, FL 32075/904-677-4358
Ultra Light Arms Co., P.O. Box 1270; 214 Price St., Granville, WV 26534/304-599-5687
United States Frame Specialists, Inc. (U.S.F.S.), P.O. Box 7762, Milwaukee, WI 53207/414-643-6387
U.S. Repeating Arms Co., P.O. Box 30-300, New Haven, CT 06511/203-789-5000
Varner Sporting Arms, Inc., 100-F N. Cobb Pkwy., Marietta, GA 30062/404-422-5468
Weatherby's, 2781 E. Firestone Blvd., South Gate, CA 90280
Weaver Arms Corp., 6265 Greenwich Dr., Suite 201, San Diego, CA 92122/619-452-2551
Dan Wesson Arms, 293 Main St., Monson, MA 01057/413-267-4081
Wichita Arms, 444 Ellis, Wichita, KS 67211/316-265-0661
Wildey Inc., P.O. Box 475, Brookfield, CT 06804/203-355-9000
Wilkinson Arms, 26884 Pearl Rd., Parma, ID 83660/208-722-6771
Winchester, (See U.S. Repeating Arms)
Wyoming Armory, Inc., Forest Pl., Bedford, WY 83112/307-883-2151

GUNS (Foreign)

Action Arms, P.O. Box 9573, Philadelphia, PA 19124/215-744-0100
American Arms, Inc., 715 E. Armour Rd., N. Kansas City, MO 64116/816-474-3161
Anschutz (See PSI)
Armes de Chasse, P.O. Box 827, Chadds Ford, PA 19317/215-388-1146 (Merkel, Mauser pistols)
Armscor Precision, 1175 Chess Dr., Suite 204, Foster City, CA 94404/415-349-3592
Arms Corp. of the Philippines (See: Armscor Precision)
Armsport, Inc., 3590 N.W. 49th St., Miami, FL 33142/305-635-7850
Bauska Mfg. Corp., P.O. Box 2270, 1694 Whalebone Dr., Kalispell, MT 59901/406-752-8082
Beeman Precision Arms, Inc., 3440-GD Airway Dr., Santa Rosa, CA 95403/707-578-7900 (FWB, Weihrauch, Unique, Cork, Hammerli firearms)
Benelli Armi, S.p.A. (See: Sile Distributors—handguns; Heckler & Koch—Shotguns)
Benson Firearms Ltd., P.O. Box 30137, Seattle, WA 98103/800-521-0714 (A. Uberti replicas)
Beretta U.S.A., 17601 Beretta Dr., Accokeek, MD 20607/301-283-2191
Charles Boswell (Gunmakers), Div. of Saxon Arms Ltd., 615 Jasmine Ave. N., Unit J, Tarpon Springs, FL 34689/813-938-4882
Bretton, 21 Rue Clement Forissier, 42-St. Etienne, France
Britarms/Berdan (Gunmakers Ltd.), See: Action Arms
BRNO (See Saki International)
Browning (Gen. Offices), Rt. 1, Morgan, UT 84050/801-876-2711
Browning, (parts & service), Rt. 4, Box 624-B, Arnold, MO 63010/314-287-6800
Century Intl. Arms Inc., 5 Federal St., St. Albans, VT 05478/802-527-1252
Ets. Chapuis, 23, rue de Montorcier, BP15, 42380 St. Bonnet-le-Chateau, France
Cimarron Arms, 9439 Katy Freeway, Houston, TX 77024 (Uberti)
Classic Doubles Int., 1001 Craig Rd., Suite 353, St. Louis, MO 63146/314-997-7281 (shotguns)
Conco Arms, P.O. Box 159, Emmaus, PA 18049/215-967-5477 (Larona)
Connecticut Valley Arms Co., 5988 Peachtree Corners East, Norcross, GA 30071/404-449-4687 (CVA)
Diana Import, 842 Vallejo St., San Francisco, CA 94133
Charles Daly (See Outdoor Sports HQ)
Dikar s. Coop. (See Connecticut Valley Arms Co.)
Dixie Gun Works, Inc., Hwy 51, South, Union City, TN 38261/901-885-0561 ("Kentucky" rifles)
Dowtin Imports, Inc., Rt. 4 Box 930A, Flagstaff, AZ 86001/602-779-1898 (G. Granger sidelock shotgun)
Dynamit Nobel-RWS Inc., 105 Stonehurst Court, Northvale, NJ 07647/201-767-1995 (Rottweil)
Peter Dyson Ltd., 29-31 Church St., Honley, Huddersfield, Yorkshire HD7 2AH, England (accessories f. antique gun collectors)
E.M.F. Co. Inc. (Early & Modern Firearms), 1900 E. Warner Ave. 1-D, Santa Ana, CA 92705/714-261-6611
Elko Arms, 28 rue Ecole Moderne, 7400 Soignes, Belgium
Euroarms of America, Inc., P.O. Box 3277, 1501 Lenoir Dr., Winchester, VA 22601/703-662-1863 (ML)
Excam Inc., 4480 E. 11 Ave., P.O. Box 3483, Hialeah, FL 33013/305-681-4661
Exel Arms of America, 14 Main St., Gardner, MA 01440/617-632-5008
F.I.E. Corp. (See Firearms Import & Export Corp.)
J. Fanzoj, P.O. Box 25, Ferlach, Austria 9170
Armi FERLIB di Libero Ferraglio, 46 Via Costa, 25063 Gardone V.T. (Brescia), Italy
Fiocchi of America, Inc., Rt. 2, Box 90-8, Ozark, MO 65721/417-725-4118
Firearms Imp. & Exp. Corp., (F.I.E.), P.O. Box 4866, Hialeah Lakes, Hialeah, FL 33014/305-685-5966
Auguste Francotte & Cie, S.A., rue de Trois Juin 109, 4400 Herstal-Liege, Belgium
Frankonia Jagd, Hofmann & Co., Postfach 6780, D-8700 Wurzburg 1, West Germany
Freeland's Scope Stands, Inc., 3737 14th Ave., Rock Island, IL 61201/309-788-7449
Frigon Guns, 627 W. Crawford, Clay Center, KS 67432/913-632-5607 (cust.-made)
Renato Gamba, S.p.A., Gardone V.T. (Brescia), Italy (See Steyr Daimler Puch of America Corp.)
Armas Garbi, Urki #12, Eibar (Guipuzcoa) Spain (shotguns, See W. L. Moore)
Glock, Inc., 5000 Highlands Pkwy. #190, Smyrna, GA 30080/404-432-1202
George Granger, 66 Cours Fauriel, 42 St. Etienne, France
Griffin & Howe, 36 West 44th St., Suite 1011, New York, NY 10036/212-921-0980 (Purdey, Holland & Holland)
Griffin & Howe, 33 Claremont Rd., Bernardsville, NJ 07924/201-766-2287
Gun South, P.O. Box 129, 108 Morrow Ave., Trussville, AL 35173/205-655-8299 (Steyr, FN, Mannlicher)
Hallowell & Co., 340 West Putnam Ave., Greenwich, CT 06830/203-869-2190 (Agents for John Rigby & Co.)
Heckler & Koch Inc., 14601 Lee Rd., Chantilly, VA 22021/703-631-2800
Heym, Friedr. Wilh., see: Paul Jaeger, Inc.; G.E. Nygren Associates, Inc.
Incor, Inc., P.O. Box 132, Addison, TX 75001/214-931-3500 (Cosmi auto shotg.)
Interarmco, See Interarms (Walther)
Interarms Ltd., 10 Prince St., Alexandria, VA 22313/703-548-1400
Interport Inc., P.O. Box 1796, St. George, UT 84770/801-628-5792
Paul Jaeger Inc., P.O. Box 449, 1 Madison Ave., Grand Junction, TN 38039/901-764-6909 (Heym)
John Jovino Co., 5 Centre Market Pl., New York, NY 10013/212-925-4881 (Terminator)
KDF, Inc., 2485 Hwy 46 No., Seguin, TX 78155/512-379-8141 (Mauser rifles)
Kassnar Imports, P.O. Box 6097, Harrisburg, PA 17112/717-652-6101
Kendall International, 418 Fithian Ave., Paris, KY 40361/606-987-6946
Keng's Firearms Specialty, 6030 Hwy 85, #222, Riverdale, GA 30274
Kimel Industries, Box 335, Matthews, NC 28105/704-821-7663
Robert Kleinguenther Firearms, P.O. Box 2020, Seguin, TX 78155/512-372-5050
Llama (See Stoeger)
MRE Dist. Inc., 19 So. Bayles Ave., Pt. Washington, NY 11050/516-883-9226
Magnum Research, Inc., P.O. Box 3221, Minneapolis, MN 55432/612-574-1868 (Israeli Galil)
Mandall Shtg. Suppl., 3616 N. Scottsdale Rd., Scottsdale, AZ 85252/602-945-2553
Mannlicher (See Steyr Daimler Puch of Amer.)
Mauser-Werke Oberndorf, P. O. Box 1349, 7238 Oberndorf/Neckar, West Germany
Mendi s. coop. (See Connecticut Valley Arms Co.)
Merkuria, FTC, Argentinska 38, 17000 Prague 7, Czechoslovakia (BRNO)
Mitchell Arms, Inc., 3411 Lake Center Dr., Santa Ana, CA 92704/714-957-5711
Mitchell Arms Corp., 116 East 16th St., Costa Mesa, CA 92627/714-548-7701 (Uberti pistols)
Wm. Larkin Moore & Co., 31360 Via Colinas, Suite 109, Westlake Village, CA 91361/818-889-4160 (Garbi, Ferlib, Piotti, Perugini Visini)
Navy Arms Co., 689 Bergen Blvd., Ridgefield, NJ 07657
G.E. Nygren Associates, Inc., P.O. Box 6188, Fort Wayne, IN 46896/219-747-9148 (Heym)
Osborne's, P.O. Box 408, Cheboygan, MI 49721/616-625-9626 (Hammerli; Tanner rifles; Korth)
Outdoor Sports Headquarters, Inc., 967 Watertower Lane, Dayton, OH 45449/513-865-5855 (Charles Daly shotguns)
PM Air Services Ltd., P.O. Box 1573, Costa Mesa, CA 92626/714-968-2689
PTK International, Inc., 2814 New Spring Rd., Suite 340, Atlanta, GA 30339/404-438-9699 (mil. auto rifles)
Pachmayr Gun Works, 1875 So. Mountain Ave., Monrovia, CA 91016/818-357-7771
Pacific Intl. Merch. Corp., 2215 "J" St., Sacramento, CA 95816/916-446-2737
Para-Ordnance Mfg. Inc., 3411 McNicoll Ave., Scarborough, ON M1V 2V6, Canada/416-297-7895
Parker Reproductions, 124 River Rd., Middlesex, NJ 08846/201-469-0100
Parker-Hale, Bisleyworks, Golden Hillock Rd., Sparbrook, Birmingham B11 2PZ, England
Perazzi U.S.A. Inc., 206 S. George St., Rome, NY 13440/315-337-8566
Poly Technologies, Inc. (See PTK International, Inc.)
Precision Sales Intl. Inc., PSI, P.O. Box 1776, Westfield, MA 01086/413-562-5055 (Anschutz)
Precision Sports, P.O. Box 708, Kellogg Rd., Cortland, NY 13045/607-756-2851 (Parker-Hale)
Proofmark, Ltd., P.O. Box 183, Alton, IL 62002/618-463-0120 (Bettinsoli shotguns)
Quality Arms, Inc., Box 19477, Houston, TX 77224/713-870-8377 (Bernardelli; Ferlib; Bretton shotguns)
Quantetics Corp., Imp.-Exp. Div., 582 Somerset St. W., Ottawa, Ont. K1R 5K2 Canada/613-237-0242 (Unique pistols-Can. only)
Rahn Gun Works, Inc., 470 Market SW, Box 33, Grand Rapids, MI 49503/616-235-0634
Ravizza Carlo Caccia Pesca, s.r.l., Via Melegnano 6, 20122 Milano, Italy
Rottweil, (See Dynamit Nobel)
S.A.E., Inc. (See: Spain America Enterprises)
Saki International, 19800 Center Ridge Rd., Rocky River, OH 44116/216-331-3533
Samco Enterprises, Inc., 6995 N.W. 43rd St., Miami, FL 33166/305-593-9782
Sauer (See Sigarms)
Savage Industries, Inc., Springdale Rd., Westfield, MA 01085/413-562-2361
Thad Scott, P.O. Box 412; Hwy 82 West, Indianola, MS 38751/601-887-5929 (Perugini Visini; Bertuzzi; Mario Beschi shotguns)
Don L. Shrum's Cape Outfitters, Rt. 2 Box 437-C, Cape Girardeau, MO 63701/314-335-4103
Sigarms Inc., 470 Spring Park Pl., Unit 900, Herndon, VA 22070/703-481-6660
Sile Distributors, 7 Centre Market Pl., New York, NY 10013/212-925-4111
Ernie Simmons Enterprises, 719 Highland Ave., Lancaster, PA 17603/717-392-0021 (SKB shotguns)
Franz Sodia Jagdgewehrfabrik, Schulhausgasse 14, 9170 Ferlach, (Karnten) Austria
Southern Gun & Tackle Distributors, 13490 N.W. 45th Ave., Opa-Locka (Miami), FL 33054/305-685-8451
Spain America Enterprises Inc., 8581 N.W. 54th St., Miami, FL 33166/305-593-5173
Sportarms of Florida, 5555 N.W. 36 Ave., Miami, FL 33142/305-635-2411
Springfield Armory, 420 W. Main St., Geneseo, IL 61254/309-944-5631 (Bernardelli)
Steyr-Daimler-Puch, Gun South, Inc., Box 6607, 7605 Eastwood Mall, Birmingham, AL 35210/800-821-3021 (rifles)
Stoeger Industries, 55 Ruta Ct., S. Hackensack, NJ 07606/201-440-2700
Taurus International Mfg. Inc., P.O. Box 558567, Ludlam Br., Miami, FL 33155/305-662-2529
Tradewinds, Inc., P.O. Box 1191, Tacoma, WA 98401
Uberti USA, Inc., 41 Church St., New Milford, CT 06776/203-355-8827
Ignacio Ugartechea, Apartado 21, Eibar, Spain
Valmet Sporting Arms Div., 55 Ruta Ct., S. Hackensack, NJ 07606 (sporting types)
Verney-Carron, B.P. 72, 54 Boulevard Thiers, 42002 St. Etienne Cedex, France
Perugini Visini & Co. s.r.l., Via Camprelle, 126, 25080 Nuvolera (Bs.), Italy
Waffen-Frankonia, see: Frankonia Jagd
Weatherby's, 2781 Firestone Blvd., So. Gate, CA 90280/213-569-7186
Weaver Arms Corp., 6265 Greenwich Dr., Suite 201, San Diego, CA 92122/619-452-2551
Whittington Arms, Box 489, Hooks, TX 75561
Winchester, Olin Corp., 120 Long Ridge Rd., Stamford, CT 06904
Zavodi Crvena Zastava (See Interarms)

GUNS (Air)

Air Rifle Specialists, 311 East Water St., Elmira, NY 14901/607-734-7340
Beeman Precision Arms, Inc., 3440-GD Airway Dr., Santa Rosa, CA 95403/707-578-7900 (Feinwerkbau, Weihrauch, Webley)
Benjamin Air Rifle Co., 2600 Chicory Rd., Racine, WI 53403/414-554-7900
Brass Eagle Inc., 3876 Midhurst Lane, Mississauga, Ont. L4Z 1C7, Canada/416-848-4844 (paint ball guns)
The Command Post, Inc., P.O. Box 1500, Crestview, FL 32536/904-682-2492 (airsoft, air and paintball marking guns)
Crosman Airguns, a Coleman Co., Routes 5 and 20, E. Bloomfield, NY 14443/716-657-6161
Daisy Mfg. Co., P.O. Box 220, Rogers, AR 72756/501-636-1200
Dynamit Nobel-RWS Inc., 105 Stonehurst Ct., Northvale, NJ 07647/201-767-1995 (Dianawerk)
Fiocchi of America, Inc., Rt. 2 Box 90-8, Ozark, MO 65721/417-725-4118
Fisher Enterprises, 655 Main St. #305, Edmonds, WA 98020/206-776-4365
Great Lakes Airguns, 6175 So. Park Ave., Hamburg, NY 14075/716-648-6666
Gil Hebard Guns, Box 1, Knoxville, IL 61448
Interarms, 10 Prince, Alexandria, VA 22313 (Walther)
Kendall International, 418 Fithian Ave., Paris, KY 40361/606-987-6946 (Italian Airmatch)
Mandall Shooting Supplies, Inc., 3616 N. Scottsdale Rd., Scottsdale, AZ 85252/602-945-2553 (Cabanas line)
Marksman Products, 5622 Engineer Dr., Huntington Beach, CA 92649/714-898-7535
McMurray & Son, 109 E. Arbor Vitae St., Inglewood, CA 90301/213-412-0558 (custom airguns)
National Survival Game, Inc., Box 1439, Main St., New London, NH 03257/603-735-5151
Phoenix Arms Co., Phoenix House, Churchdale Rd., Eastbourne, East Sussex BN22 8PX, England (Jackal)
Power Line (See Daisy Mfg. Co.)
Pursuit Marketing, Inc. (PMI), 1966 Raymond Dr., Northbrook, IL 60062
Sheridan Products, Inc., 2600 Chicory Rd., Racine, WI 53403/414-554-7900
Stone Enterprises Ltd., Rt. 609, P.O. Box 335, Wicomico Church, VA 22579/804-580-5114
Target Airgun Supply, P.O. Box 428, South Gate, CA 90280/213-569-3417
Tippman Pneumatics, Inc., 4402 New Haven Ave., Fort Wayne, IN 46803/219-422-6448

GUNS & GUN PARTS, REPLICA AND ANTIQUE

Antique Arms Co., David E. Saunders, 1110 Cleveland, Monett, MO 65708/417-235-6501
Antique Gun Parts, Inc., 1118 S. Braddock Ave., Pittsburgh, PA 15218/412-241-1811 (ML)
Armsport, Inc., 3590 N.W. 49th St., Miami, FL 33142
Beeman Precision Arms, Inc., 3440-GDD Airway Dr., Santa Rosa, CA 95403/707-578-7900
Benson Firearms Ltd., P.O. Box 30137, Seattle, WA 98103/800-521-0714, Ext. 631
Cache La Poudre Rifleworks, 140 No. College Ave., Fort Collins, CO 80524/303-482-6913
Leonard Day & Sons, Inc., One Cottage St., P.O. Box 723, East Hampton, MA 01027/413-527-7990
Dixie Gun Works, Inc., Hwy 51, South, Union City, TN 38261/901-885-0561
Andy Fautheree, P.O. Box 4607, Pagosa Springs, CO 81157/303-731-5003
Federal Ordnance Inc., 1443 Porterro Ave., So. El Monte, CA 91733/213-350-4161
Jack First Distributors, Inc., 44633 Sierra Hwy., Lancaster, CA 93534/805-945-6981
Fred Goodwin, Goodwin's Gun Shop, Silver Ridge, Sherman Mills, ME 04776/207-365-4451 (Winchester rings & studs)
Gun Parts Corp. Box 2, West Hurley, NY 12491/914-679-2417
Hansen and Company, 244 Old Post Rd., Southport, CT 06490/203-259-6222
Hopkins & Allen Arms, 3 Ethel Ave., P.O. Box 217, Hawthorne, NJ 07507/201-427-1165
Terry K. Kopp, Highway 13 South, Lexington, MO 64067/816-259-2636 (restoration & pts. 1890 & 1906 Winch.)
The House of Muskets, Inc., P.O. Box 4640, Pagosa Springs, CO 81157/303-731-2295 (ML supplies; catalog $3)
Liberty Antique Gunworks, 19 Key St., P.O. Box 183GD, Eastport, ME 04631/207-853-2327 (S&W only; ctlg. $5)
Log Cabin Sport Shop, 8010 Lafayette Rd., Lodi, OH 44254/216-948-1082 (ctlg. $30)
Edw. E. Lucas, 32 Garfield Ave., East Brunswick, NJ 08816/201-251-1526 (45/70 Springfield parts; some Sharps, Spencer parts)
Lyman Products Corp., Middlefield, CT 06455
Tommy Munsch Gunsmithing, Rt. 2, Box 248, Little Falls, MN 56345/612-632-6695 (Winchester obsolete parts only; list $1.50; oth. inq. SASE)
Precise Metalsmithing Ent., James L. Wisner, 146 Curtis Hill Rd., Chehalis, WA 98532/206-748-3743 (pre '68-M70 Winchester)
Ram Line, Inc., 15611 W. 6th Ave., Golden, CO 80401/303-279-0886
S&S Firearms, 88-21 Aubrey Ave., Glendale, NY 11385/718-497-1100
Sarco, Inc., 323 Union St., Stirling, NJ 07980/201-647-3800
Shiloh Rifle Mfg. Co., Inc., P.O. Box 279; 201 Centennial Dr., Big Timber, MT 59011/406-932-4454
South Bend Replicas, Inc., 61650 Oak Rd., South Bend, IN 46614/219-289-4500 (ctlg. $6)
C. H. Stoppler, 1426 Walton Ave., New York, NY 10452 (miniature guns)
Stott's Creek Armory Inc., R 1 Box 70, Morgantown, IN 46160/317-878-5489
Uberti USA, Inc., 41 Church St., New Milford, CT 06776/203-355-8827
Upper Missouri Trading Co., 304 Harold St., Crofton, NE 68730/402-388-4844
Weisz Antique Gun Parts, P.O. Box 311, Arlington, VA 22210/703-243-9161
W. H. Wescombe, P.O. Box 488, Glencoe, CA 95232 (Rem. R.B. parts)

GUNS, SURPLUS—PARTS AND AMMUNITION

M. Braun, 32, rue Notre-Dame, 2440 Luxembourg, Luxembourg
Can Am Enterprises, 350 Jones Rd., Fruitland, Ont. LOR ILO, Canada/416-643-4357 (Enfield rifles; catalog $2)
Century Intl. Arms, Inc., 5 Federal St., St. Albans, VT 05478/802-527-1252
Federal Ordnance, Inc., 1443 Potrero Ave., So. El Monte, CA 91733/818-350-4161
Garcia National Gun Traders, 225 S.W. 22nd, Miami, FL 33135
Gun Parts Corp. Box 2, West Hurley, NY 12491/914-679-2417
Hansen and Company, 244 Old Post Rd., Southport, CT 06490/203-259-6222
Lever Arms Service Ltd., 2131 Burrard St., Vancouver, B.C., Canada V6J 3H8/604-736-0004
Paragon Sales & Services, Inc., P.O. Box 2022, Joliet, IL 60434 (ammunition)
Raida Intertraders S.A., Raida House, 1-G Ave. de la Couronne, B1050 Brussels, Belgium (surplus guns)
Sarco, Inc., 323 Union St., Stirling, NJ 07980/201-647-3800 (military surpl. ammo)
Sherwood Intl. Export Corp., 18714 Parthenia St., Northridge, CA 91324/818-349-7600
Southern Ammunition Co., Inc., Rte. 1, Box 6B, Latta, SC 29565/803-752-7751
Southern Armory, P.O. Box 879, Hillsville, VA 24343/703-236-7835 (modern military parts)
Springfield Sporters, Inc., R.D. 1, Penn Run, PA 15765/412-254-2626

GUNSMITHS, CUSTOM (see Custom Gunsmiths)

GUNSMITHS, HANDGUN (see Pistolsmiths)

GUNSMITH SCHOOLS

Colorado School of Trades, 1575 Hoyt, Lakewood, CO 80215/303-233-4697
Lassen Community College, P.O. Box 3000, Hiway 139, Susanville, CA 96130/916-257-6181
Robert E. Maki, School of Engraving, P.O. Box 947, Northbrook, IL 60065/312-724-8238 (firearms engraving ONLY)
Modern Gun Repair School, 2538 No. 8th St., Phoenix, AZ 85006/602-990-8346 (home study)
Montgomery Technical College, P.O. Box 787, Troy, NC 27371/919-572-3691 (also 1-yr. engraving school)
Murray State College, Gunsmithing Program, 100 Faculty Dr., Tishomingo, OK 73460/405-371-2371
North American Correspondence Schools, The Gun Pro School, Oak & Pawnee St., Scranton, PA 18515/717-342-7701
Penn. Gunsmith School, 812 Ohio River Blvd., Avalon, Pittsburgh, PA 15202/412-766-1812
Piedmont Technical College, P.O. Box 1197, Roxboro, NC 27573/919-599-1181
Pine Technical Institute, 1100 Fourth St., Pine City, MN 55063/612-629-6764
Professional Gunsmiths of America, 13 Highway Route 1, Box 224E, Lexington, MO 64067/816-259-2636
Shenandoah School of Gunsmithing, P.O. Box 300, Bentonville, VA 22610/703-743-5494
Southeastern Community College—North Campus, 1015 Gear Ave.; P.O. Drawer F, West Burlington, IA 52655/319-752-2731
Trinidad State Junior College, 600 Prospect, Trinidad, CO 81082/719-846-5631
Yavapai College, 1100 East Sheldon St., Prescott, AZ 86301/602-445-7300

GUNSMITH SUPPLIES, TOOLS, SERVICES

Don Allen, Inc., HC55, Box 326, Sturgis, SD 57785/605-347-5227 (stock duplicating machine)
Alley Supply Co., Carson Valley Industrial Park, P.O. Box 848, Gardnerville, NV 89410/702-782-3800 (JET line lathes, mills, etc.; Sweany Site-A-Line Optical bore collimator)
Anderson Mfg. Co., P.O. Box 536, 6813 S. 220th St., Kent, WA 98032/206-872-7602 (tang safe)
Armite Labs., 1845 Randolph St., Los Angeles, CA 90001/213-587-7744 (pen oiler)
B-Square Co., Box 11281, Ft. Worth, TX 76110/800-433-2909
Jim Baiar, 490 Halfmoon Rd., Columbia Falls, MT 59912 (hex screws)
Baron Technology, 62 Spring Hill Rd., Trumbull, CT 06611/203-452-0515 (chemical etching, plating)
Behlert Custom Guns, Inc., RD 2 Box 36C, Route 611 North, Pipersville, PA 18947/215-766-8680
Dennis M. Bellm Gunsmithing, Inc., dba P.O. Ackley Rifle Barrels, 2376 S. Redwood Rd., Salt Lake City, UT 84119/801-974-0697 (rifles only)
Al Biesen, W. 2039 Sinto Ave., Spokane, WA 99201 (grip caps, buttplates)
Roger Biesen, 5021 W. Rosewood, Spokane, WA 99208/509-328-9340
Blue Ridge Machinery and Tools, Inc., P.O. Box 536-GD, 2806 Putnam Ave., Hurricane, WV 25526/304-562-3538/800-872-6500 (gunsmithing lathe, mills & shop suppl.)
Briganti Custom Gun-Smithing, P.O. Box 56, 475-Route 32, Highland Mills, NY 10930/914-692-4409 (cold rust bluing, hand polishing, metal work)
Brownells, Inc., 222 W. Liberty, Montezuma, IA 50171/515-623-5401
W.E. Brownell Checkering Tools, 3356 Moraga Place, San Diego, CA 92117/619-276-6146

GUNSMITH SUPPLIES, TOOLS, SERVICES — cont'd.

Buehler Scope Mounts, 17 Orinda Way, Orinda, CA 94563/415-254-3201
Burgess Vibrocrafters, Inc. (BVI), Rte. 83, Grayslake, IL 60030
M.H. Canjar, 500 E. 45th, Denver, CO 80216/303-295-2638 (triggers, etc.)
Chapman Mfg. Co., P.O. Box 250, Rte. 17 at Saw Mill Rd., Durham, CT 06422/203-349-9228
Chicago Wheel & Mfg. Co., 1101 W. Monroe St., Chicago, IL 60607/312-226-8155 (Handee grinders)
Chopie Mfg., Inc., 700 Copeland Ave., LaCrosse, WI 54603/608-784-0926
Classic Arms Corp., P.O. Box 8, Palo Alto, CA 94302/415-321-7243 (floorplates, grip caps)
Clymer Mfg. Co., Inc., 1645 W. Hamlin Rd., Rochester Hills, MI 48309/313-541-5533 (reamers)
Dave Cook, 720 Hancock Ave., Hancock, MI 49930 (metalsmithing only)
Crouse's Country Cover, P.O. Box 160, Storrs, CT 06268/203-429-3720 (Masking Gun Oil)
Dayton-Traister Co., 4778 N. Monkey Hill Rd., Oak Harbor, WA 98277/206-675-3421 (triggers; safeties)
Dem-Bart Hand Checkering Tools, Inc., 6807 Hiway #2, Snohomish, WA 98290/206-568-7356
Dremel Mfg. Co., 4915-21st St., Racine, WI 53406 (grinders)
Chas. E. Duffy, Williams Lane, West Hurley, NY 12491
The Dutchman's Firearms Inc., 4143 Taylor Blvd., Louisville, KY 40215/502-366-0555
Peter Dyson Ltd., 29-31 Church St., Honley, Huddersfield, West Yorksh. HD7 2AH, England/0484-661062 (accessories f. antique gun coll.)
Edmund Scientific Co., 101 E. Gloucester Pike, Barrington, NJ 08007/609-547-3488
Jack First Distributors, Inc., 44633 Sierra Hwy., Lancaster, CA 93534/805-945-6981
Jerry Fisher, 1244 4th Ave. West, Kalispell, MT 59901/406-755-7093
Forster Products, Inc., 82 E. Lanark Ave., Lanark, IL 61046/815-493-6360
G. R. S. Corp., P.O. Box 748, 900 Overlander St., Emporia, KS 66801/316-343-1084 (Gravermeister; Grave Max tools)
Garrett Accur-Lt. D.F.S. Co., P.O. Box 8675, Ft. Collins, CO 80524/303-224-3067
Gilmore Pattern Works, P.O. Box 50084, Tulsa, OK 74150/918-245-9627 (Wagner safe-T-planer)
Grace Metal Prod., 115 Ames St., Elk Rapids, MI 49629/616-264-8133 (screw drivers, drifts)
Gunline Tools, 2970 Saturn St., Brea, CA 92621/714-993-5100
Gun Parts Corp., Box 2, West Hurley, NY 12491/914-679-2417
Gun-Tec, P.O. Box 8125, W. Palm Beach, Fl 33407 (files; SASE f. reply)
Half Moon Rifle Shop, 490 Halfmoon Rd., Columbia Falls, MT 59912/406-892-4409 (hex screws)
Henriksen Tool Co., Inc., P.O. Box 668, Phoenix, OR 97535/503-535-2309 (reamers)
Huey Gun Cases (Marvin Huey), P.O. Box 22456, Kansas City, MO 64113/816-444-1637 (high grade English ebony tools)
Ken Jantz Supply, 222 E. Main, Davis, OK 73030/405-369-2316
JGS Precision Tool Mfg., 1141 S. Sumner Rd., Coos Bay, OR 97420/503-267-4331
Jeffredo Gunsight Co., 1629 Via Monserate, Fallbrook, CA 92028 (trap buttplate)
Jim's Gun Shop, James R. Spradlin, 113 Arthur, Pueblo, CO 81004/719-543-9462 ("Belgian Blue" rust blues; stock fillers)
Kasenit Co., Inc., P.O. Box 726, 3 King St., Mahwah, NJ 07430/201-529-3663 (surface hardening compound)
Terry K. Kopp, Highway 13 South, Lexington, MO 64067/816-259-2636 (stock rubbing compound; rust preventive grease)
J. Korzinek, RD#2, Box 73, Canton, PA 17724/717-673-8512 (stainl. steel bluing; broch. $2)
John G. Lawson, (The Sight Shop) 1802 E. Columbia Ave., Tacoma, WA 98404/206-474-5465
Lea Mfg. Co., 237 E. Aurora St., Waterbury, CT 06720/203-753-5116
Mark Lee Supplies, P.O. Box 20379, Minneapolis, MN 55420/612-431-1727
Liberty Antique Gunworks, 19 Key St., P.O. Box 183GD, Eastport, ME 04631/207-853-2327 (spl. S&W tools)
Lock's Phila. Gun Exch., 6700 Rowland Ave., Philadelphia, PA 19149/215-332-6225
Longbranch Gun Bluing Co., 2455 Jacaranda Lane, Los Osos, CA 93402/805-528-1792
McIntyre Tools, P.O. Box 491/State Road #1144, Troy, NC 27371/919-572-2603 (shotgun bbl. facing tool)
McMillan Rifle Barrels, U.S. International, P.O Box 3427, Bryan, TX 77805/409-846-3990 (services)
Mike Marsh, Croft Cottage, Main St., Elton, Derbyshire DE4 2BY, England/062-988-6699 (gun accessories)
Meier Works, Steve Hines, Box 328, 2102-2nd Ave., Canyon, TX 79015/806-655-7806 (European accessories)
Michaels of Oregon Co., P.O. Box 13010, Portland, OR 97213/503-255-6890
Miller Single Trigger Mfg. Co., R.D. 1, Box 99, Millersburg, PA 17061/717-692-3704 (selective or non-selective f. shotguns)
Miniature Machine Co. (MMC), 210 E. Poplar St., Deming, NM 88030/505-546-2151 (screwdriver grinding fixtures)
Frank Mittermeier, 3577 E. Tremont, New York, NY 10465/212-828-3843
N&J Sales Co., Lime Kiln Rd., Northford, CT 06472/203-484-0247 (screwdrivers)
Palmgren Steel Prods., Chicago Tool & Engineering Co., 8383 South Chicago Ave., Chicago, IL 60617/312-721-9675 (vises, etc.)
Panavise Prods., Inc., 2850 E. 29th St., Long Beach, CA 90806/213-595-7621
Pilkington Gun Co., P.O. Box 1296, Muskogee, OK 74402/918-683-9418 (Q.D. scope mt.)
Redman's Rifling & Reboring, Route 3, Box 330A, Omak, WA 98841/509-826-5512 (22 RF liners)
Roto/Carve, 6509 Indian Hills Rd., Minneapolis, MN 55435/612-944-5150 (tool)

A.G. Russell Co., 1705 Hiway 71 North, Springdale, AR 72764/501-751-7341 (Arkansas oilstones)
Schaffner Mfg. Co., Emsworth, Pittsburgh, PA 15202 (polishing kits)
Seacliff International Inc., 2210 Santa Anita, So. El Monte, CA 91733/818-350-0515 (portable parts washer)
Shaw's, 9447 W. Lilac Rd., Escondido, CA 92026/619-728-7070
L.S. Starrett Co., 121 Crescent St., Athol, MA 01331/617-249-3551
Texas Platers Supply Co., 2453 W. Five Mile Parkway, Dallas, TX 75233 (plating kit)
Timney Mfg. Inc., 3065 W. Fairmount Ave., Phoenix, AZ 85017/602-274-2999 (triggers)
Stan de Treville, Box 33021, San Diego, CA 92103/619-298-3393 (checkering patterns)
Twin City Steel Treating Co., Inc. 1114 S. 3rd, Minneapolis, MN 55415/612-332-4849 (heat treating)
Walker Arms Co., Inc., Rt. 2, Box 73, Hwy. 80 W, Selma, AL 36701/205-872-6231 (tools)
Weaver Arms Co., P.O. Box 8, Dexter, MO 63841/314-568-3800 (action wrenches & transfer punches)
Will-Burt Co., 169 So. Main, Orrville, OH 44667 (vises)
Williams Gun Sight Co., 7389 Lapeer Rd., Davison, MI 48423
Wilson Arms Co., 63 Leetes Island Rd., Branford, CT 06405/203-488-7297
W.C. Wolff Co., P.O. Box 232, Ardmore, PA 19003/215-896-7500 (springs)

HANDGUN ACCESSORIES

Ajax Custom Grips, Inc., Div. of A. Jack Rosenberg & Sons, 12229 Cox Lane, Dallas, TX 75244/214-241-6302
Bob Allen Companies, 214 S.W. Jackson St., Des Moines, IA 50302/515-283-2191
American Gas & Chemical Co., Ltd., 220 Pegasus Ave., Northvale, NJ 07647/201-767-7300 (clg. lube)
Armson, Inc., P.O. Box 2130, Farmington Hills, MI 48018/313-478-2577
Armsport, Inc., 3590 N.W. 49th St., Miami, FL 33142/305-635-7850
Baramie Corp., 6250 E. 7 Mile Rd., Detroit, MI 48234 (Hip-Grip)
Bar-Sto Precision Machine, 73377 Sullivan Rd., Twentynine Palms, CA 92277/619-367-2747
Behlert Precision, RD 2 Box 63, Route 611 North, Pipersville, PA 18947/215-766-8681
Brauer Bros. Mfg. Co., 2020 Delmar Blvd., St. Louis, MO 63103/314-231-2864
Centaur Systems, Inc., 15127 NE 24th, Suite 114, Redmond, WA 98052/206-392-8472 (Quadra-Lok bbls.)
Central Specialties Co., 200 Lexington Dr., Buffalo Grove, IL 60089/312-537-3300 (trigger locks only)
D&E Magazines Mfg., P.O. Box 4876-D, Sylmar, CA 91342 (clips)
Detonics Firearms Industries, 13456 SE 27th Pl., Bellevue, WA 98005/206-747-2100
Doskocil Mfg. Co., Inc, P.O. Box 1246, Arlington, TX 75010/817-467-5116 (Gun Guard cases)
Essex Arms, Box 345, Island Pond, VT 05846/802-723-4313 (45 Auto frames)
Frielich Police Equipment, 396 Broome St., New York, NY 10013/212-254-3045 (cases)
R. S. Frielich, 211 East 21st St., New York, NY 10010/212-777-4477 (cases)
Glock, Inc., 5000 Highlands Parkway #190, Smyrna, GA 30080/404-432-1202
Gun Parts Corp., Box 2, West Hurley, NY 12491/914-679-2417
Gil Hebard Guns, 125-129 Public Square, Knoxville, IL 61448
K&K Ammo Wrist Band, R.D. #1, Box 448-CA18, Lewistown, PA 17044/717-242-2329
King's Gun Works, 1837 W. Glenoaks Blvd., Glendale, CA 91201/818-956-6010
Terry K. Kopp, Highway 13 South, Lexington, MO 64067/816-259-2636
Lee's Red Ramps, 7252 E. Ave. U-3, Littlerock, CA 93543/805-944-4487 (ramp insert kits; spring kits)
Lee Precision Inc., 4275 Hwy. U, Hartford, WI 53027 (pistol rest holders)
Liberty Antique Gunworks, 19 Key St., P.O. Box 183GD, Eastport, ME 04631/207-853-2327 (shims f. S&W revs.)
Kent Lomont, 4236 West 700 South, Poneto, IN 46781 (Auto Mag only)
Lone Star Gunleather, 1301 Brushy Bend Dr., Round Rock, TX 78681/512-255-1805
Los Gatos Grip & Specialty Co., P.O. Box 1850, Los Gatos, CA 95030 (custommade)
MTM Molded Prods. Co., 3370 Obco Ct., Dayton, OH 45414/513-890-7461
Millett Industries, 16131 Gothard St., Huntington Beach, CA 92647/714-842-5575
No-Sho Mfg. Co., 10727 Glenfield Ct., Houston, TX 77096/713-723-5332
Jim Noble Co., 1305 Columbia St., Vancouver, WA 98660/206-695-1309
Omega Sales, Inc., P.O. Box 1066, Mt. Clemens, MI 48403/313-469-6727
Harry Owen (See Sport Specialties)
Pachmayr Ltd., 1875 So. Mountain Ave., Monrovia, CA 91016/818-357-7771 (cases)
Pacific Intl. Mchdsg. Corp., 2215 "J" St., Sacramento, CA 95818/916-446-2737 (Vega 45 Colt comb. mag.)
Poly-Choke Div., Marble Arms Corp., 420 Industrial Park, Gladstone, MI 49837/906-428-3710 (handgun ribs)
Ranch Products, P.O. Box 145, Malinta, OH 43535 (third-moon clips)
Ransom Intl. Corp., 1040 Sandretto Dr., Suite J, Prescott, AZ 86302/602-778-7899
SSK Industries, Rt. 1, Della Dr., Bloomingdale, OH 43910/614-264-0176
Safariland Ltd., Inc., 1941 S. Walker, Monrovia, CA 91016/818-357-7902
Sile Distributors, 7 Centre Market Pl., New York, NY 10013
Robert Sonderman, 735 W. Kenton, Charleston, IL 61920/217-345-5429 (solid walnut fitted handgun cases; other woods)
Sport Specialties, (Harry Owen), Box 5337, Hacienda Hts., CA 91745/213-968-5806 (.22 rimfire adapters; .22 insert bbls. f. T/C Contender, autom. pistols)
Sportsmen's Equipment Co., 415 W. Washington, San Diego, CA 92103/619-296-1501

HANDGUN ACCESSORIES — cont'd.

Turkey Creek Enterprises, Rt. 1, Box 10, Red Oak, CA 74563/918-754-2884 (wood handgun cases)
Melvin Tyler Mfg.-Dist., 1326 W. Britton, Oklahoma City, OK 73114/405-842-8044 (grip adaptor)
Wardell Precision Handguns Ltd., Box 4132 New River Stage 1, New River, AZ 85029/602-465-7258
Whitney Sales, P.O. Box 875, Reseda, CA 91335/818-345-4212
Wilson's Gun Shop, P.O. Box 578, Rt. 3, Box 211-D, Berryville, AR 72616/501-545-3616

HANDGUN GRIPS

Ajax Custom Grips, Inc., Div. of A. Jack Rosenberg & Sons, 12229 Cox Lane, Dallas, TX 75244/214-241-6302
Altamont Mfg. Co., 510 N. Commercial St., P.O. Box 309, Thomasboro, IL 61878/217-643-3125
Art Jewel Enterprises Ltd., Eagle Business Ctr., 460 Randy Rd., Carol Stream, IL 60188/312-260-0040 (Eagle grips)
Barami Corp., 6250 East 7 Mile Rd., Detroit, MI 48234/313-891-2536
Bear Hug Grips, Inc., P.O. Box 25944, Colorado Springs, CO 80936/303-598-5675 (cust.)
Beeman Precision Arms, Inc., 3440-GD Airway Dr., Santa Rosa, CA 95403/707-578-7900 (airguns only)
Behlert Precision, RD 2 Box 63, Route 611 North, Pipersville, PA 18947/215-766-8681
Boone's Custom Ivory Grips, Inc., 562 Coyote Rd., Brinnon, WA 98320/206-796-4330
Fab-U-Grip, An-Lin Enterprises, Inc., P.O. Box 550, Vineland, NJ 08360/609-652-1089
Fitz Pistol Grip Co., P.O. Box 171, Douglas City, CA 96024/916-778-3136
Gun Parts Corp., Box 2, West Hurley, NY 12491/914-679-2417
Herrett's, Box 741, Twin Falls, ID 83303/208-733-1498
Hogue Combat Grips, P.O. Box 2038, Atascadero, CA 93423/805-466-6266 (Monogrip)
Paul Jones Munitions Systems, (See Fitz Co.)
Russ Maloni (See Russwood)
Monogrip, (See Hogue)
Monte Kristo Pistol Grip Co., Box 171, Douglas City, CA 96024/916-778-3136
Mustang Custom Pistol Grips, see: Supreme Products Co.
Pachmayr Ltd., 1875 So. Mountain Ave., Monrovia, CA 91016/818-357-7771
Robert H. Newell, 55 Coyote, Los Alamos, NM 87544/505-662-7135 (custom stocks)
Olympic Arms Inc. dba SGW, 624 Old Pacific Hwy. S.E., Olympia, WA 98503/206-456-3471
A. Jack Rosenberg & Sons, 12229 Cox Lane, Dallas, TX 75234/214-241-6302 (Ajax)
Royal Ordnance Works Ltd., P.O. Box 3254, Wilson, NC 27893/919-237-0515
Russwood Custom Pistol Grips, P.O. Box 460, East Aurora, NY 14052/716-842-6012 (cust. exotic woods)
Jean St. Henri, 6525 Dume Dr., Malibu, CA 90265/213-457-7211 (custom)
Sile Dist., 7 Centre Market Pl., New York, NY 10013/212-925-4111
Sports Inc., P.O. Box 683, Park Ridge, IL 60068/312-825-8952 (Franzite)
Supreme Products Co., 1830 S. California Ave., Monrovia, CA 91016/800-423-7159/818-357-5359
R. D. Wallace, Star Rte. 1 Box 76, Grandin, MO 63943/314-593-4773 (cust. only)
Wayland Prec. Wood Prods., Box 1142, Mill Valley, CA 94942/415-381-3543
Wilson's Gun Shop, P.O. Box 578, Rt. 3, Box 211-D, Berryville, AR 72616/501-545-3616

HEARING PROTECTORS

AO Safety Prods., Div. of American Optical Corp., 14 Mechanic St., Southbridge, MA 01550/617-765-9711 (ear valves, ear muffs)
Bausch & Lomb, 635 St. Paul St., Rochester, NY 14602
Bilsom Interntl., Inc., 11800 Sunrise Valley Dr., Reston, VA 22091/703-620-3950 (ear plugs, muffs)
David Clark Co., Inc., 360 Franklin St., P.O. Box 15054, Worcester, MA 01615/617-756-6216
Gun Parts Corp., Box 2, West Hurley, NY 12491/914-679-2417
Marble Arms Corp., 420 Industrial Park, Box 111, Gladstone, MI 49837/906-428-3710
North Consumer Prods. Div., 16624 Edwards Rd., P.O. Box 7500, Cerritos, CA 90702/213-926-0545 (Lee Sonic ear valves)
Safety Direct, 23 Snider Way, Sparks, NV 89431/702-354-4451 (Silencio)
Smith & Wesson, 2100 Roosevelt Ave., Springfield, MA 01101
Willson Safety Prods. Div., P.O. Box 622, Reading, PA 19603 (Ray-O-Vac)

HOLSTERS & LEATHER GOODS

Alessi Holsters, Inc., 2465 Niagara Falls Blvd., Tonawanda, NY 14150/716-691-5615
Bob Allen Companies, 214 S.W. Jackson, Des Moines, IA 50315/515-283-2191
American Enterprises, 649 Herbert, El Cajon, CA 92020/619-588-1222
American Sales & Mfg. Co., P.O. Box 677, Laredo, TX 78040/512-723-6893
Andy Arratoonian, The Cottage, Sharow, Ripon HG4 5BP, England (0765-5858)
Rick M. Bachman (see Old West Reproductions)
Bang-Bang Boutique, 720 N. Flagler Dr., Fort Lauderdale, FL 33304/305-463-7910
Barami Corp., 6250 East 7 Mile Rd., Detroit, MI 48234/313-891-2536
Beeman Precision Arms, Inc., 3440-GD Airway Dr., Santa Rosa, CA 95403/707-578-7900 (airguns only)
Behlert Precision, RD 2 Box 63, Route 611 North, Pipersville, PA 18947/215-766-8681
Bianchi International Inc., 100 Calle Cortez, Temecula, CA 92390/714-676-5621
Ted Blocker's Custom Holsters, 409 West Bonita Ave. San Dimas, CA 91773/714-599-4415
Border Guns & Leather, Box 1423, Deming, NM 88031 (Old West cust.)
Boyt Co., Div. of Welsh Sptg., P.O. Box 220, Iowa Falls, IA 51026/515-648-4626
Brauer Bros. Mfg. Co., 2020 Delmar, St. Louis, MO 63103/314-231-2864
Browning, Rt. 4, Box 624-B, Arnold, MO 63010
J.M. Bucheimer Co., P.O. Box 280, Airport Rd., Frederick, MD 21701/301-662-5101
Buffalo Leather Goods, Inc., 100 E. Church St., El Dorado, AR 71730
Cathey Enterprises, Inc., 3423 Milam Dr., P.O. Box 2202, Brownwood, TX 76804/915-643-2553
Cattle Baron Leather Co., Dept. GD9, P.O. Box 100724, San Antonio, TX 78201/512-697-8900 (ctlg. $3)
Chace Leather Prods., Longhorn Div., 507 Alden St., Fall River, MA 02722/617-678-7556
Cherokee Gun Accessories, 4127 Bay St., Suite 226, Fremont, CA 94538/415-471-5770
China IM/EX, P.O. Box 27573, San Francisco, CA 94127/415-661-2212
Chas. Clements, Handicrafts Unltd., 1741 Dallas St., Aurora, CO 80010/303-364-0403
Dart Manufacturing Co., 4012 Bronze Way, Dallas, TX 75237/214-333-4221
Davis Leather Co., G. Wm. Davis, 3930 Valley Blvd., Unit F, Walnut, CA 91789/714-598-5620
DeSantis Holster & Leather Co., 140 Denton Ave., New Hyde Park, NY 11040/516-354-8000
El Paso Saddlery, P.O. Box 27194, El Paso, TX 79926/915-544-2233
Ellwood Epps Northern Ltd., 210 Worthington St. W., North Bay, Ont. P1B 3B4, Canada (custom made)
GALCO Gun Leather, 4311 W. Van Buren, Phoenix, AZ 85043/602-233-0596
Glock, Inc., 5000 Highlands Pkwy. #190, Smyrna, GA 30080/404-432-1202 (holsters)
Gould & Goodrich Leather Inc., E. McNeil St.; P.O. Box 1479, Lillington, NC 27546/919-893-2071 (licensed mfgr. of S&W leather products)
Gun Parts Corp., Box 2, West Hurley, NY 12491/914-679-2417
High North Products, P.O. Box 2, Antigo, WI 54409/715-623-5117 (1-oz. Mongoose gun sling)
Ernie Hill Speed Leather, 3128 S. Extension Rd., Mesa, AZ 85202/602-831-1919
Holster Outpost, 649 Herbert St., El Cajon, CA 92020/619-588-1222
Horseshoe Leather Prods., (See Andy Arratoonian)
Hoyt Holster Co., Inc., P.O. Box 69, Coupeville, WA 98239/206-678-6640
Don Hume, Box 351, Miami, OK 74355/918-542-6604
Hunter Corp., 3300 W. 71st Ave., Westminster, CO 80030/303-427-4626
John's Custom Leather, 525 S. Liberty St., Blairsville, PA 15717/412-459-6802
Jumbo Sports Prods., P.O. Box 280, Airport Rd., Frederick, MD 21701
Kane Products, Inc., 5572 Brecksville Rd., Cleveland, OH 44131/216-524-9962 (GunChaps)
Kirkpatrick Leather Co., P.O. Box 3150, Laredo, TX 78044/512-723-6631
Kolpin Mfg. Inc., P.O. Box 231, Berlin, WI 54923/414-361-0400
George Lawrence Co., 1435 N.W. Northrup, Portland, OR 97209/503-228-8244
Lone Star Gunleather, 1301 Brushy Bend Dr., Round Rock, TX 78681/512-255-1805
Michael's of Oregon, Co., P.O. Box 13010, Portland, OR 97213/503-255-6890 (Uncle Mike's)
No-Sho Mfg. Co., 10727 Glenfield Ct., Houston, TX 77096/713-723-5332
Jim Noble Co., 1305 Columbia St., Vancouver, WA 98660/206-695-1309 (Supreme quick-draw shoulder holster, etc.)
Kenneth L. Null-Custom Concealment Holsters, R.D. #5, Box 197, Hanover, PA 17331 (See Seventrees)
Old West Reproductions, R. M. Bachman, 1840 Stag Lane, Kalispell, MT 59901/406-755-6902 (ctlg. $3)
Orient-Western, P.O. Box 27573, San Francisco, CA 94127
Pony Express Sport Shop Inc., 1606 Schoenborn St., Sepulveda, CA 91343/818-895-1231
Red Head Brand Corp., 4949 Joseph Hardin Dr., Dallas, TX 75236/214-333-4141
Rogers Holsters Co., Inc., 1736 St. Johns Bluff Rd., Jacksonville, FL 32216/904-641-9434
Roy's Custom Leather Goods, Hwy. 1325 & Rawhide Rd., P.O. Box G, Magnolia, AR 71753/501-234-1566
Safariland Leather Products, 1941 So. Walker Ave., Monrovia, CA 91016/818-357-7902
Safety Speed Holster, Inc., 910 So. Vail, Montebello, CA 90640/213-723-4140
Schulz Industries, 16247 Minnesota Ave., Paramount, CA 90723/213-439-5903
Sile Distr., 7 Centre Market Pl., New York NY 10013/212-925-4111
Smith & Wesson Leather (See Gould & Goodrich)
Milt Sparks, Box 187, Idaho City, ID 83631/208-392-6695 (broch. $2)
Strong Holster Co., 105 Maplewood Ave., Gloucester, MA 01931/617-281-3300
Torel, Inc., 1053 N. South St., P.O. Box 592, Yoakum, TX 77995/512-293-2341 (gun slings)
Triple-K Mfg. Co., 2222 Commercial St., San Diego, CA 92113/619-232-2066
Uncle Mike's (See Michaels of Oregon)
Viking Leathercraft, Inc., 2248-2 Main St., Chula Vista, CA 92011/619-429-8050
Walt Whinnery, 1947 Meadow Creek Dr., Louisville, KY 40218/502-458-4361
Wild Bill Cleaver, Rt. 4, Box 462, Vashon, WA 98070 (antique holstermaker)
Wildlife Leather Inc., P.O. Box 339, Merrick, NY 11566/516-378-8588 (lea. gds. w. outdoor themes)
Zeus International, P.O. Box 953, Tarpon Springs, FL 33589/813-863-5029 (all leather shotshell belt)

HUNTING AND CAMP GEAR, CLOTHING, ETC.

API Outdoors Inc., 602 Kimbrough Dr., Tallulah, LA 71282/318-574-4903
Bob Allen Co., 214 S.W. Jackson, Des Moines, IA 50315/515-283-2191/800-247-8048
Eddie Bauer, 15010 NE 36th St., Redmond, WA 98052
L. L. Bean, Freeport, ME 04032
Bear Archery, R.R. 4, 4600 Southwest 41st Blvd., Gainesville, FL 32601/904-376-2327 (Himalayan backpack)
Big Beam, Teledyne Co., 290 E. Prairie St., Crystal Lake, IL 60014 (lamp)
Browning, Rte. 1, Morgan, UT 84050
Challanger Mfg. Co., Box 550, Jamaica, NY 11431 (glow safe)
Chippewa Shoe Co., P.O. Box 2521, Ft. Worth, TX 76113/817-332-4385 (boots)
Coleman Co., Inc., 250 N. St. Francis, Wichita, KS 67201
Danner Shoe Mfg. Co., P.O. Box 22204, Portland, OR 97222/503-653-2920 (boots)
DEER-ME Prod. Co., Box 34, Anoka, MN 55303/612-421-8971 (tree steps)
Dunham Co., P.O. Box 813, Brattleboro, VT 05301/802-254-2316 (boots)
Durango Boot, see: Georgia/Northlake
Frankonia Jagd, Hofmann & Co., Postfach 6780, D-8700 Wurzburg 1, West Germany
Game-Winner, Inc., 2625 Cumberland Parkway, Suite 220, Atlanta, GA 30339/404-434-9210 (camouflage suits; orange vests)
Gander Mountain, Inc., P.O. Box 128, Hwy. "W", Wilmot, WI 53192/414-862-2344
Georgia/Northlake Boot Co., P.O. Box 10, Franklin, TN 37064/615-794-1556 (Durango)
Gun Club Sportswear, Box 477, Des Moines, IA 50302
Bob Hinman Outfitters, 1217 W. Glen, Peoria, IL 61614
Hunter's Specialties, Inc., 5285 Rockwell Dr. N.E., Cedar Rapids, IA 52402/319-395-0321
Kenko Intl. Inc., 8141 West I-70 Frontage Rd. No., Arvada, CO 80002/303-425-1200 (footwear & socks)
Langenberg Hat Co., P.O. Box 1860, Washington, MO 63090/314-239-1860
Liberty Trouser Co., 2301 First Ave. North, Birmingham, AL 35203/205-251-9143
Life Knife Inc., P.O. Box 771, Santa Monica, CA 90406/213-821-6192
Marathon Rubber Prods. Co. Inc., 510 Sherman St., Wausau, WI 54401/715-845-6255 (rain gear)
Marble Arms Corp., 420 Industrial Park, Gladstone, MI 49837
Northlake Boot Co., 1810 Columbia Ave., Franklin, TN 37064/615-794-1556
The Orvis Co., 10 River Rd., Manchester, VT 05254/802-362-3622 (fishing gear; clothing)
P.A.S.T. (Precision Action Sports Technologies), 210 Park Ave., Columbia, MO 65203/314-449-7278 (shooting shirts)
Precise International, 3 Chestnut St., Suffern, NY 10901/914-357-6200
Pyromid, Inc., 625 Ellis St., Suite 209, Mountain View, CA 94043/415-964-6991 (portable camp stove)
Ranger Mfg. Co., Inc., 1536 Crescent Dr., Augusta GA 30919/404-738-3469 (camouflage suits)
Ranger Rubber Co., 1100 E. Main St., Endicott, NY 13760/607-757-4260 (boots)
Red Ball, 100 Factory St., Nashua, NH 03060/603-881-4420 (boots)
Red Head Brand Corp., 4949 Joseph Hardin Dr., Dallas, TX 75236/214-333-4141
Refrigiwear, Inc., 71 Inip Dr., Inwood, Long Island, NY 11696
Re-Heater Inc., 96302 S. Western Ave. #5, Lomita, CA 90717 (re-usable portable heat pack)
SanLar Co., N3784 Liberty St., Sullivan, WI 53178/414-593-8086 (huntg. sweatsuits, camouflage clothing)
Servus Rubber Co., 1136 2nd St., P.O. Box 3610 Rock Island, IL 61204 (footwear)
Teledyne Co., Big Beam, 290 E. Prairie St., Crystal Lake, IL 60014
10-X Mfg. Products Group, 2828 Forest Lane, Suite 1107, Dallas, TX 75234/214-243-4016
Thermos Div., KST Co., Norwich, CT 06361 (Pop Tent)
Norm Thompson, 1805 N.W. Thurman St., Portland, OR 97209
Tink's Safariland Hunting Corp., P.O. Box NN, McLean, VA 22101/703-356-0622 (camouflage rain gear)
Utica Duxbak Corp., 1745 S. Acoma St., Denver, CO 80223/303-778-0324
Waffen-Frankonia, see: Frankonia Jagd
Walker Shoe Co., P.O. Box 1167, Asheboro, NC 27203-1167/919-625-1380 (boots)
Wolverine Boots & Shoes Div., Wolverine World Wide, 9341 Courtland Dr., Rockford, MI 49351/616-866-1561 (footwear)
Woolrich Woolen Mills, Mill St., Woolrich, PA 17779/717-769-6464

KNIVES AND KNIFEMAKER'S SUPPLIES—FACTORY and MAIL ORDER

Alcas Cutlery Corp., 1116 E. State St., Olean, NY 14760/716-372-3111 (Cutco)
Atlanta Cutlery, Box 839, Conyers, GA 30207/404-922-3700 (mail order, supplies)
L. L. Bean, 386 Main St., Freeport, ME 04032/207-865-3111 (mail order)
Benchmark Knives (See Gerber)
Boker USA, Inc., 14818 West 6th Ave., Suite #17A, Golden, CO 80401/303-279-5997
Bowen Knife Co., P.O. Box 590, Blackshear, GA 31516/912-449-4794
Browning, Rt. 1, Morgan, UT 84050/801-876-2711
Buck Knives, Inc., P.O. Box 1267; 1900 Weld Blvd., El Cajon, CA 92022/619-449-1100 or 800-854-2557
Camillus Cutlery Co., 52-54 W. Genesee St., Camillus, NY 13031/315-672-8111 (Sword Brand)
W. R. Case & Sons Cutlery Co., Owens Way, Bradford, PA 16701/814-368-4123
Cattle Baron Leather Co., P.O. Box 100724, Dept. GD9, San Antonio, TX 78201/512-697-8900 (ctlg. $3)
Charter Arms Corp., 430 Sniffens Lane, Stratford, CT 06497/203-377-8080 (Skatchet)
Chicago Cutlery Co., 5420 N. County Rd. 18, Minneapolis, MN 55428/612-533-0472
E. Christopher Firearms Co., Inc., Route 128 & Ferry St., Miamitown, OH 45041/513-353-1321 (supplies)
Chas. Clements, Handicraft Unltd., 1741 Dallas St., Aurora, CO 80010/303-364-0403 (exotic sheaths)
Collins Brothers Div. (belt-buckle knife), See Bowen Knife Co.
Colonial Knife Co., P.O. Box 3327, Providence, RI 02909/401-421-1600 (Master Brand)
Compass Industries, Inc., 104 East 25th St., New York, NY 10010/212-473-2614
Crosman Blades™, The Coleman Co., 250 N. St. Francis, Wichita, KS 67201
Custom Knifemaker's Supply (Bob Schrimsher), P.O. Box 308, Emory, TX 75440/214-473-3330
Custom Purveyors, Maureen Devlet's, P.O. Box 886, Fort Lee, NJ 07024/201-886-0196 (mail order)
Damascus-USA, P.O. Box 220, Howard, CO 81233/719-942-3527
Dixie Gun Works, Inc., P.O. Box 130, Union City, TN 38261/901-885-0700 (supplies)
Eze-Lap Diamond Prods., Box 2229, 15164 Weststate St., Westminster, CA 92683/714-847-1555 (knife sharpeners)
Gerber Legendary Blades, 14200 S.W. 72nd Ave., Portland, OR 99223/503-639-6161
Gutmann Cutlery Co., Inc., 120 S. Columbus Ave., Mt. Vernon, NY 10553/914-699-4044
H & B Forge Co., Rte. 2 Geisinger Rd., Shiloh, OH 44878/419-895-1856 (throwing knives, tomahawks)
Russell Harrington Cutlery, Inc., Subs. of Hyde Mfg. Co., 44 River St., Southbridge, MA 01550/617-765-0201 (Dexter, Green River Works)
J. A. Henckels Zwillingswerk, Inc., 9 Skyline Dr., Hawthorne, NY 10532/914-592-7370
Indian Ridge Traders (See Koval Knives)
Ken Jantz Supply, 222 E. Main, Davis, OK 73030/405-369-2316 (supplies)
Jet-Aer Corp., 100 Sixth Ave., Paterson, NJ 07524/201-278-8300
KA-BAR Cutlery Inc., 5777 Grant Ave., Cleveland, OH 44105/216-271-4000
KA-BAR Knives, Collectors Division, 434 No. 9th St., Olean, NY 14760/716-372-5611
Kershaw Knives/Kai Cutlery USA Ltd., Stafford Bus. Pk., 25300 SW Parkway, Wilsonville, OR 97070/503-636-0111
Knifeco, P.O. Box 5271, Hialeah Lakes, FL 33014/305-635-2411
Knife and Gun Finishing Supplies, P.O. Box 13522, Arlington, TX 76013/817-274-1282
Koval Knives/IRT, P.O. Box 26155, Columbus, OH 43226/614-888-6486 (supplies)
Lamson & Goodnow Mfg. Co., 45 Conway St., Shelburne Falls, MA 03170/413-625-6331
Lansky Sharpeners, P.O. Box 800, Buffalo, NY 14221/716-634-6333 (sharpening devices)
Life Knife Inc., P.O. Box 771, Santa Monica, CA 90406/ 213-821-6192
Linder Solingen Knives, 4401 Sentry Dr., Tucker, GA 30084/404-939-6915
Al Mar Knives, Inc., P.O. Box 1626, 5755 SW Jean Rd., Suite 101, Lake Oswego, OR 97034/503-635-9229
Matthews Cutlery, 4401 Sentry Dr., Tucker, GA 30084/404-939-6915 (mail order)
R. Murphy Co., Inc., 13 Groton-Harvard Rd., P.O. Box 376, Ayer, MA 01432/617-772-3481 (StaySharp)
Nordic Knives, 1643-C Copenhagen Dr., Solvang, CA 93463 (mail order)
Normark Corp., 1710 E. 78th St., Minneapolis, MN 55423/612-869-3291
Ontario Knife, Queen Cutlery Co., P.O. Box 500, Franklinville, NY 14737/716-676-5527 (Old Hickory)
Parker Cutlery, 6928 Lee Highway, Chattanooga, TN 37415/615-894-1782
Plaza Cutlery Inc., 3333 Bristol, #161, South Coast Plaza, Costa Mesa, CA 92626/714-549-3932 (mail order)
Precise International, 3 Chestnut St., Suffern, NY 10901/914-357-6200
Queen Cutlery Co., 507 Chestnut St., Titusville, PA 16354/800-222-5233
R & C Knives and Such, P.O. Box 1047, Manteca, CA 95336/209-239-3722 (mail order; ctlg. $2)
Randall-Made Knives, Box 1988, Orlando, FL 32802/305-855-8075 (ctlg. $1)
Rigid Knives, P.O. Box 816, Hwy. 290E, Lake Hamilton, AR 71951/501-525-1377
A. G. Russell Co., 1705 Hiwy. 471 No., Springdale, AR 72764/501-751-7341
Bob Sanders, 2358 Tyler Lane, Louisville, KY 40205/502-454-3338 (Swedish Bahco steel)
San Diego Knives, P.O. Box 326, Lakeside, CA 92040/619-561-5900
Schrade Cutlery Corp., 1776 Broadway, New York, NY 10019/212-757-1814
Sheffield Knifemakers Supply, P.O. Box 141, Deland, FL 32720/904-775-6453
Smith & Wesson, 2100 Roosevelt Ave., Springfield, MA 01101/413-781-8300
Jesse W. Smith Saddlery, N. 307 Haven St., Spokane, WA 99202/509-534-3229 (sheathmakers)
Swiss Army Knives, Inc., P.O. Box 846, Shelton, CT 06484/203-929-6391
Tekna, 1075 Old County Rd., Belmont, CA 94002/415-592-4070
Thompson/Center, P.O. Box 2426, Rochester, NH 03867/603-332-2394
Tru-Balance Knife Co., 2155 Tremont Blvd., N.W., Grand Rapids, MI 49504/616-453-3679
Utica Cutlery Co., 820 Noyes St., Utica, NY 13503/315-733-4663 (Kutmaster)
Valor Corp., 5555 N.W. 36th Ave., Miami, FL 33142/305-633-0127
Wenoka Cutlery, P.O. Box 8238, West Palm Beach, FL 33407/305-845-6155
Western Cutlery Co., 1800 Pike Rd., Longmont, CO 80501/303-772-5900
Walt Whinnery, Walts Cust. Leather, 1947 Meadow Creek Dr., Louisville, KY 40218/502-458-4361 (sheathmaker)
Wyoming Knife Co., 101 Commerce Dr., Ft. Collins, CO 80524/303-224-3454

LABELS, BOXES, CARTRIDGE HOLDERS

Corbin Mfg. & Supply, Inc., P.O. Box 2659, White City, OR 97503/503-826-5211
Del Rey Products, P.O. Box 91561, Los Angeles, CA 90009/213-823-0494
E-Z Loader, Del Rey Products, P.O. Box 91561, Los Angeles, CA 90009
Hunter Co., Inc., 3300 W. 71st Ave., Westminster, Co 80030/303-472-4626
Peterson Label Co., P.O. Box 186, 23 Sullivan Dr., Redding Ridge, CT 06876/203-938-2349 (cartridge box labels; Targ-Dots)

LOAD TESTING and PRODUCT TESTING, (CHRONOGRAPHING, BALLISTIC STUDIES)

Accuracy Systems Inc., 15205 N. Cave Creek Rd., Phoenix, AZ 85032/602-971-1991
Ballistic Research, Tom Armbrust, 1108 W. May Ave., McHenry, IL 60050/815-385-0037 (ballistic studies, pressure & velocity)
Ballistics Research Group, Kayusoft Intl., Star Route, Spray, OR 97874/503-462-3934 (computer software "Computer Shooter")
W.W. Blackwell, 9826 Sagedale, Houston, TX 77089/ 713-484-0935 (computer program f. internal ball. f. rifle cartridges; "Load from a Disk")
Corbin Applied Technology, P.O. Box 2171, White City, OR 97503/503-826-5211
D&H Precision Tooling, 7522 Barnard Mill Rd., Ringwood IL 60072/815-653-9611 (Pressure testing equipment)
H-S Precision, Inc., 112 N. Summit, Prescott, AZ 86302/602-445-0607
Hutton Rifle Ranch, P.O. Box 45236, Boise, ID 83711/208-384-5461 (ballistic studies)
Kent Lomont, 4236 West 700 South, Poneto, IN 45781/219-694-6792 (handguns, handgun ammunition)
Plum City Ballistics Range, Norman E. Johnson, Rte. 1, Box 29A, Plum City, WI 54761/715-647-2539
Quartz-Lok, 13137 N. 21st Lane, Phoenix, AZ 85029/602-863-2729
Russell's Rifle Shop, Rte. 5, Box 92, Georgetown, TX 78626/512-778-5338 (load testing and chronographing to 300 yds.)
John M. Tovey, 4710 - 104th Lane NE, Circle Pines, MN 55014/612-786-7268
H. P. White Laboratory, Inc., 3114 Scarboro Rd., Street, MD 21154/301-838-6550

MISCELLANEOUS

Action, Left-Hand, David Gentry Custom Gunmaker, 314 N. Hoffman, P.O. Box 1440, Belgrade, MT 59714/406-388-4867
Action, Mauser-style only, Crandall Tool & Machine Co., 1545 N. Mitchell St., Cadillac, MI 49601/616-775-5562
Action, Single Shot, Miller Arms, Inc., P.O. Box 260, St. Onge, SD 57779 (deHaas-Miller)
Activator, B.M.F. Activator, Inc., P.O. Box 262364, Houston, TX 77207/713-477-8442
Adapters for Subcalibers, Harry Owen, P.O. Box 5337, Hacienda Hts., CA 91745/818-968-5806
Airgun Accessories, Beeman Precision Arms, Inc., 3440-GD Airway Dr., Santa Rosa, CA 95403/707-578-7900 (Beeman Pell seat, Pell Size, etc.)
Air Gun Combat Game Supplies, The Ultimate Game Inc., P.O. Box 1856, Ormond Beach, FL 32075/904-677-4358 (washable pellets, marking pistols/rifles)
Archery, Bear, R.R. 4, 4600 Southwest 41st Blvd., Gainesville, FL 32601/904-376-2327
Arms Restoration, Jenkins Enterprises, Inc., 12317 Locksley Lane, Auburn, CA 95603/916-823-9652
Assault Rifle Accessories, Cherokee Gun Accessories, 4127 Bay St. Suite 226, Fremont, CA 94538/415-471-5770
Assault Rifle Accessories, Feather Enterprises, 2500 Central Ave., Boulder, CO 80301/303-442-7021
Assault Rifle Accessories, Ram-Line, Inc., 15611 W. 6th Ave., Golden, CO 80401/303-279-0886 (folding stock)
Bedding Kit, Fenwal, Inc., Resins Systems Div., 50 Main St., Ashland, MA 01721 (Tru-Set)
Belt Buckles, Herrett's Stocks, Inc., Box 741, Twin Falls, ID 83303/208-733-1498 (laser engr. hardwood)
Belt Buckles, Pilgrim Pewter Inc., R.D. 2, Tully, NY 13159/607-842-6431
Benchrest & Accuracy Shooters Equipment, Bob Pease Accuracy, P.O. Box 787, Zipp Road, New Braunfels, TX 78130/512-625-1342
Benchrest Rifles & Accessories, Robert W. Hart & Son Inc., 401 Montgomery St., Nescopeck, PA 18635/717-752-3655
Bore Collimator, Alley Supply Co., P.O. Box 848, Gardnerville, NV 89410/702-782-3800 (Sweany Site-A-Line optical collimator)
Bull-Pup Conversion Kits, Bull-Pup Industries Inc., P.O. Box 187, Pioneertown, CA 92268/619-228-1949
Cannons, South Bend Replicas Ind., 61650 Oak Rd., S. Bend, IN 44614/219-289-4500 (ctlg. $6)
Cartridge Adapters, Sport Specialties, Harry Owen, Box 5337, Hacienda Hts., CA 91745/213-968-5806 (ctlg. $3)
Case Gauge, Plum City Ballistics Range, Rte. 1, Box 29A, Plum City, WI 54761/715-647-2539
Cased, high-grade English tools, Marvin Huey Gun Cases, P.O. Box 22456, Kansas City, MO 64113/816-444-1637 (ebony, horn, ivory handles)
Cherry Converter, Amimex Inc., 2660 John Montgomery Dr., Suite #3, San Jose, CA 95148/408-923-1720 (shotguns)
Clips, D&E Magazines Mfg., P.O. Box 4876-D, Sylmar, CA 91342 (handgun and rifle)
Computer & PSI Calculator, Hutton Rifle Ranch, P.O. Box 45236, Boise, ID 83711/208-384-5461
Computer Systems, Corbin Applied Technology, P.O. Box 2171, White City, OR 97503/503-826-5211 (software, books f. ballistic research)
Convert-A-Pell, Jett & Co., Inc., RR#3 Box 167-B, Litchfield, IL 62056/217-324-3779
Crossbows, Barnett International, 1967 Gunn Highway, Odessa, FL 33552/813-920-2241
Damascus Steel, Damascus-USA, P.O. Box 220, Howard, CO 81233/719-942-3527
Deer Drag, D&H Prods. Co., Inc., 465 Denny Rd., Valencia, PA 16059/412-898-2840
Dehumidifiers, Buenger Enterprises, P.O. Box 5286, Oxnard, CA 93030/805-985-0541
Dehumidifiers, Hydrosorbent Products, Box 675D, Rye NY 10580 (silica gel dehumidifier)
Dryer, Thermo-Electric, Golden-Rod, Buenger Enterprises, Box 5286, Oxnard, CA 93030/805-985-0541
E-Z Loader, Del Rey Prod., P.O. Box 91561, Los Angeles, CA 90009/213-823-04494 (f. 22-cal. rifles)
Ear-Valve, North Consumer Prods. Div., 16624 Edwards Rd., Cerritos, CA 90702/213-926-0545 (Lee-Sonic)
Embossed Leather Belts, Wallets, Wildlife Leather, Inc., P.O. Box 339, Merrick, NY 11566/516-378-8588 (outdoor themes)
Farrsight, Farr Studio, 1231 Robinhood Rd., Greenville, TN 37743/615-638-8825 (sighting aids for handgunners—clip on aperture)
Firearms Training, Ballistics Research Group, Kayusoft Intl., Star Route, Spray, Or 97874/503-462-3934 (computer software "Computer Shooter")
Game Hoist, Cam Gear Ind., P.O. Box 1002, Kalispell, MT 59901 (Sportsmaster 500 pocket hoist)
Game Scent, Buck Stop Lure Co., Inc., 3600 Grow Rd., Box 636, Stanton, MI 48888/517-762-5091
Game Scent, Pete Rickard, Inc., Rte. 1, Box 209B, Cobleskill, NY 12043/518-234-2731 (Indian Buck lure)
Game Scent, Tink's Safariland Hunting Corp., P.O. Box NN, McLean, VA 22101/703-356-0622 (buck lure)
Gas Pistol, Penguin Ind., Inc., Airport Industrial Mall, Coatesville, PA 19320/215-384-6000
Grip Caps, Classic Arms Corp., P.O. Box 8, Palo Alto, CA 94301/415-321-7243
Gun Bedding Kit, Fenwal, Inc., Resins System Div., 50 Main St., Ashland, MA 01721/617-881-2000
Gun Covers, E. Christopher Firearms Co., Inc., Route 128 & Ferry St., Miamitown, OH 45041/513-353-1321 (Gunnysox)
Gun Jewelry, Sid Bell Originals, R.D. 2, Box 219, Tully, NY 13159/607-842-6431 (jewelry for sportsmen)
Gun Jewelry, Pilgrim Pewter Inc., R.D. 2, Box 219, Tully, NY 13159/607-842-6431
Gun Jewelry, Sports Style Assoc., 148 Hendricks Ave., Lynbrook, NY 11563
Gun photographer, Mustafa Bilal, 5429 Russell Ave. NW, Suite 202, Seattle, WA 98107/206-782-4164
Gun photographer, John Hanusin, 3306 Commercial, Northbrook, IL 60062/312-564-2706
Gun photographer, Intl. Photographic Assoc., Inc., 4500 E. Speedway, Suite 90, Tucson, AZ 85712/602-326-2941
Gun photographer, Charles Semmer, 7885 Cyd Dr., Denver, CO 80221/303-429-6947
Gun photographer, Weyer Photo Services, Ltd., 333-14th St., Toledo, OH 43624/419-241-5454
Gun photographer, Steve White, 1920 Raymond Dr., Northbrook, IL 60062/312-564-2720
Gun Safety, Gun Alert Covers, Master Products, Inc., P.O. Box 8474, Van Nuys, CA 91409/818-365-0864
Gun Sling, La Paloma Marketing, 4210 E. LaPaloma Dr., Tucson, AZ 85718/602-881-4750 (Pro-sling system)
Gun Slings, Torel, Inc., 1053 N. South St., Yoakum, TX 77995
Gun Vise, Pflumm Gun Mfg. Co., 6139 Melrose Lane, Shawnee, KS 66203/913-268-3105
Hand Exerciser, Action Products, Inc., 22 No. Mulberry St., Hagerstown, MD 21740/301-797-1414
Horsepac, Yellowstone Wilderness Supply, P.O. 129, West Yellowstone, MT 59758/406-646-7613
Horsepacking Equipment/Saddle Trees, Ralide West, P.O. Box 998, 299 Firehole Ave., West Yellowstone, WY 59758/406-646-7612
Hugger Hooks Co., 3900 Easley Way, Golden, CO 80403/303-279-6160
Insect Repellent, Armor, Div. of Buck Stop, Inc., 3015 Grow Rd., Stanton, MI 48888
Insert Chambers, GTM Co., Geo. T. Mahaney, 15915B E. Main St., La Puente, CA 91744 (shotguns only)
Insert Barrels and Cartridge Adapters, Sport Specialties, Harry Owen, Box 5337, Hacienda Hts., CA 91745/213-968-5806 (ctlg. $3)
Knife Sharpeners, Lansky Sharpeners, P.O. Box 800, Buffalo, NY 14221/716-634-6333
Laser Aim, Laser Aim, Inc., 100 S. Main St., Box 581, Little Rock, AR 72203
Laser Aim, Laser Devices, Inc., #5 Hangar Way, Watsonville, CA 95076/408-722-8300
Locks, Gun, Bor-Lok Prods., 105 5th St., Arbuckle, CA 95912
Locks, Gun, Master Lock Co., 2600 N. 32nd St., Milwaukee, WI 53245
Lugheads, Floorplate Overlays, Sid Bell Originals, Inc., RD 2, Box 219, Tully, NY 13159/607-842-6431
Lug Recess Insert, P.P.C. Corp., 625 E. 24th St. Paterson, NJ 07514
Magazines, San Diego Knives, P.O. Box 326, Lakeside, CA 92040/619-561-5900 (auto pist., rifles)
Magazines, Mitchell Arms Inc., 3411 Lake Center Dr., Santa Ana, CA 92704/714-957-5711 (stainless steel)
Magazines, Ram-Line, Inc., 15611 W. 6th Ave., Golden, CO 80401/303-279-0886
Miniature Cannons, Karl J. Furr, 76 East, 350 North, Orem, UT 84057/801-225-2603 (replicas; Gatling guns)
Miniature Guns, Tom Konrad, P.O. Box 118, Shandon, OH 45063/513-738-1379

MISCELLANEOUS — cont'd.

Monte Carlo Pad, Hoppe Division, Penguin Ind., Airport Industrial Mall, Coatesville, PA 19320/215-384-6000
Old Gun Industry Art, Hansen and Company, 244 Old Post Rd., Southport, CT 06490/203-259-6222
Police Batons & Accessories, Armament Systems and Procedures, Inc., P.O. Box 1794, Appleton, WI 54913/414-731-7075
Powderhorns, Frontier, 2910 San Bernardo, Laredo, TX 78040/512-723-5409
Powderhorns, Tennessee Valley Mfg., P.O. Box 1125, Corinth, MS 38834
Practice Ammunition, Hoffman New Ideas Inc., 821 Northmoor Rd., Lake Forest, IL 60045/312-234-4075
Practice Wax Bullets, Brazos Arms Co., 7314 Skybright Lane, Houston, TX 77095/713-463-0826
Ram Line, Inc., 15611 W. 6th Ave., Golden, CO 80401/303-279-0886 (accessories)
Ransom Handgun Rests, Ransom Intl. Corp., P.O. Box 3845, Prescott, AZ 86302/602-778-7899
Reloader's Record Book, Reloaders Paper Supply, Don Doerkson, P.O. Box 556, Hines, OR 97738/503-573-7060
Rifle Magazines, Butler Creek Corp., 290 Arden Dr., Belgrade, MT 59714/406-388-1356 (30-rd. Mini-14)
Rifle Magazines, Condor Mfg. Inc., 415 & 418 W. Magnolia Ave., Glendale, CA 91204/818-240-1745 (25-rd. 22-cal.)
Rifle Magazines, Miller Gun Works, P.O. Box 1053, 1440 Peltier Dr., Point Roberts, WA 98281/206-945-7014 (30-cal. M1 15&30-round)
Rifle Slings, Bianchi International, 100 Calle Cortez, Temecula, CA 92390/714-676-5621
Rifle Slings, Butler Creek Corp., 290 Arden Dr., Belgrade, MT 59714/406-388-1356
Rifle Slings, Chace Leather Prods., Longhorn Div., 507 Alden St., Fall River, MA 02722/617-678-7556
Rifle Slings, High North Products, P.O. Box 2, Antigo, WI 54409/715-623-5117 (1-oz. Mongoose gun sling)
Rifle Slings, John's Cust. Leather, 525 S. Liberty St., Blairsville, PA 15717/412-459-6802
Rifle Slings, Kirkpatrick Leather Co., P.O. Box 3150, Laredo, TX 78044/512-723-6631
Rifle Slings, Schulz Industr., 16247 Minnesota Ave., Paramount, CA 90723/213-439-5903
RIG, NRA Scoring Plug, Rig Products, 87 Coney Island Dr., Sparks, NV 89431/702-331-5666
Rubber Cheekpiece, W. H. Lodewick, 2816 N.E. Halsey, Portland, OR 97232/503-284-2554
Rust Prevention, Rusteprufe Laboratories, Rte. 5, Sparta, WI 54656/608-269-4144
Saddle Rings, Studs, Fred Goodwin, Sherman Mills, ME 04776
Safeties, William E. Harper, The Great 870 Co., P.O. Box 6309. El Monte, CA 91734/213-579-3077 (f. Rem. 870P)
Safeties, Williams Gun Sight Co., 7389 Lapeer Rd., Davison, MI 48423
Safety Slug, Glaser Safety Slug, P.O. Box 8223, Foster City, CA 94404/415-345-7677
Sav-Bore, Saunders Sptg. Gds., 338 Somerset St., N. Plainfield, NJ 07060
Scrimshaw, Henry "Hank" Bonham, 218 Franklin Ave., Seaside Heights, NJ 08751/201-793-8309
Scrimshaw, Boone Trading Co., 562 Coyote Rd., Brinnon, WA 98320/206-796-4330
Scrimshaw, G. Marek, P.O. Box 213, Westfield, MA 01086/413-568-9816
Sharpening Stones, A. G. Russell Co., 1705 Hiway 71 North, Springdale, AR 72764/501-751-7341 (Arkansas Oilstones)
Shell Catcher, Condor Mfg. Inc., 415 & 418 W. Magnolia Ave., Glendale, CA 91204/818-240-1745
Shooting Coats, 10-X Products Group, 2828 Forest Lane, Suite 1107, Dallas, TX 75234/214-243-4016
Shooting Glasses, American Optical Corp., 14 Mechanic St., Southbridge, MA 01550/617-765-9711
Shooting Glasses, Bausch & Lomb, Inc., 42 East Ave., Rochester, NY 14603/800-828-5423 (Ray Ban®)
Shooting Glasses, Bilsom Intl., Inc., 11800 Sunrise Valley Dr., Reston, VA 22091/703-620-3950
Shooting Glasses, Willson Safety Prods. Division, P.O. Box 622, Reading, PA 19603
Shooting Gloves, James Churchill Glove Co., Box 298, Centralia, WA 98531 (singles only, right or left)
Shooting Range Equipment, Caswell Internatl. Corp., 1221 Marshall St. N.E., Minneapolis, MN 55413/612-379-2000
Shotgun Barrel, Pennsylvania Arms Co., Box 128, Duryea, PA 18642/717-457-4014 (rifled)
Shotgun bore, Custom Shootg. Prods., 8505 K St., Omaha, NE 68127
Shotgun Converter, Amimex Inc., 2660 John Montgomery Dr., Suite #3, San Jose, CA 95148/408-923-1720
Shotgun Ribs, Poly-Choke Div., Marble Arms Corp., 420 Industrial Park, Gladstone, MI 49837/906-428-3710
Shotgun Sight, bi-ocular, Trius Prod., Box 25, Cleves, OH 45002
Shotgun Specialist, Moneymaker Guncraft, 1420 Military Ave., Omaha, NE 68131/402-556-0226 (ventilated, free-floating ribs)
Shotshell Adapter, PC Co., 5942 Secor Rd., Toledo, OH 43623/419-472-6222 (Plummer 410 converter)
Shotshell Adapter, Jesse Ramos, P.O. Box 7105, La Puente, CA 91744/818-369-6384 (12 ga./410 converter)
Snap Caps, Edwards Recoil Reducer, 269 Herbert St., Alton, IL 62002/618-462-3257
Springs, W. C. Wolff Co., P.O. Box 232, Ardmore, PA 19003/215-896-7500
Stock Duplicating Machine, Don Allen, Inc., HC55, Box 326, Sturgis, SD 47785/605-347-5227
Supersound, Edmund Scientific Co., 101 E. Gloucester Pike, Barrington, NJ 08007/609-547-3488 (safety device)
Swivels, Michaels, P.O. Box 13010, Portland, OR 97213/503-255-6890
Swivels, Sile Dist., 7 Centre Market Pl., New York, NY 10013/212-925-4111
Swivels, Williams Gun Sight Co., 7389 Lapeer Rd., Davison, MI 48423
Tomahawks, H&B Forge Co., Rt. 2, Shiloh, OH 44878/419-896-2075
Tree Stand, Climbing, API Outdoors Inc., 602 Kimbrough Dr., Tallulah, LA 71282/318-574-4903
Tree Steps, Deer Me Products Co., Box 34, 1208 Park St., Anoka, MN 55303/612-421-8971
Trophies, V.H. Blackinton & Co., P.O. Box 1300, 221 John L. Dietsch Blvd., Attleboro Falls, MA 02763/617-699-4436
Trophies, F. H. Noble & Co., 888 Tower Rd., Mundelein, IL 60060
Walking Sticks, Life Knife Inc., P.O. Box 771, Santa Monica, CA 90406/213-821-6192
Warning Signs, Delta Ltd., P.O. Box 777, Mt. Ida, AR 71957
World Hunting Info., J/B Adventures & Safaris, Inc., 6312 S. Fiddlers Green Circle, Suite 330N, Englewood CO 80111/303-771-0977
World Hunting Info., Wayne Preston, Inc., 3444 Northhaven Rd., Dallas, TX 75229/214-358-4477

MUZZLE-LOADING GUNS, BARRELS or EQUIPMENT

Luther Adkins, Box 281, Shelbyville, IN 46176/317-392-3795 (breech plugs)
Allen Firearms Co., 2879 All Trades Rd., Santa Fe, NM 87501/505-471-6090
Anderson Mfg. Co., P.O. Box 536, Kent, WA 98032/206-872-7602 (Flame-N-Go fusil; Accra-Shot)
Antique Gun Parts, Inc., 1118 S. Braddock Ave., Pittsburgh, PA 15218/412-241-1811 (parts)
Armoury, Inc., Rte. 202, New Preston, CT 06777
Armsport, Inc., 3590 N.W. 49th St., Miami, FL 33142/305-635-7850
B-Square Co., P.O. Box 11281, Ft. Worth, TX 76109/817-923-0964
Bauska Mfg. Corp., P.O. Box 2270, 1694 Whalebone Dr., Kalispell, MT 59901/406-752-8082
Beaver Lodge, 9245 16th Ave. S.W., Seattle, WA 98106/206-763-1698 (cust. ML)
Beeman Precision Arms, Inc., 3440-GDD Airway Dr., Santa Rosa, CA 95403/707-578-7900
Benson Firearms Ltd., P.O. Box 30137, Seattle, WA 98103/800-521-0714 (A. Uberti replicas)
Blackhawk East, Box 2274, Loves Park, IL 61131 (blackpowder)
Blackhawk Mtn., Box 210, Conifer, CO 80433 (blackpowder)
Blackhawk West, Box 285, Hiawatha, KS 66434 (blackpowder)
Blue and Gray Prods., Inc. RD #6, Box 362, Wellsboro, PA 16901/717-724-1383 (equipment)
Butler Creek Corp., 290 Arden Dr., Belgrade, MT 59714/406-388-1356 (poly & maxi patch)
Cache La Poudre Rifleworks, 140 N. College, Ft. Collins, CO 80524/303-482-6913 (custom muzzleloaders)
R. MacDonald Champlin, P.O. Box 693, Manchester, NH 03105/603-483-8557 (custom muzzleloaders)
Cheney Firearms Co., P.O. Box 321, Woods Cross, UT 84087 (rifles)
Chopie Mfg. Inc., 700 Copeland Ave., LaCrosse, WI 54601/608-784-0926 (nipple wrenches)
Connecticut Valley Arms Co. (CVA), 5988 Peachtree East, Norcross, GA 30071/404-449-4687 (kits also)
Cumberland Knife & Gun Works, 5661 Bragg Blvd., Fayetteville, NC 28303/919-867-0009
Earl T. Cureton, Rte. 2, Box 388, Willoughby Rd., Bulls Gap, TN 37711/615-235-2854 (powder horns)
Homer L. Dangler, Box 254, Addison, MI 49220/517-547-6745
Leonard Day & Sons, Inc., One Cottage St., P.O. Box 723, East Hampton, MA 01027/413-527-7990
Denver Arms, Ltd., P.O. Box 4640, Pagosa Springs, CO 81157/303-731-2295 (S.A.S.E.)
Dixie Gun Works, Inc., P.O. Box 130, Union City, TN 38261
Peter Dyson Ltd., 29-31 Church St., Honley, Huddersfield, W. Yorksh. HD7 2AH, England/0484-661062 (acc. f. ML shooter replicas)
EMF, Co., Inc., 1900 E. Warner Ave. 1-D, Santa Ana, CA 92705/714-261-6611
Euroarms of America, Inc., P.O. Box 3277, 1501 Lenoir Dr., Winchester, VA 22601/703-662-1863
F.P.F. Co., P.O. Box 211, Van Wert, OH 45891 (black powder accessories)
Andy Fautheree, P.O. Box 4607, Pagosa Springs, CO 81157/303-731-5003 (cust. ML guns; must send SASE)
Ted Fellowes, Beaver Lodge, 9245 16th Ave. S.W., Seattle, WA 98106/206-763-1698 (cust. ML)
Marshall F. Fish. Rt. 22 N., Box 2439, Westport, NY 12993/518-962-4897 (antique ML repairs)
The Flintlock Muzzle Loading Gun Shop, 1238 "G" So. Beach Blvd., Anaheim, CA 92804/714-821-6655
Forster Prods., 82 E. Lanark Ave., Lanark, IL 61046/815-493-6360
Frontier, 2910 San Bernardo, Laredo, TX 78040/512-723-5409 (powderhorns)
Getz Barrel Co., Box 88, Beavertown, PA 17813/717-658-7263 (barrels)
GOEX, Inc., Belin Plant, Moosic, PA 18507/717-457-6724 (black powder)
A. R. Goode, 4125 N.E. 28th Terr., Ocala, FL 32670/904-622-9575 (ML rifle barrels)
Guncraft Inc., 117 W. Pipeline, Hurst, TX 76053/817-282-1464
Gun Parts Corp., Box 2, West Hurley, NY 12491/914-679-2417
The Gun Works, 236 Main St., Springfield, OR 97477/503-741-4118 (supplies)
Hatfield Rifle Works, 2020 Calhoun, St. Joseph, MO 64501/816-279-8688 (squirrel rifle)
Hopkins & Allen, 3 Ethel Ave., P.O. Box 217, Hawthorne, NJ 07507/201-427-1165
The House of Muskets, Inc., P.O. Box 4640, Pagosa Springs, CO 81157/303-731-2295 (ML bbls. & supplies; catalog $3)
Steven Dodd Hughes, P.O. Box 11455, Eugene, OR 97440/503-485-8869 (cust. guns; ctlg. $3)
Al Hunkeler, Buckskin Machine Works, 3235 So. 358th St., Auburn, WA 98001/206-927-5412 (ML guns)

MUZZLE-LOADING GUNS, BARRELS or EQUIPMENT — cont'd.

Jennings-Hawken, 326½-4th St. N.W., Winter Haven, FL 33880
Jerry's Gun Shop, 9220 Odgen Ave., Brookfield, IL 60513/312-485-5200
Wm. Large Gun & Mach. Shop, R.R. #243, Box 189B, Ironton, OH 45638/614-532-5298
Leding Loader, R.R. #1, Box 645, Ozark, AR 72949 (conical ldg. acc. f. ML)
Lever Arms Serv. Ltd., 2131 Burrard St., Vancouver, BC V6J 3H8/604-736-0004, Canada
Log Cabin Sport Shop, 8010 Lafayette Rd., Lodi, OH 44254/216-948-1082 (ctlg. $3)
Loven-Pierson Inc., 4 W. Main, P.O. Box 377, Apalachin, NY 13732/607-625-2303
Lyman Products Corp., Rte. 147, Middlefield, CT 06455
McCann's Muzzle-Gun Works, 200 Federal City Rd., Pennington, NJ 08534/609-737-1707
McKeown's Sporting Arms, R.R. 4, Pekin, IL 61554/309-347-3559 (E-Z load rev. stand)
Maurer Arms, 2154-16th St., Akron, OH 44314/216-745-6864 (cust. muzzleloaders)
Michigan Arms Corp., 363 Elmwood, Troy, MI 48083/313-583-1518
Modern Muzzleloading, Inc., Highway 136 East, P.O. Box 130, Lancaster, MO 63548/816-457-2125
Mountain State Muzzleloading Supplies, Inc., Box 154-1, Rt. #2 Williamstown, WV 26187/304-375-7842
Muzzleload Magnum Products (MMP), Rt. 6 Box 384, Harrison, AR 72601/501-741-5019
Muzzleloaders Etc., Inc., Jim Westberg, 9901 Lyndale Ave. S., Bloomington, MN 55420/612-884-1161
Muzzle Loaders, Inc., 9566 Old Keene Mill Rd., Burke, VA 22015/703-866-0990
Navy Arms Co., 689 Bergen Blvd., Ridgefield, NJ 07657/201-945-2500
Newman Gunshop, 119 Miller Rd., Agency, IA 52530/515-937-5775 (custom ML rifles)
October Country, P.O. Box 969, Hayden Lake, ID 83835
Oregon Trail Riflesmiths, Inc., P.O. Box 51, Mackay, ID 83251/208-588-2527
Ox-Yoke Originals Inc., 34 W. Main St., Milo, ME 04463/800-231-8313 (dry lubr. patches)
A. W. Peterson Gun Shop, 1693 Old Hwy. 441 N., Mt. Dora, FL 32757
Phyl-Mac, 609 N.E. 104th Ave., Vancouver, WA 98664/206-256-0579
R.V.I., P.O. Box 1439 Stn. A, Vancouver, B.C. V6C 1AO, Canada/604-524-3214 (high grade BP acc.)
Richland Arms, 321 W. Adrian St., Blissfield, MI 49228
H. M. Schoeller, 569 So. Braddock Ave., Pittsburgh, PA 15221
Tyler Scott, Inc., 8170 Corporate Park Dr., Suite 141, Cincinnati, OH 45242/513-489-2209 (Shooter's choice black solvent; patch lube)
C. Sharps Arms Co., Inc., P.O. Box 885, Big Timber, MT 59011/406-932-4353
Sile Distributors, 7 Centre Market Pl., New York, NY 10013/213-925-4111
C. E. Siler Locks, 7 Acton Woods Rd., Candler, NC 28715/704-667-9991 (flint locks)
South Bend Replicas, Inc., 61650 Oak Rd., South Bend, IN 46614/219-289-4500 (ctlg. $6)
The Swampfire Shop, 1693 Old Hwy. 441 N., Mt. Dora, FL 32757/904-383-0595
Tennessee Valley Mfg., P.O. Box 1125, Corinth, MS 38834 (powderhorns)
Ten-Ring Precision, Inc., 1449 Blue Crest Lane, San Antonio, TX 78232/512-494-3063
Traditions, Inc., 452 Main St.; P.O. Box 235, Deep River, CT 06417/203-526-9555 (guns, kits, accessories)
Trail Guns Armory, 1422 E. Main, League City, TX 77573/713-332-5833
Uberti USA, Inc., 41 Church St., New Milford, CT 06776/203-355-8827
Upper Missouri Trading Co., 304 Harold St., Crofton, NE 68730/402-388-4844
Warren Muzzle Loading, Hwy. 21, Ozone, AR 72854 (black powder accessories)
Fred Wells, Wells Sport Store, 110 N. Summit St., Prescott, AZ 86301/602-445-3655
W. H. Wescomb, P.O. Box 488, Glencoe, CA 95232/209-293-7010 (parts)
Williamson-Pate Gunsmith Serv., 117 W. Pipeline, Hurst, TX 76053/817-282-1464
Winchester Sutler, HC 38 Box 1000, Winchester, VA 22601/703-888-3595 (haversacks)
Winter & Associates, 239 Hillary Dr., Verona, PA 15147/412-795-4124 (Olde Pennsylvania ML accessories)

PISTOLSMITHS

Accuracy Gun Shop, Lance Martini, 3651 University Ave., San Diego, CA 92104/619-282-8500
Accuracy Systems, Inc., 15205 N. Cave Creek Rd., Phoenix, AZ 85032/602-971-1991
Accuracy Unlimited, 16036 N. 49 Ave., Glendale, AZ 85306/602-978-9089
Ahlman's Inc., R.R. #1 Box 20, Morristown, MN 55052/507-685-4243
Alpha Precision, Inc., Rte. 1, Box 35-1, Preston Rd., Good Hope, GA 30641/404-267-6163
American Pistolsmiths Guild, Rt. 1, Della Dr., Bloomingdale, OH 43910/614-264-0176
Ann Arbor Rod and Gun Co., 1946 Packard Rd., Ann Arbor, MI 48104/313-769-7866
Armament Gunsmithing Co., Inc., 525 Route 22, Hillside, NJ 07205/201-686-0960
Armson, Inc., P.O. Box 2130, Farmington Hills, MI 48018/313-478-2577
Richard W. Baber, Alpine Gun Mill, 1507 W. Colorado Ave., Colorado Springs, CO 80904/303-634-4867
Baer Custom Guns, 1725 Minesite Rd., Allentown, PA 18103/215-398-2362 (accurizing 45 autos and Comp II Syst.; cust. XP100s, P.P.C. rev.)

Bain & Davis Sptg. Gds., 307 E. Valley Blvd., San Gabriel, CA 91776/213-573-4241
Bar-Sto Precision Machine, 73377 Sullivan Rd., Twentynine Palms, CA 92277/619-367-2747(S.S. bbls. f. 45 ACP)
Barta's Gunsmithing, 10231 US Hwy. #10, Cato, WI 54206/414-732-4472
R. J. Beal, Jr., 170 W. Marshall Rd., Lansdowne, PA 19050/215-259-1220 (conversions, SASE f. inquiry)
Behlert Precision, RD 2 Box 63, Route 611 North, Pipersville, PA 18947/215-766-8681 (short actions)
Bell's Custom Shop, 3309 Mannheim Rd., Franklin Park, IL 60131/312-678-1900
Bowen Classic Arms Corp., P.O. Box 67, Louisville, TN 37777/615-984-3583
C. T. Brian, 2723 W. Hunt St., Decatur, IL 62526/217-429-2290
Brown's Gun Shop, Ed Brown, Rte. 2 Box 2922, Perry, MO 63462/314-565-3261
Leo Bustani, P.O. Box 8125, W. Palm Beach, FL 33407/305-622-2710
F. Bob Chow, Gun Shop, Inc., 3185 Mission, San Francisco, CA 94110/415-282-8358
Dick Campbell, 20000 Silver Ranch Rd., Conifer, CO 80433/303-697-9150 (PPC guns; custom)
Cellini's, Francesca Inc., 3115 Old Ranch Rd., San Antonio, TX 78217/512-826-2584
The Competitive Pistol Shop, John Henderson, 5233 Palmer Dr., Ft. Worth, TX 76117/817-834-8479
D&D Gun Shop, 363 Elmwood, Troy, MI 48083/313-583-1512
Davis Co., 2793 Del Monte St., West Sacramento, CA 95691/916-372-6789
Leonard Day & Sons, Inc., One Cottage St., P.O. Box 723, East Hampton, MA 01027/413-527-7990
Dilliott Gunsmithing, Inc., Rte. 3, Box 340, Dandridge, TN 37725
Dominic DiStefano, 4303 Friar Lane, Colorado Springs, CO 80907/303-599-3366 (accurizing)
Duncan's Gunworks Inc., 1619 Grand Ave., San Marcos, CA 92069/619-727-0515
Dan Dwyer, 915 W. Washington, San Diego, CA 92103/619-296-1501
Englishtown Sptg. Gds. Co., Inc., David J. Maxham, 38 Main St., Englishtown, NJ 07726/201-446-7717
Ferris Firearms, 1827 W. Hildebrand, San Antonio, TX 78201/512-734-0304
Jack First Distributors, Inc., 44633 Sierra Hwy., Lancaster, CA 93534/805-945-6981
Fountain Prods., 492 Prospect Ave., W. Springfield, MA 01089/413-781-4651
Frielich Police Equipment, 396 Broome St., New York, NY 10013/212-254-3045
Gilman-Mayfield, 1552 N. 1st., Fresno, CA 93703/209-237-2500
Keith Hamilton, P.O. Box 871, Gridley, CA 95948/916-846-2361
Gil Hebard Guns, Box 1, Knoxville, IL 61448
Richard Heinie, 821 E. Adams, Havana, IL 62644/309-543-4535
James W. Hoag, 8523 Canoga Ave., Suite C, Canoga Park, CA 91304/818-998-1510
Campbell H. Irwin, Hartland Blvd. (Rt. 20), East Hartland, CT 06027/203-653-3901
Paul Jaeger, Inc., P.O. Box 449, 1 Madison Ave., Grand Junction, TN 38039/901-764-6909
J. D. Jones, Rt. 1, Della Dr., Bloomingdale, OH 43910/614-264-0176
Reeves C. Jungkind, 5805 N. Lamar Blvd., Austin, TX 78752/512-442-1094
L. E. Jurras & Assoc., P.O. Box 680, Washington, IN 47501/812-254-7698
Ken's Gun Specialties, Rt. 1, Box 147, Lakeview, AR 72642/501-431-5606
Benjamin Kilham, Kilham & Co., Main St., Box 37, Lyme, NH 03768/603-795-4112
Terry K. Kopp, Highway 13 South, Lexington, MO 64067/816-259-2636 (rebblg., conversions)
LaFrance Specialties, P.O. Box 178211, San Diego, CA 92117/619-293-3373
Nelson H. Largent, Silver Shield's Inc., 7614 #1 Lemhi, Boise, ID 83709
William R. Laughridge, Cylinder & Slide Shop, 515 E. Military Ave., Fremont, NE 68025/402-721-4277
John G. Lawson, The Sight Shop, 1802 E. Columbia Ave., Tacoma, WA 98404/206-474-5465
Kent Lomont, 4236 West South, Poneto, IN 46781/219-694-6792 (Auto Mag only)
George F. Long, 1500 Rogue River Hwy., Ste. F, Grants Pass, OR 97527/503-476-7552
Mac's .45 Shop, Box 2028, Seal Beach, CA 90740/213-438-5046
Mag-na-port International, Inc., 41302 Executive Drive, Mt. Clemens, MI 48045/313-469-6727
Robert A. McGrew, 3315 Michigan Ave., Colorado Springs, CO 80910/303-636-1940
Philip Bruce Mahony, 1-223 White Hollow Rd., Lime Rock, CT 06039/203-435-9341
Rudolf Marent, 9711 Tiltree, Houston, TX 77075/713-946-7028 (Hammerli)
Elwyn H. Martin, Martin's Gun Shop, 937 So. Sheridan Blvd., Lakewood, CO 80226/303-922-2184
John V. Martz, 8060 Lakeview Lane, Lincoln, CA 95648/916-645-2250 (cust. German Lugers & P-38s)
Alan C. Marvel, 3922 Madonna Rd., Jarrettsville, MD 21084/301-557-7270
Maryland Gun Works, Ltd., TEC Bldg., 10097 Tyler Pl. #8, Ijamsville, MD 21754/301-831-8456
Mullis Guncraft, 3518 Lawyers Road East, Monroe, NC 28110/704-283-8789
William Neighbor, Bill's Gun Repair, 1007 Burlington St., Mendota, IL 61342/815-539-5786
Nu-Line Guns, 1053 Caulks Hill Rd., Harvester, MO 63303/314-441-4501
Nygord Precision Products, P.O. Box 8394, La Crescenta, CA 91214/818-352-3027
Pachmayr Ltd., 1875 So. Mountain Ave., Monrovia, CA 91016/818-357-7771
Frank J. Paris, 13945 Minock Dr., Redford, MI 48239/313-255-0888
Paterson Gunsmithing, 438 Main St., Paterson, NJ 07502/201-345-4100
Phillips & Bailey, Inc., 815A Yorkshire St., Houston, TX 77022/713-699-4288
J. Michael Plaxco, Rt. 1, Box 203, Roland, AR 72135/501-868-9787
Power Custom, Inc., P.O. Box 1604, Independence, MO 64055/816-833-3102
Precision Specialties, 131 Hendom Dr., Feeding Hills, MA 01030/413-786-3365

PISTOLSMITHS — cont'd.

RPS Gunshop,11 So. Haskell St., Central Point, OR 97502/503-664-5010
Roberts Custom Guns (Dayton Traister Co.), 4778 N. Monkey Hill Rd., Oak Harbor, WA 98277/206-675-3421
Bob Rogers Gunsmithing, P.O. Box 305; 344 S. Walnut St., Franklin Grove, IL 61031/815-456-2685 (custom)
SSK Industries (See: J. D. Jones)
L. W. Seecamp Co., Inc., Box 255, New Haven, CT 06502/203-877-3429
Harold H. Shockley, 204 E. Farmington Rd., Hanna City, IL 61536/309-565-4524
Hank Shows, dba The Best, 1078 Alice Ave., Ukiah, CA 95482/707-462-9060
Spokhandguns Inc., Vern D. Ewer, P.O. Box 370, 1206 Fig St., Benton City, WA 99320/509-588-5255
Sportsmens Equipmt. Co., 915 W. Washington, San Diego, CA 92103/619-296-1501 (specialty limiting trigger motion in autos)
James R. Steger, 1131 Dorsey Pl., Plainfield, NJ 07062
Irving O. Stone, Jr., 73377 Sullivan Rd., Twentynine Palms, CA 92277/619-367-2747
Victor W. Strawbridge, 6 Pineview Dr., Dover Pt., Dover, NH 03820
A. D. Swenson's 45 Shop, P.O. Box 606, Fallbrook, CA 92028
Randall Thompson, 654 Lela Pl., Grand Junction, CO 81504/303-434-4971
"300" Gunsmith Service, 4655 Washington St., Denver, CO 80216/303-295-2437
Timney Mfg. Co., 3065 W. Fairmount Ave., Phoenix, AZ 85017/602-274-2999
Trapper Gun, 18717 East 14 Mile Rd., Fraser, MI 48026/313-792-0134
Dennis A. "Doc" & Bud Ulrich, D.O.C. Specialists, 2209 So. Central Ave., Cicero, IL 60650/312-652-3606
Vic's Gun Refinishing, 6 Pineview Dr., Dover, NH 03820/603-742-0013
Walters Industries, 6226 Park Lane, Dallas, TX 75225/214-691-5150
Wardell Precision Handguns Ltd., Box 4132 New River Stage 1, New River, AZ 85029/602-465-7258
Wilson's Gun Shop, P.O. Box 578, Rt. 3, Box 211-D, Berryville, AR 72616/501-545-3616
Wisner's Gun Shop Inc., P.O. Box 58; Hiway 6, Adna, WA 98552/206-748-8942

REBORING AND RERIFLING

P.O. Ackley (See Dennis M. Bellm Gunsmithing, Inc.)
Amimex Inc., 3174 Stimson Way, San Jose, CA 95135/408-274-7816
Barnes Custom Shop, dba Barnes Bullets Inc., P.O. Box 215, American Fork, UT 84003
Bauska Mfg. Corp., P.O. Box 2270, 1694 Whalebone Dr., Kalispell, MT 59901/406-752-8082
Dennis M. Bellm Gunsmithing Inc., 2376 So. Redwood Rd., Salt Lake City, UT 84119/801-974-0697 (price list $3; rifle only)
A. R. Goode, 4125 N.E. 28th Terr., Ocala, FL 32760/904-622-9575
H-S Precision, Inc., 112 N. Summit, Prescott, AZ 86302/602-445-0607
Terry K. Kopp, Highway 13 South, Lexington, MO 64067/816-259-2636 (Invis-A-Line bbl.; relining)
LaBounty Precision Reboring, P.O. Box 186, 7968 Silver Lk. Rd., Maple Falls, WA 98266/206-599-2047
Matco, Inc., 126 E. Main St., No. Manchester, IN 46962/219-982-8282
Nu-Line Guns, 1053 Caulks Hill Rd., Harvester, MO 63303/314-441-4500
Redman's Reboring & Rerifling, Route 3, Box 330A, Omak, WA 98841/509-826-5512
Ridgetop Sporting Goods, P.O. Box 306; 42907 Hilligoss Ln. East, Eatonville, WA 98328/206-832-6422
Siegrist Gun Shop, 8752 Turtle Rd., Whittemore, MI 48770/517-873-3929
Snapp's Gunshop, 6911 E. Washington Rd., Clare, MI 48617
J. W. Van Patten, P.O. Box 145, Foster Hill, Milford, PA 18337/717-296-7069
Robt. G. West, 3973 Pam St., Eugene, OR 97402/503-689-6610 (barrel relining)

RELOADING TOOLS AND ACCESSORIES

Activ Industries, Inc., P.O. Box F, 100 Zigor Rd., Kearneysville, WV 25430/304-725-0451 (plastic hulls, wads)
Advance Car Mover Co., Inc., Rowell Div., P.O. Box 1181, 112 N. Outagamie St., Appleton, WI 54912/414-734-1878 (bottom pour lead casting ladles)
American Products Co., 14729 Spring Valley Rd., Morrison, IL 61270/815-772-3336 (12-ga. shot wad)
Ammo Load Inc., 1560 E. Edinger, Suite G, Santa Ana, CA 92705/714-558-8858
Arcadia Machine & Tool (AMT), 536 No. Vincent Ave. Covina, CA 91722/818-915-7803 (Autoscale)
Ballistic Products, Inc., P.O. Box 408, 2105 Daniels St., Long Lake, MN 55356/612-473-1550 (f. shotguns)
Benson Ballistics, Box 3796, Mission Viejo, CA 92690
Colorado Sutlers Arsenal, Box 991, Granby, CO 80446/303-887-2813
B-Square Eng. Co., Box 11281, Ft. Worth, TX 76110/800-433-2909
Ballistic Prods., P.O. Box 488, 2105 Shaughnessy Circle, Long Lake, MN 55356/612-473-1550
Ballistic Research Industries (BRI), 2825 S. Rodeo Gulch Rd. #8, Soquel, CA 95073/408-476-7981 (shotgun slugs)
Belding & Mull, Inc., P.O. Box 428, 100 N. 4th St., Philipsburg, PA 16866/814-342-0607
Berdon Machine Co., P.O. Box 9457, Yakima, WA 98909/509-453-0374 (metallic press)
Bonanza (See: Forster Products)
C-H Tool & Die Corp., 106 N. Harding St., Owen, WI 54460/715-229-2146
Camdex, Inc., 2330 Alger, Troy, MI 48083/313-528-2300
Carbide Die & Mfg. Co., Inc., P.O. Box 226, Covina, CA 91723/213-337-2518
Carter Gun Works, 2211 Jefferson Pk. Ave., Charlottesville, VA 22903
Cascade Cartridge, Inc., (See: Omark)
Cascade Shooters, 63990 Deschutes Mkt. Rd., Bend, OR 97701/503-382-1257 (bull. seating depth gauge)
Chevron Case Master, R.R. 1, Ottawa, IL 61350
Mrs. Lester Coats, 416 Simpson Ave., No. Bend, OR 97459/503-756-6995 (lead wire core cutter)
Colorado Shooter's Supply, P.O. Box 132, Fruita, CO 81521/303-858-9191 (Hoch cust. bull. moulds)
Colorado Sutlers Arsenal, Box 991, Granby, CO 80446/303-887-2813
Container Development Corp., 424 Montgomery St., Watertown, WI 53094
Continental Kite & Key Co., (CONKKO) P.O. Box 40, Broomall, PA 19008/215-356-0711 (primer pocket cleaner)
Cooper-Woodward, 8073 Canyon Ferry Rd., Helena, MT 59601/406-475-3321 (Perfect Lube)
Corbin Mfg. & Supply Inc., 600 Industrial Circle, P.O. Box 2659, White City, OR 97503/503-826-5211
Custom Products, RD #1, Box 483A, Saegertown, PA 16443/814-763-2769 (decapping tool, dies, etc.)
J. Dewey Mfg. Co., 186 Skyview Dr., Southbury, CT 06488/203-264-3064
Dillon Precision Prods., Inc., 7442 E. Butherus Dr., Scottsdale, AZ 85260/602-948-8009
Efemes Enterprises, Box 691, Colchester, VT 05446 (Berdan decapper)
Fitz, Box 171, Douglas City, CA 96024 (Fitz Flipper)
Flambeau Prods. Corp., 15981 Valplast Rd., Middlefield, OH 44062/216-632-1631
Forster Products Inc., 82 E. Lanark Ave., Lanark IL 61046/815-493-6360
Francis Tool Co., P.O. Box 7861, Eugene, OR 97401/503-345-7457 (powder measure)
Freechec' (See: Paco)
Geo. M. Fullmer, 2499 Mavis St., Oakland, CA 94601/415-533-4193 (seating die)
Hanned Precision, P.O. Box 2888, Sacramento, CA 95812/916-381-0986 (22-SGB tool)
Hart Products, Rob W. Hart & Son Inc., 401 Montgomery St., Nescopeck, PA 18635/717-752-3655
Hensley & Gibbs, P.O. Box 10, Murphy, OR 97533 (bullet moulds)
Richard Hoch, The Gun Shop, 62778 Spring Creek Rd., Montrose, CO 81401/303-249-3625 (custom Schuetzen bullet moulds)
Hoffman New Ideas Inc., 821 Northmoor Rd., Lake Forest, IL 60045/312-234-4075 (spl. gallery load press)
Hollywood Loading Tools (See M & M Engineering)
Hornady Mfg. Co., P.O. Drawer 1848, Grand Island, NE 68802/308-382-1390
Hulme see: Marshall Enterprises (Star case feeder)
Huntington, 601 Oro Dam Blvd., Oroville, CA 95965/916-534-1210 (Compact Press)
JACO Precision Co., 11803 Indian Head Dr., Austin, TX 78753/512-836-44180 (JACO precision neck turner)
Javelina Products, Box 337, San Bernardino, CA 92402 (Alox beeswax)
Neil Jones, RD #1, Box 483A, Saegertown, PA 16433/814-763-2769 (decapping tool, dies)
Paul Jones Munitions Systems (See Fitz Co.)
King & Co., Edw. R. King, Box 1242, Bloomington, IL 61701
Lage Uniwad Co., 1814 21st St., Eldora, IA 50627/515-858-2364 (Universal Shotshell Wad)
Leding Loader, R.R. #1, Box 645, Ozark, AR 72949 (conical loadg. acc. f. ML)
Lee Custom Engineering, Inc. (See Mequon Reloading Corp.)
Lee Precision, Inc., 4275 Hwy. U, Hartford, WI 53027/414-673-3075
L. L. F. Die Shop, 1281 Highway 99 N., Eugene, OR 97402/503-688-5753
Ljutic Industries Inc., P.O. Box 2117, 732 N. 16th Ave., Yakima, WA 98907/509-248-0476 (plastic wads)
Lock's Phila. Gun Exch., 6700 Rowland, Philadelphia, PA 19149/215-332-6225
Lyman Products Corp., Rte. 147, Middlefield, CT 06455
McKillen & Heyer Inc., 37603 Arlington Dr., Box 627, Willoughby, OH 44094/216-942-2491 (case gauge)
Paul McLean, 2670 Lakeshore Blvd., W., Toronto, Ont. M8V 1G8 Canada/416-259-3060 (Universal Cartridge Holder)
MEC, Inc. (See Mayville Eng. Co.)
M&M Engineering, 10642 Arminta St., Sun Valley, CA 91352/818-842-8376
MMP, R.R. 6 Box 384, Harrison, AR 72601/501-741-5019 (Tri-Cut trimmer; Power powder trickler)
MTM Molded Products Co., 3370 Obco Ct., P.O. Box 14117, Dayton, OH 45414/513-890-7461
Magma Eng. Co., P.O. Box 161, Queen Creek, AZ 85242/602-987-9008
Marquart Precision Co., P.O. Box 1740, Prescott, AZ 86302/602-445-5646 (precision case-neck turning tool)
Marshall Enterprises, 792 Canyon Rd., Redwood City, CA 94062/415-365-1230 (Hulme autom. case feeder f. Star rel.)
Mayville Eng. Co., 715 South St., Mayville, WI 53050/414-387-4500 (shotshell loader)
Mequon Reloading Corp., P.O. Box 253, Mequon, WI 53092/414-673-3060
Metallic Casting & Copper Corp. (MCC), 214 E. Third St., Mt. Vernon, NY 10550/914-664-1311
Midway Arms Inc., 7450 Old Highway 40 West, Columbia, MO 65201/314-445-9521 (cartridge boxes)
Mo's Competitor Supplies, P.A.S., 34 Delamar Dr., Brookfield, CT 06804 (neck turning tool)
Multi-Scale Charge Ltd., 55 Maitland St. Suite 310, Toronto, Ont. M4Y 1C9, Canada/416-276-6292
Necromancer Industries, Inc., 14 Communications Way, West Newton, PA 15089/412-872-8722 (Compucaster automated bull. casting machine)
Non-Toxic Components, Inc., P.O. Box 4202, Portland, OR 97208/503-226-7110
Normington Co., Box 6, Rathdrum, ID 83858 (powder baffles)
Northeast Industrial Inc., N.E.I., P.O. Box 4204, 405 N. Canyon Blvd., Canyon City, OR 97820/503-575-2513 (bullet mould)
Ohaus Scale, (See RCBS)
Old Western Scrounger, 12924 Hwy. A-12, Montague, CA 96064/916-459-5445 (Press f. 50-cal. B.M.G round)
Omark Industries, Box 856, Lewiston, ID 83501/208-746-2351

RELOADING TOOLS AND ACCESSORIES — cont'd.

P&P Tool Co., 125 W. Market St., Morrison, IL 61270/815-772-7618 (12-ga. shot wad)
Pacific Tool Co., P.O. Box 2048, Ordnance Plant Rd., Grand Island, NE 68801/308-384-2308
Paco, Box 17211, Tucson, AZ 85731 (Freechec' tool for gas checks)
Pak-Tool, Roberts Products, 25238 S. E. 32nd, Issaquah, WA 98027/206-392-8172
Pflumm Gun Mfg., 6139 Melrose Ln., Shawnee, KS 66203/913-268-3105 (Drawer Vise)
Pitzer Tool Co., RR #3, Box 50, Winterset, IA 50273/515-462-4268 (bullet lubricator & sizer)
Plum City Ballistics Range, Norman E. Johnson, Rte. 1, Box 29A, Plum City, WI 54761/715-647-2539
Ponsness-Warren, P.O. Box 8, Rathdrum, ID 83858/208-687-2231
Marian Powley, 27131 183 Ave., Eldridge, IA 52748/319-285-9214
Quinetics Corp., P.O. Box 29007, San Antonio, TX 78229/516-684-8561 (kinetic bullet puller)
RCBS (See Omark Industries)
R.D.P. Tool Co. Inc., 49162 McCoy Ave., East Liverpool, OH 43920/216-385-5129 (progressive loader)
Ransom Intl. Corp., P.O. Box 3845, 1040 Sandretto Dr., Suite J, Prescott, AZ 86302/602-778-7899 (Grandmaster progr. loader)
Redding Inc., 1089 Starr Rd., Cortland, NY 13045/607-753-3331
Reloaders Paper Supply, Don Doerksen, P.O. Box 556, Hines, OR 97738/503-573-7060 (reloader's record book)
Rochester Lead Works, 76 Anderson Ave., Rochester, NY 14607/716-442-8500 (leadwire)
Rorschach Precision Prods., P.O. Box 151613, Irving, TX 75015/214-790-3487 (carboloy bull. dies)
SAECO (See Redding)
SSK Industries, Rt. 1, Della Drive, Bloomingdale, OH 43910/614-264-0176
Sandia Die & Cartridge Co., Rte. 5, Box 5400, Albuquerque, NM 87123/505-298-5729
Vernon C. Seeley, Box 6, Osage, WY 82723/307-465-2264 (Osage arbor press)
Shannon Associates, P.O. Box 32737, Oklahoma City, OK 73123
Shooters Accessory Supply, (See Corbin Mfg. & Supply)
Jerry Simmons, 715 Middlebury St., Goshen, IN 46526/219-533-8546 (Pope de- & recapper)
J. A. Somers Co., P.O. Box 49751, Los Angeles, CA 90049 (Jasco)
Sport Flite Mfg., Inc., P.O. Box 1082, Bloomfield Hills, MI 48303/313-647-3747 (swaging dies)
Star Machine Works, 418 10th Ave., San Diego, CA 92101/619-232- 3216
Stuart Products, Inc., P.O. Box 1587, Easley, SC 29641/803-859-9360 (sight vise)
Trammco, Inc., P.O. Box 1258, Bellflower, CA 90706/213-428-5250 (Electra-Jacket bullet plater)
Trico Plastics, 590 S. Vincent Ave., Azusa, CA 91702
Tru Square Metal Products, 640 First St. S.W., P.O. Box 585, Auburn, WA 98002/206-833-2310 (Thumler's tumbler case polishers; Ultra Vibe 18)
Vibra-Tek Co., 1844 Arroya Rd., Colorado Springs, CO 80906/303-634-8611 (brass polisher; Brite Rouge)
Weatherby, Inc., 2781 Firestone Blvd., South Gate, CA 90280/213-569-7186
Weaver Arms Ltd., P.O. Box 3316, Escondido, CA 92025/619-746-2440 (progr. loader)
Webster Scale Mfg. Co., P.O. Box 188, Sebring, FL 33870/813-385-6362
Whitetail Design & Engineering Ltd., 9421 E. Mannsiding Rd., Clare, MI 48617/517-386-3932 (Match Prep primer pocket tool)
Whits Shooting Stuff, P.O. Box 1340, Cody, WY 82414
L. E. Wilson, Inc. P.O. Box 324, 404 Pioneer Ave., Cashmere, WA 98815/509-782-1328

RESTS—BENCH, PORTABLE, ETC.

Armor Metal Products, P.O. Box 4609, Helena, MT 59604/406-442-5560 (portable shooting bench)
B-Square Co., P.O. Box 11281, Ft. Worth, TX 76109/800-433-2909
Cravener's Gun Shop, 1627 - 5th Ave., Ford City, PA 16226/412-763-8312
Decker Shooting Products, 1729 Laguna Ave., Schofield, WI 54476/715-359-5873 (rifle rests)
The Gun Case, 11035 Maplefield, El Monte, CA 91733
Joe Hall's Shooting Products, Inc., 443 Wells Rd., Doylestown, PA 18901/215-345-6354 (adj. portable)
Harris Engineering, Inc., Barlow, KY 42024/502-334-3633 (bipods)
Rob. W. Hart & Son, 401 Montgomery St., Nescopeck, PA 18635
Tony Hidalgo, 12701 S.W. 9th Pl., Davie, FL 33325/305-476-7645 (adj. shooting seat)
J. B. Holden Co., 295 W. Pearl, P.O. Box 320, Plymouth, MI 48170/313-455-4850
Hoppe's Div., Penguin Industries, Inc., Airport Industrial Mall, Coatesville, PA 19320/251-384-6000 (bench rests and bags)
Metro Straight-Shooter, 38 Livonia Ave., Brooklyn, NY 11212/800-443-7734 (shooting bench)
Protektor Model Co., 7 Ash St., Galeton, PA 16922/814-435-2442 (sandbags)
Ransom Intl. Corp., 1040 Sandretto Dr., Suite J, P.O. Box 3845, Prescott, AZ 86302/602-778-7899 (handgun rest)
San Angelo Mfg. Co., 1841 Industrial Ave., San Angelo, TX 76904/915-655-7126
Sharpshooter's Rest, Box 70, Cleveland, MO 64734/816-331-5113 (portable)
Suter's, Inc., House of Guns, 332 N. Tejon, Colorado Springs, CO 80902/303-635-1475
Turkey Creek Enterprises, Rt. 1, Box 65, Red Oak, OK 74563/918-754-2884 (portable shooting rest)
Wichita Arms, 444 Ellis, Wichita, KS 67211/316-265-06612

RIFLE BARREL MAKERS

P.O. Ackley Rifle Barrels (See Dennis M. Bellm Gunsmithing Inc.)
Amimex Inc., 3174 Stimson Way, San Jose, CA 95135/408-274-7816
Jim Baiar, 490 Halfmoon Rd., Columbia Falls, MT 59912/406-892-4409
Bauska Mfg. Corp., P.O. Box 2270, 1694 Whalebone Dr., Kalispell, MT 59901/406-752-8082
Dennis M. Bellm Gunsmithing Inc., 2376 So. Redwood Rd., Salt Lake City, UT 84119/801-974-0697; price list $3 (new rifle bbls., incl. special & obsolete)
Leo Bustani, P.O. Box 8125, West Palm Beach, FL 33407/305-622-2710 (Win.92 take-down; Trapper 357-44 mag. bbls.; SASE f. reply)
Ralph L. Carter, Carter's Gun Shop, 225 G St., Penrose, CO 81240/303-372-6240
J. A. Clerke Co., P.O. Box 627, Pearblossom, CA 93553/805-945-0714
Competition Arms, Inc., 1010 S. Plumer Ave., Tucson, AZ 85719/602-792-1075
Charles P. Donnelly & Son, Siskiyou Gun Works, 405 Kubli Rd., Grants Pass, OR 97527/503-846-6604
Douglas Barrels, Inc., 5504 Big Tyler Rd., Charleston, WV 25313/304-776-1341
David Gentry Custom Gunmaker, 314 N. Hoffman, P.O. Box 1440, Belgrade, MT 59714/406-388-4867
Getz Barrel Co., Box 88, Beavertown, PA 17813/717-658-7263
A. R. Goode, 4125 N.E. 28th Terr., Ocala, FL 32670/904-622-9575
H-S Precision, Inc., 112 N. Summit, Prescott, AZ 86302/602-445-0607
Half Moon Rifle Shop, 490 Halfmoon Rd., Columbia Falls, MT 59912/406-892-4409
Hart Rifle Barrels, Inc., RD 2, Lafayette, NY 13084/315-677-9841
Hastings, Box 224, 822-6th St., Clay Center, KS 67432/913-632-3169 (shotguns ONLY)
Jackalope Gun Shop, 1048 S. 5th St., Douglas, WY 82633/307-358-3441
Terry K. Kopp, Highway 13 South, Lexington, MO 64067/816-259-2636 (22-cal. blanks)
Krieger Barrels, Inc., N114 W18697 Clinton Dr., Germantown, WI 53022/414-255-9593
Lilja Precision Rifle Barrels, Inc., 245 Compass Creek Rd., P.O. Box 372, Plains, MT 59859/406-826-3084
Marquart Precision Co., P.O. Box 1740, Prescott, AZ 86302/602-445-5646
Matco, Inc., 126 E. Main St., No. Manchester, IN 46962/219-982-8282
McMillan Rifle Barrels U.S. International, P.O. Box 3427, Bryan, TX 77805/409-846-3990
Nu-Line Guns, 1053 Caulks Hill Rd., Harvester, MO 63303/314-441-4500
Olympic Arms Inc. dba SGW, 624 Old Pacific Hwy. S.E., Olympia, WA 98503/206-456-3471
John T. Pell Octagon Barrels, (KOGOT), 410 College Ave., Trinidad, CO 81082/719-846-9406
Pence Precision Barrels, RR #2 RD 900S, So. Whitley, IN 48787/219-839-4745
Pennsylvania Arms Co., Box 128, Duryea, PA 18642/717-457-4014 (rifled shotgun bbl. only)
Redman's Rifling & Reboring, Rt. 3, Box 330A, Omak, WA 98841/509-826-5512
Rocky Mountain Rifle Works, Ltd., 1707 14th St., Boulder, CO 80302/303-449-9189
Sanders Cust. Gun Serv., 2358 Tyler Lane, Louisville, KY 40205
Gary Schneider, 12202 N. 62d Pl., Scottsdale, AZ 85254/602-948-2525
SGW, Inc., D. A. Schuetz, 624 Old Pacific Hwy. S.E., Olympia, WA 98503/206-456-3471
E. R. Shaw, dba Small Arms Mfg. Co., Thoms Run Rd. & Prestley, Bridgeville, PA 15017/412-221-4343 (also shotgun bbls.)
Shilen Rifles, Inc., 205 Metro Park Blvd., Ennis, TX 75119/214-875-5318
Shiloh Rifle Mfg. Co., Inc., P.O. Box 279; 201 Centennial Dr., Big Timber, MT 59011/406-932-4454
W. C. Strutz, Rifle Barrels, Inc., P.O. Box 611, Eagle River, WI 54521/715-479-4766
Fred Wells, Wells Sport Store, 110 N. Summit St., Prescott, AZ 86301/602-445-3655
Bob Williams, P.O. Box 143, Boonsboro, MD 21713
Wilson Arms, 63 Leetes Island Rd., Branford, CT 06405/203-488-7297

SCOPES, MOUNTS, ACCESSORIES, OPTICAL EQUIPMENT

A.R.M.S., Inc. (Atlantic Research Marketing Systems), 230 W. Center St., West Bridgewater, MA 02379/617-584-7816 (mounts)
Action Arms Ltd., P.O. Box 9573, Philadelphia, PA 19124/215-744-0100
Adco International, 1 Wyman St., Woburn, MA 01801/617-938-8060 (InterAims Mark V sight)
Aimpoint U.S.A., 203 Elden St., Suite 302, Herndon, VA 22070/703-471-6828 (electronic sight)
Aimtech (See L&S Technologies)
Alley Suppl. Co., P.O. Box 848, Gardnerville, NV 89410/702-782-3800
American Arms, Inc., P.O. Box 27163, Salt Lake City, UT 84127/801-972-5006
The American Import Co., 1453 Mission, San Francisco, CA 94103/415-863-1506
Anderson Mfg. Co., P.O. Box 536, 6813 S. 220th St., Kent, WA 98032/206-872-7602 (lens cap)
Armsport, Inc., 3590 N.W. 49th St., Miami, FL 33122/305-635-7850
Armson, Inc., P.O. Box 2130, Farmington Hills, MI 48018/313-478-2577 (O.E.G.)
Avin Industries Lasersight, 1847 Camino Palmero, Hollywood, CA 90046/213-851-9816 (Laser aiming system)
B-Square Co., Box 11281, Ft. Worth, TX 76109/800-433-2909 (Mini-14 mount)
Bausch & Lomb Inc., 42 East Ave., Rochester, NY 14603/800-828-5423

SCOPES, MOUNTS, ACCESSORIES, OPTICAL EQUIPMENT — cont'd.

Beeman Precision Arms, Inc., 3440-GD Airway Dr., Santa Rosa, CA 95403/707-578-7900 (airguns only)
Bennett, 561 Delaware, Delmar, NY 12054/518-439-1862 (mounting wrench)
Browning Arms, Rt. 4, Box 624-B, Arnold, MO 63010
Buehler Scope Mounts, 17 Orinda Highway, Orinda, CA 94563/415-254-3201
Burris Co. Inc., 331 E. 8th St., Box 1747, Greeley, CO 80632/303-356-1670
Bushnell, 300 N. Lone Hill Ave., San Dimas, CA 91773/714-592-8000
Butler Creek Corp., 290 Arden Dr., Belgrade, MT 59714/406-388-1356 (lens caps)
Clear View Mfg. Co., Inc., 413 So. Oakley St., Fordyce, AR 71742/501-352-8557 (SEE-THR mounts)
Colt Firearms, P.O. Box 1868, Hartford, CT 06101/203-236-6311
Compass Instr. & Optical Co., Inc., 104 E. 25th St., New York, NY 10010
Conetrol Scope Mounts, Hwy 123 South, Seguin, TX 78155
Cougar Optics, Box 115, Groton, NY 13073/607-898-5747
D&H Prods. Co., Inc., 465 Denny Rd., Valencia, PA 16059/412-898-2840 (lens covers)
Del-Sports Inc., Main St., Margaretville, NY 12455/914-586-4103 (Kahles scopes; EAW mts.)
Dickson (See American Import Co.)
Dynamit Nobel-RWS, Inc., 105 Stonehurst Court, Northvale, NJ 07647/201-767-1995
Europtik, Ltd., P.O. Box 319, Dunmore, PA 18509/717-347-6049
Flaig's, Babcock Blvd., Millvale, PA 15209
Freeland's Scope Stands, Inc., 3737 14th, Rock Island, IL 61201/309-788-7449
Griffin & Howe, Inc., 36 West 44th St., Suite 1011, New York, NY 10036/212-921-0980
Griffin & Howe, 33 Claremont Rd., Bernardsville, NJ 07924/201-766-2287
Gun Parts Corp., Box 2, West Hurley, NY 12491/914-679-2419
Heckler & Koch, Inc., 14601 Lee Rd., Chantilly, VA 22021/703-631-2800
H.J. Hermann Leather Co., Rt. 1, P.O. Box 525, Skiatook, OK 74070/918-396-1226 (lens caps)
J.B. Holden Co., 295 W. Pearl, P.O. Box 320, Plymouth, MI 48170/313-455-4850
Imatronic Lasersight, P.O. Box 520, Batavia, IL 60510/312-879-0020 (Laser Sight)
Interarms, 10 Prince St., Alexandria, VA 22313
Paul Jaeger, Inc., P.O. Box 449, 1 Madison Ave., Grand Junction, TN 38039/901-764-6909 (Schmidt & Bender; EAW mts., Noble)
Jason Empire Inc., 9200 Cody, P.O. Box 14930, Overland Park, KS 66214/913-888-0220
Kahles of America, Div. of Del-Sports, Inc., Main St., Margaretville, NY 12455/914-586-4103
Kassnar Imports, Inc., P.O. Box 6097, Harrisburg, PA 17112/717-652-6101
Kenko Intl. Inc., 8141 West I-70 Frontage Rd. No., Arvada, CO 80002/303-425-1200 (optical equipment)
KenPatable Ent. Inc., P.O. Box 19422, Louisville, KY 40219/502-239-5447
Kilham & Co., Main St., Box 37, Lyme, NY 03768/603-795-4112 (Hutson handgun scopes)
Kowa Optimed, Inc., 20001 S. Vermont Ave., Torrance, CA 90502/213-327-1913
Kris Mounts, 108 Lehigh St., Johnstown, PA 15905
Kwik Mount (See KenPatable)
Kwik-Site, 5555 Treadwell, Wayne, MI 48184/313-326-1500
L&S Technologies, Inc., P.O. Box 223, Thomasville, GA 31799 (mount system f. handguns)
Laser Devices, Inc., #5 Hangar Way, Watsonville, CA 95076/408-722-8300 (Laser Sight)
Lasersight Inc., 1847 Camino Palmero, Hollywood, CA 90046/213-851-9816 (Laser aiming system)
E. Leitz, Inc., 24 Link Dr., Rockleigh, NJ 07647/201-767-1100
Leupold & Stevens Inc., P.O. Box 688, Beaverton, OR 97075/503-646-9171
Jake Levin and Son, Inc., 9200 Cody, Overland Park, KS 66214
W.H. Lodewick, 2816 N.E. Halsey, Portland, OR 97232/503-284-2554 (scope safeties)
Lyman Products Corp., Route 147, Middlefield, CT. 06455
Mandall Shooting Supplies, 7150 E. 4th St., Scottsdale, AZ 85252
Marble Arms Co., 420 Industrial Park, Gladstone, MI 49837/906-428-3710
Marlin Firearms Co., 100 Kenna Dr., New Haven, CO 06473
Michaels of Oregon, P.O. Box 13101, Portland, OR 97213 (QD scope covers)
Military Armament Corp., P.O. Box 111, Mt. Zion Rd., Lingleville, TX 76461 (Leatherwood)
Millett Industries, 16131 Gothard St., Huntington Beach, CA 92647/714-842-5575 (mounts)
Mirador Optical Corp., P.O. Box 11614, Marina Del Rey, CA 90295/213-821-5587
Mitchell Arms, Inc., 3411 Lake Center Dr., Santa Ana, CA 92704/714-957-5711
Nikon Inc., 623 Stewart Ave., Garden City, NY 11530/516-222-0200
North American Specialties, 10700 Logan Ave., Suite B, Costa Mesa, CA 92627/714-979-4867 (Leatherwood scopes)
Olympic Arms Inc. dba SGW, 624 Old Pacific Hwy. S.E., Olympia, WA 98503/206-456-3471 (mounts)
Omark Industries (See Weaver)
Orchard Park Enterprise, P.O. Box 563, Orchard Park, NY 14127/716-662-2255 (Saddleproof mounts only)
Pachmayr Ltd., 1875 So. Mountain Ave., Monrovia, CA 91016/818-357-7771
PaycheX Industries, 520 Moore St., Albion, NY 14411/716-589-7787 (mounts)
Pentax Corp., 35 Inverness Dr. E., Englewood CO 80112/303-799-8000 (riflescopes)
Pilkington Gun Co., P.O. Box 1296, Muskogee, OK 74402/918-693-9418 (Q. D. mt.)
Pioneer Marketing & Research Inc., 216 Haddon Ave. Suite 522, Westmont, NJ 08108/609-854-2424 (German Steiner binoculars; scopes)
Ram Line, Inc., 15611 W. 6th Ave., Golden, CO 80401/303-279-0886 (see-thru mt. f. Mini-14)
Ranging, Inc., Routes 5 & 20, East Bloomfield, NY 14443/716-657-6161
Ray-O-Vac, Willson Prod. Div., P.O. Box 622, Reading, PA 19603 (shooting glasses)
Redfield Gun Sight Co., 5800 E. Jewell Ave., Denver, CO 80224/303-757-6411
S & K Mfg. Co., Box 247, Pittsfield, PA 16340/814-563-7808 (Insta-Mount)
SSK Industries, Rt. 1, Della Dr., Bloomingdale, OH 43910/614-264-0176 (bases)
Sanders Cust. Gun Serv., 2358 Tyler Lane, Louisville, KY 40205 (MSW)
Schmidt & Bender, see: Paul Jaeger, Inc.
Seattle Binocular & Scope Repair Co., P.O. Box 46094, Seattle, WA 98146
Shepherd Scope Ltd., Box 189, Waterloo, NE 68069/402-779-2424
Sherwood Intl. Export Corp., 18714 Parthenia St., Northridge, CA 91324/818-349-7600 (mounts)
Shooters Supply, 1120 Tieton Dr., Yakima, WA 98902/509-452-1181 (mount f. M14/M1A rifles)
W.H. Siebert, 22720 S.E. 56th St., Issaquah, WA 98027
Simmons Outdoor Corp., 14205 S.W. 119 Ave., Miami, FL 33186/305-252-0477
Spacetron Inc., Box 84, Broadview, IL 60155(bore lamp)
Springfield Armory, Inc., 420 W. Main St., Genesco, IL 61254/309-944-5631
Steiner binoculars (See Pioneer Marketing & Research)
Stoeger Industries, 55 Ruta Ct., S. Hackensack, NJ 07606/201-440-2700
Supreme Lens Covers, (See Butler Creek) (lens caps)
Swarovski Optik,Div. of Swarovski America Ltd., One Kenny Dr., Cranston, RI 02920/401-463-6400
Swift Instruments, Inc., 952 Dorchester Ave., Boston, MA 02125
Tasco Sales, Inc., 7600 N.W. 26th St., Miami, FL 33122/305-591-3670
Tele-Optics, 5514 W. Lawrence Ave., Chicago, IL 60630/312-283-7757 (optical equipment repair services only; binoculars)
Tele-Optics Inc., P.O. Box 176, 219 E. Higgins Rd., Gilberts, IL 60136/312-426-7444 (spotting scopes)
Thompson/Center Arms, Farmington Rd., P.O. Box 5002, Rochester, NH 03867/603-332-2394 (handgun scope)
Tradewinds, Inc., Box 1191, Tacoma, WA 98401
Trijicon rifle scopes (See Armson, Inc.)
John Unertl Optical Co., 1224 Freedom Rd., Mars, PA 16046/412-776-9700
United Binocular Co., 9043 S. Western Ave., Chicago, IL 60620
Wasp Shooting Systems, Box 241, Lakeview, AR 72642/501-431-5606 (mtg. system f. Ruger Mini-14 only)
Weatherby's, 2781 Firestone, South Gate, CA 90280/213-569-7186
Weaver, Omark Industries, Box 856, Lewiston, ID 83501/208-746-2351
Weaver Scope Repair Service, 1121 Larry Mahan Dr., Suite B, El Paso, TX 79925/915-593-1005
Wide View Scope Mount Corp., 26110 Michigan Ave., Inkster, MI 48141/313-274-1238
Williams Gun Sight Co., 7389 Lapeer Rd., Davison, MI 48423
Boyd Williams Inc., 8701-14 Mile Rd. (M-57),Cedar Springs, MI 49319 (BR)
Carl Zeiss Inc.,Consumer Prods. Div., Box 2010, 1015 Commerce St., Petersburg, VA 23803/804-861-0033

SIGHTS, METALLIC

Accur-Sites, The Jim J. Tembelis Co., Inc., P.O. Box 114, 216 Loper Ct.,Neenah, WI 54956/414-722-0039 (shotgun)
Alley Supply Co., P.O. Box 848, Gardnerville, NV 89410/702-782-3800
Armson, Inc., P.O. Box 2130, Farmington Hills, MI 48018/313-478-2577
Beeman Precision Arms, Inc., 3440-GDD Airway Dr., Santa Rosa, CA 95403/707-578-7900
Behlert Custom Sights, Inc., RD 2 Box 63, Route 611 North, Pipersvifle, PA 18947/215-766-8681
Bo-Mar Tool & Mfg. Co., Rt. 12, Box 405, Longview, TX 75605/214-759-4784
Burris Co., Inc., 331-8th St., P.O. Box 1747, Greeley, CO 80632/303-356-1670
Cherokee Gun Accessories, 4127 Bay St., Suite 226, Fremont, CA 94538/415-471-5770 (Tritium Tacsight)
J. A. Clerke Co., P.O. Box 627, Pearblossom, CA 93553/805-945-0714
Farr Studio, 1231 Robinhood Rd., Greeneville, TN 37743/615-638-8825 (sighting aids—clip-on aperture; the Farr Sight; the Concentrator)
Andy Fautheree, P.O. Box 4607, Pagosa Springs, CO 81157/303-731-5003 ("Calif. Sight" f. ML; must send SASE)
Freeland's Scope Stands, Inc., 3734-14th Ave., Rock Island, IL 61201/309-788-7449
Gun Parts Corp., Box 2, West Hurley, NY 12491/914-679-2417
Paul Jaeger, Inc., P.O. Box 449, 1 Madison Ave., Grand Junction, TN 38039/901-764-6909
James W. Lofland, 2275 Larkin Rd., Boothwyn, PA 19061/215-485-0391 (single shot replica)
Hester Bros. Wholesale Co. (HESCO), Rt. 4, Greenville Rd., Highway 109, La Grange, GA 30240/404-884-4057
Innovision Enterprises, 728 Skinner Dr., Kalamazoo, MI 49001/616-382-1681 (Slug Sights)
Lyman Products Corp., Rte. 147, Middlefield, CT 06455
MMC Co., Inc., 210 E. Poplar, Deming, NM 88030
Marble Arms Corp., 420 Industrial Park, Box 111, Gladstone, MI 49837/906-428-3710
Meprolight Night Sights (See Hester Bros.)
Merit Corp., Dept. GD, P.O. Box 9044, Schenectady, NY 12309/518-346-1420
Millett Ind., 16131 Gothard St., Huntington Beach, CA 92647/714-842-5575
Miniature Mach. Co., 210 E. Poplar, Deming, NM 88030/505-546-2151 (MMC)
Omega Sales, Inc., P.O. Box 1066, Mt. Clemens, MI 48043/313-469-6727
Poly Choke Div., Marble Arms Corp., 420 Industrial Park, Gladstone, MI 49837/906-428-3710
Redfield Gun Sight Co., 5800 E. Jewell St., Denver, CO 80224/303-757-6411
Simmons Gun Specialties, Inc., 700 S. Rodgers Rd., Olathe, KS 66062/913-782-3131
Slug Site Co., Ozark Wilds, Versailles, MO 65084/314-378-6430
Tradewinds, Inc., Box 1191, Tacoma, WA 98401
Wichita Arms, 444 Ellis, Wichita, KS 67211/316-265-0661
Williams Gun Sight Co., 7389 Lapeer Rd., Davison, MI 48423

STOCKS (Commercial and Custom)

Ahlman's Inc., R.R. 1, Box 20, Morristown, MN 55052
Don Allen Inc., HC55, Box 326, Sturgis, SD 57785/605-347-5227
Angelo & Little Custom Gun Stock Wood, N 4026 Sargent St. Spokane, WA 99212/509-926-0794 (blanks only)
Ann Arbor Rod and Gun Co., 1946 Packard Rd., Ann Arbor, MI 48104/313-769-7866
Anton Custom Gunstocks, owner Paul D. Hillmer, 7251 Hudson Heights, Hudson, IA 50643/319-988-3941
Bain & Davis Sporting Goods, Walter H. Little, 307 E. Valley Blvd., San Gabriel, CA 91776/213-283-7449 (cust.)
Joe J. Balickie, Custom Stocks, Rte. 2, Box 56-G, Apex, NC 27502/919-362-5185
Bartas Gunsmithing, 10231 U.S.H.#10, Cato, WI 54206/414-732-4472
Donald Bartlett, 31829-32nd Pl. S.W., Federal Way, WA 98023/206-927-0726
Beeman Precision Arms, Inc., 3440GD Airway Dr., Santa Rosa, CA 95403/707-578-7900 (airguns only)
Dennis M. Bellm Gunsmithing, Inc., 2376 So. Redwood Rd., Salt Lake City, UT 84119/801-974-0697
Al Biesen, West 2039 Sinto Ave., Spokane, WA 99201
Roger Biesen, 5021 W. Rosewood, Spokane, WA 99208/509-328-9340
Stephen L. Billeb, Box 1176, Big Piney, WY 83113/307-276-5627
E.C. Bishop & Son Inc., 119 Main St., Box 7, Warsaw MO 65355/816-438-5121
Gregg Boeke, Rte. 2, Box 149, Cresco, IA 52136/319-547-3746 (cust.)
John M. Boltin, P.O. Box 644, Estill, SC 29918/803-625-4111
Kent Bowerly, Metolious Meadows Dr., H.C.R. Box 1903, Camp Sherman, OR 97730/503-595-6028 (custom)
Larry D. Brace, 771 Blackfoot Ave., Eugene, OR 97404/503-688-1278
Garnet D. Brawley, P.O. Box 668, Prescott, AZ 86301/602-445-4768 (cust.)
Frank Brgoch, #1580 South 1500 East, Bountiful, UT 84010/801-295-1885
A. Briganti, 475 Rt. 32, Highland Mills, NY 10930/914-692-4409
Brown Precision Co., P.O. Box 270GD; 7786 Molinos Ave., Los Molinos, CA 96055/916-384-2506
Jack Burres, 10333 San Fernando Road, Pacoima, CA 91331/818-899-8000 (English, Claro, Bastogne Paradox walnut blanks only)
Calico Hardwoods, Inc., 1648 Airport Blvd., Windsor, CA 95492/707-546-4045 (blanks)
Lou Camilli, 4700 Oahu Dr. N.E., Albuquerque, NM 87111/505-293-5259
Dick Campbell, 20000 Silver Ranch Rd., Conifer, CO 80433/303-697-9150 (custom)
Kevin Campbell, 10152 Trinidad, El Paso, TX 79925/915-592-5496 (cust.)
Larry T. Caudill, 1025A Palomas Dr. S.E., Albuquerque, NM 87108/505-255-2515 (custom)
Shane Caywood, P.O. Box 321, Minocqua, WI 54548/715-356-5414 (cust.)
Winston Churchill, Twenty Mile Stream Rd., RFD, Box 29B, Proctorsville, VT 05153
J. A. Clerke Co., P.O. Box 627, Pearblossom, CA 93553/805-945-0714
Clinton River Gun Serv., Inc., 30016 S. River Rd., Mt. Clemens, MI 48045/313-468-1090
Charles H. Coffin, 3719 Scarlet Ave., Odessa, TX 79762/915-366-4729
Jim Coffin, 250 Country Club Lane, Albany, OR 97321/503-928-4391
David Costa, 94 Orient Ave., Arlington, MA 02174/617-643-9571 (cust.)
Reggie Cubriel, 15610 Purple Sage, San Antonio, TX 78255/512-695-3364 (cust. stockm.)
Custom Gun Guild, 2646 Church Dr., Doraville, GA 30340/404-455-0346
D&D Gun Shop, 363 Elmwood, Troy, MI 48083/313-583-1512 (cust.)
Dahl's Custom Stocks, Rt. 4, Box 558, Lake Geneva, WI 53147/414-248-2464
Homer L. Dangler, Box 254, Addison, MI 49220/517-547-6745
Sterling Davenport, 9611 E. Walnut Tree Dr., Tucson, AZ 85715/602-749-5590
Jack Dever, 8520 N.W. 90, Oklahoma City, OK 73132/405-721-6393
R.H. "Dick" Devereaux, D.D. Custom Rifles, 5240 Mule Deer Dr., Colorado Springs, CO 80919/719-548-8468
William Dixon, Buckhorn Gun Works, Rte. 4 Box 1230, Rapid City, SD 57702/605-787-6289
Dowtin Gunworks (DGW), Rt. 4 Box 930A, Flagstaff, AZ 86001/602-779-1898 (cust.)
Dowtin Imports, Inc., Rt. 4 Box 930A, Flagstaff, AZ 86001/602-779-1989 (blanks—French, Turkish, Kashmir)
Duncan's Gunworks Inc., 1619 Grand Ave., San Marcos, CA 92069/619-727-0515 (cust.)
D'Arcy A. Echols, 164 W. 580 S., Providence, UT 84332/801-753-2367 (cust.)
Jere Eggleston, P.O. Box 50238, Columbia, SC 29250/803-799-3402 (cust.)
Bob Emmons, 238 Robson Road, Grafton, OH 44044 (custom)
Englishtown Sporting Goods Co., Inc., David J. Maxham, 38 Main St., Englishtown, NJ 07726/201-446-7717 (custom)
Ken Eyster Heritage Gunsmiths Inc., 6441 Bishop Rd., Centerburg, OH 43011/614-625-6131 (cust.)
Reinhart Fajen Inc., 1000 Red Bud Dr., P.O. Box 338, Warsaw, MO 65355/816-438-5111
Ted Fellowes, Beaver Lodge, 9245 16th Ave. S.W., Seattle WA 98106/206-763-1698 (cust. ML)
Fiberlite, 601 Lockwood, Houston, TX 77011/713/924-3600 (synthetic)
Fiberpro Inc., 3636 California St., San Diego, CA 92101/619-295-7703 (blanks; fiberglass; Kevlar)
Jerry A. Fisher, 1244-4th Ave. W., Kalispell, MT 59901/406-755-7093
Flaig's Inc., 2200 Evergreen Rd., Millvale, PA 15209/412-821-1717
Flynn's Cust. Guns, P.O. Box 7461, Alexandria, LA 71301/318-455-7130
Donald E. Folks. 205 W. Lincoln St., Pontiac, IL 61764/815-844-7901 (custom trap, Skeet, livebird stocks)
Larry L. Forster, Box 212, 220 First St. N.E., Gwinner, ND 58040/701-678-2475
Fountain Prods., 492 Prospect Ave., W. Springfield, MA 01089 (cust.)
Frank's Custom Rifles, 7521 E. Fairmount Pl., Tucson, AZ 85715/602-885-3901
Freeland's Scope Stands, Inc., 3737 14th Ave., Rock Island, IL 61201/309-788-7449
Game Haven Gunstocks, 13750 Shire Rd., Wolverine, MI 49799/616-525-8238 (Kevlar riflestocks)
Garrett Accur-Lt. D.F.S. Co., P.O. Box 8675, Fort Collins, CO 80524/303-224-3067 (fiberglass)
K. Genecco Gun Works, 10512 Lower Sacramento Rd., Stockton, CA 95210/209-951-0706
Dale Goens, Box 224, Cedar Crest, NM 87008
Goodling's Gunsmithing, R.D.#1, Box 1007, Spring Grove, PA 17632/717-225-3350 (cust.)
Gordie's Gun Shop, Gordon Mulholland, 1401 Fulton St., Streator, IL 61364/815-672-7202 (cust.)
Gary Goudy, 263 Hedge Rd., Menlo Park, CA 94025/415-322-1338 (cust.)
Charles E. Grace, 10144 Elk Lake Rd., Williamsburg, MI 49690/616-264-9483
Roger M. Green & J. Earl Bridges, 435 E. Birch, P.O. Box 984, Glenrock, WY 82637/307-436-9804 (Teyssier French walnut blanks)
Greene's Machine Carving, 17200 W. 57th Ave., Golden, CO 80403 (blanks & custom)
Griffin & Howe, 36 West 44th St., Suite 1011, New York, NY 10036/212-921-0980
Griffin & Howe, 33 Claremont Rd., Bernardsville, NJ 07924/201-766-2287
Guncraft, Inc., 117 W. Pipeline, Hurst, TX 76053/817-282-1464
Gun Parts Corp., Box 2, West Hurley, NY 12491/914-679-2417 (commercial)
Harper's Custom Stocks, 928 Lombrano St., San Antonio, TX 78207/512-732-5780
Robert W. Hart & Son, Inc., 401 Montgomery St., Nescopeck, PA 18635/717-752-3655 (cust.)
Hubert J. Hecht, Waffen-Hecht, P.O. Box 2635, Fair Oaks, CA 95628/916-966-1020
Heppler's Gun Shop, 6000 B Soquel Ave., Santa Cruz, CA 95062/408-475-1235
Keith M. Heppler, 540 Banyan Circle, Walnut Creek, CA 94598/415-934-3509 (cust. rifle)
Warren Heydenberk, Box 354 RD4, Quakertown, PA 18951/215-538-2682
Klaus Hiptmayer, P.O. Box 136, Eastman, Que., J0E 1P0 Canada/514-297-2492
Hoenig & Rodman, 6521 Morton Dr., Boise, ID 83705/208-375-1116 (stock duplicating machine)
Hollis Gun Shop, 917 Rex St., Carlsbad, NM 88220
Corey O. Huebner, 3604 S. 3rd W., Missoula, MT 59801/406-721-9647 (cust.)
Paul Jaeger, Inc., P.O. Box 449, 1 Madison Ave., Grand Junction, TN 38039/901-764-6909
Robert L. Jamison, Rt. 4, Box 200, Moses Lake, WA 98837/509-762-2659 (cust. target)
Jenkins Enterprises, Inc., 12317 Locksley Lane, Auburn, CA 95603/916-823-9652 (custom)
Jim's Gun Shop, James R. Spradlin, 113 Arthur, Pueblo, CO 81004/719-543-9462 (cust.)
Johnson Wood Products, I.D. Johnson & Sons, Rte. #1, Strawberry Point, IA 52076/319-933-4930 (blanks)
Neal G. Johnson, Gunsmithing, Inc., 111 Marvin Dr., Hampton, VA 23666/804-838-8091
David Kartak, SRS Box 3042, South Beach, OR 97366/503-867-4951 (custom)
Don Klein, Rt. 2, P.O. Box 277, Camp Douglas, WI 54618/608-427-6948 (cust.)
Kenneth J. Klingler, P.O. Box 141; Thistle Hill, Cabot, VT 05647/802-426-3811 (carving only)
Richard Knippel, 825 Stoddard Ave., Modesto, CA 95350/209-529-6205 (cust.)
Harry Lawson Co., 3328 N. Richey Blvd., Tucson, AZ 85716/602-326-1117
Frank LeFever Arms & Sons, Inc., R.D.#1, Box 31, Lee Center, NY 13363/315-337-6722
Al Lind, 7821 76th Ave. S.W., Tacoma, WA 98498/206-584-6361 (cust.)
MPI Stocks, P.O. Box 03266, 7011 N. Reno Ave., Portland, OR 97203/503-289-8025 (fiberglass)
Monte Mandarino, 136 Fifth Ave. West, Kalispell, MT 59901/406-257-6208
Dennis McDonald, 8359 Brady St., Peosta, IA 52068/319-556-7940 (cust.)
Stan McFarland, 2221 Idella Ct., Grand Junction, CO 81505/303-243-4704
Bill McGuire, 1600 N. Eastmont Ave., East Wenatchee, WA 98801/509-884-6021
George E. Mathews & Son, Inc., 10224 S. Paramount Blvd., Downey, CA 90241/213-862-6719
Maurer Arms, Carl R. Maurer, 2154-16th St., Akron, OH 44314/216-745-6864
John E. Maxson, 3507 Red Oak Lane, Plainview, TX 79072/806-293-9042
Meadow Industries, P.O. Box 450, Marlton, NJ 08053/609-953-0922
R. M. Mercer, 216 S. Whitewater Ave., Jefferson, WI 53549/414-674-3839
Robt. U. Milhoan & Son, Rt. 3, Elizabeth, WV 26143
Miller Arms, Inc., D. E. Miller, P.O. Box 260, St. Onge, SD 57779/605-578-1790
Miller Gun Works, S.A. Miller, P.O. Box 1053, 1440 Peltier Dr., Point Roberts, WA 98281/206-945-7014
Earl Milliron Custom Guns & Stocks, 1249 N.E. 166th Ave., Portland, OR 97230/503-252-3725
Mitchell Arms, Inc., 3411 Lake Center Dr., Santa Ana, CA 92704/714-957-5711
Monell Custom Guns, Red Mill Road, RD#2, Box 96, Pine Bush, NY 12566/914-744-3021 (custom)
J.W. Morrison Custom Rifles, 4015 W. Sharon, Phoenix, AZ 85029
New England Arms Co., Lawrence Lane, Kittery Point, ME 03905/207-439-0593
Paul R. Nickels, P.O. Box 71043, Las Vegas, NV 89170/702-798-7533
Ted Nicklas, 5504 Hegel Rd., Goodrich, MI 48438/313-797-4493 (custom)
Jim Norman, Custom Gunstocks, 14281 Cane Rd., Valley Center, CA 92082/619-749-6252
Vic Olson, 5002 Countryside Dr., Imperial, MO 63052/314-296-8086 (custom)
Maurice Ottmar, Box 657, 113 E. Fir, Coulee City, WA 99115/509-632-5717
Pachmayr Gun Works, 1220 S. Grand Ave., Los Angeles, CA 90015 (blanks and custom jobs)
Pasadena Gun Center, 206 E. Shaw, Pasadena, TX 77506/713-472-0417
Paulsen Gunstocks, Rte. 71, Box 11, Chinook, MT 59523/406-357-3403 (blanks)
Wallace E. Reiswig, Claro Walnut Gunstock Co., 1235 Stanley Ave., Chico, CA 95928/916-342-5188 (California walnut blanks)
Don Robinson, Pennsylvania Hse., 36 Fairfax Crescent, Southowram, Halifax, W. Yorksh. HX3 9SW, England (blanks only)
Bob Rogers Gunsmithing, P.O. Box 305, 344 S. Walnut St., Franklin Grove, IL 61031/815-456-2685

STOCKS (Commercial and Custom) . . . cont'd.

Royal Arms, 1210 Bert Acosta, El Cajon, CA 92020/619-448-5466
Sanders Cust. Gun Serv., 2358 Tyler Lane, Louisville, KY 40205 (blanks)
Roy Schaefer, 965 W. Hilliard Lane, Eugene, OR 97404/503-688-4333 (commercial blanks)
Schwartz Custom Guns, 9621 Coleman Rd., Haslett, MI 48840/517-339-8939
David W. Schwartz, 2505 Waller St., Eau Claire, WI 54701/715-832-1735
Butch Searcy Co., 15 RD 3804, Farmington, NM 87401/505-327-3419 (cust.)
Shaw's, The Finest in Guns, 9447 W. Lilac Rd., Escondido, CA 92026/619-728-7070 (custom only)
Dan A. Sherk, 9701-17th St., Dawson Creek, B.C. V1G 4H7, Canada/604-782-5630 (custom)
Shogun Mfg. Co., 336 S. 300 East, Provo, UT 84601/801-377-0348 (Convert-A-Stock)
Hank Shows, The Best,1078 Alice Ave., Ukiah, CA 95482/707-462-9060
Sile Dist., 7 Centre Market Pl., New York, NY 10013/213-925-4111
Six Enterprises, 6564 Hidden Creek Dr., San Jose, CA 95120/408-268-8296 (fiberglass)
Ed Sowers, 8331 DeCelis Pl., Unit C, Sepulveda, CA 91343/818-893-1233 (custom hydro-coil gunstocks)
Fred D. Speiser, 2229 Dearborn, Missoula, MT 59801/406-549-8133
Sport Serv. Ctr., 2364 N. Neva, Chicago, IL 60635/312-889-1114 (custom)
Sportsmen's Equip. Co., 915 W. Washington, San Diego, CA 92103/714-296-1501 (carbine conversions)
Keith Stegall, Box 696, Gunnison, CO 81230
Talmage Enterprises, 451 Phantom Creek Lane, P.O. Box 512, Meadview, AZ 86444/602-564-2380
Tiger-Hunt, Michael D. Barton, P.O. Box 214, Jerome, PA 15937/814-479-2215 (curly maple stock blanks)
Trevallion Gunstocks, R.1, Box 39, Kittery Point, ME 03905/207-439-6822 (cust.)
Trinko's Gun Service, 1406 E. Main St., Watertown, WI 53094/414-261-5175
James C. Tucker, 205 Trinity St., Woodland, CA 95695/916-662-3109 (cust.)
Milton van Epps, Rt. 69-A, Parish, NY 13131/315-625-7251
Gil Van Horn, P.O. Box 207, Llano, CA 93544
John Vest, P.O. Box 1552, Susanville, CA 96130/916-257-7228 (classic rifles)
Vic's Gun Refinishing, 6 Pineview Dr., Dover, NH 03820/603-742-0013
Ed von Atzigen, The Custom Shop, 890 Cochrane Cres., Peterborough, Ont. K9H 5N3, Canada/705-742-6693 (cust.)
R. D. Wallace, Star Rt. 1, Box 76, Grandin, MO 63943/314-593-4773 (cust.)
Weatherby's, 2781 Firestone, South Gate, CA 90280/213-569-7186
Cecil Weems, P.O. Box 657, Mineral Wells, TX 76067/817-325-1462
Frank R. Wells, 7521 E. Fairmount Pl., Tucson, AZ 85715/602-885-3901
Fred Wells, 110 N. Summit St., Prescott, AZ 86301/602-445-3655
Terry Werth, 1203 Woodlawn Rd., Lincoln, IL 62656/217-732-1300 (cust.)
Robert G. West, 3973 Pam St., Eugene, OR 97402/503-689-6610
Western Gunstocks Mfg. Co., 550 Valencia School Rd., Aptos, CA 95003
Duane Wiebe, P.O. Box 497, Lotus, CA 95651
Bob Williams, P.O. Box 143, Boonsboro, MD 21713
Williamson-Pate Gunsmith Service, 117 W. Pipeline, Hurst, TX 76053/817-282-1464
Jim Windish, 2510 Dawn Dr., Alexandria, VA 22306/703-765-1994 (walnut blanks)
David W. Wills, 2776 Brevard Ave., Montgomery, AL 36109/305-272-8446
Robert M. Winter, R.R. 2, Box 484, Menno, SD 57045/605-387-5322
Wisner's Gun Shop Inc., P.O. Box 58; Hiway 6, Adna, WA 98552/206-748-8942
Mike Yee, 29927-56 Pl. S., Auburn, WA 98001/206-839-3991
Russell R. Zeeryp, 1601 Foard Dr., Lynn Ross Manor, Morristown, TN 37814
Dean A. Zollinger, Rt. 2, Box 135-A, Rexburg, ID 83440/208-356-6167

TARGETS, BULLET & CLAYBIRD TRAPS

Beeman Precision Arms, Inc., 3440-GD Airway Dr., Santa Rosa, CA 95403/707-578-7900 (airguns only)
Caswell International Corp. Inc., 1221 Marshall St. N.E., Minneapolis, MN 55413/612-379-2000 (target carriers; commercial shooting ranges)
J.G. Dapkus Co., P.O. Box 180, Cromwell, CT 06416/203-632-2308 (live bullseye targets)
Data-Targ, (See Rocky Mountain Target Co.)
Detroit-Armor Corp., Detroit Bullet Trap Div., 2233 N. Palmer Dr., Schaumburg, IL 60103/312-397-4070 (Shooting Ranges)
The Dutchman's Firearms Inc., 4143 Taylor Blvd., Louisville, KY 40215/502-366-0555
Ellwood Epps Northern Ltd., 210 Worthington St., W., North Bay, Ont. P1B 3B4, Canada (hand traps)
Hunterjohn, P.O. Box 477, St. Louis, MO 63166 (shotgun patterning target)
Jaro Manuf., 206 E. Shaw, Pasadena, TX 77506/713-472-0417 (paper targets)
Millard F. Lerch, Box 163, 10842 Front St., Mokena, IL 60448 (bullet target)
MCM (Mathalienne de Construction Mecanique), P.O. Box 18, 17160 Matha, France (claybird traps)
MTM Molded Prods. Co., 3370 Obco Ct., Dayton, OH 45414/513-890-7461
Maki Industries, 26-10th St. S.E., Medicine Hat, AB T1A 1P7, Canada/403-526-7997 (X-Spand Target System)
Outers Laboratories, Div. of Omark Industries, Rte. 2, Onalaska, WI 54650/608-783-1515 (claybird traps)
Peterson Instant Targets, Inc., P.O. Box 755, Bethel, CT 06801/203-791-0456 (paste-ons; Targ-Dots)
Phillips Enterprises, Inc., 3600 Sunset Ave., Ocean, NJ 07712/201-493-3191 (portable target holder)
Remington Arms Co., 1007 Market St., Wilmington, DE 19898 (claybird traps)
Rocky Mountain Target Co., P.O. Box 700, Black Hawk, SD 57718/605-787-5946 (Data-Targ)
Julio Santiago, P.O. Box O, Rosemount, MN 55068/612-890-7631 (targets)
Sheridan Products, Inc., 2600 Chicory Rd., Racine, WI 54303/414-554-7900 (traps)
Trius Prod., Box 25, Cleves, OH 45002/513-914-5682 (claybird, can thrower)

U.S. Repeating Arms Co., P.O. Box 30-300, New Haven, CT 06511/203-789-5000 (claybird traps)
Winchester, Olin Corp., 120 Long Ridge Rd., Stamford, CT 06904

TAXIDERMY

Jack Atcheson & Sons, Inc., 3210 Ottawa St., Butte, MT. 59701
Dough's Taxidermy Studio, Doug Domedion, 5112 Edwards Rd., Medina, NY 14103/716-798-4022 (deer head specialist)
Jonas Bros., Inc., 1037 Broadway, Denver, CO 80203 (catlg. $2)
Kulis Freeze-Dry Taxidermy, 725 Broadway Ave., Bedford, OH 44146
Mark D. Parker, 8811 Rogers Rd., Longmont, CO 80501/303-772-0214

TRAP & SKEET SHOOTERS EQUIP.

The American Import Co., 1453 Mission St., San Francisco, CA 94103/415-863-1506 (Targetthrower; claybird traps)
Anton Custom Gunstocks, owner Paul D. Hillmer, 7251 Hudson Heights, Hudson, IA 50643/319-988-3941
Briley Mfg. Co., 1085-B Gessner, Houston, TX 77055/713-932-6995 (choke tubes)
C&H Research, 115 Sunnyside Dr., Lewis, KS 67552/316-324-5445 (Mercury recoil suppressor)
D&H Prods. Co., Inc., 465 Denny Rd., Valencia, PA 16059/412-898-2840 (snap shell)
Euroarms of America, Inc., 1501 Lenoir Dr.; P.O. Box 3277, Winchester, VA 22601/703-662-1863
Frigon Guns, 627 W. Crawford, Clay Center, KS 67432/913-632-5607
Griggs Products, P.O. Box 789; 270 S. Main St., Suite 103, Bountiful, UT 84010/801-295-9696 (recoil redirector)
Ken Eyster Heritage Gunsmiths, Inc., 6441 Bishop Rd., Centerburg, OH 43011/614-625-6131 (shotgun competition choking)
Hoppe Division, Penguin Inds. Inc., Airport Mall, Coatesville, PA 19320/215-384-6000 (Monte Carlo pad)
Hunter Co., Inc., 3300 W. 71st Ave., Westminster, CO 80030/303-427-4626
Ljutic Industries Inc., P.O. Box 2117; 732 N 16th Ave., Yakima, WA 98907/509-248-0476
MCM (Mathalienne de Construction de Mecanique), P.O. Box 18, 17160 Matha, France (claybird traps)
Meadow Industries, P.O. Box 450, Marlton, NJ 08053/609-953-0922 (stock pad, variable; muzzle rest)
Wm. J. Mittler, 290 Moore Dr., Boulder Creek, CA 95006/408-338-3376 or 408-438-7331 (shotgun choke specialist)
Moneymaker Guncraft, 1420 Military Ave., Omaha, NE 68131/402-556-0226 (free-floating, ventilated ribs)
William J. Nittler, 111 Bean Creek Rd., Scotts Valley, CA 95066/408-438-7331 (shotgun barrel repairs)
Jim Noble Co., 1305 Columbia St., Vancouver, WA 98660/206-695-1309
Outers Laboratories, Div. of Omark Industries, Route 2, Onalaska, WI 54650/608-783-1515 (trap, claybird)
Protektor Model Co., 7 Ash St., Galeton, PA 16922/814-435-2442
Remington Arms Co., P.O. Box 1939, Bridgeport, Ct. 06601 (trap, claybird)
Daniel Titus, Shooting Specialties, 872 Penn St., Bryn Mawr, PA 19010/215-525-8829 (hullbag)
Trius Products, Box 25, Cleves, OH 45002/513-941-5682 (can thrower; trap, claybird)
Winchester-Western, New Haven, CT 06504 (trap, claybird)
Zeus International, P.O. Box 953, Tarpon Springs, FL 34688/813-863-5029

TRIGGERS, RELATED EQUIP.

Brownells, Inc., 222 W. Liberty, Montezuma, IA 50171/515-623-5401
M.H. Canjar Co., 500 E. 45th Ave., Denver, CO 80216/303-295-2638 (triggers)
Central Specialties Co., 200 Lexington Dr., Buffalo Grove, IL 60089/312-537-3300 (trigger locks only)
Crown City Arms, Inc., P.O. Box 550, Cortland, NY 13045/607-753-8238
Custom Products, Neil A. Jones, RD #1, Box 483A, Saegertown, PA 16433/814-763-2769 (trigger guard)
Cycle Dynamics Inc., 74 Garden St., Feeding Hills, MA 01030/413-786-0141
Dayton-Traister Co., 4778 N. Monkey Hill Rd., Oak Harbor, WA 98277/206-675-3421 (triggers)
Electronic Trigger Systems, 4124 Thrushwood Lane, Minnetonka, MN 55345/612-935-7829
Flaig's, 2200 Evergreen Rd., Millvale, PA 15209/412-821-1717 (trigger shoes)
Gun Parts Corp., Box 2, West Hurley, NY 12491/914-679-2419
Bill Holmes, Rt. 2, Box 242, Fayetteville, AR 72701/501-521-8958 (trigger release)
Neil A. Jones, see: Custom Products
Meier Works, Steve Hines, Box 328, Canyon, TX 79015/806-655-7806 (shotgun trigger guard)
Miller Single Trigger Mfg. Co., R.D. 1, Box 99, Millersburg, PA 17061/717-692-3704 (selective or non-selective f. shotguns)
Bruce A. Nettestad, Rt. 1, Box 140, Pelican Rapids, MN 56572/218-863-4301 (trigger guards)
Pachmayr Ltd., 1875 So. Mountain Ave., Monrovia, CA 91016/818-357-7771 (trigger shoe)
Pacific Tool Co., P.O. Box 2048, Ordnance Plant Rd., Grand Island, NE 68801 (trigger shoe)
Serrifile Inc., P.O. Box 508, Littlerock, CA 93543/805-945-0713
Timney Mfg. Co., 3065 W. Fairmount Ave., Phoenix, AZ 85017/602-274-2999 (triggers)
Melvin Tyler Mfg.-Dist., 1326 W. Britton Rd., Oklahoma City, OK 73114/405-842-8044 (trigger shoe)
U.S.F.S. (United States Frame Specialists), P.O. Box 7762, Milwaukee, WI 53207/414-643-6387
Williams Gun Sight Co., 7389 Lapeer Rd., Davison, MI 48423 (trigger shoe)